Statistical
Record
OF Black
America

ISSN 1051-8002

R

Statistical Record OF Black America

Jessie Carney Smith and
Carrell P. Horton, Editors

GALE

DETROIT · NEW YORK · TORONTO · LONDON

ie Carney Smith and Carrell P. Horton, *Editors*

Editorial Code and Data, Inc. Staff

Gary Alampi, *Programmer Analyst*
Joyce Piwowarski, *Programmer*

Gale Research Staff

Anna Sheets, *Developmental Editor*
Linda Hubbard, *Managing Editor, Multicultural Team*

Mary Beth Trimper, *Production Director*
Shanna Heilveil, *Production Assistant*

C. J. Jonik, *Desktop Publisher*

⊗™ This book is printed on acid-free paper that meets the minimum requirements of American National Standard for Information Sciences-Permanence Paper for Printed Library Materials, ANSI Z39.48-1984.

♲ This book is printed on recycled paper that meets Environmental Protection Agency Standards.

ISBN 0-8103-9252-6
ISSN 1051-8002

10 9 8 7 6 5 4 3 2 1

TABLE OF CONTENTS

Abbreviations xliii
Preface xlv

CHAPTER 1 - ATTITUDES, VALUES, AND BEHAVIOR 1
Attitudes 1

Table 1   Drug-Related: Percent Who Think Obtaining Selected Drugs is "Fairly Easy" or "Very Easy," by Age Group and Race/Ethnic Origin: 1991, 1992, and 1993-I 1

Table 2   Drug-Related: Percent Who Think Obtaining Selected Drugs is "Fairly Easy" or "Very Easy," by Age Group and Race/Ethnic Origin: 1991, 1992, and 1993-II 2

Table 3   Race-Related: Blacks' Expectation of Black President or Vice President in Next 20 Years: 1995 3

Table 4   Race-Related: Blacks' Feeling of Obligation to Help Blacks Viewed as Less Educationally and/or Economically Advantaged 3

Table 5   Race-Related: Blacks' Preference For or Against Predominantly Black College for Their Children: 1995 4

Table 6   Race-Related: Change in Employment Opportunities for Blacks in Past 5 Years: 1995 4

Table 7   Race-Related: Effects of Racism on Blacks' Ability to Achieve Career Goals: 1995 5

Table 8   School-Related: Blacks' Judgments on Desegregation's Effect on Children's Education 5

Table 9   School-Related: Distribution of Undergraduates' Educational Aspirations, by Race/Ethnic Origin: 1989-90 6

Table 10   School-Related: Percent of 4th, 8th, and 12th Graders Who Like Science (1990) and Mathematics (1992), by Race/Ethnic Origin 7

Behavior 7

Table 11   Crime/Violence-Related: High School Students' Attitudes and Behavior Related to Crime and Violence at School (in percentages), by Race/Ethnic Origin: 1993-I 7

Table 12   Crime/Violence-Related: High School Students' Attitudes and Behavior Related to Crime and Violence at School (in percentages), by Race/Ethnic Origin: 1993-II 8

Table 13   Crime/Violence-Related: High School Students' Suicide-Related Behavior, by Race/Ethnic Origin: 1993-I 9

Table 14   Crime/Violence-Related: High School Students' Suicide-Related Behavior, by Race/Ethnic Origin: 1993-II 9

Table 15   Crime/Violence-Related: Recent Weapon Carrying by High School Students, by Race/Ethnic Origin: 1993 10

Table 16   Drug-Related: Distribution (in Percentages) of Days of Alcohol Use in Past Month, by Demographic Characteristics: 1993 10

CHAPTER 1 - ATTITUDES, VALUES, AND BEHAVIOR continued:

Table 17   Drug-Related: High School Students Reporting Drug-Related Behavior on School Property, by Gender and Race/Ethnic Origin (in percentages)-Part I: 1993 11

Table 18   Drug-Related: High School Students Reporting Drug-Related Behavior on School Property, by Gender and Race/Ethnic Origin (in percentages)-Part II: 1993 11

Table 19   Drug-Related: High School Students' Lifetime and/or Current Use of Alcohol and Marijuana, by Gender and Race/Ethnic Origin (in percentages)-Part 1: 1993 12

Table 20   Drug-Related: High School Students' Lifetime and/or Current Use of Alcohol and Marijuana, by Gender and Race/Ethnic Origin (in percentages)-Part 2: 1993 12

Table 21   Drug-Related: High School Students' Lifetime and/or Current Use of Cocaine, Crack/Freebase, Illegal Steroids, and Drug Injections, by Gender and Race/Ethnic Origin (in percentages)-Part 1: 1993 13

Table 22   Drug-Related: High School Students' Lifetime and/or Current Use of Cocaine, Crack/Freebase, Illegal Steroids, and Drug Injections, by Gender and Race/Ethnic Origin (in percentages)-Part 2: 1993 13

Table 23   Drug-Related: Mean Age at First Use of Cigarettes, Alcohol, Marijuana, and Cocaine, by Race/Ethnic Origin: 1988-1993 14

Table 24   Drug-Related: Percent Distribution of Number of Cigarettes Smoked in Past Month, by Race/Ethnic Origin: 1993 15

Table 25   Drug-Related: Percent Reporting Alcohol Use in Past Month Among Those Under 21 and 21 and Over, by Race/Ethnic Origin: 1993 16

Table 26   Drug-Related: Percent Reporting Any Use of Illicit Drugs in Lifetime, Past Year, Past Month, by Age Group and Race/Ethnic Origin: 1992 and 1993 16

Table 27   Drug-Related: Percent Reporting Heavy Use of Alcohol in Past Month, by Age Group and Race/Ethnic Origin: 1993 17

Table 28   Drug-Related: Percent Reporting Nonmedical Use of Prescription Drugs in Lifetime, Past Year, Past Month, by Age Group and Race/Ethnic Origin: 1993 . . . 18

Table 29   Drug-Related: Percent Reporting Nonmedical Use of Stimulants, Sedatives, Tranquilizers, and Analgesics in Past Month, by Race/Ethnic Origin: 1993 18

Table 30   Drug-Related: Percent Reporting Seeing "Drunk" or "High on Drugs" Persons in Neighborhood, by Age Group and Race/Ethnic Origin: 1992 and 1993 19

Table 31   Drug-Related: Percent Reporting Use of Alcohol in Lifetime, Past Year, Past Month, by Age Group, Gender, and Race/Ethnic Origin: 1993 20

Table 32   Drug-Related: Percent Reporting Use of Cigarettes in Lifetime, Past Year, Past Month, by Age Group, Gender, and Race/Ethnic Origin: 1993 21

Table 33   Drug-Related: Percent Reporting Use of Cocaine in Lifetime, Past Year, Past Month, by Age Group, Gender, and Race/Ethnic Origin: 1993 22

Table 34   Drug-Related: Percent Reporting Use of Crack in Lifetime, Past Year, by Age Group and Race/Ethnic Origin: 1993 23

Table 35   Drug-Related: Percent Reporting Use of Hallucinogens in Lifetime, Past Year, by Age Group and Race/Ethnic Origin: 1993 23

Table 36   Drug-Related: Percent Reporting Use of Inhalants in Lifetime, by Age Group and Race/Ethnic Origin: 1993 24

Table 37   Drug-Related: Percent Reporting Use of Marijuana in Lifetime, Past Year, Past Month, by Age Group, Gender, and Race/Ethnic Origin: 1993 24

Table 38   Drug-Related: Percent Reporting Use of PCP and Heroin in Lifetime, by Age Group and Race/Ethnic Origin: 1993 25

CHAPTER 1 - ATTITUDES, VALUES, AND BEHAVIOR continued:

Table 39   Drug-Related: Percent Reporting Use of Smokeless Tobacco in Lifetime, Past Year, Past Month, by Age Group, Gender, and Race/Ethnic Origin: 1993 26

Table 40   Drug-Related: Percent Reporting Use of Steroids and Ice in Lifetime, by Race/Ethnic Origin: 1993 27

Table 41   Drug-Related: Percent Reporting Using Drugs with Needles in Lifetime, by Age Group and Race/Ethnic Origin: 1993 27

Table 42   Drug-Related: Percent Who Report Seeing Drugs Sold in Neighborhood, by Age Group and Race/Ethnic Origin: 1992 and 1993 28

Table 43   Drug-Related: Percent in "Big Cities" Reporting Illicit Drug Use in Past Year, by Race/Ethnic Origin: 1993 28

Table 44   Drug-Related: Percent of Black 15-44-Year-Old Women Reporting Drug Use, by Residential Area and Age Group-Part I: 1993 29

Table 45   Drug-Related: Percent of Black 15-44-Year-Old Women Reporting Drug Use, by Residential Area and Age Group-Part II: 1993 30

Table 46   Drug-Related: Percent of Current Alcohol Drinkers Among Persons 18 and Over, by Age Group and Race/Ethnic Origin: 1985 and 1990 30

Table 47   Drug-Related: Percent of Eighth Graders and High School Seniors Reporting Use of Cigarettes, Marijuana, and Cocaine in Past Month, by Race: 1980-1994 . . . 31

Table 48   Drug-Related: Percent of Eighth Graders and High School Seniors Reporting Use of Inhalants and Alcohol in Past Month, and Binge Drinking in Past 2 weeks, by Race: 1980-1994 32

Table 49   Drug-Related: Percent of Heavy Alcohol Drinkers Among Current Drinkers 18 and Over, by Age Group and Race/Ethnic Origin: 1985 and 1990 33

Table 50   Drug-Related: Percent of People Reporting Driving Under the Influence of Alcohol or Illegal Drugs in Past Year, by Age Group and Race: 1993 34

Table 51   Drug-Related: Percent of Youth 12-21 Reporting Lifetime, or Past Month Use of Alcohol, Marijuana, Cocaine, and Crack-Cocaine, by Age Group, Gender, and Race/Ethnic Origin-Part I: 1992 36

Table 52   Drug-Related: Percent of Youth 12-21 Reporting Lifetime, or Past Month Use of Alcohol, Marijuana, Cocaine, and Crack-Cocaine, by Age Group, Gender, and Race/Ethnic Origin-Part II: 1992 37

Table 53   Drug-Related: Percent of Youth Drug Users and Nonusers Reporting Selected Risk Behaviors, by Race/Ethnic Origin-Part I: 1992 37

Table 54   Drug-Related: Percent of Youth Drug Users and Nonusers Reporting Selected Risk Behaviors, by Race/Ethnic Origin-Part II: 1992 38

Table 55   Drug-Related: Percent of Youth Drug Users and Nonusers Reporting Selected Risk Behaviors, by Race/Ethnic Origin-Part III: 1992 39

Table 56   Drug-Related: Percent of Youth in National Longitudinal Survey of Youth Reporting Marijuana and Cocaine Use in Lifetime, Past Year, Past Month, by Race: 1984, 1988, and 1992 39

Table 57   Drug-Related: Summary Table – Use of Any Drugs and Selected Specific Drugs in Past Month, by Age Group and Race/Ethnic Origin (in percentages): 1991-1993 40

Table 58   Drug-Related: Total Lifetime, Annual, 30-day, and Daily Use of Alcohol - Effect and Amount, by Grade Level and Race/Ethnic Origin (in percentages): 1994 41

Table 59   Drug-Related: Total Lifetime, Annual, 30-day, and Daily Use of Cigarettes, Smokeless Tobacco, and Steroids, by Grade Level and Race/Ethnic Origin (in percentages): 1994 42

CHAPTER 1 - ATTITUDES, VALUES, AND BEHAVIOR continued:

Table 60   Drug-Related: Total Lifetime, Annual, 30-day, and Daily Use of Cocaine, by Grade Level and Race/Ethnic Origin (in percentages): 1994 43

Table 61   Drug-Related: Total Lifetime, Annual, 30-day, and Daily Use of Heroin, Other Opiates, Stimulants, Barbiturates, and Tranquilizers, by Grade Level and Race/Ethnic Origin (in percentages)-Part I: 1994 43

Table 62   Drug-Related: Total Lifetime, Annual, 30-day, and Daily Use of Heroin, Other Opiates, Stimulants, Barbiturates, and Tranquilizers, by Grade Level and Race/Ethnic Origin (in percentages)-Part II: 1994 44

Table 63   Drug-Related: Total Lifetime, Annual, 30-day, and Daily Use of Marijuana, Inhalants, Hallucinogens, and LSD, by Grade Level and Race/Ethnic Origin (in percentages): 1994 45

Table 64   Drug-Related: Trends in Percent of Female 18-and-Over Current Cigarette Smokers, by Age Group and Race: 1965-1993 46

Table 65   Drug-Related: Trends in Percent of Female 25-and-Over Current Cigarette Smokers, by Years of Education and Race: 1974-1993 47

Table 66   Drug-Related: Trends in Percent of Male 18-and-Over Current Cigarette Smokers, by Age Group and Race: 1965-1993 48

Table 67   Drug-Related: Trends in Percent of Male 25-and-Over Current Cigarette Smokers, by Years of Education and Race: 1974-1993 49

Table 68   Relationships: Dropout Status of 12-21-Year Olds Who Reported Using Marijuana and Cocaine in Past 30 Days, by Race/Ethnic Origin (in percentages): 1992 50

Values 51

Table 69   1980 High School Sophomores in 1992: Percent of 1980 High School Sophomore Cohort Reporting Specific Values, by Race/Ethnic Origin: 1992 51

CHAPTER 2 - BUSINESS AND ECONOMICS 52

Banks, Financial Institutions, Finances 52

Table 70   Financial Companies: Characteristics, 1995 52

Table 71   Financial Companies: Top 25: Summary, 1995 54

Table 72   Investment Banks: Issues, 1995 54

Business Comparisons 55

Table 73   Black-Owned Firms: Comparison of Firms in Ten Largest Cities and States, 1992 55

Table 74   Black-Owned Firms: Comparisons of Firms in Ten Largest Counties and States, 1992 55

Table 75   Black-Owned Firms: Comparisons of Firms in Ten Largest Metropolitan Areas and States, 1992 56

Business Growth and Sales 56

Table 76   Black-Owned Firms: Average Receipts by Industry Division, 1992 56

Table 77   Black-Owned Firms: Increase by Legal Form of Organization, 1987 to 1992 57

Table 78   Sales by Industry 57

Business Location 58

Table 79   Black-Owned Firms: Statistics by State, 1992 and 1987. Part 1 58

Table 80   Black-Owned Firms: Statistics by State, 1992 and 1987. Part 2 60

Businesses 62

Table 81   Automobile Dealers: 50 Companies Below the 50 Leaders, 1994 62

Insurance Companies 65

Table 82   Insurance Companies: Characteristics of Top 15, 1995 65

CHAPTER 2 - BUSINESS AND ECONOMICS continued:
Table 83   Insurance Companies: Top 15, 1995 66
Leading Businesses 66
Table 84   Automobile Dealers: Top 50 Companies, 1994 66
Table 85   Black-Owned Firms: Top Industry Receipt Leaders, 1992 69
Table 86   Franchisors Ranked by Black-Owned Outlets 70
Table 87   Top Ten Employment Leaders, 1994 71
Table 88   Top Ten Growth Leaders, 1994 71
Table 89   Top Twenty Franchises 72
Legal Form of Organization 72
Table 90   Black-Owned Businesses: Legal Form of Organization, 1992 72
Types of Businesses 73
Table 91   Black-Owned Firms: Industry Division for Regions and States, 1992. Part 1 - New England 73
Table 92   Black-Owned Firms: Industry Division for Regions and States, 1992. Part 2 - Middle Atlantic 74
Table 93   Black-Owned Firms: Industry Division for Regions and States, 1992. Part 3 - East North Central 75
Table 94   Black-Owned Firms: Industry Division for Regions and States, 1992. Part 4 - West North Central 76
Table 95   Black-Owned Firms: Industry Division for Regions and States, 1992. Part 5- South Atlantic 78
Table 96   Black-Owned Firms: Industry Division for Regions and States, 1992. Part 6- East South Central 80
Table 97   Black-Owned Firms: Industry Division for Regions and States, 1992. Part 7- West South Central 81
Table 98   Black-Owned Firms: Industry Division for Regions and States, 1992. Part 8- Mountain 82
Table 99   Black-Owned Firms: Industry Division for Regions and States, 1992. Part 9- Pacific 84
Table 100 Black-Owned Firms: Major Industry Groups, 1992 and 1987. Part 1 85
Table 101 Black-Owned Firms: Major Industry Groups, 1992 and 1987. Part 2 88
Table 102 Black-Owned Firms: Percent Distribution by Industry Division, 1992 91
Table 103 Farm Operators: Tenure and Characteristics: 1987 and 1992 92
Table 104 Industrial/Service Companies: 50 Companies Ranked in Sales Below the 50 Leaders: 1994. 92
Table 105 Industrial/Service Companies: Top 50 in Sales: 1994 95

CHAPTER 3 - CRIME, LAW ENFORCEMENT, AND LEGAL JUSTICE 98
Crime 98
Table 106 Drug-Related: Percent of Inmates Whose Most Serious Offense was Drug-Related, by Race/Ethnic Origin: 1986 and 1991 98
Table 107 Juvenile Cases: Type of Offense in Juvenile Cases Disposed by Juvenile Courts, by Race/Ethnic Origin: 1992 98
Table 108 Juvenile Offenders: Distribution of Juvenile Offenders, by Type of Offense and Race/Ethnic Origin: 1992 99
Table 109 Murder: Murder/Manslaughter Offenders per 100,000 in Each Group, by Race: 1976-1993 100
Table 110 Murder: Percent of Murder/Manslaughter Offenders, by Age Group and Race/Ethnic Origin: 1976-1993 (Aggregate) 101

CHAPTER 3 - CRIME, LAW ENFORCEMENT, AND LEGAL JUSTICE continued:

Table 111   Murder: Percent of Murder/Manslaughter Offenders, by Race: 1976-1993 101

Table 112   Relationships: Murder/Manslaughter, Victim/Offender Relationships, by Race: 1993 102

Table 113   Suicides per 100,000 in Each Age Group, by Age Group, Gender and Race: Selected Years, 1950-1992 103

Table 114   Victims: Age and Gender of Murder Victims, by Race: 1993 103

Table 115   Victims: Handgun Victimization Rate, by Gender, Age and Race: 1987-1992 . . . 104

Table 116   Victims: Percent Distribution of Age Group of Murder/Manslaughter Victims, by Race: 1976-1993 (Aggregate) 105

Table 117   Victims: Percent of Households Victimized, by Type of Crime and Race: 1992 . . . 105

Table 118   Victims: Percent of Victims of Homicide at Workplace, by Race/Ethnic Origin: 1993 106

Table 119   Victims: Percentage Distribution of School Victimizations of High School Seniors, by Type of Victimization and Race/Ethnic Origin: 1976-1993 106

Table 120   Victims: Rape, Robbery, and Assault Victimization Rates, by Race/Ethnic Origin: 1992 107

Table 121   Victims: Single-Offender Rates for Victimizations of Women, by Relationship to Victim and Victim's Race/Ethnic Origin: 1992-93 108

Table 122   Victims: Trends in Number of Homicide Victims and Homicide Rate, by Gender and Race: 1970-1992 108

Table 123   Victims: Victims of Substantiated and Indicated Child Abuse and Neglect, by Race/Ethnic Origin: 1990-1993 109

Law Enforcement 110

Table 124   Arrests: Number and Percent of Persons Arrested, by Charge and Race: 1993 . . . 110

Table 125   Officers Slain: Percent Distribution of Identified Slayers of Law Enforcement Officers, by Race: 1984-1993 (Aggregate) and 1993 111

Table 126   Officers Slain: Percent Distribution of Law Enforcement Officers Slain, by Race: 1978-1993-I 111

Table 127   Officers Slain: Percent Distribution of Law Enforcement Officers Slain, by Race: 1978-1993-II 112

Table 128   Prison Staff: Age Group and Education of Federal Bureau of Prisons Corrections Officers, by Race/Ethnic Origin: 1994 112

Table 129   Prison Staff: Length of Employment of Federal Bureau of Prisons Staff, by Gender and Race/Ethnic Origin: 1994 113

Table 130   Prison Staff: Staff in Federal Bureau of Prisons Facilities, by Education, Gender, and Race/Ethnic Origin: 1994 114

Table 131   Prison Staff: Staff of Federal Prisons, by Region, Gender, and Race/Ethnic Origin: 1994 114

Table 132   Prison Staff: Total Staff in Federal Bureau of Prisons Facilities, by Gender, Age Group, and Race/Ethnic Origin: 1994 115

Table 133   Prisoners: Drug Abuse Among Jail Inmates in Month Before Their Offense, by Race/Ethnic Origin: 1989 116

Table 134   Prisoners: Federal Prisoners' Place of Confinement, by Race/Ethnic Origin: 1994 116

Table 135   Prisoners: History of Drug Use Among State Prisoners, by Race/Ethnic Origin (in percentages): 1991 117

Table 136   Prisoners: Number and Percent of State and Federal Prisoners, by Race/Ethnic Origin: 1993 117

Table 137   Prisoners: Percent Distribution of Persons Newly Committed to Prison, by Race/Ethnic Origin: 1992 118

CHAPTER 3 - CRIME, LAW ENFORCEMENT, AND LEGAL JUSTICE continued:

Table 138   Prisoners: Percent of Violent and Nonviolent First-Timers and Recidivists in State Prisons, by Race: 1991 119

Table 139   Prisoners: Race of Federal Prisoners: 1990-1994 119

Table 140   Prisoners: Trends in Number of Jail Inmates, by Race/Ethnic Origin: 1978-1994 . . . 120

Table 141   Prisoners: Trends in Number of State and Federal Prisoners, by Gender and Race: 1980-1994 120

Table 142   Prisoners: Violent State Prisons Whose Victims were Intimates, by Race/Ethnic Origin: 1991 121

Table 143   Relationships: Drug Arrests of Blacks in Relation to Black Population Characteristics: c. 1993 121

Table 144   Relationships: Trends in Number of State and Federal Prisoners per 100,000 U.S. Residents, by Gender and Race: 1980-1994 122

Legal Justice 123

Table 145   Court Officers: Racial/Ethnic Distribution of Appointees to U.S. Courts of Appeals Judgeships: 1963-1994. Part 1 123

Table 146   Court Officers: Racial/Ethnic Distribution of Appointees to U.S. Courts of Appeals Judgeships: 1963-1994. Part 2 123

Table 147   Executions: Prisoners Executed by Order of Civil Courts, by Race: 1930-1993 . . . 124

Table 148   Felony Offenders: Most Serious Offense of Felons Convicted by State Courts, by Race: 1992 125

Table 149   Felony Offenders: Percent of Felony Defendants Failing to Appear in Court, by Race/Ethnic Origin: 1992 126

Table 150   Felony Offenders: Percent of Felony Offenders Released and Rearrested, by Race/Ethnic Origin: 1992 126

Table 151   Juvenile Cases: Percent Distribution of Juvenile Case Outcomes, by Case Category and Race: 1992 127

Table 152   Juvenile Cases: Percent Distribution of Outcome of Juvenile Court Cases, by Type of Offense and Race: 1992 128

Table 153   Offenders: Racial/Ethnic Distribution of Convicted Defendants, by Type of Offense: 1992 128

Table 154   Offenders: Racial/Ethnic Distribution of Felons Convicted and Incarcerated in 1992, by Type of Offense 129

Table 155   Pretrials: Percent of Federal Defendants Released/Detained After Pretrial, by Race: 1992 130

Table 156   Pretrials: U.S. District Court Pretrials and Their Outcomes, by Race: 1992 130

Table 157   Relationships: Blacks in Prison, Black Drug Users and Black/White Convictions for Drug Use, c. 1995. 131

Table 158   Sentences: Average Federal Sentences for Similar Crimes, by Court District and Race: 1992-93 132

Table 159   Sentences: Average Federal Sentences for Similar Crimes, by Region and Race: 1992-93 134

Table 160   Sentences: Average Length of Sentence in U.S. District Courts, by Type of Offense and Race: 1992 134

Table 161   Sentences: Maximum Length of Sentences, by Most Serious Offense and Race: 1992 135

Table 162   Sentences: Prisoners Sentenced to Death, by Race: 1980-1993 136

Table 163   Time Served/Parole: Average Time Served in State Prisons, by Most Serious Offense, Gender, and Race: 1992 136

Table 164   Time Served/Parole: Percent Distribution of Offenders Under Parole Supervision, by Offense and Race/Ethnic Origin: 1992 137

CHAPTER 3 - CRIME, LAW ENFORCEMENT, AND LEGAL JUSTICE continued:

Table 165 Time Served/Parole: Percent Distribution of Persons Discharged from Parole, by Method of Discharge and Race/Ethnic Origin: 1992 139

CHAPTER 4 - EDUCATION 140

Adult Education 140

Table 166 Relationships: Reasons for Participation in Adult Education, by Race/Ethnic Origin: 1990-91 140

Educational Attainment 141

Table 167 Number/Percent: Graduation and Degree Status (in percentages), by Race/Ethnic Origin: 1994 141

Table 168 Relationships: Educational Attainment of 18-24-Year-Olds, by Race/Ethnic Origin: 1990 141

Table 169 Trends in High School and College Graduation (in percentages), by Race/Ethnic Origin: 1960-1994 142

Elementary and Secondary 143

Table 170 Achievement: College-Bound High School Graduates Meeting Criteria for College Admission, by Race/Ethnic Origin: 1992 143

Table 171 Achievement: Mathematics Proficiency Levels of 4th, 8th, and 12th Graders, by Race/Ethnic Origin: 1992 144

Table 172 Achievement: Trends in Mathematics Proficiency Test Scores of 9-, 13-, and 17-Year-Olds, by Race/Ethnic Origin: 1977-78 - 1991-92 145

Table 173 Achievement: Trends in Reading Proficiency Test Scores of 9-, 13-, and 17-Year-Olds, by Race/Ethnic Origin: 1979-80 - 1991-92 146

Table 174 Achievement: Trends in Science Proficiency Test Scores of 9-, 13-, and 17-Year-Olds, By Race/Ethnic Origin: 1976-77 - 1991-92 147

Table 175 Achievement: Trends in Writing Proficiency Test Scores of 4th, 8th, and 12th Graders, By Race/Ethnic Origin: 1983-84 - 1991-92 148

Table 176 Aspirations: Recommendations of College for High School Sophomores, by Source of Recommendation and Race of Student: 1990 149

Table 177 Curriculum: Mathematics and Science Courses Taken by High School Graduates (in percentages), by Race: 1982 and 1992 149

Table 178 Curriculum: Percent Distribution of 12th Graders Taking or Not Taking Algebra and Calculus, by Race/Ethnic Origin: 1992 150

Table 179 Curriculum: Semesters of High School Mathematics Taken (in Percentages), by Grade and Race/Ethnic Origin: 1992 150

Table 180 Dropouts: Status Dropout Rate and Family Income Among 16-24-Year-Olds, by Race/Ethnic Origin: 1992 151

Table 181 Dropouts: Status Dropouts in Relation to Population, by Race/Ethnic Origin: 1993 151

Table 182 Dropouts: Trends in Age Group of High School Dropouts, by Race/Ethnic Origin: 1970-1993 152

Table 183 Dropouts: Trends in Event and Status Dropouts, by Gender and Race/Ethnic Origin: 1973-1993 152

Table 184 Employee Job Categories: Distribution of Job Levels in Public Schools, by Race: 1982 and 1992 153

Table 185 Employee Job Categories: Participation Rates of White and Minority Employees in U.S. Elementary and Secondary School Districts: 1975-76 and 1992-93 154

Table 186 Enrollment: State-by-State Public Elementary and Secondary Enrollment, by Race/Ethnicity: Alabama-Mississippi, Fall 1986 and Fall 1992 155

CHAPTER 4 - EDUCATION continued:

Table 187 Enrollment: State-by-State Public Elementary and Secondary Enrollment, by Race/Ethnicity: Missouri-Wyoming, Fall 1986 and Fall 1992 156

Table 188 High School Graduates: Rate and Method of High School Completion Among 21- and 22-Year-Olds, by Race/Ethnic Origin (in percentages): 1990-1993 157

Table 189 School Choice: Attendance at Chosen or Assigned School for Students in Grades 3-12, by Race/Ethnic Origin: 1993 157

Table 190 Segregation/Integration: Percent of Black Students Attending White-Majority Schools, in the Most and Least Integrated States: c. 1995 158

Table 191 Teachers: Teaching Experience and Salary of Private School Elementary and Secondary Teachers, by Race/Ethnic Origin: 1990-91 159

Higher Education 160

Table 192 Colleges and Universities: Number Colleges and Enrollment, by State and Race/Ethnic Origin, Part I-Alabama-Mississippi: 1992 160

Table 193 Colleges and Universities: Number Colleges and Enrollment, by State and Race/Ethnic Origin, Part II-Missouri-Wyoming: 1992 161

Table 194 Colleges and Universities: Percentage Distribution of Undergraduate Enrollment in Less than 2-, 2-, and 4-Year Institutions, by Race/Ethnic Origin: 1989-90 162

Table 195 Colleges and Universities: Percentage Distribution of Undergraduate Enrollment in Public and Private Institutions, by Race/Ethnic Origin: 1989-90 . . 162

Table 196 Colleges and Universities: Trends in Enrollment in 2-Year Institutions, by Race/Ethnic Origin: 1980-1992 163

Table 197 Colleges and Universities: Trends in Enrollment in 4-Year Institutions, by Race/Ethnic Origin: 1980-1992 164

Table 198 Degrees: Percentage Distribution of Doctorates Conferred, by Field (1993) and Race/Ethnic Origin: 1980 and 1993 165

Table 199 Degrees: State-by-State Distribution of Associate Degrees Awarded, by Race/Ethnic Group: Alabama-Mississippi, 1992-93 165

Table 200 Degrees: State-by-State Distribution of Associate Degrees Awarded, by Race/Ethnic Group: Missouri-Wyoming, 1992-93 166

Table 201 Degrees: State-by-State Distribution of Bachelor's Degrees Awarded, by Race/Ethnic Group: Alabama-Mississippi, 1992-93 168

Table 202 Degrees: State-by-State Distribution of Bachelor's Degrees Awarded, by Race/Ethnic Group: Missouri-Wyoming, 1992-93 169

Table 203 Degrees: State-by-State Distribution of Doctorate Degrees Awarded, by Race/Ethnic Group: Alabama-Mississippi, 1992-93 170

Table 204 Degrees: State-by-State Distribution of Doctorate Degrees Awarded, by Race/Ethnic Group: Missouri-Wyoming, 1992-93 171

Table 205 Degrees: State-by-State Distribution of First-Professional Degrees Awarded, by Race/Ethnic Group: Alabama-Mississippi, 1992-93 172

Table 206 Degrees: State-by-State Distribution of First-Professional Degrees Awarded, by Race/Ethnic Group: Missouri-Wyoming, 1992-93 173

Table 207 Degrees: State-by-State Distribution of Master's Degrees Awarded, by Race/Ethnic Group: Alabama-Mississippi, 1992-93 174

Table 208 Degrees: State-by-State Distribution of Master's Degrees Awarded, by Race/Ethnic Group: Missouri-Wyoming, 1992-93 175

Table 209 Degrees: Trends in Associate's and Bachelor's Degrees Earned, by Race/Ethnic Origin: 1981-1992 176

Table 210 Degrees: Trends in First Professional Degrees Earned, by Race/Ethnic Origin: 1981-1992 176

CHAPTER 4 - EDUCATION continued:

Table 211   Degrees: Trends in Master's and Doctor's Degrees Earned, by Race/Ethnic Origin: 1981-1992 177

Table 212   Enrollment: Enrollment and Enrollment Change in Public and Private Institutions, by Race/Ethnic Origin: 1990-1993 177

Table 213   Enrollment: Enrollment and Enrollment Change, by Level of Study and Race/Ethnic Origin: 1990-1993 178

Table 214   Enrollment: Enrollment of Full-Time Students in Public and Private Institutions, by Race/Ethnic Origin: 1991-1993 179

Table 215   Enrollment: Enrollment of Part-Time Students in Public and Private Institutions, by Race/Ethnic Origin: 1991-1993 180

Table 216   Enrollment: Female Enrollment at 2- and 4-Year Institutions, by Race/Ethnic Origin: 1991-1993 181

Table 217   Enrollment: Full-Time Enrollment at 2- and 4-Year Institutions, by Race/Ethnic Origin: 1991-1993 182

Table 218   Enrollment: Higher Education Enrollment, by Gender and Race/Ethnic Origin: 1991-1993 182

Table 219   Enrollment: Male Enrollment at 2- and 4-Year Institutions, by Race/Ethnic Origin: 1991-1993 183

Table 220   Enrollment: Male and Female Full-Time Students at Higher Education Institutions, by Race/Ethnic Origin: 1991-1993 184

Table 221   Enrollment: Male and Female Part-Time Students at Higher Education Institutions, by Race/Ethnic Origin: 1991-1993 185

Table 222   Enrollment: Part-Time Enrollment at 2- and 4-Year Institutions, by Race/Ethnic Origin: 1991-1993 185

Table 223   Enrollment: State-by-State Enrollment in Higher Education, by Race/Ethnic Origin: Alabama-Mississippi, 1993 186

Table 224   Enrollment: State-by-State Enrollment in Higher Education, by Race/Ethnic Origin: Missouri-Wyoming, 1993 187

Table 225   Enrollment: State-by-State Minority Percent of Total Enrollment in Higher Education, by Race/Ethnic Group: Alabama-Mississippi, Fall 1986 and Fall 1992-I 188

Table 226   Enrollment: State-by-State Minority Percent of Total Enrollment in Higher Education, by Race/Ethnic Group: Alabama-Mississippi, Fall 1986 and Fall 1992-II 189

Table 227   Enrollment: State-by-State Minority Percent of Total Enrollment in Higher Education, by Race/Ethnic Group: Missouri-Wyoming, Fall 1986 and Fall 1992-I 190

Table 228   Enrollment: State-by-State Minority Percent of Total Enrollment in Higher Education, by Race/Ethnic Group: Missouri-Wyoming, Fall 1986 and Fall 1992-II 191

Table 229   Enrollment: Trends in Characteristics of College Enrollment, by Race: 1978-1992 193

Table 230   Enrollment: Trends in College Enrollment of 16-24-Year-Olds Who Completed High School in Preceding 12 Months, by Race: 1960-1992 194

Table 231   Enrollment: Trends in College Enrollment, by Age and Race/Ethnic Origin: 1975-1993 195

Table 232   Enrollment: Trends in Enrollment at 2- and 4-Year Institutions, by Race/Ethnic Origin: 1984-1993 195

Table 233   Enrollment: Trends in Enrollment in Public and Private Institutions, by Race/Ethnic Origin: 1984-1993 197

CHAPTER 4 - EDUCATION continued:

Table 234 Enrollment: Trends in Higher Education Enrollment, by Level of Study and Race/Ethnic Origin: 1984-1993 198

Table 235 Enrollment: Trends in Percent of Enrollment in Higher Education, by Race/Ethnic Origin: 1980-1992 199

Table 236 Enrollment: Trends in Percent of Female Enrollment in Higher Education, by Race/Ethnic Origin: 1980-1992 199

Table 237 Enrollment: Trends in Percent of Male Enrollment in Higher Education, by Race/Ethnic Origin: 1980-1992 200

Table 238 Faculty: Participation Rates of Minority and White U.S. Higher Education Faculty: 1975-76 and 1991-92 200

Table 239 Faculty: White and Minority Tenure Status of U.S. Higher Education Faculty: 1975-76 and 1991-92 201

Table 240 Fields of Study: Percentage Distribution of Undergraduates' Major Fields, by Race/Ethnic Origin: 1989-90 201

Table 241 Financing College: Average Cost of Postsecondary Education, by Race/Ethnic Origin: 1990 to 1991 202

Table 242 Financing College: Percentage Distribution of Family Income Percentile Ranks of Undergraduate College Students, by Race/Ethnic Origin: 1989-90 203

Table 243 HBCUs: Racial/Ethnic Origin Percentage Distribution of Undergraduates at HBCUs: 1989-90 204

Table 244 HBCUs: Trends in Federal Funding for Science and Engineering: 1985-1992 . . . 204

Table 245 HBCUs: Trends in Science and Engineering Research and Development Expenditures, by Funding Source and Field: 1985-1992 206

Table 246 HBCUs: Trends in Source and Amount of Non-Federal Funding for Science and Engineering: 1985-1992 207

Table 247 Older Undergraduates: Percent Distribution of Degree Programs of Older (24 or Over) Undergraduates, by Race/Ethnic Origin: 1989-90 209

Table 248 Older Undergraduates: Percent Distribution of Financial Aid to Older (24 or Over) Undergraduates, by Aid Type and Race/Ethnic Origin: 1989-90 209

Table 249 Older Undergraduates: Percent Distribution of Hours/Week Older (24 or Over) Undergraduates Worked while in School, by Race/Ethnic Origin: 1989-90 . . 210

Table 250 Older Undergraduates: Percent Distribution of Older (24 or Over) Undergraduates' Attendance at Public/Private, 4-Year/Less than 4-Year Institutions, by Race/Ethnic Origin: 1989-90 210

Table 251 Older Undergraduates: Percent Distribution of Older (24 or Over) Undergraduates' Fields of Study, by Race/Ethnic Origin: 1989-90 211

Table 252 Older Undergraduates: Percent Distribution of Older (24 or Over) Undergraduates' "Very Important" Reasons for Choice of Institution, by Race/Ethnic Origin: 1989-90 211

Table 253 Older Undergraduates: Percent Distribution of Time Older (24 or Over) Undergraduates Spent in School, by Race/Ethnic Origin: 1989-90 212

Table 254 Persistence: Minority Students Enrolling in College Immediately After Graduation Who were Still There 3 Years Later, by Race/Ethnic Origin: 1982-83 and 1989-90 212

Table 255 Persistence: Persistence Status of 1989-90 Minority Undergraduates Aspiring to a Bachelor's Degree: 1992 213

Table 256 Persistence: Persistence Status of 1989-90 Minority Undergraduates Aspiring to an Associate Degree: 1992 213

Table 257 Persistence: Persistence Status of Postsecondary Students Who Aspired to a Vocational Certificate: 1992 214

CHAPTER 4 - EDUCATION continued:

Table 258 Relationships: Enrollment, by Type of College and Student Employment Status (in percentages), by Race/Ethnic Origin: 1987 and 1993 214

Table 259 Relationships: Length of Time from High School Graduation to Bachelor's Degree, by Gender and Race/Ethnic Origin: 1993 215

Table 260 Students: Percent Distribution of Age Category of Undergraduates, by Race/Ethnic Origin: 1989-90 215

Table 261 Students: Percent Distribution of Minority Undergraduates' Reasons for Choice of Institution: 1989-90 216

Marriage Characteristics 217

Table 262 1980 High School Sophomores in 1992: Average Number of Higher Education Institutions Attended Before Attainment of Degree or Certificate by 1980 High School Sophomores, by Type of Degree and Race/Ethnic Origin: 1992 217

Table 263 1980 High School Sophomores in 1992: Average Time (in Months) from First Higher Education Enrollment to Attainment of Degree or Certificate by 1980 High School Sophomores, by Race/Ethnic Origin: 1992 217

Table 264 1980 High School Sophomores in 1992: Major Activity Reported (in Percentages) by 1980 High School Sophomore Cohorts, by Race/Ethnic Origin: 1992 218

Table 265 1980 High School Sophomores in 1992: Percent Distribution of 1980 High School Sophomore Cohort's Highest Level of Educational Attainment, by Race/Ethnic Origin: 1992 219

Table 266 1980 High School Sophomores in 1992: Percent Distribution of Educational Attainment of 1980 High School Sophomores Who Delayed College Entry, by Race/Ethnic Origin: 1992 219

Table 267 1980 High School Sophomores in 1992: Percent Distribution of Educational Attainment of 1980 High School Sophomores Who Entered Higher Education Immediately After High School Graduation, by Race/Ethnic Origin: 1992 220

Preprimary 220

Table 268 Enrollment: Trends in Preprimary Enrollment and Enrollment Rate, by Race/Ethnic Origin: 1970-1993 220

Relationships 221

Table 269 Computer Use: Students Using Computers at Home and at School, by Educational Level (1984) and Race/Ethnic Origin (1984 and 1993) 221

Table 270 Education and Employment: Unemployed High School Graduates and Dropouts, by Race: 1980-1993 222

Table 271 Enrollment and Age: Enrollment and Enrollment in Nursery School and Above, by Race/Ethnic Origin: 1980, 1990, and 1993 223

Table 272 Literacy: Adult Average Prose Literacy, by Age Category and Race/Ethnic Origin: 1992 224

Table 273 Literacy: Adult Average Prose Literacy, by Educational Level and Race/Ethnic Origin: 1992 224

Table 274 Students and Graduates: Percent Distribution of High School Students, Graduates, and Nongraduates, by Gender and Race/Ethnic Origin: 1975 and 1993 225

Test Scores 225

Table 275 SAT Scores: Average 1994 SAT Scores, in Comparison to Scores in 1993 and 1976, by Race/Ethnic Origin 225

Table 276 SAT Scores: Characteristics of Students Who Took the SAT in 1994, by Race/Ethnic Origin 226

CHAPTER 5 - HEALTH AND MEDICAL CARE 228

Deaths 228

Table 277   Drug-Related: Drugs Noted Most Often by Medical Examiners, by Decedent's Race/Ethnic Origin: 1993 228

Table 278   Drug-Related: Percent of Accidental or Suicide Deaths that were Drug-Related, by Race/Ethnic Origin: 1993 229

Diseases/Illnesses/Conditions 230

Table 279   AIDS: Adult and Adolescent Men with AIDS, by Type of Exposure and Race/Ethnic Origin: Through December, 1994 230

Table 280   AIDS: Adult and Adolescent Women with AIDS, by Type of Exposure and Race/Ethnic Origin: Through December, 1994 230

Table 281   AIDS: Trends in Number/Percent of Diagnosed AIDS Cases, by Age Group, Gender, and Race/Ethnic Origin: 1985-1994 231

Table 282   AIDS: Trends in Transmission Category of AIDS Cases Diagnosed for Persons 13 and Over, by Race/Ethnic Origin: 1985-1994 232

Table 283   Acute Conditions: Number and Rate of Acute Conditions, by Race: 1993 233

Table 284   Cancer: Trends in 5-Year Relative Survival Rates for Selected Cancer Sites, by Race: 1974-1990 234

Table 285   Cancer: Trends in Percent Distribution of Cancer Rates (Age-Adjusted) of Females for Selected Cancer Sites, by Race: 1973-1991 235

Table 286   Cancer: Trends in Percent Distribution of Cancer Rates (Age-Adjusted) of Males for Selected Cancer Sites, by Race: 1973-1991 236

Table 287   Cancer: Trends in Prostate and Breast Cancer 5-Year Relative Survival Rates, by Race: 1974-1976, 1977-1979, 1980-1982, and 1983-1990 237

Table 288   Cholesterol: Trends (in percentages) in Cholesterol Levels and Mean Levels of Persons 20-74 Years Old, by Gender and Race/Ethnic Origin: 1960-1991 . . . 237

Table 289   Hypertension: Trends in Percent of Persons 20-74 Years Old with Hypertension, by Gender and Race/Ethnic Origin: 1960-1991 238

Table 290   Weight: Trends in Percent of Overweight Persons 20-74 Years Old, by Gender and Race/Ethnic Origin: 1960-1991 240

Health Care Facilities 242

Table 291   Hospitals: Characteristics of Amount of Service Provided in Short-Stay Hospitals, by Race: 1964, 1990, and 1993 242

Table 292   Nursing Home/Personal Home Care: Trends in Number of Nursing Home and Personal Home Care Residents and Rate per 1,000 Population Among Persons 65 and Over, by Age Group and Race: 1963-1985 242

Health Insurance 243

Table 293   Coverage: Details of Government and Private Health Insurance Coverage, by Race/Ethnic Origin: 1987-1993 243

Table 294   Coverage: Number and Percent of Persons Covered for All, Part, or None of a 32-month Period, by Type of Insurance and Race/Ethnic Origin: 1990-1992 . . . 244

Table 295   Coverage: Percent of Poor People and All People Without Health Insurance, by Race/Ethnic Origin: 1993 244

Table 296   Coverage: Trends in Type of Coverage of Persons 65 and Over, by Race/Ethnic Origin (in percentages): 1980-1993 245

Table 297   Coverage: Trends in Type of Coverage of Persons Under 65, by Race/Ethnic Origin (in percentages): 1980-1993 246

Table 298   Relationships: Medicaid Coverage Among Persons Above and Below Poverty Level, by Race/Ethnic Origin: 1988-1993 247

xvii

CHAPTER 5 - HEALTH AND MEDICAL CARE continued:

Health Status 247
  Table 299   Activity Limitations: Percent Distribution of Activity Limitation Due to Chronic
              Conditions, by Age Group and Race: 1990 and 1993 247
  Table 300   Disabilities: Total and Per Person Days of Disability, by Race/Ethnic Origin:
              1970-1993-I 248
  Table 301   Disabilities: Total and Per Person Days of Disability, by Race/Ethnic Origin:
              1970-1993-II 249
  Table 302   Ratings: Trends in Percent of Persons Who Rate Their Health as "Fair" or
              "Poor," by Age Group and Race: 1987-1993 249

Health-Related Behavior 250
  Table 303   Drugs and Drug Abuse: Percent Reporting Treatment for Substance Abuse in
              Past Year, by Race/Ethnic Origin: 1993 250
  Table 304   Drugs and Drug Abuse: Percent of Pregnant Women Who Live in Metropolitan
              Areas and Use Drugs, by Race/Ethnic Origin: 1994 251
  Table 305   Preventive Acts: Percent of 19-35-Month-Old Children Vaccinated, by Race:
              1992 and 1993 252

Medical Care 253
  Table 306   Costs: Average Total and Specific Expenditures for Health Care, by
              Race/Ethnic Origin: 1985-1993 253
  Table 307   Dentists: Trends in Number of Dental Visits and Percent Distribution of Time
              Interval Since Last Visit, by Race: 1964, 1983, and 1989 254
  Table 308   Emergency Treatment: Characteristics of Emergency Room Episodes that are
              Drug-Related, by Gender and Race/Ethnic Origin: 1993 254
  Table 309   Emergency Treatment: Frequency of Drugs Mentioned Most Often by
              Emergency Departments (in percentages), by Race/Ethnic Origin: 1993 255
  Table 310   Emergency Treatment: Incidence of Emergency Room Episodes for Cocaine
              Use, by Age Group and Race/Ethnic Origin: 1988-1993 256
  Table 311   Emergency Treatment: Incidence of Emergency Room Episodes for
              Heroin/Morphine Use, by Age Group and Race/Ethnic Origin: 1988-1993 257
  Table 312   Emergency Treatment: Percent Distribution of Emergency Room Episodes for
              Use of Selected Drugs, by Race/Ethnic Origin: 1993 258
  Table 313   Emergency Treatment: Total Visits to Emergency Rooms and Visits per 100
              Persons, by Race: 1993 259
  Table 314   Emergency Treatment: Trends in Female Emergency Room Episodes Related
              to Cocaine Use, by Age Group and Race/Ethnic Origin: 1985-1993 259
  Table 315   Emergency Treatment: Trends in Male Emergency Room Episodes Related to
              Cocaine Use, by Age Group and Race/Ethnic Origin: 1985-1993 260
  Table 316   Emergency Treatment: Trends in Number of Drug-Related Emergency
              Department Episodes, by Age Group and Race/Ethnic Origin: 1988-1993 261
  Table 317   Patients: Home and Hospice Care Patients, by Race: 1993 262
  Table 318   Patients: Visits to Hospital Outpatient Departments, by Race: 1992 263
  Table 319   Physicians: Characteristics of Office Visits to Physicians, by Physician Specialty
              and Patient Race: 1985 and 1992 264
  Table 320   Physicians: Trends in Number of Physician Contacts per Person, by Age Group
              and Race: 1987-1993 264
  Table 321   Physicians: Trends in Percent of Office Visits to Selected Medical
              Specialists – Part I, by Race: 1975-1992 265
  Table 322   Physicians: Trends in Percent of Office Visits to Selected Medical
              Specialists – Part II, by Race: 1975-1992 266

CHAPTER 5 - HEALTH AND MEDICAL CARE continued:

Table 323   Physicians: Trends in Percent of Office Visits to Selected Medical Specialists – Part III, by Race: 1975-1992 266

Table 324   Physicians: Trends in Percent of Physician Office Visits Resulting in Drug Prescription, by Physician Specialty and Patient Race: 1975-1992 267

Table 325   Physicians: Trends in Physician Office Visits, by Race: 1975-1992 267

Table 326   Physicians: Trends in Time Interval Since Last Physician Contact, by Age Group and Race: 1964, 1990, and 1993 268

Table 327   Special Treatment: Trends in Percent of Persons in Specialty Substance Abuse Treatment, by Race/Ethnic Origin: 1980-1992 269

Pregnancies 269

Table 328   Relationships: Trends in Percent of Expectant Mothers Who Smoked During Pregnancy, by Race/Ethnic Origin: 1989-1992 269

CHAPTER 6 - HOUSING 271

Central Cities 271

Table 329   Introductory Characteristics of Householders 271

Characteristics 272

Table 330   Housing Units: Introductory Characteristics: Black Occupied Housing, 1993 . . . 272

Costs of Housing 273

Table 331   Costs: Selected Characteristics. Part 1-A 273

Table 332   Costs: Selected Characteristics. Part 1-B 276

Table 333   Costs: Selected Characteristics. Part 2-A 278

Table 334   Costs: Selected Characteristics. Part 2-B 281

Table 335   Costs: Selected Characteristics. Part 3-A 283

Table 336   Costs: Selected Characteristics. Part 3-B 286

Table 337   Selected Housing Costs: Black-Occupied Units 289

Elderly Occupants 291

Table 338   Building Condition: Elderly Householder 291

Table 339   Equipment Failures: Elderly Householder 293

Table 340   Equipment and Plumbing: Elderly Householder 295

Table 341   Fuels: Elderly Householder 298

Table 342   Household Composition: Elderly Householder. Part 1 300

Table 343   Household Composition: Elderly Householder. Part 2 302

Table 344   Housing Costs: Monthly for Elderly Householder 304

Table 345   Housing Costs: Selected Characteristics for Elderly Householder 307

Table 346   Housing Quality: Elderly Householder 309

Table 347   Income Characteristics: Elderly Householder 311

Table 348   Introductory Characteristics: Elderly Householder 313

Table 349   Mortgage Characteristics: Elderly Householder. Part 1 316

Table 350   Mortgage Characteristics: Elderly Householder. Part 2 318

Table 351   Movers: Elderly Householder 320

Table 352   Neighborhoods: Elderly Householder 322

Table 353   Reasons for Move: Elderly Householder 325

Table 354   Repairs and Improvements: Elderly Householder 327

Table 355   Unit and Lot Size: Elderly Householder 330

Table 356   Value and Price: Elderly Householder 332

Equipment and Plumbing 334

Table 357   Equipment and Plumbing: Black-Occupied Housing, 1993 334

Table 358   Failures in Equipment: Black-Occupied Housing 336

CHAPTER 6 - HOUSING continued:

Families in Households 338
Table 359   Families in Households: Female Householders, Part 1-A 338
Table 360   Families in Households: Female Householders, Part 1-B 341
Table 361   Families in Households: Male Householders, Part 1-A 344
Table 362   Families in Households: Male Householders, Part 1-B 346
Table 363   Families in Households: Type and Tenure 349
Table 364   Families in Households: Type, Age of Own Children, Age, and Race. Part 1-A . . . 352
Table 365   Families in Households: Type, Age of Own Children, Age, and Race. Part 1-B . . . 355
Table 366   Families in Households: Type, Age of Own Children, Age, and Race. Part 2-A . . . 358
Table 367   Families in Households: Type, Age of Own Children, Age, and Race. Part 2-B . . . 360
Fuels 363
Table 368   House Fuels: Black-Occupied Units 363
Household Composition 365
Table 369   Household Composition: Black-Occupied Units 365
Household Vehicles 367
Table 370   Household Vehicles by Annual Mileage, Fuel Consumption, and Fuel
                    Expenditures: 1991 367
Table 371   Household Vehicles by Model Year and Fuel Efficiency: 1991 368
Householders, Mobility 369
Table 372   Householders: Previous Residence of Recent Movers 369
Table 373   Householders: Reasons for Move 371
Table 374   Persons in Previous and Current Residence 373
Table 375   Structure Type of Previous and Current Residence 374
Housing Conditions 375
Table 376   Height and Condition of Building: Black-Occupied Units 375
Housing Indicators 377
Table 377   Indicators of Quality: Black-Occupied Units 377
Housing Size 378
Table 378   Rooms in Unit: Income and Costs. Part 1 378
Table 379   Rooms in Unit: Income and Costs. Part 2 381
Table 380   Square Footage: Household and Unit Size 384
Table 381   Unit and Lot Size: Black-Occupied Units 386
Improvements 388
Table 382   Repairs, Improvements and Alterations 388
Income Characteristics 390
Table 383   Families and Primary Individuals: Income, Part 1-1 390
Table 384   Families and Primary Individuals: Income, Part 1-2 393
Table 385   Families and Primary Individuals: Income, Part 2-1 395
Table 386   Families and Primary Individuals: Income, Part 2-2 397
Table 387   Families and Primary Individuals: Income, Part 3-1 400
Table 388   Families and Primary Individuals: Income, Part 3-2 403
Table 389   Income Characteristics: Black-Occupied Units 406
Metropolitan Areas 408
Table 390   Metropolitan Areas: Black Householders in the Top 50 Metro Areas:
                    Characteristics, 1990 408
Table 391   Metropolitan Areas: Black Householders in the Top 50 Metro Areas: Home
                    Value and Rent, 1990 410
Mortgages 412
Table 392   Mortgage Characteristics: Owner Occupied Units, Part 1 412

CHAPTER 6 - HOUSING continued:

    Table 393   Mortgage Characteristics: Owner Occupied Units, Part 2 414

Physical Characteristics 416

    Table 394   Telephone Subscribers: 1984 and 1994 416

Residential Neighborhoods 417

    Table 395   Neighborhoods: Black Occupied Units 417

Subfamilies 420

    Table 396   Subfamilies: Type, Race, and Characteristics-1 420

    Table 397   Subfamilies: Type, Race, and Characteristics-2 422

Suburbs 424

    Table 398   Introductory Characteristics: Householders Outside Metropolitan Statistical
             Areas-1 424

    Table 399   Introductory Characteristics: Householders Outside Metropolitan Statistical
             Areas-2 424

    Table 400   Introductory Characteristics: Suburban Householders-1 425

    Table 401   Introductory Characteristics: Suburban Householders-2 426

Tenure 426

    Table 402   Tenure: Select Financial Characteristics of Householder. Part 1-1 426

    Table 403   Tenure: Select Financial Characteristics of Householder. Part 1-2 429

    Table 404   Tenure: Select Financial Characteristics of Householder. Part 1-3 431

Tenure in Housing 434

    Table 405   Occupied Housing by Race of Householder: 1920-1993 434

Values 435

    Table 406   Values: Owner Occupied Housing by Select Characteristics 435

    Table 407   Values: Select Characteristics. Part 1-1 436

    Table 408   Values: Select Characteristics. Part 1-2 439

    Table 409   Values: Select Characteristics. Part 2-1 441

    Table 410   Values: Select Characteristics. Part 2-2 444

    Table 411   Values: Select Characteristics. Part 3-1 446

    Table 412   Values: Select Characteristics. Part 3-2 448

CHAPTER 7 - INCOME, SPENDING, AND WEALTH 451

Expenditures 451

    Table 413   Buying Power: Black Consumer Buying Power in the Top 10 States, According
             to Amount: 1994 451

    Table 414   Total Expenditures: Mean Consumer Expenditures, by Race: 1993 452

Income/Earnings 453

    Table 415   Income: Aggregate and Mean Household Money Income, by Householder Age,
             Region, Household Size, and Race/Ethnic Origin: 1993 453

    Table 416   Income: Family and Nonfamily Median Money Income, by Family Type and
             Race/Ethnic Origin: 1993 454

    Table 417   Income: Percent Distribution of Family and Nonfamily Household Money
             Income, by Race/Ethnic Origin: 1993 455

    Table 418   Income: Percent Distribution of Household Money Income at Each Quintile and
             Top 5%, by Race/Ethnic Origin: 1993 456

    Table 419   Income: Percentage Distribution of Individual Money Income in Constant
             (1993) Dollars, by Race/Ethnic Origin: 1993 456

    Table 420   Income: Sources of Income Among the Elderly, by Race/Ethnic Origin: 1992 . . . 457

    Table 421   Income: Trends in Household Median Money Income in Current and Constant
             (1993) Dollars, by Race/Ethnic Origin: 1970-1993 457

CHAPTER 7 - INCOME, SPENDING, AND WEALTH continued:

    Table 422   Income: Trends in Median Income and Percent Distribution of Household
                Money Income in Constant (1993) Dollars, by Race/Ethnic Origin: 1970-1993 . . . 458

    Table 423   Income: Trends in Per Capita Money Income in Current and Constant (1993)
                Dollars, by Race/Ethnic Origin: 1970-1993 459

    Table 424   Relationships: Average Monthly Income, by Educational Attainment and
                Race/Ethnic Origin: 1993 460

    Table 425   Relationships: Full-Time Workers' (25 and Over) Median Earnings, by Gender,
                Educational Attainment, and Race: 1993 460

    Table 426   Salaries/Earnings: Full-Time Workers – Numbers and Median Weekly Earnings,
                by Gender and Race/Ethnic Origin: 1983-1994 461

    Table 427   Salaries/Earnings: Wage Earners at or Below $4.25/hr., by Race/Ethnic Origin:
                1994 461

    Table 428   Salaries: White and Minority Average Annual Salary of Non-Postal Federal
                Employees, Worldwide: 1991 462

    Table 429   Salaries: White and Minority Median Annual Salary of U.S. State and Local
                Government Employees, 1974 and 1991 463

  Poverty 464

    Table 430   Duration: Duration of Poverty in 1990-1991 Period, for Individuals, by
                Race/Ethnic Origin 464

    Table 431   Number/Percent: Individuals Below Poverty Level, by Income Definition and
                Race/Ethnic Origin: 1993 464

    Table 432   Number/Percent: Trends in Number and Percent of Individuals Below Poverty
                Level, by Race/Ethnic Origin: 1960-1993 465

    Table 433   Number/Percent: Trends in Persons/Families Below Poverty Level, by
                Race/Ethnic Origin (in percentages): 1973-1993 466

    Table 434   Number/Percent: Trends in Poverty Among Persons 65 and Over, by
                Race/Ethnic Origin: 1970-1993 467

    Table 435   Relationships: Age and Region of Persons Below Poverty Level, by Race/Ethnic
                Origin: 1993 468

    Table 436   Relationships: Effect of Social Security on Poverty, by Race: 1992 468

    Table 437   Relationships: Percent Going Into and Coming Out of Poverty, by Race/Ethnic
                Origin: 1991 to 1992 469

CHAPTER 8 - LABOR AND EMPLOYMENT 470

  Discouraged Workers 470

    Table 438   Discouraged Workers: Civilian Labor Force, 1992 470

  Displaced Workers 471

    Table 439   Displaced Workers: by Selected Characteristics: 1994 471

  Employers and Employment 472

    Table 440   Employment, by Industry: 1970-1994 472

  Employment and Unemployment 473

    Table 441   Employed and Unemployed: Full- and Part-time Workers by Age, Gender, and
                Race 473

  Employment in State and Local Governments 474

    Table 442   Employment Rates in State and Local Governments: Full-Time 474

    Table 443   Employment Rates in the State and Local Governments: Administrative and
                Professional Jobs 474

    Table 444   State and Local Government Employment by Gender and Population Group:
                Trends 1973-1991, Part 1 475

CHAPTER 8 - LABOR AND EMPLOYMENT continued:

Table 445   State and Local Government Employment by Gender and Population Group: Trends 1973-1991, Part 2 475

Table 446   State and Local Government Employment by Gender, Minorities, and Job Category: Trends, 1973-1991 476

Table 447   State and Local Government Employment by Population Group: Trends, 1973-1991 477

Employment in the Federal Government 478

Table 448   Employment Rates in the Federal Government 478

Table 449   Employment Rates in the Federal Government: Civilian Administrative and Professional 479

Employment in the Private Sector 479

Table 450   Employment Participation Rates in Major Private Industries: Whites, Minorities, and Women 479

Table 451   Employment Rates in the Private Sector: Managerial and Professional Jobs 480

Table 452   Private Sector Employment Rates of Minorities and Women by Job Category: 1966, 1978, and 1992 481

Table 453   Private Sector Employment Rates: by Gender and Race 1966-1992, Part 1 482

Table 454   Private Sector Employment Rates: by Gender and Race 1966-1992, Part 2 483

Table 455   Private Sector Total Employment Rates: Trends, 1966-1992 484

Labor Force 485

Table 456   Civilian Employment: Characteristics of the Civilian Noninstitutional Population. Part 1 485

Table 457   Civilian Employment: Characteristics of the Civilian Noninstitutional Population. Part 2 486

Table 458   Civilian Employment: Characteristics of the Civilian Noninstitutional Population. Part 3 488

Table 459   Civilian Employment: Employment Status of the Noninstitutional Population by Race, Gender, and Age 489

Table 460   Civilian Employment: School Enrollment and Characteristics of the Noninstitutional Population 16 to 24 Years of Age. Part 1-Enrolled 490

Table 461   Civilian Employment: School Enrollment and Characteristics of the Noninstitutional Population 16 to 24 Years of Age. Part 2-Not Enrolled 491

Table 462   Civilian Labor Force: Educational Level and Characteristics, 1970-1991 493

Table 463   Civilian Labor Force: Educational Level and Characteristics, 1992-1994 493

Table 464   Civilian Labor Force: Employment Status and Characteristics: 1994 494

Table 465   Civilian Labor Force: Employment Status of the Population by Race, Gender, and Age, Seasonally Adjusted. Part 1-1 495

Table 466   Civilian Labor Force: Employment Status of the Population by Race, Gender, and Age, Seasonally Adjusted. Part 1-2 496

Table 467   Civilian Labor Force: Employment Status of the Population by Race, Gender, and Age, Seasonally Adjusted. Part 2-1 497

Table 468   Civilian Labor Force: Employment Status of the Population by Race, Gender, and Age, Seasonally Adjusted. Part 2-2 498

Table 469   Civilian Labor Force: Employment Status of the Population by Race, Gender, and Age, Seasonally Adjusted. Part 3-1 500

Table 470   Civilian Labor Force: Employment Status of the Population by Race, Gender, and Age, Seasonally Adjusted. Part 3-2 501

Table 471   Civilian Labor Force: Employment Status of the Population: 1960-1994 502

Table 472   Civilians: School Enrollment and Labor Force: 1980 and 1993 503

CHAPTER 8 - LABOR AND EMPLOYMENT continued:

Table 473	Families Employed: Married-Couple Families in the Labor Force. Part 1-1	504
Table 474	Families Employed: Married-Couple Families in the Labor Force. Part 1-2	505
Table 475	Families Employed: Married-Couple Families in the Labor Force. Part 2-1	507
Table 476	Families Employed: Married-Couple Families in the Labor Force. Part 2-2	508
Table 477	Labor Force Participation: Wives with Husbands Present: 1975-1994	510
Table 478	Multiple Jobholders: Characteristics by Gender: 1994	510
Table 479	Multiple Jobholders: Rate, Race, and Hispanic Origin-1	511
Table 480	Multiple Jobholders: Rate, Race, and Hispanic Origin-2	511

Labor Force Projections 512

Table 481	Civilian Labor Force: Participation Rates and Projections: 1970-2005. Part 1	512
Table 482	Civilian Labor Force: Participation Rates and Projections: 1970-2005. Part 2	513

Occupations 514

Table 483	Employed Persons: Employment by Occupation, Race, and Gender, 1994-95	514
Table 484	Employed Persons: Nonagricultural Industries, 1996	515
Table 485	Occupational Employment in Private Industry: Accounting, Auditing and Bookkeeping Services	516
Table 486	Occupational Employment in Private Industry: Aeronautical Guidance and Navigation Systems	516
Table 487	Occupational Employment in Private Industry: Agriculture, Forestry, and Fishing	517
Table 488	Occupational Employment in Private Industry: Aircraft and Parts	518
Table 489	Occupational Employment in Private Industry: All Industries	519
Table 490	Occupational Employment in Private Industry: Amusement and Recreation Services	519
Table 491	Occupational Employment in Private Industry: Automobile Rental and Leasing	520
Table 492	Occupational Employment in Private Industry: Bakery Products	521
Table 493	Occupational Employment in Private Industry: Beverages	522
Table 494	Occupational Employment in Private Industry: Business Services	522
Table 495	Occupational Employment in Private Industry: Combination Utility Services	523
Table 496	Occupational Employment in Private Industry: Commercial Banks	524
Table 497	Occupational Employment in Private Industry: Commercial Printing	525
Table 498	Occupational Employment in Private Industry: Communication Equipment	525
Table 499	Occupational Employment in Private Industry: Computer Programming and Data Processing	526
Table 500	Occupational Employment in Private Industry: Computer and Office Equipment	527
Table 501	Occupational Employment in Private Industry: Construction	528
Table 502	Occupational Employment in Private Industry: Construction and Related Machinery	528
Table 503	Occupational Employment in Private Industry: Converted Paper and Paperboard Products	529
Table 504	Occupational Employment in Private Industry: Dairy Products	530
Table 505	Occupational Employment in Private Industry: Department Stores	531
Table 506	Occupational Employment in Private Industry: Drugs	532
Table 507	Occupational Employment in Private Industry: Eating and Drinking Places	532
Table 508	Occupational Employment in Private Industry: Electric Lighting and Wiring Equipment	533
Table 509	Occupational Employment in Private Industry: Electric Services	534
Table 510	Occupational Employment in Private Industry: Electrical Goods	535
Table 511	Occupational Employment in Private Industry: Electronic Components and Accessories	536

CHAPTER 8 - LABOR AND EMPLOYMENT continued:

Table 512   Occupational Employment in Private Industry: Engineering and Architectural Services 537

Table 513   Occupational Employment in Private Industry: Family Clothing Stores 537

Table 514   Occupational Employment in Private Industry: Finance, Insurance, and Real Estate 538

Table 515   Occupational Employment in Private Industry: Fire, Marine, and Casualty Insurance 539

Table 516   Occupational Employment in Private Industry: Gas Production and Distribution . . 540

Table 517   Occupational Employment in Private Industry: Groceries and Related Products . . 541

Table 518   Occupational Employment in Private Industry: Grocery Stores 542

Table 519   Occupational Employment in Private Industry: Health Insurance and Medical Service Plans 543

Table 520   Occupational Employment in Private Industry: Health Services 544

Table 521   Occupational Employment in Private Industry: Home Health Care Services 545

Table 522   Occupational Employment in Private Industry: Hospitals 546

Table 523   Occupational Employment in Private Industry: Hotels, Motels, and Tourist Courts 547

Table 524   Occupational Employment in Private Industry: Household Appliances 548

Table 525   Occupational Employment in Private Industry: Household Furniture 548

Table 526   Occupational Employment in Private Industry: Industrial Inorganic Chemicals . . . 549

Table 527   Occupational Employment in Private Industry: Insurance Agents, Brokers and Service 550

Table 528   Occupational Employment in Private Industry: Knitting Mills 551

Table 529   Occupational Employment in Private Industry: Legal Services 552

Table 530   Occupational Employment in Private Industry: Life Insurance 553

Table 531   Occupational Employment in Private Industry: Lumber and Building Materials . . 554

Table 532   Occupational Employment in Private Industry: Machinery, Equipment, and Supplies 555

Table 533   Occupational Employment in Private Industry: Management and Public Relations Services 556

Table 534   Occupational Employment in Private Industry: Manufacturing – Durable Goods . . 557

Table 535   Occupational Employment in Private Industry: Manufacturing – Nondurable Goods 557

Table 536   Occupational Employment in Private Industry: Meat Products 558

Table 537   Occupational Employment in Private Industry: Medical Instruments and Supplies 559

Table 538   Occupational Employment in Private Industry: Metalworking Machinery 560

Table 539   Occupational Employment in Private Industry: Millwork, Plywood and Structural Members 561

Table 540   Occupational Employment in Private Industry: Mining 562

Table 541   Occupational Employment in Private Industry: Miscellaneous Food and Related Products 563

Table 542   Occupational Employment in Private Industry: Motor Vehicles and Automotive Equipment 563

Table 543   Occupational Employment in Private Industry: Motor Vehicles and Equipment . . 564

Table 544   Occupational Employment in Private Industry: Nursing and Personal Care Facilities 565

Table 545   Occupational Employment in Private Industry: Occupational Distribution 566

Table 546   Occupational Employment in Private Industry: Participation Rates 567

CHAPTER 8 - LABOR AND EMPLOYMENT continued:

Table 547   Occupational Employment in Private Industry: Personnel Supply Services 567
Table 548   Occupational Employment in Private Industry: Petroleum Refining 568
Table 549   Occupational Employment in Private Industry: Plastic Materials and Synthetics . . 569
Table 550   Occupational Employment in Private Industry: Preserved Fruits and Vegetables . . 570
Table 551   Occupational Employment in Private Industry: Professional and Commercial
                Equipment 571
Table 552   Occupational Employment in Private Industry: Public Warehousing and Storage . . 572
Table 553   Occupational Employment in Private Industry: Publishing and Printing 573
Table 554   Occupational Employment in Private Industry: Railroads 574
Table 555   Occupational Employment in Private Industry: Refrigeration and Service
                Machinery 574
Table 556   Occupational Employment in Private Industry: Research, Development and
                Testing Services 575
Table 557   Occupational Employment in Private Industry: Residential Services 576
Table 558   Occupational Employment in Private Industry: Retail Trade 577
Table 559   Occupational Employment in Private Industry: Savings Institutions 578
Table 560   Occupational Employment in Private Industry: Scheduled Air Transportation . . 579
Table 561   Occupational Employment in Private Industry: Security Brokers 579
Table 562   Occupational Employment in Private Industry: Ship and Boat Building and
                Repairing 580
Table 563   Occupational Employment in Private Industry: Shopping Goods Stores 581
Table 564   Occupational Employment in Private Industry: Telephone Communication . . . 582
Table 565   Occupational Employment in Private Industry: Transportation and Public
                Utilities 583
Table 566   Occupational Employment in Private Industry: Trucking and Courier Services . . 584
Table 567   Occupational Employment in Private Industry: Weaving Mills, Cotton 584
Table 568   Occupational Employment in Private Industry: Wholesale Trade 585
Table 569   Occupations of the Employed: Characteristics, 1994 586
Unemployment 587
Table 570   Unemployed Persons: Cause and Race, 1994-95 587
Table 571   Unemployed Persons: Duration 588
Table 572   Unemployed Persons: Marital Status, Race, Age, and Gender, 1994-95 589
Table 573   Unemployed Workers: Trends, 1980-1994 590
Table 574   Unemployment Rates by Population Group: 1980 and 1992 591
Table 575   Unemployment Rates: Selected Unemployment Rates, by Race, 1985-1995 . . . 591
Table 576   Unemployment Rates: Trends by Sex and Race: 1970-1991 592
Table 577   Unemployment Rates: Unemployed Workers by Month, Race, Hispanic
                Origin-1 593
Table 578   Unemployment Rates: Unemployed Workers by Month, Race, Hispanic
                Origin-2 594
Table 579   Unemployment and Unemployment Rates: Trends by Education, Sex, Race, and
                Hispanic Origin: 1992-1994 594
Unions 595
Table 580   Labor Unions by Selected Characteristics: 1983 and 1994. Part 1 595
Table 581   Labor Unions by Selected Characteristics: 1983 and 1994. Part 2 596
Work Schedules 597
Table 582   Varied Schedules: Workers on Flexible and Shift Schedules: 1995 to 1991 597
Work at Home 597
Table 583   Workers Doing Job-Related Work at Home: 1991 597

CHAPTER 8 - LABOR AND EMPLOYMENT continued:

Workers and Computers 598
    Table 584   Workers Using Computers on the Job: 1993 598

CHAPTER 9 - MISCELLANY 599
  Arts and Entertainment 599
    Table 585   Arts Activities: Attendance Rates, 1992 599
    Table 586   Arts Activities: Participation Rates, 1992 600
  Military and Military Affairs 600
    Table 587   Personnel: Profile of the Ready Reserve, by Gender and Race/Ethnic Origin:
           1990-1993 600
  Multimedia Audience-Summary 601
    Table 588   Multimedia Audiences: 1994 601
  Religion 602
    Table 589   Religious Bodies: Characteristics of Black Churches and Organizations 602
  Television Production 602
    Table 590   Production Costs: Prime-Time Black Shows 602

CHAPTER 10 - POLITICS AND ELECTIONS 604
  Elected Officials 604
    Table 591   Black Elected Officials: Distribution by Office, 1970-1993, and Region and State,
           1993 604
    Table 592   Elected Officials: Characteristics of Members of Congress, 1981-1995. Part 1 . . . 606
    Table 593   Elected Officials: Characteristics of Members of Congress, 1981-1995. Part 2 . . . 607
    Table 594   Elected Officials: Local Officials, by Gender, Race, Hispanic Origin, and Type
           of Government, 1992 608
  Male Officials 609
    Table 595   Male County Officials by Race and Ethnicity, Part 1 609
    Table 596   Male County Officials by Race and Ethnicity, Part 2 609
    Table 597   Male Municipal Officials by Race and Ethnicity, Part 1 610
    Table 598   Male Municipal Officials by Race and Ethnicity, Part 2 611
  Political Parties 612
    Table 599   Political Party Identification: Adult Attachment, 1972-1994, and Selected
           Characteristics, 1994 612
  Voters and Voting 612
    Table 600   Voting and Registration: Indicators for 1980 High School Sophomores
           Registered and Voting, Selected Years, 1984-1992 612
    Table 601   Voting-Age Population: Registered and Voted, 1980-1994. Part 1 614
    Table 602   Voting-Age Population: Registered and Voted, 1980-1994. Part 2 614
    Table 603   Voting-Age Population: Registered and Voted, 1980-1994. Part 3 615
  Women Officials 615
    Table 604   Female County Officials by Race and Ethnicity, Part 1 615
    Table 605   Female County Officials by Race and Ethnicity, Part 2 616
    Table 606   Female Municipal Officials by Race and Ethnicity, Part 1 616
    Table 607   Female Municipal Officials by Race and Ethnicity, Part 2 617

CHAPTER 11 - POPULATION 618
  Ancestry 618
    Table 608   Top 15 Ancestry Groups: 1990 618

CHAPTER 11 - POPULATION continued:

Black Households 619
    Table 609   Black Households: Characteristics, March 1994 619
    Table 610   Black Nonfamily Households: Characteristics, March 1994. Part 1 620
    Table 611   Black Nonfamily Households: Characteristics, March 1994. Part 2 622
Black Owner Households 624
    Table 612   Black Owner Households: Age 624
    Table 613   Black Owner Households: Characteristics. Part 1. 625
    Table 614   Black Owner Households: Characteristics. Part 2. 626
Black Renter Households 627
    Table 615   Black Renter Households: Age 627
    Table 616   Black Renter Households: Characteristics. Part 1. 629
    Table 617   Black Renter Households: Characteristics. Part 2. 630
Characteristics 631
    Table 618   Native and Foreign-Born: Selected Characteristics of Natives and Foreign-Born
            Population by Citizenship and Year of Entry, 1994 631
    Table 619   Population Changes: Components of Population Changes, 1990 to 1993, and
            Projections, 1995 and 2000 632
    Table 620   Resident Population: Age and Hispanic Origin: 1980 to 1994. Part 1 633
    Table 621   Resident Population: Age and Hispanic Origin: 1980 to 1994. Part 2 635
    Table 622   Resident Population: Age, Gender, Race, and Hispanic Origin of the
            Population: 1950 to 1992. Part 1 636
    Table 623   Resident Population: Age, Gender, Race, and Hispanic Origin of the
            Population: 1950 to 1992. Part 2 638
Children and Parents 639
    Table 624   Population Characteristics: Children Under 18 Years Old, by Presence of
            Parents: 1970 to 1994 639
Distribution 640
    Table 625   Population by Region: Resident Population, Region and Division, 1960 to 1994 . . 640
Household Characteristics 642
    Table 626   All-Black Households: Age 642
    Table 627   All-Black Households: Characteristics. Part 1. 643
    Table 628   All-Black Households: Characteristics. Part 2. 644
    Table 629   Households by Type, Age, and Size: March 1994. Part 1 645
    Table 630   Households by Type, Age, and Size: March 1994. Part 2 647
    Table 631   Households by Type, Age, and Size: March 1994. Part 1-1 - Northeast 648
    Table 632   Households by Type, Age, and Size: March 1994. Part 1-2 - Northeast 649
    Table 633   Households by Type, Age, and Size: March 1994. Part 2-1 - Midwest 650
    Table 634   Households by Type, Age, and Size: March 1994. Part 2-2 - Midwest 651
    Table 635   Households by Type, Age, and Size: March 1994. Part 3-1 - South 653
    Table 636   Households by Type, Age, and Size: March 1994. Part 3-2 - South 654
    Table 637   Households by Type, Age, and Size: March 1994. Part 4-1 - West 655
    Table 638   Households by Type, Age, and Size: March 1994. Part 4-2 - West 656
Marital Status 658
    Table 639   Marital Status: Gender, Race, and Hispanic Origin: 1970 to 1994 658
    Table 640   Marital Status: Married Couples of Same or Mixed Races and Origins: 1970 to
            1994 659
    Table 641   Marital Status: Number and Percent of Unmarried Women by Age and Race,
            1960 to 1992 660

CHAPTER 11 - POPULATION continued:

Mobility 661

Table 642   Geographical Mobility: Characteristics of Movers Within and Between
Metropolitan and Nonmetroplitan Areas, 1993 661

Table 643   Geographical Mobility: Detailed Mobility of Family Householders:
Characteristics. Part 1-1 662

Table 644   Geographical Mobility: Detailed Mobility of Family Householders:
Characteristics. Part 1-2 663

Table 645   Geographical Mobility: Detailed Mobility of Family Householders:
Characteristics. Part 2-1 664

Table 646   Geographical Mobility: Detailed Mobility of Family Householders:
Characteristics. Part 2-2 665

Table 647   Geographical Mobility: Detailed Mobility of Householders, by Race and
Income. Part 1-1 666

Table 648   Geographical Mobility: Detailed Mobility of Householders, by Race and
Income. Part 1-2 667

Table 649   Geographical Mobility: Detailed Mobility of Householders, by Race and
Income. Part 2-1 668

Table 650   Geographical Mobility: Detailed Mobility of Householders, by Race and
Income. Part 2-2 669

Table 651   Geographical Mobility: Detailed Mobility of Householders, by Race and
Income. Part 3-1 670

Table 652   Geographical Mobility: Detailed Mobility of Householders, by Race and
Income. Part 3-2 671

Table 653   Geographical Mobility: Detailed Mobility of Persons 16 Years and Over, by
Race, Gender, and Labor Force Status. Part 1-1 672

Table 654   Geographical Mobility: Detailed Mobility of Persons 16 Years and Over, by
Race, Gender, and Labor Force Status. Part 1-2 673

Table 655   Geographical Mobility: Detailed Mobility of Persons 16 Years and Over, by
Race, Gender, and Labor Force Status. Part 2-1 675

Table 656   Geographical Mobility: Detailed Mobility of Persons 16 Years and Over, by
Race, Gender, and Labor Force Status. Part 2-2 676

Table 657   Geographical Mobility: Detailed Mobility of Persons 16 Years and Over, by
Race, Gender, and Labor Force Status. Part 3-1 677

Table 658   Geographical Mobility: Detailed Mobility of Persons 16 Years and Over, by
Race, Gender, and Labor Force Status. Part 3-2 678

Table 659   Geographical Mobility: Detailed Mobility of Persons 25 Years and Over, by
Race, Age, and Education. Part 1-1 679

Table 660   Geographical Mobility: Detailed Mobility of Persons 25 Years and Over, by
Race, Age, and Education. Part 1-2 681

Table 661   Geographical Mobility: Detailed Mobility of Persons 25 Years and Over, by
Race, Age, and Education. Part 2-1 682

Table 662   Geographical Mobility: Detailed Mobility of Persons 25 Years and Over, by
Race, Age, and Education. Part 2-2 684

Table 663   Geographical Mobility: Detailed Mobility of Persons 25 Years and Over, by
Race, Age, and Education. Part 3-1 685

Table 664   Geographical Mobility: Detailed Mobility of Persons 25 Years and Over, by
Race, Age, and Education. Part 3-2 687

Table 665   Geographical Mobility: Detailed Mobility, by Household and Family Status,
Region, and Race and Hispanic Origin. Part 1-1 688

CHAPTER 11 - POPULATION continued:

Table 666   Geographical Mobility: Detailed Mobility, by Household and Family Status, Region, and Race and Hispanic Origin. Part 1-2 689

Table 667   Geographical Mobility: Detailed Mobility, by Household and Family Status, Region, and Race and Hispanic Origin. Part 2-1 690

Table 668   Geographical Mobility: Detailed Mobility, by Household and Family Status, Region, and Race and Hispanic Origin. Part 2-2 691

Table 669   Geographical Mobility: Detailed Mobility, by Household and Family Status, Region, and Race and Hispanic Origin. Part 3-1 692

Table 670   Geographical Mobility: Detailed Mobility, by Household and Family Status, Region, and Race and Hispanic Origin. Part 3-2 693

Table 671   Geographical Mobility: Detailed Mobility, by Household and Family Status, Region, and Race and Hispanic Origin. Part 4-1 694

Table 672   Geographical Mobility: Detailed Mobility, by Household and Family Status, Region, and Race and Hispanic Origin. Part 4-2 695

Table 673   Geographical Mobility: Detailed Mobility, by Household and Family Status, Region, and Race and Hispanic Origin. Part 5-1 696

Table 674   Geographical Mobility: Detailed Mobility, by Household and Family Status, Region, and Race and Hispanic Origin. Part 5-2 697

Table 675   Geographical Mobility: Detailed Mobility, by Household and Family Status, Region, and Race and Hispanic Origin. Part 6-1 698

Table 676   Geographical Mobility: Detailed Mobility, by Household and Family Status, Region, and Race and Hispanic Origin. Part 6-2 699

Table 677   Geographical Mobility: Detailed Mobility, by Household and Family Status, Region, and Race. Part 1-1 700

Table 678   Geographical Mobility: Detailed Mobility, by Household and Family Status, Region, and Race. Part 1-2 701

Table 679   Geographical Mobility: Detailed Mobility, by Household and Family Status, Region, and Race. Part 2-1 702

Table 680   Geographical Mobility: Detailed Mobility, by Household and Family Status, Region, and Race. Part 2-2 703

Table 681   Geographical Mobility: Detailed Mobility, by Household and Family Status, Region, and Race. Part 3-1 704

Table 682   Geographical Mobility: Detailed Mobility, by Household and Family Status, Region, and Race. Part 3-2 705

Table 683   Geographical Mobility: Detailed Mobility, by Race, Gender, and Age. Part 1-1 . . . 706

Table 684   Geographical Mobility: Detailed Mobility, by Race, Gender, and Age. Part 1-2 . . . 707

Table 685   Geographical Mobility: Detailed Mobility, by Race, Gender, and Age. Part 2-1 . . . 708

Table 686   Geographical Mobility: Detailed Mobility, by Race, Gender, and Age. Part 2-2 . . . 709

Table 687   Geographical Mobility: Detailed Mobility, by Race, Gender, and Age. Part 3-1 . . . 710

Table 688   Geographical Mobility: Detailed Mobility, by Race, Gender, and Age. Part 3-2 . . . 711

Table 689   Geographical Mobility: Detailed Mobility, by Selected Characteristics. Part 1-1 . . 713

Table 690   Geographical Mobility: Detailed Mobility, by Selected Characteristics. Part 1-2 . . 713

Table 691   Geographical Mobility: Detailed Mobility, by Selected Characteristics. Part 2-1 . . 714

Table 692   Geographical Mobility: Detailed Mobility, by Selected Characteristics. Part 2-2 . . 714

Table 693   Geographical Mobility: Frequency Distribution of Selected Characteristics by Type of Move, 1993 715

Table 694   Geographical Mobility: General Mobility of Family Householders, by Race, Hispanic Origin and Type of Householder, and Presence of Children. Part 1 . . . 715

Table 695   Geographical Mobility: General Mobility of Family Householders, by Race, Hispanic Origin and Type of Householder, and Presence of Children. Part 2 . . . 716

CHAPTER 11 - POPULATION continued:

Table 696   Geographical Mobility: General Mobility of Householder, by Race, Gender, and Household Income. Part 1-1 717

Table 697   Geographical Mobility: General Mobility of Householder, by Race, Gender, and Household Income. Part 1-2 719

Table 698   Geographical Mobility: General Mobility of Householder, by Race, Gender, and Household Income. Part 2-1 720

Table 699   Geographical Mobility: General Mobility of Householder, by Race, Gender, and Household Income. Part 2-2 721

Table 700   Geographical Mobility: General Mobility of Householder, by Race, Gender, and Household Income. Part 3-1 722

Table 701   Geographical Mobility: General Mobility of Householder, by Race, Gender, and Household Income. Part 3-2 723

Table 702   Geographical Mobility: General Mobility of Persons 16 Years and Over, by Race, Gender, and Labor Force Status 724

Table 703   Geographical Mobility: General Mobility of Persons 25 Years and Over, by Race, Age, and Education 725

Table 704   Geographical Mobility: General Mobility, By Selected Characteristics. Part 1 . . . 727

Table 705   Geographical Mobility: General Mobility, By Selected Characteristics. Part 2 . . . 727

Table 706   Geographical Mobility: General Mobility, by Household and Family Status, Region, Race, and Hispanic Origin. Part 1 728

Table 707   Geographical Mobility: General Mobility, by Household and Family Status, Region, Race, and Hispanic Origin. Part 2 729

Table 708   Geographical Mobility: General Mobility, by Household and Family Status, Region, Race, and Hispanic Origin. Part 3 730

Table 709   Geographical Mobility: General Mobility, by Race. Part 1 731

Table 710   Geographical Mobility: General Mobility, by Race. Part 2 732

Table 711   Geographical Mobility: General Mobility, by Race. Part 3 733

Table 712   Geographical Mobility: Inmigrants, Outmigrants, and Net Migration for Large MSA's: Characteristics-1 734

Table 713   Geographical Mobility: Inmigrants, Outmigrants, and Net Migration for Large MSA's: Characteristics-2 736

Table 714   Geographical Mobility: Inmigrants, Outmigrants, and Net Migration for Regions, by Select Characteristics-1 737

Table 715   Geographical Mobility: Inmigrants, Outmigrants, and Net Migration for Regions, by Select Characteristics-2 739

Table 716   Geographical Mobility: Inmigration, Outmigration, and Net Migration for MSA's and Nonmetropolitan Areas: Characteristics. Part 1 740

Table 717   Geographical Mobility: Inmigration, Outmigration, and Net Migration for MSA's and Nonmetropolitan Areas: Characteristics. Part 2 741

Table 718   Geographical Mobility: Inmigration, Outmigration, and Net Migration for MSA's and Nonmetropolitan Areas: Characteristics. Part 3 743

Table 719   Geographical Mobility: Inmigration, Outmigration, and Net Migration for MSA's and Nonmetropolitan Areas: Characteristics. Part 4 744

Table 720   Geographical Mobility: Inmigration, Outmigration, and Net Migration for MSA's and Nonmetropolitan Areas: Characteristics. Part 5 745

Table 721   Geographical Mobility: Migration Flows Between Regions, by Selected Characteristics-1 746

Table 722   Geographical Mobility: Migration Flows Between Regions, by Selected Characteristics-2 747

CHAPTER 11 - POPULATION continued:

Table 723   Geographical Mobility: Mobility and Region of Residence, by Race. Part 1 749
Table 724   Geographical Mobility: Mobility and Region of Residence, by Race. Part 2 750
Table 725   Geographical Mobility: Mobility and Region of Residence, by Race. Part 3 751
Table 726   Geographical Mobility: Mobility and Region of Residence, by Race. Part 4 752
Table 727   Geographical Mobility: Mobility and Region of Residence, by Race. Part 5 753
Table 728   Geographical Mobility: Movers Within and Between States and Regions by Selected Characteristics-1 754
Table 729   Geographical Mobility: Movers Within and Between States and Regions by Selected Characteristics-2 755
Table 730   Geographical Mobility: Movers Within the Same MSA/PMSA by Selected Characteristics, 1993 757
Table 731   Geographical Mobility: Rates by Selected Characteristics, 1993 757
Table 732   Geographical Mobility: Size and Type of Area at Both Dates, by Race. Part 1-1 . . 758
Table 733   Geographical Mobility: Size and Type of Area at Both Dates, by Race. Part 1-2 . . 759
Table 734   Geographical Mobility: Size and Type of Area at Both Dates, by Race. Part 2-1 . . 760
Table 735   Geographical Mobility: Size and Type of Area at Both Dates, by Race. Part 2-2 . . 761
Table 736   Geographical Mobility: Sunbelt Mobility, by Selected Characteristics-1 762
Table 737   Geographical Mobility: Sunbelt Mobility, by Selected Characteristics-2 762
Projections 763
Table 738   Population Projections: Hispanic and Non-Hispanic Population. By Age and Gender: 1995 to 2025 763
Table 739   Population Projections: Race and Status, 1995 to 2010 765
Table 740   Resident Population: Projected Trends, 1995 to 2025 767
Resident Population 768
Table 741   Characteristics: Percent Distribution and Median Age, 1850-1994 and Projections, 1995-2050 768
Table 742   Characteristics: Selected Characteristics of the Population, 1790-1994 and Projections, 1995-2050 769
Table 743   Resident Population: Age and Race: 1980 to 1994. Part 1 770
Table 744   Resident Population: Age and Race: 1980 to 1994. Part 2 772
Table 745   Resident Population: Hispanic Origin Status, 1980-1994, and Projections, 1995-2050 773
Table 746   Resident Population: Race, 1980-1994, and Projections, 1995-2050 775
Table 747   Resident Population: Race, Hispanic Origin, and Single Years of Age: 1994. Part 1 777
Table 748   Resident Population: Race, Hispanic Origin, and Single Years of Age: 1994. Part 2 779
Social and Economic Characteristics 781
Table 749   Social and Economic Characteristics: Black and White Population: 1980 to 1994 . . 781

CHAPTER 12 - SOCIAL AND HUMAN SERVICES 783
Child Support and Alimony 783
Table 750   Child Support: Selected Characteristics of Custodial Parents: 1991 783
Government Assistance Programs 784
Table 751   Participants in Selected Means-Tested Government Assistance Programs: 1987 to 1991 784
Table 752   Public Assistance: Food Stamp Mothers and Nonfood Stamp Mothers: Characteristics: Summer 1993 785
Table 753   Public Assistance: Percentage of Persons Aged 25-35 Receiving AFDC or Public Assistance by Years of Schooling: 1972-92 785

CHAPTER 12 - SOCIAL AND HUMAN SERVICES continued:

Pension Coverage of Workers 786
    Table 754   Pensions Plan Coverage: Workers by Selected Characteristics: 1993 786
Uninsured 787
    Table 755   Percent of Persons Under 65 Years of Age Who are Uninsured, by Family
               Income: 1993 787
    Table 756   Percent of Persons Under 65 Years of Age Who are Uninsured: Characteristics:
               1993 788
Volunteer Workers 788
    Table 757   Adult Volunteer Workers: 1993 788
Work Disability 789
    Table 758   Persons With Work Disability: Selected Characteristics, 1992 789
Work Disability and Assistance Programs 790
    Table 759   Work Disability: Selected Characteristics of Persons, 1993 790

CHAPTER 13 - SPORTS AND LEISURE 791
Leisure 791
    Table 760   Activities: Percent of Persons Participating in Various Leisure Activities: 1992 . . . 791
    Table 761   Expenditures: Money Spent per Consumer Unit for Entertainment and
               Reading, by Race: 1985-1993 792
    Table 762   Hunting/Guns: Percent of Gun Ownership, by Race: 1974-1993 792
Leisure Sports 793
    Table 763   Golf: Black Participation in Leisure Golf During the 1980s: 1980-1989 793
    Table 764   Golf: Growth in Black Participation in Leisure Golf: 1984-1989 793
Sports 794
    Table 765   College Basketball: College Sports' Top 95-96 Players   794
    Table 766   College Basketball: All-Time Final Four Super Teams 794
    Table 767   College Basketball: Institutions with Black Head Coaches in the NCAA Division
               I Men's Basketball Tournament: 1995 795
    Table 768   College Football: Football Digest's College All-Americans: 1995   . . . 795
    Table 769   NCAA Affiliates: NCAA Awards: 1995 796
    Table 770   NCAA Affiliates: Percent of African-American Players and Head Coaches in
               NCAA Football and Men's Basketball: 1992 796
    Table 771   Professional Baseball: 1995 Batting and Pitching Leaders 797
    Table 772   Professional Baseball: 1995 Home Run Leaders 798
    Table 773   Professional Baseball: 1995 League Leaders 798
    Table 774   Professional Baseball: 1995 Players who Led the Pack in Selected Categories . . . 799
    Table 775   Professional Baseball: African-American Head Coaches and Player Positions in
               Major League Baseball: 1993 799
    Table 776   Professional Baseball: Individual World Series Leaders: 1903-1994 800
    Table 777   Professional Baseball: Leaders in Single World Series 800
    Table 778   Professional Baseball: MVP, Cy Young, and Rookie-of-the-Year Awards, by
               Decade-I 801
    Table 779   Professional Baseball: MVP, Cy Young, and Rookie-of-the-Year Awards, by
               Decade-II . . . . : 802
    Table 780   Professional Baseball: Most World Series Home Runs for All Series 802
    Table 781   Professional Baseball: Personnel Whose Uniform Numbers Have Been Retired,
               by League and Team 803
    Table 782   Professional Baseball: Players 15 Years or More with One Team 804
    Table 783   Professional Baseball: Players with the Most RBIs per 100 At-Bats 804

CHAPTER 13 - SPORTS AND LEISURE continued:

Table 784	Professional Baseball: Prolific Home Run Hitters Among Retired and Active Players	805
Table 785	Professional Baseball: Season Leaders in Regular Games: 1990-1993	805
Table 786	Professional Baseball: World Series 400 Hitters, by Decade: 1900-1993	806
Table 787	Professional Baseball: World Series Honors: 1955-1995	806
Table 788	Professional Baseball: World Series Leading Batters, by Decade: 1900-1993	807
Table 789	Professional Baseball: World Series Pitchers Who Had 10 or More Strikeouts in a Series Game, by Decade: 1903-1980	808
Table 790	Professional Basketball: 1994-95 Holders of NBA Highs and Lows, by Category	808
Table 791	Professional Basketball: 1994-95 NBA Season Leaders, by Category	809
Table 792	Professional Basketball: 1994-95 Top Tenners, by Category	810
Table 793	Professional Basketball: ABA Career Leaders, by Category: 1968-1976	810
Table 794	Professional Basketball: African-American Head Coaches and Player Positions in the National Basketball Association: 1993	811
Table 795	Professional Basketball: All-Star Game Statistics and Records	811
Table 796	Professional Basketball: Basketball Hall-of-Famers, by Decade of Election: 1959-1995	812
Table 797	Professional Basketball: Continental Basketball Association Records and Leaders, by Category	813
Table 798	Professional Basketball: NBA Award Winners: 1994-95	813
Table 799	Professional Basketball: NBA Career Leaders, by Category	814
Table 800	Professional Basketball: NBA Playoff Leaders, by Category, through 1995	814
Table 801	Professional Basketball: Top Statistical Leaders in Men's NCAA Tournaments: 1957-1995	815
Table 802	Professional Football: AFC and NFC Individual Leaders: 1995	816
Table 803	Professional Football: African-American Head Coaches and Player Positions in the National Football League: 1992	816
Table 804	Professional Football: All-Madden Hall of Fame (1992-1995) and 1995 All-Madden Team	817
Table 805	Professional Football: Decade Players of the Year According to *Football Digest*: 1973-1995	818
Table 806	Professional Football: First Team All Pros, According to Football Digest: 1995	819
Table 807	Professional Football: NFL Passing, Rushing, and Receiving Yearly Leaders, by Decade: 1932-1994	819
Table 808	Professional Football: NFL Scoring, Field Goal, and Punt Return Yearly Leaders, by Decade: 1932-1994	820
Table 809	Professional Football: NFL Scoring, Kickoff Return, Punting, and Interception Yearly Leaders, by Decade: 1932-1994	821
Table 810	Professional Football: NFL Single Season Individual All-Time Records, by Record Category	821
Table 811	Professional Football: Super Bowl Fumbles, Yards Gained, and Sacks Records	822
Table 812	Professional Football: Super Bowl Passing and Pass Receiving Records	822
Table 813	Professional Football: Super Bowl Service, Scoring, and Rushing Records	823

CHAPTER 14 - THE FAMILY 825

Children 825

Table 814	1980 High School Sophomores in 1992: Percent Distribution of Number of Children of 1980 High School Sophomore Cohort, by Race/Ethnic Origin: 1992	825
Table 815	Living Arrangements: Parent(s) with Whom Children Under 18 Live, by Age of Parent(s) and Race/Ethnic Origin: 1994-I	826

CHAPTER 14 - THE FAMILY continued:

Table 816 Living Arrangements: Parent(s) with Whom Children Under 18 Live, by Age of Parent(s) and Race/Ethnic Origin: 1994-II 826

Table 817 Living Arrangements: Parent(s) with Whom Children Under 18 Live, by Educational Attainment and Employment Status of Parent(s), and Race/Ethnic Origin: 1994-I 827

Table 818 Living Arrangements: Parent(s) with Whom Children Under 18 Live, by Educational Attainment and Employment Status of Parent(s), and Race/Ethnic Origin: 1994-II 828

Table 819 Living Arrangements: Parent(s) with Whom Children Under 18 Live, by Family Income, Home Tenure, and Race/Ethnic Origin: 1994-I 828

Table 820 Living Arrangements: Parent(s) with Whom Children Under 18 Live, by Family Income, Home Tenure, and Race/Ethnic Origin: 1994-II 829

Table 821 Poverty: Trends in Children Living in Poverty, by Race/Ethnic Origin: 1970-1993 830

Table 822 Relationships: Age of Own Black Children in Families, by Age of Householder: 1994. Part 1 831

Table 823 Relationships: Age of Own Black Children in Families, by Age of Householder: 1994. Part 2 832

Table 824 Relationships: Age of Own Black Children in Family Groups, by Householder's Educational Attainment: 1994 833

Table 825 Relationships: Age of Own Children in All Black Families and Families with Householders Under 45, by Family Type: 1994 834

Table 826 Relationships: Age of Own Children in Black Families, in Relation to Family Type and Residence Area: 1994 835

Table 827 Relationships: Own Black Children Under 18, in Families, by Subfamily Type: 1994 836

Family Types 837

Table 828 Heads/Householders: Trends in Married Couple, Male-Headed, and Female-Headed Households, by Race/Ethnic Origin: 1970-1994 837

Table 829 Relationships: Age and Gender in Black Female-Headed Families, by Age of Householder: 1994 838

Table 830 Relationships: Age and Gender in Black Male-Headed Families, by Age of Householder: 1994 839

Table 831 Relationships: Age and Gender in Black Married-Couple Families, by Age of Householder: 1994 840

Table 832 Relationships: Age and Gender of All Black Family Members, by Age of Householder: 1994 840

Table 833 Relationships: Age of Black Family Members, in Relation to Family Type and Residence Area: 1994 841

Table 834 Relationships: Size of Black Families in Relation to Family Type and Householder's Educational Attainment: 1994 842

Table 835 Relationships: Size of Black Families, in Relation to Family Type and Age of Householder: 1994. Part 1 844

Table 836 Relationships: Size of Black Families, in Relation to Family Type and Age of Householder: 1994. Part 2 845

Table 837 Relationships: Size of Black Family Members, in Relation to Family Type and Residence Area: 1994 847

Table 838 Single Parents: Age Characteristics of Members of Black Single-Parent Families, by Gender of Parent: 1994. Part 1 848

CHAPTER 14 - THE FAMILY continued:

Table 839   Single Parents: Age Characteristics of Members of Black Single-Parent
Families, by Gender of Parent: 1994. Part 2 849

Table 840   Single Parents: Age of Householder in Black Single-Parent Families, by Gender
of Parent: 1994. Part 1 851

Table 841   Single Parents: Age of Householder in Black Single-Parent Families, by Gender
of Parent: 1994. Part 2 853

Table 842   Single Parents: Characteristics of Black and White One-Parent Families:
1970-1994 856

Table 843   Single Parents: Family Size in Black Single-Parent Families, by Gender of
Parent: 1994. Part 1 857

Table 844   Single Parents: Family Size in Black Single-Parent Families, by Gender of
Parent: 1994. Part 2 859

Table 845   Subfamilies: Age of Reference Person in Black Subfamilies: 1994 860

Table 846   Subfamilies: Family Groups with Children Under 18, by Family Type and
Race/Ethnic Origin 1994 861

Table 847   Subfamilies: Number Parents Present in Families with Children Under 18, by
Race/Ethnic Origin: 1970-1994 862

Table 848   Subfamilies: Percentage Distribution of Family Type in Families with Children,
by Race/Ethnic Origin: 1970-1994 863

Table 849   Subfamilies: Size of Black Subfamilies, by Subfamily Type: 1994 864

Income 864

Table 850   Money Income: Family Income at Selected Points in the Income Distribution in
Constant (1993) Dollars, in 1980 and 1993, by Race 864

Table 851   Money Income: Median Family Income, by Region, Family Type, Number
Earners and Race/Ethnic Origin: 1993 865

Table 852   Money Income: Percent Distribution of Family Income, by Region and
Race/Ethnic Origin: 1993 866

Table 853   Money Income: Percent of Family in Each Income Quintile and Top 5%, by
Race/Ethnic Origin: 1993 867

Table 854   Money Income: Trends in Distribution of Family Income, in Constant (1993)
Dollars, by Race/Ethnic Origin: 1970-1993 867

Table 855   Money Income: Trends in Family Median Income, in Current and Constant
(1993) Dollars, by Race/Ethnic Origin: 1970-1993 868

Table 856   Poverty: Families in Poverty in 1993, by Family Size, Householder's Education
and Work Experience, and Race/Ethnic Origin 869

Table 857   Poverty: Trends in Percent of Families Below Poverty Level, by Race/Ethnic
Origin: 1960 - 1993 870

Table 858   Relationships: Family Median Income, by Family Type and Householder's Race:
1993 871

Table 859   Relationships: Married Couples' Median Income, by Work Experience of
Husbands and Wives and Race/Ethnic Origin: 1993 872

Table 860   Relationships: Trends in Median Family Earnings, by Family Type, Number
Earners, and Race/Ethnic Origin: 1980-1993 873

Marriage Characteristics 874

Table 861   1980 High School Sophomores in 1992: Percent Distribution of Number of
Marriages of 1980 High School Sophomore Cohort, by Race/Ethnic Origin:
1992 874

Table 862   Age of Spouses: Age of Husband in Black Married-Couple Families, by Age of
Wife: 1994. Part 1 874

CHAPTER 14 - THE FAMILY continued:

Table 863   Age of Spouses: Age of Husband in Black Married-Couple Families, by Age of Wife: 1994. Part 2 875

Table 864   Marital Status: Marital Status in Black Subfamilies: 1994 876

Table 865   Race of Spouses: Race of Wife, by Race of Husband in Married-Couple Families, by Subfamily Type and Race/Ethnic Origin: 1994 877

CHAPTER 15 - VITAL STATISTICS 879

Abortions 879

Table 866   Abortions, by Selected Characteristics: 1985-1991 879

Table 867   Legal Abortion Ratios and Patient Characteristics: 1973-1992 880

Birth Control 880

Table 868   Methods of Contraception for Women 15-44 Years Old: 1982, 1988, and 1990 . . . 880

Birth Projections 883

Table 869   Birth Projections: Lifetime Births Expected by Women 18 to 34 Years Old: 1992 . . 883

Table 870   Birth Projections: Percent Distribution Per 1,000 Wives: 1971-1992. Part 1 . . . 883

Table 871   Birth Projections: Percent Distribution Per 1,000 Wives: 1971-1992. Part 2 . . . 884

Table 872   Birth Projections: Percent Distribution Per 1,000 Wives: 1971-1992. Part 3 . . . 885

Table 873   Lifetime Births Expected by Married Women: Trends, Part 1 885

Table 874   Lifetime Births Expected by Married Women: Trends, Part 2 886

Birth Rates 888

Table 875   Birth Rates: Estimated Birth Rate for Unmarried Women by Education, Age, Race, and Hispanic Origin of Mother, 1992 888

Table 876   Birth Rates: First Birth Rates for Unmarried Women by Age and Race of Mother, 1980-92 889

Table 877   Birth Rates: First Birth Rates for Unmarried Women by Age of Mother, 1940-92, and Age of Mother and Race, 1940, 1950, and 1955-92 891

Births 892

Table 878   Births: Number and Percent Distribution of Births by Adequacy of Prenatal Care to Marital Status and Race of Mother, 1992 892

Table 879   Births: Percent Low Birthweight, by Smoking Status, Age, and Race of Mother: 1992 893

Table 880   Births: Percent of Births to Mother with Adequate Prenatal Care by Education, Age, Race, and Marital Status of Mother, 1992 893

Table 881   Births: Percent of Mothers Gaining Less Than 16 Pounds During Pregnancy, by Education, Age, Marital Status, and Race, 1992 894

Table 882   Births: Percent of Mothers Who Smoked During Pregnancy by Age, Marital Status, and Race, 1992 895

Table 883   Live Births and Crude Birth Rates: Trends 896

Table 884   Live Births by Race and Hispanic Origin of Mother: 1970-82 897

Table 885   Live Births in Metropolitan Areas 898

Table 886   Live Births: Drinking Status of Mother During Pregnancy: 1992 899

Table 887   Live Births: Education of Mothers Who Smoked During Pregnancy: 1992 899

Table 888   Low-birth Live Births among Mothers Twenty Years of Age and Over, by Race, Hispanic Origin, and Educational Attainment: 1989-92 900

Table 889   Low-birth Live Births by Race and Hispanic Origin of Mother and Smoking Status: 1970-92. Part 1 902

Table 890   Low-birth Live Births by Race and Hispanic Origin of Mother and Smoking Status: 1970-92. Part 2 904

Table 891   Maternal Age and Marital Status for Live Births by Race and Hispanic Origin of Mother: 1970-92. Part 1 906

CHAPTER 15 - VITAL STATISTICS continued:

Table 892   Maternal Age and Marital Status for Live Births by Race and Hispanic Origin of Mother: 1970-92. Part 2 908

Table 893   Maternal Education for Live Births: Characteristics and Trends: 1970-92. Part 1 . . 910

Table 894   Maternal Education for Live Births: Characteristics and Trends: 1970-92. Part 2 . . 912

Table 895   Women Giving Birth: Black Children Ever Born Per 1,000 Women and Percent Childless: Characteristics. Part 1 913

Table 896   Women Giving Birth: Black Children Ever Born Per 1,000 Women and Percent Childless: Characteristics. Part 2 914

Table 897   Women Giving Birth: Black Children Ever Born Per 1,000 Women and Percent Childless: Characteristics. Part 3 915

Table 898   Women Giving Birth: Black Children Ever Born Per 1,000 Women and Percent Childless: Characteristics. Part 4 916

Table 899   Women Giving Birth: Black Women Who Have Had a Child in the Last Year Per 1,000 Women: Characteristics. Part 1 918

Table 900   Women Giving Birth: Black Women Who Have Had a Child in the Last Year Per 1,000 Women: Characteristics. Part 2 919

Table 901   Women Giving Birth: Characteristics of Women Who Had a Child in the Last Year: 1992 920

Table 902   Women Giving Birth: Distribution of Women and Average Number of Children Ever Born: Characteristics. Part 1 921

Table 903   Women Giving Birth: Distribution of Women and Average Number of Children Ever Born: Characteristics. Part 2 922

Table 904   Women Giving Birth: Number and Percent of Births to Unmarried Women by Race and Hispanic Origin of Mother, 1992. Part 1 924

Table 905   Women Giving Birth: Number and Percent of Births to Unmarried Women by Race and Hispanic Origin of Mother, 1992. Part 2 925

Table 906   Women Giving Birth: Number and Percent of Births to Unmarried Women by Race and Hispanic and Non-Hispanic Origin of Mother, 1992 927

Table 907   Women Giving Birth: Number of Births to Unmarried Women by Age of Mother and Race: 1940 and 1950-92. Part 1 928

Table 908   Women Giving Birth: Number of Births to Unmarried Women by Age of Mother and Race: 1940 and 1950-92. Part 2 929

Table 909   Women Giving Birth: Percent of Births to Mothers with Less Than 12 Years of School, 1992 930

Table 910   Women Giving Birth: Percentage of Unmarried Women Who Had a Child in the Last Year: 1990-1994 931

Table 911   Women Giving Birth: Ratios of Births to Unmarried Women by Age of Mother and Race: 1940 and 1950-92. Part 1 932

Table 912   Women Giving Birth: Ratios of Births to Unmarried Women by Age of Mother and Race: 1940 and 1950-92. Part 2 933

Table 913   Women Giving Birth: Unmarried Women by Child's Race and Mother's Age: 1970-1992 934

Table 914   Women Giving Birth: Unmarried Women by Women's Age and Race, 1992 935

Table 915   Women Giving Birth: Women Who Had a Child in the Last Year Per 1,000 Women: Characteristics, June 1994 936

Table 916   Women Giving Birth: Women Who Had a Child in the Last Year and Children Ever Born: June 1994 937

Table 917   Women Giving Birth: Women Who Had a Child in the Last Year and Their Percentage Employed: Selected Characteristics, 1990 and 1994 938

CHAPTER 15 - VITAL STATISTICS continued:

Table 918   Women Without Children: Childless Women and Children Ever Born: 1992 938
Births and Birth Rates 940
Table 919   Births and Birth Rates: Trends: 1970-1992 940
Birthweight 941
Table 920   Birthweight: Percent Low Birthweight by Age, Marital Status, and Race of Mother, 1992. Part 1 941
Table 921   Birthweight: Percent Low Birthweight by Age, Marital Status, and Race of Mother, 1992. Part 2 942
Table 922   Birthweight: Percent Low Birthweight by Age, Smoking Status, Marital Status, and Race of Mother, 1992 942
Table 923   Low-Birthweight Live Births by Geographical Division and State: 1980-82, 1985-87, and 1990-92 943
Table 924   Very Low-Birthweight Live Births by Geographical Division and State: 1980-82, 1985-87, and 1990-92 945
Breastfeeding 947
Table 925   Breastfeeding by Mothers 14-55 Years of Age: 1970-71 to 1986-87 947
Death Rates 948
Table 926   Causes of Deaths: Accidents and Violence, 1990-1992 948
Table 927   Death Rates: Age Adjusted by Cause: Trends. Part 1 948
Table 928   Death Rates: Age Adjusted by Cause: Trends. Part 2 950
Table 929   Death Rates: Age, Gender, and Race: 1970-1993 952
Table 930   Death Rates: Age-Adjusted Death Rates by Race, Gender, Region, and Urbanization, 1980-82, 1984-86, and 1990-92. Part 1 953
Table 931   Death Rates: Age-Adjusted Death Rates by Race, Gender, Region, and Urbanization, 1980-82, 1984-86, and 1990-92. Part 2 954
Table 932   Death Rates: Cause of Death, 1980-1992 955
Table 933   Death Rates: Causes, by Gender, Race, and Hispanic Origin: Trends, 1950-92. Part 1 956
Table 934   Death Rates: Causes, by Gender, Race, and Hispanic Origin: Trends, 1950-92. Part 2 958
Table 935   Death Rates: Infant, Maternal, and Neonatal Death Rates and Fetal Mortality Ratios, by Race: 1970-1992. Part 1 960
Table 936   Death Rates: Infant, Maternal, and Neonatal Death Rates and Fetal Mortality Ratios, by Race: 1970-1992. Part 2 961
Table 937   Death Rates: Provisional Death Rates For All Causes, 1992-93 962
Table 938   Death Rates: Trends in Deaths by Sex, Race, and Age, 1987-92 963
Table 939   Death Rates: Trends in Deaths by Breast Malignancies, 1950-1992 965
Table 940   Death Rates: Trends in Deaths by Cerebrovascular Diseases, 1950-1992. Part 1 . 966
Table 941   Death Rates: Trends in Deaths by Cerebrovascular Diseases, 1950-1992. Part 2 . 968
Table 942   Death Rates: Trends in Deaths by Chronic Obstructive Pulmonary Diseases, 1950-1992 970
Table 943   Death Rates: Trends in Deaths by Firearm-Related Injuries, 1970-92 971
Table 944   Death Rates: Trends in Deaths by Heart Diseases, 1950-1992. Part 1 973
Table 945   Death Rates: Trends in Deaths by Heart Diseases, 1950-1992. Part 2 975
Table 946   Death Rates: Trends in Deaths by Homicide and Legal Intervention, 1950-92. Part 1 977
Table 947   Death Rates: Trends in Deaths by Homicide and Legal Intervention, 1950-92. Part 2 979
Table 948   Death Rates: Trends in Deaths by Malignant Neoplasms, 1950-1992. Part 1 . . . 981

CHAPTER 15 - VITAL STATISTICS continued:

Table 949   Death Rates: Trends in Deaths by Malignant Neoplasms, 1950-1992. Part 2 982
Table 950   Death Rates: Trends in Deaths by Motor Vehicle Accidents, 1950-1992. Part 1 . . . 984
Table 951   Death Rates: Trends in Deaths by Motor Vehicle Accidents, 1950-1992. Part 2 . . . 987
Table 952   Death Rates: Trends in Deaths by Respiratory System Malignancies, 1950-1992 . . 989
Table 953   Death Rates: Trends in Suicides, 1950-92. Part 1 990
Table 954   Death Rates: Trends in Suicides, 1950-92. Part 2 992
Table 955   Maternal Deaths: Maternal Mortality Rates, 1950-1992 994
Deaths 996
Table 956   AIDS Deaths: Trends, 1982-1994 996
Table 957   Causes of Death: Death by Firearms, by Race and Gender: 1980-1992 996
Table 958   Causes of Death: Deaths and Death Rates for Alcohol-Induced Causes, by Race
            and Gender: 1980-1992 997
Table 959   Causes of Death: Deaths and Death Rates for Drug-Induced Causes, by Race
            and Gender: 1980-1992 998
Table 960   Causes of Death: Trends and Characteristics of Death by Suicide, 1980-1992.
            Part 1 998
Table 961   Causes of Death: Trends and Characteristics of Death by Suicide, 1980-1992.
            Part 2 999
Table 962   Causes of Deaths: Age and Leading Cause: 1992 1000
Table 963   Causes of Deaths: Characteristics: 1992 1000
Table 964   Causes of Deaths: Firearm Mortality Among Children, Youth, and Young
            Adults: 1992 1001
Table 965   Deaths and Death Rates: Age, Gender, and Race: 1970-1993 1002
Table 966   Deaths: Leading Causes of Deaths and Number of Deaths, 1980 and 1982. Part
            1 1003
Table 967   Deaths: Leading Causes of Deaths and Number of Deaths, 1980 and 1982. Part
            2 1005
Table 968   Deaths: Years of Potential Life Lost Before Age 65 for Selected Causes: Trends,
            1970-92. Part 1 1007
Table 969   Deaths: Years of Potential Life Lost Before Age 65 for Selected Causes: Trends,
            1970-92. Part 2 1008
Fertility 1010
Table 970   Fertility Indicators: Characteristics of Never-Married Women 14 to 44 Years
            Old: 1990 and 1994 1010
Table 971   Fertility Rates and Live-Birth Order: 1950-93 1010
Table 972   Fertility Rates: Totals, and Intrinsic Rate of Natural Increase: 1960-1992 1012
Table 973   Fertility Rates: Trends and Projections, 1994, 2010 1013
Fetal and Infant Deaths 1014
Table 974   Fetal Death Rates: Mortality Rates by Race, Geographic Division and States:
            Trends 1014
Table 975   Infant Deaths: Mortality Rates by Race and State: 1980-1992 1016
Infant Mortality 1018
Table 976   Infant Mortality Rates by Race, Region, and State: 1980-82, 1985-87, and
            1990-92 1018
Table 977   Infant Mortality Rates by Race: 1970-92 1020
Table 978   Infant Mortality Rates for Mothers Twenty Years of Age and Over:
            Characteristics: 1983-88 1021
Table 979   Infant, Neonatal, and Postneonatal Mortality Rates by Race and Hispanic
            Origin of Mother, 1960 and 1983-88 1022

CHAPTER 15 - VITAL STATISTICS continued:

Infant, Fetal, and Perinatal Deaths 1024

    Table 980   Infant, Fetal, and Perinatal Deaths: Mortality Rates by Race: Trends 1024

Life Expectancy 1026

    Table 981   Life Expectancy: Expectancy of Life at Birth, 1970-1993, and Projections,

               1995-2010 1026

    Table 982   Life Expectancy: Life and Death Expectancy By Gender and Age: 1992 1027

    Table 983   Life Expectancy: Selected Life Table Values: 1979 to 1992 1029

    Table 984   Life Expectancy: Trends, 1900-1993 1030

    Table 985   Life Expectancy: Trends, 1970-92 1032

Live Births 1033

    Table 986   Birth Rates: Live Order and Race, 1970-1992 1033

    Table 987   Live Births: Percent and Characteristics, 1990, 1992 1034

    Table 988   Live Births: State of Birth, 1992 1035

Marital Status 1037

    Table 989   Marriage and Divorce: Characteristics of Marriage Experience for Women:

               1980 and 1990 1037

    Table 990   Marriage and Divorce: Dissolution of Marriage and Remarriage of Women:

               1988 1038

Neonatal Deaths 1039

    Table 991   Neonatal Deaths: Mortality Rates by Race, Geographic Division and States:

               Trends 1039

Postneonatal Deaths 1041

    Table 992   Postneonatal Deaths: Mortality Rates by Race, Geographic Division and States:

               Trends 1041

Pregnancies 1043

    Table 993   Pregnancies: Age of Woman and Race: 1991 1043

Prenatal Care 1044

    Table 994   Mothers with Early Prenatal Care by Race of Mother: 1970-92 1044

    Table 995   Prenatal Care for Live Births by Race and Hispanic Origin of Mother: 1970-92.

               Part 1 1045

    Table 996   Prenatal Care for Live Births by Race and Hispanic Origin of Mother: 1970-92.

               Part 2 1047

Reference Sources 1049

Index 1055

Abbreviations

ACT	American College Testing
AP	Advanced Placement
CMSA	Consolidated Metropolitan Statistical Area
EOEI	Equal Opportunity Educational Institutions
GRE	Graduate Record Exam
HBCU	Historically Black Colleges and Universities
HIED	Higher Education
MCAT	Medical College Admission Test
MSA	Metropolitan Statistical Area
NAACP	National Association for the Advancement of Colored People
NAEP	National Assessment of Educational Progress
NAFEO	National Association for Equality of Opportunity in Higher Education
NRC	National Research Council
PBI	Predominantly Black Institutions
PMSA	Primary Metropolitan Statistical Area
PWI	Predominantly White Institutions
TBI	Traditionally Black Institutions
TWI	Traditionally White Institutions
SAT	Scholastic Aptitude Test
SEF	Southern Education Foundation
SREB	Southern Regional Education Board
UNCF	United Negro College Fund

PREFACE

Each new edition of *Statistical Record of Black America* is both an adventure and a revelation. The adventure lies in searching the published literature for the most informative and most accurate information that can be found. The revelation comes when we have completed our search and can take time to see what the accumulated information tells us about the issues in American society that appear to be important to those who assemble the data, as well as how minorities—particularly black Americans—relate to these issues in comparison to each other and to the total population. Each of the past editions has revealed that if the distribution of tables in the chapters is any indication, the issues that are important in America fluctuate with some regularity, because there has been a different distribution in each edition. The present edition is no exception to this pattern. The most glaring indication of difference this time appears in the much smaller number of tables in an area that has always had minimum representation: the military. The difference is also reflected, however, in the greater number of tables that were found in publications dealing with special populations or special topics—the elderly, drug use and abuse, older undergraduates, the status of 1980 high school sophomores, and domestic violence are examples. The distribution in this fourth edition may also be partly due to the state of the economy and the costs of printing, which have caused some government publications to be issued later than usual, scaled down in coverage, or discontinued altogether.

All is not lost. Tables gathered from both private and public sources increasingly tend to include more analyses within them, relating basic number counts to more and more of the factors that may be associated with how those counts are distributed. Thus, the first edition of this book almost always included both race and gender as separate subgroups for analysis; specialized chapters would also include additional related factors—for example, the income chapter might present data by work status and occupation; the education chapter would include type of college and other variables; the family chapter might present data by gender of household head. In this fourth edition, it is more common than not to see any one of the factors that on its face relates to a particular chapter used as an analytic factor in any number of other chapters. Today's information, as collected by the demographers, epidemiologists, and research scientists, is designed to do much more than report counts: It is an invitation to examine possible explanations of why the counts are as they are.

We repeat a friendly caution to our readers. Given the plurality of analytic subgroups that any given table may include, the choice of exactly where to place a table is necessarily somewhat arbitrary. Where, for example, should a table on educational achievement by income level and marital status be placed? In the Education chapter, the Income chapter, or the Family chapter? We have guidelines that help us make these decisions, but we urge you to use the index carefully to assure that you are aware of every possible location of a table on a topic of interest to you. We also remind you that many of the tables we present have much more data in them than the space limitations of this volume will allow; many of the original tables are also presented with accompanying text. Referral to the original source is highly encouraged when more detailed information is desired.

HOW TO USE THIS BOOK

Chapters and subheadings within the chapters are a first guide to locating material. The index provides additional entry into the book.

There is a deliberate attempt not to duplicate material from one edition to the next unless it is a question of updating tables. Therefore, it is sometimes worthwhile to consult the earlier editions, which may present data in a different light or even in some cases may contain the latest material on some matters. Greater historical depth, going back to earliest times, is also available in the companion volume *Historical Statistics of Black America* (1995).

Space limitations have meant that tables are not always reprinted in their entirety. More complete information in terms of such items as span of years and related vaiables may be available in the original source. Users are therefore urged to consult the original sources if greater detail is needed.

All tables present numerical data exactly as presented in the original source. Data on the same major variable may lead to different interpretations when two or more tables are compared. The nature of the samples used and the time of data collection are important considerations when seeking to reconcile differences.

ACKNOWLEDGMENTS

Statistical Record of Black America has over the years built a loyal and enthusiastic cote-rie of friends and supporters who understand our project and help us to do our best for those who use these volumes. Some recurring and familiar contributors to our efforts in-clude Dr. Henry Ponder, recently retired Fisk president, who made it possible for us to use the vast resources and facilities at Fisk; Dr. George Neely, Jr., Fisk executive vice-presi-dent; Fisk staff members Jackie London, John Henderson, Charles Reece, and Rick Smith; and members of the Fisk University Library Staff, whose routines were often dis-rupted by our activities. We are grateful to these persons, without whom the task could not have been completed.

- Jessie Carney Smith, University Librarian and William and Camille Cosby Professor in the Humanities, Fisk University

- Carrell Peterson Horton, Director, Division of the Social Sciences, Fisk University

Statistical Record OF Black America

Chapter 1
ATTITUDES, VALUES, AND BEHAVIOR

Attitudes

★ 1 ★

Drug-Related: Percent Who Think Obtaining Selected Drugs is "Fairly Easy" or "Very Easy," by Age Group and Race/Ethnic Origin: 1991, 1992, and 1993-I

Drug of use and race/ethnicity	Age (years)								
	12-17			18-25			26-34		
	1991	1992	1993	1991	1992	1993	1991	1992	1993
Marijuana									
White	53.3	50.0	1.5	81.0	79.5	80.1	76.0[1]	72.2	73.1
Black	57.3	58.2	59.6	79.6	79.5	75.4	70.2	69.9	67.4
Hispanic	53.3	49.5[1]	56.0	66.2	67.7	64.8	62.1	60.6	61.2
Other	45.9	44.6	41.1	62.3	60.6	*	54.8[1]	45.4	36.8
Cocaine or crack-cocaine									
White	30.9	28.0	29.2	48.5[1]	46.4	43.7	51.9[2]	46.4	45.3
Black	56.4	56.1	52.6	73.2[1]	74.5[2]	66.6	65.8	66.5	64.8
Hispanic	39.1	36.7	35.1	51.3	49.0	47.9	49.3	46.6	48.6
Other	30.7	31.3	20.1	40.2	28.5	30.8	32.8	28.6	28.0
Heroin									
White	21.1	20.1	19.7	20.7[2]	23.3	22.2	25.6	25.6	23.9
Black	32.2	32.1	29.0	40.0	41.1[2]	32.5	40.2	43.4	39.1
Hispanic	25.3	23.7	24.7	33.4	31.0	30.2	31.3	30.8	34.0
Other	16.5	21.2	11.8	23.6	17.0	18.0	16.6	18.5	22.0

Source: "Percentage Reporting that Obtaining Drugs is Fairly Easy or Very Easy, by Age and Race/Ethnicity: 1991-93,"*Drug Use Among Ethnic Minorities*, 1995, p. 21. Primary source: 1991-93 National Household Survey on Drug Abuse, Substance Abuse and Mental Health Services Administration, preliminary data, June 1994. *Notes:* * Low precision, no estimate reported. 1. Difference between estimate in this cell and corresponding estimate for 1993 is statistically significant at the .05 level. 2. Difference between estimate in this cell and corresponding estimate for 1993 is statistically significant at the .01 level.

★ 2 ★

Attitudes

Drug-Related: Percent Who Think Obtaining Selected Drugs is "Fairly Easy" or "Very Easy," by Age Group and Race/Ethnic Origin: 1991, 1992, and 1993-II

Drug of use and race/ethnicity	Age (years)					
	35+			Total		
	1991	1992	1993	1991	1992	1993
Marijuana						
White	55.5[1]	52.6	50.3	62.5[2]	59.4	58.2
Black	63.8	58.6	60.0	57.0	64.3	64.0
Hispanic	53.4[2]	45.9	44.5	57.9[1]	53.9	54.0
Other	32.6	43.0	31.7	44.2	46.5	37.7
Cocaine or crack-cocaine						
White	38.0[1]	35.1	33.8	41.3[2]	38.0	36.6
Black	59.0	52.3	55.7	62.5	59.4	58.9
Hispanic	42.5[1]	33.7	35.8	45.3[1]	40.1	41.1
Other	25.5	22.6	*	30.3	25.6	24.4
Heroin						
White	28.8[1]	25.6	25.1	26.4	24.8	24.0
Black	44.2[1]	38.5	37.4	41.0[2]	39.0	35.7
Hispanic	33.9[2]	26.1	26.5	32.0	27.8	28.7
Other	18.8	18.6	*	18.9	18.6	18.2

Source: "Percentage Reporting that Obtaining Drugs is Fairly Easy or Very Easy, by Age and Race/Ethnicity: 1991-93,"*Drug Use Among Ethnic Minorities*, 1995, p. 21. Primary source: 1991-93 National Household Survey on Drug Abuse, Substance Abuse and Mental Health Services Administration, preliminary data, June 1994. *Notes:* * Low precision, no estimate reported. 1. Difference between estimate in this cell and corresponding estimate for 1993 is statistically significant at the .05 level. 2. Difference between estimate in this cell and corresponding estimate for 1993 is statistically significant at the .01 level.

★ 3 ★

Attitudes

Race-Related: Blacks' Expectation of Black President or Vice President in Next 20 Years: 1995

	Total	Sex	
		Male	Female
Black President			
Yes	34.0%	32.1%	35.5%
No	63.1	65.5	61.1
No answer	2.9	2.4	3.4
Black Vice President			
Yes	70.9%	70.2%	71.4%
No	25.9	27.0	25.0
No answer	3.1	2.7	3.6

Source: "Do You expect to See a Black President or Vice President in the Next 20 Years?," *Black Enterprise* 26 (August 1995), p. 72. Primary source: *Black Enterprise* research, 1995. Published by permission.

★ 4 ★

Attitudes

Race-Related: Blacks' Feeling of Obligation to Help Blacks Viewed as Less Educationally and/or Economically Advantaged

	Percent				
		Education			
	Total	Postgrad Degree	Some Postgrad Study	College Grad	1-3 Years College
Yes	90.1	93.6	89.1	88.6	88.3
No	7.7	5.3	9.8	8.1	8.9
No answer	2.2	1.1	1.1	3.3	2.8

Source: "Do You Feel You Have a Moral Obligation to Help Those Blacks who are Educationally and/or Economically Disadvantaged?," *Black Enterprise* 26 (August 1995), [no p. Number]. Primary source: *Black Enterprise* research, 1995. Published by permission.

★ 5 ★

Attitudes

Race-Related: Blacks' Preference For or Against Predominantly Black College for Their Children: 1995

	Percent							
	Total	Age			Education			
		Under 35	35-49	50+	Post-grad Degree	Some Post-grad Study	College Grad	1-3 Years College
Yes	59.5	54.1	63.5	59.3	61.9	56.3	55.1	63.7
No	36.5	42.7	32.1	36.2	32.8	39.9	41.5	33.1
No answer	4.0	3.2	4.4	4.5	5.3	3.8	3.3	3.2

Source: "Would You Prefer that Your Child Go to a Predominantly Black College?," *Black Enterprise* 26 (August 1995), p. 68. Primary source: *Black Enterprise* research, 1995. Published by permission.

★ 6 ★

Attitudes

Race-Related: Change in Employment Opportunities for Blacks in Past 5 Years: 1995

	Total	Education			
		Postgrad Degree	Some Postgrad Study	College Grad	1-3 Years College
Increased	24.5%	21.4%	26.2%	24.6%	27.8%
Decreased	46.6	50.0	46.4	46.0	41.9
Remained the same	28.4	28.3	26.2	29.0	29.4
No answer	0.5	0.3	1.1	0.4	0.8

Source: "Do You Think Employment Opportunities have Increased, Decreased, or Remained the Same for Blacks in the Past Five Years?," *Black Enterprise* 26 (August 1995), p. 66. Primary source: *Black Enterprise* research, 1995. Published by permission.

★ 7 ★

Attitudes

Race-Related: Effects of Racism on Blacks' Ability to Achieve Career Goals: 1995

	Percent						
		Age			Household income		
	Total	Under 35	35-49	50+	Under $35K	$35K-$74K	$75K+
Yes, a great deal	24.2	16.0	25.1	32.4	23.2	25.5	24.0
Yes, somewhat	48.9	47.7	51.1	47.1	45.3	48.2	52.3
No	26.1	35.8	23.6	18.9	30.2	25.9	23.4
Don't know	0.7	0.6	0.2	1.6	1.4	0.4	0.3

Source: "Do You Feel that Racism has Held You Back in Terms of Achieving Your Career Goals (e.g., Promotions, Merit Increases, Recognition)?," *Black Enterprise* 26 (August 1995), p. 66. Primary source: *Black Enterprise* research, 1995. Published by permission.

★ 8 ★

Attitudes

School-Related: Blacks' Judgments on Desegregation's Effect on Children's Education

	Percent						
		Age			Household income		
	Total	Under 35	35-49	50+	Under $35K	$35K-$74K	$75K+
Better	37.0	44.8	34.1	33.0	40.4	35.0	36.7
Worse	47.7	41.9	49.3	51.6	39.3	50.7	51.4
Same	12.7	9.9	14.8	12.5	17.5	11.9	9.5
No answer	2.6	3.5	1.7	2.9	2.8	2.3	2.3

Source: "It has Been 40 Years since Schools have Been Desegregated. Do you think education for Children is Better, Worse or the Same as it was Before?" *Black Enterprise* 26 (August 1995), p. 72. Primary source: *Black Enterprise* research, 1995. Published by permission.

★9★

Attitudes

School-Related: Distribution of Undergraduates' Educational Aspirations, by Race/Ethnic Origin: 1989-90

	1989-90 degree objective		Educational aspirations		
	Less than bachelor's	Bachelor's degree	Less than bachelor's	Bachelor's degree	Advanced degree
Total	61.8	38.2	15.1	32.6	52.2
Race-ethnicity					
American Indian/Alaskan Native	75.8	24.1	15.7	37.3	46.9
Asian/Pacific Islander	60.5	39.5	9.7	31.7	58.5
Black, non-Hispanic	69.6	30.4	16.2	29.9	53.7
Hispanic	68.8	31.3	18.0	31.8	50.0
White, non-Hispanic	59.9	40.1	15.0	33.0	51.9
Racial-ethnic subgroup Asian					
Asian Indian	62.8	37.2	4.2	16.2	79.4
Chinese	51.1	48.9	8.7	25.1	66.0
Japanese	61.1	38.9	10.2	35.8	53.9
Korean	49.0	51.0	0.4	23.7	75.7
Pacific Islander	68.8	31.2	13.9	43.5	42.5
Vietnamese	50.4	49.6	12.1	34.2	53.5
Other or unspecified	62.7	37.3	11.3	32.5	56.1
Racial-ethnic subgroup Hispanic					
Cuban	59.2	40.8	7.5	11.4	81.0
Mexican	76.8	23.3	20.7	36.6	42.5
Puerto Rican	45.4	54.6	11.1	28.9	59.8
Other or unspecified	67.5	32.5	17.6	28.0	54.3

Source: "Percentage Distribution of Undergraduates According to their Current Degree Objectives and their Ultimate Educational Aspirations, by Race- Ethnicity, 1989-90," U.S. Department of Education, National Center for Education Statistics, *Minority Undergraduate Participation in Postsecondary Education*, June, 1995, p. 20. Primary source: U.S. Department of Education, National Center for Education Statistics, 1989-90 National Postsecondary Student Aid Study (NPSAS:90), Undergraduate Data Analysis System. *Note:* Percentages may not sum to 100 due to rounding.

★ 10 ★

Attitudes

School-Related: Percent of 4th, 8th, and 12th Graders Who Like Science (1990) and Mathematics (1992), by Race/Ethnic Origin

Subject and Grade	Race/ethnicity				
	Asian	Hispanic	Black	White	American Indian
Science					
Fourth	78	76	75	81	80
Eighth	70	71	70	67	71
Twelfth	69	68	60	66	71
Mathematics					
Fourth	80	72	74	71	66
Eighth	65	55	64	56	51
Twelfth	64	55	55	49	50

Source: "Percent of Students who Like Science and Mathematics, by Race/Ethnicity and Grade," U.S. Department of Education, National Center for Education Statistics, *Understanding Racial-Ethnic Differences in Secondary School Science and Mathematics Achievement*, February, 1995, p. 34. Primary source: U.S. Department of Education, National Center for Education Statistics, National Assessment of Educational Progress, "1990 Science Assessment and 1992 Mathematics Assessment."

Behavior

★ 11 ★

Crime/Violence-Related: High School Students' Attitudes and Behavior Related to Crime and Violence at School (in percentages), by Race/Ethnic Origin: 1993-I

	Felt too unsafe to go to school[1]			Carried a weapon on school property[2]			Threatened or injured with a weapon on school property[3]		
	Total	Male	Female	Total	Male	Female	Total	Male	Female
National	4.4%	4.3%	4.4%	11.8%	17.9%	5.1%	7.3%	9.2%	5.4%
Race/ethnicity White, non-Hispanic	3.0	2.9	3.1	10.9	17.7	3.4	6.3	8.1	4.4

[Continued]

★ 11 ★

Crime/Violence-Related: High School Students' Attitudes and Behavior Related to Crime and Violence at School (in percentages), by Race/Ethnic Origin: 1993-I

[Continued]

	Felt too unsafe to go to school[1]			Carried a weapon on school property[2]			Threatened or injured with a weapon on school property[3]		
	Total	Male	Female	Total	Male	Female	Total	Male	Female
Black, non-Hispanic	7.1	7.0	7.3	15.0	18.2	11.9	11.2	12.6	9.8
Hispanic	10.1	10.4	9.8	13.3	20.2	6.6	8.6	10.7	6.4

Source: "High School Students Reporting Engaging in Violence-Related Behaviors in School, by Sex, Race, Ethnicity, and Grade Level, United States, 1993," *Sourcebook of Criminal Justice Statistics, 1994,* p. 275. Primary source: Laura Kann et al., "Youth Risk Behavior Surveillance-United States, 1993." CDC Surveillance Summaries, *Morbidity and Mortality Weekly Report* 44 No. SS-1 (Washington, DC: USGPO, Mar. 24, 1995). p. 29. Table adapted by SOURCEBOOK staff. *Notes:* These data are from the 1993 national school-based survey conducted as part of the Youth Risk Behavior Surveillance System (YRBSS). The data were collected and analyzed by the U.S. Department of Health and Human Services, Centers for Disease Control and Prevention. 1. On 1 or more of the 30 days preceding the survey. 2. A weapon such as a gun, knife, or club. 3. One or more times during the 12 months preceding the survey.

★ 12 ★

Behavior

Crime/Violence-Related: High School Students' Attitudes and Behavior Related to Crime and Violence at School (in percentages), by Race/Ethnic Origin: 1993-II

	In a physical fight on school property[1]			Property stolen or deliberately damaged on school property[1]		
	Total	Male	Female	Total	Male	Female
National	16.2%	23.5%	8.6%	32.7%	37.0%	28.1%
Race/ethnicity						
White, non-Hispanic	15.0	22.5	6.8	32.0	35.9	27.7
Black, non-Hispanic	22.0	28.6	15.5	35.5	39.2	31.8
Hispanic	17.9	24.1	11.7	32.2	36.7	27.6

Source: "High School Students Reporting Engaging in Violence-Related Behaviors in School, by Sex, Race, Ethnicity, and Grade Level, United States, 1993," *Sourcebook of Criminal Justice Statistics, 1994,* p. 275. Primary source: Laura Kann et al., "Youth Risk Behavior Surveillance-United States, 1993." CDC Surveillance Summaries, *Morbidity and Mortality Weekly Report* 44 No. SS-1 (Washington, DC: USGPO, Mar. 24, 1995). p. 29. Table adapted by SOURCEBOOK staff. *Notes:* These data are from the 1993 national school-based survey conducted as part of the Youth Risk Behavior Surveillance System (YRBSS). The data were collected and analyzed by the U.S. Department of Health and Human Services, Centers for Disease Control and Prevention. 1. One or more times during the 12 months preceding the survey.

★ 13 ★

Behavior

Crime/Violence-Related: High School Students' Suicide-Related Behavior, by Race/Ethnic Origin: 1993-I

	Thought seriously about attempting suicide			Made a suicide plan		
	Total	Male	Female	Total	Male	Female
National	24.1%	18.8%	29.6%	19.0%	15.3%	22.9%
Race ethnicity						
White, non-Hispanic	24.2	19.1	29.7	19.1	15.7	22.8
Black, non-Hispanic	19.9	15.4	24.5	16.0	12.4	19.5
Hispanic	26.0	17.9	34.1	20.0	13.7	26.6

Source: "High School Students Reporting Suicidal Thoughts and Suicidal Behavior in Last 12 Months, by Sex, Race, Ethnicity, and Grade Level, United States, 1993," *Sourcebook of Criminal Justice Statistics, 1994,* p. 344. Primary source: Laura Kann et al. "Youth Risk Behavior Surveillance-United States, 1993," CDC Surveillance Summaries *Morbidity and Mortality Weekly Report* 44 No. SS-1 (Washington, DC: USGPO, Mar. 24, 1995), p. 32. Table adapted by SOURCEBOOK staff.

★ 14 ★

Behavior

Crime/Violence-Related: High School Students' Suicide-Related Behavior, by Race/Ethnic Origin: 1993-II

	Attempted suicide one or more times			Suicide attempt required medical attention		
	Total	Male	Female	Total	Male	Female
National	8.6%	5.0%	12.5%	2.7%	1.6%	3.8%
Race ethnicity						
White, non-Hispanic	7.7	4.4	11.3	2.4	1.4	3.6
Black, non-Hispanic	8.4	5.4	11.2	3.0	2.0	4.0
Hispanic	13.6	7.4	19.7	3.7	2.0	5.5

Source: "High School Students Reporting Suicidal Thoughts and Suicidal Behavior in Last 12 Months, by Sex, Race, Ethnicity, and Grade Level, United States, 1993," *Sourcebook of Criminal Justice Statistics, 1994,* p. 344. Primary source: Laura Kann et al. "Youth Risk Behavior Surveillance-United States, 1993," CDC Surveillance Summaries *Morbidity and Mortality Weekly Report* 44 No. SS-1 (Washington, DC: USGPO, Mar. 24, 1995), p. 32. Table adapted by SOURCEBOOK staff.

★ 15 ★

Behavior

Crime/Violence-Related: Recent Weapon Carrying by High School Students, by Race/Ethnic Origin: 1993

	Carried a weapon in the last 30 days[1]			Carried a gun in the last 30 days		
	Total	Male	Female	Total	Male	Female
National	22.1%	34.3%	9.2%	7.9%	13.7%	1.8%
Race ethnicity						
White, non-Hispanic	20.6	33.4	6.9	6.8	12.0	1.2
Black, non-Hispanic	28.5	38.2	18.9	12.3	20.9	3.8
Hispanic	24.4	37.3	11.5	10.1	17.0	3.1

Source: "High School Students Reporting Having Carried a Weapon or a Gun in Last 30 Days, by Sex, Race, Ethnicity, and Grade Level, United States, 1993," *Sourcebook of Criminal Justice Statistics, 1994,* p. 275. Primary source: Laura Kann et al., "Youth Risk Behavior Surveillance—United States, 1993." CDC Surveillance Summaries, *Morbidity and Mortality Weekly Report* 44 No. SS-1 (Washington, DC, USGPO, Mar. 24, 1995), p. 23. Table adapted by SOURCEBOOK staff. *Note:* 1. A weapon such as a gun, knife, or club.

★ 16 ★

Behavior

Drug-Related: Distribution (in Percentages) of Days of Alcohol Use in Past Month, by Demographic Characteristics: 1993

Demographic Characteristic	(Unweighted N)	Days of Use			
		None	1-4	5-19	20-30
Total	(25,777)	52.0	26.2	14.4	7.5
Race/Ethnicity[1]					
White	(12,175)	48.8	27.2	15.5	8.5
Black	(6,003)	64.6	19.3	11.1	5.0
Hispanic	(6,692)	55.7	27.9	12.1	4.3

Source: "Percentage Distribution of Days of Alcohol Use in the Past Month, by Demographic Characteristics: 1993," *National Household Survey on Drug Abuse: Main Findings 1993,* June, 1995, p. 105. Primary source: Office of Applied Studies, SAMHSA, National Household Survey on Drug Abuse, 1993. *Notes:* Only past-month alcohol users who reported the number of days they used alcohol during the past 30 days are included in this table. 1. The category "other" for Race/Ethnicity is not included.

★ 17 ★
Behavior

Drug-Related: High School Students Reporting Drug-Related Behavior on School Property, by Gender and Race/Ethnic Origin (in percentages)-Part I: 1993

Category	Cigarette use on school property[1]			Smokeless tobacco use on school property[2]		
	Female	Male	Total	Female	Male	Total
Race/ethnicity						
White, non-Hispanic	14.5	14.7	14.5	0.9	16.0	8.7
	(+2.3)[6]	(+2.8)	(+2.4)	(+0.4)	(+2.8)	(+1.7)
Black, non-Hispanic	4.5	7.3	5.9	0.1	2.8	1.4
	(+1.7)	(+2.8)	(+1.7)	(+0.1)	(+1.7)	(+0.9)
Hispanic	11.6	10.6	11.1	0.2	4.4	2.3
	(+3.1)	(+2.7)	(+2.4)	(+0.2)	(+1.8)	(+0.9)

Source: "Percentage of High School Students who Reported Engaging in Drug- Related Behaviors on School Property, by Sex, Race/Ethnicity, and Grade Level: United States, Youth Risk Behavior Survey, 1993," *Drug Use Among Ethnic Minorities*, 1995, p. 37. Primary source: 1993 Youth Risk Behavior Surveillance System, Centers for Disease Control and Prevention, 1995. *Notes:* 1. Used cigarettes on 1 or more days during the 30 days preceding the survey. 2. Used chewing tobacco or snuff during the 30 days preceding the survey. 3. Used alcohol on 1 or more days during the 30 days preceding the survey. 4. Used marijuana 1 or more times during the 30 days preceding the survey. 5. During the 12 months preceding the survey. 6. 95-percent confidence interval.

★ 18 ★
Behavior

Drug-Related: High School Students Reporting Drug-Related Behavior on School Property, by Gender and Race/Ethnic Origin (in percentages)-Part II: 1993

Category	Alcohol use on school property[3]			Marijuana use on school property[4]			Offered, sold, or given an illegal drug on school property[5]		
	Female	Male	Total	Female	Male	Total	Female	Male	Total
Race/ethnicity									
White, non-Hispanic	3.6	5.5	4.6	2.8	7.1	5.0	18.9	28.8	24.1
	(+1.1)	(+1.0)	(+0.9)	(+0.9)	(+2.0)	(+1.4)	(+3.2)	(+3.6)	(+3.3)
Black, non-Hispanic	5.1	8.7	8.9	4.5	10.1	7.3	14.8	20.3	17.5
	(+2.5)	(+2.2)	(+1.9)	(+2.6)	(+2.9)	(+2.4)	(+2.8)	(+4.4)	(+2.9)
Hispanic	6.2	7.3	6.8	4.9	10.0	7.5	25.8	41.5	34.1
	(+1.7)	(+2.0)	(+1.7)	(+2.5)	(+2.7)	(+2.2)	(+4.0)	(+5.3)	(+3.1)

Source: "Percentage of High School Students who Reported Engaging in Drug- Related Behaviors on School Property, by Sex, Race/Ethnicity, and Grade Level: United States, Youth Risk Behavior Survey, 1993," *Drug Use Among Ethnic Minorities*, 1995, p. 37. Primary source: 1993 Youth Risk Behavior Surveillance System, Centers for Disease Control and Prevention, 1995. *Notes:* 1. Used cigarettes on 1 or more days during the 30 days preceding the survey. 2. Used chewing tobacco or snuff during the 30 days preceding the survey. 3. Used alcohol on 1 or more days during the 30 days preceding the survey. 4. Used marijuana 1 or more times during the 30 days preceding the survey. 5. During the 12 months preceding the survey. 6. 95-percent confidence interval.

★ 19 ★

Behavior

Drug-Related: High School Students' Lifetime and/or Current Use of Alcohol and Marijuana, by Gender and Race/Ethnic Origin (in percentages)-Part 1: 1993

Category	Lifetime alcohol use[1]			Current alcohol use[2]			Episodic heavy drinking[3]		
	Female	Male	Total	Female	Male	Total	Female	Male	Total
Race/Ethnicity									
White, non-Hispanic	82.4	81.0	81.7	48.6	51.1	49.8	29.3	35.6	32.6
	(+1.9)[6]	(+1.9)	(+1.5)	(+3.1)	(+2.8)	(+2.5)	(+2.6)	(+2.5)	(+2.1)
Black, non-Hispanic	76.1	82.0	80.0	37.1	48.2	42.5	13.3	25.1	19.1
	(+4.6)	(+3.6)	(+3.0)	(+4.8)	(+4.0)	(+3.6)	(+2.3)	(+3.9)	(+2.9)
Hispanic	82.2	84.9	83.5	46.9	55.0	50.8	27.6	39.4	33.4
	(+4.0)	(+4.2)	(+3.3)	(+5.9)	(+8.4)	(+5.5)	(+4.7)	(+4.7)	(+3.9)

Source: "Percentage of High School Students who Drank Alcohol or Used Marijuana, by Sex, Race/Ethnicity, and Grade Level: United States, Youth Risk Behavior Survey, 1993," *Drug Use Among Ethnic Minorities,* 1995, p. 35. Primary source: 1993 Youth Risk Behavior Surveillance System, Centers for Disease Control and Prevention, 1995. *Notes:* 1. Ever had at least one drink of alcohol. 2. Used alcohol on 1 or more of the 30 days preceding the survey. 3. Used 5 or more drinks of alcohol on at least 1 occasion on 1 or more of the 30 days preceding the survey. 4. Ever used marijuana. 5. Used marijuana 1 or more times during the 30 days preceding the survey. 6. 95-percent confidence level.

★ 20 ★

Behavior

Drug-Related: High School Students' Lifetime and/or Current Use of Alcohol and Marijuana, by Gender and Race/Ethnic Origin (in percentages)-Part 2: 1993

Category	Lifetime marijuana use[4]			Current marijuana use[5]		
	Female	Male	Total	Female	Male	Total
Race/Ethnicity						
White, non-Hispanic	29.3	36.0	32.7	14.7	19.7	17.3
	(+4.3)	(+4.3)	(+4.0)	(+2.4)	(+3.8)	(+2.8)
Black, non-Hispanic	26.3	41.1	33.6	13.0	24.3	18.6
	(+5.5)	(+5.7)	(+5.4)	(+3.4)	(+4.3)	(+3.6)
Hispanic	29.5	41.5	35.4	15.7	23.2	19.4
	(+5.6)	(+4.3)	(+3.3)	(+4.5)	(+4.5)	(+2.8)

Source: "Percentage of High School Students who Drank Alcohol or Used Marijuana, by Sex, Race/Ethnicity, and Grade Level: United States, Youth Risk Behavior Survey, 1993," *Drug Use Among Ethnic Minorities,* 1995, p. 35. Primary source: 1993 Youth Risk Behavior Surveillance System, Centers for Disease Control and Prevention, 1995. *Notes:* 1. Ever had at least one drink of alcohol. 2. Used alcohol on 1 or more of the 30 days preceding the survey. 3. Used 5 or more drinks of alcohol on at least 1 occasion on 1 or more of the 30 days preceding the survey. 4. Ever used marijuana. 5. Used marijuana 1 or more times during the 30 days preceding the survey. 6. 95-percent confidence level.

★ 21 ★

Behavior

Drug-Related: High School Students' Lifetime and/or Current Use of Cocaine, Crack/Freebase, Illegal Steroids, and Drug Injections, by Gender and Race/Ethnic Origin (in percentages)-Part 1: 1993

Category	Lifetime cocaine use[1]			Current cocaine use[2]			Lifetime crack or freebase use[3]		
	Female	Male	Total	Female	Male	Total	Female	Male	Total
Race/ethnicity									
White, non-Hispanic	3.9	5.3	4.6	1.2	2.0	1.6	2.0	2.6	2.3
	(+1.0)[6]	(+1.2)	(+0.9)	(+0.4)	(+0.8)	(+0.6)	(+0.5)	(+1.0)	(+0.6)
Black, non-Hispanic	1.2	1.9	1.6	0.5	1.5	1.0	0.6	1.6	1.1
	(+0.6)	(+1.1)	(+0.5)	(+0.3)	(+1.0)	(+0.6)	(+0.4)	(+1.0)	(+0.6)
Hispanic	10.4	12.1	11.3	3.0	6.2	4.6	5.5	7.1	6.3
	(+2.2)	(+3.1)	(+1.8)	(+1.7)	(+1.8)	(+1.5)	(+2.0)	(+2.0)	(+1.4)

Source: "Percentage of High School Students who Used Cocaine, Crack-Cocaine or Freebase, or Illegal Steroids, and Percentage who Injected Illegal Drugs, by Sex, Race/Ethnicity, and Grade Level: United States, Youth Risk Behavior Survey, 1993," *Drug Use Among Ethnic Minorities*, 1995, p. 37. Primary source: 1993 Youth Risk Behavior Surveillance System, Centers for Disease Control and Prevention, 1995. *Notes:* 1. Ever tried any form of cocaine, including powder, crack-cocaine, or freebase. 2. Used cocaine 1 or more times during the 30 days preceding the survey. 3. Ever used crack-cocaine or freebase. 4. Ever used illegal steroids 5. Ever injected illegal drugs. Respondents were classified as injecting drug users only if they (a) reported injecting drug use not prescribed by a physician and (b) answered "one or more" to any of these questions: "During your life, how many times have you used any form of cocaine including powder, crack, or freebase?"; "During your life, how many times have you used any other type of illegal drugs such as LSD, PCP, ecstacy, mushrooms, speed, ice, heroin, or pills without a doctor's prescription?"; or "During your life, how many times have you taken steroid pills or shots without a doctor's prescription?" 6. 95-percent confidence interval.

★ 22 ★

Behavior

Drug-Related: High School Students' Lifetime and/or Current Use of Cocaine, Crack/Freebase, Illegal Steroids, and Drug Injections, by Gender and Race/Ethnic Origin (in percentages)-Part 2: 1993

Category	Lifetime illegal steroid use[4]			Lifetime injecting drug use[5]		
	Female	Male	Total	Female	Male	Total
Race/ethnicity						
White, non-Hispanic	1.0	2.8	1.9	0.7	1.8	1.3
	(+0.8)	(+0.7)	(+0.5)	(+0.3)	(+0.7)	(+0.3)

[Continued]

★ 22 ★

Drug-Related: High School Students' Lifetime and/or Current Use of Cocaine, Crack/Freebase, Illegal Steroids, and Drug Injections, by Gender and Race/Ethnic Origin (in percentages)-Part 2: 1993

[Continued]

Category	Lifetime illegal steroid use[4]			Lifetime injecting drug use[5]		
	Female	Male	Total	Female	Male	Total
Black, non-Hispanic	0.8	4.0	2.4	0.4	1.4	0.9
	(+0.5)	(+1.6)	(+0.8)	(+0.5)	(+1.1)	(+0.6)
Hispanic	2.6	3.4	3.0	1.1	1.8	1.5
	(+1.4)	(+1.0)	(+0.8)	(+0.6)	(+0.8)	(+0.5)

Source: "Percentage of High School Students who Used Cocaine, Crack-Cocaine or Freebase, or Illegal Steroids, and Percentage who Injected Illegal Drugs, by Sex, Race/Ethnicity, and Grade Level: United States, Youth Risk Behavior Survey, 1993," *Drug Use Among Ethnic Minorities*, 1995, p. 37. Primary source: 1993 Youth Risk Behavior Surveillance System, Centers for Disease Control and Prevention, 1995. *Notes:* 1. Ever tried any form of cocaine, including powder, crack-cocaine, or freebase. 2. Used cocaine 1 or more times during the 30 days preceding the survey. 3. Ever used crack-cocaine or freebase. 4. Ever used illegal steroids 5. Ever injected illegal drugs. Respondents were classified as injecting drug users only if they (a) reported injecting drug use not prescribed by a physician and (b) answered "one or more" to any of these questions: "During your life, how many times have you used any form of cocaine including powder, crack, or freebase?"; "During your life, how many times have you used any other type of illegal drugs such as LSD, PCP, ecstacy, mushrooms, speed, ice, heroin, or pills without a doctor's prescription?"; or "During your life, how many times have you taken steroid pills or shots without a doctor's prescription?" 6. 95-percent confidence interval.

★ 23 ★

Behavior

Drug-Related: Mean Age at First Use of Cigarettes, Alcohol, Marijuana, and Cocaine, by Race/Ethnic Origin: 1988-1993

Drug and race/ethnicity	1988	1990	1991	1993
Cigarettes				
White	11.5	11.6	11.4	11.8
Black	11.1	10.8	11.3	11.8
Hispanic	12.3	11.7	12.0	12.0
Alcohol				
White	13.1	12.8	12.6	12.9
Black	12.9	13.3	12.9	13.2
Hispanic	13.3	12.8	12.8	13.0
Marijuana				
White	13.5	13.3	14.4	13.9
Black	13.1	13.4	13.7	14.0
Hispanic	13.4	14.1	13.1	13.7
Cocaine				
White	14.9	15.1	14.3	14.6

[Continued]

★ 23 ★

Drug-Related: Mean Age at First Use of Cigarettes, Alcohol, Marijuana, and Cocaine, by Race/Ethnic Origin: 1988-1993
[Continued]

Drug and race/ethnicity	1988	1990	1991	1993
Black	14.0	12.5	14.0	14.5
Hispanic	15.1	3.9	14.4	14.3

Source: "Average Age at First Use of Cigarettes, Alcohol, Marijuana, and Cocaine for Youth Ages 12-17, by Race/Ethnicity: 1988, 1990, 1991, and 1993," *Drug Use Among Ethnic Minorities*, 1995, p. 31. Primary source: National Household Survey on Drug Abuse, Substance Abuse and Mental Health Services Administration, 1988-93.

★ 24 ★
Behavior

Drug-Related: Percent Distribution of Number of Cigarettes Smoked in Past Month, by Race/Ethnic Origin: 1993

Demographic Characteristic	(Unweighted N)	Past Month Use[1]		
		None	Less Than a Pack a Day	A Pack or More a Day
Total	(26,130)	76.6	70.6	12.8
Race/Ethnicity[2]				
White	(12,328)	76.0	9.2	14.8
Black	(6,096)	77.5	14.7	7.8
Hispanic	(6,781)	79.8	14.8	5.5

Source: "Percentage Distribution of Amount of Past-Month Cigarette Use, by Demographic Characteristics: 1993," *National Household Survey on Drug Abuse: Main Findings 1993*, June, 1995, p. 122. Primary source: Office of Applied Studies, SAMHSA, National Household Survey on Drug Abuse, 1993. *Notes:* Only past-month cigarette users who reported the number of cigarettes they smoked per day during the past 30 days are included in this table. 1. Less than a pack a day is defined as averaging 15 cigarettes or less per day in the past month. A pack a day or more is defined as averaging 16 or more cigarettes per day in the last month. 2. The category "other" for Race/Ethnicity is not included.

★ 25 ★

Behavior

Drug-Related: Percent Reporting Alcohol Use in Past Month Among Those Under 21 and 21 and Over, by Race/Ethnic Origin: 1993

| Demographic Characteristic | Age Group (Years) | | | | Total (N=26,155) | |
| | Under 21 (N=8,923) | | 21 and Older (N=17,232) | | | |
	Any Use	Heavy Use	Any Use	Heavy Use	Any Use	Heavy Use
Total	27.4	4.2	52.9	5.5	49.0	5.3
Race/Ethnicity[1]						
White	29.6	5.0	55.8	5.8	52.2	5.7
Black	20.3	0.9	40.9	5.2	36.7	4.3
Hispanic	25.7	4.8	50.0	5.3	44.8	5.2

Source: "Percentage of Those Under 21 and 21 and Older Reporting Alcohol Use and Heavy Alcohol Use in the Past Month, by Demographic Characteristics: 1993," *National Household Survey on Drug Abuse: Main Findings 1993*, June, 1995, p. 107. Primary source: Office of Applied Studies, SAMHSA, National Household Survey on Drug Abuse, 1993. *Notes:* Heavy use is defined as drinking five or more drinks per occasion on 5 or more days in the past 30 days. 1. The category "other" for Race/Ethnicity is not included.

★ 26 ★

Behavior

Drug-Related: Percent Reporting Any Use of Illicit Drugs in Lifetime, Past Year, Past Month, by Age Group and Race/Ethnic Origin: 1992 and 1993

| Race/Ethnicity[1] | Age Group (Years) | | | | | | | | | |
| | 12-17 | | 18-25 | | 26-34 | | 35+ | | Total | |
	1992	1993	1992	1993	1992	1993	199	1993	1992	1993
Lifetime										
White	16.9	18.0	56.3	56.5	65.7	66.9	28.7	30.7	37.7	38.9
Black	15.1	14.5	42.3	37.8	51.4	50.8	28.7	30.7	33.6	33.5
Hispanic	17.6	21.6	39.2	40.9	44.3	44.4	20.7	23.1	29.2	31.2
Past Year										
White	12.1	13.5	28.7	29.7	19.1	18.1	5.3	6.2	11.3	11.8
Black	9.9	11.0	22.2	19.0	18.1	19.0	5.8	7.7	11.5	12.1
Hispanic	12.7	17.6[3]	20.0	21.3	15.1	11.7[2]	4.1	6.8[2]	10.8	12.2
Past Month										
White	6.1	6.3	13.7	15.2	10.6	8.6	2.2	2.5	5.5	5.5

[Continued]

★ 26 ★

Drug-Related: Percent Reporting Any Use of Illicit Drugs in Lifetime, Past Year, Past Month, by Age Group and Race/Ethnic Origin: 1992 and 1993

[Continued]

Race/Ethnicity[1]	Age Group (Years)									
	12-17		18-25		26-34		35+		Total	
	1992	1993	1992	1993	1992	1993	199	1993	1992	1993
Black	6.1	6.5	12.1	10.3	10.3	11.2	3.5	4.0	6.6	6.8
Hispanic	7.1	9.3	10.2	9.8	7.8	5.6	1.3	4.0[3]	5.3	6.2

Source: "Trends in Percentage Reporting Use of Any Illicit Drug in Their Lifetime, by Age Group and Demographic Characteristics: 1992 and 1993,: "Trends in Percentages Reporting Use of Any Illicit drug in the Past Year, by Age Group and Demographic Characteristics: 1992 and 1993," and "Trends in Percentage Reporting Use of Any Illicit Drug in the Past Month, by Age Group and Demographic Characteristics: 1992 and 1993," *National Household Survey on Drug Abuse: Main Findings 1993*, June 1995, pp. 37-39. Primary source: Office of Applied Studies, SAMHSA, National Household Survey on Drug Abuse, 1992 and 1993. *Notes:* Any illicit drug use is use of marijuana or hashish, cocaine (including crack), inhalants, hallucinogens (including PCP), heroin, or nonmedical use of psychotherapeutics at least once. 1. The category "other" for Race/Ethnicity is not included. 2. Difference between 1992 and 1993 statistically significant at the .05 level. 3. Difference between 1992 and 1993 statistically significant at the .01 level.

★ 27 ★

Behavior

Drug-Related: Percent Reporting Heavy Use of Alcohol in Past Month, by Age Group and Race/Ethnic Origin: 1993

Demographic Characteristic	Age Group (Years)				Total
	12-17	18-25	26-34	35+	
Total	1.3	10.4	7.3	4.2	5.3
Race/Ethnicity[1]					
White	1.3	12.7	8.1	4.3	5.7
Black	0.3	3.8	5.8	4.9	4.3
Hispanic	2.2	7.7	6.1	4.6	5.2

Source: "Percentage Reporting Heavy Alcohol Use in the Past Month, by Age Group and Demographic Characteristics: 1993," *National Household Survey on Drug Abuse: Main Findings 1993*, June, 1995, p. 106. Primary source: Office of Applied Studies, SAMHSA, National Household Survey on Drug Abuse, 1993. *Notes:* Heavy use is defined as drinking five or more drinks per occasion on 5 or more days in the past 30 days. 1. The category "other" for Race/Ethnicity is not included.

★ 28 ★

Behavior

Drug-Related: Percent Reporting Nonmedical Use of Prescription Drugs in Lifetime, Past Year, Past Month, by Age Group and Race/Ethnic Origin: 1993

Race/Ethnicity[1]	Age Group (Years)				Total
	12-17	18-25	26-34	35+	
Total	5.9	14.2	17.2	9.4	11.1
Lifetime					
White	6.6	17.2	20.2	9.7	12.2
Black	3.8	6.2	6.6	7.3	6.5
Hispanic	5.7	8.5	11.3	6.7	8.0
Past Year					
White	4.1	9.0	6.4	2.5	4.1
Black	1.3	3.2	2.7	2.2	2.3
Hispanic	4.1	3.7	3.9	2.2	3.2
Past month					
White	1.3	3.5	2.1	0.7	1.3
Black	0.7	0.8	1.0	1.0	0.9
Hispanic	1.6	2.1	1.3	1.0	1.4

Source: "Percentage Reporting Nonmedical Use of Any Prescription-Type Psychotherapeutic in their Lifetime, by Age Group and Demographic Characteristics: 1993," "Percentage Reporting Nonmedical Use of Any Prescription-Type Psychotherapeutic in the Past Year, by Age Group and Demographic Characteristics," and "Percentage reporting Nonmedical Use of Any Prescription-Type Psychotherapeutic in the Past Month, by Age Group and Demographic Characteristics," *National Household Survey on Drug Abuse: Main Findings 1993*, June, 1995, pp. 86-88. Primary source: Office of Applied Studies, SAHMSA, National Household Survey on Drug Abuse, 1993. *Notes:* Psychotherapeutic drugs are any prescription-type stimulant, sedative, tranquilizer, or analgesic used for nonmedical reasons; over-the-counter drugs are not included. 1. The category "other" for Race/Ethnicity is not included.

★ 29 ★

Behavior

Drug-Related: Percent Reporting Nonmedical Use of Stimulants, Sedatives, Tranquilizers, and Analgesics in Past Month, by Race/Ethnic Origin: 1993

Demographic Characteristic	Type of Psychotherapeutic Drug			
	Stimulants	Sedatives	Tranquilizers	Analgesics
Total	0.3	0.3	0.3	0.7
Race/Ethnicity[1]				
White	0.4	0.3	0.3	0.7

[Continued]

★ 29 ★

Drug-Related: Percent Reporting Nonmedical Use of Stimulants, Sedatives, Tranquilizers, and Analgesics in Past Month, by Race/Ethnic Origin: 1993
[Continued]

Demographic Characteristic	Type of Psychotherapeutic Drug			
	Stimulants	Sedatives	Tranquilizers	Analgesics
Black	0.3	0.1	0.3	0.4
Hispanic	0.2	0.2	0.4	0.8

Source: "Percentage Reporting Nonmedical Use of Specific Types of Psychotherapeutic Drugs in the Past Month, by Demographic Characteristics: 1993," *National Household Survey on Drug Abuse: Main Findings 1993,* June, 1995, p. 93. Primary source: Office of Applied Studies, SAHMSA, National Household Survey on Drug Abuse, 1993. *Note:* 1. The category "other" for Race/Ethnicity is not included.

★ 30 ★
Behavior

Drug-Related: Percent Reporting Seeing "Drunk" or "High on Drugs" Persons in Neighborhood, by Age Group and Race/Ethnic Origin: 1992 and 1993

Race/Ethnicity and Sex	Age (years)								Total	
	12-17		18-25		26-34		35+			
	1992	1993	1992	1993	1992	1993	1992	1993	1992	1993
Total	38.7	40.9	48.5	47.6	38.2	37.6	28.8[1]	25.2	34.2	32.1
Race/Ethnicity										
White	34.2	36.5	46.0	45.7	35.1	34.9	25.8[2]	21.9	30.8	28.4
Black	55.7	58.4	64.4[2]	58.2	53.6	50.9	48.6	47.0	53.2	51.2
Hispanic	43.5	46.7	48.3	52.2	44.7	42.8	38.4	38.0	42.4	43.0
Other	37.0	37.0	38.1	33.4	30.2	[1]	25.6	18.8	29.8	26.1

Source: "Percentage Reporting Seeing People who are Drunk or High on Drugs in the Neighborhood Occasionally or More Often, by Age, Sex, and Race/Ethnicity: 1992-93," *Drug Use Among Ethnic Minorities,* 1995, p.23. Primary source: 1992-93 National Household Survey on Drug Abuse, Substance Abuse and Mental Health Services Administration, preliminary data, June 1994. *Notes:* 1. Low precision, no estimate reported. 2. Difference between estimate in this cell and corresponding estimate for 1993 is statistically significant at the .05 level.

★ 31 ★

Behavior

Drug-Related: Percent Reporting Use of Alcohol in Lifetime, Past Year, Past Month, by Age Group, Gender, and Race/Ethnic Origin: 1993

Race/Ethnicity[1] and Sex	Age Group (Years)				
	12-17	18-25	26-34	35+	Total
(Unweighted N)					
White male	(1,508)	91,164)	(1,818)	(1,226)	(5,716)
Black male	(842)	(507)	(749)	(455)	(2,553)
Hispanic male	(1,038)	(802)	(913)	(573)	(3,326)
White female	(1,450)	(1,394)	(2,231)	(1,687)	(6,762)
Black female	(891)	(674)	(1,254)	(811)	(3,630)
Hispanic female	(973)	(760)	(1,106)	(729)	(3,568)
A. Used Alcohol in Their Lifetime					
White male	42.1	90.7	96.4	95.2	89.5
Black male	33.9	76.4	87.8	89.9	78.7
Hispanic male	43.9	85.1	95.0	95.3	85.9
White female	45.7	92.5	94.6	84.0	83.5
Black female	28.9	75.5	81.0	78.2	72.3
Hispanic female	38.5	70.1	78.2	71.4	68.2
B. Used Alcohol in the Past Year					
White male	35.3	83.4	86.8	74.6	74.0
Black male	26.7	67.1	74.1	57.0	57.3
Hispanic male	36.9	78.6	82.5	75.8	72.4
White female	39.9	85.0	83.5	60.9	65.8
Black female	24.1	63.3	65.3	42.0	47.8
Hispanic female	32.5	57.7	62.0	53.4	53.2
C. Used Alcohol in the Past Month					
White male	19.1	69.1	72.6	60.7	59.7
Black male	15.6	53.1	61.1	48.4	46.6
Hispanic male	20.3	61.4	69.0	63.4	58.2
White female	19.4	61.7	60.1	43.3	46.2
Black female	10.6	38.0	49.3	25.6	30.4
Hispanic female	14.6	37.3	42.1	32.2	32.9

Source: "Percentage Reporting Alcohol Use in Their Lifetime, the Past Year, and the Past Month, by Age Group, Race/Ethnicity, and Sex: 1993," *National Household Survey on Drug Abuse: Main Findings 1993,*June, 1995, p. 104. Primary source: Office of Applied Studies, SAMHSA, National Household Survey on Drug Abuse, 1993. *Note:* 1. The category "other" for Race/Ethnicity is not included.

★ 32 ★

Behavior

Drug-Related: Percent Reporting Use of Cigarettes in Lifetime, Past Year, Past Month, by Age Group, Gender, and Race/Ethnic Origin: 1993

Race/Ethnicity[1] and Sex	Age Group (Years)				Total
	12-17	18-25	26-34	35+	
(Unweighted N)					
White male	(1,508)	(1,164)	(1,818)	(1,226)	(5,716)
Black male	(842)	(507)	(749)	(455)	(2,553)
Hispanic male	(1,038)	(802)	(913)	(573)	(3,326)
White female	(1,450)	(1,394)	(2,231)	(1,687)	(6,762)
Black female	(891)	(674)	(1,254)	(811)	(3,630)
Hispanic female	(973)	(760)	(1,106)	(729)	(3,565)
A. Used Cigarettes in Their Lifetime					
White male	36.2	73.0	79.6	88.6	79.8
Black male	23.0	49.6	74.2	76.3	63.4
Hispanic male	36.1	66.3	72.3	76.0	67.5
White female	39.5	72.7	77.7	74.0	71.5
Black female	19.4	44.0	61.0	67.3	56.5
Hispanic female	29.8	48.5	51.9	49.7	47.3
B. Used Cigarettes in the Past Year					
White male	20.3	44.4	36.9	31.5	33.0
Black male	8.8	23.4	37.4	30.2	27.2
Hispanic male	18.9	40.8	35.7	31.3	32.5
White female	23.0	41.5	35.7	23.0	27.3
Black female	7.9	20.5	1.9	30.4	26.4
Hispanic female	17.5	24.3	25.9	22.2	22.8
C. Used Cigarettes in the Past Month					
White male	10.6	33.4	31.6	26.8	26.9
Black male	3.5	17.6	32.9	26.5	22.7
Hispanic male	9.6	31.2	30.2	24.4	25.0
White female	11.4	31.9	30.6	20.5	22.8
Black female	4.5	15.3	28.6	29.2	23.9
Hispanic female	7.0	19.1	19.0	18.9	17.3

Source: "Percentage Reporting Cigarette Use in Their Lifetime, the past Year, and the Past Month, by Age Group, Race/Ethnicity, and Sex: 1993" *National Household Survey on Drug Abuse: Main Findings 1993*, June, 1995, p. 121. Primary source: Office of Applied Studies, SAMHSA, National Household Survey on Drug Abuse, 1993. *Note:* 1. The category "other" for Race/Ethnicity is not included.

★ 33 ★
Behavior

Drug-Related: Percent Reporting Use of Cocaine in Lifetime, Past Year, Past Month, by Age Group, Gender, and Race/Ethnic Origin: 1993

Race/Ethnicity[1] and Sex	Age Group (Years)				Total
	12-17	18-25	26-34	35+	
Unweighted N					
White male	(1,508)	(1,164)	(1,818)	(1,226)	(5,716)
Black male	(842)	(507)	(749)	(455)	(2,553)
Hispanic male	(1,038)	(802)	(913)	(573)	(3,326)
White female	(1,450)	(1,394)	(2,231)	(1,687)	(6,762)
Black female	(891)	(674)	(1,254)	(811)	(3,630)
Hispanic female	(973)	(760)	(1,106)	(729)	(3,568)
A. Used Cocaine in Their Lifetime					
White male	0.7	14.8	33.2	12.4	15.2
Black male	0.5	9.7	23.5	14.6	13.3
Hispanic male	2.6	13.7	23.1	7.6	11.8
White female	1.3	13.0	24.9	5.1	9.0
Black female	0.9	4.1	10.9	6.3	6.2
Hispanic female	2.4	10.6	13.3	4.5	7.3
B. Used Cocaine in the Past Year					
White male	0.6	6.5	6.5	1.4	2.9
Black male	0.4	2.2	8.0	5.6	4.7
Hispanic male	1.5	8.7	4.7	2.5	4.1
White female	0.8	4.1	2.4	0.3	1.2
Black female	0.3	2.2	3.1	0.9	1.4
Hispanic female	2.0	4.3	2.4	0.9	2.0
C. Used Cocaine in the Past Month					
White male	0.4	1.7	1.6	0.3	0.7
Black male	0.4	0.5	3.0	2.7	2.0
Hispanic male	0.9	3.4	1.3	1.0	1.5
White female	0.3	1.4	0.2	0.1	0.3
Black female	0.2	1.9	0.8	0.4	0.7
Hispanic female	1.1	0.8	.08	0.4	0.7

Source: "Percentage Reporting Cocaine Use in Their Lifetime, the Past Year, and the Past Month, by Age Group, Race/Ethnicity, and Sex: 1993," *National Household Survey on Drug Abuse: Main Findings 1993*, June, 1995, p. 65. Primary source: Office of Applied Studies, SAMHSA, National Household Survey on Drug Abuse, 1993. *Note:* 1. The category "other" for Race/Ethnicity is not included.

★ 34 ★
Behavior

Drug-Related: Percent Reporting Use of Crack in Lifetime, Past Year, by Age Group and Race/Ethnic Origin: 1993

Race/Ethnicity[1] Characteristic	Age Group (Years)				Total
	12-17	18-25	26-34	35+	
Lifetime					
White	0.2	4.0	3.8	0.7	1.6
Black	0.3	2.1	7.2	3.3	3.4
Hispanic	1.2	3.5	3.2	0.9	2.0
Past Year					
White	0.2	1.0	0.5	0.1	0.3
Black	0.3	1.1	3.0	1.7	1.6
Hispanic	0.5	1.2	0.7	0.2	0.6

Source: "Percentage Reporting Crack Use in Their Lifetime, by Age Group and Demographic Characteristics: 1993," and "Percentage Reporting Crack Use in the Past Year, by Age Group and Demographic Characteristics: 1993," *National Household Survey on Drug Abuse: Main Findings 1993*, June, 1995, pp. 68-69. Primary source: Office of Applied Studies, SAMHSA, National Household Survey on Drug Abuse, 1993. *Note:* 1. The category "other" for Race/Ethnicity is not included.

★ 35 ★
Behavior

Drug-Related: Percent Reporting Use of Hallucinogens in Lifetime, Past Year, by Age Group and Race/Ethnic Origin: 1993

Race/Ethnicity[1]	Age Group (years)				Total
	12-17	18-25	26-34	35+	
Lifetime					
White	3.1	15.8	19.6	7.3	10.1
Black	0.2	1.9	5.3	3.1	3.0
Hispanic	4.1	7.8	6.7	5.1	5.9
Past Year					
White	2.3	6.4	1.5	0.1	1.3
Black	0.2	0.6	0.6	0.1	0.3
Hispanic	2.4	2.4	0.5	2	0.9

Source: "Percentage Reporting Inhalant Use of Any Hallucinogens in Their Lifetime, by Age Group and Demographic Characteristics: 1993," and "Percentage Reporting Use of Any Hallucinogens in the Past Month, by Age Group and Demographic Characteristics," *National Household Survey on Drug Abuse: Main Findings 1993*, June 1995, pp. 78-79. Primary source: Office of Applied Studies, SAMHSA, National Household Survey on Drug Abuse, 1993. *Notes:* 1. The category "other" for Race/Ethnicity is not included. 2. Low precision; no estimate reported.

★ 36 ★

Behavior

Drug-Related: Percent Reporting Use of Inhalants in Lifetime, by Age Group and Race/Ethnic Origin: 1993

Demographic characteristic	Age Group (years)				
	12-17	18-25	26-34	35+	Total
Total	5.9	9.9	9.4	2.8	5.3
Race/Ethnicity[1]					
White	6.5	12.4	11.5	2.8	5.8
Black	1.7	2.0	4.0	3.1	2.9
Hispanic	7.7	7.2	5.0	3.0	4.9

Source: "Percentage Reporting Inhalant Use in Their Lifetime, by Age Group and Demographic Characteristics: 1993," *National Household Survey on Drug Abuse: Main Findings 1993*, June 1995, p. 76. Primary source: Office of Applied Studies, SAMHSA, National Household Survey on Drug Abuse, 1993. *Note:* 1. The category "other" for Race/Ethnicity is not included.

★ 37 ★

Behavior

Drug-Related: Percent Reporting Use of Marijuana in Lifetime, Past Year, Past Month, by Age Group, Gender, and Race/Ethnic Origin: 1993

Race/Ethnicity[1] and Sex	Age Group (Years)				
	12-17	18-25	26-34	35+	Total
(Unweighted N)					
White male	(1,508)	(1,164)	(1,818)	(1,226)	(5,716)
Black male	(842)	(507)	(749)	(455)	(2,553)
Hispanic male	(1,038)	(802)	(913)	(573)	(3,326)
White female	(1,450)	(1,394)	(2,231)	(1,687)	(6,762)
Black female	(891)	(674)	(1,254)	(811)	(3,630)
Hispanic female	(973)	(760)	(1,106)	(729)	(3,568)
A. Used Marijuana in Their Lifetime					
White Male	11.4	53.3	68.6	34.7	40.7
Black male	13.6	41.7	57.1	39.2	39.1
Hispanic male	19.6	44.0	49.8	27.2	34.8
White female	11.2	52.5	61.7	21.1	30.8
Black female	8.2	27.5	43.6	19.4	24.0
Hispanic female	11.5	31.8	34.4	14.0	21.4

[Continued]

★ 37 ★

Drug-Related: Percent Reporting Use of Marijuana in Lifetime, Past Year, Past Month, by Age Group, Gender, and Race/Ethnic Origin: 1993

[Continued]

Race/Ethnicity[1] and Sex	Age Group (Years)				Total
	12-17	18-25	26-34	35+	

B. Used Marijuana in the Past Year

White male	10.0	31.0	18.4	5.2	11.3
Black male	12.3	21.9	20.5	9.7	14.2
Hispanic male	16.7	25.2	11.1	6.3	12.7
White female	9.6	20.1	10.2	2.3	6.4
Black female	6.9	12.2	12.9	4.1	7.4
Hispanic female	9.5	11.9	7.0	3.0	6.4

C. Used Marijuana in the Past Month

White male	4.8	18.7	9.4	2.2	5.9
Black male	7.2	14.0	13.5	4.6	8.2
Hispanic male	8.5	11.2	74.4	3.4	5.9
White female	4.3	6.4	4.2	1.3	2.7
Black female	4.4	5.2	7.0	1.3	3.4
Hispanic female	4.8	4.1	3.8	2.6	3.4

Source: "Percentage Reporting Marijuana Use in Their Lifetime, the Past Year, and the Past Month, by Age Group, Race/Ethnicity, and Sex: 1993," *National Household Survey on Drug Abuse: Main Findings 1993,* June 1995, p. 49. Primary source: Office of Applied Studies, SAMHSA, National Household Survey on Drug Abuse, 1993. *Note:* 1. The category "other" for Race/Ethnicity is not included.

★ 38 ★

Behavior

Drug-Related: Percent Reporting Use of PCP and Heroin in Lifetime, by Age Group and Race/Ethnic Origin: 1993

Race/Ethnicity[1] Characteristic	Age Group (Years)				Total
	12-17	18-25	26-34	35+	
Total	0.2	0.7	1.6	1.2	1.1
Heroin					
White	0.2	0.7	1.6	0.9	0.9
Black	0.1	1.0	1.9	3.0	2.1
Hispanic	0.7	0.6	1.8	1.7	1.4

Source: "Percentage Reporting Heroin Use in Heir Lifetime, by Age Group and Demographic Characteristics: 1993" and "Percentage Reporting PCP Use in Their Lifetime, by Age Group and Demographic Characteristics," *National Household Survey on Drug Abuse: Main Findings 1993,* June, 1995, pp. 80-81. Primary source: Office of Applied Studies, SAMHSA, National Household Survey on Drug Abuse, 1993. *Note:* 1. The category "other" for Race/Ethnicity is not included.

★ 39 ★
Behavior

Drug-Related: Percent Reporting Use of Smokeless Tobacco in Lifetime, Past Year, Past Month, by Age Group, Gender, and Race/Ethnic Origin: 1993

Race/Ethnicity[2] and Sex	Age Group (Years)				
	12-17	18-25	26-34	35+	Total
(Unweighted N)					
White male	(1,508)	(1,164)	(1,818)	(1,226)	(5,716)
Black male	(842)	(507)	(749)	(455)	(2,553)
Hispanic male	(1,038)	(802)	(913)	(573)	(2,326)
White female	(1,450)	(1,394)	(2,231)	(1,687)	(6,762)
Black female	(891)	(674)	(1,254)	(811)	(3,630)
Hispanic female	(973)	(760)	(1,106)	(729)	(3,568)
A. Used Smokeless Tobacco in Their Lifetime					
White male	19.1	44.1	41.9	21.4	27.7
Black male	1.9	10.2	12.2	13.5	11.0
Hispanic male	9.0	16.3	13.9	11.4	12.6
White female	3.4	6.8	4.2	1.6	2.8
Black female	0.4	0.9	3.3	7.0	4.5
Hispanic female	1.1	[1]	0.5	0.5	0.9
B. Used Smokeless Tobacco in Past Year					
White male	10.9	22.3	14.5	4.8	9.3
Black male	0.5	3.1	1.5	3.3	2.5
Hispanic male	5.4	5.4	2.6	2.7	3.6
White female	1.4	1.5	0.4	0.1	0.4
Black female	0.3	[1]	0.1	1.9	1.1
Hispanic female	0.9	0.2	[1]	[1]	0.2
C. Used Smokeless Tobacco in the Past Month					
White male	5.2	16.9	11.8	4.0	7.2
Black male	0.3	2.2	0.4	3.3	2.1
Hispanic male	1.8	3.6	1.8	1.6	2.1
White female	[1]	0.2	0.1	0.1	0.1
Black female	[1]	[1]	0.1	1.9	1.0
Hispanic female	[1]	[1]	[1]	[1]	[1]

Source: "Percentage Reporting Smokeless Tobacco Use in Their Lifetime, the Past Year, and the Past Month, by Age Group, Race/Ethnicity, and Sex: 1993," *National Household Survey on Drug Abuse: Main Findings1993*, June, 1995, p. 127. Primary source: Office of Applied Studies, SAMHSA, National Household Survey on Drug Abuse, 1993. *Notes:* 1. Low precision; no estimates reported. 2. The category "other" for Race/Ethnicity is not included.

★ 40 ★
Behavior

Drug-Related: Percent Reporting Use of Steroids and Ice in Lifetime, by Race/Ethnic Origin: 1993

Demographic Characteristic	Use in Lifetime	
	Anabolic Steroids	Ice[2]
Total	0.4	0.7
Number of users (in 1000s)	746	1,352
Race/Ethnicity[1]		
White	0.4	0.6
Black	0.3	0.4
Hispanic	0.5	0.8

Source: "Percentage Reporting Anabolic Steroid and Ice Use in their Lifetime, by Age Group and Demographic Characteristics: 1993," *National Household Survey on Drug Abuse: Main Findings 1993*, June, 1995, p. 162. Primary source: Office of Applied Studies, SAMHSA, National Household Survey on Drug Abuse, 1993. *Notes:* 1. The category "other" for Race/Ethnicity is not included. 2. Question asked was: Now, let's talk about a form of methamphetamine that can be smoked, say in a cigarette or pipe. Have you ever used the smokable form of methamphetamine called "Ice"?

★ 41 ★
Behavior

Drug-Related: Percent Reporting Using Drugs with Needles in Lifetime, by Age Group and Race/Ethnic Origin: 1993

Demographic Characteristic	Age Group (Years)				Total
	12-17	18-25	16-34	35+	
Total	0.3	1.4	2.7	1.2	1.4
Race/Ethnicity[1]					
White	0.2	1.7	3.1	0.9	1.3
Black	0.3	0.5	2.0	3.3	2.2
Hispanic	0.6	1.1	2.3	1.5	1.5

Source: "Percentage Reporting Drug Use with Needles in Their Lifetime, by Age Group and Demographic Characteristics: 1993," *National Household Survey on Drug Abuse: Main Findings 1993*, June, 1995, p. 149. Primary source: Office of Applied Studies, SAMHSA, National Household Survey on Drug Abuse, 1993. *Notes:* Needle use is derived from specific questions about use of cocaine, heroin, or amphetamines with a needle, and from general questions about needle use with other drugs. The 1992 and 1993 estimates are based on a more extensive set of questions about needle use available in the 1992 and 1993 NHSDA and are not comparable to those published in the 1988 Main Findings report. 1. The category "other" for Race/Ethnicity is not included.

★ 42 ★

Behavior

Drug-Related: Percent Who Report Seeing Drugs Sold in Neighborhood, by Age Group and Race/Ethnic Origin: 1992 and 1993

Race/ethnicity and sex	Age (years)								Total	
	12-17		18-25		26-34		35+			
	1992	1993	1992	1993	1992	1993	1992	1993	1992	1993
Total	14.6	14.7	19.0	18.6	14.9	14.2	9.7	8.1	12.4	11.3
Race/ethnicity										
White	7.4	7.8	12.5	12.9	9.9	9.5	6.5[2]	4.4	8.0	6.7
Black	41.2	42.7	48.1	45.6	39.3	35.8	31.2	33.2	37.0	37.0
Hispanic	23.9	22.2	27.7	26.3	23.4	22.7	19.4	17.6	22.5	21.1
Other	10.0	9.4	9.9	[1]	10.2	[1]	5.5	4.3	7.6	7.3

Source: "Percentage Reporting Seeing People Selling Drugs in the Neighborhood Occasionally or More Often, by Age, Sex, and Race/Ethnicity: 1992-93," *Drug Use Among Ethnic Minorities,* 1995, p. 22. Primary source: 1992-93 National Household Survey on Drug Abuse, Substance Abuse and Mental Health Services Administration, preliminary data, June 1994. *Notes:* 1. Low precision, no estimate reported. 2. Difference between estimate in this cell and corresponding estimate for 1993 is statistically significant at the .05 level.

★ 43 ★

Behavior

Drug-Related: Percent in "Big Cities" Reporting Illicit Drug Use in Past Year, by Race/Ethnic Origin: 1993

Demographic Characteristic	MSA					
	Chicago	Denver	Los Angeles	Miami	New York	Washington, DC
Total	11.9	16.9	13.0	5.8	10.9	12.0
Race/Ethnicity[1]						
White	12.7	17.0	15.2	6.1	11.6	14.1
Black	14.8	16.6	19.4	4.7	9.7	10.8
Hispanic	8.3	18.6	12.8	6.1	11.5	6.8

Source: "Percentage in the Oversampled MSA's Reporting Use of Any Illicit Drug in the Past Year, by Demographic Characteristics: 1993," *National Household Survey on Drug Abuse: Main Findings 1993,* June, 1995, p. 170. Primary source: Office of Applied Studies, SAMHSA, National Household Survey on Drug Abuse, 1993. *Note:* 1. The category "other" for Race/Ethnicity is not included.

★ 44 ★

Behavior

Drug-Related: Percent of Black 15-44-Year-Old Women Reporting Drug Use, by Residential Area and Age Group-Part I: 1993

Age	Race/ethnicity	Population density	Any illicit drug			Marijuana		
			Lifetime	Past year	Past month	Lifetime	Past year	Past month
All (15-44)	All	Total U.S.	48.9	14.1	6.3	45.4	10.5	4.5
		Metro	49.1	13.9	6.4	45.9	10.7	4.6
		Nonmetro	48.1	14.8	5.8	43.5	9.8	3.9
	Black, non-Hispanic	Total U.S.	38.9	12.9	6.9	34.8	10.7	5.2
		Metro	41.5	13.5	7.3	37.9	11.5	5.6
		Nonmetro	[1]	[1]	5.0	19.4	6.2	3.1
15-24	All	Total U.S.	41.0	21.1	8.7	35.6	16.4	6.4
		Metro	41.4	21.0	9.3	36.4	16.4	6.8
		Nonmetro	39.9	21.7	6.7	32.9	16.7	5.2
	Black, non-Hispanic	Total U.S.	27.1	14.5	6.9	21.8	11.4	5.5
		Metro	28.1	16.3	7.5	23.2	12.9	6.6
		Nonmetro	23.0	[1]	[1]	15.8	[1]	[1]

Source: "Percentage of Women of Childbearing Age (15-44) Using Drugs, by Age, Race/Ethnicity, and Population Density: 1993," *Drug Use Among Ethnic Minorities*, 1995, pp. 67-68. Primary source: National Household Survey on Drug Abuse, Substance Abuse and Mental Health Services Administration, 1993. *Note:* 1. Low precision, no estimate reported.

★ 45 ★

Behavior

Drug-Related: Percent of Black 15-44-Year-Old Women Reporting Drug Use, by Residential Area and Age Group-Part II: 1993

Age	Race/ethnicity	Population density	Cocaine			Cigarettes		
			Lifetime	Past year	Past month	Lifetime	Past year	Past month
All (15-44)	All	Total U.S.	14.4	2.2	0.7	68.3	33.1	27.3
		Metro	14.7	2.2	0.6	67.3	32.2	26.3
		Nonmetro	13.2	2.3	0.8	72.0	36.3	31.1
	Black, non-Hispanic	Total U.S.	8.5	2.2	1.2	56.4	28.2	24.6
		Metro	8.8	2.1	0.9	57.5	28.6	24.9
		Nonmetro	7.0	1	1	50.9	26.0	22.9
15-24	All	Total U.S.	8.1	3.2	1.2	58.6	33.3	23.9
		Metro	8.4	3.2	1.3	57.1	31.4	22.6
		Nonmetro	7.2	3.3	0.6	63.4	39.1	28.0
	Black, non-Hispanic	Total U.S.	3.5	1.9	1.7	38.2	16.7	11.8
		Metro	2.9	1.5	1.2	38.7	15.9	11.4
		Nonmetro	1	1	1	1	1	1

Source: "Percentage of Women of Childbearing Age (15-44) Using Drugs, by Age, Race/Ethnicity, and Population Density: 1993," *Drug Use Among Ethnic Minorities*, 1995, pp. 67-68. Primary source: National Household Survey on Drug Abuse, Substance Abuse and Mental Health Services Administration, 1993. *Note:* 1. Low precision, no estimate reported.

★ 46 ★

Behavior

Drug-Related: Percent of Current Alcohol Drinkers Among Persons 18 and Over, by Age Group and Race/Ethnic Origin: 1985 and 1990

[Data are based on household interviews of a sample of the civilian noninstitutionalized population].

Alcohol consumption, race, Hispanic origin, and age	Both sexes		Male		Female	
	1985	1990	1985	1990	1985	1990
Percent current drinkers among all persons						
All races:						
18-44 years	72.8	67.5	82.4	77.1	63.8	58.3
18-24 years	71.8	63.7	79.5	71.7	64.5	56.1
25-44 years	73.4	68.8	83.5	78.9	63.5	59.0
45 years and over	55.5	51.3	67.4	63.8	45.6	40.8
45-64 years	62.2	57.6	72.2	68.4	53.0	47.6
65 years and over	44.3	41.4	58.2	55.6	34.7	31.3

[Continued]

★ 46 ★

Drug-Related: Percent of Current Alcohol Drinkers Among Persons 18 and Over, by Age Group and Race/Ethnic Origin: 1985 and 1990

[Continued]

Alcohol consumption, race, Hispanic origin, and age	Both sexes		Male		Female	
	1985	1990	1985	1990	1985	1990
White, non-Hispanic:						
18-44 years	76.9	72.7	85.0	80.4	68.9	65.1
18-24 years	77.9	71.5	84.9	77.5	71.0	65.7
25-44 years	76.5	73.1	85.0	81.2	68.2	65.0
45 years and over	57.6	53.8	69.0	65.5	48.2	44.0
45-64 years	65.2	61.0	74.1	70.6	56.9	52.2
65 years and over	45.8	43.3	59.6	57.1	36.2	33.3
Black, non-Hispanic:						
18-44 years	59.0	51.5	72.2	68.1	48.2	37.9
45 years and over	41.5	36.0	57.1	51.3	29.9	24.5
Hispanic:						
18-44 years	58.7	55.7	73.2	71.3	45.6	42.0
45 years and over	48.5	43.4	64.3	63.3	35.4	27.8

Source: "Alcohol Consumption by Persons 18 Years of Age and Over, According to Sex, Race, Hispanic Origin, and Age: United States, 1985 and 1990," *Health, United States, 1994*, 1995, p. 162. Primary source: Data computed by the Alcohol Epidemiologic Data System of the National Institute on Alcohol Abuse and Alcoholism from data in the National Health Interview Survey compiled by the Division of Health Interview Statistics, National Center for Health Statistics, Centers for Disease Control and Prevention. *Notes:* Current drinkers consumed 12 or more drinks in a single year and at least 1 drink in the past year.

★ 47 ★

Behavior

Drug-Related: Percent of Eighth Graders and High School Seniors Reporting Use of Cigarettes, Marijuana, and Cocaine in Past Month, by Race: 1980-1994

Substance, sex, race, and grade in school	1980	1984	1986	1988	1990	1992	1994
Cigarettes							
All seniors	30.5	29.3	29.6	28.7	29.4	27.8	31.2
White	31.0	31.0	32.0	32.3	32.5	31.8	35.9
Black	25.2	17.6	14.6	12.8	12.0	8.2	11.0
All eighth graders	-	-	-	-	-	15.5	18.6
White	-	-	-	-	-	17.4	19.8
Black	-	-	-	-	-	5.3	9.6
Marijuana							
All seniors	33.7	25.2	23.4	18.0	14.0	11.9	19.0
White	34.2	25.3	24.6	19.9	15.6	13.1	20.1
Black	26.5	22.8	16.6	9.8	5.2	5.6	15.9
All eighth graders	-	-	-	-	-	3.7	7.8

[Continued]

★ 47 ★

Drug-Related: Percent of Eighth Graders and High School Seniors Reporting Use of Cigarettes, Marijuana, and Cocaine in Past Month, by Race: 1980-1994

[Continued]

Substance, sex, race, and grade in school	1980	1984	1986	1988	1990	1992	1994
White	-	-	-	-	-	3.5	6.7
Black	-	-	-	-	-	1.9	6.2
Cocaine							
All seniors	5.2	5.8	6.2	3.4	1.9	1.3	1.5
White	5.4	6.0	6.4	3.7	1.8	1.2	1.5
Black	2.0	2.4	2.7	1.4	0.5	0.5	0.6
All eighth graders	-	-	-	-	-	0.7	1.0
White	-	-	-	-	-	0.6	0.9
Black	-	-	-	-	-	0.4	0.3

Source: "Use of Selected Substances in the Past Month and Binge Drinking in the Past 2 Weeks, by High school Seniors and Eighth Graders, by Sex and Race: United States, 1980-94 (in percentages)," *Drug Use Among Ethnic Minorities*, 1995, p. 43. Primary source: National Institute on Drug Abuse, Monitoring the Future Study, annual surveys (adapted from National Center for Health Statistics, 1995). *Notes:* - Data not available. Monitoring the Future study excludes high school dropouts (about 15 percent of the age group during the 1980s) and absentees (about 16-19 percent of high school students). High school dropouts and absentees exhibit higher drug usage than those included in the survey. Estimates of the use of substances from the National Household Survey on Drug Abuse and the Monitoring the Future study differ because of different methodologies, sampling frames, and tabulation categories. Data are based on a survey of high school seniors and eighth graders in the coterminous United States.

★ 48 ★

Behavior

Drug-Related: Percent of Eighth Graders and High School Seniors Reporting Use of Inhalants and Alcohol in Past Month, and Binge Drinking in Past 2 weeks, by Race: 1980-1994

Substance, sex, race, and grade in school	1980	1984	1986	1988	1990	1992	1994
Inhalants							
All seniors	1.4	1.9	2.5	2.6	2.7	2.3	2.7
White	1.4	2.0	2.7	2.9	3.0	2.4	2.9
Black	1.0	1.2	1.5	1.8	1.5	1.5	1.8
All eighth graders							
White	-	-	-	-	-	4.9	5.8
Black	-	-	-	-	-	5.0	6.1
Alcohol[1]							
All seniors							
White	75.8	72.1	70.2	69.5	62.2	56.0	54.8
Black	47.7	42.1	40.4	40.9	32.9	29.5	33.1
All eighth graders							
White	-	-	-	-	-	27.3	25.4
Black	-	-	-	-	-	19.2	20.2

[Continued]

★ 48 ★

Drug-Related: Percent of Eighth Graders and High School Seniors Reporting Use of Inhalants and Alcohol in Past Month, and Binge Drinking in Past 2 weeks, by Race: 1980-1994

[Continued]

Substance, sex, race, and grade in school	1980	1984	1986	1988	1990	1992	1994
Binge drinking[2]							
All seniors							
White	44.6	42.9	40.5	38.8	36.2	31.3	31.7
Black	17.0	14.8	16.1	14.9	11.6	10.8	14.2
All eighth graders							
White	-	-	-	-	-	12.9	13.4
Black	-	-	-	-	-	9.3	11.8

Source: "Use of Selected Substances in the Past Month and Binge Drinking in the Past 2 Weeks, by High school Seniors and Eighth Graders, by Sex and Race: United States, 1980-94 (in percentages)," *Drug Use Among Ethnic Minorities*, 1995, pp. 44-45. Primary source: National Institute on Drug Abuse, Monitoring the Future Study, annual surveys (adapted from National Center for Health Statistics, 1995). *Notes:* - Data not available. Monitoring the Future study excludes high school dropouts (about 15 percent of the age group during the 1980) and absentees (about 16-19 percent of high school students). High school dropouts and absentees exhibit higher drug usage than those included in the survey. Estimates of the use of substances from the National Household Survey on Drug Abuse and the Monitoring the Future study differ because of different methodologies, sampling frames, and tabulation categories. Data are based on a survey of high school seniors and eighth graders in the coterminous United States. 1. In 1993 the alcohol question was changed to indicate that a "drink" meant "more than a few sips." 1993 data are based on a half sample. 2. Five or more drinks in a row at least once in the prior 2-week period.

★ 49 ★

Behavior

Drug-Related: Percent of Heavy Alcohol Drinkers Among Current Drinkers 18 and Over, by Age Group and Race/Ethnic Origin: 1985 and 1990

[Data are based on household interviews of a sample of the civilian noninstitutionalized population].

Alcohol consumption, race, Hispanic origin, and age	Both sexes		Male		Female	
	1985	1990	1985	1990	1985	1990
Level of alcohol consumption in						
Percent distribution of current drinkers						
All drinking levels	100.0	100.0	100.0	100.0	100.0	100.0
None	21.6	24.1	18.0	20.3	26.1	29.1
Light	37.1	39.4	30.9	33.9	44.7	46.4
Moderate	29.5	27.4	34.0	32.3	24.0	21.1
Heavier	11.8	9.1	17.2	13.6	5.3	3.4
Percent heavier drinkers among current drinkers						
All races:						
18-44 years	11.0	8.5	16.6	13.0	4.2	2.8
18-24 years	12.2	8.8	18.3	13.8	5.0	2.7
25-44 years	10.6	8.4	16.0	12.7	3.8	2.9
45 years and over	13.3	10.3	18.2	14.7	7.4	4.6

[Continued]

★ 49 ★

Drug-Related: Percent of Heavy Alcohol Drinkers Among Current Drinkers 18 and Over, by Age Group and Race/Ethnic Origin: 1985 and 1990

[Continued]

Alcohol consumption, race, Hispanic origin, and age	Both sexes		Male		Female	
	1985	1990	1985	1990	1985	1990
45-64 years	13.2	9.9	18.1	14.4	7.2	4.1
65 years and over	13.6	11.0	18.4	15.3	7.9	5.5
White, non-Hispanic:						
18-44 years	11.2	8.5	17.1	13.2	4.0	2.8
18-24 years	13.3	9.9	20.4	16.0	5.2	3.0
25-44 years	10.4	8.1	16.0	12.4	3.6	2.7
45 years and over	13.4	10.4	18.2	15.0	7.6	4.7
45-64 years	13.2	10.0	18.0	14.6	7.3	4.2
65 years and over	13.9	11.3	18.7	15.8	8.3	5.7
Black, non-Hispanic:						
18-44 years	9.6	10.3	13.4	14.7	5.1	3.9
45 years and over	10.3	7.7	16.2	10.1	[1]	[1]
Hispanic:						
18-44 years	10.6	7.9	15.2	11.3	[1]	[1]
45 years and over	15.7	12.1	[1]	17.2	[1]	[1]

Source: "Alcohol Consumption by Persons 18 Years of Age and Over, According to Sex, Race, Hispanic Origin, and Age: United States, 1985 and 1993," *Health, United States, 1994,* 1995, p. 162. Primary source: Data computed by the Alcohol Epidemiologic Data System of the National Institute on Alcohol Abuse and Alcoholism from data in the National Health Interview Survey compiled by the Division of Health Interview Statistics, National Center for Health Statistics, Centers for Disease Control and Prevention. *Notes:* 1. Estimates based on fewer than 30 subjects are not shown. Current drinkers consumed 12 or more drinks in a single year and at least 1 drink in the past year. For current drinkers, drinking levels are classified according to the average daily consumption of absolute alcohol (ethanol), in ounces, in the previous 2-week period, assuming 0.5 ounce ethanol per drink, as follows: none; light, .01-.21; moderate, .22-.99; and heavier, 1.00 or more. This corresponds to up to 3, 4-13, and 14 or more drinks per week for light, moderate, and heavier drinkers.

★ 50 ★

Behavior

Drug-Related: Percent of People Reporting Driving Under the Influence of Alcohol or Illegal Drugs in Past Year, by Age Group and Race: 1993

Race	Sex	Age	Percentage
All	All	All	7.9
		12-17	4.0
		18-25	15.9
		26-34	15.8
		35+	15.8
All	Male	All	11.7
		12-17	3.9
		18-25	21.1

[Continued]

★ 50 ★

Drug-Related: Percent of People Reporting Driving Under the Influence of Alcohol or Illegal Drugs in Past Year, by Age Group and Race: 1993

[Continued]

Race	Sex	Age	Percentage
		26-34	20.3
		35+	8.0
All	Female	All	4.4
		12-17	4.2
		18-25	10.6
		26-34	11.4
		35+	1.0
White	All	All	8.7
		12-17	4.7
		18-25	18.8
		26-34	18.8
		35+	4.4
White	Male	All	12.7
		12-17	4.1
		18-25	24.0
		26-34	24.1
		35+	8.3
White	Female	All	4.9
		12-17	5.4
		18-25	13.6
		26-34	13.7
		35+	0.9
Black	All	All	5.5
		12-17	0.6
		18-25	8.8
		26-34	6.0
		35+	5.5

[Continued]

★ 50 ★

Drug-Related: Percent of People Reporting Driving Under the Influence of Alcohol or Illegal Drugs in Past Year, by Age Group and Race: 1993

[Continued]

Race	Sex	Age	Percentage
Black	Male	All	9.2
		12-17	1.0
		18-25	14.5
		26-34	10.1
		35+	9.6
Black	Female	All	2.5
		12-17	0.2
		18-25	4.0
		26-34	2.8
		35+	2.4

Source: "Percentage of People Having driven a Vehicle Under the Influence of Alcohol or Illegal Drugs in the Past 12 Months, by Race, Sex, and Age," *Drug Use Among Ethnic Minorities*, 1995, p. 61. Primary source: National Household Survey on Drug Abuse, Substance and Mental Health Services Administration, 1993.

★ 51 ★

Behavior

Drug-Related: Percent of Youth 12-21 Reporting Lifetime, or Past Month Use of Alcohol, Marijuana, Cocaine, and Crack-Cocaine, by Age Group, Gender, and Race/Ethnic Origin-Part I: 1992

Sex and age	ALCOHOL						MARIJUANA					
	Lifetime			Past month			Lifetime			Past month		
	White	Black	Hispanic	White	Black	Hispanic	White	Black	Hispanic	White	Black	Hispanic
Male												
12-15	44.5	39.2	47.8	23.1	19.8	27.6	8.9	6.5	12.1	4.5	2.4	6.1
16-17	78.7	70.0	73.9	52.1	40.0	49.2	31.7	26.9	30.8	17.3	14.3	18.4
18-21	90.0	84.7	81.8	71.6	63.2	63.8	51.5	43.8	41.0	19.9	21.9	15.2
Female												
12-15	46.3	38.5	43.4	25.2	16.2	23.7	8.7	5.6	6.0	3.9	1.5	2.3
16-17	78.5	60.6	72.7	50.0	34.1	39.6	31.7	24.9	30.9	12.5	6.1	12.1
18-21	90.5	85.3	75.2	67.9	57.3	49.2	50.5	35.5	30.0	16.3	10.3	11.7

Source: "Prevalence Among Youth Ages 12-21 of Alcohol, Marijuana, Cocaine, or Crack-Cocaine Use in Their Lifetime or in the Past Month, by Age, Sex, and Race/Ethnicity: Youth Risk Behavior survey, 1992 (in percentages)," *Drug Use Among Ethnic Minorities*, 1995, p. 41. Primary source: National Health Interview Survey, Youth Risk Behavior Survey, Centers for Disease Control and Prevention, 1992.

★ 52 ★
Behavior

Drug-Related: Percent of Youth 12-21 Reporting Lifetime, or Past Month Use of Alcohol, Marijuana, Cocaine, and Crack-Cocaine, by Age Group, Gender, and Race/Ethnic Origin-Part II: 1992

| Sex and age | COCAINE | | | | | | CRACK-COCAINE | | |
| | Lifetime | | | Past month | | | Lifetime | | |
	White	Black	Hispanic	White	Black	Hispanic	White	Black	Hispanic
Male									
12-15	0.7	[1]	2.2	[1]	-	1.2	0.1	[1]	1.3
16-17	4.8	[1]	5.0	1.9	[1]	[1]	2.3	[1]	[1]
18-21	13.3	6.5	16.9	2.5	1.6	4.6	6.9	3.2	7.2
Female									
12-15	1.2	-	0.4	0.6	-	[1]	1.1	-	-
16-17	3.5	-	7.3	[1]	-	[1]	2.0	-	3.3
18-21	12.7	4.1	9.1	1.7	2.1	[1]	4.9	1.9	5.9

Source: "Prevalence Among Youth Ages 12-21 of Alcohol, Marijuana, Cocaine, or Crack-Cocaine Use in Their Lifetime or in the Past Month, by Age, Sex, and Race/Ethnicity: Youth Risk Behavior survey, 1992 (in percentages)," *Drug Use Among Ethnic Minorities*, 1995, p. 41. Primary source: National Health Interview Survey, Youth Risk Behavior Survey, Centers for Disease Control and Prevention, 1992. *Notes:* - No respondents. 1. Low precision, no estimate reported.

★ 53 ★
Behavior

Drug-Related: Percent of Youth Drug Users and Nonusers Reporting Selected Risk Behaviors, by Race/Ethnic Origin-Part I: 1992

Drug, type of use, and race/ethnicity	Fight in last 12 months	Carried a weapon in last 30 days	Rarely wears seatbelt	Multiple sex partners during last 3 months	Ridden in car while driver is drinking	Used drugs or alcohol before last sexual encounter	Used no condom during last sexual encounter
Marijuana							
Lifetime use							
White	43.6	19.6	26.6	19.9	48.0	21.2	62.2
Black	55.7	27.8	35.5	34.7	52.3	22.5	56.7
Hispanic	53.2	28.6	28.2	25.0	50.0	21.4	60.9
Other	52.2	23.9	24.8	25.7	45.2	18.7	62.4
No lifetime use							
White	33.7	12.8	12.5	4.5	15.6	2.7	48.9
Black	47.3	12.1	18.0	17.4	18.7	2.7	33.4
Hispanic	36.0	10.1	16.9	5.8	16.3	2.3	52.2
Other	29.8	7.4	12.5	6.2	10.6	2.3	37.3
Used last 30 days							
White	54.1	26.4	28.8	29.6	62.5	31.4	57.8
Black	70.0	42.5	45.6	53.7	60.8	36.4	54.9
Hispanic	66.8	42.8	34.3	39.2	61.7	33.2	63.3
Other	64.5	21.9	29.1	30.4[1]	56.8	36.9	59.3

[Continued]

★ 53 ★

Drug-Related: Percent of Youth Drug Users and Nonusers Reporting Selected Risk Behaviors, by Race/Ethnic Origin-Part I: 1992

[Continued]

Drug, type of use, and race/ethnicity	Fight in last 12 months	Carried a weapon in last 30 days	Rarely wears seatbelt	Multiple sex partners during last 3 months	Ridden in car while driver is drinking	Used drugs or alcohol before last sexual encounter	Used no condom during last sexual encounter
No use last 30 days							
White	34.3	13.3	15.1	6.9	20.3	5.1	55.6
Black	47.1	13.1	19.6	18.3	22.9	4.3	39.1
Hispanic	37.1	11.3	17.9	7.6	20.1	3.9	54.4
Other	32.3	9.9	14.0	9.2	14.9	3.5	46.4

Source: "Proportion of Youth Engaging in Risk Behaviors, by Drug Users and Nonusers and Race/Ethnicity: 1992 Youth Risk Behavior Survey (in percentages)," *Drug Use Among Ethnic Minorities*, 1995, p. 58. Primary source: National Health Interview Survey, Youth Risk Behavior Study, Centers for Disease Control and Prevention, 1992. *Note:* 1. Based on five or fewer respondents in numerator.

★ 54 ★

Behavior

Drug-Related: Percent of Youth Drug Users and Nonusers Reporting Selected Risk Behaviors, by Race/Ethnic Origin-Part II: 1992

Drug, type of use, and race/ethnicity	Fight in last 12 months	Carried a weapon in last 30 days	Rarely wears seatbelt	Multiple sex partners during last 3 months	Ridden in car while driver is drinking	Used drugs or alcohol before last sexual encounter	Used no condom during last sexual encounter
Cocaine							
Lifetime use							
White	52.8	25.0	40.3	23.6	61.5	32.9	74.1
Black	63.5	39.8	52.4	46.6	77.8	45.5	64.7
Hispanic	59.2	30.3	30.0	31.7	62.6	33.7	70.8
Other	70.6	36.7	42.7	[1]	49.6	32.1[2]	73.0
No lifetime use							
White	35.5	14.2	15.2	9.1	22.6	6.5	53.6
Black	48.7	14.6	21.0	21.3	24.4	5.8	40.0
Hispanic	38.2	13.1	18.8	9.3	21.3	4.8	53.6
Other	31.5	9.6	13.2	10.1	14.9	3.4	43.0
Used last 30 days							
White	63.6	44.7	48.0	41.8	79.2	44.7	70.7
Black	84.8	46.1	54.6	55.8	90.9	76.6	52.7
Hispanic	68.2	61.5	34.6	44.3	88.2	47.6	68.3
Other	-	46.7[2]	[1]	-	30.5[2]	-	[1]
No use last 30 days							
White	36.3	14.4	16.4	9.7	24.5	7.7	55.8
Black	48.8	15.0	21.5	21.7	25.3	6.2	40.9
Hispanic	39.2	13.5	19.3	10.6	23.3	5.9	55.6
Other	33.2	10.7	14.5	10.3	16.6	5.0	47.0

Source: "Proportion of Youth Engaging in Risk Behaviors, by Drug Users and Nonusers and Race/Ethnicity: 1992 Youth Risk Behavior Survey (in percentages)," *Drug Use Among Ethnic Minorities*, 1995, p. 59. Primary source: National Health Interview Survey, Youth Risk Behavior Study, Centers for Disease Control and Prevention, 1992. *Notes:* - No respondents. 1. Low precision, no estimate reported. 2. Based on five or fewer respondents in numerator.

★ 55 ★
Behavior

Drug-Related: Percent of Youth Drug Users and Nonusers Reporting Selected Risk Behaviors, by Race/Ethnic Origin-Part III: 1992

Drug, type of use, and race/ethnicity	Fight in last 12 months	Carried a weapon in last 30 days	Rarely wears seatbelt	Multiple sex partners during last 3 months	Ridden in car while driver is drinking	Used drugs or alcohol before last sexual encounter	Used no condom during last sexual encounter
Crack							
Lifetime use							
White	60.0	31.2	46.7	28.3	64.3	34.4	74.3
Black	56.2	48.0	33.9	54.0	81.9	50.8	45.6
Hispanic	63.9	35.7	32.3	41.0	71.2	41.6	71.0
Other	77.4	40.0	47.4	[1]	54.3	35.5	75.3
No lifetime use							
White	35.9	14.3	15.9	9.5	23.9	7.4	55.0
Black	49.0	14.8	21.6	21.5	25.0	6.2	40.9
Hispanic	38.8	13.5	19.1	10.0	22.6	5.5	54.8
Other	31.5	9.8	13.3	10.0	15.0	3.4	43.1
No Marijuana or Cocaine Use							
Last 30 days							
White	34.4	13.3	15.2	5.1	20.3	5.1	55.6
Black	47.0	13.1	19.8	18.8	22.8	4.5	39.4
Hispanic	36.7	11.5	18.0	7.7	20.3	3.8	54.4
Other	32.4	10.4	16.9	10.0	15.2	3.7	46.7

Source: "Proportion of Youth Engaging in Risk Behaviors, by Drug Users and Nonusers and Race/Ethnicity: 1992 Youth Risk Behavior Survey (in percentages)," *Drug Use Among Ethnic Minorities*, 1995, p. 60. Primary source: National Health Interview Survey, Youth Risk Behavior Study, Centers for Disease Control and Prevention, 1992. *Note:* 1. Low precision, no estimate reported.

★ 56 ★
Behavior

Drug-Related: Percent of Youth in National Longitudinal Survey of Youth Reporting Marijuana and Cocaine Use in Lifetime, Past Year, Past Month, by Race: 1984, 1988, and 1992

Drug and Race	1984			1988			1992		
	Lifetime	Past year	Past month	Lifetime	Past year	Past month	Lifetime	Past year	Past month
Marijuana									
White, non-Hispanic	65.8	38.2	22.4	69.4	23.5	12.9	64.2	14.8	8.8
Black, non-Hispanic	57.7	35.7	23.6	59.1	21.2	11.9	51.2	11.9	6.0
Other	55.7	35.8	20.0	61.0	20.4	12.4	52.4	12.6	9.3
Cocaine									
White, non-Hispanic	19.4	12.3	4.9	32.4	11.0	3.3	29.9	4.0	1.3
Black, non-Hispanic	10.2	7.0	3.0	21.8	8.7	3.6	19.0	5.6	2.2
Other	18.1	10.6	3.5	31.3	11.8	2.9	28.4	4.2	1.5

Source: "Percentage of National Longitudinal Survey of Youth Cohort Admitting to Use of Marijuana and Cocaine, by Race and Year: 1984, 1988, and 1992," *Drug Use Among Ethnic Minorities*, 1995, p. 42. Primary source: National Longitudinal Survey of Youth, Bureau of Labor Statistics, 1993.

★ 57 ★

Behavior

Drug-Related: Summary Table – Use of Any Drugs and Selected Specific Drugs in Past Month, by Age Group and Race/Ethnic Origin (in percentages): 1991-1993

Type of drug	12-17	18-25	26-34	35+	Total
Any illicit drug					
White[2]	6.3	15.2	8.6	2.5	5.5
Black[2]	6.5	10.3	11.2	4.0	6.8
Hispanic[1]	9.3	9.8	5.6	4.0	6.2
American Indian[3]/					
Alaska Native	11.3	20.8	15.6	6.5	11.3
Asian/Pacific[3]					
Islander	3.1	6.0	4.9	0.8	2.8
Marijuana					
White[2]	4.5	12.5	6.8	1.7	4.2
Black[2]	5.8	9.2	9.9	2.7	5.6
Hispanic[2]	6.7	7.8	4.1	2.9	4.7
American Indian[3]/					
Alaska Native	6.7	14.3	13.2	[1]	8.6
Asian/Pacific[3]					
Islander	1.6	3.1	3.2	0.3	1.5
Cocaine					
White[2]	0.3	1.6	0.9	0.2	0.5
Black[2]	0.3	1.3	1.8	1.4	1.3
Hispanic[2]	1.0	2.1	1.1	0.7	1.1
American Indian[3]/					
Alaska Native	[1]	1.4	3.3	[1]	3.1
Asian/ Pacific[3]					
Islander	0.1	1.2	0.2	[1]	0.3
Alcohol					
White[2]	19.2	65.3	66.3	51.5	52.7
Black[2]	13.1	45.0	54.5	35.5	37.6
Hispanic[2]	17.5	49.9	56.0	47.1	45.6
American Indian[3]/					
Alaska Native	23.0	56.1	64.9	51.1	50.7
Asian/Pacific[3]					
Islander	10.5	38.4	38.9	34.6	3.3
Heavy alcohol					
White[2]	4.0	23.8	25.2	25.4	23.2
Black[2]	3.8	15.5	28.3	17.9	17.6
Hispanic[2]	4.9	19.0	20.1	18.7	17.2
American Indian[3]/					
Alaska Native	5.0	7.0	9.1	5.9	6.6
Asian/Pacific[3]					
Islander	0.5	2.1	1.7	0.7	1.1
Cigarettes					
White[2]	11.0	32.7	31.1	23.4	24.7
Black[2]	4.0	16.3	30.5	28.0	23.4
Hispanic[2]	8.4	25.5	24.8	21.5	21.2
American Indian[3]/					
Alaska Native	17.9	33.0	44.1	44.2	38.7

[Continued]

★ 57 ★

Drug-Related: Summary Table – Use of Any Drugs and Selected Specific Drugs in Past Month, by Age Group and Race/Ethnic Origin (in percentages): 1991-1993

[Continued]

Type of drug	12-17	18-25	26-34	35+	Total
Asian/Pacific[3] Islander	4.8	20.7	21.1	16.7	16.9

Source: "Prevalence of Past-Month Drug Use in the United States, by Age, Sex, and Race/Ethnicity: 1991-93 (in percentages)," *Drug Use Among Ethnic Minorities*, 1995, p. 19. Primary source: National Household Survey on Drug Abuse, Substance Abuse and Mental Health Services Administration, 1991-93. *Notes:* 1. Low precision, no estimate reported. 2. 1993 National Household Survey on Drug Abuse data. 3. 1991-93 National Household Survey on Drug Abuse data.

★ 58 ★

Behavior

Drug-Related: Total Lifetime, Annual, 30-day, and Daily Use of Alcohol - Effect and Amount, by Grade Level and Race/Ethnic Origin (in percentages): 1994

Grade	Alcohol			Been drunk			5+ drinks[1]		
	8th	10th	12th	8th	10th	12th	8th	10th	12th
Lifetime									
White	54.7	72.0	83.1	26.4	49.7	67.5	-	-	-
Black	55.1	68.1	71.4	21.5	36.0	44.0	-	-	-
Hispanic	63.3	72.7	80.4	31.7	46.6	58.9	-	-	-
Annual									
White	46.6	65.4	76.6	19.0	40.8	56.7	-	-	-
Black	40.7	56.2	59.8	12.8	23.2	27.8	-	-	-
Hispanic	54.2	63.2	71.7	22.1	34.7	42.9	-	-	-
30-day									
White	25.3	40.4	54.0	8.4	22.0	34.0	-	-	-
Black	19.4	29.7	33.8	5.6	10.1	14.1	-	-	-
Hispanic	33.5	37.7	45.9	10.8	17.0	23.0	-	-	-
Daily									
White	0.8	1.6	3.1	-	-	-	12.9	24.5	31.5
Black	1.2	1.2	2.6	-	-	-	11.8	14.0	14.4
Hispanic	1.7	1.8	3.8	-	-	-	22.3	24.2	24.3

Source: "Prevalence of Lifetime, Annual, 30-Day, and Daily Prevalence of Use of Selected Drugs, by Race/Ethnicity for 8th, 10th, and 12th graders: 1994 (in percentages)," *Drug Use Among Ethnic Minorities*, 1995, p. 34. Primary source: The Monitoring the Future Study, the University of Michigan. *Notes:* - Data not available. 1. This measure refers to use of five or more drinks in a row in the past two weeks.

★ 59 ★

Behavior

Drug-Related: Total Lifetime, Annual, 30-day, and Daily Use of Cigarettes, Smokeless Tobacco, and Steroids, by Grade Level and Race/Ethnic Origin (in percentages): 1994

Grade	Cigarettes			Smokeless tobacco[8]			Steroids[6]		
	8th	10th	12th	8th	10th	12th	8th	10th	12th
Lifetime									
White	46.0	58.9	65.6	21.8	33.2	36.6	1.7	1.7	2.0
Black	37.1	39.6	44.4	10.0	10.8	11.1	1.5	1.6	2.4
Hispanic	54.2	56.5	61.7	15.6	16.5	21.8	2.0	1.9	2.9
Annual									
White	-	-	-	-	-	-	1.0	1.0	1.1
Black	-	-	-	-	-	-	0.8	0.8	1.8
Hispanic	-	-	-	-	-	-	1.1	1.3	1.7
30-day									
White	18.9	27.8	35.2	8.1	12.5	13.8	0.4	0.5	0.6
Black	8.7	9.8	10.9	3.2	2.3	1.9	0.5	0.5	1.3
Hispanic	21.3	19.4	23.6	5.0	4.3	5.4	0.6	0.7	0.8
Daily									
White	9.7	16.5	22.9	-	-	-	-	-	-
Black	2.6	3.8	4.9	-	-	-	-	-	-
Hispanic	9.0	8.1	10.6	-	-	-	-	-	-

Source: "Prevalence of Lifetime, Annual, 30-Day, and Daily Prevalence of Use of Selected Drugs, by Race/Ethnicity for 8th, 10th, and 12th graders: 1994 (in percentages)," *Drug Use Among Ethnic Minorities*, 1995, p. 34. Primary source: The Monitoring the Future Study, the University of Michigan. *Notes:* - Data not available. 1. Data from two years have been combined to increase subgroup sample sizes. 2. 12th grade only: Data based on five of six questionnaire forms. N is five-sixths of N indicated. 3. Unadjusted for known underreporting of certain drugs. 4. 12th grade only: Data based on four of six questionnaire forms. N is four-sixths of N indicated. 5. Only drug use which was not under a doctor's orders is included here. 6. 12th grade only: Data based on two of six questionnaire forms. N is two-sixths of N indicated. 7. This measure refers to use of five or more drinks in a row in the past two weeks. 8. Data based on one questionnaire form. N is one-half of N indicated for 8th and 10th grades and one-sixth of N indicated for 12th grade.

★ 60 ★

Behavior

Drug-Related: Total Lifetime, Annual, 30-day, and Daily Use of Cocaine, by Grade Level and Race/Ethnic Origin (in percentages): 1994

Grade	Cocaine			Crack-Cocaine		
	8th	10th	12th	8th	10th	12th
Lifetime						
White	2.7	3.6	6.0	1.7	1.8	2.8
Black	1.4	1.4	1.5	1.1	1.0	1.2
Hispanic	7.5	7.9	9.9	4.2	3.5	4.1
Annual						
White	1.6	2.2	3.5	1.0	1.1	1.6
Black	0.7	1.	0.9	0.5	0.8	0.9
Hispanic	4.5	4.9	5.4	2.1	1.9	2.4
30-day						
White	0.9	1.3	0.4	0.4	0.5	0.6
Black	0.6	0.5	0.3	0.3	0.5	0.7
Hispanic	1.8	2.3	1.3	1.3	0.7	1.2
Daily						
White	-	-	-	-	-	-
Black	-	-	-	-	-	-
Hispanic	-	-	-	-	-	-

Source: "Prevalence of Lifetime, Annual, 30-Day, and Daily Prevalence of Use of Selected Drugs, by Race/Ethnicity for 8th, 10th, and 12th graders: 1994 (in percentages," *Drug Use Among Ethnic Minorities*, 1995, pp. 32-33. Primary source: The Monitoring the Future Study, the University of Michigan. *Note:* - Data not available.

★ 61 ★

Behavior

Drug-Related: Total Lifetime, Annual, 30-day, and Daily Use of Heroin, Other Opiates, Stimulants, Barbiturates, and Tranquilizers, by Grade Level and Race/Ethnic Origin (in percentages)-Part I: 1994

Grade	Heroin			Other opiates			Stimulants		
	8th	10th	12th	8th	10th	12th	8th	10th	12th
Lifetime									
White	1.5	1.4	1.2	-	-	7.4	12.4	16.2	17.9
Black	1.2	0.8	0.5	-	-	2.5	7.4	6.8	5.5
Hispanic	2.8	1.5	0.9	-	-	4.4	14.3	13.1	11.5
Annual									
White	0.8	0.8	0.5	-	-	4.3	8.1	11.0	10.4
Black	0.6	0.6	0.3	-	-	1.5	3.9	4.0	3.4

[Continued]

★ 61 ★

Drug-Related: Total Lifetime, Annual, 30-day, and Daily Use of Heroin, Other Opiates, Stimulants, Barbiturates, and Tranquilizers, by Grade Level and Race/Ethnic Origin (in percentages)-Part I: 1994

[Continued]

Grade	Heroin			Other opiates			Stimulants		
	8th	10th	12th	8th	10th	12th	8th	10th	12th
Hispanic	1.5	1.5	0.5	-	-	2.2	8.6	7.7	6.4
30-day									
White	0.4	.04	0.2	-	-	1.6	3.8	4.8	4.5
Black	.03	0.4	.03	-	-	0.8	2.0	2.0	1.6
Hispanic	0.7	0.3	0.3	-	-	0.9	4.1	3.0	2.8
Daily									
White	-	-	-	-	-	-	-	-	-
Black	-	-	-	-	-	-	-	-	-
Hispanic	-	-	-	-	-	-	-	-	-

Source: "Prevalence of Lifetime, Annual, 30-Day, and Daily Prevalence of Use of Selected Drugs, by Race/Ethnicity for 8th, 10th, and 12th graders: 1994 (in percentages)," *Drug Use Among Ethnic Minorities*, 1995, p. 33. Primary source: The Monitoring the Future Study, the University of Michigan. *Note:* - Data not available.

★ 62 ★

Behavior

Drug-Related: Total Lifetime, Annual, 30-day, and Daily Use of Heroin, Other Opiates, Stimulants, Barbiturates, and Tranquilizers, by Grade Level and Race/Ethnic Origin (in percentages)-Part II: 1994

Grade	Barbiturates			Tranquilizers		
	8th	10th	12th	8th	10th	12th
Lifetime						
White	-	-	7.5	4.2	5.8	7.2
Black	-	-	2.6	2.8	2.2	2.2
Hispanic	-	-	5.2	6.6	6.0	6.0
Annual						
White	-	-	4.3	2.2	3.6	4.2
Black	-	-	1.5	1.2	0.9	1.1
Hispanic	-	-	2.6	3.4	3.1	2.4
30-day						
White	-	-	1.7	1.0	1.4	1.4
Black	-	-	0.9	0.5	0.6	0.5
Hispanic	-	-	1.1	1.5	1.0	0.8
Daily						
White	-	-	-	-	-	-

[Continued]

★ 62 ★

Drug-Related: Total Lifetime, Annual, 30-day, and Daily Use of Heroin, Other Opiates, Stimulants, Barbiturates, and Tranquilizers, by Grade Level and Race/Ethnic Origin (in percentages)-Part II: 1994

[Continued]

Grade	Barbiturates			Tranquilizers		
	8th	10th	12th	8th	10th	12th
Black	-	-	-	-	-	-
Hispanic	-	-	-	-	-	-

Source: "Prevalence of Lifetime, Annual, 30-Day, and Daily Prevalence of Use of Selected Drugs, by Race/Ethnicity for 8th, 10th, and 12th graders: 1994 (in percentages)," *Drug Use Among Ethnic Minorities*, 1995, p. 33. Primary source: The Monitoring the Future Study, the University of Michigan. *Note:* - Data not available.

★ 63 ★

Behavior

Drug-Related: Total Lifetime, Annual, 30-day, and Daily Use of Marijuana, Inhalants, Hallucinogens, and LSD, by Grade Level and Race/Ethnic Origin (in percentages): 1994

Grade	Marijuana			Inhalants			Hallucinogens			LSD		
	8th	10th	12th	8th	10th	12th	8th	10th	12th	8th	10th	12th
Lifetime												
White	12.9	27.2	38.3	20.8	19.2	20.1	4.3	8.0	12.8	3.7	7.2	12.1
Black	13.2	22.1	29.4	11.1	8.8	6.5	1.1	1.5	1.6	1.0	1.2	1.3
Hispanic	23.3	33.5	36.6	21.6	16.9	15.2	6.3	8.6	9.8	5.7	7.5	9.0
Annual												
White	10.0	22.6	30.2	12.4	9.6	8.6	2.8	5.6	8.6	2.5	5.0	8.0
Black	8.9	15.3	20.7	5.3	3.3	2.4	0.6	1.1	1.2	0.5	0.9	0.9
Hispanic	18.1	25.1	25.7	12.5	9.0	5.5	4.0	5.7	5.8	3.6	5.0	5.4
30-day												
White	5.6	13.4	18.4	6.0	3.7	2.8	1.3	2.3	3.3	1.0	2.0	0.7
Black	5.0	9.8	13.1	2.8	1.6	1.5	0.4	0.7	0.8	0.3	0.6	0.3
Hispanic	12.1	15.6	14.9	6.1	3.4	2.3	1.8	2.2	2.0	1.5	1.8	2.2
Daily												
White	0.4	1.6	3.2	-	-	-	-	-	-	-	-	-
Black	0.4	0.8	2.0	-	-	-	-	-	-	-	-	-
Hispanic	1.1	1.9	2.0	-	-	-	-	-	-	-	-	-

Source: "Prevalence of Lifetime, Annual, 30-Day, and Daily Prevalence of Use of Selected Drugs, by Race/Ethnicity for 8th, 10th, and 12th graders: 1994 (in percentages)," *Drug Use Among Ethnic Minorities*, 1995, p. 32. Primary source: The Monitoring the Future Study, the University of Michigan. *Note:* - Data not available.

★ 64 ★

Behavior

Drug-Related: Trends in Percent of Female 18-and-Over Current Cigarette Smokers, by Age Group and Race: 1965-1993

[Data are based on household interviews of a sample of the civilian noninstitutionalized population].

Sex, race, and age	1965	1974	1979	1983	1985	1987	1988	1990	1991	1992	1993
	Percent of persons 18 years of age and over										
All persons											
18 years and over, age adjusted	42.3	37.2	33.5	32.2	30.0	28.7	27.9	25.4	25.4	26.4	25.0
18 years and over, crude	42.4	37.1	33.5	32.1	30.1	28.8	28.1	25.5	25.6	26.5	25.0
All females											
18 years and over, age adjusted	34.0	32.5	30.3	29.9	28.2	26.7	26.0	23.1	23.6	24.8	22.7
18 years and over, crude	33.9	32.1	29.9	29.5	27.9	26.5	25.7	22.8	23.5	24.6	22.5
18-24 years	38.1	34.1	33.8	35.5	30.4	26.1	26.3	22.5	22.4	24.9	22.9
25-34 years	43.7	38.8	33.7	32.6	32.0	31.8	31.3	28.2	28.4	30.1	27.3
35-44 years	43.7	39.8	37.0	33.8	31.5	29.6	27.8	24.8	27.6	27.3	27.4
45-64 years	32.0	33.4	30.7	31.0	29.9	28.6	27.7	24.8	24.6	26.1	23.0
65 years and over	9.6	12.0	13.2	13.1	13.5	13.7	12.8	11.5	12.0	12.4	10.5
White:											
18 years and over, age adjusted	34.3	32.3	30.6	30.1	28.3	27.2	26.2	23.9	24.2	25.7	23.7
18 years and over, crude	34.0	31.7	30.1	29.4	27.7	26.7	25.7	23.4	23.7	25.1	23.1
18-24 years	38.4	34.0	34.5	36.5	31.8	27.8	27.5	25.4	25.1	28.5	26.8
25-34 years	43.4	38.6	34.1	32.2	32.0	31.9	31.0	28.5	28.4	31.5	28.4
35-44 years	43.9	39.3	37.2	34.8	31.0	29.2	28.3	25.0	27.0	27.6	27.3
45-64 years	32.7	33.0	30.6	30.6	29.7	29.0	27.7	25.4	25.3	25.8	23.4
65 years and over	9.8	12.3	13.8	13.2	13.3	13.9	12.6	11.5	12.1	12.6	10.5
Black:											
18 years and over, age adjusted	32.1	35.9	30.8	31.8	30.7	27.2	27.1	20.4	23.1	23.9	19.8
18 years and over, crude	33.7	36.4	31.1	32.2	31.0	28.0	27.8	21.2	24.4	24.2	20.8
18-24 years	37.1	35.6	31.8	32.0	23.7	20.4	21.8	10.0	11.8	10.3	8.2
25-34 years	47.8	42.2	35.2	38.0	36.2	35.8	37.2	29.1	32.4	26.9	24.7
35-44 years	42.8	46.4	37.7	32.7	40.2	35.3	27.6	25.5	35.3	32.4	31.5
45-64 years	25.7	38.9	34.2	36.3	33.4	28.4	29.5	22.6	23.4	30.9	21.3
65 years and over	7.1	8.9	8.5	13.1	14.5	11.7	14.8	11.1	9.6	11.1	10.2

Source: "Current Cigarette Smoking by Persons 18 Years of Age and Over, According to Sex, Race, and Age: United States Selected Years 1965-93," *Health, United States, 1994,* 1995, p. 155. Primary source: Centers for Disease Control and Prevention, National Center for Health Statistics, Division of Health Interview Statistics: Data from the National Health Interview Survey; data computed by the Division of Health and Utilization Analysis from data compiled by the Division of Health Interview Statistics. *Notes:* Data for 1992 and beyond are not strictly comparable with data for earlier years.

★ 65 ★

Behavior

Drug-Related: Trends in Percent of Female 25-and-Over Current Cigarette Smokers, by Years of Education and Race: 1974-1993

[Data are based on household interviews of a sample of the civilian noninstitutionalized population].

Sex, race, and education	1974	1979	1983	1985	1987	1988	1990	1991	1992	1993
	Percent of persons 25 years of age and over, age adjusted									
All persons[1]	37.1	33.3	31.7	30.2	29.1	28.4	25.6	26.0	26.5	24.8
Less than 12 years	43.8	41.1	40.8	41.0	40.6	39.4	36.7	37.4	36.7	35.8
12 years	36.4	33.7	33.6	32.1	31.8	31.8	29.3	29.7	30.7	28.3
13-15 years	35.8	33.2	30.3	29.7	27.2	26.4	23.5	24.7	24.6	24.5
16 or more years	27.5	22.8	20.7	18.6	16.7	16.3	14.1	13.9	15.3	13.6
All females[1]	32.2	29.6	28.8	27.8	26.9	25.9	23.2	23.9	24.8	22.7
Less than 12 years	36.8	35.0	35.3	36.7	36.1	34.5	32.1	33.0	32.4	31.0
12 years	32.5	29.9	30.9	29.6	29.2	29.1	26.3	27.1	28.7	26.7
13-15 years	30.2	30.0	27.5	26.7	26.0	24.1	21.1	22.5	23.3	21.8
16 or more years	26.1	22.5	19.2	17.4	16.1	15.3	13.6	12.8	14.6	12.4
White females[1]	31.9	29.8	28.8	27.6	27.0	25.9	23.6	24.0	25.1	23.1
Less than 12 years	37.0	36.1	35.5	37.1	37.0	35.2	33.6	33.7	33.1	31.7
12 years	32.1	29.9	30.9	29.4	29.4	29.3	26.8	27.5	29.5	27.6
13-15 years	30.5	30.6	28.0	27.1	26.2	23.8	21.4	22.3	23.6	21.9
16 or more years	25.8	21.9	18.9	16.8	16.4	15.1	13.7	13.3	14.2	12.5
Black females[1]	35.9	30.6	31.8	32.1	28.6	28.2	22.6	25.5	26.8	22.2
Less than 12 years	36.4	31.9	36.9	39.2	35.0	33.9	26.8	33.3	33.2	29.8
12 years	41.9	33.0	35.2	32.23	28.1	30.1	24.0	26.0	25.9	23.9
13-15 years	33.2	28.8[2]	26.5	23.7	27.2	26.8	23.1	24.8	27.0	22.7
16 or more years	35.2[2]	43.4[2]	38.7[2]	27.5	19.5	22.2	16.9	14.4	25.8[2]	13.3[2]

Source: "Age-Adjusted Prevalence of Current Cigarette Smoking by Persons 25 Years of Age and Over, According to Sex, Race, and Education: United States Selected Years 1974-93," *Health, United States, 1994,* 1995, p. 156. Primary source: Data computed by the Centers for Disease Control and Prevention, National Center for Health Statistics, Division of Health and Utilization Analysis from data compiled by the Division of Health Interview Statistics. *Notes:* Data for 1992 and beyond are not strictly comparable with data for earlier years. 1. Includes unknown education. 2. These age-adjusted percents should be considered unreliable because of small sample size. For age groups where percent smoking was 0 or 100 the age-adjustment procedure was modified to substitute the percent from the next lower education group.

★ 66 ★
Behavior

Drug-Related: Trends in Percent of Male 18-and-Over Current Cigarette Smokers, by Age Group and Race: 1965-1993

[Data are based on household interviews of a sample of the civilian noninstitutionalized population].

Sex, race, and age	1965	1974	1979	1983	1985	1987	1988	1990	1991	1992	1993
All Males											
18 years and over, age adjusted	51.6	42.9	37.2	34.7	32.1	31.0	30.1	28.0	27.5	28.2	27.5
18 years and over, crude	51.9	43.1	37.5	35.1	32.6	31.2	30.8	28.4	28.1	28.6	27.7
White:											
18 years and over, age adjusted	50.8	41.7	36.5	34.1	31.3	30.4	29.5	27.6	27.0	28.0	27.0
18 years and over, crude	51.1	41.9	36.8	34.5	31.7	30.5	30.1	28.0	27.4	28.2	27.0
18-24 years	53.0	40.8	34.3	32.5	28.4	29.2	26.7	27.4	25.1	30.0	30.4
25-34 years	60.1	49.5	43.6	38.6	37.3	33.8	35.4	31.6	32.1	33.5	29.9
35-44 years	57.3	50.1	41.3	40.8	36.6	36.2	35.8	33.5	32.1	30.9	31.2
45-64 years	51.3	41.2	38.3	35.0	32.1	32.4	30.0	28.7	28.0	28.1	27.8
65 years and over	27.7	24.3	20.5	20.6	18.9	16.0	16.9	13.7	14.2	14.9	12.5
Black:											
18 years and over, age adjusted	59.2	54.0	44.1	41.3	39.9	39.0	36.5	32.2	34.7	32.0	33.2
18 years and over, crude	60.4	54.3	44.1	40.6	39.9	39.0	36.5	32.5	35.0	32.2	32.7
18-24 years	62.8	54.9	40.2	34.2	27.2	24.9	18.6	21.3	15.0	16.2	19.9
25-34 years	68.4	58.5	47.5	39.9	45.6	44.9	41.6	33.8	39.4	29.5	30.7
35-44 years	67.3	61.5	48.6	45.5	45.0	44.0	42.5	42.0	44.4	47.5	36.9
45-64 years	57.9	57.8	50.0	44.8	46.1	44.3	43.2	36.7	42.0	35.4	42.4
65 years and over	36.4	29.7	26.2	38.9	27.7	30.3	29.8	21.5	24.3	28.3	27.9

Source: "Current Cigarette Smoking by Persons 18 Years of Age and Over, According to Sex, Race, and Age: United States Selected Years 1965-93," *Health, United States, 1994,* 1995, p. 155. Primary source: Centers for Disease Control and Prevention, National Center for Health Statistics, Division of Health Interview Statistics: Data from the National Health Interview Survey; data computed by the Division of Health and Utilization Analysis from data compiled by the Division of Health Interview Statistics. *Notes:* Data for 1992 and beyond are not strictly comparable with data for earlier years.

★ 67 ★

Behavior

Drug-Related: Trends in Percent of Male 25-and-Over Current Cigarette Smokers, by Years of Education and Race: 1974-1993

[Data are based on household interviews of a sample of the civilian noninstitutionalized population].

Sex, race, and education	1974	1979	1983	1985	1987	1988	1990	1991	1992	1993
	Percent of persons 25 years of age and over, age adjusted									
All persons[1]	37.1	33.3	31.7	30.2	29.1	28.4	25.6	26.0	26.5	24.8
Less than 12 years	43.8	41.1	40.8	41.0	40.6	39.4	36.7	37.4	36.7	35.8
12 years	36.4	33.7	33.6	32.1	31.8	31.8	29.3	29.7	30.7	28.3
13-15 years	35.8	33.2	30.3	29.7	27.2	26.4	23.5	24.7	24.6	24.5
16 or more years	27.5	22.8	20.7	18.6	16.7	16.3	14.1	13.9	15.3	13.6
All males[1]	43.0	37.6	35.1	32.9	31.5	31.1	28.3	28.4	28.2	27.2
Less than 12 years	52.4	48.1	47.2	46.0	45.7	44.9	41.8	42.4	41.2	41.0
12 years	42.6	39.1	37.4	35.6	35.2	35.2	33.2	32.9	33.3	30.5
13-15 years	41.6	36.5	33.0	33.0	28.4	29.0	25.9	27.2	26.1	27.4
16 or more years	28.6	23.1	21.8	19.7	17.3	17.2	14.6	14.8	15.8	14.6
White males[1]	41.9	36.9	34.5	1.9	0.6	30.1	27.7	27.3	27.6	26.3
Less than 12 years	51.6	48.0	47.9	45.2	45.3	44.8	41.7	41.8	41.4	39.7
12 years	42.2	38.6	37.1	34.8	34.6	34.2	33.0	32.4	32.9	29.7
13-15 years	41.4	36.4	32.6	32.3	28.0	28.2	25.4	26.0	25.9	26.9
16 or more years	28.1	22.8	21.1	19.2	17.4	17.1	14.5	14.7	15.0	14.1
Black males[1]	53.8	44.9	42.8	42.5	41.9	40.3	34.5	38.8	35.3	36.0
Less than 12 years	58.3	50.1	46.0	51.1	49.4	45.3	41.4	47.8	44.5	47.2
12 years	51.2[2]	48.4	47.2	41.9	43.6	48.3	37.4	39.6	38.7	36.4
13-15 years	45.7[2]	39.3	44.7	42.3	32.4	34.8	28.3	32.7	27.0	30.1
16 or more years	41.9[2]	37.9[2]	31.3[2]	32.0[2]	20.9	21.5	20.6	18.3	26.9[2]	16.0[2]

Source: "Age-Adjusted Prevalence of Current Cigarette Smoking by Persons 25 Years of Age and Over, According to Sex, Race, and Education: United States Selected Years 1974-93," *Health, United States, 1994*, 1995, p. 156. Primary source: Data computed by the Centers for Disease Control and Prevention, National Center for Health Statistics, Division of Health and Utilization Analysis from data compiled by the Division of Health Interview Statistics. *Notes:* Data for 1992 and beyond are not strictly comparable with data for earlier years. 1. Includes unknown education. 2. These age-adjusted percents should be considered unreliable because of small sample size. For age groups where percent smoking was 0 or 100 the age-adjustment procedure was modified to substitute the percent from the next lower education group.

★ 68 ★

Behavior

Relationships: Dropout Status of 12-21-Year Olds Who Reported Using Marijuana and Cocaine in Past 30 Days, by Race/Ethnic Origin (in percentages): 1992

Race/ethnicity	Age	Dropout status	Marijuana past 30 days	Cocaine past 30 days
White	12-15	Nondropout	4.02	0.34
		Dropout	4.12	[1]
	16-21	Nondropout	15.93	1.61
		Dropout	27.60	4.12
Black	12-15	Nondropout	1.21	-
		Dropout	16.21	-
	16-21	Nondropout	13.24	1.00
		Dropout	20.80	4.40
Hispanic	12-15	Nondropout	3.96	0.81
		Dropout	[1]	[1]
	16-21	Nondropout	14.92	2.89
		Dropout	11.56	2.83
Other	12-15	Nondropout	4.56	[1]
		Dropout	[1]	[1]
	16-21	Nondropout	5.85	-
		Dropout	[1]	-

Source: "Prevalence of Past-Month Drug Use for Youth Ages 12-21, by Age, Dropout Status, Type of Drug Used, and Race/Ethnicity: 1992 Youth Risk Behavior Survey (in percentages)" *Drug Use Among Ethnic Minorities*, 1995, p. 57. Primary source: National Health Interview Survey, Youth Risk Behavior Survey, Centers for Disease Control and Prevention, National Center for Health Statistics, 1992. *Note:* 1. Low precision, no estimate reported. - No respondents.

Values

★ 69 ★

1980 High School Sophomores in 1992: Percent of 1980 High School Sophomore Cohort Reporting Specific Values, by Race/ Ethnic Origin: 1992

Student characteristics	Success in their work	Steady work	Money	Strong friendships	Making their children better off
Total	95.9	95.6	55.6	95.2	96.5
Race-ethnicity					
Native American/					
Alaska Native	97.4	93.5	57.7	96.3	96.8
Asian/Pacific Islander	95.9	97.6	58.3	98.2	97.1
Black	96.3	96.5	66.0	85.1	98.1
Hispanic	97.1	95.6	61.5	92.2	98.4
White	95.7	95.4	52.9	97.2	96.0

Source: "Percentage of 1980 High School Sophomores who Reported in 1992 that They Valued the Specified Items in Their Lives, by Selected Characteristics," *Educational Attainment of 1980 High School Sophomores by 1992,* March 1995, p. 62. Primary source: U.S. Department of Education, Office of Educational Research and Improvement, National Center for Education Statistics. Statistical Analysis Report. *High School and Beyond: Educational Attainment of 1980 High School Sophomores by 1992; 1992 Descriptive Summary of 1980 High School Sophomores 12 Years Later.* NCES 95-304. Washington, DC: U.S. Government Printing Office, March, 1995.

Chapter 2
BUSINESS AND ECONOMICS

Banks, Financial Institutions, Finances

★ 70 ★

Financial Companies: Characteristics, 1995

Company	This Year	Last Year	Location	Chief Executive	Year Started	Staff	Assets[1]	Capital[1]	Deposits[1]	Loans[1]
Carver Federal Savings Bank	1	1	New York, New York	Thomas L. Clark Jr.	1948	103	362.808	34.090	246.839	51.152
Independence Federal Savings Bank	2	2	Washington, D.C.	William B. Fitzgerald	1968	68	255.125	14.166	200.927	155.687
Industrial Bank of Washington	3	4	Washington, D.C.	B. Doyle Mitchell Jr.	1934	134	230,498	14.416	215.122	94.138
Seaway National Bank of Chicago	4	3	Chicago, Illinois	Walter E. Grady	1965	215	230.157	17.100	190.174	61.617
Family Savings Bank, FSB	5	5	Los Angeles, California	Wayne-Kent Bradshaw	1948	75	171.985	9.031	135.857	145.555
Independence Bank Of Chicago	6	6	Chicago, Illinois	Alvin J. Boutte	1964	116	140.700	12.300	126.500	42.800
Drexel National Bank	7	7	Chicago, Illinois	Alvin J. Boutte	1989	90	134.918	7.106	127.162	37.610
Citizens Trust Bank	8	9	Atlanta, Georgia	William L. Gibbs	1921	133	133.043	9.387	122.175	69.507
First Texas Bank	9	8	Dallas, Texas	William E. Stahnke	1975	52	130.128	13.838	115.174	48.672
Liberty Bank and Trust Co.	10	13	New Orleans, Louisiana	Alden J. McDonald Jr.	1972	117	114.904	8.161	100.973	74.214
Mechanics and Farmers Bank	11	10	Durham, North Carolina	Julia W. Taylor	1908	80	114.698	12.577	100.375	73.004
City National Bank of New Jersey	12	19	Newark, New Jersey	Louis E. Prezeau	1973	59	111.062	5.588	163.941	24.938
Founders National Bank of Los Angeles	13	14	Los Angeles, California	Carlton J. Jenkins	1991	80	106.415	8.373	93.867	55.594

[Continued]

★ 70 ★

Financial Companies: Characteristics, 1995

[Continued]

Company	This Year	Last Year	Location	Chief Executive	Year Started	Staff	Assets[1]	Capital[1]	Deposits[1]	Loans[1]
The Harbor Bank of Maryland	14	22	Baltimore, Maryland	Joseph Haskins Jr.	1982	51	106.069	10.881	94.726	57.643
Illinois Service Federal S&L Assn.	15	11	Chicago, Illinois	Thelma J. Smith	1934	34	104.491	7.598	92.670	62.275
Broadway Federal Savings and Loan Assn.	16	12	Los Angeles, California	Paul C. Hudson	1946	44	99.466	5.091	92.137	86.245
United Bank of Philadelphia	17	18	Philadelphia, Pennsylvania	Emma C. Chappell	1992	75	95.274	7.504	87.454	63.749
Consolidated Bank and Trust Co.	18	15	Richmond, Virginia	Vernard W. Henley	1903	66	88.567	5.902	81.680	46.033
Tri-State Bank of Memphis	19	17	Memphis, Tennessee	Jesse H. Turner Jr.	1946	71	84.804	8.127	75.904	36.090
First Independence National Bank of Detroit	20	20	Detroit, Michigan	Richard W. Shealey	1970	65	83.969	4.940	73.865	37.187
Citizens Federal Savings Bank	21	16	Birmingham, Alabama	Bunny Stokes Jr.	1957	32	81.515	7.397	72.899	62.029
Boston Bank of Commerce	22	21	Boston, Massachusetts	Ronald A. Homer	1982	41	78.025	3.515	67.400	58.372
The Douglass Bank	23	-	Kansas City, Kansas	Ron Wiley	1983	25	66.140	4.237	61.207	13.486
Dryades Savings Bank, FSB	24	-	New Orleans, Louisiana	Virgil Robinson	1994	35	65.810	4.830	60.599	10.565
First Tuskegee Bank	25	24	Tuskegee, Alabama	James Wright	1894	40	51.247	3.814	41.176	37.409

Source: "B.E. Financial Companies," *Black Enterprise* 25 (June 1995), p. 163. Published by permission. *Notes:* 1. In millions of dollars, to nearest thousand. Ranked by assets as of December 31, 1994. Prepared by B.E. Research. Reviewed by Mitchell/Titus & Co.

★ 71 ★

Banks, Financial Institutions, Finances

Financial Companies: Top 25: Summary, 1995

Black-Owned Financial Institutions	1993	1994	Percent Change
Number of employees	1,741	1,901	9.19%
Assets[1]	$2,881.685	$3,241.818	12.50
Capital[1]	204.935	239.969	17.10
Deposits[1]	2,522.233	2,840.803	12.63
Loans[1]	1,469.769	1,505.571	2.44

Source: "1995 Top 25 Financial Institutions Summary," *Black Enterprise* 25 (June 1995), p. 158. Published by permission. *Notes:* 1. In millions of dollars to the nearest thousand. Prepared by B.E. Research. Reviewed by Mitchell/Titus & Co.

★ 72 ★

Banks, Financial Institutions, Finances

Investment Banks: Issues, 1995

Company	Rank	Last Year	Location	Chief Executive	Year Started	Senior-managed Issues[1] (Millions of dollars)	Co-managed issues[1] (Billions of dollars)
Grisby Brandford & Co. Inc.	1	2	San Francisco, CA	Calvin B. Grigsby	1981	633.8	17,792.1
Pryor, McClendon, Counts & Co.	2	1	Philadelphia, PA	Malcolmn D. Pryor	1981	194.8	17,611.2
WR Lazard & Co	3	4	New York, NY	M.A. Eubanks, K.E. Glover	1985	207.6	15,654.2
M.R. Beal & Co.	4	3	New York, NY	Bernard B. Beal	1988	77.1	10,336.8
Utendahl Capital Partners L.P.	5	10	New York, NY	John O. Utendahl	1992	946.9	5,360.2
Apex Securities Inc.	6	9	Houston, TX	Richard M. Ramirez	1987	4.6	4,408.9
Blaylock & Partners LP.	7	-	New York, NY	Ronald E. Baylock	1993	50.0	2,881.4
Chapman Co.	8	5	Baltimore, MD	Nathan A. Chapman Jr.	1986	1.5	2,744.0
Howard Gary & Co.	9	6	Miami, FL	Howard V. Gary	1980	739.7	2,405.9
Charles A. Bell Securities Corp.	10	7	San Francisco, CA	Charles A. Bell	1986	15.9	1,641.8
Sturdivant & Co. Inc.	11	12	Clementon, NJ	Albert A. Sturdivant	1988	[2]	1,270.6
Doley Securities Inc.	12	14	New Orleans, LA	Harold E. Doley	1976	[2]	1,072.2
United Daniels Securities Inc.	13	11	New York, NY	Wilie L. Daniels	1984	2.2	691.9
I.C. Rideau, Lyons Co. Inc.	14	15	Los Angeles, CA	Lamar Lyons	1985	14.7	485.8
Powell Capital Markets Inc.	15	-	Newark, NJ	Arthur F. Powell	1990	133.5	334.8

Source: "B.E. Investment Banks," *Black Enterprise* 25 (June 1995), p. 189. Published by permission. Primary source: Securities Data Co., Inc., Newark, N.J., 1994. *Notes:* 1. This is for all issues including municipal, agency, corporate and mortgage-backed securities for the year ending Dec. 31, 1994. 2. These investment banks did not participate as senior managers for municipal, agency, corporate and mortgage-backed securities for the year ending Dec. 31, 1994.

Business Comparisons

★ 73 ★

Black-Owned Firms: Comparison of Firms in Ten Largest Cities and States, 1992

City	Firms (number)	Receipts ($1,000)	State	Firms (number)	Receipts ($1,000)	Percent city to State	
						Firms	Receipts
New York, NY	35,120	1,466,994	New York	51,312	2,267,600	68	65
Los Angeles, CA	15,371	2,628,903	California	68,968	5,478,365	22	48
Chicago, IL	15,328	1,087,267	Illinois	28,433	1,773,293	54	61
Houston, TX	13,592	537,490	Texas	50,008	2,339,221	27	23
District of Columbia	10,111	451,861	District of Columbia	(X)	(X)	(X)	(X)
Detroit, MI	9,275	486,092	Michigan	19,695	1,268,426	47	38
Baltimore, MD	7,542	233,164	Maryland	35,758	1,241,530	21	19
Philadelphia, PA	7,183	549,414	Pennsylvania	15,917	1,133,581	45	48
Dallas, TX	7,071	330,354	Texas	50,008	2,339,221	14	14
Atlanta, GA	5,762	280,701	Georgia	38,264	1,677,083	15	17

Source: "Comparison of Black-Owned Firms in 10 Largest Cities with Black-Owned Firms in State: 1992," *Survey of Minority-Owned Business Enterprises-Black*, p. 4. Primary source: *Survey of Minority-Owned Businesses-Black*, 1992 Economic Census, MB92-1. Washington, D.C.: Government Printing Office, January 1996. *Note:* X = Not applicable.

★ 74 ★

Business Comparisons

Black-Owned Firms: Comparisons of Firms in Ten Largest Counties and States, 1992

County	Firms (number)	Receipts ($1,000)	State	Firms (number)	Receipts ($1,000)	Percent city to State	
						Firms	Receipts
Los Angeles, CA	32,645	3,618,047	California	68,968	5,478,365	47	66
Cook, IL	21,937	1,370,987	Illinois	28,433	1,773,293	77	77
Harris, TX	16,536	707,032	Texas	50,008	2,339,221	33	30
Prince George's, MD	14,770	423,729	Maryland	35,758	1,241,530	41	34
Kings, NY	13,372	394,468	New York	51,312	2,267,600	26	17
District of Columbia	10,111	451,861	District of Columbia	(X)	(X)	(X)	(X)
Fulton, GA	8,667	364,214	Georgia	38,264	1,677,083	23	22
Queens, NY	8,630	270,684	New York	51,312	2,267,600	17	12
Dekalb, IL	8,085	408,842	Illinois	28,433	1,773,293	28	23
Baltimore, MD	7,542	233,164	Maryland	35,758	1,241,530	21	19

Source: "Comparison of Black-Owned Firms in 10 Largest Counties with Black- Owned Firms in States: 1992," *Survey of Minority-Owned Business Enterprises-Black*, p. 4. Primary source: *Survey of Minority-Owned Businesses-Black*, 1992 Economic Census, MB92-1. Washington, D.C.: Government Printing Office, January 1996. *Note:* X = Not applicable.

★ 75 ★

Business Comparisons

Black-Owned Firms: Comparisons of Firms in Ten Largest Metropolitan Areas and States, 1992

MA	Firms (number)	Receipts ($1,000)	State	Firms (number)	Receipts ($1,000)	Percent MA to State	
						Firms	Receipts
New York, NY PMSA	39,404	1,691,590	New York	51,312	2,267,600	77	75
Washington, DC-MD-VA-WV MSA	37,988	1,706,734	District of Columbia	(X)	(X)	(X)	(X)
Los Angeles-Long Beach, CA PMSA	32,645	3,618,047	California	68,968	5,478,365	47	66
Chicago, IL PMSA	24,644	1,602,489	Illinois	28,433	1,773,293	87	90
Atlanta, GA MSA	23,488	1,049,164	Georgia	38,264	1,677,083	61	63
Houston, TX PMSA	18,840	831,642	Texas	50,008	2,339,221	38	36
Philadelphia, PA-NJ PMSA	13,956	1,109,837	Pennsylvania	15,917	1,133,581	88	98
Detroit, MI PMSA	13,910	947,118	Michigan	19,695	1,268,426	71	75
Baltimore, MD PMSA	12,492	495,684	Maryland	35,758	1,241,530	35	40
Dallas, TX PMSA	11,395	865,080	Texas	50,008	2,339,221	23	37

Source: "Comparison of Black-Owned Firms in 10 Largest Metropolitan Areas with Black-Owned Firms in States: 1992," *Survey of Minority-Owned Business Enterprises-Black,* p. 4. Primary source: *Survey of Minority-Owned Businesses-Black,* 1992 Economic Census, MB92-1. Washington, D.C.: Government Printing Office, January 1996. *Notes:* X = Not applicable. PMSA = Primary metropolitan statistical area; MSA = metropolitan statistical area.

Business Growth and Sales

★ 76 ★

Black-Owned Firms: Average Receipts by Industry Division, 1992

	Black	All
All firms	51	192
Agriculture services, forestry, fishing, and mining	32	139
Construction	61	167
Manufacturing	126	872
Transportation and public utilities	50	186
Wholesale trade	389	1,190
Retail trade	80	291
Finance, insurance, and real estate	92	166
Services	33	84
Industries not classified	16	29

Source: "Average Receipts Per Firm by Industry Division for Black-Owned Firms Compared to All U.S. Firms: 1992," *Survey of Minority-Owned Business Enterprises-Black,* p. 7. Primary source: *Survey of Minority-Owned Businesses-Black,* 1992 Economic Census, MB92-1. Washington, D.C.: Government Printing Office, January 1996.

★ 77 ★

Business Growth and Sales

Black-Owned Firms: Increase by Legal Form of Organization, 1987 to 1992

Legal form of organization	Black-owned firms	All U.S. firms
Individual proprietorships	45.9	20.4
Partnerships	30.8	65.1
Subchapter S corporations	74.5	71.6

Source: "Percent Increase by Legal Form of Organization for Black-Owned Firms Compared to All U.S. Firms: 1987 to 1992," *Survey of Minority-Owned Business Enterprises-Black,* p. 3. Primary source: *Survey of Minority-Owned Businesses-Black,* 1992 Economic Census, MB92-1. Washington, D.C.: Government Printing Office, January 1996.

★ 78 ★

Business Growth and Sales

Sales by Industry

Company	Sales	Percent
Automobile dealers	$4,983.747	(42.6%)
Construction	393,332	(3.4%)
Engineering	167,564	(1.4%)
Food & beverage	2,768.213	(23.6%)
Health & Beauty Aids	240,900	(2.1%)
Media	920.654	(7.9%)
Manufacturing	682.810	(5.8%)
Technology	882.692	(7.5%)
Other (Computers, Commodities, Entertainment, Health Care, Security, Maintenance, Transportation)	671.288	(5.7%)

Source: "B.E. 100's Sales by Industry," *Black Enterprise* 25 (June 1995), p. 90. Published by permission. *Notes:* In millions of dollars to the nearest thousand. Prepared by B.E. Research.

Business Location

★ 79 ★

Black-Owned Firms: Statistics by State, 1992 and 1987. Part 1

[Detail may not add to total because or rounding. For meaning of abbreviations and symbols, see introductory text. For explanation of terms, see appendix A.]

Geographical area	1992					
	All firms		Firms with paid employees			
	Firms (number) A	Sales and receipts ($1,000) B	Firms (number) C	Sales and receipts ($1,000) D	Employees (number) E	Annual payroll ($1,000) F
United States	620,912	32,197,361	64,478	22,589,676	345,193	4,806,624
Alabama	14,707	534,692	1,989	343,331	6,827	81,710
Alaska	739	39,137	78	28,871	855	10,633
Arizona	2,936	137,721	328	99,734	1,274	16,326
Arkansas	5,738	232,850	646	160,875	1,952	21,691
California	68,968	5,478,365	6,875	4,155,861	43,292	732,136
Colorado	4,372	295,305	431	242,385	2,955	43,655
Connecticut	5,714	292,369	544	188,098	2,400	40,466
Delaware	2,060	156,880	243	125,503	2,352	22,763
District of Columbia	10,111	451,861	787	313,107	4,277	88,431
Florida	40,371	2,265,451	4,435	1,601,641	22,978	320,116
Georgia	38,264	1,677,083	4,095	1,103,546	18,744	253,026
Hawaii	717	27,382	42	16,794	211	2,513
Idaho	152	24,532	28	23,079	119	2,311
Illinois	28,433	1,773,293	2,694	1,272,218	17,972	345,569
Indiana	8,349	710,971	1,260	599,379	6,894	95,907
Iowa	1,106	75,521	141	64,082	604	8,734
Kansas	3,078	92,295	291	50,991	1,088	13,012
Kentucky	5,097	250,855	522	198,117	2,452	29,686
Louisiana	20,312	774,132	2,086	487,065	8,626	90,944
Maine	235	25,439	45	21,925	293	3,244
Maryland	35,758	1,241,530	2,543	734,155	31,450	227,305
Massachusetts	7,225	427,948	567	307,974	3,692	83,650
Michigan	19,695	1,268,426	2,147	860,556	13,727	202,061
Minnesota	2,785	283,392	332	211,664	2,845	44,532
Mississippi	14,067	504,945	1,891	300,535	5,699	54,676
Missouri	9,973	403,289	1,089	276,594	4,879	56,084
Montana	113	6,504	15	5,311	124	1,626
Nebraska	1,350	61,523	154	46,833	950	9,621
Nevada	1,736	113,338	161	84,299	1,570	20,320
New Hampshire	326	46,369	46	40,182	228	5,101

[Continued]

★ 79 ★

Black-Owned Firms: Statistics by State, 1992 and 1987. Part 1
[Continued]

| Geographical area | 1992 | | | | | |
| | All firms | | Firms with paid employees | | | |
	Firms (number) A	Sales and receipts ($1,000) B	Firms (number) C	Sales and receipts ($1,000) D	Employees (number) E	Annual payroll ($1,000) F
New Jersey	20,137	1,239,325	1,970	880,252	9,989	199,195
New Mexico	925	60,631	96	45,190	591	7,122
New York	51,312	2,267,600	4,033	1,385,469	16,070	301,625
North Carolina	29,221	893,369	3,479	530,720	11,166	115,873
North Dakota	117	7,845	14	5,201	105	1,024
Ohio	22,690	1,096,178	2,328	807,206	11,604	147,470
Oklahoma	4,621	190,517	510	134,555	2,027	24,574
Oregon	1,447	100,644	196	83,726	1,066	16,038
Pennsylvania	15,917	1,133,581	1,922	870,766	12,366	223,020
Rhode Island	857	65,252	110	50,353	1,154	16,541
South Carolina	18,343	672,514	2,485	435,256	9,464	105,246
South Dakota	111	10,307	20	9,160	91	860
Tennessee	14,920	555,015	1,686	326,870	5,955	65,861
Texas	50,008	2,339,221	4,861	1,604,853	23,745	285,195
Utah	354	45,246	54	41,444	269	5,445
Vermont	139	7,202	33	5,691	109	1,358
Virginia	26,100	1,211,173	2,958	892,170	20,992	267,017
Washington	4,575	257,073	595	200,651	3,601	46,716
West Virginia	1,093	42,228	127	32,941	559	7,379
Wisconsin	3,446	323,743	488	278,266	2,858	40,322
Wyoming	97	5,301	10	4,230	85	897

Source: "Statistics for Black-Owned Firms by State: 1992 and 1987," *Survey of Minority-Owned Business Enterprises-Black,* p. 10. Primary source: *Survey of Minority-Owned Businesses-Black,* 1992 Economic Census, MB92-1. Washington, D.C.: Government Printing Office, January 1996.

★ 80 ★

Business Location

Black-Owned Firms: Statistics by State, 1992 and 1987. Part 2

[Detail may not add to total because or rounding. For meaning of abbreviations and symbols, see introductory text. For explanation of terms, see appendix A.]

Geographical area	1987[1] All firms		Relative standard error of estimate (percent)[2] for column-			
	Firms (number) G	Sales and receipts ($1,000) H	A	B	C	D
United States	424,165	19,762,876	-	2	1	3
Alabama	10,085	439,966	-	2	1	2
Alaska	507	14,444	-	3	3	5
Arizona	1,811	91,439	1	17	10	23
Arkansas	4,392	214,596	1	3	2	4
California	47,728	2,364,024	-	2	2	2
Colorado	2,871	105,849	1	7	11	8
Connecticut	4,061	225,718	1	6	6	7
Delaware	1,399	77,701	2	12	7	15
District of Columbia	8,275	411,941	1	4	3	5
Florida	25,527	1,211,648	1	15	4	22
Georgia	21,283	1,179,730	-	4	3	6
Hawaii	399	12,310	-	24	8	40
Idaho	94	4,776	3	1	16	1
Illinois	19,011	1,100,204	1	3	4	4
Indiana	5,867	349,643	1	7	6	8
Iowa	703	44,795	2	7	11	9
Kansas	2,323	154,448	1	3	3	3
Kentucky	3,738	120,201	1	4	3	4
Louisiana	15,331	531,548	-	13	3	21
Maine	131	5,151	2	6	11	7
Maryland	21,678	719,715	-	5	4	9
Massachusetts	4,761	251,946	1	5	8	7
Michigan	13,708	701,335	1	4	5	6
Minnesota	1,448	124,915	1	8	6	4
Mississippi	9,667	531,929	-	1	1	-
Missouri	7,832	336,094	1	3	2	4
Montana	77	6,944	10	8	-	-
Nebraska	863	30,826	2	13	6	17
Nevada	1,002	38,608	1	23	9	31
New Hampshire	229	31,198	1	-	7	-
New Jersey	14,556	995,614	1	6	6	9
New Mexico	587	27,133	2	9	4	10
New York	36,289	1,886,038	-	3	4	5

[Continued]

★ 80 ★

Black-Owned Firms: Statistics by State, 1992 and 1987. Part 2
[Continued]

Geographical area	1987[1] All firms		Relative standard error of estimate (percent)[2] for column-			
	Firms (number) G	Sales and receipts ($1,000) H	A	B	C	D
North Carolina	19,487	746,112	-	2	1	2
North Dakota	57	1,207	13	20	11	1
Ohio	15,983	625,665	1	4	4	5
Oklahoma	3,461	93,903	1	6	7	7
Oregon	848	34,146	3	10	15	13
Pennsylvania	11,728	747,417	1	5	5	6
Rhode Island	489	18,209	4	7	11	7
South Carolina	12,815	444,201	-	1	1	2
South Dakota	63	4,832	1	-	7	-
Tennessee	10,423	386,078	-	4	2	3
Texas	35,725	1,084,014	-	17	3	25
Utah	202	8,615	5	1	-	-
Vermont	98	6,682	-	-	-	-
Virginia	18,781	810,569	-	3	3	4
Washington	2,583	175,671	1	8	8	10
West Virginia	727	38,930	2	2	2	3
Wisconsin	2,381	190,696	1	30	7	35
Wyoming	81	3,512	-	-	-	-

Source: "Statistics for Black-Owned Firms by State: 1992 and 1987," *Survey of Minority-Owned Business Enterprises-Black*, p. 10. Primary source: *Survey of Minority-Owned Businesses-Black*, 1992 Economic Census, MB92-1. Washington, D.C.: Government Printing Office, January 1996. *Notes:* 1. The 1987 data were tabulated from administrative records; therefore, relative standard errors are not applicable. See Comparability of 1987 and 1992 Data in the introductory text. 2. For explanation of relative standard errors, see Reliability of Estimates in the introductory text.

Businesses

★ 81 ★

Automobile Dealers: 50 Companies Below the 50 Leaders, 1994

Company	This Year	Last Year	Location	Chief Executive	Year Started	Staff	Type of Business	Sales[1]
Heritage Cadillac Inc.	51	49	Forest Park, Georgia	Ernst M. Hodge	1991	47	GM	32.843
Dick Gidron Cadillac & Ford Inc.	52	29	Bronx, New York	Richard D. Gidron	1992	65	GM/Ford	32.650
Gulf Freeway Pontiac-GMC Truck	53	34	Houston, Texas	Carl L. Barnett Sr.	1991	72	GM	32.618
Noble Ford-Mercury Inc.	54	55	Indianola, Iowa	Dimaggio Nichols	1985	65	Ford	32.053
Advantage Ford Lincoln-Mercury Inc	55	-	Connersville, Indiana	Princeton Grace	1990	34	Ford	32.000
Wood River Ford/ Lincoln-Mercury Inc	56	-	Wood River, Illinois	Willie J. Forte	1990	63	Ford	31.931
Tony March Buick-GMC Truck Inc	57	60	Hartford, Connecticut	Anthony March	1985	74	GM	31.900
Dearborn Pontiac Nissan Inc.	58	-	Dearborn, Michigan	William Perkins	1993	47	GM/Nissan	30.376
Cumberland C/P Inc	59	70	Fayetteville, North Carolina	Bill Turner	1992	52	Chrysler	30.134
Chino Hills Ford Sales Inc	60	65	Chino, California	Timothy L. Woods	1982	65	Ford	29.967
Quality Ford Inc	61	50	W. Des Moines, Iowa	Franklin D. Greene	1989	69	Ford	29.958
Empire Ford Inc.	62	52	Spokane, Washington	Nathaniel D. Greene	1986	68	Ford	29.600
Deerbrook Forest Chrysler-Plymouth Inc	63	41	Kingwood, Texas	Ezzard Dale Early	1987	62	Chrysler	28.856
Coastal Ford Inc.	64	51	Mobile, Alabama	Delmont O. Dapremont Jr	1984	80	Ford	28.700
Knox Ford Inc.	65	80	Muldraugh, Kentucky	Henry Shaw	1985	41	Ford	28.451
Ray Wilkinson Buick-Cadillac-Isuzu Inc	65	-	Racine, Wisconsin	Raymond M.Wilkinson	1984	34	GM	28.451

[Continued]

★ 81 ★

Automobile Dealers: 50 Companies Below the 50 Leaders, 1994

[Continued]

Company	This Year	Last Year	Location	Chief Executive	Year Started	Staff	Type of Business	Sales[1]
Barron Chevrolet-Geo Inc.	67	59	Danvers, Massachusetts	Reginald Barron	1984	75	GM	28.100
Puget Sound Chrysler-Plymouth Inc	68	69	Renton, Washington	B. Edward Fitzpatrick	1986	54	Chrysler	28.000
R.H. Peters Chevrolet Inc	68	53	Hurricane, West Virginia	R.H. Peters Jr.	1982	52	GM	28.000
Harris Olds-GMC Truck Inc	70	-	Schaumburg, Illinois	Robert L. Harris Jr.	1988	66	GM	27.000
Brookdale Dodge Inc	71	-	Brooklyn Center, Minnesota	Perry Watson III	1993	67	Chrysler	26.893
Fairfax Pontiac- GMC Truck	72	-	Fairfax, Virginia	Roland J. Walton	1992	71	GM	26.512
Conway Ford Inc	73	73	Conway, South Carolina	Samuel H. Frink	1986	62	Ford	26.247
Broadway Ford Inc	74	63	Edmond, Oklahoma	LeMon Henderson	1981	52	Ford	26.000
Fairway Ford of Auguata Inc	75	48	Augusta, Georgia	James H. Brown	1989	60	Ford	25.428
West Covina Lincoln- Mercury Inc	76	58	West Covina, California	Boyd Harrison Jr.	1986	45	Ford	25.089
Hub City Ford-Mercury Inc	77	-	Crestview, Florida	Leon Daggs Jr	1986	48	Ford	25.000
Mike Branker Buick Inc	77	-	Lincoln, Nebraska	Julian Michael Branker	1985	80	GM/Hyundai/ Nissan	25.000
All American Ford Inc	79	89	Saginaw, Michigan	Laval Perry	1988	70	Ford	24.600
Highland Lincoln- Mercury Inc.	80	66	Highland, Indiana	Nathaniel Z. Cain Jr	1989	45	Ford	24.518
Kemper Dodge Inc	81	64	Cincinnati, Ohio	Paul C. Keels	196	46	Chrysler	24.497
Fred Jones Pontiac-GMC Truck Inc	82	76	Brookfield, Wisconsin	Frederick E. Jones	1984	53	GM	24.152
Prestige Pontiac-Oldsmobile	83	79	Mount Morris, Michigan	Gregory Jackson	1988	55	GM	23.752
Red Bluff Ford-Mercury Inc.	84	78	Red Bluff,					

[Continued]

★ 81 ★

Automobile Dealers: 50 Companies Below the 50 Leaders, 1994

[Continued]

Company	This Year	Last Year	Location	Chief Executive	Year Started	Staff	Type of Business	Sales[1]
			California	Phillip G. Price	1989	46	Ford	23.637
Durand Chevrolet-GEO-Pontiac-Olds Inc.	85	89	Durand, Michigan	Michael Johnson	1991	48	GM	23.500
Southwest Ford Sales Inc.	86	68	Oklahoma City, Oklahoma	Roger L. Williams	1990	79	Ford	23.216
Vision Ford Lincoln-Mercury Inc.	87	77	Alamogordo, New Mexico	Wayne Martin	1989	69	Ford	23.126
Denton Motors Inc DBA/Denton C/P	88	-	Denton, Texas	Edward H. Smith	1992	48	Chrysler/Ford/Isuzu	23.009
Winter Haven Ford Inc.	89	74	Winter Haven, Florida	Johnny Mac Brown	1989	46	Ford	22.510
Thorton Buick Inc D/B/A Coult Buick	90	-	Cherry Hill, New Jersey	Otis J. Thorton	1993	41	GM	22.349
Beddingfield Buick-GMC Truck-BMW Inc	91	71	Decatur, Illinois	Edward C. Beddingfield	1989	45	GM/BMW	22.309
Shamrock Lincoln-Mercury-Nissan-Saab Inc	92	93	Mishawaka, Indiana	Theodore Williams Jr.	1988	44	Ford/Saab/Nissan	22.064
Davis Oldsmobile D/B/A/ Stephens Olds-Honda	93	-	Blooington, Indiana	Richard O. Davis	1993	60	GM/Honda	22.000
Laurel Ford Lincoln-Mercury Inc.	94	83	Laurel, Mississippi	Jimmy L. Walker	1992	50	Ford	21.882
Vicksburg Chrysler-Plymouth-Dodge Inc.	95	100	Vicksburg, Michigan	Monti M. Long	1990	45	Chrysler	21.865
Hilltop Ford Inc	96	-	Denison, Texas	Larry Turner	1986	50	Ford	21.850
Plaza Ford-Lincoln-Mercury Inc	97	98	Lexington, North Carolina	Archie Kindle	1987	50	Ford	21.837
Royal Dodge Inc	98	88	Woodbury, New Jersey	Clarence A. Jackson	1989	39	Chrysler	21.293
Huntsville Dodge Inc	99	91	Huntsville, Alabama	Ellenae L. Henry-Fairhurst	1992	43	Chrysler	21.000
Mountain Home Ford-Lincoln-Mercury Inc	99	57	Mountain Home, Idaho	Robert E. Montgomery	1988	35	Ford	21.000

Source: "Automobile Dealer 100," *Black Enterprise* 25 (June 1995), pp. 114, 118, 120. Published by permission. *Notes:* 1. In millions of dollars, to nearest thousand. As of Dec. 31, 1994. Prepared by B.E. Research. Reviewed by Mitchell/Titus & Co.

Insurance Companies

★ 82 ★

Insurance Companies: Characteristics of Top 15, 1995

Company/Location	This Year	Last Year	Chief Executive	Year Started	Staff	Statutory Assets[1]	Insurance Reserves[1]	Premium In Force[1]	Net Investment Income[1]	Income[1]
North Carolina Mutual Life Insurance Co. Durham, North Carolina	1	1	Bert Collins	1899	780	228.683	136.333	9,214.130	57.415	12.175
Atlanta Life Insurance Co. Atlanta, Georgia	2	2	Don M. Royster Sr.	1905	500	149.282	118.997	2,478.000	25.363	9.343
Golden State Mutual Life Insurance Co. Los Angeles, California	3	3	Larkin Teasley	1925	297	102.477	80.048	3,816.090	15.695	8.732
Universal Life Insurance Co. Memphis, Tennessee	4	4	Robert L. Gholson Jr.	1923	600	65.104	56.073	922.366	2.274	4.067
Chicago Metropolitan Assurance Co. Chicago, Illinois	5	5	Josephine King	1927	134	55.895	35.722	1,415.763	20.852	2.200
Booker T. Washington Insurance Co. Birmingham, Alabama	6	6	Kirkwood R. Balton	1932	175	44.559	37.166	1,143.334	10.950	2.472
Protective Industrial Ins. Co. of Alabama Inc Birmingham, Alabama	7	7	Paul E. Harris	1923	90	14.192	10.650	71.741	2.651	0.753
Winnfield Life Insurance Co. Natchitoches, Louisiana	8	8	Ben D. Johnson	1936	25	6.889	7.861	26.288	1.782	0.524
Williams-Progressive Life & Accident Ins. Co. Opelousas, Louisiana	9	9	Borel C. Dauphin	1947	54	6.440	5.366	34.726	1.261	0.471
Golden Circle Life Insurance Co. Brownsville, Tennessee	10	10	William D. Rawls Sr.	1958	75	6.368	4.255	23.384	1.473	0.559
Reliable Life Insurance Co. Monroe, Louisiana	11	11	Joseph H. Miller Jr.	1940	100	5.441	3.932	30.953	1.484	0.145
Wright Mutual Insurance Co. Detroit, Michigan	12	13	Carl B. Bolden Jr.	1942	36	4.578	3.656	46.086	1.038	0.206
Gertrude Geddes Willis Life Ins. Co. New Orleans, Louisiana	13	12	Joseph O. Misshore Jr.	1941	65	3.971	4.103	41.103	1.203	0.259

[Continued]

★ 82 ★

Insurance Companies: Characteristics of Top 15, 1995

[Continued]

Company/Location	This Year	Last Year	Chief Executive	Year Started	Staff	Statutory Assets[1]	Insurance Reserves[1]	Premium In Force[1]	Net Investment Income[1]	Income[1]
Majestic Life Insurance Co. New Orleans, Louisiana	14	14	Ceilia Roberts	1947	25	3.429	0.962	11.135	0.434	0.194
Benevolent Life Insurance Co. Inc.	15	15	Granville L. Smith	1934	70	3.006	2.075	14.807	0.61	0.104

Source: "B.E. Insurance Companies," *Black Enterprise* 25 (June 1995), p. 165. Published by permission. *Notes:* 1. In millions of dollars, to nearest thousand. Ranked as of December 31, 1994. Prepared by B.E. Research. Reviewed by Mitchell/Titus & Co.

★ 83 ★

Insurance Companies

Insurance Companies: Top 15, 1995

Black-Owned Insurance Companies	1993	1994	Percent Change
Number of employees	3,043	3,026	-.56%
Assets[1]	$698.407	$700.314	.27%
Capital Reserves	$499.118	$507.199	1.62%
Insurance in Force[1]	$20,268.965	$19,289.906	-4.83%
Premium Income[1]	$158.798	$162.506	2.34%
Net Investment Income[1]	$45.705	$42.204	-7.66%

Source: "1995 Top 15 Insurance Companies Summary," *Black Enterprise* 25 (June 1995), p. 160. Published by permission. *Notes:* 1. In millions of dollars, to the nearest thousand. Prepared by B.E. Research. Reviewed by Mitchell/Titus & Co.

Leading Businesses

★ 84 ★

Automobile Dealers: Top 50 Companies, 1994

Company	This Year	Last Year	Location	Chief Executive	Year Started	Staff	Type of Business	Sales[1]
Trainer Oldsmobile-Cadillac-Pontiac-GMC Truck Inc.	1	1	Warner Robbins, Georgia	James E. Trainer	1991	5	GM	482.344
Alan Young Buick-GMC Truck Inc	2	4	Fort Worth, Texas	Alan Young	1979	78	GM	218.325

[Continued]

★ 84 ★

Automobile Dealers: Top 50 Companies, 1994
[Continued]

Company	This Year	Last Year	Location	Chief Executive	Year Started	Staff	Type of Business	Sales[1]
Mel Farr Automotive Group	3	3	Oak Park, Michigan	Mel Farr	1975	350	Ford/Toyota/ Volkswagen/Mazda	218.000
Pennsula Pontiac-Oldsmobile Inc	4	6	Torrance, California	Cecil B. Willis	1979	48	GM	177.693
S & J Enterprises	5	5	Charlotte, North Carolina	Sam Johnson	1973	285	Ford/Subaru	164.865
Chicago Truck Center D/B/A GMC-White GMC Truck Center	6	-	Chicago, Illinois	Robert L. Hatcher	1993	84	GM/Volvo	157.881
Avis Ford Inc	7	9	Southfield, Michigan	Walter E. Douglas Sr.	1986	120	Ford	94.399
Shack-Woods & Associates	8	8	Yucca Valley, California	William E. Shack Jr.	1977	260	Ford	90.257
Al Smith Chevrolet-Oldsmobile Inc.	9	-	Brighton, Colorado	Alvin Smith	1986	23	GM	86.236
University Motors	10	7	Athens, Georgia	Ronald Hill	1991	80	Ford/Mazda	84.324
Brandon Dodge Inc	11	25	Tampa, Florida	Sanford L. Woods	1989	120	Chrysler/Toyota	82.126
Harrell Enterprise	12	24	Memphis, Tennessee	H. Steve Harrell	1987	211	Chrysler/Ford/GM	81.562
The Baranco Automotive Group	13	10	Decatur, Georgia	Gregory T. Baranco	1978	170	GM/Ford/Acura	77.697
Armstrong Enterprises	14	46	Hollywood, Florida	William J. Armstrong	1990	114	Ford/Toyota	77.000
Rountree Olds-Cadillac Co. Inc	15	13	Shreveport, Louisiana	Lonnie M. Bennett	1991	140	GM/Isuzu	63.231
Fred J. Poe Automotive Group	16	38	Southgate, Michigan	Fred J. Poe	1993	131	GM	61.850
Martin Automotive Group	17	15	Bowling Green, Kentucky	Cornelius A. Martin	1985	115	GM/Chrysler	60.765
Metrolina Dodge Inc.	18	12	Charlotte, North Carolina	Reginald T. Hubbard	1986	109	Chrysler	59.239
Village Ford of Lewisville	19	22	Lewisville, Texas	Charles E. Bankston	1992	109	Ford	58.318
32 Ford Mercury Inc	20	17	Batavia, Ohio	Clarence Warren	1990	84	Ford	55.473
Bob Ross Buick, Mercedes, GMC Inc	21	19	Centerville, Ohio	Robert P. Ross	1974	49	Chrysler	51.719
Midfield Dodge Inc.	22	75	Midfield, Alabama	Jordan A. Frazier	1989	49	Chrysler	51.719

[Continued]

★ 84 ★

Automobile Dealers: Top 50 Companies, 1994

[Continued]

Company	This Year	Last Year	Location	Chief Executive	Year Started	Staff	Type of Business	Sales[1]
Taylor Companies	23	85	Arlington, Washington	Henry F. Taylor	1981	127	GM/Ford	51.176
Leader Motors Inc.	24	18	St. Louis, Missouri	Jesse Morrow	1983	95	Ford	50.703
Southside Ford Truck Sales Inc	25	16	Chicago, Illinois	Carl Statham	1984	77	Ford	46.876
Bradley Automotive Group	26	39	Ann Arbor, Michigan	James H. Bradley Jr.	1973	93	GM	46.200
Tropical Ford Inc.	26	14	Orlando, Florida	Hamilton W. Massey	1985	100	Ford	46.200
Mike Pruitt's Lima Ford Inc	28	56	Lima, Ohio	Michael Pruitt	1990	77	Ford	46.101
Bob Johnson Chevrolet Inc	29	28	Rochester, New York	Robert Johnson	1981	70	GM	42.549
Cabell Motors Inc	30	27	Houston, Texas	Enos M. Cabell Jr.	1992	110	GM/Mazda	41.645
Wilson Automotive Group	31	44	Jackson, Tennessee	Sidney Wilson Jr.	1990	120	GM/Hyundai/ Chrysler/Ford	41.018
Macon Chrysler- Plymouth Inc.	32	20	Macon, Georgia	James B. Jones	1978	31	Chrysler	40.832
J.H. Mitchell Enterprises	33	23	Lynchburg, Virginia	James H. Mitchell	1981	85	Ford	40.700
Varsity Ford Lincoln- Mercury Inc.	34	26	Bryan, Texas	Tony Majors	1988	65	Ford	40.520
Northwestern Dodge Inc.	35	31	Ferndale, Michigan	Theresa Jones	1980	70	Chrysler	39.700
Duryea Ford Inc.	36	42	Brockport, New York	Jesse Thompson	1985	85	Ford/Toyota	39.000
Spalding Ford-Lincoln- Mercury Inc.	37	37	Griffin, Georgia	Alan M. Reeves	1981	79	Ford	38.879
Legacy Ford Inc.	38	33	McDonough, Georgia	Emanuel Jones	1992	65	Ford	38.261
Glynn Smith Chevrolet-GEO Jeep Eagle	39	-	Opelika, Alabama	Ronnie Ware	1992	62	Chrysler/GM	38.133
Orville Beckford Ford-Mercury Inc.	40	32	Milton, Florida	Orville Beckford	1992	71	Ford	37.479
Landmark Ford of Niles Inc.	41	67	Niles, Illinois	Larry T. Brown	1991	90	Ford	36.579
Republic Ford Inc.	42	45	Republic, Missouri	Franklin D. Greene	1983	64	Ford	36.530

[Continued]

★ 84 ★

Automobile Dealers: Top 50 Companies, 1994

[Continued]

Company	This Year	Last Year	Location	Chief Executive	Year Started	Staff	Type of Business	Sales[1]
Ferndale Honda Inc.	43	54	Ferndale, Michigan	Barbara J. Wilson	1983	37	Honda	36.400
Team Ford Inc.	44	30	Sioux City, Iowa	Arthur P. Silva	1986	100	Ford	36.200
Conyers Riverside Ford Inc.	45	47	Detroit, Michigan	Nathan G. Conyers	1970	88	Ford	36.100
Prestige Ford Inc.	46	61	Eustis, Florida	Irving J. Matthews	1991	61	Ford	35.786
Cardinal Dodge Inc.	47	62	Louisville, Kentucky	Winston R. Pittman	1988	98	Chrysler/GM	35.134
University Ford of Peoria Inc.	48	36	Peoria, Illinois	James L. Oliver	1985	82	Ford	34.969
Sidney Moncrief Pontiac-Buick-GMC Truck Inc.	49	21	Sherwood, Arkansas	Sidney A. Moncrief	1987	78	GM	34.219
Campus Ford Inc.	50	40	Okemos, Michigan	Wendell Barron	1986	88	Ford	33.000

Source: "Automobile Dealer 100," *Black Enterprise* 25 (June 1995), pp. 111-112, 114. Published by permission. *Notes:* 1. In millions of dollars, to nearest thousand. As of Dec. 31, 1994. Prepared by B.E. Research. Reviewed by Mitchell/Titus & Co.

★ 85 ★

Leading Businesses

Black-Owned Firms: Top Industry Receipt Leaders, 1992

Industry	Receipts (Millions dollars)
SERVICES	11,057
Health services	2,859
Business services	2,371
Personal services	1,469
Engineering, accounting, research management, and related services	1,353
Amusement and recreation services	665
RETAIL TRADE	6,968
Automotive dealers and gasoline service stations	2,384
Eating and drinking places	1,786
Miscellaneous retail	1,247
Food stores	978
Apparel and accessory stores	204

[Continued]

★ 85 ★

Black-Owned Firms: Top Industry Receipt Leaders, 1992

[Continued]

Industry	Receipts (Millions dollars)
FINANCE, INSURANCE, AND REAL ESTATE	3,777
Depository institutions	(D)
Real estate	1,553
Insurance agents, brokers, and service	308
Holding and other investment offices	(D)
Security and commodity brokers	(D)
WHOLESALE TRADE	2,944
Wholesale trade-nondurable goods	1,837
Wholesale trade-durable goods	1,107
CONSTRUCTION	2,651
Special trade contractors	1,466
General building contractors	840
Subdividers and developers, n.e.c.	189
Heavy construction contractors	156

Source: "Top Industry Receipt Leaders for Black-Owned Firms: 1992," *Survey of Minority-Owned Businesses Enterprises-Black,* p. 2. Primary source: *Survey of Minority-Owned Businesses-Black,* 1992 Economic Census, MB92-1. Washington, D.C.: Government Printing Office, January 1996. *Notes:* D = Withheld to avoid disclosing data for individual companies; data are included in higher-level totals.

★ 86 ★

Leading Businesses

Franchisors Ranked by Black-Owned Outlets

Company	Rank	Type	Black units	Total units	Black % of units	Start-up cost
Coverall North America	1	Commercial cleaning	1,101	3,352	32.85	$3,600-$37,100
McDonald's Corp	2	Fast food	694	9,796	7.08	$422,600-$651,350
Subway Sandwiches & Salads	3	Submarine sandwiches	317	10,646	2.98	$74,000-199,300
D & K Enterprises Inc.	4	Personalized children's books and products	218	1,986	10.98	$2,500-$4,995
O.P.E.N. America Inc.	5	Janitorial/commercial cleaning	203	589	34.47	$4,400 & up
KFC Corp.	6	Fast food	155	5,129	3.02	$125,000
Mister Softee Inc.	7	Mobile soft ice cream units	91	782	11.64	$20,000-$30,000
Wendy's International Inc.	8	Fast food	75	3,983	1.88	$250,000
The Southland Corp. (7 Eleven)	9	Retail convenience stores	75	5,500	1.36	$13,000-$223,700
General Nutrition Center Inc.	10	Retail nutritional stores	53	2,241	2.37	$100,000-$125,000

Source: "Franchisors Ranked by Black-Owned Outlets," *Black Enterprise* 26 (September 1995), p. 64. Published by permission.

★ 87 ★

Leading Businesses

Top Ten Employment Leaders, 1994

Company	Location	Employees[2]	1994 Sales[1]	Employee-to-sales-Ratio[2]
TLC Beatrice International Holdings Inc.	New York, N.Y.	4,200	$1,800.000	1:429
Johnson Publishing Co., Inc.	Chicago, Ill.	2,662	$306.608	1:115
Envirotest Systems Corp.	Phoenix, Ariz.	2,576	$96.395	1:37
The Bartech Group	Livonia, Mich.	1,800	$63.000	1:35
La-Van Hawkins Inner City Foods	Atlanta, Ga.	1,500	$39.136	1:26
RMS Technologies Inc.	Marlton, N.J.	1,300	$121.000	1:93
V&J Foods Inc.	Milwaukee, Wis.	1,300	$30.000	1:23
Thompson Hospitality LP.	Reston, Va.	1,250	$29.000	1:23
H&J Russell & Co.	Atlanta, Ga.	1,219	$154.700	1:127
The Gourmet Companies	Atlanta, Ga.	1,100	$38.000	1:35

Source: "Top Ten Employment Leaders," *Black Enterprise* 25 (June 1995), p. 94. Published by permission. *Notes:* 1. In millions of dollars to the nearest thousand. 2. In thousands of dollars. As of Dec. 31, 1994.

★ 88 ★

Leading Businesses

Top Ten Growth Leaders, 1994

Company	Location	1994 Sales[1]	1993 Sales[1]	Percent Increase
Taylor Companies	Arlington, Wash.	$51.176	$18.793	172.3%
Armstrong Enterprises	Hollywood, Fla.	$77.000	$30.000	156.7%
Midfield Dodge Inc.	Midfield, Ala.	$51.719	$20.783	148.9%
La-Van Hawkins Inner City Foods	Atlanta, Ga.	$39.136	$16.547	136.5%
Brandon Dodge Inc.	Tampa, Fla.	$82.126	$37.173	120.9%
Harrell enterprises	Memphis, Tenn.	$81.562	$37.338	118.4%
Rush Communications	New York, N.Y.	$65.000	$31.000	109.7%
Fred J. Poe Automotive Group	Southgate, Mich.	$61.850	$31.715	95.0%
Pulsar Data Systems Inc.	New Castle, Del.	$137.000	$79.100	73.2%
Solo Construction Corp.	N. Miami Beach, Fla.	$30.251	$17.536	72.5%

Source: "Top Ten Growth Leaders," *Black enterprise* 25 (June 1995), p. 94. Published by permission. *Notes:* 1. In millions of dollars to the nearest thousand. Prepared by B.E. research. reviewed by Mitchell/Titus & Co.

★ 89 ★

Leading Businesses

Top Twenty Franchises

Company	Location	Type	Black Owned Units	Fee	Start-up costs
Accent Hair Salons Inc.	Dayton, Ohio	Hair Salons	8	$20,000	$140,000
American Leak detection	Palm Springs, Calif.	Water, sewer, gas, leak detection	3	$45,000	$85,000
Blimpie International Inc.	Atlanta, Ga.	Fast food	34	$18,000	$100,000-$150,000
Computertots	Great Falls, Va.	Children's computer classes	7	$25,900	$31,700-37,000
Coverall North America	San Diego, Calif.	Commercial cleaning	1,101	$3,250-$33,600	$3,600-$37,100
D&K Enterprises Inc.	Carrollton, Texas	Personalized children's books	218	$100	$2,500-$4,995
GNC Franchising Inc.	Pittsburgh, Pa.	Retail nutrition stores	53	$25,000	$100,000-$125,000
Goodyear Tire Centers	Akron, Ohio	Tires & automotive services	21	$15,000	$100,000 +
Jackson Hewitt Tax Service	Virginia Beach, Va.	Computerized tax service	31	$17,500	$30,000
KFC Corp.	Louisville, Ky.	Fast food	155	$25,000	$125,000
Lawn Doctor Inc.	Holmdel, N.J.	Automated lawn care	3	$0	$22,500
Mail Boxes Etc.	San Diego, Calif.	Postal, business and communications services	20	$24,950	$95,000-$125,000
O.P.E.N. America Inc.	Phoenix, Ariz.	Commercial cleaning	203	$3,900 +	$4,400 +
Padgett Business Services	Athens, Ga.	Tax services	15	$22,500	$50,000
P.J.'s USA Inc.	New Orleans, La.	Retail coffee	1	$16,000	$120,000
RACS International Inc.	Indianapolis, Ind.	Commercial cleaning	10	$3,500-$32,560	$900-$11,600
Subway Salads and Sandwiches	Milford, Conn.	Fast food	317	$10,000	$74,600-$199,300
The Southland Corp. (7 Eleven)	Dallas, Texas	Retail convenience stores	75	$80,000	$13,000-223,700
Travel Network	Englewoods Cliffs, N.J.	Travel agency	37	$9,995-$29,000	$1,000-$75,000
Wendy's International Inc.	Dublin, Ohio	Fast food	75	$25,000	$250,000

Source: "B.E.'s 20 Best Franchises," *Black Enterprise* 26 (September 1995), p. 67. Published by permission.

Legal Form of Organization

★ 90 ★

Black-Owned Businesses: Legal Form of Organization, 1992

Legal form of organization	Black-owned firms	
	Firms (thousands)	Receipts ($1,000,000)
All industries	621	32.2
Individual proprietorships	584	16.0
Partnerships	15	4.0
Subchapter S corporations	22	12.2

Source: "Black-Owned Businesses by Legal Form of Organization: 1992," *Survey of Minority-Owned Business Enterprises-Black,* p. 2. Primary source: *Survey of Minority Owned Businesses-Black,* 1992 Economic Census, MB92-1. Washington, D.C.: Government Printing Office, January 1996.

Types of Businesses

★ 91 ★

Black-Owned Firms: Industry Division for Regions and States, 1992. Part 1 - New England

[Detail may not add to total because of rounding. This table is based on the 1987 SIC system. For meaning of abbreviations and symbols, see introductory text. For explanation of terms, see appendix A.]

Geographic area and industry division	All firms		Firms with paid employees				Relative standard error of estimate (percent)[1] for column-			
	Firms (number) A	Sales and receipts ($1,000) B	Firms (number) C	Sales and receipts ($1,000) D	Employees (number) E	Annual payroll ($1,000) F	A	B	C	D
Connecticut	5,714	292,300	544	188,098	2,409	40,466	1	6	6	7
Agricultural services, forestry, fishing, and mining	49	2,337	3	(D)	(D)	(D)	-	-	-	(D)
Construction	420	15,672	65	8,134	82	1,684	5	12	21	21
Manufacturing	68	7,844	10	6,980	124	2,832	17	2	-	-
Transportation and public utilities	447	34,854	25	21,532	132	3,666	3	8	-	-
Wholesale trade	73	21,162	9	23,431	42	1,236	16	1	-	-
Retail trade	900	71,925	131	52,782	621	8,930	4	10	20	13
Finance, insurance, and real estate	368	38,279	14	(D)	(D)	(D)	9	21	7	(D)
Services	3,076	92,513	281	55,261	1,167	16,706	1	13	7	22
Industries not classified	313	3,782	6	(D)	(D)	(D)	-	-	-	(D)
Maine	225	25,439	45	21,925	293	3,244	2	6	11	7
Agricultural services, forestry, fishing, and mining	8	126	2	(D)	(D)	(D)	-	-	-	(D)
Construction	22	1,428	6	955	12	209	-	-	-	-
Manufacturing	5	10	-	-	-	-	-	-	-	-
Transportation and public utilities	9	(D)	2	(D)	(D)	(D)	-	(D)	-	(D)
Wholesale trade	9	(D)	2	(D)	(D)	(D)	-	(D)	-	(D)
Retail trade	38	3,707	14	2,721	107	668	13	43	36	59
Finance, insurance, and real estate	14	(D)	1	(D)	(D)	(D)	-	(D)	-	(D)
Services	119	3,747	16	2,545	63	662	-	-	-	-
Industries not classified	11	(D)	2	(D)	(D)	(D)	-	(D)	-	(D)
Massachusetts	7,225	427,948	567	307,974	3,692	83,650	1	5	6	7
Agricultural services, forestry, fishing, and mining	49	2,765	7	706	8	152	3	41	-	-
Construction	404	25,418	66	20,086	185	5,911	3	1	-	-
Manufacturing	92	26,689	9	25,458	188	3,954	-	-	-	-
Transportation and public utilities	562	29,022	20	19,338	189	6,179	2	2	-	-
Wholesale trade	80	19,183	7	16,132	112	3,372	-	-	-	-
Retail trade	825	74,142	80	58,756	774	8,709	3	15	17	19
Finance, insurance, and real estate	357	40,708	39	21,461	178	3,534	10	35	42	56
Services	4,492	203,727	329	144,829	2,053	51,749	1	7	11	9
Industries not classified	363	6,294	10	1,229	4	91	3	2	-	-
New Hampshire	326	46,369	46	40,182	228	5,101	1	-	7	-
Agricultural services, forestry, fishing, and mining	5	(D)	-	-	-	-	-	(D)	-	-
Construction	28	1,706	6	1,275	32	341	-	-	-	-
Manufacturing	9	(D)	3	(D)	(D)	(D)	-	(D)	-	(D)
Transportation and public utilities	12	(D)	1	(D)	(D)	(D)	-	(D)	-	(D)
Wholesale trade	6	(D)	3	(D)	(D)	(D)	-	(D)	-	(D)
Retail trade	86	3,434	14	2,540	44	551	5	5	24	7
Finance, insurance, and real estate	11	(D)	2	(D)	(D)	(D)	-	(D)	-	(D)
Services	172	10,696	17	7,004	71	1,860	-	-	-	-
Industries not classified	17	(D)	-	-	-	-	-	(D)	-	-
Rhode Island	867	85,252	110	80,363	1,154	16,541	4	7	11	7
Agricultural services, forestry, fishing, and mining	8	(D)	1	(D)	(D)	(D)	-	(D)	-	(D)
Construction	58	13,839	10	(D)	(D)	(D)	-	-	-	(D)
Manufacturing	18	(D)	4	(D)	(D)	(D)	-	(D)	-	(D)
Transportation and public utilities	44	(D)	2	(D)	(D)	(D)	28	(D)	-	(D)
Wholesale trade	11	(D)	2	(D)	(D)	(D0	-	(D)	-	(D)
Retail trade	142	12,259	40	9,940	202	1,756	8	24	21	30
Finance, insurance, and real estate	86	2,625	6	436	5	70	27	49	64	66
Services	443	28,638	45	23,032	842	9,751	4	8	17	8
Industries not classified	45	786	-	-	-	-	-	-	-	-

[Continued]

★ 91 ★

Black-Owned Firms: Industry Division for Regions and States, 1992. Part 1 - New England

[Continued]

Geographic area and industry division	All firms		Firms with paid employees				Relative standard error of estimate (percent)[1] for column-			
	Firms (number) A	Sales and receipts ($1,000) B	Firms (number) C	Sales and receipts ($1,000) D	Employees (number) E	Annual payroll ($1,000) F	A	B	C	D
Vermont	139	7,202	33	5,691	100	1,358	-	-	-	-
Agricultural services, forestry, fishing, and mining	4	(D)	4	(D)	(D)	(D)	-	(D)	-	(D)
Construction	6	(D)	4	(D)	(D)	(D)	-	(D)	-	(D)
Manufacturing	6	(D)	2	(D)	(D)	(D)	-	(D)	-	(D)
Transportation and public utilities	5	(D)	1	(D)	(D)	(D)	-	(D)	-	(D)
Wholesale trade	3	1,251	5	1,194	12	122	-	-	-	-
Retail trade	23	2,287	8	(D)	(D)	(D)	-	-	-	(D)
Finance, insurance, and real estate	4	(D)	1	(D)	(D)	(D)	-	(D)	-	(D)
Services	79	(D)	8	(D)	(D)	(D)	-	(D)	-	(D)
Industries not classified	4	(D)	-	-	-	-	-	(D)		

Source: "Statistics for Black-Owned Firms by Industry for States: 1992," *Survey of Minority-Owned Business Enterprises-Black,* pp.11-17. Primary source: *Survey of Minority-Owned Businesses-Black,* 1992 Economic Census, MB92-1. Washington, D.C.: Government Printing Office, January 1996. Adapted by editors. *Notes:* For explanation of relative standard errors, see Reliability of Estimates in the introductory text. D = Withheld to avoid disclosing data for individual companies; data are included in higher-level totals.

★ 92 ★

Types of Businesses

Black-Owned Firms: Industry Division for Regions and States, 1992. Part 2 - Middle Atlantic

[Detail may not add to total because of rounding. This table is based on the 1987 SIC system. For meaning of abbreviations and symbols, see introductory text. For explanation of items see appendix A.]

Geographic area and industry division	All firms		Firms with paid employees				Relative standard error of estimate (percent)[1] for column-			
	Firms (number) A	Sales and receipts ($1,000) B	Firms (number) C	Sales and receipts ($1,000) D	Employees (number) E	Annual payroll ($1,000) F	A	B	C	D
New Jersey	20,137	1,239,325	1,970	880,252	9,969	199,195	1	6	6	9
Agricultural services, forestry, fishing, and mining	160	4,933	21	2,018	35	574	2	17	-	-
Construction	1,066	45,342	176	27,513	413	7,257	3	12	14	18
Manufacturing	232	54,624	34	49,963	340	8,275	5	2	-	-
Transportation and public utilities	2,279	191,802	179	126,084	1,265	27,761	2	10	20	16
Wholesale trade	285	89,596	41	79,604	177	5,412	9	17	47	18
Retail trade	2,650	242,049	394	183,947	2,934	29,812	3	11	15	14
Finance, insurance, and real estate	1,684	120,128	94	88,812	588	10,237	4	53	31	72
Services	10,648	470,715	1,008	320,365	4,227	109,619	1	7	7	10
Industries not classified	1,133	20,137	23	1,947	11	247	1	-	-	-
New York	51,312	2,267,600	4,033	1,385,469	16,070	301,625	-	3	4	5
Agricultural services, forestry, fishing, and mining	196	5,420	20	2,364	71	616	6	8	-	-
Construction	2,639	164,469	323	121,510	1,129	24,584	2	9	10	11
Manufacturing	672	79,905	74	70,013	732	17,715	5	2	26	2
Transportation and public utilities	5,885	173,910	246	47,019	583	12,744	1	10	16	39
Wholesale trade	736	245,625	209	227,900	603	19,474	8	12	25	13
Retail trade	5,755	399,355	870	306,253	3,769	41,077	2	6	10	7
Finance, insurance, and real estate	3,139	275,045	298	164,225	1,069	31,516	3	20	18	31
Services	28,955	868,092	1,939	441,280	8,031	152,779	-	3	5	5
Industries not classified	3,331	55,779	55	4,906	82	1,141	1	5	28	30
Pennsylvania	15,917	1,133,581	1,922	870,766	12,366	223,020	1	5	5	6
Agricultural services, forestry, fishing, and mining	111	3,358	18	1,906	35	333	3	5	-	-
Construction	984	71,161	154	52,455	671	12,776	3	7	14	6
Manufacturing	227	61,861	71	60,220	575	11,587	13	8	39	8
Transportation and public utilities	924	62,275	85	38,144	775	15,891	2	31	19	51
Wholesale trade	207	76,898	64	69,329	369	5,997	11	24	32	26
Retail trade	2,467	228,192	484	176,681	3,053	28,445	3	10	12	12

[Continued]

★ 92 ★

Black-Owned Firms: Industry Division for Regions and States, 1992. Part 2 - Middle Atlantic

[Continued]

Geographic area and industry division	All firms		Firms with paid employees				Relative standard error of estimate (percent)[1] for column-			
	Firms (number) A	Sales and receipts ($1,000) B	Firms (number) C	Sales and receipts ($1,000) D	Employees (number) E	Annual payroll ($1,000) F	A	B	C	D
Finance, insurance, and real estate	1,070	83,062	106	59,928	459	7,906	5	43	27	59
Services	8,758	528,084	918	410,368	6,401	139,892	1	4	6	5
Industries not classified	1,170	18,691	21	1,735	28	193	2	12	-	-

Source: "Statistics for Black-Owned Firms by Industry for States: 1992," *Survey of Minority-Owned Business Enterprises-Black*, pp. 11-17. Primary source: *Survey of Minority-Owned Businesses-Black*, 1992 Economic Census, MB92-1. Washington, D.C.: Government Printing Office, January 1996. Adapted by the editors. *Notes:* For explanation of relative standard errors, see Reliability of Estimates in the introductory text.

★ 93 ★

Types of Businesses

Black-Owned Firms: Industry Division for Regions and States, 1992. Part 3 - East North Central

[Detail may not add to total because of rounding. This table is based on the 1987 SIC system. For meaning of abbreviations and symbols, see introductory text. For explanation of items see appendix A.]

Geographic area and industry division	All firms		Firms with paid employees				Relative standard error of estimate (percent)[1] for column-			
	Firms (number) A	Sales and receipts ($1,000) B	Firms (number) C	Sales and receipts ($1,000) D	Employees (number) E	Annual payroll ($1,000) F	A	B	C	D
Illinois	28,433	1,773,293	2,694	1,272,218	17,972	345,569	1	3	4	4
Agricultural services, forestry, fishing, and mining	205	17,124	46	13,332	314	3,405	64	65	55	83
Construction	1,317	97,453	232	79,538	643	25,175	3	4	13	5
Manufacturing	332	133,438	51	123,922	1,106	28,528	6	3	-	-
Transportation and public utilities	2,640	118,480	165	56,066	1,566	21,971	1	15	17	31
Wholesale trade	362	155,712	58	145,204	601	13,719	6	20	20	21
Retail trade	4,209	346,675	716	271,714	5,419	47,624	2	7	9	9
Finance, insurance, and real estate	2,698	261,119	223	169,980	1,728	34,052	3	9	19	8
Services	14,636	610,488	1,138	407,206	6,580	170,725	1	5	6	8
Industries not classified	2,033	32,806	65	5,256	14	370	1	6	32	40
Indiana	8,349	710,971	1,260	599,379	6,894	95,907	1	7	6	8
Agricultural services, forestry, fishing, and mining	76	1,175	9	696	12	196	-	-	-	-
Construction	643	96,844	164	85,556	865	18,060	5	25	16	26
Manufacturing	107	19,567	15	18,227	284	5,831	15	2	-	-
Transportation and public utilities	448	31,663	30	14,028	144	3,309	5	19	-	-
Wholesale trade	128	128,033	69	126,882	291	8,868	21	22	39	23
Retail trade	1,413	250,408	303	233,046	2,366	25,429	3	8	13	46
Finance, insurance, and real estate	589	36,510	90	23,706	287	3,483	6	33	25	18
Services	4,446	140,973	541	96,315	2,640	30,551	1	11	8	16
Industries not classified	497	5,798	38	922	6	180	4	3	55	16
Michigan	19,895	1,268,426	2,147	860,556	13,727	202,061	1	4	5	6
Agricultural services, forestry, fishing, and mining	219	8,156	41	6,696	105	1,567	8	67	40	82
Construction	998	93,653	163	64,342	723	18,144	3	23	10	31
Manufacturing	265	62,691	68	59,883	792	18,249	12	19	39	20
Transportation and public utilities	1,121	88,939	152	65,250	1,111	16,390	4	32	22	43
Wholesale trade	271	75,163	56	69,547	392	6,749	10	9	39	9
Retail trade	3,045	372,614	453	335,010	4,785	40,450	2	6	10	6
Finance, insurance, and real estate	1,454	58,824	116	31,385	246	3,282	4	30	19	55
Services	10,859	439,273	1,055	225,552	5,544	96,939	1	5	7	11
Industries not classified	1,462	69,115	42	2,891	30	290	1	-	-	-
Ohio	22,690	1,096,178	2,328	807,206	11,804	147,470	1	4	4	5
Agricultural services, forestry, fishing, and mining	224	8,642	34	4,914	90	1,329	2	10	-	-

[Continued]

★ 93 ★

Black-Owned Firms: Industry Division for Regions and States, 1992. Part 3 - East North Central

[Continued]

Geographic area and industry division	All firms		Firms with paid employees				Relative standard error of estimate (percent)[1] for column-			
	Firms (number) A	Sales and receipts ($1,000) B	Firms (number) C	Sales and receipts ($1,000) D	Employees (number) E	Annual payroll ($1,000) F	A	B	C	D
Construction	1,565	144,144	324	126,724	1,161	22,411	2	14	9	16
Manufacturing	239	46,560	47	43,878	423	9,550	7	13	26	14
Transportation and public utilities	1,439	65,475	135	31,645	515	8,383	1	1	13	2
Wholesale trade	300	172,969	70	163,661	291	7,361	8	6	31	6
Retail trade	3,023	211,962	406	172,844	3,341	23,079	1	7	8	9
Finance, insurance, and real estate	1,773	113,626	233	82,802	1,041	13,003	4	28	19	38
Services	12,707	313,623	1,047	178,540	4,726	62,039	1	3	5	6
Industries not classified	1,420	19,176	33	2,199	14	316	1	1	-	-
Wisconsin	3,446	323,743	488	276,266	2,858	40,322	1	30	7	35
Agricultural services, forestry, fishing, and mining	23	2,377	6	2,093	-	641	18	78	70	88
Construction	218	36,548	82	33,841	306	12,738	13	37	35	40
Manufacturing	53	2,901	9	1,695	23	315	24	54	50	78
Transportation and public utilities	236	11,731	36	5,676	118	1,218	3	11	17	22
Wholesale trade	23	5,847	5	(D)	(D)	(D)	-	-	-	(D)
Retail trade	739	214,244	138	201,111	1,283	14,236	1	45	7	48
Finance, insurance, and real estate	239	4,620	20	1,473	32	306	11	19	-	-
Services	1,759	42,972	174	26,060	1,068	10,204	-	2	4	3
Industries not classified	158	2,504	18	(D)	(D)	(D)	-	-	-	(D)

Source: "Statistics for Black-Owned Firms by Industry for States: 1992," *Survey of Minority-Owned Business Enterprises-Black*, pp. 11-17. Primary source: *Survey of Minority-Owned Businesses-Black*, 1992 Economic Census, MB92-1. Washington, D.C.: Government Printing Office, January 1996. Adapted by the editors. *Notes:* For explanation of relative standard errors, see Reliability of Estimates in the introductory text. D = Withheld to avoid disclosing data for individual companies; data are included in higher-level totals.

★ 94 ★

Types of Businesses

Black-Owned Firms: Industry Division for Regions and States, 1992. Part 4 - West North Central

[Detail may not add to total because of rounding. This table is based on the 1987 SIC system. For meaning of abbreviations and symbols, see introductory text. For explanation of items see appendix A.]

Geographic area and industry division	All firms		Firms with paid employees				Relative standard error of estimate (percent)[1] for column-			
	Firms (number) A	Sales and receipts ($1,000) B	Firms (number) C	Sales and receipts ($1,000) D	Employees (number) E	Annual payroll ($1,000) F	A	B	C	D
Minnesota	2,795	263,392	332	211,584	2,845	44,532	1	8	6	4
Agricultural services, forestry, fishing, and mining	18	1,387	4	(D)	(D)	(D)	8	2	-	(D)
Construction	103	16,047	36	14,835	173	4,114	8	15	23	16
Manufacturing	42	23,679	9	23,199	244	7,633	-	-	-	-
Transportation and public utilities	201	7,129	9	3,080	84	1,294	-	-	-	-
Wholesale trade	52	25,196	10	24,653	93	2,966	7	18	35	18
Retail trade	285	90,808	62	85,318	1,088	11,615	3	4	12	4
Finance, insurance, and real estate	178	22,572	26	6,644	86	441	16	36	29	51
Services	1,756	95,287	172	52,571	1,052	15,967	1	23	8	8
Industries not classified	151	1,488	4	(D)	(D)	(D)	-	-	-	(D)
Missouri	9,973	403,289	1,089	276,594	4,879	56,084	1	3	2	4
Agricultural services, forestry, fishing, and mining	109	1,992	19	1,220	40	241	-	-	-	-
Construction	582	26,947	102	20,648	269	5,498	2	22	10	29
Manufacturing	87	2,588	9	1,699	22	296	-	-	-	-
Transportation and public utilities	830	24,933	57	12,489	221	2,754	-	-	-	-
Wholesale trade	110	20,215	15	17,901	79	1,835	11	-	-	-
Retail trade	1,492	134,592	245	114,154	1,450	12,545	2	2	4	2

[Continued]

|

★ 94 ★

Black-Owned Firms: Industry Division for Regions and States, 1992. Part 4 - West North Central

[Continued]

Geographic area and industry division	All firms		Firms with paid employees				Relative standard error of estimate (percent)[1] for column-			
	Firms (number) A	Sales and receipts ($1,000) B	Firms (number) C	Sales and receipts ($1,000) D	Employees (number) E	Annual payroll ($1,000) F	A	B	C	D
Finance, insurance, and real estate	826	20,587	77	9,791	147	1,920	4	13	14	18
Services	5,467	161,566	543	96,136	2,643	30,837	1	5	4	8
Industries not classified	668	9,869	22	556	8	157	2	12	-	-
Iowa	1,106	75,521	141	64,082	604	8,734	2	7	11	9
Agricultural services, forestry, fishing, and mining	15	(D)	3	(D)	(D)	(D)	-	(D)	-	(D)
Construction	55	2,191	13	1,769	27	462	4	14	16	17
Manufacturing	22	7,064	11	8,720	68	1,520	43	77	86	81
Transportation and public utilities	49	9,680	9	8,724	28	554	-	-	-	-
Wholesale trade	14	(D)	2	(D)	(D)	(D)	-	(D)	-	(D)
Retail trade	139	25,515	16	(D)	(D)	(D)	1	1	9	(D)
Finance, insurance, and real estate	68	(D)	4	284	3	45	24	(D)	-	-
Services	675	18,163	81	11,675	309	3,275	2	7	15	11
Industries not classified	69	704	2	(D)	(D)	(D)	-	-	-	(D)
Kansas	3,078	92,295	291	50,991	1,068	13,012	1	3	3	3
Agricultural services, forestry, fishing, and mining	52	(D)	7	(D)	(D)	(D)	3	(D)	-	(D)
Construction	187	14,966	35	9,707	104	2,462	7	20	19	16
Manufacturing	35	(D)	3	(D)	(D)	(D)	34	(D)	-	(D)
Transportation and public utilities	148	8,495	18	4,548	78	955	-	-	-	-
Wholesale trade	32	1,318	5	788	6	91	-	-	-	-
Retail trade	425	18,055	55	10,926	207	2,179	-	-	-	-
Finance, insurance, and real estate	151	2,625	9	(D)	(D)	(D)	8	1	-	(D)
Services	1,834	36,014	154	18,128	620	5,916	1	1	4	1
Industries not classified	215	3,975	7	285	2	34	5	21	-	-
North Dakota	117	7,845	14	5,201	106	1,024	13	20	11	1
Agricultural services, forestry, fishing, and mining	18	(D)	1	(D)	(D)	(D)	83	(D)	-	(D)
Construction	2	(D)	1	(D)	(D)	(D)	-	(D)	-	(D)
Manufacturing	-	-	-	-	-	-	-	-	-	-
Transportation and public utilities	5	(D)	1	(D)	(D)	(D)	-	(D)	-	(D)
Wholesale trade	3	(D)	-	-	-	-	-	(D)	-	-
Retail trade	14	(D)	1	(D)	(D)	(D)	-	(D)	-	(D)
Finance, insurance, and real estate	2	(D)	1	(D)	(D)	(D)	-	(D)	-	(D)
Services	70	(D)	9	(D)	(D)	(D)	2	(D)	17	(D)
Industries not classified	3	(D)	-	-	-	-	-	(D)	-	-
Nebraska	1,360	61,523	154	46,833	950	9,621	2	13	6	17
Agricultural services, forestry, fishing, and mining	14	(D)	3	(D)	(D0	(D)	-	(D)	-	(D)
Construction	49	1,793	8	1,395	27	2934	-	-	-	-
Manufacturing	8	(D)	1	(D)	(D)	(D)	-	(D)	-	(D)
Transportation and public utilities	36	1,243	3	(D)	(D)	(D)	-	-	-	(D)
Wholesale trade	19	8,258	9	6,133	39	875	17	12	36	13
Retail trade	189	24,016	46	21,967	472	2,977	3	29	14	32
Finance, insurance, and real estate	102	5,059	9	1,997	15	510	23	40	27	58
Services	853	21,416	72	14,148	385	4,795	2	17	9	25
Industries not classified	80	(D)	4	(D)	(D)	(D)	-	(D)	-	(D)
South Dakota	111	10,397	20	9,160	91	860	1	-	7	-
Agricultural services, forestry, fishing, and mining	2	(D)	-	-	-	-	-	(D)	-	-
Construction	13	319	3	(D)	(D)	(D)	-	-	-	(D)
Manufacturing	2	(D)	1	(D)	(D)	(D)	-	(D)	-	(D)
Transportation and public utilities	8	(D)	3	(D)	(D)	(D)	-	(D)	-	(D)
Wholesale trade	2	(D)	2	(D)	(D)	(D)	-	(D)	-	(D)
Retail trade	14	(D)	2	(D)	(D)	(D)	-	(D)	-	(D)
Finance, insurance, and real estate	4	(D)	-	-	-	-	-	(D)	-	-

[Continued]

★ 94 ★

Black-Owned Firms: Industry Division for Regions and States, 1992. Part 4 - West North Central
[Continued]

Geographic area and industry division	All firms		Firms with paid employees				Relative standard error of estimate (percent)[1] for column-			
	Firms (number) A	Sales and receipts ($1,000) B	Firms (number) C	Sales and receipts ($1,000) D	Employees (number) E	Annual payroll ($1,000) F	A	B	C	D
Services	62	1,228	9	662	33	201	2	1	16	2
Industries not classified	4	11	-	-	-	-	-	-	-	-

Source: "Statistics for Black-Owned Firms by Industry for States: 1992," *Survey of Minority-Owned Business Enterprises-Black*, pp. 11-17. Primary source: *Survey of Minority-Owned Businesses-Black*, 1992 Economic Census, MB92-1. Washington, D.C.: Government Printing Office, January 1996. Adapted by the editors.
Notes: For explanation of relative standard errors, see Reliability of Estimates in the introductory text. D = Withheld to avoid disclosing data for individual companies; data are included in higher-level totals.

★ 95 ★

Types of Businesses

Black-Owned Firms: Industry Division for Regions and States, 1992. Part 5- South Atlantic

[Detail may not add to total because of rounding. This table is based on the 1987 SIC system. For meaning of abbreviations and symbols, see introductory text. For explanation of items see appendix A.]

Geographic area and industry division	All firms		Firms with paid employees				Relative standard error of estimate (percent)[1] for column-			
	Firms (number) A	Sales and receipts ($1,000) B	Firms (number) C	Sales and receipts ($1,000) D	Employees (number) E	Annual payroll ($1,000) F	A	B	C	D
Delaware	2,060	156,880	243	125,503	2,352	22,763	2	12	7	15
Agricultural services, forestry, fishing, and mining	45	2,214	12	1,945	79	1,162	-	-	-	-
Construction	151	6,013	29	4,044	60	1,255	2	24	8	35
Manufacturing	19	(D)	1	(D)	(D)	(D)	-	(D)	-	(D)
Transportation and public utilities	205	9,485	31	(D)	(D)	(D)	1	7	7	(D)
Wholesale trade	27	(D)	14	(D)	(D)	(D)	26	(D)	51	(D)
Retail trade	311	36,147	46	28,813	917	6,941	7	50	25	63
Finance, insurance, and real estate	113	(D)	7	(D)	(D)	(D)	14	(D)	-	(D)
Services	1,061	29,747	100	18,802	1,128	9,220	2	5	9	7
Industries not classified	129	(D)	4	105	1	20	-	(D)	-	-
District of Columbia	10,111	451,861	787	313,107	4,277	88,431	1	4	3	5
Agricultural services, forestry, fishing, and mining	48	1,430	8	1,057	30	282	3	-	-	-
Construction	422	18,015	56	12,887	152	3,692	3	8	10	12
Manufacturing	64	1,280	4	425	15	109	-	-	-	-
Transportation and public utilities	1,779	41,885	69	20,800	462	7,715	1	20	22	40
Wholesale trade	74	47,848	16	47,319	149	4,096	6	7	27	7
Retail trade	960	80,398	126	66,000	797	8,308	2	10	8	9
Finance, insurance, and real estate	632	36,023	41	15,786	165	7,989	7	33	19	20
Services	5,473	214,382	453	146,636	2,502	56,094	1	3	4	4
Industries not classified	658	10,601	14	2,198	6	147	-	-	-	-
Florida	40,371	2,265,451	4,435	1,601,841	22,978	320,116	1	15	4	22
Agricultural services, forestry, fishing, and mining	1,673	58,362	308	34,253	971	10,101	2	13	8	21
Construction	3,234	171,962	669	114,555	1,972	26,541	2	6	6	5
Manufacturing	497	69,873	119	63,403	1,189	16,367	7	29	27	32
Transportation and public utilities	3,063	197,144	280	112,818	3,466	40,911	1	40	11	70
Wholesale trade	811	229,527	179	200,106	764	18,600	9	19	27	21
Retail trade	4,947	728,800	755	647,612	6,346	71,177	2	46	10	52
Finance, insurance, and real estate	2,390	112,674	206	37,604	619	10,861	3	17	19	23
Services	20,829	646,109	1,840	387,726	7,619	125,134	1	4	6	7
Industries not classified	3,127	51,000	78	3,565	31	422	1	10	-	-
Georgia	38,264	1,677,083	4,095	1,103,546	18,744	253,026	-	4	3	6
Agricultural services, forestry, fishing, and mining	693	17,836	101	10,836	292	3,776	2	29	16	48
Construction	3,523	185,511	770	135,423	2,371	30,974	1	5	5	6
Manufacturing	691	100,705	157	91,098	1,228	17,475	3	6	14	7

[Continued]

★ 95 ★

Black-Owned Firms: Industry Division for Regions and States, 1992. Part 5- South Atlantic
[Continued]

Geographic area and industry division	All firms		Firms with paid employees				Relative standard error of estimate (percent)[1] for column-			
	Firms (number) A	Sales and receipts ($1,000) B	Firms (number) C	Sales and receipts ($1,000) D	Employees (number) E	Annual payroll ($1,000) F	A	B	C	D
Transportation and public utilities	2,679	269,807	244	203,027	2,484	39,215	2	2	14	3
Wholesale trade	373	43,201	54	34,540	238	5,438	6	4	32	3
Retail trade	5,198	337,658	691	254,698	4,284	33,144	1	3	7	4
Finance, insurance, and real estate	2,531	110,729	151	27,993	503	7,459	3	16	18	36
Services	20,017	568,350	1,816	337,120	7,260	114,558	1	12	5	20
Industries not classified	2,559	43,286	111	8,811	84	986	1	8	16	39
Maryland	36,758	1,241,530	2,543	734,155	31,450	227,306	-	5	4	9
Agricultural services, forestry, fishing, and mining	406	11,454	82	7,307	117	2,065	8	21	35	30
Construction	1,815	112,477	335	73,270	1,612	19,102	2	8	10	4
Manufacturing	278	15,490	21	11,823	88	1,597	4	1	-	-
Transportation and public utilities	4,204	108,864	230	29,489	579	8,715	1	1	-	-
Wholesale trade	362	90,390	27	83,487	291	10,267	6	1	-	-
Retail trade	4,206	203,895	383	149,654	2,634	19,986	1	7	14	8
Finance, insurance, and real estate	2,644	65,763	109	25,010	315	7,682	2	8	19	3
Services	19,755	605,143	1,324	352,396	25,802	157,562	-	10	6	17
Industries not classified	2,085	28,053	31	1,719	12	329	1	1	-	-
North Carolina	29,221	893,369	3,479	830,729	11,166	115,873	-	2	1	2
Agricultural services, forestry, fishing, and mining	787	13,795	100	7,669	219	2,711	-	-	-	-
Construction	2,924	115,075	696	77,327	2,241	23,243	1	3	3	3
Manufacturing	533	32,806	114	27,175	368	4,546	4	7	9	8
Transportation and public utilities	1,978	90,290	223	39,266	623	7,948	1	2	3	3
Wholesale trade	311	40,878	51	33,963	194	3,414	4	18	15	22
Retail trade	4,417	207,116	540	144,610	1,984	18,053	1	2	5	3
Finance, insurance, and real estate	1,666	36,127	104	10,205	144	1,799	4	12	8	9
Services	14,887	335,397	1,571	186,495	5,340	55,632	-	4	2	5
Industries not classified	1,719	21,884	80	4,010	52	527	-	-	-	-
South Carolina	18,343	672,514	2,485	435,258	9,484	105,246	-	1	1	2
Agricultural services, forestry, fishing, and mining	425	8,905	66	4,027	124	963	-	10	-	-
Construction	2,351	99,977	646	73,781	2,290	21,554	1	3	2	4
Manufacturing	362	50,681	117	45,080	735	7,312	5	6	3	7
Transportation and public utilities	1,237	55,522	156	17,721	292	3,975	-	2	3	8
Wholesale trade	145	10,146	19	8,398	126	1,911	8	21	7	26
Retail trade	3,370	195,215	405	142,167	1,461	13,421	1	1	4	2
Finance, insurance, and real estate	884	25,415	56	9,820	111	1,527	4	18	6	6
Services	8,244	206,213	923	129,125	4,253	53,552	4	18	6	6
Industries not classified	1,324	20,440	97	5,138	72	1,031	1	3	11	11
Virginia	26,100	1,211,173	2,958	892,170	20,992	267,017	-	3	3	4
Agricultural services, forestry, fishing, and mining	545	11,891	81	6,744	158	2,041	3	22	19	39
Construction	2,198	113,236	485	77,458	1,334	18,717	2	17	6	23
Manufacturing	494	33,624	118	24,781	287	5,722	6	13	21	9
Transportation and public utilities	2,494	97,613	374	43,660	878	8,195	2	8	12	17
Wholesale trade	249	93,202	57	90,038	685	13,112	10	18	41	19
Retail trade	3,556	252,317	382	209,477	5,228	41,871	1	8	11	10
Finance, insurance, and real estate	1,496	39,052	96	10,348	191	2,473	4	16	18	20
Services	13,456	550,462	1,320	427,594	12,213	174,504	1	3	5	4
Industries not classified	1,610	19,776	47	2,070	17	382	-	-	-	-
West Virginia	1,083	42,228	127	32,941	559	7,379	2	2	2	3
Agricultural services, forestry, fishing, and mining	21	(D)	4	(D)	(D)	(D)	10	(D)	-	(D)
Construction	79	3,525	19	2,620	48	699	15	9	-	-
Manufacturing	15	(D)	3	(D)	(D)	(D)	-	(D)	-	(D)
Transportation and public utilities	35	(D)	6	(D)	(D)	(D)	-	(D)	-	(D)
Wholesale trade	4	(D)	1	(D)	(D)	(D)	-	(D)	-	(D)
Retail trade	146	8,518	23	7,337	113	945	9	-	-	-
Finance, insurance, and real estate	45	(D)	2	(D)	(D)	(D)	26	(D)	-	(D)

[Continued]

★ 95 ★

Black-Owned Firms: Industry Division for Regions and States, 1992. Part 5- South Atlantic
[Continued]

Geographic area and industry division	All firms		Firms with paid employees				Relative standard error of estimate (percent)[1] for column-			
	Firms (number) A	Sales and receipts ($1,000) B	Firms (number) C	Sales and receipts ($1,000) D	Employees (number) E	Annual payroll ($1,000) F	A	B	C	D
Services	671	16,719	67	11,602	311	3,227	3	5	4	8
Industries not classified	76	(D)	2	(D)	(D)	(D)	-	(D)	-	(D)

Source: "Statistics for Black-Owned Firms by Industry for States: 1992," *Survey of Minority-Owned Business Enterprises-Black*, pp. 11-17. Primary source: *Survey of Minority-Owned Businesses-Black*, 1992 Economic Census, MB92-1. Washington, D.C.: Government Printing Office, January 1996. Adapted by the editors. *Notes:* For explanation of relative standard errors, see Reliability of Estimates in the introductory text. D = Withheld to avoid disclosing data for individual companies; data are included in higher-level totals.

★ 96 ★

Types of Businesses

Black-Owned Firms: Industry Division for Regions and States, 1992. Part 6- East South Central

[Detail may not add to total because of rounding. This table is based on the 1987 SIC system. For meaning of abbreviations and symbols, see introductory text. For explanation of items see appendix A.]

Geographic area and industry division	All firms		Firms with paid employees				Relative standard error of estimate (percent)[1] for column-			
	Firms (number) A	Sales and receipts ($1,000) B	Firms (number) C	Sales and receipts ($1,000) D	Employees (number) E	Annual payroll ($1,000) F	A	B	C	D
Alabama	14,707	534,692	1,969	343,331	8,827	81,710	-	2	1	2
Agricultural services, forestry, fishing, and mining	320	6,953	46	4,330	120	996	1	10	3	15
Construction	1,641	87,828	365	64,203	1,171	12,421	1	7	1	8
Manufacturing	554	66,994	148	58,304	853	17,449	1	6	2	7
Transportation and public utilities	651	30,034	108	13,694	276	3,941	1	6	8	12
Wholesale trade	104	14,671	18	11,548	100	1,603	2	15	11	19
Retail trade	2,396	118,765	341	75,877	1,458	9,451	1	2	2	2
Finance, insurance, and real estate	611	14,694	56	6,636	105	1,151	3	12	6	13
Services	7,397	178,755	862	106,506	2,683	34,203	-	2	2	4
Industries not classified	1,030	15,997	44	2,235	60	491	-	-	-	-
Kentucky	5,097	250,855	522	196,117	2,452	29,886	1	4	3	4
Agricultural services, forestry, fishing, and mining	125	(D)	22	(D)	(D)	(D)	2	(D)	6	(D)
Construction	389	16,022	75	11,906	168	3,030	2	9	8	12
Manufacturing	55	(D)	5	(D)	(D)	(D)	21	(D)	27	(D)
Transportation and public utilities	255	58,639	24	(D)	(D)	(D)	5	5	11	(D)
Wholesale trade	51	14,288	11	13,196	72	1,071	23	29	18	31
Retail trade	701	88,597	119	77,725	790	7,017	3	8	7	9
Finance, insurance, and real estate	260	7,172	28	4,584	71	802	8	16	9	24
Services	2,858	54,406	233	32,874	1,074	10,850	1	4	4	6
Industries not classified	405	(D)	6	(D)	(D)	(D)	-	(D)	-	(D)
Mississippi	14,067	504,945	1,891	300,535	5,899	54,676	-	1	1	-
Agricultural services, forestry, fishing, and mining	332	5,252	48	2,046	67	585	-	1	-	-
Construction	1,740	67,515	367	43,091	996	9,867	1	3	-	-
Manufacturing	999	39,735	176	26,062	406	4,727	1	-	2	-
Transportation and public utilities	892	43,141	132	16,468	261	2,948	2	3	5	2
Wholesale trade	114	50,024	23	48,097	236	3,271	-	-	-	-
Retail trade	2,441	126,160	402	72,326	1,323	8,069	1	1	1	-
Finance, insurance, and real estate	574	16,134	59	7,151	86	826	4	20	-	-
Services	5,914	139,187	639	82,116	2,300	23,086	-	1	1	-
Industries not classified	1,061	17,797	45	3,158	24	296	1	-	10	-
Tennessee	14,920	555,015	1,686	326,870	5,955	65,861	-	4	2	3
Agricultural services, forestry, fishing, and mining	259	7,131	47	5,070	138	1,283	-	-	-	-
Construction	1,481	51,089	283	30,734	697	8,408	1	7	2	12
Manufacturing	176	4,850	22	2,561	49	572	-	-	-	-

[Continued]

★ 96 ★

Black-Owned Firms: Industry Division for Regions and States, 1992. Part 6- East South Central

[Continued]

Geographic area and industry division	All firms		Firms with paid employees				Relative standard error of estimate (percent)[1] for column-			
	Firms (number) A	Sales and receipts ($1,000) B	Firms (number) C	Sales and receipts ($1,000) D	Employees (number) E	Annual payroll ($1,000) F	A	B	C	D
Transportation and public utilities	730	31,893	67	10,039	232	2,543	2	5	5	11
Wholesale trade	169	54,691	24	50,077	197	3,096	10	6	14	7
Retail trade	2,369	119,343	353	82,884	1,400	10,801	1	4	6	5
Finance, insurance, and real estate	847	32,553	71	13,081	207	2,652	3	20	6	5
Services	7,865	239,884	779	130,644	3,013	36,183	-	8	2	4
Industries not classified	1,024	13,580	40	1,780	23	324	-	-	-	-

Source: "Statistics for Black-Owned Firms by Industry for States: 1992," *Survey of Minority-Owned Business Enterprises-Black,* pp. 11-17. Primary source: *Survey of Minority-Owned Businesses-Black,* 1992 Economic Census, MB92-1. Washington, D.C.: Government Printing Office, January 1996. Adapted by the editors. *Notes:* For explanation of relative standard errors, see Reliability of Estimates in the introductory text. D = Withheld to avoid disclosing data for individual companies; data are included in higher-level totals.

★ 97 ★

Types of Businesses

Black-Owned Firms: Industry Division for Regions and States, 1992. Part 7- West South Central

[Detail may not add to total because of rounding. This table is based on the 1987 SIC system. For meaning of abbreviations and symbols, see introductory text. For explanation of items see appendix A.]

Geographic area and industry division	All firms		Firms with paid employees				Relative standard error of estimate (percent)[1] for column-			
	Firms (number) A	Sales and receipts ($1,000) B	Firms (number) C	Sales and receipts ($1,000) D	Employees (number) E	Annual payroll ($1,000) F	A	B	C	D
Arkansas	5,738	232,850	646	160,875	1,952	21,691	1	3	2	4
Agricultural services, forestry, fishing, and mining	170	2,423	12	428	20	147	7	27	-	-
Construction	505	15,685	90	9,810	212	2,083	-	2	2	4
Manufacturing	295	18,490	48	13,685	155	2,213	1	7	5	9
Transportation and public utilities	356	16,300	50	7,504	171	2,060	1	1	5	2
Wholesale trade	48	10,309	8	9,697	26	390	4	55	25	59
Retail trade	943	100,923	122	85,719	457	5,765	2	2	7	2
Finance, insurance, and real estate	207	3,580	17	1,284	20	285	-	-	-	-
Services	2,780	58,150	279	31,588	882	8,625	1	3	4	5
Industries not classified	435	6,989	21	1,159	9	124	-	-	-	-
Louisiana	20,312	774,132	2,066	487,065	8,626	90,944	-	13	3	21
Agricultural services, forestry, fishing, and mining	623	21,234	81	15,514	130	2,186	3	2	33	1
Construction	2,339	64,483	385	32,085	723	8,990	1	3	5	5
Manufacturing	429	122,867	87	116,050	508	7,580	4	82	16	87
Transportation and public utilities	2,069	87,201	190	34,299	856	10,018	1	13	12	32
Wholesale trade	189	24,760	19	20,526	70	1,185	9	3	-	-
Retail trade	2,995	166,238	402	109,628	1,648	12,800	1	9	9	13
Finance, insurance, and real estate	1,012	28,842	61	13,681	1,42	2,055	3	12	-	-
Services	9,326	241,088	846	142,327	4,533	45,879	-	3	4	4
Industries not classified	1,330	19,420	37	2,975	16	251	1	-	-	-
Oklahoma	4,621	190,517	510	134,555	2,027	24,574	1	6	7	7
Agricultural services, forestry, fishing, and mining	147	3,455	14	899	15	173	3	22	-	-
Construction	276	39,998	65	36,858	318	5,596	4	9	15	10
Manufacturing	51	4,033	4	3,814	63	2,012	-	-	-	-
Transportation and public utilities	180	7,894	22	2,845	52	562	6	19	33	51
Wholesale trade	48	7,955	7	(D)	(D)	(D)	-	-	-	(D)
Retail trade	666	49,842	97	41,599	565	4,679	2	3	14	4
Finance, insurance, and real estate	289	11,773	35	9,412	23	701	6	66	48	82
Services	2,855	61,368	263	29,811	971	10,840	1	13	9	8

[Continued]

★ 97 ★

Black-Owned Firms: Industry Division for Regions and States, 1992. Part 7- West South Central

[Continued]

Geographic area and industry division	All firms		Firms with paid employees				Relative standard error of estimate (percent)[1] for column-			
	Firms (number) A	Sales and receipts ($1,000) B	Firms (number) C	Sales and receipts ($1,000) D	Employees (number) E	Annual payroll ($1,000) F	A	B	C	D
Industries not classified	308	4,201	3	(D)	(D)	(D)	-	-	-	(D)
Texas	50,008	2,339,221	4,861	1,804,853	23,745	285,195	-	17	3	25
Agricultural services, forestry, fishing, and mining	1,123	40,733	128	22,004	380	4,540	2	7	18	11
Construction	3,209	144,821	636	87,248	1,244	21,975	2	11	6	14
Manufacturing	1,098	78,755	131	53,955	544	12,216	3	28	15	40
Transportation and public utilities	4,810	164,294	278	37,598	619	8,227	-	3	7	14
Wholesale trade	887	572,243	162	556,890	645	11,758	7	68	26	69
Retail trade	7,217	447,985	847	343,540	7,635	72,237	1	15	6	19
Finance, insurance, and real estate	2,567	95,227	243	53,083	631	8,527	2	6	14	3
Services	26,109	749,461	2,359	444,492	11,984	145,015	-	9	4	15
Industries not classified	3,189	45,703	78	6,043	83	899	1	2	-	-

Source: "Statistics for Black-Owned Firms by Industry for States: 1992," *Survey of Minority-Owned Business Enterprises-Black*, pp. 11-17. Primary source: *Survey of Minority-Owned Businesses-Black*, 1992 Economic Census, MB92-1. Washington, D.C.: Government Printing Office, January 1996. Adapted by the editors. *Notes:* For explanation of relative standard errors, see Reliability of Estimates in the introductory text. D = Withheld to avoid disclosing data for individual cmpanies; data are included in higher-level totals.

★ 98 ★

Types of Businesses

Black-Owned Firms: Industry Division for Regions and States, 1992. Part 8- Mountain

[Detail may not add to total because of rounding. This table is based on the 1987 SIC system. For meaning of abbreviations and symbols, see introductory text. For explanation of items see appendix A.]

Geographic area and industry division	All firms		Firms with paid employees				Relative standard error of estimate (percent)[1] for column-			
	Firms (number) A	Sales and receipts ($1,000) B	Firms (number) C	Sales and receipts ($1,000) D	Employees (number) E	Annual payroll ($1,000) F	A	B	C	D
Arizona	2,936	137,721	328	99,734	1,274	16,326	1	17	10	23
Agricultural services, forestry, fishing, and mining	55	841	8	(D)	(D)	(D)	-	-	-	(D)
Construction	107	3,819	32	3,065	65	1,491	14	22	48	28
Manufacturing	41	4,393	12	3,814	49	645	22	79	75	91
Transportation and public utilities	171	7,986	38	5,137	69	1,335	12	28	47	44
Wholesale trade	43	37,364	13	36,412	48	1,555	22	60	72	61
Retail trade	379	23,687	39	17,808	302	2,740	-	-	-	-
Finance, insurance, and real estate	210	7,378	18	4,242	39	599	5	-	-	-
Services	1,777	49,621	164	28,184	681	7,793	1	7	11	13
Industries not classified	154	2,631	5	(D)	(D)	(D)	-	-	-	(D)
Colorado	4,372	295,305	431	242,385	2,955	43,655	1	7	11	8
Agricultural services, forestry, fishing, and mining	50	(D)	7	(D)	(D)	(D)	4	(D)	-	(D)
Construction	168	28,537	25	25,784	99	3,206	7	4	-	-
Manufacturing	71	(D)	25	(D)	(D)	(D)	28	(D)	81	(D)
Transportation and public utilities	245	(D)	14	(D)	(D)	(D)	-	(D)	-	(D)
Wholesale trade	42	12,306	5	11,767	39	720	-	-	-	-
Retail trade	680	46,083	95	37,496	738	6,830	4	25	27	31
Finance, insurance, and real estate	360	8,965	23	(D)	(D)	(D)	7	7	-	(D)
Services	2,523	83,247	233	56,961	1,636	23,294	2	19	16	28
Industries not classified	233	(D)	4	59	-	20	5	(D)	-	-
Idaho	152	24,532	28	23,079	119	2,311	3	1	16	1
Agricultural services, forestry, fishing, and mining	5	(D)	1	(D)	(D)	(D)	-	(D)	-	(D)
Construction	13	(D)	3	(D)	(D)	(D)	-	(D)	-	(D)
Manufacturing	-	(D)	-	-	-	-	-	-	-	-
Transportation and public utilities	1	(D)	-	-	-	-	-	(D)	-	-

[Continued]

★ 98 ★

Black-Owned Firms: Industry Division for Regions and States, 1992. Part 8- Mountain
[Continued]

Geographic area and industry division	All firms		Firms with paid employees				Relative standard error of estimate (percent)[1] for column-			
	Firms (number) A	Sales and receipts ($1,000) B	Firms (number) C	Sales and receipts ($1,000) D	Employees (number) E	Annual payroll ($1,000) F	A	B	C	D
Wholesale trade	2	(D)	-	-	-	-	-	(D)	-	-
Retail trade	21	(D)	7	(D)	(D)	(D)	-	(D)	-	(D)
Finance, insurance, and real estate	12	(D)	3	(D)	(D)	(D)	-	(D)	-	(D)
Services	85	2,338	13	1,543	38	364	5	8	34	11
Industries not classified	13	(D)	1	(D)	(D)	(D)	-	(D)	-	(D)
Montana	113	6,504	15	5,311	124	1,626	10	8	-	-
Agricultural services, forestry, fishing, and mining	-	-	-	-	-	-	-	-	-	-
Construction	4	(D)	3	(D)	(D)	(D)	-	(D)	-	(D)
Manufacturing	1	(D)	1	(D)	(D)	(D)	-	(D)	-	(D)
Transportation and public utilities	4	(D)	-	-	-	-	-	(D)	-	-
Wholesale trade	3	(D)	3	(D)	(D)	(D)	-	(D)	-	(D)
Retail trade	19	(D)	4	(D)	(D)	(D)	-	(D)	-	(D)
Finance, insurance, and real estate	20	(D)	1	(D)	(D)	(D)	58	(D)	-	(D)
Services	55	(D)	2	(D)	(D)	(D)	-	(D)	-	(D)
Industries not classified	7	(D)	1	(D)	(D)	(D)	-	(D)	-	(D)
Nevada	1,738	113,338	161	84,299	1,570	20,320	1	23	9	31
Agricultural services, forestry, fishing, and mining	34	(D)	6	283	7	48	4	(D)	-	-
Construction	72	5,161	12	3,367	35	824	16	14	-	-
Manufacturing	8	(D)	1	(D)	(D)	(D)	-	(D)	-	(D)
Transportation and public utilities	51	1,178	4	123	4	36	-	-	-	-
Wholesale trade	24	2,581	2	(D)	(D)	(D)	-	-	-	(D)
Retail trade	248	20,921	38	18,115	393	2,841	3	0	17	-
Finance, insurance, and real estate	158	3,513	11	1,498	23	398	-	-	-	-
Services	1,041	77,612	85	59,240	1,094	16,149	2	34	14	44
Industries not classified	100	(D)	2	(D)	(D)	(D)	-	(D)	-	(D)
New Mexico	925	80,831	96	45,190	591	7,122	2	9	4	10
Agricultural services, forestry, fishing, and mining	14	(D)	1	(D)	(D)	(D)	10	(D)	-	(D)
Construction	56	8,272	15	4,634	83	1,120	21	16	-	-
Manufacturing	18	(D)	5	(D)	(D)	(D)	12	(D)	44	(D)
Transportation and public utilities	24	(D)	3	(D)	(D)	(D)	-	(D)	-	(D)
Wholesale trade	16	(D)	1	(D)	(D)	(D)	-	(D)	-	(D)
Retail trade	173	26,435	26	23,799	319	3,440	2	17	13	19
Finance, insurance, and real estate	58	4,294	3	212	4	47	21	80	-	-
Services	535	10,014	42	4,519	110	1,206	-	-	-	-
Industries not classified	33	450	-	-	-	-	-	-	-	-
Utah	354	45,246	54	41,444	269	5,445	5	1	-	-
Agricultural services, forestry, fishing, and mining	2	(D)	1	(D)	(D)	(D)	-	(D)	-	(D)
Construction	11	(D)	4	(D)	(D)	(D)	-	(D)	-	(D)
Manufacturing	3	(D)	-	-	-	-	-	(D)	-	-
Transportation and public utilities	17	(D)	7	(D)	(D)	(D)	-	(D)	-	(D)
Wholesale trade	7	137	-	-	-	-	-	-	-	-
Retail trade	54	2,905	12	2,410	36	302	-	-	-	-
Finance, insurance, and real estate	19	(D)	4	(D)	(D)	(D)	-	(D)	-	(D)
Services	217	8,130	24	5,931	107	1,647	8	8	-	-
Industries not classified	24	(D)	2	(D)	(D)	(D)	-	(D)	-	(D)
Wyoming	97	5,301	10	4,230	85	897	-	-	-	-
Agricultural services, forestry, fishing, and mining	-	-	-	-	-	-	-	-	-	-
Construction	7	(D)	1	(D)	(D)	(D)	-	(D)	-	(D)
Manufacturing	1	(D)	-	-	-	-	-	(D)	-	-
Transportation and public utilities	6	(D)	-	-	-	-	-	(D)	-	-
Wholesale trade	2	(D)	1	(D)	(D)	(D)	-	(D)	-	(D)
Retail trade	13	(D)	3	(D)	(D)	(D)	-	(D)	-	(D)
Finance, insurance, and real estate	3	(D)	2	(D)	(D)	(D)	-	(D)	-	(D)

[Continued]

★ 98 ★

Black-Owned Firms: Industry Division for Regions and States, 1992. Part 8- Mountain
[Continued]

Geographic area and industry division	All firms		Firms with paid employees				Relative standard error of estimate (percent)[1] for column-			
	Firms (number) A	Sales and receipts ($1,000) B	Firms (number) C	Sales and receipts ($1,000) D	Employees (number) E	Annual payroll ($1,000) F	A	B	C	D
Services	61	(D)	2	(D)	(D)	(D)	-	(D)	-	(D)
Industries not classified	4	(D)	1	(D)	(D)	(D)	-	(D)	-	(D)

Source: "Statistics for Black-Owned Firms by Industry for States: 1992," *Survey of Minority-Owned Business Enterprises-Black*, pp. 11-17. Primary source: *Survey of Minority-Owned Businesses-Black*, 1992 Economic Census, MB92-1. Washington, D.C.: Government Printing Office, January 1996. Adapted by the editors. *Notes:* For explanation of relative standard errors, see Reliability of Estimates in the introductory text. D = Withheld to avoid disclosing data for individual companies; data are included in higher-level totals.

★ 99 ★

Types of Businesses

Black-Owned Firms: Industry Division for Regions and States, 1992. Part 9- Pacific

[Detail may not add to total because of rounding. This table is based on the 1987 SIC system. For meaning of abbreviations and symbols, see introductory text. For explanation of items see appendix A.]

Geographic area and industry division	All firms		Firms with paid employees				Relative standard error of estimate (percent)[1] for column-			
	Firms (number) A	Sales and receipts ($1,000) B	Firms (number) C	Sales and receipts ($1,000) D	Employees (number) E	Annual payroll ($1,000) F	A	B	C	D
Alaska	739	39,137	78	28,871	855	10,633	-	3	3	5
Agricultural services, forestry, fishing, and mining	23	(D)	2	(D)	(D)	(D)	-	(D)	-	(D)
Construction	29	2,813	9	1,427	7	232	-	-	-	-
Manufacturing	6	(D)	3	(D)	(D)	(D)	-	(D)	-	(D)
Transportation and public utilities	42	1,134	1	(D)	(D)	(D)	-	-	-	(D)
Wholesale trade	16	1,936	3	1,715	23	235	9	62	48	70
Retail trade	116	9,281	13	8,135	259	3,887	-	-	-	-
Finance, insurance, and real estate	20	639	2	(D)	(D)	(D)	-	-	-	(D)
Services	463	22,262	43	16,300	545	5,961	-	2	5	3
Industries not classified	24	(D)	2	(D)	(D)	(D)	-	(D)	-	(D)
California	65,968	5,476,365	6,875	4,155,861	43,292	732,136	-	2	2	2
Agricultural services, forestry, fishing, and mining	742	33,916	116	24,327	348	4,948	4	20	20	26
Construction	2,997	345,558	643	281,380	2,671	44,124	2	22	7	27
Manufacturing	1,064	113,905	195	94,970	1,249	29,061	4	6	20	6
Transportation and public utilities	3,501	194,165	327	93,800	1,493	21,599	1	1	-	-
Wholesale trade	936	319,320	110	288,483	897	25,149	3	-	-	-
Retail trade	9,385	717,192	1,136	562,684	8,203	80,216	1	2	5	2
Finance, insurance, and real estate	5,933	2,009,418	373	1,824,009	7,884	203,945	2	1	8	-
Services	41,149	1,684,727	3,865	979,158	20,510	322,334	-	3	3	4
Industries not classified	3,262	60,163	110	7,051	36	760	1	4	-	-
Hawaii	717	27,382	42	16,794	211	2,513	-	24	8	40
Agricultural services, forestry, fishing, and mining	8	89	-	-	-	-	-	-	-	-
Construction	21	(D)	2	(D)	(D)	(D)	-	(D)	-	(D)
Manufacturing	11	(D)	1	(D)	(D)	(D)	-	(D)	-	(D)
Transportation and public utilities	23	(D)	1	(D)	(D)	(D)	-	(D)	-	(D)
Wholesale trade	16	10,607	4	9,942	52	912	11	62	42	67
Retail trade	119	4,361	7	2,407	14	161	-	-	-	-
Finance, insurance, and real estate	59	1,104	2	(D)	(D)	(D)	-	-	-	(D)
Services	422	9,443	24	4,096	137	1,376	1	5	11	11
Industries not classified	36	770	1	(D)	(D)	(D)	-	-	-	(D)
Oregon	1,447	100,644	196	83,726	1,066	16,036	3	10	15	13
Agricultural services, forestry, fishing, and mining	20	171	2	(D)	(D)	(D)	-	-	-	(D)
Construction	69	10,264	30	9,529	126	1,518	29	72	66	77
Manufacturing	45	3,598	7	2,643	22	478	27	18	50	10
Transportation and public utilities	52	2,073	4	(D)	(D)	(D)	-	-	-	(D)
Wholesale trade	70	25,165	24	24,602	125	3,284	31	21	76	21

[Continued]

★ 99 ★

Black-Owned Firms: Industry Division for Regions and States, 1992. Part 9- Pacific
[Continued]

Geographic area and industry division	All firms		Firms with paid employees				Relative standard error of estimate (percent)[1] for column-			
	Firms (number) A	Sales and receipts ($1,000) B	Firms (number) C	Sales and receipts ($1,000) D	Employees (number) E	Annual payroll ($1,000) F	A	B	C	D
Retail trade	186	25,123	36	22,703	218	2,321	4	6	19	7
Finance, insurance, and real estate	79	1,568	7	732	7	71	15	26	47	55
Services	865	32,008	83	22,801	546	8,125	2	16	11	22
Industries not classified	81	673	-	-	-	-	-	-	-	-
Washington	4,575	257,073	595	200,661	3,901	46,716	1	8	8	10
Agricultural services, forestry, fishing, and mining	47	2,224	10	1,977	40	467	-	-	-	-
Construction	192	31,743	75	29,343	809	8,588	13	52	30	56
Manufacturing	70	1,747	5	639	7	81	-	-	-	-
Transportation and public utilities	215	8,327	13	4,659	59	1,036	7	2	-	-
Wholesale trade	78	39,781	12	37,493	161	4,601	-	-	-	-
Retail trade	752	71,122	166	64,606	1,077	9,177	5	15	23	17
Finance, insurance, and real estate	403	10,225	34	2,974	50	771	8	18	41	31
Services	2,626	88,503	273	58,502	1,396	21,942	1	5	7	7
Industries not classified	192	3,401	7	459	2	53	-	-	-	-

Source: "Statistics for Black-Owned Firms by Industry for States: 1992," *Survey of Minority-Owned Business Enterprises-Black,* pp. 11-17. Primary source: *Survey of Minority-Owned Businesses-Black,* 1992 Economic Census, MB92-1. Washington, D.C.: Government Printing Office, January 1996. Adapted by the editors. *Notes:* For explanation of relative standard errors, see Reliability of Estimates in the introductory text. D = Withheld to avoid disclosing data for individual companies; data are included in higher-level totals.

★ 100 ★

Types of Businesses

Black-Owned Firms: Major Industry Groups, 1992 and 1987. Part 1

[Detail may not add to total because of rounding. This table is based on the 1987 SIC system. For meaning of abbreviations and symbols, see introductory text. For explanation of terms see appendix A.]

Major industry group	1992					
	All firms		Firms with paid employees			
	Firms (number) A	Sales and receipts ($1,000) B	Firms (number) C	Sales and receipts ($1,000) D	Employees (number) E	Annual payroll ($1,000) F
All industries	620,912	32,197,361	64,478	22,589,676	345,193	4,806,624
Agricultural services, forestry, and fishing	9,820	265,089	1,491	159,119	3,904	45,547
Agricultural services	8,771	244,356	1,426	155,105	3,822	44,668
Forestry	371	8,550	47	2,555	60	581
Fishing, hunting, and trapping	678	12,183	18	1,459	22	298
Mining	490	65,621	51	46,000	293	6,454
Metal mining	21	620	2	(D)	(D)	(D)
Coal mining	14	10,778	6	10,730	73	2,272
Oil and gas extraction	424	49,224	37	32,716	187	3,497
Nonmetallic minerals, except fuels	31	4,999	7	(D)	(D)	(D)
Construction	43,381	2,651,356	8,798	1,962,727	26,545	447,362
General building contractors	6,023	840,456	1,715	697,311	6,077	104,932
Heavy construction contractors	730	156,055	241	146,986	1,234	28,068

[Continued]

85

★ 100 ★

Black-Owned Firms: Major Industry Groups, 1992 and 1987. Part 1
[Continued]

Major industry group	1992 All firms Firms (number) A	1992 All firms Sales and receipts ($1,000) B	1992 Firms with paid employees Firms (number) C	1992 Firms with paid employees Sales and receipts ($1,000) D	1992 Firms with paid employees Employees (number) E	1992 Firms with paid employees Annual payroll ($1,000) F
Special trade contractors	36,057	1,465,642	6,759	987,598	20,117	293,863
Subdividers and developers, n.e.c.	571	189,203	82	130,832	1,117	20,498
Manufacturing	10,469	1,319,193	1,958	1,155,011	12,977	251,322
Food and kindred products	364	203,986	67	200,378	1,272	23,629
Tobacco products	-	-	-	-	-	-
Textile mill products	102	28,331	42	27,924	310	5,385
Apparel and other textile products	1,054	82,592	92	74,018	1,267	18,387
Lumber and wood products	3,793	248,306	842	177,569	2,249	26,453
Furniture and fixtures	300	35,130	55	31,196	699	8,409
Paper and allied products	147	23,272	13	22,032	345	5,618
Printing and publishing	2,365	180,062	380	145,474	1,855	42,409
Chemicals and allied products	26	64,281	13	63,894	459	14,341
Petroleum and coal products	15	3,346	1	(D)	(D)	(D)
Rubber and miscellaneous plastics products	36	81,418	20	81,213	808	18,165
Leather and leather products	79	8,126	20	7,450	119	1,727
Stone, clay, and glass products	279	32,421	47	30,453	279	6,716
Primary metal industries	73	6,661	9	(D)	(D)	(D)
Fabricated metal products	432	91,041	96	84,158	974	21,390
Industrial machinery and equipment	372	69,820	110	62,736	570	19,605
Electronic and other electric equipment	194	66,713	28	64,856	645	16,478
Transportation equipment	37	32,201	13	27,745	218	4,880
Instruments and related products	26	20,547	20	20,486	447	8,934
Miscellaneous manufacturing industries	774	40,940	90	27,691	373	7,008
Transportation and public utilities	49,095	2,498,102	4,072	1,305,091	20,308	308,376
Local and interurban passenger transit	15,974	462,237	637	195,242	6,067	66,246
Trucking and warehousing	25,756	1,346,941	2,778	538,453	7,336	116,437
Water transportation	97	10,265	10	8,545	151	4,324
Transportation by air	145	7,288	13	5,466	131	1,524
Pipelines, except natural gas	-	-	-	-	-	-
Transportation services	4,882	160,875	335	74,011	1,335	25,327
Communications	1,517	400,528	198	383,885	4,906	88,883
Electric, gas, and sanitary services	724	109,968	101	99,490	381	5,634
Wholesale trade	7,550	2,944,321	1,510	2,745,412	8,649	203,544
Wholesale trade-durable goods	4,088	1,107,372	927	1,016,558	4,744	105,620
Wholesale trade-nondurable goods	3,461	1,836,949	583	1,728,854	3,904	97,923

[Continued]

★ 100 ★

Black-Owned Firms: Major Industry Groups, 1992 and 1987. Part 1
[Continued]

Major industry group	1992					
	All firms		Firms with paid employees			
	Firms (number) A	Sales and receipts ($1,000) B	Firms (number) C	Sales and receipts ($1,000) D	Employees (number) E	Annual payroll ($1,000) F
Retail trade	86,840	6,967,644	12,096	5,591,522	82,931	760,051
Building materials and garden supplies	855	139,679	208	116,176	961	16,387
General merchandise stores	1,198	46,636	95	23,882	275	2,804
Food stores	8,466	979,773	1,915	635,336	6,741	61,312
Automotive dealers and service stations	4,040	2,384,443	1,127	2,250,442	8,222	146,850
Apparel and accessory stores	6,391	203,985	796	125,457	1,836	18,020
Furniture and homefurnishings stores	2,677	180,560	514	128,120	1,320	16,404
Eating and drinking places	13,882	1,785,569	4,571	1,590,634	54,393	404,464
Miscellaneous retail	49,381	1,246,999	2,870	721,475	9,183	93,809
Finance, insurance, and real estate	40,924	3,777,171	3,194	2,771,537	17,606	380,056
Depository institutions	53	(D)	51	(D)	(D)	(D)
Nondepository institutions	501	63,478	93	40,989	321	10,793
Security and commodity brokers	1,161	(D)	114	(D)	(D)	(D)
Insurance carriers	10	2,627	9	(D)	(D)	(D)
Insurance agents, brokers, and service	12,199	308,003	1,414	158,469	2,534	35,944
Real estate[4]	24,187	1,552,796	1,400	792,740	7,614	127,428
Holding and other investment offices[6]	2,814	(D)	114	(D)	(D)	(D)
Services	332,981	11,057,136	30,081	6,773,932	169,248	2,393,563
Hotels and other lodging places	1,657	207,731	431	168,897	5,057	45,161
Personal services	76,988	1,468,760	5,240	583,994	20,004	184,961
Business services	80,330	2,371,433	6,774	1,576,771	72,130	705,681
Auto repair services and parking	14,814	551,800	2,244	313,519	5,370	72,871
Miscellaneous repair services	5,691	169,785	605	95,795	2,203	32,520
Motion pictures	1,916	85,727	170	60,315	690	14,413
Amusement and recreation services	23,786	664,978	996	300,042	3,670	93,076
Health services	43,860	2,858,582	6,164	2,010,937	29,578	601,966
Legal services	7,016	551,363	1,732	391,175	4,500	110,680
Educational services	7,309	70,718	297	30,926	1,294	15,287
Social services	35,391	582,275	3,356	304,435	12,009	111,769
Museums, botanical, zoological gardens	-	-	-	-	-	-
Engineering and management services	29,916	1,352,798	1,940	916,084	12,399	399,943

[Continued]

★ 100 ★

Black-Owned Firms: Major Industry Groups, 1992 and 1987. Part 1
[Continued]

Major industry group	1992					
	All firms		Firms with paid employees			
	Firms (number) A	Sales and receipts ($1,000) B	Firms (number) C	Sales and receipts ($1,000) D	Employees (number) E	Annual payroll ($1,000) F
Services, n.e.c.	4,307	121,187	130	21,043	344	5,237
Industries not classified	39,363	651,727	1,226	79,325	731	10,350

Source: "Statistics for Black-Owned Firms by Major Industry Group: 1992 and 1987," *Survey of Minority - Owned Business Enterprises-Black*, p. 9. Primary source: *Survey of Minority-Owned Businesses-Black*, 1992 Economic Census, MB92-1. Washington, D.C.: Government Printing Office, January 1996. *Notes:* D = Withheld to avoid disclosing data for individual companies; data are included in higher-level totals. 1. In 1987, industry classification for firm data were based on the 1972 SIC manual; the 1992 data are based on the 1987 SIC manual. The 1987 data were tabulated from administrative records; therefore relative standard errors are not applicable. See Comparability of 1987 and 1992 Data in the introductory text. 2. For explanation of relative standard errors, see Reliability of Estimates in the introductory text. 3. The 1987 data for industries 11 (anthracite mining) and 12 (bituminous coal and lignite mining) have been combined into SIC code 12 (coal mining) for comparability to the 1987 SIC system. 4. Excludes 6552 which is included in construction industries. 5. The 1987 data excluded 673 (Trusts) and 679 (Miscellaneous investing).

★ 101 ★

Types of Businesses

Black-Owned Firms: Major Industry Groups, 1992 and 1987. Part 2

[Detail may not add to total because of rounding. This table is based on the 1987 SIC system. For meaning of abbreviations and symbols, see introductory text. For explanation of terms see appendix A.]

Major industry group	1987[1] All firms		Relative standard error of estimate percent for column-			
	Firms (number) G	Sales and receipts ($1,000) H	A	B	C	D
All industries	424,165	19,762,876	-	2	1	3
Agricultural services, forestry, and fishing	7,316	216,742	1	7	4	11
Agricultural services	6,155	189,980	1	7	5	11
Forestry	417	11,416	-	-	-	-
Fishing, hunting, and trapping	744	15,346	-	-	-	-
Mining	322	54,071	2	4	-	-
Metal mining	6	75	12	12	-	(D)
Coal mining	9	3,988	-	-	-	-
Oil and gas extraction	270	39,946	3	5	-	-
Nonmetallic minerals, except fuels	34	10,039	10	24	-	(D)
Construction	36,763	2,174,399	-	4	2	5
General building contractors	6,285	635,702	1	8	3	9
Heavy construction contractors	638	155,949	5	13	14	14
Special trade contractors	29,631	1,313,819	-	3	2	4

[Continued]

★ 101 ★

Black-Owned Firms: Major Industry Groups, 1992 and 1987. Part 2
[Continued]

Major industry group	1987[1] All firms		Relative standard error of estimate percent for column-			
	Firms (number) G	Sales and receipts ($1,000) H	A	B	C	D
Subdividers and developers, n.e.c.	209	68,929	12	25	31	34
Manufacturing	8,004	1,023,104	1	8	4	9
Food and kindred products	286	60,595	4	49	23	50
Tobacco products	-	-	-	-	-	-
Textile mill products	74	9,954	20	27	48	28
Apparel and other textile products	552	64,671	3	3	21	3
Lumber and wood products	3,720	211,281	1	3	4	4
Furniture and fixtures	226	29,812	7	56	38	63
Paper and allied products	55	26,230	-	-	-	-
Printing and publishing	1,394	126,488	3	13	12	16
Chemicals and allied products	65	57,468	-	-	-	-
Petroleum and coal products	1	(D)	82	94	-	(D)
Rubber and miscellaneous plastics products	71	11,844	-	-	-	-
Leather and leather products	42	5,187	20	8	79	6
Stone, clay, and glass products	193	30,428	1	3	3	3
Primary metal industries	54	8,122	-	-	-	(D)
Fabricated metal products	338	116,191	8	8	23	9
Industrial machinery and equipment	271	45,711	10	6	29	6
Electronic and other electric equipment	136	113,567	6	1	5	1
Transportation equipment	57	69,685	32	16	16	12
Instruments and related products	31	11,291	60	32	78	33
Miscellaneous manufacturing industries	438	(D)	5	16	30	19
Transportation and public utilities	36,958	1,573,342	-	4	3	7
Local and interurban passenger transit	11,566	218,209	-	18	9	42
Trucking and warehousing	19,663	1,010,229	-	3	3	6
Water transportation	83	9,042	12	6	-	-
Transportation by air	117	11,485	11	5	11	2
Pipelines, except natural gas	-	-	-	-	-	-
Transportation services	4,053	222,757	1	8	9	15
Communications	896	81,785	3	7	21	7
Electric, gas, and sanitary services	580	19,835	5	3	18	3
Wholesale trade	5,519	1,327,479	2	13	7	14
Wholesale trade-durable goods	2,792	628,729	2	5	9	6
Wholesale trade-nondurable goods	2,727	698,750	3	21	11	23

[Continued]

★ 101 ★

Black-Owned Firms: Major Industry Groups, 1992 and 1987. Part 2
[Continued]

Major industry group	1987[1] All firms		Relative standard error of estimate percent for column-			
	Firms (number) G	Sales and receipts ($1,000) H	A	B	C	D
Retail trade	66,229	5,889,654	-	5	2	6
Building materials and garden supplies	650	190,291	5	10	18	10
General merchandise stores	1,064	44,343	1	3	7	5
Food stores	8,952	1,001,462	1	3	4	4
Automotive dealers and service stations	3,690	2,155,680	2	15	5	15
Apparel and accessory stores	3,061	140,187	1	10	8	16
Furniture and homefurnishings stores	2,108	187,063	2	11	9	15
Eating and drinking places	11,834	1,084,468	1	5	3	5
Miscellaneous retail	34,870	1,086,160	-	3	4	5
Finance, insurance, and real estate	26,989	804,252	1	3	4	4
Depository institutions	35	17,402	39	(D)	41	(D)
Nondepository institutions	45	13,429	8	25	35	28
Security and commodity brokers	711	22,723	3	(D)	23	(D)
Insurance carriers	36	6,220	-	-	-	(D)
Insurance agents, brokers, and service	7,956	188,690	1	3	4	4
Real estate[4]	15,552	505,936	1	7	7	11
Holding and other investment offices[6]	30	2,492	3	(D)	24	(D)
Services	209,547	6,120,084	-	1	1	2
Hotels and other lodging places	1,734	128,256	3	30	10	36
Personal services	56,772	959,696	-	2	2	4
Business services	59,177	1,570,161	-	3	2	5
Auto repair services and parking	11,801	426,584	1	4	4	7
Miscellaneous repair services	5,197	154,027	1	14	7	24
Motion pictures	733	61,911	2	14	20	19
Amusement and recreation services	13,250	502,847	-	5	6	8
Health services	30,026	1,350,606	-	3	2	4
Legal services	4,920	336,218	1	3	3	4
Educational services	3,561	64,545	1	5	13	12
Social services	13,210	224,137	-	3	2	7
Museums, botanical, zoological gardens	-	-	-	-	-	-
Engineering and management services	(X)	(X)	-	3	5	4

[Continued]

★ 101 ★

Black-Owned Firms: Major Industry Groups, 1992 and 1987. Part 2
[Continued]

Major industry group	1987[1] All firms		Relative standard error of estimate percent for column-			
	Firms (number) G	Sales and receipts ($1,000) H	A	B	C	D
Services, n.e.c.	9,166	341,096	3	10	23	26
Industries not classified	26,518	579,749	-	1	3	5

Source: "Statistics for Black-Owned Firms by Major Industry Group: 1992 and 1987," *Survey of Minority - Owned Business Enterprises-Black,* p. 9. Primary source: *Survey of Minority-Owned Businesses-Black,* 1992 Economic Census, MB92-1. Washington, D.C.: Government Printing Office, January 1996. *Notes:* D = Withheld to avoid disclosing data for individual companies; data are included in higher-level totals. X - Not applicable. 1. In 1987, industry classification for firm data were based on the 1972 SIC manual; the 1992 data are based on the 1987 SIC manual. The 1987 data were tabulated from administrative records; therefore relative standard errors are not applicable. See Comparability of 1987 and 1992 Data in the introductory text. 2. For explanation of relative standard errors, see Reliability of Estimates in the introductory text. 3. The 1987 data for industries 11 (anthracite mining) and 12 (bituminous coal and lignite mining) have been combined into SIC code 12 (coal mining) for comparability to the 1987 SIC system. 4. Excludes 6552 which is included in construction industries. 5. The 1987 data excluded 673 (Trusts) and 679 (Miscellaneous investing).

★ 102 ★

Types of Businesses

Black-Owned Firms: Percent Distribution by Industry Division, 1992

Types of businesses	Percentage
Manufacturing	1.7
Construction	7.0
Mining	0.1
Agricultural services, forestry, and fishing	1.6
Industries not classified	6.3
Transportation and public utilities	7.9
Wholesale trade	1.2
Retail trade	14.0
Finance, insurance, and real estate	6.6
Services	53.6

Source: "Percent Distribution of Black-Owned Firms by Industry Division: 1992," *Survey of Minority-Owned Business Enterprises-Black,* p. 6. Primary source: *Survey of Minority-Owned Businesses-Black,* 1992 Economic Census, MB92-1. Washington, D.C.: Government Printing Office, January 1996.

★ 103 ★

Types of Businesses

Farm Operators: Tenure and Characteristics: 1987 and 1992

[**In thousands, except as indicated**. See also *Historical Statistics, Colonial Times to 1970*, series K 82-113].

CHARACTERISTIC	ALL FARMS		FARMS WITH SALES OF $10,000 AND OVER	
	1987	1992	1987	1992
Total operators	2,088	1,925	1,060	1,019
White	2,043	1,882	1,046	1,003
Black	23	19	4	5
American Indian, Eskimo, and Aleut	7	8	2	3
Asian or Pacific Islander	8	8	5	5
Other	7	8	2	3
Operators of Hispanic origin[1]	17	21	6	8
Female	132	145	42	50

Source: "Farm Operators-Tenure and Characteristics: 1987 and 1992." U.S. Bureau of the Census, *Statistical Abstract of the United States*, 115th ed., 1995, p. 671. Primary source: U.S. Bureau of the Census, *Census of Agriculture: 1987*, vol. 1; and *1992*, vol. 1. *Note:* 1. Operators of Hispanic origin may be of any race.

★ 104 ★

Types of Businesses

Industrial/Service Companies: 50 Companies Ranked in Sales Below the 50 Leaders: 1994.

Company	This Year	Last Year	Location	Chief Executive	Year Started	Staff	Type of Business	Sales[1]
Calhoun Food Supermarket	51	36	Montgomery, Alabama	Greg Calhoun	1984	256	Supermarket	33.785
Dudley Products Inc.	52	46	Kernersville, North Carolina	Joe Louis Dudley Sr.	1967	475	Beauty products manufacturer & cosmetology university	32.500
O.J. Transport Co.	53	59	Detroit, Michigan	John A. James	1971	280	Transportation service	32.258
Yancy Minerals	54	52	Woodbridge, Connecticut	Earl J. Yancy	1977	14	Industrial metals, minerals & coal distributors	32.000
H.F. Henderson Industries Inc.	55	64	West Caldwell, New Jersey	Henry F. Henderson Jr.	1954	145	Industrial process controls & defense electronics	31.550
Solo Construction Corp.	56	90	N. Miami Beach, Florida	Randy L. Pierson Herron L. Pierson	1978	127	General engineering construction	30.251
V & J Foods Inc.	57	70	Milwaukee, Wisconsin	Valerie Daniels-Carter	1984	1,300	Burger King fast foods	30.000
Restoration Supermarket Corp.	58	63	Brooklyn, New York	Roderick B. Mitchell	1977	170	Supermarket & drugstore	29.300
Queen City Broadcasting Inc.	59	56	New York, New York	J. Bruce Llewellyn	1985	130	Network TV affiliates	29.000

[Continued]

★ 104 ★

Industrial/Service Companies: 50 Companies Ranked in Sales Below the 50 Leaders: 1994.
[Continued]

Company	This Year	Last Year	Location	Chief Executive	Year Started	Staff	Type of Business	Sales[1]
Thompson Hospitality L.P.	59	44	Reston, Virginia	Warren M. Thompson	1992	1,250	Restaurant & food service	29.000
Regal Plastics Co. Inc.	61	68	Roseville, Michigan	Forest J. Farmer	1985	350	Custom plastic injection molding	28.800
Westside Distributors	62	40	South Gate, California	Edison R. Lara Sr.	1974	90	Beer & snack foods distributor	28.512
Perfection Industrial	63	-	Kansas City, Missouri	James R. Roath	1976	48	Distributor of medical & industrial supplies	28.280
Inner City Broadcasting Corp.	64	52	New York, New York	Pierre Sutton	1972	205	Radio, TV, Cable TV franchise	27.900
Edge Systems Inc.	65	51	Aurora, Illinois	Sam Bishop	1985	60	Computer systems integration; turnkey computer systems	27.250
Washington Cable Supply Inc.	66	-	Lanham, Maryland	William Parker Jr.	1984	40	Serving the electrical, utility, & telecommunications industries	27.000
Dick Griffey Productions	67	57	Hollywood, California	Dick Griffey	1975	211	Entertainment	26.750
Advance Inc.	68	65	Arlington, Virginia	Dennis Brownlee	1980	300	Computer systems integration; telecommunications	26.100
Cimarron Express Inc.	69	57	Genoa, Ohio	Glenn G. Grady	1984	70	Contract carrier	26.000
Dual Inc.	70	75	Arlington, Virginia	J. Fred Dual Jr.	1983	340	Engineering & technical services	25.776
Premium Distributors Inc of Washington, D.C.	71	59	Washington, D.C.	Henry Neloms	1984	80	Beverage distributor	25.400
Earl G. Graves Ltd.	72	72	New York, New York	Earl G. Graves	1970	70	Magazine publishing	24.807
Navcom Systems Inc.	73	67	Manassas, Virginia	Elijah "Zeke" Jackson	1986	178	Engineering design; integration; manufacturing/assembly	24.600
Powers & Sons Construction Co. Inc.	74	-	Gary, Indiana	Mamon Powers Sr.	1967	100	Construction	24.517
Bronner Brothers	75	75	Atlanta, Georgia	Bernard Bronner	1947	250	Hair care products manufacturer	23.500
Lundy Enterprises	76	69	New Orleans, Louisiana	Larry Lundy	1992	1,000	Pizza Hut restaurants	23.400
Urban Organization Inc.	77	87	Miami, Florida	Jacque E. Thermilus	1988	200	General contracting & construction management	23.005
Terry Manufacturing Co. Inc.	78	77	Roanoke, Alabama	Roy Terry	1963	300	Apparel manufacturer	23.000
Exemplar Manufacturing Co.	79	-	Ypsilanti, Michigan	Anthony L. Snoddy	197	140	Auto parts manufacturer	22.176
Texcom Inc.	80	84	Landover, Maryland	Clemon H. Wesley	1982	290	Telecommunications, systems integration engineering, maintenance	21.298
Engineered Plastic Products Inc.	81	-	Roseville, Michigan	Gerald D. Edwards	1987	185	Injection molded plastic components for auto industry	21.200
Consolidated Beverage Corp.	82	82	New York,				Beverage wholesaler,	

[Continued]

★ 104 ★

Industrial/Service Companies: 50 Companies Ranked in Sales Below the 50 Leaders: 1994.
[Continued]

Company	This Year	Last Year	Location	Chief Executive	Year Started	Staff	Type of Business	Sales[1]
			New York	Albert N. Thompson	1978	21	exporter & importer	21.100
Resource Computer Systems One	83	88	Columbus, Ohio	Stampp W. Corbin	1992	23	Computer hardware & software	21.000
Red River Shipping Corp.	84	-	Rockville, Maryland	John P. Morris III	1983	50	Transportation (ocean)	20.801
Parks Sausage Co.	85	71	Baltimore, Maryland	Raymond Haysbert Sr.	1951	206	Sausage manufacturer	20.742
GB Tech Inc.	86	-	Houston, Texas	Gale E. Burkett	1985	339	Science & engineering	20.038
American Urban Radio Networks	87	96	New York, New York	Sydney Small Ronald Davenport	1973	65	Radio network; radio station; telemarketing	20.000
G & C Equipment Corp.	87	99	Gardena, California	Gene Hale	1981	10	Sale, leasing & rental of heavy construction equipment	20.000
Specialized Packaging International Inc.	89	95	Hamden, Connecticut	Carlton L. Highsmith	1983	10	Package design, engineering & brokerage	19.660
C.H. James & Son Holdings Inc.	90	-	Charleston, West Virginia	Charles H. James III	1883	110	Wholesale food distribution/ produce processing	19.200
Crown Energy Inc.	91	85	Chicago, Illinois	Charles Harrison	1987	6	Distributor of petroleum products	19.000
Mid-Delta Home Health Inc.	91	83	Belzoni, Mississippi	Clara Taylor Reed	1978	420	Home health care; medical equipment & supplies	19.000
Ozanne Construction Co. Inc.	91	85	Cleveland, Ohio	Leroy Ozanne	1956	135	General construction & construction management	19.000
Systems Engineering & Management Associates Inc.	94	74	Alexandria, Virginia	James C. Smith	1985	265	ADP technical support services	18.800
Dynamic Concepts Inc.	95	77	Washington, D.C.	Pedro Alfonso	1979	431	Telecommunication support, optical imaging & facilities management	18.600
UBM INC	96	92	Chicago, Illinois	S. Jiles, P. King & S. Dabadghao	1975	55	General construction & construction management	18.200
Black River Mfg. Inc.	97	-	Port Huron, Michigan	Isaac Lang Jr.	1977	145	Auto parts manufacturer	18.000
Marriott Production Inc.	97	-	Cappell, Texas	Tony Wilson	1983	9	Entertainment & sports managemnet	18.000
TCM Construction Inc.	97	-	Minneapolis, Minnesota	Donald Crowther	1980	42	General contractor	18.000
Spiral Inc.	100	-	Chandler, Arizona	Reggie Fowler	1989	25	Packaging suppliers in grocery industry	17.900

Source: "B.E. Industrial/Service 100," *Black Enterprise* 25 (June 1995), pp. 104, 106, 108. Published by permission. *Notes:* 1. In millions of dollars, to nearest thousand. As of Dec. 31, 1994. Prepared by B.E. Research. Reviewed by Mitchell/Titus & Co.

★ 105 ★

Types of Businesses

Industrial/Service Companies: Top 50 in Sales: 1994

Company	This Year	Last Year	Location	Chief Executive	Year Started	Staff	Type of Business	Sales[1]
TLC Beatrice International Holdings Inc.	1	1	New York, New York	Loida N. Lewis	1987	4,200	International food	1,800.000
Johnson Publishing Co. Inc.	2	2	Chicago, Illinois	John H. Johnson	1942	2,662	Publishing; broadcasting; TV production; cosmetics; hair care	306.608
Philadelphia Coca-Cola Bottling Co. Inc.	3	3	Philadelphia, Pennsylvania	J. Bruce Llewellyn	1985	1,000	Soft-drinks bottling	305.000
H.J. Russell & Co.	4	4	Atlanta, Georgia	Herman J. Russell	1952	1,219	Construction; communications; airport concessions	154.700
Pulsar Data Systems Inc.	5	14	New Castle, Delaware	William S. Davis Sr.	1982	132	Systems integration; office automation; computer reseller	137.000
RMS Technologies Inc.	6	5	Marlton, New Jersey	David W. Huggins	1977	1,300	Computer and technical services	121.000
The Anderson-Dubose Co.	7	6	Solon, Ohio	Warren Anderson	1991	85	Food distributor	118.000
Gold Line Refining Ltd.	8	7	Houston, Texas	Earl Thomas	1990	58	Oil refinery	108.564
Uniworld Group Inc.	9	16	New York, New York	Byron E. Lewis	1969	98	Advertising; public relations; event marketing; TV Programming	104.080
Bet Holdings Inc.	10	18	Washington, D.C.	Robert L. Johnson	1980	450	Cable television network; magazine publishing	97.500
Soft Sheen Products Inc.	11	9	Chicago, Illinois	Edward G. Gardner	1964	382	Hair care products manufacturer	97.200
Envirotest Systems Corp.	12	11	Phoenix, Arizona	Chester C. Davenport	1990	2,576	Vehicle emissions testing	96.395
The Bing Group	13	12	Detroit, Michigan	David Bing	1980	237	Steel processing; metal stamping distribution	93.461
Mays Chemical Co. Inc.	14	20	Indianapolis, Indiana	William G. Mays	1980	101	Industrial chemical distributors	88.900
Midwest Stamping Inc.	15	-	Bowling Green, Ohio	Ronald L. Thompson	1993	450	Metal stamping & assemblies	83.000
Burrell Communications Group	16	17	Chicago, Illinois	Thomas J. Burrell	1971	105	Advertising; public relations; consumer promotions; entertainment	80.790
Essence Communications Inc.	17	19	New York, New York	Edward Lewis	1969	102	Magazine publishing; TV production; direct-mail catalog	77.505
Granite Broadcasting Corp.	18	30	New York, New York	W. Don Cornwell	1988	555	Network TV affiliates	76.213
Marco International Inc.	19	-	Greenwich, Connecticut	William Webb Jr.	1989	60	Manufacturer of computer memory modules	75.000
Stop Shop and Save	20	21	Baltimore, Maryland	Henry T. Baines Edward Hunt	1978	515	Supermarkets	68.000
Wesley Industries Inc.	21	23	Flint, Michigan	Delbert W. Mullens	1983	685	Industrial coatings & grey iron foundry products	67.800
Drew Pearson Companies	22	15	Addison, Texas	Drew Pearson Kenneth W. Shead	1985	107	Sports licensing & sportswear manufacturing	65.000
Rush Communications	22	49	New York, New York	Russell Simmons	1990	65	Music; music publishing; TV, film, radio production; fashion	65.000

[Continued]

95

★ 105 ★

Industrial/Service Companies: Top 50 in Sales: 1994

[Continued]

Company	This Year	Last Year	Location	Chief Executive	Year Started	Staff	Type of Business	Sales[1]
The Bartech Group	24	-	Livonia, Michigan	Jon E. Barfield	1954	1,800	Contract employment; staffing services	63.000
Trumark Inc.	25	24	Lansing, Michigan	Carlton L. Guthrie	1985	360	Metal stampings; manufacturing; welding	60.000
Sylvest Management Systems Corp.	26	37	Lanham, Maryland	Gary S. Murray	1987	85	Computer systems & engineering	59.000
Sayers Computer Source	27	32	Mt. Prospect, Illinois	Gale Sayers	1984	70	Computer hardware & software supplier; networking	55.100
African Development Public Investment Corp.	28	22	Hollywood, California	Dick Griffey	1985	10	African commodities & oil trading	54.739
Surface Protection Industries Intl.	29	27	Los Angeles, California	Robert C. Davidson Jr.	1978	200	Paint & specialty coatings manufacturer	51.000
Active Transportation Co.	30	-	Louisville, Kentucky	Charlie W. Johnson	1987	300	Transports trucks & automobiles from manufacturer to dealer	50.000
The Mingo Group	31	25	New York, New York	Samuel J. Chisholm	1977	36	Advertising & public relations	49.251
Metters Industries Inc.	32	41	McLean, Virginia	Samuel Metters	1981	580	Systems engineering; software development mgt.	49.000
Pepsi Cola of Washington, D.C., LP.	33	26	Washington, D.C.	Earl G. Graves	1990	150	Soft-drink distributor	48.438
Community Foods Inc T/A Super Pride Markets	34	28	Baltimore, Maryland	Oscar A. Smith Jr.	1970	400	Supermarkets	47.000
Luster Products Co.	35	29	Chicago, Illinois	Jory Luster	1957	313	Hair care products manufacturer & distributor	46.000
Thacker Engineering Inc.	36	35	Atlanta, Georgia	Floyd G. Thacker	1970	191	Construction; construction management; engineering	44.740
Beauchamp Distributing Co.	37	43	Campton, California	Patrick L. Beauchamp	1971	115	Beverage distributor	44.200
Capsonic Group Inc. Div. of Gabriel Inc.	38	31	Elgin, Illinois	James Liautaud	1968	350	Designs & manufacturers composite (metal/plastic) components	43.000
Karl Kani Infinity	38	-	Los Angeles, California	Karl Kani	1989	14	Men's wear, outerwear, boy's wear, footwear & licensing	43.000
Pro-Line Corp.	40	34	Dallas, Texas	Comer J. Catrell	1970	286	Hair care products manufacturer & distributor	41.700
R.O.W. Sciences Inc.	41	49	Rockville, Maryland	Ralph Williams	1983	540	Biomedical & health services; research	41.448
The Maxima Corp.	42	33	Lanham, Maryland	Joshua I. Smith	1978	812	Systems engineering & computer facilities management	41.250
Advantage Enterprises Inc.	43	45	Toledo, Ohio	Levi Cook Jr.	1980	400	Project integrator for health care & construction	40.919
Grimes Oil Co. Inc.	44	37	Boston, Massachusetts	Calvin M. Grimes	1940	15	Petroleum products distributor	40.000
La-Van Hawkins Inner City Foods	45	93	Atlanta, Georgia	La-Van Hawkins	1991	1,500	Checkers Drive-In restaurants	39.136
Digital Systems			Arlington,				Nuclear, environmental, marine	

[Continued]

★ 105 ★

Industrial/Service Companies: Top 50 in Sales: 1994
[Continued]

Company	This Year	Last Year	Location	Chief Executive	Year Started	Staff	Type of Business	Sales[1]
Research Inc.	46	54	Virginia	Willie Woods	1988	310	maintenance & combat engineering	38.668
The Gourmet Companies	47	39	Atlanta, Georgia	Nathaniel Goldston III	1975	1,100	Food srevice; golf facilities management	38.000
Integrated Steel Inc.	48	59	Detroit, Michigan	Geralda L. Dodd	1990	250	Automotive stamping & steel sales & processing	37.597
Integrated Systems Analysts Inc.	49	42	Arlington, Virginia	C. Michael Gooden	1980	553	Systems engineering; computer systems services	34.600
Am-Pro Protective Agency Inc.	50	47	Columbia, South Carolina	John E. Brown	1982	1,092	Security Guard Service	34.000

Source: "B.E. Industrial/Service 100," *Black Enterprise* 25 (June 1995), pp. 99- 100, 104. Published by permission. *Notes:* 1. In millions of dollars, to nearest thousand. As of Dec. 31, 1994. Prepared by B.E. Research. Reviewed by Mitchell/Titus & Co.

Chapter 3
CRIME, LAW ENFORCEMENT, AND LEGAL JUSTICE

Crime

★ 106 ★

Drug-Related: Percent of Inmates Whose Most Serious Offense was Drug- Related, by Race/Ethnic Origin: 1986 and 1991

Type of crime	White		Black		Other race		Hispanic	
	1991	1986	1991	1986	1991	1986	1991	1986
Violent	49	50	47	59	54	62	39	52
Property	30	36	22	29	28	29	21	26
Drug	12	8	25	7	10	6	33	16
Public-order	8	6	5	4	8	3	8	5
Number	248,705	177,187	321,217	202,872	16,627	11,381	117,632	56,505

Source: "Percentage of Inmates Having Committed Drug Crimes as Their Most Serious Offense, by Race/Ethnicity: 1986 and 1991," *Drug Use Among Ethnic Minorities,* 1995, p. 92. Primary source: Survey of State Prison Inmates, Bureau of Justice Statistics, 1991.

★ 107 ★

Crime

Juvenile Cases: Type of Offense in Juvenile Cases Disposed by Juvenile Courts, by Race/Ethnic Origin: 1992

Type of offense	Race[1]		
	White	Black	Other[2]
All offenses	100%	100%	100%
Person	17.8	26.4	18.0
Property	61.0	48.8	62.6

[Continued]

★ 107 ★

Juvenile Cases: Type of Offense in Juvenile Cases Disposed by Juvenile Courts, by Race/Ethnic Origin: 1992

[Continued]

Type of offense	Race[1]		
	White	Black	Other[2]
Drug	3.9	7.2	3.2
Public-order	17.3	17.7	16.2

Source: "Type of Offenses in Cases Disposed by Juvenile Courts, by Characteristics of Juvenile Offenders: United States, 1992," *Sourcebook of Criminal Justice Statistics, 1994,* p. 498. Jeffrey A. Butts et al. "Juvenile Court Statistics 1992" (Pittsburgh, PA: National Center for Juvenile Justice, 1994). Machine-readable data file. Table constructed by SOURCEBOOK staff. *Notes:* 1. Subcategories may not add to total because of rounding. 2. Includes persons having origin in any of the original peoples of North America the Far East, Southeast Asia, the Indian Subcontinent, or the Pacific Islands. Nearly all Hispanics were included in the "white" racial category.

★ 108 ★
Crime

Juvenile Offenders: Distribution of Juvenile Offenders, by Type of Offense and Race/Ethnic Origin: 1992

	Type of offense[1]				
	All offenses (N=1,471,200)	Person (N=301,000)	Property (N=842,200)	Drug (N=72,100)	Public-order (N=255,900)
Total	100%	100%	100%	100%	100%
Race					
White	65.3	56.7	69.5	52.0	65.1
Black	31.1	40.1	26.5	45.7	31.6
Other[2]	3.6	3.2	3.9	2.3	3.3

Source: "Characteristics of Juvenile Offenders in Cases Disposed by Juvenile Courts, by Type of Offense, United States, 1992," *Sourcebook of Criminal Justice Statistics, 1994,* p. 497. Primary source: Jeffrey A Butts et al. "Juvenile Court Statistics 1992" (Pittsburgh, PA National Center for Juvenile Justice, 1994) Machine- readable data file. Table constructed by SOURCEBOOK staff. *Notes:* These data were collected by the National Center for Juvenile Justice (NCJJ) for the U.S. Department of Justice, Office of Juvenile Justice and Delinquency Prevention. The data are gathered from courts with juvenile jurisdiction in participating States. 1. Subcategories may not add to total because of rounding. 2. Includes persons having origin in any of the original peoples of North America, the Far East, Southeast Asia, the Indian Subcontinent, or the Pacific Islands. Nearly all Hispanics were included in the "white" racial category.

★ 109 ★

Crime

Murder: Murder/Manslaughter Offenders per 100,000 in Each Group, by Race: 1976-1993

	Race	
	White	Black
1976	4.3	37.8
1977	4.0	34.8
1978	4.4	35.8
1979	4.5	36.6
1980	5.0	33.4
1981	4.6	36.5
1982	4.6	32.1
1983	4.3	28.2
1984	4.2	22.8
1985	4.2	26.5
1986	4.0	29.3
1987	3.8	24.7
1988	3.7	30.0
1989	3.8	28.0
1990	4.4	30.5
1991	4.3	35.4
1992	4.2	33.0
1993	3.9	33.5

Source: "Rate (per 100,000 Persons in Each Group) of Offenders Committing Murder and Nonnegligent Manslaughter, by Age, Sex, and Race of Offender: United States, 1976-93)," *Sourcebook of Criminal Justice Statistics, 1994*, p. 342. Primary source: Table provided to SOURCEBOOK staff by James Alan Fox, College of Criminal Justice, Northeastern University.

★ 110 ★
Crime

Murder: Percent of Murder/Manslaughter Offenders, by Age Group and Race/Ethnic Origin: 1976-1993 (Aggregate)

Characteristics of offender	Age of offender		
	14 to 17 years	18 to 24 years	25 years and older
Race			
White	43.7	44.8	51.3
Black	54.2	53.2	46.8
Other	2.0	1.9	1.9

Source: "Characteristics of Murder and Nonnegligent Manslaughter Offenders and Offenses, by Age of Offender: United States, 1976-93 (Aggregate)," *Sourcebook of Criminal Justice Statistics, 1994,* p. 341. Primary source: Table provided to SOURCEBOOK staff by James Alan Fox, College of Criminal Justice, Northeastern University. *Note:* Percents may not add to 100 because of rounding.

★ 111 ★
Crime

Murder: Percent of Murder/Manslaughter Offenders, by Race: 1976-1993

	Offender characteristics Race		
	White (%)	Black (%)	Other (%)[1]
1976	46.3	51.9	1.7
1977	47.7	50.4	1.9
1978	47.8	50.5	1.7
1979	48.9	48.9	2.2
1980	49.8	48.8	1.4
1981	49.7	48.8	1.5
1982	50.3	47.8	1.8
1983	51.5	46.5	2.0
1984	53.9	44.2	1.9
1985	51.7	46.2	2.1
1986	50.4	47.5	2.2
1987	50.5	47.6	1.9
1988	47.6	50.7	1.8
1989	47.1	51.1	1.8
1990	47.0	51.5	1.5
1991	44.4	53.6	2.1

[Continued]

★ 111 ★

Murder: Percent of Murder/Manslaughter Offenders, by Race: 1976-1993
[Continued]

	Offender characteristics Race		
	White (%)	Black (%)	Other (%)[1]
1992	42.8	54.9	2.3
1993	43.0	54.8	2.2

Source: "Characteristics of Murder and Nonnegligent Manslaughter Offenders Known to Police: United States, 1976-93)," *Sourcebook of Criminal Justice Statistics, 1994*, p. 342. Primary source: Table constructed from data provided to SOURCEBOOK staff by James Alan Fox, College of Criminal Justice, Northeastern University. *Notes:* Data have been revised by the Source and may differ from previous editions of SOURCEBOOK. These data include only those incidents for which age, sex, and race of the offender were available. 1. Includes American Indians, Asians, Pacific Islanders, and all other races.

★ 112 ★
Crime

Relationships: Murder/Manslaughter, Victim/Offender Relationships, by Race: 1993

Characteristics of victim	Total victims/ offenders	Characteristics of offender Race			
		White	Black	Other	Unknown
Total	11,721	5,062	6,299	214	146
Race					
White	5,648	4,686	849	58	55
Black	5,782	304	5,393	18	67
Other	240	61	40	137	2
Unknown	51	11	17	1	22

Source: "Murders and Nonnegligent Manslaughters Known to Police, by Race and Sex of Victim and Offender: United States, 1993," *Sourcebook of Criminal Justice Statistics, 1994*, p. 343. Primary source: U.S. Department of Justice, Federal Bureau of Investigation, *Crime in the United States, 1993* (Washington, DC: USGPO, 1994), p. 17. *Notes:* These data pertain only to the 11,721 murders and non-negligent manslaughters that involved a single offender and a single victim.

★ 113 ★
Crime

Suicides per 100,000 in Each Age Group, by Age Group, Gender and Race: Selected Years, 1950-1992

Age groups	Total	Race			Race and sex					
					White		Black		Other	
		White	Black	Other	Male	Female	Male	Female	Male	Female
10 to 14 years	1.7	1.8	1.2	0.7	2.6	1.0	2.0	0.4	1.1	0.2
15 to 19 years	10.8	11.2	8.4	11.4	18.4	3.7	14.8	1.9	17.4	5.0
20 to 24 years	14.9	15.6	11.7	13.8	26.6	4.0	21.2	2.4	21.1	6.2
25 to 29 years	14.2	14.9	11.2	10.1	25.0	4.5	20.4	2.7	15.4	5.0
30 to 34 years	14.8	15.7	11.8	8.1	25.0	6.1	21.0	3.8	12.4	4.0
35 to 39 years	15.1	16.2	10.0	8.0	25.5	6.8	18.0	3.0	12.3	4.1
40 to 44 years	15.1	16.3	9.1	6.9	24.0	7.7	15.5	3.6	9.7	4.4
45 to 49 years	14.7	15.8	7.8	7.7	23.9	7.7	12.7	3.7	11.0	4.8
50 to 54 years	14.7	15.9	6.6	7.8	24.1	8.1	12.0	2.2	9.3	6.5
55 to 59 years	14.7	16.3	4.4	5.1	25.8	7.3	7.9	1.7	7.9	2.6
60 to 64 years	15.0	16.1	6.7	6.9	26.3	7.0	12.5	2.3	8.3	5.9
65 to 69 years	15.6	16.8	5.9	7.2	29.5	6.4	10.8	2.4	8.2	5.6
70 to 74 years	17.5	18.7	6.3	7.7	35.1	6.2	13.2	1.7	13.8	3.0
75 to 79 years	21.6	23.1	6.6	12.6	48.0	6.5	16.3	1.0	17.4	9.0
80 to 84 years	24.6	25.9	8.3	24.6	61.6	6.7	22.3	1.0	41.2	11.1
85 years of age and older	21.9	23.2	7.1	13.0	67.6	6.3	17.1	3.0	22.2	7.1

Source: "Suicide Rate per 100,000 in Each Age Group) for Persons 10 Years of Age and Older, by Age Group, Sex, and Race, United States, 1992," *Sourcebook of Criminal Justice Statistics, 1994*, p. 344. Primary source: Table constructed by SOURCEBOOK staff from data provided by the U.S. Department of Health and Human Services, Centers for Disease Control and Prevention. *Notes:* These data are based on information from all death certificates filed in the 50 States and the District of Columbus. The mortality data files are maintained by the National Center for Health Statistics at the Centers for Disease Control and Prevention. Rates were calculated from decennial census counts from the U.S. Bureau of the Census. The rates for 1992 were calculated from postcensal population estimates from the U.S. Bureau of the Census.

★ 114 ★
Crime

Victims: Age and Gender of Murder Victims, by Race: 1993

AGE	Total	Race			
		White	Black	Other	Unknown
Total	23,271	10,709	11,795	563	204
Percent distribution	100.0	46.0	50.7	2.4	0.9
Under 18 yrs. old	2,697	1,187	1,411	81	18
18 yrs. old and over	20,250	9,387	10,266	473	124
Infant (under 1 yr. old)	272	135	118	10	9
1 to 4 yrs. old	459	217	225	16	1
5 to 9 yrs. old	173	101	61	10	1

[Continued]

★ 114 ★

Victims: Age and Gender of Murder Victims, by Race: 1993
[Continued]

AGE	Total	Race			
		White	Black	Other	Unknown
10 to 14 yrs. old	387	185	194	8	-
15 to 19 yrs. old	3,084	1,125	1,857	81	21
20 to 24 yrs. old	4,355	1,597	2,656	78	24
25 to 29 yrs. old	3,466	1,451	1,921	74	20
30 to 34 yrs. old	3,083	1,444	1,541	86	12
35 to 39 yrs. old	2,318	1,143	1,108	56	11
40 to 44 yrs. old	1,620	800	753	52	15
45 to 49 yrs. old	1,077	649	389	28	11
50 to 54 yrs. old	717	443	244	21	9
55 to 59 yrs. old	465	299	149	13	4
60 to 64 yrs. old	393	253	130	9	1
65 to 69 yrs. old	319	209	102	7	1
70 to 74 yrs. old	292	194	93	4	1
75 yrs. old and over	467	329	136	1	1
Age unknown	324	135	118	9	62

Source: "Murder Victims, by Age, Sex, and Race: 1993," *Statistical Abstract of the United States: 1995.* 1995, p. 202. Primary source: U.S. Federal Bureau of Investigation, *Crime in the United States,* annual. *Note:* - Represents zero.

★ 115 ★
Crime

Victims: Handgun Victimization Rate, by Gender, Age and Race: 1987-1992

[Number of victimization rates per 1,000 population. Rates do not include murder or nonnegligent manslaughter committed with handguns. Based on National Crime Victimization Survey].

AGE OF VICTIM	MALE VICTIMS			FEMALE VICTIMS		
	Total[1]	White	Black	Total[1]	White	Black
All ages	4.9	3.7	14.2	2.1	1.6	5.8
12 to 15 yrs. old	5.0	3.1	14.1	2.5	2.1	4.7
16 to 19 yrs. old	14.2	9.5	39.7	5.1	3.6	13.4
20 to 24 yrs. old	11.8	9.2	29.4	4.3	3.5	9.1
25 to 34 yrs. old	5.7	4.9	12.3	3.1	2.1	9.0
35 to 49 yrs. old	3.3	2.7	8.7	1.7	1.4	3.3
50 to 64 yrs. old	1.5	1.2	3.5	0.8	0.7	1.6
65 yrs. old and older	0.8	0.6	3.7	0.3	0.2	2.3

Source: "Handgun Crime Victimization Rate, by Sex, Race, and Age: 1987-1992 Period," *Statistical Abstract of the United States: 1995,* 1995, p. 205. Primary source: U.S. Bureau of Justice Statistics, *Guns and Crime,* Crime Data Brief, NCJ-147003. *Note:* 1. Includes persons of other races not shown separately.

★ 116 ★

Crime

Victims: Percent Distribution of Age Group of Murder/ Manslaughter Victims, by Race: 1976-1993 (Aggregate)

Characteristics of victim	Age of victim		
	14 to 17 years	18 to 24 years	25 years and older
Race			
White	47.2	46.9	53.6
Black	50.9	51.2	44.4
Other	1.9	1.9	2.0

Source: "Characteristics of Murder and Manslaughter Victims and Offenses, by Age of Victim: United States, 1976-93 (Aggregate)," *Sourcebook of Criminal Justice Statistics, 1994,* p. 341. Primary source: Table provided to SOURCEBOOK staff by James Alan Fox, College of Criminal Justice, Northeastern University.

★ 117 ★

Crime

Victims: Percent of Households Victimized, by Type of Crime and Race: 1992

[A household is considered "touched by crime" if during the year it experienced a burglary, auto theft or household theft, or if a household member was raped, robbed, or assaulted, or a victim of personal theft, no matter where the crime occurred. Data based on the National Crime Victimization Survey].

TYPE OF CRIME	1992			
	Number (1,000)	Percent touched		
		Total[1]	White	Black
Total[2]	22,093	22.6	21.9	27.2
Violent crime	4,888	5.0	4.8	7.1
Rape	149	0.2	0.2	0.1
Robbery	998	1.0	0.9	2.2
Assault	3,975	4.1	4.0	5.1
Theft	15,343	15.7	15.5	17.1
Burglary	4,116	4.2	4.0	5.8
Motor vehicle theft	1,947	2.0	1.8	3.3

Source: "Households Touched by Crime, 1990 and 1992, and by Characteristics, 1992," *Statistical Abstract of the United States: 1995,* 1995, p. 205. Primary source: U.S. Bureau of Justice Statistics, *Crime and the Nation's Households, 1992. Notes:* 1. Includes other races not shown separately. 2. Types of crime will not add to "total" since each household may report as many crime categories as experienced.

★ 118 ★

Crime

Victims: Percent of Victims of Homicide at Workplace, by Race/Ethnic Origin: 1993

	Homicides	
	Number	Percent[1]
Total	1,063	100%
Race[2]		
White	694	65.3
Black	169	15.9
Hispanic	178	16.7
Asian or Pacific Islander	120	11.3
American Indian, Aleut, or Eskimo	6	0.6
Other	74	7.0

Source: "Workplace Homicides, by Victim Characteristics, Type of Event, and Circumstances: United States, 1993)," *Sourcebook of Criminal Justice Statistics, 1994,* p. 343. Primary source: Guy Toscano and Janice Windau, "The Changing Character of Fatal Work Injuries," *Monthly Labor Review* (Washington, DC: U.S. Department of Labor, October 1994), pp. 24-28. Guy Toscano and William Weber, "Violence in the Workplace," *Compensation and Working Conditions* (Washington, DC: U.S. Department of Labor, April 1995), p. 1. and p. 7; and data provided by U.S. Department of Labor, Bureau of Labor Statistics. Table adapted by SOURCEBOOK staff. Reprinted by permission. *Notes:* These data were collected through the 1993 Census of Fatal Occupational Injuries conducted by the Bureau of Labor Statistics in cooperation with numerous Federal and State agencies. 1. Detail may not add to total because of rounding. 2. Persons identified as Hispanic may be of any race, therefore detail may not add to total.

★ 119 ★

Crime

Victims: Percentage Distribution of School Victimizations of High School Seniors, by Type of Victimization and Race/Ethnic Origin: 1976-1993

Year	Had Something stolen		Property deliberately damaged		Injured with a weapon		Threatened with a weapon		Injured without a weapon		Threatened without a weapon	
	White	Black	White	Black	White	Black	White	Black	White	Black	White	Black
1976	38.9	35.9	25.1	30.1	5.0	7.8	11.4	16.3	13.2	14.3	21.2	24.2
1977	40.4	32.8	24.3	21.0	4.0	8.1	11.0	19.7	10.6	11.4	20.2	24.2
1978	38.8	32.4	25.7	21.2	3.9	7.2	11.2	13.3	11.5	14.4	20.4	17.5
1979	34.6	27.2	24.5	20.8	4.0	8.1	11.1	16.5	11.7	9.8	20.3	17.9
1980	34.3	33.1	25.3	21.9	3.5	9.9	9.5	17.8	10.3	14.9	19.0	20.0
1981	40.1	39.2	30.4	29.8	5.1	13.4	13.4	23.7	13.8	19.1	23.6	25.0
1982	37.9	42.0	25.6	25.4	4.2	4.5	11.1	15.9	11.8	11.7	21.3	19.5
1983	39.4	39.2	25.0	23.1	4.3	5.6	11.9	14.8	13.4	13.2	23.9	24.5
1984	38.4	35.3	24.3	21.8	3.2	6.0	10.9	16.7	12.1	13.3	23.0	24.4
1985	39.3	35.2	26.6	28.0	5.4	8.9	11.6	22.6	13.6	18.2	24.5	25.2
1986	41.1	36.3	25.7	24.5	4.9	6.9	12.6	15.7	14.5	12.8	25.7	22.7
1987	42.1	39.4	27.0	25.0	4.4	5.6	11.2	17.5	15.4	15.4	25.4	20.2

[Continued]

★ 119 ★

Victims: Percentage Distribution of School Victimizations of High School Seniors, by Type of Victimization and Race/Ethnic Origin: 1976-1993

[Continued]

Year	Had Something stolen		Property deliberately damaged		Injured with a weapon		Threatened with a weapon		Injured without a weapon		Threatened without a weapon	
	White	Black	White	Black	White	Black	White	Black	White	Black	White	Black
1988	41.4	46.6	27.4	25.8	3.9	9.0	11.3	22.2	13.5	16.6	24.3	27.7
1989	39.4	46.4	26.0	28.9	4.9	11.3	12.0	24.1	13.7	17.8	24.5	21.0
1990	41.6	42.2	28.9	26.1	4.6	10.0	12.0	16.0	13.6	10.0	26.1	21.7
1991	41.4	44.3	28.4	24.6	5.3	9.6	15.7	20.2	15.4	17.1	26.5	27.5
1992	36.2	44.2	25.7	28.3	4.5	5.2	12.3	19.4	12.7	13.6	25.5	20.5
1993	41.6	46.0	25.8	26.3	4.3	6.4	13.8	23.5	11.0	11.5	23.8	22.3

Source: "Percentage of High School Seniors who Reported Being Victimized at School, by Type of Victimization and Race/Ethnicity: 1976-93," *Crime in the Schools*, National Center for Education Statistics, August, 1995, [no p. No.] Primary source: University of Michigan, Survey Research Center, Institute for Social Research, *Monitoring the Future* Study.

★ 120 ★

Crime

Victims: Rape, Robbery, and Assault Victimization Rates, by Race/Ethnic Origin: 1992

[Rate per 1,000 persons age 12 years or older. Based on the National Crime Victimization Survey].

ITEM	Total	Rape	Robbery	Assault			Larceny-theft
				Total	Aggravated	Simple	
Total	91.2	0.7	5.9	25.5	9.0	16.5	59.2
White	88.7	0.6	4.7	24.6	7.8	16.8	58.8
Black	110.8	1.3	15.6	33.5	18.3	15.2	60.4
Other	88.3	-	5.1	18.6	5.3	13.3	64.6
Hispanic	100.1	0.6	10.6	26.9	10.0	16.8	61.9
Non-Hispanic	90.3	0.7	5.4	25.3	8.9	16.4	58.9

Source: "Personal Crimes—Victimization Rate, by Type of Crime and Characteristics, 1992," *Statistical Abstract of the United States: 1995*, 1995, p. 204. Primary source: U.S. Bureau of Justice Statistics, *Criminal Victimization in the United States*, annual. *Note:* - Represents or rounds to zero.

★ 121 ★

Crime

Victims: Single-Offender Rates for Victimizations of Women, by Relationship to Victim and Victim's Race/Ethnic Origin: 1992-93

Victim characteristic	Average annual rate of violent victimizations per 1,000 females age 12 or older				
	Total	Intimate	Other relative	Acquaint-ance/friend	Stranger
Crimes of violence	36.1	9.3	2.8	12.9	7.4
Race					
White	35.2	9.1	2.6	12.5	7.1
Black	44.6	10.9	3.5	17.2	9.5
Other	27.8	6.5	4.5	8.4	5.7
Ethnicity					
Hispanic	33.9	7.3	3.2	10.0	9.0
Non-Hispanic	36.3	9.4	2.8	13.2	7.2

Source: "Average Annual Rate of Violent Victimizations of Women by a Lone Offender, by Victim Characteristics and Victim-Offender Relationship, 1992- 93," *Violence Against Women: Estimates from the Redesigned Survey,* Bureau of Justice Statistics Special Report, August, 1995, p. 4. *Notes:* Rates of violence for this table include rapes, sexual assaults, robberies, and aggravated and simple assaults from the NCVS. Rates exclude homicide victimizations. Relationship-specific rates do not add to the total because some victims did not identify their relationship to the offender.

★ 122 ★

Crime

Victims: Trends in Number of Homicide Victims and Homicide Rate, by Gender and Race: 1970-1992

[**Rate per 100,000 resident population in specified group.** Excludes deaths to nonresidents of the United States. Beginning 1980, deaths classified according to the ninth revision of the *International Classification of Diseases;* for earlier years, classified according to revision in use at the time].

YEAR	HOMICIDE VICTIMS					HOMICIDE RATE[2]				
	Total[1]	White		Black		Total[1]	White		Black	
		Male	Female	Male	Female		Male	Female	Male	Female
1970	16,848	5,865	1,938	7,265	1,569	8.3	6.8	2.1	67.6	13.3
1980	24,278	10,381	3,177	8,385	1,898	10.7	10.9	3.2	66.6	13.5
1981	23,646	9,941	3,125	8,312	1,825	10.3	10.4	3.1	64.8	12.7
1982	22,358	9,260	3,179	7,730	1,743	9.6	9.6	3.1	59.1	12.0
1983	20,191	8,355	2,880	6,822	1,672	8.6	8.6	2.8	51.4	11.3
1984	19,796	8,171	2,956	6,563	1,677	8.4	8.3	2.9	48.7	11.2
1985	19,893	8,122	3,041	6,616	1,666	8.3	8.2	2.9	48.4	11.0
1986	21,731	8,567	3,123	7,634	1,861	9.0	8.6	3.0	55.0	12.1
1987	21,103	7,979	3,149	7,518	1,969	8.7	7.9	3.0	53.3	12.6
1988	22,032	7,994	3,072	8,314	2,089	9.0	7.9	2.9	58.0	13.2

[Continued]

★ 122 ★

Victims: Trends in Number of Homicide Victims and Homicide Rate, by Gender and Race: 1970-1992
[Continued]

YEAR	HOMICIDE VICTIMS					HOMICIDE RATE[2]				
	Total[1]	White		Black		Total[1]	White		Black	
		Male	Female	Male	Female		Male	Female	Male	Female
1989	22,909	8,337	2,971	8,888	2,074	9.2	8.2	2.8	61.1	12.9
1990	24,932	9,147	3,006	9,981	2,163	10.0	9.0	2.8	69.2	13.5
1991	26,513	9,581	3,201	10,628	2,330	10.5	9.3	3.0	72.0	14.2
1992	25,488	9,456	3,012	10,131	2,187	10.0	9.1	2.8	67.5	13.1

Source: "Homicide Victims, by Race and Sex: 1970 to 1992," *Statistical Abstract of the United States: 1995,* 1995, p. 202. Primary source: National Center for Health Statistics, *Vital Statistics of the United States,* annual, and unpublished data. *Notes:* 1. Includes races not shown separately. 2. Rate based on enumerated population figures as of April 1 for 1970, 1980 and 1990; July 1 estimates for other years.

★ 123 ★
Crime

Victims: Victims of Substantiated and Indicated Child Abuse and Neglect, by Race/Ethnic Origin: 1990-1993

[Based on reports alleging child abuse and neglect that were referred for investigation by the respective child protective services agency in each State. The report period may be either calendar or fiscal year. The majority of States provided duplicated counts. Also, varying number of States reported the various characteristics presented below].

ITEM	1990		1991		1992		1993	
	Number	Percent	Number	Percent	Number	Percent	Number	Percent
RACE/ETHNIC GROUP OF VICTIM[2]								
Victims, total	775,409	100.0	818,527	99.9	956,248	100.0	916,185	100.0
White	424,470	54.7	454,059	55.5	509,111	53.2	497,913	54.3
Black	197,400	25.5	218,044	26.6	242,357	25.3	229,596	25.1
Asian and Pacific Islander	6,408	0.8	6,585	0.8	7,139	0.7	7,775	0.8
American Indian, Eskimo, and Aleut	10,283	1.3	10,873	1.3	12,782	1.3	13,657	1.5
Other races	11,749	1.5	12,982	1.6	15,094	1.6	13,659	1.5
Hispanic origin	73,132	9.4	77,985	9.5	89,426	9.4	85,026	9.3
Unknown	51,967	6.7	37,999	4.6	80,339	8.4	68,559	7.5

Source: "Child Abuse and Neglect Cases Substantiated and Indicated—Victim Characteristics: 1990 to 1993," *Statistical Abstract of the United States: 1995,* 1995, p. 215. Primary source: U.S. Department of Health and Human Services, National Center on Child Abuse and Neglect, National Child Abuse and Neglect Data System. *Working Paper 2, 1991 Summary Data Component;* May 1993; *Child Maltreatment- 1992,* May 1994; and *Child Maltreatment-1993,* April 1995. *Notes:* 1. More than one type of maltreatment may be substantiated per child. 2. Some States were unable to report on the number of Hispanic victims, thus it is probable that nationwide the percentage of Hispanic victims is higher.

Law Enforcement

★ 124 ★

Arrests: Number and Percent of Persons Arrested, by Charge and Race: 1993

[Represents arrests (not charges) reported by 10,509 agencies with a total 1993 population of 213,093,000 as estimated by FBI].

OFFENSE CHARGED	TOTAL ARRESTS (1,000)					PERCENT DISTRIBUTION				
	Total	White	Black	American Indian or Alaskan Native	Asian or Pacific Islander	Total	White	Black	American Indian or Alaskan Native	Asian or Pacific Islander
Total	11,742	7,855	3,647	126	113	100.0	66.9	31.1	1.1	1.0
Serious crimes[1]	2,419	1,482	884	23	31	100.0	61.3	36.5	0.9	1.3
Murder and nonnegligent manslaughter	20	8	12	(Z)	(Z)	100.0	40.7	57.6	0.6	1.1
Forcible rape	32	18	13	(Z)	(Z)	100.0	56.9	41.3	1.0	0.8
Robbery	153	56	95	1	2	100.0	36.5	62.1	0.4	1.0
Aggravated assault	441	258	175	4	4	100.0	58.4	39.8	0.9	1.0
Burglary	338	227	104	3	4	100.0	67.2	30.9	0.9	1.0
Larceny/theft	1,249	807	412	13	18	100.0	64.6	33.0	1.0	1.4
Motor vehicle theft	169	96	68	2	3	100.0	57.1	40.3	0.9	1.7
Arson	16	12	4	(Z)	(Z)	100.0	74.6	23.5	0.9	0.9
All other nonserious crimes:										
Other assaults	963	606	336	12	9	100.0	62.9	34.9	1.2	1.0
Forgery and counterfeiting	89	56	32	1	1	100.0	63.0	35.4	0.6	1.0
Fraud	335	209	123	2	2	100.0	62.3	36.6	0.5	0.7
Embezzlement	11	7	3	(Z)	(Z)	100.0	67.4	31.0	0.4	1.2
Stolen property-buying, receiving, possessing	135	75	57	1	1	100.0	56.1	42.3	0.6	1.1
Vandalism	261	195	60	3	3	100.0	74.8	22.9	1.1	1.2
Weapons; carrying, possessing, etc.	224	124	96	1	2	100.0	55.4	43.0	0.5	1.1
Prostitution and commercialized vice	89	55	32	1	1	100.0	62.0	35.9	0.6	1.5
Sex offenses (except forcible rape and prostitution)	88	67	18	1	1	100.0	77.0	20.9	1.0	1.1
Drug abuse violations	968	578	380	4	5	100.0	59.8	39.3	0.4	0.5
Gambling	15	7	7	(Z)	1	100.0	48.2	46.9	0.4	4.6
Offenses against family and children	89	58	28	1	2	100.0	65.6	31.2	1.3	2.0
Driving under the influence	1,227	1,070	130	16	11	100.0	87.2	10.6	1.3	0.9
Liquor laws	417	353	53	10	3	100.0	84.5	12.6	2.3	0.6
Drunkenness	604	482	108	13	2	100.0	79.7	17.8	2.1	0.3
Disorderly conduct	607	392	204	8	3	100.0	64.6	33.6	1.3	0.5
Vagrancy	25	14	10	(Z)	(Z)	100.0	56.6	41.2	1.9	0.4
All other offenses (except traffic)	2,928	1,833	1,039	28	27	100.0	62.6	35.5	1.0	0.9
Suspicion	12	6	6	(Z)	(Z)	100.0	46.9	52.0	0.6	0.5
Curfew and loitering law violations	85	67	15	1	2	100.0	78.8	18.1	1.1	2.0
Runaways	151	118	26	2	5	100.0	78.1	17.2	1.3	3.4

Source: "Persons Arrested, by Charge and Race: 1993," *Statistical Abstract of the United States: 1995,* 1995, p. 206. Primary source: U.S. Federal Bureau of Investigation, *Crime in the United States,* annual. *Notes:* Z Less than 500. 1. Includes arson.

★ 125 ★

Law Enforcement

Officers Slain: Percent Distribution of Identified Slayers of Law Enforcement Officers, by Race: 1984-1993 (Aggregate) and 1993

Characteristics of persons identified	1984 to 1993		1993	
	Number	Percent	Number	Percent
Total	942	100%	83	100%
Race				
White	507	54	36	43
Black	410	44	47	57
Other[1]	25	3	0	0

Source: "Persons Identified in the Killing of Law Enforcement Officers, by Demographic Characteristics and Prior Record: United States, 1984-93 (Aggregate) and 1993," *Sourcebook of Criminal Justice Statistics, 1994*, p. 360. Primary source: U.S. Department of Justice, Federal Bureau of Investigation, *Law Enforcement Officers Killed and Assaulted, 1993*, FBI Uniform Crime Reports (Washington, DC: USGPO, 1995), p. 36. Table constructed by SOURCEBOOK staff. *Note:* 1. Includes Asian, Pacific Islander, American Indian, and Alaskan Native.

★ 126 ★

Law Enforcement

Officers Slain: Percent Distribution of Law Enforcement Officers Slain, by Race: 1978-1993-I

Characteristics of officers killed	1978 (N=93)	1979 (N=106)	1980 (N=104)	1981 (N=91)	1982 (N=92)	1983 (N=80)	1984 (N=72)	1985 (N=78)
Race								
White	91%	88%	86%	85%	84%	84%	85%	88%
Black	9	9	13	14	15	13	14	10
Other[1]	0	3	0	1	1	4	1	1

Source: "Percent Distribution of Law Enforcement Officers Killed, by Selected Characteristics of Officers: United States, 1978-93," *Sourcebook of Criminal Justice Statistics, 1994*, p. 359. Primary source: U.S. Department of Justice, Federal Bureau of Investigation, *Law Enforcement Officers Killed, 1978*, p. 22; *1979*, p. 22; *1980*, p. 23; *1987*, p. 18; FBI Uniform Crime Reports (Washington, DC USGPO); *Law Enforcement Officers Killed and Assaulted, 1982*, FBI Uniform Crime Reports (Washington, DC: U.S. Department of Justice, 1983), p. 20. *Law Enforcement Officers Killed and Assaulted, 1983*, p. 20. *1984*, p. 20. FBI Uniform Crime Reports (Washington, DC USGPO), *Law Enforcement Officers Killed and Assaulted, 1985*, FBI Uniform Crime Reports (Washington, DC; U.S. Department of Justice, 1986), p. 21. *Law Enforcement Officers Killed and Assaulted, 1986*, p. 22; *1987*, p. 20; *1988*, p. 20, *1989*, p. 21; *1990*, p. 20, *1991*, p. 31, *1991*, p. 35, *1993*, p. 35; FBI Uniform Crime Reports (Washington, DC; USGPO). Table constructed by SOURCEBOOK staff. *Notes:* Percents may not add to 100 because of rounding. 1. Includes Asian, Pacific Islander, American Indian, and Alaskan Native.

★ 127 ★

Law Enforcement

Officers Slain: Percent Distribution of Law Enforcement Officers Slain, by Race: 1978-1993-II

Characteristics of officers killed	1986 (N=66)	1987 (N=73)	1988 (N=78)	1989 (N=66)	1990 (N=65)	1991 (N=71)	1992 (N=62)	1993 (N=70)
Race								
White	89%	90%	91%	89%	80%	87%	82%	86%
Black	11	10	9	11	18	13	16	14
Other[1]	0	0	0	0	2	0	2	0

Source: "Percent Distribution of Law Enforcement Officers Killed, by Selected Characteristics of Officers: United States, 1978-93," *Sourcebook of Criminal Justice Statistics, 1994,* p. 359. Primary source: U.S. Department of Justice, Federal Bureau of Investigation, *Law Enforcement Officers Killed, 1978,* p. 22; *1979,* p. 22; *1980,* p. 23; *1987,* p. 18; FBI Uniform Crime Reports (Washington, DC USGPO); *Law Enforcement Officers Killed and Assaulted, 1982,* FBI Uniform Crime Reports (Washington, DC: U.S. Department of Justice, 1983), p. 20. *Law Enforcement Officers Killed and Assaulted, 1983,* p. 20. *1984,* p. 20. FBI Uniform Crime Reports (Washington, DC USGPO), *Law Enforcement Officers Killed and Assaulted, 1985,* FBI Uniform Crime Reports (Washington, DC; U.S. Department of Justice, 1986), p. 21. *Law Enforcement Officers Killed and Assaulted, 1986,* p. 22; *1987,* p. 20; *1988,* p. 20, *1989,* p. 21; *1990,* p. 20, *1991,* p. 31, *1991,* p. 35, *1993,* p. 35; FBI Uniform Crime Reports (Washington, DC; USGPO). Table constructed by SOURCEBOOK staff. *Notes:* Percents may not add to 100 because of rounding. 1. Includes Asian, Pacific Islander, American Indian, and Alaskan Native.

★ 128 ★

Law Enforcement

Prison Staff: Age Group and Education of Federal Bureau of Prisons Corrections Officers, by Race/Ethnic Origin: 1994

	Total		Race and ethnicity							
			White		Black		Hispanic		Other[2]	
	Number	Percent[1]	Number	Percent[1]	Number	Percent[1]	Number	Percent[1]	Number	Percent[1]
Total	10,879	100.0%	6,940	100.0%	2,483	100.0%	1,244	100.0%	212	100.0%
Sex										
Male	9,653	88.7	6,344	91.4	1,996	80.4	1,120	90.0	193	91.0
Female	1,226	11.3	596	8.6	487	19.6	124	10.0	18	9.0
Age										
18 to 24 years	330	3.0	229	3.3	55	2.2	38	3.1	8	3.8
25 to 29 years	2,633	24.2	1,713	24.7	576	23.2	295	23.7	49	23.1
30 to 34 years	3,625	33.3	2,207	31.8	885	35.6	471	37.9	62	29.2
35 to 39 years	2,631	24.2	1,658	23.9	610	24.6	310	24.9	53	25.0
40 to 44 years	1,033	9.5	701	10.1	226	9.1	82	6.6	24	11.3
45 to 49 years	505	4.6	357	5.1	96	3.9	39	3.1	13	6.1
50 to 55 years	86	0.8	57	0.8	21	0.8	5	0.4	3	1.4
56 years and older	36	0.3	18	0.3	14	0.6	4	0.3	0	X
Education										
High school	4,673	43.0	3,018	43.5	1,014	40.8	545	43.8	96	45.3
Technical school	437	4.0	300	4.3	81	3.3	51	4.1	4	2.4

[Continued]

★ 128 ★

Prison Staff: Age Group and Education of Federal Bureau of Prisons Corrections Officers, by Race/Ethnic Origin: 1994
[Continued]

	Total		Race and ethnicity							
			White		Black		Hispanic		Other[2]	
	Number	Percent[1]	Number	Percent[1]	Number	Percent[1]	Number	Percent[1]	Number	Percent[1]
Some college	3,871	35.6	2,427	35.0	856	34.5	503	40.4	85	40.1
College degree	1,663	15.3	1,050	15.1	463	18.6	126	10.1	24	11.3
Some graduate school	118	1.1	79	1.1	29	1.2	10	0.8	0	X
Professional degree	19	0.2	11	0.2	6	0.2	2	0.2	0	X
Master's degree	98	0.9	55	0.8	34	1.4	7	0.6	2	0.9

Source: "Characteristics of Federal Bureau of Prisons Correctional Officers, by Race and Ethnicity, 1994," *Sourcebook of Criminal Justice Statistics, 1994*, p. 112. Primary source: U.S. Department of Justice, Federal Bureau of Prisons, *Federal Bureau of Prisons Annual Statistical Report Calendar Year 1994* (Washington, DC; U.S. Department of Justice, 1995), pp. 74, 76. *Notes:* 1. Percents may not sum to total because of rounding. 2. Includes Asians and Native Americans.

★ 129 ★
Law Enforcement

Prison Staff: Length of Employment of Federal Bureau of Prisons Staff, by Gender and Race/Ethnic Origin: 1994

	Total		Race and ethnicity							
			White		Black		Hispanic		Other[2]	
	Number	Percent[1]	Number	Percent[1]	Number	Percent[1]	Number	Percent[1]	Number	Percent[1]
Total	26,761	100.0%	18,535	100.0%	4,953	100.0%	2,517	100.0%	755	100.0%
Length of employment										
Male	19,646	73.4	13,898	75.0	3,228	65.2	1,969	78.2	551	73.0
Less than 1 year	1,868	7.0	1,187	6.4	358	7.2	236	9.4	87	11.5
1 to 2 years	3,536	13.2	2,266	12.2	662	13.4	499	19.8	109	14.4
3 to 4 years	4,139	15.5	2,874	15.5	666	13.4	485	19.3	114	15.1
5 to 9 years	5,325	19.9	3,878	20.9	849	17.1	433	17.2	165	21.9
10 to 14 years	2,057	7.7	1,555	8.4	314	6.3	150	6.0	38	5.0
15 to 19 years	1,774	6.6	1,363	7.4	262	5.3	123	4.9	26	3.4
20 years or more	947	3.5	775	4.2	117	2.4	43	1.7	12	1.6
Female	7,115	26.6	4,637	25.0	1,726	34.8	548	21.8	204	27.0
Less than 1 year	839	3.1	505	2.7	204	4.1	91	3.6	39	5.2
1 to 2 years	1,342	5.0	850	4.6	318	6.4	128	5.1	46	6.1
3 to 4 years	1,774	6.6	1,121	6.0	445	9.0	151	6.0	57	7.5
5 to 9 years	1,988	7.4	1,324	7.1	491	9.9	125	5.0	48	6.4
10 to 14 years	645	2.4	460	2.5	155	3.1	21	0.8	9	1.2
15 to 19 years	361	1.3	262	1.4	73	1.5	23	0.9	3	0.4
20 years or more	166	0.6	115	0.6	40	0.8	9	0.4	2	0.3

Source: "Employment Characteristics of Federal Bureau of Prisons Staff, by Race, Ethnicity, and Sex, 1994," *Sourcebook of Criminal Justice Statistics, 1994*, p. 113. Primary source: U.S. Department of Justice, Federal Bureau of Prisons, *Federal Bureau of Prisons Annual Statistical Report Calendar Year 1994* (Washington, DC; U.S. Department of Justice, 1995), pp. 68, 69. *Notes:* 1. Percents may not sum to total because of rounding. 2. Includes Asians and Native Americans.

★ 130 ★

Law Enforcement

Prison Staff: Staff in Federal Bureau of Prisons Facilities, by Education, Gender, and Race/Ethnic Origin: 1994

	Total		Race and ethnicity							
			White		Black		Hispanic		Other[2]	
	Number	Percent[1]	Number	Percent[1]	Number	Percent[1]	Number	Percent[1]	Number	Percent[1]
Total	26,761	100.0%	18,535	100.0%	4,954	100.0%	2,517	100.0%	755	100.0%
Education										
High school	8,712	32.6	6,106	32.9	1,560	31.5	858	34.1	188	24.9
Technical school	1,288	4.8	984	5.3	204	4.1	83	3.3	17	2.3
Some college	8,377	31.3	5,692	30.7	1,587	32.0	910	36.2	188	24.9
College degree	5,263	19.7	3,671	19.8	1,124	22.7	336	13.3	132	17.5
Some graduate school	784	2.9	576	3.1	137	2.8	52	2.1	19	2.5
Professional degree	506	1.9	214	1.2	61	1.2	125	5.0	106	14.0
Master's degree	1,439	5.4	1,022	5.5	254	5.1	100	4.0	63	8.3
Ph. D. degree	392	1.5	270	1.5	27	0.5	53	2.1	42	5.6

Source: "Characteristics of Federal Bureau of Prisons Staff, by Race and Ethnicity, 1994," *Sourcebook of Criminal Justice Statistics, 1994,* p. 112. Primary source: U.S. Department of Justice, Federal Bureau of Prisons, *Federal Bureau of Prisons Annual Statistical Report Calendar Year 1994* (Washington, DC; U.S. Department of Justice, 1995), pp. 61, 63. *Notes:* These data refer to staff who are in current pay status and exclude staff who are on leave without pay. 1. Percents may not sum to total because of rounding. 2. Includes Asians and Native Americans.

★ 131 ★

Law Enforcement

Prison Staff: Staff of Federal Prisons, by Region, Gender, and Race/Ethnic Origin: 1994

	Total		Race and ethnicity							
			White		Black		Hispanic		Other[2]	
	Number	Percent[1]	Number	Percent[1]	Number	Percent[1]	Number	Percent[1]	Number	Percent[1]
Total	26,761	100.0%	18,535	100.0%	4,954	100.0%	2,517	100.0%	755	100.0%
Region										
Male	19,646	73.4	13,898	75.0	3,228	65.2	1,969	78.2	551	73.0
Central Office/Training Centers[3]	782	2.9	616	3.3	113	2.3	27	1.1	26	3.4
Northeast	3,941	14.7	3,085	16.6	455	9.2	319	12.7	82	10.9
North Central	3,924	14.7	3,199	17.3	405	8.2	234	9.3	86	11.4
Mid-Atlantic	2,993	11.2	2,300	12.4	574	11.6	80	3.2	39	5.2
Southeast	2,754	10.3	1,449	7.8	813	16.4	407	16.2	85	11.3
South Central	2,783	10.4	1,751	9.4	434	8.8	500	19.9	98	13.0
West	2,469	9.2	1,498	8.1	434	8.8	402	16.0	135	17.9
Female	7,115	26.6	4,637	25.0	1,726	34.8	548	21.8	204	27.0
Central Office/Training Centers[3]	719	2.7	392	2.1	300	6.1	19	0.8	8	1.1
Northeast	1,106	4.1	771	4.2	216	4.4	91	3.6	28	3.7
North Central	1,276	4.6	1,044	5.6	149	3.0	55	2.2	28	3.7
Mid-Atlantic	1,119	4.2	809	4.4	277	5.6	22	0.9	11	1.5
Southeast	956	3.6	466	2.5	358	7.2	100	4.0	32	4.2

[Continued]

★ 131 ★

Prison Staff: Staff of Federal Prisons, by Region, Gender, and Race/Ethnic Origin: 1994
[Continued]

	Total		Race and ethnicity							
			White		Black		Hispanic		Other[2]	
	Number	Percent[1]	Number	Percent[1]	Number	Percent[1]	Number	Percent[1]	Number	Percent[1]
South Central	1,107	4.1	670	3.6	250	5.0	149	5.9	38	5.0
West	832	3.1	485	2.6	176	3.6	112	4.4	59	7.8

Source: "Employment Characteristics of Federal Bureau of Prisons Staff, by Race, Ethnicity, and Sex, 1994," *Sourcebook of Criminal Justice Statistics, 1994*, p. 113. Primary source: U.S. Department of Justice, Federal Bureau of Prisons, *Federal Bureau of Prisons Annual Statistical Report Calendar Year 1994* (Washington, DC; U.S. Department of Justice, 1995), pp. 68, 69. *Notes:* 1. Percents may not sum to total because of rounding. 2. Includes Asians and Native Americans. 3. Central Office is located in Washington, DC. The Federal Training Centers are located in Glynco, Georgia and Aurora, Colorado.

★ 132 ★

Law Enforcement

Prison Staff: Total Staff in Federal Bureau of Prisons Facilities, by Gender, Age Group, and Race/Ethnic Origin: 1994

	Total		Race and ethnicity							
			White		Black		Hispanic		Other[2]	
	Number	Percent[1]	Number	Percent[1]	Number	Percent[1]	Number	Percent[1]	Number	Percent[1]
Total	26,761	100.0%	18,535	100.0%	4,954	100.0%	2,517	100.0%	755	100.0%
Sex										
Male	19,646	73.4	13,898	75.0	3,228	65.2	1,969	78.2	551	73.0
Female	7,115	26.6	4,637	25.0	1,726	34.8	548	21.8	204	27.0
Age										
Less than 18 years	1	B	0	X	1	B	0	X	0	X
18 to 24 years	662	2.5	447	2.4	144	2.9	54	2.1	17	2.3
25 to 29 years	4,597	17.2	3,149	17.0	888	17.9	465	18.5	95	12.6
30 to 34 years	7,432	27.8	4,912	26.5	1,563	31.6	785	31.1	173	22.9
35 to 39 years	6,760	25.3	4,620	24.9	1,269	25.6	669	26.6	202	26.8
40 to 44 years	3,771	14.1	2,706	14.6	614	12.4	306	12.2	145	19.2
45 to 49 years	2,451	9.2	1,897	10.2	319	6.4	168	6.7	67	8.9
50 to 55 years	803	3.0	68	3.3	111	2.2	50	2.0	34	4.5
56 years and older	284	1.1	196	1.1	45	0.9	21	0.8	22	2.9

Source: "Characteristics of Federal Bureau of Prisons Staff, by Race and Ethnicity, 1994," *Sourcebook of Criminal Justice Statistics, 1994*, p. 112. Primary source: U.S. Department of Justice, Federal Bureau of Prisons, *Federal Bureau of Prisons Annual Statistical Report Calendar Year 1994* (Washington, DC; U.S. Department of Justice, 1995), pp. 61, 63. *Notes:* These data refer to staff who are in current pay status and exclude staff who are on leave without pay. X = Not applicable. B = base less than 75,000. 1. Percents may not sum to total because of rounding. 2. Includes Asians and Native Americans.

★ 133 ★

Law Enforcement

Prisoners: Drug Abuse Among Jail Inmates in Month Before Their Offense, by Race/Ethnic Origin: 1989

Race/ethnicity	Percent of jail inmates who in the month before the offense used		
	Cocaine or crack-cocaine	Another drug	No drug
White non-Hispanic	35.2	50.2	42.6
Black non-Hispanic	45.2	29.6	36.7
Hispanic	18.0	17.0	17.5
Other	1.6	3.3	3.1

Source: "Percentage of Convicted Jail Inmates who had Used Cocaine or Crack- Cocaine, Another Drug, or No Drugs in the Month Before Their Offense, by Race/Ethnicity: 1989," *Drug Use Among Ethnic Minorities*, 1995, p. 89. Primary source: Survey of Inmates in Local Jails, Bureau of Justice Statistics, 1989.

★ 134 ★

Law Enforcement

Prisoners: Federal Prisoners' Place of Confinement, by Race/ Ethnic Origin: 1994

	Total		Prisoners confined in:			
			Bureau of Prisons facilities		Contract facilities[2]	
	Number	Percent[1]	Number	Percent	Number	Percent
Total	94,558	100.0%	85,097	100.0%	9,461	100.0%
Race						
White	58,403	61.8	51,408	60.4	6,995	73.9
Black	33,448	35.4	31,289	36.8	2,159	22.8
Other[3]	2,707	2.9	2,400	2.8	307	3.2
Ethnicity						
Hispanic	25,226	26.7	21,893	25.7	3,333	35.2
Non-Hispanic[3]	69,332	73.3	63,204	74.3	6,128	64.8

Source: "Characteristics of Federal Prisoners, by Type of Facility: United States, 1994," *Sourcebook of Criminal Justice Statistics, 1994*, p. 558. Primary source: U.S. Department of Justice, Federal Bureau of Prisons, *Federal Bureau of Prisons Annual Statistical Report Calendar Year 1994* (Washington, DC: U.S. Department of Justice, 1995), pp. 9, 10. *Notes:* 1. Percents may not sum to total because of rounding. 2. Facilities operated by an entity other than the Federal Bureau of Prisons that house Bureau prisoners under contract, e.g., community corrections centers. 3. Includes Asians and Native Americans.

★ 135 ★

Law Enforcement

Prisoners: History of Drug Use Among State Prisoners, by Race/Ethnic Origin (in percentages): 1991

Type of drug	Ever used drugs			Used drugs in the month before the offense			Used drugs daily in the month before the offense			Under the influence at time of the offense		
	White[1]	Black[1]	Hispanic	White[1]	Black[1]	Hispanic	White[1]	Black[1]	Hispanic	White[1]	Black[1]	Hispanic
Any drug	79.9	78.9	80.1	49.4	49.0	53.6	38.2	33.7	37.8	32.4	28.8	33.6
Marijuana	77.0	73.0	69.4	36.3	30.1	28.6	24.8	19.1	17.8	13.4	10.6	9.3
Cocaine/crack-cocaine	48.9	48.1	55.3	20.3	28.1	29.1	13.3	17.8	16.8	11.4	17.0	14.9
Cocaine	47.9	41.0	53.1	17.9	20.6	26.0	11.3	12.4	14.1	9.4	10.8	12.3
Crack	16.4	23.5	18.2	6.5	13.8	8.0	4.7	9.2	5.5	2.9	7.3	3.4
Heroin/opiates	27.0	20.0	35.6	7.9	7.5	19.6	6.1	5.2	15.4	4.8	4.1	13.1
Heroin	23.1	19.0	34.7	6.8	7.2	18.8	5.4	5.0	14.9	4.5	4.1	13.1
Other opiates	14.5	4.9	10.3	2.4	0.8	2.6	1.4	0.4	1.6	0.6	0.1	0.2
Stimulates	49.4	15.9	23.5	14.4	2.6	5.7	9.6	1.3	3.2	5.9	0.6	1.9
Amphetamines	44.6	14.6	20.0	9.2	2.1	3.6	5.9	1.1	1.7	2.2	0.4	0.6
Methamphetamines	28.4	4.0	12.3	9.4	0.7	3.8	6.1	0.4	2.6	3.9	0.1	1.5
Hallucinogens	42.3	14.2	27.0	5.7	1.8	4.4	1.8	1.0	1.8	2.4	0.8	1.7
LSD	40.6	8.0	21.5	4.8	0.6	2.1	1.2	0.2	0.5	1.7	0.2	0.7
PCP	18.6	10.2	16.1	1.6	1.5	2.8	0.7	0.8	1.4	0.8	0.7	1.2
Depressants	38.2	14.2	20.0	6.8	1.7	3.1	3.7	0.8	1.3	2.0	0.3	0.5
Barbiturates	32.6	12.3	17.5	6.2	1.6	2.6	3.4	0.7	1.1	1.8	0.3	0.4
Methaqualone	29.0	7.0	11.5	1.6	0.2	1.0	0.7	0.1	0.3	0.3	0.0	0.1

Source: "Drug Use History of State Prison Inmates, by Type of Drug and Race/Ethnicity: 1991 (in percentages)," *Drug Use Among Ethnic Minorities*, 1995, p. 90. Primary source: Survey of State Prison Inmates, Bureau of Justice Statistics, 1991. *Note:* 1. Includes white, non-Hispanic and black non-Hispanic inmates.

★ 136 ★

Law Enforcement

Prisoners: Number and Percent of State and Federal Prisoners, by Race/Ethnic Origin: 1993

Race/Hispanic origin	Number	Percent
White non-Hispanics	333,100	35.8
Black non-Hispanics	410,800	44.1
Hispanics	163,500	17.6
Other[1]	24,000	2.6

Source: "Sentenced State and Federal Inmates, 1993," *Prisoners in 1994*, Bureau of Justice Statistics Bulletin, August, 1995, p. 9. *Notes:* Data were estimated using yearend population counts and the 1991 State and Federal inmate surveys. 1. Includes Asians, Pacific Islanders, American Indians, and Alaska Natives.

★ 137 ★

Law Enforcement

Prisoners: Percent Distribution of Persons Newly Committed to Prison, by Race/Ethnic Origin: 1992

Most serious offense	All new court commitments	Race[2]			Hispanic[4]
		White	Black	Other[3]	
Number of admissions	286,164	117,936	143,168	2,542	38,935
All offenses[1]	100%	100%	100%	100%	100%
Violent offenses	28.6	28.3	28.5	40.5	28.1
Homicide	4.1	4.0	4.1	6.4	4.2
Murder and nonnegligent manslaughter	2.8	2.5	3.0	4.7	3.3
Murder	2.4	2.1	2.5	4.0	2.4
Nonnegligent manslaughter	0.5	0.4	0.5	0.7	0.9
Negligent manslaughter	1.2	1.4	1.1	1.7	0.9
Unspecified homicide	0.1	0.1	0.1	0.0	(5)
Kidnaping	0.6	0.7	0.5	1.5	0.6
Rape	2.3	3.1	1.6	3.9	2.1
Other sexual assault	3.4	5.9	1.5	4.4	2.8
Robbery	9.9	6.5	12.6	10.7	10.2
Assault	7.5	7.1	7.7	12.0	7.7
Other violent	0.7	0.9	0.5	1.7	0.5
Property offenses	31.2	37.6	27.3	30.4	21.6
Burglary	13.3	16.6	10.8	14.8	11.4
Larceny-theft	8.1	9.1	7.9	6.8	4.5
Motor vehicle theft	2.5	2.9	2.1	2.7	3.2
Arson	0.6	0.8	0.4	0.6	0.3
Fraud	3.8	4.9	3.2	2.7	0.9
Stolen property	2.1	2.2	2.2	1.2	0.9
Other property	0.9	1.0	0.8	1.6	0.4
Drug offenses	30.4	21.6	36.3	15.3	41.3
Possession	6.7	3.7	8.7	2.8	6.8
Trafficking	18.8	13.9	21.7	9.6	29.2
Other drug	4.8	4.0	5.9	3.0	5.2
Public-order offenses	8.8	11.2	7.1	12.5	7.5
Weapons	2.4	1.7	2.9	1.7	2.5
Driving while intoxicated	2.6	4.9	0.8	6.5	3.9
Other public-order	3.8	4.7	3.4	4.3	1.2
Other offenses	1.1	1.3	0.8	1.3	1.5

Source: "New Court Commitments to Prisons in 38 States, by Offense, Sex, Race, and Hispanic Origin: United States, 1992," *Sourcebook of Criminal Justice Statistics, 1994,* p. 553. Primary source: U.S. Department of Justice, Bureau of Justice Statistics, *National Corrections Reporting Programs, 1992,* NCJ-145862 (Washington, DC: U.S. Department of Justice, 1994), p. 17. *Notes:* 1. Detail may not add to total because of rounding. 2. Includes persons of Hispanic origin. 3. Includes American Indians, Alaska Natives, Asians, and Pacific Islanders. 4. Includes persons of all races. 5. Less than 0.05 percent.

★ 138 ★

Law Enforcement

Prisoners: Percent of Violent and Nonviolent First-Timers and Recidivists in State Prisons, by Race: 1991

[Violent/nonviolent refers to the current or past criminal offense for which the inmate is or was incarcerated. Data based on a sample survey of 13,986 inmates; subject to sampling variability].

CHARACTERISTIC	CRIMINAL HISTORY OF PRISON INMATES								
	Total	First-timers			Recidivists[1]				
		Total	Non-violent	Violent	Total	Non-violent	Prior violent	Current violent only	Current and prior violent
Prison inmates, total	697,853	134,131	45,559	88,572	563,722	223,117	88,689	131,289	120,626
Percent of total	100.0	19.2	6.5	12.7	80.8	32.0	12.7	18.8	17.3
Percent distribution	100.0	100.0	100.0	100.0	100.0	100.0	100.0	100.0	100.0
White	49.0	52.6	50.9	53.4	48.2	52.9	40.1	50.4	42.9
Black	47.5	43.6	45.7	42.6	48.4	43.7	56.5	45.6	54.0
Other races	3.5	3.8	3.4	4.0	3.5	3.4	3.4	4.0	3.1

Source: "State Prison Inmates, by Criminal History and Selected Characteristics of the Inmate: 1991," *Statistical Abstract of the United States: 1995,* 1995, p. 218. *Notes:* 1. An individual who has been previously sentenced to probation or incarceration as a juvenile or adult.

★ 139 ★

Law Enforcement

Prisoners: Race of Federal Prisoners: 1990-1994

	1990		1991		1992		1993		1994	
	Number	Percent[1]	Number	Percent[1]	Number	Percent[1]	Number	Percent[1]	Number	Percent[1]
Total	65,347	100.0%	71,608	100.0%	79,859	100.0%	89,129	100.0%	94,558	100.0%
Race										
White	43,191	66.1	46,868	65.5	51,932	65.0	56,536	63.4	58,403	61.8
Black	20,495	31.4	22,727	31.7	25,763	32.3	30,169	33.8	33,448	35.4
Other[2]	1,661	2.5	2,013	2.8	2,164	2.7	2,424	2.7	2,707	2.9
Ethnicity										
Hispanic	17,520	26.8	19,086	26.7	21,667	27.1	24,262	27.2	25,226	26.7
Non-Hispanic	47,827	73.2	52,522	73.3	58,192	72.9	64,867	72.8	69,332	73.3

Source: "Characteristics of Federal Prisoners: United States, 1990-94," *Sourcebook of Criminal Justice Statistics, 1994,* p. 557. Primary source: U.S. Department of Justice, Federal Bureau of Prisons, *Federal Bureau of Prisons Annual Statistical Report Calendar Year 1990,* pp. 9, 10; *1991,* pp. 9, 10, 12; *1992,* pp. 9, 10, 12; *1993,* p. 9, 10, 12; *1994,* pp. 9, 10, 12 (Washington, DC; U.S. Department of Justice). Table adapted by SOURCEBOOK staff. *Notes:* These data include Federal Bureau of Prisons designated population only, which refers to prisoners who have been assigned to a facility. 1. Percents may not sum to total because of rounding.

★ 140 ★

Law Enforcement

Prisoners: Trends in Number of Jail Inmates, by Race/Ethnic Origin: 1978-1994

[Excludes Federal and State persons or other correctional institutions; institutions exclusively for juveniles; State-operated jails in Alaska, Connecticut, Delaware, Hawaii, Rhode Island, and Vermont; and other facilities which retain persons for less than 48 hours. As of **June 30**. For 1978 and 1988, data based on National Jail Census; for other years, based on sample survey and subject to sampling variability].

CHARACTERISTIC	1978	1985	1988	1989	1990	1991	1992	1993	1994
Total inmates[1]	158,394	256,615	343,569	395,553	405,320	426,479	444,584	459,804	490,442
White[2]	89,418	151,403	166,302	201,732	186,989	190,333	191,362	239,500	255,800
Black[2]	65,104	102,646	141,979	185,910	174,335	187,618	195,156	214,100	227,000
Other races[2]	3,872	2,566	3,932	7,911	5,321	5,391	5,831	6,200	7,600
Hispanic[3]	16,349	35,926	51,455	55,377	57,449	60,129	62,961	69,200	75,500
Non-Hispanic	142,045	220,689	292,114	340,176	347,871	366,350	381,623	390,600	414,942

Source: "Jail Inmates, by Race and Detention Status: 1978 to 1994," *Statistical Abstract of the United States: 1995*, 1995, p. 217. Primary source: U.S. Bureau of Justice Statistics, *Profile of Jail Inmates, 1978 and 1989: Jail Inmates*, annual; and *1988 Census of Local Jails. Notes:* 1. For 1985, 1989-1994, includes juveniles not shown separately by sex, and for 1988 and 1990-1994 includes 31,356, 38,675, 43,138, 52,235, 66,249, and 93,058 persons, respectively, of unknown race not shown separately. 2. For 1993 and 1994, data are estimated and rounded to nearest 100. 3. Hispanic persons may be of any race. Data for 1993 and 1994 are estimated and rounded to nearest 100.

★ 141 ★

Law Enforcement

Prisoners: Trends in Number of State and Federal Prisoners, by Gender and Race: 1980-1994

Year	Number of sentenced prisoners[1]						
	Total	Male			Female		
		All[2]	White	Black	All[2]	White	Black
1980	315,974	303,643	159,500	140,600	12,331	5,900	6,300
1985	480,568	459,223	242,700	210,500	21,345	10,800	10,200
1990	739,980	699,416	346,700	344,300	40,564	20,000	20,100
1991	789,610	745,808	363,600	372,200	43,802	20,900	22,200
1992	846,277	799,776	387,600	401,200	46,501	22,100	23,700
1993	932,266	878,298	418,900	445,400	53,968	25,200	27,900
1994	1,012,463	952,585	-	-	59,878	-	-
Percent change, 1980-94	220%	214%	-	-	386%	-	-

Source: "Number of Sentenced Prisoners Under State or Federal Jurisdiction, by Sex and Race, 1980, 1985, 1990-94," *Prisoners in 1994*, Bureau of Justice Statistics Bulletin, August, 1995, p. 8. *Notes:* Sentenced prisoners are those with a sentence of more than 1 year. - Not available. 1. The numbers for sex and race were estimated and rounded to the nearest 100. For men and women the total number of sentenced prisoners was multiplied by the proportion black or white of the total population in each group. The reported racial distribution was used to estimate unreported data. 2. Includes sentenced prisoners of other races.

★ 142 ★

Law Enforcement

Prisoners: Violent State Prisons Whose Victims were Intimates, by Race/Ethnic Origin: 1991

Prisoner characteristics	Percent of violent State prisoners who victimized	
	Intimates	Nonintimates
Race and ethnicity		
White	47	37
Black	40	47
Hispanic	10	14
Other	3	3

Source: "What are the characteristics of violent prisoners who victimized intimates?" *Violence Between Intimates,* November 1994, p. 7. Primary source: BJS Survey of Inmates in State Correctional Facilities, 1991.

★ 143 ★

Law Enforcement

Relationships: Drug Arrests of Blacks in Relation to Black Population Characteristics: c. 1993

Blacks as a percentage of each group in 1993.

	Percent
U.S. Population	13.0
Monthly drug users	13.0
Arrests for drug possession	35.0

Source: "A Closer Look: Drug Arrests," *The New York Times,* October 5, 1995, p. A18. Primary source: The Sentencing Project (figure for percentage of drug users from the National Institute on Drug Abuse). Published by permission.

★ 144 ★

Law Enforcement

Relationships: Trends in Number of State and Federal Prisoners per 100,000 U.S. Residents, by Gender and Race: 1980-1994

Year	Number of sentenced prisoners per 100,000 residents of relevant sex and racial group						
	Total[1]	Male			Female		
		All	White	Black	All	White	Black
1980	139	275	168	1,111	11	6	45
1985	202	397	246	1,559	17	10	68
1990	297	575	339	2,376	32	19	125
1992	332	643	371	2,675	36	20	142
1993	359	698	398	2,920	41	23	165
1994	387	746	-	-	45	-	-

Source: "Estimated Number of Sentenced Prisoners in State or Federal Prisons per 100,000 U.S. Residents, by Sex and Race, 1980, 1985, 1990-94," *Prisoners in 1994*, Bureau of Justice Statistics Bulletin, August, 1995, p. 8. *Notes:* Sentenced prisoners are those with a sentence of more than 1 year. Rates by sex and race are based on estimates of the U.S. resident population on July 1 of each year. - Not available. 1. Includes sentenced prisoners of other races. Rates for sentenced prisoners are based on the U.S. resident population on December 31 of each year.

Legal Justice

★ 145 ★

Court Officers: Racial/Ethnic Distribution of Appointees to U.S. Courts of Appeals Judgeships: 1963-1994. Part 1

	President Johnson's appointees 1963-68 (N=40)	President Nixon's appointees 1969-74 (N=45)	President Ford's appointees 1974-76 (N=12)	President Carter's appointees 1977-80 (N=56)	President Reagan's first term appointees 1981-84 (N=31)	President Reagan's second term appointees 1985-88 (N=47)	President Bush's appointees 1989-92 (N=37)	President Clinton's appointees 1993-94 (N=18)
Ethnicity								
White	95	97.8	100	78.6	93.5	100	89.2	72.2
Black	5	0	0	16.1	3.2	0	5.4	16.7
Hispanic	0	0	0	3.6	3.2	0	5.4	11.1
Asian	0	2.2	0	1.8	0	0	0	0.0

Source: "Characteristics of Presidential Appointees to U.S. Courts of Appeals Judgeships, by Presidential Administration, 1963-94," *Sourcebook of Criminal Justice Statistics, 1994,* p. 68. Primary source: Sheldon Goldman, "Reagan's Judicial Legacy: Completing the Puzzle and Summing Up," *Judicature* 72 (April-May 1989), pp. 323, 324. Table 3; and "Judicial Selection Under Clinton: A Midterm Examination," *Judicature* 78 (May-June 1995), p. 287. Table adapted by SOURCEBOOK staff. Reprinted by permission. *Notes:* Percents may not add to 100 because of rounding. These data were compiled from a variety of sources. Primarily used were questionnaires completed by judicial nominees for the U.S. Senate Judiciary Committee, transcripts of the confirmation hearing conducted by the Committee, and personal interviews. In addition, an investigation was made of various biographical directories including *The American Bench* (Sacramento: R.B. Forster), *Who's Who in American Politics* (New York: Bowker), *Martindale-Hubbell Law Directory* (Summit, NJ: Martindale-Hubbell, Inc.), national and regional editions of *Who's Who, The Judicial Staff Directory* (1994 edition), and local newspaper articles.

★ 146 ★

Legal Justice

Court Officers: Racial/Ethnic Distribution of Appointees to U.S. Courts of Appeals Judgeships: 1963-1994. Part 2

	President Johnson's appointees 1963-68 (N=122)	President Nixon's appointees 1969-74 (N=179)	President Ford's appointees 1974-76 (N=52)	President Carter's appointees 1977-80 (N=202)	President Reagan's first term appointees 1981-84 (N=129)	President Reagan's second term appointees 1985-88 (N=161)	President Bush's appointees 1989-92 (N=148)	President Clinton's appointees 1993-94 (N=107)
Ethnicity								
White	93.4	95.5	88.5	78.7	93	91.9	89.2	64.5
Black	4.1	3.4	5.8	13.9	0.8	3.1	6.8	25.2
Hispanic	2.5	1.1	1.9	6.9	5.4	4.3	4	8.4

[Continued]

★ 146 ★

Court Officers: Racial/Ethnic Distribution of Appointees to U.S. Courts of Appeals Judgeships: 1963-1994. Part 2

[Continued]

	President Johnson's appointees 1963-68 (N=122)	President Nixon's appointees 1969-74 (N=179)	President Ford's appointees 1974-76 (N=52)	President Carter's appointees 1977-80 (N=202)	President Reagan's first term appointees 1981-84 (N=129)	President Reagan's second term appointees 1985-88 (N=161)	President Bush's appointees 1989-92 (N=148)	President Clinton's appointees 1993-94 (N=107)
Asian	0	0	3.9	0.5	0.8	0.6	0	0.9
Native American	NA	NA	NA	0	0	0	0	0.9

Source: "Characteristics of Presidential Appointees to U.S. Courts of Appeals Judgeships, by Presidential Administration, 1963-94," *Sourcebook of Criminal Justice Statistics, 1994,* p. 69. Primary source: Sheldon Goldman, "Reagan's Judicial Legacy: Completing the Puzzle and Summing Up," *Judicature* 72 (April-May 1989), pp. 320, 321. and "Judicial Selection Under Clinton: A Midterm Examination," *Judicature* 78 (May-June 1995), p. 281. Table adapted by SOURCEBOOK staff. Reprinted by permission. *Note:* Percents may not add to 100 because of rounding.

★ 147 ★

Legal Justice

Executions: Prisoners Executed by Order of Civil Courts, by Race: 1930-1993

[Excludes executions by military authorities. The Army (including the Air Force) carried out 160 (148 between 1942 and 1950; 3 each in 1954, 1955, and 1957; and 1 each in 1958, 1959, and 1961). Of the total, 106 were executed for murder (including 21 involving rape), 53 for rape, and 1 for desertion. The Navy carried out no executions during the period].

YEAR OR PERIOD	Total[1]	White	Black	EXECUTED FOR MURDER			EXECUTED FOR RAPE			EXECUTED OTHER OFFENSES[2]		
				Total[1]	White	Black	Total[1]	White	Black	Total[1]	White	Black
All years	4,089	1,864	2,154	3,564	1,777	1,718	455	48	405	70	39	31
1930 to 1939	1,667	827	816	1,514	803	687	125	10	115	28	14	14
1940 to 1949	1,284	490	781	1,064	458	595	200	19	179	20	13	7
1950 to 1959	717	336	376	601	316	280	102	13	89	14	7	7
1960 to 1967	191	98	93	155	87	68	28	6	22	8	5	3
1968 to 1976	-	-	-	-	-	-	-	-	-	-	-	-
1977 to 1981	4	4	-	4	4	-	-	-	-	-	-	-
1982	2	1	1	2	1	1	-	-	-	-	-	-
1983	5	4	1	5	4	1	-	-	-	-	-	-
1984	21	13	8	21	13	8	-	-	-	-	-	-
1985	18	11	7	18	11	7	-	-	-	-	-	-
1986	18	11	7	18	11	7	-	-	-	-	-	-
1987	25	13	12	25	13	12	-	-	-	-	-	-
1988	11	6	5	11	6	5	-	-	-	-	-	-
1989	16	8	8	16	8	8	-	-	-	-	-	-
1990	23	16	7	23	16	7	-	-	-	-	-	-
1991	14	7	7	14	7	7	-	-	-	-	-	-
1992	31	19	11	31	19	11	-	-	-	-	-	-
1993	38	23	14	38	23	14	-	-	-	-	-	-

Source: "Prisoners Executed Under Civil Authority: 1930 to 1993," *Statistical Abstract of the United States: 1995,* 1995, p. 220. Primary source: Through 1978. U.S. Law Enforcement Assistance Administration; thereafter, U.S. Bureau of Justice Statistics, *Correctional Populations in the United States,* annual. *Notes:* - Represents zero. 1. Includes races other than White or Black. 2. Includes 25 armed robbery, 20 kidnaping, 11 burglary, 8 espionage (6 in 1942 and 2 in 1953), and 5 aggravated assault.

★ 148 ★
Legal Justice

Felony Offenders: Most Serious Offense of Felons Convicted by State Courts, by Race: 1992

Most serious conviction offense	Estimated total number of convictions	Total (%)	Percent of convicted felons who were: Race		
			White (%)	Black (%)	Other (%)
All offenses	893,630	100	52	47	1
Violent offenses	165,099	100	48	50	2
Murder[1]	12,548	100	41	58	1
Rape	21,655	100	86	30	4
Robbery	51,878	100	34	65	1
Aggravated assault	58,969	100	50	48	2
Other violent[2]	20,049	100	72	27	1
Property offenses	297,494	100	58	41	1
Burglary	114,630	100	60	39	1
Larceny[3]	119,000	100	57	42	1
Fraud[4]	63,864	100	57	42	1
Drug offenses	280,232	100	44	55	1
Possession	109,426	100	44	55	1
Trafficking	170,806	100	44	55	1
Weapons offenses	26,422	100	39	60	1
Other offenses[5]	124,383	100	64	34	2

Source: "Felony Offenders Convicted in State Courts, by Offense, Sex, Race, and Age: United States, 1992," *Sourcebook of Criminal Justice Statistics, 1994*, p. 486. Primary source: U.S. Department of Justice, Bureau of Justice Statistics, *Felony Sentences in State Courts, 1992*, Bulletin NCJ-151167 (Washington, DC: U.S. Department of Justice, January 1995), p. 2. p. 5. Table adapted by SOURCEBOOK staff. *Notes:* 1. Includes nonnegligent manslaughter. 2. Includes offenses such as negligent manslaughter, sexual assault, and kidnaping. 3. Includes motor vehicle theft. 4. Includes forgery and embezzlement. 5. Composed of nonviolent offenses such as receiving stolen property and vandalism.

★ 149 ★

Legal Justice

Felony Offenders: Percent of Felony Defendants Failing to Appear in Court, by Race/Ethnic Origin: 1992

Defendant characteristics	Number of defendants	Total (%)	Percent making all scheduled court appearances (%)	Percent failing to appear in court[1]		
				Total (%)	Returned to court (%)	Remained a fugitive (%)
All released defendants	33,484	100	75	25	17	8
Race						
Black	17,701	100	73	27	19	9
White	12,525	100	79	21	14	7
Other	395	100	85	15	10	5
Race/Hispanic origin[2]						
Non-Hispanic						
Black	12,566	100	72	28	19	8
White	7,166	100	81	19	13	6
Other	391	100	86	14	9	5
Hispanic, any race	5,885	100	70	30	17	13

Source: "Released Felony Defendants who Failed to Make a Scheduled Court Appearance in the 78 Largest Counties, by Selected Defendant Characteristics: United States, 1992," *Sourcebook of Criminal Justice Statistics, 1994,* p. 495. Primary source: U.S. Department of Justice, Bureau of Justice Statistics, *Pretrial Release of Felony Defendants, 1992,* Bulletin NCJ-148818 (Washington, DC: U.S. Department of Justice, November 1994), p. 10. *Notes:* Detail may not add to total because of rounding. Data on court appearance record for the current case were available for 99 percent of cases involving a defendant released prior to case disposition. All defendants who failed to appear in court and were not returned to court within the 1-year study period were counted as fugitives. Some of these defendants may have been returned to the court at a later date. 1. Failure to appear occurs when a court issues a bench warrant for a defendant's arrest because he or she has missed a scheduled court appearance. 2. Data on race combined with Hispanic origin were available for 77 percent of defendants.

★ 150 ★

Legal Justice

Felony Offenders: Percent of Felony Offenders Released and Rearrested, by Race/Ethnic Origin: 1992

Defendant characteristics	Number of defendants	Percent of released felony defendants			
		Not rearrested	Rearrested		
			Total	Felony	Misdemeanor
All released defendants	30,051	86%	14%	10%	3%
Race					
Black	15,830	85	15	12	4
White	11,329	89	11	8	3
Other	365	95	5	5	0

[Continued]

★ 150 ★

Felony Offenders: Percent of Felony Offenders Released and Rearrested, by Race/Ethnic Origin: 1992

[Continued]

Defendant characteristics	Number of defendants	Percent of released felony defendants			
		Not rearrested	Rearrested		
			Total	Felony	Misdemeanor
Race/Hispanic origin[1]					
Non-Hispanic					
Black	11,292	85	15	11	4
White	6,313	91	9	7	3
Other	361	94	6	6	0
Hispanic, any race	5,126	84	16	12	4

Source: "Felony Defendants Rearrested while On Pretrial Release in the 78 Largest Counties, by Selected Defendant Characteristics: 1992," *Sourcebook of Criminal Justice Statistics, 1994,* p. 496. Primary source: U.S. Department of Justice, Bureau of Justice Statistics, *Pretrial Release of Felony Defendants, 1992,* Bulletin NC-J-148818 (Washington, DC: U.S. Department of Justice, November 1994)p. 11. *Notes:* Detail may not add to total because of rounding. Rearrest data were collected for 1 year. Rearrests occurring after the end of this 1-year study period are not included in the table. Information on rearrests in jurisdictions other than the one granting the pretrial release was not always available. Rearrest data were available for 94 percent of released defendants. 1. Data on race combined with Hispanic origin were available for 77 percent of defendants.

★ 151 ★

Legal Justice

Juvenile Cases: Percent Distribution of Juvenile Case Outcomes, by Case Category and Race: 1992

	Delinquency cases		Petitioned cases			Adjudicated cases		
	Detained prior to juvenile court disposition	Petitioned	Adjudicated delinquent	Waived to adult court	Placed out of home	Placed on probation	Dismissed	Other[1]
Total	20.1%	50.6%	57.5%	1.6%	28.4%	57.2%	3.8%	10.7%
Race								
White	17.7	47.0	58.2	1.2	25.4	58.3	3.3	13.0
Black	25.0	58.1	55.5	2.2	33.4	55.8	5.0	5.8

Source: "Juvenile Court Case Outcomes, by Characteristics of Juvenile Offenders: United States, 1992," *Sourcebook of Criminal Justice Statistics, 1994,* p. 498. Primary source: Jeffrey A. Butts et al. "Juvenile Court Statistics 1992" (Pittsburgh, PA: National Center for Juvenile Justice, 1994), Machine- readable data file. Table constructed by SOURCEBOOK staff. *Notes:* Care should be exercised when interpreting race differences because reported statistics do not control for variations in the seriousness of the offense or the prior criminal history of the juvenile. The racial category "other" comprised a small number of cases and was therefore omitted. 1. Includes dispositions such as fined, restitution, community service, and referrals out-side the court for services with minimal or no further court involvement anticipated.

★ 152 ★

Legal Justice

Juvenile Cases: Percent Distribution of Outcome of Juvenile Court Cases, by Type of Offense and Race: 1992

	Delinquency cases		Petitioned cases		Adjudicated cases			
	Detained prior to juvenile court dis-position (%)	Petitioned (%)	Adjudicated delinquent (%)	Waived to adult court (%)	Placed out of home (%)	Placed on probation (%)	Dismissed (%)	Other[1] (%)
Person								
White	21.4	50.6	54.5	1.8	28.9	56.7	3.8	10.6
Black	27.5	60.7	51.3	3.1	35.0	53.7	5.2	6.1
Property								
White	14.7	45.3	58.8	1.3	21.5	61.1	2.9	14.4
Black	20.7	53.4	56.3	1.5	31.5	58.2	4.7	5.5
Drug								
White	25.7	50.6	62.2	1.0	26.8	57.4	5.2	10.5
Black	46.7	80.5	58.3	4.6	35.8	51.4	6.0	6.8
Public-order								
White	22.6	48.1	59.6	0.6	34.2	51.1	3.3	11.4
Black	24.2	58.2	58.1	1.2	34.3	55.2	5.1	5.4

Source: "Juvenile Court Case Outcomes, by Type of Offense and Race of Juvenile Offender: United States, 1992," *Sourcebook of Criminal Justice Statistics, 1994,* p. 499. Primary source: Jeffrey A. Butts et al., "Juvenile Court Statistics 1992" (Pittsburgh, PA: National Center for Juvenile Justice, 1994). Machine- readale data file. Table constructed by SOURCEBOOK staff. *Notes:* 1. Includes dispositions such as fines, restitution, community service, and referrals outside the court for services with minimal or no further court involvement anticipated.

★ 153 ★

Legal Justice

Offenders: Racial/Ethnic Distribution of Convicted Defendants, by Type of Offense: 1992

Offender characteristics[1]	Total number of defendants	Percent of offenders convicted of:							
		All offenses	Felonies						Mis-demeanors
			Violent offenses	Property offenses		Drug offenses	Public-order offenses		
				Fraudulent	Other		Regulatory	Other	
Race									
White	20,084	63.3	54.8	66.8	65.8	60.5	81.1	66.7	63.1
Black	10,300	32.5	33.7	29.3	30.7	36.4	14.5	28.8	31.4
Other	1,349	4.3	11.6	3.9	3.4	3.0	4.5	4.5	5.5

[Continued]

★ 153 ★

Offenders: Racial/Ethnic Distribution of Convicted Defendants, by Type of Offense: 1992

[Continued]

Offender characteristics[1]	Total number of defendants	Percent of offenders convicted of:							Mis-demeanors
		All offenses	Felonies						
			Violent offenses	Property offenses		Drug offenses	Public-order offenses		
				Fraudulent	Other		Regulatory	Other	
Ethnicity									
Hispanic	7,846	22.8	6.5	8.6	7.3	31.2	18.7	29.2	19.4
Non-Hispanic	26,572	77.2	93.5	91.4	92.7	68.8	81.3	70.8	80.6

Source: "Defendants Convicted in U.S. District Courts, by Offense and Characteristics: United States, 1992," *Sourcebook of Criminal Justice Statistics, 1994,* p. 451. Primary source: U.S. Department of Justice, Bureau of Justice Statistics, *Compendium of Federal Justice Statistics, 1992,* NCJ-148949 (Washington, DC: U.S. Department of Justice, 1995), p. 39. *Notes:* This table was created by matching the Administrative Office master data files with the United States Sentencing Commission monitoring system files, which include records for sentences imposed under guidelines only. Juvenile offenders are not subject to guidelines and are not included in tables showing offender characteristics. Tables indicate the number of records for which relevant data were available. 1. Defendant characteristics are not directly comparable with prior years.

★ 154 ★

Legal Justice

Offenders: Racial/Ethnic Distribution of Felons Convicted and Incarcerated in 1992, by Type of Offense

Offender characteristics[1]	Total number of offenders	Of all offenders convicted in cases terminated in 1992, the percent who were incarcerated for:							Mis-demeanors
		All offenses	Violent offenses	Property offenses		Drug offenses	Public-order offenses		
				Fraudulent	Other		Regulatory	Other	
All offenders[2]	52,348	65.6%	93.3%	54.5%	58.1%	91.0%	45.2%	76.5%	16.2%
Race									
White	20,084	75.9	93.8	59.3	62.7	90.9	48.6	77.9	25.8
Black	10,300	80.8	97.0	56.0	55.5	94.5	61.8	86.8	25.5
Other	1,349	73.5	92.4	47.7	52.5	92.1	58.8	74.6	20.2
Ethnicity									
Hispanic	7,846	87.2	94.7	58.0	54.8	96.0	55.6	84.4	53.3
Non-Hispanic	26,572	75.1	94.7	57.8	60.0	90.9	49.9	79.6	20.6

Source: "Offenders Sentenced to Incarceration in U.S. District Courts, by Offense and Characteristics: United States, 1992," *Sourcebook of Criminal Justice Statistics, 1994,* p. 453. Primary source: U.S. Department of Justice, Bureau of Justice Statistics, *Compendium of Federal Justice Statistics, 1992,* NCJ-148949 (Washington, DC: U.S. Department of Justice, 1995), p. 48. *Notes:* Offenders are classified by the most serious offense of conviction. 1. Offender characteristics are not directly comparable with prior years. 2. Includes offenders of whom characteristics were unknown.

★ 155 ★

Legal Justice

Pretrials: Percent of Federal Defendants Released/ Detained After Pretrial, by Race: 1992

Defendant characteristics	Number of defendants	Defendants released		Defendants detained	
		Number	Percent	Number	Percent
All defendants	49,834	30,838	61.9%	28,483	57.2%
Race					
White	33,713	21,379	63.4	18,717	55.5
Black	13,391	7,741	57.8	8,183	61.1
Other	2,730	1,718	62.9	1,583	58.0
Ethnicity					
Hispanic	13,389	5,241	39.1	11,006	82.2
Non-Hispanic	35,871	25,380	70.78	17,078	47.6

Source: "Pretrial Release and Detention Status of Federal Defendants in U.S. District Courts, by Characteristics: United States, 1992," *Sourcebook of Criminal Justice Statistics, 1994,* p. 444. Primary source: U.S. Department of Justice, Bureau of Justice Statistics, *Compendium of Federal Justice Statistics, 1992,* NCJ-148949 (Washington, DC: U.S. Department of Justice, 1995), pp. 25, 27. *Notes:* "Released" defendants includes some defendants who were also detained prior to trial; "detained" defendants includes some defendants who were also released prior to trial. Total includes defendants for whom release status data were unavailable.

★ 156 ★

Legal Justice

Pretrials: U.S. District Court Pretrials and Their Outcomes, by Race: 1992

Defendant characteristics	Number of defendants	Pretrial detention hearings held		Defendants ordered detained	
		Number	Percent	Number	Percent
All defendants[1]	49,834	19,527	39.2%	14,519	29.1%
Race					
White	33,713	12,167	36.1	8,780	26.0
Black	13,391	6,264	46.6	4,914	36.7
Other	2,730	1,096	40.1	825	30.2

Source: "Federal Pretrial Detention Hearings and Defendants Ordered Detained in U.S. District Courts, by Characteristics: United States, 1992," *Sourcebook of Criminal Justice Statistics, 1994,* p. 444. Primary source: U.S. Department of Justice, Bureau of Justice Statistics, *Compendium of Federal Justice Statistics, 1992,* NCJ-148949 (Washington, DC: U.S. Department of Justice, 1995), p. 29. *Note:* 1. Includes defendants for whom characteristics were unknown.

★ 157 ★

Legal Justice

Relationships: Blacks in Prison, Black Drug Users and Black/White Convictions for Drug Use, c. 1995.

	Percent
Young, Black, Male and Doing Time-- Percent of men age 20 to 29 in state and federal prisons, jail, probation, parole on any given day	
Black	32
White	7
Blacks and Drugs-- Blacks constitute 12% of the total population of the U.S., yet receive disproportionate share of police and judicial attention	
Users	13
Arrests	35
Convictions	55
Sentences	74
CRACK: Who's using and Who's Getting Busted-- Blacks constitute 12% of the total population of the U.S.	
White use	46
Black use	38
White convictions	3.5
Black convictions	90

Source: "Criminal Justice: A Study in Black and White," *The Crisis*, Vol. 103, No. 1, January, 1996, p. 14. Primary source: The Sentencing Project. Published by permission.

★ 158 ★

Legal Justice

Sentences: Average Federal Sentences for Similar Crimes, by Court District and Race: 1992-93

District	Black average sentence	White average sentence	Difference in months
Missouri-East	41.6	29.3	12.3
Louisiana-East	40.5	32.8	7.8
California-North	36.5	28.7	7.7
Iowa-South	43.3	35.6	7.7
Indiana-South	44.8	37.3	7.6
Mississippi-South	37.4	29.8	7.6
Tennessee-East	40.1	32.5	7.6
Delaware	38.5	31.0	7.6
Florida-South	41.4	34.0	7.4
Rhode Island	47.7	40.5	7.3
Pennsylvania-West	35.8	28.6	7.2
Wisconsin-East	45.0	38.1	6.9
Wisconsin-West	42.1	35.7	6.4
Illinois-South	43.8	37.5	6.3
Pennsylvania-Middle	36.3	30.3	6.0
Louisiana-West	41.0	35.0	6.0
Alabama-Middle	39.5	33.5	6.0
New York-North	35.0	29.1	5.9
New Jersey	33.9	28.0	5.9
Colorado	37.7	31.9	5.8
Texas-North	41.6	36.1	5.5
Mississippi-North	37.2	31.8	5.4
Michigan-East	40.1	34.7	5.4
Oklahoma-North	39.1	34.3	4.8
Indiana-North	37.4	32.6	4.8
Pennsylvania-East	28.3	23.7	4.6
Alaska	37.0	32.5	4.5
Alabama-North	32.1	28.0	4.0
North Carolina-East	38.7	34.7	4.0
West Virginia-North	38.7	34.7	4.0
Maryland	35.7	31.9	3.8
Florida-Middle	36.0	32.3	3.7
Ohio-North	36.3	32.8	3.5
South Carolina	34.5	31.2	3.3
Tennessee-Middle	39.8	36.6	3.2
Arizona	31.3	28.1	3.2
Tennessee-West	35.5	32.4	3.1
California-Central	36.5	33.7	2.8
West Virginia-South	37.9	35.2	2.7
Arkansas-East	36.6	34.0	2.6
Illinois-Central	37.0	34.6	2.5
Oklahoma-West	33.6	31.4	2.2
Ohio-South	31.8	29.6	2.2
New York-East	33.5	31.7	1.8

[Continued]

★ 158 ★

Sentences: Average Federal Sentences for Similar Crimes, by Court District and Race: 1992-93
[Continued]

District	Black average sentence	White average sentence	Difference in months
California-East	35.1	33.4	1.7
Illinois-North	33.1	31.5	1.6
California-South	29.9	28.6	1.4
Utah	34.4	33.0	1.3
Texas-East	37.8	36.5	1.2
Georgia-North	37.8	36.6	1.1
New York-West	35.1	34.2	0.9
Virginia-West	33.0	32.3	0.8
North Carolina-West	28.6	27.9	0.6
District of Columbia	36.1	35.6	0.5
Oregon	37.1	36.6	0.5
Connecticut	30.1	29.7	0.5
Louisiana-Middle	38.2	37.8	0.4
Texas-South	35.6	35.3	0.3
Texas-West	36.6	36.3	0.3
Kansas	37.4	37.1	0.3
Georgia-South	34.7	34.4	0.3
Nevada	36.8	36.6	0.2
Kentucky-East	34.5	34.5	0.0
New York-South	28.0	27.6	-0.4
Virginia-East	35.3	36.0	-0.7
Alabama-South	32.9	33.7	-0.8
Minnesota	30.5	31.4	-0.9
Missouri-West	32.3	33.6	-1.3
New Mexico	32.4	34.1	-1.7
Florida-North	29.9	31.7	-1.8
Washington-West	28.3	30.2	-1.9
North Carolina-Middle	36.1	38.0	-1.9
Massachusetts	26.7	28.8	-2.1
Georgia-Middle	35.7	37.9	-2.2
Nebraska	27.7	32.2	-4.5
Kentucky-West	27.6	32.6	-5.0
Michigan-West	27.6	33.9	-6.3

Source: "Sentencing Disparity by District," *The Tennessean*, September 24, 1995, p. 17A. Primary source: U.S. Sentencing Commission. Published by permission. *Note:* Districts with fewer than 30 convictions against black criminals.

★ 159 ★

Legal Justice

Sentences: Average Federal Sentences for Similar Crimes, by Region and Race: 1992-93

Nationally, the racial disparity in federal sentencing is smallest in the South. The disparity is greatest in the West and Midwest.

	In months			
	West	Midwest	South	Northeast
White	31	34	35	32
Black	35	38	36	35
Disparity	4	4	1	3

Source: "Sentencing Disparity by Region: Federal Sentences Nationwide," *The Tennessean,* September 24, 1995, p. 17A. Primary source: U.S. Sentencing Commission. Published by permission.

★ 160 ★

Legal Justice

Sentences: Average Length of Sentence in U.S. District Courts, by Type of Offense and Race: 1992

[In months].

Offender characteristics[1]	All offenses	Average sentence length for offenders convicted of:						Mis-demeanors
		Felonies						
		Violent offenses	Property offenses		Drug offenses	Public-order offenses		
			Fraudulent	Other		Regulatory	Other	
All offenders[2]	62.6	94.8	21.3	27.6	84.1	28.8	45.1	9.4
Race								
White	56.8	92.4	20.4	28.0	73.8	27.6	42.4	12.6
Black	84.1	103.9	17.3	20.6	106.9	36.0	65.9	13.5
Other	60.8	76.1	16.7	22.9	77.2	20.8	47.0	8
Ethnicity								
Hispanic	63.2	84.9	15.9	20.0	80.5	19.6	26.8	16.7
Non-Hispanic	66.3	94.7	19.7	26.2	87.2	30.2	56.7	11.4

Source: "Average Sentence Length Imposed on Offenders Sentenced to Incarceration in U.S. District Courts, by Offense and Characteristics: United States, 1992," *Sourcebook of Criminal Justice Statistics, 1994,* p. 458. Primary source: U.S. Department of Justice, Bureau of Justice Statistics, *Compendium of Federal Justice Statistics, 1992,* NCJ-148949 (Washington, DC: U.S. Department of Justice, 1995), p. 39. *Notes:* Data exclude corporations, offenders sentenced to life sentences, and indeterminate sentences for youthful or drug offenders; and include prison portion of split or mixed sentences. 1. Offender characteristics are not directly comparable with prior years. 2. Includes offenders for whom these characteristics were unknown.

★ 161 ★
Legal Justice

Sentences: Maximum Length of Sentences, by Most Serious Offense and Race: 1992

Most serious offense	All[1]	Maximum sentence length (in months)									
		Median[2]	Mean[3]	Male				Female			
				White		Black		White		Black	
				Median	Mean	Median	Mean	Median	Mean	Median	Mean
All offenses	100%	48	67	36	64	48	73	36	51	36	52
Violent offenses	28.4	72	104	61	99	75	113	60	95	60	86
Homicide	4.2	240	188	180	162	288	221	144	139	144	152
Murder and nonnegligent manslaughter	2.8	433	240	1,188	225	420	286	300	189	228	179
Murder	2.3	Life	279	Life	275	1,176	295	Life	231	271	200
Nonnegligent manslaughter	0.5	132	152	120	118	156	174	109	123	121	145
Negligent manslaughter	1.3	96	122	72	103	120	150	60	95	85	119
Unspecified homicide	0.1	240	192	300	183	240	201	210	167	(4)	(4)
Kidnaping	0.6	96	123	84	114	120	141	60	98	96	102
Rape	2.1	120	144	108	143	120	153	120	156	(4)	(4)
Other sexual assault	3.5	72	99	72	101	72	99	72	103	72	107
Robbery	10.0	72	99	60	93	72	105	54	83	60	80
Assault	7.4	48	74	42	66	60	81	48	75	36	58
Other violent	0.7	48	60	36	55	60	68	36	45	42	57
Property offenses	30.8	36	53	36	54	36	54	30	43	24	40
Burglary	12.9	48	65	48	65	48	67	36	60	36	52
Larceny-theft	8.1	24	40	27	42	24	41	24	36	24	34
Motor vehicle theft	2.3	36	41	36	40	36	44	24	33	30	31
Arson	0.6	60	81	60	79	60	92	60	72	54	75
Fraud	3.7	36	47	36	50	36	46	36	44	30	46
Stolen property	2.3	36	45	36	46	36	45	30	38	24	35
Other property	0.9	36	42	36	42	36	42	24	29	24	29
Drug offenses	30.8	40	58	36	51	48	63	32	46	36	50
Possession	5.5	36	53	36	46	48	57	29	38	36	48
Trafficking	20.0	48	61	36	53	48	68	36	50	36	56
Other drug	5.3	24	48	24	47	36	51	24	40	24	35
Public-order offenses	9.0	24	38	24	35	30	42	24	34	24	34
Weapons	2.5	36	45	30	39	36	47	27	31	24	33
Driving while intoxicated	2.6	24	28	24	29	24	26	24	29	24	22
Other public-order	3.8	2.4	40	24	40	24	41	24	36	24	35
Other offenses	1.1	24	45	24	40	30	53	24	43	24	38

Source: "Maximum Sentence Length for New Court Commitments to Prisons in 38 States, by Offense, Sex, and Race: United States, 1992," *Sourcebook of Criminal Justice Statistics, 1994*, p. 555. Primary source: U.S. Department of Justice, Bureau of Justice Statistics, *National Corrections Reporting Program, 1992*, NCJ-145862 (Washington, DC: U.S. Department of Justice, 1994), pp. 22, 26. Table adapted by SOURCEBOOK staff. *Notes:* Data on maximum sentence length were reported for 90.0 percent of the 284,020 new court commitments with a total sentence of more than 1 year for whom the most serious offense was reported. Data on white males are based on 99,174 cases: black males, 116,858 cases; white females, 8,885 cases; and black females, 12,250 cases. "Maximum sentence length" is the sentence length that an offender may be required to serve for the most serious offense. 1. Detail may not add to total because of rounding. 2. Includes sentences of life without parole, life plus additional years, life, and death. 3. Excludes sentences of life without parole, life plus additional years, life, and death. 4. Fewer than 10 cases.

★ 162 ★

Legal Justice

Sentences: Prisoners Sentenced to Death, by Race: 1980-1993

[Prisoners reported under sentence of death by civil authorities. The term "under sentence of death" begins when the court pronounces the first sentence of death for a capital offense].

STATUS	1980	1984	1985	1986	1987	1988	1989	1990	1991	1992	1993
Under sentence of death, Jan. 1.	595	1,209	1,420	1,575	1,800	1,967	2,117	2,243	2,346	2,465	2,580
Received death sentence[1,2]	203	296	281	297	299	296	251	244	266	265	282
White	125	173	165	164	190	196	133	147	163	147	146
Black	77	119	114	123	106	91	114	94	101	114	130
Under sentence of death, Dec. 31[1]	688	1,420	1,575	1,800	1,967	2,117	2,243	2,346	2,466	2,575	2,718
White	425	809	896	1,006	1,128	1,238	1,308	1,368	1,450	1,508	1,566
Black	268	595	664	750	813	853	898	940	1,016	1,029	1,109

Source: "Movement of Prisoners Under Sentence of Death: 1980 to 1993," *Statistical Abstract of the United States: 1995,* 1995, p. 220. Primary source: U.S. Bureau of Justice Statistics, *Capital Punishment,* annual. *Note:* 1. Includes races other than White or Black.

★ 163 ★

Legal Justice

Time Served/Parole: Average Time Served in State Prisons, by Most Serious Offense, Gender, and Race: 1992

Most serious offense	Percent of releases[1]	Time served in prison by first release from State prison (in months)									
		Median	Mean	Male				Female			
				White		Black		White		Black	
				Median	Mean	Median	Mean	Median	Mean	Median	Mean
All offenses	100.0%	13	22	13	21	14	23	10	15	10	15
Violent offenses	24.6	24	37	23	35	26	40	20	30	19	30
Homicide	2.6	46	64	38	56	56	73	34	48	39	53
Murder and nonnegligent manslaughter	1.5	70	85	66	83	74	92	58	66	56	67
Murder	1.0	84	96	83	96	94	104	69	75	81	81
Nonnegligent manslaughter	0.5	53	61	45	53	55	64	33	42	37	49
Negligent manslaughter	1.1	26	36	24	31	32	44	21	30	30	38
Unspecified homicide	(2)	23	25	16	18	31	32	21	21	4	4
Kidnaping	0.4	31	45	25	38	36	53	25	32	51	45
Rape	1.7	47	59	42	54	55	68	44	42	45	49
Other sexual assault	2.8	24	30	25	31	22	30	24	28	26	23
Robbery	9.9	27	39	26	39	28	40	18	26	18	26
Assault	6.5	16	24	15	23	16	24	16	23	13	18
Other violent	0.6	16	21	14	20	19	25	11	16	13	20
Property offenses	34.0	11	17	11	18	11	18	8	12	7	11
Burglary	14.5	14	22	14	21	16	23	11	15	11	16
Larceny-theft	9.3	8	13	9	13	9	14	8	11	7	10
Motor vehicle theft	2.4	11	14	11	13	11	13	8	10	5	8
Arson	0.7	18	26	17	26	21	29	15	23	12	18
Fraud	4.1	9	14	10	15	9	14	8	12	7	11

[Continued]

★ 163 ★

Time Served/Parole: Average Time Served in State Prisons, by Most Serious Offense, Gender, and Race: 1992

[Continued]

Most serious offense	Percent of releases[1]	Time served in prison by first release from State prison (in months)									
		Median	Mean	Male				Female			
				White		Black		White		Black	
				Median	Mean	Median	Mean	Median	Mean	Median	Mean
Stolen property	2.1	9	14	10	15	9	14	7	11	6	9
Other property	0.9	7	12	7	12	7	12	7	10	7	12
Drug offenses	30.7	12	16	13	16	12	16	10	13	10	13
Possession	7.4	10	15	10	14	10	15	8	11	8	12
Trafficking	18.6	14	18	14	17	14	17	12	14	12	15
Other drug	4.7	8	13	10	14	9	13	7	10	7	9
Public-order offenses	9.5	8	13	8	12	8	14	7	10	9	12
Weapons	2.3	11	17	11	16	11	17	11	13	8	12
Driving while intoxicated	3.3	7	9	8	10	4	6	6	7	4	8
Other public-order	4.0	8	14	8	14	9	15	8	12	9	12
Other offenses	1.2	11	16	10	16	11	18	11	14	10	11

Source: "Time Served by First Releases from State Prisons in 38 States, by Offense, Sex, and Race, United States, 1992," Sourcebook of Criminal Justice Statistics, 1994, p. 555. Primary source: U.S. Department of Justice, Bureau of Justice Statistics, National Corrections Reporting Program, 1992, NCJ-145862 (Washington, DC: U.S. Department of Justice, 1994), pp. 38, 45. Table adapted by SOURCEBOOK staff. Notes: Data are based on 219,610 first releases with a total sentence of more than 1 year for whom the most serious offense, sex, and time served were reported. Data on white males are based on 76,741 cases; black males, 87,711 cases; white females, 7,336 cases; and black females, 9,477 cases. All data exclude persons released from prison by escape, death, transfer, appeal, or detainer. 1. Detail may not add to total because of rounding. 2. Less than 0.05 percent.

★ 164 ★

Legal Justice

Time Served/Parole: Percent Distribution of Offenders Under Parole Supervision, by Offense and Race/Ethnic Origin: 1992

Most serious offense	All entries[1]	Race[2]			Hispanic[4]
		White	Black	Other[3]	
Number of parole entries	176,564	72,111	86,717	1,674	29,350
All offenses	100%	100%	100%	100%	100%
Violent offenses	25.2	23.6	26.7	32.1	22.7
Homicide	2.7	2.7	2.7	4.4	2.3
Murder and nonnegligent manslaughter	1.7	1.5	1.8	2.3	1.5
Murder	1.1	1.2	1.0	1.2	0.7
Nonnegligent manslaughter	0.6	0.4	0.8	0.7	0.8
Negligent manslaughter	0.0	0.4	0.6	0.7	0.8
Unspecified homicide	0.0	0.0	0.0	0.0	5
Kidnaping	0.4	0.5	0.3	1.0	0.3
Rape	1.7	2.1	1.4	2.3	1.4
Other sexual assault	2.5	4.1	1.3	3.2	2.1

[Continued]

★ 164 ★

Time Served/Parole: Percent Distribution of Offenders Under Parole Supervision, by Offense and Race/Ethnic Origin: 1992

[Continued]

Most serious offense	All entries[1]	Race[2]			Hispanic[4]
		White	Black	Other[3]	
Robbery	10.7	7.0	13.7	7.9	10.1
Assault	6.6	6.4	6.8	11.6	6.0
Other violent	0.6	0.8	0.5	1.7	0.5
Property offenses	32.7	38.2	29.8	36.4	23.8
Burglary	14.8	17.9	12.4	17.9	13.2
Larceny-theft	8.4	9.1	8.6	8.4	4.8
Motor vehicle theft	2.7	3.1	2.4	3.6	3.0
Arson	0.6	0.9	0.4	0.3	0.3
Fraud	3.9	5.0	3.5	3.2	1.1
Stolen property	1.6	1.3	1.7	1.6	1.1
Other property	0.7	0.8	0.6	1.4	0.3
Drug offenses	31.1	23.3	35.4	15.0	43.4
Possession	8.2	4.9	10.4	3.5	7.0
Trafficking	19.3	14.3	21.3	8.5	30.8
Other drug	3.7	4.1	3.7	3.0	5.6
Public-order offenses	9.8	13.2	7.4	15.2	8.4
Weapons	2.2	1.5	2.6	1.8	2.5
Driving while intoxicated	3.7	7.0	1.2	8.4	5.0
Other public-order	3.9	4.7	3.6	5.0	1.0
Other offenses	1.2	1.7	0.8	1.2	1.6

Source: "Entries to Parole Supervision from Prisons in 38 States, by Offense, Sex, Race, and Hispanic Origin: United States, 1992," *Sourcebook of Criminal Justice Statistics, 1994,* p. 579. Primary source: U.S. Department of Justice, Bureau of Justice Statistics, *National Corrections Reporting Program, 1992,* NCJ-145862 (Washington, DC: U.S. Department of Justice, 1994), p. 56. *Notes:* Data on most serious offense were reported for 90.8 percent of the 182,141 State parole entries who entered prison with a sentence of more than 1 year. For methodology and offense within categories. 1. Detail may not add to total because of rounding. 2. Includes persons of Hispanic origin. 3. Includes American Indians, Alaska Natives, Asians, and Pacific Islanders. 4. Includes persons of all races. 5. Less than 0.05 percent.

★ 165 ★
Legal Justice

Time Served/Parole: Percent Distribution of Persons Discharged from Parole, by Method of Discharge and Race/Ethnic Origin: 1992

Method of parole discharge	All discharges	Race[2]			Hispanic[4]
		White	Black	Other[3]	
Number of discharges	216,710	96,811	98,682	1,589	38,766
All methods	100%	100%	100%	100%	100%
Successful completion	49.3	50.7	48.6	55.6	41.8
Absconder	1.0	0.9	1.2	0.6	0.7
Return to jail or prison[5]	47.8	46.5	48.4	42.4	55.8
Transfer	0.2	0.2	0.2	0.4	0.1
Death	1.1	1.0	1.1	0.8	1.2
Other	0.6	0.7	0.5	0.2	0.4

Source: "Parole Discharges in 29 States, by Method of Parole Discharge, Sex, Race, and Hispanic Origin: United States, 1992," *Sourcebook of Criminal Justice Statistics, 1994,* p. 580. Primary source: U.S. Department of Justice, Bureau of Justice Statistics, *National Corrections Reporting Program, 1992,* NCJ-145862 (Washington, DC: U.S. Department of Justice, 1994), p. 67. *Notes:* Data were reported for 97.8 percent of the 221,552 State parole discharges who entered prison with a sentence of more than 1 year and include those on supervised release even if not technically termed "parole." 1. Detail may not add to total because of rounding. 2. Includes persons of Hispanic origin. 3. cludes American Indians, Alaska Natives, Asians, and Pacific Islanders. 4. Includes persons of all races. 5. Includes those returned to prison with a new sentence, technical parole violations, and those returned pending parole revocation of a new charge.

Chapter 4
EDUCATION

Adult Education

★ 166 ★

Relationships: Reasons for Participation in Adult Education, by Race/Ethnic Origin: 1990-91

[For the civilian noninstitutional population 17 years and over not enrolled full-time in elementary or secondary school at the time of the survey. Adult education is considered any part-time enrollment in any educational activity at any time in the prior 12 months. Based on a telephone survey and subject to sampling error].

CHARACTERISTIC	Adult population (1,000)	PARTICIPANTS IN ADULT EDUCATION					
		Number taking adult ed. courses (1,000)	Percent of total	Reason for taking course (percent)[1]			
				Personal/ social	Advanced on the job	Train for a new job	Complete degree or diploma
Total	181,800	57,391	32	30	60	9	13
Race/ethnicity:							
White[2]	143,144	47,401	33	30	62	8	13
Black[2]	20,141	4,586	23	30	53	14	13
Hispanic	13,804	4,032	29	31	48	16	12
Other races[2]	4,711	1,371	29	32	51	8	17

Source: "Participation in Adult Education: 1990-91," *Statistical Abstract of the United States: 1995,* 1995, p. 194. Primary source: U.S. National Center for Education Statistics, *Adult Education Profile for 1990-91;* and unpublished data. *Notes:* 1. Reason for taking at least one course (includes duplication). Excludes "to improve basic skills," cited by no more than 4 percent of participants. 2. Non-Hispanic.

Educational Attainment

★ 167 ★

Number/Percent: Graduation and Degree Status (in percentages), by Race/Ethnic Origin: 1994

[For persons 25 years old and over. As of **March**. Based on Current Population Survey].

CHARACTERISTICS	Population (1,000)	PERCENT OF POPULATION--					
		Not a high school graduate	High school graduate	With some college, but no degree	With an associate's degree[1]	With a bachelor's degree	With an advanced degree
Total persons	164,512	19.1	34.4	17.4	7.0	14.7	7.5
Race: White	139,760	18.0	34.5	17.5	7.1	15.1	7.9
Black	18,103	27.1	36.2	17.5	6.3	9.5	3.4
Other	6,648	21.0	26.0	14.3	6.3	22.0	10.4
Hispanic origin: Hispanic	13,714	46.7	26.2	13.3	4.7	6.2	2.9
Non-Hispanic	150,798	16.6	35.1	17.7	7.2	15.5	7.9

Source: "Years of School Completed, by Selected Characteristic: 1994," *Statistical Abstract of the United States: 1995,* 1995, p. 158. Primary source: U.S. Bureau of the Census, unpublished data. *Note:* 1. Includes vocational degrees.

★ 168 ★

Educational Attainment

Relationships: Educational Attainment of 18-24-Year-Olds, by Race/ Ethnic Origin: 1990

	Population aged 18-24	1990 high school graduates	Enrolled in higher education	Completed associate's egree	Completed bachelor's degree
Total	100.0	100.0	100.0	100.0	100.0
Race-ethnicity					
American Indian/ Alaskan Native	0.7	0.5	0.8	0.8	0.4
Asian/Pacific Islander	2.7	3.3	4.2	3.0	3.7
Black, non-Hispanic	13.9	14.1	9.6	7.8	5.8
Hispanic	11.1	5.1	6.1	4.9	3.1

[Continued]

★ 168 ★

Relationships: Educational Attainment of 18-24-Year-Olds, by Race/ Ethnic Origin: 1990

[Continued]

	Population aged 18-24	1990 high school graduates	Enrolled in higher education	Completed associate's degree	Completed bachelor's degree
White, non-Hispanic	71.5	77.0	77.5	82.1	84.3
Nonresident alien	-	-	1.8	1.4	2.5

Source: "Percentage Distribution of Students in the College-Age Population and the Percentage Distribution According to Participation and Completion in Secondary and Postsecondary Education, by Race—Ethnicity: 1990," U.S. Department of Education, National Center for Education Statistics, *Minority Undergraduate Participation in Postsecondary Education*, June, 1995, p. 8. Primary source: Percentage of population 18-24 and 1990 high school graduates: U.S. Department of Commerce, Bureau of Census. Current Population Survey, October 1990; Enrollment and degree completion: U.S. Department of Education. *Digest of Education Statistics, 1993*, based on Integrated Postsecondary Education Data System (IPEDS) "Fall Enrollment and Completion" surveys, 1989-90. *Note:* - Noncitizens not presented separately.

★ 169 ★

Educational Attainment

Trends in High School and College Graduation (in percentages), by Race/Ethnic Origin: 1960-1994

[**In percent. For persons 25 years old and over. 1960, 1970, and 1980 as of April 1** based on sample data from the censuses of population. **Other years as of March** and based on the Current Population Survey].

YEAR	Total[1]	White	Black	Asian and Pacific Islander	HISPANIC[2] Total[3]	HISPANIC[2] Mexican	HISPANIC[2] Puerto Rican	HISPANIC[2] Cuban
COMPLETED 4 YEARS OF HIGH SCHOOL OR MORE								
1960	41.1	43.2	20.1	(NA)	(NA)	(NA)	(NA)	(NA)
1965	49.0	51.3	27.2	(NA)	(NA)	(NA)	(NA)	(NA)
1970	52.3	54.5	31.4	(NA)	32.1	24.2	23.4	43.9
1975	62.5	64.5	42.5	(NA)	37.9	31.0	28.7	51.7
1980	66.5	68.8	51.2	(NA)	44.0	37.6	40.1	55.3
1985	73.9	75.5	59.8	(NA)	47.9	41.9	46.3	51.1
1990	77.6	79.1	66.2	80.4	50.8	44.1	55.5	63.5
1992[4]	79.4	80.9	67.7	(NA)	52.6	45.2	60.5	62.0
1993[4]	80.2	81.5	70.4	(NA)	53.1	46.2	59.8	62.1
1994[4]	80.9	82.0	72.9	(NA)	53.3	46.7	59.4	64.1
COMPLETED 4 YEARS OF COLLEGE OR MORE								
1960	7.7	8.1	3.1	(NA)	(NA)	(NA)	(NA)	(NA)
1965	9.4	9.9	4.7	(NA)	(NA)	(NA)	(NA)	(NA)
1970	10.7	11.3	4.4	(NA)	4.5	2.5	2.2	11.1
1975	13.9	14.5	6.4	(NA)	(NA)	(NA)	(NA)	(NA)
1980	16.2	17.1	8.4	(NA)	7.6	4.9	5.6	16.2
1985	19.4	20.0	11.1	(NA)	8.5	5.5	7.0	13.7
1990	21.3	22.0	11.3	39.9	9.2	5.4	9.7	20.2
1992[4]	21.4	22.1	11.9	(NA)	9.3	6.1	8.4	18.4

[Continued]

★ 169 ★

Trends in High School and College Graduation (in percentages), by Race/Ethnic Origin: 1960-1994
[Continued]

YEAR	Total[1]	White	Black	Asian and Pacific Islander	HISPANIC[2]			
					Total[3]	Mexican	Puerto Rican	Cuban
1993[4]	21.9	22.6	12.2	(NA)	9.0	5.9	8.0	16.5
1994[4]	22.2	22.9	12.9	(NA)	9.1	6.3	9.7	16.2

Source: "Educational Attainment, by Race and Ethnicity: 1960 to 1994," *Statistical Abstract of the United States: 1995,* 1995, p. 157. Primary source: U.S. Bureau of the Census, *U.S. Census of Population, U.S. Summary.* PC80-1C1 and *Current Population Reports* P20-455, P20-459, P20-462, P20- 465RV, P20-475; and unpublished data. *Notes:* NA Not available. 1. Includes other races, not shown separately. 2. Persons of Hispanic origin may be of any race. 3. Includes persons of other Hispanic origin, not shown separately. 4. Beginning 1992, high school graduates and those with a BA degree or higher.

Elementary and Secondary

★ 170 ★

Achievement: College-Bound High School Graduates Meeting Criteria for College Admission, by Race/Ethnic Origin: 1992

	3.5+ GPA[1]	1100+ SAT[2]	4E+ 2FL[3]	Teacher Comments[4]	2 plus Activ[5]	Meet all 5 criteria
Total %	19.2	22.0	55.5	42.1	67.7	5.9
(se)	(0.92)	(1.35)	(1.76)	(1.33)	(1.34)	(0.38)
Race/Ethnicity						
Asian	29.3	27.7	59.5	48.7	68.0	8.8
	(3.70)	(3.18)	(4.29)	(4.02)	(3.79)	(1.49)
Hispanic	10.3	8.0	47.0	40.8	63.2	2.5
	(2.27)	(1.85)	(5.35)	(4.60)	(4.30)	(1.09)
Black	4.1	2.6	55.6	39.8	67.6	0.4
	(0.93)	(0.67)	(4.43)	(4.70)	(3.95)	(0.26)
White	20.9	25.0	56.1	42.1	68.1	6.5
	(1.09)	(1.61)	(1.99)	(1.54)	(1.58)	(0.44)
Amer. Indian/	5.3	2.2	23.6	25.7	57.5	0.0
Alaskan Native	(3.30)	(2.24)	(8.13)	(9.21)	(9.12)	(0.00)

Source: "Percentage of 1992 College-Bound High School Graduates Classified as Meeting Each of Five Specified Criteria Identified as Being Important to College Admissions Officers," U.S. Department of Education, National Center for Education Statistics, *Making the Cut: Who Meets Highly Selective College Entrance Criteria?,* April, 1995, p. 4. Primary source: National Education Longitudinal Study of 1988; Second Follow-up (1992), U.S. Department of Education, National Center for Education Statistics. *Notes:* 1. High School Grade Point Average (GPA) of 3.5 or higher. 2. SAT equivalent score of 1100 or higher. 3. Accumulated four credits in English, three in math, three in science, three in social studies, and two in a foreign language. 4. Positive teacher responses to series of questions regarding student. 5. Participated in two or more extra-curricular activities.

★ 171 ★

Elementary and Secondary

Achievement: Mathematics Proficiency Levels of 4th, 8th, and 12th Graders, by Race/Ethnic Origin: 1992

Race/ethnicity	Average proficiency	Percent of students at or above proficiency level		
		Advanced	Proficient	Basic
Grade Four				
Asian	231	5	30	76
Hispanic	201	0	6	37
Black	192	0	3	24
White	227	3	23	72
American Indian	209	2	10	46
Grade Eight				
Asian	288	14	44	80
Hispanic	246	1	8	39
Black	237	0	3	27
White	277	4	32	74
American Indian	254	0	9	47
Grade 12				
Asian	315	6	31	81
Hispanic	283	1	6	45
Black	275	0	3	34
White	305	2	19	72
American Indian	281	0	4	46

Source: "Average Mathematics Proficiency and Percent of Students At or Above Three Achievement Levels, by Grade and Race/Ethnicity," U.S. Department of Education, National Center for Education Statistics, *Understanding Racial- Ethnic Differences in Secondary School Science and Mathematics Achievement*, February, 1995, p. 62. Primary source: Mullis, Ina V. S., Dossey, J. A., Owen, E. H., & Phillips, G. W.(1993). *NAEP 1992 mathematics report card for the nation and the states*. Washington, DC: National Center for Education Statistics, U.S. Department of Education, p. 93.

★ 172 ★

Elementary and Secondary

Achievement: Trends in Mathematics Proficiency Test Scores of 9-, 13-, and 17-Year-Olds, by Race/Ethnic Origin: 1977-78 - 1991-92

[Based on The National Assessment of Educational Progress Tests, which are administered to a representative sample of students in public and private schools. Test scores can range from 0 to 500].

TEST AND YEAR	Total	RACE		Hispanic origin
		White[1]	Black[1]	
MATHEMATICS				
9 year olds:				
1977-78	219	224	192	203
1981-82	219	224	195	204
1985-86	222	227	202	205
1989-90	230	235	208	214
13 year olds:				
1977-78	264	272	230	238
1981-82	269	274	240	252
1985-86	269	274	249	254
1989-90	270	276	249	255
17 year olds:				
1977-78	300	306	268	276
1981-82	299	304	272	277
1985-86	302	308	279	283
1989-90	305	310	289	284
1991-92	307	312	286	292

Source: "Proficiency Test Scores for Selected Subjects, by Characteristic: 1977 to 1992," *Statistical Abstract of the United States: 1995,* 1995, p. 176. Primary source: U.S. National Center for Education Statistics, *NAEP Trends in Academic Progress,* Report No. 23-TR01, July 1994. *Note:* 1. Non-Hispanic.

★ 173 ★

Elementary and Secondary

Achievement: Trends in Reading Proficiency Test Scores of 9-, 13-, and 17-Year-Olds, by Race/Ethnic Origin: 1979-80 - 1991-92

[Based on The National Assessment of Educational Progress Tests, which are administered to a representative sample of students in public and private schools. Test scores can range from 0 to 500].

TEST AND YEAR	Total	RACE		Hispanic origin
		White[1]	Black[1]	
READING				
9 year olds:				
1979-80	215	221	189	190
1983-84	211	218	186	187
1987-88	212	218	189	194
1989-90	209	217	182	189
1991-92	211	218	185	192
13 year olds:				
1979-80	259	264	233	237
1983-84	257	263	236	240
1987-88	258	261	243	240
1989-90	257	262	242	238
1991-92	260	266	238	239
17 year olds:				
1979-80	286	293	243	264
1983-84	289	295	264	268
1987-88	290	295	274	271
1989-90	290	297	267	275
1991-92	290	297	261	271

Source: "Proficiency Test Scores for Selected Subjects, by Characteristic: 1977 to 1992," *Statistical Abstract of the United States: 1995,* 1995, p. 176. Primary source: U.S. National Center for Education Statistics, *NAEP Trends in Academic Progress,* Report No. 23-TR01, July 1994. *Note:* 1. Non-Hispanic.

★ 174 ★

Elementary and Secondary

Achievement: Trends in Science Proficiency Test Scores of 9-, 13-, and 17-Year-Olds, By Race/Ethnic Origin: 1976-77 - 1991-92

[Based on The National Assessment of Educational Progress Tests, which are administered to a representative sample of students in public and private schools. Test scores can range from 0 to 500].

TEST AND YEAR	Total	RACE		Hispanic origin
		White[1]	Black[1]	
SCIENCE				
9 year olds:				
1976-77	220	230	175	192
1981-82	221	229	187	189
1985-86	224	232	196	199
1989-90	229	238	196	206
13 year olds:				
1976-77	247	256	208	213
1981-82	250	257	217	226
1985-86	251	259	222	226
1989-90	255	264	226	232
1991-92	258	267	224	238
17 year olds:				
1976-77	290	298	240	262
1981-82	283	293	235	249
1985-86	289	298	253	259
1989-90	290	301	253	262
1991-92	294	304	256	270

Source: "Proficiency Test Scores for Selected Subjects, by Characteristic: 1977 to 1992," *Statistical Abstract of the United States: 1995*, 1995, p. 176. Primary source: U.S. National Center for Education Statistics, *NAEP Trends in Academic Progress.* Report No. 23-TR01, July 1994. *Note:* 1. Non-Hispanic.

★ 175 ★

Elementary and Secondary

Achievement: Trends in Writing Proficiency Test Scores of 4th, 8th, and 12th Graders, By Race/Ethnic Origin: 1983-84 - 1991-92

[Based on The National Assessment of Educational Progress Tests, which are administered to a representative sample of students in public and private schools. Test scores can range from 0 to 500].

TEST AND YEAR	Total	RACE		Hispanic origin
		White[1]	Black[1]	
WRITING[2]				
4th graders:				
1983-84	204	211	182	189
1987-88	206	215	173	190
1989-90	202	211	171	184
1991-92	207	217	175	189
8th graders:				
1983-84	267	272	247	247
1987-88	264	269	246	250
1989-90	257	262	239	246
1991-92	274	279	258	265
11th graders:				
1983-84	290	297	270	259
1987-88	291	296	275	274
1989-90	287	293	268	277
1991-92	287	294	263	274

Source: "Proficiency Test Scores for Selected Subjects, by Characteristic: 1977 to 1992," *Statistical Abstract of the United States: 1995,* 1995, p. 176. Primary source: U.S. National Center for Education Statistics, *NAEP Trends in Academic Progress.* Report No. 23-TR01, July 1994. *Notes:* 1. Non-Hispanic. 2. Writing scores revised from previous years, previous writing scores were recorded on a 0 to 400 rather than 0 to 500 scale.

★ 176 ★

Elementary and Secondary

Aspirations: Recommendations of College for High School Sophomores, by Source of Recommendation and Race of Student: 1990

	White	Black
Fathers	78	69
Mothers	84	77
Guidance counselors	65	66
Teachers	65	70

Source: "Percentage of 1990 High School Sophomores for Whom College was Recommended," *The Educational Progress of Black Students,* 1995, p. 13. Primary source: NCES, High School and Beyond and National Education Longitudinal Study of 1988.

★ 177 ★

Elementary and Secondary

Curriculum: Mathematics and Science Courses Taken by High School Graduates (in percentages), by Race: 1982 and 1992

Mathematics and science courses	1982		1992	
	White	Black	White	Black
Any mathematics	99.1	99.6	99.7	99.1
Remedial mathematics	27.0	54.4	14.6	30.9
Algebra II	40.5	26.2	59.2	40.9
Geometry	53.9	30.3	72.6	60.4
Trigonometry	13.8	6.3	22.5	13.0
Algebra II, geometry, and trigonometry	8.5	2.9	15.9	6.8
Calculus	5.0	1.4	10.7	6.9
Any science	97.7	98.6	99.5	100.0
Biology	80.1	75.3	93.5	92.2
AP/honors biology	7.5	4.5	6.5	3.2
Chemistry	34.7	22.5	58.0	45.9
AP/honors chemistry	2.9	1.6	4.2	2.3
Physics	15.3	6.8	25.9	17.6
AP/honors physics	0.9	0.8	2.9	1.4
Biology, chemistry, and physics	11.2	4.7	22.6	15.5

Source: "Percentage of High School Graduates Taking Selected Courses, *"The Educational Progress of Black Students,* 1995, p. 12. Primary source: NCES, 1987 and 1990 NAEP High School Transcript Studies, High School and Beyond Transcript Study, and National Education Longitudinal Study Transcripts, 1992.

★ 178 ★

Elementary and Secondary

Curriculum: Percent Distribution of 12th Graders Taking or Not Taking Algebra and Calculus, by Race/Ethnic Origin: 1992

Algebra course taking	Race/ethnicity			
	Asian	Hispanic	Black	White
Have not studied algebra	1	7	8	5
Only taken pre-algebra	4	9	8	5
Only taken algebra I	20	34	37	27
Taken algebra II but not beyond	45	40	38	45
Taken algebra III or pre-calculus	12	6	7	12
Taken calculus	17	4	3	5

Source: "Percent Distribution of Algebra Course Taking of the 1992 12th Graders, by Race/Ethnicity," U.S. Department of Education, National Center for Education Statistics, *Understanding Racial-Ethnic Differences in Secondary School Science and Mathematics Achievement*, February, 1995, p. 39. Primary source: U.S. Department of Education, National Center for Education Statistics, National Assessment of Educational Progress, "1992 Twelfth Grade Mathematics Assessment." *Note:* Details may not add up to 100 percent due to rounding.

★ 179 ★

Elementary and Secondary

Curriculum: Semesters of High School Mathematics Taken (in Percentages), by Grade and Race/Ethnic Origin: 1992

Number of semesters	Race/ethnicity				
	Asian	Hispanic	Black	White	American Indian
Zero to three	4	20	21	12	24
Four to five	15	19	27	18	22
Six to seven	17	30	19	26	26
Eight or more	64	30	32	44	28

Source: "Percent Distribution of the Number of Semesters of High School Mathematics Courses Taken in Grades 9 Through 12, by Race/Ethnicity," U.S. Department of Education, National Center for Education Statistics, *Understanding Racial-Ethnic Differences in Secondary School Science and Mathematics Achievement*," February, 1995, p. 39. Primary source: U.S. Department of Education, National Center for Education Statistics, National Assessment of Educational Progress, "1992 Twelfth Grade Mathematics Assessment." *Note:* Details may not add up to 100 due to rounding.

★ 180 ★

Elementary and Secondary

Dropouts: Status Dropout Rate and Family Income Among 16-24-Year-Olds, by Race/Ethnic Origin: 1992

	Total	Race/ethnicity[1]		
		White, non-Hispanic	Black, non-Hispanic	Hispanic
Total	11.0	7.7	13.7	29.4
Family income[2]				
Low income level	24.6	19.0	24.0	44.7
Middle income level	10.1	7.9	9.6	25.2
High income level	2.3	1.9	0.8	9.6

Source: "Status Dropout Rate for Youth Ages 16-24, by Income Level and Race/Ethnicity: 1992," *Drug Use Among Ethnic Minorities*, 1995, p.54. Primary source: Current Population Survey, U.S. Bureau of the Census, unpublished data, October 1992. *Notes:* 1. Not shown separately are non-Hispanics who are neither black nor white, but who are included in the total. 2. Family income in current residence. Low income is defined as the bottom 20 percent of all family incomes for 1992, middle income is defined as between 20 and 80 percent of all family incomes, and high income is defined as the top 20 percent of all family incomes.

★ 181 ★

Elementary and Secondary

Dropouts: Status Dropouts in Relation to Population, by Race/Ethnic Origin: 1993

Characteristics	Status dropout rate	Number of status dropouts (in thousands)	Population (in thousands)	Percent of all dropouts	Percent of population
Total	11.0	3,396	30,845	100.0	100.0
Race/ethnicity[1]					
White, non-Hispanic	7.9	1,707	21,499	50.3	69.7
Black, non-Hispanic	13.6	615	4,536	18.1	14.7
Hispanic	27.5	989	3,595	29.1	11.7

Source: "Rate, Number, and Distribution of Status Dropouts, by Sex, Race/Ethnicity, Family Income, Region, and Metropolitan Status: 1993," *Drug Use Among Ethnic Minorities*, 1995, p. 54. Primary source: Current Population Survey, U.S. Bureau of the Census, unpublished data, October 1993. *Notes:* Percentages may not sum to 100 percent due to rounding. 1. Not shown separately are non-Hispanics who are neither black nor white but who are included in the total.

★ 182 ★

Elementary and Secondary

Dropouts: Trends in Age Group of High School Dropouts, by Race/Ethnic Origin: 1970-1993

[As of **October. For persons 14 to 24 years old**].

AGE AND RACE	NUMBER OF DROPOUTS (1,000)					PERCENT OF POPULATION				
	1970	1980	1985	1990	1993	1970	1980	1985	1990	1993
Total dropouts[1,2]	4,670	5,212	4,456	3,854	3,472	12.2	12.0	10.6	10.1	9.2
16 to 17 years	617	709	505	418	326	8.0	8.8	7.0	6.3	4.8
18 to 21 years	2,138	2,578	2,095	1,921	1,658	16.4	15.8	14.1	13.4	12.6
22 to 24 years	1,770	1,798	1,724	1,458	1,412	18 7	15.2	14.1	13.8	12.9
White[2]	3,577	4,169	3,583	3,127	2,683	10.8	11.3	10.3	10.1	8.8
16 to 17 years	485	619	424	334	253	7.3	9.2	7.1	6.4	4.7
18 to 21 years	1,618	2,032	1,678	1,516	1,283	14.3	14.7	13.6	13.1	12.3
22 to 24 years	1,356	1,416	1,372	1,235	1,086	16.3	14.0	13.3	14.0	12.1
Black[2]	1,047	934	748	611	641	22.2	16.0	12.6	10.9	11.2
16 to 17 years	125	80	70	73	50	12.8	6.9	6.5	6.9	4.6
18 to 21 years	500	486	376	345	328	30.5	23.0	17.5	16.0	15.9
22 to 24 years	397	346	279	185	250	37.8	24.0	17.8	13.5	17.2
Hispanic[2,3]	(NA)	919	820	1,122	1,009	(NA)	29.5	23.3	26.8	22.9
16 to 17 years	(NA)	92	97	89	82	(NA)	16.6	14.6	12.9	9.9
18 to 21 years	(NA)	470	335	502	437	(NA)	40.3	29.3	32.9	28.6
22 to 24 years	(NA)	323	365	523	470	(NA)	40.6	33.9	42.8	37.8

Source: "High School Dropouts, by Age, Race, and Hispanic Origin: 1970 to 1993," *Statistical Abstract of the United States: 1995,* 1995, p. 174. Primary source: U.S. Bureau of the Census, *Current Population Reports,* P20-479; and earlier reports. *Notes:* NA Not available. 1. Includes other groups not shown separately. 2. Includes persons 14 to 15 years, not shown separately. 3. Persons of Hispanic origin may be of any race.

★ 183 ★

Elementary and Secondary

Dropouts: Trends in Event and Status Dropouts, by Gender and Race/Ethnic Origin: 1973-1993

[In percent. As of **October**].

ITEM	1973	1975	1980	1985	1986	1987[1]	1988	1989	1990	1991	1992	1993
EVENT DROPOUTS[2]												
Total[3]	6.3	5.8	6.0	5.2	4.3	4.1	4.8	4.5	4.0	4.0	4.3	4.2
White	5.7	5.4	5.6	4.8	4.2	3.7	4.7	3.9	3.8	3.7	4.1	4.1
Male	6.1	5.0	6.4	4.9	4.2	4.1	5.1	4.1	4.1	3.6	3.8	4.1
Female	5.3	5.8	4.9	4.7	4.1	3.4	4.3	3.8	3.5	3.8	4.4	4.1
Black	10.1	8.7	8.3	7.7	4.7	6.4	6.3	7.7	5.1	6.2	4.9	5.4

[Continued]

★ 183 ★

Dropouts: Trends in Event and Status Dropouts, by Gender and Race/Ethnic Origin: 1973-1993

[Continued]

ITEM	1973	1975	1980	1985	1986	1987[1]	1988	1989	1990	1991	1992	1993
Male	12.0	8.3	8.0	8.3	4.8	6.2	6.7	6.9	4.1	5.5	3.3	5.7
Female	8.4	9.0	8.5	7.2	4.6	6.4	6.0	8.6	6.0	7.0	6.7	5.0
Hispanic[4]	10.0	10.9	11.5	9.7	11.9	5.6	10.5	7.7	8.0	7.3	7.9	5.4
Male	7.9	10.1	16.9	9.3	11.7	5.0	12.3	7.6	8.7	10.4	5.8	5.7
Female	12.0	11.6	6.9	9.8	12.4	6.2	8.4	7.7	7.2	4.8	8.6	5.0
STATUS DROPOUTS[5]												
Total[3]	15.7	15.6	15.6	13.9	13.8	14.5	14.6	14.4	13.6	14.2	12.7	12.7
White	14.2	13.9	14.4	13.5	13.5	14.2	14.2	14.1	13.5	14.2	12.2	12.2
Male	13.8	13.5	15.7	14.7	14.6	15.1	15.4	15.4	14.2	15.4	13.3	13.0
Female	14.5	14.2	13.2	12.3	12.4	13.2	13.0	12.8	12.8	13.1	11.1	11.5
Black	26.5	27.3	23.5	17.6	16.6	17.0	17.7	16.4	15.1	15.6	16.3	16.4
Male	25.9	27.8	26.0	18.8	18.1	18.7	18.9	18.6	13.6	15.4	15.5	15.6
Female	27.1	26.9	21.5	16.6	15.8	15.4	16.6	14.5	16.2	15.8	17.1	17.2
Hispanic[4]	38.9	34.9	40.3	31.5	27.9	32.8	39.6	37.7	37.3	39.6	33.9	32.7
Male	36.5	32.6	42.6	35.8	37.4	34.5	40.2	40.3	39.8	44.4	38.4	34.7
Female	41.3	36.8	38.1	27.0	31.1	30.8	38.8	35.0	34.5	34.5	29.6	31.0

Source: "High School Dropouts, by Race, and Hispanic Origin: 1973 to 1993," *Statistical Abstract of the United States: 1995*, 1995, p. 173. Primary source: U.S. Bureau of the Census, *Current Population Reports*, P20-479. *Notes:* 1. Beginning 1987 reflects new editing procedures for cases with missing data on school enrollment. 2. Percent of students who dropout in a single year without completing high school. For grades 10 to 12. 3. Includes other races, not shown separately. 4. Persons of Hispanic origin may be of any race. 5. Percent of the population who have not completed high school and are not enrolled, regardless of when they dropped out. For persons 18 to 24 years old.

★ 184 ★

Elementary and Secondary

Employee Job Categories: Distribution of Job Levels in Public Schools, by Race: 1982 and 1992

[**In thousands.** Covers full-time employment. Excludes Hawaii. 1982 also excludes District of Columbia and New Jersey. 1982 based on sample survey of school districts with 250 or more students. 1992 based on sample survey of school districts with 100 or more employees].

OCCUPATION	1982			1992		
	Total	White[1]	Black[1]	Total	White[1]	Black[1]
All occupations	3,082	2,498	432	3,376	2,643	494
Officials, administrators	41	36	3	44	37	5
Principals and assistant principals	90	76	11	93	74	14
Classroom teachers[2]	1,680	1,435	186	1,862	1,565	202
Elementary schools	798	667	98	930	770	108
Secondary schools	706	619	67	693	598	67

[Continued]

★ 184 ★

Employee Job Categories: Distribution of Job Levels in Public Schools, by Race: 1982 and 1992

[Continued]

OCCUPATION	1982			1992		
	Total	White[1]	Black[1]	Total	White[1]	Black[1]
Other professional staff	235	193	35	242	199	31
Teachers aides[3]	215	146	45	351	223	76
Clinical, secretarial staff	210	177	19	236	187	27
Service workers[4]	611	434	132	547	360	138

Source: "Public School Employment: 1982 and 1992," *Statistical Abstract of the United States: 1995*, 1995, p. 166. Primary source: U.S. Equal Employment Opportunity Commission, *Elementary Secondary Staff Information (EEO-5)*, biennial. *Notes:* 1. Excludes individuals of Hispanic origin. 2. Includes other classroom teachers, not shown separately. 3. Includes technicians. 4. Includes craftworkers and laborers.

★ 185 ★

Elementary and Secondary

Employee Job Categories: Participation Rates of White and Minority Employees in U.S. Elementary and Secondary School Districts: 1975-76 and 1992-93

Job Category	School Year	Whites	Total	Blacks	Hispanics	Asians, Pacific Islanders	American Indians, Alaskan Natives
Officials and Administrators	1975-76	92.2	7.8	5.5	1.8	0.2	0.4
	1992-93	84.4	15.6	10.2	4.2	0.8	0.4
Principals	1975-76	90.2	9.7	8.0	1.3	0.1	0.3
	1992-93	81.2	18.8	13.4	4.3	0.6	0.4
Assistant Principals	1975-76	82.4	17.7	15.0	2.0	0.4	0.3
	1992-93	76.2	23.8	17.4	5.5	0.6	0.3
Elementary Classroom Teachers	1975-76	86.2	13.9	11.3	1.7	0.6	0.3
	1992-93	83.4	16.6	11.0	4.4	0.9	0.3
Secondary Classroom Teachers	1975-76	89.6	10.4	8.3	1.5	0.4	0.2
	1992-93	86.6	13.4	9.4	3.2	0.6	0.2

Source: "Full-Time Employment Participation Rates of Minorities and Women in Elementary and Secondary School Districts, U.S. Summary, 1975-76 and 1992- 93 Academic Years," *Indicators of Equal Employment Opportunity—Status and Trends*, September, 1993, p. 30. Primary source: Equal Opportunity Commission, Elementary-Secondary Staff Information (EEO-5) Reports.

★ 186 ★
Elementary and Secondary

Enrollment: State-by-State Public Elementary and Secondary Enrollment, by Race/Ethnicity: Alabama-Mississippi, Fall 1986 and Fall 1992

State or other area	Percent distribution, fall 1986						Percent distribution, fall 1992					
	Total	White[1]	Black[1]	Hispanic	Asian or Pacific Islander	American Indian/ Alaskan Native	Total	White[1]	Black[1]	Hispanic	Asian or Pacific Islander	American Indian/ Alaskan Native
United States	100.0	70.4	16.1	9.9	2.8	0.9	100.0	66.7[2]	16.5[2]	12.3[2]	3.5[2]	1.0[2]
Alabama	100.0	62.0	37.0	0.1	0.4	0.5	100.0	62.7	35.6	0.3	0.6	0.8
Alaska	100.0	65.7	4.3	1.7	3.3	25.1	100.0	66.1	4.7	2.3	4.0	23.0
Arizona	100.0	62.2	4.0	26.4	1.3	6.1	100.0	60.4	4.1	26.9	1.6	7.0
Arkansas	100.0	74.7	24.2	0.4	0.6	0.2	100.0	74.4	23.9	0.7	0.7	0.3
California	100.0	53.7	9.0	27.5	9.1	0.7	100.0	43.4	8.6	36.1	11.0	0.8
Colorado	100.0	78.7	4.5	13.7	2.0	1.0	100.0	74.5	5.4	16.8	2.4	1.0
Connecticut	100.0	77.2	12.1	8.9	1.5	0.2	100.0	73.8	12.9	10.7	2.3	0.2
Delaware	100.0	68.3	27.7	2.5	1.4	0.2	100.0	66.8	28.1	3.2	1.7	0.2
District of Columbia	100.0	4.0	91.1	3.9	0.9	0.1	100.0	4.0	89.1	5.6	1.3	[3]
Florida	100.0	65.4	23.7	9.5	1.2	0.2	100.0	60.3	24.4	13.4	1.6	0.2
Georgia	100.0	60.7	37.9	0.6	0.8	[3]	-	-	-	-	-	-
Hawaii	100.0	23.5	2.3	2.2	71.7	0.3	100.0	23.8	2.7	5.2	68.0	0.3
Idaho	100.0	92.6	0.3	4.9	0.8	1.3	-	-	-	-	-	-
Illinois	100.0	69.8	18.7	9.2	2.3	0.1	100.0	65.1	21.2	10.7	2.8	0.1
Indiana	100.0	88.7	9.0	1.7	0.5	0.1	100.0	86.2	11.0	1.9	0.7	0.1
Iowa	100.0	94.6	3.0	0.9	1.2	0.3	100.0	93.8	2.9	1.5	1.4	0.4
Kansas	100.0	85.6	7.6	4.4	1.9	0.6	100.0	84.1	8.2	5.0	1.8	0.9
Kentucky	100.0	89.2	10.2	0.1	0.5	[3]	99.9	89.7	9.5	0.2	0.5	[3]
Louisiana	100.0	56.5	41.3	0.8	1.1	0.3	100.0	52.2	45.1	1.0	1.2	0.4
Maine	100.0	98.3	0.5	0.2	0.8	0.2	-	-	-	-	-	-
Maryland	100.0	59.7	35.3	1.7	3.1	0.2	100.0	59.8	33.6	2.7	3.7	0.3
Massachusetts	100.0	83.7	7.4	6.0	2.8	0.1	100.0	79.8	8.0	8.5	3.6	0.2
Michigan	100.0	76.4	19.8	1.8	1.2	0.8	100.0	77.8	17.4	2.4	1.3	1.0
Minnesota	100.0	93.9	2.1	0.9	1.7	1.5	100.0	89.8	3.7	1.5	3.2	1.8
Mississippi	100.0	43.9	55.5	0.1	0.4	0.1	100.0	48.3	50.6	0.2	0.5	0.4

Source: "Enrollment in Public Elementary and Secondary Schools, by Race or Ethnicity and State: Fall 1986 and Fall 1992," Department of Education, National Center for Education Statistics, *State Comparisons of Education Statistics: 1969-70 to 1993-94*, p. 31. Primary source: U.S. Department of Education, Office for Civil Rights, 1986 State Summaries of Elementary and Secondary School Civil Rights Survey; and National Center for Education Statistics, Common Core of Data Survey. (This table was prepared May 1994). *Notes:* - Data not available. 1. Excludes persons of Hispanic origin. 2. Includes estimates for nonresponding states. 3. Less than 0.05 percent.

★ 187 ★

Elementary and Secondary

Enrollment: State-by-State Public Elementary and Secondary Enrollment, by Race/Ethnicity: Missouri-Wyoming, Fall 1986 and Fall 1992

State or other area	Percent distribution, fall 1986						Percent distribution, fall 1992					
	Total	White[1]	Black[1]	Hispanic	Asian or Pacific Islander	American Indian/ Alaskan Native	Total	White[1]	Black[1]	Hispanic	Asian or Pacific Islander	American Indian/ Alaskan Native
Missouri	100.0	83.4	14.9	0.7	0.8	0.2	100.0	82.6	15.5	0.8	0.9	0.2
Montana	100.0	92.7	0.3	0.9	0.5	5.5	100.0	88.0	0.5	1.4	0.7	9.4
Nebraska	100.0	91.4	4.4	2.4	0.8	1.0	100.0	88.9	5.5	3.2	1.1	1.2
Nevada	100.0	77.4	9.6	7.5	3.2	2.3	100.0	72.0	9.1	13.1	3.9	1.9
New Hampshire	100.0	98.0	0.7	0.5	0.8	0.1	100.0	97.0	0.8	1.0	1.0	0.2
New Jersey	100.0	69.1	17.4	10.7	2.7	0.1	100.0	63.7	18.7	12.6	4.9	0.1
New Mexico	100.0	43.1	2.3	45.1	0.8	8.7	100.0	40.9	2.3	45.8	0.9	10.2
New York	100.0	68.4	16.5	12.3	2.7	0.2	100.0	58.9	20.0	16.1	4.6	0.3
North Carolina	100.0	68.4	28.9	0.4	0.6	1.7	100.0	66.1	30.2	1.1	1.0	1.6
North Dakota	100.0	92.4	0.6	1.1	0.8	5.0	100.0	90.8	0.7	0.7	0.7	7.1
Ohio	100.0	83.1	15.0	1.0	0.7	0.1	100.0	83.0	14.6	1.3	1.0	0.1
Oklahoma	100.0	79.0	7.8	1.6	1.0	10.6	100.0	72.6	10.2	3.1	1.2	13.0
Oregon	100.0	89.8	2.2	3.9	2.4	1.7	100.0	87.5	2.4	5.3	3.0	1.8
Pennsylvania	100.0	84.4	12.6	1.8	1.2	0.1	100.0	81.7	13.5	3.1	1.7	0.1
Rhode Island	100.0	87.9	5.6	3.7	2.4	0.3	100.0	82.0	6.6	8.0	3.1	0.4
South Carolina	100.0	54.6	44.5	0.2	0.6	0.1	100.0	57.3	41.4	0.5	0.6	0.2
South Dakota	100.0	90.6	0.5	0.6	0.7	7.6	100.0	86.3	0.7	0.5	0.7	11.9
Tennessee	100.0	76.5	22.6	0.2	0.6	[3]	100.0	75.8	22.9	0.4	0.8	0.1
Texas	100.0	51.0	14.4	32.5	2.0	0.2	100.0	48.4	14.3	34.9	2.2	0.2
Utah	100.0	93.7	0.4	3.0	1.5	1.5	100.0	91.7	0.6	4.3	2.0	1.4
Vermont	100.0	98.4	0.3	0.2	0.6	0.6	100.0	97.7	0.6	0.3	0.6	0.8
Virginia	100.0	72.6	23.7	1.0	2.6	0.1	100.0	68.5	25.5	2.5	3.3	0.2
Washington	100.0	84.5	4.2	3.8	5.1	2.3	100.0	80.7	4.4	6.4	6.0	2.5
West Virginia	100.0	95.9	3.7	0.1	0.3	[3]	100.0	95.4	4.0	0.2	0.4	0.1
Wisconsin	100.0	86.6	8.9	1.9	1.7	1.0	100.0	84.8	8.9	2.8	2.2	1.3
Wyoming	100.0	90.7	0.9	5.9	0.6	1.9	100.0	89.6	0.9	6.1	0.7	2.6

Source: "Enrollment in Public Elementary and Secondary Schools, by Race or Ethnicity and State: Fall 1986 and Fall 1992," Department of Education, National Center for Education Statistics, *State Comparisons of Education Statistics: 1969-70 to 1993-94*, p. 31. Primary source: U.S. Department of Education, Office for Civil Rights, 1986 State Summaries of Elementary and Secondary School Civil Rights Survey; and National Center for Education Statistics, Common Core of Data Survey. (This table was prepared May 1994). *Notes:* - Data not available. 1. Excludes persons of Hispanic origin. 2. Includes estimates for nonresponding states. 3. Less than 0.05 percent.

★ 188 ★

Elementary and Secondary

High School Graduates: Rate and Method of High School Completion Among 21- and 22-Year-Olds, by Race/Ethnic Origin (in percentages): 1990-1993

Completion method	1990	1991	1992[2]	1993[2]
Total				
Completed	86.1	85.7	86.0	85.9
Diploma	81.0	81.4	80.5	80.8
Alternative	5.2	4.3	5.5	5.0
White, non-Hispanic				
Completed	90.5	90.2	90.2	89.8
Diploma	85.6	85.8	85.1	84.8
Alternative	4.9	4.3	5.1	5.0
Black, non-Hispanic				
Completed	83.3	81.2	81.0	83.8
Diploma	77.8	75.9	73.6	78.3
Alternative	5.5	5.3	7.4	5.5
Hispanic				
Completed	61.1	61.1	62.6	63.0
Diploma	56.1	57.9	56.4	57.6
Alternative	5.0	3.2	6.2	5.4

Source: "High School Completion Rates and Method of Completion for Youth Ages 21-22, by Race/Ethnicity: October 1990, 1991, 1992, and 1993 (in percentages)" *Drug Use Among Ethnic Minorities,* 1995, p. 57. Primary source: Current Population Survey, U.S. Bureau of the Census, unpublished data, October (various years). *Notes:* 1. Not shown separately are non-Hispanics who are neither black nor white but who are included in the total. 2. Numbers for these years reflect new wording of the educational attainment item in the Current Population Survey.

★ 189 ★

Elementary and Secondary

School Choice: Attendance at Chosen or Assigned School for Students in Grades 3-12, by Race/Ethnic Origin: 1993

	Total Number of Students	Percent Distribution:		
		Public, Assigned	Public, Chosen	Private
Total students	59,004,955	81%	11	8
Race/Ethnicity				
White	41,039,023	82%	8	10

[Continued]

★ 189 ★

School Choice: Attendance at Chosen or Assigned School for Students in Grades 3-12, by Race/Ethnic Origin: 1993

[Continued]

	Total Number of Students	Percent Distribution:		
		Public, Assigned	Public, Chosen	Private
Black	9,332,499	76%	20	4
Hispanic	6,557,854	80%	14	6

Source: "Students in Grades 3-12 Attending a Chosen or Assigned School by Family Characteristics," *Use of School Choice*, National Center for Educational Statistics, May, 1995, [no p. No.].

★ 190 ★

Elementary and Secondary

Segregation/Integration: Percent of Black Students Attending White-Majority Schools, in the Most and Least Integrated States: c. 1995

State	The 10 most integrated states- percent of blacks attending white- majority schools	State	The 10 most segregated states- percent of blacks attending white- majority schools
Kentucky	96	New York	15
Delaware	92	California	20
Nevada	77	Illinois	20
Nebraska	69	Michigan	20
Kansas	64	Mississippi	26
Oklahoma	58	New Jersey	27
North Carolina	56	Maryland	28
Virginia	54	Wisconsin	30
Indiana	53	Pennsylvania	31
Colorado	52	Louisiana	32

Primary source: Harvard Project on School Desegregation. Adapted by the editors from "The Tide Turns," *Time*, April 29, 1996, pp. 42-43. Published by permission.

★ 191 ★

Elementary and Secondary

Teachers: Teaching Experience and Salary of Private School Elementary and Secondary Teachers, by Race/ Ethnic Origin: 1990-91

[For school year. Based on survey and subject to sampling error].

CHARACTERISTIC	Unit	RACE/ETHNICITY		
		White[1]	Black[1]	Hispanic
Total teachers[2]	1,000	329	9	12
Highest degree held:				
Bachelor's	Percent	61.8	72.8	60.6
Master's	Percent	27.3	21.7	22.1
Education specialist	Percent	3.0	1.0	1.7
Doctorate	Percent	1.8	0.9	2.7
Full-time teaching experience:				
Less than 3 years	Percent	27.2	28.9	32.4
3 to 9 years	Percent	36.6	43.0	33.0
10 to 20 years	Percent	25.1	22.5	22.8
20 years or more	Percent	11.1	5.6	11.9
Full-time teachers	1,000	278	9	9
Earned income	Dol.	21,568	23,094	22,912
Salary	Dol.	19,709	20,333	20,740

Source: "Private Elementary and Secondary School Teachers—Selected Characteristics," *Statistical Abstract of the United States: 1995*, 1995, p. 172. Primary source: U.S. National Center for Education Statistics, *Digest of Education Statistics*, 1994. *Notes:* 1. Non-Hispanic. 2. Includes teachers with no degrees and associates degrees, not shown separately.

Higher Education

★ 192 ★

Colleges and Universities: Number Colleges and Enrollment, by State and Race/Ethnic Origin, Part I-Alabama-Mississippi: 1992

[Number of institutions beginning in academic year. Opening fall enrollment of resident and extension students attending full-time or part- time. Excludes students taking courses for credit by mail, radio, or TV and students in branches of U.S. institutions operated in foreign countries.]

STATE	Number of insti- tutions[1]	ENROLLMENT, PREL. (1,000)					
		Total	White[2]	Minority enrollment			Non- resident alien
				Total[3]	Black[2]	Hispanic	
United States	3,638	14,491	10,870	3,164	1,393	954	456
Alabama	86	231	172	54	49	1	5
Alaska	8	31	25	6	1	1	1
Arizona	40	276	209	59	9	34	8
Arkansas	34	97	80	16	14	1	2
California	322	1,977	1,115	764	140	315	96
Colorado	59	240	198	37	8	20	5
Connecticut	47	166	138	23	11	6	5
Delaware	10	43	35	7	5	1	1
District of Columbia	18	82	41	32	25	3	9
Florida	105	618	436	166	73	75	17
Georgia	115	293	211	76	65	4	6
Hawaii	17	61	17	39	1	1	5
Idaho	11	58	53	3	(Z)	1	2
Illinois	169	748	543	187	94	55	18
Indiana	78	297	260	28	17	5	8
Iowa	61	178	158	11	5	3	8
Kansas	49	169	146	17	8	4	6
Kentucky	62	188	170	15	12	1	3
Louisiana	33	204	140	59	50	4	5
Maine	31	58	55	3	1	(Z)	1
Maryland	56	268	189	71	52	5	9
Massachusetts	117	423	343	58	20	15	23
Michigan	102	560	461	83	57	10	15
Minnesota	99	273	249	18	6	3	6
Mississippi	46	124	85	36	34	(Z)	2

Source: "Colleges-Number and Enrollment, by State," *Statistical Abstract of the United States: 1995,* 1992, p. 182. Primary source: U.S. National Center for Education Statistics, *Digest of Education Statistics,* annual. *Notes:* Z Fewer than 500. 1. Branch campuses counted as separate institutions. 2. Non-Hispanic. 3. Includes other races not shown separately.

★ 193 ★

Higher Education

Colleges and Universities: Number Colleges and Enrollment, by State and Race/Ethnic Origin, Part II-Missouri-Wyoming: 1992

[Number of institutions beginning in academic year. Opening fall enrollment of resident and extension students attending full-time or part-time. Excludes students taking course for credit by mail, radio, or TV and students in branches of U.S. institutions operated in foreign countries].

STATE	Number of insti-tutions[1]	ENROLLMENT, PREL. (1,000)					Non-resident alien
		Total	White[2]	Minority enrollment			
				Total[3]	Black[2]	Hispanic	
United States	3,638	14,491	10,870	3,164	1,393	954	486
Missouri	96	297	253	36	25	4	8
Montana	19	40	34	5	(Z)	(Z)	1
Nebraska	37	123	111	9	4	2	3
Nevada	9	64	51	12	3	4	1
New Hampshire	29	64	60	3	1	1	1
New Jersey	62	342	247	82	38	26	13
New Mexico	31	99	59	39	3	29	2
New York	320	1,070	754	277	129	88	39
North Carolina	122	383	292	85	72	4	6
North Dakota	20	40	36	3	(Z)	(Z)	2
Ohio	165	573	490	67	50	7	16
Oklahoma	46	182	144	31	13	3	7
Oregon	45	167	144	17	3	4	6
Pennsylvania	220	630	537	77	46	11	17
Rhode Island	12	79	69	8	3	2	3
South Carolina	60	171	128	40	36	1	3
South Dakota	19	38	34	3	(Z)	(Z)	1
Tennessee	78	243	198	41	35	2	4
Texas	176	939	617	295	89	169	27
Utah	16	133	120	7	1	3	6
Vermont	22	37	35	1	(Z)	(Z)	1
Virginia	86	354	274	74	53	6	6
Washington	62	276	230	40	9	8	6
West Virginia	28	90	84	5	3	-	2
Wisconsin	64	308	275	26	12	6	7
Wyoming	9	32	29	2	(Z)	1	1
U.S. military[4]	10	53	40	11	5	4	1

Source: "Colleges-Number and Enrollment, by State," *Statistical Abstract of the United States: 1995*, 1992, p. 182. Primary source: U.S. National Center for Education Statistics, *Digest of Education Statistics*, annual. *Notes:* - Represents zero. Z Fewer than 500. 1. Branch campuses counted as separate institutions. 2. Non-Hispanic. 3. Includes other races not shown separately. 4. Service schools.

★ 194 ★

Higher Education

Colleges and Universities: Percentage Distribution of Undergraduate Enrollment in Less than 2-, 2-, and 4-Year Institutions, by Race/Ethnic Origin: 1989-90

	Less-than 2-year	2-year	4-year
Total	7.5	45.5	46.9
Race/ethnicity			
American Indian/Alaskan Native	9.3	57.2	33.3
Asian/Pacific Islander	4.1	49.2	46.5
Black, non-Hispanic	17.0	45.1	37.8
Hispanic	15.2	47.3	37.3
White, non-Hispanic	5.5	45.0	49.3
Racial-ethnic subgroup Asian			
Asian Indian	1.3	39.0	59.6
Chinese	1.8	44.3	53.7
Japanese	0.6	51.5	47.7
Korean	1.4	38.4	60.1
Pacific Islander	3.0	61.4	35.4
Vietnamese	1.3	53.9	44.7
Other or nonspecified	8.1	48.5	43.3
Racial-ethnic subgroup Hispanic			
Cuban	2.5	49.1	48.2
Mexican	7.4	65.5	26.9
Puerto Rican	10.8	23.8	65.3
Other or nonspecified	21.4	39.0	39.4

Source: "Percentage Distribution of Undergraduate Enrollment According to Highest Level of Institutional Offering, and by Race—Ethnicity: 1989-90," U.S. Department of Education, National Center for Education Statistics, *Minority Undergraduate Participation in Postsecondary Education,* June, 1995, p. 18. Primary source: U.S. Department of Education, National Center for Education Statistics, 1989-90 National Postsecondary Student Aid Study (NPSAS: 90), Undergraduate Data Analysis System. *Note:* Percentages may not sum to 100 due to rounding.

★ 195 ★

Higher Education

Colleges and Universities: Percentage Distribution of Undergraduate Enrollment in Public and Private Institutions, by Race/Ethnic Origin: 1989- 90

	Public	Private, not-for-profit	Private, for-profit
Total	75.6	15.7	8.5
Race-ethnicity			
American Indian/Alaskan Native	78.3	10.3	11.2

[Continued]

★ 195 ★

Colleges and Universities: Percentage Distribution of Undergraduate Enrollment in Public and Private Institutions, by Race/Ethnic Origin: 1989- 90

[Continued]

	Public	Private, not-for-profit	Private, for-profit
Asian/Pacific Islander	81.2	13.4	5.3
Black, non-Hispanic	68.1	12.0	19.8
Hispanic	68.1	16.5	15.3
White, non-Hispanic	77.1	16.4	6.4
Racial-ethnic subgroup Asian			
Asian Indian	76.3	21.3	2.3
Chinese	82.6	14.4	2.9
Japanese	88.7	9.6	1.5
Korean	77.4	20.6	1.9
Pacific Islander	86.1	8.9	4.8
Vietnamese	86.5	11.8	1.6
Other or nonspecified	76.8	13.6	9.5
Racial-ethnic subgroup Hispanic			
Cuban	77.7	16.1	6.1
Mexican	85.7	5.5	8.7
Puerto Rican	55.2	30.5	14.2
Other or nonspecified	58.4	21.5	20.0

Source: "Percentage Distribution of Undergraduate Enrollment According to Control of Institution, by Race-Ethnicity: 1989-90," U.S. Department of Education, National Center for Education Statistics, *Minority Undergraduate Participation in Postsecondary Education*, June, 1995, p. 17. Primary source: U.S. Department of Education, National Center for Education Statistics, 1989-90 National Postsecondary Student Aid Study (NPSAS:90), Undergraduate Data Analysis System. *Note:* Percentages may not sum to 100 due to rounding.

★ 196 ★

Higher Education

Colleges and Universities: Trends in Enrollment in 2-Year Institutions, by Race/Ethnic Origin: 1980-1992

	1980	1982	1984	1986	1988	1990	1992
Total	100.0	100.0	100.0	100.0	100.0	100.0	100.0
American Indian/ Alaskan Native	1.0	1.0	1.0	1.1	1.0	1.0	1.1
Asian/Pacific Islander	2.7	3.3	3.7	4.0	4.1	4.1	5.0
Black, non-Hispanic	10.4	10.3	10.1	10.0	9.7	9.8	10.5
Hispanic	5.6	6.1	6.4	7.3	7.9	8.0	9.5

[Continued]

★ 196 ★

Colleges and Universities: Trends in Enrollment in 2-Year Institutions, by Race/Ethnic Origin: 1980-1992

[Continued]

	1980	1982	1984	1986	1988	1990	1992
White, non-Hispanic	78.7	77.9	77.6	76.6	76.0	75.6	72.0
Nonresident alien	1.4	1.3	1.2	1.1	1.2	1.4	1.7

Source: "Percentage Distribution of Students Enrolled in 2-Year Institutions of Higher Education by Race-Ethnicity: Fall 1980-1992,"U.S. Department of Education, National Center for Education Statistics, *Minority Undergraduate Participation in Postsecondary Education*, June, 1995, p. 7. Primary source: U.S. Department of Education, National Center for Education Statistics, *Trends in Racial/ Ethnic Enrollment in Higher Education: Fall 1980 through Fall 1990* (NCES 92-024) and *Trends in Enrollment in Higher Education by Racial/Ethnic Category: Fall 1982 through Fall 1992* (NCES 94-104); based on Integrated Postsecondary Education Data System (IPEDS) "Fall Enrollment" surveys. *Note:* Percentages may not sum to 100 because of rounding.

★ 197 ★

Higher Education

Colleges and Universities: Trends in Enrollment in 4-Year Institutions, by Race/Ethnic Origin: 1980-1992

	1980	1982	1984	1986	1988	1990	1992
Total	100.0	100.0	100.0	100.0	100.0	100.0	100.0
American Indian/ Alaskan Native	0.5	0.5	0.5	0.5	0.5	0.6	0.6
Asian/Pacific Islander	2.1	2.5	2.9	3.3	3.6	4.0	4.7
Black, non-Hispanic	8.4	8.0	8.0	7.9	8.0	8.4	9.0
Hispanic	2.9	3.0	3.2	3.6	3.6	4.0	4.7
White, non-Hispanic	82.9	82.5	81.7	81.0	80.5	79.2	77.0
Nonresident alien	3.2	3.5	3.7	3.7	3.7	3.8	4.1

Source: "Percentage Distribution of Students Enrolled in 4-Year Institutions of Higher Education by Race-Ethnicity: Fall 1980-1992,"U.S. Department of Education, National Center for Education Statistics, *Minority Undergraduate Participation in Postsecondary Education*, June, 1995, p. 6. Primary source: U.S. Department of Education, National Center for Education Statistics, *Trends in Racial/ Ethnic Enrollment in Higher Education: Fall 1980 through Fall 1990* (NCES 92-024) and *Trends in Enrollment in Higher Education by Racial/Ethnic Category: Fall 1982 through Fall 1992* (NCES 94-104); based on Integrated Postsecondary Education Data System (IPEDS) "Fall Enrollment" surveys. *Note:* Percentages may not sum to 100 because of rounding.

★ 198 ★

Higher Education

Degrees: Percentage Distribution of Doctorates Conferred, by Field (1993) and Race/Ethnic Origin: 1980 and 1993

[In percent, except as indicated].

CHARACTERISTIC	1980, total	1993									
		All fields[1]	Engineering	Physical sciences[2]	Earth sciences	Math-ematics	Computer sciences	Biological sciences[3]	Agricultural	Social sciences[4]	Psychology
Total conferred (number)	31,020	39,754	5,696	3,682	790	1,146	878	5,090	969	3,514	3,419
RACE/ETHNICITY[5]											
Total conferred (number)	26,512	28,636	2,691	1,199	516	590	498	3,747	506	2,215	3,606
White[6]	84.7	83.8	75.1	65.2	89.9	80.7	80.3	83.9	86.4	85.0	77.6
Black[6]	4.2	4.5	1.9	3.3	1.0	1.4	1.2	2.0	3.2	6.0	3.3
Asian/Pacific[6]	4.2	7.0	19.5	21.9	4.5	13.4	15.5	9.8	5.7	3.3	14.6
Indian/Alaskan[6]	0.3	0.4	0.1	0.4	0.8	0.2	0.2	0.2	0.2	0.2	0.4
Hispanic	1.8	3.4	2.4	6.8	2.5	2.7	1.4	3.0	4.0	4.0	3.6
Other/Unknown	4.9	0.9	1.0	2.3	1.4	1.7	1.4	1.1	0.6	1.4	0.4

Source: "Doctorates Conferred, by Recipients' Characteristics," *Statistical Abstract of the United States: 1995*, 1995, p. 182. Primary source: U.S. National Science Foundation, Division of Science Resources Studies, Survey of Earned Doctorates, *Selected Data on Science and Engineering Doctorate Awards: 1993*, annual. *Notes:* 1. Includes other fields, not shown separately. 2. Astronomy, physics, and chemistry. 3. Biochemistry, botany, microbiology, physiology, zoology, and related fields. 4. Anthropology; sociology, political science, economics, international relations, and related fields. 5. Excludes those with temporary visas. 6. Non-Hispanic.

★ 199 ★

Higher Education

Degrees: State-by-State Distribution of Associate Degrees Awarded, by Race/Ethnic Group: Alabama-Mississippi, 1992-93

State or other area	Total	Total resident	Percentage distribution of resident degrees by race/ethnicity[1]							Total, non-resident alien
			Total	White non-Hispanic	Total, minority	Black non-Hispanic	Hispanic	American Indian/ Alaskan Native	Asian Pacific Islander	
United States	100.0	98.2	100.0	81.3	18.7	8.5	6.0	0.9	3.3	1.8
Alabama	100.0	99.8	100.0	79.8	20.2	18.2	0.4	0.3	1.2	0.2
Alaska	100.0	97.8	100.0	81.1	18.9	5.3	2.7	9.6	1.2	2.2
Arizona	100.0	99.1	100.0	75.4	24.6	3.5	13.6	5.4	2.1	0.9
Arkansas	100.0	99.8	100.0	87.1	12.9	10.7	0.5	0.5	1.2	0.2
California	100.0	94.2	100.0	63.7	36.3	7.2	15.9	1.2	12.1	5.8
Colorado	100.0	97.7	100.0	82.0	18.0	5.2	10.2	1.1	1.4	2.3
Connecticut	100.0	99.5	100.0	88.1	11.9	6.9	3.5	0.1	1.4	0.5
Delaware	100.0	99.7	100.0	87.9	12.1	8.9	1.0	0.2	1.9	0.3
District of Columbia	100.0	98.1	100.0	20.6	79.4	68.7	5.1	0.0	5.6	1.9
Florida	100.0	97.4	100.0	77.4	22.6	8.5	11.5	0.4	2.2	2.6

[Continued]

Degrees: State-by-State Distribution of Associate Degrees Awarded, by Race/Ethnic Group: Alabama-Mississippi, 1992-93

[Continued]

State or other area	Total	Total resident	Percentage distribution of resident degrees by race/ethnicity[1]							Total, non-resident alien
			Total	White non-Hispanic	Total, minority	Black non-Hispanic	Hispanic	American Indian/ Alaskan Native	Asian Pacific Islander	
Georgia	100.0	98.8	100.0	80.4	19.6	17.3	1.0	0.2	1.1	1.2
Hawaii	100.0	98.6	100.0	34.0	66.0	4.1	2.9	0.4	58.6	1.4
Idaho	100.0	96.8	100.0	96.7	3.3	0.4	1.1	0.7	1.2	3.2
Illinois	100.0	99.6	100.0	81.9	18.1	10.5	4.9	0.3	2.5	0.4
Indiana	100.0	99.2	100.0	92.5	7.5	5.1	1.5	0.3	0.6	0.8
Iowa	100.0	98.8	100.0	96.1	3.9	1.5	0.5	0.3	1.5	1.2
Kansas	100.0	98.8	100.0	86.4	13.6	7.3	3.0	1.9	1.5	1.2
Kentucky	100.0	99.6	100.0	93.8	6.2	4.9	0.4	0.2	0.7	0.4
Louisiana	100.0	100.0	100.0	75.5	24.5	20.0	2.8	0.5	1.3	0.0
Maine	100.0	99.2	100.0	97.7	2.3	0.2	0.5	0.9	0.6	0.8
Maryland	100.0	98.7	100.0	80.0	20.0	14.9	1.8	0.6	2.7	1.3
Massachusetts	100.0	98.0	100.0	87.4	12.6	6.0	3.3	0.4	2.9	2.0
Michigan	100.0	99.1	100.0	88.3	11.7	8.6	1.3	0.7	1.1	0.9
Minnesota	100.0	99.1	100.0	94.9	5.1	1.7	1.1	1.2	1.2	0.9
Mississippi	100.0	99.7	100.0	76.7	23.3	22.1	0.3	0.6	0.3	0.3

Source: "Percentage Distribution of Associate Degrees Conferred by Institutions of Higher Education, by Race/Ethnicity and State: 1992-93," Department of Education, National Center for Education Statistics, *State Comparisons of Education Statistics: 1969-70 to 1993-94,* p. 153. Primary source: U.S. Department of Education, National Center for Education Statistics Integrated Postsecondary Education Data System (IPEDS), "Completions" survey. (This table was prepared October 1994.) *Note:* 1. Excludes degree recipients whose race was not reported.

Degrees: State-by-State Distribution of Associate Degrees Awarded, by Race/Ethnic Group: Missouri-Wyoming, 1992-93

State or other area	Total	Total resident	Percentage distribution of resident degrees by race/ethnicity[1]							Total, non-resident alien
			Total	White, non-Hispanic	Total minority	Black, non-Hispanic	Hispanic	American Indian/ Alaskan Native	Asian Pacific Islander	
United States	100.0	98.2	100.0	81.3	18.7	8.5	6.0	0.9	3.3	1.8
Missouri	100.0	99.3	100.0	87.9	12.1	9.6	1.0	0.7	0.8	0.7
Montana	100.0	97.7	100.0	79.1	20.9	0.1	1.0	19.1	0.6	2.3
Nebraska	100.0	99.7	100.0	95.0	5.0	2.6	1.0	0.6	0.8	0.3
Nevada	100.0	98.6	100.0	85.3	14.7	5.7	4.7	1.8	2.6	1.4
New Hampshire	100.0	99.5	100.0	97.4	2.6	0.7	0.7	0.3	0.8	0.5

[Continued]

★ 200 ★

Degrees: State-by-State Distribution of Associate Degrees Awarded, by Race/Ethnic Group: Missouri-Wyoming, 1992-93
[Continued]

State or other area	Total	Total resident	Percentage distribution of resident degrees by race/ethnicity[1]							Total, non-resident alien
			Total	White, non-Hispanic	Total minority	Black, non-Hispanic	Hispanic	American Indian/ Alaskan Native	Asian Pacific Islander	
New Jersey	100.0	97.1	100.0	82.6	17.4	8.9	5.4	0.1	3.0	2.9
New Mexico	100.0	98.9	100.0	59.5	40.5	2.1	29.7	7.8	0.8	1.1
New York	100.0	98.1	100.0	75.6	24.4	12.4	8.3	0.4	3.3	1.9
North Carolina	100.0	99.6	100.0	84.5	15.5	12.8	0.7	1.0	1.1	0.4
North Dakota	100.0	99.9	100.0	90.5	9.5	0.6	0.2	7.9	0.9	0.1
Ohio	100.0	99.4	100.0	90.3	9.7	7.8	0.9	0.4	0.6	0.6
Oklahoma	100.0	99.5	100.0	82.8	17.2	6.3	1.8	7.6	1.5	0.5
Oregon	100.0	98.2	100.0	90.3	9.7	1.2	2.0	1.1	5.3	1.8
Pennsylvania	100.0	99.3	100.0	90.6	9.4	6.9	1.2	0.2	1.2	0.7
Rhode Island	100.0	97.2	100.0	90.3	9.7	5.1	2.5	0.5	1.6	2.8
South Carolina	100.0	99.3	100.0	79.4	20.6	18.6	0.6	0.3	1.0	0.7
South Dakota	100.0	98.7	100.0	91.7	8.3	0.7	0.8	6.6	0.3	1.3
Tennessee	100.0	99.4	100.0	87.1	12.9	11.3	0.7	0.3	0.7	0.6
Texas	100.0	99.0	100.0	69.6	30.4	10.0	17.8	0.4	2.2	1.0
Utah	100.0	96.3	100.0	92.5	7.5	0.6	2.1	1.3	3.6	3.7
Vermont	100.0	99.4	100.0	98.3	1.7	0.5	0.6	0.3	0.2	0.6
Virginia	100.0	99.4	100.0	82.1	17.9	12.6	1.7	0.2	3.5	0.6
Washington	100.0	95.4	100.0	87.7	12.3	2.9	2.4	1.2	5.7	4.6
West Virginia	100.0	99.5	100.0	95.6	4.4	3.2	0.2	0.4	0.6	0.5
Wisconsin	100.0	99.8	100.0	92.2	7.8	3.4	2.7	0.9	0.8	0.2
Wyoming	100.0	98.9	100.0	92.3	7.7	1.0	3.9	1.2	1.6	1.1
U.S. Service Schools	-	-	-	-	-	-	-	-	-	-

Source: "Percentage Distribution of Associate Degrees Conferred by Institutions of Higher Education, by Race/Ethnicity and State: 1992-93," Department of Education, National Center for Education Statistics, *State Comparisons of Education Statistics: 1969-70 to 1993-94*, p. 153. Primary source: U.S. Department of Education, National Center for Education Statistics, Integrated Postsecondary Education Data System (IPEDS), "Completions" survey. (This table was prepared October 1994). *Notes:* 1. Excludes degree recipients whose race was not reported. - Data not available or not applicable.

★ 201 ★

Higher Education

Degrees: State-by-State Distribution of Bachelor's Degrees Awarded, by Race/Ethnic Group: Alabama-Mississippi, 1992-93

State or other area	Total	Total resident	Percentage distribution of resident degrees by race/ethnicity[1]							Total, non-resident alien
			Total	White non-Hispanic	Total, minority	Black non-Hispanic	Hispanic	American Indian/ Alaskan Native	Asian Pacific Islander	
United States	100.0	97.2	100.0	84.0	16.0	6.9	4.0	0.5	4.5	2.8
Alabama	100.0	98.4	100.0	82.2	17.8	16.0	0.7	0.4	0.8	1.6
Alaska	100.0	96.9	100.0	86.9	13.1	2.3	2.3	6.2	2.3	3.1
Arizona	100.0	96.6	100.0	85.6	14.4	2.2	7.6	1.6	2.9	3.4
Arkansas	100.0	97.7	100.0	87.7	12.3	9.9	0.7	0.6	1.2	2.3
California	100.0	95.0	100.0	66.8	33.2	4.4	10.8	1.0	17.1	5.0
Colorado	100.0	98.2	100.0	88.9	11.1	2.0	5.6	0.8	2.7	1.8
Connecticut	100.0	97.3	100.0	88.4	11.6	4.4	3.2	0.3	3.8	2.7
Delaware	100.0	99.1	100.0	88.7	11.3	8.4	0.8	0.2	1.8	0.9
District of Columbia	100.0	91.0	100.0	59.2	40.8	31.2	3.5	0.2	5.9	9.0
Florida	100.0	96.7	100.0	77.9	22.1	8.9	10.3	0.2	2.6	3.3
Georgia	100.0	98.0	100.0	80.1	19.9	16.7	1.1	0.1	2.0	2.0
Hawaii	100.0	89.4	100.0	29.9	70.1	1.6	1.4	0.4	66.8	10.6
Idaho	100.0	97.5	100.0	94.9	5.1	0.7	2.5	0.5	1.5	2.5
Illinois	100.0	98.1	100.0	83.8	16.2	7.7	3.2	0.3	5.0	1.9
Indiana	100.0	97.9	100.0	92.4	7.6	4.1	1.5	0.2	1.8	2.1
Iowa	100.0	96.7	100.0	95.5	4.5	1.8	1.0	0.2	1.5	3.3
Kansas	100.0	96.2	100.0	92.9	7.1	2.6	2.1	0.7	1.8	3.8
Kentucky	100.0	98.4	100.0	93.9	6.1	4.7	0.4	0.2	0.8	1.6
Louisiana	100.0	98.0	100.0	74.5	25.5	21.8	1.9	0.3	1.5	2.0
Maine	100.0	97.8	100.0	96.4	3.6	1.1	0.7	0.3	1.5	2.2
Maryland	100.0	97.5	100.0	78.4	21.6	13.8	1.9	0.3	5.6	2.5
Massachusetts	100.0	95.2	100.0	87.8	12.2	3.7	2.8	0.3	5.4	4.8
Michigan	100.0	96.8	100.0	89.3	10.7	6.2	1.5	0.5	2.5	3.2
Minnesota	100.0	97.8	100.0	95.5	4.5	1.2	0.7	0.4	2.2	2.2
Mississippi	100.0	98.1	100.0	75.7	24.3	22.6	0.9	0.2	0.7	1.9

Source: "Percentage Distribution of Bachelor's Degrees Conferred by Institutions of Higher Education, by Race/Ethnicity and State: 1992-93," Department of Education, National Center for Education Statistics, *State Comparisons of Education Statistics: 1969-70 to 1993-94*, p. 154. Primary source: U.S. Department of Education, National Center for Education Statistics, Integrated Postsecondary Education Data System (IPEDS), "Completions" survey. (This table was prepared October 1994.) *Note:* 1. Excludes degree recipients whose race was not reported.

★ 202 ★

Higher Education

Degrees: State-by-State Distribution of Bachelor's Degrees Awarded, by Race/Ethnic Group: Missouri-Wyoming, 1992-93

State or other area	Total	Total resident	Percentage distribution of resident degrees by race/ethnicity[1]							Total, non-resident alien
			Total	White, non-Hispanic	Total minority	Black, non-Hispanic	Hispanic	American Indian/ Alaskan Native	Asian Pacific Islander	
United States	100.0	97.2	100.0	84.0	16.0	6.9	4.0	0.5	4.5	2.8
Missouri	100.0	97.9	100.0	90.7	9.3	5.4	1.8	0.3	1.8	2.1
Montana	100.0	96.1	100.0	96.0	4.0	0.3	0.9	2.2	0.6	3.9
Nebraska	100.0	97.3	100.0	95.2	4.8	2.1	1.2	0.3	1.3	2.7
Nevada	100.0	96.1	100.0	88.5	11.5	3.2	4.1	0.7	3.5	3.9
New Hampshire	100.0	98.1	100.0	95.8	4.2	1.3	1.0	0.4	1.5	1.9
New Jersey	100.0	97.2	100.0	80.6	19.4	8.0	5.6	0.2	5.6	2.8
New Mexico	100.0	98.7	100.0	70.0	30.0	1.9	24.7	2.3	1.2	1.3
New York	100.0	97.0	100.0	79.8	20.2	8.6	5.7	0.3	5.7	3.0
North Carolina	100.0	98.9	100.0	81.6	18.4	15.3	0.7	0.7	1.7	1.1
North Dakota	100.0	97.7	100.0	96.5	3.5	0.5	0.5	1.6	1.0	2.3
Ohio	100.0	97.7	100.0	92.0	8.0	5.3	0.9	0.2	1.6	2.3
Oklahoma	100.0	95.7	100.0	85.7	14.3	5.9	1.5	5.3	1.6	4.3
Oregon	100.0	94.8	100.0	89.8	10.2	1.5	2.3	1.2	5.1	5.2
Pennsylvania	100.0	98.1	100.0	91.5	8.5	4.3	1.2	0.1	2.9	1.9
Rhode Island	100.0	96.7	100.0	91.5	8.5	2.9	2.2	0.2	3.1	3.3
South Carolina	100.0	98.8	100.0	82.7	17.3	15.6	0.5	0.1	1.0	1.2
South Dakota	100.0	98.5	100.0	97.2	2.8	0.6	0.4	1.5	0.4	1.5
Tennessee	100.0	98.9	100.0	88.0	12.0	9.5	0.6	0.2	1.6	1.1
Texas	100.0	97.6	100.0	77.5	22.5	6.2	12.2	0.3	3.7	2.4
Utah	100.0	95.2	100.0	96.0	4.0	0.6	1.4	0.5	1.4	4.8
Vermont	100.0	97.7	100.0	95.4	4.6	1.1	1.6	0.2	1.7	2.3
Virginia	100.0	98.4	100.0	82.3	17.7	12.4	1.3	0.3	3.8	1.6
Washington	100.0	96.7	100.0	86.9	13.1	1.9	2.5	1.3	7.4	3.3
West Virginia	100.0	98.3	100.0	95.1	4.9	3.0	0.5	0.1	1.2	1.7
Wisconsin	100.0	97.7	100.0	94.8	5.2	1.8	1.0	0.5	1.9	2.3
Wyoming	100.0	97.4	100.0	95.4	4.6	0.5	2.5	0.9	0.6	2.6
U.S. Service Schools	100.0	99.0	100.0	83.9	16.1	5.3	5.0	0.8	5.0	1.0

Source: "Percentage Distribution of Bachelor's Degrees Conferred by Institutions of Higher Education, by Race/Ethnicity and State: 1992-93," Department of Education, National Center for Education Statistics, *State Comparisons of Education Statistics: 1969-70 to 1993-94*, p. 154. Primary source: U.S. department of Education, National Center for Education Statistics, Integrated Postsecondary Education Data System (IPEDS), "Completions" survey. (This table was prepared October 1994). *Note:* 1. Excludes degree recipients whose race was not reported.

★ 203 ★

Higher Education

Degrees: State-by-State Distribution of Doctorate Degrees Awarded, by Race/Ethnic Group: Alabama-Mississippi, 1992-93

| State or other area | Total | Total resident | Percentage distribution of resident degrees by race/ethnicity[1] | | | | | | | Total, non-resident alien |
			Total	White non-Hispanic	Total, minority	Black non-Hispanic	Hispanic	American Indian/ Alaskan Native	Asian Pacific Islander	
United States	100.0	72.2	100.0	87.4	12.6	4.4	2.7	0.4	5.1	27.8
Alabama	100.0	70.0	100.0	91.8	8.2	5.7	0.4	-	2.1	30.0
Alaska	100.0	70.0	100.0	100.0	-	-	-	-	-	30.0
Arizona	100.0	74.2	100.0	88.3	11.7	2.3	3.1	0.6	5.7	25.8
Arkansas	100.0	87.6	100.0	89.9	10.1	2.0	3.0	3.0	2.0	12.4
California	100.0	75.2	100.0	82.5	17.5	3.1	4.7	0.4	9.3	24.8
Colorado	100.0	72.7	100.0	92.1	7.9	2.1	2.4	0.8	2.6	27.3
Connecticut	100.0	72.5	100.0	89.9	10.1	2.4	2.4	-	5.3	27.5
Delaware	100.0	68.1	100.0	93.9	6.1	4.1	-	-	2.0	31.9
District of Columbia	100.0	69.8	100.0	71.0	29.0	21.1	3.4	-	4.4	30.2
Florida	100.0	81.9	100.0	83.8	16.2	9.4	4.3	0.4	2.1	18.1
Georgia	100.0	77.0	100.0	84.4	15.6	10.5	1.7	0.1	3.2	23.0
Hawaii	100.0	96.7	100.0	44.8	55.2	0.7	-	-	54.5	3.3
Idaho	100.0	59.3	100.0	100.0	-	-	-	-	-	40.7
Illinois	100.0	70.9	100.0	88.3	11.7	4.2	2.3	0.1	5.1	29.1
Indiana	100.0	66.3	100.0	90.8	9.2	2.5	1.9	0.8	4.0	33.7
Iowa	100.0	59.9	100.0	88.8	11.2	3.9	1.7	-	5.6	40.1
Kansas	100.0	66.7	100.0	90.4	9.6	4.0	1.2	-	4.4	33.3
Kentucky	100.0	76.5	100.0	93.6	6.4	1.6	1.2	1.2	2.4	23.5
Louisiana	100.0	74.1	100.0	87.1	12.9	2.8	3.5	0.6	6.0	25.9
Maine	100.0	100.0	100.0	96.9	3.1	-	-	-	3.1	-
Maryland	100.0	68.4	98.5	85.3	13.2	5.8	2.0	-	5.2	31.6
Massachusetts	100.0	70.3	100.0	88.5	11.5	3.6	3.3	0.5	4.1	29.7
Michigan	100.0	64.5	100.0	86.6	13.4	5.0	3.2	0.1	5.1	35.5
Minnesota	100.0	67.3	100.0	93.8	6.2	0.7	0.9	0.7	3.9	32.7
Mississippi	100.0	72.1	100.0	86.4	13.6	9.8	0.9	-	2.8	27.9

Source: "Percentage Distribution of Doctor's Degrees Conferred by Institutions of Higher Education, by Race/Ethnicity and State: 1992-93," Department of Education, National Center for Education Statistics, *State Comparisons of Education Statistics: 1969-70 to 1993-94*, p. 157. Primary source: U.S. Department of Education, National Center for Education Statistics Integrated Postsecondary Education Data System (IPEDS), "Completions" survey. (This table was prepared October 1994.) *Notes:* - Data not available or not applicable. 1. Excludes degree recipients whose race was not reported.

Higher Education

Degrees: State-by-State Distribution of Doctorate Degrees Awarded, by Race/Ethnic Group: Missouri-Wyoming, 1992-93

State or other area	Total	Total resident	Percentage distribution of resident degrees by race/ethnicity[1]							Total, non-resident alien
			Total	White, non-Hispanic	Total minority	Black, non-Hispanic	Hispanic	American Indian/ Alaskan Native	Asian Pacific Islander	
United States	100.0	72.2	100.0	87.4	12.6	4.4	2.7	0.4	5.1	27.8
Missouri	100.0	78.4	100.0	90.8	9.2	4.2	1.3	0.5	3.3	21.6
Montana	100.0	68.0	100.0	97.1	2.9	-	-	2.9	-	32.0
Nebraska	100.0	73.1	100.0	96.6	3.4	0.6	0.6	-	2.3	26.9
Nevada	100.0	68.6	100.0	91.7	8.3	-	4.2	-	4.2	31.4
New Hampshire	100.0	70.7	100.0	100.0	-	-	-	-	-	29.3
New Jersey	100.0	68.1	100.0	85.9	14.1	4.1	3.0	0.2	6.8	31.9
New Mexico	100.0	78.8	100.0	86.8	13.2	2.1	10.0	0.5	0.5	21.2
New York	100.0	69.4	100.0	86.9	13.1	3.8	3.2	0.1	6.0	30.6
North Carolina	100.0	78.5	100.0	89.4	10.6	5.0	2.1	0.5	3.0	21.5
North Dakota	100.0	76.7	100.0	94.6	5.4	-	-	1.8	3.6	23.3
Ohio	100.0	72.4	100.0	86.3	13.7	7.6	2.0	0.4	3.7	27.6
Oklahoma	100.0	76.9	100.0	89.4	10.6	3.8	1.9	1.6	3.4	23.1
Oregon	100.0	63.5	100.0	96.4	3.6	1.3	1.0	-	1.3	36.5
Pennsylvania	100.0	70.0	100.0	88.6	11.4	4.3	2.1	0.4	4.7	30.0
Rhode Island	100.0	65.5	100.0	92.6	7.4	1.1	1.1	1.7	3.4	34.5
South Carolina	100.0	74.7	100.0	91.4	8.6	6.9	0.7	0.3	0.7	25.3
South Dakota	100.0	82.7	100.0	88.4	11.6	4.7	-	7.0	-	17.3
Tennessee	100.0	85.2	100.0	87.7	12.3	6.9	1.0	0.2	4.3	14.8
Texas	100.0	72.6	100.0	86.7	13.3	3.2	3.4	0.3	6.4	27.4
Utah	100.0	54.5	100.0	95.6	4.4	0.5	1.1	0.5	2.2	45.5
Vermont	100.0	86.8	100.0	100.0	-	-	-	-	-	13.2
Virginia	100.0	79.9	10.0	93.0	7.0	4.4	0.9	.3	1.5	20.1
Washington	100.0	74.8	100.0	88.1	11.9	2.0	2.4	0.7	6.8	25.2
West Virginia	100.0	78.4	100.0	95.4	4.6	2.3	1.1	-	1.1	21.6
Wisconsin	100.0	67.2	100.0	90.5	9.5	2.7	2.3	0.2	4.4	32.8
Wyoming	100.0	71.7	100.0	97.0	3.0	-	-	3.0	-	28.3
U.S. Service Schools	100.0	68.8	90.9	90.9	-	-	-	-	9.1	31.3

Source: "Percentage Distribution of Doctor's Degrees Conferred by Institutions of Higher Education, by Race/Ethnicity and State: 1992-93," Department of Education, National Center for Education Statistics, *State Comparisons of Education Statistics: 1969-70 to 1993-94*, p. 157. Primary source: U.S. Department of Education, National Center for Education Statistics, Integrated Postsecondary Education Data System (IPEDS), "Completions" survey. (This table was prepared October 1994). *Notes:* 1. Excludes degree recipients whose race was not reported. - Data not available or not applicable.

★ 205 ★

Higher Education

Degrees: State-by-State Distribution of First-Professional Degrees Awarded, by Race/Ethnic Group: Alabama-Mississippi, 1992-93[1]

State or other area	Total	Total resident	Percentage distribution of resident degrees by race/ethnicity[2]							Total, non-resident alien
			Total	White non-Hispanic	Total, minority	Black non-Hispanic	Hispanic	American Indian/ Alaskan Native	Asian Pacific Islander	
United States	100.0	97.9	100.0	82.8	17.2	5.6	4.1	0.5	7.0	2.1
Alabama	100.0	99.8	100.0	88.4	11.6	7.3	1.2	0.9	2.2	0.2
Alaska	-	-	-	-	-	-	-	-	-	-
Arizona	100.0	99.5	100.0	78.1	21.9	3.7	10.7	1.9	5.6	0.5
Arkansas	100.0	100.0	100.0	94.0	6.0	2.7	1.1	0.4	1.8	-
California	100.0	97.7	100.0	72.1	27.9	4.2	7.2	0.7	15.8	2.3
Colorado	100.0	99.6	100.0	86.4	13.6	2.3	6.6	0.9	3.9	0.4
Connecticut	100.0	98.4	100.0	81.3	18.7	7.5	4.7	0.6	5.9	1.6
Delaware	100.0	100.0	100.0	94.3	5.7	2.2	2.6	-	0.9	-
District of Columbia	100.0	96.4	100.0	73.5	26.5	14.9	4.3	0.2	7.0	3.6
Florida	100.0	99.3	100.0	81.7	18.3	5.0	10.3	0.1	2.8	0.7
Georgia	100.0	98.5	100.0	84.8	15.2	9.4	2.0	0.2	3.7	1.5
Hawaii	100.0	61.1	100.0	26.0	74.0	-	-	-	74.0	38.9
Idaho	100.0	98.6	100.0	95.0	5.0	0.7	1.4	-	2.9	1.4
Illinois	100.0	97.3	100.0	80.9	19.1	4.9	4.1	0.3	9.9	2.7
Indiana	100.0	98.1	100.0	90.9	9.1	3.2	2.3	0.2	3.3	1.9
Iowa	100.0	96.7	100.0	88.7	11.3	3.6	3.2	0.5	3.9	3.3
Kansas	100.0	99.7	100.0	86.2	13.8	2.9	6.5	1.0	3.4	0.3
Kentucky	100.0	98.5	100.0	95.3	4.7	2.4	0.4	-	2.0	1.5
Louisiana	100.0	99.3	100.0	82.3	17.7	8.8	4.1	0.1	4.7	0.7
Maine	100.0	98.8	100.0	95.8	4.2	0.6	1.2	-	2.4	1.2
Maryland	100.0	99.0	100.0	77.3	22.7	12.8	1.5	0.1	8.3	1.0
Massachusetts	100.0	96.7	100.0	82.7	17.3	4.8	3.5	0.4	8.5	3.3
Michigan	100.0	96.2	100.0	84.7	15.3	7.4	2.3	0.6	5.0	3.8
Minnesota	100.0	94.2	100.0	90.6	9.4	2.5	1.6	0.4	4.9	5.8
Mississippi	100.0	99.4	100.0	94.0	6.0	5.2	0.4	-	0.4	0.6

Source: "Percentage Distribution of First-Professional Degrees Conferred by Institutions of Higher Education, by Race/Ethnicity and State: 1992-93," Department of Education, National Center for Education Statistics, *State Comparisons of Education Statistics: 1969-70 to 1993-94,* p. 156. Primary source: U.S. Department of Education, National Center for Education Statistics, Integrated Postsecondary Education Data System (IPEDS), "Completions" survey. (This table was prepared October 1994.) *Notes:* - Data not available or not applicable. 1. Includes degrees which require at least 6 years of college work for completion (including at least 2 years of professional training). 2. Excludes degree recipients whose race was not reported.

★ 206 ★
Higher Education

Degrees: State-by-State Distribution of First-Professional Degrees Awarded, by Race/Ethnic Group: Missouri-Wyoming, 1992-93[1]

| State or other area | Total | Total resident | Percentage distribution of resident degrees by race/ethnicity[2] | | | | | | | Total, non-resident alien |
			Total	White non-Hispanic	Total, minority	Black non-Hispanic	Hispanic	American Indian/ Alaskan Native	Asian Pacific Islander	
United States	100.0	97.9	100.0	82.8	17.2	5.6	4.1	0.5	7.0	2.1
Missouri	100.0	98.1	100.0	88.4	11.6	2.8	2.5	0.5	5.8	1.9
Montana	100.0	100.0	100.0	89.7	10.3	-	1.5	8.8	-	-
Nebraska	100.0	98.6	100.0	89.1	10.9	2.4	2.5	0.4	5.7	1.4
Nevada	100.0	100.0	100.0	90.0	10.0	-	2.0	-	8.0	-
New Hampshire	100.0	98.5	10.0	91.1	8.9	1.0	1.6	1.6	4.7	1.5
New Jersey	100.0	98.9	100.0	77.5	22.5	9.3	5.3	0.1	7.7	1.1
New Mexico	100.0	100.0	100.0	65.2	34.8	2.2	21.9	8.4	2.2	-
New York	100.0	98.6	100.0	82.3	17.7	5.7	4.2	0.2	7.6	1.4
North Carolina	100.0	97.0	100.0	86.1	13.9	9.7	0.8	0.7	2.7	3.0
North Dakota	100.0	99.3	100.0	91.4	8.6	0.7	1.4	4.3	2.1	0.7
Ohio	100.0	98.3	100.0	88.2	11.8	5.7	1.4	0.3	4.4	1.7
Oklahoma	100.0	99.5	100.0	88.9	11.1	3.0	1.8	3.9	2.3	0.5
Oregon	100.0	96.8	100.0	89.2	10.8	2.0	2.1	0.6	6.0	3.2
Pennsylvania	100.0	98.8	100.0	84.3	15.7	5.3	2.6	0.2	7.5	1.2
Rhode Island	100.0	100.0	100.0	72.8	27.2	8.6	3.7	-	14.8	-
South Carolina	100.0	98.2	100.0	90.7	9.3	5.4	1.0	0.2	2.7	1.8
South Dakota	100.0	97.7	10.0	97.6	2.4	-	0.8	1.6	-	2.3
Tennessee	100.0	96.7	100.0	84.2	15.8	11.8	1.2	0.1	2.8	3.3
Texas	100.0	98.0	100.0	79.8	20.2	5.6	8.0	0.5	6.1	2.0
Utah	100.0	95.9	100.0	90.5	9.5	0.4	4.2	1.4	3.5	4.1
Vermont	100.0	97.9	100.0	91.5	8.5	-	1.1	1.1	6.4	2.1
Virginia	100.0	99.0	100.0	85.5	14.5	7.9	1.1	0.1	5.4	1.0
Washington	100.0	99.2	100.0	86.9	13.1	1.6	2.4	1.8	7.3	0.8
West Virginia	100.0	99.4	100.0	90.3	9.7	3.1	0.9	0.6	5.0	0.6
Wisconsin	100.0	98.4	100.0	86.6	13.4	2.8	4.8	0.9	4.8	1.6
Wyoming	100.0	100.0	100.0	96.9	3.1	1.6	1.6	-	-	-
U.S. Service Schools	100.0	100.0	100.0	84.5	15.5	4.5	5.2	0.6	5.2	-

Source: "Percentage Distribution of First-Professional Degrees Conferred by Institutions of Higher Education, by Race/Ethnicity and State: 1992-93," Department of Education, National Center for Education Statistics, *State Comparisons of Education Statistics: 1969-70 to 1993-94*, p. 156. Primary source: U.S. Department of Education, National Center for Education Statistics, Integrated Postsecondary Education Data System (IPEDS), "Completions" survey. (This table was prepared October 1994.) *Notes:* - Data not available or not applicable. 1. Includes degrees which require at least 6 years of college work for completion (including at least 2 years of professional training). 2. Excludes degree recipients whose race was not reported.

Higher Education

Degrees: State-by-State Distribution of Master's Degrees Awarded, by Race/Ethnic Group: Alabama-Mississippi, 1992-93

State or other area	Total	Total resident	Percentage distribution of resident degrees by race/ethnicity[1]							Total, non-resident alien
			Total	White non-Hispanic	Total, minority	Black non-Hispanic	Hispanic	American Indian/ Alaskan Native	Asian Pacific Islander	
United States	100.0	87.5	100.0	85.9	14.1	6.1	3.3	0.4	4.3	12.5
Alabama	100.0	91.3	100.0	86.1	13.9	11.2	1.1	0.1	1.5	8.7
Alaska	100.0	87.1	100.0	92.3	7.7	1.6	0.3	4.5	1.3	12.9
Arizona	100.0	80.7	100.0	86.4	13.6	3.0	7.3	1.4	2.0	19.3
Arkansas	100.0	95.7	100.0	89.7	10.3	7.1	0.7	0.5	2.0	4.3
California	100.0	84.7	100.0	76.6	23.4	4.8	6.7	0.6	11.3	15.3
Colorado	100.0	90.3	100.0	91.8	8.2	1.7	3.6	0.5	2.4	9.7
Connecticut	100.0	86.8	100.0	92.8	7.2	3.0	2.0	0.1	2.0	13.2
Delaware	100.0	88.6	1000.0	86.7	13.3	9.9	1.2	0.8	1.3	11.4
District of Columbia	100.0	79.3	100.0	74.9	25.1	13.8	3.2	0.5	7.6	20.7
Florida	100.0	91.0	100.0	81.3	18.7	7.4	9.1	0.2	2.0	9.0
Georgia	100.0	91.7	100.0	83.2	16.8	13.0	1.3	0.2	2.3	8.3
Hawaii	100.0	93.8	100.0	43.5	56.5	1.5	1.6	0.8	52.6	6.3
Idaho	100.0	90.8	100.0	95.6	4.4	0.3	2.4	0.7	1.0	9.2
Illinois	100.0	88.8	100.0	85.1	14.9	7.9	2.1	0.4	4.5	11.2
Indiana	100.0	86.9	100.0	92.0	8.0	3.7	1.7	0.2	2.4	13.1
Iowa	100.0	82.8	100.0	94.9	5.1	1.7	1.6	0.4	1.4	17.2
Kansas	100.0	87.0	100.0	91.8	8.2	2.8	1.7	0.7	3.1	13.0
Kentucky	100.0	93.6	100.0	95.1	4.9	3.4	0.4	0.1	1.0	6.4
Louisiana	100.0	85.5	100.0	80.3	19.7	14.1	2.2	0.4	3.0	14.5
Maine	100.0	97.2	100.0	97.6	2.4	0.4	0.3	0.6	1.1	2.8
Maryland	100.0	89.0	100.0	83.9	16.1	9.9	1.8	0.2	4.1	11.0
Massachusetts	100.0	83.4	100.0	88.4	11.6	4.2	2.6	0.3	4.5	16.6
Michigan	100.0	86.0	100.0	85.4	14.6	8.7	1.8	0.4	3.7	14.0
Minnesota	100.0	91.8	100.0	95.9	4.1	1.4	0.8	0.3	1.6	8.2
Mississippi	100.0	89.2	100.0	83.5	16.5	14.3	0.3	0.2	1.8	10.8

Source: "Percentage Distribution of Master's Degrees Conferred by Institutions of Higher Education, by Race/Ethnicity and State: 1992-93," Department of Education, National Center for Education Statistics, *State Comparisons of Education Statistics: 1969-70 to 1993-94*, p. 155. Primary source: U.S. Department of Education, National Center for Education Statistics, Integrated Postsecondary Education Data System (IPEDS), "Completions" survey. (This table was prepared October 1994.) *Note:* 1. Excludes degree recipients whose race was not reported.

Higher Education

Degrees: State-by-State Distribution of Master's Degrees Awarded, by Race/Ethnic Group: Missouri-Wyoming, 1992-93

State or other area	Total	Total resident	Percentage distribution of resident degrees by race/ethnicity[1]							Total, non-resident alien
			Total	White non-Hispanic	Total, minority	Black non-Hispanic	Hispanic	American Indian/ Alaskan Native	Asian Pacific Islander	
United States	100.0	87.5	100.0	85.9	14.1	6.1	3.3	0.4	4.3	12.5
Missouri	100.0	91.6	100.0	86.5	13.5	7.9	2.2	0.4	2.9	8.4
Montana	100.0	88.6	100.0	96.3	3.7	0.2	0.2	2.4	0.9	11.4
Nebraska	100.0	92.2	100.0	95.6	4.4	1.8	0.8	0.2	1.6	7.8
Nevada	100.0	90.1	100.0	91.8	8.2	2.0	2.6	0.1	3.4	9.9
New Hampshire	100.0	93.0	100.0	97.1	2.9	1.2	0.7	-	0.9	7.0
New Jersey	100.0	84.1	100.0	85.4	14.6	5.1	3.3	0.2	6.0	15.9
New Mexico	100.0	88.7	100.0	77.7	22.3	1.2	18.1	1.9	1.0	11.3
New York	100.0	86.5	100.0	82.8	17.2	7.4	4.4	0.2	5.2	13.5
North Carolina	100.0	92.9	100.0	87.2	12.8	9.2	0.9	0.5	2.3	7.1
North Dakota	100.0	90.0	100.0	94.0	6.0	0.5	0.5	1.2	3.8	10.0
Ohio	100.0	86.5	100.0	90.8	9.2	5.7	1.4	0.3	1.8	13.5
Oklahoma	100.0	81.4	100.0	88.0	12.0	4.3	1.3	4.4	2.0	18.6
Oregon	100.0	82.5	100.0	92.9	7.1	1.2	1.6	0.7	3.6	17.5
Pennsylvania	100.0	87.8	100.0	90.8	9.2	4.6	1.0	0.3	3.5	12.2
Rhode Island	100.0	85.2	100.0	93.2	6.8	2.7	1.5	0.1	2.5	14.8
South Carolina	100.0	89.4	100.0	90.0	10.0	7.9	0.9	0.3	1.0	10.6
South Dakota	100.0	83.9	100.0	95.2	4.8	1.6	-	2.5	0.8	16.1
Tennessee	100.0	95.5	100.0	88.1	11.9	6.6	0.7	0.2	4.3	4.5
Texas	100.0	86.2	100.0	82.0	18.0	5.8	8.1	0.3	3.8	13.8
Utah	100.0	86.0	100.0	96.4	3.6	0.6	1.6	0.3	1.1	14.0
Vermont	100.0	91.9	100.0	97.1	2.9	1.1	1.3	0.3	0.1	8.1
Virginia	100.0	93.4	100.0	88.6	11.4	7.5	1.2	0.1	2.6	6.6
Washington	100.0	89.2	100.0	90.0	10.0	1.8	2.5	0.8	4.9	10.8
West Virginia	100.0	93.1	100.	96.2	3.8	2.1	0.7	0.6	0.4	6.9
Wisconsin	100.0	87.6	100.0	94.7	5.3	1.8	1.1	0.5	1.8	12.4
Wyoming	100.0	83.2	100.0	97.4	2.6	0.7	0.7	0.4	0.7	16.8
U.S. Service Schools	100.0	-	-	-	-	-	-	-	-	100.0

Source: "Percentage Distribution of Master's Degrees Conferred by Institutions of Higher Education, by Race/Ethnicity and State: 1992-93," Department of Education, National Center for Education Statistics, *State Comparisons of Education Statistics: 1969-70 to 1993-94*, p. 155. Primary source: U.S. Department of Education, National Center for Education Statistics, Integrated Postsecondary Education Data System (IPEDS), "Completions" survey. (This table was prepared October 1994.) *Notes:* 1. Excludes degree recipients whose race was not reported. - Data not available or not applicable.

★ 209 ★

Higher Education

Degrees: Trends in Associate's and Bachelor's Degrees Earned, by Race/Ethnic Origin: 1981-1992

[For **school year ending in year shown.** Data exclude some institutions not reporting field of study and are slight undercounts of degrees awarded].

LEVEL OF DEGREE AND RACE/ETHNICITY	TOTAL					PERCENT DISTRIBUTION		
	1981	1985	1990	1991	1992	1981	1985	1992
Associate's degrees, total	410,174	429,815	450,263	462,030	494,387	100.0	100.0	100.0
White, non-Hispanic	339,167	355,343	369,580	376,081	400,530	82.7	82.7	81.0
Black, non-Hispanic	35,330	35,791	35,327	37,657	39,411	8.5	8.3	8.0
Hispanic	17,800	19,407	22,195	24,251	26,905	4.3	4.5	5.4
Asian or Pacific Islander	8,650	9,914	13,482	13,725	15,596	2.1	2.3	3.2
American Indian/Alaskan Native	2,584	2,953	3,530	3,672	4,008	0.6	0.7	0.8
Nonresident alien	6,643	6,407	6,149	6,644	7,937	1.6	1.5	1.6
Bachelor's degrees, total	934,800	968,311	1,048,631	1,081,280	1,129,833	100.0	100.0	100.0
White, non-Hispanic	807,319	826,106	884,376	904,062	936,771	86.4	85.3	82.9
Black, non-Hispanic	60,673	57,473	61,063	65,341	72,326	6.5	5.9	6.4
Hispanic	21,832	25,874	32,844	36,612	40,761	2.3	2.7	3.6
Asian or Pacific Islander	18,794	25,395	39,248	41,618	46,720	2.0	2.6	4.1
American Indian/Alaskan Native	3,593	4,246	4,392	4,513	5,176	0.4	0.4	0.5
Nonresident alien	22,589	29,217	26,708	29,134	28,079	2.4	3.0	2.5

Source: "Degrees Earned, by Level and Race/Ethnicity: 1981 to 1992," *Statistical Abstract of the United States: 1995,* 1995, p. 192. Primary source: U.S. National Center for Education Statistics, *Digest of Education Statistics,* annual.

★ 210 ★

Higher Education

Degrees: Trends in First Professional Degrees Earned, by Race/Ethnic Origin: 1981-1992

[For **school year ending in year shown.** Data exclude some institutions not reporting field of study and are slight undercounts of degrees awarded].

LEVEL OF DEGREE AND RACE/ETHNICITY	TOTAL					PERCENT DISTRIBUTION		
	1981	1985	1990	1991	1992	1981	1985	1992
First-professional degrees, total	71,340	71,057	70,744	71,515	72,129	100.0	100.0	100.0
White, non-Hispanic	64,551	63,219	60,240	60,327	59,800	90.5	89.0	82.9
Black, non-Hispanic	2,931	3,029	3,410	3,575	3,560	4.1	4.3	4.9
Hispanic	1,541	1,884	2,427	2,527	2,766	2.2	2.7	3.8
Asian or Pacific Islander	1,456	1,816	3,362	3,755	4,455	2.0	2.6	6.2
American Indian/Alaskan Native	192	248	257	261	296	0.3	0.3	0.4
Nonresident alien	669	861	1,048	1,070	1,252	0.9	1.2	1.7

Source: "Degrees Earned, by Level and Race/Ethnicity: 1981 to 1992," *Statistical Abstract of the United States: 1995,* 1995, p. 192. Primary source: U.S. National Center for Education Statistics, *Digest of Education Statistics,* annual.

★ 211 ★

Higher Education

Degrees: Trends in Master's and Doctor's Degrees Earned, by Race/Ethnic Origin: 1981-1992

[For **school year ending in year shown.** Data exclude some institutions not reporting field of study and are slight undercounts of degrees awarded].

LEVEL OF DEGREE AND RACE/ETHNICITY	TOTAL					PERCENT DISTRIBUTION		
	1981	1985	1990	1991	1992	1981	1985	1992
Master's degrees, total	294,183	280,421	322,465	328,645	348,682	100.0	100.0	100.0
White, non-Hispanic	241,216	223,628	251,690	255,281	268,371	82.0	79.7	77.0
Black, non-Hispanic	17,133	13,939	15,446	16,139	18,116	5.8	5.0	5.2
Hispanic	6,461	6,864	7,950	8,386	9,358	2.2	2.4	2.7
Asian or Pacific Islander	6,282	7,782	10,577	11,180	12,658	2.1	2.8	3.6
American Indian/Alaskan Native	1,034	1,256	1,101	1,136	1,273	0.4	0.4	0.4
Nonresident alien	22,057	26,952	35,701	36,523	38,906	7.5	9.6	11.2
Doctor's degrees, total	32,839	32,307	38,113	38,547	40,090	100.0	100.0	100.0
White, non-Hispanic	25,908	23,934	25,880	25,328	25,813	78.9	74.1	64.4
Black, non-Hispanic	1,265	1,154	1,153	1,211	1,223	3.9	3.6	3.1
Hispanic	456	677	788	732	811	1.4	2.1	2.0
Asian or Pacific Islander	877	1,106	1,235	1,459	1,559	2.7	3.4	3.9
American Indian/Alaskan Native	130	119	99	102	118	0.4	0.4	0.3
Nonresident alien	4,203	5,317	8,958	9,715	10,566	12.8	16.5	26.4

Source: "Degrees Earned, by Level and Race/Ethnicity: 1981 to 1992," *Statistical Abstract of the United States: 1995,* 1995, p. 192. Primary source: U.S. National Center for Education Statistics, *Digest of Education Statistics,* annual.

★ 212 ★

Higher Education

Enrollment: Enrollment and Enrollment Change in Public and Private Institutions, by Race/Ethnic Origin: 1990-1993

	Number, in thousands				Percentage change			
					1990 to 1991	1991 to 1992	1992 to 1993	1990 to 1993
	1990	1991	1992	1993				
Control of institution and race/ethnicity								
All institutions	13,819	14,359	14,486	14,306	3.9	0.9	-1.2	3.5
White, non-Hispanic	10,722	10,990	10,875	10,604	2.5	-1.0	-2.5	-1.1
Black, non-Hispanic	1,247	1,335	1,393	1,410	7.1	4.3	1.3	13.1
Hispanic	782	867	955	989	10.8	10.2	3.6	26.4
Asian or Pacific Islander	572	637	697	724	11.3	9.4	3.9	26.5
American Indian or Alaskan Native	103	114	119	122	10.6	4.9	2.0	18.4
Nonresident alien	391	416	448	457	6.4	7.5	2.0	16.7

[Continued]

★ 212 ★

Enrollment: Enrollment and Enrollment Change in Public and Private Institutions, by Race/Ethnic Origin: 1990-1993

[Continued]

	Number, in thousands				Percentage change			
	1990	1991	1992	1993	1990 to 1991	1991 to 1992	1992 to 1993	1990 to 1993
Public	10,845	11,310	11,385	11,189	4.3	0.7	-1.7	3.2
White, non-Hispanic	8,385	8,622	8,493	8,227	2.8	-1.5	-3.1	-1.9
Black, non-Hispanic	976	1,053	1,100	1,114	7.9	4.5	1.3	14.1
Hispanic	671	742	822	851	10.5	10.8	3.5	26.8
Asian or Pacific Islander	461	516	566	586	12.0	9.6	3.6	27.2
American Indian or Alaskan Native	90	100	103	106	10.8	3.2	2.9	17.7
Nonresident alien	260	275	300	304	5.9	8.8	1.6	17.1
Private	2,974	3,049	3,102	3,117	2.5	1.7	0.5	4.8
White, non-Hispanic	2,237	2,368	2,382	2,377	1.3	0.6	-0.2	1.7
Black, non-Hispanic	271	282	292	296	4.2	3.7	1.3	9.4
Hispanic	111	125	133	138	12.2	6.6	3.8	24.0
Asian or Pacific Islander	111	121	131	138	8.4	8.5	5.2	23.7
American Indian or Alaskan Native	12	14	16	15	9.0	18.0	-4.0	23.5
Nonresident Alien	131	141	148	152	7.3	5.0	2.9	16.0

Source: "Total Enrollment and Percent of Change in Institutions of Higher Education, by Control of Institution, Level of Study, and Race/Ethnicity: 50 States and the District of Columbia, Fall 1990 through Fall 1993," U.S. Department of Education, National Center for Education Statistics, *Enrollment in Higher Education: Fall 1984 Through Fall 1993*, April, 1995, p. 1. Primary source: U.S. Department of Education, National Center for Education Statistics, Integrated Postsecondary Education Data System, "Fall Enrollment" surveys for 1990, 1991, 1992, and 1993. *Notes:* 1992 data may differ from that in prior publications due to corrections and the addition of late data. Detail may not sum to total due to rounding.

★ 213 ★

Higher Education

Enrollment: Enrollment and Enrollment Change, by Level of Study and Race/Ethnic Origin: 1990-1993

Level of Study and race/ethnicity	Number, in thousands				Percentage of change			
	1990	1991	1992	1993	1990 to 1991	1991 to 1992	1992 to 1993	1990 to 1993
All institutions	13,819	14,359	14,486	14,306	3.9	0.9	-1.2	3.5
Undergraduate enrollment	11,959	12,439	12,357	12,324	4.0	0.8	-1.7	3.1
White, non-Hispanic	9,273	9,508	9,387	9,103	2.5	-1.3	-3.0	-1.8
Black, non-Hispanic	1,147	1,229	1,280	1,288	7.1	4.2	0.6	12.3
Hispanic	725	804	888	918	11.0	10.4	3.4	26.7
Asian or Pacific Islander	501	559	613	634	11.6	9.7	3.4	26.6
American Indian or Alaskan Native	95	106	111	113	10.8	4.8	1.7	18.1
Nonresident alien	219	234	258	268	6.8	10.4	4.0	22.6

[Continued]

★ 213 ★

Enrollment: Enrollment and Enrollment Change, by Level of Study and Race/Ethnic Origin: 1990-1993

[Continued]

Level of Study and race/ethnicity	Number, in thousands				Percentage of change			
					1990 to 1991	1991 to 1992	1992 to 1993	1990 to 1993
	1990	1991	1992	1993				
Graduate enrollment	1,586	1,639	1,669	1,689	3.3	1.8	1.2	6.5
White, non-Hispanic	1,228	1,258	1,267	1,275	2.4	0.7	0.6	3.8
Black, non-Hispanic	84	89	94	102	6.0	5.7	8.2	21.3
Hispanic	47	51	55	58	8.0	8.4	5.4	23.4
Asian or Pacific Islander	53	58	62	65	8.3	6.7	6.0	22.6
American Indian or Alaskan Native	6	7	7	7	7.3	5.5	4.7	18.5
Nonresident alien	167	177	184	182	5.8	3.7	-1.0	8.7
First-professional enrollment	274	281	281	292	2.3	0.1	4.1	6.7
White, non-Hispanic	222	224	221	226	0.9	-1.5	2.4	1.8
Black, non-Hispanic	16	17	18	20	7.8	5.4	11.0	26.2
Hispanic	11	11	12	13	5.4	4.6	6.8	17.7
Asian or Pacific Islander	19	21	23	25	10.9	8.0	11.2	33.2
American Indian or Alaskan Native	1	1	1	2	11.6	14.7	14.0	45.9
Nonresident alien	5	6	6	7	6.0	8.3	10.6	27.0

Source: "Total Enrollment and Percent of Change in Institutions of Higher Education, by Control of Institution, Level of Study, and Race/Ethnicity: 50 States and the District of Columbia, Fall 1990 through Fall 1993," U.S. Department of Education, National Center for Education Statistics, *Enrollment in Higher Education: Fall 1984 Through Fall 1993*, April , 1995, p. 1. Primary source: U.S. Department of Education, National center for Education Statistics, Integrated Postsecondary Education Data System, "Fall Enrollment" surveys for 1990, 1991, 1992, and 1993. *Notes:* 1992 data may differ from that in prior publications due to corrections and the addition of late data. Detail may not sum to total due to rounding.

★ 214 ★

Higher Education

Enrollment: Enrollment of Full-Time Students in Public and Private Institutions, by Race/Ethnic Origin: 1991-1993

Control of institution and race/ethnicity	Number			Percentage Distribution		
	1991	1992	1993	1991	1992	1993
Public	5,974,577	6,010,875	5,962,562	100.0	100.0	100.0
White, non-Hispanic	4,527,091	4,474,077	4,368,008	75.8	74.4	73.3
Black, non-Hispanic	569,439	589,269	603,169	9.5	9.8	10.1
Hispanic	346,232	376,885	395,860	5.8	6.3	6.6
Asian or Pacific Islander	287,821	311,039	328,698	4.8	5.2	5.5
American Indian or Alaskan Native	51,703	54,762	56,928	0.9	0.9	1.0
Nonresident alien	192,291	204,843	209,899	3.2	3.4	3.5
Private	2,140,752	2,150,243	2,165,178	100.0	100.0	100.0
White, non-Hispanic	1,618,414	1,606,189	1,607,032	75.6	74.7	74.2

[Continued]

★ 214 ★

Enrollment: Enrollment of Full-Time Students in Public and Private Institutions, by Race/Ethnic Origin: 1991-1993

[Continued]

Control of institution and race/ethnicity	Number			Percentage Distribution		
	1991	1992	1993	1991	1992	1993
Black, non-Hispanic	208,508	211,571	212,346	9.7	9.8	9.8
Hispanic	93,504	97,819	103,498	4.4	4.5	4.8
Asian or Pacific Islander	94,434	102,371	107,837	4.4	4.8	5.0
American Indian or Alaskan Native	9,457	10,452	10,537	0.4	0.5	0.5
Nonresident alien	116,435	121,841	123,928	5.4	5.7	5.7

Source: "Full-Time Enrollment in Institutions of Higher Education, by Control of Institution and Race/Ethnicity: 50 States and the District of Columbia, Fall 1991 through Fall 1993," U.S. Department of Education, National Center for Education Statistics, *Enrollment in Higher Education: Fall 1984 Through Fall 1993,* April, 1995, p. 4. Primary source: U.S. Department of Education, National Center for Education Statistics, Integrated Postsecondary Education System, "Fall Enrollment" surveys for 1991, 1992, and 1993. *Notes:* Data for 1992 may differ from that in prior publications due to corrections and the addition of late data. Detail may not sum to total due to rounding.

★ 215 ★

Higher Education

Enrollment: Enrollment of Part-Time Students in Public and Private Institutions, by Race/Ethnic Origin: 1991-1993

Control of institution and race/ethnicity	Number			Percentage Distribution		
	1991	1992	1993	1991	1992	1993
Public	5,334,986	5,373,692	5,226,526	100.0	100.0	100.0
White, non-Hispanic	4,095,122	4,019,140	3,858,575	76.8	74.8	73.8
Black, non-Hispanic	484,015	511,082	511,099	9.1	9.5	9.8
Hispanic	395,831	445,359	455,411	7.4	8.3	8.7
Asian or Pacific Islander	228,480	254,789	257,536	4.3	4.7	4.9
American Indian or Alaskan Native	48,490	48,594	49,430	0.9	0.9	0.9
Nonresident alien	83,048	94,728	94,475	1.6	1.8	1.8
Private	908,638	951,505	951,392	1000	100.0	100.0
White, non-Hispanic	749,149	775,407	770,131	82.4	81.5	80.9
Black, non-Hispanic	73,426	80,734	83,686	8.1	8.5	8.8
Hispanic	31,005	34,848	34,191	3.4	3.7	3.6
Asian or Pacific Islander	26,416	28,741	30,053	2.9	3.0	3.2
American Indian or Alaskan Native	4,063	5,507	4,786	0.4	0.6	0.5
Nonresident alien	24,579	26,268	28,545	2.7	2.8	3.0

Source: "Part-Time Enrollment in Institutions of Higher Education, by Control of Institution and Race/Ethnicity: 50 States and the District of Columbia, Fall 1991 through Fall 1993," U.S. Department of Education, National Center for Education Statistics, *Enrollment in Higher Education: Fall 1984 Through Fall 1993,* April, 1995, p. 4. Primary source: U.S. Department of Education, National Center for Education Statistics, Integrated Postsecondary Education Data System, "Fall Enrollment" surveys for 1991, 1992, and 1993. *Notes:* Data for 1992 may differ from that in prior publications due to corrections and the addition of late data. Detail may not sum to total due to rounding.

Higher Education

Enrollment: Female Enrollment at 2- and 4-Year Institutions, by Race/Ethnic Origin: 1991-1993

Level of study and race/ethnicity	Number			Percentage distribution		
	1991	1992	1993	1991	1992	1993
All institutions	7,857,109	7,962,799	7,877,942	100.0	100.0	100.0
White, non-Hispanic	6,027,568	5,990,545	5,847,742	76.7	75.2	74.2
Black, non-Hispanic	818,381	855,865	867,369	10.4	10.7	11.0
Hispanic	476,027	527,237	547,581	6.1	6.6	7.0
Asian or Pacific Islander	312,035	345,494	361,104	4.0	4.3	4.6
American Indian or Alaskan Native	66,097	69,078	70,537	0.8	0.9	0.9
Nonresident alien	157,001	174,580	183,609	2.0	2.2	2.3
4-year institutions	4,607,119	4,653,685	4,657,534	58.6	58.4	59.1
White, non-Hispanic	3,607,936	3,594,738	3,550,120	45.9	45.1	45.1
Black, non-Hispanic	458,255	477,203	490,518	5.8	6.0	6.2
Hispanic	206,560	223,306	236,432	2.6	2.8	3.0
Asian or Pacific Islander	183,536	197,658	210,040	23	2.5	2.7
American Indian or Alaskan Native	29,289	31,103	33,035	0.4	0.4	0.4
Nonresident alien	121,543	129,677	137,389	1.5	1.6	1.7
2-year institutions	3,249,990	3,309,114	3,220,408	41.4	41.6	40.9
White, non-Hispanic	2,419,632	2,395,807	2,297,622	30.8	30.1	29.2
Black, non-Hispanic	360,126	378,662	376,851	4.6	4.8	4.8
Hispanic	269,467	303,931	311,149	3.4	3.8	3.9
Asian or Pacific Islander	128,499	147,836	151,064	1.6	1.9	1.9
American Indian or Alaskan Native	36,808	37,975	37,502	0.5	0.5	0.5
Nonresident alien	35,458	44,903	46,220	0.5	0.6	0.6

Source: "Female Enrollment in Institutions of Higher Education, by Level of Institution and Race/Ethnicity: 50 States and the District of Columbia, Fall 1991 through Fall 1993," U.S. Department of Education, National Center for Education Statistics, *Enrollment in Higher Education: Fall 1984 Through Fall 1993*, April, 1995, p. 6. Primary source: U.S. Department of Education, National Center for Education Statistics, Integrated Postsecondary Education Data System, "Fall Enrollment" surveys for 1991, 1992, and 1993. *Notes:* Data for 1992 may differ from that in prior publications due to corrections and the addition of late data. Detail may not sum to total due to rounding.

★ 217 ★

Higher Education

Enrollment: Full-Time Enrollment at 2- and 4-Year Institutions, by Race/Ethnic Origin: 1991-1993

Level of institution and race/ethnicity	Number			Percentage distribution		
	1991	1992	1993	1991	1992	1993
4-year institutions	6,040,799	6,081,112	6,084,421	100.0	100.0	100.0
White, non-Hispanic	4,641,652	4,601,738	4,548,211	76.8	75.7	74.8
Black, non-Hispanic	538,170	561,759	574,720	8.9	9.2	9.4
Hispanic	265,296	285,914	303,898	4.4	4.7	5.0
Asian or Pacific Islander	291,122	312,514	329,982	4.8	5.1	5.4
American Indian or Alaskan Native	35,521	38,304	41,598	0.6	0.6	0.7
Nonresident alien	269,038	280,883	286,012	4.5	4.6	4.7
2-year institutions	2,074,530	2,080,006	2,043,319	100.0	100.0	100.0
White, non-Hispanic	1,503,853	1,478,528	1,426,829	72.5	71.1	69.8
Black, non-Hispanic	239,777	239,081	240,795	11.6	11.5	11.8
Hispanic	174,440	188,790	195,460	8.4	9.1	9.6
Asian or Pacific Islander	91,133	100,896	106,553	4.4	4.9	5.2
American Indian or Alaskan Native	25,639	26,910	25,867	1.2	1.3	1.3
Nonresident alien	39,688	45,801	47,815	1.9	2.2	2.3

Source: "Full-Time Enrollment in Institutions of Higher Education, by Level of Institution and Race/Ethnicity: 50 States and District of Columbia, Fall 1991 through Fall 1993," U.S. Department of Education, National Center for Education Statistics, *Enrollment in Higher Education: Fall 1984 Through Fall 1993*, April, 1995, p. 7. Primary source: U.S. Department of Education, National Center for Education Statistics, Integrated Postsecondary Education Data System, "Fall Enrollment" surveys for 1991, 1992, and 1993. *Notes:* Data for 1992 may differ from that in prior publications due to corrections and the addition of late data. Detail may not sum to total due to rounding.

★ 218 ★

Higher Education

Enrollment: Higher Education Enrollment, by Gender and Race/Ethnic Origin: 1991-1993

Sex and Race/Ethnicity	Number			Percentage Distribution		
	1991	1992	1993	1991	1992	1993
All Students	14,358,953	14,486,315	14,305,658	N/A	N/A	N/A
Male	6,501,844	6,523,516	6,427,716	100.0	100.0	100.0
White, non-Hispanic	4,962,208	4,884,268	4,756,004	76.3	74.9	74.0
Black, non-Hispanic	517,007	536,791	542,931	8.0	8.2	8.4
Hispanic	390,545	427,674	441,379	6.0	6.6	6.9
Asian or Pacific Islander	325,116	351,446	363,020	5.0	5.4	5.6
American Indian or Alaskan Native	47,616	50,237	51,144	0.7	0.8	0.8

[Continued]

★ 218 ★

Enrollment: Higher Education Enrollment, by Gender and Race/Ethnic Origin: 1991-1993

[Continued]

Sex and Race/Ethnicity	Number			Percentage Distribution		
	1991	1992	1993	1991	1992	1993
Nonresident alien	259,352	273,100	273,238	4.0	4.2	4.3
Female	7,857,109	7,962,799	7,877,942	100.0	100.0	100.0
White, non-Hispanic	6,027,568	5,990,545	5,847,742	76.7	75.2	74.2
Black, non-Hispanic	818,381	855,865	867,369	10.4	10.7	11.0
Hispanic	476,027	527,237	547,581	6.1	6.6	7.0
Asian or Pacific Islander	312,035	345,494	361,104	4.0	4.3	4.6
American Indian or Alaskan Native	66,097	69,078	70,537	0.8	0.9	0.9
Nonresident alien	157,001	174,580	183,609	2.0	2.2	2.3

Source: "Total Enrollment in Institutions of Higher Education, by Sex and Race/Ethnicity: 50 States and the District of Columbia, Fall 1991 through Fall 1993," U.S. Department of Education, National Center for Education Statistics, *Enrollment in Higher Education: Fall 1984 Through Fall 1993*, April, 1995, p. 8. Primary source: U.S. Department of Education, National Center for Education Statistics, Integrated Postsecondary Education Data System, "Fall Enrollment" surveys for 1991, 1992, and 1993. *Notes:* Data for 1992 may differ from that in prior publications due to corrections and the addition of late data. Detail may not sum to total due to rounding. N/A - Not applicable.

★ 219 ★

Higher Education

Enrollment: Male Enrollment at 2- and 4-Year Institutions, by Race/Ethnic Origin: 1991-1993

Level of study and race/ethnicity	Number			Percentage distribution		
	1991	1992	1993	1991	1992	1993
All institutions	6,501,844	6,523,516	6,427,716	100.0	100.0	100.0
White, non-Hispanic	4,962,208	4,884,268	4,756,004	76.3	74.9	74.0
Black, non-Hispanic	517,007	536,791	542,931	8.0	8.2	8.4
Hispanic	390,545	427,674	441,379	6.0	6.6	6.9
Asian or Pacific Islander	325,116	251,446	363,020	5.0	5.4	5.6
American Indian or Alaskan Native	47,616	50,237	51,144	0.7	0.8	0.8
Nonresident alien	259,352	273,100	273,238	4.0	4.2	4.3
4-year institutions	4,099,934	4,110,240	4,082,257	63.1	63.0	63.5
White, non-Hispanic	3,183,017	3,148,890	3,093,074	49.0	48.3	48.1
Black, non-Hispanic	299,503	313,825	320,751	4.6	4.8	5.0
Hispanic	176,310	186,616	195,692	2.7	2.9	3.0
Asian or Pacific Islander	197,952	209,785	219,035	3.0	3.2	3.4
American Indian or Alaskan Native	21,858	23,768	25,471	0.3	0.4	0.4
Nonresident alien	221,294	227,356	228,234	3.4	3.5	3.6
2-year institutions	2,401,910	2,413,276	2,345,459	36.9	37.0	36.5

[Continued]

★ 219 ★

Enrollment: Male Enrollment at 2- and 4-Year Institutions, by Race/Ethnic Origin: 1991-1993
[Continued]

Level of study and race/ethnicity	Number			Percentage distribution		
	1991	1992	1993	1991	1992	1993
White, non-Hispanic	1,779,191	1,735,378	1,662,930	27.4	26.6	25.9
Black, non-Hispanic	217,504	222,966	222,180	3.3	3.4	3.5
Hispanic	214,235	241,058	245,687	3.3	3.7	3.8
Asian or Pacific Islander	127,164	141,661	143,985	2.0	2.2	2.2
American Indian or Alaskan Native	25,758	26,469	25,673	0.4	0.4	0.4
Nonresident alien	38,058	45,744	45,004	0.6	0.7	0.7

Source: "Male Enrollment in Institutions of Higher Education, by Level of Institution and Race/Ethnicity: 50 States and the District of Columbia, Fall 1991 through Fall 1993," U.S. Department of Education, National Center for Education Statistics, *Enrollment in Higher Education: Fall 1984 Through Fall 1993*, April, 1995, p. 6. Primary source: U.S. Department of Education, National Center for Education Statistics, Integrated Postsecondary Education Data System, "Fall Enrollment" surveys for 1991, 1992, and 1993. *Notes:* Data for 1992 may differ from that in prior publications due to corrections and the addition of late data.

★ 220 ★

Higher Education

Enrollment: Male and Female Full-Time Students at Higher Education Institutions, by Race/Ethnic Origin: 1991-1993

Sex and race/ethnicity	Number			Percentage distribution		
	1991	1992	1993	1991	1992	1993
Male	3,929,375	3,926,441	3,890,603	100.0	100.0	100.0
White, non-Hispanic	2,986,796	2,938,055	2,876,033	76.0	74.8	73.9
Black, non-Hispanic	318,291	325,349	330,710	8.1	8.3	8.5
Hispanic	201,918	217,397	226,567	5.1	5.5	5.8
Asian or Pacific Islander	198,669	212,698	222,801	5.1	5.4	5.7
American Indian or Alaskan Native	26,905	28,806	29,921	0.7	0.7	0.8
Nonresident alien	196,796	204,136	204,571	5.0	5.2	5.3
Female	4,185,954	4,234,677	4,237,137	100.0	100.0	100.0
White, non-Hispanic	3,158,709	3,142,211	3,099,007	75.5	74.2	73.1
Black, non-Hispanic	459,656	475,491	484,805	11.0	11.2	11.4
Hispanic	237,818	257,307	272,791	5.7	6.1	6.4
Asian or Pacific Islander	183,586	200,712	213,734	4.4	4.7	5.0
American Indian or Alaskan Native	34,2855	36,408	37,544	0.8	0.9	0.9
Nonresident alien	111,930	122,548	129,256	2.7	2.9	3.1

Source: "Full-Time Enrollment in Institutions of Higher Education, by Sex and Race/Ethnicity: 50 States and the District of Columbia, Fall 1991 through Fall 1993," U. S. Department of Education, National Center for Education Statistics, *Enrollment in Higher Education: Fall 1984 Through Fall 1993*, April, 1995, p. 9. Primary source: U.S. Department of Education, National Center for Education Statistics, Integrated Postsecondary Education Data System, "Fall Enrollment" surveys for 1991, 1992, and 1993. *Notes:* Data for 1992 may differ from that in prior publications due to corrections and the addition of late data. Detail may not sum to total due to rounding.

★ 221 ★

Higher Education

Enrollment: Male and Female Part-Time Students at Higher Education Institutions, by Race/Ethnic Origin: 1991-1993

Sex and race/ethnicity	Number			Percentage distribution		
	1991	1992	1993	1991	1992	1993
Male	2,572,469	2,597,075	2,537,113	100.0	100.0	100.0
White, non-Hispanic	1,975,412	1,946,213	1,879,971	76.8	74.9	74.1
Black, non-Hispanic	198,716	211,442	212,221	7.7	8.1	8.4
Hispanic	188,627	210,277	214,812	7.3	8.1	8.5
Asian or Pacific Islander	126,447	138,748	140,219	4.9	5.3	5.5
American Indian or Alaskan Native	20,711	21,431	21,223	0.8	0.8	0.8
Nonresident alien	62,556	68,964	68,667	2.4	2.7	2.7
Female	3,671,155	3,728,122	3,640,805	100.0	100.0	100.0
White, non-Hispanic	2,868,859	2,848,334	2,748,735	78.1	76.4	75.5
Black, non-Hispanic	358,725	380,374	382,564	9.8	10.2	10.5
Hispanic	238,209	269,930	274,790	6.5	7.2	7.5
Asian or Pacific Islander	128,449	144,782	147,370	3.5	3.9	4.0
American Indian or Alaskan Native	31,842	32,670	32,993	0.9	0.9	0.9
Nonresident alien	45,071	52,032	54,353	1.2	1.4	1.5

Source: "Part-Time Enrollment in Institutions of Higher Education, by Sex and Race/Ethnicity: 50 States and the District of Columbia, Fall 1991 through Fall 1993," U.S. Department of Education, National Center for Education Statistics, *Enrollment in Higher Education: Fall 1984 through Fall 1993*, April, 1995, p. 9. Primary source: U.S. Department of Education, National Center for Education Statistics, Integrated Postsecondary education Data System, "Fall Enrollment" surveys for 1991, 1992, and 1993. *Notes:* Data for 1992 may differ from that in prior publications due to corrections and the addition of late data. Detail may not sum to total due to rounding.

★ 222 ★

Higher Education

Enrollment: Part-Time Enrollment at 2- and 4-Year Institutions, by Race/Ethnic Origin: 1991-1993

Level of institution and race/ethnicity	Number			Percentage Distribution		
	1991	1992	1993	1991	1992	1993
4-year institutions	2,666,254	2,682,813	2,655,370	100.0	100.0	100.0
White, non-Hispanic	2,149,301	2,141,890	2,094,983	80.6	79.8	78.9
Black, non-Hispanic	219,588	229,269	236,549	8.2	8.5	8.9
Hispanic	117,574	124,008	128,226	4.4	4.6	4.8
Asian or Pacific Islander	90,366	94,929	99,093	3.4	3.5	3.7
American Indian or Alaskan Native	15,626	16,567	16,908	0.6	0.6	0.6
Nonresident alien	73,799	76,150	79,611	2.8	2.8	3.0

[Continued]

★ 222 ★

Enrollment: Part-Time Enrollment at 2- and 4-Year Institutions, by Race/Ethnic Origin: 1991-1993

[Continued]

Level of institution and race/ethnicity	Number			Percentage Distribution		
	1991	1992	1993	1991	1992	1993
2-year institutions	3,577,370	3,642,384	3,522,548	100.0	100.0	100.0
White, non-Hispanic	2,694,970	2,652,657	2,533,723	75.3	72.8	71.9
Black, non-Hispanic	337,853	362,547	358,236	9.4	10.0	10.2
Hispanic	309,262	356,199	361,376	8.6	9.8	10.3
Asian or Pacific Islander	164,530	188,601	188,496	4.6	5.2	5.4
American Indian or Alaskan Native	36,927	37,534	37,308	1.0	1.0	1.1
Nonresident alien	33,828	44,846	43,409	0.9	1.2	1.2

Source: "Part-Time Enrollment in Institutions of Higher Education, by Level of Institution and Race/Ethnicity: 50 States and the District of Columbia, Fall 1991 through Fall 1993," U.S. Department of Education Statistics, *Enrollment in Higher Education: Fall 1984 Through Fall 1993*, April, 1995, p. 7. Primary source: U.S. Department of Education, National Center for Education Statistics, Integrated Postsecondary Education Data System, "Fall Enrollment" surveys for 1991, 1992, and 1993. *Notes:* Data for 1992 may differ from that in prior publications due to corrections and the addition of late data. Detail may not sum to total due to rounding.

★ 223 ★

Higher Education

Enrollment: State-by-State Enrollment in Higher Education, by Race/Ethnic Origin: Alabama-Mississippi, 1993

State	Total	White, non-Hispanic	Black, non-Hispanic	Hispanic	Asian or Pacific Islander	American Indian or Alaskan Native	Nonresident alien
50 states and D.C.	14,305,658	10,603,746	1,410,300	988,960	724,124	121,681	456,847
Alabama	266,972	197,437	55,833	4,163	3,142	1,428	4,969
Alaska	30,638	24,421	1,306	791	832	2,665	623
Arizona	272,300	202,042	9,294	35,718	7,625	10,422	7,199
Arkansas	99,262	80,285	14,204	652	1,012	779	2,330
California	1,838,172	981,070	133,614	323,131	292,441	20,403	87,513
Colorado	244,044	199,158	8,085	20,884	7,285	2,893	5,739
Connecticut	163,230	134,086	11,458	6,985	5,104	422	5,175
Delaware	43,528	35,424	5,456	661	948	148	891
District of Columbia	81,916	41,065	24,850	2,886	4,144	196	8,775
Florida	623,403	433,723	75,424	77,292	16,572	2,590	17,802
Georgia	302,844	213,261	70,987	4,269	6,534	784	7,009
Hawaii	62,871	17,290	1,613	1,443	36,776	285	5,464
Idaho	58,768	53,752	390	1,468	883	734	1,541
Illinois	734,089	529,185	91,130	55,721	37,525	2,385	18,143
Indiana	294,685	257,136	17,539	5,752	4,774	1,079	8,405
Iowa	172,797	153,417	4,979	2,435	3,303	545	8,118
Kansas	171,325	146,536	7,941	4,341	3,468	2,421	6,618
Kentucky	187,332	168,389	12,454	1,073	1,797	595	3,024
Louisiana	201,987	137,023	50,074	4,526	3,644	1,071	5,649

[Continued]

★ 223 ★

Enrollment: State-by-State Enrollment in Higher Education, by Race/Ethnic Origin: Alabama-Mississippi, 1993
[Continued]

State	Total	White, non-Hispanic	Black, non-Hispanic	Hispanic	Asian or Pacific Islander	American Indian or Alaskan Native	Nonresident alien
Maine	56,294	53,838	464	255	595	518	624
Maryland	272,912	189,145	53,869	5,797	14,191	987	8,923
Massachusetts	420,127	335,563	21,344	15,810	21,601	1,613	24,196
Michigan	568,210	462,897	60,662	10,920	13,672	4,473	15,586
Minnesota	268,118	241,946	6,016	3,275	8,002	2,403	6,476
Mississippi	122,408	83,462	34,959	523	905	423	2,136

Source: "Fall Enrollment in Institutions of Higher Education, by State and Race/Ethnicity: 50 States and the District of Columbia, Fall 1993," U.S. Department of Education, National Center for Education Statistics, *Enrollment in Higher Education: Fall 1984 Through Fall 1993,* April, 1995, p. 13. Primary source: U.S. Department of Education, National Center for Education Statistics, Integrated Postsecondary Education Data System, "Fall Enrollment" survey, 1993.

★ 224 ★

Higher Education

Enrollment: State-by-State Enrollment in Higher Education, by Race/Ethnic Origin: Missouri-Wyoming, 1993

State	Total	White, non-Hispanic	Black, non-Hispanic	Hispanic	Asian or Pacific Islander	American Indian or Alaskan Native	Nonresident alien
50 states and D.C.	14,305,658	10,603,746	1,410,300	988,960	724,124	121,681	456,847
Missouri	297,062	249,403	25,682	4,212	5,704	1,339	10,722
Montana	39,557	33,956	153	394	314	3,555	1,185
Nebraska	115,523	104,954	3,322	2,105	1,566	854	2,722
Nevada	63,947	50,859	3,125	3,873	3,207	979	1,904
New Hampshire	64,043	60,003	939	854	1,022	288	937
New Jersey	343,029	245,151	38,146	26,955	18,203	962	13,612
New Mexico	101,460	58,836	2,489	30,069	1,397	6,749	1,920
New York	1,069,018	743,956	132,146	91,452	58,380	3,500	39,584
North Carolina	371,280	281,031	71,137	3,853	6,299	3,389	5,571
North Dakota	40,316	35,616	263	229	282	2,102	1,824
Ohio	563,274	477,650	49,983	7,754	10,074	1,841	15,972
Oklahoma	183,342	142,680	13,002	3,592	3,563	12,762	7,743
Oregon	165,834	140,855	2,711	4,943	8,539	2,339	6,447
Pennsylvania	621,228	528,595	46,315	9,671	18,335	1,303	17,009
Rhode Island	77,407	66,784	3,057	2,441	2,492	259	2,374
South Carolina	174,302	130,396	36,933	1,297	1,990	496	3,190
South Dakota	38,166	34,723	312	191	331	1,682	927
Tennessee	244,936	198,786	35,843	2,124	3,061	651	4,471
Texas	942,178	609,184	89,307	175,973	36,505	4,091	27,118
Utah	138,139	123,496	988	3,513	2,784	1,440	5,918
Vermont	36,415	34,226	355	417	471	143	803

[Continued]

★ 224 ★

Enrollment: State-by-State Enrollment in Higher Education, by Race/Ethnic Origin: Missouri-Wyoming, 1993
[Continued]

State	Total	White, non-Hispanic	Black, non-Hispanic	Hispanic	Asian or Pacific Islander	American Indian or Alaskan Native	Nonresident alien
Virginia	348,535	265,467	53,682	6,483	15,228	1,110	6,565
Washington	279,845	230,388	9,902	8,487	20,020	4,653	6,395
West Virginia	88,852	82,063	3,433	433	870	161	1,892
Wisconsin	309,036	275,022	12,853	5,818	6,472	2,321	6,550
Wyoming	30,702	28,115	277	1,056	240	450	564

Source: "Fall Enrollment in Institutions of Higher Education, by State and Race/Ethnicity: 50 States and the District of Columbia, Fall 1993," U.S. Department of Education, National Center for Education Statistics, *Enrollment in Higher Education: Fall 1984 Through Fall 1993,* April, 1995, p. 13. Primary source: U.S. Department of Education, National Center for Education Statistics, Integrated Postsecondary Education Data System, "Fall Enrollment" survey, 1993.

★ 225 ★

Higher Education

Enrollment: State-by-State Minority Percent of Total Enrollment in Higher Education, by Race/Ethnic Group: Alabama-Mississippi, Fall 1986 and Fall 1992-I

State or other area	Total minority			Black			Hispanic		
	Fall 1980	Fall 1990	Fall 1993	Fall 1980	Fall 1990	Fall 1993	Fall 1980	Fall 1990	Fall 1993
United States	16.5	20.1	23.4	9.4	9.3	10.2	4.0	5.8	7.1
Alabama	23.1	21.7	24.8	22.0	20.1	22.8	0.4	0.5	0.7
Alaska	11.1	17.4	18.6	2.5	3.7	4.4	1.0	2.2	2.6
Arizona	15.3	20.4	23.8	2.8	3.0	3.5	7.6	11.6	13.5
Arkansas	16.7	15.5	17.2	15.0	13.7	14.7	0.3	0.5	0.7
California	26.7	34.5	44.0	8.2	6.8	7.6	9.7	13.4	18.5
Colorado	10.8	14.1	16.4	2.9	3.0	3.3	5.7	7.7	8.8
Connecticut	8.1	12.4	15.1	5.0	6.1	7.3	1.7	3.4	4.4
Delaware	12.6	14.7	16.9	11.1	11.4	12.8	0.8	1.3	1.6
District of Columbia	39.7	42.5	43.9	34.8	34.3	34.0	2.0	3.4	3.9
Florida	19.9	24.6	28.4	10.6	10.7	12.5	8.1	11.5	12.8
Georgia	20.7	23.1	27.9	19.2	200	24.0	0.7	1.1	1.4
Hawaii	69.6	68.1	69.9	1.3	2.9	2.8	2.7	2.0	2.5
Idaho	4.4	5.0	6.1	0.6	0.6	0.7	1.5	2.0	2.6
Illinois	16.6	24.2	26.1	11.6	12.5	12.7	2.5	6.9	7.8
Indiana	8.5	9.1	10.2	6.4	5.7	6.1	1.2	1.6	2.0
Iowa	4.1	5.2	6.8	2.4	2.5	3.0	0.6	1.0	1.5
Kansas	7.7	9.5	11.0	4.3	4.3	4.8	1.5	2.2	2.6
Kentucky	8.4	7.4	8.6	7.2	6.0	6.8	0.4	0.4	0.6
Louisiana	25.8	28.5	30.2	23.3	24.6	25.5	1.6	1.9	2.3

[Continued]

★ 225 ★

Enrollment: State-by-State Minority Percent of Total Enrollment in Higher Education, by Race/Ethnic Group: Alabama-Mississippi, Fall 1986 and Fall 1992-I
[Continued]

State or other area	Total minority			Black			Hispanic		
	Fall 1980	Fall 1990	Fall 1993	Fall 1980	Fall 1990	Fall 1993	Fall 1980	Fall 1990	Fall 1993
Maine	1.2	2.3	3.3	0.4	0.5	0.8	0.2	0.3	0.5
Maryland	21.8	24.3	28.5	18.0	17.5	20.7	1.4	1.9	2.1
Massachusetts	6.6	12.2	15.2	3.6	4.7	5.4	1.5	3.2	4.0
Michigan	13.0	14.4	16.2	10.3	10.2	11.0	1.2	1.6	2.0
Minnesota	3.1	5.2	7.5	1.2	1.7	2.3	0.5	0.8	1.3
Mississippi	30.5	29.1	30.6	29.7	27.9	29.1	0.3	0.3	0.4

Source: "Enrollment in Public Elementary and Secondary Schools, by Race or Ethnicity and State: Fall 1986 and Fall 1992," Department of Education, National Center for Education Statistics, *State Comparisons of Education Statistics: 1969-70 to 1993-94*, p. 117. Primary source: U.S. Department of Education, National Center for Education Statistics, Integrated Postsecondary Education Data System (IPEDS), "Fall Enrollment" surveys. (This table was prepared January 1995.) *Notes:* Percentages based on U.S. resident enrollment (total enrollment less enrollment of nonresident aliens). Some data revised from previously published figures.

★ 226 ★

Higher Education

Enrollment: State-by-State Minority Percent of Total Enrollment in Higher Education, by Race/Ethnic Group: Alabama-Mississippi, Fall 1986 and Fall 1992-II

State or other area	Asian/Pacific Islander			American Indian/Alaskan Native		
	Fall 1980	Fall 1990	Fall 1993	Fall 1980	Fall 1990	Fall 1993
United States	2.4	4.3	5.2	0.7	0.8	0.9
Alabama	0.5	0.8	0.9	0.2	0.3	0.5
Alaska	1.2	2.5	2.8	6.4	9.0	8.9
Arizona	1.3	2.4	2.9	3.6	3.4	3.9
Arkansas	0.7	0.8	1.0	0.7	0.5	0.8
California	7.5	13.1	16.7	1.3	1.2	1.2
Colorado	1.4	2.4	3.0	0.7	1.0	1.2
Connecticut	1.0	2.6	3.2	0.3	0.3	0.3
Delaware	0.6	1.7	2.2	0.1	0.2	0.3
District of Columbia	2.5	4.5	5.7	0.4	0.4	0.3
Florida	1.0	2.1	2.7	0.3	0.3	0.4
Georgia	0.7	1.7	2.2	0.2	0.2	0.3
Hawaii	65.3	62.8	64.1	0.3	0.4	0.5
Idaho	1.4	1.4	1.5	0.9	1.0	1.3
Illinois	2.2	4.5	5.2	0.4	0.3	0.3
Indiana	0.7	1.4	1.7	0.3	0.3	0.4

[Continued]

★ 226 ★

Enrollment: State-by-State Minority Percent of Total Enrollment in Higher Education, by Race/Ethnic Group: Alabama-Mississippi, Fall 1986 and Fall 1992-II

[Continued]

State or other area	Asian/Pacific Islander			American Indian/Alaskan Native		
	Fall 1980	Fall 1990	Fall 1993	Fall 1980	Fall 1990	Fall 1993
Iowa	0.8	1.5	2.0	0.4	0.3	0.3
Kansas	0.6	1.7	2.1	1.3	1.2	1.5
Kentucky	0.6	0.8	1.0	0.3	0.3	0.3
Louisiana	0.6	1.5	1.9	0.2	0.5	0.5
Maine	0.3	0.7	1.1	0.4	0.7	0.9
Maryland	2.1	4.5	5.4	0.3	0.3	0.4
Massachusetts	1.3	4.1	5.5	0.2	0.3	0.4
Michigan	0.9	1.9	2.5	0.5	0.6	0.8
Minnesota	1.0	2.0	3.1	0.5	0.8	0.9
Mississippi	0.3	0.6	0.8	0.2	0.3	0.4

Source: "Enrollment in Public Elementary and Secondary Schools, by Race or Ethnicity and State: Fall 1986 and Fall 1992," Department of Education, National Center for Education Statistics, *State Comparisons of Education Statistics: 1969-70 to 1993-94,* p. 117. Primary source: U.S. Department of Education, National Center for Education Statistics, Integrated Postsecondary Education Data System (IPEDS), "Fall Enrollment" surveys. (This table was prepared January 1995.) *Notes:* Percentages based on U.S. resident enrollment (total enrollment less enrollment of nonresident aliens). Some data revised from previously published figures.

★ 227 ★

Higher Education

Enrollment: State-by-State Minority Percent of Total Enrollment in Higher Education, by Race/Ethnic Group: Missouri-Wyoming, Fall 1986 and Fall 1992-I

State or other area	Total minority			Black			Hispanic		
	Fall 1980	Fall 1990	Fall 1993	Fall 1980	Fall 1990	Fall 1993	Fall 1980	Fall 1990	Fall 1993
United States	16.5	20.1	23.4	9.4	9.3	10.2	4.0	5.8	7.1
Missouri	11.1	11.4	12.9	9.1	8.2	9.0	0.8	1.2	1.5
Montana	5.7	8.4	11.5	0.4	0.3	0.4	0.4	0.8	1.0
Nebraska	5.4	5.6	7.0	3.0	2.5	2.9	1.0	1.4	1.9
Nevada	13.8	16.3	18.0	6.9	4.8	5.0	3.2	5.6	6.2
New Hampshire	2.9	3.7	4.9	1.6	1.1	1.5	0.6	0.8	1.4
New Jersey	16.4	22.4	25.6	10.2	10.6	11.6	4.3	6.9	8.2
New Mexico	31.7	37.5	40.9	2.2	2.6	2.5	24.8	28.1	30.2
New York	19.3	25.4	27.8	10.9	12.1	12.9	5.5	7.9	8.9
North Carolina	21.2	21.1	23.2	19.4	17.9	19.5	0.4	0.7	1.1
North Dakota	3.4	6.4	7.5	0.5	0.7	0.7	0.2	0.5	0.6
Ohio	11.2	11.4	12.7	9.5	8.7	9.1	0.7	1.0	1.4

[Continued]

★ 227 ★

Enrollment: State-by-State Minority Percent of Total Enrollment in Higher Education, by Race/Ethnic Group: Missouri-Wyoming, Fall 1986 and Fall 1992-I

[Continued]

State or other area	Total minority			Black			Hispanic		
	Fall 1980	Fall 1990	Fall 1993	Fall 1980	Fall 1990	Fall 1993	Fall 1980	Fall 1990	Fall 1993
Oklahoma	12.2	16.1	18.7	6.2	7.0	7.4	1.1	1.6	2.0
Oregon	5.7	8.8	11.6	1.0	1.4	1.7	1.1	2.0	3.1
Pennsylvania	9.5	11.3	12.5	7.6	7.5	7.7	0.8	1.3	1.6
Rhode Island	5.9	8.2	11.0	3.4	3.4	4.1	1.4	2.1	3.3
South Carolina	23.4	21.6	23.8	22.3	19.9	21.6	0.5	0.6	0.8
South Dakota	6.2	7.3	6.8	1.0	0.7	0.8	0.8	0.3	0.5
Tennessee	16.4	15.9	17.3	15.4	14.1	14.9	0.4	0.6	0.9
Texas	23.6	29.6	33.4	9.5	9.2	9.8	12.7	16.9	19.2
Utah	4.5	5.5	6.6	0.6	0.6	0.7	1.5	1.9	2.7
Vermont	2.0	4.2	3.9	1.1	1.1	1.0	0.5	1.2	1.2
Virginia	17.0	19.2	22.4	14.7	14.3	15.7	0.7	1.4	1.9
Washington	8.6	12.7	15.7	2.2	2.9	3.6	1.5	2.4	3.1
West Virginia	4.9	5.2	5.6	4.0	3.8	3.9	0.3	0.4	0.5
Wisconsin	6.0	7.6	9.1	3.5	3.6	4.2	1.0	1.6	1.9
Wyoming	4.0	5.9	6.7	0.8	0.9	0.9	1.7	2.9	3.5
U.S. Service Schools	13.5	16.6	21.7	11.1	13.2	9.3	1.2	1.7	7.1

Source: "Enrollment in Public Elementary and Secondary Schools, by Race or Ethnicity and State: Fall 1986 and Fall 1992," Department of Education, National Center for Education Statistics, *State Comparisons of Education Statistics: 1969-70 to 1993-94*, p. 117. Primary source: U.S. Department of Education, National Center for Education Statistics, Integrated Postsecondary Education Data System (IPEDS), "Fall Enrollment" surveys. (This table was prepared January 1995.) *Notes:* Percentages based on U.S. resident enrollment (total enrollment less enrollment of nonresident aliens). Some data revised from previously published figures.

★ 228 ★

Higher Education

Enrollment: State-by-State Minority Percent of Total Enrollment in Higher Education, by Race/Ethnic Group: Missouri-Wyoming, Fall 1986 and Fall 1992-II

State or other area	Asian/Pacific Islander			American Indian/Alaskan Native		
	Fall 1980	Fall 1990	Fall 1993	Fall 1980	Fall 1990	Fall 1993
United States	2.4	4.3	5.2	0.7	0.8	0.9
Missouri	0.9	1.6	2.0	0.3	0.4	0.5
Montana	0.3	0.3	0.8	4.5	6.9	9.3
Nebraska	0.7	1.1	1.4	0.6	0.7	0.8
Nevada	2.2	4.2	5.2	1.5	1.7	1.6
New Hampshire	0.4	1.3	1.6	0.3	0.4	0.5

[Continued]

★ 228 ★

Enrollment: State-by-State Minority Percent of Total Enrollment in Higher Education, by Race/Ethnic Group: Missouri-Wyoming, Fall 1986 and Fall 1992-II

[Continued]

State or other area	Asian/Pacific Islander			American Indian/Alaskan Native		
	Fall 1980	Fall 1990	Fall 1993	Fall 1980	Fall 1990	Fall 1993
New Jersey	1.6	4.6	5.5	0.3	0.2	0.3
New Mexico	0.8	1.3	1.4	3.9	5.5	6.8
New York	2.3	5.0	5.7	0.5	0.3	0.3
North Carolina	0.6	1.6	1.7	0.7	0.9	0.9
North Dakota	0.3	0.8	0.7	2.4	4.4	5.5
Ohio	0.7	1.4	1.8	0.3	0.3	0.3
Oklahoma	1.1	1.7	2.0	3.9	5.7	7.3
Oregon	2.6	4.2	5.4	1.0	1.1	1.5
Pennsylvania	0.9	2.3	3.0	0.2	0.2	0.2
Rhode Island	1.0	2.5	3.3	0.2	0.3	0.3
South Carolina	0.5	1.0	1.2	0.1	0.2	0.3
South Dakota	0.3	0.6	0.9	4.2	5.7	4.5
Tennessee	0.4	1.0	1.3	0.2	0.2	0.3
Texas	1.1	3.2	4.0	0.4	0.3	0.4
Utah	1.2	1.9	2.1	1.1	1.1	1.1
Vermont	0.3	1.6	1.3	0.1	0.4	0.4
Virginia	1.3	3.3	4.5	0.2	0.2	0.3
Washington	3.6	6.0	7.3	1.3	1.5	1.7
West Virginia	0.4	0.8	1.0	0.2	0.2	0.2
Wisconsin	0.8	1.7	2.1	0.7	0.7	0.8
Wyoming	0.5	0.6	0.8	.09	1.4	1.5
U.S. Service Schools	1.0	1.5	4.3	0.1	0.2	1.0

Source: "Enrollment in Public Elementary and Secondary Schools, by Race or Ethnicity and State: Fall 1986 and Fall 1992," Department of Education, National Center for Education Statistics, *State Comparisons of Education Statistics: 1969-70 to 1993-94*, p. 117. Primary source: U.S. Department of Education, National Center for Education Statistics, Integrated Postsecondary Education Data System (IPEDS), "Fall Enrollment" surveys. (This table was prepared January 1995.) *Notes:* Percentages based on U.S. resident enrollment (total enrollment less enrollment of nonresident aliens). Some data revised from previously published figures.

★ 229 ★

Higher Education

Enrollment: Trends in Characteristics of College Enrollment, by Race: 1978-1992

[**In thousands. As of fall.** Totals may differ from other tables because of adjustments to underreported and nonreported racial/ethnic data. Nonresident alien students are not distributed among racial/ethnic groups].

CHARACTERISTIC	1978	1980	1984	1988	1990	1991, est.	1992, prel.
Total	11,231.2	12,086.8	12,233.0	13,043.1	13,819.5	14,359.0	14,491.2
White[1]	9,194.0	9,833.0	9,814.7	10,283.2	10,723.0	10,989.8	10,870.0
Male	4,613.1	4,772.9	4,689.9	4,711.6	4,861.3	4,962.2	4,882.5
Female	4,580.9	5,060.1	5,124.7	5.571.6	5,861.7	6,027.6	5,987.6
Public	7,136.1	7,656.1	7,542.4	7,963.8	8,385.4	8,622.2	8,486.9
Private	2,057.9	2,176.9	2,272.3	2,319.4	2,337.6	2,367.5	2,383.1
2-year	3,166.9	3,558.5	3,514.3	3,701.5	3,954.3	4,198.8	4,123.1
4-year	6,027.1	6,274.5	6,300.4	6,581.6	6,768.7	6,791.0	6,746.9
Undergraduate	7,870.6	8,480.7	8,484.0	8,906.7	9,272.6	9,507.7	9,380.6
Graduate	1,094.1	1,104.7	1,087.3	1,153.2	1,228.4	1,258.0	1,268.4
First professional	229.3	247.7	243.4	223.2	222.0	224.0	220.9
Black[1]	1,054.4	1,106.8	1,075.8	1,129.6	1,247.1	1,335.4	1,393.5
Male	453.3	463.7	436.7	442.7	484.7	517.0	537.1
Female	601.1	643.0	639.0	686.9	762.4	818.4	856.4
Public	839.5	876.1	844.0	881.1	976.5	1,053.4	1,101.1
Private	214.9	230.7	231.8	248.5	270.6	281.9	292.4
2-year	442.6	472.5	458.7	473.3	524.3	577.6	602.0
4-year	611.8	634.3	617.0	656.3	722.8	757.8	791.5
Undergraduate	966.5	1,018.5	994.9	1,038.8	1,147.2	1,229.3	1,281.2
Graduate	76.4	75.1	67.4	76.5	83.9	88.9	94.1
First professional	11.4	12.8	13.4	14.3	16.0	17.2	18.2

Source: "College Enrollment, by Selected Characteristics: 1978 to 1992," *Statistical Abstract of the United States: 1995*, 1995, p. 179. Primary source: U.S. National Center for Education Statistics, *Digest of Education Statistics*, annual. *Note:* 1. Non-Hispanic.

★ 230 ★

Higher Education

Enrollment: Trends in College Enrollment of 16-24-Year-Olds Who Completed High School in Preceding 12 Months, by Race: 1960-1992

[For persons 16 to 24 who graduated from high school in the preceding 12 months. Includes persons receiving GED's. Based on surveys and subject to sampling error].

YEAR	NUMBER OF HIGH SCHOOL GRADUATES (1,000)			PERCENT ENROLLED IN COLLEGE[2]		
	Total[1]	White	Black	Total	White	Black
1960	1,679	1,565	(NA)	45.1	45.8	(NA)
1961	1,763	1,612	(NA)	48.0	49.5	(NA)
1962	1,838	1,660	(NA)	49.0	50.6	(NA)
1963	1,741	1,615	(NA)	45.0	45.6	(NA)
1964	2,145	1,964	(NA)	48.3	49.2	(NA)
1965	2,659	2,417	(NA)	50.9	51.7	(NA)
1966	2,612	2,403	(NA)	50.1	51.7	(NA)
1967	2,525	2,267	(NA)	51.9	53.0	(NA)
1968	2,606	2,303	(NA)	55.4	56.6	(NA)
1969	2,842	2,538	(NA)	53.3	55.2	(NA)
1970	2,757	2,461	(NA)	51.8	52.0	(NA)
1971	2,872	2,596	(NA)	53.4	54.0	(NA)
1972	2,961	2,614	(NA)	49.2	49.4	(NA)
1973	3,059	2,707	(NA)	46.6	48.1	(NA)
1974	3,101	2,736	(NA)	47.5	47.1	(NA)
1975	3,186	2,825	(NA)	50.7	51.2	(NA)
1976	2,987	2,640	320	48.8	48.9	41.9
1977	3,140	2,768	335	50.6	50.7	49.5
1978	3,161	2,750	352	50.1	50.1	45.7
1979	3,160	2,776	324	49.3	49.6	45.4
1980	3,089	2,682	361	49.3	49.9	41.8
1981	3,053	2,626	359	53.9	54.6	42.9
1982	3,100	2,644	384	50.6	52.0	36.5
1983	2,964	2,496	392	52.7	55.0	38.5
1984	3,012	2,514	438	55.2	57.9	40.2
1985	2,666	2,241	333	57.7	59.4	42.3
1986	2,786	2,307	386	53.8	56.0	36.5
1987	2,647	2,207	337	56.8	56.6	51.9
1988	2,673	2,187	382	58.9	60.7	45.0
1989	2,454	2,051	337	59.6	60.4	52.8
1990	2,355	1,921	341	59.9	61.5	46.3
1991	2,276	1,867	320	62.4	64.6	45.6
1992	2,398	1,900	353	61.7	63.4	47.9

Source: "College Enrollment of Recent High School Graduates: 1960 to 1992," *Statistical Abstract of the United States: 1995,* 1995, p. 178. Primary source: U.S. Department of Education Statistics, *Digest of Education Statistics,* 1994. *Notes:* NA Not available. 1. Includes other races, not shown separately. 2. As of October.

★ 231 ★

Higher Education

Enrollment: Trends in College Enrollment, by Age and Race/Ethnic Origin: 1975-1993

[**In thousands.** As of **October** for the civilian noninstitutional population, 14 years and over. Based on the Current Population Survey].

CHARACTERISTIC	1975	1980	1985	1986[1]	1987	1988	1989	1990	1991	1992	1993
Total[2]	10,880	11,387	12,524	12,651	12,719	13,116	13,180	13,621	14,057	14,035	13,898
White[3]	9,546	9,925	10,781	10,707	10,731	11,140	11,243	11,488	11,686	11,710	11,434
18 to 24 years	6,116	6,334	6,500	6,307	6,483	6,659	6,631	6,635	6,813	6,916	6,783
25 to 34 years	2,147	2,328	2,604	2,617	2,468	2,448	2,597	2,698	2,661	2,582	2,505
35 years old and over	1,031	1,051	1,448	1,609	1,584	1,896	1,868	2,023	2,107	2,053	2,068
Male	5,263	4,804	5,103	5,074	5,104	5,078	5,136	5,235	5,304	5,210	5,222
Female	4,284	5,121	5,679	5,632	5,627	6,063	6,107	6,253	6,382	6,499	6,212
Black[3]	1,099	1,163	1,263	1,359	1,351	1,321	1,287	1,393	1,477	1,424	1,545
18 to 24 years	665	688	734	812	823	752	835	894	828	886	861
25 to 34 years	248	289	295	330	341	330	275	258	373	302	386
35 years old and over	152	156	213	198	155	206	146	207	257	208	284
Male	523	476	552	580	587	494	480	587	629	527	636
Female	577	686	712	779	764	827	807	807	848	897	909
Hispanic origin[3,4]	411	443	580	794	739	747	754	748	830	918	995
18 to 24 years	295	315	375	458	455	450	453	435	516	586	602
25 to 34 years	103	118	189	231	204	191	170	168	196	214	249
35 years old and over	(NA)	(NA)	(NA)	89	73	93	114	130	109	102	129
Male	218	222	279	377	390	355	353	364	347	388	442
Female	193	221	299	417	349	391	401	384	483	530	553

Source: "College Enrollment, by Sex, Age, Race, and Hispanic Origin: 1975 to 1993," *Statistical Abstract of the United States: 1995,* 1995, p. 180. Primary source: U.S. Bureau of the Census, *Current Population Reports,* P20-479; and earlier reports. *Notes:* NA Not available. 1. Revised. Beginning 1986, based on a revised edit and tabulation package. 2. Includes other races not shown separately. 3. Includes persons 14 to 17 years old, not shown separately. 4. Persons of Hispanic origin may be of any race.

★ 232 ★

Higher Education

Enrollment: Trends in Enrollment at 2- and 4-Year Institutions, by Race/Ethnic Origin: 1984-1993

Level of institution and race/ethnicity	Number, in thousands						
	1984	1986	1988	1990	1991	1992	1993
All institutions	12,235	12,504	13,043	13,819	14,359	14,486	14,306
4-year institutions	7,707	7,824	8,175	8,579	8,707	8,764	8,740
2-year institutions	4,528	4,680	4,868	5,240	5,652	5,722	5,566

[Continued]

★ 232 ★

Enrollment: Trends in Enrollment at 2- and 4-Year Institutions, by Race/ Ethnic Origin: 1984-1993

[Continued]

Level of institution and race/ethnicity	Number, in thousands						
	1984	1986	1988	1990	1991	1992	1993
Percentage Distribution							
All institutions	100.0	100.0	100.0	100.0	100.0	100.0	100.0
White, non-Hispanic	80.2	79.3	78.8	77.6	76.5	75.1	74.1
Black, non-Hispanic	8.8	8.7	8.7	9.0	9.3	9.6	9.9
Hispanic	4.4	4.9	5.2	5.7	6.0	6.6	6.9
Asian or Pacific Islander	3.2	3.6	3.8	4.1	4.4	4.8	5.1
American Indian or Alaskan Native	0.7	0.7	0.7	0.7	0.8	0.8	0.9
Nonresident alien	2.7	2.8	2.8	2.8	2.9	3.1	3.2
4-year institutions	63.0	62.6	62.7	62.1	60.6	60.5	61.1
White, non-Hispanic	51.5	50.7	50.5	49.0	47.3	46.6	46.4
Black, non-Hispanic	5.0	4.9	5.0	5.2	5.3	5.5	5.7
Hispanic	2.0	2.2	2.3	2.6	2.7	2.8	3.0
Asian or Pacific Islander	1.8	2.1	2.3	2.6	2.7	2.8	3.0
American Indian or Alaskan Native	0.3	0.3	0.3	0.3	0.4	0.4	0.4
Nonresident alien	2.3	2.3	2.3	2.3	2.4	2.5	2.6
2-year institutions	37.0	37.4	37.3	37.9	39.4	39.5	38.9
White, non-Hispanic	28.7	28.7	28.4	28.6	29.2	28.5	27.7
Black, non-Hispanic	3.8	3.7	3.6	3.8	4.0	4.2	4.2
Hispanic	2.4	2.7	2.9	3.1	3.4	3.8	3.9
Asian or Pacific Islander	1.4	1.5	1.5	1.6	1.8	2.0	2.1
American Indian or Alaskan Native	0.4	0.4	0.4	0.4	0.4	0.4	0.4
Nonresident alien	0.4	0.4	0.5	0.5	0.5	0.6	0.6

Source: "Total Enrollment in Institutions of Higher Education, by Level of Institution and Race/Ethnicity: 50 States and the District of Columbia, Fall 1984 through Fall 1993," U.S. Department of Education, National Center for Education Statistics, *Enrollment in Higher Education: Fall 1984 Through Fall 1993*, April 1995, p. 5. Primary source: U.S. Department of Education, National Center for Education Statistics, Higher Education General Information Survey, "Fall Enrollment and Compliance Report of Institutions of Higher Education" (1984) and Integrated Postsecondary Education Data System, "Fall Enrollment" surveys for 1986, 1988, 1990, 1991, 1992, and 1993. *Notes:* Because of underreporting/nonreporting of racial/ethnic data, data prior to 1986 were estimated, when possible. Also 1992 data may differ from that in prior publications due to corrections and the addition of late data. Detail may not sum to total due to rounding.

★ 233 ★

Higher Education

Enrollment: Trends in Enrollment in Public and Private Institutions, by Race/Ethnic Origin: 1984-1993

Control of institution and race/ethnicity	Number, in thousands						
	1984	1986	1988	1990	1991	1992	1993
All institutions	12,235	12,504	13,043	13,819	14,359	14,486	14,306
Public	9,458	9,714	10,156	10,845	11,310	11,385	11,189
Private	2,777	2,790	2,887	2,974	3,049	3,102	3,117

	Percentage Distribution						
All institutions	100.0	100.0	100.0	100.0	100.0	100.0	100.0
White, non-Hispanic	80.2	79.3	78.8	77.6	76.5	75.1	74.1
Black, non-Hispanic	8.8	8.7	8.7	9.0	9.3	9.6	9.9
Hispanic	4.4	4.9	5.2	5.7	6.0	6.6	6.9
Asian or Pacific Islander	3.2	3.6	3.8	4.1	4.4	4.8	5.1
American Indian or Alaskan Native	0.7	0.7	0.7	0.7	0.8	0.8	0.9
Nonresident alien	2.7	2.8	2.8	2.8	2.9	3.1	3.2
Public	77.3	77.7	77.9	78.5	78.8	78.6	78.2
White, non-Hispanic	61.7	61.2	61.1	60.7	60.0	58.6	57.5
Black, non-Hispanic	6.9	6.8	6.8	7.1	7.3	7.6	7.8
Hispanic	3.7	43	4.5	4.9	5.2	5.7	6.0
Asian or Pacific Islander	2.6	3.0	3.1	3.3	3.6	3.9	4.1
American Indian or Alaskan Native	0.6	0.6	0.6	0.7	0.7	0.7	0.7
Nonresident alien	1.8	1.8	1.8	1.9	1.9	2.1	2.1
Private	22.7	22.3	22.1	21.5	21.2	21.4	21.8
White, non-Hispanic	18.6	18.1	17.8	16.9	16.5	16.4	16.6
Black, non-Hispanic	1.9	1.8	1.9	2.0	2.0	2.0	2.1
Hispanic	0.6	0.7	0.7	0.8	0.9	0.9	1.0
Asian or Pacific Islander	0.5	0.6	0.7	0.8	0.8	0.9	1.0
American Indian or Alaskan Native	0.1	0.1	0.1	0.1	0.1	0.1	0.1
Nonresident alien	0.9	1.0	0.9	1.0	1.0	1.0	1.1

Source: "Total Enrollment in Institutions of Higher Education, by Control of Institution and Race/Ethnicity: 50 States and the District of Columbia, Fall 1990 through Fall 1993," U.S. Department of Education, National Center for Education Statistics, *Enrollment in Higher Education: Fall 1984 Through Fall 1993*, April, 1995, p. 2. Primary source: U.S. Department of Education, National Center for Education Statistics, Higher Education General Information Survey, "Fall Enrollment and Compliance Report of Institutions of Higher Education" (1984) and Integrated Postsecondary Education Data System, "Fall Enrollment" surveys for 1986, 1988, 1990, 1991, 1992, and 1993. *Notes:* Because of underreporting/nonreporting of racial/ethnic data, data prior to 1986 were estimated, when possible. Also, 1992 data may differ from that in prior publications due to corrections and the addition of late data. Detail may not sum to total due to rounding.

★ 234 ★

Higher Education

Enrollment: Trends in Higher Education Enrollment, by Level of Study and Race/Ethnic Origin: 1984-1993

Level of study and race/ethnicity	Number, in thousands						
	1984	1986	1988	1990	1991	1992	1993
Undergraduate enrollment	10,610	10,798	11,304	11,959	12,439	12,537	12,324
Graduate enrollment	1,344	1,435	1,472	1,586	1,639	1,669	1,689
First-professional enrollment	278	270	267	274	281	281	292

	Percentage Distribution						
Undergraduate enrollment	100.0	100.0	100.0	100.0	100.0	100.0	100.0
White, non-Hispanic	80.0	79.3	78.8	77.5	76.4	74.9	73.9
Black, non-Hispanic	9.4	9.2	9.2	9.6	9.9	10.2	10.5
Hispanic	4.7	5.2	5.6	6.1	6.5	7.1	7.4
Asian or Pacific Islander	3.2	3.6	3.9	4.2	4.5	4.9	5.1
American Indian or Alaskan Native	0.7	.08	0.8	0.8	0.9	0.9	0.9
Nonresident alien	2.0	1.9	1.8	1.8	1.9	2.1	2.2
Graduate enrollment	100.0	100.0	100.0	100.0	100.0	100.0	100.0
White, non-Hispanic	80.9	78.9	78.4	77.4	76.7	75.9	75.5
Black, non-Hispanic	5.0	5.0	5.2	5.3	5.4	5.6	6.0
Hispanic	2.4	3.2	2.7	3.0	3.1	3.3	3.4
Asian or Pacific Islander	2.8	3.0	3.1	3.4	3.5	3.7	3.9
American Indian or Alaskan Native	0.4	0.4	0.4	0.4	0.4	0.4	0.4
Nonresident alien	8.6	9.5	10.3	10.5	10.8	11.0	10.8
First-professional enrollment	100.0	100.0	100.0	100.0	100.0	100.0	100.0
White, non-Hispanic	87.4	85.3	83.6	81.0	79.8	78.5	77.3
Black, non-Hispanic	4.8	5.2	5.4	5.8	6.1	6.5	6.9
Hispanic	2.9	3.4	3.5	4.0	4.1	4.3	4.4
Asian or Pacific Islander	3.4	4.2	5.4	6.9	7.4	8.0	8.6
American Indian or Alaskan Native	0.4	0.4	0.4	0.4	0.5	0.5	0.6
Nonresident alien	1.2	1.5	1.8	2.0	2.0	2.2	2.4

Source: "Total Enrollment in Institutions of Higher Education, by Level of Study and Race/Ethnicity: 50 States and the District of Columbia, Fall 1984 through Fall 1993," U.S. Department of Education, National Center for Education Statistics, *Enrollment in Higher Education: Fall 1984 Through Fall 1993*, April 1995, p. 10. Primary source: U.S. department of Education, National Center for Education Statistics, Higher Education General Information Survey "Fall Enrollment and Compliance Report of Institutions of Higher Education" (1984) and Integrated Postsecondary Education Data System "Fall Enrollment" surveys for 1986, 1988, 1988, 1990, 1991, 1992, and 1993. *Notes:* Because of underreporting/nonreporting of racial/ethnic data, data prior to 1986 were estimated, when possible. Also, 1992 data may differ slightly from that in prior publications due to corrections and the addition of late data. Due to rounding, detail may not add to totals.

★ 235 ★

Higher Education

Enrollment: Trends in Percent of Enrollment in Higher Education, by Race/Ethnic Origin: 1980-1992

	1980	1982	1984	1986	1988	1990	1992
Total	100.0	100.0	100.0	100.0	100.0	100.0	100.0
American Indian/ Alaskan Native	0.7	0.7	0.7	0.7	0.7	0.7	0.8
Asian/Pacific Islander	2.4	2.8	3.2	3.6	3.8	4.0	4.8
Black, non-Hispanic	9.2	8.9	8.8	8.7	8.7	8.9	9.6
Hispanic	3.9	4.2	4.4	4.9	5.2	5.5	6.6
White, non-Hispanic	81.4	80.7	80.2	79.3	78.8	77.9	75.0
Nonresident alien	2.5	2.7	2.7	2.8	2.8	2.9	3.2

Source: "Percentage Distribution of All Students Enrolled in Higher Education by Race/Ethnicity: Fall 1980-1992," U.S. Department of Education, National Center for Education Statistics, *Minority Undergraduate Participation in Postsecondary Education*, June, 1995, p. 3. Primary source: U.S. Department of Education, National Center for Education Statistics, *Trends in Racial/Ethnic Enrollment in Higher Education: Fall 1980 through Fall 1992* (NCES 92-024) and *Trends in Enrollment in Higher Education, by Racial/Ethnic Category: Fall 1982 through Fall 1992* (NCES 94- 104); based on Integrated Postsecondary Education Data System (IPEDS) "Fall Enrollment" surveys. *Note:* Percentages may not sum to 100 because of rounding.

★ 236 ★

Higher Education

Enrollment: Trends in Percent of Female Enrollment in Higher Education, by Race/Ethnic Origin: 1980-1992

	1980	1982	1984	1986	1988	1990	1992
Total	100.0	100.0	100.0	100.0	100.0	100.0	100.0
American Indian/ Alaskan Native	0.7	0.8	0.7	0.8	0.8	0.8	0.9
Asian/Pacific Islander	2.2	2.5	2.8	3.2	3.4	3.6	4.3
Black, non-Hispanic	10.3	10.1	10.0	9.8	9.8	10.0	10.8
Hispanic	3.9	4.1	4.4	5.0	5.3	5.5	6.6
White, non-Hispanic	81.4	80.9	80.4	79.7	79.1	78.1	75.2
Nonresident alien	1.5	1.6	1.6	1.7	1.8	2.0	2.3

Source: "Percentage Distribution of All Female Students Enrolled in Higher Education by Race—Ethnicity: Fall 1980-1992," U.S. Department of Education, National Center for Education Statistics, *Minority Undergraduate Participation in Postsecondary Education*, June, 1995, p. 5. Primary source: U.S. Department of Education, National Center for Education Statistics, *Trends in Racial/Ethnic Enrollment in Higher Education: Fall 1980 through Fall 1990* (NCES 92-024) and *Trends in Enrollment in Higher Education by Racial/Ethnic Category: Fall 1982 through Fall 1992* (NCES 94- 104); based on Integrated Postsecondary Education Data System (IPEDS) "Fall Enrollment" surveys. *Note:* Percentages may not sum to 100 because of rounding.

★ 237 ★

Higher Education

Enrollment: Trends in Percent of Male Enrollment in Higher Education, by Race/Ethnic Origin: 1980-1992

	1980	1982	1984	1986	1988	1990	1992
Total	100.0	100.0	100.0	100.0	100.0	100.0	100.0
American Indian/ Alaskan Native	0.6	0.7	0.6	0.7	0.7	0.7	0.8
Asian or Pacific Islander	2.6	3.2	3.6	4.1	4.3	4.6	5.4
Black, Non-Hispanic	7.9	7.6	7.5	7.4	7.4	7.6	8.2
Hispanic	4.0	4.2	4.3	4.9	5.2	5.5	6.5
White, Non-Hispanic	81.3	80.5	80.0	79.0	78.6	77.6	74.8
Nonresident Alien	3.6	3.8	3.9	4.0	3.9	4.0	4.3

Source: "Percentage Distribution of All Male Students Enrolled in Higher Education by Race—Ethnicity: Fall 1980-1992," U.S. Department of Education, National Center for Education Statistics, *Minority Undergraduate Participation in Postsecondary Education*, June, 1995, p. 4. Primary source: U.S. Department of Education, National Center for Education Statistics, *Trends in Racial/Ethnic Enrollment in Higher Education: Fall 1980 through Fall 1990* (NCES 92-024) and *Trends in Enrollment in Higher Education, by Racial/Ethnic category: Fall 1982 through Fall 1992* (NCES 94- 104); based on Integrated Postsecondary Education Data System (IPEDS) "Fall Enrollment" surveys. *Note:* Percentages may not sum to 100 because of rounding.

★ 238 ★

Higher Education

Faculty: Participation Rates of Minority and White U.S. Higher Education Faculty: 1975-76 and 1991-92

Academic Year	Whites	Minorities				
		Total	Blacks	Hispanics	Asians, Pacific Islanders	American Indians, Alaskan Natives
1975-76	91.7	8.3	4.4	1.4	2.2	0.2
1991-92	87.7	12.3	4.7	2.2	5.1	0.3

Source: "Full-Time Employment Participation Rates of Minorities and Women in Higher Education Faculty, U.S. Summary, 1975-76 and 1991-92 Academic Years," *Indicators of Equal Employment Opportunity—Status and Trends*, September, 1993, p. 32. Primary source: *Equal Employment Opportunity Commission, Higher Education Staff Information* (EEO-6) *Reports.*

★ 239 ★

Higher Education

Faculty: White and Minority Tenure Status of U.S. Higher Education Faculty: 1975-76 and 1991-92

Tenure Status	Academic Year	Whites	Minorities				
			Total	Blacks	Hispanics	Asians, Pacific Islanders	American Indians, Alaskan Natives
Tenured	1975-76	53.5	39.2	36.0	41.4	44.2	38.0
	1991-92	52.5	39.3	38.4	42.3	38.9	38.6
Non-Tenured On-Track	1975-76	28.4	36.5	39.3	35.6	31.7	33.3
	1991-92	20.9	27.7	27.5	27.5	28.1	24.2
Other Non-Tenured	1975-76	18.1	24.4	24.7	23.0	24.1	28.6
	1991-92	26.6	33.0	34.0	30.2	33.0	37.1

Source: "Tenure Status of Minorities and Women in Higher Education Full-Time Faculty, U.S. Summary, 1975-76 and 1991-92 Academic Years," *Indicators of Equal Employment Opportunity—Status and Trends*, September, 1993, p. 34. Primary source: *Equal Employment Opportunity Commission, Higher Education Staff Information* (EEO-6) *Reports.*

★ 240 ★

Higher Education

Fields of Study: Percentage Distribution of Undergraduates' Major Fields, by Race/Ethnic Origin: 1989-90

	Humanities social science	Math/ science/ engineering/ computing	Education	Business manage-ment	Health	Vocational/ technical	Other technical prof.
Total	21.5	16.6	6.9	23.7	8.6	6.4	15.9
Race-ethnicity							
American Indian/Alaskan Native	20.4	17.4	8.6	20.1	8.8	7.0	17.5
Asian/Pacific Islander	20.6	29.4	2.4	24.2	6.9	5.0	11.1
Black, non-Hispanic	14.2	14.6	4.1	28.4	8.9	7.7	21.9
Hispanic	17.8	18.4	6.2	25.9	6.3	8.5	16.7
White, non-Hispanic	23.0	15.9	7.7	22.8	9.0	6.0	15.2
Racial-ethnic subgroup Asian							
Asian Indian	11.3	44.0	3.0	12.8	12.8	9.6	6.2
Chinese	19.5	42.7	0.8	20.3	4.1	1.0	11.3
Japanese	33.4	13.0	4.0	26.6	5.0	3.4	14.3
Korean	29.8	35.7	0.5	15.6	5.2	0.2	12.8
Pacific Islander	19.7	20.9	4.4	23.6	16.4	9.2	5.5
Vietnamese	16.9	36.5	1.8	31.6	5.4	1.0	6.5

[Continued]

★ 240 ★

Fields of Study: Percentage Distribution of Undergraduates' Major Fields, by Race/Ethnic Origin: 1989-90

[Continued]

	Humanities social science	Math/ science/ engineering/ computing	Education	Business manage- ment	Health	Vocational/ technical	Other technical prof.
Other or nonspecified	18.5	25.8	2.4	26.9	5.0	7.0	14.0
Racial-ethnic subgroup Hispanic							
Cuban	38.3	15.9	1.0	24.5	5.8	1.1	13.0
Mexican	16.3	18.0	9.4	23.5	7.1	10.9	14.4
Puerto Rican	18.2	21.3	5.4	25.0	7.9	6.3	15.6
Other or nonspecific	17.7	18.3	4.7	24.4	5.7	7.7	18.2

Source: "Percentage Distribution of Undergraduates' Major Field of Study by Race—Ethnicity: 1989-90," U.S. Department of Education, National Center for Education Statistics, *Minority Undergraduate Participation in Postsecondary Education*, June, 1995, p. 19. Primary source: U.S. Department of Education, National Center for Education Statistics 1989-90 National Postsecondary Student Aid Study (NPSAS:90), Undergraduate Data Analysis System. *Note:* Percentages may not sum to 100 due to rounding.

★ 241 ★

Higher Education

Financing College: Average Cost of Postsecondary Education, by Race/Ethnic Origin: 1990 to 1991

Race/ethnicity	Costs
White, not Hispanic	2,691
Black, not Hispanic	2,552
Hispanic (of any race)	1,882
Other races, not Hispanic	3,203

Source: "Average Postsecondary Schooling Costs: 1990 to 1991," *Population Profile of the United States: 1995*, 1995, p. 20.

★ 242 ★

Higher Education

Financing College: Percentage Distribution of Family Income Percentile Ranks of Undergraduate College Students, by Race/Ethnic Origin: 1989-90

	Total family income, 1988 percentile rank		
	25th or lower	26th-75th	76th or higher
Total	24.9	49.9	25.0
Race-ethnicity			
American Indian/Alaskan Native	30.2	52.8	16.9
Asian/Pacific Islander	34.5	42.4	23.0
Black, non-Hispanic	40.5	47.5	11.9
Hispanic	39.2	46.8	13.9
White, non-Hispanic	20.6	51.0	28.2
Racial-ethnic subgroup Asian			
Asian Indian	33.4	34.8	31.6
Chinese	37.0	35.0	27.9
Japanese	19.8	43.4	36.6
Korean	24.8	47.4	27.7
Pacific Islander	20.0	54.9	25.0
Vietnamese	68.3	24.4	7.2
Other or nonspecified	37.3	44.7	17.8
Racial-ethnic subgroup Hispanic			
Cuban	17.3	45.6	37.0
Mexican	32.3	51.1	16.4
Puerto Rican	42.9	40.4	16.6
Other or nonspecified	44.2	45.0	10.7

Source: "Percentage Distribution of Undergraduates According to Their Family Income Percentile Rankings by Race—Ethnicity: 1989-90," U.S. Department of Education, National Center for Education Statistics, *Minority Undergraduate Participation in Postsecondary Education,* June, 1995, p. 15. Primary source: U.S. Department of Education, National Center for Education Statistics, 1989-90 National Postsecondary Student Aid Study (NPSAS:90), Undergraduate Data Analysis System. *Note:* Percentages may not sum to 100 due to rounding.

★ 243 ★

Higher Education

HBCUs: Racial/Ethnic Origin Percentage Distribution of Undergraduates at HBCUs: 1989-90

	Attend HBCU		Percent racial-ethnic distribution attending HBCUs
	All under-graduates	Undergraduates in public or private, not-for-profit institutions in fall 1990	
Total	1.4	1.5	100.0
Race-ethnicity			
American Indian/ Alaskan Native	2.2	2.8	1.2
Asian/Pacific Islander	0.7	0.6	2.7
Black, non-Hispanic	11.7	14.1	74.7
Hispanic	1.1	1.4	6.5
White, non-Hispanic	0.2	0.2	14.9

Source: "Percentage of Undergraduates Enrolled In Historically Black Colleges or Universities (HBCU) and the Percentage Distribution of Students, by Race-Ethnicity: 1989-90," U.S. Department of Education, National Center for Education Statistics, *Minority Undergraduate Participation in Postsecondary Education,* June 1995, p. 21. Primary source: U.S. Department of Education, National Center for Education Statistics, 1989-90 National Postsecondary Student Aid Study (NPSAS:90), Undergraduate Data Analysis System. *Note:* Percentages may not sum to 100 due to rounding.

★ 244 ★

Higher Education

HBCUs: Trends in Federal Funding for Science and Engineering: 1985-1992

[Dollars in thousands]

Field	1985	1986	1987	1988	1989	1990	1991	1992
Total	57,873	60,910	61,572	75,998	106,548	117,200	122,080	146,707
Engineering, total	4,372	4,911	4,331	5,665	8,008	11,839	12,295	16,034
Aeronautical and astronautical	243	256	350	382	123	119	170	423
Chemical	140	158	123	554	586	747	791	852
Civil	184	130	585	811	880	647	278	1,314
Electrical	962	1,031	1,381	1,358	1,906	2,075	3,173	3,446
Mechanical	878	1,279	1,480	1,964	2,787	3,106	3,616	5,467
Metallurgical and materials[1]	--	--	--	--	--	1,375	1,178	245
Other, n.e.c.	1,965	2,057	412	596	1,726	3,770	3,089	4,287
All sciences, total	53,501	55,999	57,241	70,333	98,540	105,361	109,785	130,673

[Continued]

★ 244 ★

HBCUs: Trends in Federal Funding for Science and Engineering: 1985-1992
[Continued]

Field	1985	1986	1987	1988	1989	1990	1991	1992
Physical sciences	10,483	10,956	11,756	11,940	17,706	21,729	21,490	24,498
Astronomy	16	26	12	27	0	0	164	367
Chemistry	6,936	6,989	6,347	7,633	10,292	10,731	10,368	11,057
Physics	3,331	3,708	5,269	4,279	7,291	10,829	10,540	12,678
Other, n.e.c.	200	233	128	1	123	169	418	396
Environmental sciences	1,270	1,278	1,392	1,641	1,408	1,334	2,078	2,020
Atmospheric	19	0	0	3	129	105	104	212
Earth sciences	316	245	239	250	248	252	150	556
Oceanography	297	348	206	372	2	22	0	74
Other, n.e.c.	638	685	947	1,016	1,029	955	1,824	1,178
Mathematical sciences	889	955	269	188	486	676	1,281	2,637
Computer sciences	428	525	801	1,088	2,037	1,930	4,523	3,477
Life sciences	36,552	36,896	38,740	50,360	71,199	72,802	74,556	90,808
Agricultural sciences	16,993	17,778	16,774	21,039	30,388	29,667	34,013	40,125
Biological sciences	12,488	11,914	14,865	21,825	31,534	33,352	32,700	39,848
Medical sciences	6,409	6,431	6,065	6,641	8,902	9,338	6,878	9,946
Other, n.e.c.	662	773	1,036	855	375	265	965	889
Psychology	213	343	589	452	1,108	1,240	1,263	1,597
Social sciences	3,153	4,135	2,238	3,932	3,649	4,923	4,212	4,777
Economics	1,247	522	203	548	755	1,296	2,137	2,570
Political science	713	697	364	438	556	433	83	160
Sociology	769	764	162	185	442	649	1,488	1,478
Other, n.e.c.	424	2,152	1,509	2,761	1,886	2,545	504	569
Other sciences, n.e.c.	513	911	1,456	732	947	727	382	859

Source: "Federally Financed R&D Expenditures at Historically Black Colleges and Universities, by Science and Engineering Field: Fiscal Years 1985-92," U.S. Department of Education, National Center for Education Statistics, *Academic Science and Engineering: R&D Expenditures, Fiscal Year 1992,* 1994, p. 41. Primary source: National Science Foundations/SRS, Survey of Scientific and Engineering Expenditures at Universities and Colleges. *Notes:* 1. Data for metallurgical and materials engineering were not collected separately prior to fiscal year 1990.

★ 245 ★

Higher Education

HBCUs: Trends in Science and Engineering Research and Development Expenditures, by Funding Source and Field: 1985-1992

[Dollars in thousands]

Source and field	1985	1986	1987	1988	1989	1990	1991	1992
Total	63,115	72,577	74,822	93,818	130,728	142,452	150,305	177,899
Source of funds:								
Federal Government	57,873	60,910	61,572	75,998	106,548	117,200	122,080	146,707
State and local governments	1,150	1,163	2,528	4,475	6,883	6,931	6,505	9,053
Industry	1,377	1,797	1,637	3,292	3,966	5,332	3,102	4,145
Institutional funds	1,867	7,223	7,884	8,392	12,086	11,035	13,744	14,096
All other sources	848	1,484	1,201	1,661	1,245	1,954	4,874	3,898
Field:								
Engineering total	5,077	6,898	6,400	7,814	10,529	13,645	16,889	20,733
Aeronautical and astronautical	250	263	371	410	226	119	170	423
Chemical	140	220	184	607	660	1,014	1,171	1,114
Civil	191	134	906	1,340	1,198	1,022	1,231	2,475
Electrical	1,119	1,467	2,123	1,915	2,763	2,530	4,133	4,144
Mechanical	1,002	1,619	1,912	2,224	3,108	3,412	4,484	7,142
Metallurgical and materials[1]	--	--	--	--	--	1,375	1,345	245
Other, n.e.c.	2,375	3,195	904	1,318	2,574	4,173	4,355	5,190
All sciences, total	58,038	65,679	68,422	86,004	120,199	128,807	133,416	157,166
Physical sciences	11,425	13,345	13,717	14,350	21,133	25,990	25,449	29,294
Astronomy	16	26	12	27	0	0	164	367
Chemistry	7,514	8,950	7,828	9,332	12,111	12,426	11,740	11,959
Physics	3,622	4,136	5,749	4,990	8,856	13,331	13,071	16,560
Other, n.e.c.	273	233	128	1	166	233	474	408
Environmental sciences	1,741	1,829	2,111	2,401	2,642	4,090	3,923	3,318
Atmospheric	21	0	0	3	388	625	542	667
Earth sciences	350	286	303	328	526	461	211	668
Oceanography	305	381	208	397	27	48	25	98
Other, n.e.c.	1,065	1,162	1,600	1,673	1,701	2,956	3,145	1,885
Mathematical sciences	922	1,444	311	244	728	948	1,574	3,407
Computer sciences	441	572	895	1,223	2,426	2,540	5,276	4,068
Life sciences	39,010	42,247	44,679	57,828	82,574	84,153	88,942	105,722
Agricultural sciences	18,190	18,999	18,538	22,1458	34,112	33,715	38,745	44,769
Biological sciences	13,038	13,214	16,573	25,822	36,322	37,908	37,468	45,602
Medical sciences	7,089	9,215	8,514	8,998	11,024	11,765	10,584	12,542
Other, n.e.c.	693	819	1,054	860	1,116	765	2,145	2,809
Psychology	221	352	628	494	1,494	1,706	1,336	2,053

[Continued]

★ 245 ★

HBCUs: Trends in Science and Engineering Research and Development Expenditures, by Funding Source and Field: 1985-1992
[Continued]

Source and field	1985	1986	1987	1988	1989	1990	1991	1992
Social sciences	3,737	4,929	4,488	8,536	8,032	7,906	5,693	8,002
Economics	1,310	634	290	838	864	1,528	2,404	2,847
Political science	870	930	651	1,095	1,200	1,028	159	364
Sociology	934	975	649	2,059	1,673	2,081	2,373	2,469
Other, n.e.c.	623	2,390	2,898	4,544	4,295	3,269	757	2,322
Other sciences, n.e.c.	541	961	1,593	928	1,170	1,474	1,223	1,302

Source: "R&D Expenditures at Historically Black Colleges and Universities, by Source of Funds and Science and Engineering Field: Fiscal Years 1985-92," U.S. Department of Education, National Center for Education Statistics, *Academic Science and Engineering: R&D Expenditures, Fiscal Year 1992, 1994,* p. 40. Primary source: National Science Foundation/SRS, Survey of Scientific and Engineering Expenditures at Universities and Colleges. *Notes:* 1. Data for metallurgical and materials engineering were not collected separately prior to fiscal year 1990.

★ 246 ★

Higher Education

HBCUs: Trends in Source and Amount of Non-Federal Funding for Science and Engineering: 1985-1992

[Dollars in thousands]

Source and field	1985	1986	1987	1988	1989	1990	1991	1992
Total	5,242	11,667	13,250	17,820	24,180	25,252	28,225	31,192
Source of funds:								
State and local governments	1,150	1,163	2,528	4,475	6,883	6,931	6,505	9,053
Industry	1,377	1,797	1,637	3,292	3,966	5,332	3,102	4,145
Institutional funds	1,867	7,223	7,884	8,392	12,086	11,035	13,744	14,096
All other sources	848	1,484	1,201	1,661	1,245	1,954	4,874	3,898
Field:								
Engineering, total	705	1,987	2,069	2,149	2,521	1,806	4,594	4,699
Aeronautical and astronautical	7	7	21	28	103	0	0	0
Chemical	0	62	61	53	74	267	380	262
Civil	7	4	321	529	318	375	953	1,161
Electrical	157	436	742	557	857	455	960	698
Mechanical	124	340	432	260	321	306	868	1,675
Metallurgical and materials[1]	--	--	--	--	--	0	167	0
Other, n.e.c.	410	1,138	492	722	848	403	1,266	903
All sciences, total	4,537	9,680	11,181	15,671	21,659	23,446	23,631	26,493
Physical sciences	942	2,389	1,961	2,410	3,427	4,261	3,959	4,796
Astronomy	0	0	0	0	0	0	0	0

[Continued]

★ 246 ★

HBCUs: Trends in Source and Amount of Non-Federal Funding for Science and Engineering: 1985-1992
[Continued]

Source and field	1985	1986	1987	1988	1989	1990	1991	1992
Chemistry	578	1,961	1,481	1,699	1,819	1,695	1,372	902
Physics	291	428	480	711	1,565	2,502	2,531	3,882
Other, n.e.c.	73	0	0	0	43	64	56	12
Environmental sciences	471	551	719	760	1,234	2,756	1,845	1,298
Atmospheric	2	0	0	0	259	520	438	455
Earth sciences	34	41	64	78	278	209	61	112
Oceanography	8	33	2	25	25	26	25	24
Other, n.e.c.	427	477	653	657	672	2,001	1,321	707
Mathematical sciences	33	489	42	56	242	272	293	770
Computer sciences	13	47	94	135	389	610	753	591
Life sciences	2,458	5,351	5,939	7,468	11,375	11,351	14,386	14,914
Agricultural sciences	1,197	1,221	1,764	1,109	3,724	4,048	4,732	4,644
Biological sciences	550	1,300	1,708	3,997	4,788	4,376	4,768	5,754
Medical sciences	680	2,784	2,449	2,357	2,122	2,427	3,706	2,596
Other, n.e.c.	31	46	18	5	741	500	1,180	1,920
Psychology	8	9	39	42	386	466	73	456
Social sciences	584	794	2,250	4,604	4,383	2,983	1,481	3,225
Economics	63	112	87	290	109	232	267	277
Political science	157	233	287	657	634	595	76	204
Sociology	165	211	487	1,874	1,231	1,432	885	991
Other, n.e.c.	199	238	1,389	1,783	2,409	724	253	1,753
Other sciences, n.e.c.	28	50	137	196	223	747	841	443

Source: "Non-Federal R&D Expenditures at Historically Black Colleges and Universities, by Source of Funds and Science and Engineering Field: Fiscal Years 1985-92," U.S. Department of Education, National Center for Education Statistics, *Academic Science and Engineering: R&D Expenditures, Fiscal Year 1992,* 1994, p. 42. Primary source: National Science Foundations/SRS, Survey of Scientific and Engineering Expenditures at Universities and Colleges. *Notes:* 1. Data for metallurgical and materials engineering were not collected separately prior to fiscal year 1990.

★ 247 ★

Higher Education

Older Undergraduates: Percent Distribution of Degree Programs of Older (24 or Over) Undergraduates, by Race/Ethnic Origin: 1989-90

	Associate's degree	Bachelor's degree	Undergraduate certificate	Other undergraduate
Total	33.1	24.3	16.9	25.7
Race-ethnicity				
American Indian or Native Alaskan	41.5	20.4	22.4	15.7
Asian/Pacific Islander	24.7	24.0	15.7	35.6
Black, non-Hispanic	35.9	19.2	20.6	24.3
Hispanic	28.1	23.6	22.9	25.4
White, non-Hispanic	33.5	25.1	15.8	25.5

Source: "Percentage Distribution of Older Undergraduates According to Degree Programs, by Selected Characteristics: 1989-90," U.S. Department of Education, National Center for Education Statistics, *Profile of Older Undergraduates: 1989-90*, April, 1995, p. 30. Primary source: U.S. Department of Education, National Center for Education Statistics, 1989-90 National Postsecondary Student Aid Study (NPSAS:90), Data Analysis System. *Note:* Details may not add to totals because of rounding.

★ 248 ★

Higher Education

Older Undergraduates: Percent Distribution of Financial Aid to Older (24 or Over) Undergraduates, by Aid Type and Race/Ethnic Origin: 1989-90

	Any aid		Grants		Loans		Employer aid	
	Average percent	Amount	Average percent	Amount	Average percent	Amount	Average percent	Amount
Total	38.7	$2,970	34.0	$1,714	14.9	$3,183	8.6	$765
Race-ethnicity								
American Indian or Native Alaskan	48.9	3,621	43.8	2,257	14.7	3,642	4.3	-
Asian/Pacific Islander	23.8	3,643	21.1	2,330	7.9	3,399	3.0	-
Black, non-Hispanic	49.9	3,154	43.7	1,905	21.6	2,905	4.6	753
Hispanic	45.9	3,141	39.7	1,886	18.3	3,241	5.1	636
White, non-Hispanic	37.0	2,879	32.6	1,626	13.9	3,226	9.9	761

Source: "Percentage of Older Undergraduates with Any Aid, Grants, Loans, and Employer Aid, by Selected Characteristics: 1989-90," U.S. Department of Education, National Center for Education Statistics, *Profile of Older Undergraduates: 1989-90*, April, 1995, pp. 36-37. Primary source: U.S. Department of Education, National Center for Education Statistics, 1989-90 National Postsecondary Aid Study (NPSAS:90), Data Analysis System.

★ 249 ★

Higher Education

Older Undergraduates: Percent Distribution of Hours/Week Older (24 or Over) Undergraduates Worked while in School, by Race/Ethnic Origin: 1989-90

	None	1-19	20-29	30-39	40 or more
Total	25.2	7.8	8.9	11.8	46.3
Race-ethnicity					
American Indian or Native Alaskan	22.0	11.3	6.4	9.4	50.9
Asian/Pacific Islander	31.9	8.2	9.6	10.2	40.1
Black, non-Hispanic	27.8	6.2	9.3	13.7	43.1
Hispanic	26.4	4.6	9.9	12.0	47.2
White, non-Hispanic	24.4	8.2	8.8	11.6	47.0

Source: "Percentage Distribution of Older Undergraduates According to Hours Worked Per Week While Enrolled, by Selected Characteristics: 1989-90," U.S. Department of Education, National Center for Education Statistics, *Profile of Older Undergraduates: 1989-90,* April, 1995, p. 35. Primary source: U.S. Department of Education, National Center for Education Statistics, 1989-90 National Postsecondary Student Aid Study (NPSAS:90), Data Analysis System. *Note:* Details may not add to totals because of rounding.

★ 250 ★

Higher Education

Older Undergraduates: Percent Distribution of Older (24 or Over) Undergraduates' Attendance at Public/Private, 4-Year/Less than 4-Year Institutions, by Race/Ethnic Origin: 1989-90

	Public		Private, not-for-profit		Private, for-profit
	Less-than 4-year	4-year	Less-than 4-year	4-year	
Total	58.7	22.0	1.6	9.4	8.3
Race-ethnicity					
American Indian or Native Alaskan	63.2	20.7	0.8	6.7	8.6
Asian/Pacific Islander	63.2	22.2	1.0	7.3	6.3
Black, non-Hispanic	54.8	17.4	2.2	8.2	17.4
Hispanic	53.8	18.4	3.1	10.8	14.0
White, non-Hispanic	59.4	23.1	1.4	9.6	6.4

Source: "Percentage Distribution of Undergraduates According to Type of Institution, by Age: 1989-90," U.S. Department of Education, National Center for Education Statistics, *Profile of Older Undergraduates: 1989-90,* April 1995, p. 29. Primary source: U.S. Department of Education, National Center for Education Statistics, 1989-90 National Postsecondary Student Aid Study (NPSAS:90), Data Analysis System. *Note:* Details may not add to totals because of rounding.

★ 251 ★

Higher Education

Older Undergraduates: Percent Distribution of Older (24 or Over) Undergraduates' Fields of Study, by Race/Ethnic Origin: 1989-90

	Liberal arts/ Humanities/ arts	Social/ behavior science	Life science	Physical science	Math	Computer information tech.	Engineering	Education	Business/ management	Health	Vocational/ tech.	Other tech./ prof.
Total	14.0	4.2	1.5	1.2	0.9	5.8	6.4	7.7	24.1	10.6	8.0	15.7
Race-ethnicity												
American Indian or Native Alaskan	22.9	1.0	1.9	3.7	0.0	4.5	10.5	7.2	20.2	13.0	4.8	10.2
Asian/Pacific Islander	15.8	2.6	1.8	0.5	3.0	13.0	12.2	4.0	22.7	7.5	6.8	10.1
Black, non-Hispanic	9.3	3.2	2.2	0.9	0.7	5.2	5.2	5.0	27.7	11.2	8.3	21.1
Hispanic	14.7	3.5	1.3	0.3	1.3	6.2	6.3	7.3	24.3	5.6	11.8	17.5
White, non-Hispanic	14.4	4.5	1.4	1.4	0.8	5.4	6.3	8.3	23.6	11.1	7.7	15.0

Source: "Percentage of Older Undergraduates According to Field of Study, by Selected Characteristics: 1989-90," U.S. Department of Education, National Center for Education Statistics, *Profile of Older Undergraduates: 1989-90*, April, 1995, pp. 33-34. Primary source: U.S. Department of Education, National Center for Education Statistics, 1989-90 National Postsecondary Aid Study (NPSAS:90), Data Analysis System. *Note:* Details may not add to total because of rounding.

★ 252 ★

Higher Education

Older Undergraduates: Percent Distribution of Older (24 or Over) Undergraduates' "Very Important" Reasons for Choice of Institution, by Race/Ethnic Origin: 1989-90

	Offered course of study wanted	Could work while attending	Could live at home	Institution had a good reputation	Institution was close to home	Good reputation for placing grads	Tuition less than others	Could finish in shorter time	Obtained financial aid
Total	78.6	63.0	68.5	49.9	53.6	30.3	36.5	36.9	23.5
Race-ethnicity									
American Indian or Native Alaskan	82.2	69.1	74.4	71.4	49.2	38.1	45.6	26.8	25.4
Asian/Pacific Islander	72.5	50.8	59.5	48.1	55.9	35.0	38.1	39.8	23.3
Black, non-Hispanic	86.9	67.7	67.6	59.4	52.1	44.1	32.6	48.4	38.5
Hispanic	78.5	66.2	68.1	54.1	56.4	39.6	48.8	42.0	29.5
White, non-Hispanic	77.8	62.6	69.0	48.2	53.5	27.4	34.4	25.0	21.0

Source: "Percentage of Older Undergraduates who Identified Various Considerations as 'Very Important' in Their Choice of Institution, by Selected Characteristics: 1989-90," U.S. Department of Education, National Center for Education Statistics, *Profile of Older Undergraduates: 1989-90*, April, 1995, pp. 32-33. Primary source: U.S. Department of Education, National Center for Education Statistics, 1989-90 National Postsecondary Aid Study (NPSAS:90), Data Analysis System.

★ 253 ★

Higher Education

Older Undergraduates: Percent Distribution of Time Older (24 or Over) Undergraduates Spent in School, by Race/Ethnic Origin: 1989-90

	Full-time	At least half-time	Less than half-time
Total	31.3	27.5	41.2
Race-ethnicity			
American Indian or Native Alaskan	40.0	27.5	32.6
Asian/Pacific Islander	30.4	27.5	42.1
Black, non-Hispanic	41.6	28.3	30.1
Hispanic	36.2	29.6	34.3
White, non-Hispanic	29.3	27.1	43.5

Source: "Percentage Distribution of Older Undergraduates According to Attendance Status, by Selected Characteristics: 1989-90," U.S. Department of Education, National Center for Education Statistics, *Profile of Older Undergraduates: 1989-90,* April, 1995, p. 31. Primary source: U.S. Department of Education, National Center for Education Statistics, 1989-90 National Postsecondary Student Aid Study (NPSAS:90), Data Analysis System. *Note:* Details may not add to totals because of rounding.

★ 254 ★

Higher Education

Persistence: Minority Students Enrolling in College Immediately After Graduation Who were Still There 3 Years Later, by Race/Ethnic Origin: 1982-83 and 1989-90

Race/ethnicity	1982-83	1989-90
Asian or Pacific Islander	90.7	89.9
Black, non-Hispanic	62.1	70.7
Hispanic	76.0	71.2
White, non-Hispanic	79.8	74.4

Source: "Percentage of 1982-83 and 1989-90 Beginning Postsecondary Students who Initially Enrolled in a 4-Year Institution the Fall After Their High School Graduation, and who were Enrolled in May 3 Years Later," U.S. Department of Education, National Center for Education Statistics, *Minority Undergraduate Participation in Postsecondary Education,* June, 1995, p. 35. Primary source: U.S. Department of Education, National Center for Education Statistics, 1989-90. Beginning Postsecondary Student Survey, first follow-up (1992), and High School and Beyond Student Survey (1982). *Notes:* Students who interrupted their education and reenrolled are included if they were enrolled in May of their third year.

★ 255 ★

Higher Education

Persistence: Persistence Status of 1989-90 Minority Undergraduates Aspiring to a Bachelor's Degree: 1992

Race/ethnicity	Left school with no degree	Interrupted and reenrolled	Continuously enrolled[1]
Asian or Pacific Islander	11.8	19.3	68.8
Black, non-Hispanic	26.3	23.3	50.3
Hispanic	26.2	27.7	46.0
White, non-Hispanic	24.4	17.8	57.6

Source: "Percentage of 1989-90 Beginning Postsecondary Students Who Reported a Bachelor's Degree as Their Current Degree Objective, According to Their Persistence Status as of Spring 1992, by Race-Ethnicity," U.S. Department of Education, National Center for Education Statistics, *Minority Undergraduate Participation in Postsecondary Education*, June, 1995, p. 27. Primary source: U.S. Department of Education, National Center for Education Statistics, 1989-90. Beginning Postsecondary Student Survey, first followup (1992). *Notes:* Percentages may not sum to 100 due to rounding. 1. This category includes a small percentage (1.5 percent) who reported completing the degree.

★ 256 ★

Higher Education

Persistence: Persistence Status of 1989-90 Minority Undergraduates Aspiring to an Associate Degree: 1992

Race/ethnicity	Left school with no degree	Still enrolled or reenrolled	Completed
Black, non-Hispanic	52.8	39.2	7.8
Hispanic	28.4	54.9	16.6
White, non-Hispanic	47.1	40.0	12.7

Source: "Percentage of 1989-90 Beginning Postsecondary Students who Reported an Associate's Degree as Their Current Objective, According to Their Persistence Status as of Spring 1992, by Race-Ethnicity," U.S. Department of Education, National Center for Education Statistics, *Minority Undergraduate Participation in Postsecondary Education*, June 1995, p. 28. Primary source: U.S. Department of Education, National Center for Education Statistics, 1989-90. Beginning Postsecondary Student Survey, first followup (1992). *Note:* Percentages may not sum to 100 due to rounding.

★ 257 ★

Higher Education

Persistence: Persistence Status of Postsecondary
Students Who Aspired to a Vocational Certificate: 1992

Race/ethnicity	Left school with no certificate	Still enrolled	Completed
Black, non-Hispanic	51.1	4.9	43.9
Hispanic	58.4	9.1	32.3
White, non-Hispanic	42.9	4.3	52.7

Source: "Percentage of 1989-90 Beginning Postsecondary Students who Reported a Vocational Certificate as Their Current Education Objective, According to Their Persistence Status as of Spring 1992, by Race-Ethnicity," U.S. Department of Education, National Center for Education Statistics, *Minority Undergraduate Participation in Postsecondary Education,* June, 1995, p. 30. Primary source: U.S. Department of Education, National Center for Education Statistics, 1989-90. Beginning Postsecondary Student Survey, first followup (1992). *Note:* Percentages may not sum to 100 due to rounding.

★ 258 ★

Higher Education

Relationships: Enrollment, by Type of College and Student Employment Status (in percentages), by Race/Ethnic Origin: 1987 and 1993

[In thousands, except percent. As of October. Based on the Current Population Survey].

CHARACTERISTIC	Total population	ENROLLED IN COLLEGE					PERCENT EMPLOYED		
		Total	Type of school			Percent enrolled full-time	Total	Full-time	Part-time
			2-year	4-year	Graduate school				
Total, 1987[1]	190,058	12,719	3,648	6,656	2,415	62.6	60.4	31.7	28.7
White	162,757	10,731	3,039	5,617	2,075	61.6	62.2	32.6	29.6
Black	21,520	1,351	422	748	181	66.3	50.5	28.6	21.9
Hispanic origin[2]	13,687	739	307	342	90	57.3	65.5	37.0	28.6
Total, 1993[1]	197,652	13,898	4,196	7,311	2,391	64.9	59.7	30.8	28.9
White	167,086	11,434	3,431	5,990	2,013	63.6	62.4	31.5	30.9
Black	23,003	1,545	530	833	182	65.7	49.2	33.2	16.0
Hispanic origin[2]	16,329	995	446	451	98	61.0	60.5	30.7	29.8

Source: "College Population, by Selected Characteristics: 1987 and 1993," *Statistical Abstract of the United States: 1995,* 1995, p. 180. Primary source: U.S. Bureau of the Census, *Current Population Reports,* P20-443 and P20-479. *Notes:* 1. Includes other races, not shown separately. 2. Persons of Hispanic origin may be of any race.

★ 259 ★

Higher Education

Relationships: Length of Time from High School Graduation to Bachelor's Degree, by Gender and Race/Ethnic Origin: 1993

[As of **spring**. Based on Survey of Income and Program Participation].

CHARACTERISTIC	Total with bachelor's degrees (1,000)	YEARS TO BA DEGREE FROM END OF HIGH SCHOOL						Mean duration[1]
		Number (1,000)			Percent			
		4 years or less	5 years or less	6 years or less	4 years or less	5 years or less	6 years or less	
All persons	36,787	15,624	23,810	27,334	42.5	64.7	74.3	6.29
Male	19,351	7,321	11,695	13,827	37.8	60.4	71.5	6.28
Female	17,436	8,302	12,115	13,508	47.6	69.5	77.5	6.30
White	32,279	14,161	21,201	24,235	43.9	65.7	75.1	6.24
Male	17,258	6,717	10,537	12,411	38.9	61.1	71.9	6.22
Female	15,021	7,444	10,664	11,824	49.6	71.0	78.7	6.26
Black	2,314	713	1,258	1,473	30.8	54.4	63.7	7.19
Male	926	264	493	570	28.5	53.2	61.6	6.98
Female	1,388	448	764	904	32.3	55.0	65.1	7.33
Hispanic origin[1]	1,367	363	689	852	26.6	50.4	62.3	6.79
Male	693	187	308	407	27.0	44.4	58.7	7.06
Female	674	176	381	445	26.1	56.5	66.0	6.50

Source: "Time Spent Earning Bachelor's Degree, by Selected Characteristics: 1993," *Statistical Abstract of the United States: 1995,* 1995, p. 189. Primary source: U.S. Bureau of the Census, unpublished data. *Note:* 1. Persons of Hispanic origin may be of any race.

★ 260 ★

Higher Education

Students: Percent Distribution of Age Category of Undergraduates, by Race/Ethnic Origin: 1989-90

	Under 24	24-29	30-34	35-39	40-44	45-49	50 or older
Total	57.7	16.7	8.9	6.7	4.7	2.7	2.6
Race-ethnicity							
American Indian	52.8	11.6	13.2	11.1	5.3	4.0	2.0
Asian/Pacific Islander	63.2	18.5	6.8	4.3	4.2	2.0	1.1
Black, non-Hispanic	51.9	20.3	11.1	7.3	4.8	2.7	1.9

[Continued]

★ 260 ★

Students: Percent Distribution of Age Category of Undergraduates, by Race/Ethnic Origin: 1989-90
[Continued]

	Under 24	24-29	30-34	35-39	40-44	45-49	50 or older
Hispanic	59.6	19.4	9.1	6.2	2.5	1.5	1.6
White, non-Hispanic	57.9	15.9	8.6	6.8	4.9	2.9	3.0

Source: "Percentage Distribution of Undergraduates According to Age, by Gender, Race-Ethnicity, and Type of Institution: 1989-90," U.S. Department of Education, National Center for Education Statistics, *Profile of Older Undergraduates: 1989-90*, April, 1995, p. 6. Primary source: U.S. Department of Education, National Center for Education Statistics, 1989-90 National Postsecondary Student Aid Study (NPSAS:90), Data Analysis System. *Note:* Details may not add to totals because of rounding.

★ 261 ★

Higher Education

Students: Percent Distribution of Minority Undergraduates' Reasons for Choice of Institution: 1989-90

Race/ethnicity	Good reputation placing graduates	Good reputation of school	Offered courses wanted	Better chance getting job at school	Can attend school and work	Can graduate in shorter time	Got financial aid needed	Can live at home	Friends attended
Total	65.9	83.2	91.9	28.4	71.1	56.7	35.8	62.1	22.1
Race-ethnicity									
American Indian/Alaskan Native	67.1	89.6	91.1	35.8	77.1	53.3	41.4	63.4	21.7
Asian/Pacific Islander	67.7	79.8	88.8	37.4	65.1	60.8	37.7	65.1	32.8
Black, non-Hispanic	69.3	82.8	93.3	38.3	75.4	64.1	56.6	66.9	18.8
Hispanic	70.4	82.2	91.6	34.1	77.7	62.5	42.3	73.1	24.4
White, non-Hispanic	65.0	83.4	91.9	26.1	70.3	55.1	32.8	60.3	21.6
Racial-ethnic subgroup Asian									
Asian Indian	68.8	80.8	81.9	25.6	49.5	47.2	34.4	65.7	23.0
Chinese	67.8	78.4	93.7	38.7	52.4	57.7	36.1	60.3	31.3
Japanese	58.0	71.6	87.6	27.3	52.3	49.3	14.0	64.3	33.1
Korean	70.6	86.0	82.6	41.0	65.4	61.7	38.7	51.3	26.2
Pacific Islander	67.1	83.7	91.1	34.7	82.5	68.6	36.9	82.7	38.4
Vietnamese	72.6	78.6	92.5	63.3	76.4	65.6	66.2	64.3	34.5
Other or nonspecified	69.6	80.6	85.6	33.4	69.2	65.3	40.2	61.1	34.6
Racial-ethnic subgroup Hispanic									
Cuban	62.6	76.0	83.3	35.5	64.2	47.3	32.1	69.3	15.4
Mexican	67.8	79.8	91.4	33.0	81.0	63.6	40.4	73.3	27.6
Puerto Rican	80.4	85.4	94.5	38.5	67.8	62.3	63.7	75.8	21.8
Other or nonspecified	71.7	85.4	91.8	34.0	77.7	62.8	39.4	72.5	21.6

Source: "Percentage of Undergraduates who Reported Various Reasons for Choosing Their Postsecondary Institution as Somewhat or Very Important, by Race- Ethnicity: 1989-90," U.S. Department of Education, National Center for Education Statistics, *Minority Undergraduate Participation in Postsecondary Education*, June 1995, p. 23. Primary source: U.S. Department of Education, National Center for Education Statistics, 1989-90 National Postsecondary Student Aid Study (NPSAS: 90), Undergraduate Data Analysis System. *Note:* Percentages may not sum to 100 due to rounding.

██

Marriage Characteristics

██

★ 262 ★

1980 High School Sophomores in 1992: Average Number of Higher Education Institutions Attended Before Attainment of Degree or Certificate by 1980 High School Sophomores, by Type of Degree and Race/Ethnic Origin: 1992

Student characteristics	Certificate	Associate's	Bachelor's
Total	1.5	1.5	1.7
Race-ethnicity			
Native American/Alaska Native	1.4	-	-
Asian/Pacific Islander	1.6	1.7	1.9
Black	1.6	1.5	1.6
Hispanic	1.6	1.6	1.8
White	1.5	1.5	1.8

Source: "Average Number of Postsecondary Institutions Attended Prior to Degree Attainment by High School Sophomores, by Type of Degree and Selected Characteristics," *Educational Attainment of 1980 High School Sophomores by 1992,* March 1995, p. 38. Primary source: U.S. Department of Education, Office of Educational Research and Improvement, National Center for Education Statistics. Statistical Analysis Report. *High School and Beyond: Educational Attainment of 1980 High School Sophomores by 1992; 1992 Descriptive Summary of 1980 High School Sophomores 12 Years Later.* NCES 95-304. Washington, DC: U.S. Government Printing Office, March, 1995. National Center for Education Statistics, High School & Beyond: 1980 Sophomore Cohort, 1980-1992. *Note:* - Sample size is too small for a reliable estimate.

★ 263 ★

Marriage Characteristics

1980 High School Sophomores in 1992: Average Time (in Months) from First Higher Education Enrollment to Attainment of Degree or Certificate by 1980 High School Sophomores, by Race/Ethnic Origin: 1992

Student characteristics	Percentage who attained certificate	Average months to certificate	Percentage who attained associate's	Average months to associate's	Percentage who attained bachelor's	Average months to bachelor's
Total	12.1	29.7	9.4	36.8	22.4	55.7
Race-ethnicity						
Native American/Alaska Native	12.2	33.0	5.2	-	6.4	-
Asian/Pacific Islander	7.4	-	8.1	40.5	42.5	59.0
Black	17.0	31.5	5.2	40.2	11.1	57.3

[Continued]

★ 263 ★

1980 High School Sophomores in 1992: Average Time (in Months) from First Higher Education Enrollment to Attainment of Degree or Certificate by 1980 High School Sophomores, by Race/Ethnic Origin: 1992

[Continued]

Student characteristics	Percentage who attained certificate	Average months to certificate	Percentage who attained associate's	Average months to associate's	Percentage who attained bachelor's	Average months to bachelor's
Hispanic	12.2	28.7	7.9	45.3	9.3	60.0
White	11.1	29.5	10.4	35.3	25.9	55.3

Source: "Percentage of 1980 High School Sophomores Attaining Degrees and Average Number of Months Between First Enrollment and Attainment of Degrees, by Type of Degree and Selected Characteristics," *Educational Attainment of 1980 High School Sophomores by 1992*, March 1995, p. 35. Primary source: U.S. Department of Education, Office of Educational Research and Improvement, National Center for Education Statistics. Statistical Analysis Report. *High School and Beyond: Educational Attainment of 1980 High School Sophomores by 1992; 1992 Descriptive Summary of 1980 High School Sophomores 12 Years Later*. NCES 95-304. Washington, DC: U.S. Government Printing Office, March, 1995. National Center for Education Statistics, High School & Beyond: 1980 Sophomore Cohort, 1980-1992. *Notes:* - Sample size is too small for a reliable estimate. The percentage of students at each attainment level does not necessarily match the percentage distributions by highest degree because students can have earned degrees other than their highest degree.

★ 264 ★

Marriage Characteristics

1980 High School Sophomores in 1992: Major Activity Reported (in Percentages) by 1980 High School Sophomore Cohorts, by Race/Ethnic Origin: 1992

Student characteristics	Working	Layoff	Looking for work	Taking break	Training program	Vocational/ technical courses	Undergraduate academic courses	Graduate/ professional courses	Active duty/armed forces
Total	79.3	1.3	3.9	2.9	0.2	2.0	5.4	3.3	0.8
Race-ethnicity									
Native American/Alaska Native	77.0	1.6	7.1	2.2	0.0	1.2	4.7	3.4	0.2
Asian/Pacific Islander	75.7	0.3	3.1	7.3	0.8	2.0	5.4	6.3	1.1
Black	73.3	1.2	7.6	3.9	0.7	2.4	6.0	1.6	1.5
Hispanic	77.4	1.8	4.6	2.5	0.2	2.0	5.3	1.4	0.9
White	80.6	1.2	3.0	2.8	0.2	1.9	5.5	3.8	0.7

Source: "Percentage of 1980 High School Sophomores by Highest Degree Attained Through 1992, by Selected Characteristics," *Educational Attainment of 1980 High School Sophomores by 1992*, March 1995, p. 21. Primary source: U.S. Department of Education, Office of Educational Research and Improvement, National Center for Education Statistics. Statistical Analysis Report. *High School and Beyond: Educational Attainment of 1980 High School Sophomores by 1992; 1992 Descriptive Summary of 1980 High School Sophomores 12 Years Later*. NCES 95-304. Washington, DC: U.S. Government Printing Office, March, 1995. National Center for Education Statistics, High School & Beyond: 1980 Sophomore Cohort, 1980-1992. *Notes:* - Sample size is too small for a reliable estimate. Percentages may not sum to 100 percent due to rounding.

★ 265 ★

Marriage Characteristics

1980 High School Sophomores in 1992: Percent Distribution of 1980 High School Sophomore Cohort's Highest Level of Educational Attainment, by Race/Ethnic Origin: 1992

Student characteristics	Less than high school	High school	Certificate	Associate's	Bachelor's	Master's	Professional	Doctorate
Race-ethnicity								
Native American/Alaska Native	17.8	58.2	11.8	5.0	6.7	0.5	0.0	0.0
Asian/Pacific Islander	0.6	40.9	6.9	6.2	32.7	4.7	7.5	0.7
Black	6.9	59.6	16.3	5.2	10.0	1.5	0.5	0.2
Hispanic	11.9	59.6	11.2	7.3	9.0	0.6	0.3	0.0
White	4.9	49.1	10.1	8.4	23.1	3.2	1.0	0.2

Source: "Percentage of 1980 High School Sophomores by Highest Degree Attained Through 1992, by Selected Characteristics," *Educational Attainment of 1980 High School Sophomores by 1992*, March 1995, p. 31. Primary source: U.S. Department of Education, Office of Educational Research and Improvement, National Center for Education Statistics. Statistical Analysis Report. *High School and Beyond: Educational Attainment of 1980 High School Sophomores by 1992; 1992 Descriptive Summary of 1980 High School Sophomores 12 Years Later.* NCES 95-304. Washington, DC: U.S. Government Printing Office, March, 1995. National Center for Education Statistics, High School & Beyond: 1980 Sophomore Cohort, 1980-1992. *Note:* Percentages may not sum to 100 percent due to rounding.

★ 266 ★

Marriage Characteristics

1980 High School Sophomores in 1992: Percent Distribution of Educational Attainment of 1980 High School Sophomores Who Delayed College Entry, by Race/Ethnic Origin: 1992

Student characteristics	High school	Certificate	Associate's	Bachelor's	Advanced degree
Total	53.8	24.2	11.8	9.2	1.1
Race-ethnicity					
Native American/Alaska Native	72.2	15.0	8.8	4.0	0.0
Asian/Pacific Islander	72.1	11.5	9.2	7.3	0.0
Black	54.8	29.7	8.3	6.6	0.6
Hispanic	57.6	27.9	10.4	3.9	0.2
White	52.6	23.1	12.3	10.7	1.4

Source: "Percentage Distribution of 1980 High School Sophomores who Delayed Entry into Postsecondary Education by Highest Degree Attained Through 1992, by Selected Characteristics," *Educational Attainment of 1980 High School Sophomores by 1992*, March 1995, p. 33. Primary source: U.S. Department of Education, Office of Educational Research and Improvement, National Center for Education Statistics. Statistical Analysis Report. *High School and Beyond: Educational Attainment of 1980 High School Sophomores by 1992; 1992 Descriptive Summary of 1980 High School Sophomores 12 Years Later.* NCES 95-304. Washington, DC: U.S. Government Printing Office, March, 1995. National Center for Education Statistics, High School & Beyond: 1980 Sophomore Cohort, 1980-1992. National Center for Education Statistics, High School & Beyond: 1980 Sophomore Cohort, 1980-1992. *Notes:* Percentages may not sum to 100 percent due to rounding. Students who enrolled in postsecondary education after November 1982 were defined as delayed entrants.

★ 267 ★

Marriage Characteristics

1980 High School Sophomores in 1992: Percent Distribution of Educational Attainment of 1980 High School Sophomores Who Entered Higher Education Immediately After High School Graduation, by Race/Ethnic Origin: 1992

Student characteristics	High school	Certificate	Associate's	Bachelor's	Advanced degree
Total	29.6	10.0	12.2	40.3	7.9
Race-ethnicity					
Native American/Alaska Native	38.0	23.1	10.1	26.3	2.6
Asian/Pacific Islander	23.6	5.9	6.5	45.3	18.6
Black	43.8	19.4	8.6	23.3	4.9
Hispanic	43.1	11.4	16.0	26.5	2.9
White	27.0	8.7	12.4	43.5	8.5

Source: "Percentage Distribution of 1980 High School Sophomores who Enrolled in Postsecondary Education Immediately After High School by Highest Degree Attained Through 1992, by Selected Characteristics," *Educational Attainment of 1980 High School Sophomores by 1992,* March 1995, p. 32. Primary source: U.S. Department of Education, Office of Educational Research and Improvement, National Center for Education Statistics. Statistical Analysis Report. *High School and Beyond: Educational Attainment of 1980 High School Sophomores by 1992; 1992 Descriptive Summary of 1980 High School Sophomores 12 Years Later.* NCES 95-304. Washington, DC: U.S. Government Printing Office, March, 1995. National Center for Education Statistics, High School & Beyond: 1980 Sophomore Cohort, 1980-1992. *Notes:* - Sample size is too small for a reliable estimate. Students who enrolled in postsecondary education before November 1982 were defined as immediate entrants. Percentages may not sum to 100 percent due to rounding.

Preprimary

★ 268 ★

Enrollment: Trends in Preprimary Enrollment and Enrollment Rate, by Race/Ethnic Origin: 1970-1993

[As of **October.** Civilian noninstitutional population. Includes public and nonpublic nursery school and kindergarten programs. Excludes 5 year olds enrolled in elementary school. Based on Current Population Survey].

ITEM	1970	1975	1980	1985	1989	1990	1991	1992	1993
NUMBER OF CHILDREN (1,000)									
Population, 3 to 5 years old	10,949	10,183	9,284	10,733	11,038	11,207	11,370	11,544	11,954
Total enrolled	4,104	4,954	4,878	5,865	6,026	6,659	6,334	6,403	6,581
White	3,443	4,105	3,994	4,757	4,911	5,389	5,104	5,137	5,224
Black	586	731	725	919	872	986	928	966	1,011
Hispanic[2]	(NA)	(NA)	370	496	520	642	675	728	657

[Continued]

★ 268 ★

Enrollment: Trends in Preprimary Enrollment and Enrollment Rate, by Race/Ethnic Origin: 1970-1993
[Continued]

ITEM	1970	1975	1980	1985	1989	1990	1991	1992	1993
ENROLLMENT RATE									
Total enrolled[1]	37.5	48.6	52.5	54.6	54.6	59.4	55.7	55.5	55.1
White	37.8	48.6	52.7	54.7	55.0	59.7	56.2	55.8	55.7
Black	34.9	48.1	51.8	55.8	54.2	57.8	53.1	55.1	52.7
Hispanic[2]	(NA)	(NA)	43.3	43.3	41.6	49.0	46.4	48.4	43.9

Source: "Preprimary School Enrollment-Summary: 1970 to 1993," *Statistical Abstract of the United States: 1995*, 1995, p. 160. Primary source: U.S. Bureau of the Census, *Current Population Reports*, P20-479. *Notes:* NA Not available. 1. Includes races not shown separately. 2. Persons of Hispanic origin may be of any race. The method of identifying Hispanic children was changed in 1980 from allocation based on status of mother to status reported for each child. The number of Hispanic children using the new method is larger.

Relationships

★ 269 ★

Computer Use: Students Using Computers at Home and at School, by Educational Level (1984) and Race/Ethnic Origin (1984 and 1993)

[**In percent**. As of **October**. Based on the Current Population Survey and subject to sampling error].

CHARACTERISTIC	1984, total	1993					
		Total	Prekinder-garten and kindergarten	Grades 1-8	Grades 9-12	1st to 4th year of college	5th or later year of college
USING COMPUTERS AT SCHOOL							
Total	27.3	59.0	26.2	68.9	58.2	55.2	52.1
Race/ethnicity:							
White[1]	30.0	61.6	29.4	73.7	59.9	54.9	49.8
Black[1]	16.8	51.5	16.5	56.5	54.5	56.9	57.9
Hispanic	18.6	52.3	19.2	58.4	54.1	51.9	53.7
Other	28.6	59.0	23.5	65.7	57.3	60.9	69.4
USING COMPUTERS AT HOME							
Total	11.5	27.0	15.6	24.7	28.7	32.8	52.6
Race/ethnicity:							
White[1]	13.7	32.8	19.4	31.4	35.9	36.0	53.6
Black[1]	4.9	10.9	4.2	9.0	10.4	19.4	48.1
Hispanic	3.6	10.4	5.7	7.5	9.8	22.0	52.2
Other	9.0	28.7	17.0	23.2	37.0	33.0	47.1

[Continued]

★ 269 ★

Computer Use: Students Using Computers at Home and at School, by Educational Level (1984) and Race/Ethnic Origin (1984 and 1993)

[Continued]

CHARACTERISTIC	1984, total	1993					
		Total	Prekinder-garten and kindergarten	Grades 1-8	Grades 9-12	1st to 4th year of college	5th or later year of college
USING COMPUTERS AT HOME FOR SCHOOL WORK							
Total	4.6	14.9	0.6	10.8	20.9	23.1	36.6
Race/ethnicity:							
White[1]	5.4	18.2	0.8	13.8	26.5	25.7	37.8
Black[1]	2.3	5.7	(NA)	4.0	6.9	11.5	30.1
Hispanic	1.4	5.6	(NA)	2.9	6.7	15.9	36.8
Other	3.8	16.0	1.1	9.3	27.0	23.7	29.2

Source: "Student Use of Computers: 1984 and 1993," *Statistical Abstract of the United States, 1995,* 1995, p. 170. Primary source: U.S. National Center for Statistics, *Digest of Education Statistics,* 1994. *Notes:* NA Not available. 1. Non-Hispanic.

★ 270 ★

Relationships

Education and Employment: Unemployed High School Graduates and Dropouts, by Race: 1980-1993

[**In thousands, except percent. As of October.** For civilian noninstitutional population 16 to 24 years old. Based on Current Population Survey].

EMPLOYMENT STATUS, SEX, AND RACE	GRADUATES[1]				DROPOUTS[2]			
	1980	1985	1990	1993	1980	1985	1990	1993
Civilian population	11,622	10,381	8,370	6,819	5,254	4,323	3,800	3,390
In labor force	9,795	8,825	7,107	5,652	3,549	2,920	2,506	2,084
Percent of population	84.3	85.0	84.9	82.9	67.5	67.5	66.0	61.5
Employed	8,567	7,707	6,279	4,969	2,651	2,165	1,993	1,658
Percent of labor force	87.5	87.3	88.3	87.9	74.7	74.1	79.5	79.6
Unemployed	1,228	1,118	828	683	898	755	513	426
Unemployment rate, total[3]	12.5	12.7	11.7	12.1	25.3	25.9	20.5	20.4
White	10.8	9.8	9.0	10.6	21.6	23.6	17.0	18.3
Black	26.1	29.4	26.0	21.1	43.9	41.5	43.3	34.4
Not in labor force	1,827	1,556	1,262	1,167	1,705	1,403	1,294	1,305
Percent of population	15.7	15.0	15.1	17.1	32.5	32.5	34.1	38.5

Source: "Employment Status of High School Graduates and School Dropouts: 1980 to 1993," *Statistical Abstract of the United States: 1995,* 1995, p. 174. Primary source: U.S. Bureau of Labor Statistics, Bulletin 2307, *News,* USDL 94-252, May 20, 1994, and unpublished data. *Notes:* 1. For persons not enrolled in college who have completed 4 years of high school only. 2. For persons not in regular school and who have not completed the 12th grade nor received a general equivalency degree. 3. Includes other races not shown separately.

★ 271 ★
Relationships

Enrollment and Age: Enrollment and Enrollment in Nursery School and Above, by Race/Ethnic Origin: 1980, 1990, and 1993

[As of **October.** Covers civilian noninstitutional population enrolled in nursery school and above. Based on Current Population Survey].

AGE	WHITE			BLACK			HISPANIC ORIGIN[1]		
	1980	1990	1993	1980	1990	1993	1980	1990	1993
ENROLLMENT									
Total 3 to 34 years old	47,673	48,899	49,985	8,251	8,854	9,470	4,263	6,073	6,689
3 and 4 years old	1,844	2,700	2,581	371	452	526	172	249	275
5 and 6 years old	4,781	5,750	5,784	904	1,129	1,139	491	835	844
7 to 13 years old	19,585	20,076	20,739	3,598	3,832	4,081	2,009	2,794	2,991
14 and 15 years old	6,038	5,265	5,572	1,088	1,023	1,111	568	739	793
16 and 17 years old	5,937	4,858	5,060	1,047	962	1,024	454	592	727
18 and 19 years old	3,199	3,271	3,242	494	596	600	226	329	355
20 and 21 years old	2,206	2,402	2,295	242	305	308	111	213	260
22 to 24 years old	1,669	1,781	2,091	196	274	262	93	121	170
25 to 29 years old	1,473	1,706	1,537	187	162	269	84	130	159
30 to 34 years old	942	1,090	1,083	124	119	149	54	72	116
35 years old and over	1,104	2,096	2,167	186	238	321	(NA)	145	149
ENROLLMENT RATE									
Total 3 to 34 years old	48.9	49.5	51.1	53.9	51.9	53.6	49.8	47.4	48.9
3 and 4 years old	36.3	44.9	40.8	38.2	41.6	39.8	28.5	29.8	26.8
5 and 6 years old	95.8	96.5	95.5	95.4	96.3	94.6	94.5	94.8	93.8
7 to 13 years old	99.2	99.6	99.5	99.4	99.8	99.5	99.2	99.4	99.4
14 and 15 years old	98.3	99.1	98.9	97.9	99.2	98.5	94.3	99.0	97.6
16 and 17 years old	88.6	92.5	94.1	90.6	91.7	94.7	81.8	85.4	88.3
18 and 19 years old	46.3	57.1	61.7	45.7	55.2	57.7	37.8	44.1	50.0
20 and 21 years old	31.9	41.0	44.0	23.4	28.4	30.0	19.5	27.2	31.8
22 to 24 years old	16.4	20.2	23.3	13.6	20.0	18.1	11.7	9.9	13.7
25 to 29 years old	9.2	9.9	9.8	8.8	6.1	10.4	6.9	6.3	7.7
30 to 34 years old	6.3	5.9	5.9	6.8	4.4	5.5	5.1	3.6	5.1
35 years old and over	1.3	2.1	2.1	1.8	2.1	2.6	(NA)	2.1	1.9

Source: "School Enrollment, by Race, Hispanic Origin, and Age: 1980 to 1993," *Statistical Abstract of the United States: 1995,* 1995, p. 155. Primary source: U.S. Bureau of the Census, *Current Population Reports,* P20-479; and earlier reports. *Notes:* NA Not available. 1. Persons of Hispanic origin may be of any race.

★ 272 ★

Relationships

Literacy: Adult Average Prose Literacy, by Age Category and Race/Ethnic Origin: 1992

Numbers are standardized test scores. Range or average not given in source table.

Race/ethnicity	Total	Age					
		16-18	19-24	25-39	40-54	55-64	65 and over
Total	272	271	280	284	286	260	230
White	286	284	295	303	300	273	240
Black	237	248	254	251	235	212	187
Hispanic	215	237	238	215	211	192	170

Source: "Average Prose Literacy of Adults, by Age and Race/Ethnicity: 1992," *Adult Literacy,* National Center for Educational Statistics, January, 1995. Primary source: U.S. Department of Education, National Center for Education Statistics, *Adult Literacy in America; A First Look at the National Adult Literacy Survey,* 1993.

★ 273 ★

Relationships

Literacy: Adult Average Prose Literacy, by Educational Level and Race/Ethnic Origin: 1992

Numbers are standardized test scores. Range or average not given in source table.

Race/ethnicity	Total	Age					
		16-18	19-24	25-39	40-54	55-64	65 and over
Total	272	271	280	284	286	260	230
White	286	284	295	303	300	273	240
Black	237	248	254	251	235	212	187
Hispanic	215	237	238	215	211	192	170

Source: "Average Prose Literacy of Adults, by Level of Educational Attainment and Race/Ethnicity: 1992," *Adult Literacy,* National Center for Educational Statistics, January, 1995. Primary source: U.S. Department of Education, National Center for Education Statistics, *Adult Literacy in America; A First Look at the National Adult Literacy Survey,* 1993.

★ 274 ★

Relationships

Students and Graduates: Percent Distribution of High School Students, Graduates, and Nongraduates, by Gender and Race/Ethnic Origin: 1975 and 1993

[As of **October. For persons 18 to 21 years old.** For civilian noninstitutional population. Based on the Current Population Survey].

CHARACTERISTIC	TOTAL PERSONS 18 TO 21 YEARS OLD (1,000)		PERCENT DISTRIBUTION							
			Enrolled in high school		High school graduates				Not high school graduates	
					Total		In college			
	1975	1993	1975	1993	1975	1993	1975	1993	1975	1993
Total[1]	15,693	13,169	5.7	7.6	78.0	78.2	33.5	42.9	16.3	12.6
White	13,448	10,466	4.7	8.0	80.6	79.7	34.6	44.9	14.7	12.3
Black	1,997	2,067	12.5	14.4	60.4	69.6	24.9	29.4	27.0	15.9
Hispanic[2]	899	1,526	12.0	11.3	57.2	59.7	24.4	28.6	30.8	28.6
Male[1]	7,584	6,521	7.4	11.6	76.6	75.4	35.4	40.6	15.9	13.0
White	6,545	5,212	6.2	10.1	79.7	77.1	36.9	42.6	14.1	12.7
Black	911	986	15.9	18.8	55.0	65.1	23.9	25.9	29.0	16.0
Hispanic[2]	416	736	17.3	13.3	54.6	56.2	25.2	25.4	27.9	30.4
Female[1]	8,109	6,648	4.2	6.8	79.2	81.0	31.8	45.3	16.6	12.2
White	6,903	5,255	3.2	5.8	81.4	82.3	32.4	47.1	15.3	11.8
Black	1,085	1,081	9.7	10.4	65.0	73.8	25.8	32.7	25.4	15.7
Hispanic[2]	484	790	7.6	9.7	59.3	62.8	23.6	31.5	33.1	27.1

Source: "Enrollment Status, by Race, Hispanic Origin, and Sex: 1975 and 1993," *Statistical Abstract of the United States: 1995*, 1995, p. 174. Primary source: U.S. Bureau of the Census, *Current Population Reports*, P20-479; and earlier reports. *Notes:* 1. Includes other races not shown separately. 2. Persons of Hispanic origin may be of any race.

Test Scores

★ 275 ★

SAT Scores: Average 1994 SAT Scores, in Comparison to Scores in 1993 and 1976, by Race/Ethnic Origin

Ethnic Group	1994	Change from 1976[1]	Change from 1993
SAT Verbal			
American Indian	396	+8	-4
Asian American	416	+2	+1
Black	352	+20	-1
Mexican American	372	+1	-2
Puerto Rican	367	+3	0

[Continued]

★ 275 ★

SAT Scores: Average 1994 SAT Scores, in Comparison to Scores in 1993 and 1976, by Race/Ethnic Origin

[Continued]

Ethnic Group	1994	Change from 1976[1]	Change from 1993
Other Hispanic	383	NA	-1
White	443	-8	-1
Other	425	+15	+3
All Students	423	-8	-1
All Men	425	-8	-3
All Women	421	-9	+1
SAT Math			
American Indian	441	+21	-6
Asian American	535	+17	0
Black	388	+34	0
Mexican American	427	+17	-1
Puerto Rican	411	+10	+2
Other Hispanic	435	NA	+2
White	495	+2	+1
Other	480	+22	+3
All Students	479	+7	+1
All Men	501	+4	-1
All Women	460	+14	+3

Source: "1994 SAT Averages by Ethnic Group, Compared with 1976 and 1993," *College-Bound Seniors, National Report: 1994 Profile of SAT and Achievement Test Takers,"* 1994, p. iv. Published by permission. *Notes:* 1. The first year for which SAT scores by ethnic group are available is 1976. The SDQ question on ethnic background was changed in 1987 to include the "Other Hispanic" category.

★ 276 ★

Test Scores

SAT Scores: Characteristics of Students Who Took the SAT in 1994, by Race/Ethnic Origin

	NUMBER OF SAT TAKERS	PERCENT	% MALE/ FEMALE	SAT-V MEAN	SAT-M MEAN
ALL STUDENTS	1,050,386	100	47/53	423	479
ETHNIC GROUP					
American Indian/Alaskan Native	8,150	1	47/53	396	441
Asian/Asian Amer./Pacific Isl.	81,097	9	49/51	416	535
Black/African American	102,679	11	41/59	352	388

[Continued]

★ 276 ★

SAT Scores: Characteristics of Students Who Took the SAT in 1994, by Race/Ethnic Origin
[Continued]

	NUMBER OF SAT TAKERS	PERCENT	% MALE/ FEMALE	SAT-V MEAN	SAT-M MEAN
Hispanic/Latino:					
Mexican/Mexican American	35,397	4	44/56	372	427
Puerto Rican	13,036	1	43/57	367	411
Other Hispanic/Latino	29,395	3	44/56	383	435
White	662,107	69	47/53	443	495
Other	22,198	2	46/54	425	480
No response	96,327				

Source: "1994 Profiles," *College-Bound Seniors, National Report: 1994 Profile of SAT and Achievement Test Takers,"* 1994, p. 6. Primary source: The College Board. Published by permission.

Chapter 5
HEALTH AND MEDICAL CARE

Deaths

★ 277 ★

Drug-Related: Drugs Noted Most Often by Medical Examiners, by Decedent's Race/Ethnic Origin: 1993

Drug name	Rank	Percent of total episodes
White decedents		
Heroin/morphine[1]	1	41.3
Alcohol-in-combination	2	39.3
Cocaine	3	32.5
Codeine	4	12.3
Diazepam	5	10.5
Methamphetamine/speed	6	6.3
D-Propoxyphene	7	6.2
Amitriptyline	8	6.1
Marijuana/hashish	9	5.9
Diphenhydramine	10	5.4
Black decedents		
Cocaine	1	69.7
Heroin/morphine[1]	2	45.1
Alcohol-in-combination	3	39.7
Codeine	4	10.6
Methadone	5	5.2
Quinine	6	4.4
Marijuana/hashish	7	4.3
Amitriptyline	8	3.5
Lidocaine	9	3.2
Diphenhydramine	10	3.1

[Continued]

★ 277 ★

Drug-Related: Drugs Noted Most Often by Medical Examiners, by Decedent's Race/Ethnic Origin: 1993
[Continued]

Drug name	Rank	Percent of total episodes
Hispanic decedents		
Heroin/morphine[1]	1	60.5
Cocaine	2	51.0
Alcohol-in-combination	3	47.7
Codeine	4	11.4
Methadone	5	7.8
Marijuana/hashish	6	5.3
PCP/PCP combinations	7	4.8
Methamphetamine	8	4.1
Lidocaine	9	2.5
Amphetamine	10	2.5

Source: "Drugs Mentioned Most Frequently by Medical Examiners in 1993, by Sex and Race/ Ethnicity of Decedent," *Drug Use Among Ethnic Minorities*, 1995, p. 83. Primary source: Drug Abuse Warning Network, Substance Abuse and Mental Health Services Administration, APril 1994 provisional data file. *Notes:* Percentages are based on raw medical examiner drug abuse case counts of 5,596 male decedents and 1,880 female decedents. Total raw medical examiner drug abuse case counts included 85 decedents ages 6-17, 732 decedents ages 18-25, 2,170 decedents ages 26-34, and 4,521 decedents age 35 and older. Drugs with fewer than 10 mentions are excluded. 1. Includes opiates not specified as to type.

★ 278 ★
Deaths

Drug-Related: Percent of Accidental or Suicide Deaths that were Drug- Related, by Race/Ethnic Origin: 1993

	Accidental	Suicide
Black	62.9	7.8
Hispanic	80.5	11.1
White	51.8	26.7

Source: "Manner of Drug-Related Death, by Race/Ethnicity, DAWN Medical Examiner Data: 1993," *Drug Use Among Ethnic Minorities*, 1995, p. 85. Primary source: Drug Abuse Warning Network, Substance Abuse and Mental Health Services Administration, April 1994 provisional data file. *Notes:* DAWN = Drug Abuse Warning Network. Percentages do not sum to 100.0 within race/ ethnic groups.

Diseases/Illnesses/Conditions

★ 279 ★

AIDS: Adult and Adolescent Men with AIDS, by Type of Exposure and Race/Ethnic Origin: Through December, 1994

Exposure	White, not Hispanic		Black, not Hispanic		Hispanic		Asian/Pacific Islander		American Indian/ Alaska Native		Cumulative totals[1]	
	No.	%	No.	%	No.	%	No.	%	No.	%	No.	%
Men who have sex with men	153,150	(77)	44,597	(40)	28,232	(45)	2,085	(78)	544	(61)	228,954	(61)
Injecting drug use	16,632	(8)	40,580	(37)	23,911	(38)	120	(4)	110	(12)	81,491	(22)
Men who have sex with men and inject drugs	15,503	(8)	8,479	(8)	4,275	(7)	84	(3)	155	(17)	28,521	(8)
Hemophilia/coagulation disorder	2,848	(1)	338	(0)	285	(0)	41	(2)	24	(3)	3,545	(1)
Heterosexual contact	2,374	(1)	5,876	(5)	2,320	(4)	49	(2)	12	(1)	10,641	(3)
Receipt of blood transfusion, blood Components, or tissue	2,711	(1)	790	(1)	443	(1)	84	(3)	7	(1)	4,047	(1)
Risk not reported or identified	5,604	(3)	10,298	(9)	3,468	(6)	204	(8)	36	(4)	19,690	(5)
Total	198,822	(100)	110,958	(100)	62,934	(100)	2,667	(100)	888	(100)	376,889	(100)

Source: "Male Adult/Adolescent AIDS Cases, by Exposure Category and Race/Ethnicity, Cumulative Totals Through December, 1994," *Drug Use Among Ethnic Minorities,* 1995, p. 76. Primary source: Centers for Disease Control and Prevention, 1995. *Note:* 1. Includes 620 men whose race/ethnicity is unknown.

★ 280 ★

Diseases/Illnesses/Conditions

AIDS: Adult and Adolescent Women with AIDS, by Type of Exposure and Race/Ethnic Origin: Through December, 1994

Exposure	White, not Hispanic		Black, not Hispanic		Hispanic		Asian/Pacific Islander		American Indian/Alaska Native		Cumulative totals[1]	
	No.	%	No.	%	No.	%	No.	%	No.	%	No.	%
Injecting drug use	6,141	(43)	16,069	(50)	5,519	(46)	48	(17)	79	(50)	27,902	(48)
Hemophilia/coagulation disorder	65	(0)	25	(0)	6	(0)	1	(0)	-	-	97	(0)
Heterosexual contact	5,207	(37)	10,481	(33)	5,125	(43)	129	(44)	56	(35)	21,021	(36)
Receipt of blood transfusion, blood Components, or tissue	1,551	(11)	776	(2)	413	(3)	68	(23)	10	(6)	2,819	(5)
Risk not reported or identified	1,202	(8)	4,470	(14)	846	(7)	44	(15)	14	(9)	6,589	(11)
Total	14,186	(100)	31,821	(100)	11,909	(100)	290	(100)	159	(100)	58,428	(100)

Source: "Female Adult/Adolescent AIDS Cases, by Exposure Category and Race/Ethnicity, Cumulative Totals Through December, 1994," *Drug Use Among Ethnic Minorities,* 1995, p. 76. Primary source: Centers for Disease Control and Prevention, (1995). *Note:* 1. Includes 83 women whose race/ethnicity is unknown.

★ 281 ★

Diseases/Illnesses/Conditions

AIDS: Trends in Number/Percent of Diagnosed AIDS Cases, by Age Group, Gender, and Race/Ethnic Origin: 1985-1994

[Data are based on reporting by State health departments].

Age at diagnosis, sex, race, and Hispanic origin	All years[1] Percent distribution	Number, by year of report								January-September 1994	12 months ending September 30, 1994 Cases per 100,000 population[2]
		All years[1]	1985	1988	1989	1990	1991	1992	1993		
All races	...	410,532	8,190	30,716	33,643	41,761	43,771	45,961	103,463	61,301	30.7
Male											
All males, 13 years and over	100.0	352,092	7,539	27,106	29,666	36,475	37,722	39,223	86,469	49,887	64.3
White, not Hispanic	54.6	192,158	4,781	16,041	17,543	21,000	20,675	20,899	43,892	23,211	39.6
Black, not Hispanic	30.2	106,167	1,713	7,188	8,055	10,300	11,149	12,209	28,714	18,089	214.1
Hispanic	14.1	49,786	986	3,637	3,737	4,773	5,467	5,625	12,782	7,954	111.5
American Indian[3]	0.2	841	6	38	61	78	84	102	289	135	26.0
Asian or Pacific Islander[4]	0.7	2,528	49	162	216	262	259	285	670	397	16.3
13-19 years	0.3	1,184	31	84	92	106	98	94	362	186	...
20-29 years	17.6	61,926	1,471	5,393	5,694	6,813	6,457	6,387	14,456	7,622	...
30-39 years	46.3	162,922	3,619	12,669	13,940	16,885	17,481	18,014	39,513	22,932	...
40-49 years	25.3	89,238	1,656	6,127	6,846	8,977	9,657	10,392	23,382	13,750	...
50-59 years	7.7	27,047	602	1,993	2,247	2,664	2,909	3,097	6,590	4,031	...
60 years and over	2.8	9,775	160	840	847	1,030	1,120	1,239	2,166	1,366	...
Female											
All females, 13 years and over	100.0	52,778	520	3,040	3,380	4,560	5,373	5,980	16,113	10,693	12.6
White, not Hispanic	25.5	13,448	141	860	944	1,225	1,352	1,479	4,077	2,437	3.7
Black, not Hispanic	57.0	30,092	280	1,655	1,903	2,561	3,110	3,409	9,193	6,318	63.6
Hispanic	16.5	8,728	96	492	499	736	863	1,023	2,670	1,854	26.4
American Indian[3]	0.3	152	2	6	9	9	11	17	57	35	6.3
Asian or Pacific Islander[4]	0.5	279	1	22	16	19	25	39	96	40	1.4
13-19 years	1.1	586	4	22	29	63	55	55	194	134	...
20-29 years	23.6	12,462	174	768	889	1,105	1,219	1,381	3,692	2,308	...
30-39 years	46.7	24,657	233	1,512	1,625	2,109	2,542	2,747	7,654	4,838	...
40-49 years	19.3	10,194	45	412	506	787	998	1,244	3,269	2,524	...
50-59 years	5.6	2,941	27	151	171	276	338	338	871	610	...
60 years and over	3.7	1,938	37	175	160	220	221	215	433	279	...
Children											
All children, under 13 years	100.0	5,662	131	570	597	726	676	758	881	721	1.9
White, not Hispanic	19.8	1,122	26	148	114	160	147	129	146	102	0.4
Black, not Hispanic	59.1	3,348	86	307	339	389	408	483	538	478	8.1
Hispanic	20.0	1,130	19	111	137	169	114	139	184	131	2.6
American Indian[3]	0.3	17	-	-	2	4	2	3	3	-	0.2
Asian or Pacific Islander[4]	0.6	32	-	4	3	4	4	1	5	8	0.5

[Continued]

★ 281 ★

AIDS: Trends in Number/Percent of Diagnosed AIDS Cases, by Age Group, Gender, and Race/Ethnic Origin: 1985-1994

[Continued]

Age at diagnosis, sex, race, and Hispanic origin	All years[1] Percent distribution	Number, by year of report								January-September 1994	12 months ending September 30, 1994 Cases per 100,000 population[2]
		All years[1]	1985	1988	1989	1990	1991	1992	1993		
Under 1 year	38.6	2,183	56	192	241	288	255	318	324	233	...
1-12 years	61.4	3,479	75	378	356	438	421	440	557	488	...

Source: "Acquired Immunodeficiency Syndrome (AIDS) Cases, According to Age at Diagnosis, Sex, Detailed Race, and Hispanic Origin: United States, 1985- 94," *Health, United States, 1994,* 1995, p. 147. Primary source: Centers for Disease Control and Prevention, National Center for Infectious Diseases, Division of HIV/AIDS. *Notes:* The AIDS case reporting definitions were expanded in 1985, 1987, and 1993. Excludes residents of U.S. territories. Data are updated periodically because of reporting delays. Data for all years have been updated through September 30, 1994. Data as of December 31, 1994, are available in the Centers for Disease Control and Prevention, HIV/AIDS Surveillance Report Year-End edition, February, 1995. 1. Includes cases prior to 1985. 2. Computed using resident population estimates for 1993 based on extrapolation from 1990 census counts from the U.S. Bureau of the Census. 3. Includes Aleut and Eskimo. 4. Includes Chinese, Japanese, Filipino, Hawaiian and part Hawaiian, and other Asian or Pacific Islander.

★ 282 ★

Diseases/Illnesses/Conditions

AIDS: Trends in Transmission Category of AIDS Cases Diagnosed for Persons 13 and Over, by Race/Ethnic Origin: 1985-1994

[Data are based on reporting by State health departments].

Race, Hispanic origin, sex, and transmission category	Percent distribution All years[1]	Number, by year of report								
		All years[1]	1985	1988	1989	1990	1991	1992	1993	January-September 1994
All races	100.0	404,870	8,059	30,146	33,046	41,035	43,095	45,203	102,582	60,580
White, not Hispanic	100.0	205,606	4,922	16,901	18,487	22,225	22,027	22,378	47,969	25,648
Men who have sex with men	72.1	148,216	4,016	12,714	13,841	16,699	16,202	16,095	32,327	16,615
Injecting drug use	10.6	21,788	246	1,468	1,691	2,058	2,302	2,521	6,519	3,514
Men who have sex with men and injecting drug use	7.2	14,899	401	1,259	1,411	1,513	1,625	1,571	3,440	1,516
Hemophilia/coagulation disorder	1.4	2,850	58	246	236	282	252	252	887	301
Heterosexual contact[2]	3.5	7,142	33	371	437	649	728	900	2,323	1,388
Sex with injecting drug user	1.6	3,311	18	215	259	354	373	425	971	538
Transfusion[3]	2.1	4,229	125	596	511	521	407	386	631	289
Undetermined[4]	3.2	6,482	43	247	360	503	511	653	1,842	2,025
Black, not Hispanic	100.0	136,259	1,993	8,843	9,958	12,861	14,259	15,618	37,907	24,407
Men who have sex with men	31.4	42,762	788	3,092	3,596	4,500	4,667	5,126	10,632	6,215
Injecting drug use	39.8	54,194	742	3,752	4,042	5,187	5,802	6,074	15,534	9,323
Men who have sex with men and injecting drug use	5.9	8,050	158	669	705	847	893	930	2,036	956
Hemophilia/coagulation disorder	0.3	355	4	27	18	27	36	37	121	63
Heterosexual contact[2]	11.2	15,300	88	590	786	1,214	1,588	2,067	5,122	3,312
Sex with injecting drug user	5.9	7,977	65	454	597	858	1,014	1,191	2,194	1,207

[Continued]

★ 282 ★

AIDS: Trends in Transmission Category of AIDS Cases Diagnosed for Persons 13 and Over, by Race/Ethnic Origin: 1985-1994

[Continued]

Race, Hispanic origin, sex, and transmission category	Percent distribution All years[1]	Number, by year of report								
		All years[1]	1985	1988	1989	1990	1991	1992	1993	January-September 1994
Transfusion[3]	1.1	1,517	31	145	138	172	147	146	348	222
Undetermined[4]	10.3	14,081	182	568	673	914	1,126	1,238	4,114	4,316
Hispanic	100.0	58,514	1,082	4,129	4,236	5,509	6,330	6,648	15,452	9,808
Men who have sex with men	42.3	24,755	546	1,796	1,989	2,468	2,837	2,941	6,041	3,469
Injecting drug use	36.2	21,176	388	1,631	1,450	2,028	2,273	2,297	5,807	3,482
Men who have sex with men and injecting drug use	5.3	3,087	81	268	249	299	345	366	758	328
Hemophilia/coagulation disorder	0.4	249	7	21	22	26	21	28	61	41
Heterosexual contact[2]	8.1	4,712	27	228	249	374	424	569	1,560	1,068
Sex with injecting drug user	4.5	2,625	24	186	193	282	294	351	733	379
Transfusion[3]	1.1	636	7	56	57	82	68	78	143	82
Undetermined[4]	6.7	3,899	26	129	220	232	362	369	1,082	1,338

Source: "Acquired Immunodeficiency Syndrome (AIDS) Cases, According to Race, Hispanic Origin, Sex, and Transmission Category for Persons 13 Years of Age and Over at Diagnosis: United States, 1985-94," *Health, United States, 1994*, 1995 pp. 148-149. Primary source: Centers for Disease Control and Prevention, National Center for Infectious Diseases, Division of HIV/AIDS. *Notes:* The AIDS case reporting definitions were expanded in 1985, 1987, and 1993. Excludes residents of U.S. territories. Data are updated periodically because of reporting delays. Data for all years have been updated through September 30, 1994. Data as of December 31, 1994, are available in the Centers for Disease Control and Prevention, HIV/AIDS Surveillance Report Year-End edition, February 1995. 1. Includes cases prior to 1985. 2. Includes persons who have had heterosexual contact with a person with human immunodeficiency virus (HIV) infection or at risk of HIV infection. 3. Receipt of blood transfusion, blood components, or tissue. 4. Includes persons for whom risk information is incomplete (because of death, refusal to be interviewed, or loss to followup), persons still under investigation, men reported only to have had heterosexual contact with prostitutes, and interviewed persons for whom no specific risk is identified.

★ 283 ★

Diseases/Illnesses/Conditions

Acute Conditions: Number and Rate of Acute Conditions, by Race: 1993

[Covers civilian noninstitutional population. Estimates include only acute conditions which were medically attended or caused at least 1 day of restricted activity. Based on National Health Interview Survey].

YEAR AND CHARACTERISTIC	NUMBER OF CONDITIONS (mil.)					RATE PER 100 POPULATION				
	Interactive and parasitic	Respiratory		Digestive system	Injuries	Infective and parasitic	Respiratory		Digestive system	Injuries
		Common cold	Influenza				Common cold	Influenza		
1993, total[1]	54.3	68.2	132.6	16.1	62.1	21.3	26.8	52.2	6.3	24.4
White	47.1	56.1	117.9	13.1	52.9	22.3	26.6	55.8	6.2	25.0
Black	5.9	9.5	9.6	2.7	7.5	18.3	29.6	29.9	8.5	23.4

Source: "Acute Conditions, by Type: 1970 to 1993," *Statistical Abstract of the United States: 1995*, 1995, p. 141. Primary source: U.S. National Center for Health Statistics, *Vital and Health Statistics*, series 10, No. 190, and earlier reports; and unpublished data. *Note:* 1. Includes other races and unknown income not shown separately.

★ 284 ★

Diseases/Illnesses/Conditions

Cancer: Trends in 5-Year Relative Survival Rates for Selected Cancer Sites, by Race: 1974-1990

[Data are based on the Surveillance, Epidemiology, and End Results Program's population-based registries in Atlanta, Detroit, Seattle-Puget Sound, San Francisco-Oakland, Connecticut, Iowa, New Mexico, Utah, and Hawaii].

Sex and site	All races				White				Black			
	1974-76	1977-79	1980-82	1983-90	1974-76	1977-79	1980-82	1983-90	1974-76	1977-79	1980-82	1983-90
						Percent of patients						
Male												
All sites	40.8	43.1	45.0	49.0	41.9	44.3	46.3	50.8	31.3	32.1	34.0	35.7
Oral cavity and pharynx	52.2	51.1	50.6	49.5	54.3	53.4	53.8	52.5	31.2	30.8	25.8	28.5
Esophagus	3.6	4.7	6.0	8.6	4.3	5.6	6.7	9.9	2.1	2.4	4.6	5.5
Stomach	13.9	15.3	16.3	16.6	13.2	14.4	15.2	15.5	15.5	14.6	18.5	16.9
Colon	49.4	51.4	55.4	60.9	49.8	51.7	55.8	62.0	44.1	45.4	46.5	49.2
Rectum	47.4	48.6	50.1	57.3	47.8	49.6	51.2	58.2	34.1	38.0	36.1	46.7
Pancreas	3.0	2.3	2.7	2.7	3.1	2.3	2.6	2.4	1.4	2.8	3.7	4.5
Lung and bronchus	11.1	11.8	12.0	12.0	11.0	12.0	12.2	12.1	11.0	8.9	10.9	10.6
Prostate gland	66.7	70.9	73.1	79.6	67.7	71.9	74.3	81.3	58.0	62.1	64.4	66.4
Urinary bladder	73.7	76.4	79.1	82.0	74.5	76.9	79.8	82.6	54.1	62.4	62.3	66.0
Non-Hodgkin's lymphoma	46.9	45.6	49.9	49.9	47.7	46.2	50.6	50.6	43.1	43.2	47.5	42.1
Leukemia	33.1	35.9	37.1	38.4	33.5	36.8	38.3	39.9	32.6	29.0	29.8	29.3
Female												
All sites	56.7	56.0	56.0	58.6	57.4	56.8	56.8	59.8	46.8	46.3	45.6	45.5
Colon	50.6	53.6	55.0	59.0	50.8	53.7	55.3	59.9	46.6	49.8	50.7	50.1
Rectum	49.4	50.8	53.9	58.0	49.7	51.4	54.6	58.7	49.3	38.6	40.7	50.6
Pancreas	2.1	2.7	3.4	3.8	2.1	2.4	3.0	3.5	3.1	4.8	5.9	5.3
Lung and bronchus	15.6	17.0	16.0	15.8	15.8	17.1	16.1	16.2	13.1	17.0	15.4	12.3
Melanoma of skin	84.7	85.8	87.6	89.3	84.8	86.1	87.6	· 89.4	-	-	-	77.9
Breast	74.3	74.5	76.2	80.4	74.9	75.2	76.9	81.6	62.9	62.8	65.7	65.8
Cervix uteri	68.5	67.7	66.9	67.4	69.2	68.8	67.7	69.9	63.5	61.9	60.4	56.4
Corpus uteri	87.7	84.9	81.4	83.2	88.6	86.2	82.7	84.9	60.4	57.5	53.7	55.2
Ovary	36.5	38.1	38.9	41.8	36.3	37.5	38.7	41.6	40.1	39.8	37.6	38.4
Non-Hodgkin's lymphoma	47.3	50.6	52.4	54.6	47.3	50.5	52.7	55.0	54.1	59.2	53.3	49.5

Source: "Five-Year Relative Cancer Survival rates for Selected Sites, According to Race and Sex: Selected Geographic Areas, 1974-76, 1977-79, 1980-92, and 1983-90," *Health, United States, 1994*, 1995, p. 152. Primary source: National Cancer Institute, National Institutes of Health, Cancer Statics Branch, Bethesda, Md. 20892. *Notes:* Rates are based on followup patients through 1991. The rate is the ratio of the observed survival rate for the patient group to the expected survival rate for persons in the general population similar to the patient group with respect to age, sex, race, and calendar year of observation. It estimates the chance of surviving the effects of cancer.

★ 285 ★
Diseases/Illnesses/Conditions

Cancer: Trends in Percent Distribution of Cancer Rates (Age-Adjusted) of Females for Selected Cancer Sites, by Race: 1973-1991

[Data are based on the Surveillance, Epidemiology, and End Results Program's population-based registries in Atlanta, Detroit, Seattle-Puget Sound, San Francisco-Oakland, Connecticut, Iowa, New Mexico, Utah, and Hawaii].

Race, sex, and site	Number of new cases per 100,000 population[2]									Estimated annual percent change[1]
	1973	1975	1980	1985	1987	1988	1989	1990	1991	
White female										
All sites	294.0	309.2	309.7	341.3	350.0	346.4	345.3	350.2	347.8	0.9
Colon and rectum	41.6	42.8	44.6	45.7	41.0	39.9	40.7	39.8	38.0	-0.4
Colon	30.2	30.8	32.8	33.8	30.1	29.3	29.9	29.8	28.2	-0.3
Rectum	11.4	12.0	11.7	11.9	10.9	10.6	10.8	10.0	9.8	-0.8
Pancreas	7.4	7.1	7.3	8.1	7.5	7.6	7.4	7.7	7.3	0.2
Lung and bronchus	17.8	21.8	28.2	35.8	39.5	41.3	40.7	41.9	42.8	4.8
Melanoma of skin	5.9	6.9	9.2	10.3	11.1	10.5	10.8	10.6	11.5	3.5
Breast	84.1	89.3	87.1	106.3	116.8	113.3	109.2	112.8	113.6	1.8
Cervix uteri	12.8	11.1	9.1	7.6	7.4	7.9	8.1	8.3	7.5	-2.5
Corpus uteri	29.4	33.5	25.2	23.1	22.6	21.2	22.1	22.9	22.0	-2.3
Ovary	14.6	14.4	13.9	15.0	14.5	15.5	16.1	15.9	15.7	0.5
Non-Hodgkin's lymphoma	7.5	8.4	9.2	11.3	11.4	12.1	11.8	12.6	12.0	2.7
Black female										
All sites	282.6	295.8	304.8	323.5	327.0	335.6	322.5	339.0	334.0	1.1
Colon and rectum	41.1	43.1	49.5	45.9	48.2	45.8	44.4	49.3	45.5	0.9
Colon	29.5	32.5	40.9	36.0	37.3	36.4	34.1	38.8	37.2	1.2
Rectum	11.6	10.6	8.6	10.0	10.9	9.5	10.3	10.4	8.3	-0.3
Pancreas	11.6	11.8	13.0	11.3	14.9	14.4	11.0	10.6	12.4	0.5
Lung and bronchus	20.9	20.6	34.0	40.7	38.5	42.8	45.4	46.3	49.0	4.9
Breast	68.8	78.3	74.1	92.6	90.3	98.4	88.6	97.2	95.1	1.9
Cervix uteri	29.7	27.9	19.0	15.9	15.2	15.2	13.2	13.6	12.9	-4.3
Corpus uteri	15.0	17.2	14.2	15.2	13.3	14.0	16.4	14.5	14.2	-0.3
Ovary	10.4	10.1	10.0	10.1	10.2	10.7	10.7	10.3	10.0	0.2
Non-Hodgkin's lymphoma	5.5	4.1	6.0	7.0	8.0	7.1	7.7	9.1	8.3	4.0

Source: "Age-Adjusted Cancer Incidence Rates for Selected Sites, According to Sex and Race: Selected Geographic Areas, Selected Years 1973-91," *Health, United States, 1994*, 1995, p. 151. Primary source: National Cancer Institute, National Institutes of Health, Cancer Statistics Branch, Bethesda, Md. 20892. *Notes:* 1. The estimated annual percent change has been calculated by fitting a linear regression model to the natural logarithm of the yearly rates from 1973-91. 2. Age adjusted by the direct method to the 1970 U.S. population.

★ 286 ★

Diseases/Illnesses/Conditions

Cancer: Trends in Percent Distribution of Cancer Rates (Age-Adjusted) of Males for Selected Cancer Sites, by Race: 1973-1991

[Data are based on the Surveillance, Epidemiology, and End Results Program's population-based registries in Atlanta, Detroit, Seattle-Puget Sound, San Francisco-Oakland, Connecticut, Iowa, New Mexico, Utah, and Hawaii].

Race, sex, and site	Number of new cases per 100,000 population[2]									Estimated annual percent change[1]
	1973	1975	1980	1985	1987	1988	1989	1990	1991	
White male										
All sites	363.2	378.6	405.7	428.3	452.3	448.1	453.7	470.2	494.5	1.4
Oral cavity and pharynx	17.5	18.2	16.8	16.7	17.2	15.4	15.3	15.9	15.3	-0.8
Esophagus	4.8	4.8	4.9	5.3	5.4	5.3	5.1	6.1	5.6	1.0
Stomach	13.9	12.5	12.3	10.5	10.4	10.6	10.7	9.3	9.5	-1.8
Colon and rectum	54.1	55.0	58.4	63.3	61.0	59.3	58.7	58.4	56.3	0.3
Colon	34.7	36.1	39.2	43.3	41.8	40.8	40.1	39.9	39.3	0.7
Rectum	19.4	19.0	19.3	20.0	19.2	18.4	18.6	18.5	17.0	-0.4
Pancreas	12.7	12.4	11.0	10.7	10.5	10.5	10.1	9.9	9.6	-1.1
Lung and bronhcus	72.2	75.7	82.1	81.8	83.8	81.7	80.4	79.7	77.9	0.4
Prostate	62.3	68.8	78.4	86.3	101.6	104.4	110.0	129.2	159.2	4.0
Urinary bladder	27.2	28.6	31.3	30.9	33.4	32.8	32.0	31.8	31.6	0.9
Non-Hodgkin's lymphoma	10.3	11.4	12.6	15.8	18.2	18.0	18.3	19.1	19.5	3.9
Leukemia	14.3	14.2	14.5	14.3	14.1	13.7	13.9	12.9	12.5	-0.5
Black male										
All sites	441.6	437.8	509.6	529.9	546.1	538.7	536.8	564.6	597.9	1.6
Oral cavity and pharynx	16.8	17.3	23.1	22.5	26.0	23.0	24.1	24.8	20.7	1.8
Esophagus	13.0	17.4	16.4	19.4	18.1	16.7	15.7	19.9	15.1	0.3
Stomach	25.9	19.9	21.4	18.4	20.7	20.0	18.3	189.0	20.2	-0.9
Colon and rectum	42.6	47.5	63.7	60.4	61.3	57.8	64.1	59.9	61.7	1.7
Colon	31.5	34.5	46.0	46.6	47.5	42.8	48.9	46.2	45.9	1.9
Rectum	11.1	13.0	17.7	13.8	13.7	15.0	15.1	13.7	15.7	1.0
Pancreas	15.8	15.4	17.6	19.8	16.0	16.9	13.1	15.5	14.4	-0.6
Lung and bronchus	105.1	101.2	131.2	131.3	124.0	125.9	122.1	118.2	122.0	1.2
Prostate gland	106.4	111.3	126.0	132.6	145.7	146.0	145.4	166.6	209.6	2.8
Urinary bladder	10.7	13.7	14.5	15.8	17.4	14.2	14.1	14.9	14.7	1.0
Non-Hodgkin's lymphoma	9.0	7.1	9.3	9.9	9.4	13.3	11.6	13.8	15.6	3.8
Leukemia	12.0	12.5	13.1	12.9	13.8	10.8	13.0	10.7	9.5	-0.4

Source: "Age-Adjusted Cancer Incidence Rates for Selected Sites, According to Sex and Race: Selected Geographic Areas, Selected Years 1973-91," *Health, United States, 1994,* 1995, p. 151. Primary source: National Cancer Institute, National Institutes of Health, Cancer Statistics Branch, Bethesda, Md. 20892. *Notes:* 1. The estimated annual percent change has been calculated by fitting a linear regression model to the natural logarithm of the yearly rates from 1973-91. 2. Age adjusted by the direct method to the 1970 U.S. population.

★ 287 ★

Diseases/Illnesses/Conditions

Cancer: Trends in Prostate and Breast Cancer 5-Year Relative Survival Rates, by Race: 1974-1976, 1977-1979, 1980-1982, and 1983-1990

Year	Prostate		Breast	
	White	Black	White	Black
1974-76	67.7	58.0	74.9	62.9
1977-79	71.9	62.1	75.2	62.8
1980-82	74.3	64.4	76.9	65.7
1983-90	81.3	66.4	81.6	65.8

Source: "Five-Year Relative Survival Rates for Prostate and Breast Cancers by Race: Selected Geographic Areas, 1974-76, 1977-79, 1980-82, and 1983-90," *Health, United States, 1994,* 1995, pp. 20, 50. Primary source: National Institutes of Health, National Center Institute, Surveillance, Epidemiology, and End Results Program.

★ 288 ★

Diseases/Illnesses/Conditions

Cholesterol: Trends (in percentages) in Cholesterol Levels and Mean Levels of Persons 20-74 Years Old, by Gender and Race/Ethnic Origin: 1960-1991

[Data are based on physical examinations of a sample of the civilian noninstitutionalized population].

Sex, age, race, and Hispanic origin[1]	Percent of population with high serum cholesterol				Mean serum cholesterol level, mg/dL			
	1960-62	1971-74	1976-80[2]	1988-91	1960-62	1971-74	1976-80[2]	1988-91
20-74 years, age adjusted								
Both sexes	31.8	27.2	26.3	19.7	220	214	213	205
Male	28.7	25.8	24.6	19.0	217	213	211	205
Female	34.5	28.2	27.6	20.2	222	215	214	205
White male	29.4	25.9	24.6	19.3	218	213	211	205
White female	35.1	28.1	28.0	20.3	223	215	214	205
Black male	24.5	25.1	24.1	16.5	210	212	208	200
Black female	30.7	29.2	24.9	20.7	216	217	213	205
White, non-Hispanic male	-	-	24.7	19.1	-	-	211	205
White, non-Hispanic female	-	-	28.3	20.0	-	-	214	205
Black, non-Hispanic male	-	-	24.0	16.6	-	-	208	201
Black, non-Hispanic female	-	-	24.9	20.7	-	-	214	205
Mexican-American male	-	-	18.8	20.3	-	-	207	207
Mexican-American female	-	-	20.0	19.4	-	-	207	205

[Continued]

★ 288 ★

Cholesterol: Trends (in percentages) in Cholesterol Levels and Mean Levels of Persons 20-74 Years Old, by Gender and Race/Ethnic Origin: 1960-1991

[Continued]

Sex, age, race, and Hispanic origin[1]	Percent of population with high serum cholesterol				Mean serum cholesterol level, mg/dL			
	1960-62	1971-74	1976-80[2]	1988-91	1960-62	1971-74	1976-80[2]	1988-91
20-74 years, crude								
Both sexes	33.6	28.2	26.8	19.7	222	216	213	205
Male	30.7	26.8	24.9	19.0	220	214	211	205
Female	36.3	29.6	28.5	20.3	225	217	215	205
White male	31.4	26.9	25.0	19.6	221	215	211	206
White female	37.5	29.8	29.2	20.8	227	217	216	206
Black male	26.7	25.1	23.9	15.3	214	212	208	198
Black female	29.9	28.8	23.7	18.1	216	216	212	201
White, non-Hispanic male	-	-	25.1	19.6	-	-	211	206
White, non-Hispanic female	-	-	29.8	20.9	-	-	216	206
Black, non-Hispanic male	-	-	23.7	15.4	-	-	208	199
Black, non-Hispanic female	-	-	23.7	18.2	-	-	212	202
Mexican-American male	-	-	16.6	17.6	-	-	203	202
Mexican-American female	-	-	16.5	15.6	-	-	202	200

Source: "Serum Cholesterol Levels Among Persons 20 Years of Age and Over, According to Sex, Age, Race, and Hispanic Origin: United States, 1960-62, 1971-74, 1976-80, 1988-91," *Health, United States, 1994,* 1995, p. 164. Primary source: Centers for Disease Control and Prevention, National Center for Health Statistics, Division of Health Examination Statistics: Unpublished data. *Notes:* High serum cholesterol is defined as greater than or equal to 240 mg/dL (6.20 mmol/L). Risk levels have been defined by the National Cholesterol Education Program Expert Panel on Detection, Evaluation and Treatment of High Blood Cholesterol in Adults, Nov. 1987 (Archives of Internal Medicine: January 1988, 148: 36-69). 1. The race groups, white and black, include persons of Hispanic and non-Hispanic origin. Conversely, persons of Hispanic origin may be of any race. 2. Data for Mexican-Americans are for 1982-84.

★ 289 ★

Diseases/Illnesses/Conditions

Hypertension: Trends in Percent of Persons 20-74 Years Old with Hypertension, by Gender and Race/Ethnic Origin: 1960-1991

[Data are based on physical examinations of a sample of the civilian noninstitutionalized population].

Sex, age, race, and Hispanic origin[1]	Percent of population			
	1960-62	1971-74	1976-80[2]	1988-91
20-74 years, age adjusted				
Both sexes[3]	36.9	38.3	39.0	23.4
Male	40.0	42.4	44.0	26.3

[Continued]

★ 289 ★

Hypertension: Trends in Percent of Persons 20-74 Years Old with Hypertension, by Gender and Race/Ethnic Origin: 1960-1991
[Continued]

Sex, age, race, and Hispanic origin[1]	Percent of population			
	1960-62	1971-74	1976-80[2]	1988-91
Female[3]	33.7	34.3	34.0	20.3
White male	39.3	41.7	43.5	25.1
White female[3]	31.7	32.4	32.3	19.0
Black male	48.1	51.8	48.7	37.4
Black female[3]	50.8	50.3	47.5	31.3
White, non-Hispanic male	-	-	43.9	25.4
White, non-Hispanic female[3]	-	-	32.1	18.9
Black, non-Hispanic male	-	-	48.7	37.3
Black, non-Hispanic female[3]	-	-	47.6	31.4
Mexican-American male	-	-	25.0	26.9
Mexican-American female[3]	-	-	21.8	20.8
27-74 years, crude				
Both sexes[3]	39.0	39.7	39.7	23.5
Male	41.7	43.3	44.0	25.7
Female[3]	36.6	36.5	35.6	21.3
White male	41.0	42.8	43.8	25.0
White female[3]	34.9	34.9	34.2	20.4
Black male	50.5	52.1	47.4	34.3
Black female[3]	52.0	50.2	46.1	28.7
White, non-Hispanic male	-	-	44.3	25.8
White, non-Hispanic female[3]	-	-	34.4	20.7
Black, non-Hispanic males	-	-	47.5	34.2
Black, non-Hispanic females[3]	-	-	46.1	29.0

[Continued]

★ 289 ★

Hypertension: Trends in Percent of Persons 20-74 Years Old with Hypertension, by Gender and Race/Ethnic Origin: 1960-1991

[Continued]

Sex, age, race, and Hispanic origin[1]	Percent of population			
	1960-62	1971-74	1976-80[2]	1988-91
Mexican-American male	-	-	18.8	19.6
Mexican-American female[3]	-	-	16.7	14.9

Source: "Hypertension Among Persons 20 Years of Age and Over, According to Sex, Age, race, and Hispanic Origin: United States, 1960-62, 1971-74, 1976-80, 1988-91," Health, United States, 1994, 1995, p. 163. Primary source: Centers for Disease Control and Prevention, National Center for Health Statistics, Division of Health Examination Statistics: Unpublished data. Notes: A person with hypertension is defined by either having elevated blood pressure (systolic pressure of at least 140 mmHg or diastolic pressure of at least 90 mmHg) or taking antihypertensive medication. Percents are based on a single measurement of blood pressure to provide comparable data across the 4 time periods. In 1976-80, 31.3 percent of persons 20-74 years of age had hypertension, based on the average of 3 blood pressure measurements, in contrast to 39.7 percent when a single measurement is used. 1. The race groups, white and black, include persons of Hispanic and non-Hispanic origin. Conversely, persons of Hispanic origin may be of any race. 2. Data for Mexican Americans are for 1982-84. 3. Excludes pregnant women.

★ 290 ★

Diseases/Illnesses/Conditions

Weight: Trends in Percent of Overweight Persons 20-74 Years Old, by Gender and Race/Ethnic Origin: 1960-1991

[Data are based on physical examinations of a sample of the civilian noninstitutionalized population].

Sex, age, race, and Hispanic origin[1]	Percent of population			
	1960-62	1971-74	1976-80[2]	1988-91
20-74 years, age adjusted				
Both sexes	24.4	24.9	25.4	33.3
Male	22.9	23.6	24.0	31.6
Female[3]	25.6	25.9	26.5	35.
White male	23.1	23.8	24.2	32.0
White female[3]	23.5	24.0	24.4	33.5
Black male	22.2	24.3	25.7	31.5
Black female[3]	41.7	42.9	44.3	49.6
White, non-Hispanic male	-	-	24.1	32.1
White, non-Hispanic female[3]	-	-	23.9	32.4
Black, non-Hispanic male	-	-	25.6	31.5
Black, non-Hispanic female[3]	-	-	44.1	49.5
Mexican-American male	-	-	31.0	39.5

[Continued]

★ 290 ★

Weight: Trends in Percent of Overweight Persons 20-74 Years Old, by Gender and Race/Ethnic Origin: 1960-1991
[Continued]

Sex, age, race, and Hispanic origin[1]	Percent of population			
	1960-62	1971-74	1976-80[2]	1988-91
Mexican-American female[3]	-	-	41.4	47.9
27-74 years, crude				
Both sexes	25.5	25.5	25.7	33.7
Male	23.4	24.0	24.2	31.7
Female[3]	27.4	27.0	27.1	35.6
White male	23.7	24.2	24.4	32.4
White female[3]	25.4	25.2	25.1	34.3
Black male	22.5	24.5	25.7	31.2
Black female[3]	43.0	43.2	43.7	49.1
White, non-Hispanic male	-	-	24.4	32.7
White, non-Hispanic female[3]	-	-	24.8	33.3
Black, non-Hispanic males	-	-	25.6	31.2
Black, non-Hispanic females[3]	-	-	43.4	49.1
Mexican-American male	-	-	29.5	35.6
Mexican-American female[3]	-	-	39.1	47.1

Source: "Overweight Persons 20 Years of Age and Over, According to Sex, Age, Race, and Hispanic Origin: United States, 1960-62, 1971-74, 1976-80, 1988- 91," *Health, United States, 1994,* 1995, p. 165. Primary source: Centers for Disease Control and Prevention, National Center for Health Statistics, Division of Health Examination Statistics: Unpublished data. *Notes:* Overweight is defined for men as body mass index greater than or equal to 27.8 kilograms per meter squared, and for women as body mass index greater than or equal to 27.3 kilograms per meter squared. These cut points were used because they represent the sex-specific 85th percentiles for persons 20-29 years of age in the 1976-80 National Health and Nutrition Examination Survey. Height was measured without shoes; two pounds are deducted from data for 1960-62 to allow for weight of clothing. 1. The race groups, white and black, include persons of Hispanic and non-Hispanic origin. Conversely, persons of Hispanic origin may be of any race. 2. Data for Mexican Americans are for 1982-84. 3. Excludes pregnant women.

Health Care Facilities

★ 291 ★

Hospitals: Characteristics of Amount of Service Provided in Short-Stay Hospitals, by Race: 1964, 1990, and 1993

[Data are based on household interviews of a sample of the civilian noninstitutionalized population].

Race[1]	Number per 1,000 population						Number of days		
	Discharges			Days of care			Average length of stay		
	1964	1990	1993	1964	1990	1993	1964	1990	1993
Total[1,2]	109.1	91.0	88.1	970.9	607.1	539.2	8.9	6.7	6.1
White	112.4	89.5	86.0	961.4	580.9	508.2	8.6	6.5	5.9
Black[3]	84.0	112.0	111.7	1,062.9	875.9	848.0	12.7	7.8	7.6

Source: "Discharges, Days of Care, and Average Length of Stay in Short-Stay Hospitals, According to Selected Patient Characteristics: United States, 1964, 1990, and 1993," *Health, United States, 1994*, 1995, p. 178. Primary source: Centers for Disease Control and Prevention, National Center for Health Statistics, Division of Health Interview Statistics: Data from the National Health Interview Survey. *Notes:* Excludes deliveries. 1. Age adjusted. 2. Includes all other races not shown separately and unknown family income. 3. 1964 data include all other races.

★ 292 ★

Health Care Facilities

Nursing Home/Personal Home Care: Trends in Number of Nursing Home and Personal Home Care Residents and Rate per 1,000 Population Among Persons 65 and Over, by Age Group and Race: 1963-1985

[Data are based on a sample of nursing homes].

Age and race[4]	Residents				Residents per 1,000 population[1]			
	1963	1973-74[2]	1977[3]	1985	1963	1973-74[2]	1977[3]	1985
White	431,700	920,600	1,059,900	1,227,400	26.6	46.9	48.9	47.7
65-74 years	84,400	150,100	187,500	187,800	8.1	12.5	14.2	12.3
75-84 years	202,000	369,700	443,200	473,600	41.7	60.3	67.0	59.1
85 years and over	145,400	400,800	429,100	566,000	157.7	270.	234.2	228.7
Black	13,800	37,700	60,800	82,000	10.3	22.0	30.7	35.0
65-74 years	5,200	12,200	22,000	22,500	5.9	11.1	17.6	15.4

[Continued]

★ 292 ★

Nursing Home/Personal Home Care: Trends in Number of Nursing Home and Personal Home Care Residents and Rate per 1,000 Population Among Persons 65 and Over, by Age Group and Race: 1963-1985

[Continued]

Age and race[4]	Residents				Residents per 1,000 population[1]			
	1963	1973-74[2]	1977[3]	1985	1963	1973-74[2]	1977[3]	1985
75-84 years	5,300	13,400	19,700	30,600	13.8	26.7	33.4	45.3
85 years and over	3,300	12,100	19,100	29,000	41.8	105.7	133.6	141.5

Source: "Nursing Home and Personal Home Care Residents 65 years of Age and Over and Rate per 1000 Population, According to Age, Sex, and Race: United States, 1963, 1973-74, 1977, and 1985," *Health, United States, 1994,* 1995, p. 191. Primary source: Centers for Disease Control and Prevention: Wunderlich GS. Characteristics of residents in institutions for the aged and chronically ill, United States, April-June 1963. National Center for Health Statistics. Vital Health Stat 12(2). 1965; Zappolo A. Characteristics, social contracts, and activities of nursing home residents, United States, 1973-74 National Nursing Home Survey. National Center for Health Statistics. Vital Health Stat 13(27). 1977; Hing E. Characteristics of nursing home residents, health status, and care received: National Nursing Home Survey, United States May-December 1977. National Center for Health Statistics. Vital Health Stat 13(51). 1981; and Hing E, Sekscenski E, Strahan G. The National Nursing Home Survey: 1985 summary for the United States. National Center for Health Statistics. Vital Health Stat 13(97). 1985. U.S. Bureau of the Census: Preliminary estimates of the population of the United States by age, sex, and race: 1970-1981. Current Population Reports. Series P-25, No. 917. Washington. U.S. Government Printing Office, July 1982. *Notes:* 1. Residents per 1,000 population for 1973-74 and 1977 will differ from those presented in the sources because the rates have been recomputed using revised census estimates for these years. 2. Excludes residents in personal care or domiciliary care homes. 3. Includes residents in domiciliary care homes. 4. For data years 1973-74 and 1977, all Hispanics were included in the white category. For 1963 black includes other races.

Health Insurance

★ 293 ★

Coverage: Details of Government and Private Health Insurance Coverage, by Race/Ethnic Origin: 1987-1993

[Persons as of following year for coverage in the year shown. Government health insurance includes Medicare, Medicaid, and military plans. Based on Current Population Survey].

CHARACTERISTIC	NUMBER (mil.)							PERCENT			
	Total persons	Covered by private or Government health insurance					Not covered by health insurance	Covered by private or Government health insurance		Medicaid	Not covered by health insurance
		Total[1]	Private		Government			Total[1]	Private		
			Total	Group health[2]	Medicare	Medicaid					
1993, total[3,4]	259.8	220.0	182.4	148.3	33.1	31.7	39.7	84.7	70.2	12.2	15.3
Race:											
White	215.2	184.7	158.6	128.9	29.3	20.6	30.5	85.8	73.7	9.6	14.2
Black	33.0	26.3	16.6	13.7	3.1	9.3	6.8	79.5	50.2	28.1	20.5
Hispanic origin[5]	26.6	18.2	12.0	10.0	1.6	6.3	8.4	68.4	45.1	23.7	31.6

Source: "Health Insurance Coverage Status, by Selected Characteristics: 1987 to 1993," *Statistical Abstract of the United States: 1995,* 1995, p. 118. Primary source: U.S. Bureau of the Census, March Supplement to the Current Population Survey, unpublished data. *Notes:* 1. Includes other Government insurance, not shown separately. Persons with coverage counted only once in total, even though they may have been covered by more than one type of policy. 2. Related to employment of self or other family members. 3. Beginning 1992, data based on 1990 census adjusted population controls. 4. Includes other races not shown separately. 5. Persons of Hispanic origin may be of any race.

★ 294 ★

Health Insurance

Coverage: Number and Percent of Persons Covered for All, Part, or None of a 32-month Period, by Type of Insurance and Race/Ethnic Origin: 1990-1992

[Data represent persons covered by Government or private health insurance coverage during a 32-month period, beginning October 1989. Based on Survey of Income and Program Participation].

CHARACTERISTIC	All persons (mil.)	COVERED BY INSURANCE (mil.)				PERCENT COVERED BY INSURANCE			
		Government or private			Private for entire period	Government or private			Private for entire period
		For entire period	For part of the period	No coverage		For entire period	For part of the period	No coverage	
Total	235.8	176.2	50.6	8.9	152.3	74.7	21.5	3.8	64.8
White	198.6	151.9	39.6	7.0	135.8	76.5	19.9	3.5	68.4
Black	29.0	18.5	9.0	1.5	12.0	64.0	31.0	5.1	41.5
Hispanic[1]	18.6	9.7	7.0	1.9	6.7	52.0	37.8	10.1	36.1

Source: "Health Insurance Coverage, by Selected Characteristic: 1990-92," *Statistical Abstract of the United States: 1995,* 1995, p. 119. Primary source: U.S. Bureau of the Census, *Current Population Reports,* series P70- 37; and unpublished data. *Note:* 1. Persons of Hispanic origin may be of any race.

★ 295 ★

Health Insurance

Coverage: Percent of Poor People and All People Without Health Insurance, by Race/Ethnic Origin: 1993

Race/ethnicity	All persons	Poor persons
White	14.2	31.3
Black	20.5	23.5
Hispanic origin (of any race)	31.6	40.8

Source: "Percent Without Health Insurance, by Selected Characteristics: 1993," *Population Profile of the United States: 1995,* 1995, p. 37.

★ 296 ★

Health Insurance

Coverage: Trends in Type of Coverage of Persons 65 and Over, by Race/Ethnic Origin (in percentages): 1980-1993

[Data are based on household interviews of a sample of the civilian noninstitutionalized population].

Characteristic	Percent of population											
	Medicare and private insurance				Medicare and Medicaid[1]				Medicare only[2]			
	1980	1984	1989	1993[3]	1980	1984	1989	1993[3]	1980	1984	1989	1993[3]
Total[4,5]	64.4	70.9	73.5	75.5	8.1	5.4	5.7	5.2	22.7	20.0	16.8	15.3
Race[4]												
White	68.3	74.4	77.3	79.1	6.6	4.0	4.5	4.2	21.0	18.5	14.7	13.2
Black	26.5	38.1	39.3	43.6	23.3	19.9	16.5	13.3	40.6	35.4	7.9	36.2
Hispanic origin[4]												
All Hispanic	-	-	38.8	38.1	-	-	20.4	23.6	-	-	24.1	31.7
Mexican American	-	-	33.5	30.2	-	-	23.5	15.7	-	-	26.7	45.8
Puerto Rican	-	-	18.5[6]	6.3[6]	-	-	30.6[6]	21.9[6]	-	-	27.6[6]	59.0
Cuban	-	-	45.7	59.0	-	-	20.6[6]	39.7	-	-	23.7[6]	3.2[6]
Other Hispanic	-	-	49.5	42.6	-	-	13.0	19.1[6]	-	-	19.2	27.9

Source: "Health Care Coverage for Persons 65 Years of Age and Over, According to Type of Coverage and Selected Characteristics: United States, 1980, 1984, 1989, and 1993," *Health, United States, 1994,* 1995, p. 241. Primary source: Centers for Disease Control and Prevention, National Center for Health Statistics, Division of Health Interview Statistics and Division of Health and Utilization Analysis: Data are from the National Health Interview Survey. *Notes:* Percents do not add to 100 because the percent without Medicare is not shown, and because persons with Medicare, private insurance, and Medicaid appear in both columns. 1980 denominators include persons with unknown health insurance (less than 1.0 percent). In 1993, 4.4 percent of all persons 65 years of age and over had no Medicare, but only 0.7 percent were without health insurance. 1. Includes persons receiving Aid to Families with Dependent Children or Supplemental Security Income or those with current Medicaid cards. 2. Includes persons not covered by private insurance or Medicaid and a small proportion of persons with other types of coverage, such as CHAMPUS or public assistance. 3. The questionnaire design changed in 1993 compared with previous years. The direction of health care coverage change is consistent with data from the Current Population Survey. 4. Age adjusted. 5. Includes all other races not shown separately. 6. Relative standard error greater than 30 percent.

★ 297 ★

Health Insurance

Coverage: Trends in Type of Coverage of Persons Under 65, by Race/Ethnic Origin (in percentages): 1980-1993

[Data are based on household interviews of a sample of the civilian noninstitutionalized population].

Characteristic	Private insurance				Medicaid[1]				Not covered[2]			
	1980	1984	1989	1993[3]	1980	1984	1989	1993[3]	1980	1984	1989	1993[3]
	Percent of population											
Total[4,5]	78.8	76.9	76.6	71.3	5.9	6.0	6.4	9.7	12.5	15.4	15.7	17.3
Race[4]												
White	81.9	80.0	79.7	75.1	3.9	4.1	4.5	7.1	11.4	14.2	14.5	16.2
Black	60.1	58.9	59.2	61.1	17.9	17.5	17.1	23.3	19.0	22.3	22.0	23.2
Hispanic origin[4]												
All Hispanic	-	-	50.6	48.6	-	-	10.5	16.2	-	-	31.3	34.2
Mexican American	-	-	46.5	44.6	-	-	9.5	14.8	-	-	38.1	39.5
Puerto Rican	-	-	43.8	45.8	-	-	21.9	30.3	-	-	21.4	21.0
Cuban	-	-	66.7	68.6	-	-	7.0	15.0	-	-	20.7	16.9
Other Hispanic	-	-	58.5	56.4	-	-	8.4	12.2	-	-	23.0	31.1

Source: "Health Care Coverage for Persons Under 65 Years of Age, According to Type of Coverage and Selected Characteristics: United States, 1980, 1984, 1989, and 1993," *Health, United States, 1994,* 1995, p. 240. Primary source: Centers for Disease Control and Prevention, National Center for Health Statistics, Division of Health Interview Statistics and Division of Health and Utilization Analysis: Data from the National Health Interview Survey; and U.S. Bureau of the Census: Money Income of Households, Families, and Persons in the United States. Series P-60. Annual reports for 1989-93. Washington. U.S. Government Printing Office. *Notes:* Percents do not add to 100 because the percent with other types of health insurance (e.g., Medicare, military) is not shown, and because persons with both private insurance and Medicaid appear in both columns. 1980 denominators include persons with unknown health insurance (1.0 percent). Estimates in this table differ slightly from estimates based on the Current Population Survey (CPS) conducted by the Bureau of the Census. The direction of change in the percents shown in his table is consistent with data from the CPS. 1. Includes persons receiving Aid to Families with Dependent Children or Supplemental Security Income or those with current Medicaid cards. 2. Includes persons not covered by private insurance, Medicaid, Medicare, or military plans. 3. July 1 to Dec. 31, 1993. The questionnaire design changed in 1993 compared with previous years. In 1993 among the civilian noninstitutionalized population 39.7 million persons under age 65 were not covered by private insurance, Medicaid, Medicare, or military plans. An additional 0.2 million noninstitutionalized elderly persons were uninsured. 4. Age adjusted. 5. Includes all other races not shown separately and unknown family income.

★ 298 ★

Health Insurance

Relationships: Medicaid Coverage Among Persons Above and Below Poverty Level, by Race/Ethnic Origin: 1988-1993

[**In thousands, except percent.** Represents number of persons as of March of following year who were enrolled at any time in year shown. Person did not have to receive medical care paid for by Medicaid in order to be counted].

POVERTY STATUS	1993				65 years and over
	Total[1]	White	Black	Hispanic[2]	
Persons covered, total	31,537	20,513	9,213	6,272	2,709
Below poverty level	18,801	11,070	6,692	3,872	1,031
Above poverty level	12,736	9,443	2,521	2,400	1,678
Percent of population covered	12.2	9.5	28.0	23.6	8.8
Below poverty level	47.9	42.2	61.5	47.6	27.5
Above poverty level	5.8	5.0	11.4	13.0	6.2

Source: "Medicaid—Selected Characteristics of Persons Covered: 1988 to 1993," *Statistical Abstract of the United States: 1995,* 1995, p. 116. Primary source: U.S. Bureau of the Census, *Current Population Reports,* P60-188, earlier reports; and unpublished data. *Notes:* 1. Includes other races not shown separately. 2. Persons of Hispanic origin may be of any race.

Health Status

★ 299 ★

Activity Limitations: Percent Distribution of Activity Limitation Due to Chronic Conditions, by Age Group and Race: 1990 and 1993

[Data are based on household interviews of a sample of the civilian noninstitutionalized population].

Characteristic	Total with limitation of activity		Limited but not in major activity		Limited in amount or kind of major activity		Unable to carry on major activity	
	1990	1993	1990	1993	1990	1993	1990	1993
	Percent of population							
Total[1,2]	12.9	14.6	4.1	4.4	5.0	5.9	3.9	4.3
Race and age								
White[1]	12.8	14.4	4.2	4.5	5.0	5.9	3.6	4.0
Under 15 years	4.7	6.1	1.3	1.7	3.0	3.8	0.4	0.6
15-44 years	8.5	10.4	2.7	3.3	3.6	4.3	2.2	2.8
45-64 years	21.2	22.5	5.8	5.3	7.6	8.8	7.9	8.5
65-74 years	33.2	34.0	13.4	13.8	9.8	10.2	10.0	9.9
75 years and over	42.9	45.1	19.2	20.1	14.7	16.8	9.0	8.1

[Continued]

★ 299 ★

Activity Limitations: Percent Distribution of Activity Limitation Due to Chronic Conditions, by Age Group and Race: 1990 and 1993
[Continued]

Characteristic	Total with limitation of activity		Limited but not in major activity		Limited in amount or kind of major activity		Unable to carry on major activity	
	1990	1993	1990	1993	1990	1993	1990	1993
Black[1]	15.5	17.8	3.8	4.1	5.3	6.5	6.5	7.2
Under 15 years	5.3	7.4	1.2	1.9	3.4	4.5	0.7	0.9
15-44 years	9.4	11.2	2.2	2.7	3.4	3.7	3.9	4.8
45-64 years	28.1	33.0	5.7	6.0	7.7	9.8	14.8	17.1
65-74 years	41.6	40.0	12.4	12.8	11.5	12.8	17.6	14.4
75 years and over	50.9	52.0	16.2	11.3	17.6	25.0	17.0	15.6

Source: "Limitation of Activity Caused by Chronic Conditions, According to Selected Characteristics: United States, 1990 and 1993," Health, United States, 1994, 1995, p. 153. Primary source: Centers for Disease Control and Prevention, National Center for Health Statistics, Division of Health Interview Statistics: Data from the National Health Interview Survey. Notes: 1. Age adjusted. 2. Includes all other races not shown separately.

★ 300 ★

Health Status

Disabilities: Total and Per Person Days of Disability, by Race/ Ethnic Origin: 1970-1993-I

[Covers civilian noninstitutional population. Beginning 1985, the levels of estimates may not be comparable to estimates for 1970-1980 because the later data are based on a revised questionnaire and field procedures. Based on National Health Interview Survey].

ITEM	TOTAL DAYS OF DISABILITY (millions)					
	1970	1980	1985	1990	1992	1993
Restricted-activity days[1]	2,913	4,165	3,453	3,669	4,096	4,346
White[2]	2,526	3,518	2,899	3,057	3,384	2,598
Black[2]	365	580	489	536	586	616
Hispanic[3]	(NA)	(NA)	228	(NA)	(NA)	(NA)

Source: "Days of Disability, by Type and Selected Characteristics: 1970 to 1993," Statistical Abstract of the United States: 1995, 1995, p. 136. Primary source: U.S. National Center for Health Statistics, Vital and Health Statistics, series 10, No. 190; and earlier reports and unpublished data. Notes: NA Not available. 1. A day when a person cuts down on his activities for more than half a day because of illness or injury includes bed-disability, work-loss, and school-loss days. Total includes other races, not shown separately. 2. Beginning 1980, race was determined by asking the household respondent to report his race. In earlier years the racial classification of respondents was determined by interviewer observation. 3. Persons of Hispanic origin may be of any race.

★ 301 ★

Health Status

Disabilities: Total and Per Person Days of Disability, by Race/Ethnic Origin: 1970-1993-II

[Covers civilian noninstitutional population. Beginning 1985, the levels of estimates may not be comparable to estimates for 1970-1980 because the later data are based on a revised questionnaire and field procedures. Based on National Health Interview Survey].

ITEM	DAYS PER PERSON					
	1970	1980	1985	1990	1992	1993
Restricted-activity days[1]	14.6	19.1	14.8	14.9	16.3	17.1
White[2]	14.4	18.7	14.5	14.8	16.2	17.0
Black[2]	16.2	22.7	17.4	17.7	18.6	19.2
Hispanic[3]	(NA)	(NA)	13.2	(NA)	(NA)	(NA)

Source: "Days of Disability, by Type and Selected Characteristics: 1970 to 1993," *Statistical Abstract of the United States: 1995*, 1995, p. 136. Primary source: U.S. National Center for Health Statistics, *Vital and Health Statistics*, series 10, No. 190; and earlier reports and unpublished data. *Notes:* NA Not available. 1. A day when a person cuts down on his activities for more than half a day because of illness or injury includes bed-disability, work-loss, and school-loss days. Total includes other races, not shown separately. 2. Beginning 1980, race was determined by asking the household respondent to report his race. In earlier years the racial classification of respondents was determined by interviewer observation. 3. Persons of Hispanic origin may be of any race.

★ 302 ★

Health Status

Ratings: Trends in Percent of Persons Who Rate Their Health as "Fair" or "Poor," by Age Group and Race: 1987-1993

[Data are based on household interviews of a sample of the civilian noninstitutionalized population].

Characteristic	Percent with fair or poor health						
	1987	1988	1989	1990	1991	1992	1993
Total[1,2]	9.5	9.4	9.1	8.9	9.3	9.7	9.7
Race and age							
White[1]	8.5	8.85	8.2	8.1	8.6	8.9	8.8
Under 15 years	2.0	2.4	2.0	1.9	2.1	2.5	2.4
15-44 years	4.6	4.8	4.9	4.8	5.2	5.7	5.9
45-64 years	15.6	15.3	14.5	14.6	15.4	15.5	15.3
65-74 years	26.8	24.8	24.5	23.9	24.6	24.1	23.4
75 years and over	33.2	32.3	30.8	30.7	32.4	31.9	31.0
Black[1]	16.7	16.4	15.9	15.1	15.1	16.3	16.8
Under 15 years	4.1	4.6	4.4	4.8	4.5	4.4	4.9
15-44 years	10.5	9.9	10.2	9.9	9.7	10.7	11.1
45-64 years	32.9	30.9	29.6	28.3	27.2	30.9	32.0

[Continued]

★ 302 ★

Ratings: Trends in Percent of Persons Who Rate Their Health as "Fair" or "Poor," by Age Group and Race: 1987-1993
[Continued]

Characteristic	Percent with fair or poor health						
	1987	1988	1989	1990	1991	1992	1993
65-74 years	42.9	46.8	44.7	38.4	41.2	42.1	41.1
75 years and over	52.4	50.8	45.2	42.9	48.2	48.4	48.2

Source: "Respondent-Assessed Health Status, According to Selected Characteristics: United States, 1987-93," *Health, United States, 1994,* 1995, p. 154. Primary source: Centers for Disease Control and Prevention, National Center for Health Statistics, Division of Health Interview Statistics: Data from the National Health Interview Survey. *Notes:* 1. Age adjusted. 2. Includes all other races not shown separately and unknown family income.

Health-Related Behavior

★ 303 ★

Drugs and Drug Abuse: Percent Reporting Treatment for Substance Abuse in Past Year, by Race/Ethnic Origin: 1993

Demographic Characteristic	Received			
	Drug Abuse Treatment[1]	Alcohol Abuse Treatment[2]	Any Substance Abuse Treatment[3]	(Unweighted N)
Total	0.6	0.9	1.2	(26,443)
Number Receiving (in 1,000s)	1,260	1,771	2,578	(26,443)
Race/Ethnicity[4]				
White	0.5	0.9	1.2	(12,447)
Black	1.0	0.9	1.5	(6,176)
Hispanic	0.6	1.0	1.3	(6,886)

Source: "Percentage Reporting Having Received Treatment in the Past Year for Drug or Alcohol Abuse, by Demographic Characteristics: 1993," *National Household Survey on Drug Abuse: Main Findings 1993,* June, 1995, p. 159. Primary source: Office of Applied Studies, SAMHSA, National Household Survey on Drug Abuse, 1993. *Notes:* The unweighted Ns for alcohol abuse treatment and drug abuse treatment are slightly smaller than those shown for any substance abuse treatment because of differing patterns of nonresponse across the demographic groups. 1. This category may include some individuals who have also received alcohol abuse treatment. 2. This category may include some individuals who have also received other drug abuse treatment. 3. This category includes individuals who have received alcohol abuse treatment, drug abuse treatment, or both. 4. The category "other" for Race/Ethnicity is not included.

★ 304 ★

Health-Related Behavior

Drugs and Drug Abuse: Percent of Pregnant Women Who Live in Metropolitan Areas and Use Drugs, by Race/Ethnic Origin: 1994

Drug and type of use	White, non-Hispanic		Black, non-Hispanic		Hispanic	
	Estimate	95% C.I.[2]	Estimate	95% C.I.	Estimate	95% C.I.
Illicit drug use or nonmedical use of psychotherapeutics						
Any illicit drug use[3]	4.4	2.8 - 6.8	12.6	9.3 - 16.9	4.6	3.0 - 7.1
Marijuana	2.8	1.6 - 4.8	5.2	3.4 - 7.8	1.5	0.6 - 4.0
Cocaine	0.4	0.1 - 1.3	5.1	3.3 - 7.7	0.7	0.2 - 2.7
Crack-cocaine	0.3	0.1 - 1.3	4.6	2.9 - 7.1	0.1	0.0 - 2.1
Other cocaine	0.1	0.0 - 0.6	0.7	0.2 - 2.3	0.6	0.1 - 2.8
Methamphetamine	0.2	0.0 - 0.8	0.1	0.0 - 1.9	(no)	(no) - (no)
Heroin	0.0	0.0 - 0.7	0.2	0.0 - 2.0	(no)	(no) - (no)
Methadone	0.1	0.0 - 0.6	0.2	0.0 - 1.8	(no)	(no) - (no)
Inhalants	0.3	0.1 - 0.9	0.5	0.1 - 1.9	0.5	0.1 - 2.8
Hallucinogens	0.1	0.0 - 0.7	0.4	0.1 - 1.9	0.7	0.2 - 2.3
Nonmedical use of any pschyotherapeutics[4]	1.2	0.7 - 2.2	3.4	1.9 - 6.0	1.8	0.8 - 3.9
Amphetamines	0.1	0.0 - 0.6	(no)	(no) - (no)	(no)	(no) - (no)
Sedatives	0.0	0.0 - 0.7	1.1	0.3 - 4.0	0.4	0.1 - 1.8
Tranquilizers	0.0	0.0 - 0.7	[1]	[1]	0.2	0.0 - 1.7
Analgesics	1.1	0.5 - 2.1	2.5	1.4 - 4.5	1.3	0.5 - 3.3
Alcohol	25.1	21.2 - 29.3	16.3	12.4 - 21.0	8.6	5.3 - 13.8
Cigarettes	25.0	22.6 - 27.7	22.0	17.0 - 28.1	5.5	3.7 - 8.2
Medical use of any psychotherapeutics[5]	11.0	7.7 - 15.6	9.4	6.3 - 13.7	6.1	3.9 - 9.5
Amphetamines	0.3	0.1 - 0.8	0.4	0.1 - 2.0	0.3	0.1 - 1.7
Sedatives	4.1	2.2 - 7.3	2.6	1.3 - 5.1	1.4	0.5 - 4.3
Tranquilizers	1.0	0.5 - 1.9	0.9	0.2 - 4.1	1.0	0.3 - 3.4
Analgesics	8.6	5.8 - 12.5	7.6	5.2 - 10.9	4.2	2.6 - 6.6

Source: "Estimated Use by Women in Metropolitan Areas of Selected Substances During Pregnancy, by Race/Ethnicity (in percentages)," *Drug Use Among Ethnic Minorities,* 1995, p. 70. Primary source: National Pregnancy and Health Survey, National Institute on Drug Abuse, 1994. *Notes:* 1. Low precision, no estimate reported. (no) = No reported use, C.I. not computed. 0.0 = Estimate <0.05, rounded to 0.0 with valid C.I. 2. "C.I." stands for confidence interval. 3. Use of marijuana, cocaine (all forms), methamphetamine, heroin, methadone, inhalants, hallucinogens, or nonmedical use of psychotherapeutics during pregnancy. 4. Nonmedical use of any prescription amphetamines, sedatives, tranquilizers, or analgesics during pregnancy. 5. Medical use of any prescription amphetamines, sedatives, tranquilizers, or analgesics during pregnancy.

★ 305 ★

Health-Related Behavior

Preventive Acts: Percent of 19-35-Month-Old Children Vaccinated, by Race: 1992 and 1993

[Data are based on household interviews of a sample of the civilian noninstitutionalized population].

Vaccination and year	Total	Race	
		White	Black
All respondents			
DTP[1,2]:			
1992	83.0	84.8	74.7
1993	88.2	89.4	82.6
Polio[2]:			
1992	72.4	74.1	62.7
1993	78.9	79.8	73.4
Measles-containing[3]:			
1992	82.5	83.6	77.9
1993	78.9	79.8	73.4
HIB[5]:			
1992	28.2	29.1	25.5
1993	55.0	57.0	44.8
Combined series[6]:			
1992	55.3	55.9	50.9
1993	67.1	68.4	61.8
Respondents consulting vaccination records or reporting no vaccinations[6]			
DTP[1,2]:			
1992	86.8	87.8	84.6
1993	86.5	88.3	78.0
Polio[2]:			
1992	74.1	75.0	66.4
1993	73.7	74.7	67.4
Measles-containing[3]:			
1992	84.5	85.0	85.8
1993	83.2	84.2	80.8
HIB[4]:			
1992	23.1	24.3	18.1
1993	62.2	64.4	46.5

[Continued]

★ 305 ★

Preventive Acts: Percent of 19-35-Month-Old Children Vaccinated, by Race: 1992 and 1993

[Continued]

Vaccination and year	Total	Race White	Race Black
Combined series[5]:			
1992	56.7	58.2	50.7
1993	59.9	62.2	48.9

Source: "Vaccinations of Children 19-35 Months of Age for Selected Diseases, According to Race, Poverty Status, and Residence in Metropolitan Statistical Area (MSA): United States, 1992 and 1993," *Health, United States, 1994,* 1995, p. 145. Primary source: Centers for Disease Control and Prevention: Data computed by the National Immunization Program, Center for Prevention Services from data compiled by the Division of Health Interview Statistics, National Center for Health Statistics. *Notes:* In 1992 refusals and unknowns were omitted (15-17 percent for DTP, polio, or MMR vaccines; 9 percent for HIB). In 1993 refusals and unknowns were omitted (13 percent for DTP, polio, or MMR vaccines; 8 percent for HIB). 1. Diphtheria-tetanus-pertussis. 2. Three doses or more. 3. Respondents were asked about measles-containing or MMR (Measles-Mumps-Rubella) vaccines. 4. Haemophilus b, 3 or more doses. The percent of children 19-35 months of age who received 3 or more doses of HIB vaccine is artificially low in 1992 and to a lesser degree in 1993 because universal infant vaccination with a 3-4 dose series was not recommended until October 1990. 5. The combined series consisted of 4 doses of DTP vaccine, 3 doses of polio vaccine, and 1 dose of a measles-containing vaccine. 6. Data are based on respondents who either consulted records for all of the vaccination questions or reported no vaccinations (35.8 percent of white and 23.0 percent of black respondents in 1992, and 38.1 percent of white and 29.6 percent of black respondents in 1993).

Medical Care

★ 306 ★

Costs: Average Total and Specific Expenditures for Health Care, by Race/Ethnic Origin: 1985-1993

[In dollars, except percent].

ITEM	HEALTHCARE, TOTAL Amount	HEALTHCARE, TOTAL Percent of total expenditures	Health insurance	Medical services	Drugs and medical supplies[1]	PERCENT DISTRIBUTION Health insurance	PERCENT DISTRIBUTION Medical services	PERCENT DISTRIBUTION Drugs and medical supplies[1]
Race:								
White and other	1,890	5.9	842	621	427	44.6	32.9	22.6
Black	894	4.3	480	211	202	53.7	23.6	22.6

Source: "Average Annual Expenditures per Consumer Unite for Health Care: 1985 to 1993," *Statistical Abstract of the United States: 1995,* 1995, p. 117. Primary source: Bureau of Labor Statistics, *Consumer Expenditure Survey,* annual. *Note:* 1. Includes prescription and nonprescription drugs.

★ 307 ★

Medical Care

Dentists: Trends in Number of Dental Visits and Percent Distribution of Time Interval Since Last Visit, by Race: 1964, 1983, and 1989

[Data are based on household interviews of a sample of the civilian noninstitutionalized population].

Race	Number per person Dental visits			Percent of population								
				Interval since last dental visit[1]						Never visited dentist		
				Less than 1 year			2 years or more					
	1964	1983	1989	1964	1983	1989	1964	1983	1989	1964	1983	1989
Total[2,3,4]	1.6	1.9	2.1	42.7	55.3	57.7	28.7	24.1	21.4	15.5	7.7	6.4
White	1.7	2.0	2.3	45.3	57.5	60.0	27.8	23.0	20.2	13.8	7.2	6.1
Black[5]	0.8	1.2	1.2	22.3	41.1	44.0	37.6	32.2	29.5	28.0	10.3	7.7

Source: "Dental Visits and Interval Since Last Visit, According to Selected Patient Characteristics: United States, 1964, 1983, and 1989," *Health, United states, 1994,* 1995, p. 177. Primary source: Centers for Disease Control and Prevention, National Center for Health Statistics, Division of Health Interview Statistics: Data from the National Interview Survey. *Notes:* 1. Percent not shown for an interval of 1 year-less than 2 years. Denominators exclude persons with unknown interval (5.2 percent in 1989). 2. Age adjusted. 3. Includes all other races not shown separately. 4. Data for 1983 and 1989 are shown for ages 2 years and over because children under 2 years of age rarely visit a dentist. For 1964 data for children under 2 years of age are included. 5. 1964 data are for all other races.

★ 308 ★

Medical Care

Emergency Treatment: Characteristics of Emergency Room Episodes that are Drug-Related, by Gender and Race/Ethnic Origin: 1993

Episode characteristic	Males			Females		
	White	Black	Hispanic	White	Black	Hispanic
Drug concomitance						
Single-drug episodes	45.5	45.9	55.0	48.2	57.1	58.3
Multi-drug episodes	54.5	54.1	45.0	51.8	42.9	41.7
Patient disposition						
Treated and released	45.0	55.6	60.6	35.2	51.0	51.9
Admitted to hospital	54.6	40.7	33.6	61.9	46.0	44.1
Other	4.6	3.7	5.8	3.0	3.0	4.0

Source: "Percentage of DAWN Emergency Room Drug Abuse Episodes, by Selected Episode Characteristics, Sex, and Race/Ethnicity: 1993," *Drug Use Among Ethnic Minorities,* 1995, p. 82. Primary source: Drug Abuse Warning Network, Substance Abuse and Mental Health Services Administration, April 1994 provisional file. *Note:* DAWN = Drug Abuse Warning Network.

★ 309 ★

Medical Care

Emergency Treatment: Frequency of Drugs Mentioned Most Often by Emergency Departments (in percentages), by Race/Ethnic Origin: 1993

Primary source: Drug Abuse Warning Network, Substance Abuse and Mental Health Services Administration, April 1994 provisional data file.

Drug name	Rank	Percent of total episodes
White patients		
Alcohol-in-combination	1	29.9
Cocaine	2	13.1
Acetaminophen	3	9.2
Heroin/morphine	4	9.2
Alprazolam	5	5.7
Marijuana/hashish	6	5.5
Asprin	7	5.2
Ibuprofen	8	4.5
Diazepam	9	3.8
Lorazepam	10	3.6
Black patients		
Cocaine	1	54.2
Alcohol-in-combination	2	36.4
Heroin/morphine	3	18.3
Marijuana/hashish	4	8.0
Acetaminophen	5	4.2
Ibuprofen	6	2.8
PCP/PCP combinations	7	2.2
Asprin	8	1.9
Unspecified Benzodiazepine	9	1.2
Amitriptyline	10	1.0
Hispanic patients		
Alcohol-in-combination	1	27.0
Cocaine	2	25.6
Heroin/morphine	3	23.4
Acetaminophen	4	8.1
Marijuana/hashish	5	5.5
Asprin	6	3.9
Ibuprofen	7	3.6
PCP/PCP combinations	8	3.3

[Continued]

★ 309 ★

Emergency Treatment: Frequency of Drugs Mentioned Most Often by Emergency Departments (in percentages), by Race/Ethnic Origin: 1993

[Continued]

Drug name	Rank	Percent of total episodes
Methamphetamine/speed	9	2.8
Alprazolam	10	2.2

Source: "Drugs Mentioned Most Frequently by Emergency Departments in 1992, by Sex and Race/Ethnicity of Patient," *Drug Use Among Ethnic Minorities*, 1995, p. 78. *Notes:* These estimates are based on a representative sample of non-Federal hospitals with 24-hour emergency rooms in the coterminous United States. Percentages are based on weighted emergency room episode estimates of 235,643 white patients; 122,880 black patients; and 42,174 Hispanic patients.

★ 310 ★

Medical Care

Emergency Treatment: Incidence of Emergency Room Episodes for Cocaine Use, by Age Group and Race/Ethnic Origin: 1988-1993

Race/ethnicity and age	1988	1989	1990	1991	1992	1993[1]
TOTAL						
Total	101,578	110,013	80,355	101,188	119,843	123,317
6+	101,349	109,601	80,185	100,695	119,476	122,893
6-34	79,715	83,973	57,131	70,113	78,188	76,382
12-17	2,755	2,544	1,859	2,138	1,534	1,583
18-25	32,322	31,600	19,614	21,766	23,883	22,077
26-34	44,632	49,818	35,639	46,137	52,760	52,715
35+	21,634	25,628	23,054	30,582	41,288	46,512
White	34,350	38,349	24,100	29,198	31,927	33,050
6+	34,284	38,200	24,076	29,095	31,879	32,890
6-34	28,488	31,191	18,063	22,435	22,665	23,410
12-17	1,217	1,389	1,059	1,021	468	715
18-25	12,741	12,425	6,563	8,077	8,268	8,237
26-34	14,530	17,372	10,434	13,275	13,923	14,456
35+	5,796	7,008	6,013	6,660	9,214	9,480
Black	48,761	51,052	43,010	56,106	69,123	69,045
6+	48,687	50,883	42,918	55,772	68,907	68,897
6-34	36,321	36,805	29,179	35,994	42,134	39,097
12-17	686	613	413	447	341	344
18-25	13,525	12,453	9,016	9,710	10,596	9,417
26-34	22,105	23,735	19,741	25,829	31,190	29,331
35+	12,366	14,078	13,739	19,778	26,774	29,799

[Continued]

★ 310 ★

Emergency Treatment: Incidence of Emergency Room Episodes for Cocaine Use, by Age Group and Race/Ethnic Origin: 1988-1993

[Continued]

Race/ethnicity and age	1988	1989	1990	1991	1992	1993[1]
Hispanic	9,388	9,710	6,628	9,012	11,824	12,178
6+	9,369	9,695	6,606	8,993	11,789	12,147
6-34	7,455	7,392	5,106	6,656	8,713	8,224
12-17	474	395	206	388	536	380
18-25	3,221	3,290	2,443	2,473	3,369	2,666
26-34	3,760	3,705	2,455	3,795	4,808	5,177
35+	1,914	2,303	1,499	2,337	3,075	3,923

Source: "Estimated Numbers of DAWN Emergency Department Mentions for Cocaine, by Race/Ethnicity and Age: 1988-93," *Drug Use Among Ethnic Minorities*, 1995, p. 80. Primary source: Drug Abuse Warning Network, Substance Abuse and Mental Health Services Administration, 1988-92 data files. *Notes:* DAWN=Drug Abuse Warning Network. 1. April 1994 provisional data file.

★ 311 ★

Medical Care

Emergency Treatment: Incidence of Emergency Room Episodes for Heroin/Morphine Use, by Age Group and Race/Ethnic Origin: 1988-1993

Race/ethnicity and age	1988	1989	1990	1991	1992	1993[1]
TOTAL						
Total	38,063	41,656	33,884	35,898	48,003	62,965
6+	37,916	41,468	33,818	35,754	47,878	62,854
6-34	22,383	22,519	17,967	18,445	22,502	29,323
12-17	135	168	182	182	232	282
18-25	5,187	5,094	4,654	4,704	5,860	7,912
26-34	17,060	17,251	13,127	13,559	16,409	21,127
35+	15,533	18,949	15,850	17,310	25,376	33,531
White	16,977	17,644	13,667	13,367	17,926	23,140
6+	16,896	17,574	13,649	13,272	17,893	23,118
6-34	10,797	10,225	7,610	7,763	8,580	11,935
12-17	39	*	*	*	*	*
18-25	2,430	2,078	1,892	2,075	2,454	3,643
26-34	8,327	8,046	5,628	5,583	6,026	8,122
35+	6,099	7,350	6,039	5,509	9,313	11,183
Black	13,475	13,338	12,313	15,175	18,600	23,332
6+	13,441	13,255	12,282	15,144	18,550	23,290
6-34	6,559	5,618	5,503	6,495	7,733	8,883
12-17	34	40	54	29	29	33
18-25	1,191	1,031	1,092	1,407	1,878	2,275
26-34	5,334	4,546	4,357	4,951	5,826	6,576

[Continued]

★ 311 ★

Emergency Treatment: Incidence of Emergency Room Episodes for Heroin/Morphine Use, by Age Group and Race/Ethnic Origin: 1988-1993

[Continued]

Race/ethnicity and age	1988	1989	1990	1991	1992	1993[1]
35+	6,882	7,637	6,779	8,758	10,817	14,406
Hispanic	5,094	7,307	5,195	5,118	8,519	11,159
6+	5,084	7,302	5,190	5,112	8,508	11,146
6-34	3,503	4,811	3,486	3,164	4,794	6,262
12-17	50	26	29	39	*	54
18-25	1,159	1,516	1,278	950	1,217	1,321
26-34	2,294	3,269	2,179	2,176	3,489	4,886
35+	1,581	2,491	1,704	1,949	3,714	4,884

Source: "Estimated Numbers of DAWN Emergency Department Mentions for Heroin/Morphine, by Race/Ethnicity and Age: 1988-93," *Drug Use Among Ethnic Minorities*, 1995, p. 81. Primary source: Drug Abuse Warning Network, Substance Abuse and Mental Health Services Administration, 1988-92 data files. *Notes:* DAWN=Drug Abuse Warning Network. * Low precision, no estimate reported. 1. April 1994 provisional data file.

★ 312 ★

Medical Care

Emergency Treatment: Percent Distribution of Emergency Room Episodes for Use of Selected Drugs, by Race/Ethnic Origin: 1993

Percent and type of drug	Race/Ethnicity		
	White	Black	Hispanic
Percent of total DAWN ER episodes	54.0	27.3	10.2
Percent of ER drug mentions			
Heroin/morphine	36.8	37.1	17.7
Methadone	45.2	26.6	18.9
PCP/PCP combinations	26.8	42.4	23.9
Cocaine	26.8	56.0	9.9
Marijuana/hashish	47.2	34.9	9.0
Methamphetamine/speed	72.1	3.3	13.4

Source: "A Comparison of the Race/Ethnicity Distribution for Total DAWN Emergency Room Episodes with the Race/Ethnicity Distribution for Selected Drug Mentions: 1993," *Drug Use Among Ethnic Minorities*, 1995, p. 82. Primary source: Drug Abuse Warning Network, Substance Abuse and Mental Health Services Administration, April 1994 provisional file. *Notes:* DAWN=Drug Abuse Warning Network. Percentages do not sum to 100 due to exclusion of data for patients of other and unknown races/ethnicities.

★ 313 ★
Medical Care

Emergency Treatment: Total Visits to Emergency Rooms and Visits per 100 Persons, by Race: 1993

[An emergency room is a hospital facility staffed by physicians for the provision of providing outpatient services to patients whose conditions require immediate attention and is staffed 24 hours a day. Data are for non-Federal short stay or general hospitals. Based on the National Hospital Ambulatory Care Survey and subject to sampling error].

CHARACTERISTIC	NUMBER OF VISITS (1,000)				VISITS PER 100 PERSONS			
	Total	Urgent[1]	Non-urgent	Injury-related	Total	Non-Urgent[1]	Injury-urgent	related
All visits[2]	92,814	42,048	50,766	37,712	36.5	16.5	20.0	14.8
Race:								
White	72,354	33,531	38,823	30,859	34.2	15.9	18.4	14.6
Black	18,464	7,849	10,615	6,096	57.6	24.5	33.1	19.0

Source: "Hospital Emergency Room Visits: 1993," *Statistical Abstract of the United States: 1995,* 1995, p. 129. Primary source: U.S. National Center for Health Statistics, unpublished data. *Notes:* 1. Patient requires immediate attention. 2. Includes other races, not shown separately.

★ 314 ★
Medical Care

Emergency Treatment: Trends in Female Emergency Room Episodes Related to Cocaine Use, by Age Group and Race/Ethnic Origin: 1985-1993

[Data are weighted national estimates based on a sample of emergency rooms].

Age, sex, race, and Hispanic origin	Number of episodes								
	1985	1986	1987	1988	1989	1990	1991	1992	1993
All races, both sexes[1]									
All ages[2]	28,801	51,636	91,596	101,578	110,013	80,355	101,189	119,843	123,317
6-17 years	1,004	1,807	2,544	2,760	2,555	1,877	2,210	1,546	1,590
18-25 years	9,356	17,365	29,329	32,322	31,600	19,614	21,766	23,883	22,077
26-34 years	12,895	22,965	40,923	44,632	49,818	35,639	46,137	52,760	52,715
35 years and over	5,495	9,311	18,466	21,634	25,628	23,054	30,582	41,288	46,512
White, non-Hispanic female									
All ages[2]	4,111	6,833	10,907	10,843	13,226	8,331	9,541	10,132	11,359
6-17 years	338	502	601	682	505	486	529	204	332
18-25 years	1,690	2,931	4,641	4,601	4,802	2,663	2,765	2,817	2,924
26-34 years	1,757	2,778	4,574	4,166	5,846	3,636	4,427	4,571	5,495
35 years and over	323	601	1,083	1,377	2,009	1,539	1,808	2,531	2,534

[Continued]

★ 314 ★

Emergency Treatment: Trends in Female Emergency Room Episodes Related to Cocaine Use, by Age Group and Race/Ethnic Origin: 1985-1993

[Continued]

Age, sex, race, and Hispanic origin	Number of episodes								
	1985	1986	1987	1988	1989	1990	1991	1992	1993
Black, non-Hispanic female									
All ages[2]	3,959	7,413	15,578	16,518	17,657	14,833	19,149	22,687	22,248
6-17 years	91	113	319	304	249	177	210	100	134
18-25 years	1,249	2,519	5,062	5,302	4,954	3,820	3,892	4,247	3,726
26-34 years	1,927	3,555	7,551	7,751	8,705	7,418	9,481	11,078	10,405
35 years and over	686	1,206	2,623	3,138	3,659	3,369	5,512	7,198	7,939
Hispanic female									
All ages[2]	781	1,282	1,911	2,469	2,556	1,719	2,356	3,074	3,437
6-17 years	38	84	100	113	93	64	183	193	173
18-25 years	349	551	752	1,097	853	634	616	815	695
26-34 years	298	486	862	904	992	663	1,044	1,324	1,483
35 years and over	95	158	195	355	613	357	513	732	1,084

Source: "Cocaine-Related Emergency Room Episodes, According to Age, Sex, Race, and Hispanic Origin: United States, 1985-93," *Health, United States, 1994*, 1995, p. 161. Primary source: Substance Abuse and Mental Health Services Administration, Drug Abuse Warning Network. *Notes:* 1. Includes other races and unknown race, Hispanic origin, and/or sex. Percent other and unknown ranges from 7-11 percent of episodes. 2. Includes unknown age.

★ 315 ★

Medical Care

Emergency Treatment: Trends in Male Emergency Room Episodes Related to Cocaine Use, by Age Group and Race/Ethnic Origin: 1985-1993

[Data are weighted national estimates based on a sample of emergency rooms].

Age, sex, race, and Hispanic origin	Number of episodes								
	1985	1986	1987	1988	1989	1990	1991	1992	1993
All races, both sexes[1]									
All ages[2]	28,801	51,636	91,596	101,578	110,013	80,355	101,189	119,843	123,317
6-17 years	1,004	1,807	2,544	2,760	2,555	1,877	2,210	1,546	1,590
18-25 years	9,356	17,365	29,329	32,322	31,600	19,614	21,766	23,883	22,077
26-34 years	12,895	22,965	40,923	44,632	49,818	35,639	46,137	52,760	52,715
35 years and over	5,495	9,311	18,466	21,634	25,628	23,054	30,582	41,288	46,512
White, non-Hispanic male									
All ages[2]	7,540	13,695	21,112	23,372	24,789	15,512	19,385	21,360	21,418

[Continued]

★ 315 ★

Emergency Treatment: Trends in Male Emergency Room Episodes Related to Cocaine Use, by Age Group and Race/Ethnic Origin: 1985-1993
[Continued]

Age, sex, race, and Hispanic origin	Number of episodes								
	1985	1986	1987	1988	1989	1990	1991	1992	1993
6-17 years	354	597	765	531	885	527	486	264	377
18-25 years	2,785	5,181	7,389	8,096	7,455	3,810	5,284	5,297	5,273
26-34 years	3,236	5,830	9,172	10,306	11,397	6,724	8,777	9,175	8,896
35 years and over	1,149	2,079	3,741	4,396	4,967	4,432	4,747	6,585	6,850
Black, non-Hispanic male									
All ages[2]	8,159	14,633	29,068	31,891	33,070	27,745	36,597	46,064	46,497
6-17 years	94	262	383	386	365	241	244	246	211
18-25 years	1,714	3,500	7,306	8,107	7,430	5,104	5,743	6,308	5,643
26-34 years	3,888	6,900	13,285	14,212	14,862	12,160	16,232	19,952	18,807
35 years and over	2,444	3,929	8,022	9,146	10,342	10,202	14,110	19,416	21,742
Hispanic male									
All ages[2]	2,041	3,297	4,960	6,752	7,067	4,821	6,571	8,683	8,693
6-17 years	38	118	179	356	300	144	201	336	203
18-25 years	720	1,076	1,612	2,088	2,406	1,774	1,831	2,535	1,961
26-34 years	849	1,492	2,066	2,815	2,690	1,758	2,723	3,457	3,676
35 years and over	432	598	1,097	1,478	1,662	1,125	1,801	2,332	2,826

Source: "Cocaine-Related Emergency Room Episodes, According to Age, Sex, Race, and Hispanic Origin: United States, 1985-93," *Health, United States, 1994,* 1995, p. 161. Primary source: Substance Abuse and Mental Health Services Administration, Drug Abuse Warning Network. *Notes:* 1. Includes other races and unknown race, Hispanic origin, and/or sex. Percent other and unknown ranges from 7-11 percent of episodes. 2. Includes unknown age.

★ 316 ★

Medical Care

Emergency Treatment: Trends in Number of Drug-Related Emergency Department Episodes, by Age Group and Race/Ethnic Origin: 1988-1993

Race/ethnicity and age	1988	1989	1990	1991	1992	1993[1]
TOTAL						
Total	403,578	425,904	371,208	393,968	433,493	466,897
6+	402,017	424,727	370,251	392,725	432,457	465,650
6-34	295,301	301,872	254,297	261,873	277,887	292,814
12-17	54,206	55,299	49,109	47,494	46,822	51,334
18-25	114,753	111,707	92,236	92,410	96,307	99,794
26-34	125,657	133,510	111,980	121,354	133,506	140,234
35+	106,716	122,855	115,954	130,852	154,570	172,835

[Continued]

★ 316 ★

Emergency Treatment: Trends in Number of Drug-Related Emergency Department Episodes, by Age Group and Race/Ethnic Origin: 1988-1993
[Continued]

Race/ethnicity and age	1988	1989	1990	1991	1992	1993[1]
White	230,527	243,862	217,191	221,541	235,643	252,023
6+	229,929	243,333	216,827	221,025	235,329	251,326
6-34	167,238	171,470	148,581	148,215	151,810	161,610
12-17	37,321	37,770	33,602	32,999	32,301	35,184
18-25	64,619	63,345	52,767	52,876	54,835	56,041
26-34	64,860	69,468	61,503	62,009	64,143	69,361
35+	62,691	71,863	68,247	72,810	83,519	89,716
Black	96,319	97,480	88,317	106,914	122,880	127,293
6+	95,952	97,142	87,910	106,464	122,448	127,060
6-34	69,143	68,101	58,184	67,237	74,686	73,456
12-17	6,004	6,218	6,122	5,382	5,949	5,188
18-25	25,917	23,928	20,174	22,267	22,641	23,107
26-34	37,101	37,714	31,700	39,495	45,769	45,029
35+	26,809	29,041	29,726	39,227	47,762	53,603
Hispanic	33,983	38,743	29,834	33,082	42,174	47,624
6+	33,841	38,686	29,764	32,965	42,044	47,538
6-34	26,352	29,062	22,074	23,546	29,604	32,089
12-17	4,296	5,162	3,856	4,059	4,455	5,833
18-25	10,812	11,597	9,432	8,886	10,812	11,310
26-34	11,202	12,234	8,752	10,511	14,044	14,688
35+	7,489	9,624	7,691	9,419	12,440	15,449

Source: "Estimated Numbers of DAWN Emergency Episodes, by Race/Ethnicity and Age: 1988-93," *Drug Use Among Ethnic Minorities*, 1995, p. 79. Primary source: Drug Abuse Warning Network, Substance Abuse and Mental Health Services Administration, 1988-92 data files. *Notes:* DAWN=Drug Abuse Warning Network. 1. April 1994 provisional data file.

★ 317 ★
Medical Care

Patients: Home and Hospice Care Patients, by Race: 1993

[See headnote, table 199].

ITEM	CURRENT PATIENTS[1]			DISCHARGES[2]		
	Total	Home health agency	Hospice	Total	Home health agency	Hospice
Total (1,000)	1,501.3	1,451.2	50.1	3,945.1	3,688.0	257.2

PERCENT DISTRIBUTION

Race:						
White	68.5	68.0	80.4	68.2	67.5	79.3

[Continued]

★ 317 ★

Patients: Home and Hospice Care Patients, by Race: 1993
[Continued]

ITEM	CURRENT PATIENTS[1]			DISCHARGES[2]		
	Total	Home health agency	Hospice	Total	Home health agency	Hospice
Black	13.6	13.7	9.1	9.7	9.8	9.1
Other or unknown	18.0	18.3	10.6	22.1	22.8	11.6

Source: "Home Health and Hospice Care Patients, by Selected Characteristics: 1993," *Statistical Abstract of the United States: 1995,* 1995, p. 132. Primary source: U.S. National Center for Health Statistics, unpublished data. *Notes:* 1. Patients on the rolls of the agency as of midnight the day prior to the survey. 2. Patients removed from the rolls of the agency during the 12 months prior to the day of the survey. A patient could be included more than once if the individual had more than one episode of care during the year.

★ 318 ★

Medical Care

Patients: Visits to Hospital Outpatient Departments, by Race: 1992

[An outpatient department is a hospital facility where nonurgent ambulatory care is provided under the supervision of a physician. Data exclude clinics where only ancillary services, such as radiology, are provided. Based on the National Ambulatory Care Survey and subject to sampling error].

CHARACTERISTIC	Number of visits (1,000)	Percent distribution	Visits per 100 persons
All visits	56,605	100.0	22.5
Race:			
White	42,034	74.3	20.1
Black	12,549	22.2	39.9
Asian/Pacific Islander	1,609	2.8	(NA)
American Indian/Eskimo/Aleut	414	0.7	(NA)

Source: "Hospital Outpatient Department Visits: 1992," *Statistical Abstract of the United States: 1995,* 1995, p. 129. Primary source: U.S. National Center for Health Statistics, *Advanced Data,* No. 248, March 9, 1994. *Note:* NA Not available.

★ 319 ★

Medical Care

Physicians: Characteristics of Office Visits to Physicians, by Physician Specialty and Patient Race: 1985 and 1992

[Data are based on reporting by a sample of office-based physicians].

Race	All specialties		General and family practice		Internal medicine		Pediatrics		Obstetrics and gynecology		All others	
	1985	1992	1985	1992	1985	1992	1985	1992	1985	1992	1985	1992
Percent of visits that are patient's first visit												
Total	16.9	14.7	14.1	10.8	15.3	9.1	12.8	10.8	14.2	11.8	21.6	22.0
White	16.6	14.6	13.6	10.7	15.4	9.0	12.2	10.5	14.2	11.0	21.2	21.6
Black	18.2	15.6	16.0	12.7	12.1	9.9	16.5	12.6	12.8	18.6	24.8	23.4
Percent of visits lasting 10 minutes or less[2]												
Total	38.7	33.1	43.2	40.4	24.4	19.1	47.6	40.5	39.9	44.5	36.6	27.1
White	39.3	32.1	44.2	39.0	23.9	15.7	48.9	39.2	41.0	46.1	37.0	26.8
Black	42.9	36.8	47.0	43.5	34.1	37.0	45.3	41.9	34.6	30.3	43.1	27.9
Percent of visits with return visit scheduled												
Total	61.5	61.6	50.8	48.1	64.9	64.3	49.4	47.9	75.7	77.8	69.4	71.9
White	61.2	61.5	50.2	46.8	64.1	61.8	49.2	47.7	74.4	78.2	69.4	72.7
Black	65.5	64.0	57.2	62.4	74.9	76.2	53.0	51.9	84.2	74.9	70.2	63.4

Source: "Office Visits to Physicians, According to Selected Patient and Visit Characteristics and Physician Specialty: United States, 1985 and 1992," *Health, United States, 1994,* 1995, pp. 175-176. Primary source: Centers for Disease Control and Prevention, National Center for Health Statistics: Data from the National Ambulatory Medical care Survey. *Notes:* 1. Relative standard error greater than 30 percent. In 1985 the survey excluded Alaska and Hawaii. Beginning in 1989 the survey included all 50 States. Specialty information based on the physician's self-designated primary area of practice. General and family practice includes family practice, and beginning in 1992 family practice and geriatric medicine. Internal medicine is comprised of general internal medicine and excludes all subspecialties. Pediatrics and obstetrics and gynecology include physicians practicing in the general field and subspecialties. Some numbers in this table have been revised and differ from previous editions of *Health, United States.* 2. Excludes visits of 0 minutes in duration (no face-to-face physician contact).

★ 320 ★

Medical Care

Physicians: Trends in Number of Physician Contacts per Person, by Age Group and Race: 1987-1993

[Data are based on household interviews of a sample of the civilian noninstitutionalized population].

Characteristic	Physician contacts per person						
	1987	1988	1989	1990	1991	1992	1993
Total[1,2]	5.4	5.3	5.3	5.5	5.6	5.9	6.0
Race and age							
White[1]	5.5	5.5	5.5	5.6	5.8	6.0	6.0
Under 5 years	7.1	7.6	7.1	7.1	7.4	7.3	7.5

[Continued]

★ 320 ★

Physicians: Trends in Number of Physician Contacts per Person, by Age Group and Race: 1987-1993
[Continued]

Characteristic	Physician contacts per person						
	1987	1988	1989	1990	1991	1992	1993
5-14 years	3.5	3.6	3.8	3.5	3.7	3.7	3.9
15-44 years	4.7	4.8	4.8	4.9	4.9	5.0	5.1
45-64 years	6.4	6.1	6.2	6.4	6.6	7.2	7.0
65-74 years	8.4	8.3	8.0	8.5	9.4	9.6	9.7
75 years and over	9.7	9.3	9.7	10.1	12.1	12.0	12.2
Black[1]	5.1	4.8	4.9	5.1	5.2	5.9	6.0
Under 5 years	5.1	4.6	5.3	5.6	6.0	5.6	6.2
5-14 years	2.3	2.2	2.3	2.2	2.1	2.3	2.4
15-44 years	4.2	4.2	3.9	4.2	4.0	5.3	4.7
45-64 years	7.3	6.6	6.3	7.1	7.5	7.8	8.7
65-74 years	8.6	9.1	10.0	9.2	7.3	10.9	11.5
75 years and over	10.8	8.7	12.7	10.4	15.7	13.7	13.1

Source: "Physician Contacts, According to Selected Patient Characteristics: United States, 1987-93," *Health, United States, 1994,* 1995, p. 169. Primary source: Centers for Disease Control and Prevention, National Center for Health Statistics, Division of Health Interview Statistics: Data from the National Health Interview Survey. *Notes:* 1. Age adjusted. 2. Includes all other races not shown separately.

★ 321 ★

Medical Care

Physicians: Trends in Percent of Office Visits to Selected Medical Specialists – Part I, by Race: 1975-1992

[Data are based on reporting by a sample of office-based physicians].

Characteristic	Percent distribution						
	All specialties	General and family practice			Internal medicine		
		1975	1982	1992	1975	1985	1992
Total	100.0	41.3	30.5	28.8	10.9	11.6	13.2
Race							
White	100.0	40.8	30.0	28.7	11.1	11.8	12.5
Black	100.0	46.9	35.4	29.1	9.9	10.4	16.2

Source: "Office Visits to Physicians, Percent Distribution According to Selected Patient Characteristics and Physician Specialty: United States, 1975, 1985, and 1992," *Health, United States, 1994,* 1995, p. 174. Primary source: Centers for Disease Control and Prevention, National Center for Health Statistics, Division of Health Care Statistics: Data from the National Ambulatory Medical Care Survey. *Notes:* Rates are based on the civilian noninstitutionalized population. In 1975 and 1985 the survey excluded Alaska and Hawaii. Beginning in 1989 the survey included all 50 States. Specialty information based on the physician's self-designated primary area of practice. General and family practice includes general practice, general family practice, and beginning in 1992 the subspecialty of family practice geriatric medicine. Internal medicine is comprised of general internal medicine and excludes all subspecialties. Pediatrics includes physicians practicing in the general field and sub-specialties.

★ 322 ★

Medical Care

Physicians: Trends in Percent of Office Visits to Selected Medical Specialists – Part II, by Race: 1975-1992

[Data are based on reporting by a sample of office-based physicians].

Characteristic	Percent distribution					
	Pediatrics			Obstetrics and gynecology		
	1975	1982	1992	1975	1985	1992
Total	8.2	11.4	12.6	8.5	8.9	9.0
Race						
White	8.2	11.4	11.6	8.2	8.7	9.2
Black	8.0	11.3	18.9	11.9	9.9	8.6

Source: "Office Visits to Physicians, Percent Distribution According to Selected Patient Characteristics and Physician Specialty: United States, 1975, 1985, and 1992," *Health, United States, 1994,* 1995, p. 174. Primary source: Centers for Disease Control and Prevention, National Center for Health Statistics, Division of Health Care Statistics: Data from the National Ambulatory Medical Care Survey. *Notes:* Rates are based on the civilian noninstitutionalized population. In 1975 and 1985 the survey excluded Alaska and Hawaii. Beginning in 1989 the survey included all 50 States. Specialty information based on the physician's self-designated primary area of practice. General and family practice includes general practice, general family practice, and beginning in 1992 the subspecialty of family practice geriatric medicine. Internal medicine is comprised of general internal medicine and excludes all subspecialties. Pediatrics includes physicians practicing in the general field and sub-specialties.

★ 323 ★

Medical Care

Physicians: Trends in Percent of Office Visits to Selected Medical Specialists – Part III, by Race: 1975-1992

[Data are based on reporting by a sample of office-based physicians].

Characteristic	Percent distribution											
	General surgery			Opthalmology			Orthopedic surgery			All others		
	1975	1985	1992	1975	1985	1992	1975	1985	1992	1975	1985	1992
Total	7.3	4.7	3.2	4.4	6.3	6.1	3.4	5.0	5.0	16.0	21.7	22.2
Race												
White	7.5	4.6	3.1	4.3	6.4	6.4	3.5	5.0	5.2	16.5	22.3	23.1
Black	6.1	6.2	3.5	3.2	4.7	4.2	2.8	4.8	3.6	11.0	17.2	15.8

Source: "Office Visits to Physicians, Percent Distribution According to Selected Patient Characteristics and Physician Specialty: United States, 1975, 1985, and 1992," *Health, United States, 1994,* 1995, p. 174. Primary source: Centers for Disease Control and Prevention, National Center for Health Statistics, Division of Health Care Statistics: Data from the National Ambulatory Medical Care Survey. *Notes:* Rates are based on the civilian noninstitutionalized population. In 1975 and 1985 the survey excluded Alaska and Hawaii. Beginning in 1989 the survey included all 50 States. Specialty information based on the physician's self-designated primary area of practice.

★ 324 ★

Medical Care

Physicians: Trends in Percent of Physician Office Visits Resulting in Drug Prescription, by Physician Specialty and Patient Race: 1975-1992

[Data are based on reporting by a sample of office-based physicians].

Characteristic	Percent of visits with drug administered or prescribed							
	All specialties		General and family practice		Internal medicine		Pediatrics	
	1985	1992	1985	1992	1985	1992	1985	1992
Total	61.2	63.8	72.7	75.5	77.4	79.3	66.8	68.9
Race								
White	60.6	62.5	71.8	74.1	77.3	79.2	66.3	67.7
Black	67.2	71.3	78.6	84.6	80.2	81.1	70.3	70.5

Source: "Office Visits to Physicians and Percent of Visits with Drug Prescribed, According to Selected Patient Characteristics and Physician Specialty: United States, Selected Years, 1975-92," *Health, United States, 1994,* 1995, p. 173. Primary source: Centers for Disease Control and Prevention, National Center for Health Statistics, Division of Health Care Statistics: Data from the National Ambulatory Medical Care Survey. *Notes:* Rates are based on the civilian noninstitutionalized population. In 1975 and 1985 the survey excluded Alaska and Hawaii. Beginning in 1989 the survey included all 50 States. Specialty information based on the physician's self-designated primary area of practice. General and family practice includes general practice, general family practice, and beginning in 1992 the subspecialty of family practice geriatric medicine. Internal medicine is comprised of general internal medicine and excludes all subspecialties. Pediatrics includes physicians practicing in the general field and sub-specialties.

★ 325 ★

Medical Care

Physicians: Trends in Physician Office Visits, by Race: 1975-1992

[Data are based on reporting by a sample of office-based physicians].

Characteristic	All specialties							
	Visits per person				Number of visits in thousands			
	1975	1985	1990	1992	1975	1985	1990	1992
Total	2.7	2.7	2.9	3.0	567,600	636,386	704,604	762,045
Race								
White	2.8	2.9	2.9	3.1	508,672	572,507	597,306	653,851
Black	1.9	1.9	2.1	2.6	46,716	52,143	52,317	82,599

Source: "Office Visits to Physicians and Percent of Visits with Drug Prescribed, According to Selected Patient Characteristics and Physician Specialty: United States, Selected Years, 1975-92," *Health, United States, 1994,* 1995, p. 173. Primary source: Centers for Disease Control and Prevention, National Center for Health Statistics, Division of Health Care Statistics: Data from the National Ambulatory Medical Care Survey. *Notes:* Rates are based on the civilian noninstitutionalized population. In 1975 and 1985 the survey excluded Alaska and Hawaii. Beginning in 1989 the survey included all 50 States.

★ 326 ★

Medical Care

Physicians: Trends in Time Interval Since Last Physician Contact, by Age Group and Race: 1964, 1990, and 1993

[Data are based on household interviews of a sample of the civilian noninstitutionalized population].

Characteristic	Total	Percent distribution[2]								
		Less than 1 year			1 year-less than 2 years			2 years or more[1]		
		1964	1990	1993	1964	1990	1993	1964	1990	1993
Total[3,4]	100.0	66.9	78.2	79.0	14.0	10.1	9.7	19.1	11.7	11.4
Race and age										
White[3]	100.0	68.1	78.7	79.1	13.8	9.9	9.5	18.1	11.5	11.4
Under 15 years	100.0	-	83.6	85.0	-	10.3	9.5	-	6.1	5.6
15-44 years	100.0	-	73.9	73.4	-	11.4	11.2	-	14.8	15.4
45-64 years	100.0	-	77.3	78.0	-	8.7	8.5	-	14.1	13.5
65-74 years	100.0	-	86.0	86.5	-	5.0	5.0	-	9.0	8.6
75 years and over	100.0	-	89.3	90.6	-	4.2	3.8	-	6.5	5.6
Black[3,5]	100.0	58.3	77.5	79.3	15.1	11.0	10.6	26.6	11.6	10.1
Under 15 years	100.0	-	79.9	83.3	-	12.6	10.9	-	7.5	5.8
15-44 years	100.0	-	72.3	74.1	-	12.7	12.7	-	15.0	13.2
45-64 years	100.0	-	80.2	80.2	-	8.0	8.4	-	11.8	11.4
65-74 years	100.0	-	84.4	86.3	-	5.9	6.2	-	9.7	7.4
75 years and over	100.0	-	89.4	89.0	-	3.4[6]	3.2[6]	-	7.3	7.9

Source: "Interval Since Last Physician Contact, According to Selected Patient Characteristics: United States, 1964, 1990, and 1993," *Health, United States, 1994,* 1995, p. 172. Primary source: Centers for Disease Control and Prevention, National Center for Health Statistics, Division of Health Interview Statistics: Data from the National Health Interview Survey. *Notes:* 1. Includes persons who never visited a physician. 2. Denominator excludes persons with unknown interval. 3. Age adjusted. 4. Includes all other races not shown separately. 5. 1964 data included in all other races. 6. Relative standard error greater than 30 percent.

★ 327 ★

Medical Care

Special Treatment: Trends in Percent of Persons in Specialty Substance Abuse Treatment, by Race/Ethnic Origin: 1980-1992

Race/ethnicity	Percent (by year)						
	1980	1982	1987	1989	1990	1991	1992
White, non-Hispanic	62.7	64.2	65.6	62.6	61.8	61.5	59.8
Black, non-Hispanic	20.6	20.5	19.4	20.6	20.7	21.2	21.6
Hispanic	13.4	12.3	12.4	13.8	14.4	14.1	14.6
Asian or Pacific Islander	0.4	.04	0.5	0.6	0.9	0.9	0.8
American Indian/Alaska Native	2.9	2.7	1.7	2.0	1.8	1.8	1.3

Source: "Percentage Representation of Race/Ethnicity in Specialty Substance Abuse Treatment: 1980, 1982, 1987, 1990, 1991, and 1992," *Drug Use Among Ethnic Minorities*, 1995, p. 84. Primary source: National Drug and Alcoholism Treatment Unit Survey, Substance Abuse and Mental Health Services Administration.

Pregnancies

★ 328 ★

Relationships: Trends in Percent of Expectant Mothers Who Smoked During Pregnancy, by Race/Ethnic Origin: 1989-1992

[Data are based on the National Vital Statistics System].

Characteristic of mother	Percent of mothers who smoked[1]			
	1989	1990	1991	1992
Race of mother[2]				
All races	19.5	18.4	17.8	16.9
White	20.4	19.4	18.8	17.9
Black	17.1	15.9	14.6	13.8
American Indian or Alaskan Native	23.0	22.4	22.6	22.5
Asian or Pacific Islander[3]	5.7	5.5	5.2	4.8
Chinese	2.7	2.0	1.9	1.7
Japanese	8.2	8.0	7.5	6.6
Filipino	5.1	5.3	5.3	4.8
Hawaiian and part Hawaiian	19.3	21.0	19.4	18.5
Other Asian or Pacific Islander	4.2	3.8	3.8	3.6
Hispanic origin of mother[4]				
Hispanic origin (selected States)	8.0	6.7	6.3	5.8
Mexican American	6.3	5.3	4.8	4.3
Puerto Rican	14.5	13.6	13.2	12.7

[Continued]

★ 328 ★

Relationships: Trends in Percent of Expectant Mothers Who Smoked During Pregnancy, by Race/Ethnic Origin: 1989-1992
[Continued]

Characteristic of mother	Percent of mothers who smoked[1]			
	1989	1990	1991	1992
Cuban	6.9	6.4	6.2	5.9
Central and South American	3.6	3.0	2.8	2.6
Other and unknown Hispanic	12.1	10.8	10.7	10.1
Non-Hispanic white (selected States)	21.7	21.0	20.5	19.7
Non-Hispanic black (selected States)	17.2	15.9	14.6	13.8

Source: "Mothers who Smoked Cigarettes During Pregnancy, According to Mother's Detailed Race, Hispanic Origin, Educational Attainment, and Age," *Health, United States, 1994,* 1995, p. 76. Primary source: Centers for Disease Control and Prevention, National Center for Health Statistics: Data computed by the Division of Health and Utilization Analysis from data compiled by the Division of Vital Statistics. *Notes:* The race groups, white and black, included persons of Hispanic and non- Hispanic origin. Conversely, persons of Hispanic origin may be of any race. 1. Excludes live births for whom smoking status of mother is unknown. 2. Includes data for 43 States and the District of Columbia (DC) in 1989, 45 States and DC in 1991-92. Excludes data for California, Indiana, New York, and South Dakota (1989-92), Oklahoma (1989-90), and Louisiana and Nebraska (1989), which did not require the reporting of mother's tobacco use during pregnancy on the birth certificate. 3. Maternal tobacco use during pregnancy was not reported on the birth certificates of California, and New York, which during 1989-91 together accounted for 43-66 percent of the births in each Asian subgroup (except Hawaiian). 4. Includes data for 42 States and DC in 1989, 44 States and DC in 1990, and 45 States and DC in 1991-92. Excludes data for California, Indiana, New Hampshire, New York, and South Dakota (1989-92), Oklahoma (1989-90), and Louisiana and Nebraska (1989), which did not require the reporting of either Hispanic origin of mother or tobacco use during pregnancy on the birth certificate.

Chapter 6
HOUSING

★ 329 ★

Introductory Characteristics of Householders

[Numbers in thousands. Consistent with the 1990 Census. ... means not applicable or sample too small. - means zero or rounds to zero].

	Race and Origin					
	White	Non-Hispanic	Hispanic	Black	Other	Total Hispanic
Total occupied units	21,581	18,826	2,755	6,523	1,734	3,352
Tenure						
Owner	11,735	10,733	1,002	2,375	533	1,088
Renter	9,846	8,093	1,753	4,147	1,201	2,264
Housing unit characteristics						
New construction, 4 yrs.	655	581	74	75	75	81
Mobile homes	303	283	20	17	7	20
Physical problems						
Severe	446	342	104	209	89	148
Moderate	952	642	309	623	100	358
Household characteristics						
Moved in past year	4,343	3,651	691	1,326	489	875
Below poverty level	3,071	2,228	844	2,242	423	1,061
Regions						
Northeast	4,131	3,643	488	1,493	584	818
Midwest	4,832	4,616	216	1,683	211	271
South	6,826	5,802	1,024	2,796	195	1,101
West	5,792	4,765	1,027	552	744	1,161

Source: "Introductory Characteristics—in Central Cities—Occupied Units." *American Housing Survey for the United States in 1993*, February 1995, p. 376.

Characteristics

★ 330 ★

Housing Units: Introductory Characteristics: Black Occupied Housing, 1993

[Numbers in thousands. Consistent with the 1990 Census. ... means not applicable or sample too small. - means zero or rounds to zero.]

Characteristic	Total occupied units	Tenure		Housing characteristics				Household characteristics		
		Owner	Renter	New construction 4 yrs.	Mobile homes	Physical problems		Elderly (65+)	Moved in past year	Below poverty level
						Severe	Moderate			
Total	11,128	4,788	6,340	334	337	385	1,154	1,825	2,162	3,555
Tenure										
Owner occupied	4,788	4,788	...	192	252	137	450	1,153	239	1,001
Percent of all occupied	43.0	100.0	...	57.4	74.9	35.6	39.0	63.2	11.1	28.2
Renter occupied	6,340	...	6,340	142	85	248	704	672	1,923	2,554
Race and Origin										
White	...	...	...	...	...	...	...	...	...	...
Non-Hispanic	...	...	...	...	...	...	...	...	...	...
Hispanic	...	...	...	...	...	...	...	...	...	...
Black	11,128	4,788	6,340	334	337	385	1,154	1,825	2,162	3,555
Other	...	...	...	...	...	...	...	...	...	...
Total Hispanic	188	51	138	7	5	15	6	20	51	72
Units in Structure										
1, detached	5,232	3,875	1,358	165	...	185	634	1,097	529	1,379
1, attached	1,015	421	594	30	...	21	110	155	232	343
2 to 4	1,627	151	1,476	30	...	56	158	186	430	636
5 to 9	953	25	928	17	...	34	72	64	303	365
10 to 19	762	20	741	33	...	11	38	51	306	247
20 to 49	532	13	519	9	...	31	44	53	153	196
50 or more	671	32	639	12	...	39	46	173	155	260
Mobile home or trailer	337	252	85	38	337	8	53	45	54	129
Cooperatives and Condominiums										
Cooperatives	114	42	72	-	-	10	7	14	19	24
Condominiums	211	86	125	6	-	8	8	17	48	40
Year Structure Built[1]										
1990 to 1994	307	170	138	307	35	-	10	27	123	46
1985 to 1989	556	246	309	27	51	7	17	33	158	108
1980 to 1984	686	285	401	...	51	10	20	75	133	161
1975 to 1979	891	350	540	...	70	11	40	68	190	258
1970 to 1974	1,254	490	764	...	84	25	106	166	263	400
1960 to 1969	1,819	789	1,030	...	43	78	175	255	371	549
1950 to 1959	1,481	718	763	...	2	45	200	295	242	538
1940 to 1949	1,302	603	699	...	-	48	201	276	187	458
1930 to 1939	1,021	427	594	...	-	44	149	243	173	388
1920 to 1929	774	313	461	...	-	35	113	169	118	278

[Continued]

★ 330 ★

Housing Units: Introductory Characteristics: Black Occupied Housing, 1993

[Continued]

Characteristic	Total occupied units	Tenure		New construction 4 yrs.	Mobile homes	Physical problems		Elderly (65+)	Moved in past year	Below poverty level
		Owner	Renter			Severe	Moderate			
1919 or earlier	1,038	396	641	...	-	83	124	218	203	369
Median	1960	1959	1960	...	1978	1946	1950	1950	1964	1955

Source: "Introductory Characteristics—Occupied Units with Black Householder," *American Housing Survey for the United States in 1993*, p. 190. *Note:* 1. For mobile home, oldest category is 1939 or earlier.

Costs of Housing

★ 331 ★

Costs: Selected Characteristics. Part 1-A

[Numbers in thousands. Consistent with the 1990 Census. ... means not applicable or sample too small. - means zero or rounds to zero.]

Characteristic	Total	Less than $100	$100 to $199	$200 to $299	$300 to $399	$400 to $499	$500 to $599	$600 to $699
Total	11,128	419	1,373	1,443	1,520	1,372	1,159	938
Units in structure								
1, detached	5,232	153	641	753	607	502	422	417
1, attached	1,015	36	133	137	125	107	88	82
2 to 4	1,627	33	135	219	311	274	197	140
5 to 9	953	49	94	105	162	153	119	89
10 to 19	762	59	77	48	124	131	124	76
20 to 49	532	17	52	28	105	104	90	54
50 or more	671	41	150	91	55	70	81	76
Mobile home or trailer	337	31	91	62	31	29	37	5
Year Structure Built[1]								
1990 to 1994	307	4	30	32	21	14	25	19
1985 to 1989	556	4	35	38	44	56	70	61
1980 to 1984	686	19	63	72	77	98	69	70
1975 to 1979	891	30	109	72	123	145	90	73
1970 to 1974	1,254	37	173	155	141	165	144	138
1960 to 1969	1,819	111	221	185	238	197	219	154
1950 to 1959	1,481	61	206	219	223	160	122	102
1940 to 1949	1,302	86	192	220	196	143	108	84
1930 to 1939	1,021	49	139	163	156	137	106	77
1920 to 1929	774	13	92	119	118	106	91	69

[Continued]

★ 331 ★

Costs: Selected Characteristics. Part 1-A

[Continued]

Characteristic	Total	Less than $100	$100 to $199	$200 to $299	$300 to $399	$400 to $499	$500 to $599	$600 to $699
1919 or earlier	1,038	4	114	167	184	151	113	91
Median	1960	1959	1957	1952	1955	1959	1962	1963
Rooms								
1 room	121	2	20	30	30	10	11	5
2 rooms	168	7	32	49	29	19	12	14
3 rooms	1,283	61	228	176	266	202	148	71
4 rooms	2,535	151	328	348	411	388	312	204
5 rooms	2,754	142	346	361	342	374	256	253
6 rooms	2,194	46	276	269	245	217	238	231
7 rooms	1,132	6	99	143	126	84	118	92
8 rooms	546	-	33	46	36	34	41	43
9 rooms	221	-	7	12	17	27	15	16
10 rooms or more	175	2	4	10	19	18	8	9
Median	5.0	4.4	4.7	4.8	4.6	4.7	4.9	5.2
Bedrooms								
None	193	5	31	58	32	24	20	11
1	1,740	70	294	224	367	297	210	109
2	3,753	197	424	517	561	543	425	350
3	4,124	124	501	50	450	393	392	393
4 or more	1,319	24	123	145	110	115	111	76
Median	2.5	2.2	2.4	2.4	2.1	2.2	2.3	2.5
Complete bathrooms								
None	120	19	32	27	16	3	-	3
1	6,895	361	1,026	1,055	1,117	1,013	800	480
1 and one-half	1,778	30	177	174	223	200	167	228
2 or more	2,335	9	138	186	164	155	192	226
Main Heating Equipment								
Warm air furnace	5,300	147	491	700	724	656	558	495
Steam or water system	1,931	64	181	187	286	246	271	201
Electric heat pump	846	8	69	51	101	125	93	86
Built-in electric units	679	28	95	61	134	84	73	48
Floor, wall, or other built-in hot air units without ducts	741	41	149	93	90	91	49	69
Room heaters with flue	373	18	99	91	47	40	15	4
Room heaters without flue	585	63	148	155	59	61	35	-
Portable electric heaters	112	14	21	22	10	18	5	6
Stoves	236	27	74	38	22	17	21	9

[Continued]

★ 331 ★

Costs: Selected Characteristics. Part 1-A
[Continued]

Characteristic	Total	Less than $100	$100 to $199	$200 to $299	$300 to $399	$400 to $499	$500 to $599	$600 to $699
Fireplaces with inserts	21	-	2	-	-	-	7	-
Fireplaces without inserts	25	2	2	8	2	4	6	-
Other	157	3	37	29	18	11	7	14
None	124	5	6	10	27	19	19	7
Source of Water								
U								
Public system or private company	10,439	364	1,218	1,321	1,451	1,336	1,109	890
Well serving 1 to 5 units	547	46	138	101	56	29	45	27
Drilled	400	42	88	80	37	14	33	25
Dug	122	4	44	17	13	12	12	2
Not reported	25	-	7	4	5	2	-	-
Other	142	9	17	21	14	7	5	21
Means of Sewage Disposal								
Public sewer	9,964	327	1,091	1,245	1,405	1,278	1,091	878
Septic tank, cesspool, chemical toilet	1,113	73	271	192	115	94	67	61
Other	51	19	10	7	-	-	-	-
Main House Heating Fuel								
Housing units with heating fuel	11,004	414	1,367	1,434	1,493	1,353	1,140	932
Electricity	2,922	81	306	283	410	443	319	275
Piped gas	5,945	233	679	819	812	670	594	493
Bottled gas	362	37	88	73	46	33	24	11
Fuel oil	1,242	18	147	153	165	169	149	136
Kerosene or other liquid fuel	174	13	43	51	25	12	9	-
Coal or coke	21	6	-	2	6	-	-	-
Wood	297	22	90	46	27	21	37	13
Solar energy	-	-	-	-	-	-	-	-
Other	42	3	14	6	2	5	8	3

Source: "Housing Costs by Selected Characteristics - Occupied Units with Black Householder," *American Housing Survey for the United States in 1993,* p. 241. *Note:* 1. For mobile home, oldest category is 1939 or older.

★ 332 ★

Costs of Housing

Costs: Selected Characteristics. Part 1-B

[Numbers in thousands. Consistent with the 1990 Census. ... means not applicable or sample too small. - means zero or rounds to zero.]

Characteristic	$700 to $799	$800 to $999	$1,000 to $1,499	$1,500 or more	No cash rent	Mortgage payment not reported	Median excluding no cash rent
Total	610	667	501	156	473	496	424
Units in structure							
1, detached	291	396	372	123	158	397	437
1, attached	74	63	68	10	36	55	428
2 to 4	94	67	20	18	109	10	421
5 to 9	54	28	10	3	78	8	415
10 to 19	35	44	11	-	30	3	443
20 to 49	19	26	6	-	31	-	447
50 or more	37	42	11	2	9	5	384
Mobile home or trailer	4	2	2	-	21	22	241
Year Structure Built[1]							
1990 to 1994	34	39	39	21	-	27	666
1985 to 1989	56	58	62	23	9	40	610
1980 to 1984	43	70	48	-	22	36	485
1975 to 1979	59	58	41	12	43	35	449
1970 to 1974	69	54	36	19	59	64	436
1960 to 1969	114	117	79	27	74	84	439
1950 to 1959	73	65	73	18	90	68	379
1940 to 1949	49	78	33	10	46	57	352
1930 to 1939	46	37	36	5	45	24	380
1920 to 1929	43	36	17	18	23	30	417
1919 or earlier	23	56	36	3	62	34	402
Median	1966	1965	1967	1969	1957	1964	...
Rooms							
1 room	-	9	2	-	2	-	323
2 rooms	2	-	2	-	2	-	289
3 rooms	26	36	8	3	50	9	355
4 rooms	110	93	25	3	130	32	387
5 rooms	191	130	59	9	182	109	411
6 rooms	139	166	132	35	63	137	474
7 rooms	97	105	104	23	24	111	534
8 rooms	25	86	101	29	14	57	717
9 rooms	11	27	29	26	5	30	697
10 rooms or more	10	15	38	28	-	13	809
Median	5.4	5.9	6.7	7.7	4.8	6.2	...

[Continued]

★ 332 ★

Costs: Selected Characteristics. Part 1-B
[Continued]

Characteristic	$700 to $799	$800 to $999	$1,000 to $1,499	$1,500 or more	No cash rent	Mortgage payment not reported	Median excluding no cash rent
Bedrooms							
None	-	9	2	-	2	-	306
1	33	44	13	5	60	14	367
2	227	162	67	10	199	71	408
3	299	323	252	54	162	281	468
4 or more	51	129	167	87	49	131	546
Median	2.7	2.9	3.2	3.5+	2.4	3.1	...
Complete bathrooms							
None	-	2	-	-	14	2	204
1	205	240	92	18	325	163	368
1 and one-half	146	120	90	24	65	134	493
2 or more	259	305	318	115	69	199	684
Main Heating Equipment							
Warm air furnace	295	354	289	83	191	318	451
Steam or water system	104	136	93	51	51	61	478
Electric heat pump	76	78	60	8	45	48	525
Built-in electric units	57	23	15	2	46	12	394
Floor, wall, or other built-in hot air units without ducts	46	28	28	8	32	17	370
Room heaters with flue	13	14	-	-	32	-	259
Room heaters without flue	4	10	2	-	36	13	237
Portable electric heaters	5	1	-	-	5	5	277
Stoves	3	-	-	-	26	2	211
Fireplaces with inserts	-	4	3	-	-	5	...
Fireplaces without inserts	-	-	-	-	-	-	...
Other	2	10	5	3	3	15	307
None	6	8	6	2	6	2	448
Source of Water							
Public system or private company	591	631	485	150	434	459	431
Well serving 1 to 5 units	13	12	10	6	32	33	257
Drilled	8	10	10	6	19	28	259
Dug	3	-	-	-	13	2	236
Not reported	2	2	-	-	-	3	...
Other	5	24	5	-	7	5	445

[Continued]

★ 332 ★

Costs: Selected Characteristics. Part 1-B

[Continued]

Characteristic	$700 to $799	$800 to $999	$1,000 to $1,499	$1,500 or more	No cash rent	Mortgage payment not reported	Median excluding no cash rent
Means of Sewage Disposal							
Public sewer	577	610	473	146	419	425	439
Septic tank, cesspool, chemical toilet	33	57	28	11	40	73	282
Other	-	-	-	-	14	-	...
Main House Heating Fuel							
Housing units with heating fuel	603	659	495	154	467	495	423
Electricity	213	173	124	17	160	117	455
Piped gas	329	393	307	118	203	296	427
Bottled gas	2	13	3	-	14	17	254
Fuel oil	55	74	58	20	46	52	453
Kerosene or other liquid fuel	-	2	-	-	13	7	243
Coal or coke	-	-	-	-	6	-	...
Wood	3	4	3	-	26	6	244
Solar energy	-	-	-	-	-	-	...
Other	2	-	-	-	-	-	...

Source: "Housing Costs by Selected Characteristics - Occupied Units with Black Householder," *American Housing Survey for the United States in 1993*, p. 241. *Note:* 1. For mobile home, oldest category is 1939 or older.

★ 333 ★

Costs of Housing

Costs: Selected Characteristics. Part 2-A

[Numbers in thousands. Consistent with the 1990 Census. ... means not applicable or sample too small. - means zero or rounds to zero.]

Characteristic	Total	Less than $100	$100 to $199	$200 to $299	$300 to $399	$400 to $499	$500 to $599	$600 to $699
Cooking Fuel								
With cooking fuel	11,061	416	1,367	1,416	1,503	1,364	1,157	938
Electricity	4,656	118	513	506	608	625	496	441
Piped gas	5,905	251	732	810	830	698	624	482
Bottled gas	478	45	116	94	61	38	36	16
Kerosene or other liquid fuel	12	-	3	4	4	-	-	-
Coal or coke	-	-	-	-	-	-	-	-
Wood	2	-	2	-	-	-	-	-
Other	8	2	-	3	-	3	-	-

[Continued]

★ 333 ★

Costs: Selected Characteristics. Part 2-A
[Continued]

Characteristic	Total	Less than $100	$100 to $199	$200 to $299	$300 to $399	$400 to $499	$500 to $599	$600 to $699
Persons								
1 person	3,024	165	590	480	525	354	268	188
2 persons	2,832	86	320	388	416	386	299	267
3 persons	2,242	78	215	297	244	275	243	203
4 persons	1,665	55	140	157	182	167	176	152
5 persons	801	22	59	63	87	102	110	78
6 persons	320	8	26	39	34	37	32	26
7 persons or more	244	5	22	19	32	50	31	23
Median	2.4	2.0	1.8	2.1	2.1	2.4	2.6	2.6
Household Composition by Age of Householder								
2-or-more person households	8,104	254	783	963	995	1,017	891	750
Married-couple families, no nonrelatives	3,300	23	244	353	385	312	330	311
Under 25 years	81	5	7	8	29	10	14	-
25 to 29 years	227	-	14	18	42	33	18	30
30 to 34 years	438	4	25	34	31	40	49	40
35 to 44 years	927	5	19	35	63	105	133	104
45 to 64 years	1,194	5	91	129	143	97	97	113
65 years and over	433	4	88	128	77	28	19	24
Other male householder	925	15	62	103	100	142	142	110
Under 45 years	583	7	37	50	52	89	107	82
45 to 64 years	213	4	8	24	23	39	19	18
65 years and over	130	4	17	29	24	15	16	9
Other female householder	3,878	216	476	507	510	563	419	330
Under 45 years	2,520	169	280	287	334	369	278	214
45 to 64 years	941	37	107	119	107	159	104	92
65 years and over	417	10	89	101	69	36	37	23
1-person households	3,024	165	590	480	525	354	268	188
Male householder	1,461	77	223	219	275	182	148	101
Under 45 years	748	30	52	98	170	115	71	79
45 to 64 years	449	27	86	64	72	47	56	19
65 years and over	263	21	85	58	32	20	22	3
Female householder	1,563	88	367	261	250	172	120	87
Under 45 years	476	8	31	48	110	70	68	39
45 to 64 years	505	25	98	100	61	64	40	34
65 years and over	582	55	238	114	80	38	11	13
Own Never Married Children Under 18 Years Old								
No own children under 18 years old	6,717	229	987	1,036	1,047	789	638	545
With own children under 18 years	4,412	190	386	407	473	583	520	394

[Continued]

★ 333 ★

Costs: Selected Characteristics. Part 2-A
[Continued]

Characteristic	Total	Less than $100	$100 to $199	$200 to $299	$300 to $399	$400 to $499	$500 to $599	$600 to $699
Under 6 years only	950	54	79	95	133	100	103	84
1	572	16	40	43	82	76	74	64
2	287	31	33	36	28	15	26	16
3 or more	91	6	6	16	23	9	3	4
6 to 17 years only	2,462	87	198	207	240	346	321	213
1	1,338	40	102	117	117	216	176	127
2	770	26	74	61	68	76	97	66
3 or more	354	21	22	30	55	55	48	20
Both age groups	999	48	109	105	100	136	97	97
2	446	23	31	44	47	46	45	51
3 or more	554	25	78	61	53	90	52	45
Income of Families and Primary Individuals								
Less than $5,000	1,556	196	324	230	180	149	83	51
$5,000 to $9,999	1,956	129	525	400	281	228	130	70
$1,000 to $14,999	1,328	29	144	253	303	212	151	76
$15,000 to $19,999	1,221	31	123	144	272	232	134	99
$20,000 to $24,999	966	14	86	131	141	143	147	109
$25,000 to $29,999	884	3	61	103	105	141	148	77
$30,000 to $34,999	583	10	28	55	70	70	76	97
$35,000 to $39,999	500	3	22	20	45	65	87	78
$40,000 to $49,999	750	2	30	58	37	57	115	122
$50,000 to $59,999	475	2	12	19	23	40	41	65
$60,000 to $79,999	510	-	11	19	41	25	25	68
$80,000 to $99,999	194	-	-	5	5	5	12	14
$100,000 to $119,999	87	-	5	5	13	-	5	12
$120,000 or more	117	-	3	2	5	5	5	-
Median	17,963	5,516	8,454	11,817	14,946	17,097	22,754	29,091

Source: "Housing Costs by Selected Characteristics - Occupied Units with Black Householder," *American Housing Survey for the United States in 1993*, p. 242.

★ 334 ★

Costs of Housing

Costs: Selected Characteristics. Part 2-B

[Numbers in thousands. Consistent with the 1990 Census. ... means not applicable or sample too small. - means zero or rounds to zero.]

Characteristic	$700 to $799	$800 to $999	$1,000 to $1,499	$1,500 or more	No cash rent	Mort-gage pay-ment not re-ported	Median exclud-ing no cash rent
Cooking Fuel							
With cooking fuel	610	667	501	156	466	496	425
Electricity	311	309	263	40	201	226	459
Piped gas	299	348	231	117	233	252	413
Bottled gas	-	10	7	-	34	20	254
Kerosene or other liquid fuel	-	-	-	-	-	-	-
Coal or coke	-	-	-	-	-	-	-
Wood	-	-	-	-	-	-	-
Other	-	-	-	-	-	-	-
Persons							
1 person	86	97	58	7	112	94	333
2 persons	154	183	97	36	90	110	427
3 persons	138	163	109	32	126	119	460
4 persons	123	118	139	63	83	109	520
5 persons	61	61	67	10	33	48	525
6 persons	41	26	15	5	23	7	501
7 persons or more	6	19	15	3	7	12	469
Median	3.0	2.8	3.4	3.6	2.8	2.9	-
Household Composition by Age of Householder							
2-or-more person households	523	570	443	149	361	404	466
Married-couple families, no nonrelatives	281	315	288	114	90	255	549
Under 25 years	3	-	-	-	5	-	359
25 to 29 years	21	24	8	-	18	3	491
30 to 34 years	49	46	49	10	25	37	613
35 to 44 years	101	94	121	59	34	54	658
45 to 64 years	92	136	94	43	5	148	557
65 years and over	16	14	16	2	4	13	291
Other male householder	71	69	42	9	30	31	507
Under 45 years	51	40	33	-	20	14	537
45 to 64 years	17	21	7	9	8	16	490
65 years and over	3	8	2	-	2	2	357
Other female householder	172	187	113	26	241	118	409
Under 45 years	121	106	78	9	207	68	414
45 to 64 years	44	71	33	12	22	33	446
65 years and over	7	10	2	5	12	16	294

[Continued]

★ 334 ★

Costs: Selected Characteristics. Part 2-B

[Continued]

Characteristic	$700 to $799	$800 to $999	$1,000 to $1,499	$1,500 or more	No cash rent	Mortgage payment not reported	Median excluding no cash rent
1-person households	86	97	58	7	112	94	333
Male householder	40	42	29	7	72	45	356
Under 45 years	28	33	20	4	34	16	400
45 to 64 years	11	9	7	-	26	25	332
65 years and over	2	-	2	8	12	6	230
Female householder	46	54	29	-	40	49	308
Under 45 years	31	33	8	-	21	10	438
45 to 64 years	13	17	19	-	8	26	321
65 years and over	2	4	2	-	10	13	194
Own Never Married Children Under 18 Years Old							
No own children under 18 years old	301	377	245	71	169	283	384
With own children under 18 years	309	290	256	85	304	215	484
Under 6 years only	53	56	39	13	114	28	444
1	28	44	24	6	54	20	489
2	21	12	15	8	41	5	370
3 or more	4	-	-	-	18	2	332
6 to 17 years only	189	181	163	54	99	161	506
1	82	122	74	35	36	93	507
2	78	44	70	17	40	54	534
3 or more	29	15	19	2	23	15	455
Both age groups	67	52	54	17	91	26	458
2	32	21	22	16	50	19	496
3 or more	35	31	33	1	41	7	439
Income of Families and Primary Individuals							
Less than $5,000	30	38	12	-	216	48	255
$5,000 to $9,999	24	15	16	5	93	40	264
$1,000 to $14,999	52	31	3	2	46	26	367
$15,000 to $19,999	50	44	25	6	38	25	404
$20,000 to $24,999	43	62	16	5	24	45	454
$25,000 to $29,999	67	72	24	9	30	43	494
$30,000 to $34,999	51	49	40	-	11	26	552
$35,000 to $39,999	64	54	25	10	-	27	594
$40,000 to $49,999	75	100	76	11	10	57	635
$50,000 to $59,999	57	96	59	13	2	47	720
$60,000 to $79,999	65	66	120	19	2	50	762
$80,000 to $99,999	20	21	49	31	-	32	987

[Continued]

★ 334 ★

Costs: Selected Characteristics. Part 2-B
[Continued]

Characteristic	$700 to $799	$800 to $999	$1,000 to $1,499	$1,500 or more	No cash rent	Mortgage payment not reported	Median excluding no cash rent
$100,000 to $119,999	4	7	8	18	-	11	690
$120,000 or more	7	12	29	27	-	22	1,144
Median	33,319	37,070	52,325	77,703	6,063	34,264	-

Source: "Housing Costs by Selected Characteristics - Occupied Units with Black Householder," *American Housing Survey for the United States in 1993*, p. 242.

★ 335 ★

Costs of Housing

Costs: Selected Characteristics. Part 3-A

[Numbers in thousands. Consistent with the 1990 Census. ... means not applicable or sample too small. - means zero or rounds to zero.]

Characteristic	Total	Less than $100	$100 to $199	$200 to $299	$300 to $399	$400 to $499	$500 to $599	$600 to $699
OWNER OCCUPIED UNITS								
Total	4,788	178	687	668	487	357	381	363
Value								
Less than $10,000	217	51	84	34	22	11	2	3
$10,000 to $19,999	317	28	111	69	37	13	22	8
$20,000 to $29,999	450	27	110	99	76	38	36	25
$30,000 to $39,999	498	21	117	89	68	70	46	24
$40,000 to $49,999	526	11	79	99	61	70	65	49
$50,000 to $59,999	461	9	37	67	49	28	67	72
$60,000 to $69,999	436	11	42	69	27	46	27	67
$70,000 to $79,999	327	9	31	40	34	25	18	36
$80,000 to $99,999	533	9	34	40	33	26	50	43
$100,000 to $119,999	277	2	14	23	23	18	32	17
$120,000 to $149,999	312	-	11	15	25	5	4	3
$150,000 to $199,999	264	-	10	17	22	4	8	10
$200,000 to $249,999	91	-	2	2	8	3	4	2
$250,000 to $299,999	37	-	-	2	-	-	-	2
$300,000 or more	41	-	4	2	2	-	2	2
Median	58,372	23,835	33,300	44,333	46,775	46,488	52,958	60,103

[Continued]

★ 335 ★

Costs: Selected Characteristics. Part 3-A
[Continued]

Characteristic	Total	Less than $100	$100 to $199	$200 to $299	$300 to $399	$400 to $499	$500 to $599	$600 to $699
Ratio of Value to Current Income[2]								
Less than 1.5	1,615	57	216	210	166	112	158	171
1.5 to 1.9	572	15	63	79	49	40	40	62
2.0 to 2.4	495	14	47	66	40	51	38	38
2.5 to 2.9	369	7	40	44	35	7	27	20
3.0 to 3.9	455	13	61	78	46	40	39	21
4.0 to 4.9	279	19	46	23	33	17	14	15
5.0 or more	872	42	184	157	108	76	54	33
zero or negative income	130	11	30	11	11	13	10	2
Median	2.1	2.4	2.5	2.3	2.3	2.2	1.8	1.6
Monthly Payment for Principal and Interest								
Less than $100	115	-	23	43	20	19	3	7
$100 to $199	387	-	5	65	154	100	40	9
$200 to $249	219	-	-	3	55	75	59	19
$250 to $299	180	-	-	-	18	72	48	24
$300 to $349	176	-	-	-	-	26	93	37
$350 to $399	143	-	-	-	-	8	67	53
$400 to $449	200	-	-	-	-	-	14	114
$450 to $499	139	-	-	-	-	-	11	45
$500 to $599	257	-	-	-	-	-	-	28
$600 to $699	205	-	-	-	-	-	-	-
$700 to $799	135	-	-	-	-	-	-	-
$800 to $999	161	-	-	-	-	-	-	-
$1,000 to $1,249	87	-	-	-	-	-	-	-
$1,250 to $1,499	42	-	-	-	-	-	-	-
$1,500 or more	41	-	-	-	-	-	-	-
Not reported	498	...	...	...	...	...	...	...
Median	406	...	...	119	167	221	309	408
Average Monthly Cost Paid for Real Estate Taxes								
Less than $25	1,517	162	439	235	147	125	124	73
$25 to $49	1,040	14	171	212	136	85	96	93
$50 to $74	702	2	63	95	61	65	60	87
$75 to $99	455	-	14	78	54	32	26	33
$100 to $149	502	-	-	44	68	31	44	44
$150 to $199	199	-	-	3	17	12	15	10
$200 or more	373	-	-	-	5	8	16	22
Median	46	25-	25-	37	43	41	42	55

[Continued]

★ 335 ★

Costs: Selected Characteristics. Part 3-A
[Continued]

Characteristic	Total	Less than $100	$100 to $199	$200 to $299	$300 to $399	$400 to $499	$500 to $599	$600 to $699
Purchase Price								
Home purchased or built	4,395	113	562	599	463	348	370	357
Less than $10,000	539	45	194	160	38	33	14	12
$10,000 to $19,999	883	19	153	195	170	89	85	42
$20,000 to $29,999	499	2	26	44	106	90	83	52
$30,000 to $39,999	389	2	23	31	30	58	73	45
$40,000 to $49,999	309	-	12	14	10	21	34	83
$50,000 to $59,999	252	-	5	23	2	3	27	52
$60,000 to $69,999	205	-	9	5	9	5	11	46
$70,000 to $79,999	155	-	2	2	9	5	3	8
$80,000 to $99,999	227	-	3	2	3	5	3	-
$100,000 to $119,999	71	-	-	-	4	-	-	-
$120,000 to $149,999	106	-	-	2	-	-	-	-
$150,000 to $199,999	50	-	2	-	3	-	-	-
$200,000 to $249,999	27	-	-	-	-	-	-	-
$250,000 to $299,999	13	-	-	-	-	-	-	-
$300,000 or more	18	-	-	-	-	-	2	-
Not reported	654	45	132	121	79	40	36	17
Median	29,003	10000-	11,339	14,026	19,055	23,553	28,239	42,250
Received as inheritance or gift	213	59	87	33	7	4	8	6
Not reported	180	6	38	35	17	5	2	-
RENTER OCCUPIED UNITS								
Total	6,340	240	686	776	1,033	1,014	778	575
Rent Reductions								
No subsidy or income reporting	4,398	22	162	438	829	862	678	518
Rent control	120	-	5	12	17	15	37	15
No rent control	4,276	22	157	427	812	844	640	503
Reduced by owner	210	-	5	33	40	29	19	12
Not reduced by owner	4,060	22	152	391	772	815	621	488
Owner reduction not reported	5	-	-	3	-	-	-	3
Rent control not reported	3	-	-	-	-	3	-	-
Owned by public housing authority	939	158	304	149	116	66	34	12
Other, Federal subsidy	609	57	168	124	52	36	20	5
Other, State or local subsidy	186	3	33	38	15	16	9	14
Other, income verification	127	-	14	18	19	27	22	11
Subsidy or income verification not reported	80	-	4	8	2	8	15	15

Source: "Housing Costs by Selected Characteristics - Occupied Units with Black Householder," *American Housing Survey for the United States in 1993*, p. 243. *Notes:* 1. For mobile home, oldest category is 1939 or earlier. 2. Beginning with 1989 this item uses current income in its calculation.

★ 336 ★

Costs of Housing

Costs: Selected Characteristics. Part 3-B

[Numbers in thousands. Consistent with the 1990 Census. ... means not applicable or sample too small. - means zero or rounds to zero.]

Characteristic	$700 to $799	$800 to $999	$1,000 to $1,499	$1,500 or more	No cash rent	Mortgage payment not reported	Median excluding no cash rent
OWNER OCCUPIED UNITS							
Total	251	383	386	151	...	496	435
Value							
Less than $10,000	-	2	-	-	...	9	164
$10,000 to $19,999	-	5	3	-	...	23	212
$20,000 to $29,999	5	5	2	-	...	27	275
$30,000 to $39,999	5	12	4	-	...	41	302
$40,000 to $49,999	19	16	7	-	...	48	380
$50,000 to $59,999	42	33	5	3	...	48	525
$60,000 to $69,999	50	41	17	2	...	37	519
$70,000 to $79,999	32	16	12	-	...	30	554
$80,000 to $99,999	53	100	69	5	...	72	692
$100,000 to $119,999	17	33	64	3	...	31	668
$120,000 to $149,999	10	39	111	37	...	52	1,082
$150,000 to $199,999	16	24	64	44	...	45	990
$200,000 to $249,999	2	5	24	24	...	15	1,206
$250,000 to $299,999	-	5	2	19	...	6	...
$300,000 or more	-	3	-	13	...	13	...
Median	71,415	83,380	122,425	177,615	...	75,214	...
Ratio of Value to Current Income[2]							
Less than 1.5	91	126	121	16	...	172	465
1.5 to 1.9	37	53	52	20	...	61	522
2.0 to 2.4	36	57	37	22	...	47	515
2.5 to 2.9	26	36	61	25	...	42	622
3.0 to 3.9	22	26	42	26	...	40	422
4.0 to 4.9	5	32	21	17	...	37	406
5.0 or more	27	50	45	25	...	72	315
zero or negative income	7	2	6	-	...	26	300
Median	1.9	2.1	2.2	2.8	...	2.0	...
Monthly Payment for Principal and Interest							
Less than $100	-	-	-	-	...	...	280
$100 to $199	13	-	-	-	...	...	380
$200 to $249	2	3	2	-	...	...	469

[Continued]

★ 336 ★

Costs: Selected Characteristics. Part 3-B

[Continued]

Characteristic	$700 to $799	$800 to $999	$1,000 to $1,499	$1,500 or more	No cash rent	Mortgage payment not reported	Median excluding no cash rent
$250 to $299	12	6	-	-	...	...	500
$300 to $349	8	7	5	-	...	...	567
$350 to $399	15	-	-	-	...	...	596
$400 to $449	42	27	3	-	...	...	676
$450 to $499	41	37	5	-	...	...	733
$500 to $599	92	112	23	3	...	...	816
$600 to $699	13	128	65	-	...	...	941
$700 to $799	-	38	93	4	...	...	1,157
$800 to $999	-	5	142	13	...	...	1,264
$1,000 to $1,249	-	-	46	41	...	...	1,475
$1,250 to $1,499	-	-	-	42	...	...	...
$1,500 or more	-	-	-	41	...	...	...
Not reported	...	...	...	...	...	498	...
Median	483	591	796	1,315	...	...	...
Average Monthly Cost Paid for Real Estate Taxes							
Less than $25	35	49	27	5	...	98	246
$25 to $49	59	55	22	4	...	93	356
$50 to $74	49	78	44	8	...	88	533
$75 to $99	36	63	71	9	...	38	614
$100 to $149	32	75	81	21	...	61	675
$150 to $199	18	35	49	13	...	26	862
$200 or more	21	27	91	90	...	94	1,229
Median	66	79	118	200+	...	66	...
Purchase Price							
Home purchased or built	249	378	376	151	...	430	471
Less than $10,000	7	6	5	-	...	25	211
$10,000 to $19,999	20	36	12	3	...	58	326
$20,000 to $29,999	17	20	10	6	...	44	455
$30,000 to $39,999	29	41	23	8	...	27	551
$40,000 to $49,999	40	42	17	5	...	30	658
$50,000 to $59,999	51	46	23	-	...	21	707
$60,000 to $69,999	36	48	24	2	...	12	736
$70,000 to $79,999	24	45	40	3	...	16	881
$80,000 to $99,999	13	57	104	8	...	30	1,061
$100,000 to $119,999	-	8	29	12	...	17	1,253
$120,000 to $149,999	-	7	59	28	...	9	1,330
$150,000 to $199,999	-	2	13	27	...	3	...

[Continued]

★ 336 ★

Costs: Selected Characteristics. Part 3-B

[Continued]

Characteristic	$700 to $799	$800 to $999	$1,000 to $1,499	$1,500 or more	No cash rent	Mortgage payment not reported	Median excluding no cash rent
$200,000 to $249,999	-	-	2	25	...	-	...
$250,000 to $299,999	-	-	2	8	...	2	...
$300,000 or more	-	3	-	8	...	5	...
Not reported	13	20	12	8	...	130	270
Median	51,014	57,787	85,424	146,293	...	38,469	...
Received as inheritance or gift	-	2	4	-	...	2	153
Not reported	2	3	6	-	...	66	237
RENTER OCCUPIED UNITS							
Total	358	284	115	6	473	...	420
Rent Reductions							
No subsidy or income reporting	342	252	106	6	181	...	476
Rent control	12	2	3	-	-	...	528
No rent control	329	250	106	6	181	...	475
Reduced by owner	11	-	3	-	58	...	395
Not reduced by owner	319	250	103	6	123	...	478
Owner reduction not reported	-	-	-	-	-	...	...
Rent control not reported	-	-	-	-	-	...	...
Owned by public housing authority	5	12	2	-	82	...	189
Other,Federal subsidy	10	-	-	-	137	...	209
Other, State or local subsidy	2	-	-	-	55	...	275
Other, income verification	-	7	-	-	8	...	429
Subsidy or income verification not reported	-	13	5	-	10	...	584

Source: "Housing Costs by Selected Characteristics - Occupied Units with Black Householder," *American Housing Survey for the United States in 1993*, p. 243. *Notes:* 1. For mobile home, oldest category is 1939 or earlier. 2. Beginning with 1989 this item uses current income in its calculation.

★ 337 ★

Costs of Housing

Selected Housing Costs: Black-Occupied Units

[Numbers in thousands. Consistent with the 1990 Census. ... means not applicable or sample too small. - means zero or rounds to zero.]

Characteristics	Total occupied units	Tenure		Housing unit characteristics			
		Owner	Renter	New construction 4 yrs.	Mobile homes	Physical problems	
						Severe	Moderate
Total	11,128	4,788	6,340	334	337	385	1,154
MONTHLY HOUSING COSTS							
Less than $100	419	178	240	4	31	31	84
$100 to $199	1,373	687	686	30	91	63	236
$200 to $249	722	360	362	11	26	26	104
$250 to $299	721	307	414	22	35	24	124
$300 to $349	658	286	373	10	14	16	70
$350 to $399	862	202	661	15	17	46	83
$400 to $449	717	179	539	4	19	29	84
$450 to $499	654	178	476	13	10	14	68
$500 to $599	1,159	381	778	25	37	18	105
$600 to $699	938	363	575	22	5	33	32
$700 to $799	610	251	358	34	4	15	25
$800 to $999	667	383	284	41	2	15	28
$1,000 to $1,249	369	281	88	40	2	13	22
$1,250 to $1,499	132	104	27	7	-	-	2
$1,500 or more	156	151	6	24	-	-	3
No cash rent	473	...	473	-	21	33	64
Mortgage payment not reported	498	498	...	32	22	7	19
Median (excludes no cash rent)	423	435	418	678	248	362	295
Median Monthly Housing Costs for Owners							
Monthly costs including all mortgages plus maintenance costs	464	464	...	831	198	279	235
Monthly costs excluding 2nd and subsequent mortgages and maintenance costs	415	415	...	764	193	269	226
Monthly Housing Costs as Percent of Current Income[1]							
Less than 5 percent	140	120	20	9	21	4	16
5 to 9 percent	629	494	135	24	37	19	57
10 to 14 percent	1,077	649	428	27	44	24	83
15 to 19 percent	1,280	604	677	28	27	43	118
20 to 24 percent	1,299	550	749	47	29	39	103
25 to 29 percent	1,105	395	710	55	25	39	111
30 to 34 percent	913	313	600	30	13	18	97
35 to 39 percent	599	177	422	20	24	31	59

[Continued]

★ 337 ★

Selected Housing Costs: Black-Occupied Units
[Continued]

Characteristics	Total occupied units	Tenure		Housing unit characteristics			
		Owner	Renter	New construction 4 yrs.	Mobile homes	Severe	Moderate
40 to 49 percent	795	277	519	32	10	38	103
50 to 59 percent	551	179	372	10	9	16	65
60 to 69 percent	348	113	235	-	10	8	51
70 to 99 percent	539	147	392	10	11	23	97
100 percent or more[2]	634	168	465	10	19	24	81
Zero or negative income	248	104	144	-	15	18	32
No cash rent	473	...	473	-	21	33	64
Mortgage payment not reported	498	498	...	32	22	7	19
Median (excludes 3 previous lines)	27	22	31	26	22	29	32
Median (excludes 4 lines before medians)	26	21	29	26	20	28	30
Nonrelatives' Shared Housing Costs							
Nonrelatives in housing units	435	93	342	11	12	25	48
Less than $100 per month	175	38	137	7	8	14	17
$100 to $199	47	21	26	-	2	2	8
$200 to $299	79	5	74	-	-	5	11
$300 to $399	50	7	43	4	-	-	2
$400 or more per month	41	9	32	-	2	-	7
Not reported	44	14	30	-	-	3	2
Median	144	109	173	...	...	...	...
Monthly Cost Paid for Electricity							
Electricity used	11,125	4,786	6,338	334	337	381	1,154
Less than $25	754	174	580	15	18	43	96
$25 to $49	2,909	939	1,970	74	55	99	408
$50 to $74	2,386	1,196	1,191	88	103	71	244
$75 to $99	1,445	909	537	58	52	51	121
$100 to $149	1,228	727	501	61	70	19	65
$150 to $199	414	287	127	15	18	9	28
$200 or more	240	167	73	17	9	3	17
Median	61	73	49	71	72	52	49
Included in rent, other fee, or obtained free	1,748	388	1,360	6	12	88	174
Monthly Cost Paid for Piped Gas							
Piped gas used	7,817	3,340	4,477	158	65	266	864
Less than $25	1,725	586	1,139	42	21	49	252
$25 to $49	2,012	959	1,054	60	24	57	245
$50 to $74	1,265	782	483	20	12	22	108
$75 to $99	499	320	179	13	-	29	34
$100 to $149	345	231	114	6	2	10	15
$150 to $199	95	76	19	-	-	-	7

[Continued]

★ 337 ★

Selected Housing Costs: Black-Occupied Units

[Continued]

Characteristics	Total occupied units	Tenure		Housing unit characteristics			
		Owner	Renter	New construction 4 yrs.	Mobile homes	Physical problems	
						Severe	Moderate
$200 or more	115	88	28	4	2	3	13
Median	41	49	34	38	35	40	34
Included in rent, other fee, or obtained free	1,760	298	1,462	13	3	97	189
Average Monthly Cost Paid for Fuel Oil							
Fuel oil used	1,524	472	1,051	16	12	114	124
Less than $25	172	64	108	-	2	9	8
$25 to $49	170	94	76	3	2	9	16
$50 to $74	159	109	50	-	4	2	5
$75 to $99	104	62	43	-	4	3	18
$100 to $149	75	64	11	-	-	2	3
$150 to $199	30	25	4	-	-	-	-
$200 or more	27	8	19	-	-	3	-
Median	54	63	41	...	...	39	55
Included in rent, other fee, or obtained free	785	46	739	13	-	85	74

Source: "Selected Housing Costs - Occupied Units with Black Householder," *American Housing Survey for the United States in 1993*, p. 216. *Notes:* 1. Beginning with 1989, this item uses current income in its calculation. 2. May reflect a temporary situation, living off savings, or response error.

Elderly Occupants

★ 338 ★

Building Condition: Elderly Householder

[Numbers in thousands. Consistent with the 1990 Census. ...means not applicable or sample too small. - means zero or rounds to zero.]

Characteristics	Total occupied units	Household characteristics	
		Black	Hispanic
Total	20,438	1,825	696
Stories in Structure[1]			
1	537	55	28
2	1,170	121	75
3	1,198	110	28
4 to 6	769	91	31

[Continued]

★ 338 ★

Building Condition: Elderly Householder
[Continued]

Characteristics	Total occupied units	Household characteristics	
		Black	Hispanic
7 or more	820	149	56
Common Stairways			
Multiunits, 2 or more floors	3,957	472	190
No common stairways	665	82	22
With common stairways	2,934	359	162
No loose steps	2,794	343	155
Railings not loose	2,601	325	134
Railings loose	85	7	13
No railings	81	7	8
Status of railings not reported	26	5	-
Loose steps	127	13	5
Railings not loose	107	13	5
Railings loose	14	-	-
No railings	4	-	-
Status of railings not reported	2	-	-
Status of steps not reported	13	2	2
Status of stairways not reported	358	32	5
External Building Conditions[1,2]			
Sagging roof	-	-	-
Missing roofing material	13	-	-
Hole in roof	-	-	-
Could not see roof	522	73	30
Missing bricks, siding, other outside wall material	23	3	3
Sloping outside walls	4	2	-
Boarded up windows	11	7	-
Broken windows	13	8	-
Bars on widows	83	22	11
Foundation crumbling or has open crack or hole	24	8	-
Could not see foundation	184	33	10
None of the above	3,358	384	167
Could not observe or not reported	537	44	18
Site Placement			
Mobile homes	1,266	45	28
First site	866	25	18
Moved from another site	240	18	3
Don't know	124	-	5

[Continued]

★ 338 ★

Building Condition: Elderly Householder
[Continued]

Characteristics	Total occupied units	Household characteristics	
		Black	Hispanic
Not reported	36	2	2
Previous Occupancy			
Unit built 1980 or later	2,522	135	65
Not previously occupied	1,561	51	40
Not reported	254	29	7

Source: "Height and Condition of Building—Occupied Units with Elderly Householder." *American Housing Survey for the United States in 1993*, February 1995, p. 316. *Notes:* 1. Limited to multiunit structures. 2. Figures may not add to total because more than one category may apply.

★ 339 ★

Elderly Occupants

Equipment Failures: Elderly Householder

[Numbers in thousands. Consistent with the 1990 Census. ...means not applicable or sample too small. - means zero or rounds to zero.]

Characteristics	Total occupied units	Household characteristics	
		Black	Hispanic
Total	20,438	1,825	696
Water Supply Stoppage			
With hot and cold piped water	20,373	1,798	696
No stoppage in last 3 months	19,562	1,719	665
With stoppage in last 3 months	693	45	17
No stoppage lasting 6 hours or more	349	15	8
1 time lasting 6 hours or more	222	18	8
2 times	43	-	-
3 times	22	4	-
4 times or more	13	-	-
Number of times not reported	44	9	-
Stoppage not reported	119	34	14
Flush Toilet Breakdowns			
With one or more flush toilets	20,384	1,799	696
With at least one working toilet at all times in last 3 months	19,477	1,644	654
None working some time in last 3 months	844	150	42
No breakdowns lasting 6 hours or more	295	38	12
1 time lasting 6 hours or more	389	63	19

[Continued]

★ 339 ★

Equipment Failures: Elderly Householder
[Continued]

Characteristics	Total occupied units	Household characteristics	
		Black	Hispanic
2 times	66	16	2
3 times	16	7	3
4 times or more	16	2	2
Number of times not reported	64	24	4
Breakdowns not reported	63	5	-
Sewage Disposal Breakdowns			
With public sewer	15,601	1,532	621
No breakdowns in last 3 months	15,386	1,493	610
With breakdowns in last 3 months	215	38	11
No breakdowns lasting 6 hours or more	87	14	2
1 time lasting 6 hours or more	100	17	9
2 times	26	7	-
3 times	-	-	-
4 times or more	2	-	-
With septic tank or cesspool	4,796	272	75
No breakdowns in last 3 months	4,728	261	73
With breakdowns in last 3 months	70	11	2
No breakdowns lasting 6 hours or more	19	2	-
1 time lasting 6 hours or more	47	9	2
2 times	2	-	-
3 times	-	-	-
4 times or more	2	-	-
Heating Problems			
With heating equipment and occupied last winter	19,805	1,774	664
Not uncomfortable cold for 24 hours or more last winter	18,846	1,638	602
Uncomfortable cold for 24 hours or more last winter[1]	906	131	56
Equipment breakdowns	224	41	18
No breakdowns lasting 6 hours or more	21	3	6
1 time lasting 6 hours or more	136	23	5
2 times	33	6	4
3 times	8	-	-
4 times or more	11	7	-
Number of times not reported	14	2	2
Other causes	706	97	45
Utility interruption	295	15	8

[Continued]

★ 339 ★

Equipment Failures: Elderly Householder
[Continued]

Characteristics	Total occupied units	Household characteristics	
		Black	Hispanic
Inadequate heating capacity	125	25	13
Inadequate insulation	63	16	11
Other	197	31	13
Not reported	29	10	-
Reason for discomfort not reported	5	-	-
Discomfort not reported	53	5	5
Electric fuses and Circuit Breakers			
With electrical wiring	20,433	1,825	696
No fuses or breakers blown in last 3 mo.	18,500	1,634	650
With fuses or breakers blown in last 3 mo.	1,761	173	38
1 time	1,107	86	20
2 times	287	37	5
3 times	147	12	4
4 times or more	91	23	7
Number of times not reported	129	17	3
Problem not reported or don't know	172	17	8

Source: "Failures in Equipment—Occupied Units with Elderly Householder." *American Housing Survey for the United States in 1993,* February 1995, p. 324. *Notes:* 1. Other causes and equipment breakdowns may not add to total as both may be reported.

★ 340 ★
Elderly Occupants

Equipment and Plumbing: Elderly Householder

[Numbers in thousands. Consistent with the 1990 Census. ...means not applicable or sample too small. - means zero or rounds to zero.]

Characteristics	Total occupied units	Household characteristics	
		Black	Hispanic
Total	20,438	1,825	696
Equipment[1]			
Lacking complete kitchen facilities	207	36	4
With complete kitchen (sink, refrigerator and burners)	20,231	1,788	692
Kitchen sink	20,308	1,800	694
Refrigerator	20,391	1,822	695
Less than 5 years old	5,958	587	223
Age not reported	165	29	9

[Continued]

★ 340 ★

Equipment and Plumbing: Elderly Householder
[Continued]

Characteristics	Total occupied units	Household characteristics	
		Black	Hispanic
Burners and oven	20,345	1,812	694
Less than 5 years old	4,374	468	176
Age not reported	209	22	11
Burners only	34	8	-
Less than 5 years old	7	-	-
Age not reported	7	5	-
Oven only	9	-	-
Less than 5 years old	7	-	-
Age not reported	-	-	-
Neither burners nor oven	50	5	3
Dishwasher	8,644	263	191
Less than 5 years old	2,385	80	49
Age not reported	85	16	5
Washing machine	16,117	1,173	483
Less than 5 years old	4,228	347	173
Age not reported	116	18	5
Clothes dryer	13,956	708	330
Less than 5 years old	3,174	230	97
Age not reported	101	13	-
Disposal in kitchen sink	7,349	282	215
Less than 5 years old	2,490	87	100
Age not reported	157	19	11
Air conditioning:			
Central	8,560	432	250
1 room unit	4,087	502	132
2 room units	1,572	140	50
3 room units or more	628	67	30
Main Heating Equipment			
Warm-air furnace	10,772	775	230
Steam or hot water system	3,261	339	103
Electric heat pump	1,489	37	58
Built-in electric units	1,481	84	59
Floor, wall, or other built-in hot air units without ducts	1,070	145	89
Room heaters with flue	568	110	21
Room heaters without flue	430	165	48
Portable electric heaters	167	32	16
Stoves	570	81	20
Fireplaces with inserts	133	4	11
Fireplaces without inserts	35	8	3
Other	350	36	25
None	113	9	14

[Continued]

★ 340 ★

Equipment and Plumbing: Elderly Householder

[Continued]

Characteristics	Total occupied units	Household characteristics	
		Black	Hispanic
Other Heating Equipment			
With other heating equipment[1]	5,274	332	127
Warm-air furnace	195	17	6
Steam or hot water system	38	2	-
Electric heat pump	46	-	3
Built-in electric units	446	11	8
Floor, wall, or other built-in hot-air units without ducts	115	2	2
Room heaters with flue	213	17	2
Room heaters without flue	305	67	7
Portable electric heaters	1,460	137	51
Stoves	688	26	18
Fireplaces with inserts	788	19	7
Fireplaces with no inserts	1,393	49	36
Other	170	7	2
Plumbing			
With all plumbing facilities	20,049	1,763	686
Lacking some plumbing facilities[1]	47	9	-
No hot piped water	21	4	-
No bathtub nor shower	32	5	-
No flush toilet	11	3	-
No plumbing facilities for exclusive use	342	53	11
Source of Water			
Public system or private company	17,580	1,653	649
Well serving 1 to 5 units	2,522	140	25
Drilled	2,169	105	21
Dug	274	31	1
Not reported	79	4	2
Other	336	32	23
Means of Sewage Disposal			
Public sewer	15,601	1,532	621
Septic tank, cesspool, chemical toilet	4,798	272	75
Other	39	21	-

Source: "Selected Equipment and Plumbing—Occupied Units with Elderly Householder." *American Housing Survey for the United States in 1993*, February 1995, p. 320. *Notes:* 1. Figures may not add to total because more than one category may apply to a unit.

★ 341 ★

Elderly Occupants

Fuels: Elderly Householder

[Numbers in thousands. Consistent with the 1990 Census. ...means not applicable or sample too small. - means zero or rounds to zero.]

Characteristics	Total occupied units	Household characteristics	
		Black	Hispanic
Total	20,438	1,825	696
Main House Heating Fuel			
Housing units with heating fuel	20,325	1,816	682
Electricity	4,699	254	196
Piped gas	10,406	1,053	349
Bottled gas	1,050	128	18
Fuel oil	2,937	243	74
Kerosene or other liquid fuel	230	34	2
Coal or coke	74	7	2
Wood	799	94	35
Solar energy	11	-	1
Other	120	4	5
Other House Heating Fuels			
With other heating fuels[1]	3,210	215	70
Electricity	1,217	92	39
Piped gas	147	13	5
Bottled gas	131	17	3
Fuel oil	124	10	2
Kerosene or other liquid fuel	150	42	-
Coal or coke	48	2	-
Wood	1,433	46	27
Solar energy	9	-	-
Other	86	2	-
Not reported	145	12	8
Cooking Fuel			
With cooking fuel	20,379	1,820	694
Electricity	12,019	591	278
Piped gas	7,150	1,052	387
Bottled gas	1,093	168	23
Kerosene or other liquid fuel	75	7	3
Coal or coke	12	-	-
Wood	7	2	3
Other	22	-	-
Water Heating Fuel			
With hot piped water	20,373	1,796	696
Electricity	7,561	515	200

[Continued]

★ 341 ★

Fuels: Elderly Householder
[Continued]

Characteristics	Total occupied units	Household characteristics	
		Black	Hispanic
Piped gas	10,351	1,074	418
Bottled gas	770	82	20
Fuel oil	1,439	119	49
Kerosene or other liquid fuel	75	4	2
Coal or coke	19	-	2
Wood	4	-	-
Solar energy	67	2	4
Other	87	2	-
Central Air Conditioning Fuel			
With central air conditioning	8,560	432	250
Electricity	7,701	369	227
Piped gas	741	59	18
Other	117	4	5
Clothes Dryer Fuel			
With clothes dryer	13,956	706	330
Electricity	10,524	484	224
Piped gas	3,215	213	106
Other	216	11	-
Units Using Each Fuel[1]			
Electricity	20,433	1,825	696
All-electric units	3,825	164	129
Piped gas	12,475	1,304	521
Bottled gas	1,905	229	36
Fuel oil	3,501	284	94
Kerosene or other liquid fuel	418	84	2
Coal or coke	125	9	2
Wood	2,231	139	62
Solar energy	78	2	4
Other	259	9	5

Source: "Fuels—Occupied Units with Elderly Householder." *American Housing Survey for the United States in 1993,* February 1995, p. 322. *Notes:* 1. Figures may not add to total because more than one category may apply to a unit.

★ 342 ★

Elderly Occupants

Household Composition: Elderly Householder. Part 1

[Numbers in thousands. Consistent with the 1990 Census. ...means not applicable or sample too small. - means zero or rounds to zero.]

Characteristics	Total occupied units	Household characteristics	
		Black	Hispanic
Own Never Married Children Under 18 Years Old			
No own children under 18 years	20,305	1,801	682
With own children under 18 years	133	23	15
Under 6 years only	16	5	-
1	13	2	-
2	2	2	-
3 or more	-	-	-
6 to 17 years only	110	19	13
1	78	8	11
2	18	11	2
3 or more	13	-	-
Both age groups	7	-	2
2	5	-	2
3 or more	2	-	-
Persons Other Than Spouse or Children[1]			
With other relatives	3,600	614	203
Single adult offspring 18 to 29	478	96	30
Single adult offspring 30 years of age or over	1,912	297	107
Households with three generations	309	71	34
Households with 1 subfamily	495	105	46
Subfamily householder age under 30	120	34	15
30 to 64	366	68	31
65 and over	8	2	-
Households with 2 or more subfamilies	17	4	7
Households with other types of relatives	1,375	314	79
With non-relatives	440	85	14
Co-owners or co-renters	83	13	6
Lodgers	158	42	7
Unrelated children, under 18 years old	128	23	-
Other non-relatives	164	29	4
One or more secondary families	25	12	-
2-person households, none related to each other	327	45	8
3-8 person households, none related to each other	28	5	-

[Continued]

★ 342 ★

Household Composition: Elderly Householder. Part 1
[Continued]

Characteristics	Total occupied units	Household characteristics	
		Black	Hispanic
Years of School Completed by Householder			
No school years completed	134	23	52
Elementary:			
less than 8 years	2,037	583	197
8 years	2,348	242	71
High school:			
1 to 3 years	3,341	397	96
4 years	6,895	359	158
College:			
1 to 3 years	2,696	115	62
4 years or more	2,967	106	61
Median	12.3	9.5	9.6
Year Householder Moved into Unit			
1990 to 1994	2,927	268	126
1985 to 1989	2,812	228	105
1980 to 1984	1,906	157	77
1975 to 1979	1,969	174	80
1970 to 1974	1,853	190	79
1960 to 1969	3,629	402	95
1950 to 1959	3,299	258	81
1940 to 1949	1,375	108	35
1939 or earlier	665	41	18
Median	1973	1973	1977
Household Moves and Formation in Last Year			
Total with a move in last year	1,272	132	61
Household all moved here from one unit	855	70	37
Householder of previous unit did not move here	66	5	5
Householder of previous unit moved here	765	65	29
Householder of previous unit not reported	24	-	3
Household moved here from two or more units	25	3	-
No previous householder moved here	4	-	-
1 previous householder moved here	5	3	-
2 or more previous householders moved here	14	-	-
Previous householder(s) not reported	2	-	-
Some already here, rest moved in	390	57	24

[Continued]

★ 342 ★

Household Composition: Elderly Householder. Part 1
[Continued]

Characteristics	Total occupied units	Household characteristics	
		Black	Hispanic
No previous householder moved here	105	23	13
1 or more previous householders moved here	234	24	11
Previous householder(s) not reported	51	10	-
Number of previous units not reported	2	2	-

Source: "Household Composition—Occupied Units with Elderly Householder." *American Housing Survey for the United States in 1993*, February 1995, p. 332. *Notes:* 1. Figures may not add to total because more than one category may apply.

★ 343 ★
Elderly Occupants

Household Composition: Elderly Householder. Part 2

[Numbers in thousands. Consistent with the 1990 Census. ...means not applicable or sample too small. - means zero or rounds to zero.]

Characteristics	Total occupied units	Household characteristics	
		Black	Hispanic
Population in housing units	35,396	3,540	1,414
Total	20,438	1,825	696
Persons			
1 person	8,984	845	283
2 persons	9,340	598	281
3 persons	1,368	190	67
4 persons	395	106	21
5 persons	202	49	22
6 persons	76	17	6
7 persons or more	73	20	16
Median	1.6	1.6	1.7
Number of Single Children Under 18 Years Old			
None	19,558	1,593	619
1	558	127	45
2	206	66	16
3	78	23	7
4	19	6	5
5	14	7	5
6 or more	6	2	-
Median	.5-	.5-	.5-

[Continued]

★ 343 ★

Household Composition: Elderly Householder. Part 2
[Continued]

Characteristics	Total occupied units	Household characteristics	
		Black	Hispanic
Persons 65 Years Old and Over			
None	...	...	...
1 person	13,164	1,423	491
2 persons or more	7,274	402	205
Age of Householder			
Under 25 years	...	...	...
25 to 29 years	...	...	...
30 to 34 years	...	...	...
35 to 44 years	...	...	...
45 to 54 years	...	...	...
55 to 64 years	...	...	...
65 to 74 years	11,456	1,071	411
75 years and over	8,981	754	285
Median	74	74	73
Household Composition by Age of Householder			
2-or-more person households	11,454	980	413
Married-couple families, no nonrelatives	8,692	433	278
Under 25 years	...	...	...
25 to 29 years	...	...	...
30 to 34 years	...	...	...
35 to 44 years	...	...	...
45 to 64 years	...	...	...
65 years and over	8,692	433	278
Other male householder	861	130	37
Under 45 years	...	...	...
45 to 64 years	...	...	...
65 years and over	861	130	37
Other female householder	1,901	417	99
Under 45 years	...	...	...
45 to 64 years	...	...	...
65 years and over	1,901	417	99
1-person households	8,984	845	283
Male householder	1,941	263	65
Under 45 years	...	...	...
45 to 64 years	...	...	...
65 years and over	1,941	263	65
Female householder	7,043	582	218
Under 45 years	...	...	...

[Continued]

★ 343 ★

Household Composition: Elderly Householder. Part 2

[Continued]

Characteristics	Total occupied units	Household characteristics	
		Black	Hispanic
45 to 64 years	...	...	...
65 years and over	7,043	582	218

Source: "Household Composition—Occupied Units with Elderly Householder." *American Housing Survey for the United States in 1993,* February 1995, p. 330.

★ 344 ★

Elderly Occupants

Housing Costs: Monthly for Elderly Householder

[Numbers in thousands. Consistent with the 1990 Census. ...means not applicable or sample too small. - means zero or rounds to zero.]

Characteristics	Total occupied units	Household characteristics	
		Black	Hispanic
Total	20,438	1,825	696
Monthly Housing Costs			
Less than $100	626	93	36
$100 to $199	4,963	517	181
$200 to $249	2,762	225	64
$250 to $299	2,182	204	36
$300 to $349	1,801	174	57
$350 to $399	1,267	108	38
$400 to $449	1,061	80	33
$450 to $499	832	56	47
$500 to $599	1,215	105	24
$600 to $699	833	72	45
$700 to $799	504	30	26
$800 to $999	600	36	30
$1,000 to $1,249	318	15	16
$1,250 to $1,499	141	10	3
$1,500 or more	272	10	9
No cash rent	469	40	17
Mortgage payment not reported	593	49	34
Median (exclude no cash rent)	281	258	305
Median Monthly Housing Costs for Owners			
Monthly costs including all mortgages plus maintenance costs	276	262	262

[Continued]

Housing Costs: Monthly for Elderly Householder
[Continued]

Characteristics	Total occupied units	Household characteristics	
		Black	Hispanic
Monthly costs excluding 2nd and subsequent mortgages and maintenance costs	261	248	244
Monthly Housing Costs as Percent of Current Income[1]			
Less than 5 percent	570	21	11
5 to 9 percent	2,590	116	65
10 to 14 percent	3,164	177	87
15 to 19 percent	2,767	190	81
20 to 24 percent	1,988	159	45
25 to 29 percent	1,774	179	58
30 to 34 percent	1,383	206	35
35 to 39 percent	985	109	51
40 to 49 percent	1,213	152	49
50 to 59 percent	698	125	30
60 to 69 percent	571	88	45
70 to 99 percent	729	97	41
100 percent or more[2]	780	102	35
Zero or negative income	165	15	11
No cash rent	469	40	17
Mortgage payment not reported	593	49	34
Median (excludes 3 previous lines)	21	30	27
Median (excludes 4 lines before medians)	20	29	26
Nonrelatives' Shared Housing Costs			
Nonrelatives in housing units	158	42	7
Less than $100 per month	76	11	4
$100 to $199	26	9	-
$200 to $299	19	5	3
$300 to $399	9	5	-
$400 or more per month	10	-	-
Not reported	17	13	-
Median	100-	...	...
Monthly Cost Paid for Electricity			
Electricity used	20,433	1,825	696
Less than $25	2,124	184	95
$25 to $49	6,223	500	205
$50 to $74	4,672	410	130
$75 to $99	2,484	229	79
$100 to $149	1,848	130	38

[Continued]

★ 344 ★

Housing Costs: Monthly for Elderly Householder
[Continued]

Characteristics	Total occupied units	Household characteristics	
		Black	Hispanic
$150 to $199	546	33	25
$200 or more	365	27	15
Median	54	54	49
Included in rent, other fee, or obtained free	2,171	312	110
Monthly Cost Paid for Piped Gas			
Piped gas used	12,475	1,304	521
Less than $25	2,759	288	220
$25 to $49	4,234	290	136
$50 to $74	2,132	265	18
$75 to $99	836	83	33
$100 to $149	385	66	5
$150 to $199	120	30	2
$200 or more	72	11	2
Median	40	45	25-
Included in rent, other fee, or obtained free	1,937	271	104
Average Monthly Cost Paid for Fuel Oil			
Fuel oil used	3,501	284	94
Less than $25	352	45	9
$25 to $49	689	50	2
$50 to $74	776	42	11
$75 to $99	473	17	7
$100 to $149	407	35	-
$150 to $199	110	6	3
$200 or more	63	6	5
Median	63	53	66
Included in rent, other fee, or free	632	83	58

Source: "Selected Housing Costs—Occupied Units with Elderly Householder." *American Housing Survey for the United States in 1993*, February 1995, p. 340. *Notes:* 1. Beginning with 1989, this item uses current income in its calculation. 2. May reflect a temporary situation, living off savings, or response error.

★ 345 ★

Elderly Occupants

Housing Costs: Selected Characteristics for Elderly Householder

[Numbers in thousands. Consistent with the 1990 Census. ... means not applicable or sample too small. - means zero or rounds to zero.]

Characteristic	Total occupied units	Household characteristics	
		Black	Hispanic
Property Insurance			
Property insurance paid	16,473	1,118	363
Median per month	28	26	33
Monthly Costs Paid for Selected Utilities and Fuels			
Water paid separately	10,987	886	319
Median	20	20	24
Trash paid separately	7,311	334	221
Median	12	11	14
Bottled gas paid separately	1,666	180	28
Median	46	46	...
Other fuel paid separately	1,824	161	53
Median	15	17	16
OWNER OCCUPIED UNITS			
Total	15,767	1,153	448
Cost and Ownership Sharing			
Ownership shared by person not living here	527	41	23
Costs shared by person not living here	35	2	2
Costs not shared	492	39	21
Cost sharing not reported	-	-	-
Ownership not shared	15,051	1,102	412
Costs shared by person not living here	58	14	7
Costs not shared	14,948	1,088	405
Cost sharing not reported	45	-	-
Ownership sharing not reported	189	10	13
Monthly Payment for Principal and Interest			
Less than $100	181	53	19
$100 to $199	505	86	13
$200 to $249	261	25	15
$250 to $299	228	28	11
$300 to $349	184	25	9
$350 to $399	146	9	10
$400 to $449	135	12	6
$450 to $499	89	10	2

[Continued]

★ 345 ★

Housing Costs: Selected Characteristics for Elderly Householder
[Continued]

Characteristic	Total occupied units	Household characteristics	
		Black	Hispanic
$500 to $599	129	11	6
$600 to $699	97	4	2
$700 to $799	79	9	6
$800 to $999	108	13	6
$1,000 to $1,249	68	5	2
$1,250 to $1,499	40	-	-
$1,500 or more	52	2	2
Not reported	593	49	34
Median	295	215	282
Average Monthly Cost Paid for Real Estate Taxes			
Less than $25	3,689	506	133
$25 to $49	3,020	282	125
$50 to $74	2,305	133	45
$75 to $99	1,654	78	49
$100 to $149	2,147	87	37
$150 to $199	1,188	24	22
$200 or more	1,765	43	36
Median	63	31	43
Annual Taxes Paid Per $1,000 Value			
Less than $5	3,654	413	173
$5 to $9	4,080	278	118
$10 to $14	3,132	165	66
$15 to $19	1,727	107	19
$20 to $24	1,152	70	19
$25 or more	2,023	119	53
Median	10	8	7
Routine Maintenance in Last Year			
Less than $25 per month	12,049	873	341
$25 to $49	1,716	161	49
$50 to $74	407	19	10
$75 to $99	424	29	20
$100 to $149	212	11	4
$150 to $199	171	2	-
$200 or more per month	223	19	2
Not reported	564	39	22
Median	25-	25-	25-

[Continued]

★ 345 ★

Housing Costs: Selected Characteristics for Elderly Householder
[Continued]

Characteristic	Total occupied units	Household characteristics	
		Black	Hispanic
Condominium and Cooperative Fee			
Fee paid by owners	752	2	18
Less than $25 per month	11	-	2
$25 to $49	10	-	-
$50 to $74	50	-	2
$75 to $99	80	-	2
$100 to $149	195	-	-
$150 to $199	180	2	7
$200 or more per month	184	-	3
Not reported	42	-	-
Median	153	...	...

Source: "Selected Housing Costs—Occupied Unites with Elderly Householder," *American Housing Survey for the United States in 1993*, February 1995, p. 342.

★ 346 ★

Elderly Occupants

Housing Quality: Elderly Householder

[Numbers in thousands. Consistent with the 1990 Census. ...means not applicable or sample too small. - means zero or rounds to zero.]

Characteristics	Total occupied units	Household characteristics	
		Black	Hispanic
Total	20,438	1,825	696
Selected Amenities[1]			
Porch, deck, balcony, or patio	15,690	1,304	485
Not reported	32	-	3
Telephone available	19,672	1,684	648
Usable fireplace	5,544	256	140
Separate dining room	8,844	706	290
With 2 or more living rooms or recreation rooms, etc.	6,206	361	138
Garage or carport included with home	12,987	655	380
Not included	7,401	1,164	309
Offstreet parking included	5,480	732	187
Offstreet parking not reported	60	4	3
Garage or carport not reported	50	5	7

[Continued]

★ 346 ★

Housing Quality: Elderly Householder
[Continued]

Characteristics	Total occupied units	Household characteristics	
		Black	Hispanic
Cars and Trucks Available			
No cars, trucks, or vans	4,017	746	227
Other households without cars	769	55	39
1 car with or without trucks or vans	11,438	793	314
2 cars	3,678	189	97
3 or more cars	537	41	19
With cars, no trucks or vans	11,975	831	339
1 truck or van with or without cars	3,875	226	110
2 or more trucks or vans	571	22	21
Owner or Manager on Property			
Rental, multiunit[2]	3,360	476	188
Owner or manager lives on property	1,231	110	74
Neither owner nor manager lives on property	2,130	366	114
Selected Deficiencies[1]			
Signs of rats in last 3 months	393	135	41
Holes in floors	188	61	22
Open cracks or holes (interior)	573	168	42
Broken plaster or peeling paint (interior)	537	136	46
No electrical wiring	4	-	-
Exposed wiring	352	58	34
Rooms without electric outlets	325	68	18
Water Leakage During Last 12 Months			
No leakage from inside structure	18,971	1,595	635
With leakage from inside structure[1]	1,447	227	61
Fixtures backed up or overflowed	453	85	25
Pipes leaked	674	115	30
Other or unknown (includes not reported)	355	36	8
Interior leakage not reported	20	3	-
No leakage from outside structure	17,273	1,496	607
With leakage from outside structure	3,140	324	90
Roof	1,283	212	61
Basement	1,220	57	9
Walls, closed windows, or doors	454	52	12

[Continued]

★ 346 ★

Housing Quality: Elderly Householder
[Continued]

Characteristics	Total occupied units	Household characteristics	
		Black	Hispanic
Other or unknown (includes not reported)	330	24	12
Exterior leakage not reported	25	5	-

Source: "Housing Quality—Occupied Units with Elderly Householder." *American Housing Survey for the United States in 1993,* February 1995, p. 326. *Notes:* 1. Figures may not add to total because more than one category may apply to a unit. 2. Two or more units of any tenure in the structure.

★ 347 ★
Elderly Occupants

Income Characteristics: Elderly Householder

[Numbers in thousands. Consistent with the 1990 Census. ...means not applicable or sample too small. - means zero or rounds to zero.]

Characteristics	Total occupied units	Household characteristics	
		Black	Hispanic
Total	20,438	1,825	696
Household Income			
Less than $5,000	1,154	224	57
$5,000 to $9,999	4,491	687	238
$10,000 to $14,999	3,547	292	125
$15,000 to $19,999	2,318	221	53
$20,000 to $24,999	1,964	125	48
$25,000 to $29,999	2,215	98	39
$30,000 to $34,999	1,152	42	29
$35,000 to $39,999	786	38	22
$40,000 to $49,999	937	32	33
$50,000 to $59,999	604	17	17
$60,000 to $79,999	588	25	18
$80,000 to $99,999	252	11	5
$100,000 to $119,999	167	7	4
$120,000 or more	264	5	9
Median	17,216	10,015	12,154
As percent of poverty level:			
Less than 50 percent	707	143	33
50 to 99	2,624	594	163
100 to 149	3,813	411	174
150 to 199	2,861	223	85
200 percent or more	10,433	454	241

[Continued]

★ 347 ★

Income Characteristics: Elderly Householder

[Continued]

Characteristics	Total occupied units	Household characteristics	
		Black	Hispanic
Income of Families and Primary Individuals			
Less than $5,000	1,183	235	59
$5,000 to $9,999	4,539	695	240
$10,000 to $14,999	3,544	285	122
$15,000 to $19,999	2,307	213	51
$20,000 to $24,999	1,956	126	48
$25,000 to $29,999	2,215	101	39
$30,000 to $34,999	1,142	41	31
$35,000 to $39,999	789	38	26
$40,000 to $49,999	914	29	30
$50,000 to $59,999	595	17	17
$60,000 to $79,999	578	23	16
$80,000 to $99,999	250	11	5
$100,000 to $119,999	167	7	4
$120,000 or more	259	5	9
Median	17,065	9,970	11,989
Income Sources of Families and Primary Individuals			
Wages and salaries	4,965	454	216
Wages and salaries were majority of income - 2 or more people each earned over 20%	2,529	262	125
of wages and salaries	692	81	46
Business, farm, or ranch	1,686	42	28
Social Security or pensions	19,571	1,697	627
Interest	12,819	395	247
Stock owner(s)	4,670	56	63
Rental income	1,974	137	59
With lodger(s)	158	42	7
Welfare or SSI	953	320	89
Alimony or child support	115	6	8
Other	1,621	159	68
Amount of Savings and Investments			
Income of $25,000 or less	14,251	1,576	531
No savings or investments	5,257	1,100	323
$25,000 or less	5,365	349	127
More than $25,000	2,112	43	38
Not reported	1,517	85	44

[Continued]

★ 347 ★

Income Characteristics: Elderly Householder
[Continued]

Characteristics	Total occupied units	Household characteristics	
		Black	Hispanic
Food Stamps			
Income of $25,000 or less	14,251	1,576	531
Family members received food stamps	991	366	111
Did not receive food stamps	12,668	1,170	402
Not reported	593	40	18
Rent Reductions			
No subsidy or income reporting	3,245	355	154
Rent control	203	22	9
No rent control	3,038	333	145
Reduced by owner	300	31	15
Not reduced by owner	2,733	302	128
Owner reduction not reported	6	-	3
Rent control not reported	4	-	-
Owned by public housing authority	692	192	42
Other, Federal subsidy	388	67	12
Other, state or local subsidy	75	18	16
Other, income verification	195	19	15
Subsidy or income verification not reported	76	20	10

Source: "Income Characteristics—Occupied Units with Elderly Householder." *American Housing Survey for the United States in 1993*, February 1995, p. 338.

★ 348 ★

Elderly Occupants

Introductory Characteristics: Elderly Householder

[Numbers in thousands. Consistent with the 1990 Census. ...means not applicable or sample too small. - means zero or rounds to zero.]

Characteristics	Total occupied units	Household characteristics	
		Black	Hispanic
Total	20,438	1,825	696
Tenure			
Owner occupied	15,767	1,153	448
Percent of all occupied	77.1	63.2	64.3
Renter occupied	4,671	672	248

[Continued]

★ 348 ★

Introductory Characteristics: Elderly Householder

[Continued]

Characteristics	Total occupied units	Household characteristics	
		Black	Hispanic
Race and Origin			
White	18,329	...	642
Non-Hispanic	17,687	...	...
Hispanic	642	...	642
Black	1,825	1,825	20
Other	285	...	34
Total Hispanic	696	20	696
Units in Structure			
1, detached	13,681	1,097	408
1, attached	999	155	42
2 to 4	1,476	186	70
5 to 9	613	64	16
10 to 19	499	51	28
20 to 49	629	53	39
50 or more	1,274	173	66
Mobile home or trailer	1,266	45	28
Cooperatives and Condominiums			
Cooperatives	219	14	9
Condominiums	923	17	26
Year Structure was Built[1]			
1990 to 1994	525	27	23
1985 to 1989	929	33	19
1980 to 1984	1,067	75	23
1975 to 1979	1,737	68	73
1970 to 1974	2,014	166	83
1960 to 1969	3,315	255	108
1950 to 1959	3,789	295	128
1940 to 1949	2,145	276	80
1930 to 1939	1,435	243	81
1920 to 1929	1,262	169	46
1919 or earlier	2,219	218	32
Median	1958	1950	1959
Metropolitan/Nonmetropolitan Areas			
Inside metropolitan statistical areas	14,885	1,469	606
In central cities	6,039	1,138	318
Suburbs	8,846	330	288

[Continued]

★ 348 ★

Introductory Characteristics: Elderly Householder
[Continued]

Characteristics	Total occupied units	Household characteristics	
		Black	Hispanic
Outside metropolitan statistical areas	5,553	356	91
Regions			
Northeast	4,540	340	122
Midwest	4,976	342	40
South	7,048	1,006	262
West	3,874	138	272
Urbanized Areas			
Inside urbanized areas	11,674	1,322	525
In central cities of (P)MSA's	5,935	1,128	314
Urban fringe	5,739	194	211
Outside urbanized areas	8,764	503	172
Other urban	3,036	197	90
Rural	5,729	306	82
Place Size			
Less than 2,500 persons	1,276	40	13
2,500 to 9,999 persons	2,345	93	77
10,000 to 19,999 persons	1,988	133	50
20,000 to 49,999 persons	2,632	178	95
50,000 to 99,999 persons	1,851	100	99
100,000 to 249,999 persons	1,261	204	66
250,000 to 499,999 persons	998	200	70
500,000 to 999,999 persons	885	226	35
1,000,000 persons or more	1,361	345	105

Source: "Introductory Characteristics—Occupied Units with Elderly Householder." *American Housing Survey for the United States in 1993,* February 1995, p. 314. *Note:* 1. For mobile home, oldest category is 1939 or older.

★ 349 ★

Elderly Occupants

Mortgage Characteristics: Elderly Householder. Part 1

[Numbers in thousands. Consistent with the 1990 Census. ... means not applicable or sample too small. - means zero or rounds to zero.]

Characteristics	Total occupied units	Household characteristics	
		Black	Hispanic
Total	15,767	1,153	448
Mortgages currently on Property			
None, owned free and clear	12,873	811	306
With mortgage or land contract	2,894	342	142
One mortgage or land contract	2,553	293	124
Two mortgages	189	40	2
Three or more mortgages	4	-	-
Number of mortgages not reported	148	9	16
OWNERS WITH ONE OR MORE MORTGAGES			
Total	2,894	342	142
Type of Primary Mortgage			
FHA	290	84	13
VA	188	27	4
Farmers Home Administration	38	13	-
Other types	2,098	187	90
Don't know	102	19	13
Not reported	178	12	20
Lower Cost State and Local Mortgages			
State or local program used	262	75	15
Not used	2,444	256	107
Not reported	188	11	20
Mortgage Origination			
Placed new mortgage(s)	2,417	284	122
Primary obtained when property acquired	1,481	172	87
Obtained later	926	112	35
Date not reported	11	-	-
Assumed	137	11	2
Wrap-around	-	-	-
Combination of the above	182	37	2
Origin not reported	158	9	16

[Continued]

★ 349 ★

Mortgage Characteristics: Elderly Householder. Part 1
[Continued]

Characteristics	Total occupied units	Household characteristics	
		Black	Hispanic
Payment Plan of Primary Mortgage			
Fixed payment, self amortizing	1,970	230	97
Adjustable rate mortgage	195	9	7
Adjustable term mortgage	17	2	-
Graduated payment mortgage	13	2	-
Balloon	24	-	-
Other	42	14	-
Combination of the above	17	-	-
Not reported	616	84	38
Payment Plan of Secondary Mortgage			
Units with two or more mortgages	193	40	2
Fixed payment, self amortizing	84	16	-
Adjustable rate mortgage	23	4	-
Adjustable term mortgage	6	-	-
Graduated payment mortgage	-	-	-
Balloon	-	-	-
Other	-	-	-
Combination of the above	11	-	-
Not reported	68	19	2
Lenders of Primary and Secondary Mortgages			
Only borrowed from farm(s)	2,510	280	101
Only borrowed from seller	40	11	4
Only borrowed from other individual(s)	52	11	15
Borrowed from a farm and seller	5	-	-
Borrowed from a firm and other individual	9	5	-
Borrowed from seller and other individual	-	-	-
One or both sources not reported	279	37	22
Items Included in Primary Mortgage Payment			
Principal and interest only	1,469	147	70
Property taxes	1,101	150	44
Property insurance	894	152	35
Other	78	11	5
Not reported	252	25	26

[Continued]

★ 349 ★

Mortgage Characteristics: Elderly Householder. Part 1

[Continued]

Characteristics	Total occupied units	Household characteristics	
		Black	Hispanic
Year Primary Mortgage Originated			
1990 to 1994	857	57	48
1985 to 1989	568	72	34
1980 to 1984	269	21	10
1975 to 1979	396	73	6
1970 to 1974	299	45	16
1960 to 1969	240	46	7
1950 to 1959	32	4	-
1949 or earlier	5	-	-
Not reported	226	23	21
Median	1986	1979	1988

Source: "Mortgage Characteristics-Occupied Units with Elderly Householder." *American Housing Survey for the United States in 1993,* February 1995, p. 348.

★ 350 ★

Elderly Occupants

Mortgage Characteristics: Elderly Householder. Part 2

[Numbers in thousands. Consistent with the 1990 Census. ...means not applicable or sample too small. - means zero or rounds to zero.]

Characteristics	Total occupied units	Household characteristics	
		Black	Hispanic
OWNERS WITH ONE OR MORE MORTGAGES			
Term of Primary Mortgage at Origination or Assumption			
Less than 8 years	47	2	15
8 to 12 years	63	6	3
13 to 17 years	198	7	8
18 to 22 years	152	8	5
23 to 27 years	146	9	10
28 to 32 years	911	128	44
33 years or more	54	17	-
Variable	102	7	5
Not reported	1,220	143	54
Median	29	30	28

[Continued]

★ 350 ★

Mortgage Characteristics: Elderly Householder. Part 2

[Continued]

Characteristics	Total occupied units	Household characteristics	
		Black	Hispanic
Remaining Years Mortgaged			
Less than 8 years	693	106	45
8 to 12	462	45	11
13 to 17	405	50	18
18 to 22	174	9	11
23 to 27	205	24	10
28 to 32	235	14	12
33 years or more	-	-	-
Variable	132	7	6
Not reported	587	86	28
Median	12	10	12
Current Interest Rate			
Less than 6 percent	108	10	5
6 to 7.9	298	12	14
8 to 9.9	450	26	26
10 to 11.9	121	16	2
12 to 13.9	43	2	-
14 to 15.9	21	3	-
16 to 17.9	2	-	-
18 to 19.9	2	2	-
20 percent or more	-	-	-
Not reported	1,849	271	94
Median	8.5	9.0	8.3
Total Outstanding Principal Amount			
Less than $10,000	278	33	15
$10,000 to $19,999	212	14	8
$20,000 to $29,999	130	7	8
$30,000 to $39,999	129	10	6
$40,000 to $49,999	86	2	8
$50,000 to $59,999	61	-	-
$60,000 to $69,999	26	-	-
$70,000 to $79,999	25	2	-
$80,000 to $99,999	35	2	2
$100,000 to $119,999	27	-	-
$120,000 to $149,999	14	-	2
$150,000 to $199,999	15	-	-
$200,000 to $249,999	2	-	-
$250,000 to $299,999	3	-	-
$300,000 or more	2	-	-
Not reported	1,849	271	94

[Continued]

★ 350 ★

Mortgage Characteristics: Elderly Householder. Part 2

[Continued]

Characteristics	Total occupied units	Household characteristics	
		Black	Hispanic
Median	22,486	11,696	21,935
Current Total Loan as Percent of Value			
Less than 20 percent	395	32	23
30 to 39	244	21	6
40 to 59	177	9	14
60 to 79	141	9	4
80 to 89	25	-	-
90 to 99	34	-	2
100 percent or more	30	-	-
Not reported	1,849	271	94
Median	30.5	23.2	23.8

Source: "Mortgage Characteristics—Occupied Units with Elderly Householder." *American Housing Survey for the United States in 1993*, February 1995, p. 350.

★ 351 ★

Elderly Occupants

Movers: Elderly Householder

[Numbers in thousands. Consistent with the 1990 Census. ...means not applicable or sample too small. - means zero or rounds to zero.]

Characteristics	Total occupied units	Household characteristics	
		Black	Hispanic
UNITS WHERE HOUSEHOLDER MOVED DURING PAST YEAR			
Total	884	75	37
Location of Previous Unit			
Inside same (P)MSA	407	48	29
In central city(s)	169	38	13
Not in central city(s)	238	10	17
Inside different (P)MSA in same state	98	4	3
In central city(s)	41	4	-
Not in central city(s)	56	-	3
Inside different (P)MSA in different state	127	8	5

[Continued]

★ 351 ★

Movers: Elderly Householder
[Continued]

Characteristics	Total occupied units	Household characteristics	
		Black	Hispanic
In central city(s)	57	5	5
Not in central city(s)	70	3	-
Outside any metropolitan area	245	13	-
Same state	181	11	-
Different state	65	2	-
Different nation	7	2	-
Structure Type of Previous Residence			
Moved within United States	878	73	37
House	476	25	10
Apartment	329	48	27
Mobile home	63	-	-
Other	10	-	-
Tenure of Previous Residence			
House, apt., mobile home in United States	868	73	37
Owner occupied	413	7	4
Renter occupied	455	66	33
Persons - Previous residence			
House, apt., mobile home in United States	868	73	37
1 person	361	36	13
2 persons	367	19	13
3 persons	75	15	7
4 persons	19	-	-
5 persons	11	-	2
6 persons	9	-	-
7 persons or more	4	-	-
Not reported	22	2	3
Median	1.7	1.5-	...
Previous Home Owned or Rented by Someone Who Moved Here			
House, apt., mobile home in United States	868	73	37
Owned or rented by mover	779	65	29
Owned or rented by other	62	5	5

[Continued]

★ 351 ★

Movers: Elderly Householder
[Continued]

Characteristics	Total occupied units	Household characteristics	
		Black	Hispanic
By a relative	37	3	2
By a nonrelative	22	2	-
Not reported	3	-	3
Not reported	27	2	3
Change in Housing Costs			
House, apt., mobile home in United States	868	73	37
Increased with move	324	30	11
Stayed about the same	219	20	13
Decreased	262	16	8
Don't know	47	5	3
Not reported	16	2	3

Source: "Previous Unit of Recent Movers—Occupied Units with Elderly Householder." *American Housing Survey for the United States in 1993*, February 1995, p. 334.

★ 352 ★

Elderly Occupants

Neighborhoods: Elderly Householder

[Numbers in thousands. Consistent with the 1990 Census. ...means not applicable or sample too small. - means zero or rounds to zero.]

Characteristics	Total occupied units	Household characteristics	
		Black	Hispanic
Total	20,438	1,825	696
Overall Opinion of Neighborhood			
1 (worst)	230	57	13
2	150	18	3
3	164	18	17
4	241	46	12
5	1,366	221	39
6	756	109	39
7	1,451	137	45
8	3,973	331	157
9	2,515	177	59
10 (best)	9,006	637	293
No neighborhood	231	6	5
Not reported	354	66	16

[Continued]

★ 352 ★

Neighborhoods: Elderly Householder
[Continued]

Characteristics	Total occupied units	Household characteristics	
		Black	Hispanic
Neighborhood Conditions			
With neighborhood	19,853	1,752	676
No problems	14,113	1,136	480
With problems[1]	5,681	603	189
Crime	846	179	28
Noise	1,203	135	58
Traffic	969	55	47
Litter or housing deterioration	812	116	23
Poor city or county services	187	32	9
Undesirable commercial, institutional, industrial	273	16	12
People	1,834	194	56
Other	1,555	156	44
Type of problem not reported	77	11	-
Presence of problems not reported	60	14	7
Description of Area Within 300 Feet[1,2]			
Single-family detached houses	1,803	212	82
Only single-family detached	...	...	...
single-family attached or 1 to 3 story multiunit	2,684	322	131
4 to 6 story multiunit	817	95	55
7 stories or more multiunit	509	75	48
Mobile homes	26	3	-
Residential parking lots	1,392	206	74
Commercial, institutional, or industrial	1,276	158	50
Body of water	246	20	6
Open space, park, woods, farm, or ranch	844	104	37
4+ lane highway, railroad, or airport	375	56	16
Other	280	50	24
Not observed or not reported	470	35	13
Age of Other Residential Buildings Within 300 Feet[2]			
Older	451	55	22
About the same	2,708	309	139
Newer	104	12	13
Very mixed	544	86	29
No other residential buildings	213	26	2
Not reported	473	40	13

[Continued]

★ 352 ★

Neighborhoods: Elderly Householder

[Continued]

Characteristics	Total occupied units	Household characteristics	
		Black	Hispanic
Mobile Homes in Group			
Mobile homes	1,266	45	28
1 to 6	670	45	14
7 to 20	53	-	-
21 or more	544	-	13
Other Buildings Vandalized or With Interior Exposed[2]			
None	3,710	392	187
1 building	72	19	6
More than 1 building	91	57	5
No buildings within 300 feet	104	12	-
Not reported	516	47	20
Bars on Windows of Buildings[2]			
With other buildings within 300 feet	3,874	469	199
No bars on windows	3,235	287	140
1 building with bars	111	21	4
2 or more buildings with bars	503	155	55
Not reported	25	5	-
Condition of Streets[2]			
No repairs needed	3,216	340	149
Minor repairs needed	713	133	48
Major repairs needed	57	18	9
No streets within 300 feet	52	5	-
Not reported	455	32	13
Trash, Litter, or Junk on Streets or any Properties[2]			
None	3,235	292	140
Minor accumulation	768	178	65
Major accumulation	46	26	-
Not reported	445	32	13

Source: "Household Composition—Occupied Units with Elderly Householder." *American Housing Survey for the United States in 1993,* February 1995, p. 328. *Notes:* 1. Figures may not add to total because more than one category may apply to a unit. 2. Limited to multiunit structures.

★ 353 ★

Elderly Occupants

Reasons for Move: Elderly Householder

[Numbers in thousands. Consistent with the 1990 Census. ...means not applicable or sample too small. - means zero or rounds to zero.]

Characteristics	Total occupied units	Household characteristics	
		Black	Hispanic
RESPONDENT MOVED DURING PAST YEAR			
Total	950	88	41
Reasons for Leaving Previous Unit[1]			
Private displacement	44	7	-
Owner to move into unit	4	-	-
To be converted to condominium or cooperative	-	-	-
Closed for repairs	-	-	-
Other	19	3	-
Not reported	21	4	-
Government displacement	8	-	1
Government wanted building or land	2	-	-
Unit unfit for occupancy	-	-	-
Other	1	-	1
Not reported	5	-	-
Disaster loss (fire, flood, etc.)	6	2	-
New job or job transfer	16	-	-
To be closer to work/school/other	36	2	3
Other, financial/employment related	42	2	-
To establish own household	35	5	-
Needed larger house or apartment	42	7	3
Married	6	-	-
Widowed, divorced or separated	87	5	-
Other, family/person related	245	14	6
Wanted better home	79	19	7
Change from owner to renter	53	-	-
Change from renter to owner	12	3	3
Wanted lower rent or maintenance	106	12	6
Other housing related reasons	125	6	7
Other	266	25	15
Not reported	37	9	3
Choice of Present Neighborhood[1]			
Convenient to job	28	2	2
Convenient to friends or relatives	324	19	15
Convenient to leisure activities	51	-	3
Convenient to public transportation	43	2	2
Good schools	4	-	-
Other public services	29	2	2

[Continued]

★ 353 ★

Reasons for Move: Elderly Householder
[Continued]

Characteristics	Total occupied units	Household characteristics	
		Black	Hispanic
Looks/design of neighborhood	161	10	2
House was most important consideration	187	17	7
Other	344	44	18
Not reported	43	9	3
Neighborhood Search			
Looked at just this neighborhood	528	46	24
Looked at other neighborhood(s)	377	32	14
Not reported	45	9	3
Choice of Present Home[1]			
Financial reasons	278	27	10
Room layout/design	202	7	7
Kitchen	7	-	-
Size	168	13	9
Exterior appearance	67	5	2
Yard/trees/view	75	2	-
Quality of construction	58	5	2
Only one available	88	10	6
Other	375	35	13
Home Search			
Now in house	383	29	16
Looked at only this unit	22	2	-
Looked at houses or mobile homes only	259	15	8
Looked at apartments too	75	5	5
Search not reported	26	7	3
Now in mobile home	103	2	3
Looked at only this unit	11	-	-
Looked at houses or mobile homes only	38	2	-
Looked at apartments too	50	-	3
Search reported	5	-	-
Now in apartment	465	56	23
Looked at only this unit	72	8	-
Looked at apartments only	70	12	2
Looked at houses or mobile homes too	307	34	20
Search not reported	15	2	-
Recent Mover Comparison to Previous Home			
Better home	388	47	25

[Continued]

★ 353 ★

Reasons for Move: Elderly Householder
[Continued]

Characteristics	Total occupied units	Household characteristics	
		Black	Hispanic
Worse home	169	6	5
About the same	349	25	8
Not reported	44	9	3
Recent Mover Comparison to Previous Neighborhood			
Better neighborhood	301	33	24
Worse neighborhood	119	9	-
About the same	397	26	8
Same neighborhood	88	10	6
Not reported	46	9	3

Source: "Reason for Move and Choice of Current Residence—Occupied Units with Elderly Householder." *American Housing Survey for the United States in 1993*, February 1995, p. 336. *Notes:* 1. Figures may not add to total because more than one category may apply to a unit.

★ 354 ★

Elderly Occupants

Repairs and Improvements: Elderly Householder

[Numbers in thousands. Consistent with the 1990 Census. ...means not applicable or sample too small. - means zero or rounds to zero.]

Characteristics	Total occupied units	Household characteristics	
		Black	Hispanic
Total	15,767	1,153	448
Repairs, Improvements, Alterations in Last 2 Years			
Roof replaced (all or part)	2,589	236	84
Mostly done by household	363	26	12
Mostly done by others	2,188	207	69
Workers not reported	38	3	3
Costing $500 or more	1,806	157	64
Costing less than $500	428	50	12
Cost not reported	355	6	8
Roof replacement not reported	161	6	8
Additions built	315	26	18
Mostly done by household	88	-	7
Mostly done by others	217	24	10

[Continued]

★ 354 ★

Repairs and Improvements: Elderly Householder
[Continued]

Characteristics	Total occupied units	Household characteristics	
		Black	Hispanic
Workers not reported	10	2	-
Costing $500 or more	242	14	18
Costing less than $500	29	12	-
Cost not reported	44	-	-
Additions not reported	140	6	8
Kitchen remodeled or added	764	65	19
Mostly done by household	222	7	2
Mostly done by others	536	58	17
Workers not reported	6	-	-
Costing $500 or more	532	45	13
Costing less than $500	124	15	4
Cost not reported	109	5	2
Kitchen remodeled or added not reported	132	2	8
Bathroom remodeled or added	810	68	36
Mostly done by household	259	17	14
Mostly done by others	539	51	21
Workers not reported	13	-	-
Costing $500 or more	481	44	19
Costing less than $500	218	22	6
Cost not reported	112	2	10
Bathroom remodeled or added not reported	140	2	8
Siding replaced or added	644	35	17
Mostly done by householder	112	9	6
Mostly done by others	523	26	9
Workers not reported	9	-	3
Costing $500 or more	436	28	5
Costing less than $500	113	-	6
Cost not reported	96	7	6
Siding replaced or added not reported	141	2	8
Storm doors/windows bought and installed	1,333	125	20
Mostly done by householder	349	17	7
Mostly done by others	970	108	11
Workers not reported	14	-	3
Costing $500 or more	564	56	10
Costing less than $500	603	50	2
Cost not reported	166	18	8
Storm doors/windows bought and installed not reported	136	2	8

[Continued]

★ 354 ★

Repairs and Improvements: Elderly Householder
[Continued]

Characteristics	Total occupied units	Household characteristics	
		Black	Hispanic
Major equipment replaced or added	1,313	50	37
Mostly done by householder	134	2	6
Mostly done by others	1,157	48	29
Workers not reported	22	-	3
Costing $500 or more	1,023	34	22
Costing less than $500	162	12	9
Cost not reported	129	5	5
Major equipment replaced or added not reported	165	7	11
Insulation added	483	28	17
Mostly done by household	127	5	2
Mostly done by others	328	20	9
Workers not reported	28	2	6
Costing $500 or more	108	3	2
Costing less than $500	230	14	7
Cost not reported	146	11	8
Insulation added not reported	166	2	11
Other major work[1]	2,166	162	59
Mostly done by household	373	22	10
Mostly done by others	1,733	138	46
Workers not reported	59	2	3
Other major work not reported	170	4	16
Government Subsidy for Repairs			
Units with major repairs the last 2 years	6,647	503	182
Received low-interest loan or grant	145	30	4
No low-interest loan or grant	6,360	457	176
Not reported	142	16	2

Source: "Repairs, Improvements, and Alterations—Occupied Units with Elderly Householder." *American Housing Survey for the United States in 1993*, February 1995, p. 352. *Notes:* 1. Includes other major repairs, alterations, or improvements totaling over $500 each.

★355★

Elderly Occupants

Unit and Lot Size: Elderly Householder

[Numbers in thousands. Consistent with the 1990 Census. ...means not applicable or sample too small. - means zero or rounds to zero.]

Characteristics	Total occupied units	Household characteristics	
		Black	Hispanic
Total	20,438	1,825	696
Rooms			
1 room	109	16	8
2 rooms	242	36	23
3 rooms	1,973	262	87
4 rooms	3,763	367	172
5 rooms	5,147	440	174
6 rooms	4,557	371	115
7 rooms	2,496	191	73
8 rooms	1,231	75	27
9 rooms	524	33	16
10 rooms or more	396	31	3
Median	5.3	5.0	4.8
Bedrooms			
None	222	29	16
1	2,789	323	129
2	7,324	592	270
3	7,813	647	226
4 or more	2,291	234	55
Median	2.5	2.4	2.3
Complete Bathrooms			
None	130	36	3
1	10,277	1,220	425
1 and one-half	3,625	307	92
2 or more	6,406	261	177
Square Footage of Unit			
Single detached and mobile homes	14,948	1,142	436
Less than 500	165	22	17
500 to 749	624	118	27
750 to 999	1,480	163	57
1,000 to 1,499	3,907	314	102
1,500 to 1,999	3,062	188	95
2,000 to 2,499	1,998	86	47
2,500 to 2,999	1,082	31	17
3,000 to 3,999	956	37	20
4,000 or more	570	39	14

[Continued]

★ 355 ★

Unit and Lot Size: Elderly Householder
[Continued]

Characteristics	Total occupied units	Household characteristics	
		Black	Hispanic
Not reported	1,104	145	41
Median	1,622	1,311	1,473
Lot Size			
Less than one-eighth acre	1,829	199	83
One-eighth up to one-quarter acre	3,253	183	119
One-quarter up to one-half acre	2,265	136	45
One-half up to one acre	1,376	67	19
1 to 4 acres	2,075	171	33
5 to 9 acres	320	10	-
10 acres or more	1,059	41	5
Don't know	2,465	283	110
Not reported	1,303	208	65
Median	.36	.29	.20
Persons Per Room			
0.50 or less	18,856	1,520	572
0.51 to 1.00	1,498	282	104
1.01 to 1.50	80	17	16
1.51 or more	24	5	5
Square Feet Per Person			
Single detached and mobile homes	14,948	1,142	436
Less than 200	100	25	21
200 to 299	308	80	18
300 to 399	530	99	22
400 to 499	824	83	11
500 to 599	955	71	32
600 to 699	1,213	84	55
700 to 799	1,200	106	33
800 to 899	944	67	49
900 to 999	1,057	63	29
1,000 to 1,499	3,430	170	69
1,500 or more	3,282	150	55
Not reported	1,104	145	41
Median	980	753	811

Source: "Size of Unit and Lot—Occupied Units with Elderly Householder." *American Housing Survey for the United States in 1993*, February 1995, p. 318.

★ 356 ★

Elderly Occupants

Value and Price: Elderly Householder

Characteristic	Total occupied units	Household characteristics	
		Black	Hispanic
Total	15,767	1,153	448
Value			
Less than $10,000	425	45	9
$10,000 to $19,999	769	113	17
$20,000 to $29,999	897	161	11
$30,000 to $39,999	1,075	148	42
$40,000 to $49,999	1,408	120	42
$50,000 to $59,999	1,233	91	41
$60,000 to $69,999	1,302	109	37
$70,000 to $79,999	1,248	68	28
$80,000 to $99,999	1,901	99	56
$100,000 to $119,999	1,236	60	23
$120,000 to $149,999	1,239	57	33
$150,000 to $199,999	1,393	51	49
$200,000 to $249,999	619	15	11
$250,000 to $299,999	402	7	31
$300,000 or more	620	9	19
Median	76,202	49,112	79,021
Ratio of Value to Current Income[1]			
Less than 1.5	2,395	211	59
1.5 to 1.9	1,170	74	15
2.0 to 2.4	1,313	105	31
2.5 to 2.9	1,208	82	24
3.0 to 3.9	2,247	152	44
4.0 to 4.9	1,591	101	37
5.0 or more	5,707	417	235
Zero or negative income	137	11	3
Median	3.8	3.7	5.0+
Other Activities on Property[2]			
Commercial establishment	212	6	9
Medical or dental office	73	-	2
Neither	15,508	1,147	439
Year Unit Acquired			
1990 to 1994	1,095	40	38
1985 to 1989	1,635	61	50
1980 to 1984	1,231	59	35
1975 to 1979	1,619	116	56
1970 to 1974	1,568	126	44

[Continued]

★ 356 ★

Value and Price: Elderly Householder
[Continued]

Characteristic	Total occupied units	Household characteristics	
		Black	Hispanic
1960 to 1969	3,281	335	82
1950 to 1959	3,203	229	75
1940 to 1949	1,335	114	34
1939 or earlier	380	30	13
Not reported	420	44	20
Median	1968	1965	1971
First Time Owners			
First home ever owned	5,814	751	211
Not first home	9,710	386	218
Not reported	243	17	19
Purchase Price			
Home purchased or built	14,726	1,025	417
Less than $10,000	2,687	279	81
$10,000 to $19,999	3,387	289	86
$20,000 to $29,999	1,621	81	37
$30,000 to $39,999	1,134	57	40
$40,000 to $49,999	774	31	23
$50,000 to $59,999	573	13	18
$60,000 to $69,999	428	14	14
$70,000 to $79,999	321	10	13
$80,000 to $99,999	448	7	14
$100,000 to $119,999	219	4	3
$120,000 to $149,999	264	5	3
$150,000 to $199,999	247	-	9
$200,000 to $249,999	76	-	5
$250,000 to $299,999	43	-	2
$300,000 or more	60	3	-
Not reported	2,444	232	66
Median	20,411	14,078	22,140
Received as inheritance or gift	621	83	11
Not reported	420	44	20
Major Source of Down Payment			
Home purchased or built	14,726	1,025	417
Sale of previous home	4,968	127	94
Savings or cash on hand	6,503	571	218
Sale of other investment	96	-	2
Borrowing, other than mortgage on this property	548	57	27
Inheritance or gift	189	15	2

[Continued]

★ 356 ★

Value and Price: Elderly Householder
[Continued]

Characteristic	Total occupied units	Household characteristics	
		Black	Hispanic
Land where building built used for financing	79	10	-
Other	625	47	23
No down payment	1,228	134	34
Not reported	491	64	17

Source: "Value, Price, and Source of down Payment-Occupied Units with Elderly Householder." *American Housing Survey for the United States in 1993*, February 1995, p. 346. *Notes:* 1. Beginning with 1989 this item uses current income in its calculation. 2. Figures may not add to total because more than one category may apply to a unit.

Equipment and Plumbing

★ 357 ★

Equipment and Plumbing: Black-Occupied Housing, 1993

[Numbers in thousands. Consistent with the 1990 Census. ... means not applicable or sample too small. - means zero or rounds to zero.]

Characteristic	Total occupied units	Tenure		Housing unit characteristics			
		Owner	Renter	New construction 4 yrs.	Mobile homes	Physical problems	
						Severe	Moderate
Total	11,128	4,788	6,340	334	337	385	1,154
Equipment[1]							
Lacking complete kitchen facilities	193	59	133	-	5	78	106
With complete kitchen (sink, refrigerator and burners)	10,935	4,729	6,207	334	332	306	1,048
Kitchen sink	11,022	4,744	6,278	334	337	318	1,114
Refrigerator	11,046	4,777	6,269	334	334	354	1,102
Less than 5 years old	4,263	1,819	2,444	283	142	115	370
Age not reported	278	36	242	-	5	10	10
Burners and oven	11,044	4,775	6,268	334	335	356	1,107
Less than 5 years old	3,489	1,508	1,981	294	114	109	271
Age not reported	274	40	234	5	3	-	19
Burners only	17	8	9	-	2	3	5
Less than 5 years old	3	-	2	-	-	-	3
Age not reported	5	5	-	-	2	3	2
Oven only	1	-	1	-	-	-	1
Less than 5 years old	1	-	1	-	-	-	1
Age not reported	-	-	-	-	-	-	-
Neither burners nor oven	67	5	62	-	-	26	41
Dishwasher	3,019	1,536	1,483	215	35	53	74

[Continued]

★ 357 ★

Equipment and Plumbing: Black-Occupied Housing, 1993
[Continued]

Characteristic	Total occupied units	Tenure		Housing unit characteristics			
				New construction 4 yrs.	Mobile homes	Physical problems	
		Owner	Renter			Severe	Moderate
Less than 5 years old	1,068	547	522	199	9	19	26
Age not reported	150	21	128	5	4	-	3
Washing machine	6,716	4,175	2,542	266	226	163	621
Less than 5 years old	2,733	1,555	1,178	208	97	42	225
Age not reported	103	35	68	-	-	9	8
Clothes dryer	5,127	3,394	1,733	244	154	96	337
Less than 5 years old	2,027	1,219	808	183	59	16	131
Age not reported	82	26	56	4	4	5	8
Disposal in kitchen sink	3,169	1,216	1,954	194	7	55	97
Less than 5 years old	1,136	455	682	173	-	16	28
Age not reported	196	21	174	-	-	-	7
Air conditioning:							
Central	3,841	1,866	1,974	261	125	50	88
1 room unit	2,503	1,002	1,501	34	117	82	376
2 room units	1,001	570	431	2	35	36	129
3 room units or more	295	222	73	-	-	9	26
Main Heating Equipment							
Warm-air furnace	5,300	2,602	2,698	201	197	110	270
Steam or hot water system	1,931	591	1,340	9	-	115	146
Electric heat pump	846	367	479	69	35	10	22
Built-in electric units	679	156	523	24	9	5	22
Floor, wall, or other built-in hot air units without ducts	741	256	485	14	19	7	58
Room heaters with flue	373	171	202	-	12	25	27
Room heaters without flue	585	306	279	7	35	42	543
Portable electric heaters	112	45	67	4	9	7	15
Stoves	236	145	91	-	12	35	18
Fireplaces with inserts	21	19	2	3	2	-	-
Fireplaces without inserts	25	17	8	-	-	3	6
Other	157	84	73	3	3	14	14
None	124	31	93	-	4	11	13
Plumbing							
With all plumbing facilities	10,906	4,688	6,217	334	333	162	1,154
Lacking some plumbing facilities[1]	45	7	38	-	-	45	-
No hot piped water	12	4	7	-	-	12	-
No bathtub nor shower	33	2	30	-	-	33	-
No flush toilet	36	2	34	-	-	36	-
No plumbing facilities for exclusive use	177	93	84	-	4	177	-

[Continued]

★ 357 ★

Equipment and Plumbing: Black-Occupied Housing, 1993
[Continued]

| Characteristic | Total occupied units | Tenure | | Housing unit characteristics | | | |
| | | Owner | Renter | New construction 4 yrs. | Mobile homes | Physical problems | |
						Severe	Moderate
Source of Water							
Public system or private company	10,439	4,269	6,170	299	222	318	1,047
Well serving 1 to 5 units	547	451	96	32	113	48	88
Drilled	400	341	59	25	67	32	64
Dug	122	88	35	7	42	16	23
Not reported	25	23	2	-	4	-	-
Other	142	68	74	3	2	18	19
Means of Sewage Disposal							
Public sewer	9,964	3,864	6,100	281	113	304	937
Septic tank, cesspool, chemical toilet	1,113	894	219	53	224	30	217
Other	51	30	21	-	-	51	-

Source: "Selected Equipment and Plumbing—Occupied Units with Black Householder," *American Housing Survey for the United States in 1993*, February 1995, p. 196. *Notes:* 1. Figures may not add to total because more than one category may apply to a unit.

★ 358 ★

Equipment and Plumbing

Failures in Equipment: Black-Occupied Housing

[Numbers in thousands. Consistent with the 1990 Census. ... means not applicable or sample too small. - means zero or rounds to zero.]

| Characteristic | Total occupied units | Tenure | | Housing unit characteristics | | | |
| | | Owner | Renter | New construction 4 yrs. | Mobile homes | Physical problems | |
						Severe	Moderate
Total	11,128	4,788	6,340	334	337	385	1,154
Water Supply Stoppage							
With hot and cold piped water	11,063	4,754	6,309	334	337	319	1,154
No stoppage in last 3 months	10,481	4,628	5,853	334	311	261	1,034
With stoppage in last 3 months	446	86	360	-	21	45	77
No stoppage lasting 6 hours or more	137	31	106	-	9	3	12
1 time lasting 6 hours or more	191	42	149	-	12	22	33
2 times	35	-	35	-	-	7	11
3 times	28	-	28	-	-	7	4
4 times or more	21	-	21	-	-	3	4
Number of times not reported	34	13	21	-	-	3	12
Stoppage not reported	137	40	96	-	5	14	43

[Continued]

★ 358 ★

Failures in Equipment: Black-Occupied Housing

[Continued]

Characteristic	Total occupied units	Tenure		Housing unit characteristics			
		Owner	Renter	New construction 4 yrs.	Mobile homes	Physical problems	
						Severe	Moderate
Flush Toilet Breakdowns							
With one or more flush toilets	11,039	4,756	6,283	334	337	295	1,154
With at least one working toilet at all times in last 3 months	10,081	4,518	5,562	325	307	228	895
None working some time in last 3 months	906	230	676	9	28	55	259
No breakdowns lasting 6 hours or more	190	43	147	-	6	6	28
1 time lasting 6 hours or more	425	128	297	2	4	23	91
2 times	134	29	105	4	8	9	24
3 times	47	5	43	-	3	2	45
4 times or more	61	10	51	3	-	14	47
Number of times not reported	50	16	34	-	8	-	23
Breakdowns not reported	52	8	44	-	2	12	-
Sewage Disposal Breakdowns							
With public sewer	9,964	3,864	6,100	281	113	304	937
No breakdowns in last 3 months	9,732	3,773	5,959	281	113	280	902
With breakdowns in last 3 months	233	91	142	-	-	24	35
No breakdowns lasting 6 hours or more	44	14	31	-	-	6	7
1 time lasting 6 hours or more	120	51	69	-	-	8	17
2 times	44	15	29	-	-	6	2
3 times	14	7	7	-	-	2	5
4 times or more	10	4	6	-	-	-	3
With septic tank or cesspool	1,113	894	219	53	224	30	217
No breakdowns in last 3 months	1,059	849	210	53	217	21	206
With breakdowns in last 3 months	54	45	9	-	8	10	9
No breakdowns lasting 6 hours or more	12	12	-	-	3	7	-
1 time lasting 6 hours or more	36	29	7	-	4	-	7
2 times	4	4	-	-	-	2	-
3 times	-	-	-	-	-	-	-
4 times or more	2	-	2	-	-	-	2
Heating Problems							
With heating equipment and occupied last winter	10,005	4,844	5,361	279	316	358	1,063
Not uncomfortably cold for 24 hours or more last winter	8,910	4,368	4,604	253	283	203	871
Uncomfortable cold for 24 hours or more last winter[1]	1,077	333	744	26	33	156	212
Equipment breakdowns	385	94	291	10	12	111	62
No breakdown lasting 6 hours or more	19	10	9	-	-	3	-
1 time lasting 6 hours or more	163	60	103	8	9	9	25
2 times	91	11	80	4	3	8	17
3 times	27	-	27	-	-	27	-
4 times or more	59	12	47	-	-	59	-
Number of times not reported	25	-	25	-	-	4	19

[Continued]

★ 358 ★

Failures in Equipment: Black-Occupied Housing
[Continued]

Characteristic	Total occupied units	Tenure		Housing unit characteristics			
		Owner	Renter	New construction 4 yrs.	Mobile homes	Physical problems	
						Severe	Moderate
Other causes	744	251	493	16	23	59	168
Utility interruption	127	89	38	9	15	3	17
Inadequate heating capacity	251	68	184	-	3	33	54
Inadequate insulation	128	16	112	-	-	10	38
Other	209	71	138	7	5	13	52
Not reported	29	7	22	-	-	-	7
Reason for discomfort not reported	9	2	6	-	-	2	-
Discomfort not reported	18	5	13	-	-	-	-
Electric Fuses and Circuit Breakers							
With electric wiring	11,126	4,786	6,340	334	337	383	1,154
No fuses or breakers blown in last 3 mo.	9,483	4,022	5,461	309	285	253	922
With fuses or breakers blown in last 3 mo.	1,539	726	813	25	51	122	224
1 time	721	352	369	12	40	26	93
2 times	328	168	161	4	-	37	54
3 times	163	66	97	6	5	15	31
4 times or more	249	99	150	-	4	41	35
Number of times not reported	78	41	37	3	2	5	10
Problem not reported or don't know	104	38	66	-	-	7	9

Source: "Failures in Equipment—Occupied Units with Black Householder," *American Housing Survey for the United States in 1993*, February 1995, p. 200. *Notes:* 1. Other causes and equipment breakdowns may not add to total as both may be reported.

Families in Households

★ 359 ★

Families in Households: Female Householders, Part 1-A

[Numbers in thousands except for averages and medians.]

Characteristic	Total	Age of householder					
		Under 20 years	20 to 24 years	25 to 29 years	30 to 34 years	35 to 39 years	40 to 44 years
BLACK-OTHER FAMILIES, FEMALE HOUSEHOLDER							
Tenure							
Families	3,825	58	359	498	657	643	440
Owner families	1,102	4	10	38	93	165	160

[Continued]

★ 359 ★

Families in Households: Female Householders, Part 1-A
[Continued]

Characteristic	Total	Age of householder					
		Under 20 years	20 to 24 years	25 to 29 years	30 to 34 years	35 to 39 years	40 to 44 years
Renter families	2,722	54	350	460	563	478	280
Size of Family							
Families	3,825	58	359	498	657	643	440
Two persons	1,362	29	153	133	186	194	172
Three persons	1,193	19	100	149	226	215	135
Four persons	657	11	67	112	119	122	67
Five persons	340	-	26	73	63	62	29
Six persons	129	-	10	19	22	21	23
Seven or more persons	144	-	2	13	40	30	15
Total persons	12,977	134	990	1,622	2,193	2,096	1,531
Average per family	3.39	(B)	2.76	3.26	3.34	3.26	3.48
Age of Own Children							
Families	3,825	58	359	498	657	643	440
With own children of any age	3,465	56	339	478	635	633	406
Under 25 years	3,004	56	339	478	633	633	396
Under 18 years	2,630	56	336	478	633	574	315
Under 12 years	2,021	56	336	470	563	344	159
Under 6 years	1,277	56	328	363	314	152	39
Under 3 years	708	52	246	177	147	57	14
Under 1 year	202	25	85	36	36	16	2
Six to 17 years	2,018	-	52	351	554	538	304
Total own children	7,021	68	526	1,012	1,407	1,267	899
Under 25 years	5,965	68	526	1,012	1,405	1,267	870
Under 18 years	4,907	68	523	1,012	1,393	1,017	562
Under 12 years	3,320	68	523	962	964	464	218
Under 6 years	1,715	68	471	522	415	159	44
Under 3 years	802	55	268	217	170	58	14
Under 1 year	192	19	75	39	39	15	2
Six to 17 years	3,192	-	52	491	978	858	518
Own Children Selected Ages							
Families with own children under 18	2,630	56	336	478	63	574	315
Under 6 only	613	56	285	127	79	36	11
Some under 6 and some 6 to 17	664	-	43	236	235	116	29
Six to 17 only	1,354	-	8	115	319	422	276
Total members	8,689	124	924	1,569	2,137	1,901	1,155

[Continued]

★ 359 ★

Families in Households: Female Householders, Part 1-A
[Continued]

Characteristic	Total	Age of householder					
		Under 20 years	20 to 24 years	25 to 29 years	30 to 34 years	35 to 39 years	40 to 44 years
Average per family	3.30	(B)	2.75	3.28	3.37	3.31	3.67
Own Children Under 18							
Families	3,825	58	359	498	657	643	440
Without own children under 18	1,194	2	23	20	24	69	125
With own children under 18	2,630	56	336	478	633	574	315
One under 18	1,068	29	154	133	184	234	157
Two under 18	871	19	105	153	232	200	117
Three under 18	417	8	55	109	114	94	23
Four under 18	188	-	21	62	56	33	15
Five under 18	48	-	-	15	25	7	2
Six or more under 18	38	-	-	6	22	6	2
Total own children under 18	4,907	68	523	1,012	1,393	1,017	562
Average per family	1.28	(B)	1.46	2.03	2.12	1.58	1.28
Average per family with children	1.87	(B)	1.55	2.12	2.20	1.77	1.78
Own Children 6 to 17 Years							
Families	3,825	58	359	498	657	643	440
Without own children 6 to 17 years	1,807	58	308	147	103	105	136
With own children 6 to 17 years	2,018	-	52	351	554	538	304
One child 6 to 17 years	1,064	-	45	193	241	256	160
Two children 6 to 17 years	632	-	5	107	193	187	106
Three children 6 to 17 years	246	-	-	45	74	79	35
Four or more children 6 to 17 years	76	-	2	6	47	16	3
Total children 6 to 17 years	3,192	-	52	491	978	858	518
Average per family	.83	(B)	.14	.99	1.49	1.33	1.18
Own Children 12 to 17 Years							
Families	3,825	58	359	498	657	643	440
Without own children 12 to 17 years	2,608	58	359	443	322	225	209
With own children 12 to 17 years	1,217	-	-	55	335	418	232
One child 12 to 17 years	885	-	-	50	247	280	152
Two children 12 to 17 years	269	-	-	5	70	109	68
Three children 12 to 17 years	52	-	-	-	15	22	12
Four or more children 12 to 17 years	10	-	-	-	3	7	-
Total own children 12 to 17 years	1,587	-	-	50	430	552	344
Average per family	.42	(B)	-	.10	.65	.86	.78

[Continued]

★ 359 ★

Families in Households: Female Householders, Part 1-A
[Continued]

Characteristic	Total	Age of householder					
		Under 20 years	20 to 24 years	25 to 29 years	30 to 34 years	35 to 39 years	40 to 44 years
Own Children 6 to 11 Years							
Families	3,825	58	359	498	657	643	440
Without own children 6 to 11 years	2,531	58	308	167	230	367	304
With own children 6 to 11 years	1,293	-	52	331	426	276	137
One child 6 to 11 years	889	-	45	193	275	209	110
Two children 6 to 11 years	338	-	5	105	127	63	24
Three children 6 to 11 years	47	-	-	29	14	4	-
Four or more children 6 to 11 years	20	-	2	4	11	-	3
Total own children 6 to 11 years	1,605	-	52	441	548	306	174
Average per family	.42	(B)	.14	.89	.84	.48	.39

Source: "Families by Type, Age of Own Children and Age, Race and Hispanic Origin of Householder: March 1994," Steve W. Rawlings and Arlene F. Saluter, *Household and Family Characteristics: March 1995*, pp. 23-24. *Note:* B = less than 75,000.

★ 360 ★

Families in Households

Families in Households: Female Householders, Part 1-B

[Numbers in thousands except for averages and medians.]

Characteristic	Age of householder					
	45 to 54 years	55 to 64 years	65 to 74 years	75 to 84 years	85 years and over	Median age
BLACK-OTHER FAMILIES, FEMALE HOUSEHOLDER						
Tenure						
Families	533	301	208	105	22	37.6
Owner families	222	181	134	76	19	48.1
Renter families	310	120	74	29	3	34.4
Size of Family						
Families	533	301	208	105	22	37.6
Two persons	218	118	90	59	11	39.7
Three persons	169	83	53	37	7	37.4
Four persons	60	49	42	6	1	35.8
Five persons	45	28	10	2	2	35.6
Six persons	20	10	5	-	-	38.3
Seven or more persons	22	13	8	1	-	37.8
Total persons	1,978	1,169	832	359	72	(X)

[Continued]

★ 360 ★

Families in Households: Female Householders, Part 1-B
[Continued]

Characteristic	Age of householder					
	45 to 54 years	55 to 64 years	65 to 74 years	75 to 84 years	85 years and over	Median age
Average per family	3.71	3.88	4.00	3.42	(B)	(X)
Age of Own Children						
Families	533	301	208	105	22	37.6
With own children of any age	469	228	146	59	15	36.8
Under 25 years	371	83	12	-	2	35.0
Under 18 years	201	29	6	-	2	33.5
Under 12 years	75	14	3	-	-	31.3
Under 6 years	14	9	2	-	-	28.5
Under 3 years	9	6	-	-	-	26.6
Under 1 year	1	-	-	-	-	24.5
Six to 17 years	190	23	4	-	2	35.5
Total own children	964	458	288	114	19	(X)
Under 25 years	664	127	24	-	1	(X)
Under 18 years	282	41	8	-	1	(X)
Under 12 years	98	20	3	-	-	(X)
Under 6 years	24	11	2	-	-	(X)
Under 3 years	13	6	-	-	-	(X)
Under 1 year	2	-	-	-	-	(X)
Six to 17 years	259	30	6	-	1	(X)
Own Children Selected Ages						
Families with own children under 18	201	29	6	-	2	33.5
Under 6 only	11	6	2	-	-	24.4
Some under 6 and some 6 to 17	3	2	-	-	-	31.1
Six to 17 only	187	21	4	-	2	37.8
Total members	734	119	18	-	9	(X)
Average per family	3.65	(B)	(B)	(B)	(B)	(X)
Own Children Under 18						
Families	533	301	208	105	22	37.6
Without own children under 18	332	272	202	105	20	55.1
With own children under 18	201	29	6	-	2	33.5
One under 18	152	19	4	-	2	35.7
Two under 18	33	10	1	-	-	33.4
Three under 18	14	-	-	-	-	31.6
Four under 18	2	-	-	-	-	31.0
Five under 18	-	-	-	-	-	(B)
Six or more under 18	1	-	-	-	-	(B)

[Continued]

★ 360 ★

Families in Households: Female Householders, Part 1-B
[Continued]

Characteristic	Age of householder					
	45 to 54 years	55 to 64 years	65 to 74 years	75 to 84 years	85 years and over	Median age
Total own children under 18	282	41	8	-	1	(X)
Average per family	.53	.14	.04	-	(B)	(X)
Average per family with children	1.40	(B)	(B)	(B)	(B)	(X)
Own Children 6 to 17 Years						
Families	533	301	208	105	22	37.6
Without own children 6 to 17 years	343	278	204	105	20	46.2
With own children 6 to 17 years	190	23	4	-	2	35.5
One child 6 to 17 years	146	19	2	-	2	36.0
Two children 6 to 17 years	29	4	1	-	-	35.3
Three children 6 to 17 years	14	-	-	-	-	35.3
Four or more children 6 to 17 years	1	-	-	-	-	33.2
Total children 6 to 17 years	259	30	6	-	1	(X)
Average per family	.49	.10	.03	-	(B)	(X)
Own Children 12 to 17 Years						
Families	533	301	208	105	22	37.6
Without own children 12 to 17 years	378	284	205	105	20	37.7
With own children 12 to 17 years	155	17	3	-	2	37.6
One child 12 to 17 years	138	16	1	-	2	37.6
Two children 12 to 17 years	14	2	1	-	-	37.7
Three children 12 to 17 years	3	-	-	-	-	(B)
Four or more children 12 to 17 years	-	-	-	-	-	(B)
Total own children 12 to 17 years	184	21	4	-	1	(X)
Average per family	.35	.07	.02	-	(B)	(X)
Own Children 6 to 11 Years						
Families	533	301	208	105	22	37.6
Without own children 6 to 11 years	470	293	207	105	22	42.2
With own children 6 to 11 years	63	8	1	-	-	33.1
One child 6 to 11 years	48	8	1	-	-	33.8
Two children 6 to 11 years	15	-	-	-	-	32.3
Three children 6 to 11 years	-	-	-	-	-	(B)
Four or more children 6 to 11 years	-	-	-	-	-	(B)
Total own children 6 to 11 years	75	8	2	-	-	(X)
Average per family	.14	.03	.01	-	(B)	(X)

Source: "Families by Type, Age of Own Children and Age, Race and Hispanic Origin of Householder: March 1994," Steve W. Rawlings and Arlene F. Saluter, *Household and Family Characteristics: March 1995*, pp. 23-24. *Note:* B - less than 75,000; X - Not applicable.

★ 361 ★

Families in Households

Families in Households: Male Householders, Part 1-A

[Numbers in thousands except for averages and medians.]

Characteristic	Total	Age of householder					
		Under 20 years	20 to 24 years	25 to 29 years	30 to 34 years	35 to 39 years	40 to 44 years
BLACK-OTHER FAMILIES, MALE HOUSEHOLDER							
Tenure							
Families	450	6	33	67	91	70	45
Owner families	166	-	9	16	23	25	19
Renter families	284	6	24	51	68	45	26
Size of Family							
Families	450	6	33	67	91	70	45
Two persons	251	4	19	30	40	40	28
Three persons	109	3	9	28	20	18	12
Four persons	74	-	5	6	31	7	3
Five persons	11	-	-	2	-	5	-
Six persons	-	-	-	-	-	-	-
Seven or more persons	6	-	-	-	-	-	2
Total persons	1,327	20	89	189	264	207	134
Average per family	2.95	(B)	(B)	(B)	2.89	(B)	(B)
Age of Own Children							
Families	450	6	33	67	91	70	45
With own children of any age	313	-	12	42	76	54	28
Under 25 years	266	-	12	40	76	54	28
Under 18 years	238	-	12	40	76	48	19
Under 12 years	186	-	12	40	69	33	11
Under 6 years	117	-	12	32	48	15	3
Under 3 years	87	-	12	28	34	10	2
Under1 year	30	-	-	6	15	8	1
Six to 17 years	154	-	-	16	46	36	17
Total own children	509	-	12	66	131	83	45
Under 25 years	431	-	12	62	131	83	45
Under 18 years	375	-	12	62	131	78	31
Under 12 years	282	-	12	62	115	42	16
Under 6 years	157	-	12	47	68	18	4
Under 3 years	97	-	12	30	39	12	2
Under 1 year	34	-	-	7	17	9	1
Six to 17 years	218	-	-	15	64	60	27

[Continued]

★ 361 ★

Families in Households: Male Householders, Part 1-A
[Continued]

Characteristic	Total	Age of householder					
		Under 20 years	20 to 24 years	25 to 29 years	30 to 34 years	35 to 39 years	40 to 44 years
Own Children Selected Ages							
Families with own children under 18	238	-	12	40	76	48	19
Under 6 only	84	-	12	24	30	13	2
Some under 6 and some 6 to 17	33	-	-	8	18	3	-
Six to 17 only	122	-	-	8	28	33	17
Total members	659	-	24	104	213	143	54
Average per family	2.76	(B)	(B)	(B)	2.80	(B)	(B)
Own Children Under 18							
Families	450	6	33	67	91	70	45
Without own children under 18	212	6	21	27	15	22	26
With own children under 18	238	-	12	40	76	48	19
One under 18	144	-	9	20	34	31	15
Two under 18	63	-	3	17	20	13	4
Three under 18	29	-	-	3	22	2	1
Four under 18	3	-	-	-	-	3	-
Five under 18	-	-	-	-	-	-	-
Six or more under 18	-	-	-	-	-	-	-
Total own children under 18	375	-	12	62	131	78	31
Average per family	.83	(B)	(B)	(B)	1.44	(B)	(B)
Average per family with children	1.57	(B)	(B)	(B)	1.73	(B)	(B)
Own Children 6 to 17 Years							
Families	450	6	33	67	91	70	45
Without own children 6 to 17 years	296	6	33	51	45	34	28
With own children 6 to 17 years	154	-	-	16	46	36	17
One child 6 to 17 years	115	-	-	16	28	24	13
Two children 6 to 17 years	29	-	-	-	13	7	3
Three children 6 to 17 years	8	-	-	-	5	2	1
Four or more children 6 to 17 years	3	-	-	-	-	3	-
Total children 6 to 17 years	218	-	-	15	64	60	27
Average per family	.48	(B)	(B)	(B)	.70	(B)	(B)
Own Children 12 to 17 Years							
Families	450	6	33	67	91	70	45
Without own children 12 to 17 years	381	6	33	67	74	50	35
With own children 12 to 17 years	69	-	-	-	17	20	11

[Continued]

★ 361 ★

Families in Households: Male Householders, Part 1-A

[Continued]

Characteristic	Total	Age of householder					
		Under 20 years	20 to 24 years	25 to 29 years	30 to 34 years	35 to 39 years	40 to 44 years
One child 12 to 17 years	55	-	-	-	15	10	10
Two children 12 to 17 years	14	-	-	-	2	10	-
Three children 12 to 17 years	1	-	-	-	-	-	1
Four or more children 12 to 17 years	-	-	-	-	-	-	-
Total own children 12 to 17 years	93	-	-	-	16	36	15
Average per family	.21	(B)	()	(B)	.18	(B)	(B)
Own Children 6 to 11 Years							
Families	450	6	33	67	91	70	45
Without own children 6 to 11 years	349	6	33	51	52	50	36
With own children 6 to 11 years	102	-	-	16	39	20	9
One child 6 to 11 years	81	-	-	16	27	16	7
Two children 6 to 11 years	21	-	-	-	11	4	1
Three children 6 to 11 years	-	-	-	-	-	-	-
Four or more children 6 to 11 years	-	-	-	-	-	-	-
Total own children 6 to 11 years	125	-	-	15	47	24	12
Average per family	.28	(B)	(B)	(B)	.52	(B)	(B)

Source: "Families by Type, Age of Own Children and Age, Race and Hispanic Origin of Householder: March 1994," Steve W. Rawlings and Arlene F. Saluter, *Household and Family Characteristics: March 1995*, pp. 24-25. *Note:* B - less than 75,000; X - Not applicable.

★ 362 ★

Families in Households

Families in Households: Male Householders, Part 1-B

[Numbers in thousands except for averages and medians.]

Characteristic	Age of householder					
	45 to 54 years	55 to 64 years	65 to 74 years	75 to 84 years	85 years and over	Median age
BLACK-OTHER FAMILIES, MALE HOUSEHOLDER						
Tenure						
Families	63	25	31	13	5	36.9
Owner families	26	10	22	9	5	42.3
Renter families	37	15	9	4	-	34.5
Size of Family						
Families	63	25	31	13	5	36.9

[Continued]

★ 362 ★

Families in Households: Male Householders, Part 1-B
[Continued]

Characteristic	Age of householder					
	45 to 54 years	55 to 64 years	65 to 74 years	75 to 84 years	85 years and over	Median age
Two persons	39	21	18	11	2	39.1
Three persons	11	-	2	2	3	33.5
Four persons	9	4	9	-	-	(B)
Five persons	1	-	2	-	-	(B)
Six persons	-	-	-	-	-	(B)
Seven or more persons	3	-	-	-	-	(B)
Total persons	194	68	102	42	18	(X)
Average per family	(B)	(B)	(B)	(B)	(B)	(X)
Age of Own Children						
Families	63	25	31	13	5	36.9
With own children of any age	52	17	22	9	2	37.5
Under 25 years	43	12	2	-	-	35.5
Under 18 years	33	8	1	-	-	34.4
Under 12 years	17	4	-	-	-	33.0
Under 6 years	7	-	-	-	-	31.5
Under 3 years	2	-	-	-	-	30.6
Under 1 year	-	-	-	-	-	(B)
Six to 17 years	30	8	1	-	-	37.1
Total own children	92	24	34	17	6	(X)
Under 25 years	81	15	2	-	-	(X)
Under 18 years	52	8	1	-	-	(X)
Under 12 years	32	3	-	-	-	(X)
Under 6 years	8	-	-	-	-	(X)
Under 3 years	2	-	-	-	-	(X)
Under 1 year	-	-	-	-	-	(B)
Six to 17 years	44	8	1	-	-	(X)
Own Children Selected Ages						
Families with own children under 18	33	8	1	-	-	34.4
Under 6 only	3	-	-	-	-	31.0
Some under 6 and some 6 to 17	3	-	-	-	-	(B)
Six to 17 only	27	8	1	-	-	38.7
Total members	101	19	2	-	-	(X)
Average per family	(B)	(B)	(B)	(B)	(B)	(X)
Own Children Under 18						
Families	63	25	31	13	5	36.9

[Continued]

★ 362 ★

Families in Households: Male Householders, Part 1-B
[Continued]

Characteristic	Age of householder					
	45 to 54 years	55 to 64 years	65 to 74 years	75 to 84 years	85 years and over	Median age
Without own children under 18	30	17	30	13	5	42.8
With own children under 18	33	8	1	-	-	34.4
One under 18	27	6	1	-	-	36.3
Two under 18	5	2	-	-	-	(B)
Three under 18	2	-	-	-	-	(B)
Four under 18	-	-	-	-	-	(B)
Five under 18	-	-	-	-	-	(B)
Six or more under 18	-	-	-	-	-	(B)
Total own children under 18	52	8	1	-	-	(X)
Average per family	(B)	(B)	(B)	(B)	(B)	(X)
Average per family with children	(B)	(B)	(B)	(B)	(B)	(X)
Own Children 6 to 17 Years						
Families	63	25	31	13	5	36.9
Without own children 6 to 17 years	34	17	30	13	5	36.8
With own children 6 to 17 years	30	8	1	-	-	37.1
One child 6 to 17 years	26	6	1	-	-	37.8
Two children 6 to 17 years	4	2	-	-	-	(B)
Three children 6 to 17 years	-	-	-	-	-	(B)
Four or more children 6 to 17 years	-	-	-	-	-	(B)
Total children 6 to 17 years	44	8	1	-	-	(X)
Average per family	(B)	(B)	(B)	(B)	(B)	(X)
Own Children 12 to 17 Years						
Families	63	25	31	13	5	36.9
Without own children 12 to 17 years	47	21	30	13	5	36.0
With own children 12 to 17 years	16	4	1	-	-	(B)
One child 12 to 17 years	16	2	1	-	-	(B)
Two children 12 to 17 years	-	2	-	-	-	(B)
Three children 12 to 17 years	-	-	-	-	-	(B)
Four or more children 12 to 17 years	-	-	-	-	-	(B)
Total own children 12 to 17 years	20	5	1	-	-	(X)
Average per family	(B)	(B)	(B)	(B)	(B)	(X)
Own Children 6 to 11 Years						
Families	63	25	31	13	5	36.9
Without own children 6 to 11 years	50	21	31	13	5	38.1
With own children 6 to 11 years	14	4	-	-	-	34.4
One child 6 to 11 years	10	4	-	-	-	34.4

[Continued]

★ 362 ★

Families in Households: Male Householders, Part 1-B

[Continued]

| Characteristic | Age of householder | | | | | |
	45 to 54 years	55 to 64 years	65 to 74 years	75 to 84 years	85 years and over	Median age
Two children 6 to 11 years	4	-	-	-	-	(B)
Three children 6 to 11 years	-	-	-	-	-	(B)
Four or more children 6 to 11 years	-	-	-	-	-	(B)
Total own children 6 to 11 years	24	3	-	-	-	(X)
Average per family	(B)	(B)	(B)	(B)	(B)	(X)

Source: "Families by Type, Age of Own Children and Age, Race and Hispanic Origin of Householder: March 1994," Steve W. Rawlings and Arlene F. Saluter, *Household and Family Characteristics: March 1995*, pp. 24-25. *Note:* B - less than 75,000; X - Not applicable.

★ 363 ★

Families in Households

Families in Households: Type and Tenure

[Numbers in thousands except for averages and medians.]

| Characteristic | Owner | | | | Renter | | | |
| | | | Other families | | | | Other families | |
	Total	Married-couple families	Male house-holder	Female house-holder	Total	Married-couple families	Male house-holder	Female house-holder
BLACK FAMILIES								
Metropolitan-Nonmetropolitan								
Residence								
Families	3,756	2,487	166	1,102	4,233	1,227	284	2,722
In MSA's	3,098	2,059	153	885	3,741	1,083	257	2,400
Central cities	1,843	1,137	101	606	2,540	637	152	1,752
Ring	1,254	923	52	280	1,201	447	105	649
MSA's of 2,500,000 or more	1,335	887	67	381	1,686	491	109	1,086
Central cities	785	482	49	254	1,208	297	65	846
Ring	550	405	18	127	478	194	44	240
MSA's of 1,000,000 to 2,499,999	711	469	22	220	924	253	46	626
Central cities	465	261	16	189	565	113	24	428
Ring	246	209	6	31	359	140	22	197
MSA's of 250,000 to 999,999	747	495	47	204	808	234	71	504
Central cities	424	274	28	123	534	144	45	345
Ring	322	222	19	82	274	90	26	158
MSA's of 249,999 or less	305	208	17	80	322	106	32	185
Central cities	169	121	8	41	232	82	19	132
Ring	136	87	9	40	90	23	13	53
Not in MSA's	658	428	13	217	492	143	27	322
Units in Structure								
Families	3,756	2,487	166	1,102	4,233	1,227	284	2,722

[Continued]

★ 363 ★

Families in Households: Type and Tenure
[Continued]

Characteristic	Owner				Renter			
	Total	Married-couple families	Other families		Total	Married-couple families	Other families	
			Male house-holder	Female house-holder			Male house-holder	Female house-holder
One unit	3,023	2,014	120	888	1,224	422	83	719
Two units	93	54	5	34	519	141	31	347
Three or four units	46	32	3	12	362	71	22	268
Five to nine units	49	36	5	8	637	152	45	440
Ten or more units	38	14	2	22	1,021	305	66	650
Size of Family								
Families	3,756	2,487	166	1,102	4,233	1,227	284	2,722
Two persons	1,299	769	96	434	1,402	319	154	928
Three persons	947	585	35	327	1,236	297	74	865
Four persons	847	642	25	180	842	316	49	477
Five persons	367	282	4	82	422	157	7	258
Six persons	177	128	-	49	160	81	-	80
Seven or more persons	118	82	5	31	171	57	-	113
Total persons	13,621	9,178	505	3,937	14,329	4,467	823	9,040
Average per family	3.63	3.69	3.04	3.57	3.39	3.64	2.89	3.32
Members Under 18								
Families	3,756	2,487	166	1,102	4,233	1,227	284	2,722
No members under 18	1,666	1,175	81	410	790	386	74	330
One member under 18	917	551	51	315	1,335	277	122	936
Two members under 18	733	489	18	225	1,092	313	60	719
Three members under 18	281	174	6	101	588	152	24	412
Four members under 18	110	66	9	35	269	65	3	200
Five members under 18	33	20	-	13	83	21	-	62
Six or more members under 18	16	12	-	5	75	12	-	63
Total members	3,961	2,505	152	1,304	6,846	1,708	331	4,807
Average per family	1.05	1.01	.91	1.18	1.62	1.39	1.16	1.77
Members 18 to 64								
Families	3,756	2,487	166	1,102	4,233	1,227	284	2,722
No members 18 to 64	292	241	3	48	60	35	4	21
One member 18 to 64	794	215	89	490	2,123	26	176	1,921
Two members 18 to 64	1,774	1,354	59	362	1,638	990	82	565
Three members 18 to 64	624	463	13	148	329	132	19	177
Four members 18 to 64	211	163	2	46	68	32	3	32
Five or members 18 to 64	62	52	-	10	16	10	-	6

[Continued]

★ 363 ★

Families in Households: Type and Tenure
[Continued]

Characteristic	Owner				Renter			
	Total	Married-couple families	Other families		Total	Married-couple families	Other families	
			Male house-holder	Female house-holder			Male house-holder	Female house-holder
Total members 18 to 64	8,306	5,701	294	2,311	7,189	2,643	467	4,080
Average per family	2.21	2.29	1.77	2.10	1.70	2.15	1.64	1.50
Members 65 and Over								
Families	3,756	2,487	166	1,102	4,233	1,227	284	2,722
No members 65 and over	2,845	1,892	112	840	3,996	1,149	263	2,584
One member 65 and over	503	241	48	214	190	41	18	131
Two members 65 and over	388	337	6	45	46	37	3	6
Three or more members 65 and over	21	17	-	4	1	-	-	1
Total members 65 and over	1,353	973	59	322	294	115	25	153
Average per family	.36	.39	.35	.29	.07	.09	.09	.06
Own Children, Selected Ages								
Families with own children under 18	1,640	1,113	59	468	3,152	811	180	2,162
Under 6 only	193	144	12	37	913	265	72	575
Some under 6 and some 6 to 17	322	245	12	65	839	219	21	598
Six to 17 only	1,125	724	36	366	1,401	327	86	988
Total members	6,725	4,934	174	1,617	11,002	3,445	485	7,072
Average per family	4.10	4.43	(B)	3.45	3.49	4.25	2.70	3.27
Own Children Under 18								
Families	3,756	2,487	166	1,102	4,233	1,227	284	2,722
Without own children under 18	2,115	1,374	107	634	1,081	416	105	560
With own children under 18	1,640	1,113	59	468	3,152	811	180	2,162
One own child under 18	742	483	36	224	1,240	288	108	844
Two own children under 18	580	397	15	168	1,050	298	48	704
Three own children under 18	220	163	6	52	535	146	23	366
Four own children under 18	78	52	2	24	222	57	1	165
Five own children under 18	10	10	-	-	61	13	-	48
Six or more own children under 18	9	7	-	2	44	8	-	36
Total own children under 18	2,943	2,035	101	808	5,940	1,567	274	4,099
Average per family	.78	.82	.61	.73	1.40	1.28	.96	1.51
Average per family with children	1.79	1.83	(B)	1.73	1.88	1.93	1.53	1.90

[Continued]

★ 363 ★

Families in Households: Type and Tenure

[Continued]

Characteristic	Owner				Renter			
	Total	Married-couple families	Other families		Total	Married-couple families	Other families	
			Male house-holder	Female house-holder			Male house-holder	Female house-holder
Own Children Under 6								
Families	3,756	2,487	166	1,102	4,233	1,227	284	2,722
Without own children under 6	3,241	2,098	143	1,000	2,482	743	191	1,548
With own children under 6	515	389	23	103	1,751	484	93	1,174
One own child under 6	418	317	18	83	1,075	293	58	724
Two own children under 6	83	58	5	19	506	152	33	321
Three own children under 6	9	9	-	-	135	26	3	107
Four or more own children under 6	5	5	-	-	35	13	-	22
Total own children under 6	605	459	31	116	2,400	675	126	1,599
Average per family	.16	.18	.19	.10	.57	.55	.44	.59
Average per family with children	1.17	1.18	(B)	1.13	1.37	1.39	1.35	1.36
Own Children Under 3								
Families	3,756	2,487	166	1,102	4,233	1,227	284	2,722
Without own children under 3	3,508	2,285	157	1,066	3,175	918	206	2,051
With own children under 3	248	203	9	37	1,058	308	78	671
One own child under 3	228	185	9	34	846	257	67	523
Two or more own children under 3	20	18	-	3	212	52	11	149
Total own children under 3	260	209	10	41	1,199	352	86	761
Average per family	.07	.08	.06	.04	.28	.29	.30	.28
Average per family with children	1.05	1.03	(B)	(B)	1.13	1.14	1.10	1.13

Source: "Families, by Type, Tenure, and Race and Hispanic Origin of Householder: March 1994," Steve W. Rawlings and Arlene F. Saluter, *Household and Family Characteristics: March 1995*, pp. 9-10. *Note:* B = Base less than 75,000.

★ 364 ★

Families in Households

Families in Households: Type, Age of Own Children, Age, and Race. Part 1-A

[Numbers in thousands except for averages and medians.]

Characteristic	Total	Age of householder					
		Under 20 years	20 to 24 years	25 to 29 years	30 to 34 years	35 to 39 years	40 to 44 years
BLACK-ALL FAMILIES							
Tenure							
Families	7,989	65	510	882	1,181	1,178	1,006

[Continued]

★ 364 ★

Families in Households: Type, Age of Own Children, Age, and Race. Part 1-A

[Continued]

| Characteristic | Total | Age of householder | | | | | |
		Under 20 years	20 to 24 years	25 to 29 years	30 to 34 years	35 to 39 years	40 to 44 years
Owner families	3,756	5	43	136	307	456	553
Renter families	4,233	60	466	746	874	722	453
Size of Family							
Families	7,989	65	510	882	1,181	1,178	1,006
Two persons	2,701	32	209	234	286	289	293
Three persons	2,164	22	150	272	329	320	246
Four persons	1,688	11	97	211	328	299	231
Five persons	790	-	41	104	128	148	127
Six persons	338	-	10	45	46	66	67
Seven or more persons	289	-	3	18	63	56	43
Total persons	27,950	156	1,446	2,904	4,132	4,205	3,790
Average per family	3.50	(B)	2.84	3.29	3.50	3.57	3.77
Age of Own Children							
Families	7,989	65	510	882	1,181	1,178	1,006
With own children of any age	6,234	57	425	762	1,082	1,096	851
Under 25 years	5,456	57	424	761	1,077	1,096	837
Under 18 years	4,793	57	421	761	1,077	1,020	711
Under 12 years	3,647	57	421	751	975	704	418
Under 6 years	2,266	57	409	614	592	355	159
Under 3 years	1,306	53	325	355	317	163	63
Under 1 year	417	25	108	107	89	62	17
Six to 17 years	3,687	-	63	472	895	90	656
Total own children	12,804	68	653	1,522	2,292	2,216	1,935
Under 25 years	10,967	68	652	1,518	2,280	2,215	1,898
Under 18 years	8,884	68	649	1,518	2,265	1,880	1,335
Under 12 years	5,966	68	649	1,453	1,691	1,039	621
Under 6 years	3,005	68	587	867	778	413	191
Under 3 years	1,460	56	358	402	352	184	70
Under 1 year	420	19	101	110	94	64	22
Six to 17 years	5,879	-	63	651	1,488	1,466	1,144
Own Children, Selected Ages							
Families with own children under 18	4,793	57	421	761	1,077	1,020	711
Under 6 only	1,105	57	358	289	183	120	55
Some under 6 and some 6 to 17	1,161	-	51	325	410	235	104
Six to 17 only	2,526	-	12	147	485	665	552

[Continued]

★ 364 ★

Families in Households: Type, Age of Own Children, Age, and Race. Part 1-A
[Continued]

Characteristic	Total	Age of householder					
		Under 20 years	20 to 24 years	25 to 29 years	30 to 34 years	35 to 39 years	40 to 44 years
Total members	17,727	126	1,212	2,610	3,883	3,791	2,932
Average per family	3.70	(B)	2.88	3.43	3.60	3.72	4.13
Own Children Under 18							
Families	7,989	65	510	882	1,181	1,178	1,006
Without own children under 18	3,196	9	89	121	104	158	295
With own children under 18	4,793	57	421	761	1,077	1,020	711
One under 18	1,983	30	200	246	303	385	310
Two under 18	1,630	19	129	262	432	370	263
Three under 18	755	8	70	143	208	182	93
Four under 18	301	-	21	84	79	64	39
Five under 18	70	-	-	17	29	11	3
Six or more under 18	53	-	-	9	26	8	4
Total own children under 18	8,884	68	649	1,518	2,265	1,880	1,335
Average per family	1.11	(B)	1.27	1.72	1.92	1.60	1.33
Average per family with children	1.85	(B)	1.54	1.99	2.10	1.84	1.88
Own Children 6 to 17 Years							
Families	7,989	65	510	882	1,181	1,178	1,006
Without own children 6 to 17 years	4,302	65	447	410	286	278	350
With own children 6 to 17 years	3,687	-	63	472	895	900	656
One child 6 to 17 years	1,985	-	57	276	417	421	324
Two children 6 to 17 years	1,128	-	5	136	305	309	227
Three children 6 to 17 years	445	-	-	46	126	141	93
Four or more children 6 to 17 years	129	-	2	14	47	29	11
Total own children 6 to 17 years	5,879	-	63	651	1,488	1,466	1,144
Average per family	.74	(B)	.12	.74	1.26	1.24	1.14
Own Children 12 to 17 Years							
Families	7,989	65	510	882	1,181	1,178	1,006
Without own children 12 to 17 years	5,789	65	510	814	724	537	521
With own children 12 to 17 years	2,200	-	-	68	457	641	484
One child 12 to 17 years	1,602	-	-	57	341	436	321
Two children 12 to 17 years	482	-	-	11	94	163	132
Three children 12 to 17 years	99	-	-	-	19	34	31
Four or more children 12 to 17 years	16	-	-	-	3	7	-
Total own children 12 to 17 years	2,918	-	-	65	574	840	713
Average per family	.37	(B)	-	.07	.49	.71	.71

[Continued]

★ 364 ★

Families in Households: Type, Age of Own Children, Age, and Race. Part 1-A
[Continued]

| Characteristic | Total | Age of householder | | | | | |
		Under 20 years	20 to 24 years	25 to 29 years	30 to 34 years	35 to 39 years	40 to 44 years
Own children 6 to 11 Years							
Families	7,989	65	510	882	1,181	1,178	1,006
Without own children 6 to 11 years	5,623	65	447	436	456	649	671
With own children 6 to 11 years	2,366	-	63	446	725	529	335
One child 6 to 11 years	1,667	-	57	275	481	389	259
Two children 6 to 11 years	580	-	5	134	205	121	63
Three children 6 to 11 years	89	-	-	29	28	15	10
Four or more children 6 to 11 years	30	-	2	9	11	5	3
Total own children 6 to 11 years	2,960	-	63	587	913	626	431
Average per family	.37	(B)	.12	.66	.77	.53	.43

Source: "Families, by Type, Age of Own Children and Age, Race and Hispanic Origin of Householder: March 1994," Steve W. Rawlings and Arlene F. Saluter, *Household and Family Characteristics: March 1995*, pp. 21-22. *Note:* B = less than 75,000.

★ 365 ★
Families in Households

Families in Households: Type, Age of Own Children, Age, and Race. Part 1-B

[Numbers in thousands except for averages and medians.]

| Characteristic | Age of householder | | | | | |
	45 to 54 years	55 to 64 years	65 to 74 years	75 to 84 years	85 years and over	Median age
BLACK-ALL FAMILIES						
Tenure						
Families	1,379	844	613	290	41	40.9
Owner families	864	618	507	233	33	49.0
Renter families	516	226	106	57	8	34.8
Size of Family						
Families	1,379	844	613	290	41	40.9
Two persons	461	380	294	197	26	45.2
Three persons	399	210	165	60	11	40.0
Four persons	264	134	100	14	1	38.3
Five persons	130	63	30	16	2	39.1
Six persons	61	27	16	-	-	40.1
Seven or more persons	64	30	9	4	-	40.6
Total persons	5,179	3,031	2,126	862	120	(X)
Average per family	3.76	3.59	3.47	2.97	(B)	(X)

[Continued]

★ 365 ★

Families in Households: Type, Age of Own Children, Age, and Race. Part 1-B
[Continued]

Characteristic	Age of householder					
	45 to 54 years	55 to 64 years	65 to 74 years	75 to 84 years	85 years and over	Median age
Age of Own Children						
Families	1,379	844	613	290	41	40.9
With own children of any age	1,069	482	300	95	16	38.6
Under 25 years	914	229	49	10	2	36.9
Under 18 years	606	118	20	1	2	35.4
Under 12 years	265	47	10	-	-	33.1
Under 6 years	59	15	7	-	-	30.5
Under 3 years	19	8	3	-	-	28.9
Under 1 year	8	-	-	-	-	28.5
Six to 17 years	577	109	13	1	2	37.3
Total own children	2,278	1,014	614	186	25	(X)
Under 25 years	1,816	407	96	16	1	(X)
Under 18 years	937	198	31	1	1	(X)
Under 12 years	357	74	11	-	-	(X)
Under 6 years	74	21	7	-	-	(X)
Under 3 years	26	8	4	-	-	(X)
Under 1 year	9	-	-	-	-	(X)
Six to 17 years	863	178	24	1	1	(X)
Own Children, Selected Ages						
Families with own children under 18	606	118	20	1	2	35.4
Under 6 only	29	9	7	-	-	27.4
Some under 6 and some 6 to 17	30	7	-	-	-	32.5
Six to 17 only	547	103	13	1	2	39.7
Total members	2,511	572	78	4	9	(X)
Average per family	4.15	4.85	(B)	(B)	(B)	(X)
Own Children Under 18						
Families	1,379	844	613	290	41	40.9
Without own children under 18	774	726	594	288	39	56.6
With own children under 18	606	118	20	1	2	35.4
One under 18	420	73	13	1	2	37.8
Two under 18	115	36	4	-	-	34.7
Three under 18	45	3	3	-	-	33.7
Four under 18	13	-	-	-	-	32.9
Five under 18	6	5	-	-	-	(B)
Six or more under 18	7	-	-	-	-	(B)
Total own children under 18	937	198	31	1	1	(X)

[Continued]

★ 365 ★

Families in Households: Type, Age of Own Children, Age, and Race. Part 1-B
[Continued]

Characteristic	Age of householder					
	45 to 54 years	55 to 64 years	65 to 74 years	75 to 84 years	85 years and over	Median age
Average per family	.68	.24	.05	-	(B)	(X)
Average per family with children	1.55	1.68	(B)	(B)	(B)	(X)
Own Children 6 to 17 Years						
Families	1,379	844	613	290	41	40.9
Without own children 6 to 17 years	802	734	601	288	39	49.0
With own children 6 to 17 years	577	109	13	1	2	37.3
One child 6 to 17 years	409	72	6	1	2	37.9
Two children 6 to 17 years	112	30	4	-	-	36.9
Three children 6 to 17 years	34	3	3	-	-	36.8
Four or more children 6 to 17 years	23	3	-	-	-	35.3
Total own children 6 to 17 years	863	178	24	1	1	(X)
Average per family	.63	.21	.04	-	(B)	(X)
Own Children 12 to 17 Years						
Families	1,379	844	613	290	41	40.9
Without own children 12 to 17 years	932	753	604	288	39	42.3
With own children 12 to 17 years	447	91	9	1	2	39.5
One child 12 to 17 years	366	76	2	1	2	39.6
Two children 12 to 17 years	66	12	4	-	-	39.2
Three children 12 to 17 years	9	3	3	-	-	39.5
Four or more children 12 to 17 years	6	-	-	-	-	(B)
Total own children 12 to 17 years	580	124	20	1	1	(X)
Average per family	.42	.15	.03	-	(B)	(X)
Own children 6 to 11 Years						
Families	1,379	844	613	290	41	40.9
Without own children 6 to 11 years	1,152	807	610	290	41	45.7
With own children 6 to 11 years	228	37	3	-	-	34.6
One child 6 to 11 years	173	29	3	-	-	35.3
Two children 6 to 11 years	48	4	-	-	-	33.7
Three children 6 to 11 years	6	2	-	-	-	32.9
Four or more children 6 to 11 years	-	1	-	-	-	(B)
Total own children 6 to 11 years	283	54	4	-	-	(X)
Average per family	.21	.06	.01	-	(B)	(X)

Source: "Families, by Type, Age of Own Children and Age, Race and Hispanic Origin of Householder: March 1994," Steve W. Rawlings and Arlene F. Saluter, *Household and Family Characteristics: March 1995*, pp. 21-22. *Note:* B - less than 75,000; X = Not applicable.

★ 366 ★
Families in Households

Families in Households: Type, Age of Own Children, Age, and Race. Part 2-A

[Numbers in thousands except for averages and medians].

Characteristic	Total	Age of householder					
		Under 20 years	20 to 24 years	25 to 29 years	30 to 34 years	35 to 39 years	40 to 44 years
BLACK MARRIED-COUPLE FAMILIES							
Tenure							
Families	3,714	1	117	317	433	465	520
Owner families	2,487	1	24	82	190	266	374
Renter families	1,227	-	93	234	243	199	146
Size of Family							
Families	3,714	1	117	317	433	465	520
Two persons	1,068	-	37	71	60	55	93
Three persons	882	1	41	95	83	87	98
Four persons	957	-	24	92	179	170	161
Five persons	439	-	15	29	65	82	98
Six persons	209	-	-	26	24	45	44
Seven or more persons	139	-	-	5	23	26	26
Total persons	13,645	2	367	1,093	1,676	1,900	2,125
Average per family	3.67	(B)	3.13	3.45	3.87	4.09	4.08
Age of Own Children							
Families	3,714	1	117	317	433	465	520
With own children of any age	2,456	1	73	243	371	409	417
Under 25 years	2,186	1	73	243	368	409	414
Under 18 years	1,924	1	73	243	368	397	376
Under 12 years	1,440	1	73	240	343	327	248
Under 6 years	873	1	69	219	230	188	117
Under 3 years	511	1	66	151	137	96	48
Under 1 year	185	-	23	66	38	38	13
Six to 17 years	1,515	-	12	105	295	326	334
Total own children	5,273	1	115	444	754	866	992
Under 25 years	4,571	1	114	444	744	864	982
Under 18 years	3,602	1	114	444	741	785	743
Under 12 years	2,364	1	114	429	613	533	388
Under 6 years	1,133	1	14	298	295	237	143
Under 3 years	561	1	78	156	143	114	55
Under 1 year	194	-	26	64	38	40	19
Six to 17 years	2,469	-	11	146	446	548	600

[Continued]

★ 366 ★

Families in Households: Type, Age of Own Children, Age, and Race. Part 2-A
[Continued]

Characteristic	Total	Age of householder					
		Under 20 years	20 to 24 years	25 to 29 years	30 to 34 years	35 to 39 years	40 to 44 years
Own Children, Selected Ages							
Families with own children under 18	1,924	1	73	243	368	397	376
Under 6 only	409	1	61	138	73	72	42
Some under 6 and some 6 to 17	464	-	8	81	157	116	75
Six to 17 only	1,050	-	4	24	138	210	259
Total members	8,379	2	264	937	1,533	1,747	1,724
Average per family	4.36	(B)	(B)	3.86	4.16	4.40	4.58
Own Children Under 18							
Families	3,714	1	117	317	433	465	520
Without own children under 18	1,790	-	45	74	65	67	144
With own children under 18	1,924	1	73	243	368	397	376
One under 18	771	1	36	93	85	120	139
Two under 18	696	-	22	92	179	157	141
Three under 18	309	-	15	31	73	86	69
Four under 18	110	-	-	22	23	29	24
Five under 18	23	-	-	2	5	4	1
Six or more under 18	16	-	-	3	3	2	2
Total own children under 18	3,602	1	114	444	741	785	743
Average per family	.97	(B)	.97	1.40	1.71	1.69	1.43
Average per family with children	1.87	(B)	(B)	1.83	2.01	1.98	1.97
With Own Children 6 to 17 Years							
Families	3,714	1	117	317	433	465	520
Without own children 6 to 17 years	2,199	1	106	212	138	139	186
With own children 6 to 17 years	1,515	-	12	105	295	326	334
One child 6 to 17 years	806	-	12	66	149	141	151
Two children 6 to 17 years	467	-	-	29	99	115	117
Three children 6 to 17 years	191	-	-	2	47	59	58
Four or more children 6 to 17 years	51	-	-	8	-	10	8
Total own children 6 to 17 years	2,469	-	11	146	446	548	600
Average per family	.66	(B)	.09	.46	1.03	1.18	1.15
Own Children 12 to 17 Years							
Families	3,714	1	117	317	433	465	520
Without own children 12 to 17 years	2,800	1	117	304	329	262	278
With own children 12 to 17 years	914	-	-	13	104	202	242

[Continued]

★ 366 ★

Families in Households: Type, Age of Own Children, Age, and Race. Part 2-A

[Continued]

Characteristic	Total	Age of householder					
		Under 20 years	20 to 24 years	25 to 29 years	30 to 34 years	35 to 39 years	40 to 44 years
One child 12 to 17 years	662	-	-	8	78	146	159
Two children 12 to 17 years	200	-	-	5	22	45	64
Three children 12 to 17 years	47	-	-	-	4	11	19
Four or more children 12 to 17 years	6	-	-	-	-	-	-
Total own children 12 to 17 years	1,238	-	-	14	128	252	355
Average per family	.33	(B)	-	.05	.30	.54	.68
Own Children 6 to 11 Years							
Families	3,714	1	117	317	433	465	520
Without own children 6 to 11 years	2,743	1	106	218	174	232	331
With own children 6 to 11 years	971	-	12	99	260	233	190
One child 6 to 11 years	697	-	12	65	179	164	142
Two children 6 to 11 years	221	-	-	29	66	54	38
Three children 6 to 11 years	43	-	-	-	14	10	10
Four or more children 6 to 11 years	10	-	-	5	-	5	-
Total own children 6 to 11 years	1,231	-	11	131	318	296	245
Average per family	.33	(B)	.09	.41	.73	.64	.47

Source: "Families, by Type, Age of Own Children and Age, Race and Hispanic Origin of Householder: March 1994," Steve W. Rawlings and Arlene F. Saluter, *Household and Family Characteristics: March 1995*, pp. 22-23. *Note:* B - less than 75,000; X = Not applicable.

★ 367 ★

Families in Households

Families in Households: Type, Age of Own Children, Age, and Race. Part 2-B

[Numbers in thousands except for averages and medians].

Characteristic	Age of householder					
	45 to 54 years	55 to 64 years	65 to 74 years	75 to 84 years	85 years and over	Median age
BLACK MARRIED-COUPLE FAMILIES						
Tenure						
Families	783	517	374	172	14	45.0
Owner families	615	427	350	148	10	49.7
Renter families	168	90	24	24	4	36.1
Size of Family						
Families	783	517	374	172	14	45.0

[Continued]

★ 367 ★

Families in Households: Type, Age of Own Children, Age, and Race. Part 2-B
[Continued]

| Characteristic | Age of householder | | | | | |
	45 to 54 years	55 to 64 years	65 to 74 years	75 to 84 years	85 years and over	Median age
Two persons	204	241	186	128	13	56.0
Three persons	220	127	110	21	1	46.5
Four persons	195	80	49	7	-	40.4
Five persons	84	35	18	14	-	41.5
Six persons	42	17	11	-	-	41.0
Seven or more persons	38	18	1	3	-	43.1
Total persons	3,007	1,794	1,192	461	30	(X)
Average per family	3.84	3.47	3.18	2.68	(B)	(X)
Age of Own Children						
Families	783	517	374	172	14	45.0
With own children of any age	548	236	132	27	-	41.6
Under 25 years	500	134	35	10	-	40.0
Under 18 years	371	81	13	1	-	38.5
Under 12 years	172	29	7	-	-	36.0
Under 6 years	38	7	5	-	-	33.2
Under 3 years	8	2	3	-	-	31.4
Under 1 year	7	-	-	-	-	30.5
Six to 17 years	357	78	8	1	-	40.3
Total own children	1,222	532	293	55	-	(X)
Under 25 years	1,070	266	70	16	-	(X)
Under 18 years	602	150	22	1	-	(X)
Under 12 years	227	52	8	-	-	(X)
Under 6 years	42	9	5	-	-	(X)
Under 3 years	10	1	4	-	-	(X)
Under 1 year	7	-	-	-	-	(X)
Six to 17 years	560	140	17	1	-	(X)
Own Children, Selected Ages						
Families with own children under 18	371	81	13	1	-	38.5
Under 6 only	14	2	5	-	-	30.3
Some under 6 and some 6 to 17	24	4	-	-	-	34.6
Six to 17 only	333	74	8	1	-	42.9
Total members	1,675	435	57	4	-	(X)
Average per family	4.52	5.39	(B)	(B)	(B)	(X)
Own Children Under 18						
Families	783	517	374	172	14	45.0

[Continued]

★ 367 ★

Families in Households: Type, Age of Own Children, Age, and Race. Part 2-B
[Continued]

Characteristic	Age of householder					
	45 to 54 years	55 to 64 years	65 to 74 years	75 to 84 years	85 years and over	Median age
Without own children under 18	412	437	361	171	14	56.9
With own children under 18	371	81	13	1	-	38.5
One under 18	241	48	7	1	-	41.8
Two under 18	77	25	3	-	-	36.8
Three under 18	29	3	3	-	-	37.1
Four under 18	12	-	-	-	-	36.7
Five under 18	6	5	-	-	-	(B)
Six or more under 18	6	-	-	-	-	(B)
Total own children under 18	62	150	22	1	-	(X)
Average per family	.77	.29	.06	.01	(B)	(X)
Average per family with children	1.62	1.85	(B)	(B)	(B)	(X)
With Own Children 6 to 17 Years						
Families	783	517	374	172	14	45.0
Without own children 6 to 17 years	426	439	367	171	14	52.7
With own children 6 to 17 years	357	78	8	1	-	40.3
One child 6 to 17 years	237	47	2	1	-	41.2
Two children 6 to 17 years	79	25	3	-	-	39.6
Three children 6 to 17 years	20	3	3	-	-	39.0
Four or more children 6 to 17 years	21	3	-	-	-	(B)
Total own children 6 to 17 years	560	140	17	1	-	(X)
Average per family	.72	.27	.04	.01	(B)	(X)
Own Children 12 to 17 Years						
Families	783	517	374	172	14	45.0
Without own children 12 to 17 years	506	448	369	171	14	47.2
With own children 12 to 17 years	276	69	6	1	-	42.8
One child 12 to 17 years	212	57	-	1	-	43.1
Two children 12 to 17 years	52	9	3	-	-	42.2
Three children 12 to 17 years	6	3	3	-	-	(B)
Four or more children 12 to 17 years	6	-	-	-	-	(B)
Total own children 12 to 17 years	376	98	14	1	-	(X)
Average per family	.48	.19	.04	.01	(B)	(X)
Own Children 6 to 11 Years						
Families	783	517	374	172	14	45.0
Without own children 6 to 11 years	632	492	372	172	14	49.7
With own children 6 to 11 years	151	25	2	-	-	37.5
One child 6 to 11 years	115	18	2	-	-	37.8

[Continued]

★ 367 ★

Families in Households: Type, Age of Own Children, Age, and Race. Part 2-B
[Continued]

| Characteristic | Age of householder | | | | | |
	45 to 54 years	55 to 64 years	65 to 74 years	75 to 84 years	85 years and over	Median age
Two children 6 to 11 years	29	4	-	-	-	36.4
Three children 6 to 11 years	6	2	-	-	-	(B)
Four or more children 6 to 11 years	-	1	-	-	-	(B)
Total own children 6 to 11 years	185	43	2	-	-	(X)
Average per family	.24	.08	.01	-	(B)	(X)

Source: "Families, by Type, Age of Own Children and Age, Race and Hispanic Origin of Householder: March 1994," Steve W. Rawlings and Arlene F. Saluter, *Household and Family Characteristics: March 1995*, pp. 22-23. *Note:* B - less than 75,000; X - Not applicable.

Fuels

★ 368 ★

House Fuels: Black-Occupied Units

[Numbers in thousands. Consistent with the 1990 Census. ... means not applicable or sample too small. - means zero or rounds to zero.]

| Characteristic | Total occupied units | Tenure | | Housing unit characteristics | | | |
| | | Owner | Renter | New construction 4 yrs. | Mobile homes | Physical problems | |
						Severe	Moderate
Total	11,128	4,788	6,340	334	337	385	1,154
Main House Heating Fuel							
Housing units with heating fuel	11,004	4,757	6,247	334	333	373	1,141
Electricity	2,922	958	1,964	177	141	43	105
Piped gas	5,945	2,832	3,113	125	45	170	708
Bottled gas	362	270	91	8	88	18	113
Fuel oil	1,242	393	849	13	12	88	102
Kerosene or other liquid fuel	174	101	73	7	27	15	89
Coal or coke	21	9	12	-	-	-	-
Wood	297	193	105	3	16	40	24
Solar energy	-	-	-	-	-	-	-
Other	42	3	40	-	3	-	-
Other House Heating Fuels							
With other heating fuels[1]	1,300	796	504	42	50	66	160
Electricity	553	307	246	15	15	37	87

[Continued]

★ 368 ★

House Fuels: Black-Occupied Units
[Continued]

Characteristic	Total occupied units	Tenure		Housing unit characteristics			
				New construction 4 yrs.	Mobile homes	Physical problems	
		Owner	Renter			Severe	Moderate
Piped gas	95	49	46	3	2	-	8
Bottled gas	38	35	2	-	-	2	6
Fuel oil	44	17	27	-	-	7	2
Kerosene or other liquid fuel	192	134	58	7	30	10	39
Coal or coke	2	-	2	-	-	-	-
Wood	401	285	117	17	5	6	27
Solar energy	3	3	-	-	-	-	-
Other	37	22	15	-	-	9	3
Not reported	68	30	37	-	2	7	7
Cooking Fuel							
With cooking fuel	11,061	4,783	6,278	334	337	359	1,113
Electricity	4,656	1,939	2,717	213	164	94	253
Piped gas	5,905	2,477	3,428	109	57	212	730
Bottled gas	478	350	128	12	110	49	129
Kerosene or other liquid fuel	12	12	-	-	3	2	-
Coal or coke	-	-	-	-	-	-	-
Wood	2	2	-	-	-	2	-
Other	8	3	5	-	3	-	-
Water Heating Fuel							
With hot piped water	11,063	4,754	6,309	334	337	319	1,154
Electricity	3,665	1,473	2,192	189	263	55	320
Piped gas	6,399	2,911	3,487	132	37	184	711
Bottled gas	254	187	67	8	34	15	63
Fuel oil	660	152	508	5	-	66	57
Kerosene or other liquid fuel	9	9	-	-	-	-	-
Coal or coke	-	-	-	-	-	-	-
Wood	-	-	-	-	-	-	-
Solar energy	16	13	2	-	-	-	-
Other	61	9	52	-	3	-	4
Central Air Conditioning Fuel							
With central air conditioning	3,841	1,866	1,974	261	125	50	88
Electricity	3,572	1,687	1,885	252	116	40	85
Piped gas	231	161	70	4	2	8	2
Other	38	19	19	5	7	2	-
Clothes Dryer Fuel							
With clothes dryer	5,127	3,394	1,733	244	154	96	337

[Continued]

★ 368 ★

House Fuels: Black-Occupied Units

[Continued]

Characteristic	Total occupied units	Tenure		Housing unit characteristics			
		Owner	Renter	New construction 4 yrs.	Mobile homes	Physical problems	
						Severe	Moderate
Electricity	3,818	2,393	1,425	223	151	68	250
Piped gas	1,282	980	302	21	3	28	86
Other	27	21	6	-	-	-	2
Units Using Each Fuel[1]							
Electricity	11,125	4,786	6,338	334	337	381	1,154
All-electric units	2,088	682	1,406	149	123	17	50
Piped gas	7,817	3,340	4,477	158	85	266	864
Bottled gas	661	472	189	14	121	56	168
Fuel oil	1,524	472	1,051	16	12	114	124
Kerosene or other liquid fuel	375	244	131	14	60	27	127
Coal or coke	23	9	14	-	-	-	-
Wood	699	477	222	20	21	47	51
Solar energy	16	13	2	-	-	-	-
Other	129	31	98	-	3	9	6

Source: "Fuels—Occupied Units with Black Householder," *American Housing Survey for the United States in 1993*, February 1995, p. 198. *Notes:* 1. Figures may not add to total because more than one category may apply to a unit.

Household Composition

★ 369 ★

Household Composition: Black-Occupied Units

[Numbers in thousands. Consistent with the 1990 Census. ... means not applicable or sample too small. - means zero or rounds to zero.]

Characteristic	Total occupied units	Tenure		Housing unit characteristics			
		Owner	Renter	New construction 4 yrs.	Mobile homes	Physical problems	
						Severe	Moderate
Population in housing units	29,884	13,726	16,158	923	1,015	1,067	3,167
Total	11,128	4,788	6,340	334	337	385	1,154
Persons							
1 person	3,024	1,007	2,017	83	70	118	334
2 persons	2,832	1,286	1,546	71	68	85	305
3 persons	2,242	973	1,269	73	91	67	176
4 persons	1,665	857	808	70	46	56	143

[Continued]

★ 369 ★

Household Composition: Black-Occupied Units
[Continued]

Characteristic	Total occupied units	Tenure		Housing unit characteristics			
				New construction	Mobile homes	Physical problems	
		Owner	Renter	4 yrs.		Severe	Moderate
5 persons	801	389	412	21	33	26	115
6 persons	320	170	150	15	24	16	37
7 persons or more	244	107	138	-	6	16	45
Median	2.4	2.6	2.2	2.7	2.8	2.4	2.3
Number of Single Children Under 18 Years Old							
None	5,861	2,684	3,177	169	149	219	619
1	2,273	1,012	1,261	66	74	56	171
2	1,759	696	1,062	74	57	67	168
3	777	260	517	13	35	13	118
4	279	82	197	11	14	11	47
5	119	36	84	-	9	13	25
6 or more	60	18	42	-	-	5	7
Median	.5-	.5-	.5-	.5-	.8	.5-	.5-
Persons 65 Years Old and Over							
None	9,076	3,475	5,600	293	280	291	874
1 person	1,637	965	672	37	54	66	230
2 persons or more	415	347	68	4	2	28	50
Age of Householder							
Under 25 years	738	46	692	11	32	23	75
25 to 29	1,100	150	950	34	44	35	89
30 to 34	1,396	344	1,052	82	48	35	121
35 to 44	2,767	1,137	1,629	108	96	107	265
45 to 54	1,844	1,017	826	32	43	47	175
55 to 64	1,459	940	519	34	29	62	169
65 to 74	1,071	674	398	21	24	34	161
75 years and over	754	479	274	12	21	41	99
Median	43	52	38	39	40	44	47
Household Composition by Age of Householder							
2-or-more person households	8,104	3,781	4,323	251	267	267	820
Married-couple families, no nonrelatives	3,300	2,248	1,052	159	127	94	242
Under 25 years	81	12	69	-	12	2	7
25 to 29 years	227	66	161	20	20	3	10
30 to 34 years	438	211	226	43	18	2	25
35 to 44 years	927	591	336	65	44	32	76

[Continued]

★ 369 ★

Household Composition: Black-Occupied Units
[Continued]

Characteristic	Total occupied units	Tenure		Housing unit characteristics			
				New construction 4 yrs.	Mobile homes	Physical problems	
		Owner	Renter			Severe	Moderate
45 to 64 years	1,194	987	208	25	26	34	72
65 years and over	433	382	52	7	6	20	52
Other male householder	925	344	581	32	22	37	125
Under 45 years	583	160	423	24	21	25	66
45 to 64 years	213	107	106	4	-	9	34
65 years and over	130	77	53	5	2	3	25
Other female householder	3,878	1,180	2,690	60	118	135	453
Under 45 years	2,520	439	2,081	38	83	96	276
45 to 64 years	941	461	480	17	20	29	104
65 years and over	417	288	128	5	15	10	73
1-person households	3,024	1,007	2,017	83	70	118	334
Male householder	1,461	382	1,079	23	39	65	186
Under 45 years	748	119	630	19	17	24	66
45 to 64 years	449	153	296	-	16	25	81
65 years and over	263	110	153	4	7	16	38
Female householder	1,563	625	939	60	31	53	148
Under 45 years	476	80	396	26	4	15	24
45 to 64 years	505	249	256	20	10	12	53
65 years and over	582	296	286	14	16	27	71

Source: "Household Composition—Occupied Units with Black Householder," *American Housing Survey for the United States in 1993*, February 1995, p. 206.

Household Vehicles

★ 370 ★

Household Vehicles by Annual Mileage, Fuel Consumption, and Fuel Expenditures: 1991

1990 HOUSEHOLD CHARACTERISTICS	VEHICLES		VEHICLE MILES TRAVELED		CONSUMPTION			EXPENDITURES	
	Total (mil.)	Percent	Total (bil.)	Percent	Total (bil. gal.)	Gallon (percent)	Btu. (quadrillion)	Total (bil. dol.)	Percent
Total	151.2	100.0	1,602	100.0	82.8	100.0	10.3	98.2	100.0
White	135.3	89.5	1,429	89.2	73.9	89.2	9.1	87.5	89.1
Black	12.8	8.4	143	8.9	7.4	8.9	0.9	8.9	9.0
Other	3.1	2.1	30	1.9	1.6	1.9	0.2	1.8	1.9

[Continued]

★ 370 ★

Household Vehicles by Annual Mileage, Fuel Consumption, and Fuel Expenditures: 1991

[Continued]

1990 HOUSEHOLD CHARACTERISTICS	VEHICLES		VEHICLE MILES TRAVELED		CONSUMPTION			EXPENDITURES	
	Total (mil.)	Percent	Total (bil.)	Percent	Total (bil. gal.)	Gallon (percent)	Btu. (quadrillion)	Total (bil. dol.)	Percent
Hispanic descent:									
Yes	9.4	6.2	95	5.9	5.2	6.3	0.6	6.1	6.3
No	141.8	93.8	1,507	94.1	77.6	93.7	9.6	92.1	93.7

Source: "Household Vehicles-Annual Mileage, Fuel Consumption, and Fuel Expenditures: 1991." U.S. Bureau of the Census, *Statistical Abstract of the United States,* 115th ed., 1995, p. 643. Primary source: U.S. Energy Information Administration, *Household Vehicles Energy Consumption,* 1991.

★ 371 ★

Household Vehicles

Household Vehicles by Model Year and Fuel Efficiency: 1991

1990 HOUSEHOLD CHARACTERISTICS	U.S. VEHICLES (mil.)					U.S. VEHICLE FUEL EFFICIENCY (mpg)				
	All model years	Model year				All model years	Model year			
		1991 to 1992	1990	1989	1986 to 1988		1991 to 1992	1990	1989	1986 to 1988
Total	151.2	5.5	10.5	12.5	39.0	19.3	21.8	21.5	21.8	22.0
White	135.3	5.1	9.4	11.1	35.8	19.3	21.8	21.4	21.6	21.9
Black	12.8	(S)	0.7	1.1	2.5	19.4	(S)	(S)	24.3	23.5
Other	3.1	(S)	(S)	(S)	0.6	19.3	(S)	(S)	(S)	(S)
Hispanic descent:										
Yes	9.4	(S)	(S)	(S)	2.3	18.3	(S)	(S)	(S)	20.1
No	141.8	5.3	10.0	12.0	36.6	19.4	21.8	21.4	21.8	22.1

Source: "U.S. Vehicle, by Model Year and Vehicle Fuel Efficiency; 1991." U.S Bureau of the Census, *Statistical Abstract of the United States,* 115th ed., 1995, p. 643. Primary source: U.S. Energy Information Administration, *Household Vehicles Energy Consumption,* 1991. *Note:* S Figure does not meet publications standards.

Householders, Mobility

★372★

Householders: Previous Residence of Recent Movers

[Numbers in thousands. Consistent with the 1990 Census. ... means not applicable or sample too small. - means zero or rounds to zero.]

Characteristic	Total occupied units	Tenure		Housing unit characteristics			
		Owner	Renter	New construction 4 yrs.	Mobile homes	Physical problems	
						Severe	Moderate
UNITS WHERE HOUSEHOLDER MOVED DURING PAST YEAR							
Total	2,162	239	1,923	125	54	36	164
Location of Previous Unit							
Inside same (P)MSA	1,568	181	1,387	71	20	20	116
In central city(s)	1,107	86	1,021	37	10	13	81
Not in central city(s)	460	94	366	34	10	7	35
Inside different (P)MSA in same state	149	14	135	16	-	5	6
In central city(s)	87	14	73	6	-	2	3
Not in central city(s)	62	-	62	10	-	2	3
Inside different (P)MSA in different state	206	20	186	28	11	3	10
In central city(s)	135	15	121	17	5	3	10
Not in central city(s)	71	6	65	11	6	-	-
Outside any metropolitan area	220	25	195	11	23	9	32
Same state	187	21	166	11	13	9	23
Different state	33	4	29	-	10	-	9
Different nation	20	-	20	-	-	-	-
Structure Type of Previous Residence							
Moved from within United States	2,142	239	1,903	125	54	36	164
House	905	133	772	59	31	18	82
Apartment	1,164	101	1,064	63	18	14	73
Mobile home	28	3	25	-	5	-	4
Other	45	4	41	3	-	5	5
Tenure of Previous Residence							
House, apt., mobile home in United States	2,097	236	1,862	122	54	31	159
Owner occupied	439	92	346	27	16	1	43
Renter occupied	1,659	143	1,515	96	38	31	116

[Continued]

★ 372 ★

Householders: Previous Residence of Recent Movers

[Continued]

Characteristic	Total occupied units	Tenure		Housing unit characteristics			
		Owner	Renter	New construction 4 yrs.	Mobile homes	Severe	Moderate
Persons - Previous Residence							
House, apt., mobile home in United States	2,097	236	1,862	122	54	31	159
1 person	279	41	239	23	4	9	29
2 persons	389	53	336	33	12	6	18
3 persons	487	48	439	29	9	4	26
4 persons	400	49	351	23	11	2	32
5 persons	181	11	170	7	4	2	13
6 persons	120	9	111	-	5	3	10
7 persons or more	139	9	130	4	4	6	6
Not reported	102	16	87	3	5	-	26
Median	3.2	2.9	3.2	2.6	3.4	...	3.3
Previous Home Owned or Rented by Someone Who Moved Here							
House, apt., mobile home in United States	2,097	236	1,862	122	54	31	159
Owned or rented by a mover	1,401	174	1,227	87	31	21	81
Owned or rented by other	613	55	558	35	14	11	55
By a relative	452	30	422	26	12	6	45
By a nonrelative	158	22	136	6	3	5	10
Not reported	3	3	-	3	-	-	-
Not reported	84	7	77	-	8	-	23
Change in Housing Costs							
House, apt., mobile home in United States	2,097	236	1,862	122	54	31	159
Increased with move	1,066	168	898	84	20	19	56
Stayed about the same	495	35	461	17	11	9	52
Decreased	426	21	405	16	17	2	28
Don't know	54	3	51	6	-	2	2
Not reported	56	9	47	-	6	-	20

Source: "Previous Unit of Recent Movers—Occupied Units with Black Householder," *American Housing Survey for the United States in 1993*, February 1995, p. 210.

★ 373 ★
Householders, Mobility

Householders: Reasons for Move

[Numbers in thousands. Consistent with the 1990 Census. ... means not applicable or sample too small. - means zero or rounds to zero.]

Characteristic	Total occupied units	Tenure		Housing unit characteristics			
				New construction	Mobile homes	Physical problems	
		Owner	Renter	4 yrs.		Severe	Moderate
RESPONDENT MOVED DURING PAST YEAR							
Total	2,208	259	1,949	125	54	40	162
Reasons for Leaving Previous Unit[1]							
Private displacement	117	17	100	8	7	3	6
Owner to move into unit	13	-	13	-	-	-	-
To be converted to condominium or cooperative	-	-	-	-	-	-	-
Closed for repairs	3	-	3	-	-	-	-
Other	44	3	42	-	3	3	-
Not reported	57	14	42	8	4	-	6
Government displacement	40	5	35	-	-	5	2
Government wanted building or land	14	-	14	-	-	3	2
Unit unfit for occupancy	-	-	-	-	-	-	-
Other	21	5	16	-	-	-	-
Not reported	5	-	5	-	-	2	-
Disaster loss (fire, flood, etc.)	20	5	16	-	2	-	2
New job or job transfer	154	7	147	15	19	-	8
To be closer to work/school/other	136	10	126	5	2	2	10
Other, financial/employment related	101	7	95	5	-	-	15
To establish own household	459	38	420	24	13	6	36
Needed larger house or apartment	396	50	346	26	4	4	19
Married	26	8	19	3	-	-	2
Widowed, divorced or separated	82	5	78	-	-	3	5
Other, family/person related	184	19	165	7	4	5	23
Wanted better home	295	32	263	15	5	7	16
Change from owner to renter	19	-	19	-	2	-	-
Change from renter to owner	86	86	-	19	2	-	-
Wanted lower rent or maintenance	152	3	150	12	-	2	15
Other housing related reasons	166	13	153	12	3	12	19
Other	345	32	313	16	3	-	22
Not reported	57	12	46	-	5	3	12
Choice of Present Neighborhood[1]							
Convenient to job	408	39	370	36	11	-	23
Convenient to friends or relatives	420	28	392	35	20	7	30
Convenient to leisure activities	46	12	34	3	-	2	3
Convenient to public transportation	110	8	102	-	-	5	16
Good schools	161	45	116	18	2	3	11

[Continued]

★ 373 ★

Householders: Reasons for Move
[Continued]

Characteristic	Total occupied units	Tenure		Housing unit characteristics			
				New construction 4 yrs.	Mobile homes	Physical problems	
		Owner	Renter			Severe	Moderate
Other public services	46	11	36	4	-	-	3
Looks/design of neighborhood	348	62	285	26	2	-	21
House was most important consideration	475	92	384	27	8	1	40
Other	827	78	749	28	20	26	65
Not reported	104	18	86	9	5	3	12
Neighborhood Search							
Looked at just this neighborhood	877	66	811	28	19	9	70
Looked at other neighborhood(s)	1,261	179	1,083	95	30	27	77
Not reported	69	14	55	3	5	3	15
Choice of Present Home[1]							
Financial reasons	874	140	734	47	22	10	79
Room layout/design	407	76	331	44	9	5	10
Kitchen	40	18	22	5	-	-	-
Size	346	49	298	35	4	2	15
Exterior appearance	135	46	90	23	4	-	1
Yard/trees/view	99	24	75	14	-	-	2
Quality of construction	81	40	41	14	7	-	-
Only one available	333	10	323	3	8	9	23
Other	636	48	588	45	13	15	46
Home Search							
Now in house	792	229	563	58	-	15	76
Looked at only this unit	45	12	33	-	-	2	6
Looked at houses or mobile homes only	449	148	300	44	-	4	43
Looked at apartments too	252	55	197	14	-	5	23
Search not reported	46	14	32	-	-	3	5
Now in mobile home	54	11	43	10	54	3	10
Looked at only this unit	4	4	-	4	4	-	-
Looked at houses or mobile homes only	17	4	14	-	17	-	2
Looked at apartments too	26	2	23	6	26	3	3
Search not reported	7	-	7	-	7	-	5
Now in apartment	1,362	19	1,343	58	-	22	76
Looked at only this unit	84	-	84	3	-	-	-
Looked at apartments only	439	7	432	11	-	4	21
Looked at houses or mobile homes too	786	12	774	41	-	18	43
Search not reported	54	-	54	3	-	-	11

[Continued]

★ 373 ★

Householders: Reasons for Move

[Continued]

Characteristic	Total occupied units	Tenure		Housing unit characteristics			
		Owner	Renter	New construction 4 yrs.	Mobile homes	Physical problems	
						Severe	Moderate
Recent Mover Comparison to Previous Home							
Better home	1,099	178	921	74	18	16	55
Worse home	375	15	360	11	9	10	58
About the same	655	52	603	38	20	10	30
Not reported	78	14	64	3	7	3	18
Recent Mover Comparison to Previous Neighborhood							
Better neighborhood	783	118	665	45	11	9	44
Worse neighborhood	326	17	309	6	13	10	34
About the same	843	108	735	58	20	14	60
Same neighborhood	180	4	176	13	6	2	9
Not reported	76	12	64	3	5	3	15

Source: "Reasons for Move and Choice of Current Residence—Occupied Units with Black Householder," *American Housing Survey for the United States in 1993*, February 1995, p. 212. *Notes:* 1. Figures may not add to total because more than one category may apply to a unit.

★ 374 ★

Householders, Mobility

Persons in Previous and Current Residence

[Numbers in thousands. Consistent with the 1990 Census. ...means not applicable or sample too small. - means zero or rounds to zero.]

Characteristics	Persons in Current Residence								
	Total occupied units	1 person	2 persons	3 persons	4 persons	5 persons	6 persons	7 persons or more	Median
RESPONDENT MOVED DURING PAST YEAR FROM HOUSE, APT., OR MOBILE HOME IN UNITED STATES									
Total	2,187	590	534	506	334	132	59	32	2.4
Persons in Respondent's Previous Residence									
1 person	292	231	40	10	7	4	-	-	.5
2 persons	398	115	238	39	2	3	2	-	1.9
3 persons	500	103	85	280	29	-	3	-	2.7
4 persons	405	57	62	61	209	12	3	2	3.6
5 persons	181	22	29	22	21	87	-	-	4.3
6 persons	119	12	23	19	27	6	31	2	3.7
7 persons or more	188	32	40	45	27	6	12	26	3.0

[Continued]

★ 374 ★

Persons in Previous and Current Residence

[Continued]

Characteristics	Persons in Current Residence								
	Total occupied units	1 person	2 persons	3 persons	4 persons	5 persons	6 persons	7 persons or more	Median
Not reported	104	18	17	32	12	15	8	3	3.0
Median	3.2	2.0	2.4	3.2	4.1	5.0	6.1	...	...

Source: "Persons in Current Residence by Persons in Previous Residence—Occupied Units with Black Householder," *American Housing Survey for the United States in 1993*, p. 250.

★ 375 ★

Householders, Mobility

Structure Type of Previous and Current Residence

[Numbers in thousands. Consistent with the 1990 Census. ... means not applicable or sample too small. - means zero or rounds to zero.]

Characteristic	Structure type of previous residence									
	Respondent moved in last 12 months					Entire household moved from same residence in last 12 months				
	Total moved from within the U.S.	House	Apartment	Mobile home	Other	Total moved from within the U.S.	House	Apartment	Mobile home	Other
UNITS WHERE RESPONDENT MOVED WITHIN THE UNITED STATES DURING PAST YEAR										
Total	2,187	921	1,193	26	48	1,819	769	999	18	34
Home Search										
Now in house	789	425	345	13	6	656	352	289	10	6
Looked at only this unit	45	21	24	-	-	37	17	20	-	-
Looked at houses or mobile homes only	445	239	198	6	3	388	214	166	6	3
Looked at apartments too	252	132	110	7	3	207	105	94	5	3
Search not reported	46	33	13	-	-	24	15	9	-	-
Now in mobile home	54	31	21	3	-	40	23	14	3	-
Looked at only this unit	4	4	-	-	-	4	4	-	-	-
Looked at houses or mobile homes only	17	5	9	3	-	16	5	7	3	-
Looked at apartments too	26	19	7	-	-	13	11	2	-	-
Search not reported	7	2	5	-	-	7	2	5	-	-
Now in apartment	1,344	465	827	10	42	1,123	394	696	5	28
Looked at only this unit	84	35	49	-	-	84	35	49	-	-
Looked at apartments only	435	190	227	3	15	358	162	188	-	8
Looked at houses or mobile homes too	772	216	524	8	25	643	179	440	5	20
Search not reported	54	24	27	-	2	38	19	18	-	-

Source: "Structure Type of Previous Residence by Home Search and Structure Type of Current Residence - Occupied Units with Black Householder," *American Housing Survey for the United States in 1993*, p. 251.

Housing Conditions

★ 376 ★

Height and Condition of Building: Black-Occupied Units

[Numbers in thousands. Consistent with the 1990 Census. ...means not applicable or sample too small. - means zero or rounds to zero.]

Characteristics	Total occupied units	Tenure		Housing unit characteristics			
		Owner	Renter	New construction 4 yrs	Mobile homes	Physical problems	
						Severe	Moderate
Total	11,128	4,788	6,340	334	337	385	1,154
Stories in Structure[1]							
1	445	17	428	28	...	9	55
2	1,619	28	1,591	39	...	24	113
3	1,180	114	1,066	25	...	38	79
4 to 6	749	55	694	9	...	71	66
7 or more	552	27	525	-	...	29	46
Stories Between Main and Apartment Entrances							
Multiunits 2 or more floors	4,100	224	3,876	73	...	161	303
None (on same floor)	1,390	88	1,302	26	...	28	103
1 (up or down)	1,175	69	1,106	15	...	41	88
2 or more (up or down)	1,323	54	1,270	32	...	91	93
Not reported	211	13	198	-	...	2	20
Common Stairways							
Multiunits, 2 or more floors	4,100	224	3,876	73	...	161	303
No common stairways	715	49	666	11	...	14	58
With common stairways	3,208	165	3,043	62	...	145	228
No loose steps	2,930	162	2,768	62	...	102	176
Railings not loose	2,640	143	2,497	57	...	93	161
Railings loose	133	5	128	5	...	9	6
No railings	130	14	116	-	...	-	4
Status of railings not reported	27	-	27	-	...	-	5
Loose steps	261	1	261	-	...	43	52
Railings not loose	179	1	178	-	...	22	25
Railings loose	62	-	62	-	...	19	19
No railings	15	-	15	-	...	-	8
Status of railings not reported	5	-	5	-	...	2	-
Status of steps not reported	17	2	14	-	...	-	-
Status of stairways not reported	176	10	167	-	...	2	17
Light Fixtures in Public Halls							
2 or more units in structure	4,544	240	4,304	101	...	171	357
No public halls	1,591	81	1,510	32	...	34	123
No light fixtures in public halls	13	-	13	-	...	-	3
All in working order	1,791	108	1,683	51	...	83	127
Some in working order	245	7	237	-	...	41	33
None in working order	4	-	4	-	...	2	-
Unable to determine if working	693	31	662	18	...	8	46
Not reported	207	13	195	-	...	2	26

[Continued]

★ 376 ★

Height and Condition of Building: Black-Occupied Units
[Continued]

Characteristics	Total occupied units	Tenure		Housing unit characteristics			
		Owner	Renter	New construction 4 yrs	Mobile homes	Physical problems	
						Severe	Moderate
Elevator on floor							
Multiunits, 2 or more floors	4,100	224	3,876	73	...	161	303
With 1 or more elevators working	690	32	658	13	...	36	53
With elevator, none in working condition	24	2	22	-	...	2	-
No elevator	3,188	177	3,011	56	...	121	232
Units 3 or more floors from main entrance	249	5	244	6	...	25	20
Foundation							
1 unit bldg. excl. mobile homes	6,247	4,295	1,951	195	...	206	744
With basement under all of building	1,947	1,476	472	40	...	48	115
With basement under part of building	335	254	81	12	...	10	8
With crawl space	2,061	1,342	718	42	...	103	469
On concrete slab	1,764	1,142	622	101	...	29	135
Other	140	81	58	-	...	16	17
External Building Conditions[1,2]							
Sagging roof	33	-	33	-	...	7	14
Missing roofing material	27	5	22	-	...	5	-
Hole in roof	5	-	5	-	...	-	5
Could not see roof	652	44	608	4	...	39	75
Missing bricks, siding, other outside wall material	92	2	90	-	...	9	17
Sloping outside walls	29	-	29	-	...	2	6
Boarded up windows	80	9	80	-	...	4	20
Broken windows	99	-	99	-	...	10	26
Bars and windows	164	11	153	-	...	7	34
Foundation crumbling or has open crack or hole	96	2	93	-	...	13	26
Could not see foundation	217	25	192	-	...	18	30
None of the above	3,371	164	3,208	87	...	108	217
Could not observe or not reported	266	12	254	10	...	2	24
Site Placement							
Mobile homes	337	252	85	38	337	8	53
First site	174	143	31	31	174	-	18
Moved from another site	105	86	19	7	105	5	20
Don't know	43	16	26	-	43	3	14
Not reported	15	8	6	-	15	-	-
Previous Occupancy							
Unit built 1980 or later	1,549	701	848	334	137	17	47
Not previously occupied	555	443	112	231	77	8	24
Not reported	280	60	220	15	8	3	21

Source: "Height and Condition of Building—Occupied Units with Black Householder," *American Housing Survey for the United States in 1993*, p. 192. *Notes:* 1. Limited to multiunit structures. 2. Figures may not add to total because more than one category may apply.

Housing Indicators

★ 377 ★

Indicators of Quality: Black-Occupied Units

[Numbers in thousands. Consistent with the 1990 Census. ...means not applicable or sample too small. - means zero or rounds to zero.]

Characteristics	Total occupied units	Tenure		Housing unit characteristics			
		Owner	Renter	New construction 4 yrs	Mobile homes	Physical problems	
						Severe	Moderate
Total	11,128	4,788	6,340	334	337	385	1,154
Selected Amenities[1]							
Porch, deck, balcony, or patio	7,497	3,730	3,767	239	144	216	801
Not reported	13	-	13	-	-	-	-
Telephone available	9,525	4,515	5,010	294	272	305	885
Usable fireplace	1,804	1,289	515	148	46	41	87
Separate dining room	4,621	2,699	1,922	182	82	104	388
With 2 or more living rooms or recreation rooms, etc.	2,164	1,759	406	96	24	48	143
Garage or carport included with home	3,641	2,594	1,047	167	23	67	235
Not included	7,438	2,181	5,257	161	312	317	919
Offstreet parking included	5,027	1,634	3,393	157	276	169	577
Offstreet parking not reported	56	-	56	-	-	3	5
Garage or carport not reported	49	13	36	6	2	-	-
Cars and Trucks Available							
No cars, trucks, or vans	3,114	579	2,536	34	74	169	451
Other households without cars	325	173	152	11	12	17	52
1 car with or without trucks or vans	5,078	2,231	2,848	137	150	130	489
2 cars	2,102	1,399	703	123	78	60	120
3 or more cars	509	407	101	29	23	9	43
With cars, no trucks or vans	6,192	2,875	3,316	223	181	167	525
1 truck or van with or without cars	1,567	1,106	461	73	75	32	164
2 or more trucks or vans	255	228	27	5	7	16	14
Owner or Manager on Property							
Rental, multiunit[2]	4,304	...	4,304	98	...	164	356
Owner or manager lives on property	1,367	...	1,367	44	...	34	65
Neither owner nor manager lives on property	2,938	...	2,938	54	...	130	291

Source: "Additional Indicators of Housing Quality—Occupied Units with Black Householder," *American Housing Survey for the United States in 1993,* February 1995, p. 202. *Notes:* 1. Figures may not add to total because more than one category may apply to a unit. 2. Two or more units of any tenure in the structure.

Housing Size

★ 378 ★

Rooms in Unit: Income and Costs. Part 1

[Numbers in thousands. Consistent with the 1990 Census. ...means not applicable or sample too small. - means zero or rounds to zero.]

Characteristics	Occupied units					
	Total	Rooms				
		1 and 2 rooms	3 and 4 rooms	5 and 6 rooms	7 rooms or more	Median
Total	11,128	289	3,818	4,948	2,073	5.1
Persons						
1 person	3,024	239	1,682	917	187	4.0
2 persons	2,832	34	1,073	1,274	451	5.0
3 persons	2,242	13	610	1,116	503	5.4
4 persons	1,665	3	304	897	461	5.7
5 persons	801	-	86	462	253	5.9
6 persons	320	-	44	151	124	6.0
7 persons or more	244	-	19	131	95	6.1
Median	2.4	1.5-	1.7	2.8	3.3	...
Rooms						
1 room	121	...	...	...	...	...
2 rooms	168	...	...	...	...	...
3 rooms	1,283	...	...	...	...	...
4 rooms	2,535	...	...	...	...	...
5 rooms	2,754	...	...	...	...	...
6 rooms	2,194	...	...	...	...	...
7 rooms	1,132	...	...	...	...	...
8 rooms	546	...	...	...	...	...
9 rooms	221	...	...	...	...	...
10 rooms or more	175	...	...	...	...	...
Median	5.0	...	...	...	...	...
Bedrooms						
None	193	193	-	-	-	2.5-
1	1,740	97	1,605	36	3	3.5
2	3,753	-	2,185	1,499	69	4.2
3	4,124	-	28	3,206	890	5.8
4 or more	1,319	-	-	207	1,112	6.5+
Median	2.5	.5-	1.6	2.8	3.5+	...
Complete Bathrooms						
None	120	36	57	28	-	3.4
1	6,895	249	3,359	2,825	462	4.4
1 and one-half	1,778	5	250	1,069	454	5.7
2 or more	2,335	-	153	1,025	1,157	6.5

[Continued]

★ 378 ★

Rooms in Unit: Income and Costs. Part 1
[Continued]

Characteristics	Occupied units					
	Total	Rooms				
		1 and 2 rooms	3 and 4 rooms	5 and 6 rooms	7 rooms or more	Median
Lot Size						
Less than one-eighth acre	689	-	102	390	197	5.7
One-eighth up to one-quarter acre	876	2	104	492	278	5.9
One-quarter up to one-half acre	637	-	53	307	277	6.2
One-half up to one acre	404	-	52	198	154	6.0
1 to 4 acres	701	2	76	393	229	5.9
5 to 9 acres	50	-	14	17	19	...
10 acres or more	109	-	22	64	23	5.5
Don't know	2,159	8	425	1,219	507	5.6
Not reported	957	9	159	532	257	5.7
Median	.32	...	.27	.29	.35	...
Income of Families and Primary Individuals						
Individuals						
Less than $5,000	1,556	59	768	599	130	4.4
$10,000 to $9,999	1,956	77	877	816	187	4.6
$10,000 to $14,999	1,328	36	532	595	165	4.8
$15,000 to $19,999	1,221	39	467	552	164	4.9
$20,000 to $24,999	966	22	353	459	131	5.0
$25,000 to $29,999	884	14	273	412	185	5.3
$30,000 to $34,999	583	15	153	277	138	5.4
$35,000 to $39,999	500	16	125	245	114	5.4
$40,000 to $49,999	750	9	171	356	214	5.6
$50,000 to $59,999	475	3	51	274	147	5.8
$60,000 to $79,999	510	-	31	234	245	6.4
$80,000 to $99,999	194	-	7	80	107	6.5+
$100,000 to $119,999	87	-	5	25	57	6.5+
$120,000 or more	117	-	6	23	89	6.5+
Median	17,963	11,198	12,481	19,202	32,729	...
Monthly Housing Costs						
Less than $100	419	10	212	189	9	4.4
$100 to $199	1,373	52	556	622	142	4.8
$200 to $249	722	1	238	330	113	5.0
$250 to $299	721	37	286	300	96	4.7
$300 to $349	658	26	247	274	111	4.9
$350 to $399	862	32	430	313	87	4.4
$400 to $449	717	12	326	297	72	4.6
$450 to $499	854	16	263	294	81	4.8
$500 to $599	1,159	23	460	493	182	4.9
$600 to $699	938	19	275	485	160	5.2
$700 to $799	610	2	135	329	143	5.5
$800 to $999	667	9	129	296	233	5.8
$1,000 to $1,249	369	2	30	157	179	6.4

[Continued]

★ 378 ★

Rooms in Unit: Income and Costs. Part 1
[Continued]

| Characteristics | Occupied units | | | | | |
| | Total | Rooms | | | | |
		1 and 2 rooms	3 and 4 rooms	5 and 6 rooms	7 rooms or more	Median
$1,250 to $1,499	132	2	3	34	93	6.5+
$1,500 or more	156	-	6	44	107	6.5+
No cash rent	473	4	181	245	43	4.9
Mortgage payment not reported	496	-	41	246	211	6.2
Median (excludes no cash rent)	423	302	380	434	603	...
Median Monthly Housing Costs for Owners						
Monthly costs including all mortgages plus maintenance costs	464	...	230	412	661	...
Monthly costs excluding 2nd and subsequent mortgages and maintenance costs	415	...	218	371	581	...
OWNER OCCUPIED UNITS						
Total	4,788	-	515	2,602	1,671	5.9
Value						
Less than $10,000	217	-	84	114	20	4.9
$10,000 to $19,999	317	-	59	205	53	5.5
$20,000 to $29,999	450	-	64	270	117	5.7
$30,000 to $39,999	498	-	50	316	132	5.8
$40,000 to $49,999	526	-	60	367	100	5.6
$50,000 to $59,999	461	-	46	298	117	5.7
$60,000 to $69,999	436	-	25	248	163	6.1
$70,000 to $79,999	327	-	20	164	144	6.3
$80,000 to $99,999	533	-	35	232	266	6.5
$100,000 to $119,999	277	-	30	122	125	6.3
$120,000 to $149,999	312	-	11	128	173	6.5+
$150,000 to $199,999	264	-	17	94	152	6.5+
$200,000 to $249,999	91	-	10	28	54	6.5+
$250,000 to $299,999	37	-	2	4	30	...
$300,000 or more	41	-	3	11	28	...
Median	58,372	...	40,285	50,966	79,398	...

Source: "Rooms in Unit by Household and Unit Size, Income, and Costs - Occupied Units with Black Householder," *American Housing Survey for the United States in 1993,* p. 230.

★ 379 ★

Housing Size

Rooms in Unit: Income and Costs. Part 2

[Numbers in thousands. Consistent with the 1990 Census. ...means not applicable or sample too small. - means zero or rounds to zero.]

Characteristics	Occupied units					
	Bedrooms					Median
	No rooms	1 room	2 rooms	3 rooms	4 rooms or more	
Total	193	1,740	3,753	4,124	1,319	2.5
Persons						
1 person	161	1,182	1,012	564	105	1.7
2 persons	20	376	1,244	966	227	2.3
3 persons	9	131	850	988	265	2.6
4 persons	3	37	418	881	326	2.9
5 persons	-	10	142	472	178	3.0
6 persons	-	3	51	145	121	3.2
7 persons or more	-	2	37	108	97	3.3
Median	1.5-	1.5-	2.2	3.0	3.7	...
Rooms						
1 room	121	-	-	-	-	.5-
2 rooms	72	97	-	-	-	.6
3 rooms	-	1,241	43	-	-	1.0
4 rooms	-	364	2,142	28	-	1.9
5 rooms	-	29	1,247	1,469	8	2.6
6 rooms	-	7	252	1,736	199	3.0
7 rooms	-	3	39	630	460	3.3
8 rooms	-	-	18	191	337	3.5+
9 rooms	-	-	3	39	179	3.5+
10 rooms or more	-	-	9	31	135	3.5+
Median	1.5-	3.1	4.4	5.8	7.5	...
Bedrooms						
None	...	...	...	...	...	...
1	...	...	...	...	...	...
2	...	...	...	...	...	...
3	...	...	...	...	...	...
4 or more	...	...	...	...	...	...
Median	...	...	...	...	...	...
Complete Bathrooms						
None	29	35	34	16	7	1.4
1	161	1,676	2,883	1,875	300	2.1
1 and one-half	2	25	482	985	282	2.9
2 or more	-	5	353	1,248	729	3.1
Lot Size						
Less than one-eighth acre	-	8	218	338	125	2.9
One-eighth up to one-quarter acre	-	18	210	484	164	2.9
One-quarter up to one-half acre	-	5	95	388	149	3.1

[Continued]

★ 379 ★

Rooms in Unit: Income and Costs. Part 2

[Continued]

Characteristics	Occupied units					
	Bedrooms					Median
	No rooms	1 room	2 rooms	3 rooms	4 rooms or more	
One-half up to one acre	-	6	79	216	103	3.0
1 to 4 acres	-	8	130	409	154	3.0
5 to 9 acres	-	2	12	23	13	...
10 acres or more	-	9	22	53	24	2.9
Don't know	3	100	664	1,086	3.5	2.8
Not reported	4	44	257	471	180	2.9
Median	...	.37	.22	.34	.38	...
Income of Families and Primary Individuals						
Less than $5,000	48	322	668	408	110	2.1
$10,000 to $9,999	40	421	730	606	158	2.2
$10,000 to $14,999	25	232	507	454	110	2.3
$15,000 to $19,999	24	225	439	410	122	2.3
$20,000 to $24,999	15	169	355	320	107	2.3
$25,000 to $29,999	10	136	259	372	107	2.6
$30,000 to $34,999	8	74	173	254	74	2.6
$35,000 to $39,999	13	55	165	212	54	2.6
$40,000 to $49,999	6	60	225	349	111	2.3
$50,000 to $59,999	3	20	116	254	83	2.9
$60,000 to $79,999	-	23	71	281	135	3.1
$80,000 to $99,999	-	-	35	109	51	3.1
$100,000 to $119,999	-	-	5	49	33	3.3
$120,000 or more	-	3	4	46	63	3.5+
Median	11,623	12,726	14,716	22,861	27,464	...
Monthly Housing Costs						
Less than $100	5	70	197	124	24	2.2
$100 to $199	31	294	424	501	123	2.4
$200 to $249	31	111	236	275	70	2.4
$250 to $299	27	113	281	225	75	2.3
$300 to $349	19	147	195	245	52	2.3
$350 to $399	13	219	367	205	58	2.0
$400 to $449	10	161	301	193	52	2.1
$450 to $499	13	136	242	200	63	2.2
$500 to $599	20	210	425	392	111	2.3
$600 to $699	11	109	350	393	76	2.5
$700 to $799	-	33	227	299	51	2.7
$800 to $999	9	44	162	323	129	2.9
$1,000 to $1,249	-	13	61	198	97	3.1
$1,250 to $1,499	2	-	6	54	70	3.5+
$1,500 or more	-	5	10	54	87	3.5+
No cash rent	2	60	199	162	49	2.4
Mortgage payment not reported	-	14	71	281	131	3.1

[Continued]

★ 379 ★

Rooms in Unit: Income and Costs. Part 2

[Continued]

Characteristics	Occupied units					
	Bedrooms					Median
	No rooms	1 room	2 rooms	3 rooms	4 rooms or more	
Median (excludes no cash rent)	305	372	407	468	546	...
Median Monthly Housing Costs for Owners						
Monthly costs including all mortgages plus maintenance costs	...	229	310	492	627	...
Monthly costs excluding 2nd and subsequent mortgages and maintenance costs	...	194	287	434	552	...
OWNER OCCUPIED UNITS						
Total	-	86	1,030	2,673	998	3.0
Value						
Less than $10,000	-	9	102	91	15	2.5
$10,000 to $19,999	-	9	112	154	41	2.7
$20,000 to $29,999	-	6	135	231	78	2.9
$30,000 to $39,999	-	10	106	289	93	3.0
$40,000 to $49,999	-	2	137	307	79	2.9
$50,000 to $59,999	-	10	101	291	59	2.9
$60,000 to $69,999	-	6	80	285	65	3.0
$70,000 to $79,999	-	5	40	219	63	3.0
$80,000 to $99,999	-	13	66	309	145	3.1
$100,000 to $119,999	-	3	64	153	57	3.0
$120,000 to $149,999	-	3	32	171	107	3.2
$150,000 to $199,999	-	6	37	121	100	3.2
$200,000 to $249,999	-	5	12	38	37	3.3
$250,000 to $299,999	-	-	4	7	26	...
$300,000 or more	-	-	3	7	32	...
Median	...	56,822	44,426	59,050	80,657	...

Source: "Rooms in Unit by Household and Unit Size, Income, and Costs - Occupied Units with Black Householder," *American Housing Survey for the United States in 1993,* p. 230.

★ 380 ★

Housing Size

Square Footage: Household and Unit Size

[Numbers in thousands. Consistent with the 1990 Census. ...means not applicable or sample too small. - means zero or rounds to zero.]

Characteristics	Total	Size of occupied detached 1-family homes and 1-family mobile homes							
		Less than 500 square feet	500 to 999 square feet	1000 to 1499 square feet	1500 to 1999 square feet	2000 to 2499 square feet	2500 to 2499 feet or more	Not reported	Median
Total	5,567	106	1,029	1,530	996	546	675	684	1,427
PERSONS									
1 person	1,055	43	311	301	142	90	70	98	1,206
2 persons	1,449	26	292	345	301	115	180	190	1,451
3 persons	1,153	17	176	356	219	119	141	124	1,451
4 persons	1,002	9	141	253	196	111	152	141	1,573
5 persons	524	6	66	150	79	72	66	85	1,491
6 persons	217	6	24	81	26	22	35	23	1,414
7 persons or more	167	-	19	45	32	17	31	23	1,631
Median	2.7	1.9	2.2	2.8	2.7	3.1	3.1	2.9	...
Rooms									
1 room	3	-	-	-	-	-	-	3	...
2 rooms	12	5	2	-	-	-	-	5	...
3 rooms	92	15	51	2	5	5	-	14	738
4 rooms	672	52	346	114	35	20	17	86	847
5 rooms	1,444	17	386	494	220	88	82	157	1,243
6 rooms	1,586	12	171	576	356	140	147	184	1,449
7 rooms	925	-	51	246	247	125	132	124	1,710
8 rooms	491	2	11	64	96	105	146	67	2,184
9 rooms	197	3	8	26	17	34	89	20	2,500+
10 rooms or more	145	-	4	7	20	28	62	24	2,500+
Median	5.9	4.1	4.8	5.8	6.2	6.7	7.2	5.9	...
Bedrooms									
None	3	-	-	-	-	-	-	3	...
1	116	28	55	2	5	6	5	15	705
2	1,360	56	512	319	162	58	86	167	1,045
3	3,002	20	415	1,026	620	292	305	323	1,440
4 or more	1,086	2	47	183	209	191	278	175	2,035
Median	2.9	1.9	2.4	2.9	3.0	3.2	3.3	3.0	...
Complete Bathrooms									
None	64	7	35	12	8	-	-	2	842
1	2,647	88	771	816	314	171	179	308	1,190
1 and one-half	1,118	-	125	338	227	123	153	152	1,543
2 or more	1,737	11	98	364	447	251	343	222	1,818
Lot Size									
Less than one-eighth acre	584	12	114	138	104	57	64	95	1,429
One-eighth up to one-quarter acre	825	8	144	232	173	82	87	100	1,455
One-quarter up to one-half acre	622	5	75	171	135	69	110	56	1,617
One-half up to one acre	399	5	60	121	78	41	56	39	1,476
1 to 4 acres	684	19	128	223	125	71	76	42	1,390
5 to 9 acres	50	3	12	5	8	8	5	11	...
10 acres or more	102	-	36	33	7	9	8	9	1,165
Don't know	1,669	40	373	467	259	127	172	232	1,327
Not reported	632	15	89	140	108	81	99	100	1,601
Median	.34	.61	.34	.38	.32	.36	.37	.23	...
Income of Families and Primary Individuals									
Less than $5,000	547	21	165	163	49	36	41	71	1,158
$5,000 to $9,999	881	33	301	240	97	45	46	119	1,097
$10,000 to $14,999	596	18	150	180	87	38	46	77	1,254
$15,000 to $19,999	566	11	107	178	86	52	61	71	1,365
$20,000 to $24,999	474	13	77	150	72	45	46	71	1,372
$25,000 to $29,999	453	5	54	138	94	60	58	44	1,540
$30,000 to $34,999	298	3	53	87	54	24	39	38	1,428
$35,000 to $39,999	289	-	41	98	64	33	30	22	1,469
$40,000 to $49,999	455	2	35	108	151	50	63	45	1,697
$50,000 to $59,999	290	-	20	69	80	51	53	18	1,796

[Continued]

★ 380 ★

Square Footage: Household and Unit Size
[Continued]

Characteristics	Total	Size of occupied detached 1-family homes and 1-family mobile homes							Median
		Less than 500 square feet	500 to 999 square feet	1000 to 1499 square feet	1500 to 1999 square feet	2000 to 2499 square feet	2500 to 2499 feet or more	Not reported	
$60,000 to $79,999	391	-	11	75	101	59	86	60	1,897
$80,000 to $99,999	143	-	9	18	29	40	27	20	2,066
$100,000 to $119,999	77	-	4	15	13	3	30	12	2,048
$120,000 or more	105	-	2	11	18	10	48	16	2,500+
Median	22,024	9,784	11,596	20,128	31,194	29,716	34,978	20,264	...
Monthly Housing Costs									
Less than $100	184	5	87	40	9	12	6	25	927
$100 to $199	732	33	233	214	100	40	32	81	1,138
$200 to $249	410	8	112	113	77	20	25	54	1,252
$250 to $299	402	15	106	103	60	26	41	52	1,265
$300 to $349	307	10	59	85	42	31	40	40	1,381
$350 to $399	331	11	70	93	57	27	16	57	1,302
$400 to $449	297	5	73	98	38	36	23	25	1,299
$450 to $499	233	-	39	88	30	15	33	29	1,361
$500 to $599	459	2	66	151	72	49	54	64	1,427
$600 to $699	422	2	34	125	106	59	64	31	1,663
$700 to $799	296	-	20	92	75	34	42	33	1,630
$800 to $999	398	5	22	87	100	53	78	52	1,792
$1,000 to $1,249	266	2	15	37	65	46	70	30	1,963
$1,250 to $1,499	109	-	-	7	34	25	28	16	2,118
$1,500 or more	123	-	3	15	23	16	50	16	2,402
No cash rent	180	8	66	59	20	9	2	16	1,067
Mortgage payment not reported	419	-	24	123	87	49	72	64	1,674
Median (excludes not cash rent)	420	259	267	413	544	577	650	394	...
Median Monthly Housing Costs for Owners									
Monthly costs including all mortgages plus maintenance costs	449	...	219	407	570	611	695	410	...
Monthly costs excluding 2nd and subsequent mortgages and maintenance costs	401	-	208	358	501	557	619	383	...
OWNER OCCUPIED UNITS									
Total	4,124	49	582	1,110	821	485	587	489	1,546
Value									
Less than $10,000	205	14	111	42	5	4	5	25	843
$10,000 to $19,999	276	4	107	66	22	12	29	36	1,070
$20,000 to $29,999	383	7	81	138	48	31	24	54	1,278
$30,000 to $39,999	424	2	50	139	96	50	48	39	1,508
$40,000 to $49,999	467	10	48	179	90	55	52	33	1,445
$50,000 to $59,999	382	2	43	144	76	54	33	29	1,456
$60,000 to $69,999	375	2	37	133	104	31	41	27	1,507
$70,000 to $79,999	300	2	27	68	87	34	35	46	1,670
$80,000 to $99,999	460	5	42	77	128	80	87	41	1,834
$100,000 to $119,999	229	-	14	33	56	37	48	40	1,912
$120,000 to $149,999	245	-	5	36	50	40	63	53	2,079
$150,000 to $199,999	240	-	12	40	36	33	80	39	2,192
$200,000 to $249,999	72	-	-	12	17	18	16	9	2,068
$250,000 to $299,999	34	-	5	-	4	7	8	9	...
$300,000 or more	34	-	-	4	-	-	19	11	...
Median	58,078	...	29,086	49,584	66,991	71,855	86,123	70,644	...

Source: "Square Footage by Household and Unit Size, Income, and Costs - Occupied Units with Black Householder," *American Housing Survey for the United States in 1993*, p. 232.

★ 381 ★

Housing Size

Unit and Lot Size: Black-Occupied Units

[Numbers in thousands. Consistent with the 1990 Census. ...means not applicable or sample too small. - means zero or rounds to zero.]

Characteristics	Total occupied units	Tenure		Housing unit characteristics			
		Owner	Renter	New construction 4 yrs	Mobile homes	Physical problems	
						Severe	Moderate
Total	11,128	4,788	6,340	334	337	385	1,154
Rooms							
1 room	121	-	121	-	-	24	12
2 rooms	168	-	168	3	-	15	26
3 rooms	1,283	62	1,221	43	9	59	110
4 rooms	2,535	452	2,083	40	117	89	331
5 rooms	2,754	1,162	1,592	78	136	85	317
6 rooms	2,194	1,440	753	62	38	71	227
7 rooms	1,132	871	261	56	30	20	83
8 rooms	546	441	104	23	7	13	32
9 rooms	221	204	17	8	-	3	14
10 rooms or more	175	155	20	20	-	4	2
Median	5.0	6.0	4.3	5.5	4.8	4.6	4.8
Bedrooms							
None	193	-	193	3	-	33	31
1	1,740	86	1,654	46	5	72	141
2	3,753	1,030	2,723	66	134	126	468
3	4,124	2,673	1,450	145	184	118	409
4 or more	1,319	998	320	73	15	36	105
Median	2.5	3.0	2.0	2.9	2.7	2.2	2.4
Complete Bathrooms							
None	120	38	82	-	-	98	9
1	6,895	1,984	4,912	98	148	198	938
1 and one-half	1,778	1,106	672	36	65	44	81
2 or more	2,335	1,661	674	200	124	44	126
Square Footage of Unit							
Single detached and mobile homes	5,569	4,127	1,442	203	337	193	687
Less than 500	106	49	58	-	20	17	26
500 to 749	370	214	156	3	81	31	91
750 to 999	662	370	291	17	111	27	129
1,000 to 1,499	1,530	1,110	420	40	60	56	200
1,500 to 1,999	996	821	175	56	18	18	78
2,000 to 2,499	546	485	60	15	-	5	29
2,500 to 2,999	304	265	39	8	-	5	24
3,000 to 3,999	231	194	37	9	-	-	10
4,000 or more	139	128	11	14	-	5	7
Not reported	684	489	194	40	46	29	93

[Continued]

★ 381 ★

Unit and Lot Size: Black-Occupied Units
[Continued]

Characteristics	Total occupied units	Tenure		Housing unit characteristics			
				New construction	Mobile homes	Physical problems	
		Owner	Renter	4 yrs		Severe	Moderate
Median	1,426	1,546	1,142	1,687	848	1,059	1,127
Lot Size							
Less than one-eighth acre	689	576	114	5	13	29	118
One-eighth up to one-quarter acre	876	717	158	38	30	21	103
One-quarter up to one-half acre	637	561	76	42	7	19	37
One-half up to one acre	404	342	62	25	31	11	36
1 to 4 acres	701	576	125	41	88	37	86
5 to 9 acres	50	50	-	-	14	2	7
10 acres or more	109	74	35	4	8	18	34
Don't know	2,159	982	1,177	72	128	46	304
Not reported	957	667	289	6	16	31	72
Median	.32	.32	.29	.46	1.65	.50	.24
Persons Per Room							
0.50 or less	6,722	3,233	3,489	232	165	184	655
0.51 to 1.00	3,961	1,425	2,536	89	143	165	418
1.01 to 1.50	369	108	262	13	25	19	73
1.51 or more	76	22	54	-	4	16	8
Square Feet Per Person							
Single detached and mobile homes	5,569	4,127	1,442	203	337	193	687
Less than 200	300	173	127	4	55	27	64
200 to 299	573	320	253	23	63	24	89
300 to 399	682	458	224	28	62	14	93
400 to 499	645	457	188	25	34	16	59
500 to 599	464	387	78	12	20	16	33
600 to 699	371	290	81	5	23	16	55
700 to 799	359	296	64	17	12	13	37
800 to 899	234	198	36	5	12	7	31
900 to 999	240	205	35	5	2	7	21
1,000 to 1,499	566	465	101	17	8	19	74
1,500 or more	450	390	60	21	-	5	38
Not reported	684	489	194	40	46	29	93
Median	552	609	411	510	344	504	487

Source: "Size of Unit and Lot-Occupied Units with Black Householder," *American Housing Survey for the United States in 1993*, p. 194.

Improvements

★ 382 ★

Repairs, Improvements and Alterations

[Numbers in thousands. Consistent with the 1990 Census. ...means not applicable or sample too small. - means zero or rounds to zero.]

Characteristics	Total occupied units	Tenure		Housing unit characteristics			
		Owner	Renter	New construction 4 yrs	Mobile homes	Severe	Moderate
Total	4,788	4,788	...	192	252	137	450
Repairs, Improvements, Alterations in Last 2 Years							
Roof replaced (all or part)	904	904	...	8	16	38	112
Mostly done by household	165	165	...	-	3	18	31
Mostly done by others	710	710	...	8	13	20	76
Workers not reported	30	30	...	-	-	-	5
Costing $500 or more	619	619	...	4	7	20	66
Costing less than $500	190	190	...	-	5	14	35
Cost not reported	96	96	...	5	5	5	10
Roof replacement not reported	83	83	...	6	7	2	9
Additions built	170	170	...	5	7	-	23
Mostly done by household	37	37	...	5	5	-	5
Mostly done by others	131	131	...	-	2	-	19
Workers not reported	2	2	...	-	-	-	-
Costing $500 or more	121	121	...	5	5	-	9
Costing less than $500	21	21	...	-	2	-	6
Cost not reported	28	28	...	-	-	-	8
Additions not reported	80	80	...	6	7	2	9
Kitchen remodeled or added	389	389	...	-	11	14	30
Mostly done by household	148	148	...	-	6	10	7
Mostly done by others	240	240	...	-	6	4	23
Workers not reported	2	2	...	-	-	-	-
Costing $500 or more	257	257	...	-	4	7	13
Costing less than $500	97	97	...	-	7	7	12
Cost not reported	35	35	...	-	-	-	5
Kitchen remodeled or added not reported	81	81	...	6	7	2	7
Bathroom remodeled or added	452	452	...	-	12	9	61
Mostly done by household	209	209	...	-	7	6	29
Mostly done by others	235	235	...	-	5	3	31
Workers not reported	7	7	...	-	-	-	-
Costing $500 or more	241	241	...	-	4	1	28
Costing less than $500	152	152	...	-	8	8	25

[Continued]

★ 382 ★

Repairs, Improvements and Alterations
[Continued]

Characteristics	Total occupied units	Tenure		Housing unit characteristics			
		Owner	Renter	New construction 4 yrs	Mobile homes	Physical problems	
						Severe	Moderate
Cost not reported	59	59	...	-	-	-	8
Bathroom remodeled or added not reported	83	83	...	9	7	2	7
Siding replaced or added	221	221	...	-	5	3	24
Mostly done by household	38	38	...	-	3	3	7
Mostly done by others	169	169	...	-	2	-	18
Workers not reported	14	14	...	-	-	-	-
Costing $500 or more	115	115	...	-	-	-	17
Costing less than $500	39	39	...	-	3	3	2
Cost not reported	68	68	...	-	2	-	5
Siding replaced or added not reported	83	83	...	6	7	2	7
Storm doors/windows bought and installed	604	604	...	3	9	15	50
Mostly done by household	160	160	...	3	7	2	14
Mostly done by others	431	431	...	-	2	13	33
Workers not reported	14	14	...	-	-	-	3
Costing $500 or more	298	298	...	3	3	8	15
Costing less than $500	215	215	...	3	7	2	25
Cost not reported	92	92	...	-	-	5	10
Storm doors/windows bought and installed not reported	884	84	...	6	10	2	11
Major equipment replaced or added	375	375	...	7	10	13	20
Mostly done by household	46	46	...	-	-	8	-
Mostly done by others	325	325	...	7	10	5	17
Workers not reported	5	5	...	-	-	-	3
Costing $500 or more	248	248	...	7	7	5	8
Costing less than $500	74	74	...	-	3	5	4
Cost not reported	54	54	...	-	-	2	8
Major equipment replaced or added not reported	88	88	...	6	7	2	7
Insulation added	235	235	...	3	6	2	32
Mostly done by household	84	84	...	-	3	2	8
Mostly done by others	137	137	...	3	-	-	16
Workers not reported	14	14	...	-	4	-	9
Costing $500 or more	40	40	...	-	-	-	1
Costing less than $500	121	121	...	3	3	2	15
Cost not reported	74	74	...	-	4	-	16
Insulation added not reported	92	92	...	6	7	2	7
Other major work[1]	804	804	...	16	12	26	59

[Continued]

★ 382 ★

Repairs, Improvements and Alterations
[Continued]

Characteristics	Total occupied units	Tenure		Housing unit characteristics			
				New construction	Mobile homes	Physical problems	
		Owner	Renter	4 yrs		Severe	Moderate
Mostly done by household	206	206	...	7	7	8	9
Mostly done by others	575	575	...	6	5	16	48
Workers not reported	21	21	...	3	-	2	2
Other major work not reported	97	97	...	6	7	2	9
Government Subsidy for Repairs							
Units with major repairs the last 2 years	2,213	2,213	...	37	56	63	196
Recovered low-interest loan or grant	108	108	...	-	2	7	6
No low-interest loan or grant	2,036	2,036	...	29	48	54	186
Not reported	88	68	...	8	7	2	4

Source: "Repairs, Improvements, and Alterations - Occupied Units with Black Householder," *American Housing Survey for the United States in 1993*, p. 228. *Notes:* 1. Includes other major repairs, alternations, or improvements totaling over $500 each.

Income Characteristics

★ 383 ★

Families and Primary Individuals: Income, Part 1-1

[Numbers in thousands. Consistent with the 1990 Census. ...means not applicable or sample too small. - means zero or rounds to zero.]

Characteristics	Total	Zero to negative	$1 to $4,999	$5,000 to $9,999	$10,000 to $14,999	$15,000 to $19,999	$20,000 to $29,999
Total	11,128	308	1,249	1,956	1,328	1,221	1,850
Units in Structure							
1, detached	5,232	131	369	803	549	509	887
1, attached	1,015	31	126	172	112	97	179
2 to 4	1,627	54	255	305	252	215	241
5 to 9	953	27	141	203	139	92	177
10 to 19	762	17	120	114	114	114	131
20 to 49	532	22	92	99	49	68	102
50 or more	671	18	106	182	65	67	92
Mobile home or trailer	337	6	39	79	47	59	40
Year Structure Built[1]							
1990 to 1994	307	3	3	48	13	24	41
1985 to 1989	556	8	33	68	51	51	90

[Continued]

★ 383 ★

Families and Primary Individuals: Income, Part 1-1
[Continued]

Characteristics	Total	Zero to negative	$1 to $4,999	$5,000 to $9,999	$10,000 to $14,999	$15,000 to $19,999	$20,000 to $29,999
1980 to 1984	686	15	56	87	90	78	120
1975 to 1979	891	31	95	143	81	109	154
1970 to 1974	1,254	22	146	242	134	141	214
1960 to 1969	1,819	51	196	276	198	175	335
1950 to 1959	1,481	50	192	264	182	178	256
1940 to 1949	1,302	28	181	273	137	150	182
1930 to 1939	1,021	34	153	182	175	106	165
1920 to 1929	774	42	69	156	121	85	123
1919 or earlier	1,038	24	125	217	146	123	170
Median	1960	1955	1955	1956	1955	1958	1961
Rooms							
1 room	121	2	33	22	16	9	15
2 rooms	168	3	21	55	20	30	21
3 rooms	1,283	62	207	340	179	155	208
4 rooms	2,535	66	433	537	353	312	418
5 rooms	2,754	90	310	518	370	299	442
6 rooms	2,194	49	150	298	225	252	429
7 rooms	1,132	12	73	139	93	97	198
8 rooms	546	12	15	31	44	41	73
9 rooms	221	5	-	9	13	17	30
10 rooms or more	175	5	6	7	14	9	17
Median	5.0	4.7	4.3	4.5	4.8	4.9	5.1
Bedrooms							
None	193	5	44	40	25	24	25
1	1,740	70	252	421	232	225	305
2	3,753	112	556	730	507	439	614
3	4,124	103	304	606	454	410	692
4 or more	1,319	17	93	158	110	122	213
Median	2.5	2.2	2.1	2.2	2.3	2.3	2.5
Complete Bathrooms							
None	120	4	32	34	10	22	15
1	6,895	224	1,021	1,533	960	803	1,100
1 and one-half	1,778	35	103	223	182	219	349
2 or more	2,335	45	93	166	176	177	387
Main Heating Equipment							
Warm-air furnace	5,300	127	500	820	569	589	931
Steam or hot water system	1,931	74	209	323	229	194	288
Electric heat pump	846	12	64	74	102	70	175
Built-in electric units	679	22	86	139	77	78	109
Floor, wall, or other built-in hot air units without ducts	741	23	104	164	117	114	104

[Continued]

★ 383 ★

Families and Primary Individuals: Income, Part 1-1

[Continued]

Characteristics	Total	Zero to negative	$1 to $4,999	$5,000 to $9,999	$10,000 to $14,999	$15,000 to $19,999	$20,000 to $29,999
Room heaters with flue	373	4	72	78	57	53	77
Room heaters without flue	585	23	117	180	97	59	65
Portable electric heaters	112	7	13	37	10	7	17
Stoves	236	4	34	86	19	26	45
Fireplaces with inserts	21	-	-	4	-	-	2
Fireplaces without inserts	25	-	-	4	10	5	-
Other	157	7	29	32	16	8	20
None	124	5	22	15	25	19	16
Source of Water							
Public system or private company	10,439	290	1,186	1,808	1,252	1,148	1,718
Well serving 1 to 5 units	547	13	47	117	62	59	122
Drilled	400	11	29	74	47	42	101
Dug	122	-	16	38	13	14	15
Not reported	25	2	2	5	2	2	6
Other	142	5	17	30	15	14	10
Means of Sewage Disposal							
Public sewer	9,964	272	1,144	1,734	1,197	1,093	1,639
Septic tank, cesspool, chemical toilet	1,113	33	86	210	124	121	207
Other	51	2	19	12	6	7	4
Main House Heating Fuel							
Housing units with heating fuel	11,004	303	1,226	1,941	1,304	1,202	1,834
Electricity	2,922	70	279	475	334	330	558
Piped gas	5,945	169	681	1,037	717	627	917
Bottled gas	362	16	63	82	35	45	44
Fuel oil	1,242	34	131	204	148	132	226
Kerosene or other liquid fuel	174	8	29	36	32	30	25
Coal and coke	21	-	-	2	6	4	6
Wood	297	4	34	96	29	27	56
Solar energy	-	-	-	-	-	-	-
Other	42	2	8	8	2	7	2

Source: "Income of Families and Primary Individuals by Selected Characteristics - Occupied Units with Black Householder," *American Housing Survey for the United States in 1993*, p. 237. *Note:* 1. For mobile home, oldest category is 1939 or earlier.

★ 384 ★

Income Characteristics

Families and Primary Individuals: Income, Part 1-2

[Numbers in thousands. Consistent with the 1990 Census. ...means not applicable or sample too small. - means zero or rounds to zero.]

Characteristics	$30,000 to $39,999	$40,000 to $59,999	$60,000 to $79,999	$80,000 to $99,999	$100,000 to $119,999	$120,000 or more	Median
Total	1,083	1,225	510	194	87	117	17,963
Units in Structure							
1, detached	553	723	385	141	77	105	22,869
1, attached	87	137	42	22	8	3	18,449
2 to 4	145	115	30	8	3	4	13,957
5 to 9	75	79	13	6	-	-	13,773
10 to 19	82	60	8	2	-	-	15,713
20 to 49	45	39	6	8	-	-	15,272
50 or more	62	50	20	4	-	5	12,270
Mobile home or trailer	35	21	6	2	-	-	14,530
Year Structure Built[1]							
1990 to 1994	42	67	30	15	9	11	35,168
1985 to 1989	65	102	41	23	5	18	27,470
1980 to 1984	96	102	32	8	-	3	21,451
1975 to 1979	82	119	47	18	2	11	19,388
1970 to 1974	123	112	80	18	9	12	17,945
1960 to 1969	192	222	103	35	17	17	20,378
1950 to 1959	126	137	42	26	14	15	16,487
1940 to 1949	126	132	45	23	7	15	16,035
1930 to 1939	80	72	27	10	13	6	14,065
1920 to 1929	77	59	27	8	5	3	14,970
1919 or earlier	75	100	35	10	5	5	15,241
Median	1963	1965	1968	1966	1959	1968	...
Rooms							
1 room	15	8	-	-	-	-	11,115
2 rooms	15	3	-	-	-	-	11,264
3 rooms	75	43	13	-	-	-	10,896
4 rooms	203	179	18	7	5	5	13,283
5 rooms	312	269	96	35	5	7	16,491
6 rooms	210	361	139	44	20	16	22,843
7 rooms	143	183	92	42	28	31	27,639
8 rooms	63	99	108	33	7	19	39,044
9 rooms	28	46	19	22	9	21	43,372
10 rooms or more	17	34	24	10	12	18	46,626
Median	5.2	5.8	6.4	6.8	7.0	7.5	...
Bedrooms							
None	22	8	-	-	-	-	11,623
1	129	80	23	-	-	3	12,726
2	338	341	71	35	5	4	14,716
3	466	603	281	109	49	46	22,647

[Continued]

★ 384 ★

Families and Primary Individuals: Income, Part 1-2
[Continued]

Characteristics	$30,000 to $39,999	$40,000 to $59,999	$60,000 to $79,999	$80,000 to $99,999	$100,000 to $119,999	$120,000 or more	Median
4 or more	128	194	135	51	33	63	27,463
Median	2.6	2.8	3.1	3.1	3.3	3.5+	...
Complete Bathrooms							
None	2	-	1	-	-	-	8,523
1	597	478	112	41	12	16	13,491
1 and one-half	198	258	122	47	20	22	23,629
2 or more	286	490	275	106	55	79	34,333
Main Heating Equipment							
Warm-air furnace	565	679	285	115	56	64	20,486
Steam or hot water system	205	233	92	46	15	24	18,379
Electric heat pump	97	143	68	17	10	15	25,773
Built-in electric units	80	59	21	4	-	5	15,999
Floor, wall, or other built-in hot air units							
without ducts	39	36	24	4	7	5	13,394
Room heaters with flue	22	9	2	-	-	-	12,927
Room heaters without flue	9	28	7	-	-	-	9,227
Portable electric heaters	16	2	-	3	-	-	9,968
Stoves	7	11	3	2	-	-	9,648
Fireplaces with inserts	3	2	7	2	-	-	...
Fireplaces without inserts	3	2	-	-	-	-	...
Other	30	13	2	-	-	-	13,226
None	9	9	-	-	-	4	14,017
Source of Water							
Public system or private company	1,037	1,154	475	181	80	110	17,979
Well serving 1 to 5 units	40	42	23	10	7	5	17,974
Drilled	29	25	23	8	7	5	19,760
Dug	9	14	-	2	-	-	12,744
Not reported	2	3	-	-	-	-	...
Other	6	29	12	2	-	3	16,675
Means of Sewage Disposal							
Public sewer	974	1,103	458	171	78	103	17,906
Septic tank, cesspool, chemical toilet	110	122	53	23	9	15	19,237
Other	-	-	-	-	-	-	...
Main House Heating Fuel							
Housing units with heating fuel	1,074	1,216	510	194	87	113	18,030
Electricity	317	357	124	41	10	29	19,599
Piped gas	561	691	305	119	60	61	17,934
Bottled gas	42	19	5	2	-	7	12,701
Fuel oil	128	127	55	28	15	13	18,908
Kerosene or other liquid fuel	2	2	10	-	-	-	12,202

[Continued]

★ 384 ★

Families and Primary Individuals: Income, Part 1-2
[Continued]

Characteristics	$30,000 to $39,999	$40,000 to $59,999	$60,000 to $79,999	$80,000 to $99,999	$100,000 to $119,999	$120,000 or more	Median
Coal and coke	-	2	-	-	-	-	...
Wood	18	16	10	4	3	-	12,479
Solar energy	-	-	-	-	-	-	...
Other	6	2	2	-	-	3	...

Source: "Income of Families and Primary Individuals by Selected Characteristics - Occupied Units with Black Householder," *American Housing Survey for the United States in 1993,* p. 237. *Note:* 1. For mobile home, oldest category is 1939 or earlier.

★ 385 ★

Income Characteristics

Families and Primary Individuals: Income, Part 2-1

[Numbers in thousands. Consistent with the 1990 Census. ...means not applicable or sample too small. - means zero or rounds to zero.]

Characteristics	Total	Zero to negative	$1 to $4,999	$5,000 to $9,999	$10,000 to $14,999	$15,000 to $19,999	$20,000 to $29,999
Cooking Fuel							
With cooking fuel	11,061	303	1,237	1,946	1,315	1,215	1,833
Electricity	4,656	99	412	720	549	511	845
Piped gas	5,905	191	738	1,104	715	632	936
Bottled gas	478	14	79	119	47	70	49
Kerosene or other liquid fuel	12	-	3	2	2	2	-
Coal and coke	-	-	...	-	-	-	-
Wood	2	-	-	-	2	-	-
Other	8	-	5	-	-	-	3
Persons							
1 person	3,024	132	399	823	364	294	521
2 persons	2,832	67	248	482	400	403	507
3 persons	2,242	39	318	275	224	242	355
4 persons	1,665	42	165	205	164	148	251
5 persons	801	20	72	90	101	66	114
6 persons	320	2	35	38	39	38	56
7 persons or more	244	5	12	43	36	29	45
Median	2.4	1.8	2.4	1.8	2.3	2.3	2.3
Household Composition by Age of Householder							
2-or-more person households	8,104	175	850	1,133	964	927	1,329
Married-couple families, no nonrelatives	3,300	58	70	183	270	340	576
Under 25 years	81	-	-	7	24	15	26
25 to 29 years	227	-	7	5	10	44	42
30 to 34 years	438	7	4	9	16	25	78

[Continued]

★ 385 ★

Families and Primary Individuals: Income, Part 2-1

[Continued]

Characteristics	Total	Zero to negative	$1 to $4,999	$5,000 to $9,999	$10,000 to $14,999	$15,000 to $19,999	$20,000 to $29,999
35 to 44 years	927	20	22	29	50	80	149
45 to 64 years	1,194	29	23	60	88	80	193
65 years and over	433	3	13	73	81	97	88
Other male householder	925	11	49	137	131	128	160
Under 45 years	583	9	38	88	64	81	98
45 to 64 years	213	2	9	20	32	27	46
65 years and over	130	-	2	29	35	21	16
Other female householder	3,878	106	731	814	563	459	593
Under 45 years	2,520	82	594	549	338	289	329
45 to 64 years	941	24	96	150	132	126	189
65 years and over	417	-	42	115	93	44	74
1-persons households	3,024	132	399	823	364	294	521
Male householder	1,461	57	154	291	181	185	280
Under 45 years	748	22	70	68	94	116	185
45 to 64 years	449	28	46	105	56	27	74
65 years and over	263	6	38	118	31	42	21
Female householder	1,563	75	245	531	183	108	241
Under 45 years	476	26	46	55	79	45	128
45 to 64 years	505	40	75	117	60	54	86
65 years and over	582	10	122	360	44	9	27
Own Never Married Children Under 18 Years Old							
No own children under 18 years	6,717	203	588	1,319	854	767	1,221
With own children under 18 years	4,412	105	661	637	474	455	628
Under 6 years only	950	23	234	132	91	95	121
1	572	19	106	57	56	76	73
2	287	4	105	43	19	14	40
3 or more	91	-	23	32	16	5	8
6 to 17 years only	2,462	61	260	348	259	260	376
1	1,338	32	117	172	148	146	204
2	770	16	102	109	67	78	110
3 or more	354	14	41	67	43	36	62
Both age groups	999	20	166	157	124	100	131
2	446	10	58	48	51	44	68
3 or more	554	10	108	109	73	56	63
Monthly Housing Costs							
Less than $100	419	16	180	129	29	31	17
$100 to $199	1,373	39	285	525	144	123	146
$200 to $249	722	22	103	208	125	77	107
$250 to $299	721	12	92	192	128	68	127
$300 to $349	658	10	56	126	142	105	103
$350 to $399	862	29	85	154	161	167	143
$400 to $449	717	29	55	133	110	123	141

[Continued]

★ 385 ★

Families and Primary Individuals: Income, Part 2-1
[Continued]

Characteristics	Total	Zero to negative	$1 to $4,999	$5,000 to $9,999	$10,000 to $14,999	$15,000 to $19,999	$20,000 to $29,999
$450 to $499	654	19	46	94	102	110	144
$500 to $599	1,159	29	54	130	151	134	295
$600 to $699	938	12	39	70	76	99	186
$700 to $799	610	14	18	24	52	50	110
$800 to $999	667	13	24	15	31	44	135
$1,000 to $1,249	369	6	3	14	-	25	22
$1,250 to $1,499	132	-	2	3	3	-	18
$1,500 or more	156	-	-	5	2	6	14
No cash rent	473	30	186	93	46	38	55
Mortgage payment not reported	498	26	22	40	26	25	88
Median (excludes no cash rent)	423	395	227	263	369	404	474
Median Monthly Housing Costs For Owners							
Monthly costs including all mortgages plus maintenance costs	464	362	206	232	316	375	424
Monthly costs excluding 2nd subsequent mortgages and maintenance costs	415	355	191	225	303	336	382

Source: "Income of Families and Primary Individuals by Selected Characteristics - Occupied Units with Black Householder," *American Housing Survey for the United States in 1993*, p. 237.

★ 386 ★

Income Characteristics

Families and Primary Individuals: Income, Part 2-2

[Numbers in thousands. Consistent with the 1990 Census. ...means not applicable or sample too small. - means zero or rounds to zero.]

Characteristics	$30,000 to $39,999	$40,000 to $59,999	$60,000 to $79,999	$80,000 to $99,999	$100,000 to $119,999	$120,000 or more	Median
Cooking Fuel							
With cooking fuel	1,079	1,225	510	194	87	117	18,004
Electricity	497	590	248	86	39	59	20,444
Piped gas	534	604	248	100	48	55	16,620
Bottled gas	46	31	14	8	-	2	12,935
Kerosene or other liquid fuel	2	-	-	-	-	-	...
Coal and coke	-	-	-	-	-	-	...
Wood	-	-	-	-	-	-	...
Other	-	-	-	-	-	-	...
Persons							
1 person	262	195	19	10	3	3	12,177
2 persons	255	257	125	54	21	12	17,714

[Continued]

★ 386 ★

Families and Primary Individuals: Income, Part 2-2

[Continued]

Characteristics	$30,000 to $39,999	$40,000 to $59,999	$60,000 to $79,999	$80,000 to $99,999	$100,000 to $119,999	$120,000 or more	Median
3 persons	246	323	124	51	7	38	20,653
4 persons	172	267	138	37	38	38	24,324
5 persons	79	124	77	28	13	16	24,420
6 persons	47	27	22	7	3	5	21,422
7 persons or more	23	32	6	5	2	5	19,371
Median	2.6	3.0	3.4	3.1	3.9	3.6	...
Household Composition by Age of Householder							
2-or-more person households	821	1,030	491	184	85	114	20,014
Married-couple families, no nonrelatives	438	665	364	161	70	106	33,497
Under 25 years	4	3	-	-	-	2	18,028
25 to 29 years	33	57	18	6	3	3	31,722
30 to 34 years	76	140	47	13	10	13	40,496
35 to 44 years	142	186	150	59	11	30	38,047
45 to 64 years	147	262	143	74	39	56	38,432
65 years and over	37	17	7	9	7	2	17,417
Other male householder	130	103	50	13	10	3	20,427
Under 45 years	92	63	33	10	8	-	21,146
45 to 64 years	24	30	156	3	3	3	23,677
65 years and over	15	11	2	-	-	-	14,885
Other female householder	253	263	77	10	5	5	12,558
Under 45 years	156	142	35	5	3	-	10,529
45 to 64 years	80	105	32	2	2	3	17,743
65 years and over	18	16	10	2	-	2	12,758
1-persons households	262	195	19	10	3	3	12,177
Male householder	171	115	11	10	3	3	16,286
Under 45 years	109	68	9	7	-	-	20,215
45 to 64 years	57	45	2	3	3	3	14,007
65 years and over	5	2	-	-	-	-	8,714
Female householder	91	80	9	-	-	-	9,343
Under 45 years	56	38	2	-	-	-	18,452
45 to 64 years	31	42	2	-	-	-	11,818
65 years and over	4	-	4	-	-	-	7,206
Own Never Married Children Under 18 Years Old							
No own children under 18 years	664	644	227	114	64	52	17,571
With own children under 18 years	420	581	283	80	23	65	18,625
Under 6 years only	65	121	44	16	-	7	14,682
1	52	84	33	11	-	4	18,180
2	10	32	11	5	-	2	8,969
3 or more	3	4	-	-	-	-	8,472
6 to 17 years only	263	337	189	50	15	44	21,142
1	148	211	91	26	9	34	22,669
2	80	93	78	23	6	8	21,229
3 or more	35	33	20	-	-	2	16,532

[Continued]

★ 386 ★

Families and Primary Individuals: Income, Part 2-2
[Continued]

Characteristics	$30,000 to $39,999	$40,000 to $59,999	$60,000 to $79,999	$80,000 to $99,999	$100,000 to $119,999	$120,000 or more	Median
Both age groups	91	124	50	14	9	14	16,631
2	45	77	24	3	5	12	21,715
3 or more	46	47	26	10	4	2	13,434
Monthly Housing Costs							
Less than $100	13	5	-	-	-	-	5,516
$100 to $199	51	42	11	-	5	3	8,454
$200 to $249	37	29	7	2	2	2	11,104
$250 to $299	38	48	12	2	2	-	12,512
$300 to $349	48	28	25	2	10	2	14,825
$350 to $399	67	31	17	3	2	3	15,052
$400 to $449	59	52	14	2	-	-	16,279
$450 to $499	77	45	11	3	-	5	18,013
$500 to $599	163	155	25	12	5	5	22,749
$600 to $699	175	187	68	14	12	-	29,244
$700 to $799	115	132	65	20	4	7	33,403
$800 to $999	103	195	66	21	7	12	36,905
$1,000 to $1,249	47	109	89	33	4	18	52,387
$1,250 to $1,499	18	26	31	16	5	10	57,018
$1,500 or more	10	24	19	31	18	27	77,703
No cash rent	11	13	2	-	-	-	6,083
Mortgage payment not reported	53	104	50	32	11	22	34,213
Median (excludes no cash rent)	574	663	762	987	690	1,112	...
Median Monthly Housing Costs For Owners							
Monthly costs including all mortgages plus maintenance costs	559	730	861	1,044	768	1,118	...
Monthly costs excluding 2nd subsequent mortgages and maintenance costs	519	629	750	944	861	1,003	...

Source: "Income of Families and Primary Individuals by Selected Characteristics - Occupied Units with Black Householder," *American Housing Survey for the United States in 1993*, p. 237.

★ 387 ★
Income Characteristics

Families and Primary Individuals: Income, Part 3-1

[Numbers in thousands. Consistent with the 1990 Census. ...means not applicable or sample too small. - means zero or rounds to zero.]

Characteristics	Total	Zero to negative	$1 to $4,999	$5,000 to $9,999	$10,000 to $14,999	$15,000 to $19,999	$20,000 to $29,999
Monthly Housing Costs as Percent of Current Income[1]							
Less than 5 percent	140	2	2	2	5	11	11
5 to 9 percent	629	-	5	13	19	58	123
10 to 14 percent	1,077	-	14	58	73	97	246
15 to 19 percent	1,280	3	25	101	78	129	257
20 to 24 percent	1,299	3	51	106	132	133	322
25 to 29 percent	1,105	-	49	191	147	191	247
30 to 34 percent	913	-	74	210	154	156	185
35 to 39 percent	599	-	27	140	123	114	136
40 to 49 percent	795	-	79	214	218	131	106
50 to 59 percent	551	-	78	211	145	56	25
60 to 69 percent	348	-	50	146	87	28	33
70 to 99 percent	539	-	146	271	57	49	10
100 percent or more[2]	634	3	433	160	18	8	8
Zero or negative income	248	240	8	-	-	-	-
No cash rent	473	30	186	93	46	38	55
Mortgage payment not reported	498	26	22	40	26	25	88
Median (excludes 3 pervious lines)	27	21	83	44	36	29	23
Median (excludes 4 lines before medians)	26	18	47	40	35	29	23
OWNER OCCUPIED UNITS							
Total	4,788	122	274	601	439	460	814
Value							
Less than $10,000	217	12	48	45	24	27	28
$10,000 to $19,999	317	5	39	73	59	25	61
$20,000 to $29,999	450	8	45	89	63	59	85
$30,000 to $39,999	498	19	27	107	46	61	87
$40,000 to $49,999	526	22	33	63	60	68	127
$50,000 to $59,999	461	12	13	58	49	37	83
$60,000 to $69,999	436	7	17	46	32	36	66
$70,000 to $79,999	327	5	17	25	25	24	78
$80,000 to $99,999	533	11	19	31	20	62	82
$100,000 to $119,999	277	2	6	25	26	23	46
$120,000 to $149,999	312	8	-	19	15	10	32
$150,000 to $199,999	264	10	9	10	15	15	23
$200,000 to $249,999	91	3	-	5	-	4	13
$250,000 to $299,999	37	-	-	-	-	4	-
$300,000 or more	41	-	-	4	7	5	3
Median	58,372	47,931	31,774	38,771	44,680	48,493	52,389
Ratio of Value to Current Income[1]							
Less than 1.5	1,615	-	24	58	81	93	229

[Continued]

★ 387 ★

Families and Primary Individuals: Income, Part 3-1
[Continued]

Characteristics	Total	Zero to negative	$1 to $4,999	$5,000 to $9,999	$10,000 to $14,999	$15,000 to $19,999	$20,000 to $29,999
1.5 to 1.9	572	-	7	27	24	61	124
2.0 to 2.4	495	-	7	29	57	55	120
2.5 to 2.9	369	-	5	33	20	31	97
3.0 to 3.9	455	-	13	64	71	66	131
4.0 to 4.9	279	-	19	58	40	59	46
5.0 or more	872	-	193	332	147	96	67
Zero or negative income	130	122	8	-	-	-	-
Median	2.1	...	5.0+	5.0+	3.5	2.9	2.2
Monthly Payment for Principal and Interest							
Less than $100	115	2	7	22	13	20	20
$100 to $199	387	7	15	57	56	68	83
$200 to $249	219	8	17	36	25	19	30
$250 to $299	180	2	9	18	16	20	43
$300 to $349	176	-	-	10	16	14	60
$350 to $399	143	2	2	8	7	21	24
$400 to $449	200	2	2	-	7	14	39
$450 to $499	139	2	2	10	14	18	10
$500 to $599	257	2	2	2	9	15	31
$600 to $699	205	2	-	2	9	9	31
$700 to $799	135	3	-	2	-	5	11
$800 to $999	161	-	-	7	2	13	12
$1,000 to $1,249	87	-	2	-	-	3	3
$1,250 to $1,499	42	-	-	2	-	-	6
$1,500 or more	41	-	-	-	-	2	3
Not reported	498	26	22	40	26	25	88
Median	406	253	225	213	236	286	322
Average Monthly Cost Paid for Rent Estate Taxes							
Less than $25	1,517	31	166	325	219	171	228
$25 to $49	1,040	35	46	136	107	99	244
$50 to $74	702	16	21	54	39	81	126
$75 to $99	455	11	12	27	23	46	72
$100 to $149	502	19	20	34	29	33	74
$150 to $199	199	5	-	10	8	7	22
$200 to more	373	5	9	16	14	23	47
Median	46	46	25-	25-	25	40	43
Purchase Price							
Home purchased or built	4,395	98	197	514	405	414	748
Less than $10,000	539	8	36	159	84	77	89
$10,000 to $19,999	883	20	42	153	106	124	176
$20,000 to $29,999	499	15	33	54	51	54	82

[Continued]

★ 387 ★

Families and Primary Individuals: Income, Part 3-1

[Continued]

Characteristics	Total	Zero to negative	$1 to $4,999	$5,000 to $9,999	$10,000 to $14,999	$15,000 to $19,999	$20,000 to $29,999
$30,000 to $39,999	389	2	10	17	33	34	89
$40,000 to $49,999	309	2	-	18	19	23	51
$50,000 to $59,999	252	5	7	4	17	25	31
$60,000 to $69,999	205	3	2	5	3	13	32
$70,000 to $79,999	155	-	2	3	3	9	23
$80,000 to $99,999	227	5	-	4	-	12	16
$100,000 to $119,999	71	3	-	-	-	-	10
$120,000 to $149,999	106	2	-	2	-	3	10
$150,000 to $199,999	50	3	3	-	2	-	-
$200,000 to $249,999	27	-	-	-	-	-	-
$250,000 to $299,999	13	-	-	-	-	-	-
$300,000 or more	18	-	-	-	-	-	3
Not reported	654	31	62	95	87	41	136
Median	29,003	24,110	17,547	13,320	17,103	18,886	24,958
Received as inheritance or gift	213	8	61	54	21	22	24
Not reported	180	16	16	34	13	24	41
RENTER OCCUPIED UNITS							
Total	6,340	185	975	1,355	889	761	1,036
Rent Reduction							
No subsidy or income reporting	4,398	128	375	696	630	615	899
Rent control	120	7	4	21	21	11	20
No rent control	4,276	121	370	675	607	603	879
Reduced by owner	210	16	30	42	28	28	40
Not reduced by owner	4,060	106	340	633	576	576	839
Owner reduction not reported	5	-	-	-	3	-	-
Rent control not reported	3	-	-	-	3	-	-
Owner by public housing authority	939	23	300	350	117	57	67
Other, Federal subsidy	609	15	183	207	95	58	25
Other, State or local subsidy	186	5	87	48	16	13	11
Other, Income verification	127	8	10	38	19	15	22
Subsidy, or income verification not reported	80	5	20	16	11	3	11

Source: "Income of Families and Primary Individuals by Selected Characteristics - Occupied Units with Black Householder," *American Housing Survey for the United States in 1993*, p. 237. *Notes:* 1. Beginning with 1989 this item uses current income in its calculation. See appendix A. 2. May reflect a temporary situation, living off savings, or response error.

★ 388 ★

Income Characteristics

Families and Primary Individuals: Income, Part 3-2

[Numbers in thousands. Consistent with the 1990 Census. ...means not applicable or sample too small. - means zero or rounds to zero.]

Characteristics	$30,000 to $39,999	$40,000 to $59,999	$60,000 to $79,999	$80,000 to $99,999	$100,000 to $119,999	$120,000 or more	Median
Monthly Housing Costs as Percent of Current Income[1]							
Less than 5 percent	19	32	19	5	17	15	50,946
5 to 9 percent	95	139	79	39	27	32	40,293
10 to 14 percent	164	203	137	48	10	26	33,071
15 to 19 percent	203	325	111	26	12	10	32,353
20 to 24 percent	220	220	79	23	3	8	27,016
25 to 29 percent	151	89	16	15	5	4	19,331
30 to 34 percent	72	52	5	3	2	-	15,602
35 to 39 percent	31	22	5	-	-	-	15,386
40 to 49 percent	32	13	2	-	-	-	12,402
50 to 59 percent	26	6	3	3	-	-	9,689
60 to 69 percent	-	3	1	-	-	-	9,246
70 to 99 percent	5	2	-	-	-	-	7,293
100 percent or more[2]	2	-	-	-	-	-	3,618
Zero or negative income	-	-	-	-	-	-	1-
No cash rent	11	13	2	-	-	-	6,083
Mortgage payment not reported	53	105	50	32	11	22	34,213
Median (excludes 3 pervious lines)	21	18	15	14	9	10	...
Median (excludes 4 lines before medians)	21	18	15	14	9	10	...
OWNER OCCUPIED UNITS							
Total	543	782	406	156	85	105	26,103
Value							
Less than $10,000	17	10	1	-	5	-	10,673
$10,000 to $19,999	20	27	9	-	-	-	13,564
$20,000 to $29,999	54	26	17	-	5	-	16,755
$30,000 to $39,999	53	75	19	2	2	-	19,097
$40,000 to $49,999	35	77	21	10	3	8	21,322
$50,000 to $59,999	81	69	46	8	3	3	27,436
$60,000 to $69,999	84	92	38	13	5	-	31,765
$70,000 to $79,999	43	74	21	4	5	5	28,592
$80,000 to $99,999	52	107	96	25	18	8	37,731
$100,000 to $119,999	40	58	26	13	5	8	32,709
$120,000 to $149,999	22	104	41	36	8	16	49,310
$150,000 to $199,999	32	44	48	21	12	24	47,883
$200,000 to $249,999	2	14	16	18	8	10	66,717
$250,000 to $299,999	2	3	7	6	5	9	...
$300,000 or more	2	2	-	-	3	15	...
Median	61,294	72,116	86,408	122,320	97,130	161,911	...
Ratio of Value to Current Income[1]							
Less than 1.5	214	419	265	93	63	76	45,174
1.5 to 1.9	114	119	50	26	7	15	33,867
2.0 to 2.4	71	90	33	18	8	7	28,294

[Continued]

★ 388 ★

Families and Primary Individuals: Income, Part 3-2
[Continued]

Characteristics	$30,000 to $39,999	$40,000 to $59,999	$60,000 to $79,999	$80,000 to $99,999	$100,000 to $119,999	$120,000 or more	Median
2.5 to 2.9	56	75	29	12	6	5	29,978
3.0 to 3.9	25	49	26	6	2	2	21,033
4.0 to 4.9	32	22	3	-	-	-	16,952
5.0 or more	29	8	-	-	-	-	8,659
Zero or negative income	-	-	-	-	-	-	1-
Median	1.7	1.5-	1.5-	1.5-	1.5-	1.5-	...
Monthly Payment for Principal and Interest							
Less than $100	13	9	5	-	-	3	18,304
$100 to $199	43	25	18	-	10	5	19,348
$200 to $249	42	30	7	5	-	-	21,575
$250 to $299	15	27	11	15	2	1	25,596
$300 to $349	18	28	17	5	7	-	27,892
$350 to $399	24	33	17	3	-	2	33,251
$400 to $449	32	62	32	5	5	-	41,110
$450 to $499	26	39	13	2	-	3	35,229
$500 to $599	58	83	29	10	4	10	41,815
$600 to $699	21	64	51	7	2	6	48,602
$700 to $799	27	40	35	5	4	2	49,552
$800 to $999	9	60	34	7	2	15	52,783
$1,000 to $1,249	10	10	12	28	10	8	81,671
$1,250 to $1,499	2	8	6	8	2	8	...
$1,500 or more	-	3	8	8	7	10	...
Not reported	53	105	50	32	11	22	34,213
Median	424	508	596	747	588	855	...
Average Monthly Cost Paid for Rent Estate Taxes							
Less than $25	152	149	46	12	3	15	15,505
$25 to $49	125	145	72	12	16	2	23,950
$50 to $74	92	142	72	30	13	16	31,393
$75 to $99	62	114	43	21	10	15	36,015
$100 to $149	44	130	71	26	13	10	39,706
$150 to $199	33	40	41	17	5	12	47,398
$200 to more	35	63	62	38	26	35	51,874
Median	49	67	83	105	105	123	...
Purchase Price							
Home purchased or built	528	754	395	153	83	105	27,593
Less than $10,000	34	40	3	5	5	-	13,980
$10,000 to $19,999	87	109	40	7	17	3	19,885
$20,000 to $29,999	63	70	44	17	7	7	25,125
$30,000 to $39,999	68	60	45	7	8	15	31,316
$40,000 to $49,999	57	80	40	5	7	5	37,022
$50,000 to $59,999	54	54	29	18	5	2	36,672
$60,000 to $69,999	25	80	31	4	5	3	45,109

[Continued]

★ 388 ★

Families and Primary Individuals: Income, Part 3-2

[Continued]

Characteristics	$30,000 to $39,999	$40,000 to $59,999	$60,000 to $79,999	$80,000 to $99,999	$100,000 to $119,999	$120,000 or more	Median
$70,000 to $79,999	32	33	31	12	5	3	43,678
$80,000 to $99,999	21	80	49	24	6	11	53,928
$100,000 to $119,999	8	27	19	2	2	-	51,297
$120,000 to $149,999	13	37	21	7	-	10	52,119
$150,000 to $199,999	3	5	11	16	2	5	...
$200,000 to $249,999	-	4	-	9	5	-	...
$250,000 to $299,999	-	3	7	-	-	3	...
$300,000 or more	-	2	-	-	3	10	...
Not reported	63	69	27	18	5	19	20,838
Median	37,073	47,916	54,592	72,624	42,499	90,172	...
Received as inheritance or gift	10	7	4	-	3	-	8,482
Not reported	5	21	8	3	-	-	17,325
RENTER OCCUPIED UNITS							
Total	541	443	104	38	2	12	13,689
Rent Reduction							
No subsidy or income reporting	509	405	89	38	2	12	18,013
Rent control	19	11	-	4	-	-	17,886
No rent control	490	394	89	34	2	12	18,027
Reduced by owner	14	5	7	2	-	-	13,156
Not reduced by owner	476	387	83	31	2	12	18,261
Owner reduction not reported	-	3	-	-	-	-	...
Rent control not reported	-	-	-	-	-	-	...
Owner by public housing authority	11	11	3	-	-	-	7,087
Other, Federal subsidy	11	13	2	-	-	-	7,575
Other, State or local subsidy	-	3	4	-	-	-	5,192
Other, Income verification	5	9	-	-	-	-	11,824
Subsidy, or income verification not reported	5	2	6	-	-	-	9,610

Source: "Income of Families and Primary Individuals by Selected Characteristics - Occupied Units with Black Householder," *American Housing Survey for the United States in 1993,* p. 237. *Notes:* 1. Beginning with 1989 this item uses current income in its calculation. See appendix A. 2. May reflect a temporary situation, living off savings, or response error.

Income Characteristics: Black-Occupied Units

[Numbers in thousands. Consistent with the 1990 Census. ...means not applicable or sample too small. - means zero or rounds to zero.]

Characteristics	Total occupied units	Tenure		Housing unit characteristics			
		Owner	Renter	New construction 4 yrs	Mobile homes	Physical problems	
						Severe	Moderate
Total	11,128	4,788	6,340	334	337	385	1,154
Household Income							
Less than $5,000	1,491	381	1,111	6	45	85	238
$5,000 to $9,999	1,899	604	1,295	46	76	86	324
$10,000 to $14,999	1,308	433	874	13	49	42	187
$15,000 to $19,999	1,187	450	737	35	60	40	116
$20,000 to $24,999	964	411	553	4	27	45	78
$25,000 to $29,999	896	402	494	31	16	22	58
$30,000 to $34,999	598	284	314	23	28	13	19
$35,000 to $39,999	528	256	272	16	4	6	31
$40,000 to $49,999	776	454	322	52	21	8	45
$50,000 to $59,999	513	337	176	34	2	17	30
$60,000 to $79,999	562	428	134	34	6	11	18
$80,000 to $99,999	196	158	38	18	2	9	8
$100,000 to $119,999	89	85	4	9	-	-	-
$120,000 or more	121	105	15	11	-	-	2
Median	18,649	26,436	14,370	37,603	14,865	12,533	10,393
As percent of poverty level:							
Less than 50 percent	1,661	385	1,276	13	45	85	261
50 to 99	1,894	616	1,278	38	84	98	320
100 to 149	1,474	583	892	34	77	62	202
150 to 199	1,203	487	716	22	41	29	98
200 percent or more	4,896	2,717	2,179	226	90	111	273
Income of Families and Primary Individuals							
Less than $5,000	1,556	397	1,160	6	47	91	245
$5,000 to $9,999	1,956	601	1,355	50	79	86	331
$10,000 to $14,999	1,328	439	889	13	47	37	187
$15,000 to $19,999	1,221	460	761	31	59	52	116
$20,000 to $24,999	966	416	550	7	27	42	82
$25,000 to $29,999	884	397	487	35	14	22	61
$30,000 to $34,999	583	284	300	27	30	13	18
$35,000 to $39,999	500	259	241	16	4	6	23
$40,000 to $49,999	750	451	298	46	19	5	40
$50,000 to $59,999	475	331	145	34	2	13	25
$60,000 to $79,999	510	406	104	30	6	9	15
$80,000 to $99,999	194	156	38	18	2	9	8
$100,000 to $119,999	87	85	2	9	-	-	-
$120,000 or more	117	105	12	11	-	-	2

[Continued]

★ 389 ★

Income Characteristics: Black-Occupied Units
[Continued]

Characteristics	Total occupied units	Tenure		Housing unit characteristics			
		Owner	Renter	New construction 4 yrs	Mobile homes	Physical problems	
						Severe	Moderate
Median	17,963	26,010	13,689	34,688	14,530	12,187	10,001
Income Sources of Families and Primary Individuals							
Wages and salaries	7,721	3,462	4,259	282	252	200	667
Wages and salaries were majority of income	7,055	3,106	3,949	274	237	172	598
2 or more people each earned over 20% of wages and salaries	2,258	1,395	863	139	100	68	154
Business, farm, or ranch	433	323	110	7	4	15	50
Social security or pensions	2,846	1,762	1,084	83	91	116	364
Interest	1,801	1,245	556	94	21	42	82
Stock dividend(s)	541	415	126	30	2	12	18
Rental income	851	436	416	28	12	30	60
With lodger(s)	435	93	342	11	12	25	48
Welfare or SSI	2,027	406	1,621	37	56	123	307
Alimony or child support	689	232	457	15	17	27	54
Other	1,573	717	856	37	61	61	178
Amount of Savings and Investments							
Income of $25,000 or less	7,217	2,394	4,823	107	259	309	973
No savings or investments	5,533	1,576	3,957	76	208	256	849
$25,000 or less	1,122	544	578	16	32	42	77
More than $25,000	89	71	18	3	-	2	-
Not reported	473	204	269	12	19	9	47
Food Stamps							
Income of $25,000 or less	7,217	2,394	4,823	107	259	309	973
Family members received food stamps	2,551	458	2,093	36	95	144	396
Did not receive food stamps	4,354	1,809	2,545	58	151	161	549
Not reported	313	128	185	12	13	5	28
Rent Reductions							
No subsidy of income reporting	4,398	...	4,398	112	84	178	561
Rent control	120	...	120	-	-	16	23
No rent control	4,276	...	4,276	112	84	162	538
Reduced by owner	210	...	210	-	6	14	43
Not reduced by owner	4,060	...	4,060	112	78	148	492
Owner reduction not reported	5	...	5	-	-	-	3
Rent control not reported	3	...	3	-	-	-	-
Owned by public housing authority	939	...	939	3	-	42	76
Other Federal subsidy	609	...	609	23	-	17	36
Other, State or local subsidy	186	...	186	4	-	8	22

[Continued]

★ 389 ★

Income Characteristics: Black-Occupied Units
[Continued]

Characteristics	Total occupied units	Tenure		Housing unit characteristics			
		Owner	Renter	New construction 4 yrs	Mobile homes	Physical problems	
						Severe	Moderate
Other, income verification	127	...	127	-	-	3	5
Subsidy or income verification not reported	80	...	80	-	-	-	4

Source: "Income Characteristics—Occupied Units with Black Householder," *American Housing Survey for the United States in 1993*, p. 214.

Metropolitan Areas

★ 390 ★

Metropolitan Areas: Black Householders in the Top 50 Metro Areas: Characteristics, 1990

Selected households and housing characteristics for Black householders: United States by inside and outside metropolitan areas and the 50 metropolitan areas (MA's) with the highest number of Black households: 1990.

	Number of Black households	Rank	Percent of all households	Percent who owned their home	Median number of persons in households	Percent who lived in a crowded home
United States	9,976,161	-	10.8	43.4	2.52	9.8
Inside metropolitan area	8,455,952	-	11.9	40.6	2.50	9.7
In central city	5,925,383	-	19.9	36.6	2.42	10.0
Not in central city	2,530,569	-	6.1	50.0	2.71	8.9
Outside metropolitan area	1,520,209	-	7.4	58.9	2.65	10.5
Top 50 MA's	6,334,069					
Atlanta, GA	253,881	7	24.0	40.4	2.52	7.8
Augusta, GA-SC	40,187	50	28.2	51.7	2.68	8.8
Baltimore, MD	206,989	9	23.5	39.4	2.55	6.3
Baton Rouge, LA	49,222	39	26.1	52.8	2.81	11.1
Birmingham, AL	84,864	20	24.6	53.3	2.51	6.3
Boston, MA	70,642	24	6.5	24.7	2.44	10.1
Buffalo, NY	42,585	45	11.3	34.2	2.16	3.2
Charleston, SC	47,439	41	26.7	57.1	2.87	9.5
Charlotte-Gastonia-Rock Hill, NC-SC	77,588	21	17.6	43.8	2.62	8.7
Chicago, IL	439,938	2	19.8	37.1	2.56	9.4
Cincinnati, OH-KY-IN	71,050	22	13.0	33.1	2.23	5.7
Cleveland, OH	131,799	14	18.5	42.2	2.30	3.4

[Continued]

★ 390 ★

Metropolitan Areas: Black Householders in the Top 50 Metro Areas: Characteristics, 1990
[Continued]

	Number of Black households	Rank	Percent of all house-holds	Percent who owned their home	Median number of persons in households	Percent who lived in a crowded home
Columbia, SC	42,435	46	26.0	50.3	2.72	8.5
Columbus, OH	58,021	33	11.1	38.9	2.32	4.5
Dallas, TX	140,359	13	14.7	37.9	2.57	12.0
Dayton-Springfield, OH	45,808	42	12.6	47.3	2.30	4.2
Detroit, MI	329,319	5	20.3	48.7	2.42	6.0
Ft. Lauderdale-Hollywood- Pompano Beach, FL	58,627	32	11.1	44.9	2.95	22.4
Fort Worth-Arlington, TX	49,044	40	9.9	43.9	2.56	10.5
Gary-Hammond, IN	40,312	49	18.7	50.8	2.50	7.0
Greensboro-Winston-Salem- High Point, NC	65,701	25	17.7	41.3	2.37	5.1
Houston, TX	209,183	8	17.6	43.1	2.53	11.1
Indianapolis, IN	61,838	31	12.9	42.5	2.36	5.9
Jacksonville, FL	61,898	30	18.0	50.2	2.50	10.9
Jackson, MS	51,671	37	36.9	54.0	2.82	12.2
Kansas City, MO-KS	70,728	23	11.7	46.7	2.38	6.5
Los Angeles- Long Beach, CA	352,679	4	11.8	36.5	2.33	14.0
Louisville, KY-IN	45,589	43	12.4	42.7	2.36	5.9
Memphis, TN-AR-MS	128,620	16	36.0	47.9	2.72	10.3
Miami-Hialeah, FL	120,321	17	17.4	43.7	2.90	25.9
Milwaukee, WI	62,092	29	11.5	30.3	2.79	8.4
Mobile, AL	42,225	47	24.3	54.8	2.75	9.5
Nashville, TN	53,671	35	14.3	41.7	2.39	6.2
Nassau-Suffolk, NY	51,737	36	6.0	61.5	3.30	11.0
New Orleans, LA	140,834	12	30.9	40.9	2.69	12.3
New York, NY	762,309	1	23.4	20.8	2.45	16.4
Newark, NJ	140,895	11	21.6	30.9	2.51	11.1
Norfolk-Virginia Beach- Newport News, VA	131,545	15	26.7	42.3	2.59	7.0
Oakland, CA	111,281	18	14.3	36.7	2.28	9.3
Orlando, FL	41,461	48	10.3	46.0	2.78	13.0
Philadelphia, PA-NJ	315,557	6	17.8	55.5	2.44	6.5
Pittsburgh, PA	63,548	27	7.7	38.9	2.22	3.5
Raleigh-Durham, NC	65,458	26	22.8	41.4	2.35	6.1
Richmond-Petersburg, VA	88,800	19	26.8	49.0	2.42	4.7
Riverside- San Bernardino, CA	53,833	34	6.2	45.5	2.88	11.5
San Diego, CA	50,219	38	5.7	28.4	2.58	12.7
San Francisco, CA	44,167	44	6.9	31.5	2.16	11.2
St. Louis, MO-IL	144,221	10	15.6	45.3	2.48	8.1

[Continued]

★ 390 ★

Metropolitan Areas: Black Householders in the Top 50 Metro Areas: Characteristics, 1990

[Continued]

	Number of Black households	Rank	Percent of all house- holds	Percent who owned their home	Median number of persons in households	Percent who lived in a crowded home
Tampa-St. Petersburg- Clearwater, FL	63,035	28	7.2	45.4	2.51	12.1
Washington, DC-MD-VA	371,387	3	25.4	41.1	2.35	8.2

Source: "The Top 50 Metro Areas—An Overview," "Housing in Metropolitan Areas—Black Households," Bureau of the Census, Statistical Brief, March 1995, p. 3.

★ 391 ★

Metropolitan Areas

Metropolitan Areas: Black Householders in the Top 50 Metro Areas: Home Value and Rent, 1990

Selected financial housing characteristics for Black and White householders: United States by inside and outside metropolitan areas and the 50 metropolitan areas (MA's) with the highest number of Black households: 1990.

	Median home value ($)		Value ratio	Median contract rent ($)	
	Blacks	Whites	Black:White	Blacks	Whites
United States	50,700	80,200	0.63	312	382
Inside metropolitan area	55,500	91,700	0.61	329	414
In central city	47,800	75,800	0.63	307	390
Not in central city	72,900	99,400	0.73	420	443
Outside metropolitan area	34,400	51,400	0.67	161	246
Top 50 MA's					
Atlanta, GA	66,700	94,000	0.71	390	476
Augusta, GA-SC	47,700	68,500	0.70	235	330
Baltimore, MD	57,100	109,900	0.52	325	453
Baton Rouge, LA	45,900	71,500	0.64	221	311
Birmingham, AL	38,900	66,200	0.59	176	307
Boston, MA	160,200	186,600	0.86	501	593
Buffalo, NY	38,500	75,200	0.51	233	312
Charleston, SC	52,800	77,600	0.68	263	373
Charlotte-Gastonia-Rock Hill, NC-SC	49,900	76,100	0.66	270	358
Chicago, IL	64,100	118,900	0.54	355	480
Cincinnati, OH-KY-IN	54,400	72,000	0.76	249	326
Cleveland, OH	45,500	77,500	0.59	261	366
Columbia, SC	53,200	78,200	0.68	287	367
Columbus, OH	50,400	73,700	0.68	291	353
Dallas, TX	57,000	86,700	0.66	352	415
Dayton-Springfield, OH	42,100	66,700	0.63	250	321
Detroit, MI	29,200	74,200	0.39	267	426

[Continued]

★ 391 ★

Metropolitan Areas: Black Householders in the Top 50 Metro Areas: Home Value and Rent, 1990
[Continued]

	Median home value ($)		Value ratio	Median contract rent ($)	
	Blacks	Whites	Black:White	Blacks	Whites
Ft. Lauderdale-Hollywood-Pompano Beach, FL	67,300	94,400	0.71	412	519
Fort Worth-Arlington, TX	47,600	74,500	0.64	325	372
Gary-Hammond, IN	34,200	62,600	0.55	222	337
Greensboro-Winston-Salem-High Point, NC	53,700	74,000	0.73	266	317
Houston, TX	43,200	70,100	0.62	296	366
Indianapolis, IN	41,000	69,300	0.59	290	355
Jacksonville, FL	41,500	72,200	0.57	284	383
Jackson, MS	42,100	69,100	0.61	218	362
Kansas City, MO-KS	37,600	68,700	0.55	272	363
Los Angeles-Long Beach, CA	143,500	246,600	0.58	522	603
Louisville, KY-IN	34,800	58,300	0.60	225	291
Memphis, TN-AR-MS	44,500	74,600	0.60	222	366
Miami-Hialeah, FL	62,800	91,900	0.68	353	445
Milwaukee, WI	40,600	78,400	0.52	305	401
Mobile, AL	38,500	60,300	0.64	158	273
Nashville, TN	57,100	78,200	0.73	282	365
Nassau-Suffolk, NY	152,600	188,800	0.81	637	692
New Orleans, LA	56,300	73,900	0.76	252	340
New York, NY	159,900	222,400	0.72	406	495
Newark, NJ	132,400	196,400	0.67	452	559
Norfolk-Virginia Beach-Newport News, VA	66,300	90,600	0.73	329	438
Oakland, CA	138,100	234,400	0.59	502	626
Orlando, FL	59,400	85,300	0.70	368	459
Philadelphia, PA-NJ	36,200	112,400	0.32	319	476
Pittsburgh, PA	36,200	55,700	0.65	225	297
Raleigh-Durham, NC	63,400	98,100	0.65	316	408
Richmond-Petersburg, VA	57,300	85,300	0.67	296	423
Riverside-San Bernardino, CA	127,900	135,400	0.94	502	502
San Diego, CA	129,700	192,900	0.67	530	581
San Francisco, CA	223,200	348,200	0.64	515	697
St. Louis, MO-IL	43,800	72,600	0.60	250	344
Tampa-St. Petersburg-Clearwater, FL	47,000	72,700	0.65	289	388
Washington, DC-MD-VA	111,700	180,500	0.62	518	684

Source: "The Top 50 Metro Areas—Home Value and Rent," "Housing in Metropolitan Areas—Black Households," Bureau of the Census, *Statistical Brief*, March 1995, p. 34.

Mortgages

★ 392 ★

Mortgage Characteristics: Owner Occupied Units, Part 1

[Numbers in thousands. Consistent with the 1990 Census. ...means not applicable or sample too small. - means zero or rounds to zero.]

Characteristics	Total occupied units	Tenure		Housing unit characteristics			
		Owner	Renter	New construction 4 yrs	Mobile homes	Physical problems	
						Severe	Moderate
Total	4,788	4,788	...	192	252	137	450
Mortgage Currently on Property							
None, owned free and clear	1,804	1,804	...	34	170	82	268
With mortgage or land contract	2,984	2,984	...	157	82	55	182
One mortgage or land contract	2,489	2,489	...	139	71	47	148
Two mortgages	389	389	...	11	3	8	22
Three or more mortgages	9	9	...	-	-	-	-
Number of mortgages not reported	97	97	...	8	8	-	12
OWNERS WITH ONE OR MORE MORTGAGES							
Total	2,984	2,984	...	157	82	55	182
Type of Primary Mortgage							
FHA	887	887	...	54	14	15	35
VA	394	394	...	32	-	10	12
Farmers Home Administration	64	64	...	3	-	-	9
Other types	1,418	1,418	...	59	55	30	111
Don't know	84	84	...	2	6	-	3
Not reported	137	137	...	8	8	-	12
Lower Cost State and Local Mortgages							
State or local program used	507	507	...	19	12	7	35
Not used	2,340	2,340	...	128	66	48	136
Not reported	138	138	...	11	5	-	11
Mortgage Origination							
Placed new mortgage(s)	2,389	2,389	...	144	69	47	144
Primary obtained when property acquired	1,909	1,909	...	136	67	40	109
Obtained later	461	461	...	8	2	7	35
Data not reported	20	20	...	-	-	-	-
Assumed	130	130	...	-	2	-	7
Wrap-around	-	-	...	-	-	-	-
Combination of the above	346	346	...	5	3	8	19
Origin not reported	119	119	...	8	8	-	12

[Continued]

★ 392 ★

Mortgage Characteristics: Owner Occupied Units, Part 1

[Continued]

Characteristics	Total occupied units	Tenure		Housing unit characteristics			
				New construction 4 yrs	Mobile homes	Physical problems	
		Owner	Renter			Severe	Moderate
Payment Plan of Primary Mortgage							
Fixed payment, self amortizing	2,292	2,292	...	125	53	47	130
Adjustable rate mortgage	163	163	...	11	-	-	9
Adjustable term mortgage	10	10	...	-	-	2	3
Graduated payment mortgage	23	23	...	3	-	-	-
Balloon	10	10	...	-	-	-	3
Other	55	55	...	-	-	-	5
Combination of the above	6	6	...	-	-	-	-
Not reported	425	425	...	19	30	5	33
Payment Plan of Secondary Mortgage							
Units with two or more mortgages	398	398	...	11	3	8	22
Fixed payment, self amortizing	207	207	...	8	-	8	10
Adjustable rate mortgage	28	28	...	2	-	-	4
Adjustable term mortgage	5	5	...	-	-	-	-
Graduated payment mortgage	-	-	...	-	-	-	-
Balloon	5	5	...	-	-	-	-
Other	5	5	...	-	-	-	-
Combination of the above	20	20	...	-	-	-	-
Not reported	129	129	...	-	3	-	8
Lenders of Primary and Secondary Mortgages							
Only borrowed from firm(s)	2,472	2,472	...	142	71	49	135
Only borrowed from seller	80	80	...	-	-	-	13
Only borrowed from other individual(s)	31	31	...	-	-	-	12
Borrowed from a firm and seller	10	10	...	-	3	-	-
Borrowed from a firm and other individual	12	12	...	-	-	-	2
Borrowed from seller and other individual	-	-	...	-	-	-	-
One or both sources not reported	379	379	...	15	8	5	20
Items Included in Primary Mortgage Payment							
Principal and interest only	773	773	...	27	46	18	84
Property taxes	1,895	1,895	...	109	11	32	79
Property insurance	1,782	1,782	...	116	22	32	79
Other	146	146	...	6	2	3	3
Not reported	188	188	...	8	8	5	12
Year Primary Mortgage Originated							
1990 to 1994	926	926	...	133	30	5	48
1985 to 1989	801	801	...	17	32	25	46
1980 to 1984	305	305	...	...	8	10	23
1975 to 1979	393	393	...	...	2	10	15

[Continued]

★ 392 ★

Mortgage Characteristics: Owner Occupied Units, Part 1
[Continued]

| Characteristics | Total occupied units | Tenure | | Housing unit characteristics | | | |
| | | Owner | Renter | New construction 4 yrs | Mobile homes | Physical problems | |
						Severe	Moderate
1970 to 1974	278	278	...	...	-	5	19
1960 to 1969	116	116	...	...	-	-	10
1950 to 1959	7	7	...	...	-	-	-
1949 or earlier	-	-	...	...	-	-	-
Not reported	160	160	...	8	10	-	22
Median	1987	1987	...	...	1989	1985	1986

Source: "Mortgage Characteristics - Occupied Units with Black Householder," *American Housing Survey for the United States in 1993*, p. 224. Notes: Figures may not add to total because more than one category may add to a unit.

★ 393 ★

Mortgages

Mortgage Characteristics: Owner Occupied Units, Part 2

[Numbers in thousands. Consistent with the 1990 Census. ...means not applicable or sample too small. - means zero or rounds to zero.]

| Characteristics | Total occupied units | Tenure | | Housing unit characteristics | | | |
| | | Owner | Renter | New construction 4 yrs | Mobile homes | Physical problems | |
						Severe	Moderate
OWNERS WITH ONE OR MORE MORTGAGES-Con.							
Term of Primary Mortgage at Origination of Assumption							
Less than 8 years	33	33	...	-	2	3	4
8 to 12 years	74	74	...	-	13	-	9
13 to 17 years	172	172	...	15	43	3	26
18 to 22 years	165	165	...	6	2	5	10
23 to 27 years	108	108	...	5	-	-	5
28 to 32 years	1,612	1,612	...	110	-	35	55
33 years or more	55	55	...	2	-	-	6
Variable	33	33	...	-	-	2	5
Not reported	733	733	...	19	22	7	61
Median	30	30	...	30	15	30	28
Remaining Years Mortgaged							
Less than 8 years	437	437	...	-	29	13	40
8 to 12	383	383	...	3	16	2	40
13 to 17	457	457	...	16	18	11	21
18 to 22	290	290	...	5	-	15	23
23 to 27	540	540	...	39	-	7	10
28 to 32	400	400	...	84	-	2	2

[Continued]

★ 393 ★

Mortgage Characteristics: Owner Occupied Units, Part 2
[Continued]

Characteristics	Total occupied units	Tenure		Housing unit characteristics			
		Owner	Renter	New construction 4 yrs	Mobile homes	Physical problems	
						Severe	Moderate
33 years or more	2	2	...	-	-	-	-
Variable	68	68	...	-	-	2	5
Not reported	407	407	...	10	19	2	41
Median	18	18	...	29	9	17	12
Current Interest Rate							
Less than 6 percent	49	49	...	5	3	-	4
6 to 7.9	243	243	...	35	2	2	8
8 to 9.9	507	507	...	48	2	8	7
10 to 11.9	259	259	...	3	-	7	7
12 to 13.9	77	77	...	-	5	-	13
14 to 15.9	21	21	...	-	-	-	-
16 to 17.9	15	15	...	7	4	-	-
18 to 19.9	2	2	...	-	-	-	-
20 percent or more	2	2	...	-	-	-	-
Not reported	1,809	1,809	...	60	66	37	143
Median	9.1	9.1	...	8.3	12.2	9.6	10.2
Total Outstanding Principal Amount							
Less than $10,000	158	158	...	-	5	2	18
$10,000 to $19,999	159	159	...	4	10	-	8
$20,000 to $29,999	155	155	...	6	-	3	5
$30,000 to $39,999	128	128	...	-	2	7	-
$40,000 to $49,999	116	116	...	-	-	3	3
$50,000 to $59,999	109	109	...	-	-	-	2
$60,000 to $69,999	85	85	...	10	-	-	-
$70,000 to $79,999	83	83	...	16	-	2	3
$80,000 to $99,999	73	73	...	27	-	-	-
$100,000 to $119,999	43	43	...	16	-	-	-
$120,000 to $149,999	26	26	...	3	-	-	-
$150,000 to $199,999	32	32	...	12	-	-	-
$200,000 to $249,999	2	2	...	-	-	-	-
$250,000 to $299,999	-	-	...	3	-	-	-
$300,000 or more	5	5	...	3	-	-	-
Not reported	1,809	1,809	...	60	66	37	143
Median	39,070	39,070	...	89,186	13,225	35,017	11,961
Current Total Loan as Percent of Value							
Less than 20 percent	158	158	...	3	3	2	13
20 to 39	178	178	...	-	3	3	6
40 to 59	205	205	...	4	2	7	5
60 to 79	251	251	...	28	4	-	10
80 to 89	175	175	...	21	-	5	2

[Continued]

★ 393 ★

Mortgage Characteristics: Owner Occupied Units, Part 2

[Continued]

Characteristics	Total occupied units	Tenure		Housing unit characteristics			
				New construction	Mobile homes	Physical problems	
		Owner	Renter	4 yrs		Severe	Moderate
90 to 99	141	141	...	42	4	-	2
100 percent or more	68	68	...	-	-	-	
Not reported	1,809	1,809	...	60	66	37	143
Median	63.7	63.7	...	36.8	59.5	49.8	41.8

Source: "Mortgage Characteristics - Occupied Units with Black Householder," *American Housing Survey for the United States in 1993*, p. 226.

Physical Characteristics

★ 394 ★

Telephone Subscribers: 1984 and 1994

CHARACTERISTIC	1984				1994			
	All races	White	Black	Hispanic[1]	All races	White	Black	Hispanic[1]
Total	92	93	80	81	94	95	86	86
Age of householder:								
15 to 24 years old[2]	77	80	58	61	84	86	74	72
25 to 54 years old	92	93	80	83	93	95	85	86
55 to 59 years old	95	96	87	87	96	96	91	89
60 to 64 years old	95	96	87	87	96	97	90	92
65 to 69 years old	96	97	88	90	97	97	92	93
70 years old and over	95	96	88	84	97	97	92	92
Household size:								
1 person	88	90	75	73	92	93	82	82
2 to 3 persons	93	95	82	82	95	96	88	87
4 to 5 persons	93	94	82	84	94	96	87	88
6 or more persons	87	90	76	79	89	91	82	83
Household level:								
Under $5,000	71	75	63	55	76	80	69	66
$5,000 to $7,499	83	86	75	70	83	85	77	73
$7,500 to $9,999	87	88	77	75	87	89	81	81
$10,000 to $12,499	90	91	81	80	90	91	82	83
$12,500 to $14,999	92	93	85	87	92	93	86	85
$15,000 to $19,999	(NA)	(NA)	(NA)	(NA)	94	94	87	88
$15,000 to $17,499	94	94	89	88	(NA)	(NA)	(NA)	(NA)
$17,500 to $19,999	95	96	92	91	(NA)	(NA)	(NA)	(NA)
$20,000 to $24,999	97	97	93	93	95	96	90	91

[Continued]

★ 394 ★

Telephone Subscribers: 1984 and 1994

[Continued]

CHARACTERISTIC	1984				1994			
	All races	White	Black	Hispanic[1]	All races	White	Black	Hispanic[1]
$25,000 to $29,999	98	98	95	96	97	97	94	92
$30,000 to $34,999	99	99	97	99	97	98	94	92
$35,000 to $39,999	99	99	98	98	98	98	94	95
$40,000 to $49,999	99	99	97	99	99	99	97	96
$50,000 to $74,999	99	100	98	100	(NA)	(NA)	(NA)	(NA)
$50,000 to $59,999	(NA)	(NA)	(NA)	(NA)	99	99	96	100
$60,000 to $74,999	(NA)	(NA)	(NA)	(NA)	99	99	100	98
$75,000 and over	99	99	97	98	99	99	99	99
Labor force status of persons, 15 years old and over[3]								
Total civilian noninstitutional population	93	94	83	83	95	96	88	87
Employed	94	95	86	86	96	96	90	89
Unemployed	82	84	75	74	88	90	81	84
Not in labor force	92	94	81	80	93	95	85	86

Source: "Percent of Households with Telephone Service: 1984 and 1994." U.S. Bureau of the Census, *Statistical Abstract of the United States,* 115th ed., 1995, p. 574. Primary source: Federal Communications Commission, *Telephone Subscribers in the U.S.* April 1995. *Notes:* NA Not available. 1. Persons of Hispanic origin may be of any race 2. 16 to 24 years old in 1984. 3. 16 years old and over in 1984.

Residential Neighborhoods

★ 395 ★

Neighborhoods: Black Occupied Units

[Numbers in thousands. Consistent with the 1990 Census. ...means not applicable or sample too small. - means zero or rounds to zero.]

Characteristics	Total occupied units	Tenure		Housing unit characteristics			
		Owner	Renter	New construction 4 yrs	Mobile homes	Physical problems	
						Severe	Moderate
Total	11,128	4,788	6,340	334	337	385	1,154
Overall Opinion of Neighborhood							
1 (worst)	560	112	448	7	5	47	106
2	201	61	140	3	2	11	27
3	292	58	234	-	-	10	42
4	360	107	253	-	11	13	28
5	1,172	410	761	15	11	51	159
6	707	259	448	17	8	28	69
7	1,347	577	770	25	18	50	117
8	2,181	1,022	1,158	81	73	36	149

[Continued]

★ 395 ★

Neighborhoods: Black Occupied Units

[Continued]

| Characteristics | Total occupied units | Tenure | | Housing unit characteristics | | | |
| | | Owner | Renter | New construction 4 yrs | Mobile homes | Physical problems | |
						Severe	Moderate
9	1,209	576	633	52	40	24	92
10 (best)	2,924	1,526	1,397	129	156	106	345
No neighborhood	27	13	14	-	4	2	3
Not reported	149	65	83	4	8	6	19
Neighborhood Conditions							
With neighborhood	10,953	4,710	6,243	330	325	376	1,132
No problems	6,151	2,765	3,386	213	273	195	625
With problems[1]	4,763	1,929	2,835	114	52	179	508
Crime	1,659	513	1,147	13	12	90	206
Noise	1,120	386	735	16	10	35	122
Traffic	598	248	350	10	4	32	65
Litter or housing deterioration	640	305	336	9	5	37	84
Poor city or county services	250	127	124	12	2	16	29
Undesirable commercial, institutional, industrial	152	50	102	3	-	6	13
People	1,712	558	1,154	35	16	60	184
Other	1,125	570	555	49	16	35	127
Type of problem not reported	77	29	48	-	-	9	6
Presence of problems not reported	39	16	22	3	-	3	-
Description of Area Within 300 Feet[1,2]							
Single-family detached houses	1,502	105	1,397	28	-	55	131
Only single-family detached	...	...	...	...	...	...	...
Single-family attached or 1 to 3 story multiunit	3,261	177	3,084	85	-	106	236
4 to 6 story multiunit	819	38	781	-	-	78	80
7 stories or more multiunit	454	31	423	2	-	40	29
Mobile homes	29	-	29	-	-	-	2
Residential parking lots	1,379	60	1,320	22	-	84	107
Commercial, institutional, or industrial	1,279	23	1,256	26	-	33	52
Body of water	131	13	118	7	-	-	4
Open space, park, woods, farm, or ranch	829	41	788	43	-	34	65
4+ lane highway, railroad, or airport	537	22	515	18	-	15	32
Other	231	12	219	9	-	9	28
Not observed or not reported	201	12	189	-	-	2	21
Age of Other Residential Buildings Within 300 Feet[2]							
Older	280	3	277	29	-	7	11
About the same	3,321	190	3,122	51	-	107	275
Newer	70	-	70	-	-	3	2
Very mixed	540	26	514	14	-	49	46
No other residential buildings	120	-	120	7	-	3	2
Not reported	212	12	200	-	-	2	21
Mobile Homes in Group							
Mobile homes	337	252	85	38	337	8	53
1 to 6	277	221	56	34	277	8	51
7 to 20	6	6	-	4	6	-	-
21 or more	53	25	28	-	53	-	2

[Continued]

★ 395 ★

Neighborhoods: Black Occupied Units
[Continued]

Characteristics	Total occupied units	Tenure		Housing unit characteristics			
		Owner	Renter	New construction 4 yrs	Mobile homes	Physical problems	
						Severe	Moderate
Other Buildings Vandalized or With Interior Exposed[2]							
None	3,573	193	3,380	86	-	100	250
1 building	173	8	165	-	-	13	19
More than 1 building	438	15	423	7	-	52	53
No building within 300 feet	76	-	76	7	-	3	-
Not reported	264	25	259	-	-	2	36
Bars on Windows of Buildings[2]							
With other buildings within 300 feet	4,184	216	3,969	94	-	165	321
No bars on windows	2,879	114	2,765	73	-	62	163
1 building with bars	158	16	141	4	-	18	5
2 or more buildings with bars	1,118	83	1,035	17	-	85	131
Not reported	29	3	27	-	-	-	2
Condition of Streets[2]							
No repairs needed	2,863	156	2,706	63	-	101	189
Minor repairs needed	1,207	53	1,154	14	-	49	100
Major repairs needed	186	7	179	4	-	14	44
No streets within 300 feet	76	10	66	-	-	3	4
Not reported	211	14	197	-	-	2	21
Trash, Litter, or Junk or Streets or any Properties[2]							
None	2,411	138	2,273	87	-	55	127
Minor accumulation	1,642	82	1,560	10	-	93	156
Major accumulation	290	8	282	4	-	20	54
Not reported	202	12	190	-	-	2	21

Source: "Neighborhood—Occupied Units with Black Householder," *American Housing Survey for the United States in 1993,* February 1995, p. 204. *Notes:* 1. Figures may not add to total because more than one category may apply to a unit. 2. Limited to multiunit structures.

Subfamilies

★ 396 ★

Subfamilies: Type, Race, and Characteristics-1

[Numbers in thousands except for averages and medians. For meaning of symbols, see text.]

Characteristic	All subfamilies				Related subfamilies			
	Total	Married-couple	Father-child	Mother-child	Total	Married-couple	Father-child	Mother-child
BLACK SUBFAMILIES								
Metropolitan-Nonmetropolitan Residence								
Total	867	99	48	719	778	95	40	644
In MSA's	747	88	40	618	666	84	33	549
Central cities	494	43	32	419	446	42	24	380
Ring	253	45	9	199	220	42	9	169
MSA's of 2,500,000 or more	391	46	22	322	359	44	19	296
Central cities	276	19	15	242	259	19	12	227
Ring	114	27	7	80	101	25	7	69
MSA's of 1,000,000 to 2,499,999	167	22	10	136	147	22	10	118
Central cities	119	17	10	92	109	17	10	83
Ring	48	5	-	43	38	5	-	33
MSA's of 250,000 to 999,999	134	8	8	118	112	6	4	102
Central cities	78	5	7	67	63	3	2	58
Ring	56	3	2	51	49	3	2	44
MSA's of 249,999 or less	55	12	-	43	47	12	-	35
Central cities	20	3	-	18	15	3	-	12
Ring	34	9	-	25	33	9	-	23
Not in MSA's	120	11	8	101	112	11	7	94
Size of Subfamily								
Total	867	99	48	719	778	95	40	644
Two persons	587	45	45	497	519	43	37	439
Three persons	178	28	3	148	163	25	3	135
Four persons	62	14	-	48	57	14	-	43
Five persons	23	7	-	17	23	7	-	17
Six persons	15	5	-	10	15	5	-	10
Seven or more persons	1	1	-	-	1	1	-	-
Total persons	2,073	290	96	1,686	1,883	279	79	1,524
Average per subfamily	2.39	2.93	(B)	2.35	2.42	2.94	(B)	2.37
Own Children Under 18								
Total	867	99	48	719	778	95	40	644
Without own children under 18	45	45	-	-	43	43	-	-
With own children under 18	822	54	48	719	735	52	40	644
One own child under 18	570	28	45	497	501	25	37	439
Two own children under 18	165	14	3	148	152	14	3	135
Three own children under 18	55	7	-	48	49	7	-	43

[Continued]

★ 396 ★

Subfamilies: Type, Race, and Characteristics-1
[Continued]

Characteristic	All subfamilies				Related subfamilies			
	Total	Married-couple	Father-child	Mother-child	Total	Married-couple	Father-child	Mother-child
Four own children under 18	21	5	-	17	21	5	-	17
Five own children under 18	11	1	-	10	11	1	-	10
Six or more children under 18	-	-	-	-	-	-	-	-
Total own children under 18	1,107	92	48	967	1,010	89	40	880
Average per subfamily	1.28	.93	(B)	1.35	1.30	.94	(B)	1.37
Average per subfamily with children	1.35	(B)	(B)	1.35	1.37	(B)	(B)	1.37
Marital Status of Reference Person								
Total	867	99	48	719	778	95	40	644
Married, spouse present	99	99	-	-	95	95	-	-
Married, spouse absent	93	-	6	87	84	-	6	78
Separated	70	-	5	65	61	-	5	56
Other	23	-	1	22	23	-	1	22
Widowed	12	-	2	10	10	-	2	8
Divorced	81	-	6	75	58	-	3	55
Never married	582	-	34	548	531	-	29	502
Age of Reference Person								
Total	867	99	48	719	778	95	40	644
15 to 19 years	134	-	9	125	131	-	9	122
20 to 24 years	214	20	1	194	195	17	-	178
25 to 29 years	178	32	20	126	159	30	20	109
30 to 34 years	147	7	1	139	132	7	1	124
35 to 39 years	95	16	7	72	77	16	2	60
40 to 44 years	52	4	8	39	38	4	5	28
45 to 49 years	11	2	-	9	11	2	-	9
50 to 54 years	18	5	2	11	16	5	2	9
55 to 59 years	6	1	-	4	6	1	-	4
60 to 64 years	2	2	-	-	2	2	-	-
65 to 74 years	5	5	-	-	5	5	-	-
75 to 84 years	6	6	-	-	6	6	-	-
85 years and over	-	-	-	-	-	-	-	-
Median	27.4	29.7	(B)	26.6	27.0	30.2	(B)	26.0

Source: "Subfamilies, by Type, Race, and Hispanic Origin of Reference Person: March 1994, " Steve W. Rawlings and Arlene F. Saluter, *Household and Family Characteristics: March 1995,* p. 129. *Note:* B = Base less than 75,000.

★ 397 ★
Subfamilies

Subfamilies: Type, Race, and Characteristics-2

[Numbers in thousands except for averages and medians. For meaning of symbols, see text.]

Characteristic	Unrelated subfamilies			
	Total	Married-couple	Father-child	Mother-child
BLACK SUBFAMILIES				
Metropolitan-Nonmetropolitan Residence				
Total	89	4	9	76
In MSA's	80	4	7	69
Central cities	48	2	7	39
Ring	32	2	-	30
MSA's of 2,500,000 or more	32	2	3	26
Central cities	18	-	3	15
Ring	14	2	-	11
MSA's of 1,000,000 to 2,499,999	20	-	-	20
Central cities	9	-	-	9
Ring	10	-	-	10
MSA's of 250,000 to 999,999	22	2	4	16
Central cities	15	2	4	9
Ring	6	-	-	6
MSA's of 249,999 or less	7	-	-	7
Central cities	6	-	-	6
Ring	1	-	-	1
Not in MSA's	8	-	1	7
Size of Subfamily				
Total	89	4	9	76
Two persons	68	2	9	58
Three persons	15	2	-	13
Four persons	5	-	-	5
Five persons	-	-	-	-
Six persons	-	-	-	-
Seven or more persons	-	-	-	-
Total persons	190	11	17	162
Average per subfamily	2.15	(B)	(B)	2.15
Own Children Under 18				
Total	89	4	9	76
Without own children under 18	2	2	-	-
With own children under 18	87	2	9	76
One own child under 18	69	2	9	58
Two own children under 18	13	-	-	13
Three own children under 18	5	-	-	5
Four own children under 18	-	-	-	-
Five own children under 18	-	-	-	-
Six or more children under 18	-	-	-	-

[Continued]

★ 397 ★

Subfamilies: Type, Race, and Characteristics-2
[Continued]

Characteristic	Unrelated subfamilies			
	Total	Married-couple	Father-child	Mother-child
Total own children under 18	97	3	8	87
Average per subfamily	1.10	(B)	(B)	1.15
Average per subfamily with children	1.12	(B)	(B)	1.15
Marital Status of Reference Person				
Total	89	4	9	76
Married, spouse present	4	4	-	-
Married, spouse absent	9	-	-	9
Separated	9	-	-	9
Other	-	-	-	-
Widowed	2	-	-	2
Divorced	23	-	4	20
Never married	51	-	5	45
Age of Reference Person				
Total	89	4	9	76
15 to 19 years	3	-	-	3
20 to 24 years	19	2	-	16
25 to 29 years	19	2	-	17
30 to 39 years	15	-	-	15
40 to 44 years	17	-	6	12
45 to 49 years	14	-	3	11
50 to 54 years	-	-	-	-
55 to 59 years	2	-	-	2
60 to 64 years	-	-	-	-
65 to 74 years	-	-	-	-
75 to 84 years	-	-	-	-
85 years and over	-	-	-	-
Median	31.3	(B)	(B)	30.6

Source: "Subfamilies, by Type, Race, and Hispanic Origin of Reference Person: March 1994, " Steve W. Rawlings and Arlene F. Saluter, *Household and Family Characteristics: March 1995*, p. 129. *Note:* B = Base less than 75,000.

Suburbs

★ 398 ★

Introductory Characteristics: Householders Outside Metropolitan Statistical Areas-1

[Numbers in thousands. Consistent with the 1990 Census. ...means not applicable or sample too small. - means zero or rounds to zero.]

Characteristics	Total occupied units	Tenure		Housing unit characteristics			
				New construction 4 yrs	Mobile homes	Physical problems	
		Owner	Renter			Severe	Moderate
Total	20,826	15,170	5,656	1,209	2,666	416	1,181
Race and Origin							
White	18,995	14,122	4,873	1,136	2,423	335	865
Non-Hispanic	18,420	13,794	4,627	1,120	2,331	327	791
Hispanic	575	328	247	15	92	9	75
Black	1,466	857	609	57	191	69	287
Other	365	192	173	17	52	11	28
Total Hispanic	615	343	272	19	103	11	78

Source: "Introductory Characteristics-Outside Metropolitan Statistical Areas- Occupied Units." *American Housing Survey for the United States in 1993,* February 1995, p. 460.

★ 399 ★

Suburbs

Introductory Characteristics: Householders Outside Metropolitan Statistical Areas-2

[Numbers in thousands. Consistent with the 1990 Census. ...means not applicable or sample too small. - means zero or rounds to zero.]

Characteristics	Household characteristics		Regions			
	Moved in past year	Below poverty level	Northeast	Midwest	South	West
Total	3,078	3,565	2,446	6,634	8,584	3,162
Race and Origin						
White	2,772	2,807	2,400	6,459	7,180	2,956
Non-Hispanic	2,675	2,639	2,372	6,405	6,964	2,679
Hispanic	96	168	29	53	216	277
Black	213	625	21	100	1,322	22

[Continued]

★ 399 ★

Introductory Characteristics: Householders Outside Metropolitan Statistical Areas-2
[Continued]

Characteristics	Household characteristics		Regions			
	Moved in past year	Below poverty level	Northeast	Midwest	South	West
Other	93	133	24	75	82	183
Total Hispanic	112	179	33	63	234	285

Source: "Introductory Characteristics-Outside Metropolitan Statistical Areas- Occupied Units." *American Housing Survey for the United States in 1993,* February 1995, p. 460.

★ 400 ★
Suburbs

Introductory Characteristics: Suburban Householders-1

[Numbers in thousands. Consistent withe the 1990 Census. ...means not applicable or sample too small. - means zero or rounds to zero.]

Characteristics	Total occupied units	Tenure		Housing unit characteristics			
		Owner	Renter	New construction 4 yrs	Mobile homes	Physical problems	
						Severe	Moderate
Total	44,060	31,438	12,623	2,976	2,663	741	1,370
Race and Origin							
White	39,453	29,021	10,432	2,646	2,511	610	1,080
Non-Hispanic	37,034	27,753	9,281	2,509	2,376	559	938
Hispanic	2,419	1,268	1,151	137	135	51	142
Black	3,140	1,556	1,584	202	129	106	244
Other	1,468	861	607	128	23	26	46
Total Hispanic	2,646	1,357	1,289	158	139	58	155

Source: "Introductory Characteristics-Suburbs-Occupied Units." *American Housing Survey for the United States in 1993,* February 1995, p. 418.

★ 401 ★

Suburbs

Introductory Characteristics: Suburban Householders-2

[Numbers in thousands. Consistent withe the 1990 Census. ...means not applicable or sample too small. - means zero or rounds to zero.]

Characteristics	Household characteristics		Regions			
	Moved in past year	Below poverty level	Northeast	Midwest	South	West
Total	6,867	4,486	10,252	9,672	14,535	9,601
Race and Origin						
White	5,899	3,613	9,556	9,068	12,443	8,386
Non-Hispanic	5,333	3,117	9,316	8,950	11,619	7,148
Hispanic	566	497	240	118	824	1,238
Black	623	688	476	466	1,784	413
Other	345	185	220	138	308	802
Total Hispanic	642	553	282	140	862	1,363

Source: "Introductory Characteristics-Suburbs-Occupied Units." *American Housing Survey for the United States in 1993,* February 1995, p. 418.

Tenure

★ 402 ★

Tenure: Select Financial Characteristics of Householder. Part 1-1

[Numbers in thousands. Consistent with the 1990 Census. ...means not applicable or sample too small. - means zero or rounds to zero.]

Characteristics	Owner occupied							
	With mortgage				With no mortgage			
	Total	Specified[1]	Not specified		Total	Specified[1]	Not specified	
			Condo or Coop	Other			Condo or Coop	Other
Total	2,984	2,677	92	216	1,804	1,466	36	302
Income of Families and Primary Individuals								
Less than $5,000	141	122	-	19	256	192	6	58
$5,000 to $9,999	217	191	7	19	384	312	-	72
$10,000 to $14,999	200	172	3	25	239	212	-	27
$15,000 to $19,999	267	218	10	38	193	157	2	34

[Continued]

★ 402 ★

Tenure: Select Financial Characteristics of Householder. Part 1-1

[Continued]

Characteristics	Owner occupied							
	With mortgage				With no mortgage			
			Not specified				Not specified	
	Total	Specified[1]	Condo or Coop	Other	Total	Specified[1]	Condo or Coop	Other
$20,000 to $24,999	251	217	5	30	165	139	5	21
$25,000 to $29,999	241	229	8	5	156	134	3	19
$30,000 to $34,999	180	159	10	10	104	66	3	35
$35,000 to $39,999	215	184	18	13	44	37	2	5
$40,000 to $49,999	351	331	2	18	100	77	8	15
$50,000 to $59,999	273	242	19	12	57	50	-	7
$60,000 to $79,999	346	329	5	12	60	54	-	6
$80,000 to $99,999	139	126	2	10	17	14	3	-
$100,000 to $119,999	68	66	-	2	17	15	-	3
$120,000 or more	95	90	2	4	10	7	3	-
Median	34,848	35,798	35,875	21,054	15,589	15,547	....	13,891
Monthly Housing Costs								
Less than $100	-	-	-	-	178	131	8	40
$100 to $199	28	28	-	-	658	523	11	124
$200 to $249	48	43	-	5	312	271	-	41
$250 to $299	63	57	2	4	245	218	-	27
$300 to $349	121	109	-	12	165	144	2	19
$350 to $399	126	117	-	9	76	61	-	15
$400 to $449	143	125	5	14	35	26	-	9
$450 to $499	157	144	-	13	22	14	3	5
$500 to $599	334	287	10	37	47	27	6	14
$600 to $699	337	305	21	11	26	21	-	5
$700 to $799	239	221	8	10	13	8	2	2
$800 to $999	363	322	14	27	19	19	-	-
$1,000 to $1,249	278	265	9	5	3	-	3	-
$1,250 to $1,499	104	97	3	5	-	-	-	-
$1,500 or more	145	124	2	18	6	3	-	3
No cash rent	...	...	...	...	...	...	...	...
Mortgage payment not reported	498	432	19	46	...	...	...	...
Median (excludes no cash rent)	666	670	698	575	210	215	....	190
Median Monthly Housing Costs For Owners								
Monthly costs including all mortgages plus maintenance costs	699	700	750	590	225	230	...	195
Monthly costs excluding 2nd and subsequent mortgages and maintenance costs	626	627	684	574	210	215	...	190
Monthly Housing Costs as Percent of Current Income[2]								
Less than 5 percent	7	7	-	-	113	82	11	21
5 to 9 percent	131	115	2	13	363	308	8	47

[Continued]

★ 402 ★

Tenure: Select Financial Characteristics of Householder. Part 1-1
[Continued]

Characteristics	Owner occupied							
	With mortgage				With no mortgage			
			Not specified				Not specified	
	Total	Specified[1]	Condo or Coop	Other	Total	Specified[1]	Condo or Coop	Other
10 to 14 percent	299	265	10	25	350	278	5	66
15 to 19 percent	402	381	5	16	202	167	3	31
20 to 24 percent	386	368	8	10	164	133	2	29
25 to 29 percent	280	255	16	9	114	101	-	14
30 to 34 percent	204	187	13	5	109	96	-	13
35 to 39 percent	129	112	2	15	48	36	-	11
40 to 49 percent	188	162	3	24	89	76	-	13
50 to 59 percent	138	117	6	15	42	38	-	4
60 to 69 percent	80	70	-	10	32	28	-	5
70 to 99 percent	115	96	8	12	32	17	-	15
100 percent or more[3]	93	78	-	15	75	63	3	9
Zero or negative income	33	33	-	1	71	43	3	25
No cash rent	...	...	...	...	...	...	...	...
Mortgage payment not reported	498	432	19	46	...	...	...	...
Median (excludes 3 previous lines)	25	25	28	37	16	16	...	16
Median (excludes 4 lines before medians)	24	24	28	24	15	15	...	15
OWNER OCCUPIED UNITS								
Total	2,984	2,677	92	216	1,804	1,466	36	302
Value								
Less than $10,000	46	14	-	32	171	60	-	110
$10,000 to $19,999	115	85	3	28	202	155	2	45
$20,000 to $29,999	211	173	5	34	238	215	8	15
$30,000 to $39,999	256	229	10	17	241	216	2	23
$40,000 to $49,999	313	287	2	23	213	169	2	42
$50,000 to $59,999	329	301	15	12	133	105	8	19
$60,000 to $69,999	299	286	8	6	137	115	3	19
$70,000 to $79,999	214	203	7	4	113	108	-	5
$80,000 to $99,999	412	375	13	25	121	106	3	11
$100,000 to $119,999	189	165	16	8	87	79	3	5
$120,000 to $149,999	259	241	6	12	54	51	-	3
$150,000 to $199,999	205	201	2	1	59	57	-	2
$200,000 to $249,999	76	64	-	11	16	10	3	2
$250,000 to $299,999	34	32	-	3	2	2	-	-
$300,000 or more	25	21	5	-	16	16	-	-
Median	67,414	68,697	74,424	38,610	42,299	45,112	...	19,141

Source: "Detailed Tenure by Financial Characteristics - Occupied Units with Black Householder," *American Housing Survey for the United States in 1993,* p. 234. *Notes:* 1. Limited to one-unit structure on less than 10 acres and no business on property. 2. Beginning with 1989 this item uses current income in its calculation. See appendix A. 3. May reflect a temporary situation, living off savings, or response error.

★ 403 ★

Tenure

Tenure: Select Financial Characteristics of Householder. Part 1-2

[Numbers in thousands. Consistent with the 1990 Census. ...means not applicable or sample too small. - means zero or rounds to zero.]

Characteristics	Renter occupied			
	All renters		Unsubsidized renters[1]	
	Specified[2]	Other	Specified[2]	Other
Total	6,305	35	4,445	33
Income of Families and Primary Individuals				
Less than $5,000	1,160	-	528	-
$5,000 to $9,999	1,346	8	706	6
$10,000 to $14,999	885	4	637	4
$15,000 to $19,999	753	7	610	7
$20,000 to $24,999	539	11	470	11
$25,000 to $29,999	487	-	430	-
$30,000 to $34,999	300	-	280	-
$35,000 to $39,999	237	4	230	4
$40,000 to $49,999	298	-	268	-
$50,000 to $59,999	145	-	140	-
$60,000 to $79,999	104	-	95	-
$80,000 to $99,999	38	-	38	-
$100,000 to $119,999	2	-	2	-
$120,000 or more	12	-	12	-
Median	13,655	...	17,881	...
Monthly Housing Costs				
Less than $100	240	-	22	-
$100 to $199	682	5	162	5
$200 to $249	362	-	179	-
$250 to $299	414	-	267	-
$300 to $349	373	-	277	-
$350 to $399	661	-	554	-
$400 to $449	539	-	453	-
$450 to $499	476	-	417	-
$500 to $599	778	-	693	-
$600 to $699	571	4	529	4
$700 to $799	358	-	342	-
$800 to $999	280	4	261	4
$1,000 to $1,249	88	-	86	-
$1,250 to $1,499	27	-	27	-
$1,500 or more	6	-	6	-
No cash rent	451	22	172	20
Mortgage payment not reported	...	...	...	...

[Continued]

★ 403 ★

Tenure: Select Financial Characteristics of Householder. Part 1-2
[Continued]

Characteristics	Renter occupied			
	All renters		Unsubsidized renters[1]	
	Specified[2]	Other	Specified[2]	Other
Median (excludes no cash rent)	418	...	477	...
Median Monthly Housing Costs For Owners				
Monthly costs including all mortgages plus maintenance costs	...	...	...	...
Monthly costs excluding 2nd and subsequent mortgages and maintenance costs	...	...	...	...
Monthly Housing Costs as Percent of Current Income[3]				
Less than 5 percent	20	-	13	-
5 to 9 percent	135	-	85	-
10 to 14 percent	424	5	324	5
15 to 19 percent	677	-	547	-
20 to 24 percent	746	2	595	2
25 to 29 percent	710	-	454	-
30 to 34 percent	595	4	357	4
35 to 39 percent	420	2	297	2
40 to 49 percent	519	-	370	-
50 to 59 percent	372	-	276	-
60 to 69 percent	235	-	181	-
70 to 99 percent	392	-	306	-
100 percent or more[4]	465	-	360	-
Zero or negative income	144	-	110	-
No cash rent	451	22	172	20
Mortgage payment not reported	...	...	...	...
Median (excludes 3 previous lines)	31	...	31	...
Median (excludes 4 lines before medians)	29	...	29	...
OWNER OCCUPIED UNITS				
Total	...	...	...	...
Value				
Less than $10,000	...	...	...	...
$10,000 to $19,999	...	...	...	...
$20,000 to $29,999	...	...	...	...
$30,000 to $39,999	...	...	...	...
$40,000 to $49,999	...	...	...	...
$50,000 to $59,999	...	...	...	...
$60,000 to $69,999	...	...	...	...
$70,000 to $79,999	...	...	...	...
$80,000 to $99,999	...	...	...	...
$100,000 to $119,999	...	...	...	...
$120,000 to $149,999	...	...	...	...
$150,000 to $199,999	...	...	...	...

[Continued]

★ 403 ★

Tenure: Select Financial Characteristics of Householder. Part 1-2

[Continued]

Characteristics	Renter occupied			
	All renters		Unsubsidized renters[1]	
	Specified[2]	Other	Specified[2]	Other
$200,000 to $249,999	...	...	...	...
$250,000 to $299,999	...	...	...	...
$300,000 or more	...	...	...	...
Median	...	...	...	...

Source: "Detailed Tenure by Financial Characteristics - Occupied Units with Black Householder," *American Housing Survey for the United States in 1993*, p. 234. *Notes:* 1. Excludes units in public housing projects, and housing units with government rent subsidies. 2. Excludes one-unit structures on 10 acres or more. 3. Beginning with 1989 this item uses current income in its calculation. See appendix A. 4. May reflect a temporary situation, living off savings, or response error.

★ 404 ★

Tenure

Tenure: Select Financial Characteristics of Householder. Part 1-3

[Numbers in thousands. Consistent with the 1990 Census. ...means not applicable or sample too small. - means zero or rounds to zero.]

Characteristics	Owner occupied							
	With mortgage				With no mortgage			
			Not specified				Not specified	
	Total	Specified[2]	Condo or Coop	Other	Total	Specified[2]	Condo or Coop	Other
OWNER OCCUPIED UNITS								
Ratio of Value to Current Income[1]								
Less than 1.5	1,069	938	28	102	547	384	18	144
1.5 to 1.9	403	368	13	21	169	125	5	39
2.0 to 2.4	353	328	6	18	142	119	6	18
2.5 to 2.9	252	220	14	18	117	109	-	8
3.0 to 3.9	270	254	7	9	185	168	-	17
4.0 to 4.9	169	148	9	12	111	102	-	8
5.0 or more	410	367	15	28	462	415	3	44
Zero or negative income	59	53	-	6	71	43	3	25
Median	2.0	2.0	2.4	1.6	2.5	2.9	...	1.5-
Average Monthly Cost Paid for Real Estate Taxes								
Less than $25	733	615	15	104	784	605	10	168
$25 to $49	581	539	12	30	459	393	10	56
$50 to $74	500	466	15	19	202	174	6	21
$75 to $99	318	279	15	24	137	115	3	20
$100 to $149	371	339	19	13	131	113	3	14
$150 to $199	161	149	5	8	38	25	3	10
$200 or more	320	289	12	19	53	40	-	13

[Continued]

★ 404 ★

Tenure: Select Financial Characteristics of Householder. Part 1-3
[Continued]

Characteristics	Owner occupied							
	With mortgage				With no mortgage			
			Not specified				Not specified	
	Total	Specified[2]	Condo or Coop	Other	Total	Specified[2]	Condo or Coop	Other
Median	59	60	82	28	31	33	...	25-
OWNERS WITH ONE OR MORE MORTGAGES **Total**	2,984	2,677	92	216	...	...	...	...
Monthly Payment for Principal and Interest								
Less than $100	115	107	2	6	...	...	...	...
$100 to $199	387	358	-	29	...	...	...	...
$200 to $249	219	183	12	24	...	...	...	...
$250 to $299	180	148	10	22	...	...	...	...
$300 to $349	176	156	2	18	...	...	...	...
$350 to $399	143	126	10	8	...	...	...	...
$400 to $449	200	180	8	12	...	...	...	...
$450 to $499	139	133	3	3	...	...	...	...
$500 to $599	257	239	3	15	...	...	...	...
$600 to $699	205	195	3	8	...	...	...	...
$700 to $799	135	117	12	6	...	...	...	...
$800 to $999	161	147	6	7	...	...	...	...
$1,000 to $1,249	87	81	-	6	...	...	...	...
$1,250 to $1,499	42	40	-	2	...	...	...	...
$1,500 or more	41	36	2	4	...	...	...	...
Not reported	498	432	19	46	...	...	...	...
Median	406	413	403	310	...	...	...	...
Type of Primary Mortgage								
FHA	887	815	28	43	...	...	...	...
VA	394	380	8	7	...	...	...	...
Farmers Home Administration	64	56	-	8	...	...	...	...
Other types	1,418	1,238	51	130	...	...	...	...
Don't know	84	75	-	9	...	...	...	...
Not reported	137	113	5	19	...	...	...	...
Mortgage Origination								
Placed new mortgage(s)	2,389	2,135	82	173	...	...	...	...
Primary obtained when property acquired	1,909	1,697	77	135	...	...	...	...
Obtained later	461	418	5	38	...	...	...	...
Date not reported	20	20	-	-	...	...	...	...
Assumed	130	119	3	9	...	...	...	...
Wrap-around	-	-	-	-	...	...	...	...
Combination of the above	346	327	3	16	...	...	...	...
Origin not reported	119	95	5	19	...	...	...	...

[Continued]

★ 404 ★

Tenure: Select Financial Characteristics of Householder. Part 1-3
[Continued]

Characteristics	Owner occupied							
	With mortgage				With no mortgage			
			Not specified				Not specified	
	Total	Specified[2]	Condo or Coop	Other	Total	Specified[2]	Condo or Coop	Other
Payment Plan of Primary Mortgage								
Fixed payment, self amortizing	2,292	2,078	65	149	...	...	...	...
Adjustable rate mortgage	163	143	8	12	...	...	...	...
Adjustable term mortgage	10	10	-	-	...	...	...	...
Graduated payment mortgage	23	23	-	-	...	...	...	...
Balloon	10	7	-	3	...	...	...	...
Other	55	52	2	-	...	...	...	...
Combination of the above	6	6	-	-	...	...	...	...
Not reported	425	356	18	51	...	...	...	...
Payment Plan of Secondary Mortgage								
Units with two or more mortgages	398	380	3	16	...	...	...	...
Fixed payment, self amortizing	207	198	-	9	...	...	...	...
Adjustable rate mortgage	28	28	-	-	...	...	...	...
Adjustable term mortgage	5	5	-	-	...	...	...	...
Graduated payment mortgage	-	-	-	-	...	...	...	...
Balloon	5	5	-	-	...	...	...	...
Other	5	3	-	2	...	...	...	...
Combination of the above	20	20	-	-	...	...	...	...
Not reported	129	122	3	4	...	...	...	...
Lenders of Primary and Secondary Mortgages								
Only borrowed from firm(s)	2,472	2,204	83	185	...	...	...	...
Only borrowed from seller	80	74	1	5	...	...	...	...
Only borrowed from other individual(s)	31	27	-	4	...	...	...	...
Borrowed from a firm and seller	10	7	-	3	...	...	...	...
Borrowed from a firm and other individual	12	12	-	-	...	...	...	...
Borrowed from seller and other individual	-	-	-	-	...	...	...	...
One or both sources not reported	379	352	8	19	...	...	...	...

Source: "Detailed Tenure by Financial Characteristics - Occupied Units with Black Householder," *American Housing Survey for the United States in 1993,* p. 235-36. *Notes:* 1. Excludes units in public housing projects, and housing units with government rent subsidies. 2. Limited to one-unit structure on less than 10 acres and no business on property.

Tenure in Housing

★ 405 ★

Occupied Housing by Race of Householder: 1920-1993

[**In thousands, except as indicated.** As of **April, except 1991,** as of **fall.** Prior to **1960,** excludes Alaska and Hawaii. Statistics on the number of occupied units are essentially comparable although identified by various terms. See also *Historical Statistics, Colonial Times to 1970,* series N 238-245].

RACE AND TENURE	1920	1930	1940	1950	1960	1970	1980	1990	1993
ALL RACES									
Occupied units, total	24,352	29,905	34,855	42,826	53,024	63,445	80,390	91,947	94,724
Owner occupied	11,114	14,280	15,196	23,560	32,797	39,886	51,795	59,025	61,252
Percent of occupied	45.6	47.8	43.6	55.0	61.9	62.9	64.4	64.2	64.7
Renter occupied	13,238	15,624	19,659	19,266	20,227	23,560	28,595	32,923	33,472
WHITE									
Occupied units, total	21,826	26,983	31,561	39,044	47,880	56,606	68,810	76,880	80,029
Owner occupied	10,511	13,544	14,418	22,241	30,823	37,005	46,671	52,433	54,878
Percent of occupied	48.2	50.2	45.7	57.0	64.4	65.4	67.8	68.2	68.6
Renter occupied	11,315	13,439	17,143	16,803	17,057	19,601	22,139	24,447	25,151
BLACK AND OTHER									
Occupied units, total	2,526	2,922	3,293	3,783	5,144	6,839	11,580	15,067	14,695
Owner occupied	603	737	778	1,319	1,974	2,881	5,124	6,592	6,374
Percent of occupied	23.9	25.2	23.6	34.9	38.4	42.1	44.2	43.8	43.4
Renter occupied	1,923	2,185	2,516	2,464	3,170	3,959	6,456	8,475	8,321

Source: "Occupied Housing Units-Tenure, by Race of Householder: 1920 to 1993." U.S. Bureau of the Census, *Statistical Abstract of the United States,* 115th ed., 1995, p. 733. Primary source: U.S. Bureau of the Census, *Census of Housing: 1960,* vol. 1; *1970,* vol. 1; *1980 Census of Housing,* vol. 1. chapter A (HC80-1-A) and *1990 Census of Housing, General Housing Characteristics,* series CH-90-1; 1993 data, *Current Housing Reports,* series H150/93, American Housing Survey in the United States.

Values

★ 406 ★

Values: Owner Occupied Housing by Select Characteristics

[Numbers in thousands. Consistent with the 1990 Census. ...means not applicable or sample too small. - means zero or rounds to zero.]

Characteristics	Total occupied units	Tenure		Housing unit characteristics				Household characteristics		
		Owner	Renter	New construction 4 yrs	Mobile homes	Physical problems		Elderly (65+)	Moved in past year	Below poverty level
						Severe	Moderate			
Total	4,788	4,788	...	192	252	137	450	1,153	239	1,001
Value										
Less than $10,000	217	217	...	4	134	14	57	45	14	107
$10,000 to $19,999	317	317	...	7	63	5	63	113	18	130
$20,000 to $29,999	450	450	...	10	19	24	76	161	18	148
$30,000 to $39,999	498	498	...	6	6	9	83	148	12	135
$40,000 to $49,999	526	526	...	15	15	20	51	120	15	122
$50,000 to $59,999	461	461	...	10	11	12	20	91	24	88
$60,000 to $69,999	436	436	...	8	5	20	22	109	21	63
$70,000 to $79,999	327	327	...	16	-	5	26	68	18	40
$80,000 to $99,999	533	533	...	31	-	18	11	99	34	62
$100,000 to $119,999	277	277	...	22	-	8	17	60	12	40
$120,000 to $149,999	312	312	...	26	-	3	13	57	30	25
$150,000 to $199,999	264	264	...	16	-	-	8	51	12	27
$200,000 to $249,999	91	91	...	5	-	-	5	15	9	8
$250,000 to $299,999	37	37	...	3	-	-	-	7	3	-
$300,000 or more	41	41	...	11	-	-	-	9	-	6
Median	58,372	58,372	...	93,002	10000-	48,453	33,599	49,112	68,970	38,528
Ratio of Value to Current Income[1]										
Less than 1.5	1,615	1,615	...	47	172	30	153	211	66	110
1.5 to 1.9	572	572	...	46	27	11	37	74	32	48
2.0 to 2.4	495	495	...	33	12	16	31	105	46	48
2.5 to 2.9	369	369	...	25	10	9	23	82	23	29
3.0 to 3.9	455	455	...	12	7	19	43	152	23	75
4.0 to 4.9	279	279	...	12	3	15	28	101	14	68
5.0 or more	872	872	...	13	5	35	123	417	27	494
Zero or negative income	130	130	...	3	15	2	13	11	8	128
Median	2.1	2.1	...	2.0	1.5-	3.1	2.5	3.7	2.2	5.0+
Other Activities on Property[2]										
Commercial establishment	52	52	...	-	5	2	11	6	-	16
Medical or dental office	8	8	...	-	-	-	-	-	-	3
Neither	4,731	4,731	...	192	248	134	439	1,147	239	982
Year Unit Acquired										
1990 to 1994	827	827	...	169	73	5	54	40	207	107
1985 to 1989	955	955	...	17	83	30	69	61	2	181
1980 to 1984	509	509	...	...	22	16	59	59	-	95
1975 to 1979	631	631	...	...	29	21	40	116	2	121
1970 to 1974	592	592	...	...	28	9	55	126	3	176
1960 to 1969	663	663	...	...	4	17	85	335	-	176
1950 to 1959	282	282	...	...	-	22	33	229	2	75
1940 to 1949	116	116	...	...	-	9	26	114	-	45
1939 or earlier	34	34	...	...	-	4	2	30	-	16
Not reported	180	180	...	...	15	2	28	44	23	64
Median	1980	1980	...	...	1987	1976	1976	1965	1990+	1976
First Time Owners										
First home ever owned	3,202	3,202	...	89	177	97	350	751	117	723
Not first home	1,453	1,453	...	97	69	37	86	386	91	236
Not reported	134	134	...	6	7	2	14	17	32	42
Purchase Price										
Home purchased or built	4,395	4,395	...	186	218	112	359	1,025	214	822
Less than $10,000	539	539	...	-	57	40	101	279	11	174

[Continued]

★ 406 ★

Values: Owner Occupied Housing by Select Characteristics

[Continued]

Characteristics	Total occupied units	Tenure		Housing unit characteristics				Household characteristics		
		Owner	Renter	New construction 4 yrs	Mobile homes	Physical problems		Elderly (65+)	Moved in past year	Below poverty level
						Severe	Moderate			
$10,000 to $19,999	883	883	...	7	74	13	82	289	20	215
$20,000 to $29,999	499	499	...	11	29	8	25	81	8	123
$30,000 to $39,999	389	389	...	10	9	3	31	57	10	44
$40,000 to $49,999	309	309	...	10	4	12	5	31	11	19
$50,000 to $59,999	252	252	...	11	11	2	6	13	28	26
$60,000 to $69,999	205	205	...	10	-	3	5	14	16	10
$70,000 to $79,999	155	155	...	15	-	-	3	10	29	2
$80,000 to $99,999	227	227	...	40	-	5	10	7	22	10
$100,000 to $119,999	71	71	...	10	-	-	-	4	3	3
$120,000 to $149,999	106	106	...	15	-	-	-	5	23	7
$150,000 to $199,999	50	50	...	13	-	-	-	-	8	8
$200,000 to $249,999	27	27	...	9	-	-	-	-	6	-
$250,000 to $299,999	13	13	...	-	-	-	-	-	-	-
$300,000 or more	18	18	...	11	-	-	-	3	-	-
Not reported	654	654	...	12	34	26	92	232	20	180
Median	29,003	29,003	...	86,074	14,716	12,249	13,959	14,078	65,778	16,810
Received as inheritance or gift	213	213	...	-	19	23	63	83	3	115
Not reported	180	180	...	6	15	2	28	44	23	64
Major Source of Down Payment										
Home purchased or built	4,395	4,395	...	186	218	1'12	359	1,025	214	822
Sale of previous home	463	463	...	37	11	10	13	127	13	44
Savings or cash on hand	2,759	2,759	...	112	127	79	183	571	159	461
Sale of other investment	14	14	...	3	2	-	-	-	3	2
Borrowing, other than mortgage on this property	193	193	...	18	21	6	37	57	4	55
Inheritance or gift	74	74	...	-	-	-	9	15	3	15
Land where building built used for financing	30	30	...	-	-	-	4	10	-	7
Other	231	231	...	4	21	2	22	47	12	51
No down payment	453	453	...	11	25	12	68	134	12	115
Not reported	179	179	...	-	11	2	24	64	8	74

Source: "Value, Purchase Price, and Source of Down Payment - Occupied Units with Black Householder," *American Housing Survey for the United States in1993*, p. 222. *Notes:* 1. Beginning with 1989 this item uses current income in its calculation. See appendix A. 2. Figures may not add to total because more than one category may apply to a unit.

★ 407 ★

Values

Values: Select Characteristics. Part 1-1

[Numbers in thousands. Consistent with the 1990 Census. ...means not applicable or sample too small. - means zero or rounds to zero.]

Characteristics	Total	Less than $30,000	$30,000 to $39,999	$40,000 to $49,999	$50,000 to $59,999	$60,000 to $79,999	$80,000 to $99,999
Total	4,788	984	498	526	461	764	533
Units in Structure							
1, detached	3,875	650	418	452	370	671	460
1, attached	421	80	41	23	43	75	47
2 to 4	151	30	23	32	16	6	13
5 to 9	25	-	3	-	5	-	8
10 to 19	20	6	2	2	-	5	3
20 to 49	13	3	-	2	5	-	-

[Continued]

★ 407 ★

Values: Select Characteristics. Part 1-1
[Continued]

Characteristics	Total	Less than $30,000	$30,000 to $39,999	$40,000 to $49,999	$50,000 to $59,999	$60,000 to $79,999	$80,000 to $99,999
50 or more	32	-	5	-	11	3	2
Mobile home or trailer	252	216	6	15	11	5	-
Year Structure Built[1]							
1990 to 1994	170	19	4	15	10	18	31
1985 to 1989	246	35	17	11	15	32	48
1980 to 1984	285	47	18	38	29	45	43
1975 to 1979	350	72	20	33	30	74	46
1970 to 1974	490	97	39	60	60	103	45
1960 to 1969	789	134	79	93	97	153	91
1950 to 1959	718	101	102	77	65	113	91
1940 to 1949	603	175	79	51	52	91	45
1930 to 1939	427	115	50	65	35	42	30
1920 to 1929	313	83	22	41	36	36	37
1919 or earlier	396	106	68	41	32	58	27
Median	1959	1951	1953	1958	1961	1963	1964
Rooms							
1 room	-	-	-	-	-	-	-
2 rooms	-	-	-	-	-	-	-
3 rooms	62	21	8	-	4	4	7
4 rooms	452	185	42	60	42	40	29
5 rooms	1,162	349	142	174	126	157	76
6 rooms	1,440	240	174	193	172	255	156
7 rooms	871	122	82	63	72	181	157
8 rooms	441	41	26	23	30	77	70
9 rooms	204	6	17	7	13	35	24
10 rooms or more	155	19	7	6	2	14	15
Median	6.0	5.3	5.8	5.7	5.8	6.2	6.5
Bedrooms							
None	-	-	-	-	-	-	-
1	86	24	10	2	10	10	13
2	1,030	348	106	137	101	120	66
3	2,673	477	289	307	291	504	309
4 or more	998	134	93	79	59	129	145
Median	3.0	2.8	3.0	2.9	2.9	3.0	3.1
Complete Bathrooms							
None	38	23	2	2	-	8	3
1	1,984	652	270	277	185	253	144
1 and one-half	1,106	156	117	133	133	218	104
2 or more	1,661	153	109	114	143	284	282

[Continued]

★ 407 ★

Values: Select Characteristics. Part 1-1
[Continued]

Characteristics	Total	Less than $30,000	$30,000 to $39,999	$40,000 to $49,999	$50,000 to $59,999	$60,000 to $79,999	$80,000 to $99,999
Main Heating Equipment							
Warm-air furnace	2,602	477	236	294	280	438	331
Steam or hot water system	591	68	47	53	54	71	42
Electric heat pump	367	33	32	37	43	83	56
Built-in electric units	156	13	25	26	18	28	25
Floor, wall, or other built-in hot air units without ducts	256	70	29	20	14	30	25
Room heaters with flue	171	59	29	20	12	19	16
Room heaters without flue	306	144	53	45	12	35	6
Portable electric heaters	45	14	7	5	8	7	2
Stoves	145	72	17	17	8	18	9
Fireplaces with inserts	19	2	2	-	2	3	8
Fireplaces without inserts	17	9	4	-	-	4	-
Other	84	19	14	9	5	17	10
None	31	4	3	-	5	13	4
Source of Water							
Public system or private company	4,269	829	468	458	418	683	465
Well serving 1 to 5 units	451	140	28	66	41	69	61
Drilled	341	101	26	45	30	54	50
Dug	88	34	2	17	9	10	7
Not reported	23	4	-	4	3	5	4
Other	68	15	2	2	2	12	7
Means of Sewage Disposal							
Public sewer	3,864	667	413	410	387	623	444
Septic tank, cesspool, chemical toilet	894	294	84	116	75	137	86
Other	30	23	-	-	-	4	3
Main House Heating Fuel							
Housing units with heating fuel	4,757	980	495	526	457	751	529
Electricity	958	126	95	116	112	215	142
Piped gas	2,832	519	307	311	273	397	316
Bottled gas	270	131	29	28	9	40	11
Fuel oil	393	54	35	31	38	68	38
Kerosene or other liquid fuel	101	54	4	22	9	7	2
Coal and coke	9	9	-	-	-	-	-
Wood	193	87	26	17	13	24	19
Solar energy	-	-	-	-	-	-	-
Other	3	-	-	-	3	-	-

Source: "Value by Selected Characteristics - Occupied Units with Black Householder," *American Housing Survey for the United States in 1933,* p. 245. *Note:* For mobile home, oldest category is 1939 or earlier.

★ 408 ★
Values

Values: Select Characteristics. Part 1-2

[Numbers in thousands. Consistent with the 1990 Census. ...means not applicable or sample too small. - means zero or rounds to zero.]

Characteristics	$100,000 to $149,999	$150,000 to $199,999	$200,000 to $249,999	$250,000 to $299,999	$300,000 or more	Median
Total	589	264	91	37	41	58,372
Units in Structure						
1, detached	474	240	72	34	34	61,395
1, attached	83	22	5	-	2	66,393
2 to 4	16	1	12	3	-	47,151
5 to 9	5	-	-	-	3	...
10 to 19	3	-	-	-	-	...
20 to 49	3	-	-	-	-	...
50 or more	6	-	3	-	2	...
Mobile home or trailer	-	-	-	-	-	30000-
Year Structure Built[1]						
1990 to 1994	41	12	5	3	11	92,242
1985 to 1989	46	19	12	8	5	85,514
1980 to 1984	49	10	-	-	6	64,506
1975 to 1979	55	10	5	2	3	65,511
1970 to 1974	37	34	8	-	7	58,115
1960 to 1969	87	35	10	10	-	59,143
1950 to 1959	94	56	18	-	-	62,335
1940 to 1949	61	18	19	4	9	49,454
1930 to 1939	42	34	8	7	-	47,540
1920 to 1929	38	18	-	-	2	52,808
1919 or earlier	39	18	5	2	-	45,803
Median	1962	1958	1957	...	...	...
Rooms						
1 room	-	-	-	-	-	...
2 rooms	-	-	-	-	-	...
3 rooms	7	8	3	-	-	54,699
4 rooms	34	9	7	2	3	39,907
5 rooms	94	29	12	2	-	45,168
6 rooms	156	65	16	2	11	56,577
7 rooms	122	47	18	5	2	70,664
8 rooms	97	49	9	12	7	86,944
9 rooms	39	35	7	10	9	99,035
10 rooms or more	39	21	20	3	9	118,015
Median	6.5	6.9	7.0	...	...	...
Bedrooms						
None	-	-	-	-	-	...
1	5	6	5	-	-	56,822
2	95	37	12	4	3	44,426
3	324	121	38	7	7	59,050

[Continued]

★ 408 ★

Values: Select Characteristics. Part 1-2
[Continued]

Characteristics	$100,000 to $149,999	$150,000 to $199,999	$200,000 to $249,999	$250,000 to $299,999	$300,000 or more	Median
4 or more	164	100	37	26	32	80,657
Median	3.1	3.2	3.3	...	...	...
Complete Bathrooms						
None	-	-	-	-	-	...
1	126	52	21	-	4	42,541
1 and one-half	150	71	13	7	5	61,298
2 or more	313	141	58	30	33	81,878
Main Heating Equipment						
Warm-air furnace	315	127	47	24	33	60,607
Steam or hot water system	147	75	25	8	-	80,730
Electric heat pump	56	17	8	2	-	69,238
Built-in electric units	12	7	-	-	2	58,122
Floor, wall, or other built-in hot air units without ducts	33	27	4	2	2	56,654
Room heaters with flue	8	7	-	-	-	38,951
Room heaters without flue	11	-	-	-	-	31,750
Portable electric heaters	2	-	-	-	-	...
Stoves	-	-	2	-	2	30,450
Fireplaces with inserts	2	-	-	-	-	...
Fireplaces without inserts	-	-	-	-	-	...
Other	2	3	3	-	2	49,926
None	-	-	2	-	-	...
Source of Water						
Public system or private company	552	239	81	37	39	59,077
Well serving 1 to 5 units	27	10	8	-	2	48,834
Drilled	22	8	6	-	-	49,645
Dug	2	2	2	-	2	44,510
Not reported	2	-	-	-	-	...
Other	10	14	2	-	-	80,245
Means of Sewage Disposal						
Public sewer	523	240	83	34	39	61,761
Septic tank, cesspool, chemical toilet	66	24	8	2	2	45,920
Other	-	-	-	-	-	...
Main House Heating Fuel						
Housing units with heating fuel	589	264	89	37	41	58,269
Electricity	100	36	8	5	4	62,875
Piped gas	407	187	55	27	32	60,294
Bottled gas	12	4	5	-	-	31,364
Fuel oil	65	37	19	5	3	71,275
Kerosene or other liquid fuel	2	-	-	-	-	30000-

[Continued]

★ 408 ★

Values: Select Characteristics. Part 1-2
[Continued]

Characteristics	$100,000 to $149,999	$150,000 to $199,999	$200,000 to $249,999	$250,000 to $299,999	$300,000 or more	Median
Coal and coke	-	-	-	-	-	...
Wood	2	-	2	-	2	33,597
Solar energy	-	-	-	-	-	...
Other	-	-	-	-	-	...

Source: "Value by Selected Characteristics - Occupied Units with Black Householder," *American Housing Survey for the United States in 1933,* p. 245. *Note:* For mobile home, oldest category in 1939 or earlier.

★ 409 ★
Values

Values: Select Characteristics. Part 2-1

[Numbers in thousands. Consistent with the 1990 Census. ...means not applicable or sample too small. - means zero or rounds to zero.]

Characteristics	Total	Less than $30,000	$30,000 to $39,999	$40,000 to $49,999	$50,000 to $59,999	$60,000 to $79,999
Cooking Fuel						
With cooking fuel	4,783	979	498	526	461	764
Electricity	1,939	303	168	229	199	400
Piped gas	2,477	515	294	259	237	314
Bottled gas	350	156	31	37	25	48
Kerosene or other liquid fuel	12	3	4	-	-	2
Coal or coke	-	-	-	-	-	-
Wood	2	2	-	-	-	-
Other	3	-	-	3	-	-
Persons						
1 person	1,007	286	122	112	93	155
2 persons	1,286	253	111	131	127	234
3 persons	973	169	122	92	103	170
4 persons	857	126	83	112	76	131
5 persons	389	68	33	39	39	40
6 persons	170	53	13	23	13	20
7 persons or more	107	28	14	16	11	14
Median	2.6	2.3	2.6	2.7	2.6	2.5
Household Composition by Age of Householder						
2-or-more person households	3,781	698	376	414	368	609
Married-couple families, no nonrelatives	2,248	356	183	249	211	349
Under 25 years	12	9	-	2	-	-
25 to 29 years	66	16	5	5	3	16
30 to 34 years	211	37	10	12	32	24

[Continued]

★ 409 ★

Values: Select Characteristics. Part 2-1

[Continued]

Characteristics	Total	Less than $30,000	$30,000 to $39,999	$40,000 to $49,999	$50,000 to $59,999	$60,000 to $79,999
35 to 44 years	591	84	47	58	55	87
45 to 64 years	987	119	73	130	86	163
65 years and over	382	90	47	40	36	60
Other male householder	344	65	42	18	34	55
Under 45 years	160	30	16	10	17	33
45 to 64 years	107	13	18	6	11	16
65 years and over	77	22	8	2	7	6
Other female householder	1,189	277	151	148	123	205
Under 45 years	439	104	66	59	43	82
45 to 64 years	461	94	53	49	60	80
65 years and over	288	79	32	40	20	42
1-person households	1,007	286	122	112	93	155
Male householder	382	110	37	40	36	66
Under 45 years	119	44	6	14	11	14
45 to 64 years	153	38	15	17	20	34
65 years and over	110	28	17	9	6	18
Female householder	625	176	85	72	57	89
Under 45 years	80	17	11	6	5	13
45 to 64 years	249	59	29	37	29	25
65 years and over	296	100	44	30	23	50
Own Never Married Children Under 18 Years Old						
No own children under 18 years	3,179	698	342	341	309	514
With own children under 18 years	1,609	285	155	185	152	250
Under 6 years only	210	29	17	17	25	41
1	140	19	12	7	20	30
2	66	7	4	10	5	11
3 or more	5	3	-	-	-	-
6 to 17 years only	1,141	202	119	147	95	181
1	648	104	67	78	56	124
2	353	50	36	55	22	48
3 or more	139	48	16	14	17	10
Both age groups	259	54	19	21	33	27
2	121	23	10	10	17	10
3 or more	138	31	10	11	16	17
Income of Families and Primary Individuals						
Less than $5,000	397	156	46	56	25	46
$5,000 to $9,999	601	207	107	63	58	71
$10,000 to $14,999	439	146	46	60	49	57
$15,000 to $19,999	460	111	61	68	36	60
$20,000 to $24,999	416	90	53	81	38	65
$25,000 to $29,999	397	83	34	45	44	80

[Continued]

★ 409 ★

Values: Select Characteristics. Part 2-1
[Continued]

Characteristics	Total	Less than $30,000	$30,000 to $39,999	$40,000 to $49,999	$50,000 to $59,999	$60,000 to $79,999
$30,000 to $34,999	284	58	36	19	36	76
$35,000 to $39,999	259	33	17	16	45	52
$40,000 to $49,999	451	42	44	48	34	93
$50,000 to $59,999	331	20	31	28	35	73
$60,000 to $79,999	406	27	19	21	46	60
$80,000 to $99,999	156	-	2	10	8	17
$100,000 to $119,999	85	9	2	3	3	10
$120,000 or more	105	-	-	8	3	5
Median	26,010	14,405	19,097	21,029	27,617	30,252
Monthly Housing Costs						
Less than $100	178	106	21	11	9	20
$100 to $199	687	305	117	79	37	73
$200 to $249	360	107	43	68	35	57
$250 to $299	307	95	46	32	32	51
$300 to $349	286	88	37	32	38	34
$350 to $399	202	46	31	30	11	27
$400 to $449	179	35	45	35	10	29
$450 to $499	178	28	25	36	18	41
$500 to $599	381	80	46	65	67	44
$600 to $699	363	36	24	49	72	103
$700 to $799	251	5	5	19	42	82
$800 to $999	383	11	12	16	33	102
$1,000 to $1,249	281	-	4	7	5	25
$1,250 to $1,499	104	5	-	-	-	5
$1,500 or more	151	-	-	-	3	2
No cash rent	...	...	...	...	...	...
Mortgage payment not reported	498	59	41	48	48	67
Median (excludes no cash rent)	435	224	301	379	525	533

Source: "Value by Selected Characteristics - Occupied Units with Black Householder," *American Housing Survey for the United States in 1993*, p. 246.

★ 410 ★

Values

Values: Select Characteristics. Part 2-2

[Numbers in thousands. Consistent with the 1990 Census. ...means not applicable or sample too small. - means zero or rounds to zero.]

Characteristics	$80,000 to $99,999	$100,000 to $149,999	$150,000 to $199,999	$200,000 to $249,999	$250,000 to $299,999	$300,000 or more	Median
Cooking Fuel							
With cooking fuel	533	589	264	91	37	41	58,426
Electricity	273	223	93	18	15	20	63,567
Piped gas	235	344	167	71	22	19	57,213
Bottled gas	24	21	4	2	-	2	36,104
Kerosene or other liquid fuel	-	2	-	-	-	-	...
Coal or coke	-	-	-	-	-	-	...
Wood	-	-	-	-	-	-	...
Other	-	-	-	-	-	-	...
Persons							
1 person	79	100	46	8	2	3	48,511
2 persons	130	161	78	38	9	14	61,769
3 persons	129	130	29	12	7	10	59,973
4 persons	102	116	67	13	15	13	64,564
5 persons	67	55	32	11	3	2	68,045
6 persons	21	18	7	3	-	-	48,276
7 persons or more	5	8	5	6	-	-	47,095
Median	2.9	2.8	2.8	2.5	...	...	...
Household Composition by Age of Householder							
2-or-more person households	454	489	218	83	34	39	61,137
Married-couple families, no nonrelatives	302	315	158	57	34	34	67,209
Under 25 years	-	-	-	-	-	-	...
25 to 29 years	10	8	-	3	-	-	65,027
30 to 34 years	42	27	15	9	-	2	71,225
35 to 44 years	82	82	56	12	13	15	71,754
45 to 64 years	121	157	81	31	17	9	70,560
65 years and over	46	41	7	2	4	7	53,679
Other male householder	70	48	10	1	-	-	64,649
Under 45 years	34	20	-	-	-	-	64,200
45 to 64 years	23	12	7	-	-	-	66,739
65 years and over	14	16	3	1	-	-	61,146
Other female householder	82	126	49	24	-	5	51,549
Under 45 years	30	37	8	10	-	-	48,417
45 to 64 years	38	57	23	5	-	2	55,777
65 years and over	14	32	18	9	-	2	48,438
1-person households	79	100	46	8	2	3	48,511
Male householder	37	28	23	3	-	3	51,152
Under 45 years	11	11	2	3	-	3	46,849
45 to 64 years	10	9	11		-	-	53,454
65 years and over	16	7	10	-	-	-	53,178
Female householder	42	72	24	5	2	-	47,119
Under 45 years	14	13	-	-	-	-	60,573
45 to 64 years	19	38	10	3	-	-	50,043

[Continued]

★ 410 ★

Values: Select Characteristics. Part 2-2
[Continued]

Characteristics	$80,000 to $99,999	$100,000 to $149,999	$150,000 to $199,999	$200,000 to $249,999	$250,000 to $299,999	$300,000 or more	Median
65 years and over	9	21	13	2	2	-	41,067
Own Never Married Children Under 18 Years Old							
No own children under 18 years	312	392	169	60	16	25	56,703
With own children under 18 years	221	197	95	31	21	17	62,141
Under 6 years only	36	34	3	5	4	-	68,507
1	29	17	3	-	2	-	67,306
2	7	17	-	2	2	-	72,299
3 or more	-	-	-	2	-	-	...
6 to 17 years only	146	138	63	22	14	14	60,771
1	72	79	37	14	8	9	63,060
2	58	47	24	3	6	5	65,604
3 or more	16	12	2	4	-	-	43,990
Both age groups	39	25	30	5	2	2	61,550
2	19	12	16	-	2	2	61,785
3 or more	21	13	14	5	-	-	61,413
Income of Families and Primary Individuals							
Less than $5,000	30	16	19	3	-	-	39,099
$5,000 to $9,999	31	44	10	5	-	4	38,771
$10,000 to $14,999	20	41	15	-	-	7	44,680
$15,000 to $19,999	62	33	15	4	4	5	48,493
$20,000 to $24,999	45	25	14	5	-	-	47,957
$25,000 to $29,999	37	53	9	8	-	3	58,180
$30,000 to $34,999	19	27	10	-	-	2	57,869
$35,000 to $39,999	35	35	22	2	2	-	67,212
$40,000 to $49,999	70	87	22	5	3	2	72,146
$50,000 to $59,999	37	75	22	9	-	-	74,082
$60,000 to $79,999	96	67	48	16	7	-	86,408
$80,000 to $99,999	25	48	21	18	6	-	116,021
$100,000 to $119,999	18	13	12	8	5	3	97,130
$120,000 or more	8	23	24	10	9	15	161,911
Median	38,251	42,246	47,793	66,717	...	...	...
Monthly Housing Costs							
Less than $100	9	2	-	-	-	-	30000-
$100 to $199	34	25	10	2	-	4	33,300
$200 to $249	18	17	10	2	-	2	44,434
$250 to $299	22	21	7	-	2	-	44,117
$300 to $349	24	18	7	5	-	2	45,612
$350 to $399	10	30	15	2	-	-	48,021
$400 to $449	14	10	2	-	-	-	42,770
$450 to $499	12	13	2	3	-	-	50,191
$500 to $599	50	36	8	4	-	2	52,958
$600 to $699	43	20	10	2	2	2	60,134

[Continued]

★ 410 ★

Values: Select Characteristics. Part 2-2

[Continued]

Characteristics	$80,000 to $99,999	$100,000 to $149,999	$150,000 to $199,999	$200,000 to $249,999	$250,000 to $299,999	$300,000 or more	Median
$700 to $799	53	27	16	2	-	-	73,289
$800 to $999	100	72	24	5	5	3	83,380
$1,000 to $1,249	64	133	34	10	-	-	113,519
$1,250 to $1,499	5	42	30	14	2	-	143,681
$1,500 or more	5	40	44	24	19	13	177,615
No cash rent	...	...	...	...	...	...	...
Mortgage payment not reported	72	84	45	15	6	13	75,724
Median (excludes no cash rent)	692	897	990	1,250	...	...	...

Source: "Value by Selected Characteristics - Occupied Units with Black Householder," *American Housing Survey for the United States in 1993,* p. 246.

★ 411 ★

Values

Values: Select Characteristics. Part 3-1

[Numbers in thousands. Consistent with the 1990 Census. ...means not applicable or sample too small. - means zero or rounds to zero.]

Characteristics	Total	Less than $30,000	$30,000 to $39,999	$40,000 to $49,999	$50,000 to $59,999	$60,000 to $79,999	$80,000 to $99,999
Median Monthly Housing Costs For Owners							
Monthly costs including all mortgages plus maintenance costs	464	236	310	406	536	566	733
Monthly costs excluding 2nd and subsequent mortgages and maintenance costs	415	224	294	363	472	494	648
Monthly Housing Costs as Percent of Current Income[1]							
Less than 5 percent	120	38	12	17	12	23	7
5 to 9 percent	494	142	69	52	33	71	52
10 to 14 percent	649	163	81	70	65	106	47
15 to 19 percent	604	92	47	66	83	119	102
20 to 24 percent	550	101	41	51	45	102	79
25 to 29 percent	395	87	47	36	33	68	40
30 to 34 percent	313	51	40	33	27	58	28
35 to 39 percent	177	47	6	28	17	29	14
40 to 49 percent	277	59	37	27	37	37	27
50 to 59 percent	179	37	13	24	14	19	22
60 to 69 percent	113	13	9	17	17	11	7
70 to 99 percent	147	23	19	19	12	28	8
100 percent or more[2]	168	41	17	18	9	19	24

[Continued]

★ 411 ★

Values: Select Characteristics. Part 3-1
[Continued]

Characteristics	Total	Less than $30,000	$30,000 to $39,999	$40,000 to $49,999	$50,000 to $59,999	$60,000 to $79,999	$80,000 to $99,999
Zero or negative income	104	32	17	19	9	7	5
No cash rent	...	...	...	...	...	...	...
Mortgage payment not reported	498	59	41	48	48	67	72
Median (excludes 3 previous lines)	22	21	21	22	21	21	21
Median (excludes 4 lines before medians)	21	20	20	22	21	21	21
Monthly Payment for Principal and Interest							
Less than $100	115	42	16	11	7	24	11
$100 to $199	387	105	53	54	51	58	27
$200 to $249	219	65	45	29	24	18	16
$250 to $299	180	32	25	39	17	28	19
$300 to $349	176	20	33	40	20	21	23
$350 to $399	143	12	15	26	29	32	22
$400 to $449	200	21	13	21	48	51	19
$450 to $499	139	2	5	18	29	44	24
$500 to $599	257	9	5	20	31	96	47
$600 to $699	205	-	2	-	18	50	59
$700 to $799	135	-	2	-	2	12	48
$800 to $999	161	3	2	5	3	7	17
$1,000 to $1,249	87	2	-	-	-	2	5
$1,250 to $1,499	42	-	-	-	-	-	2
$1,500 or more	41	-	-	-	-	2	-
Not reported	498	59	41	48	48	67	72
Median	406	208	244	298	386	441	519
Average Monthly Cost Paid for Real Estate Taxes							
Less than $25	1,517	646	228	195	125	180	64
$25 to $49	1,040	193	132	147	157	188	100
$50 to $74	702	72	71	72	71	201	102
$75 to $99	455	36	23	49	37	79	94
$100 to $149	502	25	31	27	56	72	92
$150 to $199	199	2	5	21	8	22	34
$200 or more	373	10	8	15	7	20	47
Median	46	25-	29	37	42	52	75
Purchase Price							
Home purchased or built	4,395	831	440	486	439	711	515
Less than $10,000	539	269	85	46	25	54	27
$10,000 to $19,999	883	285	111	125	97	114	58
$20,000 to $29,999	499	90	78	77	68	71	45
$30,000 to $39,999	389	17	69	78	48	82	22
$40,000 to $49,999	309	3	12	62	68	71	47
$50,000 to $59,999	252	7	-	8	59	98	46

[Continued]

★ 411 ★

Values: Select Characteristics. Part 3-1
[Continued]

Characteristics	Total	Less than $30,000	$30,000 to $39,999	$40,000 to $49,999	$50,000 to $59,999	$60,000 to $79,999	$80,000 to $99,999
$60,000 to $69,999	205	3	2	8	15	96	34
$70,000 to $79,999	155	-	-	-	3	34	78
$80,000 to $99,999	227	-	-	-	-	2	81
$100,000 to $119,999	71	3	-	-	-	-	-
$120,000 to $149,999	106	3	-	3	-	-	-
$150,000 to $199,999	50	-	-	-	-	-	2
$200,000 to $249,999	27	-	-	-	-	-	-
$250,000 to $299,999	13	-	-	-	-	-	-
$300,000 or more	18	-	-	-	-	-	-
Not reported	654	152	82	80	59	90	74
Median	29,003	12,478	18,473	24,134	30,185	38,785	54,665
Received as inheritance or gift	213	109	28	20	7	28	2
Not reported	180	44	29	20	15	25	17

Source: "Value by Selected Characteristics - Occupied Units with Black Householder," *American Housing Survey for the United States in 1933,* p. 345. *Notes:* 1. Beginning with 1989 this item current income in its calculation. See appendix A. 2. May reflect a temporary situation, living off savings, or response error.

★ 412 ★

Values

Values: Select Characteristics. Part 3-2

[Numbers in thousands. Consistent with the 1990 Census. ...means not applicable or sample too small. - means zero or rounds to zero.]

Characteristics	$100,000 to $149,999	$150,000 to $199,999	$200,000 to $249,999	$250,000 to $299,999	$300,000 or more	Median
Median Monthly Housing Costs For Owners						
Monthly costs including all mortgages plus maintenance costs	958	1,042	1,250	...	...	...
Monthly costs excluding 2nd and subsequent mortgages and maintenance costs	834	888	1,126	...	...	...
Monthly Housing Costs as Percent of Current Income[1]						
Less than 5 percent	7	2	2	-	-	45,666
5 to 9 percent	45	21	5	2	2	46,822
10 to 14 percent	74	33	6	2	2	51,717
15 to 19 percent	38	36	10	5	7	62,296
20 to 24 percent	82	23	14	10	3	67,242
25 to 29 percent	45	19	13	-	7	58,184
30 to 34 percent	48	21	2	5	...	62,041
35 to 39 percent	17	10	3	3	3	54,334

[Continued]

★ 412 ★

Values: Select Characteristics. Part 3-2
[Continued]

Characteristics	$100,000 to $149,999	$150,000 to $199,999	$200,000 to $249,999	$250,000 to $299,999	$300,000 or more	Median
40 to 49 percent	38	6	7	-	-	53,856
50 to 59 percent	22	21	4	3	-	61,939
60 to 69 percent	26	5	5	-	2	59,827
70 to 99 percent	25	10	3	-	-	60,826
100 percent or more[2]	31	7	-	-	2	59,032
Zero or negative income	8	5	3	-	-	41,621
No cash rent	...	...	...	...	...	...
Mortgage payment not reported	84	45	15	6	13	75,724
Median (excludes 3 previous lines)	25	23	25	...	...	...
Median (excludes 4 lines before medians)	24	22	25	...	...	...
Monthly Payment for Principal and Interest						
Less than $100	2	2	-	-	-	40,275
$100 to $199	26	7	4	-	-	46,469
$200 to $249	16	5	3	-	-	39,976
$250 to $299	13	6	-	-	-	48,395
$300 to $349	16	2	-	-	-	48,544
$350 to $399	2	3	2	-	-	56,695
$400 to $449	13	5	5	5	-	59,294
$450 to $499	3	13	-	-	-	66,546
$500 to $599	30	11	6	2	-	73,185
$600 to $699	67	8	-	-	-	90,828
$700 to $799	53	8	6	2	-	102,168
$800 to $999	80	37	7	-	-	126,875
$1,000 to $1,249	32	32	11	3	-	153,197
$1,250 to $1,499	8	16	6	5	5	...
$1,500 or more	4	5	12	11	8	...
Not reported	84	45	15	6	13	75,724
Median	692	853	934	...	...	...
Average Monthly Cost Paid for Real Estate Taxes						
Less than $25	47	19	10	-	2	34,913
$25 to $49	73	36	8	2	4	53,094
$50 to $74	76	28	7	2	-	66,519
$75 to $99	95	33	7	-	2	80,788
$100 to $149	113	61	11	10	2	88,314
$150 to $199	59	28	10	7	2	106,326
$200 or more	126	59	38	15	28	131,751
Median	102	114	162	...	...	...
Purchase Price						
Home purchased or built	566	254	80	37	36	60,046
Less than $10,000	26	3	-	2	2	30,080

[Continued]

★ 412 ★

Values: Select Characteristics. Part 3-2
[Continued]

Characteristics	$100,000 to $149,999	$150,000 to $199,999	$200,000 to $249,999	$250,000 to $299,999	$300,000 or more	Median
$10,000 to $19,999	52	33	8	-	-	43,607
$20,000 to $29,999	39	20	5	2	4	50,671
$30,000 to $39,999	46	14	10	2	-	56,145
$40,000 to $49,999	25	21	-	2	-	63,298
$50,000 to $59,999	26	6	-	2	-	70,591
$60,000 to $69,999	33	15	-	-	-	75,722
$70,000 to $79,999	26	10	3	-	-	90,340
$80,000 to $99,999	114	25	2	-	2	113,051
$100,000 to $119,999	47	11	7	3	-	134,746
$120,000 to $149,999	60	28	10	-	2	139,358
$150,000 to $199,999	9	35	2	-	2	...
$200,000 to $249,999	-	-	16	11	-	...
$250,000 to $299,999	-	-	3	7	3	...
$300,000 or more	-	-	-	-	18	...
Not reported	64	34	13	4	2	52,153
Median	71,724	69,410	112,408	...	...	...
Received as inheritance or gift	8	2	9	-	-	30000-
Not reported	15	8	3	-	5	48,645

Source: "Value by Selected Characteristics - Occupied Units with Black Householder," *American Housing Survey for the United States in 1933,* p. 345.
Notes: 1. Beginning with 1989 this item current income in its calculation. See appendix A. 2. May reflect a temporary situation, living off savings, or response error.

Chapter 7
INCOME, SPENDING, AND WEALTH

Expenditures

★ 413 ★

Buying Power: Black Consumer Buying Power in the Top 10 States, According to Amount: 1994

[In billions of dollars].

State	Consumer Buying Power
New York	45.8
California	33.7
Texas	26.3
Illinois	22.9
Florida	21.5
Georgia	21.4
Maryland	20.8
Michigan	18.2
New Jersey	17.8
North Carolina	17.5
Total U.S. Black buying power $399	

Source: Adapted by the editors from "Largest Black Consumer Markets," *Jet*, **86**, August 29, 1994, p. 22. Primary source: University of Georgia, Economic Forecasting. Published by permission.

★ 414 ★

Expenditures

Total Expenditures: Mean Consumer Expenditures, by Race: 1993

Item	All consumer units	White all other	Black
Expenditures, total	30,692	31,967	20,684
Food	4,399	4,517	3,399
Food at home	2,735	2,772	2,421
Food away from home	1,664	1,746	978
Alcoholic beverages	268	288	98
Housing	9,636	9,928	7,341
Shelter	5,415	5,585	4,106
Utilities, fuels, and public services	2,112	2,121	2,048
Household operations	469	496	256
Housekeeping supplies	410	427	263
Household furnishings and equipment	1,230	1,299	667
Apparel and services	1,676	1,681	1,638
Transportation	5,453	5,759	3,092
Vehicle purchases (net outlay)	2,319	2,493	981
Gasoline and motor oil	977	1,017	666
Other vehicle expenses	1,843	1,932	1,154
Public transportation	314	317	291
Health care	1,776	1,890	894
Entertainment	1,626	1,734	772
Personal care products and services	385	393	310
Reading	166	177	83
Education	455	475	305
Tobacco products and smoking supplies	268	277	198
Miscellaneous	715	751	434
Cash contribution	961	1,029	436
Personal insurance and pensions	2,908	3,067	1,685
Life and other personal insurance	399	414	284

[Continued]

★ 414 ★

Total Expenditures: Mean Consumer Expenditures, by Race: 1993
[Continued]

Item	All consumer units	White all other	Black
Pensions and Social Security	2,509	2,653	1,401
Personal taxes	2,978	3,173	1,413

Source: Adapted by the editors from "Average Annual Expenditures of All Consumer Units, by Race and Age of Householder: 1993," *Statistical Abstract of the United States: 1995*, 1995, p. 465. Primary source: U.S. Bureau of Labor Statistics, *Consumer Expenditures in 1993;* and unpublished data.

Income/Earnings

★ 415 ★

Income: Aggregate and Mean Household Money Income, by Householder Age, Region, Household Size, and Race/Ethnic Origin: 1993

CHARACTERISTIC	ALL RACES[1]		WHITE		BLACK		HISPANIC[2]	
	Aggregate income (bil. dol.)	Mean income (dollars)	Aggregate income (bil. dol.)	Mean income (dollars)	Aggregate income (bil. dol.)	Mean income (dollars)	Aggregate income (bil. dol.)	Mean income (dollars)
Total	4,022.9	41,428	3,566.1	43,285	307.2	27,229	223	30,291
Age of householder:								
15 to 24 years old	121.3	23,041	102.7	24,298	12.4	16,009	12.7	21,423
25 to 34 years old	739.6	37,510	642.1	40,020	64.4	23,455	60.9	28,666
35 to 44 years old	1,102.9	49,473	966.7	52,205	89.5	31,666	64.1	34,520
45 to 54 years old	972.9	57,770	861.0	60,106	70.8	38,159	46.4	38,042
55 to 64 years old	546.2	44,814	493.2	46,650	38.7	29,450	22.5	29,316
65 years old and over	540.2	25,965	500.5	26,761	31.4	17,782	16.3	20,459
Region:								
Northeast	882.4	45,319	792.5	46,823	58.4	30,161	36.4	27,311
Midwest	922.4	39,442	843.3	40,963	63.3	26,580	15.8	31,364
South	1,296.8	38,249	1,111.2	40,897	15.66	25,853	72.8	30,551
West	921.4	45,284	819.2	46,269	28.8	31,883	98.1	31,185
Size of household:								
One person	524.6	22,217	463.6	22,946	47.1	16,808	19.4	18,223
Two persons	1,322.5	42,374	1,214.1	44,195	77.6	26,602	48.9	29,265
Three persons	811.6	48,030	710.4	50,805	70.7	31,356	43.1	30,631
Four persons	836.6	55,516	735.4	58,306	63.4	36,018	48.0	34,042

[Continued]

★ 415 ★

Income: Aggregate and Mean Household Money Income, by Householder Age, Region, Household Size, and Race/Ethnic Origin: 1993

[Continued]

CHARACTERISTIC	ALL RACES[1]		WHITE		BLACK		HISPANIC[2]	
	Aggregate income (bil. dol.)	Mean income (dollars)	Aggregate income (bil. dol.)	Mean income (dollars)	Aggregate income (bil. dol.)	Mean income (dollars)	Aggregate income (bil. dol.)	Mean income (dollars)
Five persons	354.1	52,473	305.7	55,456	26.8	30,862	34.1	35,474
Six persons	112.1	51,259	92.0	55,575	12.3	33,978	14.9	35,576
Seven or more persons	61.2	44,401	45.1	47,388	9.2	29,373	14.7	33,937

Source: "Money Income of Households—Aggregate and Average Income, by Race, and Hispanic Origin: 1993," *Statistical Abstract of the United States: 1995,* 1995, p. 471. Primary source: U.S. Bureau of the Census, *Current Population Reports,* P60-188; and unpublished data. *Notes:* 1. Includes other races not shown separately. 2. Persons of Hispanic origin may be of any race.

★ 416 ★

Income/Earnings

Income: Family and Nonfamily Median Money Income, by Family Type and Race/Ethnic Origin: 1993

ITEM	All households	FAMILY HOUSEHOLDS				NONFAMILY HOUSEHOLDS		
		Total	Married couple	Male householder, wife absent	Female householder, husband absent	Total[1]	Single-person household	
							Male householder	Female householder
MEDIAN INCOME (dollars)								
All households	31,241	37,484	43,129	29,849	18,545	18,880	21,372	12,995
White	32,960	39,841	43,785	31,177	21,583	19,639	22,383	13,468
Black	19,533	22,221	35,409	22,000	12,423	13,857	15,983	10,082
Hispanic[2]	22,886	24,530	28,867	25,013	13,223	15,799	17,324	8,672

Source: "Money Income of Households—Median Income and Income Level, by household Type: 1993," *Statistical Abstract of the United States: 1995,* 1995, p. 471. Primary source: U.S. Bureau of the Census, *Current Population Reports,* P60-188; and unpublished data. *Notes:* 1. Includes other nonfamily households not shown separately. 2. Persons of Hispanic origin may be of any race.

★ 417 ★

Income/Earnings

Income: Percent Distribution of Family and Nonfamily Household Money Income, by Race/Ethnic Origin: 1993

TYPE OF HOUSEHOLD	Number of households (1,000)	PERCENT DISTRIBUTION									Median income (dollars)
		Under $5,000	$5,000-$9,999	$10,000-$14,999	$15,000-$24,999	$25,000-$34,999	$35,000-$49,999	$50,000-$74,999	$75,000-$99,999	$100,000 and over	
HOUSEHOLDS											
Total[1]	97,107	4.5	9.7	9.2	16.9	14.7	16.3	16.1	6.7	5.8	31,241
White	82,387	3.6	8.6	8.9	16.6	14.9	17.0	17.0	7.1	6.3	32,960
Black	11,281	10.9	18.0	11.8	19.2	13.8	12.0	9.3	3.3	1.9	19,533
Asian, Pacific Islander	2,233	5.5	8.1	7.2	14.4	12.4	12.9	20.0	10.5	9.0	38,347
Hispanic[2]	7,362	5.9	14.1	12.4	21.5	16.5	13.4	10.8	3.1	2.3	22,886
FAMILIES											
Total[1]	68,490	3.2	5.8	7.1	15.3	15.0	18.2	19.6	8.4	7.4	37,484
White	57,870	2.2	4.6	6.5	14.9	15.2	19.0	20.8	8.8	8.0	39,841
Black	7,989	9.9	14.8	11.2	18.5	14.1	13.3	11.3	4.4	2.4	22,221
Asian, Pacific Islander	1,737	4.0	5.9	6.4	12.3	11.6	13.9	22.7	12.6	10.5	45,251
Hispanic[2]	5,040	5.0	11.6	12.2	22.1	17.0	14.6	11.8	3.2	2.4	24,530
NONFAMILIES											
Total[1]	28,617	7.8	19.1	14.3	20.7	14.2	11.6	7.7	2.6	2.0	18,880
White	24,518	7.0	18.2	14.5	20.7	14.3	12.1	8.1	2.9	2.2	19,639
Black	3,292	13.2	25.8	13.1	20.8	13.0	8.6	4.4	0.7	0.5	13,857
Asian, Pacific Islander	496	10.5	15.5	10.1	22.0	15.1	9.3	10.3	3.4	4.0	21,407
Hispanic[2]	1,423	9.7	2.7	13.4	19.0	14.3	8.1	6.8	2.6	1.5	15,799

Source: "Money Income of Households—Percent Distribution, by Income Level, Race, and Hispanic Origin: 1993," *Statistical Abstract of the United States: 1995,* 1995, p. 472. Primary source: U.S. Bureau of the Census, *Current Population Reports,* P60-188; and unpublished data. *Notes:* 1. Includes other races not shown separately. 2. Persons of Hispanic origin may be of any race.

★ 418 ★

Income/Earnings

Income: Percent Distribution of Household Money Income at Each Quintile and Top 5%, by Race/Ethnic Origin: 1993

CHARACTERISTIC	Number (1,000)	PERCENT DISTRIBUTION						
		Total	Lowest fifth	Second fifth	Third fifth	Fourth fifth	Highest fifth	Top 5 percent
Total	97,107	100.0	20.0	20.0	20.0	20.0	20.0	5.0
White	82,387	100.0	17.7	19.7	20.4	21.0	21.4	5.4
Black	11,281	100.0	36.8	22.6	18.0	13.3	9.3	1.7
Hispanic origin[1]	7,362	100.0	27.9	25.6	21.4	15.1	10.0	1.8

Source: "Money Income of Households—Percent Distribution, by Income Quintile and Top 5 Percent: 1993," *Statistical Abstract of the United States: 1995*, 1995, p. 472. Primary source: U.S. Bureau of the Census, Current Population Survey, unpublished data. *Note:* 1. Persons of Hispanic origin may be of any race.

★ 419 ★

Income/Earnings

Income: Percentage Distribution of Individual Money Income in Constant (1993) Dollars, by Race/Ethnic Origin: 1993

[Constant dollars based on CPI-U-XI deflator. As of **March of following year.** For 1970, persons 14 years old and over, thereafter, 15 years old and over].

ITEM	All persons (mil.)	PERSONS WITH INCOME									Median income (dollars)
		Total (mil.)	Percent distribution								
			$1 to $2,499 or loss[1]	$2,500 to $4,999	$5,000 to $9,999	$10,000 to $14,999	$15,000 to $24,999	$25,000 to $49,999	$50,000 to $74,999	$75,000 and over	
MALE											
1993	96.8	90.2	7.0	4.9	12.1	12.4	20.8	28.8	8.7	5.2	21,102
White	82.0	77.7	6.5	4.5	11.3	12.2	20.7	29.8	9.3	5.7	21,981
Black	10.6	8.9	11.1	7.5	18.0	14.1	21.8	22.2	4.1	1.2	14,605
Hispanic[2]	9.3	8.2	7.8	7.1	20.1	18.5	23.1	18.4	3.5	1.4	13,689
FEMALE											
1993	104.0	94.4	14.1	10.9	21.4	14.4	19.1	16.5	2.6	0.9	11,046
White	86.8	79.5	14.2	10.4	21.0	14.5	19.3	16.9	2.7	1.0	11,266
Black	12.9	11.3	11.8	14.7	25.3	14.7	17.7	13.8	1.5	0.5	9,508
Hispanic[2]	9.1	7.1	16.3	14.5	27.1	15.3	15.7	9.8	1.0	0.4	8,100

Source: "Money Income of Persons—Percent Distribution, by Income Level, in Constant (1993) Dollars: 1970-1993," *Statistical Abstract of the United States: 1995*, 1995, p. 478. Primary source: U.S. Bureau of the Census, *Current Population Reports*, P60-188, and unpublished data. *Notes:* 1. Includes persons with income deficit. 2. Persons of Hispanic origin may be of any race.

★ 420 ★

Income/Earnings

Income: Sources of Income Among the Elderly, by Race/ Ethnic Origin: 1992

	White	Black	Hispanic[1]
Social Security	93	89	79
Asset income	72	26	34
Pensions[2]	48	26	26
Earnings	21	17	17
SSI	5	21	23

Source: "Receipt of Income from Sources, by Race and Hispanic Origin, *"Income of the Aged Chartbook, 1992,* December 1994, p. 14. *Notes:* 1. Persons of Hispanic origin may be of any race. 2. Includes private pensions or annuities, government employee pensions, Railroad Retirement, and IRA, Keogh, and 401(k) payments.

★ 421 ★

Income/Earnings

Income: Trends in Household Median Money Income in Current and Constant (1993) Dollars, by Race/Ethnic Origin: 1970-1993

YEAR	MEDIAN INCOME IN CURRENT DOLLARS					MEDIAN INCOME CONSTANT (1993) DOLLARS				
	All households[1]	White	Black	Asian, Pacific, Islander	Hispanic[2]	All households[2]	White	Black	Asian, Pacific Islanders	Hispanic[2]
1970	8,734	9,097	5,537	(NA)	(NA)	30,558	31,828	19,373	(NA)	(NA)
1975	11,800	12,340	7,408	(NA)	8,865	30,340	31,728	19,047	(NA)	22,793
1980	17,710	18,634	10,764	(NA)	13,651	31,095	32,805	18,899	(NA)	23,968
1981	19,074	20,153	11,309	(NA)	15,300	30,590	32,321	18,137	(NA)	24,538
1982	20,171	21,116	11,968	(NA)	15,178	30,489	31,918	18,090	(NA)	22,942
1983[3]	20,885	21,902	12,429	(NA)	15,906	30,300	31,775	18,032	(NA)	23,076
1984	22,415	23,647	13,471	(NA)	16,992	31,174	32,887	18,735	(NA)	23,632
1985	23,618	24,908	14,819	(NA)	17,465	31,717	33,450	19,901	(NA)	23,454
1986	24,897	26,175	15,080	(NA)	18,352	32,825	34,510	19,882	(NA)	24,196
1987[4]	26,061	27,458	15,672	(NA)	19,336	33,150	34,927	19,935	(NA)	24,596
1988	27,225	28,781	16,407	32,267	20,359	33,255	35,155	20,041	39,413	24,868
1989	28,906	30,406	18,083	36,102	21,921	33,685	35,433	21,073	42,070	25,545
1990	29,943	31,231	18,676	38,450	22,330	33,105	34,529	20,648	42,510	24,688
1991	30,126	31,569	18,807	36,449	22,691	31,962	33,493	19,953	38,670	24,074
1992	30,786	32,368	18,660	38,153	22,848	31,708	33,337	19,219	39,295	23,532
1992[5]	30,636	32,209	18,755	37,801	22,597	31,553	33,173	19,316	38,933	22,273
1993	31,241	32,960	19,533	38,347	22,886	31,241	32,960	19,533	38,347	22,886

Source: "Money Income of Households—Percent Distribution, by Income Level, Race, and Hispanic Origin, in Constant (1993) Dollars: 1970 to 1993," *Statistical Abstract of the United States: 1995,* 1995, p. 469. Primary source: U.S. Bureau of the Census, *Current Population Reports,* P60-188; and unpublished data. *Notes:* NA Not available. 1. Includes other races not shown separately. 2. Persons of Hispanic origin may be of any race. 3. Beginning 1983, data based on revised Hispanic population controls and not directly comparable with prior years. 4. Beginning 1987, based on revised processing procedures and not directly comparable with prior years. 5. Based on 1990 population controls.

★ 422 ★

Income/Earnings

Income: Trends in Median Income and Percent Distribution of Household Money Income in Constant (1993) Dollars, by Race/Ethnic Origin: 1970-1993

[Constant dollars based on CPI-U-XI deflator. Households as of **March** of **following year.** Based on Current Population Survey].

YEAR	Number of household (1,000)	PERCENT DISTRIBUTION							Median income (dollars)
		Under $10,000	$10,000-$14,999	$15,000-$24,999	$25,000-$34,999	$35,000-$49,999	$50,000-$74,999	$75,000 and over	
ALL HOUSEHOLDS[1]									
1970	64,778	15.0	8.5	16.9	18.0	20.4	14.8	6.4	30,558
1975	72,867	14.4	9.0	17.2	16.6	19.7	15.5	6.9	30,340
1980	82,368	14.2	9.0	17.4	15.0	19.4	16.3	8.8	31,095
1985	88,458	14.4	8.7	16.7	15.1	17.9	16.5	10.6	31,717
1990	94,312	13.4	8.6	16.4	14.7	17.7	16.6	12.6	33,105
1991	95,669	14.0	9.0	16.4	15.0	17.4	16.2	12.0	31,962
1992	96,426	14.4	9.3	16.6	14.6	17.1	16.4	11.7	31,553
1993	97,107	14.2	9.2	16.9	14.7	16.3	16.1	12.5	31,241
WHITE									
1970	57,575	13.8	8.0	16.3	18.3	21.2	15.5	6.8	31,828
1975	64,392	12.9	9.2	16.9	16.8	20.4	16.4	7.5	31,728
1980	71,872	12.4	8.5	17.0	15.2	20.1	17.2	9.5	32,805
1985	76,576	12.7	8.2	16.5	15.3	18.5	17.2	11.5	33,450
1990	80,968	11.5	8.3	16.2	15.0	18.2	17.5	13.3	34,529
1991	81,675	11.9	8.7	16.3	15.2	17.9	17.1	12.9	33,493
1992	81,795	12.2	8.9	16.4	14.8	17.6	17.4	12.6	33,173
1993	82,387	12.2	8.9	16.6	14.9	17.0	17.0	13.4	32,960
BLACK									
1970	6,180	27.2	13.0	22.2	15.4	13.1	7.4	1.7	19,373
1975	7,489	27.6	14.0	19.7	15.2	13.9	7.7	1.9	19,047
1980	8,847	28.1	13.4	20.7	12.9	13.2	9.0	2.7	18,899
1985	9,797	28.1	12.6	19.4	13.4	13.3	9.7	3.5	19,901
1990	10,671	28.2	11.3	18.3	13.2	13.8	9.6	5.5	20,648
1991	11,083	29.5	11.1	18.0	13.7	13.9	9.4	4.6	19,953
1992	11,269	29.6	12.2	18.2	13.1	13.3	9.0	4.6	19,316
1993	11,281	28.9	11.8	19.2	13.8	12.0	9.3	5.2	19,533
HISPANIC[2]									
1975	2,948	18.5	13.2	22.9	17.8	16.9	8.2	2.4	22,793
1980	3,906	18.2	12.3	22.2	15.9	16.3	11.2	4.1	23,968
1985	5,213	20.4	12.7	19.8	15.8	15.1	11.2	4.8	23,454
1990	6,220	18.6	12.9	19.1	16.3	16.3	10.8	5.9	24,688
1991	6,379	19.4	11.8	20.6	15.8	15.5	11.1	5.9	24,074

[Continued]

★ 422 ★

Income: Trends in Median Income and Percent Distribution of Household Money Income in Constant (1993) Dollars, by Race/Ethnic Origin: 1970-1993
[Continued]

YEAR	Number of household (1,000)	PERCENT DISTRIBUTION							Median income (dollars)
		Under $10,000	$10,000-$14,999	$15,000-$24,999	$25,000-$34,999	$35,000-$49,999	$50,000-$74,999	$75,000 and over	
1992	7,153	20.1	12.2	21.1	15.6	14.9	10.8	5.3	23,273
1993	7,362	20.0	12.4	21.5	16.5	13.4	10.8	5.4	22,886

Source: "Money Income of Households—Percent Distribution, by Income Level, Race, and Hispanic Origin, in Constant (1993) Dollars: 1970 to 1993," *Statistical Abstract of the United States: 1995*, 1995, p. 469. Primary source: U.S. Bureau of the Census, *Current Population Reports*, P60-188; and unpublished data. *Notes:* 1. Includes other races not shown separately. 2. Persons of Hispanic origin may be of any race. Income data for Hispanic origin households are not available prior to 1972.

★ 423 ★

Income/Earnings

Income: Trends in Per Capita Money Income in Current and Constant (1993) Dollars, by Race/Ethnic Origin: 1970-1993

[In dollars. Constant dollars based on CPI-U-X1 deflator. As of March of following year].

YEAR	CURRENT DOLLARS				CONSTANT (1993) DOLLARS			
	All races[1]	White	Black	Hispanic[2]	All races[1]	White	Black	Hispanic[2]
1970	3,177	3,354	1,869	(NA)	11,116	11,735	6,539	(NA)
1975	4,818	5,072	2,972	2,847	12,388	13,041	7,642	7,320
1980	7,787	8,233	4,804	4,865	13,672	14,455	8,435	8,542
1985[3]	11,013	11,671	6,840	6,613	14,790	15,673	9,186	8,881
1986	11,670	12,352	7,207	7,000	15,386	16,285	9,502	9,229
1987[4]	12,391	13,143	7,645	7,653	15,761	16,718	9,724	9,735
1988	13,123	13,896	8,271	7,956	16,029	16,974	10,103	9,718
1989	14,056	14,896	8,747	8,390	16,380	17,359	10,193	9,777
1990	14,387	15,265	9,017	8,424	15,906	16,877	9,969	9,313
1991	14,617	15,510	9,170	8,662	15,506	16,455	9,729	9,190
1992	15,033	15,981	9,296	8,874	15,483	16,459	9,574	9,140
1992[5]	14,847	15,785	9,239	8,591	15,291	16,258	9,516	8,848
1993	15,777	16,800	9,863	8,830	15,777	16,800	9,863	8,830

Source: "Per Capita Money Income in Current and Constant (1993) Dollars, by Race and Hispanic Origin: 1970-1993," *Statistical Abstract of the United States: 1995*, 1995, p. 479. Primary source: U.S. Bureau of the Census, *Current Population Reports*, P60-188. *Notes:* NA Not available. 1. Includes other races not shown separately. 2. Persons of Hispanic origin may be of any race. 3. Beginning 1983, data based on revised Hispanic population controls and not directly comparable with prior years. 4. Beginning 1987, data based on revised processing procedures and not directly comparable with prior years. 5. Based on 1990 population controls.

★ 424 ★

Income/Earnings

Relationships: Average Monthly Income, by Educational Attainment and Race/Ethnic Origin: 1993

[**For persons 18 years old and over.** Based on the Survey of Income and Program Participation].

CHARACTERISTIC	Total persons	LEVEL OF DEGREE								
		Not a high school graduate	High school graduate only	Some college, no degree	Vocational	Associate's	Bachelor's	Master's	Professional	Doctorate
MEAN MONTHLY INCOME (dol.)										
All persons[1]	1,687	906	1,380	1,579	1,736	1,985	2,625	3,411	5,534	4,328
Race: White	1,756	951	1,422	1,649	1,768	2,021	2,682	3,478	5,590	4,449
Black	1,192	713	1,071	1,222	1,428	1,746	2,333	2,834	3,445	3,778
Hispanic[2]	1,126	786	1,106	1,239	1,329	2,069	2,186	2,605	2,317	2,677

Source: "Mean Monthly Income, by Highest Degree Earned: 1993," *Statistical Abstract of the United States: 1995*, 1995, p. 158. Primary source: U.S. Bureau of the Census, unpublished data. *Notes:* 1. Includes other races, not shown separately. 2. Persons of Hispanic origin may be of any race.

★ 425 ★

Income/Earnings

Relationships: Full-Time Workers' (25 and Over) Median Earnings, by Gender, Educational Attainment, and Race: 1993

	Both sexes	Male	Female
Black			
High school graduate	$18,460	$20,580	$16,460
Bachelor's degree or more	$32,360	$35,850	$31,160
White, not Hispanic			
High school graduate	$24,120	$28,370	$19,850
Bachelor's degree or more	$41,090	$47,180	$32,920

Source: "Median Earnings of Year-Round, Full-Time Workers 25 Years and Over, by Educational Attainment, Sex, and Race: 1993," *Population Profile of the United States: 1995*, 1995, p. 44.

★ 426 ★

Income/Earnings

Salaries/Earnings: Full-Time Workers – Numbers and Median Weekly Earnings, by Gender and Race/Ethnic Origin: 1983-1994

[**In current dollars of usual weekly earnings.** Data represent annual averages of quarterly data. Based on Current Population Survey].

CHARACTERISTIC	NUMBER OF WORKERS (1,000)				MEDIAN WEEKLY EARNINGS (dol.)			
	1983	1985	1990	1994[1]	1983	1985	1990	1994
All workers[1]	70,976	77,002	85,082	87,379	313	343	415	467
Male	42,309	45,589	49,015	49,992	378	406	485	522
16 to 24 years old	6,702	6,956	6,313	6,040	223	240	283	294
25 years old and over	35,607	38,632	42,702	43,952	406	442	514	576
Female	28,667	31,414	36,068	37,386	252	277	348	399
16 to 24 years old	5,345	5,621	5,001	4,403	197	210	254	276
25 years old and over	23,322	25,793	31,066	32,983	267	296	370	421
White	61,739	66,481	72,637	73,500	319	355	427	484
Male	37,378	40,030	42,563	42,816	387	417	497	547
Female	24,361	26,452	30,075	30,685	254	281	355	408
Black	7,373	8,393	9,642	10,199	261	277	329	371
Male	3,883	4,367	4,909	5,009	293	304	360	400
Female	3,490	4,026	4,733	5,100	231	252	308	346
Hispanic origin[2]	(NA)	(NA)	6,903	8,274	(NA)	(NA)	307	324
Male	(NA)	(NA)	4,410	5,295	(NA)	(NA)	322	343
Female	(NA)	(NA)	2,583	2,979	(NA)	(NA)	280	305

Source: "Full-Time Wage and Salary Workers—Number and Earnings: 1983 to 1994, *Statistical Abstract of the United States: 1995*, p. 433. Primary source: U.S. Bureau of Labor Statistics, Bulletin 2307, and *Employment and Earnings*, monthly, January issues. *Notes:* NA Not available. 1. Includes other races not shown separately. 2. Persons of Hispanic origin may be of any race.

★ 427 ★

Income/Earnings

Salaries/Earnings: Wage Earners at or Below $4.25/hr., by Race/Ethnic Origin: 1994

[Annual average of monthly figures; for employed wage and salary workers. Based on Current Population Survey].

CHARACTERISTIC	NUMBER OF WORKERS[1](1,000)				PERCENT OF ALL WORKERS PAID HOURLY RATES				Median hourly earnings of workers paid hourly rates
	Total paid hourly rates	At or below $4.25			Total	At or below $4.25			
		Total	At $4.25	Below $4.25	Total	At $4.25	Below $4.25		
Total, 16 years and over[2]	66,549	4,127	2,132	1,995	6.2	3.2	3.0		$8.01
White	55,151	3,384	1,657	1,727	6.1	3.0	3.1		8.11

[Continued]

★ 427 ★

Salaries/Earnings: Wage Earners at or Below $4.25/hr., by Race/Ethnic Origin: 1994

[Continued]

CHARACTERISTIC	NUMBER OF WORKERS[1](1,000)				PERCENT OF ALL WORKERS PAID HOURLY RATES			Median hourly earnings of workers paid hourly rates
	Total paid hourly rates	At or below $4.25			At or below $4.25			
		Total	At $4.25	Below $4.25	Total	At $4.25	Below $4.25	
Black	8,586	561	356	205	6.5	4.1	2.4	7.29
Hispanic origin[3]	7,130	612	401	211	8.6	5.6	3.0	6.93

Source: "Workers Paid Hourly Rates, by Selected Characteristics: 1994, *Statistical Abstract of the United States: 1995*, p. 436. Primary source: U.S. Bureau of Labor Statistics, unpublished data. *Notes:* 1. Excludes the incorporated self-employed. 2. Includes races not shown separately. Includes a small number of multiple jobholders whose full/part-time status can not be determined for their principal job. 3. Persons of Hispanic origin may be of any race.

★ 428 ★

Income/Earnings

Salaries: White and Minority Average Annual Salary of Non-Postal Federal Employees, Worldwide: 1991

Gender and Job Category	Total All Groups	Individual Population Group				
		Whites	Blacks	Hispanics	Asians, Pacific Islanders	American Indians, Alaskan Natives
Total, All Jobs						
Men	$41,220	$42,736	$32,607	$34,825	$40,727	$34,929
Women	28,461	29,383	26,265	26,276	30,540	24,982
Administrators						
Men	44,477	45,234	40,844	39,381	40,130	42,606
Women	36,859	37,317	36,123	34,409	35,287	34,237
Professionals						
Men	49,830	50,440	44,698	45,102	48,444	43,308
Women	40,130	40,300	38,996	38,147	42,768	36,723

Source: "Average Annual Salaries of Total, Administrative and Professional Employees in Federal Government by Population Group, Worldwide, 1991," *Indicators of Equal Employment Opportunity-Status and Trends*, September, 1993, p. 50. Primary source: *U.S. Office of Personnel Management, Central Personnel Data File (CPDF), 1991.*

★ 429 ★

Income/Earnings

Salaries: White and Minority Median Annual Salary of U.S. State and Local Government Employees, 1974 and 1991

Gender and job category	Year	Total All Groups[1]	Individual Population Group				
			Whites	Blacks	Hispanics	Asians, Pacific Islanders	American Indians, Alaskan Natives
Total, All jobs							
Men	1974	$10,269	$10,586	$8,676	$8,756	$13,329	$9,474
Women		7,523	7,562	7,380	7,034	9,546	7,122
Men	1991	28,395	29,269	24,117	27,019	35,452	25,449
Women		22,669	22,885	21,672	22,180	30,434	21,461
Officials and Administrators							
Men	1974	15,039	15,070	14,572	13,879	18,429	13,596
Women		11,747	11,595	13,065	11,160	13,717	10,250
Men	1991	43,666	43,654	43,256	43,705	46,169	41,850
Women		37,019	36,443	39,502	37,039	44,913	34,696
Professionals							
Men	1974	13,289	13,334	12,210	12,508	16,232	12,497
Women		10,935	10,847	11,239	10,958	12,134	10,809
Men	1991	35,926	36,214	31,546	34,711	41,818	32,574
Women		30,778	30,655	29,818	30,805	38,388	28,367

Source: "Median Annual Salaries of Total, Administrative and Professional Full-Time Employees in State and Local Government by Population Group, U.S. Summary, 1974 and 1991," *Indicators of Equal Employment Opportunity—Status and Trends,* September, 1993, p. 48. Primary source: *Equal Employment Opportunity Commission, State and Local Government Information (EEO-4) Reports. Notes:* 1. Data for total men and women in 1974 include salaries of a small group of "other" minorities, not shown separately.

Poverty

★ 430 ★

Duration: Duration of Poverty in 1990-1991 Period, for Individuals, by Race/Ethnic Origin

[**In thousands, except percent.** Cover 2-year calendar period. Based on Survey of Income and Program Participation].

CHARACTERISTIC	PERSONS POOR IN AN AVERAGE MONTH		PERSONS POOR 2 OR MORE MONTHS		PERSONS POOR ALL 24 MONTHS OF 1990-91		Median duration of poverty spells (months)
	Number	Percent	Number	Percent	Number	Percent	
Total[1]	31,818	12.9	45,638	18.9	10,619	4.5	4.0
White	21,233	10.2	32,042	15.7	5,969	3.0	3.9
Black	9,152	30.1	11,621	39.2	4,060	13.9	5.8
Hispanic origin[2]	5,465	26.1	7,345	37.5	1,949	10.4	4.9

Source: "Monthly Measures of Poverty Status, by Selected Characteristics: 1990- 91 Period," *Statistical Abstract of the United States: 1995,* 1995, p. 483. Primary source: U.S. Bureau of the Census, *Current Population Reports,* P70-42. *Notes:* 1. Includes other characteristics not shown separately. 2. Persons of Hispanic origin may be of any race.

★ 431 ★

Poverty

Number/Percent: Individuals Below Poverty Level, by Income Definition and Race/Ethnic Origin: 1993

[Persons as of **March 1994**].

DEFINITION	NUMBER BELOW POVERTY LEVEL (1,000)				PERCENT BELOW POVERTY LEVEL			
	All races[1]	White	Black	Hispanic[2]	All races[1]	White	Black	Hispanic[2]
All persons	259,278	214,899	32,910	26,559	(X)	(X)	(X)	(X)
INCOME BEFORE TAXES								
Money income excluding capital gains[3]	35,616	23,386	10,203	7,390	13.7	10.9	31.0	27.8
Definition 1 less government money transfers	57,293	41,439	13,190	9,384	22.1	19.3	40.1	35.3
Definition 2 plus capital gains	57,070	41,198	13,210	9,353	22.0	19.2	40.1	35.2
Definition 3 plus health insurance supplements to wage or salary income[4]	55,368	39,956	12,828	9,025	21.4	18.6	39.0	34.0
INCOME AFTER TAXES								
Definition 4 less Social Security payroll taxes	57,678	41,869	13,132	9,523	22.2	19.5	39.9	35.9
Definition 5 less Federal income taxes (excluding EITC)[5]	58,049	42,149	13,201	9,601	22.4	19.6	40.1	36.2
Definition 6 plus EITC[5]	56,275	40,791	12,880	9,217	21.7	19.0	39.1	34.7
Definition 7 less State income taxes	58,581	41,027	12,945	9,235	21.8	19.1	39.3	34.8
Definition 8 plus nonmeans-tested government cash transfers[6]	38,406	25,201	10,963	7,951	14.8	11.7	33.3	29.9
Definition 9 plus value of Medicare	37,521	24,582	10,715	7,797	14.5	11.4	32.6	29.4
Definition 10 plus value of regular-price school lunches	37,506	24,567	10,715	7,794	14.5	11.4	32.6	29.3
Definition 11 plus means-tested government cash transfers	34,026	22,291	9,773	7,048	13.1	10.4	29.7	26.5
Definition 12 plus value of Medicaid	31,981	20,897	9,254	6,470	12.3	9.7	28.1	24.4

[Continued]

★ 431 ★

Number/Percent: Individuals Below Poverty Level, by Income Definition and Race/Ethnic Origin: 1993

[Continued]

DEFINITION	NUMBER BELOW POVERTY LEVEL (1,000)				PERCENT BELOW POVERTY LEVEL			
	All races[1]	White	Black	Hispanic[2]	All races[1]	White	Black	Hispanic[2]
Definition 13 plus means-tested government noncash transfers[6]	27,818	18,444	7,794	5,586	10.7	8.6	23.7	21.0
Definition 14 plus net imputed return on equity in own home[9]	25,409	16,535	7,366	5,232	9.8	7.7	22.4	19.7

Source: "Persons Below Poverty Level, by Definition of Income: 1993," *Standard Abstract of the United States: 1995,*, 1995, p. 485. Primary source: U.S. Bureau of the Census, *Current Population Reports,* P60-188. *Notes:* X Not applicable. 1. Includes other races not shown separately. 2. Persons of Hispanic origin may be of any race. 3. Official definition based on income before taxes and includes government cash transfers. 4. Employer contributions to the health insurance plans of employees. 5. Earned Income Tax Credit. 6. Includes Social Security and Railroad Retirement, veterans payments, unemployment and workers' compensation, Black Lung payments, Pell Grants, and other government educational assistance. 7. Includes AFDC and other public assistance or welfare payments. Supplemental Security Income, and veterans payments. Households must meet certain eligibility requirements in order to qualify for these benefits. 8. Includes Medicaid, food stamps, subsidies from free or reduced-price school lunches, and rent subsidies. 9. Estimated amount of income a household would receive if it chose to shift amount held as home equity into an interest bearing account.

★ 432 ★

Poverty

Number/Percent: Trends in Number and Percent of Individuals Below Poverty Level, by Race/Ethnic Origin: 1960-1993

[Persons as of **March of the following year.** Based on Current Population Survey].

YEAR	NUMBER BELOW POVERTY LEVEL (1,000)				PERCENT BELOW POVERTY LEVEL			
	All races[1]	White	Black	Hispanic[2]	All races[1]	White	Black	Hispanic[2]
1960	39,581	28,309	(NA)	(NA)	22.2	17.8	(NA)	(NA)
1966	28,510	19,290	8,867	(NA)	14.7	11.3	41.8	(NA)
1969	24,147	16,659	7,095	(NA)	12.1	9.5	32.2	(NA)
1970	25,420	17,484	7,548	(NA)	12.6	9.9	33.5	(NA)
1975	25,877	17,770	7,545	2,991	12.3	9.7	31.3	23.0
1976	24,975	16,713	7,595	2,783	11.8	9.1	31.1	26.9
1977	24,720	16,416	7,726	2,700	11.6	8.9	31.3	24.7
1978	24,497	16,259	7,625	2,607	11.4	8.7	30.6	22.4
1979[3]	26,072	17,214	8,050	2,921	11.7	9.0	31.0	21.6
1980	29,272	19,699	8,579	3,491	13.0	10.2	32.5	21.8
1981	31,822	21,553	9,173	3,713	14.0	11.1	34.2	25.7
1982	34,398	23,517	9,697	4,301	15.0	12.0	35.6	26.5
1983[4]	35,303	23,984	9,882	4,633	15.2	12.1	35.7	29.9
1984	33,700	22,955	9,490	4,806	14.4	11.5	33.8	28.0
1985	33,064	22,860	8,926	5,236	14.0	11.4	31.3	28.4
1986	32,370	22,183	8,983	5,117	13.6	11.0	31.1	29.0
1987[5]	32,221	21,195	9,520	5,422	13.4	10.4	32.4	27.3
1988	31,745	20,715	9,356	5,357	13.0	10.1	31.3	28.0
1989	31,528	20,785	9,302	5,430	12.8	10.0	30.7	26.7
1990	33,585	22,326	9,837	6,006	13.5	10.7	31.9	26.2
1991[6]	35,708	23,747	10,242	6,339	14.2	11.3	32.7	28.1

[Continued]

★ 432 ★

Number/Percent: Trends in Number and Percent of Individuals Below Poverty Level, by Race/Ethnic Origin: 1960-1993

[Continued]

YEAR	NUMBER BELOW POVERTY LEVEL (1,000)				PERCENT BELOW POVERTY LEVEL			
	All races[1]	White	Black	Hispanic[2]	All races[1]	White	Black	Hispanic[2]
1992	38,014	25,259	10,827	7,592	14.8	11.9	33.4	29.6
1993	39,265	26,226	10,877	8,126	15.1	12.2	33.1	30.6

Source: "Persons Below Poverty Level and Below 125 Percent of Poverty Level: 1960 to 1993," *Statistical Abstract of the United States: 1995,* 1995, p. 480. Primary source: U.S. Bureau of the Census, *Current Population Reports,* P60-188. *Notes:* NA Not available. 1. Includes other races not shown separately. 2. Persons of Hispanic origin may be of any race. 3. Population controls based on 1980 census. 4. Beginning 1983, data based on revised Hispanic population controls and not directly comparable with prior years. 5. Beginning 1987, data based on revised processing procedures and not directly comparable with prior years. 6. Beginning 1992, based on 1990 population controls.

★ 433 ★

Poverty

Number/Percent: Trends in Persons/Families Below Poverty Level, by Race/Ethnic Origin (in percentages): 1973-1993

[Data are based on household interviews of the civilian noninstitutionalized population].

Selected characteristics, race, and Hispanic origin	Percent below poverty									
	1973	1980[1]	1985	1987	1988	1989	1990	1991	1992	1993
All persons										
All races	11.1	13.0	14.0	13.4	13.0	12.8	13.5	14.2	14.8	15.1
White	8.4	10.2	11.4	10.4	10.1	10.0	10.7	11.3	11.9	12.2
Black	31.4	32.5	31.3	32.4	31.3	30.7	31.9	32.7	33.4	33.1
Hispanic	21.9	25.7	29.0	28.0	26.7	26.2	28.1	28.7	29.6	30.6
Mexican American	-	-	28.8	28.2	28.5	28.4	28.1	29.5	30.1	31.6
Puerto Rican	-	-	43.3	40.7	33.7	33.0	40.6	39.4	36.5	38.4
Related children under 18 years of age in families										
All races	14.2	17.9	20.1	19.7	19.0	19.0	19.9	21.1	21.6	22.0
White	9.7	13.4	15.6	14.7	14.0	14.1	15.1	16.1	16.5	17.0
Black	40.6	42.1	43.1	44.4	42.8	43.2	44.2	45.6	46.3	45.9
Hispanic	27.8	33.0	39.6	38.9	37.3	35.5	37.7	39.8	39.0	39.9
Mexican American	-	-	37.4	37.1	37.5	36.3	35.5	38.9	38.2	39.5
Puerto Rican	-	-	58.6	57.3	49.1	48.0	56.7	57.7	52.2	53.8

[Continued]

★ 433 ★

Number/Percent: Trends in Persons/Families Below Poverty Level, by Race/ Ethnic Origin (in percentages): 1973-1993
[Continued]

Selected characteristics, race, and Hispanic origin	Percent below poverty									
	1973	1980[1]	1985	1987	1988	1989	1990	1991	1992	1993
Families with female householder, no husband present, and children under 18 years of age[2]										
All races	43.2	42.9	45.4	45.5	44.7	42.8	44.5	47.1	46.2	46.1
White	35.2	35.9	38.7	38.3	38.2	36.1	37.9	39.6	39.6	39.6
Black	58.8	56.0	58.9	58.6	56.2	53.9	56.1	60.5	57.4	57.7
Hispanic	-	57.3	64.0	60.9	59.2	57.9	58.2	60.1	57.7	60.5

Source: "Persons and Families Below Poverty Level, According to Selected Characteristics, Race, and Hispanic Origin: United States, Selected Years 1973-93," *Health, United States, 1994,* 1995, p. 65. Primary source: U.S. Bureau of the Census: Income, Poverty, and Valuation of Noncash Benefits: 1993. Current Population Reports. Series P-60, No. 188. Washington. U.S. Government Printing Office, Nov. 1994. *Notes:* The race groups, white and black, include persons of both Hispanic and non-Hispanic origin. Conversely, persons of Hispanic origin may be of any race. Some numbers in this table have been revised and differ from previous editions of *Health, United States.*

★ 434 ★
Poverty

Number/Percent: Trends in Poverty Among Persons 65 and Over, by Race/Ethnic Origin: 1970-1993

[Persons as of **March of following year**].

CHARACTERISTIC	NUMBER BELOW POVERTY LEVEL (1,000)					PERCENT BELOW POVERTY LEVEL				
	1970	1979[1]	1990[2]	1992	1993	1970	1979[1]	1990[2]	1992	1993
Total[3]	4,793	3,682	3,658	3,983	3,755	24.6	15.2	12.2	12.9	12.2
White	4,011	2,911	2,707	2,992	2,939	22.6	13.3	10.1	10.9	10.7
Black	683	740	860	887	702	48.0	36.2	33.8	33.3	28.0
Hispanic[4]	(NA)	154	245	269	297	(NA)	26.8	22.5	22.0	21.4

Source: "Persons 65 Years Old and Over Below Poverty Level: 1970 to 1993," *Statistical Abstract of the United States: 1995,* 1995, p. 481. Primary source: U.S. Bureau of the Census, *Current Population Reports,* P60-188; and earlier reports. *Notes:* NA Not available. 1. Population controls based on 1980 census. 2. Beginning 1987, data based on revised processing procedures and not directly comparable with prior years. 3. Beginning 1979, includes members of unrelated subfamilies not shown separately. For earlier years, unrelated subfamily members are included in the "in families" category. 4. Persons of Hispanic origin may be of any race.

★ 435 ★

Poverty

Relationships: Age and Region of Persons Below Poverty Level, by Race/Ethnic Origin: 1993

[Persons as of **March 1994**. Based on Current Population Survey].

AGE AND REGION	NUMBER BELOW POVERTY LEVEL (1,000)				PERCENT BELOW POVERTY LEVEL			
	All races[1]	White	Black	Hispanic[2]	All races[1]	White	Black	Hispanic[2]
Total	39,265	26,226	10,877	8,126	15.1	12.2	33.1	30.6
Under 18 years old	15,727	9,752	5,125	3,873	22.7	17.8	46.1	40.9
18 to 24 years old	4,854	3,274	1,264	1,047	19.1	16.0	34.4	31.0
25 to 34 years old	5,804	3,885	1,5565	1,279	13.8	11.3	28.4	25.4
35 to 44 years old	4,415	3,001	1,156	879	10.6	8.7	23.0	23.8
45 to 54 years old	2,522	1,776	586	446	8.5	7.0	19.2	20.2
55 to 59 years old	1,057	742	254	154	9.9	8.0	23.6	20.6
60 to 64 years old	1,129	857	233	151	11.3	9.8	24.4	24.4
65 years old and over	3,755	2,939	702	297	12.2	10.7	28.0	21.4
Northeast	6,839	4,817	1,744	1,527	13.3	11.0	31.2	37.3
Midwest	8,172	5,454	2,413	476	13.4	10.3	35.9	26.5
South	15,375	8,876	6,063	2,349	17.1	12.8	33.6	28.0
West	8,879	7,080	658	3,774	15.6	14.6	25.9	30.7

Source: "Persons Below Poverty Level, by Selected Characteristics: 1993," *Statistical Abstract of the United States: 1995*, 1995, p. 481. Primary source: U.S. Bureau of the Census, *Current Population Reports*, P60-188; and unpublished data. *Notes:* 1. Includes other races not shown separately. 2. Persons of Hispanic origin may be of any race.

★ 436 ★

Poverty

Relationships: Effect of Social Security on Poverty, by Race: 1992

Race/ethnicity	Percent	
	Poor with Social Security	Kept out of poverty by Social Security
Total beneficiaries	14	38
White	12	39
Black	35	35

Source: "Social Security's Role in Reducing Poverty, by Marital Status and Race, 1992," *Income of the Aged Chartbook, 1993*, December 1994, p. 10.

★ 437 ★

Poverty

Relationships: Percent Going Into and Coming Out of Poverty, by Race/Ethnic Origin: 1991 to 1992

	Percent of persons poor in 1991 who were not poor in 1992, by demographic characteristic	Percent of persons not poor in 1991 who were poor in 1992, by demographic characteristic
Total	22	3
Race and Hispanic Origin		
White	26	3
Black	13	7
Hispanic origin	17	7

Source: "Who Passed Through the Revolving Door," Bureau of the Census, *Statistical Brief: Poverty's Revolving Door,* August 1995, [no p. No.] Primary source: U.S. Department of Commerce, Economics and Statistics Administration, Bureau of the Census. *Note:* Persons of Hispanic origin may be of any race.

Chapter 8
LABOR AND EMPLOYMENT

Discouraged Workers

★ 438 ★

Discouraged Workers: Civilian Labor Force, 1992

As of 1992, there were approximately one million discouraged workers reported in the Current Population Survey (CPS). These discouraged workers represented about 1.7 percent of the total civilian noninstitutional population, 16 years of age or older, not in the labor force. The impact of discouragement by population group can be measured by the differences in the percent distribution of the total Civilian Labor Force (CLF). The accompanying table provides the percent distribution of discouraged workers as reported in the CPS for whites, blacks, and Hispanics in 1992. For comparison purposes, the table also provides the percent distribution of the CLF for the same population that year.

Labor force status and gender	Total, all groups	Whites	Blacks	Hispanics[2]
Percent of total discouraged workers	100.0[1]	67.7	27.8	14.6
Percent of total CLF	100.0[1]	85.5	10.9	8.0
Percent of males of total discouraged workers	45.4	29.9	13.0	6.6
Percent of males of total CLF	54.5	47.1	5.4	4.8
Percent females of total discouraged workers	54.6	37.8	14.7	7.9
Percent females of total CLF	45.5	38.3	5.5	3.2

Source: "Percent Distributions of Discouraged Workers and Civilian Labor Force (CLF) by Population Group: U.S. Summary, 1992." U.S. Equal Employment Opportunity Commission, *Indicators of Equal Employment Opportunity—Status and Trends*, p. 44. Primary source: U.S. Department of Labor, Bureau of Labor Statistics, *Bulletin* 2307 and unpublished data from the *Current Population Survey* (CPS). *Notes:* 1. Percent distribution represents the number of a particular population group divided by the total of all population groups. The distributions do not sum to 100.0% by race and ethnic group because of the exclusion of Asian Americans and American Indians, and Because Hispanics are included in both the white and black population groups. 2. Hispanics may be of any race.

Displaced Workers

★ 439 ★

Displaced Workers: by Selected Characteristics: 1994

[As of **February. In percent, except total.** For persons 20 years old and over with tenure of 3 years or more who lost or left a job between January 1991 and December 1993 because of plant closing or moves, slack work, or the abolishment of their positions. Based on Current Population Survey and subject to sampling error, see source and Appendix III.]

SEX, AGE, RACE, AND HISPANIC ORIGIN	Total (1,000)	EMPLOYMENT STATUS			REASON FOR JOB LOSS		
		Employed	Unemployed	Not in the labor force	Plant or company closed down or moved	Slack work	Position or shift abolished
Total[1]	4,473	68.0	19.1	12.9	42.3	29.9	27.7
White	3,859	69.3	17.9	12.8	41.2	30.2	28.6
Male	2,291	73.4	18.4	8.2	40.2	33.1	26.6
Female	1,568	63.3	17.2	19.5	42.7	25.9	31.4
Black	427	61.5	26.1	12.4	51.4	25.3	23.3
Male	219	59.3	32.1	8.7	50.7	25.2	24.0
Female	209	63.7	19.8	16.4	52.1	25.3	22.6
Hispanic origin[2]	361	55.6	30.5	13.9	49.2	35.5	15.4
Male	243	57.8	34.0	8.1	44.9	42.0	13.1
Female	118	51.0	23.1	25.9	58.0	21.8	20.2

Source: "Displaced Workers: Selected Characteristics: 1994," *Statistical Abstract of the United States, 1995,* p. 419. Primary source: U.S. Bureau of Labor Statistics, *News,* USDL 94-434. *Notes:* 1. Includes other races, not shown separately. 2. Persons of Hispanic origin may be of any race.

Employers and Employment

★ 440 ★

Employment, by Industry: 1970-1994

[**In thousands, except percent.** See headnote, table 634. Data from 1985 to 1990, and also beginning 1994, not strictly comparable with other years due to changes in industrial classification.]

INDUSTRY	1994[1]			
	Total	Percent		
		Female	Black	Hispanic[2]
Total employed	123,060	46.0	10.4	8.8
Agriculture	3,409	25.1	4.0	16.4
Mining	669	15.7	4.5	5.5
Construction	7,493	9.6	6.4	10.5
Manufacturing	20,157	32.1	10.1	9.9
Transportation, communication, and other public utilities	8,692	28.4	13.7	7.8
Wholesale and retail trade	25,699	47.2	8.5	9.7
Wholesale trade	4,713	28.9	6.5	9.2
Retail trade	20,986	51.3	8.9	9.9
Finance, insurance, real estate	8,141	58.9	9.1	6.7
Services[3]	42,986	61.8	11.9	7.8
Business and repair services[3]	7,304	36.3	11.2	10.0
Advertising	272	52.6	5.6	4.2
Services to dwellings and buildings	849	49.2	16.4	20.3
	804	61.3	20.5	6.7
Computer and data processing	1,017	34.5	7.1	3.8
Defective/protective services	477	17.6	24.0	10.6
Automotive services	1,546	13.5	8.9	12.9
Personal services[3]	4,339	69.0	13.6	15.2
Private households	976	89.3	17.5	25.4
Hotels and lodging places	1,328	54.7	16.1	17.8
Entertainment and recreation	2,134	42.6	8.4	7.9
Professional and related services[3]	29,030	68.8	12.0	6.0
Hospitals	5,009	76.5	16.4	5.5
Health services, except hospitals	5,579	78.9	13.3	6.8
Elementary, secondary schools	6,447	74.6	11.8	7.1
Colleges and universities	2,743	52.3	9.7	4.7
Social services	3,046	81.3	17.5	7.8
Legal services	1,286	55.0	5.2	5.3
Public administration[4]	5,814	43.0	16.4	5.8

Source: "Employment, by Industry: 1970 to 1994," *Statistical Abstract of the United States, 1995*, p. 416. Primary source: U.S. Bureau of Labor Statistics, *Employment and Earnings*, monthly, January issues. *Notes:* NA Not available. 1. See footnote 2, table 626. 2. Persons of Hispanic origin may be of any race. 3. Includes industries not shown separately. 4. Includes workers involved in uniquely governmental activities, e.g., judicial and legislative.

Employment and Unemployment

★ 441 ★

Employed and Unemployed: Full- and Part-time Workers by Age, Gender, and Race

[In thousands].

Age, sex, and race	November 1995									
	Employed[1]								Unemployed	
	Full-time workers				Part-time workers				Looking for full-time work	Looking for part-time work
		At work		Not at work		At work[2]		Not at work		
	Total	35 hours or more	1 to 34 hours economic or noneconomic reasons		Total	Part time for economic reasons	Part time for noneconomic reasons			
White										
Men, 16 years and over	51,453	46,176	3,933	1,344	6,570	997	5,222	350	2,399	498
16 to 19 years	884	733	123	28	1,777	97	1,604	76	219	300
20 years and over	50,568	45,443	3,809	1,316	4,793	901	3,618	274	2,180	198
20 to 24 years	4,180	3,805	330	45	1,231	232	979	20	410	58
25 years and over	46,388	41,638	3,479	1,271	3,562	689	2,640	253	1,770	140
25 to 54 years	40,354	36,321	2,991	1,042	1,895	566	1,235	94	1,577	71
55 years and over	6,034	5,317	488	228	1,667	103	1,405	160	193	69
Women, 16 years and over	34,677	30,477	3,261	939	14,128	1,401	12,011	716	1,691	673
16 to 19 years	581	488	80	13	1,974	111	1,824	40	170	248
20 years and over	34,096	29,989	3,180	926	12,154	1,290	10,187	677	1,521	425
20 to 24 years	2,995	2,678	263	55	1,707	252	1,395	59	231	82
25 years and over	31,100	27,311	2,917	871	10,447	1,038	8,791	618	1,290	343
25 to 54 years	27,381	24,114	2,534	732	8,175	899	6,837	439	1,136	258
55 years and over	3,719	3,197	383	139	2,272	140	1,954	179	154	85
Black										
Men, 16 years and over	5,662	5,118	428	116	794	200	545	49	567	104
16 to 19 years	111	102	8	1	227	20	195	12	77	56
20 years and over	5,551	5,015	420	116	567	180	350	37	490	47
20 to 24 years	512	486	23	4	184	56	119	8	106	3
25 years and over	5,039	4,530	397	112	383	124	230	28	384	44
25 to 54 years	4,537	4,074	364	98	290	119	151	21	351	37
55 years and over	502	456	33	14	93	6	80	8	33	7
Women, 16 years and over	5,836	5,071	552	212	1,368	356	960	52	549	142
16 to 19 years	66	53	14	-	267	45	217	5	64	76
20 years and over	5,769	5,018	538	213	1,101	310	743	48	486	66
20 to 24 years	528	455	60	13	209	62	141	6	112	29
25 years and over	5,241	4,563	478	200	893	249	602	42	374	38
24 to 54 years	4,758	4,143	426	188	704	231	444	29	358	34
55 years and over	483	419	52	12	189	18	158	12	16	3

Source: "Employed and Unemployed Full-time and Part-time Workers by Age, Sex, and Race," *Employment and Earnings,* December 1995, p. 33. *Notes:* Not seasonally adjusted. 1. Employed persons are classified as full- or part-time workers based on their usual weekly hours at jobs regardless of the number of hours they are at work during the reference week. Persons absent from work are also classified according to their usual status. 2. Includes some persons at work 35 hours or more classified by their reason for working part time.

Employment in State and Local Governments

★ 442 ★

Employment Rates in State and Local Governments: Full-Time

Gender	Year	Total, All Groups	Whites	Minorities				
				Total[1]	Blacks	Hispanics	Asians, Pacific Islanders	American Indians, Alaskan Natives
Total, Both	1974	100.0	80.5	19.5	14.8	3.5	0.6	0.3
Men and women	1991	100.0	72.6	27.4	18.5	6.2	2.1	0.6
Men	1974	64.5	53.5	11.1	8.1	2.4	0.3	0.2
	1991	57.0	43.0	14.0	9.0	3.6	1.1	0.3
Women	1974	35.5	27.1	8.4	6.8	1.1	0.3	0.1
	1991	43.0	29.6	13.4	9.6	2.6	1.0	0.2

Source: "Full-Time Employment Participation Rates, State and Local Governments." U.S. equal Employment Opportunity Commission, Indicators of Equal Employment Opportunity—Status and Trends, p. 9. Primary source: Equal Employment Opportunity Commission, *State and Local Government Information (EEO-4) Reports. Notes:* 1. Data for 1974 include a small number of "other" minorities, not shown separately.

★ 443 ★

Employment in State and Local Governments

Employment Rates in the State and Local Governments: Administrative and Professional Jobs

Job category	Year	Whites	Minorities					Women
			Total[1]	Blacks	Hispanics	Asians, Pacific Islanders	American Indians, Alaskan Natives	
Officials and	1974	92.5	7.5	5.3	1.4	0.4	0.2	18.0
Administrators	1991	85.9	14.0	9.1	3.2	1.3	0.4	30.4
Professionals	1974	87.6	12.4	7.9	2.1	1.6	0.3	38.4
	1991	78.0	22.0	13.4	4.3	3.8	0.5	50.4

Source: "Full-Time Employment Participation Rates: State and Local Government Administrative Professional Jobs." U.S. Equal Employment Opportunity Commission, Indicators of Equal Employment Opportunity—Status and Trends, p. 16. Primary source: Equal Opportunity Employment Commission, *State and Local Government Information* (EEO-4) *Reports. Notes:* 1. Data for 1974 include a small number of "other" minorities, not shown separately.

★ 444 ★

Employment in State and Local Governments

State and Local Government Employment by Gender and Population Group: Trends 1973-1991, Part 1

Year	Total, All Groups		Whites		Minorities			
					Total[1]		Blacks	
	Men	Women	Men	Women	Men	Women	Men	Women
1973	65.3	34.7	54.7	27.1	10.6	7.7	7.5	6.2
1974	64.5	35.5	53.5	27.1	11.1	8.4	8.1	6.8
1975	62.5	37.5	51.1	28.4	11.3	9.1	8.1	7.3
1976	62.3	37.7	51.1	28.8	11.2	8.9	8.1	7.1
1977	62.0	38.0	50.1	28.7	11.9	9.3	8.6	7.4
1978	61.0	39.0	49.0	29.3	11.9	9.6	8.6	7.6
1979	60.3	39.7	48.3	29.7	12.0	10.1	8.5	7.9
1981	58.7	41.3	46.7	30.2	12.0	10.9	8.4	8.3
1983	59.5	40.5	46.7	29.5	12.9	10.9	8.8	8.3
1984	58.9	41.1	45.9	29.7	13.1	11.4	8.9	8.6
1985	58.9	41.1	45.7	29.5	13.2	11.6	8.9	8.7
1986	58.5	41.5	44.9	29.4	13.6	12.1	9.7	9.0
1987	58.1	41.9	44.8	29.5	13.3	12.5	8.8	9.2
1989	57.6	42.4	43.9	29.6	13.8	12.8	9.0	9.3
1990	57.2	42.8	43.3	29.6	13.9	13.2	9.0	9.5
1991	57.0	43.0	43.0	29.6	14.0	13.4	9.0	9.5

Source: "State and Local Government Total Full-Time Employment and Participation Rates of Minorities and Women by Job Category, U.S. Summary, 1973-1991." U.S. Equal Employment Opportunity Commission, *Indicators of Equal Opportunity—Status and Trends*, A-4. Primary source: *Employer Information Reports* (EEO-1) and *State and Local Government Information* (EEO-4) *Notes:* 1. Includes such other minorities as Pacific Islanders from 1973 through 1975, not shown separately.

★ 445 ★

Employment in State and Local Governments

State and Local Government Employment by Gender and Population Group: Trends 1973-1991, Part 2

Year	Minorities					
	Hispanics		Asians, Pacific Islanders[2]		American Indians, Alaskan Natives[3]	
	Men	Women	Men	Women	Men	Women
1973	2.3	1.0	0.3	0.3	0.2	0.1
1974	2.4	1.1	0.3	0.3	0.2	0.1
1975	2.5	1.3	0.3	0.3	0.2	0.1
1976	2.5	1.3	0.4	0.4	0.2	0.1
1977	2.6	1.4	0.5	0.4	0.2	0.1
1978	2.6	1.4	0.5	0.5	0.2	0.1

[Continued]

★ 445 ★

State and Local Government Employment by Gender and Population Group: Trends 1973-1991, Part 2

[Continued]

Year	Minorities					
	Hispanics		Asians, Pacific Islanders[2]		American Indians, Alaskan Natives[3]	
	Men	Women	Men	Women	Men	Women
1979	2.7	1.5	0.5	0.5	0.3	0.2
1981	2.7	1.6	0.6	0.6	0.3	0.4
1983	3.1	1.8	0.7	0.6	0.3	0.2
1984	3.2	1.9	0.7	0.7	0.3	0.2
1985	3.2	2.0	0.8	0.7	0.3	0.2
1986	3.3	2.1	0.8	0.8	0.4	0.2
1987	3.3	2.2	0.9	0.9	0.3	0.2
1989	3.5	2.4	1.0	0.9	0.3	0.2
1990	3.6	2.5	1.0	1.0	0.3	0.2
1991	3.6	2.6	1.1	1.0	0.3	0.2

Source: "State and Local Government Total Full-Time Employment and Participation Rates of Minorities and Women by Job Category, U.S. Summary, 1973-1991." U.S. Equal Employment Opportunity Commission, *Indicators of Equal Opportunity—Status and Trends*, A-4. Primary source: *Employer Information Reports* (EEO-1) and *State and Local Government Information* (EEO-4) *Notes:* 1. Includes such other minorities as Pacific Islanders from 1973 through 1975, not shown separately. 2. Excludes Pacific Islanders before 1976. 3. Excludes Alaskan Natives before 1976.

★ 446 ★

Employment in State and Local Governments

State and Local Government Employment by Gender, Minorities, and Job Category: Trends, 1973-1991

Job Category	Year	Total Full-Time Employment[1]	Participation Rates					
			Minorities					Women
			Total[1]	Blacks	Hispanics	Asians, Pacific Islanders[2]	American Indians, Alaskan Natives[3]	
Total, All Jobs	1974	3,983,855	19.5	14.8	3.5	0.6	0.3	35.5
	1991	5,458,570	27.4	18.5	6.2	2.1	0.6	43.0
Officials/Administrators	1974	211,880	7.5	5.3	1.4	0.4	0.2	18.0
	1991	304,499	14.0	9.1	3.2	1.3	0.4	30.4
Professionals	1974	656,381	12.4	7.9	2.1	1.6	0.3	38.4
	1991	1,227,176	22.0	13.4	4.3	3.8	0.5	50.4
Technicians	1974	370,606	14.3	10.3	2.6	0.9	0.3	30.3
	1991	501,092	23.9	14.8	6.0	2.6	0.5	41.4
Protective Service	1974	573,916	10.8	8.0	2.4	0.1	0.2	3.6
	1991	912,933	23.6	16.2	6.2	0.7	0.5	13.3
Para-professionals	1974	359,703	34.3	29.3	4.0	0.4	0.3	66.1

[Continued]

★ 446 ★

State and Local Government Employment by Gender, Minorities, and Job Category: Trends, 1973-1991

[Continued]

Job Category	Year	Total Full-Time Employment[1]	Participation Rates					
			Minorities					Women
			Total[1]	Blacks	Hispanics	Asians, Pacific Islanders[2]	American Indians, Alaskan Natives[3]	
	1991	402,531	39.2	31.4	5.8	1.4	0.6	72.7
Administrative Support	1974	747,340	18.4	13.5	3.6	0.8	0.2	84.7
	1991	976,326	30.0	19.5	7.7	2.2	0.6	87.6
Skilled Craft	1974	351,173	14.5	9.7	4.1	0.3	0.3	4.1
	1991	455,268	23.3	14.7	6.6	1.3	0.7	4.3
Service Maintenance	1974	172,856	35.3	28.5	6.0	0.3	0.3	14.5
	1991	678,745	42.4	31.4	9.2	1.2	0.6	20.8

Source: "State and Local Government Total Full-Time Employment and Participation Rates of Minorities and Women by Job Category, U.S. Summary, 1973-1991." U.S. Equal Employment Opportunity Commission, *Indicators of Equal Opportunity—Status and Trends*, A-6. Primary source: *Employer Information Reports* (EEO-1) and *State and Local Government Information* (EEO-4) *Notes:* 1. Includes such other minorities as Pacific Islanders from 1973 through 1975, not shown separately. 2. Excludes Pacific Islanders before 1976. 3. Excludes Alaskan Natives before 1976.

★ 447 ★

Employment in State and Local Governments

State and Local Government Employment by Population Group: Trends, 1973- 1991

Year	Total Full-Time Employment, Both Men and Women	Whites	Participation Rates				
			Minorities				
			Total[1]	Blacks	Hispanics	Asians, Pacific Islanders[2]	American Indians, Alaskan Natives[3]
1973	3,808,538	81.8	18.3	13.7	0.3	0.6	0.3
1974	3,983,855	80.5	19.5	14.8	3.5	0.6	0.3
1975	3,899,280	79.6	20.4	15.4	3.8	0.7	0.3
1976	4,369,222	79.9	20.2	15.2	3.8	0.8	0.4
1977	4,415,108	78.8	21.3	16.0	4.0	0.9	0.4
1978	4,443,984	78.3	21.5	16.2	4.0	1.0	0.3
1979	4,576,448	78.0	22.0	16.4	4.2	1.0	0.4
1981	4,665,184	77.0	23.0	16.7	4.4	1.2	0.7
1983	4,492,433	76.2	23.8	17.1	5.1	1.5	0.5
1984	4,579,737	75.5	24.6	17.5	5.1	1.5	0.5
1985	4,741,508	75.2	24.8	17.6	5.2	1.5	0.5
1986	4,779,051	74.3	25.7	18.1	5.4	1.6	0.6
1987	4,848,579	74.2	25.8	18.0	5.5	1.7	0.5
1989	5,257,431	73.5	26.6	18.3	5.9	1.9	0.5

[Continued]

★ 447 ★

State and Local Government Employment by Population Group:
Trends, 1973- 1991
[Continued]

Year	Total Full-Time Employment, Both Men and Women	Participation Rates					
		Whites	Minorities				
			Total[1]	Blacks	Hispanics	Asians, Pacific Islanders[2]	American Indians, Alaskan Natives[3]
1990	5,373,766	72.9	27.1	18.5	6.1	2.0	0.5
1991	5,458,570	72.6	27.4	18.5	6.2	2.1	0.6

Source: "State and Local Government Total Full-Time Employment and Participation Rates Population Group and Year, U.S. Summary, 1973-1991." U.S. Equal Employment Opportunity Commission, *Indicators of Equal Opportunity—Status and Trends*, A-3. Primary source: *Employer Information Reports* (EEO-1) and *State and Local Government Information* (EEO-4) *Notes:* 1. Includes such other minorities as Pacific Islanders from 1973 through 1975, not shown separately. 2. Excludes Pacific Islanders before 1976. 3. Excludes Alaskan Natives before 1976.

Employment in the Federal Government

★ 448 ★

Employment Rates in the Federal Government

Gender	Year	Total, All Groups	Whites	Minorities				
				Total	Blacks	Hispanics	Asians, Pacific Islanders	American Indians, Alaskan Natives
Total, Both	1982	100.0	76.2	23.8	15.7	4.4	2.4	1.3
Men and women	1991	100.0	73.0	26.9	16.6	5.3	3.5	1.5
Men	1982	61.8	49.3	12.5	7.2	3.0	1.6	0.7
	1991	57.4	44.7	12.6	6.5	3.2	2.1	0.7
Women	1982	38.2	26.9	11.3	8.5	1.4	0.8	0.6
	1991	42.6	28.3	14.3	10.0	2.1	1.4	0.8

Source: "Federal Government Employment Participation Rates by Population Group Worldwide, 1982 and 1991." U.S. Equal Employment Opportunity Commission, Indicators of Equal Employment Opportunity—Status and Trends, p. 12. Primary source: U.S. Office of Personnel Management, Central Personnel Data File (CPDF), 1982 and 1991.

★ 449 ★

Employment in the Federal Government

Employment Rates in the Federal Government: Civilian Administrative and Professional

Job category	Year	Whites	Minorities					Women
			Total	Blacks	Hispanics	Asians, Pacific Islanders	American Indians, Alaskan Natives	
Administrators	1982	83.4	16.6	10.7	3.5	1.4	1.0	31.0
	1991	79.2	20.8	12.8	4.6	2.2	1.2	39.5
Professionals	1982	87.3	12.7	5.9	2.5	3.5	0.8	23.5
	1991	82.5	17.4	7.6	3.5	5.4	0.9	33.7

Source: "Federal Government Employment Participation Rates of Minorities and Women in Administrative and Professional jobs, Worldwide, 1982 and 1991." U.S. Equal Employment Opportunity Commission, Indicators of Equal Employment Opportunity—Status and Trends, p. 18. Primary source: U.S. Office of Personnel Management, Central Personnel Data File (CPDF), 1982 and 1991.

Employment in the Private Sector

★ 450 ★

Employment Participation Rates in Major Private Industries: Whites, Minorities, and Women

Among all industry divisions, the services division experienced the largest increase in employment between 1983 and 1992. Minorities and women had above-average employment participation rates in this division. On the other hand, manufacturing, where minorities and women have below-average employment participation, experienced a decline in the proportion of employment covered in the EEO-1 survey. Employment participation rates for 1983 and 1992 are provided in the accompanying table by population group and majority industry division.

Major industry	Year	Whites	Minorities					Women
			Total	Blacks	Hispanics	Asians, Pacific Islanders	American Indians, Alaskan Natives	
Manufacturing	1983	81.8	18.2	10.9	5.3	1.6	0.4	32.0
	1992	78.3	21.7	11.6	6.7	2.9	0.5	33.1
Transportation/ Public Utilities	1983	82.8	17.2	11.0	4.6	1.2	0.4	31.5
	1992	78.5	21.5	12.9	6.0	2.1	0.5	32.9

[Continued]

★ 450 ★

Employment Participation Rates in Major Private Industries: Whites, Minorities, and Women

[Continued]

| Major industry | Year | Whites | Minorities | | | | | Women |
			Total	Blacks	Hispanics	Asians, Pacific Islanders	American Indians, Alaskan Natives	
Trade	1983	81.5	18.5	10.5	6.0	1.7	0.3	52.2
	1992	77.1	22.9	12.2	8.2	2.3	0.5	52.1
Finance	1983	80.6	19.4	11.5	5.1	2.5	0.3	64.4
	1992	79.0	21.0	12.0	5.2	3.5	0.3	64.7
Services	1983	77.1	22.9	14.1	5.2	3.0	0.3	62.0
	1992	73.8	26.2	14.7	7.0	4.1	0.4	62.6

Source: "Employment Participation Rates of Whites, Minorities, and Women in Major Private Industry Divisions, U.S. Summary, 1983 and 1992." U.S. Equal Employment Opportunity Commission, Indicators of Equal Employment Opportunity—Status and trends, p. 24. Primary source: Equal Employment Opportunity Commission, *Employer Information Reports* (EEO-1).

★ 451 ★

Employment in the Private Sector

Employment Rates in the Private Sector: Managerial and Professional Jobs

| Job category | Year | Whites | Minorities | | | | | Women |
			Total	Blacks	Hispanics	Asians, Pacific Islanders	American Indians, Alaskan Natives	
Officials and Managers	1966	98.2	1.8	0.9	0.6	0.2	0.1	9.3
	1978	93.1	6.9	3.7	2.0	0.8	0.4	17.3
	1992	89.4	10.8	5.3	3.2	2.0	0.3	30.5
Professionals	1966[1]	96.1	3.9	1.7	0.8	1.3	0.1	20.5
	1978	90.8	9.2	4.0	1.8	3.2	0.2	33.9
	1992	87.0	13.9	5.5	2.7	5.4	0.3	49.4

Source: "Employment Participation Rates: Private Sector Managerial and Professional Jobs." U.S. Equal Employment Opportunity Commission, Indicators of Equal Employment Opportunity—Status and Trends, p. 14. Primary source: Equal Employment Opportunity Commission, *Employer Information Reports* (EEO-1). *Notes:* 1. Because this job definition was changed in 1967, the participation rates from that year were used to make the rates comparable to the 1978 and 1992 rates.

★ 452 ★

Employment in the Private Sector

Private Sector Employment Rates of Minorities and Women by Job Category: 1966, 1978, and 1992

Job Category	Year	Total Employment[1]	Participation Rates[1]					Women
			Minorities					
			Total	Blacks	Hispanics	Asians, Pacific Islanders[2]	American Indians, Alaskan Natives	
Total, All Jobs	1966	24,887,122	11.2	8.2	2.5	0.3	0.2	31.2
	1978	36,028,647	17.9	11.2	5.0	1.3	0.4	40.0
	1992	42,257,903	22.89	12.3	7.1	3.0	0.5	46.9
Officials/Managers	1966	2,048,655	1.8	0.9	0.6	.02	0.1	9.3
	1978	3,971,933	6.9	3.7	2.0	0.8	0.4	17.3
	1992	4,883,707	10.8	5.3	3.2	2.0	0.3	30.5
Professionals	1967	1,818,604	3.9	1.7	0.8	1.3	0.1	20.5
	1978	2,963,481	9.2	4.0	1.8	3.2	0.2	33.9
	1992	5,598,954	13.9	5.5	2.7	5.4	0.3	49.4
Technicians	1967	1,086,792	6.5	4.0	1.5	0.8	0.2	22.6
	1978	1,729,051	13.8	8.2	3.3	2.0	0.4	37.5
	1992	2,457,211	19.5	10.2	4.7	4.1	0.4	45.1
Sales Workers	1966	1,792,981	4.2	2.4	1.4	0.2	0.2	38.8
	1978	3,629,481	11.5	6.8	3.4	0.9	0.3	50.7
	1992	5,499,455	19.3	10.2	6.5	2.2	0.5	56.0
Office/Clerical	1966	4,132,214	5.7	3.5	1.7	0.4	0.1	72.0
	1978	5,659,036	16.0	10.1	4.1	1.5	0.4	82.2
	1992	6,602,629	22.7	13.1	6.3	2.9	0.4	83.6
Skilled Craft	1966	3,600,064	6.0	3.6	2.0	0.2	0.2	6.4
	1978	4,391,854	13.8	8.0	4.7	0.6	0.5	8.6
	1992	3,670,493	17.8	9.1	6.5	1.6	0.6	10.4
Operatives	1966	6,477,598	14.3	10.8	3.1	0.2	0.2	27.7
	1978	7,317,451	23.9	16.1	6.5	0.8	0.5	31.9
	1992	5,960,244	28.7	16.7	8.8	2.6	0.6	31.1
Laborers	1966	2,438,778	28.1	21.3	6.1	0.2	0.4	24.0
	1978	3,006,482	31.8	19.1	11.1	1.0	0.6	33.9
	1992	2,828,630	37.5	18.5	15.8	2.5	0.7	34.0
Service Workers	1966	1,857,134	27.5	22.6	4.1	0.5	0.3	43.1
	1978	3,359,878	30.6	21.5	7.0	1.7	0.4	54.6
	1992	4,756,580	39.4	23.3	12.3	3.3	0.6	55.7

Source: "Private Sector Total Full-Time Employment and Participation Rates of Minorities and Women by Job Category, U.S. Summary, 1966, 1978, and 1992." U.S. Equal Employment Opportunity Commission, *Indicators of Equal Employment Opportunity—Status and Trends*, A-5. Primary source: *Employer Information Reports* (EEO-1) and *State and Local Government Information* (EEO-4) *Notes:* 1. Employment and participation rates are based upon consolidated reports from multi-establishment employers in all years except 1967. Includes employment mainly from those employers with at least 100 employees. 2. Excludes Pacific Islanders before 1976.

★ 453 ★

Employment in the Private Sector

Private Sector Employment Rates: by Gender and Race
1966-1992, Part 1

Year	Total, All Groups		Whites		Minorities			
					Total		Blacks	
	Men	Women	Men	Women	Men	Women	Men	Women
1966	68.8	31.2	60.9	27.8	7.8	3.4	5.7	2.4
1967	67.7	32.3	59.5	28.4	8.2	3.9	5.9	2.8
1969	66.1	33.9	57.3	29.1	8.8	4.8	6.1	3.4
1970	65.9	34.1	56.6	28.9	9.3	5.2	6.4	3.7
1971	66.1	33.9	57.4	28.8	8.8	5.1	5.9	3.6
1972	64.8	35.2	55.6	29.6	9.1	5.6	6.1	3.9
1973	63.5	36.5	53.8	30.3	9.6	6.2	6.3	4.3
1974	63.3	36.7	53.5	30.1	9.8	6.5	6.4	4.5
1975	62.7	37.3	53.3	30.7	9.5	6.6	6.0	4.5
1976	61.6	38.4	52.6	31.9	9.0	6.5	5.7	4.3
1978	60.0	40.0	49.9	32.2	10.1	7.8	6.1	5.1
1979	59.8	40.2	49.4	32.1	10.4	8.1	6.2	5.3
1980	58.7	41.3	48.3	32.9	10.4	8.4	6.0	5.4
1981	58.2	41.8	48.0	33.2	10.2	8.6	5.9	5.5
1982	57.4	42.6	47.4	33.9	10.0	8.7	5.6	5.5
1983	56.2	43.8	46.4	34.8	9.8	8.9	5.5	5.6
1984	56.1	43.9	45.9	34.7	10.2	9.2	5.6	5.8
1985	55.6	44.4	45.1	34.9	10.4	9.6	5.8	6.0
1986	54.9	45.1	44.4	35.2	10.5	9.9	5.8	6.2
1987	54.1	45.9	43.4	35.6	10.7	10.3	5.9	6.4
1988	53.9	46.1	43.0	35.6	10.9	10.5	5.9	6.5
1989	53.8	46.2	42.6	35.4	11.2	10.8	5.9	6.6
1990	53.5	46.5	42.1	35.5	11.4	11.0	5.9	6.6
1991	53.3	46.7	41.9	35.6	11.4	11.0	5.8	6.5
1992	53.1	46.9	41.5	35.7	11.6	11.2	5.8	6.6

Source: "Private Sector Participation Rates of Men and Women by Population Group and Year, U.S. Summary, 1966-1992." U.S. Equal Employment Opportunity Commission, *Indicators of Equal Employment Opportunity—Status and Trends*, A-2. Primary source: *Employer Information Reports* (EEO-1) and *State and Local Government Information* (EEO-4).

★ 454 ★

Employment in the Private Sector

Private Sector Employment Rates: by Gender and Race 1966-1992, Part 2

Year	Hispanics		Asians, Pacific Islanders[1]		American Indians, Alaskan Natives	
	Men	Women	Men	Women	Men	Women
1966	1.8	0.8	0.2	0.1	0.1	0.1
1967	1.9	0.9	0.2	0.1	0.2	0.1
1969	2.1	1.0	0.4	0.2	0.2	0.1
1970	2.4	1.2	0.3	0.2	0.2	0.1
1971	2.4	1.2	0.3	0.2	0.2	0.1
1972	2.5	1.3	0.3	0.3	0.2	0.1
1973	2.7	1.5	0.4	0.3	0.2	0.1
1974	2.8	1.5	0.4	0.4	.02	0.1
1975	2.8	1.6	0.5	0.4	0.2	0.1
1976	2.7	1.6	0.5	0.4	0.2	0.1
1978	3.1	1.9	.07	0.6	0.3	0.1
1979	3.1	2.1	0.7	0.7	0.3	0.1
1980	3.2	2.1	0.8	0.7	0.3	0.1
1981	3.3	2.3	0.8	0.8	0.2	0.1
1982	3.2	2.2	0.9	0.8	0.2	0.2
1983	3.1	2.3	1.0	0.9	0.2	0.2
1984	3.2	2.3	1.0	1.0	0.3	0.2
1985	3.3	2.4	1.1	1.0	0.2	0.2
1986	3.3	2.5	1.1	1.1	0.2	0.2
1987	3.4	2.6	1.2	1.1	0.2	0.2
1988	3.5	2.6	1.3	1.2	0.2	0.2
1989	3.8	2.8	1.4	1.3	0.2	0.2
1990	3.9	2.9	1.4	1.3	0.2	0.2
1991	4.0	2.9	1.5	1.4	0.3	0.2
1992	4.1	3.0	1.5	1.5	0.3	0.2

Source: "Private Sector Participation Rates of Men and Women by Population Group and Year, U.S. Summary, 1966-1992." U.S. Equal Employment Opportunity Commission, *Indicators of Equal Employment Opportunity—Status and Trends*, A-2. Primary source: *Employer Information Reports* (EEO-1) and *State and Local Government Information* (EEO-4). *Note:* 1. Excludes Pacific Islanders before 1976.

★ 455 ★
Employment in the Private Sector

Private Sector Total Employment Rates: Trends, 1966-1992

Year	Total Employment Both men and Women (In Thousands)	Participation rates, Both Men and Women[1]					
			Minorities				
		Whites	Total	Blacks	Hispanics	Asians, Pacific Islanders[2]	American Indians, Alaskan Natives
1966	24,887	88.8	11.2	8.2	2.5	0.3	0.2
1967	27,635	88.0	12.0	8.6	2.8	0.4	0.3
1969	28,913	86.4	13.6	9.5	3.2	0.6	0.3
1970	29,975	85.5	14.5	10.1	3.6	0.5	0.3
1971	29,285	86.1	13.9	9.5	3.5	0.6	0.3
1972	31,505	85.2	14.7	10.0	3.8	0.6	0.3
1973	33,130	84.1	15.9	10.6	4.1	0.7	0.4
1974	33,719	83.7	16.3	10.9	4.3	0.8	0.4
1975	32,692	84.0	16.0	10.5	4.3	0.9	0.4
1976	32,303	84.5	15.5	10.0	4.2	0.9	0.4
1978	36,029	82.1	17.9	11.2	5.0	1.3	0.4
1979	37,405	81.5	18.5	11.5	5.1	1.4	0.4
1980	37,182	81.2	18.7	11.4	5.4	1.5	0.5
1981	37,476	81.2	18.8	11.2	5.6	1.6	0.4
1982	36,256	81.3	18.7	11.1	5.5	1.8	0.4
1983	35,024	81.3	18.7	11.1	5.4	1.9	0.4
1984	35,909	80.6	19.4	11.4	5.5	2.0	0.5
1985	36,574	80.0	20.0	11.8	5.6	2.1	0.4
1986	37,247	79.6	20.4	12.0	5.8	2.2	0.4
1987	37,820	78.9	21.1	12.3	6.0	2.4	0.4
1988	39,099	78.6	21.4	12.4	6.2	2.4	0.4
1989	41,448	78.0	22.0	12.5	6.5	2.6	0.4
1990	42,026	77.6	22.4	12.5	6.7	2.7	0.4
1991	42,017	77.5	22.5	12.3	6.9	2.9	0.5
1992	42,258	77.2	22.8	12.3	7.1	3.0	0.5

Source: "Private Sector Total Employment and Participation Rates by Population Group and Year, U.S. Summary, 1966-1992." U.S. Equal Employment Opportunity Commission, *Indicators of Equal Employment Opportunity—Status and Trends*, A-1. Primary source: *Employer Information Reports* (EEO-1) and *State and Local Government Information* (EEO-4). *Notes:* 1. Employment and participation rates are based upon consolidated reports from multi-establishment employers in all years except 1967. Includes employment mainly from those employers with at least 100 employees. 2. Excludes Pacific Islanders before 1976.

Labor Force

★ 456 ★

Civilian Employment: Characteristics of the Civilian Noninstitutional Population. Part 1

[Numbers in thousands].

Age, sex, and race	Civilian noninstitutional population	November 1995								
		Civilian labor force								Not in labor force
		Total	Percent of population	Employed				Unemployed		
				Total	Percent of population	Agriculture	Nonagricultural industries	Number	Percent of labor force	
WHITE										
16 years and over	167,441	112,069	66.9	106,828	63.8	3,043	103,785	5,261	4.7	55,352
16 to 19 years	11,573	6,154	53.2	5,217	45.1	198	5,019	937	15.2	5,419
16 to 17 years	5,862	2,570	43.8	2,124	36.2	97	2,028	446	17.4	3,292
18 to 19 years	5,711	3,584	62.8	3,093	54.2	102	2,991	491	13.7	2,127
20 to 24 years	14,121	10,894	77.1	10,113	71.6	275	9,838	781	7.2	3,227
25 to 54 years	95,461	80,846	84.7	77,804	81.5	1,822	75,982	3,042	3.8	14,614
25 to 34 years	33,142	28,343	85.5	27,104	81.8	599	26,505	1,239	4.4	4,799
25 to 29 years	15,468	13,126	84.9	12,503	80.8	250	12,253	823	4.7	2,341
30 to 34 years	17,674	15,217	86.1	14,601	82.6	348	14,253	616	4.0	2,458
35 to 44 years	35,478	30,321	85.5	29,206	82.3	740	28,466	1,115	3.7	5,157
35 to 39 years	18,471	15,669	84.8	15,079	81.6	399	14,680	590	3.8	2,801
40 to 44 years	17,007	14,652	86.1	14,127	83.1	341	13,786	525	3.6	2,356
45 to 54 years	26,841	22,182	82.6	21,495	80.1	484	21,011	687	3.1	4,659
45 to 54 years	15,131	12,852	84.9	12,441	82.2	263	12,178	411	3.2	2,279
50 to 54 years	11,710	9,330	79.7	9,054	77.3	221	8,833	276	3.0	2,379
55 to 64 years	18,026	10,626	58.9	10,261	56.9	426	9,834	365	3.4	7,400
55 to 59 years	9,481	6,589	69.5	6,373	67.2	245	6,127	217	3.3	2,891
60 to 64 years	8,545	4,037	47.2	3,888	45.5	181	3,707	149	3.7	4,508
65 years and over	28,260	3,568	12.6	3,433	12.1	321	3,112	136	3.8	24,692
65 to 69 years	8,539	1,963	23.0	1,901	22.3	149	1,752	62	3.2	6,576
70 to 74 years	7,689	1,039	13.5	967	12.8	105	882	52	5.0	6,850
75 years and over	12,033	567	4.7	545	4.5	67	478	22	3.8	11,466
BLACK										
16 years and over	23,389	15,022	64.2	13,660	58.4	68	13,591	1,363	9.1	8,366
16 to 19 years	2,367	944	39.9	671	28.3	-	671	273	28.9	1,423
16 to 17 years	1,181	365	31.0	246	20.8	-	246	119	32.7	815
18 to 19 years	1,186	579	48.8	425	35.8	-	425	154	26.6	607
20 to 24 years	2,471	1,683	68.1	1,433	58.0	5	1,428	250	14.9	188
25 to 54 years	13,869	11,069	79.8	10,289	74.2	49	10,240	780	7.0	2,801
25 to 34 years	5,326	4,306	80.9	3,906	73.3	7	3,899	400	9.3	1,019
25 to 29 years	2,548	2,032	79.7	1,831	71.9	2	1,829	201	9.9	516
30 to 34 years	2,778	2,274	81.9	2,075	74.7	5	2,070	199	8.8	504
35 to 44 years	5,232	4,318	82.5	4,049	77.4	22	4,026	269	6.2	913
35 to 39 years	2,793	2,323	83.2	2,170	77.7	13	2,157	154	6.6	470
40 to 44 years	2,439	1,995	81.8	1,880	77.1	9	1,871	115	5.8	444
45 to 54 years	3,312	2,444	73.8	2,333	70.4	20	2,314	111	4.5	868
45 to 54 years	1,947	1,488	76.4	1,409	72.4	10	1,400	79	5.3	459
50 to 54 years	1,365	956	70.0	924	67.7	10	914	32	3.3	409

[Continued]

★ 456 ★

Civilian Employment: Characteristics of the Civilian Noninstitutional Population. Part 1

[Continued]

Age, sex, and race	Civilian noninsti-tutional population	November 1995								
		Civilian labor force								Not in labor force
		Total	Percent of population	Employed				Unemployed		
				Total	Percent of population	Agriculture	Nonagri-cultural industries	Number	Percent of labor force	
55 to 64 years	2,094	1,062	50.7	1,027	49.0	3	1,024	35	3.3	1,032
55 to 59 years	1,126	679	60.3	657	58.3	3	654	22	3.3	447
60 to 64 years	968	383	39.6	370	38.2	-	371	13	3.4	585
65 years and over	2,587	265	10.2	241	9.3	12	228	24	9.2	2,322
65 to 69 years	918	170	18.5	154	16.8	6	148	16	9.6	748
70 to 74 years	714	61	8.6	53	7.4	2	51	8	(1)	653
75 years and over	955	34	3.5	34	3.5	4	29	-	(1)	922

Source: "Employment Status off the Civilian Noninstitutional Population by Age, Sex, and Race," *Employment and Earnings,* December 1995, p. 28-29. Adapted by the editors. *Notes:* Not seasonally adjusted. 1. Data not shown where base is less than 75,000.

★ 457 ★

Labor Force

Civilian Employment: Characteristics of the Civilian Noninstitutional Population. Part 2

[Numbers in thousands].

Age, sex, and race	Civilian noninsti-tutional population	November 1995								
		Civilian labor force								Not in labor force
		Total	Percent of population	Employed				Unemployed		
				Total	Percent of population	Agriculture	Nonagri-cultural industries	Number	Percent of labor force	
WHITE										
MEN										
16 years and over	81,021	60,919	75.2	58,023	71.6	2,246	55,777	2,896	4.8	20,102
16 to 19 years	5,907	3,180	53.8	2,662	45.1	156	2,505	519	16.3	2,726
16 to 17 years	3,015	1,306	43.3	1,052	34.9	76	976	255	19.5	1,709
18 to 19 years	2,892	1,874	64.8	1,610	55.7	80	1,529	264	14.1	1,018
20 to 24 years	7,072	5,879	83.1	5,411	76.5	220	5,191	468	8.0	1,193
25 to 54 years	47,488	43,896	92.4	42,249	89.0	1,315	40,934	1,847	3.8	3,591
25 to 34 years	16,547	15,548	94.0	14,884	90.0	472	14,412	861	4.3	1,001
25 to 29 years	7,713	7,168	92.9	6,831	88.6	209	6,622	337	4.7	545
30 to 34 years	8,834	8,378	94.8	8,053	91.2	263	7,791	324	3.9	456
35 to 44 years	17,701	16,485	93.1	15,865	89.6	518	15,347	820	3.8	1,216
35 to 39 years	9,229	8,608	93.3	8,292	89.8	278	8,014	316	3.7	621
40 to 44 years	8,472	7,877	93.0	7,573	89.4	240	7,333	304	3.9	595
45 to 54 years	13,240	11,865	89.6	11,499	86.9	325	11,174	366	3.1	1,375
45 to 49 years	7,496	6,846	91.3	6,656	88.8	191	6,465	190	2.8	650
50 to 54 years	5,744	5,019	87.4	4,843	84.3	134	4,709	176	3.5	725
55 to 64 years	8,677	5,894	67.9	5,715	65.9	296	5,419	179	3.0	2,783
55 to 59 years	4,601	3,599	78.2	3,492	75.9	162	3,330	107	3.0	1,002
60 to 64 years	4,076	2,295	56.3	2,223	54.8	134	2,069	72	3.1	1,780
65 years and over	11,878	2,069	17.4	1,986	16.7	258	1,726	83	4.0	9,808

[Continued]

★ 457 ★

Civilian Employment: Characteristics of the Civilian Noninstitutional Population. Part 2

[Continued]

Age, sex, and race	Civilian noninsti-tutional population	November 1995								
		Civilian labor force								Not in labor force
		Total	Percent of population	Employed				Unemployed		
				Total	Percent of population	Agriculture	Nonagri-cultural industries	Number	Percent of labor force	
65 to 69 years	3,921	1,108	28.3	1,072	27.4	122	951	35	3.2	2,813
70 to 74 years	3,378	607	18.0	575	17.0	85	490	32	5.3	2,771
75 years and over	4,579	354	7.7	338	7.4	51	267	16	4.5	4,224
BLACK										
Men										
16 years and over	10,480	7,127	68.0	6,456	61.6	56	6,400	671	9.4	3,352
16 to 19 years	1,203	472	39.2	338	28.1	-	338	134	28.4	731
16 to 17 years	588	164	27.9	114	19.3	-	114	51	30.8	424
18 to 19 years	615	307	50.0	224	36.5	-	224	83	27.1	307
20 to 24 years	1,090	806	73.9	696	63.9	5	691	110	13.6	284
25 to 54 years	6,268	5,214	83.2	4,827	77.0	40	4,787	387	7.4	1,053
25 to 34 years	2,386	2,063	86.4	1,866	78.2	3	1,863	196	9.5	323
25 to 29 years	1,127	969	85.9	866	76.8	-	866	103	10.6	159
30 to 34 years	1,259	1,094	86.9	1,001	79.5	3	997	93	8.5	165
35 to 44 years	2,388	2,014	84.3	1,879	78.7	19	1,880	135	6.7	374
35 to 39 years	1,271	1,062	85.1	997	78.5	11	967	85	7.8	189
40 to 44 years	1,117	932	83.4	882	79.0	9	873	50	5.4	185
45 to 54 years	1,494	1,138	76.2	1,081	72.4	17	1,064	57	5.0	356
45 to 49 years	884	714	80.7	669	75.6	9	859	45	6.4	170
50 to 54 years	609	424	69.5	413	67.7	19	405	11	2.6	186
55 to 64 years	906	494	54.5	468	51.7	3	466	25	5.2	413
55 to 59 years	492	323	65.7	306	62.1	3	302	18	5.5	169
60 to 64 years	414	171	41.2	163	39.3	-	163	8	4.6	244
65 years and over	1,013	142	14.0	127	12.5	9	118	15	10.4	871
65 to 69 years	384	95	24.8	84	22.0	5	79	11	11.4	289
70 to 74 years	298	24	8.1	20	6.8	-	20	4	[1]	274
75 years and over	331	23	6.8	23	6.8	4	18	-	[1]	309

Source: "Employment Status of the Civilian Noninstitutional Population by Age, Sex, and Race," *Employment and Earnings,* December 1995, p. 28-29. Adapted by the editors. *Notes:* Not seasonally adjusted. 1. Data not shown where base is less than 75,000.

★ 458 ★

Labor Force

Civilian Employment: Characteristics of the Civilian Noninstitutional Population. Part 3

[Numbers in thousands].

Age, sex, and race	Civilian noninsti-tutional population	November 1995								Not in labor force
		Civilian labor force								
		Total	Percent of population	Employed				Unemployed		
				Total	Percent of population	Agriculture	Nonagri-cultural industries	Number	Percent of labor force	
WHITE										
WOMEN										
16 years and over	12,909	7,895	61.2	7,204	55.8	12	7,192	691	8.8	5,014
16 to 19 years	1,164	473	40.6	333	28.6	-	333	139	29.5	691
16 to 17 years	592	201	34.0	132	22.3	-	132	69	34.2	391
18 to 19 years	571	271	47.5	201	35.1	-	201	70	26.0	300
20 to 24 years	1,382	877	63.5	737	53.3	-	737	140	16.0	505
25 to 54 years	7,602	5,854	77.0	5,462	71.9	9	5,453	392	6.7	1,748
25 to 34 years	2,940	2,244	76.3	2,040	69.4	4	2,036	204	9.1	696
25 to 29 years	1,420	1,063	74.8	965	67.9	2	963	98	9.2	357
30 to 34 years	1,519	1,180	77.7	1,075	70.7	2	1,072	106	9.0	339
35 to 44 years	2,844	2,304	81.0	2,170	76.3	2	2,168	134	5.8	539
35 to 39 years	1,522	1,241	81.6	1,172	77.0	2	1,170	69	5.5	281
40 to 44 years	1,322	1,063	80.4	998	75.5	-	996	65	6.1	259
45 to 54 years	1,819	1,306	71.8	1,252	68.9	3	1,250	54	4.1	512
45 to 49 years	1,063	774	72.8	741	69.7	-	741	33	4.3	289
50 to 54 years	756	532	70.4	511	67.6	2	509	21	3.9	224
55 to 64 years	1,188	568	47.8	558	47.0	-	558	10	1.8	620
55 to 59 years	634	356	56.1	351	55.4	-	351	5	1.3	278
60 to 64 years	554	212	38.3	207	37.4	-	207	5	2.5	341
65 years and over	1,574	123	7.8	113	7.2	3	110	10	7.8	1,451
65 to 69 years	534	75	14.0	70	13.0	1	68	5	7.3	459
70 to 74 years	415	37	8.9	33	7.9	2	31	4	(1)	378
75 years and over	624	11	1.8	11	1.8	-	11	-	(1)	613
BLACK										
WOMEN										
16 years and over	12,909	7,895	61.2	7,204	55.8	12	7,192	691	8.8	5,014
16 to 19 years	1,164	473	40.6	333	28.6	-	333	139	29.5	691
16 to 17 years	592	201	34.0	132	22.3	-	132	69	34.2	391
18 to 19 years	571	271	47.5	201	35.1	-	201	70	26.0	300
20 to 24 years	1,382	877	63.5	737	53.3	-	737	140	16.0	505
25 to 54 years	7,602	5,854	77.0	5,462	71.9	9	5,453	392	6.7	1,748
25 to 34 years	2,940	2,244	76.3	2,040	69.4	4	2,036	204	9.1	696
25 to 29 years	1,420	1,063	74.8	965	67.9	2	963	96	9.2	357
30 to 34 years	1,519	1,180	77.7	1,075	70.7	2	1,072	106	9.0	339
35 to 44 years	2,844	2,304	81.0	2,170	76.3	2	2,168	134	5.8	539
35 to 39 years	1,522	1,241	81.6	1,172	77.0	2	1,170	69	5.5	281
40 to 44 years	1,322	1,063	80.4	998	75.5	-	996	85	6.1	259
45 to 54 years	1,819	1,306	71.8	1,252	68.9	3	1,250	54	4.1	512
45 to 49 years	1,063	774	72.8	741	69.7	-	741	33	4.3	289
50 to 54 years	756	532	70.4	511	67.6	2	509	21	3.9	224
55 to 64 years	1,188	568	47.8	558	47.0	-	558	10	1.8	620

[Continued]

★ 458 ★

Civilian Employment: Characteristics of the Civilian Noninstitutional Population. Part 3

[Continued]

Age, sex, and race	November 1995									
	Civilian noninsti-tutional population	Civilian labor force								Not in labor force
		Total	Percent of population	Employed				Unemployed		
				Total	Percent of population	Agriculture	Nonagri-cultural industries	Number	Percent of labor force	
55 to 59 years	634	356	56.1	351	55.4	-	351	5	1.3	278
60 to 64 years	554	212	38.3	207	37.4	-	207	5	2.5	341
65 years and over	1,574	123	7.8	113	7.2	3	110	10	7.8	1,451
65 to 69 years	534	75	14.0	70	13.0	1	68	5	7.3	459
70 to 74 years	415	37	8.9	33	7.9	2	31	4	(1)	378
75 years and over	624	11	1.8	11	1.8	-	11	-	(1)	613

Source: "Employment Status of the Civilian Noninstitutional Population by Age, Sex, and Race," *Employment and Earnings,* December 1995, pp. 28-29. Adapted by the editors. *Notes:* Not seasonally adjusted. 1. Data not shown where base is less than 75,000.

★ 459 ★

Labor Force

Civilian Employment: Employment Status of the Noninstitutional Population by Race, Gender, and Age

Employment status and race	Total		Men, 20 years and over		Women, 20 years and over		Both sexes, 16 to 19 years	
	Nov. 1994	Nov. 1995	Nov. 1994	Nov. 1995	Nov. 1994	Nov. 1995	Nov. 1994	Nov. 1995
TOTAL								
Civilian noninstitutional population	197,607	199,355	87,529	88,046	95,821	96,555	14,257	14,754
Civilian labor force	131,869	132,622	67,364	67,203	57,444	58,026	7,061	7,393
Percent of population	66.7	66.5	77.0	76.3	59.9	60.1	49.5	50.1
Employed	124,896	125,599	64,239	64,103	54,667	55,374	5,990	6,121
Agriculture	3,480	3,242	2,402	2,243	844	790	234	209
Nonagricultural industries	121,416	122,357	61,837	61,860	53,823	54,584	5,756	5,913
Unemployed	6,973	7,024	3,125	3,100	2,776	2,652	1,071	1,272
Unemployment rate	5.3	5.3	4.6	4.6	4.8	4.6	15.2	17.2
Not in labor force	65,738	66,733	20,165	20,843	38,377	38,529	7,196	7,360
White								
Civilian noninstitutional population	166,072	167,441	74,569	75,114	80,192	80,754	11,311	11,573
Civilian labor force	111,703	112,089	57,744	57,739	47,975	48,196	5,984	6,154
Percent of population	67.3	66.9	77.4	76.9	59.8	59.7	52.9	53.2
Employed	106,655	106,828	55,441	55,361	45,992	46,250	5,222	5,217
Agriculture	3,187	3,043	2,157	2,090	804	755	226	198
Nonagricultural industries	103,468	103,785	53,283	53,271	45,188	45,494	4,996	5,019
Unemployed	5,048	5,261	2,303	2,378	1,983	1,946	762	937
Unemployment rate	4.5	4.7	4.0	4.1	4.1	4.0	12.7	15.2
Not in labor force	54,369	55,352	16,825	17,375	32,217	32,558	5,327	5,419

[Continued]

★ 459 ★

Civilian Employment: Employment Status of the Noninstitutional Population by Race, Gender, and Age

[Continued]

Employment status and race	Total		Men, 20 years and over		Women, 20 years and over		Both sexes, 16 to 19 years	
	Nov. 1994	Nov. 1995	Nov. 1994	Nov. 1995	Nov. 1994	Nov. 1995	Nov. 1994	Nov. 1995
Black								
Civilian noninstitutional population	23,023	23,389	9,236	9,277	11,561	11,745	2,226	2,367
Civilian labor force	14,566	15,022	6,703	6,656	7,041	7,423	822	944
Percent of population	63.3	64.2	72.6	71.7	60.9	63.2	36.9	39.9
Employed	13,080	13,660	6,097	6,118	6,417	6,871	566	671
Agriculture	154	68	132	57	18	12	4	-
Nonagricultural industries	12,926	13,591	5,965	6,062	6,399	6,859	562	671
Unemployed	1,486	1,363	605	537	625	552	256	273
Unemployment rate	10.2	9.1	9.0	8.1	8.9	7.4	31.1	28.9
Not in labor force	8,458	8,366	2,533	2,621	4,520	4,322	1,405	1,423

Source: "Employment Status of the Civilian Noninstitutional Population by Race, Sex, and Age," *Employment and Earnings*, December 1995, p. 30. *Note:* Not seasonally adjusted.

★ 460 ★

Labor Force

Civilian Employment: School Enrollment and Characteristics of the Noninstitutional Population 16 to 24 Years of Age. Part 1-Enrolled

[Numbers in thousands].

Enrollment status, educational attainment, race, and Hispanic origin	Civilian noninsti-tutional population	November 1995								
		Civilian labor force								
		Total	Percent of population	Employed			Unemployed			
				Total	Full time	Part time	Total	Looking for full-time work	Looking for part-time work	Percent of labor force
White										
Total, 16 to 24 years	13,253	6,830	51.5	6,176	1,072	5,104	654	90	564	9.6
16 to 19 years	8,952	4,208	47.0	3,648	350	3,298	559	57	503	13.3
20 to 24 years	4,301	2,622	61.0	2,528	722	1,806	94	33	61	3.6
Men	6,680	3,375	50.5	3,002	588	2,414	373	58	315	11.0
Women	6,573	3,455	52.6	3,174	484	2,690	281	32	248	8.1
High school	6,535	2,916	44.6	2,457	141	2,315	459	47	412	15.8
College	6,718	3,914	58.3	3,720	931	2,789	194	43	151	5.0
Full-time students	5,668	2,979	52.6	2,832	378	2,454	147	23	124	4.9
Part-time students	1,050	934	88.9	887	553	334	47	20	27	5.0
Black										
Total, 16 to 24 years	2,522	919	36.4	729	149	580	190	54	136	20.7
16 to 19 years	1,800	558	31.0	413	33	380	145	25	120	26.0
20 to 24 years	722	361	50.0	316	116	200	45	29	16	12.5

[Continued]

★ 460 ★

Civilian Employment: School Enrollment and Characteristics of the Noninstitutional Population 16 to 24 Years of Age. Part 1-Enrolled

[Continued]

Enrollment status, educational attainment, race, and Hispanic origin	Civilian noninsti-tutional population	November 1995								
		Civilian labor force								
		Total	Percent of population	Employed			Unemployed			
				Total	Full time	Part time	Total	Looking for full-time work	Looking for part-time work	Percent of labor force
Men	1,244	423	34.0	345	57	288	79	26	53	18.6
Women	1,278	495	38.8	384	92	292	111	28	83	22.4
High school	1,470	438	29.8	298	20	278	140	28	112	31.9
College	1,052	481	45.7	431	129	302	50	25	24	10.4
Full-time students	849	328	38.6	287	47	240	41	18	23	12.6
Part-time students	203	153	75.3	144	82	62	9	8	1	5.7
Hispanic origin										
Total, 16 to 24 years	1,774	651	36.7	506	119	387	145	28	117	22.2
16 to 19 years	1,319	412	31.3	288	50	238	124	16	108	30.1
20 to 24 years	455	238	52.4	218	69	148	20	12	9	8.6
Men	897	337	37.6	249	61	188	89	16	72	26.2
Women	877	313	35.7	257	59	199	56	11	45	17.9
High school	1,067	307	28.7	191	20	171	116	14	101	37.7
College	707	344	48.7	315	99	216	29	13	16	8.4
Full-time students	534	212	39.6	192	45	147	19	8	11	9.2
Part-time students	172	132	76.8	123	54	68	10	5	4	7.3

Source: "Employment Status of the Civilian Noninstitutional Population 16 to 24 Years of Age by School Enrollment, Educational Attainment, Sex, Race, and Hispanic Origin," *Employment and Earnings,* December 1995, p. 31. In the summer months, the educational attainment levels of youth not enrolled in school are increased by the temporary movement of high school and college students into that group. Detail for the above race and Hispanic-origin groups will not sum to totals because data for the "other races" group are not presented and Hispanics are included in both the white and black population groups. *Note:* Not seasonally adjusted.

★ 461 ★

Labor Force

Civilian Employment: School Enrollment and Characteristics of the Noninstitutional Population 16 to 24 Years of Age. Part 2-Not Enrolled

[Numbers in thousands].

Enrollment status, educational attainment, race, and Hispanic origin	Civilian noninsti-tutional population	November 1995								
		Civilian labor force								
		Total	Percent of population	Employed			Unemployed			
				Total	Full time	Part time	Total	Looking for full-time work	Looking for part-time work	Percent of labor force
White										
Total, 16 to 24 years	12,442	10,218	82.1	9,154	7,569	1,585	1,064	940	124	10.4
16 to 19 years	2,622	1,947	74.3	1,569	1,116	453	378	333	45	19.4
20 to 24 years	9,820	8,272	84.2	7,585	6,453	1,132	687	608	79	8.3
Men	6,299	5,684	90.2	5,070	4,476	594	614	571	43	10.8
Women	6,143	4,534	73.8	4,084	3,093	991	450	369	81	9.9

[Continued]

★ 461 ★

Civilian Employment: School Enrollment and Characteristics of the Noninstitutional Population 16 to 24 Years of Age. Part 2-Not Enrolled

[Continued]

Enrollment status, educational attainment, race, and Hispanic origin	November 1995									
	Civilian noninsti-tutional population	Civilian labor force								
		Total	Percent of population	Employed			Unemployed			
				Total	Full time	Part time	Total	Looking for full-time work	Looking for part-time work	Percent of labor force
Less than a high school diploma	3,093	1,960	63.4	1,555	1,181	374	405	359	46	20.7
High school graduates, no college	5,149	4,375	85.0	3,956	3,283	673	419	381	38	9.6
Less than a bachelor's degree	2,957	2,689	90.9	2,522	2,089	433	168	132	36	6.2
College graduates	1,243	1,193	96.0	1,121	1,016	105	72	68	4	6.1
Black										
Total, 16 to 24 years	2,316	1,708	73.8	1,375	1,069	306	333	305	28	19.5
16 to 19 years	567	386	68.2	258	144	114	128	116	13	33.3
20 to 24 years	1,749	1,322	75.6	1,117	925	192	205	189	15	15.5
Men	1,048	854	81.5	689	566	123	165	158	7	19.3
Women	1,268	854	67.4	686	502	183	169	148	21	19.7
Less than a high school diploma	573	291	50.7	154	106	48	137	120	18	47.2
High school graduates, no college	1,146	905	78.9	736	558	177	169	160	9	18.7
Less than a bachelor's degree	514	435	84.6	408	331	77	27	25	2	6.1
College graduates	83	78	94.2	77	74	4	-	-	-	-
Hispanic origin										
Total, 16 to 24 years	2,730	1,919	70.3	1,657	1,385	272	262	240	22	13.7
16 to 19 years	581	333	57.3	266	195	70	67	60	7	20.2
20 to 24 years	2,149	1,586	73.8	1,391	1,190	202	195	180	15	12.3
Men	1,442	1,239	85.9	1,079	963	115	161	151	10	13.0
Women	1,288	680	52.8	578	422	157	102	89	12	14.9
Less than a high school diploma	1,308	785	60.0	665	518	146	120	118	3	15.3
High school graduates, no college	968	729	75.3	628	556	72	101	94	7	13.9
Less than a bachelor's degree	363	317	87.3	279	231	48	37	25	12	11.8
College graduates	91	88	96.6	85	80	5	3	3	-	3.2

Source: "Employment Status of the Civilian Noninstitutional Population 16 to 24 Years of Age by School Enrollment, Educational Attainment, Sex, Race, and Hispanic Origin," *Employment and Earnings,* December 1995, p. 32. In the summer months, the educational attainment levels of youth not enrolled in school are increased by the temporary movement of high school and college students into that group. Detail for the above race and Hispanic-origin groups will not sum to totals because data for the "other races" group are not presented and Hispanics are included in both the white and black population groups. *Notes:* Not seasonally adjusted. In the summer months, the educational attainment levels of youth not enrolled in school are increased by the temporary movement of high school and college students into that group. Detail for the above race and Hispanic-origin groups will not sum to totals because data for the "other races" group are not presented and Hispanics are included in both the white and black population groups.

★ 462 ★

Labor Force

Civilian Labor Force: Educational Level and Characteristics, 1970-1991

[As of **March.** For civilian noninstitutional population 25 to 64 years of age. Beginning 1992, the method of computing educational attainment data was changed. See table 630 for later data. Based on Current Population Survey; see text, section 1, and Appendix III.]

ITEM	CIVILIAN LABOR FORCE					PARTICIPATION RATE[1]				
	Total (1,000)	Percent distribution				Total	Less than high school	High school graduate	College	
		Less than high school	High school graduate	College					1-3 years	4 years or more
				1-3 years	4 years or more					
Total:[2] 1970	61,765	36.1	38.1	11.8	14.1	70.3	65.5	70.2	73.8	82.3
1980	78,010	20.6	39.8	17.6	22.0	73.9	60.7	74.2	79.5	86.1
1990	99,175	13.4	39.5	20.7	26.4	78.6	60.7	78.2	83.3	88.4
1991	100,480	13.0	39.4	21.1	26.5	78.6	60.7	78.1	83.2	88.4
White: 1970	55,044	33.7	39.3	12.2	14.8	70.1	65.2	69.7	73.3	81.9
1980	68,509	19.1	40.2	17.7	22.9	74.2	61.4	73.7	79.2	86.0
1990	85,238	12.6	39.6	20.6	27.1	79.2	62.5	78.4	83.3	88.3
1991	86,344	12.2	39.3	21.1	27.4	79.4	62.5	78.3	83.1	88.6
Black: 1970	6,721	55.5	28.2	8.0	8.3	72.0	67.1	76.8	81.0	87.4
1980	7,731	34.7	38.1	16.3	11.0	71.5	58.1	79.2	82.0	90.1
1990	10,537	19.9	42.5	22.1	15.5	74.6	54.5	78.2	84.2	92.0
1991	10,650	19.5	42.9	22.1	15.4	73.9	53.9	77.1	84.1	90.2

Source: "Civilian Labor Force and Participation Rates, by Education Attainment, Sex, and Race: 1970 to 1991," *Statistical Abstract of the United States,* 1995, p. 401. Primary source: U.S. Bureau of Labor Statistics, Bulletin 2307; and unpublished data. *Notes:* 1. Percent of the civilian population in each group in the civilian labor force. 2. Includes other races, not shown separately. For 1970, White and Black races only.

★ 463 ★

Labor Force

Civilian Labor Force: Educational Level and Characteristics, 1992-1994

[As of March. For the civilian noninstitutional population 25 to 64 years of age. See table 663 for unemployment data. Based on Current Population Survey; see text, section 1, and Appendix III.]

YEAR, SEX, AND RACE	CIVILIAN LABOR FORCE (1,000)					PARTICIPATION RATE[1]				
	Total	Percent distribution				Total	Less than high school diploma	High school graduates, no degree	Less than a bachelor's degree	College graduate
		Less than high school diploma	High school graduate, no degree	Less than a bachelor's degree	College graduate					
Total:[2]										
1992	102,387	12.2	36.2	25.2	26.4	79.0	60.3	78.3	83.5	88.4
1993	103,504	11.5	35.2	26.3	27.0	78.9	59.6	77.7	92.9	88.3
1994[3]	104,868	11.0	34.0	27.6	27.3	78.9	58.3	77.8	83.2	88.2
White:										
1992	87,656	11.3	36.1	25.5	27.1	79.8	61.5	78.7	83.8	88.7

[Continued]

★ 463 ★

Civilian Labor Force: Educational Level and Characteristics, 1992-1994
[Continued]

| YEAR, SEX, AND RACE | CIVILIAN LABOR FORCE (1,000) | | | | | PARTICIPATION RATE[1] | | | | |
| | Total | Percent distribution | | | | Total | Less than high school diploma | High school graduates, no degree | Less than a bachelor's degree | College graduate |
		Less than high school diploma	High school graduate, no degree	Less than a bachelor's degree	College graduate					
1993	88,457	10.7	35.0	26.4	27.9	79.7	61.1	78.2	83.1	88.8
1994[3]	89,009	10.5	33.7	27.7	28.1	79.8	60.3	78.3	83.5	88.5
Black:										
1992	10,936	19.2	40.3	24.9	15.6	74.4	55.4	76.9	83.4	89.1
1993	11,051	16.8	39.5	27.6	16.1	73.8	53.4	74.7	83.0	89.6
1994[3]	11,368	14.5	39.3	29.2	17.0	73.5	49.4	75.2	82.5	89.5
Hispanic:[4]										
1992	7,702	39.1	30.2	19.3	11.4	73.8	64.6	77.5	84.2	87.1
1993	8,010	38.7	29.4	21.0	10.9	73.9	64.9	76.8	84.0	87.3
1994[3]	8,984	38.6	28.7	21.5	11.1	73.2	63.9	77.5	81.9	86.3

Source: "Civilian Labor Force and Participation Rates, by Educational Attainment, Sex, Race, and Hispanic Origin: 1992 to 1994," *Statistical Abstract of the United States,* 1995, p. 401. Primary source: U.S. Bureau of Labor Statistics, unpublished data. *Notes:* 1. Percent of the civilian population in each group in the civilian labor force. 2. Includes other races, not shown separately. 3. See footnote 2, table 626. 4. Persons of Hispanic origin may be of any race.

★ 464 ★

Labor Force

Civilian Labor Force: Employment Status and Characteristics: 1994

[For civilian noninstitutional population 16 years old and over. Annual averages of monthly figures. Based on Current Population Survey; see text, section 1, and Appendix III.]

| AGE AND RACE | TOTAL (1,000) | MALE (1,000) | | | FEMALE (1,000) | | | PERCENT OF LABOR FORCE | | | |
| | | | | | | | | Employed | | Unemployed | |
		Total	Employed	Unemployed	Total	Employed	Unemployed	Male	Female	Male	Female
All workers[1]	131,056	70,817	66,450	4,367	60,239	56,610	3,629	93.8	94.0	6.2	6.0
16 to 19 years	7,481	3,896	3,156	740	3,585	3,005	580	81.0	83.8	19.0	16.2
20 to 24 years	14,131	7,540	6,771	768	6,592	5,987	605	89.8	90.8	10.2	9.2
25 to 34 years	34,353	18,854	17,411	1,113	15,499	14,545	954	94.1	93.8	5.9	6.2
35 to 44 years	35,226	18,966	18,111	855	16,259	15,488	772	95.5	95.3	4.5	4.7
45 to 54 years	24,318	12,962	12,439	522	11,357	10,908	449	96.0	96.0	4.0	4.0
55 to 64 years	11,713	6,423	6,142	281	5,289	5,085	204	95.6	96.1	4.4	3.9
65 years and over	3,834	2,176	2,089	88	1,658	1,592	66	96.0	96.0	4.0	4.0
White	111,082	60,727	57,452	3,275	50,356	47,738	2,617	94.6	94.8	5.4	5.2
16 to 19 years	6,357	3,315	2,776	540	3,042	2,622	420	83.7	86.2	16.3	13.8
20 to 24 years	11,688	6,294	5,738	555	5,394	4,997	397	91.2	92.6	8.8	7.4
25 to 34 years	28,580	15,879	15,052	827	12,702	12,049	652	94.8	94.9	5.2	5.1
35 to 44 years	29,626	16,188	15,562	626	13,439	12,880	558	96.1	95.8	3.9	4.2
45 to 54 years	21,026	11,327	10,910	417	9,699	9,338	361	96.3	96.3	3.7	3.7
55 to 64 years	10,319	5,726	5,490	236	4,593	4,423	170	95.9	96.3	4.1	3.7
65 years and over	3,486	1,998	1,925	74	1,487	1,429	58	96.3	96.1	3.7	3.9
Black	14,502	7,089	6,241	848	7,413	6,595	818	88.0	89.0	12.0	11.0
16 to 19 years	852	443	276	167	409	275	133	62.3	67.4	37.6	32.6
20 to 24 years	1,800	891	718	173	909	731	178	80.6	80.4	19.4	19.6
25 to 34 years	4,199	2,068	1,850	218	2,131	1,882	249	89.5	88.3	10.6	11.7
35 to 44 years	4,068	1,975	1,795	180	2,093	1,926	166	90.9	92.0	9.1	8.0

[Continued]

★ 464 ★

Civilian Labor Force: Employment Status and Characteristics: 1994
[Continued]

AGE AND RACE	TOTAL (1,000)	MALE (1,000)			FEMALE (1,000)			PERCENT OF LABOR FORCE			
								Employed		Unemployed	
		Total	Employed	Unemployed	Total	Employed	Unemployed	Male	Female	Male	Female
45 to 54 years	2,308	1,102	1,030	72	1,206	1,147	59	93.5	95.1	6.5	4.9
55 to 64 years	1,007	484	455	29	523	497	26	94.0	95.1	6.0	4.9
65 years and over	267	125	115	10	142	136	6	91.8	95.6	8.2	4.4
Hispanic[2]	11,975	7,210	6,530	680	4,765	4,258	508	90.6	89.3	9.4	10.7
16 to 19 years	807	463	341	121	345	268	77	73.7	77.8	26.3	22.2
20 to 24 years	1,863	1,184	1,056	128	679	587	92	89.2	86.5	10.8	13.5
25 to 34 years	3,865	2,430	2,227	203	1,435	1,290	145	91.6	89.9	8.4	10.1
35 to 44 years	2,965	1,713	1,600	113	1,252	1,137	115	93.4	89.8	6.6	9.2
45 to 54 years	1,626	922	847	75	704	648	57	91.9	92.0	8.1	8.0
55 to 64 years	698	410	379	30	288	268	21	92.6	92.9	7.4	7.1
65 years and over	151	89	79	9	62	59	2	89.5	96.4	10.5	3.6

Source: "Civilian Labor Force—Employment Status, by Sex, Race, and Age: 1994," *Statistical Abstract of the United States,* 1995, p. 407. Primary source: U.S. Bureau of Labor Statistics, *Employment and Earnings,* monthly, January 1995. *Notes:* 1. Includes other races not shown separately. 2. Persons of Hispanic origin may be of any race.

★ 465 ★
Labor Force

Civilian Labor Force: Employment Status of the Population by Race, Gender, and Age, Seasonally Adjusted. Part 1-1

[Numbers in thousands].

Employment status, race, sex, age, and Hispanic origin	1994		1995				
	Nov.	Dec.	Jan.	Feb.	Mar.	Apr.	May
WHITE							
Civilian noninstitutional population[1]	166,072	166,175	166,361	166,444	166,521	166,613	166,708
Civilian labor force	111,637	111,715	111,876	111,830	111,999	112,153	111,568
Percent of population	67.2	67.2	67.2	67.2	67.3	67.3	66.9
Employed	106,242	106,352	106,366	106,604	106,698	106,500	105,935
Employment-population ratio	64.0	64.0	63.9	64.0	64.1	63.9	63.5
Unemployed	5,395	5,363	5,510	5,226	5,301	5,653	5,633
Unemployment rate	4.8	4.8	4.9	4.7	4.7	5.0	5.0
BLACK							
Civilian noninstitutional population[1]	23,023	23,052	23,089	23,117	23,142	23,169	23,192
Civilian labor force	14,578	14,541	14,697	14,868	14,818	14,938	14,803
Percent of population	63.3	63.1	63.7	64.3	64.0	64.5	63.8
Employed	13,054	13,119	13,192	13,362	13,370	13,337	13,336
Employment-population ratio	56.7	56.9	57.1	57.8	57.8	57.6	57.5
Unemployed	1,524	1,422	1,505	1,505	1,448	1,601	1,467
Unemployment rate	10.5	9.8	10.2	10.1	9.8	10.7	9.9

[Continued]

★ 465 ★

Civilian Labor Force: Employment Status of the Population by Race, Gender, and Age, Seasonally Adjusted. Part 1-1

[Continued]

Employment status, race, sex, age, and Hispanic origin	1994		1995				
	Nov.	Dec.	Jan.	Feb.	Mar.	Apr.	May
HISPANIC ORIGIN							
Civilian noninstitutional population[1]	18,339	18,385	18,368	18,413	18,458	18,509	18,554
Civilian labor force	12,324	12,224	12,036	12,017	12,001	12,131	12,111
Percent of population	67.2	66.5	65.5	65.3	65.0	65.5	65.3
Employed	11,236	11,105	10,811	10,943	10,903	11,058	10,895
Employment-population ratio	61.3	60.4	58.9	59.4	59.1	59.7	58.7
Unemployed	1,088	1,119	1,224	1,073	1,098	1,073	1,216
Unemployment rate	8.8	9.2	10.2	8.9	9.1	8.8	10.0

Source: "Employment Status of the Civilian Noninstitutional Population by Race, Sex, and Age, and Hispanic Origin, Seasonally Adjusted," *Employment and Earnings,* December 1995, pp. 19-20. *Notes:* Detail for the above race and Hispanic groups will not sum to totals because data for the "other races" group are not presented and Hispanics are included in both the white and black population groups. 1. The population figures are not adjusted for seasonal variation.

★ 466 ★

Labor Force

Civilian Labor Force: Employment Status of the Population by Race, Gender, and Age, Seasonally Adjusted. Part 1-2

[Numbers in thousands].

Employment status, race, sex, age, and Hispanic origin	1995					
	June	July	Aug.	Sept.	Oct.	Nov.
WHITE						
Civilian noninstitutional population[1]	166,822	166,931	167,058	167,200	167,327	167,441
Civilian labor force	111,541	112,197	111,971	112,247	112,232	111,978
Percent of population	66.9	67.2	67.0	67.1	67.1	66.9
Employed	106,145	106,770	106,567	106,851	106,815	106,331
Employment-population ratio	63.7	64.0	63.8	63.9	63.8	63.5
Unemployed	5,396	5,427	5,404	5,396	5,417	5,648
Unemployment rate	4.8	4.8	4.8	4.8	4.8	5.0
BLACK						
Civilian noninstitutional population[1]	23,221	23,249	23,284	23,323	23,357	23,389
Civilian labor force	14,707	14,656	14,715	14,823	14,883	15,071
Percent of population	63.3	63.0	63.2	63.6	63.7	64.4
Employed	13,142	13,033	13,049	13,147	13,413	13,662
Employment-population ratio	56.6	56.1	56.0	56.4	57.4	58.4
Unemployed	1,565	1,623	1,666	1,676	1,470	1,409
Unemployment rate	10.6	11.1	11.3	11.3	9.9	9.4

[Continued]

★ 466 ★

Civilian Labor Force: Employment Status of the Population by Race, Gender, and Age, Seasonally Adjusted. Part 1-2

[Continued]

Employment status, race, sex, age, and Hispanic origin	1995					
	June	July	Aug.	Sept.	Oct.	Nov.
HISPANIC ORIGIN						
Civilian noninstitutional population[1]	18,604	18,653	18,702	18,752	18,800	18,845
Civilian labor force	12,229	12,323	12,383	12,456	12,504	12,437
Percent of population	65.7	66.1	66.2	66.4	66.5	66.0
Employed	11,131	11,235	11,158	11,351	11,333	11,269
Employment-population ratio	59.8	60.2	59.7	60.5	60.3	59.8
Unemployed	1,098	1,088	1,225	1,105	1,171	1,168
Unemployment rate	9.0	8.8	9.9	8.9	9.4	9.4

Source: "Employment Status of the Civilian Noninstitutional Population by Race, Sex, and Age, and Hispanic Origin, Seasonally Adjusted," *Employment and Earnings,* December 1995, pp. 19-20. *Notes:* Detail for the above race and Hispanic groups will not sum to totals because data for the "other races" group are not presented and Hispanics are included in both the white and black population groups. 1. The population figures are not adjusted for seasonal variation.

★ 467 ★

Labor Force

Civilian Labor Force: Employment Status of the Population by Race, Gender, and Age, Seasonally Adjusted. Part 2-1

[Numbers in thousands].

Employment status, race, sex, age, and Hispanic origin	1994		1995				
	Nov.	Dec.	Jan.	Feb.	Mar.	Apr.	May
WHITE							
Men, 20 years and over							
Civilian labor force	57,726	57,836	57,848	57,841	57,868	57,768	57,594
Percent of population	77.4	77.5	77.5	77.5	77.5	77.3	77.0
Employed	55,242	55,384	55,289	55,508	55,448	55,225	54,956
Employment-population ratio	74.1	74.2	74.1	74.3	74.2	73.9	73.5
Unemployed	2,484	2,452	2,559	2,333	2,420	2,544	2,638
Unemployment rate	4.3	4.2	4.4	4.0	4.2	4.4	4.6
Women, 20 years and over							
Civilian labor force	47,631	47,440	47,443	47,525	47,494	47,765	47,432
Percent of population	59.4	59.1	59.0	59.1	59.1	59.4	58.9
Employed	45,569	45,475	45,419	45,581	45,515	45,622	45,403
Employment-population ratio	56.8	56.7	56.5	56.7	56.6	56.7	56.4
Unemployed	2,062	1,965	2,024	1,944	1,978	2,143	2,028
Unemployment rate	4.3	4.1	4.3	4.1	4.2	4.5	4.3

[Continued]

★ 467 ★

Civilian Labor Force: Employment Status of the Population by Race, Gender, and Age, Seasonally Adjusted. Part 2-1

[Continued]

Employment status, race, sex, age, and Hispanic origin	1994		1995				
	Nov.	Dec.	Jan.	Feb.	Mar.	Apr.	May
BLACK							
Men, 20 years and over							
Civilian labor force	6,702	6,722	6,796	6,812	6,828	6,826	6,749
Percent of population	72.6	72.7	73.6	73.7	73.8	73.7	73.0
Employed	6,085	6,165	6,172	6,272	6,297	6,221	6,158
Employment-population ratio	65.9	66.7	66.8	67.8	68.0	67.1	66.6
Unemployed	617	557	624	540	531	605	591
Unemployment rate	9.2	8.3	9.2	7.9	7.8	8.9	8.8
Women, 20 years and over							
Civilian labor force	7,012	7,002	7,127	7,169	7,131	7,205	7,153
Percent of population	60.7	60.5	61.4	61.7	61.3	61.9	61.4
Employed	6,390	6,420	6,521	6,520	6,482	6,532	6,593
Employment-population ratio	55.3	55.5	56.2	56.1	55.7	56.1	56.6
Unemployed	622	582	606	648	649	673	559
Unemployment rate	8.9	8.3	8.5	9.0	9.1	9.3	7.8

Source: "Employment Status of the Civilian Noninstitutional Population by Race, Sex, Age, and Hispanic Origin, Seasonally Adjusted," *Employment and Earnings,* December 1995, pp. 19.

★ 468 ★

Labor Force

Civilian Labor Force: Employment Status of the Population by Race, Gender, and Age, Seasonally Adjusted. Part 2-2

[Numbers in thousands].

Employment status, race, sex, age, and Hispanic origin	1995					
	June	July	Aug.	Sept.	Oct.	Nov.
WHITE						
Men, 20 years and over						
Civilian labor force	57,592	57,618	57,559	57,790	57,707	57,673
Percent of population	77.0	76.9	76.8	77.0	76.9	76.8
Employed	55,133	55,263	55,126	55,318	55,395	55,086
Employment-population ratio	73.7	73.8	73.6	73.8	73.8	73.3
Unemployed	2,459	2,355	2,433	2,472	2,312	2,587
Unemployment rate	4.3	4.1	4.2	4.3	4.0	4.5

[Continued]

★ 468 ★

Civilian Labor Force: Employment Status of the Population by Race, Gender, and Age, Seasonally Adjusted. Part 2-2
[Continued]

Employment status, race, sex, age, and Hispanic origin	1995					
	June	July	Aug.	Sept.	Oct.	Nov.
Women, 20 years and over						
Civilian labor force	47,275	47,965	47,881	47,958	48,003	47,821
Percent of population	58.7	59.5	59.4	59.4	59.5	59.2
Employed	45,215	45,873	45,824	45,988	45,871	45,792
Employment-population ratio	56.1	56.9	56.8	57.0	56.8	56.7
Unemployed	2,060	2,092	2,057	1,970	2,131	2,030
Unemployment rate	4.4	4.4	4.3	4.1	4.4	4.2
BLACK						
Men, 20 years and over						
Civilian labor force	6,721	6,666	6,666	6,729	6,688	6,663
Percent of population	72.5	71.7	71.6	72.4	71.8	71.8
Employed	6,117	6,059	6,039	6,083	6,158	6,118
Employment-population ratio	66.0	65.2	64.9	65.4	66.1	66.0
Unemployed	604	607	627	646	530	544
Unemployment rate	9.0	9.1	9.4	9.6	7.9	8.2
Women, 20 years and over						
Civilian labor force	7,067	7,085	7,105	7,116	7,284	7,414
Percent of population	60.6	60.6	60.7	60.7	62.1	63.1
Employed	6,453	6,422	6,468	6,442	6,645	6,857
Employment-population ratio	55.3	55.0	55.3	55.0	56.6	58.4
Unemployed	614	663	636	674	638	558
Unemployment rate	8.7	9.4	9.0	9.5	8.8	7.5

Source: "Employment Status of the Civilian Noninstitutional Population by Race, Sex, Age, and Hispanic Origin, Seasonally Adjusted," *Employment and Earnings*, December 1995, pp. 19.

★ 469 ★

Labor Force

Civilian Labor Force: Employment Status of the Population by Race, Gender, and Age, Seasonally Adjusted. Part 3-1

[Numbers in thousands].

Employment status, race, sex, age, and Hispanic origin	1994		1995				
	Nov.	Dec.	Jan.	Feb.	Mar.	Apr.	May
WHITE							
Both sexes, 16 to 19 years							
Civilian labor force	6,280	6,439	6,586	6,464	6,637	6,619	6,542
Percent of population	55.5	56.9	58.1	56.9	58.3	58.0	57.2
Employed	5,431	5,493	5,658	5,515	5,734	5,653	5,575
Employment-population ratio	48.0	48.5	49.9	48.5	50.4	49.5	48.8
Unemployed	849	946	928	949	903	966	967
Unemployment rate	13.5	14.7	14.1	14.7	13.6	14.6	14.8
Men	14.3	16.0	15.0	16.1	14.7	15.3	15.2
Women	12.6	13.2	13.1	13.1	12.4	13.8	14.3
BLACK							
Both sexes, 16 to 19 years							
Civilian labor force	864	817	773	887	859	907	901
Percent of population	38.8	36.6	34.6	39.5	38.2	40.2	39.4
Employed	579	534	499	570	591	584	585
Employment-population ratio	26.0	23.9	22.3	25.4	26.3	25.9	25.6
Unemployed	285	283	275	317	268	323	317
Unemployment rate	33.0	34.6	35.5	35.7	31.2	35.6	35.1
Men	32.0	34.3	34.0	38.7	31.7	35.4	40.0
Women	34.1	35.0	37.1	32.4	30.7	35.8	30.5

Source: "Employment Status of the Civilian Noninstitutional Population by Race, Sex, Age, and Hispanic Origin, Seasonally Adjusted," *Employment and Earnings*, December 1995, pp. 19-20.

★ 470 ★

Labor Force

Civilian Labor Force: Employment Status of the Population by Race, Gender, and Age, Seasonally Adjusted. Part 3-2

[Numbers in thousands].

Employment status, race, sex, age, and Hispanic origin	1995					
	June	July	Aug.	Sept.	Oct.	Nov.
WHITE						
Both sexes, 16 to 19 years						
Civilian labor force	6,674	6,614	6,532	6,499	6,522	6,484
Percent of population	58.3	57.6	56.8	56.4	56.5	56.0
Employed	5,797	5,634	5,617	5,544	5,549	5,453
Employment-population ratio	50.6	49.1	48.8	48.1	48.0	47.1
Unemployed	877	980	914	955	973	1,031
Unemployment rate	13.1	14.8	14.0	14.7	14.9	15.9
Men	14.5	14.6	15.7	16.0	17.6	16.8
Women	11.6	15.0	12.1	13.3	12.0	15.0
BLACK						
Both sexes, 16 to 19 years						
Civilian labor force	918	905	945	978	911	994
Percent of population	40.4	39.8	41.5	42.4	39.4	42.0
Employed	571	552	542	622	610	687
Employment-population ratio	25.1	24.3	23.8	27.0	26.4	29.0
Unemployed	347	353	403	356	301	307
Unemployment rate	37.8	39.0	42.6	36.4	33.1	30.9
Men	38.7	41.6	46.3	32.7	33.6	32.0
Women	36.8	36.3	38.9	39.7	32.6	29.8

Source: "Employment Status of the Civilian Noninstitutional Population by Race, Sex, Age, and Hispanic Origin, Seasonally Adjusted," *Employment and Earnings,* December 1995, pp. 19-20.

★ 471 ★

Labor Force

Civilian Labor Force: Employment Status of the Population: 1960-1994

[**In thousands, except as indicated.** Annual averages of monthly figures. For the civilian noninstitutional population 16 years old and over. Based on Current Population Survey; see text, section 1, and Appendix III. See also *Historical Statistics, Colonial Times to 1970,* series D 11-19 and D 85-86.]

YEAR, SEX, RACE, AND HISPANIC ORIGIN	Civilian noninstitutional population	CIVILIAN LABOR FORCE						NOT IN LABOR FORCE	
		Total	Percent of population	Employed	Employment/ population ratio[1]	Unemployed		Number	Percent of population
						Number	Percent of labor force		
Total:[2]									
1960	117,245	69,628	59.4	65,778	56.1	3,852	5.5	47,617	40.6
1970	137,085	82,771	60.4	78,678	57.4	4,093	4.9	54,315	39.6
1980	167,745	106,940	63.8	99,303	59.2	7,637	7.1	60,806	36.2
1985	178,206	115,461	64.8	107,150	60.1	8,312	7.2	62,744	35.2
1990	188,049	124,787	66.4	117,914	62.7	6,874	5.5	63,262	33.6
1991	189,765	125,303	66.0	116,877	61.6	8,426	6.7	64,462	34.0
1992	191,576	126,982	66.3	117,598	61.4	9,384	7.4	64,593	33.7
1993	193,550	128,040	66.2	119,306	61.6	8,734	6.8	65,509	33.8
1994[3]	196,814	131,056	66.6	123,060	62.5	7,996	6.1	65,758	33.4
White:									
1960	105,282	61,915	58.8	58,850	55.9	3,065	5.0	43,367	41.2
1970	122,174	73,556	60.2	70,217	57.5	3,339	4.5	48,618	39.8
1980	146,122	93,600	64.1	87,715	60.0	5,884	6.3	52,523	35.9
1985	153,679	99,926	65.0	93,736	61.0	6,191	6.2	53,753	35.0
1990	160,415	107,177	66.8	102,087	63.6	5,091	4.7	53,237	33.2
1991	161,511	107,486	66.6	101,039	62.6	6,447	6.0	54,025	33.4
1992	162,658	108,526	66.7	101,479	62.4	7,047	6.5	54,132	33.3
1993	163,921	109,359	66.7	102,812	62.7	6,547	6.0	54,562	33.3
1994[3]	165,555	111,082	67.1	105,190	63.5	5,892	5.3	54,473	32.9
Black:									
1973	14,917	8,976	60.2	8,128	54.5	846	9.4	5,941	39.8
1980	17,824	10,865	61.0	9,313	52.2	1,553	14.3	6,959	39.0
1985	19,664	12,364	62.9	10,501	53.4	1,864	15.1	7,299	37.1
1990	21,300	13,493	63.3	11,966	56.2	1,527	11.3	7,808	36.7
1991	21,615	13,542	62.6	11,863	54.9	1,679	12.4	8,074	37.4
1992	21,958	13,891	63.3	11,933	54.3	1,958	14.1	8,067	36.7
1993	22,329	13,943	62.4	12,146	54.4	1,796	12.9	8,386	37.6
1994[3]	22,879	14,502	63.4	12,835	56.1	1,666	11.5	8,377	36.6
Hispanic:[4]									
1980	9,598	6,146	64.0	5,527	57.6	620	10.1	3,451	36.0
1985	11,915	7,698	64.6	6,888	57.8	811	10.5	4,217	35.4
1990	14,297	9,576	67.0	8,808	61.6	769	8.0	4,721	33.0
1991	14,770	9,762	66.1	8,799	59.6	963	9.9	5,008	33.9
1992	15,244	10,341	66.5	8,971	58.9	1,160	11.4	5,113	33.5
1993	15,753	10,377	65.9	9,272	58.9	1,104	10.6	5,377	34.1
1994[3]	18,117	11,975	66.1	10,788	59.5	1,187	9.9	6,142	33.9
Mexican:									
1986	7,377	4,941	67.0	4,387	59.5	555	11.2	2,436	33.0
1990	8,742	5,970	68.3	5,478	62.7	492	8.2	2,773	31.7
1992	9,368	6,319	67.5	5,581	59.6	739	11.7	3,049	32.5
1993	9,693	6,499	67.0	5,805	59.9	693	10.7	3,194	33.0
1994[3]	11,174	7,567	67.7	6,800	60.9	766	10.1	3,608	32.3

[Continued]

★ 471 ★

Civilian Labor Force: Employment Status of the Population: 1960-1994

[Continued]

YEAR, SEX, RACE, AND HISPANIC ORIGIN	Civilian noninsti-tutional population	CIVILIAN LABOR FORCE						NOT IN LABOR FORCE	
		Total	Percent of population	Employed	Employment/ population ratio[1]	Unemployed		Number	Percent of population
						Number	Percent of labor force		
Puerto Rican:									
1986	1,494	804	53.8	691	46.3	113	14.0	690	46.2
1990	1,546	859	55.6	780	50.5	79	9.1	687	44.4
1992	1,628	934	57.4	802	49.2	132	14.1	694	42.6
1993	1,676	950	56.7	828	49.4	122	12.8	725	43.3
1994[3]	1,854	1,026	55.4	907	48.9	119	11.6	828	44.6
Cuban:									
1986	842	570	67.7	533	63.3	36	6.4	272	32.3
1990	847	552	65.1	512	60.4	40	7.2	295	34.8
1992	867	529	61.1	488	56.3	42	7.9	337	38.9
1993	927	554	59.8	511	55.1	43	7.8	373	40.2
1994[3]	1,002	604	60.3	555	55.4	49	8.1	398	39.7

Source: "Employment Status of the Civilian Population: 1960 to 1994," *Statistical Abstract of the United States,* 1995, p. 400. Primary source: U.S. Bureau of Labor Statistics, Bulletin 2307; and *Employment and Earnings,* monthly, January issues. *Notes:* 1. Civilian employed as a percent of the civilian noninstitutional population. 2. Includes other races, not shown separately. 3. Data beginning 1994 not directly comparable with earlier years. See text, section 13, and February 1994 issue of Employment and Earnings. 4. Persons of Hispanic origin may be of any race. Includes persons of other Hispanic origin, not shown separately.

★ 472 ★

Labor Force

Civilians: School Enrollment and Labor Force: 1980 and 1993

[**In thousands, except percent. As of October.** For the civilian noninstitutional population 16 to 24 years old. Based on Current Population Survey; see text, section 1, and Appendix III.]

CHARACTERISTIC	POPULATION		CIVILIAN LABOR FORCE			EMPLOYED		UNEMPLOYED		
	1980	1993	1980, total	1993		1980	1993	1980, total	1993	
				Total	Percent[1]				Total	Rate[2]
Total, 16 to 24 years[3]	37,103	30,844	24,918	19,899	64.5	21,454	17,464	3,464	2,435	12.2
Race:										
White	13,242	12,689	6,687	6,696	52.8	5,889	5,941	798	755	11.3
Below college	6,566	5,830	3,095	2,511	43.1	2,579	2,053	516	458	18.3
College level	6,678	6,859	3,592	4,185	61.0	3,310	3,888	282	296	7.1
Black	2,028	2,195	595	686	31.3	406	469	189	217	31.7
Below college	1,282	1,323	294	288	21.8	174	167	120	121	41.9
College level	747	872	300	398	45.6	230	301	70	97	24.3
Not enrolled[3]	21,390	15,054	17,464	12,207	81.1	15,021	10,787	2,443	1,420	11.6
White	18,103	12,122	15,121	10,153	83.8	13,318	9,117	1,803	1,037	10.2
Black	2,864	2,401	2,055	1,675	69.7	1,451	1,331	604	344	20.5

Source: "School enrollment and Labor Force Status: 1980 and 1993," *Statistical Abstract of the United States,* 1995, p. 404. Primary source: U.S. Bureau of Labor Statistics, Bulletin 2307; *News,* USDL 94-252, May 20, 1994; and unpublished data. *Notes:* 1. Percent of civilian population. 2. Percent of civilian labor force in each category. 3. Includes other races, not shown separately.

★ 473 ★

Labor Force

Families Employed: Married-Couple Families in the Labor Force. Part 1-1

[Numbers in thousands except for averages and medians. For meaning of symbols, see text.]

Characteristic	All married-couple families	In labor force husband and wife				
		Total	Both employed	Only husband employed	Only wife employed	Both unemployed
BLACK MARRIED-COUPLE FAMILIES						
Metropolitan-Nonmetropolitan Residence						
Total	3,714	2,083	1,831	109	115	28
In MSA's	3,143	1,802	1,572	100	103	27
Central cities	1,773	927	805	47	61	13
Ring	1,369	875	767	53	42	13
MSA's of 2,500,000 or more	1,378	804	708	36	48	12
Central cities	779	401	355	13	26	6
Ring	599	403	353	22	22	6
MSA's of 1,000,000 to 2,499,999	723	418	360	30	24	5
Central cities	374	186	157	14	15	-
Ring	349	232	203	16	9	5
MSA's of 250,000 to 999,999	729	412	368	20	18	5
Central cities	418	233	204	11	15	3
Ring	311	180	165	9	3	3
MSA's of 249,999 or less	313	167	136	14	13	4
Central cities	203	107	89	9	6	4
Ring	111	60	47	6	7	-
Not in MSA's	571	281	259	9	12	1
Size of Family						
Total	3,714	2,083	1,831	109	115	28
Two persons	1,088	443	393	16	31	3
Three persons	882	535	472	36	20	7
Four persons	957	644	562	33	40	9
Five persons	439	290	264	14	12	-
Six persons	209	99	75	5	10	9
Seven or more persons	139	72	65	5	1	1
Total persons	13,645	7,881	6,900	432	433	117
Average per family	3.67	3.78	3.77	3.96	3.77	(B)
Own Children Under 18						
Total	3,714	2,083	1,831	109	115	28
Without own children under 18	1,790	752	672	36	39	5
With own children under 18	1,924	1,331	1,159	74	76	23
One own child under 18	771	545	482	33	26	4
Two own children under 18	696	503	435	24	34	10

[Continued]

★ 473 ★

Families Employed: Married-Couple Families in the Labor Force. Part 1-1

[Continued]

Characteristic	All married-couple families	In labor force husband and wife				
		Total	Both employed	Only husband employed	Only wife employed	Both unemployed
Three own children under 18	309	219	194	11	11	3
Four own children under 18	110	47	36	1	4	5
Five own children under 18	23	10	10	-	-	-
Six or more own children under 18	16	6	3	3	-	-
Total own children under 18	3,602	2,398	2,058	142	149	49
Average per family	97	1.15	1.12	1.30	1.30	(B)
Average per family with children	1.87	1.80	1.78	(B)	1.96	(B)

Source: "Married-Couple Families, by Labor Force Status of Husband and Wife and Race and Hispanic Origin of Householder: March 1994," Steve W. Rawlings and Arlene F. Saluter, *Household and Family Characteristics: March 1995*, p. 135. *Note:* B = Base less than 75,000.

★ 474 ★

Labor Force

Families Employed: Married-Couple Families in the Labor Force. Part 1-2

[Numbers in thousands except for averages and medians. For meaning of symbols, see text.]

Characteristic	In labor force						Husband and wife not in labor force
	Husband only			Wife only			
	Total	Employed	Unemployed	Total	Employed	Unemployed	
BLACK MARRIED-COUPLE FAMILIES							
Metropolitan-Nonmetropolitan Residence							
Total	650	620	31	357	326	31	623
In MSA's	561	537	23	284	262	22	497
Central cities	337	316	20	167	163	4	343
Ring	224	221	3	117	99	18	154
MSA's of 2,500,000 or more	227	217	10	141	126	14	206
Central cities	151	140	10	85	83	2	143
Ring	76	76	-	56	44	12	64
MSA's of 1,000,000 to 2,499,999	143	140	3	59	56	3	102
Central cities	67	67	-	38	38	-	84
Ring	77	74	3	21	18	3	19
MSA's of 250,000 to 999,999	120	112	8	69	65	4	128
Central cities	72	64	8	35	33	1	79
Ring	48	48	-	34	31	3	50

[Continued]

★ 474 ★

Families Employed: Married-Couple Families in the Labor Force. Part 1-2
[Continued]

Characteristic	In labor force						Husband and wife not in labor force
	Husband only			Wife only			
	Total	Employed	Unemployed	Total	Employed	Unemployed	
MSA's of 249,999 or less	71	68	2	16	15	-	60
Central cities	47	45	2	10	9	-	38
Ring	23	23	-	6	6	-	22
Not in MSA's	90	82	7	73	65	9	127
Size of Family							
Total	650	620	31	357	326	31	623
Two persons	156	151	5	132	129	4	357
Three persons	147	145	1	85	81	4	115
Four persons	174	162	12	68	55	13	72
Five persons	81	78	2	28	25	2	41
Six persons	62	56	6	27	25	2	21
Seven or more persons	31	27	4	18	11	7	18
Total persons	2,521	2,377	144	1,306	1,159	147	1,937
Average per family	3.88	3.84	(B)	3.66	3.55	(B)	3.11
Own Children Under 18							
Total	650	620	31	357	326	31	623
Without own children under 18	259	251	9	238	230	8	541
With own children under 18	391	369	22	119	97	22	82
One own child under 18	145	137	7	58	55	3	23
Two own children under 18	125	119	6	39	24	15	28
Three own children under 18	64	64	-	16	14	3	9
Four own children under 18	43	38	5	6	4	2	14
Five own children under 18	10	5	4	-	-	-	3
Six or more own children under 18	5	5	-	-	-	-	4
Total own children under 18	810	754	57	195	147	48	199
Average per family	1.25	1.22	(B)	.55	.45	(B)	.32
Average per family with children	2.07	2.04	(B)	1.63	1.52	(B)	2.42

Source: "Married-Couple Families, by Labor Force Status of Husband and Wife and Race and Hispanic Origin of Householder: March 1994," Steve W. Rawlings and Arlene F. Saluter, *Household and Family Characteristics: March 1995*, p. 135. *Note:* B = Base less than 75,000.

★ 475 ★

Labor Force

Families Employed: Married-Couple Families in the Labor Force. Part 2-1

[Numbers in thousands except for averages and medians. For meaning of symbols, see text.]

Characteristic	All married-couple families	In labor force husband and wife				
		Total	Both employed	Only husband employed	Only wife employed	Both unemployed
BLACK MARRIED-COUPLE FAMILIES-Con.						
Own Children, Selected Ages						
Total with own children under 18	1,924	1,331	1,159	74	76	23
Under 6 only	409	273	222	21	26	4
Some under 6 and some 6 to 17	464	292	250	12	16	14
Six to 17 only	1,050	766	687	41	33	5
Total family members	8,379	5,665	4,906	326	330	103
Average per family	4.36	4.26	4.23	(B)	4.35	(B)
Stepchildren Under 18						
Families	3,714	2,083	1,831	109	115	28
Without stepchildren under 18	3,714	2,083	1,831	109	115	28
With stepchildren under 18	-	-	-	-	-	-
Total stepchildren under 18	-	-	-	-	-	-
Average per family	-	-	-	-	-	(B)
Average per family with stepchildren	(B)	(B)	(B)	(B)	(B)	(B)
Age of Householder						
Total	3,714	2,083	1,831	109	115	28
15 to 19 years	1	1	-	-	1	-
20 to 24 years	117	68	58	10	-	-
25 to 29 years	317	208	176	12	13	7
30 to 34 years	433	333	286	22	18	6
35 to 39 years	465	337	298	9	30	1
40 to 44 years	520	406	337	27	28	14
45 to 49 years	427	296	273	12	10	-
50 to 54 years	356	225	213	6	6	-
55 to 59 years	284	124	113	7	4	-
60 to 64 years	233	57	50	1	5	-
65 to 74 years	374	22	20	2	-	-
75 to 84 years	172	6	6	-	-	-
85 years and over	14	-	-	-	-	-
Median	45.0	41.2	41.4	40.3	39.2	(B)
Family Income						
Total	3,714	2,083	1,831	109	115	28
Under $5,000	107	17	3	2	-	13
$5,000 to $9,999	214	36	15	6	7	8
$10,000 to $14,999	254	47	24	9	15	-

[Continued]

★ 475 ★

Families Employed: Married-Couple Families in the Labor Force. Part 2-1
[Continued]

Characteristic	All married-couple families	In labor force husband and wife				
		Total	Both employed	Only husband employed	Only wife employed	Both unemployed
$15,000 to $19,999	301	85	57	6	20	3
$20,000 to $24,999	350	120	88	16	15	-
$25,000 to $29,999	287	167	142	17	7	1
$30,000 to $39,999	568	324	291	19	13	-
$40,000 to $49,999	446	310	289	10	8	3
$50,000 to $74,999	706	572	532	12	26	1
$75,000 and over	482	404	389	10	4	-
Median (dollars)	35,264	47,857	50,195	29,175	25,741	(B)
Below poverty level	458	103	43	14	25	21

Source: "Married-Couple Families, by Labor Force Status of Husband and Wife and Race and Hispanic Origin of Householder: March 1994," Steve W. Rawlings and Arlene F. Saluter, *Household and Family Characteristics: March 1995*, p. 136. *Note:* B = Base less than 75,000.

★ 476 ★
Labor Force

Families Employed: Married-Couple Families in the Labor Force. Part 2-2

[Numbers in thousands except for averages and medians. For meaning of symbols, see text.]

Characteristic	In labor force						Husband and wife not in labor force
	Husband only			Wife only			
	Total	Employed	Unemployed	Total	Employed	Unemployed	
BLACK MARRIED-COUPLE FAMILIES-Con.							
Own Children, Selected Ages							
Total with own children under 18	391	369	22	119	97	22	82
Under 6 only	95	90	5	31	25	6	9
Some under 6 and some 6 to 17	125	116	9	23	17	6	24
Six to 17 only	171	163	8	65	55	10	49
Total family members	1,766	1,650	115	538	421	117	410
Average per family	4.52	4.48	(B)	4.51	4.34	(B)	4.99
Stepchildren Under 18							
Families	650	620	31	357	326	31	623
Without stepchildren under 18	650	620	31	357	326	31	623
With stepchildren under 18							
Total stepchildren under 18	-	-	-	-	-	-	-
Average per family	-	-	(B)	-	-	(B)	-

[Continued]

★ 476 ★

Families Employed: Married-Couple Families in the Labor Force. Part 2-2
[Continued]

Characteristic	In labor force						Husband and wife not in labor force
	Husband only			Wife only			
	Total	Employed	Unemployed	Total	Employed	Unemployed	
Average per family with stepchildren	(B)	(B)	(B)	(B)	(B)	(B)	(B)
Age of Householder							
Total	650	620	31	357	326	31	623
15 to 19 years	-	-	-	-	-	-	-
20 to 24 years	36	36	-	9	5	4	5
25 to 29 years	63	56	7	31	25	6	15
30 to 34 years	80	76	4	16	14	2	3
35 to 39 years	89	86	3	18	16	3	21
40 to 44 years	72	72	-	31	25	6	12
45 to 49 years	69	63	6	33	32	-	29
50 to 54 years	83	78	4	37	31	6	12
55 to 59 years	61	58	3	41	38	3	58
60 to 64 years	45	41	4	61	60	1	71
65 to 74 years	46	46	-	63	63	-	243
75 to 84 years	8	8	-	18	18	-	140
85 years and over	-	-	-	-	-	-	14
Median	44.0	43.9	(B)	55.5	57.0	(B)	68.5
Family Income							
Total	650	620	31	357	326	31	623
Under $5,000	11	7	4	12	9	3	67
$5,000 to $9,999	37	30	7	22	19	3	119
$10,000 to $14,999	47	47	-	45	40	5	115
$15,000 to $19,999	78	70	8	42	42	-	96
$20,000 to $24,999	98	98	-	53	45	8	79
$25,000 to $29,999	55	54	2	28	24	5	37
$30,000 to $39,999	115	114	1	67	61	6	62
$40,000 to $49,999	82	76	6	31	29	2	22
$50,000 to $74,999	78	76	2	32	32	-	25
$75,000 and over	49	48	1	26	26	-	3
Median (dollars)	30,002	30,272	(B)	25,876	26,663	(B)	15,568
Below poverty level	84	70	13	50	41	9	222

Source: "Married-Couple Families, by Labor Force Status of Husband and Wife and Race and Hispanic Origin of Householder: March 1994," Steve W. Rawlings and Arlene F. Saluter, *Household and Family Characteristics: March 1995*, p. 136. *Note:* B = Base less than 75,000.

★ 477 ★

Labor Force

Labor Force Participation: Wives with Husbands Present: 1975-1994

PRESENCE AND AGE OF CHILD	TOTAL			WHITE			BLACK		
	1975	1985	1994[1]	1975	1985	1994[1]	1975	1985	1994[1]
Wives, total	44.4	54.2	60.6	43.6	53.3	60.3	54.1	63.8	65.6
No children under 18	43.8	48.2	53.2	43.6	47.5	53.0	47.6	55.2	55.6
With children under 18	44.9	60.8	69.0	43.6	59.9	68.7	58.4	71.7	75.2
Under 6, total	36.7	53.4	61.7	34.7	52.1	61.2	54.9	69.6	70.6
Under 3	32.7	50.5	59.7	30.7	49.4	59.3	50.1	66.2	68.3
1 year or under	30.8	49.4	58.8	29.2	48.6	58.8	50.0	63.7	64.2
2 years	37.1	54.0	64.5	35.1	52.7	63.2	56.4	69.9	80.5
3 to 5 years	42.2	58.4	64.6	40.1	56.6	63.9	61.2	73.8	74.0
3 years	41.2	55.1	62.9	39.0	52.7	61.7	62.7	72.3	74.8
4 years	41.2	59.7	63.9	38.7	58.4	62.4	64.9	70.6	77.7
5 years	44.4	62.1	67.1	43.8	59.9	67.5	56.3	79.1	70.5
6 to 13 years	51.8	68.2	75.5	50.7	67.7	75.3	65.7	73.3	81.2
14 to 17 years	53.5	67.0	77.2	53.4	66.6	77.8	52.3	74.4	73.7

Source: "Labor Force Participation Rates for Wives, Husband Present, by Age of Own Youngest Child: 1975 to 1994," *Statistical Abstract of the United States,* 1995, p. 406. U.S. Bureau of Labor Statistics, Bulletin 2340; and unpublished data. *Note:* 1. Widowed, divorced, or separated.

★ 478 ★

Labor Force

Multiple Jobholders: Characteristics by Gender: 1994

[**Annual average of monthly figures.** For the civilian noninstitutional population 16 years old and over. Multiple jobholders are employed persons who, either 1) had jobs as wage or salary workers with two employers or more; 2) were self-employed and also held a wage and salary job; or 3) were unpaid family workers on their primary jobs but also held wage and salary job. Based on the Current Population Survey; see text, section 1, and Appendix III.]

CHARACTERISTIC	TOTAL		MALE		FEMALE	
	Number (1,000)	Percent of employed	Number (1,000)	Percent of employed	Number (1,000)	Percent of employed
Total[1]	7,260	5.9	3,924	5.9	3,336	5.9
Race and Hispanic origin:						
White	6,392	6.1	3,462	6.0	2,930	6.1
Black	630	4.9	337	5.4	293	4.4
Hispanic origin[2]	394	3.7	243	3.7	151	3.6

Source: "Multiple Jobholders: 1994," *Statistical Abstract of the United States,* 1995, p. 409. Primary source: U.S. Bureau of Labor Statistics, *Employment and Earnings,* monthly, January 1995. *Notes:* 1. Includes a small number of persons who work part time on their primary job and full time on their secondary job(s), not shown separately. Includes other races, not shown separately. 2. Persons of Hispanic origin may be of any race.

★ 479 ★

Labor Force

Multiple Jobholders: Rate, Race, and Hispanic Origin-1

[Numbers in thousands].

Characteristic	Both sexes			
	Number		Rate[1]	
	Nov. 1994	Nov. 1995	Nov. 1994	Nov. 1995
RACE AND HISPANIC ORIGIN				
White	6,590	6,709	6.2	6.3
Black	656	673	5.0	4.9
Hispanic origin	404	452	3.6	4.0

Source: "Multiple Jobholders by Selected Demographic and Economic Characteristics," *Employment and Earnings,* December 1995, p. 49. *Notes:* Not seasonally adjusted. Detail for the above race and Hispanic-origin groups will not sum to totals because data for the "other races are not presented and Hispanics are included in both the white and black population groups. 1. Multiple jobholders as a percent of all employed persons in specified group.

★ 480 ★

Labor Force

Multiple Jobholders: Rate, Race, and Hispanic Origin-2

[Numbers in thousands].

Characteristic	Men				Women			
	Number		Rate[1]		Number		Rate[1]	
	Nov. 1994	Nov. 1995	Nov. 1994	Nov. 1995	Nov. 1994	Nov. 1995	Nov. 1994	Nov. 1995
RACE AND HISPANIC ORIGIN								
White	3,576	3,582	6.2	6.2	3,014	3,128	6.2	6.4
Black	367	341	5.7	5.3	289	332	4.3	4.6
Hispanic origin	269	244	4.0	3.7	136	207	3.1	4.6

Source: "Multiple Jobholders by Selected Demographic and Economic Characteristics," *Employment and Earnings,* December 1995, p. 49. *Notes:* Not seasonally adjusted. Detail for the above race and Hispanic-origin groups will not sum to totals because data for the "other races are not presented and Hispanics are included in both the white and black population groups. 1. Multiple jobholders as a percent of all employed persons in specified group.

Labor Force Projections

★ 481 ★

Civilian Labor Force: Participation Rates and Projections: 1970-2005. Part 1

[**For civilian noninstitutional population 16 years old and over.** Annual averages of monthly figures. Rates are based on annual average civilian noninstitutional population of each specified group and represent proportion of each specified group in the civilian labor force. Based on Current Population Survey; see text, section 1, and Appendix III. See also *Historical Statistics, Colonial Times to 1970,* series D 42-48.]

RACE, SEX, AND AGE	CIVILIAN LABOR FORCE (millions)					
	1970	1980	1990	1994[1]	2000, proj.	2005, proj.
Total[2]	82.8	106.9	124.8	131.0	141.8	150.5
White	73.6	93.6	107.2	111.1	118.8	124.8
Male	46.0	54.5	59.3	60.7	63.8	66.0
Female	27.5	39.1	47.9	50.3	55.1	58.8
Black[3]	9.2	10.9	13.5	14.5	16.0	17.4
Male	5.2	5.6	6.7	7.1	7.8	8.3
Female	4.0	5.3	6.8	7.4	8.2	9.0
Hispanic[4]	(NA)	6.1	9.6	12.0	14.3	16.6
Male	(NA)	3.8	5.8	7.2	8.7	9.6
Female	(NA)	2.3	3.8	4.8	5.8	7.0

Source: "Civilian Labor Force and Participation Rates, With Projections: 1970 to 2005," *Statistical Abstract of the United States,* 1995, p. 399. Primary source: U.S. Bureau of Labor Statistics, Bulletin 2307; *Employment and Earnings,* monthly January issues; *Monthly Labor Review,* November 1993; and unpublished data. *Notes:* NA Not available. 1. See footnote 2, table 626. 2. Beginning 1980, includes other races not shown separately. 3. For 1970, Black and other. 4. Persons of Hispanic origin may be of any race.

★ 482 ★

Labor Force Projections

Civilian Labor Force: Participation Rates and Projections: 1970-2005. Part 2

[For civilian noninstitutional population 16 years old and over. Annual averages of monthly figures. Rates are based on annual average civilian noninstitutional population of each specified group and represent proportion of each specified group in the civilian labor force. Based on Current Population Survey; see text, section 1, and Appendix III. See also *Historical Statistics, Colonial Times to 1970,* series D 42-48.]

RACE, SEX, AND AGE	PARTICIPATION RATE (percent)					
	1970	1980	1990	1994[1]	2000, proj.	2005, proj.
Total[2]	60.4	63.8	66.4	66.6	68.2	68.8
White	60.2	64.1	66.8	67.1	68.7	69.3
Male	80.0	78.2	76.9	75.9	76.0	75.3
Female	42.6	51.2	57.5	58.9	61.8	63.6
Black[3]	61.8	61.0	63.3	63.4	65.5	66.2
Male	76.5	70.3	70.1	69.2	70.8	70.5
Female	49.5	53.1	57.8	58.7	61.2	62.6
Hispanic[4]	(NA)	64.0	67.0	66.2	68.0	68.4
Male	(NA)	81.4	81.2	79.2	80.2	79.5
Female	(NA)	47.4	53.0	52.9	55.8	57.3

Source: "Civilian Labor Force and Participation Rates, With Projections: 1970 to 2005," *Statistical Abstract of the United States,* 1995, p. 399. Primary source: U.S. Bureau of Labor Statistics, Bulletin 2307; *Employment and Earnings,* monthly January issues; *Monthly Labor Review,* November 1993; and unpublished data. *Notes:* NA Not available. 1. See footnote 2, table 626. 2. Beginning 1980, includes other races not shown separately. 3. For 1970, Black and other. 4. Persons of Hispanic origin may be of any race.

Occupations

★ 483 ★

Employed Persons: Employment by Occupation, Race, and Gender, 1994-95

[Percent distribution].

Occupation and race	Total		Men		Women	
	Nov. 1994	Nov. 1995	Nov. 1994	Nov. 1995	Nov. 1994	Nov. 1995
White						
Total, 16 years and over (thousands)	106,655	106,828	58,104	58,023	48,550	48,805
Percent	100.0	100.0	100.0	100.0	100.0	100.0
Managerial and professional specialty	28.8	29.6	28.0	28.7	29.8	30.7
Executive, administrative, and managerial	14.1	14.5	15.0	15.4	13.1	13.4
Professional specialty	14.7	15.1	13.0	13.3	16.7	17.3
Technical, sales, and administrative support	30.6	30.2	19.9	19.6	43.3	42.8
Technicians and related support	3.2	3.2	2.8	2.8	3.6	3.6
Sales occupations	12.6	12.8	11.6	11.9	13.7	13.9
Administrative support, including clerical	14.8	14.3	5.5	5.0	26.0	25.3
Service occupations	12.3	12.2	9.0	8.8	16.3	16.2
Private household	.6	.6	.1	.1	1.3	1.2
Protective service	1.7	1.6	2.7	2.4	.6	.5
Service, except private household and protective	10.0	10.0	6.3	6.3	14.5	14.5
Precision production, craft, and repair	11.6	11.2	19.6	18.9	2.1	1.9
Operators, fabricators, and laborers	13.6	13.8	19.0	19.5	7.2	7.1
Machine operators, assemblers, and inspectors	5.9	5.9	6.8	6.9	4.8	4.7
Transportation and material moving occupations	3.9	4.1	6.6	6.8	.8	.8
Handlers, equipment cleaners, helpers and laborers	3.8	3.9	5.6	5.8	1.6	1.6
Farming, forestry, and fishing	3.0	3.0	4.5	4.4	1.3	1.3
Black						
Total, 16 years and over (thousands)	13,080	13,660	6,402	6,456	6,678	7,204
Percent	100.0	100.0	100.0	100.0	100.0	100.0
Managerial and professional specialty	19.2	21.9	16.9	19.9	21.3	23.7
Executive, administrative, and managerial	8.3	10.1	8.1	10.2	8.4	10.0
Professional specialty	10.9	11.8	8.8	9.7	12.9	13.7
Technical, sales, and administrative support	28.3	27.9	17.6	16.5	38.6	38.2
Technicians and related support	2.8	2.6	2.4	1.7	3.1	3.4
Sales occupations	8.5	9.1	6.7	6.5	10.3	11.5
Administrative support, including clerical	17.1	16.2	8.6	8.3	25.2	23.2
Service occupations	21.1	21.3	17.7	17.1	24.3	25.1
Private household	1.0	1.1	-	.1	2.0	2.0
Protective service	3.2	3.0	5.2	5.1	1.2	1.1
Service, except private household and protective	16.9	17.2	12.5	11.9	21.1	22.0
Precision production, craft, and repair	7.9	8.1	13.2	14.7	2.8	2.1
Operators, fabricators, and laborers	22.0	19.9	31.6	30.1	12.8	10.8

[Continued]

★ 483 ★

Employed Persons: Employment by Occupation, Race, and Gender, 1994-95

[Continued]

Occupation and race	Total		Men		Women	
	Nov. 1994	Nov. 1995	Nov. 1994	Nov. 1995	Nov. 1994	Nov. 1995
Machine operators, assemblers, and inspectors	9.5	9.1	9.9	10.5	9.0	7.9
Transportation and material moving occupations	6.0	5.5	10.9	10.2	1.3	1.3
Handlers, equipment cleaners, helpers and laborers	6.5	5.3	10.8	9.4	2.5	1.6
Farming, forestry, and fishing	1.6	.8	3.0	1.6	.2	.2

Source: "Employed Persons by Occupation, Race, and Sex," *Employment and Earnings*, December 1995, p. 35. *Notes:* Not seasonally adjusted.

★ 484 ★

Occupations

Employed Persons: Nonagricultural Industries, 1996

[Numbers in thousands].

Age, sex, race, and marital status	January 1996							
	Total at work	Worked 1 to 34 hours				Worked 35 hours or more	Average hours	
		Total	For economic reasons	For noneconomic reasons			Total at work	Persons who usually work full time
				Usually work full time	Usually work part time			
Race								
White, 16 years and over	97,161	31,748	3,298	13,516	14,933	65,413	37.6	41.5
Men	52,806	12,809	1,671	6,685	4,453	39,997	40.8	43.2
Women	44,355	18,938	1,627	6,831	10,480	25,416	33.8	39.0
Black, 16 years and over	12,260	4,343	587	2,365	1,391	7,917	35.7	38.5
Men	5,817	1,628	223	925	481	4,189	38.2	40.4
Women	6,443	2,715	365	1,440	910	3,728	33.5	36.6

Source: "Persons at Work in Nonagricultural Industries by Age, Sex, Race, Marital Status, and Usual Full- or Part-time Status," *Employment and Earnings*, December 1995, p. 40. *Note:* Not seasonally adjusted.

★ 485 ★

Occupations

Occupational Employment in Private Industry: Accounting, Auditing and Bookkeeping Services

Race/ethnic group/sex	Total employment	Officials and managers	Professionals	Technicians	Sales workers	Office & clerical workers	Craft workers	Operatives	Laborers	Service workers
				NUMBER EMPLOYED						
All employees	141,640	29,382	57,722	3,589	3,613	39,811	1,646	2,862	2,264	751
Male	68,516	19,682	32,751	2,092	1,308	6,967	1,249	2,212	1,774	481
Female	73,124	9,700	24,971	1,497	2,305	32,844	397	650	490	270
White	117,587	26,915	50,475	2,966	3,039	29,057	1,317	2,016	1,388	414
Male	58,940	18,291	29,153	1,720	1,173	4,726	1,036	1,545	1,053	243
Female	58,647	8,624	21,322	1,246	1,866	24,331	281	471	335	171
Minority	24,053	2,467	7,247	623	574	10,754	329	846	876	337
Male	9,576	1,391	3,598	372	135	2,241	213	667	721	238
Female	14,477	1,076	3,649	251	439	8,513	116	179	155	99
Black	11,835	947	1,961	288	347	6,757	153	536	708	138
Male	4,039	426	860	163	58	1,287	102	444	609	90
Female	7,796	521	1,101	125	289	5,470	51	92	99	48
Hispanic	5,021	479	1,348	129	166	2,407	122	129	66	175
Male	2,090	300	736	83	54	541	83	101	56	136
Female	2,931	179	612	46	112	1,866	39	28	10	39
Asian/Pacific Islander	6,909	1,007	3,850	192	46	1,483	48	165	97	21
Male	3,314	642	1,953	117	17	389	22	111	53	10
Female	3,595	365	1,897	75	29	1,094	26	54	44	11
Am. Ind./Alaskan Native	288	34	88	14	15	107	6	16	5	3
Male	133	23	49	9	6	24	6	11	3	2
Female	155	11	39	5	9	83	0	5	2	1

Source: "Occupational Employment in Private Industry by Race/Ethnic Group/Sex, and by Industry, United States, 1994, All Industries." U.S. Equal Employment Opportunity Commission, *Job Patterns for Minorities and Women in Private Industry 1994,* p. 36. *Note:* Data for the state of Hawaii are not included.

★ 486 ★

Occupations

Occupational Employment in Private Industry: Aeronautical Guidance and Navigation Systems

Race/ethnic group/sex	Total employment	Officials and managers	Professionals	Technicians	Sales workers	Office & clerical workers	Craft workers	Operatives	Laborers	Service workers
				NUMBER EMPLOYED						
All employees	110,873	15,498	44,637	11,515	653	11,552	13,698	11,055	701	1,564
Male	80,173	13,697	36,579	9,310	510	2,464	11,428	4,579	434	1,172
Female	30,700	1,801	8,058	2,205	143	9,088	2,270	6,476	267	392
White	95,585	14,543	40,290	9,850	608	9,729	11,444	7,491	476	1,154
Male	70,987	12,955	33,390	8,050	479	1,967	9,744	3,230	308	864
Female	24,598	1,588	6,900	1,800	129	7,762	1,700	4,261	168	290

[Continued]

★ 486 ★

Occupational Employment in Private Industry: Aeronautical Guidance and Navigation Systems
[Continued]

Race/ethnic group/sex	Total employment	Officials and managers	Professionals	Technicians	Sales workers	Office & clerical workers	Craft workers	Operatives	Laborers	Service workers
Minority	15,288	955	4,347	1,665	45	1,823	2,254	3,564	225	410
Male	9,186	742	3,189	1,260	31	497	1,684	1,349	126	308
Female	6,102	213	1,158	405	14	1,326	570	2,215	99	102
Black	6,179	409	1,377	696	26	921	902	1,427	146	275
Male	3,425	306	905	493	17	245	652	515	81	211
Female	2,754	103	472	203	9	676	250	912	65	64
Hispanic	4,653	280	997	456	11	634	974	1,144	62	95
Male	2,855	218	774	355	9	192	756	440	38	73
Female	1,798	62	223	101	2	442	218	704	24	22
Asian/Pacific Islander	4,072	222	1,862	464	6	226	328	913	15	36
Male	2,685	181	1,443	376	4	55	239	361	6	20
Female	1,387	41	419	878	2	171	89	552	9	16 .
Am. Ind./Alaskan Native	384	44	111	49	2	42	50	80	2	4
Male	221	37	67	36	1	5	37	33	1	4
Female	163	7	44	13	1	37	13	47	1	0

Source: "Occupational Employment in Private Industry by Race/Ethnic Group/Sex, and by Industry, United States, 1994, All Industries." U.S. Equal Employment Opportunity Commission, *Job Patterns for Minorities and Women in Private Industry 1994*, p. 20. *Note:* Data for the state of Hawaii are not included.

★ 487 ★

Occupations

Occupational Employment in Private Industry: Agriculture, Forestry, and Fishing

Race/ethnic group/sex	Total employment	Officials and managers	Professionals	Technicians	Sales workers	Office & clerical workers	Craft workers	Operatives	Laborers	Service workers
NUMBER EMPLOYED											
All employees	193,024	15,996	5,358	4,329	2,871	11,593	21,387	40,540	87,373	3,577
Male	133,462	13,418	3,418	2,649	2,006	1,788	19,854	32,569	55,317	2,443
Female	59,562	2,578	1,940	1,680	865	9,805	1,533	7,971	32,056	1,134
White	103,774	13,605	4,764	3,553	2,614	9,854	15,858	23,707	27,598	2,221
Male	71,966	11,396	3,039	2,208	1,840	1,430	14,926	19,672	16,023	1,432
Female	31,808	2,209	1,725	1,345	774	8,424	932	4,035	11,575	789
Minority	89,250	2,391	594	776	257	1,739	5,529	16,833	59,775	1,356
Male	61,496	2,022	379	441	166	358	4,928	12,897	39,294	1,011
Female	27,754	369	215	335	91	1,381	601	3,936	20,481	345
Black	24,371	677	133	223	94	527	1,769	5,851	14,379	718
Male	14,101	531	66	103	43	92	1,386	4,226	7,158	496
Female	10,270	146	67	120	51	435	383	1,625	7,221	222
Hispanic	58,578	1,431	279	418	120	963	3,318	9,797	41,695	557
Male	43,589	1,270	199	251	89	207	3,153	7,799	30,165	456
Female	14,989	161	80	167	31	756	165	1,998	11,530	101
Asian/Pacific Islander	4,034	188	159	94	35	187	177	555	2,598	41
Male	2,252	149	101	62	28	46	144	383	1,310	29

[Continued]

★ 487 ★

Occupational Employment in Private Industry: Agriculture, Forestry, and Fishing

[Continued]

Race/ethnic group/sex	Total employment	Officials and managers	Professionals	Technicians	Sales workers	Office & clerical workers	Craft workers	Operatives	Laborers	Service workers
Female	1,782	39	58	32	7	141	33	172	1,288	12
Am. Ind./Alaskan Native	2,267	95	23	41	8	62	265	630	1,103	40
Male	1,554	72	13	25	6	13	245	489	661	30
Female	713	23	10	16	2	49	20	141	442	10

Source: "Occupational Employment in Private Industry by Race/Ethnic Group/Sex, and by Industry, United States, 1994, All Industries." U.S. Equal Employment Opportunity Commission, *Job Patterns for Minorities and Women in Private Industry 1994*, p. 2. *Note:* Data for the state of Hawaii are not included.

★ 488 ★

Occupations

Occupational Employment in Private Industry: Aircraft and Parts

Race/ethnic group/sex	Total employment	Officials and managers	Professionals	Technicians	Sales workers	Office & clerical workers	Craft workers	Operatives	Laborers	Service workers
					NUMBER EMPLOYED					
All employees	402,728	45,426	124,626	31,727	1,466	32,274	95,490	60,473	6,542	4,704
Male	314,047	40,616	102,421	25,274	1,109	7,818	86,561	42,767	3,919	3,562
Female	88,681	4,810	22,205	6,453	357	24,456	8,929	17,706	2,623	1,142
White	334,597	41,856	109,450	27,016	1,361	26,181	78,068	43,117	4,458	3,090
Male	265,128	37,589	90,958	21,728	1,050	6,053	71,695	30,991	2,619	2,445
Female	69,469	4,267	18,492	5,288	311	20,128	6,373	12,126	1,839	645
Minority	68,131	3,570	15,176	4,711	105	6,093	17,422	17,356	2,084	1,614
Male	48,919	3,027	11,463	3,546	59	1,765	14,866	11,776	1,300	1,117
Female	19,212	543	3,713	1,165	46	4,328	2,556	5,580	784	497
Black	29,668	1,344	4,598	1,714	30	3,194	8,193	8,725	925	945
Male	19,439	1,102	3,083	1,172	13	954	6,525	5,424	496	670
Female	10,229	242	1,515	542	17	2,240	1,668	3,301	429	275
Hispanic	21,168	1,074	3,482	1,360	41	1,983	6,479	5,420	776	553
Male	16,216	926	2,666	1,077	24	613	5,841	4,132	563	374
Female	4,952	148	816	283	17	1,370	638	1,288	213	179
Asian/Pacific Islander	15,341	933	6,676	1,447	29	731	2,280	2,802	343	100
Male	11,925	813	5,406	1,156	20	165	2,102	1,975	225	63
Female	3,416	120	1,270	291	9	566	178	827	118	37
Am. Ind./Alaskan Native	1,954	219	420	190	5	185	470	409	40	16
Male	1,339	186	308	141	2	33	398	245	16	10
Female	615	33	112	49	3	152	72	164	24	6

Source: "Occupational Employment in Private Industry by Race/Ethnic Group/Sex, and by Industry, United States, 1994, All Industries." U.S. Equal Employment Opportunity Commission, *Job Patterns for Minorities and Women in Private Industry 1994*, p. 20. *Note:* Data for the state of Hawaii are not included.

★ 489 ★

Occupations

Occupational Employment in Private Industry: All Industries

Race/ethnic group/sex	Total employment	Officials and managers	Professionals	Technicians	Sales workers	Office & clerical workers	Craft workers	Operatives	Laborers	Service workers
				NUMBER EMPLOYED						
All employees	37,236,561	3,971,605	5,408,840	2,239,688	4,049,128	5,608,488	3,388,016	5,673,696	2,831,000	4,066,100
Male	19,924,844	2,766,362	2,684,391	1,196,019	1,755,984	978,955	2,992,548	3,874,925	1,860,453	1,815,207
Female	17,311,717	1,205,243	2,724,449	1,043,669	2,293,144	4,629,533	395,468	1,798,771	970,547	2,250,893
White	28,216,146	3,532,213	4,613,826	1,787,233	3,194,967	4,250,387	2,769,070	3,959,036	1,719,013	2,390,401
Male	15,297,649	2,491,524	2,325,768	975,600	1,415,673	696,420	2,473,121	2,791,019	1,129,649	998,875
Female	12,918,497	1,040,689	2,288,058	811,633	1,779,294	3,553,967	295,949	1,168,017	589,364	1,391,526
Minority	9,020,415	439,392	795,014	452,455	854,161	1,358,101	618,946	1,714,660	1,111,987	1,675,699
Male	4,627,195	274,838	358,623	220,419	340,311	282,535	519,427	1,083,906	730,804	816,332
Female	4,393,220	164,554	436,391	232,036	514,850	1,075,566	99,519	630,754	381,183	859,367
Black	4,818,805	212,405	305,129	233,763	463,301	795,819	314,923	979,220	534,193	980,052
Male	2,263,490	120,976	107,110	92,247	168,091	142,920	258,823	599,226	344,602	429,495
Female	2,555,315	91,429	198,019	141,516	295,210	652,899	56,100	379,994	189,591	550,557
Hispanic	2,810,546	126,289	150,436	109,549	281,599	371,408	226,843	539,941	475,923	528,558
Male	1,641,749	85,167	76,262	65,239	124,792	87,100	198,641	371,826	326,457	306,175
Female	1,168,797	41,122	74,174	44,310	156,807	284,218	28,202	168,115	149,466	222,383
Asian/Pacific Islander	1,205,984	87,378	323,340	99,252	87,604	167,127	56,754	161,112	82,043	141,374
Male	619,350	59,444	166,996	57,254	38,655	47,254	43,803	90,333	46,685	68,926
Female	586,634	27,934	156,344	41,998	48,949	119,873	12,951	70,779	35,358	72,448
Am. Ind./Alaskan Native	185,080	13,320	16,109	9,891	21,657	23,747	20,426	34,387	19,828	25,715
Male	102,606	9,251	8,255	5,679	8,773	5,171	18,160	22,521	13,060	11,736
Female	82,474	4,069	7,854	4,212	12,884	18,576	2,266	11,866	6,768	13,979

Source: "Occupational Employment in Private Industry by Race/Ethnic Group/Sex, and by Industry, United States, 1994, All Industries." U.S. Equal Employment Opportunity Commission, *Job Patterns for Minorities and Women in Private Industry 1994.*, p. 1. *Note:* Data for the state of Hawaii are not included.

★ 490 ★

Occupations

Occupational Employment in Private Industry: Amusement and Recreation Services

Race/ethnic group/sex	Total employment	Officials and managers	Professionals	Technicians	Sales workers	Office & clerical workers	Craft workers	Operatives	Laborers	Service workers
				NUMBER EMPLOYED						
All employees	202,425	15,252	10,024	4,875	13,576	19,856	16,796	10,519	8,629	102,898
Male	109,691	9,587	5,494	3,592	4,823	4,470	12,828	7,032	7,052	54,543
Female	92,734	5,395	4,530	1,283	8,753	15,385	3,968	3,487	1,577	48,355
White	146,535	13,418	8,473	4,235	9,947	15,597	13,495	7,692	4,828	68,850
Male	78,022	8,702	4,623	3,093	3,363	3,443	10,386	5,330	3,935	35,147
Female	68,513	4,716	3,850	1,142	6,584	12,154	3,109	2,362	893	33,703

[Continued]

★ 490 ★

Occupational Employment in Private Industry: Amusement and Recreation Services

[Continued]

Race/ethnic group/sex	Total employment	Officials and managers	Professionals	Technicians	Sales workers	Office & clerical workers	Craft workers	Operatives	Laborers	Service workers
Minority	55,890	1,834	1,551	640	3,629	4,259	3,301	2,827	3,801	34,048
Male	31,669	1,155	871	499	1,460	1,027	2,442	1,702	3,117	19,396
Female	24,221	679	680	141	2,169	3,232	859	1,125	684	14,652
Black	20,639	811	407	282	980	1,776	834	1,398	1,418	12,733
Male	10,569	499	237	220	359	377	595	702	1,017	6,543
Female	10,070	312	170	62	621	1,399	239	696	401	6,170
Hispanic	24,153	658	476	193	1,406	1,768	1,629	1,057	2,135	14,831
Male	15,244	437	277	153	539	437	1,384	800	1,896	9,321
Female	8,909	221	199	40	867	1,331	245	257	239	5,510
Asian/Pacific Islander	10,275	323	630	145	1,186	651	768	321	186	6,065
Male	5,403	196	337	109	546	201	410	168	151	3,285
Female	4,872	127	293	36	640	450	358	153	35	2,780
Am. Ind./Alaskan Native	823	42	38	20	57	64	70	51	62	419
Male	453	23	20	17	16	12	53	32	53	227
Female	370	19	18	3	41	52	17	19	9	192

Source: "Occupational Employment in Private Industry by Race/Ethnic Group/Sex, and by Industry, United States, 1994, All Industries." U.S. Equal Employment Opportunity Commission, *Job Patterns for Minorities and Women in Private Industry 1994,* p. 33. *Note:* Data for the state of Hawaii are not included.

★ 491 ★

Occupations

Occupational Employment in Private Industry: Automobile Rental and Leasing

Race/ethnic group/sex	Total employment	Officials and managers	Professionals	Technicians	Sales workers	Office & clerical workers	Craft workers	Operatives	Laborers	Service workers
					NUMBER EMPLOYED					
All employees	98,568	11,707	3,487	1,324	14,705	16,821	9,791	23,662	14,636	2,435
Male	67,143	8,669	1,861	909	8,381	3,914	9,733	19,097	12,653	1,926
Female	31,425	3,038	1,626	415	6,324	12,907	58	4,565	1,983	509
White	69,080	10,186	2,957	1,045	9,548	12,281	7,844	14,793	9,267	1,159
Male	46,535	7,568	1,635	712	5,579	2,697	7,801	11,778	7,899	866
Female	22,545	2,618	1,322	333	3,969	9,584	43	3,015	1,368	293
Minority	29,488	1,521	530	279	5,157	4,540	1,947	8,869	5,369	1,276
Male	20,608	1,101	226	197	2,802	1,217	1,932	7,319	4,754	1,060
Female	8,880	420	304	82	2,355	3,323	15	1,550	615	216
Black	17,691	803	223	110	3,272	2,616	911	5,784	3,133	839
Male	11,821	567	83	66	1,639	615	905	4,557	2,717	672
Female	5,870	236	140	44	1,633	2,001	6	1,227	416	167
Hispanic	8,919	529	205	117	1,357	1,342	791	2,508	1,751	318
Male	6,719	402	97	102	847	405	783	2,227	1,578	278
Female	2,200	127	109	15	510	937	8	281	173	40
Asian/Pacific Islander	2,373	148	84	47	459	421	196	489	429	100
Male	1,761	104	38	29	279	150	196	463	409	93

[Continued]

★ 491 ★

Occupational Employment in Private Industry: Automobile Rental and Leasing

[Continued]

Race/ethnic group/sex	Total employment	Officials and managers	Professionals	Technicians	Sales workers	Office & clerical workers	Craft workers	Operatives	Laborers	Service workers
Female	612	44	46	18	180	271	0	26	20	7
Am. Ind./Alaskan Native	505	41	17	5	69	161	49	88	56	19
Male	307	28	8	0	37	47	48	72	50	17
Female	198	13	9	5	32	114	1	16	6	2

Source: "Occupational Employment in Private Industry by Race/Ethnic Group/Sex, and by Industry, United States, 1994, All Industries." U.S. Equal Employment Opportunity Commission, *Job Patterns for Minorities and Women in Private Industry 1994*, p. 32. *Note:* Data for the state of Hawaii are not included.

★ 492 ★

Occupations

Occupational Employment in Private Industry: Bakery Products

Race/ethnic group/sex	Total employment	Officials and managers	Professionals	Technicians	Sales workers	Office & clerical workers	Craft workers	Operatives	Laborers	Service workers
					NUMBER EMPLOYED					
All employees	164,053	18,230	2,943	1,732	25,828	9,029	18,899	44,583	36,817	5,992
Male	112,009	15,340	1,701	854	19,806	1,228	16,810	32,200	19,802	4,268
Female	52,044	2,890	1,242	878	6,022	7,801	2,089	12,383	17,015	1,724
White	114,921	16,180	2,550	1,421	22,078	7,169	13,522	28,925	20,177	2,899
Male	80,521	13,682	1,484	713	16,948	847	12,249	21,612	11,022	1,964
Female	34,400	2,498	1,066	708	5,130	6,322	1,273	7,313	9,155	935
Minority	49,132	2,050	393	311	3,750	1,860	5,377	15,658	16,640	3,093
Male	31,488	1,658	217	141	2,858	381	4,561	10,528	8,780	2,304
Female	17,644	392	176	170	892	1,479	816	5,070	7,860	789
Black	28,654	1,165	212	193	1,819	1,211	2,872	9,532	9,964	1,686
Male	17,210	924	105	75	1,353	243	2,296	6,026	4,996	1,192
Female	11,444	241	107	118	466	968	576	3,506	4,968	494
Hispanic	16,185	619	68	72	1,654	432	2,043	4,996	5,158	1,143
Male	11,597	524	49	42	1,284	89	1,856	3,834	3,005	914
Female	4,588	95	19	30	370	343	187	1,162	2,153	229
Asian/Pacific Islander	3,488	206	103	36	190	190	363	895	1,289	216
Male	2,194	161	56	21	153	47	327	585	672	172
Female	1,294	45	47	15	37	143	36	319	617	44
Am. Ind./Alaskan Native	805	60	10	10	87	27	99	235	229	48
Male	487	49	7	3	68	2	82	143	107	26
Female	318	11	3	7	19	25	17	92	122	22

Source: "Occupational Employment in Private Industry by Race/Ethnic Group/Sex, and by Industry, United States, 1994, All Industries." U.S. Equal Employment Opportunity Commission, *Job Patterns for Minorities and Women in Private Industry 1994*, p. 6. *Note:* Data for the state of Hawaii are not included.

★ 493 ★

Occupations

Occupational Employment in Private Industry: Beverages

Race/ethnic group/sex	Total employment	Officials and managers	Professionals	Technicians	Sales workers	Office & clerical workers	Craft workers	Operatives	Laborers	Service workers
NUMBER EMPLOYED										
All employees	157,871	21,790	10,791	3,516	25,134	16,111	16,167	46,468	13,597	4,297
Male	125,087	18,363	6,698	2,434	23,286	2,979	15,785	41,082	11,960	2,500
Female	32,784	3,427	4,093	1,082	1,848	13,132	382	5,386	1,637	1,797
White	120,546	19,298	9,244	2,637	20,011	12,635	13,419	32,310	8,089	2,903
Male	95,514	16,332	5,798	1,836	18,526	2,164	13,112	28,894	7,140	1,712
Female	25,032	2,966	3,446	801	1,485	10,471	307	3,416	949	1,191
Minority	37,325	2,492	1,547	879	5,123	3,476	2,748	14,158	5,508	1,394
Male	29,573	2,031	900	598	4,760	815	2,673	12,188	4,820	788
Female	7,752	461	647	281	363	2,661	75	1,970	688	606
Black	20,992	1,340	772	494	2,968	2,078	1,249	8,435	2,847	809
Male	16,285	1,076	410	307	2,769	467	1,201	7,151	2,480	424
Female	4,707	264	362	187	199	1,611	48	1,284	367	385
Hispanic	13,305	821	427	242	1,849	1,042	1,258	5,020	2,373	273
Male	11,100	703	284	186	1,717	263	1,240	4,449	2,089	169
Female	2,205	118	143	56	132	779	18	571	284	104
Asian/Pacific Islander	2,234	270	325	121	214	286	167	523	224	104
Male	1,614	201	191	91	190	72	164	436	199	70
Female	620	69	134	30	24	214	3	87	25	34
Am. Ind./Alaskan Native	794	61	23	22	92	70	74	180	64	208
Male	574	51	15	14	84	13	68	152	52	125
Female	220	10	8	8	8	57	6	28	12	83

Source: "Occupational Employment in Private Industry by Race/Ethnic Group/Sex, and by Industry, United States, 1994, All Industries." U.S. Equal Employment Opportunity Commission, *Job Patterns for Minorities and Women in Private Industry 1994*, p. 8. *Note:* Data for the state of Hawaii are not included.

★ 494 ★

Occupations

Occupational Employment in Private Industry: Business Services

Race/ethnic group/sex	Total employment	Officials and managers	Professionals	Technicians	Sales workers	Office & clerical workers	Craft workers	Operatives	Laborers	Service workers
NUMBER EMPLOYED										
All employees	715,709	59,488	65,806	28,474	47,424	124,530	28,482	60,831	23,521	277,153
Male	462,553	43,037	41,951	20,729	21,039	32,614	24,675	38,675	13,929	225,904
Female	253,156	16,451	23,855	7,745	26,385	91,916	3,807	22,156	9,592	51,249
White	485,550	52,006	56,170	23,061	34,028	88,811	22,331	40,077	12,060	157,006
Male	312,998	37,996	36,356	16,981	15,823	21,917	19,633	26,074	7,341	130,877
Female	172,552	14,010	19,814	6,080	18,205	66,894	2,698	14,003	4,719	26,129

[Continued]

★ 494 ★

Occupational Employment in Private Industry: Business Services
[Continued]

Race/ethnic group/sex	Total employment	Officials and managers	Professionals	Technicians	Sales workers	Office & clerical workers	Craft workers	Operatives	Laborers	Service workers
Minority	230,159	7,482	9,636	5,413	13,394	35,719	6,151	20,754	11,461	120,147
Male	149,555	5,041	5,595	3,748	5,216	10,697	5,042	12,601	6,588	95,027
Female	80,604	2,441	4,041	1,665	8,180	25,022	1,109	8,153	4,873	25,120
Black	146,356	3,948	3,753	2,789	8,421	21,684	2,778	11,525	5,600	85,858
Male	93,916	2,601	1,799	1,843	2,982	5,909	2,194	6,828	3,279	66,481
Female	52,440	1,347	1,954	946	5,439	15,775	584	4,697	2,321	19,377
Hispanic	57,309	2,156	2,244	1,453	4,058	9,213	2,569	6,010	4,496	25,110
Male	38,007	1,459	1,353	1,060	1,823	2,890	2,232	3,933	2,578	20,679
Female	19,302	697	891	393	2,235	6,323	337	2,077	1,918	4,431
Asian/Pacific Islander	23,288	1,181	3,409	1,011	728	4,242	662	2,952	1,240	7,863
Male	15,564	838	2,294	731	343	1,709	492	1,684	653	6,820
Female	7,724	343	1,115	280	385	2,533	170	1,268	587	1,043
Am. Ind./Alaskan Native	3,206	197	230	160	189	580	142	267	125	1,316
Male	2,068	143	149	114	68	189	124	156	78	1,047
Female	1,138	54	81	46	121	391	18	111	47	269

Source: "Occupational Employment in Private Industry by Race/Ethnic Group/Sex, and by Industry, United States, 1994, All Industries." U.S. Equal Employment Opportunity Commission, *Job Patterns for Minorities and Women in Private Industry 1994*, p. 32. *Note:* Data for the state of Hawaii are not included.

★ 495 ★

Occupations

Occupational Employment in Private Industry: Combination Utility Services

Race/ethnic group/sex	Total employment	Officials and managers	Professionals	Technicians	Sales workers	Office & clerical workers	Craft workers	Operatives	Laborers	Service workers
					NUMBER EMPLOYED					
All employees	95,615	13,243	15,105	9,016	327	17,459	28,733	8,734	2,103	895
Male	74,095	11,617	11,601	7,439	242	4,597	28,250	7,905	1,796	648
Female	21,520	1,626	3,504	1,577	85	12,862	483	829	307	247
White	78,381	11,956	13,280	7,676	301	12,874	24,119	6,081	1,417	677
Male	61,975	10,621	10,352	6,410	223	3,419	23,766	5,488	1,191	505
Female	16,406	1,335	2,928	1,266	78	9,455	353	593	226	172
Minority	17,234	1,287	1,825	1,340	26	4,585	4,614	2,653	686	218
Male	12,120	996	1,249	1,029	19	1,178	4,484	2,417	605	143
Female	5,114	291	576	311	7	3,407	130	236	81	75
Black	9,760	664	802	629	18	3,003	2,483	1,550	453	158
Male	6,440	473	472	482	13	703	2,399	1,401	395	102
Female	3,320	191	330	147	5	2,300	84	149	58	56
Hispanic	5,186	379	432	501	6	1,158	1,617	881	171	41
Male	4,016	333	328	373	5	386	1,588	817	154	32
Female	1,170	46	104	128	1	772	29	64	17	9
Asian/Pacific Islander	1,533	187	524	160	1	245	256	122	34	4
Male	1,135	143	400	129	0	66	252	111	31	3

[Continued]

★ 495 ★

Occupational Employment in Private Industry: Combination Utility Services

[Continued]

Race/ethnic group/sex	Total employment	Officials and managers	Professionals	Technicians	Sales workers	Office & clerical workers	Craft workers	Operatives	Laborers	Service workers
Female	398	44	124	31	1	179	4	11	3	1
Am. Ind./Alaskan Native	755	57	67	50	1	179	258	100	28	15
Male	529	47	49	45	1	23	245	88	25	6
Female	226	10	18	5	0	156	13	12	3	9

Source: "Occupational Employment in Private Industry by Race/Ethnic Group/Sex, and by Industry, United States, 1994, All Industries." U.S. Equal Employment Opportunity Commission, *Job Patterns for Minorities and Women in Private Industry 1994*, p. 24. *Note:* Data for the state of Hawaii are not included.

★ 496 ★

Occupations

Occupational Employment in Private Industry: Commercial Banks

Race/ethnic group/sex	Total employment	Officials and managers	Professionals	Technicians	Sales workers	Office & clerical workers	Craft workers	Operatives	Laborers	Service workers
					NUMBER EMPLOYED					
All employees	925,187	190,927	162,570	19,847	24,339	505,774	3,608	6,905	1,000	10,217
Male	294,942	101,256	72,519	11,528	10,172	84,195	1,983	4,451	808	8,030
Female	630,245	89,671	90,051	8,319	14,167	421,579	1,625	2,454	192	2,187
White	703,375	167,724	133,628	14,981	19,681	352,347	2,936	4,123	649	7,306
Male	234,271	91,541	61,838	8,785	8,702	52,760	1,606	2,727	532	5,780
Female	469,104	7,183	71,790	6,196	10,979	299,587	1,330	1,396	117	1,256
Minority	221,812	23,203	28,942	4,866	4,658	153,427	672	2,782	351	2,911
Male	60,671	9,715	10,681	2,743	1,470	31,435	377	1,724	276	2,250
Female	161,141	13,488	18,261	2,123	3,188	121,992	295	1,058	75	661
Black	120,047	10,772	13,344	2,264	2,681	86,833	434	1,427	227	2,065
Male	27,608	3,751	4,243	1,199	694	14,933	227	843	168	1,550
Female	92,439	7,021	9,101	1,065	1,987	71,900	207	584	59	515
Hispanic	55,803	6,537	6,791	1,151	1,128	38,484	152	675	104	681
Male	16,378	2,877	2,595	686	413	8,599	101	451	90	566
Female	39,425	3,660	4,196	465	815	29,885	51	224	14	115
Asian/Pacific Islander	42,841	5,430	8,424	1,390	652	26,092	67	645	19	122
Male	15,775	2,885	3,686	818	314	7,512	41	405	17	97
Female	27,066	2,545	4,738	572	338	18,580	26	240	2	25
Am. Ind./Alaskan Native	3,121	464	383	61	97	2,018	19	35	1	43
Male	910	202	157	40	49	391	8	25	1	37
Female	2,211	262	226	21	48	1,627	11	10	0	6

Source: "Occupational Employment in Private Industry by Race/Ethnic Group/Sex, and by Industry, United States, 1994, All Industries." U.S. Equal Employment Opportunity Commission, *Job Patterns for Minorities and Women in Private Industry 1994*, p. 28. *Note:* Data for the state of Hawaii are not included.

★ 497 ★

Occupations

Occupational Employment in Private Industry: Commercial Printing

Race/ethnic group/sex	Total employment	Officials and managers	Professionals	Technicians	Sales workers	Office & clerical workers	Craft workers	Operatives	Laborers	Service workers
				NUMBER EMPLOYED						
All employees	184,255	15,995	9,416	6,766	8,826	22,155	46,785	42,049	29,685	2,578
Male	117,223	12,571	4,927	4,202	5,577	4,219	39,313	27,770	16,945	1,699
Female	67,032	3,424	4,489	2,564	3,249	17,936	7,472	14,279	12,740	879
White	154,880	15,079	8,744	6,147	8,378	19,433	41,052	33,152	20,983	1,912
Male	98,794	11,889	4,558	3,834	5,390	3,541	34,566	21,898	11,917	1,201
Female	56,086	3,190	4,186	2,313	2,988	15,892	6,486	11,254	9,066	711
Minority	29,375	916	672	619	448	2,722	5,733	8,897	8,702	666
Male	18,429	682	369	368	187	678	4,747	5,872	5,028	498
Female	10,946	234	303	251	261	2,044	986	3,025	3,674	168
Black	14,183	417	311	283	250	1,362	2,503	4,595	4,062	400
Male	8,398	302	153	159	96	328	1,966	2,921	2,185	289
Female	5,785	115	159	124	154	1,034	537	1,674	1,877	111
Hispanic	10,767	314	150	717	133	887	2,366	3,189	3,357	200
Male	7,283	253	92	103	66	220	2,066	2,298	2,027	158
Female	3,484	61	58	68	67	667	300	891	1,330	42
Asian/Pacific Islander	3,864	148	189	146	43	421	733	960	1,168	56
Male	2,402	95	118	94	20	119	606	564	741	45
Female	1,462	53	71	52	23	302	127	396	427	11
Am. Ind./Alaskan Native	561	37	22	19	22	52	131	153	115	10
Male	346	32	7	12	5	11	109	89	75	6
Female	215	5	15	7	17	41	22	64	40	4

Source: "Occupational Employment in Private Industry by Race/Ethnic Group/Sex, and by Industry, United States, 1994, All Industries." U.S. Equal Employment Opportunity Commission, *Job Patterns for Minorities and Women in Private Industry 1994,* p. 11. *Note:* Data for the state of Hawaii are not included.

★ 498 ★

Occupations

Occupational Employment in Private Industry: Communication Equipment

Race/ethnic group/sex	Total employment	Officials and managers	Professionals	Technicians	Sales workers	Office & clerical workers	Craft workers	Operatives	Laborers	Service workers
				NUMBER EMPLOYED						
All employees	282,876	39,968	91,656	32,376	6,396	31,566	19,816	53,837	5,280	1,981
Male	178, 188	32,089	69,955	26,574	4,133	6,136	14,598	20,875	2,334	1,494
Female	104,688	7,879	21,701	5,802	2,263	25,430	5,218	32,962	2,946	487
White	220,148	35,843	76,625	24,702	5,634	24,440	15,774	32,602	3,183	1,345
Male	144,402	29,007	59,213	20,501	3,748	4,431	12,189	12,890	1,412	1,011
Female	75,746	6,836	17,412	4,201	1,886	20,009	3,585	19,712	1,771	334

[Continued]

★ 498 ★

Occupational Employment in Private Industry: Communication Equipment

[Continued]

Race/ethnic group/sex	Total employment	Officials and managers	Professionals	Technicians	Sales workers	Office & clerical workers	Craft workers	Operatives	Laborers	Service workers
Minority	62,728	4,125	15,031	7,674	762	7,126	4,042	21,235	2,097	636
Male	33,786	3,082	10,742	6,073	385	1,705	2,409	7,985	922	483
Female	28,942	1,043	4,289	1,601	377	5,421	1,633	13,250	1,175	153
Black	25,402	1,504	3,782	2,889	415	4,001	1,878	9,804	807	322
Male	11,129	998	2,353	2,160	154	825	1,031	3,042	323	243
Female	14,273	506	1,429	729	261	3,176	847	6,762	484	79
Hispanic	16,116	990	2,919	1,900	188	1,854	1,154	6,128	734	249
Male	8,737	735	2,118	1,563	123	462	783	2,404	349	200
Female	7,379	255	801	337	65	1,392	371	3,724	385	49
Asian/Pacific Islander	20,099	1,505	8,055	2,716	130	1,115	929	5,063	532	54
Male	13,286	1,248	6,072	2,221	94	384	543	2,448	242	34
Female	6,813	257	1,983	495	36	731	386	2,615	290	20
Am. Ind./Alaskan Native	1,111	126	275	169	29	156	81	240	24	11
Male	634	101	199	129	14	34	52	91	8	6
Female	477	26	76	40	15	122	29	149	16	5

Source: "Occupational Employment in Private Industry by Race/Ethnic Group/Sex, and by Industry, United States, 1994, All Industries." U.S. Equal Employment Opportunity Commission, *Job Patterns for Minorities and Women in Private Industry 1994*, p. 18. *Note:* Data for the state of Hawaii are not included.

★ 499 ★

Occupations

Occupational Employment in Private Industry: Computer Programming and Data Processing

Race/ethnic group/sex	Total employment	Officials and managers	Professionals	Technicians	Sales workers	Office & clerical workers	Craft workers	Operatives	Laborers	Service workers
					NUMBER EMPLOYED					
All employees	541,750	77,672	238,516	64,663	21,498	118,808	5,755	10,752	2,207	1,879
Male	308,023	53,721	155,102	45,493	12,704	27,100	4,643	6,557	1,497	1,206
Female	233,727	23,951	83,414	19,170	8,794	91,708	1,112	4,195	710	673
White	438,091	69,998	198,841	51,341	19,421	84,340	4,725	6,898	1,344	1,183
Male	255,231	48,878	129,871	36,542	11,685	18,290	3,881	4,342	924	818
Female	182,860	21,120	68,970	14,799	7,736	66,050	844	2,556	420	365
Minority	103,659	7,674	39,675	13,322	2,077	34,468	1,030	3,854	863	696
Male	52,792	4,843	25,231	8,951	1,019	8,810	762	2,215	573	388
Female	50,867	2,831	14,444	4,371	1,058	25,658	268	1,639	290	308
Black	45,944	3,236	11,958	6,173	1,022	20,329	511	1,800	467	448
Male	18,712	1,802	6,225	3,835	435	4,471	402	984	337	221
Female	27,232	1,434	5,733	2,338	587	15,858	109	816	130	227
Hispanic	20,036	1,655	5,357	2,779	544	8,049	288	924	262	178
Male	10,293	1,085	3,475	2,026	302	2,360	205	555	167	118
Female	9,743	570	1,882	753	242	5,689	83	369	95	60
Asian/Pacific Islander	35,418	2,559	21,601	4,017	450	5,387	203	1,023	120	58
Male	22,558	1,807	15,047	2,842	253	1,772	133	599	60	45

[Continued]

★ 499 ★

Occupational Employment in Private Industry: Computer Programming and Data Processing
[Continued]

Race/ethnic group/sex	Total employment	Officials and managers	Professionals	Technicians	Sales workers	Office & clerical workers	Craft workers	Operatives	Laborers	Service workers
Female	12,860	752	6,554	1,175	197	3,615	70	424	60	13
Am. Ind./Alaskan Native	2,261	224	759	353	61	703	28	107	14	12
Male	1,229	149	484	248	29	207	22	77	9	4
Female	1,032	75	275	105	32	496	6	30	5	8

Source: "Occupational Employment in Private Industry by Race/Ethnic Group/Sex, and by Industry, United States, 1994, All Industries." U.S. Equal Employment Opportunity Commission, *Job Patterns for Minorities and Women in Private Industry 1994*, p. 32. *Note:* Data for the state of Hawaii are not included.

★ 500 ★
Occupations

Occupational Employment in Private Industry: Computer and Office Equipment

Race/ethnic group/sex	Total employment	Officials and managers	Professionals	Technicians	Sales workers	Office & clerical workers	Craft workers	Operatives	Laborers	Service workers
				NUMBER EMPLOYED						
All employees	360,681	50,707	134,937	42,027	14,247	39,718	15,454	53,708	8,398	1,485
Male	236,215	39,693	98,148	35,484	9,669	9,687	12,183	25,880	4,378	1,093
Female	124,466	11,014	36,789	6,543	4,578	30,031	3,271	27,828	4,020	392
White	283,445	45,188	112,653	33,112	12,511	31,249	12,740	30,508	4,474	1,010
Male	190,231	35,576	82,789	28,226	8,589	7,156	10,309	14,572	2,285	729
Female	93,214	9,612	29,864	4,886	3,922	24,093	2,431	15,936	2,189	281
Minority	77,236	5,519	22,284	8,915	1,736	8,469	2,714	23,200	3,924	475
Male	45,984	4,117	15,359	7,258	1,080	2,531	1,874	11,308	2,093	364
Female	31,252	1,402	6,925	1,657	656	5,938	840	11,892	1,831	111
Black	24,885	1,609	5,132	2,325	780	4,051	1,144	8,179	1,423	242
Male	13,007	1,098	3,077	1,882	482	1,086	756	3,768	688	170
Female	11,878	511	2,055	443	298	2,965	388	4,411	735	72
Hispanic	17,463	1,184	3,529	2,268	444	2,607	803	4,944	1,502	182
Male	10,327	873	2,394	1,849	286	880	583	2,417	894	151
Female	7,136	311	1,135	419	158	1,727	220	2,527	608	31
Asian/Pacific Islander	33,594	2,564	13,256	4,165	475	1,630	723	9,783	954	44
Male	21,924	2,030	9,653	3,403	289	519	504	5,005	485	38
Female	11,670	534	3,603	762	186	1,111	219	4,778	471	6
Am. Ind./Alaskan Native	1,294	162	367	157	37	181	44	294	45	7
Male	726	116	235	124	23	46	31	118	28	5
Female	568	46	132	33	14	135	13	176	17	2

Source: "Occupational Employment in Private Industry by Race/Ethnic Group/Sex, and by Industry, United States, 1994, All Industries." U.S. Equal Employment Opportunity Commission, *Job Patterns for Minorities and Women in Private Industry 1994*, p. 17. *Note:* Data for the state of Hawaii are not included.

★ 501 ★

Occupations

Occupational Employment in Private Industry: Construction

Race/ethnic group/sex	Total employment	Officials and managers	Professionals	Technicians	Sales workers	Office & clerical workers	Craft workers	Operatives	Laborers	Service workers
				NUMBER EMPLOYED						
All employees	626,471	60,282	43,529	19,073	10,967	48,931	239,013	102,658	89,514	12,504
Male	548,920	54,662	35,912	16,638	6,871	10,305	233,326	97,632	84,291	9,283
Female	77,551	5,620	7,617	2,435	4,096	38,626	5,687	5,026	5,223	3,221
White	495,206	55,776	38,393	16,554	9,562	41,147	196,216	75,962	54,882	6,714
Male	432,451	50,766	32,093	14,548	6,243	8,556	192,020	72,173	50,930	5,123
Female	62,755	5,010	6,301	2,006	3,319	32,591	4,196	3,789	3,952	1,591
Minority	131,265	4,506	5,136	2,519	1,405	7,784	42,797	26,696	34,632	5,790
Male	116,469	3,896	3,820	2,090	628	1,749	41,306	25,459	33,361	4,160
Female	14,796	610	1,316	429	777	6,035	1,491	1,237	1,271	1,630
Black	57,645	1,540	1,396	1,086	884	4,070	18,191	12,541	15,723	2,214
Male	50,006	1,266	905	888	342	808	17,275	11,911	14,991	1,620
Female	7,639	274	491	198	542	3,262	916	630	732	594
Hispanic	59,095	1,726	1,224	843	366	2,503	20,228	11,785	171,34	3,286
Male	54,445	1,553	947	740	195	634	19,820	11,444	16,779	2,333
Female	4,650	173	277	103	171	1,869	408	341	355	953
Asian/Pacific Islander	7,934	938	2,331	457	124	952	1,498	886	534	214
Male	6,143	912	1,822	353	66	268	1,434	771	464	153
Female	1,791	126	509	104	58	684	64	115	70	61
Am. Ind./Alaskan Native	6,591	302	185	133	31	259	2,880	1,484	1,241	76
Male	5,875	265	146	109	25	39	2,777	1,333	1,127	54
Female	716	37	39	24	6	220	103	151	114	22

Source: "Occupational Employment in Private Industry by Race/Ethnic Group/Sex, and by Industry, United States, 1994, All Industries." U.S. Equal Employment Opportunity Commission, *Job Patterns for Minorities and Women in Private Industry 1994*, p. 2. *Note:* Data for the state of Hawaii are not included.

★ 502 ★

Occupations

Occupational Employment in Private Industry: Construction and Related Machinery

RACE/ETHNIC GROUP/ SEX	Total employment	Officials and managers	Professionals	Technicians	Sales workers	Office & clerical workers	Craft workers	Operatives	Laborers	Service workers
				NUMBER EMPLOYED						
All employees	135,502	15,260	16,864	9,931	3,675	12,163	28,331	42,651	5,552	1,075
Male	114,837	13,876	14,257	8,301	3,263	3,043	27,750	38,720	4,738	889
Female	20,665	1,384	2,607	1,630	412	9,120	581	3,931	814	186
White	119,081	14,409	15,767	9,127	3,510	10,872	24,532	35,725	4,242	897
Male	101,176	13,136	13,389	7,665	3,129	2,709	24,063	32,743	3,590	752
Female	17,905	1,273	2,378	1,462	381	8,163	469	2,982	652	145

[Continued]

★ 502 ★

Occupational Employment in Private Industry: Construction and Related Machinery

[Continued]

RACE/ETHNIC GROUP/ SEX	Total employ- ment	Officials and managers	Profes- sionals	Techni- cians	Sales workers	Office & clerical workers	Craft workers	Opera- tives	Laborers	Service workers
Minority	16,421	851	1,097	804	165	1,291	3,799	6,926	1,310	178
Male	13,661	740	868	636	134	334	3,687	5,977	1,148	137
Female	2,760	111	229	168	31	957	112	949	162	41
Black	8,414	290	350	344	39	754	1,671	4,201	656	109
Male	6,638	234	244	241	23	195	1,609	3,456	554	82
Female	1,776	56	106	103	16	559	62	745	102	27
Hispanic	5,034	223	210	262	85	369	1,353	2,007	477	48
Male	4,430	193	162	235	76	101	1,322	1,851	452	38
Female	604	30	48	27	9	268	31	156	25	10
Asian/Pacific Islander	2,114	265	490	154	19	108	524	448	89	17
Male	1,859	249	422	126	16	25	515	424	69	13
Female	255	16	68	28	3	83	9	24	20	4
Amind/Alaskan Native	859	73	47	44	22	60	251	270	88	4
Male	734	64	40	34	19	13	241	246	73	4
Female	125	9	7	10	3	47	10	24	15	0

Source: "Occupational Employment in Private Industry by Race/Ethnic Group/Sex, and by Industry, United States, 1994, All Industries." U.S. Equal Employment Opportunity Commission, *Job Patterns for Minorities and Women in Private Industry 1994*, p. 15. *Note:* Data for the state of Hawaii are not included.

★ 503 ★
Occupations

Occupational Employment in Private Industry: Converted Paper and Paperboard Products

RACE/ETHNIC GROUP/ SEX	Total employ- ment	Officials and managers	Profes- sional	Techni- cians	Sales workers	Office & clerical workers	Craft workers	Opera- tives	Laborers	Service workers
					NUMBER EMPLOYED					
All employees	156,032	17,263	14,277	4,360	7,165	13,618	26,043	49,595	22,155	1,556
Male	102,607	14,313	9,865	2,947	5,374	2,033	23,645	32,757	10,558	1,115
Female	53,425	2,950	4,412	1,413	1,791	11,585	2,398	16,838	11,597	441
White	121,896	16,002	12,984	3,829	6,554	12,037	21,492	34,500	13,338	1,150
Male	82,086	13,303	8,983	2,621	4,924	1,698	19,653	23,461	6,633	810
Female	39,810	2,699	4,001	1,218	1,630	10,339	1,839	11,039	6,705	340
Minority	34,136	1,261	1,293	521	611	1,581	4,551	15,095	8,817	406
Male	20,521	1,010	882	326	450	335	3,992	9,296	3,925	305
Female	13,615	251	411	195	161	1,246	559	5,799	4,892	101
Black	19,411	594	442	303	359	819	2,608	9,024	4,997	265
Male	11,025	469	275	183	275	150	2,249	5,243	1,987	194
Female	8,386	125	167	120	84	669	359	3,781	3,010	71

[Continued]

★ 503 ★

Occupational Employment in Private Industry: Converted Paper and Paperboard Products
[Continued]

RACE/ETHNIC GROUP/ SEX	Total employ- ment	Officials and managers	Profes- sional	Techni- cians	Sales workers	Office & clerical workers	Craft workers	Opera- tives	Laborers	Service workers
Hispanic	11,028	380	242	122	182	500	1,549	4,825	3,119	109
Male	7,093	312	156	90	127	105	1,387	3,205	1,625	86
Female	3,935	68	86	32	55	395	162	1,620	1,494	23
Asian/Pacific Islander	3,156	242	559	86	509	201	317	1,081	592	28
Male	2,056	193	414	48	34	58	284	738	264	23
Female	1,100	49	145	38	16	143	33	343	328	5
Amind/Alaskan Native	541	45	50	10	20	61	77	165	109	4
Male	347	36	37	5	14	22	72	110	49	2
Female	194	9	13	5	6	39	5	55	60	2

Source: "Occupational Employment in Private Industry by Race/Ethnic Group/Sex, and by Industry, United States, 1994, All Industries." U.S. Equal Employment Opportunity Commission, *Job Patterns for Minorities and Women in Private Industry 1994,* p. 11. *Note:* Data for the state of Hawaii are not included.

★ 504 ★
Occupations

Occupational Employment in Private Industry: Dairy Products

RACE/ETHNIC GROUP/ SEX	Total employ- ment	Officials and managers	Profes- sionals	Techni- cians	Sales workers	Office & clerical workers	Craft workers	Opera- tives	Laborers	Service workers
NUMBER EMPLOYED										
All employees	93,951	9,913	3,494	2,968	6,227	7,890	12,381	29,178	20,562	1,338
Male	69,123	8,241	2,100	1,451	5,031	924	11,532	25,438	13,660	746
Female	24,828	1,672	1,394	1,517	1,196	6,966	849	3,740	6,902	592
White	77,831	9,201	3,120	2,571	5,509	6,886	10,782	23,584	15,253	925
Male	57,640	7,675	1,896	1,259	4,393	765	10,074	20,744	10,320	514
Female	20,191	1,526	1,224	1,312	1,116	6,121	708	2,840	4,933	411
Minority	16,120	712	374	397	718	1,004	1,599	5,594	5,309	413
Male	11,483	566	204	192	638	159	1,458	4,694	3,340	232
Female	4,637	146	170	205	80	845	141	900	1,969	181
Black	7,482	316	120	157	383	500	584	2,757	2,423	242
Male	5,231	245	61	74	338	59	536	2,255	1,539	124
Female	2,251	71	59	83	45	441	48	502	884	118
Hispanic	6,879	259	71	129	291	335	848	2,358	2,450	138
Male	5,085	223	41	56	265	65	766	2,046	1,535	88
Female	1,794	36	30	73	26	270	82	312	915	50
Asian/Pacific Islander	1,317	103	171	95	26	125	111	326	341	19
Male	853	68	94	57	18	30	105	265	204	12
Female	464	35	77	38	8	95	6	61	137	7

[Continued]

★ 504 ★

Occupational Employment in Private Industry: Dairy Products
[Continued]

RACE/ETHNIC GROUP/ SEX	Total employment	Officials and managers	Professionals	Technicians	Sales workers	Office & clerical workers	Craft workers	Operatives	Laborers	Service workers
Amind/Alaskan Native	442	34	12	16	18	44	56	153	95	14
Male	314	30	8	5	17	5	51	128	62	8
Female	128	4	4	11	1	39	5	25	33	6

Source: "Occupational Employment in Private Industry by Race/Ethnic Group/Sex, and by Industry, United States, 1994, All Industries." U.S. Equal Employment Opportunity Commission, *Job Patterns for Minorities and Women in Private Industry 1994*, p. 6. *Note:* Data for the state of Hawaii are not included.

★ 505 ★

Occupations

Occupational Employment in Private Industry: Department Stores

Race/ethnic group/sex	Total employment	Officials and managers	Professionals	Technicians	Sales workers	Office & clerical workers	Craft workers	Operatives	Laborers	Service workers
				NUMBER EMPLOYED						
All employees	1,999,668	155,179	23,161	13,377	1,166,640	199,624	77,437	33,312	222,123	108,815
Male	626,765	78,121	11,113	6,143	268,986	27,100	32,783	21,922	132,919	47,678
Female	1,372,903	77,058	12,048	7,234	897,654	172,524	44,654	11,390	89,204	61,137
White	1,526,734	135,290	20,426	10,852	881,463	158,835	63,368	23,466	156,238	76,796
Male	466,934	68,374	9,958	4,947	199,929	20,185	26,026	15,562	89,807	32,146
Female	1,059,800	66,916	10,468	5,905	681,534	138,650	37,342	7,904	66,431	44,650
Minority	473,934	19,889	2,735	2,525	285,177	40,789	14,069	9,846	65,885	32,019
Male	159,831	9,747	1,155	1,196	69,057	6,915	6,757	6,360	43,112	15,532
Female	313,102	10,142	1,580	1,329	216,120	33,874	7,312	3,486	22,773	16,487
Black	262,261	10,890	1,169	1,412	158,212	23,344	6,876	5,106	36,922	18,330
Male	83,189	4,980	475	655	34,214	3,565	3,045	3,226	24,129	8,900
Female	179,072	5,910	694	757	123,998	19,779	3,831	1,880	12,793	9,430
Hispanic	153,826	6,225	704	687	90,767	12,995	5,364	3,504	23,089	10,491
Male	57,131	3,400	331	330	24,651	2,416	2,804	2,435	15,352	5,412
Female	96,695	2,825	373	357	66,116	10,579	2,560	1,069	7,737	5,079
Asian/Pacific Islander	43,865	2,203	770	360	28,225	3,475	1,369	992	3,897	2,574
Male	14,868	1,099	319	184	7,940	741	657	524	2,473	931
Female	28,997	1,104	451	176	20,285	2,734	712	468	1,424	1,643
Am. Ind./Alaskan Native	12,982	571	92	66	7,973	975	460	244	1,977	624
Male	4,643	268	30	27	2,252	193	251	175	1,158	289
Female	8,339	303	62	39	5,721	782	209	69	819	335

Source: "Occupational Employment in Private Industry by Race/Ethnic Group/Sex, and by Industry, United States, 1994, All Industries." U.S. Equal Employment Opportunity Commission, *Job Patterns for Minorities and Women in Private Industry 1994*, p. 26. *Note:* Data for the state of Hawaii are not included.

★ 506 ★

Occupations

Occupational Employment in Private Industry: Drugs

RACE/ETHNIC GROUP/ SEX	Total employ- ment	Officials and managers	Profes- sionals	Techni- cians	Sales workers	Office & clerical workers	Craft workers	Opera- tives	Laborers	Service workers
				NUMBER EMPLOYED						
All employees	290,702	51,263	68,028	20,658	40,390	36,313	21,450	38,773	8,305	5,522
Male	155,885	37,121	36,591	11,337	23,335	3,993	18,294	18,828	3,430	2,956
Female	134,817	14,142	31,437	9,321	17,055	32,320	3,156	19,945	4,875	2,566
White	226,274	45,240	55,194	15,474	35,060	28,740	16,242	23,369	3,785	3,170
Male	124,518	33,063	30,056	8,715	20,310	2,714	14,370	11,983	1,633	1,674
Female	101,756	12,177	25,138	6,759	14,750	26,026	1,872	11,386	2,152	1,496
Minority	64,428	6,023	12,834	3,184	5,330	7,573	5,208	15,404	4,520	2,352
Male	31,367	4,058	6,535	2,622	3,025	1,279	3,924	6,845	1,797	1,282
Female	33,061	1,965	6,299	2,562	2,305	6,294	1,284	8,559	2,723	1,070
Black	28,786	2,259	3,305	2,336	2,669	4,300	2,588	7,985	1,882	1,462
Male	12,742	1,401	1,472	1,046	1,470	566	2,004	3,346	718	719
Female	16,044	858	1,833	1,290	1,199	3,734	584	4,639	1,164	743
Hispanic	16,752	1,332	1,892	1,124	1,459	2,122	1,840	4,710	1,644	629
Male	8,423	926	974	675	833	379	1,399	2,226	611	400
Female	8,329	406	918	449	626	1,743	441	2,484	1,033	229
Asian/Pacific Islander	17,770	2,280	7,497	1,647	1,026	989	701	2,414	971	245
Male	9,630	1,626	4,002	854	621	272	458	1,184	458	155
Female	8,140	654	3,495	793	405	717	243	1,230	513	90
Amind/Alaskan Native	1,120	152	140	77	176	162	79	295	23	16
Male	572	105	87	47	101	62	63	89	10	8
Female	548	47	53	30	75	100	16	206	13	8

Source: "Occupational Employment in Private Industry by Race/Ethnic Group/Sex, and by Industry, United States, 1994, All Industries." U.S. Equal Employment Opportunity Commission, *Job Patterns for Minorities and Women in Private Industry 1994*, p. 12. *Note:* Data for the state of Hawaii are not included.

★ 507 ★

Occupations

Occupational Employment in Private Industry: Eating and Drinking Places

Race/ethnic group/sex	Total employment	Officials and managers	Professionals	Technicians	Sales workers	Office & clerical workers	Craft workers	Operatives	Laborers	Service workers
				NUMBER EMPLOYED						
All employees	1,137,957	82,510	14,172	4,283	19,926	38,169	17,941	19,822	31,635	909,499
Male	557,767	55,854	7,911	2,206	7,676	7,825	15,077	15,448	18,850	426,920
Female	580,190	26,656	6,261	2,077	12,250	30,344	2,864	4,374	12,785	482,579

[Continued]

★ 507 ★

Occupational Employment in Private Industry: Eating and Drinking Places

[Continued]

Race/ethnic group/sex	Total employment	Officials and managers	Professionals	Technicians	Sales workers	Office & clerical workers	Craft workers	Operatives	Laborers	Service workers
White	752,482	68,609	11,412	2,883	14,829	27,800	10,959	9,749	13,432	592,809
Male	329,229	46,577	6,514	1,655	6,053	5,063	9,262	7,274	7,358	239,473
Female	423,253	22,032	4,898	1,228	8,776	22,737	1,697	2,475	6,074	353,336
Minority	385,475	13,901	2,760	1,400	5,097	10,369	6,982	10,073	18,203	316,690
Male	228,538	9,277	1,397	551	1,623	2,762	5,815	8,174	11,492	187,447
Female	156,937	4,624	1,363	849	3,474	7,607	1,167	1,899	6,711	129,243
Black	192,798	7,515	1,114	850	2,514	5,390	2,060	4,682	8,408	160,265
Male	104,785	4,542	494	269	742	1,260	1,556	3,647	4,896	87,379
Female	88,013	2,973	620	581	1,772	4,130	504	1,035	3,512	72,886
Hispanic	144,357	4,287	702	316	1,593	3,248	3,349	4,037	7,933	118,892
Male	98,931	3,212	457	185	575	976	2,890	3,364	5,481	81,791
Female	45,426	1,075	245	131	1,018	2,272	459	673	2,452	37,101
Asian/Pacific Islander	37,689	1,770	863	209	832	1,543	1,442	1,214	1,603	28,213
Male	19,483	1,305	400	84	252	489	1,264	1,058	965	13,666
Female	18,206	465	463	125	580	1,054	178	156	638	14,547
Am. Ind./Alaskan Native	10,631	329	81	25	158	188	131	140	259	9,320
Male	5,339	218	46	13	54	37	105	105	150	4,611
Female	5,292	111	35	12	104	151	26	35	109	4,709

Source: "Occupational Employment in Private Industry by Race/Ethnic Group/Sex, and by Industry, United States, 1994, All Industries." U.S. Equal Employment Opportunity Commission, *Job Patterns for Minorities and Women in Private Industry 1994*, p. 27. *Note:* Data for the state of Hawaii are not included.

★ 508 ★

Occupations

Occupational Employment in Private Industry: Electric Lighting and Wiring Equipment

RACE/ETHNIC GROUP/ SEX	Total employment	Officials and managers	Professionals	Technicians	Sales workers	Office & clerical workers	Craft workers	Operatives	Laborers	Service workers
					NUMBER EMPLOYED					
All employees	94,466	8,846	5,807	3,154	2,911	7,246	12,952	36,838	15,789	923
Male	52,121	7,349	4,428	2,420	2,148	1,239	11,199	16,497	6,162	679
Female	42,345	1,497	1,379	734	763	6,007	1,753	20,341	9,627	244
White	68,235	8,109	5,242	2,640	2,739	6,057	10,651	23,432	8,738	627
Male	38,897	6,770	4,016	2,037	2,052	948	9,228	10,223	3,197	426
Female	29,338	1,339	1,226	603	687	5,109	1,423	13,209	5,541	201
Minority	26,231	737	565	514	172	1,189	2,301	13,406	7,051	296
Male	13,224	579	412	383	96	291	1,971	6,274	2,965	253
Female	13,007	158	153	131	76	898	330	7,132	4,086	43
Black	12,326	286	191	188	92	537	1,080	7,107	2,707	138
Male	5,662	202	112	139	39	74	892	2,966	1,125	113
Female	6,664	84	79	49	53	463	188	4,141	1,582	25

[Continued]

★ 508 ★

Occupational Employment in Private Industry: Electric Lighting and Wiring Equipment

[Continued]

RACE/ETHNIC GROUP/ SEX	Total employ- ment	Officials and managers	Profes- sionals	Techni- cians	Sales workers	Office & clerical workers	Craft workers	Opera- tives	Laborers	Service workers
Hispanic	10,152	234	102	153	55	476	967	4,647	3,380	138
Male	5,467	180	79	113	39	156	846	2,478	1,454	122
Female	4,685	54	23	40	16	320	121	2,169	1,926	16
Asian/Pacific Islander	3,532	189	263	163	16	160	225	1,569	929	18
Male	1,990	176	214	126	13	58	210	802	374	17
Female	1,542	13	49	37	3	102	15	767	555	1
Amind/Alaskan Native	221	28	9	10	9	16	29	83	35	2
Male	105	21	7	5	5	3	23	28	12	1
Female	116	7	2	5	4	13	6	55	23	1

Source: "Occupational Employment in Private Industry by Race/Ethnic Group/Sex, and by Industry, United States, 1994, All Industries." U.S. Equal Employment Opportunity Commission, *Job Patterns for Minorities and Women in Private Industry 1994,* p. 18. *Note:* Data for the state of Hawaii are not included.

★ 509 ★

Occupations

Occupational Employment in Private Industry: Electric Services

Race/Ethnic Group/Sex	Number employed									
	Total Employ- ment	Officials and Managers	Profes- sionals	Techni- cians	Sales workers	Office & Clerical workers	Craft workers	Opera- tives	Laborers	Service workers
All Employees	421,362	62,764	91,010	36,518	1,818	71,398	112,501	31,679	8,733	4,941
Male	323,076	55,386	70,062	30,072	997	16,993	109,905	28,569	7,451	3,641
Female	98,286	7,378	20,948	6,446	821	54,405	2,596	3,110	1,282	1,300
White	356,484	57,448	80,206	31,539	1,426	53,732	97,062	24,853	6,602	3,616
Male	279,925	51,383	62,874	26,421	837	12,514	95,020	22,491	5,680	2,705
Female	76,559	6,065	17,332	5,118	589	41,218	2,042	2,362	922	911
Minority	64,878	5,316	10,804	4,979	392	17,666	15,439	6,826	2,131	1,325
Male	43,151	4,003	7,188	3,651	160	4,479	14,885	6,078	1,771	936
Female	21,727	1,313	3,616	1,328	232	13,187	554	748	360	389
Black	38,919	2,735	4,916	2,816	209	11,565	10,044	4,475	1,250	909
Male	24,963	2,049	2,927	1,999	60	2,644	9,599	3,981	1,085	619
Female	13,956	686	1,989	817	149	8,921	445	494	165	290
Hispanic	16,523	1,428	2,493	1,396	158	4,325	4,055	1,726	623	319
Male	11,600	1,140	1,661	1,056	83	1,369	3,997	1,577	472	245
Female	4,923	288	832	340	75	2,956	58	149	151	74
Asian/Pacific Islander	6,688	924	3,051	568	17	1,330	499	164	98	37
Male	4,515	620	2,356	448	12	339	486	137	86	31

[Continued]

★ 509 ★

Occupational Employment in Private Industry: Electric Services
[Continued]

Race/Ethnic Group/Sex	Total Employment	Officials and Managers	Professionals	Technicians	Sales workers	Office & Clerical workers	Craft workers	Operatives	Laborers	Service workers
						Number employed				
Female	2,173	304	695	120	5	991	13	27	12	6
AmInd/Alaskan Native	2,748	229	344	199	8	446	841	461	160	60
Male	2,073	194	244	148	5	127	803	383	128	41
Female	675	35	100	51	3	319	38	78	32	19

Source: "Occupational Employment in Private Industry by Race/Ethnic Group/Sex, and by Industry, United States, 1994, All Industries." U.S. Equal Employment Opportunity Commission, *Job Patterns for Minorities and Women in Private Industry 1994*, p. 23. *Note:* Data for the state of Hawaii are not included.

★ 510 ★

Occupations

Occupational Employment in Private Industry: Electrical Goods

RACE/ETHNIC GROUP/SEX	Total employment	Officials and managers	Professionals	Technicians	Sales workers	Office & clerical workers	Craft workers	Operatives	Laborers	Service workers
					NUMBER EMPLOYED					
All employees	108,608	19,699	17,429	7,172	13,061	21,062	6,688	15,663	6,552	1,282
Male	66,169	14,970	11,852	6,042	8,952	4,557	5,623	9,167	4,047	959
Female	42,439	4,729	5,577	1,130	4,109	16,505	1,065	6,496	2,505	323
White	84,547	17,163	14,288	5,554	11,398	16,065	5,365	9,519	4,396	799
Male	52,879	13,095	9,812	4,705	8,012	3,303	4,678	5,970	2,698	606
Female	31,668	4,068	4,476	849	3,386	12,762	687	3,549	1,698	193
Minority	24,061	2,536	3,141	1,618	1,663	4,997	1,323	6,144	2,156	483
Male	13,290	1,875	2,040	1,337	940	1,254	945	3,197	1,349	353
Female	10,771	661	1,101	281	723	3,743	378	2,947	807	130
Black	10,547	703	797	429	874	2,452	734	3,163	1,016	379
Male	4,891	400	436	334	398	496	497	1,408	643	279
Female	5,656	303	361	95	476	1,956	237	1,755	373	100
Hispanic	6,576	585	680	439	430	1,584	359	1,630	804	65
Male	3,811	416	424	375	281	465	278	1,012	514	46
Female	2,765	169	256	64	149	1,119	81	618	290	19
Asian/Pacific Islander	6,603	1,201	1,635	722	334	892	201	1,271	311	36
Male	4,399	1,024	1,160	603	248	278	147	738	175	26
Female	2,204	177	475	119	86	614	54	533	136	10
Amind/Alaskan Native	335	47	29	28	25	69	29	80	25	3

[Continued]

★ 510 ★

Occupational Employment in Private Industry: Electrical Goods

[Continued]

RACE/ETHNIC GROUP/ SEX	Total employment	Officials and managers	Profes-sionals	Techni-cians	Sales workers	Office & clerical workers	Craft workers	Opera-tives	Laborers	Service workers
Male	189	35	20	25	13	15	23	39	17	2
Female	146	12	9	3	12	54	6	41	8	1

Source: "Occupational Employment in Private Industry by Race/Ethnic Group/Sex, and by Industry, United States, 1994, All Industries." U.S. Equal Employment Opportunity Commission, *Job Patterns for Minorities and Women in Private Industry 1994,* p. 25. *Note:* Data for the state of Hawaii are not included.

★ 511 ★

Occupations

Occupational Employment in Private Industry: Electronic Components and Accessories

Race/ethnic group/sex	Total employment	Officials and managers	Professionals	Technicians	Sales workers	Office & clerical workers	Craft workers	Operatives	Laborers	Service workers
				NUMBER EMPLOYED						
All employees	425,719	51,757	97,301	48,912	6,713	36,560	33,311	131,834	15,691	3,640
Male	249,580	42,133	74,632	37,643	4,594	7,178	22,557	51,746	6,421	2,676
Female	176,139	9,624	22,669	11,269	2,119	29,382	10,754	80,088	9,270	964
White	298,154	44,091	74,920	34,793	6,088	27,031	24,007	76,716	8,280	2,228
Male	181,392	36,114	58,251	27,412	4,247	4,733	16,890	29,481	2,586	1,678
Female	116,762	7,977	16,669	7,381	1,841	22,298	7,117	47,235	5,694	550
Minority	127,565	7,666	22,381	14,119	625	9,529	9,304	55,118	7,411	1,412
Male	68,188	6,019	16,381	10,231	347	2,445	5,667	22,265	3,835	998
Female	59,377	1,647	6,000	3,888	278	7,084	3,637	32,853	3,576	414
Black	29,521	1,295	2,983	3,020	148	2,789	2,471	13,980	2,289	546
Male	13,643	911	1,871	2,022	61	648	1,498	4,985	1,267	382
Female	15,878	384	1,112	998	87	2,141	975	8,995	1,022	164
Hispanic	42,081	2,001	4,128	4,535	194	3,769	3,701	19,845	3,248	660
Male	21,334	1,467	2,875	3,258	106	948	2,347	8,060	1,807	466
Female	20,747	534	1,253	1,277	88	2,821	1,354	11,785	1,441	194
Asian/Pacific Islander	53,522	4,122	14,971	6,320	259	2,763	2,954	20,124	1,831	178
Male	32,020	3,435	11,428	4,782	170	798	1,717	8,817	741	132
Female	21,502	687	3,543	1,538	89	1,965	1,237	11,307	1,090	46
Am. Ind./Alaskan Native	2,441	248	299	244	24	208	178	1,169	43	28
Male	1,191	206	207	169	10	51	107	403	20	18
Female	1,250	42	92	75	14	157	71	766	23	10

Source: "Occupational Employment in Private Industry by Race/Ethnic Group/Sex, and by Industry, United States, 1994, All Industries." U.S. Equal Employment Opportunity Commission, *Job Patterns for Minorities and Women in Private Industry 1994,* p. 19. *Note:* Data for the state of Hawaii are not included.

★ 512 ★

Occupations

Occupational Employment in Private Industry: Engineering and Architectural Services

Race/ethnic group/sex	Total employment	Officials and managers	Professionals	Technicians	Sales workers	Office & clerical workers	Craft workers	Operatives	Laborers	Service workers
				NUMBER EMPLOYED						
All employees	283,365	43,541	117,936	50,559	2,184	36,496	18,541	8,720	3,636	1,752
Male	211,773	38,107	95,370	41,063	1,390	6,261	17,751	7,430	3,076	1,325
Female	71,592	5,434	22,566	9,496	794	30,235	790	1,290	560	427
White	237,856	39,420	101,938	42,448	1,930	28,581	14,321	5,939	2,094	1,165
Male	179,614	34,683	82,937	34,767	1,277	4,473	13,683	5,094	1,801	899
Female	58,242	4,737	19,001	7,701	653	24,108	638	845	293	266
Minority	45,509	4,121	15,998	8,091	254	7,915	4,220	2,781	1,542	587
Male	32,159	3,424	12,433	6,296	113	1,788	4,068	2,336	1,275	426
Female	13,350	697	3,565	1,795	141	6,127	152	445	267	161
Black	16,776	1,049	3,466	3,237	130	4,247	1,844	1,460	948	395
Male	10,372	725	2,303	2,466	42	884	1,734	1,163	756	299
Female	6,404	324	1,163	771	88	3,363	110	297	192	96
Hispanic	12,606	1,045	3,116	2,297	59	2,213	2,140	1,110	469	157
Male	9,383	901	2,377	1,869	31	539	2,113	1,015	433	105
Female	3,223	144	739	428	28	1,674	27	95	36	52
Asian/Pacific Islander	14,986	1,884	9,086	2,297	61	1,287	138	154	62	17
Male	11,617	1,694	7,508	1,752	39	334	127	108	45	10
Female	3,369	190	1,578	545	22	953	11	46	17	7
Am. Ind./Alaskan Native	1,141	143	330	260	4	168	98	57	63	18
Male	787	104	245	209	1	31	94	50	41	12
Female	354	39	85	51	3	137	4	7	22	6

Source: "Occupational Employment in Private Industry by Race/Ethnic Group/Sex, and by Industry, United States, 1994, All Industries." U.S. Equal Employment Opportunity Commission, *Job Patterns for Minorities and Women in Private Industry 1994*, p. 35. *Note:* Data for the state of Hawaii are not included.

★ 513 ★

Occupations

Occupational Employment in Private Industry: Family Clothing Stores

Race/Ethnic Group/Sex	Total Employment	Officials and Managers	Professionals	Technicians	Sales workers	Office & Clerical workers	Craft workers	Operatives	Laborers	Service workers
	Number employed									
All employees	93,309	12,367	3,633	1,093	45,752	11,216	3,885	2,875	5,979	6,509
Male	29,981	5,163	1,385	589	10,470	2,780	1,819	1,018	2,882	3,875
Female	63,328	7,204	2,248	504	35,282	8,436	2,066	1,857	3,097	2,634
White	65,794	10,486	3,142	942	31,400	7,948	2,240	1,855	3,760	4,021
Male	20,252	4,424	1,161	509	7,017	1,722	979	634	1,626	2,180

[Continued]

★ 513 ★

Occupational Employment in Private Industry: Family Clothing Stores
[Continued]

Race/Ethnic Group/Sex	Number employed									
	Total Employment	Officials and Managers	Professionals	Technicians	Sales workers	Office & Clerical workers	Craft workers	Operatives	Laborers	Service workers
Female	45,542	6,062	1,981	433	24,383	6,226	1,261	1,221	2,134	1,841
Minority	27,515	1,881	491	151	14,352	3,268	1,645	1,020	2,219	2,488
Male	9,729	739	224	80	3,453	1,058	840	384	1,256	1,695
Female	17,786	1,142	267	71	10,899	2,210	805	636	963	793
Black	14,468	979	189	75	8,378	1,637	487	560	971	1,192
Male	4,647	346	73	45	1,915	457	290	171	552	798
Female	9,821	633	116	30	6,463	1,180	197	389	419	394
Hispanic	7,894	537	86	19	3,688	937	697	326	622	982
Male	3,255	239	42	10	940	404	380	142	400	698
Female	4,639	298	44	9	2,748	533	317	184	222	284
Asian/Pacific Islander	4,778	331	202	50	2,093	646	448	126	608	274
Male	1,696	140	103	22	544	188	163	67	296	175
Female	3,080	191	99	28	1,549	458	285	59	312	99
AmInd/Alaskan Native	375	34	14	7	193	48	13	8	18	40
Male	129	14	6	3	54	9	7	4	8	24
Female	246	20	8	4	139	39	6	4	10	16

Source: "Occupational Employment in Private Industry by Race/Ethnic Group/Sex, and by Industry, United States, 1994, All Industries." U.S. Equal Employment Opportunity Commission, *Job Patterns for Minorities and Women in Private Industry 1994*, p. 27. *Note:* Data for the state of Hawaii are not included.

★ 514 ★

Occupations

Occupational Employment in Private Industry: Finance, Insurance, and Real Estate

Race/Ethnic Group/Sex	Number employed									
	Total Employment	Officials and Managers	Professionals	Technicians	Sales workers	Office & Clerical workers	Craft workers	Operatives	Laborers	Service workers
All employees	2,887,150	503,655	599,417	169,541	156,040	1,324,713	21,424	25,099	14,731	72,530
Male	1,037,647	286,424	270,965	68,987	99,884	221,849	17,318	17,972	11,823	42,425
Female	1,849,503	217,231	328,452	100,554	56,156	1,102,864	4,106	7,127	2,908	30,105
White	2,261,783	448,359	503,378	133,774	135,346	954,118	16,957	15,850	9,043	44,958
Male	848,422	261,650	234,211	55,290	90,079	148,382	13,781	11,558	7,345	26,126
Female	1,413,361	186,709	269,167	78,484	45,267	805,736	3,176	4,292	1,698	18,832
Minority	625,367	55,296	96,039	35,767	20,694	370,595	4,467	9,249	5,688	27,572
Male	189,225	24,774	36,754	13,697	9,805	73,467	3,537	6,414	4,478	16,299
Female	436,142	30,522	59,285	22,070	10,889	297,128	930	2,835	1,210	11,273

[Continued]

★ 514 ★

Occupational Employment in Private Industry: Finance, Insurance, and Real Estate
[Continued]

Race/Ethnic Group/Sex	Number employed									
	Total Employ-ment	Officials and Managers	Profes-sionals	Techni-cians	Sales workers	Office & Clerical workers	Craft workers	Opera-tives	Laborers	Service workers
Black	345,387	27,111	46,546	20,307	9,503	215,426	2,232	5,035	2,930	16,297
Male	88,845	10,431	14,919	6,112	4,077	36,646	1,641	3,314	2,232	9,473
Female	256,542	16,680	31,627	14,195	5,426	178,780	591	1,721	698	6,824
Hispanic	160,164	14,605	21,241	7,381	6,756	94,044	1,752	2,828	2,427	9,130
Male	54,090	6,909	8,681	3,481	3,113	20,438	1,525	2,203	2,014	5,726
Female	106,074	7,696	12,560	3,900	3,643	73,606	227	625	413	3,404
Asian/Pacific Islander	109,984	12,357	26,766	7,499	3,819	55,886	386	1,270	274	1,727
Male	42,999	6,812	12,537	3,837	2,251	15,384	299	814	187	878
Female	66,985	5,545	14,229	3,662	1,568	40,502	87	456	87	849
AmInd/Alaskan Native	9,832	1,223	1,486	580	616	5,239	97	116	57	418
Male	3,291	622	617	267	364	999	72	83	45	222
Female	6,541	601	869	313	252	4,240	25	33	12	196

Source: "Occupational Employment in Private Industry by Race/Ethnic Group/Sex, and by Industry, United States, 1994, All Industries." U.S. Equal Employment Opportunity Commission, *Job Patterns for Minorities and Women in Private Industry 1994*, p. 4. *Note:* Data for the state of Hawaii are not included.

★ 515 ★
Occupations

Occupational Employment in Private Industry: Fire, Marine, and Casualty Insurance

Race/Ethnic Group/Sex	Number employed									
	Total Employ-ment	Officials and Managers	Profes-sionals	Techni-cians	Sales workers	Office & Clerical workers	Craft workers	Opera-tives	Laborers	Service workers
All employees	323,032	51,115	102,320	27,694	7,048	128,528	1,521	2,106	506	2,194
Male	116,650	32,335	49,097	12,885	4,092	13,821	1,305	1,344	411	1,360
Female	206,382	18,780	53,223	14,809	2,956	114,707	216	762	95	834
White	265,450	46,302	86,958	22,988	6,277	98,291	1,325	1,626	377	1,306
Male	100,898	30,062	43,119	10,974	3,823	9,634	1,142	1,025	309	810
Female	164,552	16,240	43,839	12,014	2,454	88,657	183	601	68	496
Minority	57,582	4,813	15,362	4,706	771	30,237	196	480	129	888
Male	15,752	2,273	5,978	1,911	269	4,187	163	319	102	550
Female	41,830	2,540	9,384	2,795	502	26,050	33	161	27	338
Black	32,722	2,727	8,400	2,581	443	17,632	102	257	74	506
Male	7,705	1,197	2,842	904	107	2,054	76	165	59	301
Female	25,017	1,530	5,558	1,677	336	15,578	26	92	15	205
Hispanic	13,669	1,097	3,312	929	242	7,591	51	128	42	277

[Continued]

539

★ 515 ★

Occupational Employment in Private Industry: Fire, Marine, and Casualty Insurance

[Continued]

Race/Ethnic Group/Sex	Number employed									
	Total Employ- ment	Officials and Managers	Profes- sionals	Techni- cians	Sales workers	Office & Clerical workers	Craft workers	Opera- tives	Laborers	Service workers
Male	4,173	542	1,498	475	123	1,180	48	98	32	177
Female	9,496	555	1,814	454	119	6,411	3	30	10	100
Asian/Pacific Islander	10,251	869	3,363	1,135	74	4,579	37	83	13	98
Male	3,572	462	1,511	507	33	900	33	48	11	67
Female	6,679	407	1,852	628	41	3,679	4	35	2	31
AmInd/Alaskan Native	940	120	287	61	12	435	6	12	0	7
Male	302	72	127	25	6	53	6	8	0	5
Female	638	48	160	36	6	382	0	4	0	2

Source: "Occupational Employment in Private Industry by Race/Ethnic Group/Sex, and by Industry, United States, 1994, All Industries." U.S. Equal Employment Opportunity Commission, *Job Patterns for Minorities and Women in Private Industry 1994*, p. 30. *Note:* Data for the state of Hawaii are not included.

★ 516 ★

Occupations

Occupational Employment in Private Industry: Gas Production and Distribution

Race/ethnic group/sex	Total employment	Officials and managers	Professionals	Technicians	Sales workers	Office & clerical workers	Craft workers	Operatives	Laborers	Service workers
	NUMBER EMPLOYED									
All employees	104,812	16,846	17,073	7,728	2,601	24,904	21,855	9,645	2,621	1,539
Male	71,984	13,790	10,633	6,313	1,722	5,917	21,248	8,990	2,403	968
Female	32,828	3,056	6,440	1,415	879	18,987	607	655	218	571
White	82,262	15,162	14,415	6,230	2,208	17,214	17,235	6,894	1,810	1,094
Male	57,918	12,606	9,288	5,100	1,459	3,985	16,793	6,418	1,643	626
Female	24,344	2,556	5,127	1,130	749	13,229	442	476	167	468
Minority	22,550	1,684	2,658	1,498	393	7,690	4,620	2,751	811	445
Male	14,066	1,184	1,345	1,213	263	1,932	4,455	2,572	760	342
Female	8,484	500	1,313	285	130	5,758	165	179	51	103
Black	12,235	901	1,229	491	127	4,571	2,733	1,366	598	219
Male	7,279	622	530	384	63	1,104	2,610	1,241	559	166
Female	4,956	279	699	107	64	3,467	123	125	39	53
Hispanic	7,776	517	708	727	125	2,508	1,638	1,256	175	122
Male	5,298	395	432	639	93	674	1,604	1,209	165	87
Female	2,478	122	276	88	32	1,834	34	47	10	35
Asian/Pacific Islander	1,703	200	637	176	37	451	116	60	14	12
Male	881	118	333	101	12	119	115	57	14	12
Female	822	82	304	75	25	332	1	3	0	0
Am. Ind./Alaskan Native	836	66	84	104	104	160	133	69	24	92

[Continued]

★ 516 ★

Occupational Employment in Private Industry: Gas Production and Distribution

[Continued]

Race/ethnic group/sex	Total employment	Officials and managers	Professionals	Technicians	Sales workers	Office & clerical workers	Craft workers	Operatives	Laborers	Service workers
Male	608	49	50	89	95	35	126	65	22	77
Female	228	17	34	15	9	125	7	4	2	15

Source: "Occupational Employment in Private Industry by Race/Ethnic Group/Sex, and by Industry, United States, 1994, All Industries." U.S. Equal Employment Opportunity Commission, *Job Patterns for Minorities and Women in Private Industry 1994*, p. 23. *Note:* Data for the state of Hawaii are not included.

★ 517 ★

Occupations

Occupational Employment in Private Industry: Groceries and Related Products

Race/ethnic group/sex	Total employment	Officials and managers	Professionals	Technicians	Sales workers	Office & clerical workers	Craft workers	Operatives	Laborers	Service workers
					NUMBER EMPLOYED					
All employees	317,650	39,003	11,756	5,138	57,295	37,077	14,053	77,241	66,586	9,501
Male	233,523	31,112	7,053	3,140	42,402	6,694	12,624	70,785	53,236	6,477
Female	84,127	7,891	4,703	1,998	14,893	30,383	1,429	6,456	13,350	3,024
White	247,042	35,445	10,433	4,262	51,088	31,239	10,936	55,774	42,066	5,799
Male	180,205	28,352	6,329	2,704	37,764	5,169	9,967	51,646	34,623	3,651
Female	66,837	7,093	4,104	1,558	13,324	26,070	969	4,128	7,443	2,148
Minority	70,608	3,558	1,323	876	6,207	5,838	3,117	21,467	24,520	3,702
Male	53,318	2,760	724	436	4,638	1,525	2,657	19,139	18,613	2,826
Female	17,290	798	599	440	1,569	4,313	460	2,328	5,907	876
Black	34,666	1,561	547	354	2,554	2,756	1,462	11,308	11,672	2,452
Male	27,131	1,216	281	161	1,822	710	1,218	10,504	9,383	1,836
Female	7,535	345	266	193	732	2,046	244	804	2,289	616
Hispanic	29,897	1,415	361	338	2,813	2,359	1,434	9,069	11,042	1,066
Male	22,288	1,125	211	162	2,232	618	1,261	7,768	8,042	869
Female	7,609	290	150	176	581	1,741	173	1,301	3,000	197
Asian/Pacific Islander	4,985	476	370	161	703	616	157	807	1,534	161
Male	3,132	339	204	101	496	178	121	611	976	106
Female	1,853	137	166	60	207	438	36	196	558	55
Am. Ind./Alaskan Native	1,060	106	45	23	137	107	64	283	272	23
Male	767	80	28	12	88	19	57	256	212	15
Female	293	26	17	11	49	88	7	27	60	8

Source: "Occupational Employment in Private Industry by Race/Ethnic Group/Sex, and by Industry, United States, 1994, All Industries." U.S. Equal Employment Opportunity Commission, *Job Patterns for Minorities and Women in Private Industry 1994*, p. 25. *Note:* Data for the state of Hawaii are not included.

★ 518 ★

Occupations

Occupational Employment in Private Industry: Grocery Stores

Race/Ethnic Group/Sex	Number employed									
	Total Employment	Officials and Managers	Profes-sionals	Techni-cians	Sales workers	Office & Clerical workers	Craft workers	Opera-tives	Laborers	Service workers
All employees	1,655,886	145,142	19,149	8,648	1,105,531	53,445	51,965	85,503	97,850	88,653
Male	848,714	101,318	10,491	4,118	503,881	10,098	35,382	61,461	71,907	50,058
Female	807,172	43,824	8,658	4,530	601,650	43,347	16,583	24,024	25,943	38,595
White	1,291,858	127,378	16,662	7,041	853,375	45,012	41,847	64,725	70,579	65,239
Male	647,176	89,117	9,310	3,356	379,154	7,952	27,735	45,267	51,014	34,271
Female	644,682	38,261	7,352	3,685	474,221	37,060	14,112	19,458	19,565	30,968
Minority	364,028	17,764	2,487	1,607	252,156	8,433	10,118	20,778	27,271	23,414
Male	201,538	12,201	1,181	762	124,727	2,146	7,647	16,194	20,893	15,787
Female	162,490	5,563	1,306	845	127,429	6,287	2,471	4,584	6,378	7,627
Black	191,248	8,389	965	603	140,57	3,779	4,082	9,256	12,607	11,000
Male	100,078	5,356	434	295	65,625	826	2,957	7,293	10,030	7,262
Female	91,170	3,033	531	308	74,942	2,953	1,125	1,963	2,577	3,738
Hispanic	135,281	7,001	570	767	86,520	3,545	4,789	9,958	12,273	9,858
Male	80,764	5,199	305	350	46,136	994	3,776	7,792	9,227	6,985
Female	54,517	1,802	265	417	40,384	2,551	1,013	2,166	3,046	2,873
Asian/Pacific Islander	28,587	1,861	870	198	19,029	854	950	1,132	1,597	2,096
Male	16,323	1,347	398	96	10,271	277	720	824	1,093	1,297
Female	12,264	514	472	102	8,758	577	230	308	504	799
AmInd/Alaskan Native	8,912	513	82	39	6,040	255	297	432	794	460
Male	4,373	299	44	21	2,695	49	194	285	543	243
Female	4,539	214	38	18	3,345	206	103	147	251	217

Source: "Occupational Employment in Private Industry by Race/Ethnic Group/Sex, and by Industry, United States, 1994, All Industries." U.S. Equal Employment Opportunity Commission, *Job Patterns for Minorities and Women in Private Industry 1994*, p. 27. *Note:* Data for the state of Hawaii are not included.

★ 519 ★

Occupations

Occupational Employment in Private Industry: Health Insurance and Medical Service Plans

Race/Ethnic Group/Sex	Number employed									
	Total Employment	Officials and Managers	Professionals	Technicians	Sales workers	Office & Clerical workers	Craft workers	Operatives	Laborers	Service workers
All employees	250,233	33,451	60,008	32,593	10,333	109,038	1,013	836	426	2,535
Male	65,104	16,468	18,970	7,403	5,819	13,567	825	559	275	1,218
Female	185,129	16,963	41,038	25,190	4,514	95,471	188	277	151	1,317
White	191,046	29,455	50,025	24,693	8,942	74,717	793	549	363	1,509
Male	53,035	15,060	16,255	5,935	5,147	8,578	673	369	233	785
Female	138,011	14,395	33,770	18,758	3,795	66,139	120	180	130	724
Minority	59,187	3,996	9,983	7,900	1,391	34,321	220	287	63	1,026
Male	12,069	1,408	2,715	1,468	672	4,989	152	190	42	433
Female	47,118	2,588	7,268	6,432	719	29,332	68	97	21	593
Black	38,755	2,369	5,711	5,756	793	23,103	147	186	44	646
Male	6,451	703	1,206	812	367	2,796	101	113	34	319
Female	32,304	1,666	4,505	4,944	426	20,307	46	73	10	327
Hispanic	11,340	945	1,854	1,075	433	6,642	44	76	10	261
Male	2,883	381	606	304	220	1,200	33	62	7	70
Female	5,457	564	1,248	771	213	5,442	11	14	3	191
Asian/Pacific Islander	8,118	586	2,256	938	119	4,063	20	23	8	105
Male	2,509	280	846	325	64	930	12	13	1	38
Female	5,609	306	1,410	613	55	3,133	8	10	7	67
AmInd/Alaskan Native	974	96	162	131	46	513	9	2	1	14
Male	226	44	57	27	21	63	6	2	0	6
Female	748	52	105	104	25	450	3	0	1	8

Source: "Occupational Employment in Private Industry by Race/Ethnic Group/Sex, and by Industry, United States, 1994, All Industries." U.S. Equal Employment Opportunity Commission, *Job Patterns for Minorities and Women in Private Industry 1994*, p. 30. *Note:* Data for the state of Hawaii are not included.

★ 520 ★

Occupations

Occupational Employment in Private Industry: Health Services

Race/Ethnic Group/Sex	Number employed									
	Total Employment	Officials and Managers	Profes-sionals	Techni-cians	Sales workers	Office & Clerical workers	Craft workers	Opera-tives	Laborers	Service workers
All employees	215,494	18,805	73,405	34,421	2,066	49,535	1,751	4,976	1,564	28,971
Male	49,137	7,096	16,067	7,815	585	4,791	1,278	3,293	920	7,292
Female	166,357	11,709	57,338	26,606	1,481	44,744	473	1,683	644	21,679
White	162,124	16,361	61,918	24,969	1,626	36,090	1,292	3,251	994	15,623
Male	36,229	6,240	13,269	5,472	466	3,030	959	2,163	573	4,057
Female	125,895	10,121	48,649	19,497	1,160	33,060	333	1,088	421	11,566
Minority	53,370	2,444	11,487	9,452	440	13,445	459	1,725	570	13,348
Male	12,908	856	2,798	2,343	119	1,761	319	1,130	347	3,235
Female	40,462	1,588	8,689	7,109	321	11,684	140	595	223	10,113
Black	34,139	1,399	6,127	6,132	319	8,272	268	1,260	361	10,001
Male	7,426	415	1,249	1,288	81	943	170	814	233	2,233
Female	26,713	984	4,878	4,844	238	7,329	98	446	128	7,768
Hispanic	11,148	486	1,926	1,939	88	3,606	125	331	132	2,515
Male	3,082	199	597	595	31	486	99	235	89	751
Female	8,066	287	1,329	1,344	57	3,120	26	96	43	1,764
Asian/Pacific Islander	7,104	463	3,151	1,236	28	1,338	49	100	74	665
Male	2,126	205	859	420	6	308	38	65	24	201
Female	4,978	258	2,292	816	22	1,030	11	35	50	464
AmInd/Alaskan Native	979	96	283	145	5	229	17	34	3	167
Male	274	37	93	40	1	24	12	16	1	50
Female	705	59	190	105	4	205	5	18	2	117

Source: "Occupational Employment in Private Industry by Race/Ethnic Group/Sex, and by Industry, United States, 1994, All Industries." U.S. Equal Employment Opportunity Commission, *Job Patterns for Minorities and Women in Private Industry 1994*, p. 34. *Note:* Data for the state of Hawaii are not included.

★ 521 ★

Occupations

Occupational Employment in Private Industry: Home Health Care Services

Race/Ethnic Group/Sex	Number employed									
	Total Employment	Officials and Managers	Professionals	Technicians	Sales workers	Office & Clerical workers	Craft workers	Operatives	Laborers	Service workers
All employees	107,427	6,689	34,795	8,477	1,387	16,285	367	973	2,216	36,238
Male	13,075	1,553	3,784	1,432	496	1,468	228	633	346	3,135
Female	94,352	5,136	31,011	7,045	891	14,817	139	340	1,870	33,103
White	71,886	5,949	29,607	6,276	1,031	12,223	282	664	990	14,864
Male	9,219	1,411	3,100	1,013	457	985	170	408	204	1,471
Female	62,667	4,538	26,507	5,263	574	11,238	112	256	786	13,393
Minority	35,541	740	5,188	2,201	356	4,062	85	309	1,226	21,374
Male	3,856	142	684	419	39	483	58	225	142	1,664
Female	31,685	598	4,504	1,782	317	3,579	27	84	1,084	19,710
Black	26,061	456	3,079	1,373	307	2,500	46	199	1,070	17,031
Male	2,150	54	280	181	17	248	30	131	92	1,117
Female	23,911	402	2,799	1,192	290	2,252	16	68	978	15,914
Hispanic	5,889	153	776	332	33	1,013	22	89	114	3,357
Male	921	46	156	91	12	139	19	77	34	347
Female	4,968	107	620	241	21	874	3	12	80	3,010
Asian/Pacific Islander	3,141	116	1,209	445	12	475	6	14	35	829
Male	718	38	233	134	7	91	6	12	15	182
Female	2,423	78	976	311	5	384	0	2	20	647
AmInd/Alaskan Native	450	15	124	51	4	74	11	7	7	157
Male	67	4	15	13	3	5	3	5	1	18
Female	383	11	109	38	1	69	8	2	6	139

Source: "Occupational Employment in Private Industry by Race/Ethnic Group/Sex, and by Industry, United States, 1994, All Industries." U.S. Equal Employment Opportunity Commission, *Job Patterns for Minorities and Women in Private Industry 1994*, p. 34. *Note:* Data for the state of Hawaii are not included.

★ 522 ★

Occupations

Occupational Employment in Private Industry: Hospitals

Race/Ethnic Group/Sex	Number employed									
	Total Employ-ment	Officials and Managers	Profes-sionals	Techni-cians	Sales workers	Office & Clerical workers	Craft workers	Opera-tives	Laborers	Service workers
All Employees	3,510,821	237,312	1,340,367	563,688	6,666	621,596	49,392	38,192	20,410	633,198
Male	731,739	82,146	196,837	137,684	1,380	48,174	39,232	21,332	10,671	194,283
Female	2,779,082	155,166	1,143,530	426,004	5,286	573,422	10,160	16,860	9,739	438,915
White	2,713,467	210,127	1,141,666	434,058	5,140	475,848	39,899	26,737	12,390	367,602
Male	522,278	72,787	158,814	100,431	1,056	30,370	32,473	15,390	6,517	104,440
Female	2,191,189	137,340	982,852	333,627	4,084	445,478	7,426	11,347	5,873	263,162
Minority	797,354	27,185	198,701	129,630	1,526	145,748	9,493	11,455	8,020	265,596
Male	209,461	9,359	38,023	37,253	324	17,804	6,759	5,942	4,154	89,843
Female	587,893	17,826	160,678	92,377	1,202	127,944	2,734	5,513	3,866	175,753
Black	470,955	14,599	79,479	76,600	985	94,226	5,396	7,776	5,137	186,757
Male	109,003	4,208	10,766	17,102	176	9,318	3,426	3,638	2,431	57,938
Female	361,952	10,391	68,713	59,498	809	84,908	1,970	4,138	2,706	128,819
Hispanic	164,633	6,256	30,802	27,229	330	37,155	2,788	2,542	2,208	55,323
Male	55,164	2,578	7,816	10,634	76	5,381	2,299	1,666	1,400	23,314
Female	109,469	3,678	22,986	16,595	254	31,774	489	876	808	32,009
Asian/Pacific Islander	150,158	5,783	84,766	23,622	187	12,545	1,075	975	589	20,616
Male	42,186	2,316	18,579	8,822	64	2,898	866	543	281	7,817
Female	107,972	3,467	66,187	14,800	123	9,647	209	432	308	12,799
AmInd/Alaskan Native	11,608	547	3,654	2,179	24	1,822	234	162	86	2,900
Male	3,108	257	862	695	8	207	168	95	42	774
Female	8,500	290	2,792	1,484	16	1,615	66	67	44	2,126

Source: "Occupational Employment in Private Industry by Race/Ethnic Group/Sex, and by Industry, United States, 1994, All Industries." U.S. Equal Employment Opportunity Commission, *Job Patterns for Minorities and Women in Private Industry 1994*, p. 34. *Note:* Data for the state of Hawaii are not included.

★ 523 ★

Occupations

Occupational Employment in Private Industry: Hotels, Motels, and Tourist Courts

Race/Ethnic Group/Sex	Number employed									
	Total Employ-ment	Officials and Managers	Profes-sionals	Techni-cians	Sales workers	Office & Clerical workers	Craft workers	Opera-tives	Laborers	Service workers
All Employees	719,014	66,561	17,564	6,138	24,892	86,910	37,411	22,159	24,129	433,250
Male	364,304	40,133	9,301	4,542	6,589	23,050	28,441	15,577	16,472	220,199
Female	354,710	26,428	8,263	1,596	18,303	63,860	8,970	6,582	7,657	213,051
White	399,874	54,525	13,513	4,861	18,019	59,380	25,313	11,502	9,960	202,801
Male	196,085	32,941	7,082	3,629	4,741	14,701	19,566	8,865	7,013	99,547
Female	201,789	21,584	6,431	1,232	13,278	44,679	5,747	2,637	2,947	103,254
Minority	319,140	12,036	4,051	1,277	6,873	27,530	12,098	10,657	14,169	230,449
Male	166,219	7,192	2,219	913	1,848	8,349	8,875	6,712	9,459	120,652
Female	152,921	4,844	1,832	364	5,025	19,181	3,223	3,945	4,710	109,797
Black	129,197	5,252	1,560	685	3,265	14,163	3,914	4,370	5,302	90,686
Male	60,858	2,877	750	438	630	3,670	2,920	2,622	3,394	43,557
Female	68,339	2,375	810	247	2,635	10,493	994	1,748	1,908	47,129
Hispanic	139,546	4,217	1,008	387	1,878	8,384	5,005	4,733	7,638	106,296
Male	79,398	2,707	615	332	530	2,891	4,082	3,180	5,272	59,789
Female	60,148	1,510	393	55	1,348	5,493	923	1,553	2,366	46,507
Asian/Pacific Islander	46,634	2,376	1,399	169	1,598	4,578	2,949	1,441	1,059	31,063
Male	24,213	1,512	805	114	646	1,660	1,704	829	702	16,241
Female	22,421	866	594	55	952	2,918	1,245	612	357	14,822
AmInd/Alaskan Native	3,763	189	84	36	132	405	230	113	170	2,404
Male	1,750	96	49	29	42	128	169	81	91	1,065
Female	2,013	93	35	7	90	277	61	32	79	1,339

Source: "Occupational Employment in Private Industry by Race/Ethnic Group/Sex, and by Industry, United States, 1994, All Industries." U.S. Equal Employment Opportunity Commission, *Job Patterns for Minorities and Women in Private Industry 1994*, p. 31. *Note:* Data for the state of Hawaii are not included.

★ 524 ★

Occupations

Occupational Employment in Private Industry: Household Appliances

Race/ethnic group/sex	Total employment	Officials and managers	Professionals	Technicians	Sales workers	Office & clerical workers	Craft workers	Operatives	Laborers	Service workers
				NUMBER EMPLOYED						
All employees	109,258	7,740	7,137	2,807	2,173	7,187	9,459	47,809	24,322	624
Male	67,990	6,567	5,608	2,244	1,657	1,323	8,492	29,070	12,543	486
Female	41,268	1,173	1,529	563	516	5,864	967	18,739	11,779	138
White	90,001	7,217	6,618	2,586	2,059	6,262	8,424	37,735	18,564	536
Male	58,147	6,132	5,228	2,072	1,586	1,094	7,646	24,075	9,898	416
Female	31,854	1,085	1,390	514	473	5,168	778	13,660	8,666	120
Minority	19,257	523	519	221	114	925	1,035	10,074	5,758	88
Male	9,843	435	380	172	71	229	846	4,995	2,645	70
Female	9,414	88	139	49	43	696	189	5,079	3,113	18
Black	13,511	221	223	125	43	593	696	8,388	3,158	64
Male	6,384	173	149	89	19	142	545	4,001	1,215	51
Female	7,127	48	74	36	24	451	151	4,387	1,943	13
Hispanic	4,062	101	106	56	54	265	249	1,246	1,965	20
Male	2,379	78	76	50	39	71	220	713	1,116	16
Female	1,683	23	30	6	15	194	29	533	849	4
Asian/Pacific Islander	1,377	179	176	34	15	52	66	334	519	2
Male	871	165	144	28	11	12	59	201	249	2
Female	506	14	32	6	4	40	7	133	270	0
Am. Ind./Alaskan Native	307	22	14	6	2	15	24	106	116	2
Male	209	19	11	5	2	4	22	80	65	1
Female	98	3	3	1	0	11	2	26	51	1

Source: "Occupational Employment in Private Industry by Race/Ethnic Group/Sex, and by Industry, United States, 1994, All Industries." U.S. Equal Employment Opportunity Commission, *Job Patterns for Minorities and Women in Private Industry 1994*, p. 18. *Note:* Data for the state of Hawaii are not included.

★ 525 ★

Occupations

Occupational Employment in Private Industry: Household Furniture

Race/Ethnic Group/Sex	Number employed									
	Total Employment	Officials and Managers	Professionals	Technicians	Sales workers	Office & Clerical workers	Craft workers	Operatives	Laborers	Service workers
All Employees	177,104	11,580	3,112	2,268	3,108	10,540	38,476	76,902	29,536	1,582
Male	114,969	9,551	2,077	1,593	1,878	1,460	29,691	48,850	18,639	1,230
Female	62,135	2,029	1,035	675	1,230	9,080	8,785	28,052	10,897	352
White	136,014	10,740	2,959	2,096	2,977	9,627	31,459	55,699	19,256	1,201
Male	86,594	8,848	1,979	1,461	1,806	1,234	24,185	34,591	11,540	950

[Continued]

★ 525 ★

Occupational Employment in Private Industry: Household Furniture

[Continued]

Race/Ethnic Group/Sex	Number employed									
	Total Employment	Officials and Managers	Professionals	Technicians	Sales workers	Office & Clerical workers	Craft workers	Operatives	Laborers	Service workers
Female	49,420	1,892	980	635	1,171	8,393	7,274	21,108	7,716	251
Minority	41,090	840	153	172	131	913	7,017	21,203	10,280	381
Male	28,375	703	98	132	72	226	5,506	14,259	7,099	280
Female	12,715	137	55	40	59	687	1,511	6,944	3,181	101
Black	25,521	422	65	66	47	449	4,775	13,439	6,009	249
Male	16,570	345	39	43	24	92	3,589	8,407	3,842	189
Female	8,951	77	26	23	23	357	1,186	5,032	2,167	60
Hispanic	12,892	316	42	76	65	329	1,672	6,432	3,843	117
Male	10,033	273	27	67	37	98	1,436	5,034	2,980	81
Female	2,859	43	15	9	28	231	236	1,398	863	36
Asian/Pacific Islander	2,039	70	40	26	18	94	392	1,061	330	8
Male	1,341	57	29	18	11	21	333	652	213	7
Female	698	13	11	8	7	73	59	409	117	1
AmInd/Alaskan Native	638	32	6	4	1	41	178	271	98	7
Male	431	28	3	4	0	15	148	166	64	3
Female	207	4	3	0	1	26	30	105	34	4

Source: "Occupational Employment in Private Industry by Race/Ethnic Group/Sex, and by Industry, United States, 1994, All Industries." U.S. Equal Employment Opportunity Commission, *Job Patterns for Minorities and Women in Private Industry 1994*, p. 10. *Note:* Data for the state of Hawaii are not included.

★ 526 ★

Occupations

Occupational Employment in Private Industry: Industrial Inorganic Chemicals

Race/Ethnic Group/Sex	Number employed									
	Total Employment	Officials and Managers	Professionals	Technicians	Sales workers	Office & Clerical workers	Craft workers	Operatives	Laborers	Service workers
All Employees	109,617	18,742	16,236	7,335	2,658	10,475	24,272	25,027	3,165	1,707
Male	86,844	16,668	12,245	5,545	2,115	1,399	23,077	21,815	2,690	1,290
Female	22,773	2,074	3,991	1,790	543	9,076	1,195	3,212	475	417
White	91,150	17,080	14,295	6,041	2,493	8,812	20,158	18,978	2,113	1,180
Male	73,023	15,265	10,970	4,699	1,999	1,142	19,313	16,879	1,831	925
Female	18,127	1,815	3,325	1,342	494	7,670	845	2,099	282	255
Minority	18,467	1,662	1,941	1,294	165	1,663	4,114	6,049	1,052	527

[Continued]

★ 526 ★

Occupational Employment in Private Industry: Industrial Inorganic Chemicals

[Continued]

Race/Ethnic Group/Sex	Number employed									
	Total Employment	Officials and Managers	Professionals	Technicians	Sales workers	Office & Clerical workers	Craft workers	Operatives	Laborers	Service workers
Male	13,821	1,403	1,275	846	116	257	3,764	4,936	859	365
Female	4,646	259	666	448	49	1,406	350	1,113	193	162
Black	11,389	833	676	825	77	1,034	2,841	4,076	683	344
Male	8,492	699	375	507	50	153	2,541	3,382	562	223
Female	2,897	134	301	318	27	881	300	694	121	121
Hispanic	4,613	424	367	197	56	453	1,031	1,637	301	147
Male	3,542	362	241	151	45	69	998	1,307	252	117
Female	1,071	62	126	46	11	384	33	330	49	30
Asian/Pacific Islander	1,966	336	855	243	28	131	116	198	36	23
Male	1,390	281	626	169	18	29	100	130	22	15
Female	576	55	229	74	10	102	16	68	14	8
AmInd/Alaskan Native	499	69	43	29	4	45	126	138	32	13
Male	397	61	33	19	3	6	125	117	23	10
Female	102	8	10	10	1	39	1	21	9	3

Source: "Occupational Employment in Private Industry by Race/Ethnic Group/Sex, and by Industry, United States, 1994, All Industries." U.S. Equal Employment Opportunity Commission, *Job Patterns for Minorities and Women in Private Industry 1994*, p. 12. *Note:* Data for the state of Hawaii are not included.

★ 527 ★

Occupations

Occupational Employment in Private Industry: Insurance Agents, Brokers and Service

Race/Ethnic Group/Sex	Number employed									
	Total Employment	Officials and Managers	Professionals	Technicians	Sales workers	Office & Clerical workers	Craft workers	Operatives	Laborers	Service workers
All Employees	189,554	26,499	45,441	19,299	15,038	81,113	773	698	196	497
Male	63,592	15,597	20,526	7,149	9,693	9,069	533	529	148	348
Female	125,962	10,902	24,915	12,150	5,345	72,044	240	169	48	149
White	157,557	24,318	39,553	16,057	13,315	62,686	600	528	161	339
Male	55,575	14,670	18,397	5,998	8,788	6,491	459	401	121	250
Female	101,982	9,648	21,156	10,059	4,527	56,195	141	127	40	89
Minority	31,997	2,181	5,888	3,242	1,723	18,427	173	170	35	158
Male	8,017	927	2,129	1,151	905	2,578	74	128	27	96
Female	23,980	1,254	3,759	2,091	818	15,849	99	42	8	60

[Continued]

★ 527 ★

Occupational Employment in Private Industry: Insurance Agents, Brokers and Service
[Continued]

Race/Ethnic Group/Sex	Number employed									
	Total Employ-ment	Officials and Managers	Profes-sionals	Techni-cians	Sales workers	Office & Clerical workers	Craft workers	Opera-tives	Laborers	Service workers
Black	18,751	1,244	3,343	1,917	767	11,145	99	116	8	112
Male	4,011	472	1,065	568	383	1,326	33	81	7	76
Female	14,740	772	2,278	1,349	384	9,819	66	35	1	36
Hispanic	7,441	463	1,249	656	389	4,519	53	50	21	41
Male	2,044	220	520	272	205	714	35	44	14	20
Female	5,397	243	729	384	184	3,805	18	6	7	21
Asian/Pacific Islander	5,080	381	1,173	619	484	2,390	19	4	6	4
Male	1,734	187	496	291	267	477	6	3	6	1
Female	3,346	194	677	328	217	1,913	13	1	0	3
AmInd/Alaskan Native	725	93	123	50	83	373	2	0	0	1
Male	228	48	48	20	50	61	0	0	0	1
Female	497	45	75	30	33	312	2	0	0	0

Source: "Occupational Employment in Private Industry by Race/Ethnic Group/Sex, and by Industry, United States, 1994, All Industries." U.S. Equal Employment Opportunity Commission, *Job Patterns for Minorities and Women in Private Industry 1994,* p. 30. *Note:* Data for the state of Hawaii are not included.

★ 528 ★

Occupations

Occupational Employment in Private Industry: Knitting Mills

Race/Ethnic Group/Sex	Number employed									
	Total Employ-ment	Officials and Managers	Profes-sionals	Techni-cians	Sales workers	Office & Clerical workers	Craft workers	Opera-tives	Laborers	Service workers
All Employees	124,589	7,730	1,873	2,317	1,670	6,812	12,543	78,481	11,537	1,626
Male	42,933	5,336	1,059	1,313	663	826	8,993	18,404	5,341	998
Female	81,656	2,394	814	1,004	1,007	5,986	3,550	60,077	6,196	628
White	87,778	6,928	1,725	1,996	1,504	5,945	9,882	51,111	7,534	1,153
Male	31,418	4,834	976	1,133	606	660	7,264	11,862	3,391	692
Female	56,360	2,094	749	863	898	5,285	2,618	39,249	4,143	461
Minority	36,811	802	148	321	166	867	2,661	27,370	4,003	473
Male	11,515	502	83	180	57	166	1,729	6,542	1,950	306
Female	25,296	300	65	141	109	701	932	20,828	2,053	167
Black	29,130	598	81	262	82	701	1,974	22,274	2,754	404
Male	8,720	363	43	138	34	144	1,225	5,088	1,427	258
Female	20,410	235	38	124	48	557	749	17,186	1,327	146

[Continued]

★ 528 ★

Occupational Employment in Private Industry: Knitting Mills

[Continued]

Race/Ethnic Group/Sex	Number employed									
	Total Employ-ment	Officials and Managers	Profes-sionals	Techni-cians	Sales workers	Office & Clerical workers	Craft workers	Opera-tives	Laborers	Service workers
Hispanic	4,289	116	25	27	62	120	425	2,578	888	48
Male	1,879	79	14	17	14	16	317	1,004	383	35
Female	2,410	37	11	10	48	104	108	1,574	505	13
Asian/Pacific Islander	1,961	54	39	26	14	23	154	1,507	132	12
Male	617	44	23	21	7	4	104	342	66	6
Female	1,344	10	16	5	7	19	50	1,165	66	6
AmInd/Alaskan Native	1,431	34	3	6	8	23	108	1,011	229	9
Male	299	16	3	4	2	2	83	108	74	7
Female	1,132	18	0	2	6	21	25	903	155	2

Source: "Occupational Employment in Private Industry by Race/Ethnic Group/Sex, and by Industry, United States, 1994, All Industries." U.S. Equal Employment Opportunity Commission, *Job Patterns for Minorities and Women in Private Industry 1994*, p. 9. *Note:* Data for the state of Hawaii are not included.

★ 529 ★

Occupations

Occupational Employment in Private Industry: Legal Services

Race/Ethnic Group/Sex	Number employed									
	Total Employ-ment	Officials and Managers	Profes-sionals	Techni-cians	Sales workers	Office & Clerical workers	Craft workers	Opera-tives	Laborers	Service workers
All Employees	171,922	9,496	60,368	3,040	175	96,288	418	185	62	1,890
Male	63,073	4,879	38,575	1,469	60	16,549	155	161	47	1,178
Female	108,849	4,617	21,793	1,571	115	79,739	263	24	15	712
White	138,893	8,527	55,596	2,352	82	70,885	343	63	24	1,021
Male	52,578	4,479	36,079	1,089	31	9,991	132	53	18	706
Female	86,315	4,048	19,517	1,263	51	60,894	211	10	6	315
Minority	33,029	969	4,772	688	93	25,403	75	122	38	869
Male	10,495	400	2,496	380	29	6,558	23	108	29	472
Female	22,534	569	2,276	308	64	18,845	52	14	9	397
Black	19,031	544	1,998	333	78	15,375	61	60	6	576
Male	5,594	207	957	169	27	3,860	18	46	3	307
Female	13,437	337	1,041	164	51	11,515	43	14	3	269
Hispanic	8,178	225	1,148	139	12	6,363	6	26	10	249
Male	2,779	111	685	80	1	1,733	1	26	7	135
Female	5,399	114	463	59	11	4,630	5	0	3	114

[Continued]

★ 529 ★

Occupational Employment in Private Industry: Legal Services

[Continued]

Race/Ethnic Group/Sex	Number employed									
	Total Employ-ment	Officials and Managers	Profes-sionals	Techni-cians	Sales workers	Office & Clerical workers	Craft workers	Opera-tives	Laborers	Service workers
Asian/Pacific Islander	5,469	185	1,555	211	1	3,465	6	2	4	40
Male	1,973	79	806	129	1	924	2	2	4	26
Female	3,496	106	749	82	0	2,541	4	0	0	14
AmInd/Alaskan Native	351	15	71	5	2	200	2	34	18	4
Male	149	3	48	2	0	41	2	34	15	4
Female	202	12	23	3	2	159	0	0	3	0

Source: "Occupational Employment in Private Industry by Race/Ethnic Group/Sex, and by Industry, United States, 1994, All Industries." U.S. Equal Employment Opportunity Commission, *Job Patterns for Minorities and Women in Private Industry 1994*, p. 26. *Note:* Data for the state of Hawaii are not included.

★ 530 ★

Occupations

Occupational Employment in Private Industry: Life Insurance

Race/Ethnic Group/Sex	Number employed									
	Total Employ-ment	Officials and Managers	Profes-sionals	Techni-cians	Sales workers	Office & Clerical workers	Craft workers	Opera-tives	Laborers	Service workers
All Employees	314,994	49,300	70,967	37,865	26,004	123,378	1,963	2,147	480	2,890
Male	109,049	28,420	28,620	11,932	19,275	15,470	1,732	1,553	362	1,685
Female	205,945	20,880	42,347	25,933	6,729	107,908	231	594	118	1,205
White	257,467	44,875	61,226	30,683	21,793	93,720	1,576	1,477	304	1,813
Male	92,856	26,356	25,389	9,794	16,796	10,787	1,389	1,073	226	1,046
Female	164,611	18,519	35,837	20,889	4,997	82,933	187	404	78	767
Minority	57,527	4,425	9,741	7,182	4,211	29,658	387	670	176	1,077
Male	16,193	2,064	3,231	2,138	2,479	4,683	343	480	136	639
Female	41,334	2,361	6,510	5,044	1,732	24,975	44	190	40	438
Black	34,540	2,435	5,189	4,529	1,656	19,358	170	404	91	708
Male	8,200	1,004	1,431	1,057	1,125	2,662	151	289	62	419
Female	26,340	1,431	3,758	3,472	531	16,696	19	115	29	289
Hispanic	14,247	1,039	2,397	1,569	1,517	6,985	186	198	81	275
Male	4,497	531	856	627	636	1,279	167	154	71	176
Female	9,750	508	1,541	942	881	5,706	19	44	10	99
Asian/Pacific Islander	7,816	853	2,004	995	863	2,921	24	64	2	90
Male	3,138	464	890	423	574	692	18	34	1	62
Female	4,678	389	1,114	572	289	2,229	6	30	1	48

[Continued]

★ 530 ★

Occupational Employment in Private Industry: Life Insurance
[Continued]

Race/Ethnic Group/Sex	Number employed									
	Total Employ-ment	Officials and Managers	Profes-sionals	Techni-cians	Sales workers	Office & Clerical workers	Craft workers	Opera-tives	Laborers	Service workers
AmInd/Alaskan Native	924	96	151	89	175	394	7	4	2	4
Male	358	65	54	31	144	50	7	3	2	2
Female	566	33	97	58	31	344	0	1	0	2

Source: "Occupational Employment in Private Industry by Race/Ethnic Group/Sex, and by Industry, United States, 1994, All Industries." U.S. Equal Employment Opportunity Commission, *Job Patterns for Minorities and Women in Private Industry 1994*, p. 29. *Note:* Data for the state of Hawaii are not included.

★ 531 ★

Occupations

Occupational Employment in Private Industry: Lumber and Building Materials

Race/Ethnic Group/Sex	Number employed									
	Total Employ-ment	Officials and Managers	Profes-sionals	Techni-cians	Sales workers	Office & Clerical workers	Craft workers	Opera-tives	Laborers	Service workers
All Employees	140,143	15,595	2,565	1,029	76,176	12,529	3,152	15,624	12,466	1,007
Male	93,786	12,542	1,594	767	46,453	2,975	2,932	14,512	11,247	764
Female	46,357	3,053	971	262	29,723	9,554	220	1,112	1,219	243
White	115,073	14,323	2,340	936	62,857	10,292	2,568	12,272	8,848	637
Male	77,229	11,544	1,457	693	38,881	2,448	2,393	11,382	7,943	488
Female	37,844	2,779	883	243	23,976	7,844	175	890	905	149
Minority	25,070	1,272	225	93	13,319	2,237	584	3,352	3,618	370
Male	16,557	998	137	74	7,572	527	539	3,130	3,304	276
Female	8,513	274	88	19	5,747	1,710	45	222	314	94
Black	13,413	739	120	31	7,213	1,157	287	1,804	1,877	185
Male	8,485	564	67	24	3,871	253	263	1,631	1,679	133
Female	4,928	175	53	7	3,342	904	24	173	198	52
Hispanic	8,883	394	69	40	4,516	804	236	1,195	1,504	125
Male	6,280	326	47	30	2,761	204	218	1,172	1,421	101
Female	2,603	68	22	10	1,755	600	18	23	83	24
Asian/Pacific Islander	1,694	95	33	15	1,047	185	23	123	118	55
Male	1,073	71	22	14	642	43	22	117	106	38
Female	621	24	11	1	405	142	1	6	14	17
AmInd/Alaskan Native	1,080	44	3	7	543	91	38	230	119	5

[Continued]

★ 531 ★

Occupational Employment in Private Industry: Lumber and Building Materials
[Continued]

Race/Ethnic Group/Sex	Number employed									
	Total Employment	Officials and Managers	Professionals	Technicians	Sales workers	Office & Clerical workers	Craft workers	Operatives	Laborers	Service workers
Male	719	37	1	6	298	27	36	210	100	4
Female	361	7	2	1	245	64	2	20	19	1

Source: "Occupational Employment in Private Industry by Race/Ethnic Group/Sex, and by Industry, United States, 1994, All Industries." U.S. Equal Employment Opportunity Commission, *Job Patterns for Minorities and Women in Private Industry 1994*, p. 26. *Note:* Data for the state of Hawaii are not included.

★ 532 ★

Occupations

Occupational Employment in Private Industry: Machinery, Equipment, and Supplies

RACE/ETHNIC GROUP/SEX	Total employment	Officials and managers	Professionals	Technicians	Sales workers	Office & clerical workers	Craft workers	Operatives	Laborers	Service workers
	NUMBER EMPLOYED									
All employees	160,061	21,648	19,887	14,385	17,430	25,333	24,802	21,856	8,270	6,450
Male	115,869	18,050	14,341	12,604	14,083	5,721	24,096	17,299	6,135	3,540
Female	44,192	3,598	5,546	1,781	3,347	19,612	706	4,557	2,135	2,910
White	132,446	19,892	17,382	12,077	16,001	21,284	21,231	16,179	5,373	3,027
Male	97,471	16,698	12,705	10,662	13,126	4,594	20,732	13,211	4,008	1,735
Female	34,975	3,194	4,677	1,415	2,875	16,690	499	2,968	1,365	1,292
Minority	27,615	1,756	2,505	2,308	1,429	4,049	3,571	5,677	2,897	3,423
Male	18,398	1,352	1,636	1,942	957	1,127	3,364	4,088	2,127	1,805
Female	9,217	404	869	366	472	2,922	207	1,589	770	1,618
Black	12,654	669	926	1,131	570	2,118	1,356	2,965	1,421	1,498
Male	8,018	468	505	923	346	558	1,251	2,120	996	851
Female	4,636	201	421	208	224	1,560	105	845	425	647
Hispanic	10,242	474	502	604	595	1,338	1,660	1,991	1,315	1,763
Male	7,016	366	354	529	429	383	1,581	1,492	1,014	868
Female	3,226	108	148	75	166	955	79	499	301	895
Asian/Pacific Islander	4,027	519	1,020	508	196	485	437	592	139	131
Male	2,883	441	739	427	130	163	418	384	101	80
Female	1,144	78	281	81	66	322	19	208	38	51
Amind/Alaskan Native	692	94	57	65	68	108	118	129	22	31
Male	481	77	38	63	52	23	114	92	16	6
Female	211	17	19	2	16	85	4	37	6	25

Source: "Occupational Employment in Private Industry by Race/Ethnic Group/Sex, and by Industry, United States, 1994, All Industries." U.S. Equal Employment Opportunity Commission, *Job Patterns for Minorities and Women in Private Industry 1994*, p. 25. *Note:* Data for the state of Hawaii are not included.

★ 533 ★

Occupations

Occupational Employment in Private Industry: Management and Public Relations Services

RACE/ETHNIC GROUP/ SEX	Total employment	Officials and managers	Professionals	Technicians	Sales workers	Office & clerical workers	Craft workers	Operatives	Laborers	Service workers
	NUMBER EMPLOYED									
All employees	343,862	48,739	95,220	23,820	15,078	79,050	22,135	21,738	14,836	23,246
Male	190,824	33,844	58,271	15,427	7,669	14,772	20,348	17,446	11,096	11,951
Female	153,038	14,895	36,949	8,393	7,409	64,278	1,787	4,292	3,740	11,295
White	267,685	43,391	81,340	18,647	11,736	58,066	16,964	13,995	10,592	12,954
Male	151,439	30,539	50,484	12,222	6,169	10,103	15,796	11,685	8,065	6,376
Female	116,246	12,852	30,856	6,425	5,567	47,963	1,168	2,310	2,527	6,578
Minority	76,177	5,348	13,880	5,173	3,342	20,984	5,171	7,743	4,244	10,292
Male	39,385	3,305	7,787	3,205	1,500	4,669	4,552	5,761	3,031	5,575
Female	36,792	2,043	6,093	1,968	1,842	16,315	619	1,982	1,213	4,717
Black	37,356	2,508	4,950	2,154	1,599	12,139	2,075	3,714	2,787	5,430
Male	17,432	1,379	2,371	1,113	497	2,465	1,860	2,876	2,010	2,861
Female	19,924	1,129	2,579	1,041	1,102	9,674	215	838	777	2,569
Hispanic	22,626	1,478	2,653	1,806	1,326	5,992	2,168	2,539	1,189	3,475
Male	12,661	974	1,541	1,314	806	1,377	1,966	1,883	813	1,987
Female	9,965	504	1,112	492	520	4,615	202	656	376	1,488
Asian/Pacific Islander	14,723	1,196	6,024	1,061	355	2,478	784	1,376	215	1,234
Male	8,464	837	3,731	671	166	749	592	906	162	650
Female	6,259	359	2,293	390	189	1,729	192	470	53	584
Amind/Alaskan Native	1,472	166	253	152	62	375	144	114	53	153
Male	828	115	144	107	31	78	134	96	46	77
Female	644	51	109	45	31	297	10	18	7	76

Source: "Occupational Employment in Private Industry by Race/Ethnic Group/Sex, and by Industry, United States, 1994, All Industries." U.S. Equal Employment Opportunity Commission, *Job Patterns for Minorities and Women in Private Industry 1994*, p. 36. *Note:* Data for the state of Hawaii are not included.

★ 534 ★
Occupations

Occupational Employment in Private Industry: Manufacturing – Durable Goods

Race/Ethnic Group/Sex	Number employed									
	Total Employment	Officials and Managers	Professionals	Technicians	Sales workers	Office & Clerical workers	Craft workers	Operatives	Laborers	Service workers
All Employees	6,917,248	723,109	987,197	414,035	151,402	525,934	1,140,035	2,282,281	621,940	71,315
Male	4,966,010	620,255	767,452	334,368	110,839	109,125	1,032,230	1,543,971	395,167	52,603
Female	1,951,238	102,854	219,745	79,667	40,563	416,809	107,805	738,310	226,773	18,712
White	5,511,500	661,437	855,978	345,561	141,013	443,279	950,465	1,641,142	420,898	51,727
Male	4,036,645	569,869	672,802	282,115	104,590	87,453	870,008	1,144,606	266,798	38,404
Female	1,474,855	91,568	183,176	63,446	36,423	355,826	80,457	496,536	154,100	13,323
Minority	1,405,748	61,672	131,219	68,474	10,389	82,655	189,570	641,139	201,042	19,588
Male	929,365	50,386	94,650	52,253	6,249	21,672	162,222	399,365	128,369	14,199
Female	476,383	11,286	36,569	16,221	4,140	60,983	27,348	241,774	72,673	5,389
Black	688,099	24,351	33,771	22,360	4,312	39,191	100,732	351,726	99,382	12,274
Male	445,452	19,452	21,236	16,141	2,296	9,639	85,680	219,384	62,880	8,744
Female	242,647	4,899	12,535	6,219	2,016	29,552	15,052	132,342	36,502	3,530
Hispanic	432,489	16,534	26,027	20,030	3,689	28,398	62,475	189,500	80,103	5,733
Male	296,996	13,439	18,788	15,698	2,425	7,858	54,939	125,485	53,972	4,392
Female	135,493	3,095	7,239	4,332	1,264	20,540	7,536	64,015	26,131	1,341
Asian/Pacific Islander	254,367	18,176	68,561	24,301	1,987	12,872	21,044	87,838	18,336	1,252
Male	166,077	15,317	52,612	19,087	1,276	3,673	16,918	46,889	9,454	851
Female	88,290	2,859	15,949	5,214	711	9,199	4,126	40,949	8,882	401
AmInd/Alaskan Native	30,793	2,611	2,860	1,783	401	2,194	5,319	12,075	3,221	329
Male	20,840	2,178	2,014	1,327	252	502	4,685	7,607	2,063	212
Female	9,953	433	846	456	149	1,692	634	4,468	1,158	117

Source: "Occupational Employment in Private Industry by Race/Ethnic Group/Sex, and by Industry, United States, 1994, All Industries." U.S. Equal Employment Opportunity Commission, *Job Patterns for Minorities and Women in Private Industry 1994*, p. 3. *Note:* Data for the state of Hawaii are not included.

★ 535 ★
Occupations

Occupational Employment in Private Industry: Manufacturing – Nondurable Goods

Race/Ethnic Group/Sex	Number employed									
	Total Employment	Officials and Managers	Professionals	Technicians	Sales workers	Office & Clerical workers	Craft workers	Operatives	Laborers	Service workers
All Employees	5,229,613	571,919	425,656	181,617	310,617	488,801	716,129	1,647,295	773,387	114,192
Male	3,174,251	451,433	265,066	118,500	195,263	78,815	616,176	940,402	442,827	65,769
Female	2,055,362	120,486	160,590	63,117	115,354	409,986	99,953	706,893	330,560	48,423
White	3,892,015	516,151	373,723	150,299	271,508	401,676	580,544	1,094,324	426,230	77,560

[Continued]

★ 535 ★

Occupational Employment in Private Industry: Manufacturing – Nondurable Goods
[Continued]

Race/Ethnic Group/Sex	Number employed									
	Total Employment	Officials and Managers	Profes-sionals	Techni-cians	Sales workers	Office & Clerical workers	Craft workers	Opera-tives	Laborers	Service workers
Male	2,422,198	410,521	236,044	100,186	171,873	60,211	507,419	649,657	244,830	41,457
Female	1,469,817	105,630	137,679	50,113	99,635	341,465	73,125	444,667	181,400	36,103
Minority	1,337,598	55,768	51,933	31,318	39,109	87,125	135,585	552,971	347,157	36,632
Male	752,053	40,912	29,022	18,314	23,390	18,604	118,757	290,745	197,997	24,312
Female	585,545	14,856	22,911	13,004	15,719	68,521	26,828	262,226	149,160	12,320
Black	728,404	28,286	19,452	16,641	20,489	50,075	76,625	340,358	155,049	21,429
Male	385,564	20,304	9,561	9,090	11,589	9,723	60,537	167,326	83,472	13,962
Female	342,840	7,982	9,891	7,551	8,900	40,352	16,088	173,032	71,577	7,467
Hispanic	452,952	16,154	10,502	8,049	13,579	25,529	45,232	165,373	156,663	11,871
Male	280,150	12,229	6,205	5,169	8,835	5,939	37,784	99,680	96,131	8,178
Female	172,802	3,925	4,297	2,880	4,744	19,590	7,448	65,693	60,532	3,693
Asian/Pacific Islander	129,707	9,487	20,909	5,932	3,971	9,691	10,090	37,130	29,900	2,597
Male	71,219	6,938	12,592	3,629	2,325	2,578	7,311	18,757	15,359	1,730
Female	58,488	2,549	8,317	2,303	1,646	7,113	2,779	18,373	14,541	867
AmInd/Alaskan Native	26,535	1,841	1,070	696	1,070	1,830	3,638	10,110	5,545	735
Male	15,120	1,441	664	426	641	364	3,125	4,982	3,035	442
Female	11,415	400	406	270	429	1,466	513	5,128	2,510	293

Source: "Occupational Employment in Private Industry by Race/Ethnic Group/Sex, and by Industry, United States, 1994, All Industries." U.S. Equal Employment Opportunity Commission, *Job Patterns for Minorities and Women in Private Industry 1994*, p. 3. *Note:* Data for the state of Hawaii are not included.

★ 536 ★
Occupations

Occupational Employment in Private Industry: Meat Products

Race/Ethnic Group/Sex	Number employed									
	Total Employment	Officials and Managers	Profes-sionals	Techni-cians	Sales workers	Office & Clerical workers	Craft workers	Opera-tives	Laborers	Service workers
All Employees	331,111	23,042	5,220	5,608	4,656	11,300	24,865	83,887	166,243	6,290
Male	219,948	19,739	3,382	3,149	3,712	1,948	22,477	58,857	102,050	4,634
Female	111,163	3,303	1,838	2,459	944	9,352	2,388	25,030	64,193	1,656
White	165,929	19,783	4,721	4,430	4,441	9,629	17,638	37,562	64,423	3,302
Male	112,836	17,158	3,090	2,559	3,553	1,551	16,186	27,834	38,580	2,325
Female	53,093	2,625	1,631	1,871	888	8,078	1,452	9,728	25,843	977
Minority	165,182	3,259	499	1,178	215	1,671	7,227	46,325	101,820	2,988
Male	107,112	2,581	292	590	159	397	6,291	31,023	63,470	2,309
Female	58,070	678	207	588	56	1,274	936	15,302	38,350	679

[Continued]

★ 536 ★

Occupational Employment in Private Industry: Meat Products
[Continued]

Race/Ethnic Group/Sex	Number employed									
	Total Employment	Officials and Managers	Professionals	Technicians	Sales workers	Office & Clerical workers	Craft workers	Operatives	Laborers	Service workers
Black	74,021	1,944	243	611	99	984	3,756	23,251	41,365	1,768
Male	40,212	1,423	134	245	75	246	3,144	13,298	20,396	1,251
Female	33,809	521	109	366	24	738	612	9,953	20,969	517
Hispanic	75,131	1,045	154	420	82	532	2,962	19,308	49,593	1,035
Male	57,054	933	96	257	62	105	2,718	15,273	36,692	918
Female	18,077	112	58	163	20	427	244	4,035	12,901	117
Asian/Pacific Islander	13,475	184	86	120	28	109	366	3,401	9,058	123
Male	8,174	156	52	71	19	34	320	2,190	5,235	97
Female	5,301	28	34	49	9	75	46	1,211	3,823	26
AmInd/Alaskan Native	2,555	86	16	27	6	46	143	365	1,804	62
Male	1,672	69	10	17	3	12	109	262	1,147	43
Female	883	17	6	10	3	34	34	103	657	19

Source: "Occupational Employment in Private Industry by Race/Ethnic Group/Sex, and by Industry, United States, 1994, All Industries." U.S. Equal Employment Opportunity Commission, *Job Patterns for Minorities and Women in Private Industry 1994*, p. 6. *Note:* Data for the state of Hawaii are not included.

★ 537 ★

Occupations

Occupational Employment in Private Industry: Medical Instruments and Supplies

Race/ethnic group/sex	Total employment	Officials and managers	Professionals	Technicians	Sales workers	Office & clerical workers	Craft workers	Operatives	Laborers	Service workers
	NUMBER EMPLOYED									
All employees	217,563	28,231	34,463	18,878	15,905	25,253	17,147	63,220	12,381	2,085
Male	114,853	21,253	23,349	13,698	10,993	3,706	13,229	23,028	4,248	1,349
Female	102,710	6,978	11,114	5,180	4,912	21,547	3,918	40,192	8,133	736
White	164,209	25,724	29,419	14,330	14,881	20,747	12,938	38,449	6,355	1,366
Male	90,306	19,470	20,066	10,560	10,314	2,693	10,321	13,963	2,055	864
Female	73,903	6,254	9,353	3,770	4,567	18,054	2,617	24,486	4,300	502
Minority	53,354	2,507	5,044	4,548	1,024	4,506	4,209	24,771	6,026	719
Male	24,547	1,783	3,283	3,138	679	1,013	2,908	9,065	2,193	485
Female	28,807	724	1,761	1,410	345	3,493	1,301	15,706	3,833	234
Black	15,263	728	1,016	1,053	433	1,522	1,474	7,078	1,673	286
Male	6,421	505	593	687	277	294	993	2,416	469	187
Female	8,842	223	423	366	156	1,228	481	4,662	1,204	99
Hispanic	20,840	925	1,442	1,416	390	2,105	1,924	9,478	2,781	379
Male	9,741	650	922	1,020	273	489	1,351	3,608	1,165	263
Female	11,099	275	520	396	117	1,616	573	5,870	1,616	116

[Continued]

★ 537 ★

Occupational Employment in Private Industry: Medical Instruments and Supplies

[Continued]

Race/ethnic group/sex	Total employment	Officials and managers	Professionals	Technicians	Sales workers	Office & clerical workers	Craft workers	Operatives	Laborers	Service workers
Asian/Pacific Islander	16,386	777	2,509	1,998	161	798	751	7,856	1,497	39
Male	8,035	572	1,717	1,374	103	219	526	2,954	542	28
Female	8,351	205	792	624	58	579	225	4,902	955	11
Am. Ind./Alaskan Native	865	77	77	81	40	81	60	359	75	15
Male	350	56	51	57	26	11	38	87	17	7
Female	515	21	26	24	14	70	22	272	58	8

Source: "Occupational Employment in Private Industry by Race/Ethnic Group/Sex, and by Industry, United States, 1994, All Industries." U.S. Equal Employment Opportunity Commission, *Job Patterns for Minorities and Women in Private Industry 1994*, p. 21. *Note:* Data for the state of Hawaii are not included.

★ 538 ★

Occupations

Occupational Employment in Private Industry: Metalworking Machinery

RACE/ETHNIC GROUP/ SEX	Total employ- ment	Officials and managers	Profes- sionals	Techni- cians	Sales workers	Office & clerical workers	Craft workers	Opera- tives	Laborers	Service workers
NUMBER EMPLOYED										
All employees	120,175	12,425	10,290	8,166	3,888	9,611	32,950	35,701	6,101	1,043
Male	93,463	11,100	8,638	7,065	3,287	2,238	30,790	25,853	3,643	849
Female	26,712	1,325	1,652	1,101	601	7,373	2,160	9,848	2,458	194
White	104,196	11,894	9,682	7,571	3,752	8,692	29,381	28,243	4,180	801
Male	82,614	10,636	8,165	6,572	3,196	1,950	27,744	21,164	2,538	649
Female	21,582	1,258	1,517	999	556	6,742	1,637	7,079	1,642	152
Minority	15,979	531	608	595	136	919	3,569	7,458	1,921	242
Male	10,849	464	473	493	91	288	3,046	4,689	1,105	200
Female	5,130	67	135	102	45	631	523	2,769	816	42
Black	8,704	195	215	245	40	470	1,864	4,152	1,340	183
Male	5,308	159	142	194	20	134	1,470	2,358	684	147
Female	3,396	36	73	51	20	336	394	1,794	656	36
Hispanic	4,769	146	111	177	60	275	1,119	2,371	463	47
Male	3,619	131	84	146	45	90	1,064	1,672	344	43
Female	1,150	15	27	31	15	185	55	699	119	4
Asian/Pacific Islander	2,182	166	270	155	27	131	495	824	103	11
Male	1,692	155	240	139	20	48	433	578	70	9
Female	490	11	30	16	7	83	62	246	33	2
Amind/Alaskan Native	324	24	12	18	9	43	91	111	15	1

[Continued]

★ 538 ★

Occupational Employment in Private Industry: Metalworking Machinery
[Continued]

RACE/ETHNIC GROUP/ SEX	Total employ- ment	Officials and managers	Profes- sionals	Techni- cians	Sales workers	Office & clerical workers	Craft workers	Opera- tives	Laborers	Service workers
Male	230	19	7	14	6	16	79	81	7	1
Female	94	5	5	4	3	27	12	30	8	0

Source: "Occupational Employment in Private Industry by Race/Ethnic Group/Sex, and by Industry, United States, 1994, All Industries." U.S. Equal Employment Opportunity Commission, *Job Patterns for Minorities and Women in Private Industry 1994*, p. 16. *Note:* Data for the state of Hawaii are not included.

★ 539 ★
Occupations

Occupational Employment in Private Industry: Millwork, Plywood and Structural Members

RACE/ETHNIC GROUP/ SEX	Total employ- ment	Officials and managers	Profes- sionals	Techni- cians	Sales workers	Office & clerical workers	Craft workers	Opera- tives	Laborers	Service workers
				NUMBER EMPLOYED						
All employees	100,237	6,759	1,988	1,815	2,651	5,426	19,309	31,765	29,570	954
Male	76,191	6,052	1,514	1,477	2,108	934	17,248	25,215	20,945	698
Female	24,046	707	474	338	543	4,492	2,061	6,550	8,625	256
White	81,698	6,363	1,928	1,725	2,578	5,117	16,797	24,754	21,734	702
Male	61,645	5,697	1,470	1,397	2,055	866	14,972	19,558	15,079	551
Female	20,053	666	458	328	523	4,251	1,825	5,196	6,655	151
Minority	18,539	396	60	90	73	309	2,512	7,011	7,836	252
Male	14,546	355	44	80	53	68	2,276	5,657	5,866	147
Female	3,993	41	16	10	20	241	236	1,354	1,970	105
Black	11,601	236	22	24	27	184	1,582	4,812	4,622	92
Male	8,776	208	13	18	21	41	1,404	3,798	3,214	59
Female	2,825	28	9	6	6	143	178	1,014	1,408	33
Hispanic	5,113	95	16	38	31	79	647	1,622	2,520	65
Male	4,305	90	11	36	24	19	609	1,369	2,098	49
Female	808	5	5	2	7	60	38	253	422	16
Asian/Pacific Islander	1,255	35	18	22	10	33	134	404	509	90
Male	1,010	31	16	20	4	5	128	353	416	37
Female	245	4	2	2	6	28	6	51	93	53
Amind/Alaskan Native	570	30	4	6	5	13	149	173	185	5
Male	455	26	4	6	4	3	135	137	138	2
Female	115	4	0	0	1	10	14	36	47	3

Source: "Occupational Employment in Private Industry by Race/Ethnic Group/Sex, and by Industry, United States, 1994, All Industries." U.S. Equal Employment Opportunity Commission, *Job Patterns for Minorities and Women in Private Industry 1994*, p. 9. *Note:* Data for the state of Hawaii are not included.

★ 540 ★

Occupations

Occupational Employment in Private Industry: Mining

Race/Ethnic Group/Sex	Number employed									
	Total Employment	Officials and Managers	Profes-sionals	Techni-cians	Sales workers	Office & Clerical workers	Craft workers	Opera-tives	Laborers	Service workers
All Employees	316,336	43,160	53,704	17,017	3,168	30,157	68,600	71,946	25,531	3,053
Male	263,863	39,135	40,538	13,156	2,334	5,703	67,387	69,180	24,044	2,386
Female	52,473	4,025	13,166	3,861	834	24,454	1,213	2,766	1,487	667
White	264,799	40,003	47,203	13,993	2,730	23,765	56,965	57,484	20,433	2,223
Male	222,606	36,379	36,442	10,919	2,098	4,369	56,016	55,358	19,269	1,756
Female	42,193	3,624	10,761	3,074	632	19,396	949	2,126	1,164	467
Minority	51,537	3,157	6,501	3,024	438	6,392	11,635	14,462	5,098	830
Male	41,257	2,756	4,096	2,237	236	1,334	11,371	13,822	4,775	630
Female	10,280	401	2,405	787	202	5,058	264	640	323	200
Black	17,786	933	2,283	1,139	207	3,172	3,425	4,494	1,648	485
Male	12,702	766	1,231	757	78	535	3,301	4,154	1,509	371
Female	5,084	167	1,052	382	129	2,637	124	340	139	114
Hispanic	25,122	1,446	1,840	1,245	172	2,272	6,238	8,591	3,014	304
Male	22,011	1,331	1,284	1,030	113	581	6,163	8,395	2,877	237
Female	3,111	115	556	215	59	1,691	75	196	137	67
Asian/Pacific Islander	4,101	399	2,055	407	45	613	292	190	79	21
Male	2,644	313	1,359	273	33	147	278	165	62	14
Female	1,457	86	696	134	12	466	14	25	17	7
AmInd/Alaskan Native	4,528	379	323	233	14	335	1,680	1,187	357	20
Male	3,900	346	222	177	12	71	1,629	1,108	327	8
Female	628	33	101	56	2	264	51	79	30	12

Source: "Occupational Employment in Private Industry by Race/Ethnic Group/Sex, and by Industry, United States, 1994, All Industries." U.S. Equal Employment Opportunity Commission, *Job Patterns for Minorities and Women in Private Industry 1994*, p. 2. *Note:* Data for the state of Hawaii are not included.

★ 541 ★

Occupations

Occupational Employment in Private Industry: Miscellaneous Food and Related Products

RACE/ETHNIC GROUP/ SEX	Total employ- ment	Officials and managers	Profes- sionals	Techni- cians	Sales workers	Office & clerical workers	Craft workers	Opera- tives	Laborers	Service workers
NUMBER EMPLOYED										
All employees	137,051	13,310	3,959	2,777	14,559	9,714	11,970	29,829	35,255	15,678
Male	85,082	10,475	2,169	1,332	10,745	1,624	10,112	20,636	18,568	9,421
Female	51,969	2,835	1,790	1,445	3,814	8,090	1,858	9,193	16,687	6,257
White	88,179	11,446	3,356	2,058	11,951	7,657	8,539	17,287	16,898	8,987
Male	56,107	9,037	1,859	988	8,905	1,118	7,492	12,192	9,316	5,200
Female	32,072	2,409	1,497	1,070	3,046	6,539	1,047	5,095	7,582	3,787
Minority	48,872	1,864	603	719	2,608	2,057	3,431	12,542	18,357	6,691
Male	28,975	1,438	310	344	1,840	506	2,620	8,444	9,252	4,221
Female	19,897	426	293	375	768	1,551	811	4,098	9,105	2,470
Black	20,204	738	186	308	932	751	1,596	6,265	6,344	3,084
Male	11,267	571	79	127	650	130	1,134	3,790	2,847	1,939
Female	8,937	167	107	181	282	621	462	2,475	3,497	1,145
Hispanic	20,875	697	159	222	1,346	826	1,376	4,826	8,486	2,937
Male	13,228	538	86	94	971	206	1,124	3,683	4,645	1,881
Female	7,647	159	73	128	375	620	252	1,143	3,841	1,056
Asian/Pacific Islander	7,172	386	248	180	281	431	390	1,306	3,345	605
Male	4,094	296	139	116	185	158	302	882	1,661	357
Female	3,076	90	109	64	96	273	88	424	1,684	248
Amind/Alaskan Native	621	43	10	9	49	49	69	145	182	65
Male	384	33	6	7	34	12	60	89	99	44
Female	237	10	4	2	15	37	9	56	83	21

Source: "Occupational Employment in Private Industry by Race/Ethnic Group/Sex, and by Industry, United States, 1994, All Industries." U.S. Equal Employment Opportunity Commission, *Job Patterns for Minorities and Women in Private Industry 1994*, p. 8. *Note:* Data for the state of Hawaii are not included.

★ 542 ★

Occupations

Occupational Employment in Private Industry: Motor Vehicles and Automotive Equipment

Race/ethnic group/sex	Total employment	Officials and managers	Professionals	Technicians	Sales workers	Office & clerical workers	Craft workers	Operatives	Laborers	Service workers
NUMBER EMPLOYED										
All employees	102,426	13,892	10,682	2,777	11,179	17,914	6,392	24,903	12,352	2,335
Male	71,437	11,696	7,562	2,183	8,799	4,523	5,899	19,998	8,940	1,837
Female	30,989	2,196	3,120	594	2,380	13,391	493	4,905	3,412	498

[Continued]

★ 542 ★

Occupational Employment in Private Industry: Motor Vehicles and Automotive Equipment

[Continued]

Race/ethnic group/sex	Total employment	Officials and managers	Professionals	Technicians	Sales workers	Office & clerical workers	Craft workers	Operatives	Laborers	Service workers
White	83,635	12,622	8,884	2,458	9,932	14,837	5,206	19,395	8,583	1,718
Male	58,540	10,666	6,460	1,946	8,000	3,315	4,805	15,739	6,044	1,365
Female	25,095	1,956	2,424	512	1,932	11,322	401	3,656	2,539	353
Minority	18,791	1,270	1,798	319	1,247	3,077	1,186	5,508	3,769	617
Male	12,897	1,030	1,102	237	799	1,008	1,094	4,529	2,896	472
Female	5,894	240	696	82	448	2,069	92	1,249	873	145
Black	9,564	397	568	131	622	1,576	573	3,412	1,844	441
Male	6,385	299	351	97	324	577	537	2,525	1,328	347
Female	3,179	98	217	34	298	999	36	887	516	94
Hispanic	5,824	321	377	81	525	882	496	1,611	1,393	138
Male	4,282	270	252	60	394	285	446	1,356	1,120	99
Female	1,542	51	125	21	131	597	50	255	273	39
Asian/Pacific Islander	3,026	510	832	103	76	562	87	349	480	27
Male	1,982	431	487	77	64	131	87	281	406	18
Female	1,044	79	345	26	12	431	0	68	74	9
Am. Ind./Alaskan Native	377	42	21	4	26	57	30	136	52	11
Male	248	30	12	3	17	15	24	97	42	8
Female	129	12	9	1	7	42	6	39	10	3

Source: "Occupational Employment in Private Industry by Race/Ethnic Group/Sex, and by Industry, United States, 1994, All Industries." U.S. Equal Employment Opportunity Commission, *Job Patterns for Minorities and Women in Private Industry 1994*, p. 24. *Note:* Data for the state of Hawaii are not included.

★ 543 ★

Occupations

Occupational Employment in Private Industry: Motor Vehicles and Equipment

Race/ethnic group/sex	Total employment	Officials and managers	Professionals	Technicians	Sales workers	Office & clerical workers	Craft workers	Operatives	Laborers	Service workers
					NUMBER EMPLOYED					
All employees	787,936	62,846	73,229	23,424	7,009	28,463	128,082	389,685	64,303	10,895
Male	626,386	56,593	58,803	19,391	5,938	8,393	122,716	300,479	45,000	9,073
Female	161,550	6,253	14,426	4,033	1,071	20,070	5,366	89,206	19,303	1,822
White	634,763	56,371	64,365	20,927	6,404	24,311	112,866	293,689	48,056	7,774
Male	515,994	51,006	52,222	17,480	5,503	7,096	108,650	233,526	33,986	6,525
Female	118,769	5,365	12,143	3,447	901	17,215	4,216	60,163	14,070	1,249
Minority	153,173	6,475	8,864	2,497	605	4,152	15,216	95,996	16,247	3,121
Male	110,392	5,587	6,581	1,911	435	1,297	14,066	66,953	11,014	2,548
Female	42,781	888	2,283	586	170	2,855	1,150	29,043	5,233	573
Black	112,364	4,119	4,133	1,334	226	2,765	10,421	76,158	10,516	2,692
Male	78,398	3,457	2,602	972	169	856	9,546	51,588	7,020	2,188
Female	33,966	662	1,531	362	57	1,909	875	24,570	3,496	504
Hispanic	26,502	1,014	1,059	648	269	943	3,425	14,776	4,019	349
Male	21,070	907	824	540	191	286	3,264	11,774	2,985	299

[Continued]

★ 543 ★

Occupational Employment in Private Industry: Motor Vehicles and Equipment
[Continued]

Race/ethnic group/sex	Total employment	Officials and managers	Professionals	Technicians	Sales workers	Office & clerical workers	Craft workers	Operatives	Laborers	Service workers
Female	5,432	107	235	108	78	657	161	3,002	1,034	50
Asian/Pacific Islander	11,686	1,118	3,475	410	94	307	880	3,871	1,481	50
Male	8,943	1,027	3,010	325	64	97	808	2,714	861	37
Female	2,743	91	465	85	30	210	72	1,157	620	13
Am. Ind./Alaskan Native	2,621	224	197	105	16	137	490	1,191	231	30
Male	1,981	196	145	74	11	58	448	877	148	24
Female	640	28	52	31	5	79	42	314	83	6

Source: "Occupational Employment in Private Industry by Race/Ethnic Group/Sex, and by Industry, United States, 1994, All Industries." U.S. Equal Employment Opportunity Commission, *Job Patterns for Minorities and Women in Private Industry 1994*, p. 19. *Note:* Data for the state of Hawaii are not included.

★ 544 ★
Occupations

Occupational Employment in Private Industry: Nursing and Personal Care Facilities

Race/Ethnic Group/Sex	Number employed									
	Total Employment	Officials and Managers	Professionals	Technicians	Sales workers	Office & Clerical workers	Craft workers	Operatives	Laborers	Service workers
All Employees	817,775	48,374	117,106	94,438	1,456	54,715	9,016	12,514	15,094	465,062
Male	134,249	13,937	13,022	9,046	289	4,095	4,334	5,207	5,665	78,654
Female	683,526	34,437	104,084	85,392	1,167	50,620	4,682	7,307	9,429	386,408
White	530,934	42,432	92,746	68,867	1,271	43,829	6,197	8,613	9,297	257,682
Male	79,343	12,320	10,102	6,035	239	2,790	3,222	3,657	3,198	37,780
Female	451,591	30,112	82,644	62,832	1,032	41,039	2,975	4,956	6,099	219,902
Minority	286,841	5,942	24,360	25,571	185	10,886	2,819	3,901	5,797	207,380
Male	54,906	1,617	2,920	3,011	50	1,305	1,112	1,550	2,467	40,874
Female	231,935	4,325	21,440	22,560	135	9,581	1,707	2,351	3,330	166,506
Black	201,120	3,662	11,654	18,456	118	6,468	1,929	2,423	2,744	153,666
Male	33,440	875	1,111	1,652	22	603	643	874	1,130	26,530
Female	167,680	2,787	10,543	16,804	96	5,865	1,286	1,549	1,614	127,136
Hispanic	48,752	1,102	2,654	2,917	42	2,749	677	1,034	1,974	35,603
Male	13,560	477	557	607	13	386	354	473	975	9,718
Female	35,192	625	2,097	2,310	29	2,363	323	561	999	25,885
Asian/Pacific Islander	33,336	1,021	9,641	3,833	14	1,481	187	360	1,037	15,762
Male	7,164	221	1,164	696	5	294	103	175	344	4,162
Female	26,172	800	8,477	3,137	9	1,187	84	185	693	11,600
AmInd/Alaskan Native	3,633	157	411	365	11	188	26	84	42	2,349

[Continued]

★ 544 ★

Occupational Employment in Private Industry: Nursing and Personal Care Facilities
[Continued]

Race/Ethnic Group/Sex	Number employed									
	Total Employment	Officials and Managers	Professionals	Technicians	Sales workers	Office & Clerical workers	Craft workers	Operatives	Laborers	Service workers
Male	742	44	88	56	10	22	12	28	18	464
Female	2,891	113	323	309	1	166	14	56	24	1,885

Source: "Occupational Employment in Private Industry by Race/Ethnic Group/Sex, and by Industry, United States, 1994, All Industries." U.S. Equal Employment Opportunity Commission, *Job Patterns for Minorities and Women in Private Industry 1994*, p. 33. *Note:* Data for the state of Hawaii are not included.

★ 545 ★

Occupations

Occupational Employment in Private Industry: Occupational Distribution

Race/ethnic group/sex	Total employment	Officials and managers	Professionals	Technicians	Sales workers	Office & clerical workers	Craft workers	Operatives	Laborers	Service workers
OCCUPATIONAL DISTRIBUTION										
All employees	100.0	10.7	14.5	6.0	10.9	15.1	9.1	15.2	7.6	10.9
Male	100.0	13.9	13.5	6.0	8.8	4.9	15.0	19.4	9.3	9.1
Female	100.0	7.0	15.7	6.0	13.2	26.7	2.3	10.4	5.6	13.0
White	100.0	12.5	16.4	6.3	11.3	15.1	9.8	14.0	6.1	8.5
Male	100.0	16.3	15.2	6.4	9.3	4.6	16.2	18.2	7.4	6.5
Female	100.0	8.1	17.7	6.3	13.8	27.5	2.3	9.0	4.6	10.8
Minority	100.0	4.9	8.8	5.0	9.5	15.1	6.9	19.0	12.3	18.6
Male	100.0	5.9	7.8	4.8	7.4	6.1	11.2	23.4	15.8	17.6
Female	100.0	3.7	9.9	5.3	11.7	24.5	2.3	14.4	8.7	19.6
Black	100.0	4.4	6.3	4.9	9.6	16.5	6.5	20.3	11.1	20.3
Male	100.0	5.3	4.7	4.1	7.4	6.3	11.4	26.5	15.2	19.0
Female	100.0	3.6	7.7	5.5	11.6	25.6	2.2	14.9	7.4	21.5
Hispanic	100.0	4.5	5.4	3.9	10.0	13.2	8.1	19.2	16.9	18.8
Male	100.0	5.2	4.6	4.0	7.6	5.3	12.1	22.6	19.9	18.6
Female	100.0	3.5	6.3	3.8	13.4	24.3	2.4	14.4	12.8	19.0
Asian/Pacific Islander	100.0	7.2	26.8	8.2	7.3	13.9	4.7	13.4	6.8	11.7
Male	100.0	9.6	27.0	9.2	6.2	7.6	7.1	14.6	7.5	11.1
Female	100.0	4.8	26.7	7.2	8.3	20.4	2.2	12.1	6.0	12.3
Am. Ind./Alaskan Native	100.0	7.2	8.7	5.3	11.7	12.8	11.0	18.6	10.7	13.9
Male	100.0	9.0	8.0	5.5	8.6	5.0	17.7	21.9	12.7	11.4
Female	100.0	4.9	9.5	5.1	15.6	22.5	2.7	14.4	8.2	16.9

Source: "Occupational Employment in Private Industry by Race/Ethnic Group/Sex, and by Industry, United States, 1994, All Industries." U.S. Equal Employment Opportunity Commission, *Job Patterns for Minorities and Women in Private Industry 1994.*, p. 1. *Note:* Data for the state of Hawaii are not included.

★ 546 ★

Occupations

Occupational Employment in Private Industry: Participation Rates

Race/ethnic group/sex	Total employment	Officials and managers	Professionals	Technicians	Sales workers	Office & clerical workers	Craft workers	Operatives	Laborers	Service workers
					PARTICIPATION RATE					
All employees	100.0	100.0	100.0	100.0	100.0	100.0	100.0	100.0	100.0	100.0
Male	53.5	69.7	49.6	53.4	43.4	17.5	88.3	68.3	65.7	44.6
Female	46.5	30.3	50.4	46.6	56.6	82.5	11.7	31.7	34.3	55.4
White	75.8	88.9	85.3	79.8	78.9	75.8	81.7	69.8	60.7	58.8
Male	41.1	62.7	43.0	43.6	35.0	12.4	73.0	49.2	39.9	24.6
Female	34.7	26.2	42.3	36.2	43.9	63.4	8.7	20.6	20.8	34.2
Minority	24.2	11.1	14.7	20.2	21.1	24.2	18.3	30.2	39.3	41.2
Male	12.4	6.9	6.6	9.8	8.4	5.0	15.3	19.1	25.8	20.1
Female	11.8	4.1	8.1	10.4	12.7	19.2	2.9	11.1	13.5	21.1
Black	12.9	5.3	5.6	10.4	11.4	14.2	9.3	17.3	18.9	24.1
Male	6.1	3.0	2.0	4.1	4.2	2.5	7.6	10.6	12.2	10.6
Female	6.9	2.3	3.7	6.3	7.3	11.6	1.7	6.7	6.7	13.5
Hispanic	7.5	3.2	2.8	4.9	7.0	6.6	6.7	9.5	16.8	13.0
Male	4.4	2.1	1.4	2.9	3.1	1.6	5.9	6.6	11.5	7.5
Female	3.1	1.0	1.4	2.0	3.9	5.1	0.8	3.0	5.3	5.5
Asian/Pacific Islander	3.2	2.2	6.0	4.4	2.2	3.0	1.7	2.8	2.9	3.5
Male	1.7	1.5	3.1	2.6	1.0	0.8	1.3	1.6	1.6	1.7
Female	1.6	0.7	2.9	1.9	1.2	2.1	0.4	1.2	1.2	1.8
Am. Ind./Alaskan Native	0.5	0.3	0.3	0.4	0.5	0.4	0.6	0.6	0.7	0.6
Male	0.3	0.2	0.2	0.3	0.2	0.1	0.5	0.4	0.5	0.3
Female	0.2	0.1	0.1	0.2	0.3	0.3	0.1	0.2	0.2	0.3

Source: "Occupational Employment in Private Industry by Race/Ethnic Group/Sex, and by Industry, United States, 1994, All Industries." U.S. Equal Employment Opportunity Commission, *Job Patterns for Minorities and Women in Private Industry 1994.*, p. 1. *Note:* Data for the state of Hawaii are not included.

★ 547 ★

Occupations

Occupational Employment in Private Industry: Personnel Supply Services

RACE/ETHNIC GROUP/SEX	Total employment	Officials and managers	Professionals	Technicians	Sales workers	Office & clerical workers	Craft workers	Operatives	Laborers	Service workers
					NUMBER EMPLOYED					
All employees	205,296	12,036	19,319	15,186	7,063	48,200	12,283	22,790	42,371	26,048
Male	119,524	7,584	11,073	10,328	4,051	12,330	10,873	18,258	32,689	12,338
Female	85,772	4,452	8,246	4,858	3,012	35,870	1,410	4,532	9,682	13,710
White	135,598	10,444	15,693	10,487	5,727	34,758	7,811	13,659	19,627	17,392
Male	77,189	6,698	9,198	7,484	3,358	8,566	7,200	11,342	14,971	8,372
Female	58,409	3,746	6,495	3,003	2,369	26,192	611	2,317	4,656	9,020

[Continued]

★ 547 ★

Occupational Employment in Private Industry: Personnel Supply Services

[Continued]

RACE/ETHNIC GROUP/ SEX	Total employ- ment	Officials and managers	Profes- sionals	Techni- cians	Sales workers	Office & clerical workers	Craft workers	Opera- tices	Laborers	Service workers
Minority	69,698	1,592	3,626	4,699	1,336	13,442	4,472	9,131	22,744	8,656
Male	42,335	886	1,875	2,844	693	3,764	3,673	6,916	17,718	3,966
Female	27,363	706	1,751	1,855	643	9,678	799	2,215	5,026	4,690
Black	30,969	435	1,531	1,671	457	6,469	911	3,499	11,185	4,811
Male	17,276	186	526	915	196	1,491	792	2,681	8,510	1,979
Female	13,693	249	1,005	756	261	4,978	119	818	2,675	2,832
Hispanic	29,601	838	779	1,177	763	4,934	2,954	4,359	10,491	3,306
Male	19,879	496	463	826	434	1,419	2,571	3,415	8,514	1,741
Female	9,722	342	316	351	329	3,515	383	944	1,977	1,565
Asian/Pacific Islander	7,911	227	1,109	1,794	74	1,764	547	1,186	818	392
Male	4,326	125	725	1,060	40	687	254	748	528	159
Female	3,585	102	384	734	34	1,077	293	438	290	233
Amind/Alaskan Native	1,217	92	207	57	42	275	60	87	250	147
Male	854	79	161	43	23	167	56	72	166	87
Female	363	13	46	14	19	108	4	145	84	60

Source: "Occupational Employment in Private Industry by Race/Ethnic Group/Sex, and by Industry, United States, 1994, All Industries." U.S. Equal Employment Opportunity Commission, *Job Patterns for Minorities and Women in Private Industry 1994*, p. 31. *Note:* Data for the state of Hawaii are not included.

★ 548 ★

Occupations

Occupational Employment in Private Industry: Petroleum Refining

RACE/ETHNIC GROUP/ SEX	Total employ- ment	Officials and managers	Profes- sionals	Techni- cians	Sales workers	Office & clerical workers	Craft workers	Opera- tives	Laborers	Service workers
					NUMBER EMPLOYED					
All employees	120,228	19,225	25,277	6,295	7,705	13,446	32,382	12,439	2,236	1,223
Male	90,735	16,937	18,513	4,908	3,782	1,917	30,545	11,338	1,997	798
Female	29,493	2,288	6,764	1,387	3,923	11,529	1,837	1,101	239	425
White	97,947	17,361	21,971	5,084	6,125	10,241	24,239	9,544	1,594	788
Male	75,098	15,367	16,399	4,066	3,129	1,447	23,937	8,786	1,427	540
Female	22,849	1,994	5,572	1,018	2,996	8,794	1,302	758	167	248
Minority	22,281	1,864	3,306	1,211	1,580	3,205	7,143	2,895	642	435
Male	15,637	1,570	2,114	842	653	470	6,608	2,552	570	258
Female	6,644	294	1,192	369	927	2,735	535	343	72	17
Black	12,286	977	1,285	657	1,107	1,889	4,244	1,582	340	205
Male	8,240	807	721	431	403	275	3,819	1,335	305	144
Female	4,046	170	564	226	704	1,614	425	247	35	61

[Continued]

★ 548 ★

Occupational Employment in Private Industry: Petroleum Refining
[Continued]

RACE/ETHNIC GROUP/ SEX	Total employ- ment	Officials and managers	Profes- sionals	Techni- cians	Sales workers	Office & clerical workers	Craft workers	Opera- tives	Laborers	Service workers
Hispanic	6,619	532	835	339	306	913	2,295	1,055	236	108
Male	5,077	473	582	264	138	135	2,203	999	213	70
Female	1,542	59	253	75	168	778	92	56	23	38
Asian/Pacific Islander	2,345	249	1,056	163	71	226	324	123	31	103
Male	1,602	202	724	111	53	31	319	102	23	37
Female	743	46	332	52	18	195	5	21	8	66
Amind/Alaskan Native	1,031	107	130	52	96	177	280	135	35	19
Male	718	88	87	36	59	97	267	116	29	7
Female	313	19	43	16	37	148	13	19	6	12

Source: "Occupational Employment in Private Industry by Race/Ethnic Group/Sex, and by Industry, United States, 1994, All Industries." U.S. Equal Employment Opportunity Commission, *Job Patterns for Minorities and Women in Private Industry 1994*, p. 13. *Note:* Data for the state of Hawaii are not included.

★ 549 ★
Occupations

Occupational Employment in Private Industry: Plastic Materials and Synthetics

Race/Ethnic Group/Sex	Number employed									
	Total Employ- ment	Officials and Managers	Profes- sionals	Techni- cians	Sales workers	Office & Clerical workers	Craft workers	Opera- tives	Laborers	Service workers
All Employees	117,871	14,208	16,106	9,610	2,354	8,310	25,630	33,121	7,468	1,064
Male	90,765	12,733	12,795	7,613	1,758	1,298	23,466	25,249	5,056	797
Female	27,106	1,475	3,311	1,997	596	7,012	2,164	7,872	2,412	267
White	96,082	12,891	13,992	8,178	2,179	7,074	21,306	24,699	4,990	773
Male	75,188	11,592	11,212	6,606	1,650	1,074	19,771	19,364	3,334	585
Female	20,894	1,299	2,780	1,572	529	6,000	1,535	5,335	1,656	188
Minority	21,789	1,317	2,114	1,432	175	1,236	4,324	8,422	2,478	291
Male	15,577	1,141	1,583	1,007	108	224	3,695	5,885	1,722	212
Female	6,212	176	531	425	67	1,012	629	2,537	756	79
Black	14,808	782	786	946	102	814	3,198	6,428	1,527	225
Male	10,079	659	498	617	51	144	2,652	4,279	1,020	159
Female	4,729	123	288	329	51	670	546	2,149	507	66
Hispanic	4,590	229	348	316	47	288	928	1,623	760	51
Male	3,678	208	267	266	37	53	869	1,350	586	42
Female	912	21	81	50	10	235	59	273	174	9
Asian/Pacific Islander	1,974	265	943	147	22	107	86	228	166	10
Male	1,548	240	796	106	16	22	78	179	104	7

[Continued]

★ 549 ★

Occupational Employment in Private Industry: Plastic Materials and Synthetics
[Continued]

Race/Ethnic Group/Sex	Number employed									
	Total Employment	Officials and Managers	Professionals	Technicians	Sales workers	Office & Clerical workers	Craft workers	Operatives	Laborers	Service workers
Female	426	25	147	41	6	85	8	49	62	3
AmInd/Alaskan Native	417	41	37	23	4	27	112	143	25	5
Male	272	34	22	18	4	5	96	77	12	4
Female	145	7	15	5	0	22	16	66	13	1

Source: "Occupational Employment in Private Industry by Race/Ethnic Group/Sex, and by Industry, United States, 1994, All Industries." U.S. Equal Employment Opportunity Commission, *Job Patterns for Minorities and Women in Private Industry 1994*, p. 12. *Note:* Data for the state of Hawaii are not included.

★ 550 ★
Occupations

Occupational Employment in Private Industry: Preserved Fruits and Vegetables

RACE/ETHNIC GROUP/SEX	Total employment	Officials and managers	Professionals	Technicians	Sales workers	Office & clerical workers	Craft workers	Operatives	Laborers	Service workers
	NUMBER EMPLOYED									
All employees	174,772	16,078	6,107	4,464	2,894	12,234	21,698	44,135	63,112	4,050
Male	99,299	12,834	3,424	1,862	1,992	1,661	18,568	28,187	28,162	2,609
Female	75,473	3,244	2,683	2,602	902	10,573	3,130	15,948	34,950	1,441
White	107,022	14,354	5,497	3,449	2,523	10,310	16,855	27,414	24,420	2,200
Male	63,032	11,508	3,130	1,442	1,774	1,285	14,734	17,000	10,746	1,413
Female	43,990	2,846	2,367	2,007	749	9,025	2,121	10,414	13,674	787
Minority	67,750	1,724	610	1,015	371	1,924	4,843	16,721	38,692	1,850
Male	36,267	1,326	294	420	218	376	3,834	11,187	17,416	1,196
Female	31,483	398	316	595	153	1,548	1,009	5,534	21,276	654
Black	15,077	507	188	322	246	662	1,527	4,776	6,346	503
Male	8,376	389	77	123	129	131	1,057	3,108	3,009	353
Female	6,701	118	111	199	117	531	470	1,668	3,337	150
Hispanic	46,234	839	191	525	91	940	2,846	10,702	28,878	1,222
Male	25,223	655	107	226	74	195	2,396	7,393	13,415	762
Female	21,011	184	84	299	17	745	450	3,309	15,463	460
Asian/Pacific Islander	4,963	299	209	145	25	264	221	734	2,969	97
Male	1,889	218	99	61	10	44	178	409	807	63
Female	3,074	81	110	84	15	220	43	325	2,162	34
AmInd/Alaskan Native	1,476	79	22	23	9	58	249	509	499	28

[Continued]

★ 550 ★

Occupational Employment in Private Industry: Preserved Fruits and Vegetables

[Continued]

RACE/ETHNIC GROUP/ SEX	Total employ-ment	Officials and managers	Profes-sionals	Techni-cians	Sales workers	Office & clerical workers	Craft workers	Opera-tives	Laborers	Service workers
Male	779	64	11	10	5	6	203	277	185	18
Female	697	15	11	13	4	52	46	232	314	10

Source: "Occupational Employment in Private Industry by Race/Ethnic Group/Sex, and by Industry, United States, 1994, All Industries." U.S. Equal Employment Opportunity Commission, *Job Patterns for Minorities and Women in Private Industry 1994*, p. 6. *Note:* Data for the state of Hawaii are not included.

★ 551 ★

Occupations

Occupational Employment in Private Industry: Professional and Commercial Equipment

Race/ethnic group/sex	Total employment	Officials and managers	Professionals	Technicians	Sales workers	Office & clerical workers	Craft workers	Operatives	Laborers	Service workers
				NUMBER EMPLOYED						
All employees	173,186	23,778	30,531	35,916	26,217	34,927	4,464	10,831	5,044	1,478
Male	111,117	17,590	20,067	32,331	17,441	8,445	3,643	7,040	3,660	900
Female	62,069	6,188	10,464	3,585	8,776	26,482	821	3,791	1,384	578
White	139,704	20,981	26,182	28,719	23,038	26,668	3,571	6,620	3,156	769
Male	90,508	15,540	17,393	25,869	15,569	5,679	3,006	4,604	2,330	518
Female	49,196	5,441	8,789	2,850	7,469	20,989	565	2,016	826	251
Minority	33,482	2,797	4,349	7,197	3,179	8,259	893	4,211	1,888	709
Male	20,609	2,050	2,674	6,462	1,872	2,766	637	2,436	1,330	382
Female	12,873	747	1,675	735	1,307	5,493	256	1,775	558	327
Black	15,390	1,042	1,429	3,145	1,779	4,245	280	2,086	897	487
Male	8,738	675	753	2,812	982	1,286	220	1,120	659	231
Female	6,652	367	676	333	797	2,959	60	966	238	256
Hispanic	9,730	654	871	2,229	770	2,496	306	1,577	690	137
Male	6,281	462	572	2,046	482	924	232	992	470	101
Female	3,449	192	299	183	288	1,572	74	585	220	36
Asian/Pacific Islander	7,626	1,023	1,956	1,644	543	1,320	293	496	277	74
Male	5,082	857	1,281	1,448	352	449	178	291	180	46
Female	2,544	166	675	196	191	871	115	205	97	28
Am. Ind./Alaskan Native	736	78	93	179	87	198	14	52	24	11
Male	508	56	68	156	56	107	7	33	21	4
Female	228	22	25	23	31	91	7	19	3	7

Source: "Occupational Employment in Private Industry by Race/Ethnic Group/Sex, and by Industry, United States, 1994, All Industries." U.S. Equal Employment Opportunity Commission, *Job Patterns for Minorities and Women in Private Industry 1994*, p. 24. *Note:* Data for the state of Hawaii are not included.

★ 552 ★

Occupations

Occupational Employment in Private Industry: Public Warehousing and Storage

RACE/ETHNIC GROUP/ SEX	Total employ- ment	Officials and managers	Profes- sional	Techni- cians	Sales workers	Office & clerical workers	Craft workers	Operat- ives	Laborers	Service workers
				NUMBER EMPLOYED						
All employees	171,045	15,881	5,550	2,601	11,130	26,912	13,288	46,677	44,312	4,694
Male	107,746	12,145	3,474	1,771	5,609	6,854	10,445	34,834	29,111	3,503
Female	63,299	3,736	2,076	830	5,521	20,058	2,843	11,843	15,201	1,191
White	120,469	13,841	4,900	2,172	8,782	20,690	10,735	31,212	25,685	2,452
Male	76,187	10,621	3,119	1,497	4,550	4,858	8,483	23,627	17,586	1,846
Female	44,282	3,220	1,781	675	4,232	15,832	2,252	7,585	8,099	606
Minority	50,576	2,040	650	429	2,348	6,222	2,553	15,465	18,627	2,242
Male	31,559	1,524	355	274	1,059	1,996	1,962	11,207	11,525	1,657
Female	19,017	516	295	155	1,289	4,226	591	4,258	7,102	585
Black	28,896	1,107	313	221	1,474	3,755	1,379	8,771	10,700	1,176
Male	17,297	805	140	115	587	1,179	1,015	6,088	6,517	851
Female	11,599	302	173	106	887	2,576	364	2,683	4,183	325
Hispanic	17,745	704	141	115	684	1,804	1,002	5,743	6,737	815
Male	11,866	553	84	91	360	598	834	4,460	4,292	594
Female	5,879	151	57	24	324	1,206	168	1,283	2,445	221
Asian/Pacific Islander	3,213	187	174	86	167	535	144	731	962	227
Male	1,947	133	116	64	103	166	89	492	588	196
Female	1,266	54	58	22	64	369	55	239	374	31
AmInd/Alaskan Native	722	42	22	7	23	128	28	220	228	24
Male	449	33	15	4	9	53	24	167	128	16
Female	273	9	7	3	13	75	4	53	100	8

Source: "Occupational Employment in Private Industry by Race/Ethnic Group/Sex, and by Industry, United States, 1994, All Industries." U.S. Equal Employment Opportunity Commission, *Job Patterns for Minorities and Women in Private Industry 1994*, p. 22. *Note:* Data for the state of Hawaii are not included.

★ 553 ★

Occupations

Occupational Employment in Private Industry: Publishing and Printing

Race/Ethnic Group/Sex	Number employed									
	Total Employment	Officials and Managers	Profes-sionals	Techni-cians	Sales workers	Office & Clerical workers	Craft workers	Opera-tives	Laborers	Service workers
All Employees	302,675	37,580	49,860	8,640	38,257	48,796	36,056	41,902	31,476	10,108
Male	178,536	26,097	29,731	6,271	16,192	10,533	29,256	32,922	19,752	7,782
Female	124,139	11,483	20,129	2,369	22,065	38,263	6,800	8,980	11,724	2,326
White	242,797	33,697	44,171	7,304	31,933	37,952	31,050	30,542	20,053	6,095
Male	144,060	23,639	26,912	5,314	13,553	7,950	25,265	24,234	12,628	4,565
Female	98,737	10,058	17,259	1,990	18,380	30,002	5,785	6,308	7,425	1,530
Minority	59,878	3,883	5,689	1,336	6,324	10,844	5,006	11,360	11,423	4,013
Male	34,476	2,458	2,819	957	2,639	2,583	3,991	8,688	7,124	3,217
Female	25,402	1,425	2,870	379	3,685	8,261	1,015	2,672	4,299	796
Black	36,339	2,124	2,912	631	4,072	6,793	2,628	7,042	7,363	2,774
Male	20,024	1,326	1,340	426	1,519	1,414	2,058	5,203	4,523	2,215
Female	16,315	798	1,572	205	2,553	5,379	570	1,839	2,840	559
Hispanic	16,097	1,211	1,560	419	1,656	2,839	1,737	3,004	2,776	895
Male	9,986	782	903	320	812	771	1,465	2,444	1,770	719
Female	6,111	429	657	99	844	2,068	272	560	1,006	176
Asian/Pacific Islander	6,192	394	1,082	251	466	1,043	489	1,062	1,109	296
Male	3,731	243	512	191	253	366	346	857	721	242
Female	2,461	151	570	60	213	677	143	205	388	54
AmInd/Alaskan Native	1,250	154	135	35	130	169	152	252	175	48
Male	735	107	64	20	55	32	122	184	110	41
Female	515	47	71	15	75	137	30	68	65	7

Source: "Occupational Employment in Private Industry by Race/Ethnic Group/Sex, and by Industry, United States, 1994, All Industries." U.S. Equal Employment Opportunity Commission, *Job Patterns for Minorities and Women in Private Industry 1994*, p. 11. *Note:* Data for the state of Hawaii are not included.

★ 554 ★

Occupations

Occupational Employment in Private Industry: Railroads

Race/ethnic group/sex	Total employment	Officials and managers	Professionals	Technicians	Sales workers	Office & clerical workers	Craft workers	Operatives	Laborers	Service workers
				NUMBER EMPLOYED						
All employees	225,043	24,673	7,308	3,107	3,250	25,987	99,006	40,985	14,303	6,424
Male	206,782	22,806	5,370	2,849	1,656	16,560	98,214	40,288	14,025	5,014
Female	18,261	1,867	1,938	258	1,594	9,427	792	697	278	1,410
White	185,909	22,008	6,356	2,770	2,133	21,336	86,316	32,708	9,010	3,272
Male	173,164	20,492	4,849	2,571	1,272	14,431	85,677	32,221	8,847	2,804
Female	12,745	1,516	1,507	199	861	6,905	639	487	163	468
Minority	39,134	2,665	952	337	1,117	4,651	12,690	8,277	5,293	3,152
Male	33,618	2,314	521	278	384	2,129	12,537	8,067	5,178	2,210
Female	5,516	351	431	59	733	2,522	153	210	115	942
Black	24,690	1,545	576	178	827	3,244	7,820	5,078	2,823	2,599
Male	20,402	1,281	273	133	255	1,316	7,706	4,912	2,727	1,799
Female	4,288	264	303	45	572	1,928	114	166	96	800
Hispanic	10,673	835	147	92	214	939	3,920	2,519	1,626	381
Male	9,943	796	100	82	89	595	3,891	2,485	1,614	291
Female	730	39	47	10	125	344	29	34	12	90
Asian/Pacific Islander	1,545	194	207	35	66	383	344	134	43	139
Male	1,123	149	134	32	36	163	339	129	40	101
Female	422	45	73	3	30	220	5	5	3	38
Am. Ind./Alaskan Native	2,226	91	22	32	10	85	606	546	801	33
Male	2,150	88	14	31	4	55	601	541	797	19
Female	76	3	8	1	6	30	5	5	4	14

Source: "Occupational Employment in Private Industry by Race/Ethnic Group/Sex, and by Industry, United States, 1994, All Industries." U.S. Equal Employment Opportunity Commission, *Job Patterns for Minorities and Women in Private Industry 1994*, p. 21. *Note:* Data for the state of Hawaii are not included.

★ 555 ★

Occupations

Occupational Employment in Private Industry: Refrigeration and Service Machinery

RACE/ETHNIC GROUP/ SEX	Total employment	Officials and managers	Professionals	Technicians	Sales workers	Office & clerical workers	Craft workers	Operatives	Laborers	Service workers
					NUMBER EMPLOYED					
All employees	131,652	12,519	9,801	6,780	2,599	9,259	21,058	57,388	11,459	789
Male	98,698	10,994	7,727	5,779	2,135	1,713	19,248	42,900	7,455	657
Female	32,954	1,525	2,074	1,001	464	7,546	1,810	14,398	4,004	132
White	103,000	11,667	9,012	6,140	2,466	8,260	17,292	40,022	7,519	622
Male	77,948	10,242	7,127	5,228	2,038	1,469	15,985	30,376	4,968	515
Female	25,052	1,425	1,885	912	428	6,791	1,307	9,646	2,551	107

[Continued]

★ 555 ★

Occupational Employment in Private Industry: Refrigeration and Service Machinery
[Continued]

RACE/ETHNIC GROUP/ SEX	Total employ-ment	Officials and managers	Profes-sionals	Techni-cians	Sales workers	Office & clerical workers	Craft workers	Opera-tives	Laborers	Service workers
Minority	28,652	852	789	640	133	999	3,766	17,366	3,940	167
Male	20,750	752	600	551	97	244	3,263	12,614	2,487	142
Female	7,902	100	189	89	36	755	503	4,752	1,453	25
Black	16,329	383	216	273	33	502	2,100	10,951	1,762	109
Male	11,139	333	134	230	17	128	1,721	7,368	1,115	93
Female	5,190	50	82	43	16	374	379	3,583	647	16
Hispanic	9,071	228	159	200	71	378	1,258	4,939	1,789	49
Male	7,016	201	126	171	54	89	1,157	4,030	1,146	42
Female	2,055	27	33	29	17	289	101	909	643	7
Asian/Pacific Islander	2,819	212	389	149	23	101	333	1,243	361	8
Male	2,276	195	323	133	21	25	318	1,042	213	6
Female	543	17	66	16	2	76	15	201	148	2
Amind/Alaskan Native	433	29	25	18	6	18	75	233	28	1
Male	319	23	17	17	5	2	67	174	13	1
Female	114	6	8	1	1	16	8	59	15	0

Source: "Occupational Employment in Private Industry by Race/Ethnic Group/Sex, and by Industry, United States, 1994, All Industries." U.S. Equal Employment Opportunity Commission, *Job Patterns for Minorities and Women in Private Industry 1994*, p. 17. *Note:* Data for the state of Hawaii are not included.

★ 556 ★
Occupations

Occupational Employment in Private Industry: Research, Development and Testing Services

Race/Ethnic Group/Sex	Number employed									
	Total Employ-ment	Officials and Managers	Profes-sionals	Techni-cians	Sales workers	Office & Clerical workers	Craft workers	Opera-tives	Laborers	Service workers
All Employees	321,246	47,195	136,801	43,794	3,948	50,782	14,820	14,160	2,949	6,797
Male	202,104	36,465	94,279	30,015	2,348	8,286	14,090	10,468	1,883	4,270
Female	119,142	10,730	42,522	13,779	1,600	42,496	730	3,692	1,066	2,527
White	259,973	42,099	114,176	34,820	3,480	37,264	12,168	10,123	1,866	3,977
Male	167,973	32,746	79,963	24,344	2,143	5,374	11,680	7,918	1,243	2,562
Female	92,000	9,353	34,213	10,476	1,337	31,890	488	2,205	623	1,415
Minority	61,273	5,096	22,625	8,974	468	13,518	2,652	4,037	1,083	2,820
Male	34,131	3,719	14,316	5,671	205	2,912	2,410	2,550	640	1,708
Female	27,142	1,377	8,309	3,303	263	10,606	242	1,487	443	1,112
Black	24,169	1,599	5,286	3,185	285	7,992	1,232	2,274	578	1,738
Male	11,221	993	2,697	1,908	109	1,671	1,109	1,389	354	991
Female	12,948	606	2,589	1,277	176	6,321	123	885	224	747

[Continued]

★ 556 ★

Occupational Employment in Private Industry: Research, Development and Testing Services
[Continued]

Race/Ethnic Group/Sex	Number employed									
	Total Employment	Officials and Managers	Profes-sionals	Techni-cians	Sales workers	Office & Clerical workers	Craft workers	Opera-tives	Laborers	Service workers
Hispanic	14,819	1,115	4,054	2,619	103	3,517	1,029	1,179	352	851
Male	8,670	833	2,613	1,873	49	751	947	823	207	574
Female	6,149	282	1,441	746	54	2,766	82	356	145	277
Asian/Pacific Islander	20,939	2,237	12,862	2,948	70	1,729	295	493	124	181
Male	13,469	1,777	8,749	1,736	40	449	267	275	65	111
Female	7,470	460	4,113	1,212	30	1,280	28	218	59	70
AmInd/Alaskan Native	1,346	145	423	222	10	280	96	91	29	50
Male	771	116	257	154	7	41	87	63	14	32
Female	575	29	166	68	3	239	9	28	15	18

Source: "Occupational Employment in Private Industry by Race/Ethnic Group/Sex, and by Industry, United States, 1994, All Industries." U.S. Equal Employment Opportunity Commission, *Job Patterns for Minorities and Women in Private Industry 1994*, p. 36. *Note:* Data for the state of Hawaii are not included.

★ 557 ★

Occupations

Occupational Employment in Private Industry: Residential Services

RACE/ETHNIC GROUP/SEX	Total employ-ment	Officials and managers	Profes-sionals	Techni-cians	Sales workers	Office & clerical workers	Craft workers	Opera-tives	Laborers	Service workers
					NUMBER EMPLOYED					
All employees	106,956	7,652	23,536	6,828	989	9,332	1,621	2,877	3,073	51,048
Male	28,514	2,968	5,553	1,021	212	715	1,204	1,493	1,795	13,553
Female	78,442	4,684	17,983	5,807	777	8,617	417	1,384	1,278	37,495
White	69,432	6,523	17,962	4,496	557	7,412	1,308	1,838	2,130	27,206
Male	18,046	2,579	3,875	625	163	512	988	1,036	1,274	6,994
Female	51,386	3,944	14,087	3,871	394	6,900	320	802	856	20,212
Minority	37,524	1,129	5,574	2,332	432	1,920	313	1,039	943	23,842
Male	10,468	389	1,678	396	49	203	216	457	521	6,559
Female	27,056	740	3,896	1,936	383	1,717	97	582	422	17,283
Black	28,596	816	3,872	1,826	352	1,288	180	716	572	18,974
Male	7,417	267	1,273	278	36	136	105	290	287	4,745
Female	21,179	549	2,599	1,548	316	1,152	75	426	285	14,229
Hispanic	6,092	201	928	263	31	480	100	246	278	3,565
Male	2,253	78	242	72	7	43	82	133	180	1,416
Female	3,839	123	686	191	24	437	18	113	98	2,149
Asian/Pacific Islander	2,579	87	726	233	49	137	27	73	85	1,162

[Continued]

★ 557 ★

Occupational Employment in Private Industry: Residential Services
[Continued]

RACE/ETHNIC GROUP/ SEX	Total employ- ment	Officials and managers	Profes- sionals	Techni- cians	Sales workers	Office & clerical workers	Craft workers	Opera- tives	Laborers	Service workers
Male	702	30	145	45	6	23	23	30	48	352
Female	1,877	57	581	188	43	114	4	43	37	810
Amind/Alaskan Native	257	25	48	10	0	15	6	4	8	141
Male	96	14	18	1	0	1	6	4	6	46
Female	161	11	30	9	0	14	0	0	2	95

Source: "Occupational Employment in Private Industry by Race/Ethnic Group/Sex, and by Industry, United States, 1994, All Industries." U.S. Equal Employment Opportunity Commission, *Job Patterns for Minorities and Women in Private Industry 1994*, p. 35. *Note:* Data for the state of Hawaii are not included.

★ 558 ★

Occupations

Occupational Employment in Private Industry: Retail Trade

Race/Ethnic Group/Sex	Number employed									
	Total Employ- ment	Officials and Managers	Profes- sionals	Techni- cians	Sales workers	Office & Clerical workers	Craft workers	Opera- tives	Laborers	Service workers
All Employees	6,031,868	533,859	107,879	59,792	2,779,452	487,189	196,198	232,864	463,316	1,171,319
Male	2,653,940	331,072	53,372	34,649	1,008,327	84,300	119,496	164,728	300,066	557,930
Female	3,377,928	202,787	54,507	25,143	1,771,125	402,889	76,702	68,136	163,250	613,389
White	4,518,165	464,968	93,933	48,207	2,121,356	381,763	154,268	165,453	312,874	775,343
Male	1,916,094	289,523	46,919	27,929	760,846	61,879	91,370	115,476	197,323	324,829
Female	2,602,071	175,445	47,014	20,278	1,360,510	319,884	62,898	49,977	115,551	450,514
Minority	1,513,703	68,891	13,946	11,585	658,096	105,426	41,930	67,411	150,442	395,976
Male	737,846	41,549	6,453	6,720	247,481	22,421	28,126	49,252	102,743	233,101
Female	775,857	27,342	7,493	4,865	410,615	83,005	13,804	18,159	47,699	162,875
Black	797,114	35,258	5,602	5,089	360,910	58,897	17,065	33,937	78,861	201,495
Male	358,624	19,684	2,410	2,612	125,110	10,863	10,430	23,582	53,790	110,143
Female	438,490	15,574	3,192	2,477	235,800	48,034	6,635	10,355	25,071	91,352
Hispanic	531,882	23,346	3,276	4,011	217,521	33,104	18,396	26,573	57,280	148,375
Male	292,685	15,513	1,773	2,625	90,456	7,921	13,407	20,805	39,903	100,282
Female	239,197	7,833	1,503	1,386	127,065	25,183	4,989	5,768	17,377	48,093
Asian/Pacific Islander	145,380	8,406	4,685	2,200	62,555	11,160	5,339	5,456	10,571	35,008
Male	68,595	5,271	2,083	1,306	25,582	3,145	3,539	3,839	6,693	17,137
Female	76,785	3,135	2,602	894	36,973	8,015	1,800	1,617	3,878	17,871
AmInd/Alaskan Native	39,327	1,881	383	285	17,110	2,265	1,130	1,445	3,730	11,098
Male	17,942	1,081	187	177	6,333	492	750	1,026	2,357	5,539
Female	21,385	800	196	108	10,777	1,773	380	419	1,373	5,559

Source: "Occupational Employment in Private Industry by Race/Ethnic Group/Sex, and by Industry, United States, 1994, All Industries." U.S. Equal Employment Opportunity Commission, *Job Patterns for Minorities and Women in Private Industry 1994*, p. 4. *Note:* Data for the state of Hawaii are not included.

★ 559 ★

Occupations

Occupational Employment in Private Industry: Savings Institutions

Race/Ethnic Group/Sex	Number employed									
	Total Employ-ment	Officials and Managers	Profes-sionals	Techni-cians	Sales workers	Office & Clerical workers	Craft workers	Opera-tives	Laborers	Service workers
All Employees	104,917	22,826	14,131	2,894	3,952	58,470	498	467	162	1,517
Male	31,338	11,561	5,697	1,645	1,776	8,587	292	386	146	1,248
Female	73,579	11,265	8,434	1,249	2,176	49,883	206	81	16	269
White	82,796	20,473	11,362	2,234	3,163	43,634	347	324	113	1,146
Male	25,392	10,686	4,692	1,245	1,463	5,810	192	261	106	937
Female	57,404	9,787	6,670	989	1,700	37,824	155	63	7	209
Minority	22,121	2,353	2,769	660	789	14,836	151	143	49	371
Male	5,946	875	1,005	400	313	2,777	100	125	40	311
Female	16,175	1,478	1,764	260	476	12,059	51	18	9	60
Black	9,825	987	979	234	271	6,979	54	65	28	228
Male	2,281	323	293	131	106	1,129	35	60	21	183
Female	7,544	664	686	103	165	5,850	19	5	7	45
Hispanic	7,376	775	767	191	344	5,038	76	56	18	111
Male	1,993	302	274	121	130	952	51	48	17	98
Female	5,383	473	493	70	214	4,086	25	8	1	13
Asian/Pacific Islander	4,599	538	980	224	162	2,632	11	19	3	30
Male	1,593	229	424	141	73	671	9	16	2	28
Female	3,006	309	556	83	89	1,961	2	3	1	2
AmInd/Alaskan Native	321	53	43	11	12	187	10	3	0	2
Male	79	21	14	7	4	25	5	1	0	2
Female	242	32	29	4	8	162	5	2	0	0

Source: "Occupational Employment in Private Industry by Race/Ethnic Group/Sex, and by Industry, United States, 1994, All Industries." U.S. Equal Employment Opportunity Commission, *Job Patterns for Minorities and Women in Private Industry 1994*, p. 29. *Note:* Data for the state of Hawaii are not included.

★ 560 ★

Occupations

Occupational Employment in Private Industry: Scheduled Air Transportation

Race/ethnic group/sex	Total employment	Officials and managers	Professionals	Technicians	Sales workers	Office & clerical workers	Craft workers	Operatives	Laborers	Service workers
				NUMBER EMPLOYED						
All employees	382,334	24,456	60,637	6,177	39,259	53,070	55,892	40,873	20,469	81,501
Male	222,617	17,504	54,131	4,330	10,625	15,307	52,250	35,499	13,791	19,180
Female	159,717	6,952	6,506	1,847	28,634	37,763	3,642	5,374	6,678	62,321
White	302,978	21,117	57,001	5,308	29,382	39,584	46,785	28,055	10,015	65,731
Male	178,905	15,296	51,502	3,788	8,152	11,552	44,212	24,187	7,188	13,028
Female	124,073	5,821	5,499	1,520	21,230	28,032	2,573	3,868	2,827	52,703
Minority	79,356	3,339	3,636	869	9,877	13,486	9,107	12,818	10,454	15,770
Male	43,712	2,208	2,629	542	2,473	3,755	8,038	11,312	6,603	6,152
Female	35,644	1,131	1,007	327	7,404	9,731	1,069	1,506	3,851	9,618
Black	44,242	1,785	1,502	402	5,151	8,131	4,300	7,022	8,142	7,807
Male	22,516	1,068	932	234	1,059	1,958	3,604	6,048	4,776	2,837
Female	21,726	717	570	168	4,092	6,173	696	974	3,366	4,970
Hispanic	21,007	815	1,042	199	2,693	3,132	2,376	4,290	1,634	4,826
Male	13,046	596	845	141	833	1,054	2,222	3,887	1,295	2,173
Female	7,961	219	197	58	1,860	2,078	154	403	339	2,653
Asian/Pacific Islander	12,279	621	861	215	1,830	1,914	2,172	1,207	607	2,852
Male	7,049	465	648	137	521	664	1,969	1,106	479	1,060
Female	5,230	156	213	78	1,308	1,250	203	101	128	1,792
Am. Ind./Alaskan Native	1,828	118	231	53	203	309	259	299	71	285
Male	1,101	79	204	30	60	79	243	271	53	82
Female	727	39	27	23	143	230	16	28	18	203

Source: "Occupational Employment in Private Industry by Race/Ethnic Group/Sex, and by Industry, United States, 1994, All Industries." U.S. Equal Employment Opportunity Commission, *Job Patterns for Minorities and Women in Private Industry 1994*, p. 22. *Note:* Data for the state of Hawaii are not included.

★ 561 ★

Occupations

Occupational Employment in Private Industry: Security Brokers

Race/Ethnic Group/Sex	Number employed									
	Total Employment	Officials and Managers	Professionals	Technicians	Sales workers	Office & Clerical workers	Craft workers	Operatives	Laborers	Service workers
All Employees	200,146	30,107	46,878	5,669	39,838	72,532	763	838	625	2,896
Male	114,021	21,389	28,920	3,838	33,039	23,500	681	656	414	1,584
Female	86,125	8,718	17,958	1,831	6,799	49,032	82	182	211	1,312
White	163,853	27,150	38,833	4,233	37,289	53,085	584	346	322	2,011
Male	96,969	19,545	24,330	2,849	31,237	16,948	518	271	212	1,059

[Continued]

★ 561 ★

Occupational Employment in Private Industry: Security Brokers

[Continued]

Race/Ethnic Group/Sex	Number employed									
	Total Employment	Officials and Managers	Professionals	Technicians	Sales workers	Office & Clerical workers	Craft workers	Operatives	Laborers	Service workers
Female	66,884	7,605	14,503	1,384	6,052	36,137	66	75	110	952
Minority	36,293	2,957	8,045	1,436	2,549	19,447	179	492	303	885
Male	17,052	1,844	4,590	989	1,802	6,552	163	385	202	525
Female	19,241	1,113	3,455	447	747	12,895	16	107	101	360
Black	17,007	1,251	2,700	542	921	10,621	66	246	170	490
Male	6,956	669	1,318	330	588	3,386	62	189	123	291
Female	10,051	582	1,382	212	333	7,235	4	57	47	199
Hispanic	9,506	716	1,534	292	723	5,525	102	205	126	283
Male	4,500	477	899	219	529	1,863	94	162	78	179
Female	5,006	239	635	73	194	3,622	8	43	48	104
Asian/Pacific Islander	9,430	962	3,752	574	873	3,106	9	41	4	109
Male	5,423	679	2,337	423	658	1,232	6	34	1	53
Female	4,007	283	1,415	151	215	1,874	3	7	3	56
AmInd/Alaskan Native	350	28	59	28	32	195	2	0	3	3
Male	173	19	36	17	27	71	1	0	0	2
Female	177	9	23	11	5	124	1	0	3	1

Source: "Occupational Employment in Private Industry by Race/Ethnic Group/Sex, and by Industry, United States, 1994, All Industries." U.S. Equal Employment Opportunity Commission, *Job Patterns for Minorities and Women in Private Industry 1994*, p. 29. *Note:* Data for the state of Hawaii are not included.

★ 562 ★

Occupations

Occupational Employment in Private Industry: Ship and Boat Building and Repairing

Race/ethnic group/sex	Total employment	Officials and managers	Professionals	Technicians	Sales workers	Office & clerical workers	Craft workers	Operatives	Laborers	Service workers
	NUMBER EMPLOYED									
All employees	118,520	11,962	13,186	7,090	496	5,549	53,660	17,515	7,755	1,307
Male	103,012	11,306	11,200	6,164	345	1,280	50,446	14,849	6,393	1,029
Female	15,508	656	1,986	926	151	4,269	3,124	2,666	1,362	278
White	89,473	10,831	12,147	6,338	456	4,434	37,728	12,173	4,480	886
Male	77,931	10,260	10,424	5,523	322	953	35,787	10,209	3,728	725
Female	11,542	571	1,723	815	134	3,481	1,941	1,964	752	161
Minority	29,047	1,131	1,039	752	40	1,115	15,932	5,342	3,275	421
Male	25,081	1,046	776	641	23	327	14,659	4,640	2,665	304
Female	3,966	85	263	111	17	788	1,273	702	610	117

[Continued]

★ 562 ★

Occupational Employment in Private Industry: Ship and Boat Building and Repairing
[Continued]

Race/ethnic group/sex	Total employment	Officials and managers	Professionais	Technicians	Sales workers	Office & clerical workers	Craft workers	Operatives	Laborers	Service workers
Black	22,355	899	726	578	28	951	12,838	3,425	2,521	362
Male	19,031	834	514	494	13	295	11,691	2,952	1,979	259
Female	3,324	65	212	84	15	656	1,147	500	542	103
Hispanic	4,572	143	113	84	9	97	2,055	1,433	601	37
Male	4,197	136	94	71	7	22	1,975	1,297	567	28
Female	375	7	19	13	2	75	80	136	34	9
Asian/Pacific Islander	1,789	61	181	79	3	55	876	396	124	14
Male	1,564	48	153	67	3	8	845	337	93	10
Female	225	13	28	12	0	47	31	59	31	4
Am. Ind./Alaskan Native	331	28	19	11	0	12	163	61	29	8
Male	289	28	15	9	0	2	148	54	26	7
Female	42	0	4	2	0	10	15	7	3	1

Source: "Occupational Employment in Private Industry by Race/Ethnic Group/Sex, and by Industry, United States, 1994, All Industries." U.S. Equal Employment Opportunity Commission, *Job Patterns for Minorities and Women in Private Industry 1994*, p. 20. *Note:* Data for the state of Hawaii are not included.

★ 563 ★
Occupations

Occupational Employment in Private Industry: Shopping Goods Stores

Race/Ethnic Group/Sex	Number employed									
	Total Employment	Officials and Managers	Profes-sionals	Techni-cians	Sales workers	Office & Clerical workers	Craft workers	Opera-tives	Laborers	Service workers
All Employees	118,776	15,038	8,611	3,550	53,998	20,230	1,247	4,327	6,822	4,953
Male	51,167	8,783	2,271	1,513	23,760	4,793	889	2,780	4,244	2,134
Female	67,609	6,255	6,340	2,037	30,238	15,437	358	1,547	2,578	2,819
White	89,161	13,262	7,543	2,946	39,725	14,876	918	2,659	4,314	2,918
Male	37,511	7,762	1,947	1,199	17,271	3,228	639	1,754	2,623	1,088
Female	51,650	5,500	5,596	1,747	22,454	11,648	279	905	1,691	1,830
Minority	29,615	1,776	1,068	604	14,273	5,354	329	1,668	2,508	2,035
Male	13,656	1,021	324	314	6,489	1,565	250	1,026	1,621	1,046
Female	15,959	755	744	290	7,784	3,789	79	642	887	989
Black	14,381	859	391	249	7,035	2,795	117	886	1,282	767
Male	6,230	459	112	101	3,093	702	66	500	882	315
Female	8,151	400	279	148	3,942	2,093	51	386	400	452
Hispanic	9,608	504	208	154	4,748	1,538	153	485	936	882
Male	4,737	325	76	89	2,204	471	141	344	549	538
Female	4,871	179	132	65	2,544	1,067	12	141	387	344

[Continued]

★ 563 ★

Occupational Employment in Private Industry: Shopping Goods Stores

[Continued]

Race/Ethnic Group/Sex	Number employed									
	Total Employ-ment	Officials and Managers	Profes-sionals	Techni-cians	Sales workers	Office & Clerical workers	Craft workers	Opera-tives	Laborers	Service workers
Asian/Pacific Islander	5,016	351	446	189	2,186	927	55	251	255	356
Male	2,401	204	125	118	1,041	357	41	165	168	182
Female	2,615	147	321	71	1,145	570	14	86	87	174
AmInd/Alaskan Native	610	62	23	12	304	94	4	46	35	30
Male	288	33	11	6	151	35	2	17	22	11
Female	322	29	12	6	153	59	2	29	13	19

Source: "Occupational Employment in Private Industry by Race/Ethnic Group/Sex, and by Industry, United States, 1994, All Industries." U.S. Equal Employment Opportunity Commission, *Job Patterns for Minorities and Women in Private Industry 1994*, p. 28. *Note:* Data for the state of Hawaii are not included.

★ 564 ★

Occupations

Occupational Employment in Private Industry: Telephone Communication

Race/ethnic group/sex	Total employment	Officials and managers	Professionals	Technicians	Sales workers	Office & clerical workers	Craft workers	Operatives	Laborers	Service workers
	NUMBER EMPLOYED									
All employees	744,539	130,265	78,877	44,554	49,351	261,525	155,544	19,554	2,237	2,632
Male	363,703	77,392	48,201	35,047	19,949	37,015	133,977	9,263	1,093	1,766
Female	380,836	52,873	30,676	9,507	29,402	224,510	21,567	10,291	1,144	866
White	567,272	108,853	63,951	36,954	36,465	174,341	129,536	13,837	1,883	1,452
Male	300,565	67,503	39,881	29,986	15,682	25,096	113,628	6,965	896	928
Female	266,707	41,350	24,070	6,968	20,783	149,245	15,908	6,872	987	524
Minority	177,267	21,412	14,926	7,600	12,886	87,184	26,008	5,717	354	1,180
Male	63,138	9,889	8,320	5,061	4,267	11,919	20,349	2,298	197	838
Female	114,129	11,523	6,606	2,539	8,619	75,265	5,659	3,419	157	342
Black	112,679	12,538	6,504	4,681	8,093	61,343	15,340	3,098	212	870
Male	32,856	4,963	2,954	2,851	2,322	6,658	11,106	1,272	103	627
Female	79,823	7,575	3,550	1,830	5,771	54,685	4,234	1,826	109	243
Hispanic	43,852	5,477	2,622	1,740	3,677	19,279	8,480	2,190	113	274
Male	19,738	2,977	1,595	1,370	1,451	3,831	7,421	831	78	184
Female	24,114	2,500	1,027	370	2,226	15,448	1,059	1,359	35	90
Asian/Pacific Islander	17,359	2,854	5,497	984	860	5,239	1,518	357	19	31
Male	9,025	1,647	3,604	682	407	1,226	1,257	165	11	26
Female	8,334	1,207	1,893	302	453	4,013	261	192	8	5
Am. Ind./Alaskan Native	3,377	543	303	195	256	1,323	670	72	10	5

[Continued]

★ 564 ★

Occupational Employment in Private Industry: Telephone Communication
[Continued]

Race/ethnic group/sex	Total employment	Officials and managers	Professionals	Technicians	Sales workers	Office & clerical workers	Craft workers	Operatives	Laborers	Service workers
Male	1,519	302	167	158	87	204	565	30	5	1
Female	1,858	241	136	37	169	1,119	105	42	5	4

Source: "Occupational Employment in Private Industry by Race/Ethnic Group/Sex, and by Industry, United States, 1994, All Industries." U.S. Equal Employment Opportunity Commission, *Job Patterns for Minorities and Women in Private Industry 1994*, p. 23. *Note:* Data for the state of Hawaii are not included.

★ 565 ★

Occupations

Occupational Employment in Private Industry: Transportation and Public Utilities

Race/Ethnic Group/Sex	Number employed									
	Total Employ- ment	Officials and Managers	Profes- sionals	Techni- cians	Sales workers	Office & Clerical workers	Craft workers	Opera- tives	Laborers	Service workers
All Employees	3,528,932	443,260	382,571	183,344	163,620	682,910	589,332	639,029	287,375	157,491
Male	2,388,191	332,390	276,331	148,591	65,937	151,368	553,334	557,106	239,588	63,546
Female	1,140,741	110,870	106,240	34,753	97,683	531,542	35,998	81,923	47,787	93,945
White	2,734,599	383,849	331,573	152,997	125,019	488,477	493,785	469,843	175,284	113,772
Male	1,900,030	294,411	245,722	125,619	53,055	110,840	466,943	414,972	148,691	39,777
Female	834,569	89,438	85,851	27,378	71,964	377,637	26,842	54,871	26,593	73,995
Minority	794,333	59,411	50,998	30,347	38,601	194,433	95,547	169,186	112,091	43,719
Male	488,161	37,979	30,609	22,972	12,882	40,528	86,391	142,134	90,897	23,769
Female	306,172	21,432	20,389	7,375	25,719	153,905	9,156	27,052	21,194	19,950
Black	479,310	32,963	23,212	16,326	22,347	126,008	54,332	108,521	69,970	25,631
Male	279,742	19,643	12,180	11,720	6,624	22,103	47,786	89,872	55,982	13,832
Female	199,568	13,320	11,032	4,606	15,723	103,905	6,546	18,649	13,988	11,799
Hispanic	224,508	16,530	11,674	8,950	11,123	49,078	31,163	49,285	34,109	12,596
Male	151,062	11,678	7,554	7,356	4,308	12,954	29,373	42,405	28,211	7,223
Female	73,446	4,852	4,120	1,594	6,815	36,124	1,790	6,880	5,898	5,373
Asian/Pacific Islander	71,090	8,115	14,597	3,978	4,333	15,728	6,674	7,197	5,753	4,715
Male	43,824	5,377	9,829	3,019	1,620	4,658	6,071	6,166	4,753	2,331
Female	27,266	2,738	4,768	959	2,713	11,070	603	1,031	1,000	2,384
AmInd/Alaskan Native	19,425	1,803	1,515	1,093	798	3,619	3,378	4,183	2,259	777
Male	13,533	1,281	1,046	877	330	813	3,161	3,691	1,951	383
Female	5,892	522	469	216	468	2,806	217	492	308	394

Source: "Occupational Employment in Private Industry by Race/Ethnic Group/Sex, and by Industry, United States, 1994, All Industries." U.S. Equal Employment Opportunity Commission, *Job Patterns for Minorities and Women in Private Industry 1994*, p. 3. *Note:* Data for the state of Hawaii are not included.

★ 566 ★

Occupations

Occupational Employment in Private Industry: Trucking and Courier Services

Race/ethnic group/sex	Total employment	Officials and managers	Professionals	Technicians	Sales workers	Office & clerical workers	Craft workers	Operatives	Laborers	Service workers
				NUMBER EMPLOYED						
All employees	633,158	71,590	17,033	6,117	14,866	77,156	32,294	257,850	145,875	10,377
Male	511,892	59,658	11,906	4,285	6,872	18,044	31,697	241,525	130,001	7,906
Female	121,266	11,932	5,127	1,833	7,994	59,112	597	16,325	15,874	2,471
White	481,213	60,284	15,076	5,446	11,757	60,041	26,833	203,396	91,409	6,971
Male	388,149	50,507	10,564	3,819	5,927	14,016	26,329	190,446	81,410	5,131
Female	93,064	9,777	4,512	1,627	5,830	46,025	504	12,950	9,999	1,840
Minority	151,945	11,306	1,957	671	3,109	17,115	5,461	54,454	54,466	3,406
Male	123,743	9,151	1,342	464	945	4,028	5,368	51,079	48,591	2,775
Female	28,202	2,155	615	207	2,164	13,087	93	3,375	5,875	631
Black	98,569	6,612	967	304	1,683	10,673	2,989	37,143	36,248	1,950
Male	79,693	5,247	657	188	457	2,110	2,928	34,744	31,690	1,672
Female	18,876	1,365	310	116	1,226	8,563	61	2,399	4,558	278
Hispanic	41,037	3,228	442	154	1,055	4,597	1,914	13,854	14,596	1,197
Male	32,247	2,767	302	128	353	1,245	1,896	13,103	13,549	904
Female	6,790	461	140	26	702	3,352	18	751	1,047	293
Asian/Pacific Islander	9,306	1,194	505	196	326	1,522	415	1,943	2,991	214
Male	7,339	924	355	135	118	587	408	1,830	2,812	170
Female	1,967	270	150	61	208	935	7	113	179	44
Am. Ind./Alaskan Native	3,033	272	43	17	45	323	143	1,514	631	45
Male	2,464	213	28	13	17	86	136	1,402	540	29
Female	569	59	15	4	28	237	7	112	91	16

Source: "Occupational Employment in Private Industry by Race/Ethnic Group/Sex, and by Industry, United States, 1994, All Industries." U.S. Equal Employment Opportunity Commission, *Job Patterns for Minorities and Women in Private Industry 1994*, p. 22. *Note:* Data for the state of Hawaii are not included.

★ 567 ★

Occupations

Occupational Employment in Private Industry: Weaving Mills, Cotton

Race/Ethnic Group/Sex	Number employed									
	Total Employment	Officials and Managers	Profes-sionals	Techni-cians	Sales workers	Office & Clerical workers	Craft workers	Opera-tives	Laborers	Service workers
All Employees	105,286	7,597	1,961	2,586	439	6,046	16,698	58,619	9,687	1,633
Male	58,641	6,379	1,275	1,312	284	1,094	14,619	26,125	6,590	963
Female	46,645	1,218	706	1,274	155	4,952	2,079	32,494	3,097	670
White	69,820	6,852	1,865	2,143	403	4,960	12,559	34,904	5,191	943
Male	39,528	5,777	1,209	1,091	270	775	11,228	15,070	3,519	589

[Continued]

★ 567 ★

Occupational Employment in Private Industry: Weaving Mills, Cotton

[Continued]

Race/Ethnic Group/Sex	Number employed									
	Total Employ-ment	Officials and Managers	Profes-sionals	Techni-cians	Sales workers	Office & Clerical workers	Craft workers	Opera-tives	Laborers	Service workers
Female	30,292	1,075	656	1,052	133	4,185	1,331	19,834	1,672	354
Minority	35,466	745	116	443	36	1,086	4,139	23,715	4,496	690
Male	19,113	602	66	221	14	319	3,391	11,055	3,071	374
Female	16,353	143	50	222	22	767	748	12,660	1,425	316
Black	31,388	620	89	374	21	959	3,593	21,276	3,810	646
Male	16,764	504	47	180	7	291	2,936	9,820	2,636	343
Female	14,624	116	42	194	14	668	657	11,456	1,174	303
Hispanic	2,592	77	6	50	11	93	352	1,491	490	22
Male	1,542	57	3	27	6	22	308	790	313	16
Female	1,050	20	3	23	5	71	44	701	177	6
Asian/Pacific Islander	1,143	32	16	11	3	17	146	731	169	18
Male	586	26	13	9	1	3	100	317	104	13
Female	557	6	3	2	2	14	46	414	65	5
AmInd/Alaskan Native	343	16	5	8	1	17	48	217	27	4
Male	221	15	3	5	0	3	47	128	18	2
Female	122	1	2	3	1	14	1	89	9	2

Source: "Occupational Employment in Private Industry by Race/Ethnic Group/Sex, and by Industry, United States, 1994, All Industries." U.S. Equal Employment Opportunity Commission, *Job Patterns for Minorities and Women in Private Industry 1994,* p. 8. *Note:* Data for the state of Hawaii are not included.

★ 568 ★

Occupations

Occupational Employment in Private Industry: Wholesale Trade

Race/Ethnic Group/Sex	Number employed									
	Total Employ-ment	Officials and Managers	Profes-sionals	Techni-cians	Sales workers	Office & Clerical workers	Craft workers	Opera-tives	Laborers	Service workers
All Employees	1,446,294	192,979	126,078	81,847	235,860	234,064	95,200	263,720	182,872	33,674
Male	957,789	149,965	82,341	67,238	159,075	48,949	85,371	210,958	132,720	21,172
Female	488,505	43,014	43,737	14,609	76,785	185,115	9,829	52,762	50,152	12,502
White	1,140,991	174,024	108,233	66,853	205,661	189,889	76,276	184,091	115,193	20,771
Male	758,052	135,865	71,709	55,180	141,185	36,846	69,129	151,409	83,953	12,776
Female	382,939	38,159	36,524	11,673	64,476	153,043	7,147	32,682	31,240	7,995
Minority	305,303	18,955	17,845	14,994	30,199	44,175	18,924	79,629	67,679	12,903
Male	199,737	14,100	10,632	12,058	17,890	12,103	16,242	59,549	48,767	8,396
Female	105,566	4,855	7,213	2,936	12,309	32,072	2,682	20,080	18,912	4,507

[Continued]

★ 568 ★

Occupational Employment in Private Industry: Wholesale Trade

[Continued]

Race/Ethnic Group/Sex	Number employed									
	Total Employ-ment	Officials and Managers	Profes-sionals	Techni-cians	Sales workers	Office & Clerical workers	Craft workers	Opera-tives	Laborers	Service workers
Black	144,733	7,100	5,793	6,374	14,431	21,618	8,276	42,392	31,547	7,202
Male	92,577	4,912	3,051	5,006	7,662	5,44	7,060	31,624	23,057	4,751
Female	52,156	2,188	2,742	1,368	6,769	16,164	1,216	10,768	8,490	2,451
Hispanic	114,186	5,797	3,885	4,445	11,404	15,054	8,317	30,339	30,204	4,741
Male	77,702	4,367	2,400	3,669	7,563	4,370	7,306	23,239	21,742	3,046
Female	36,484	1,430	1,485	776	3,841	10,684	1,011	7,100	8,42	1,695
Asian/Pacific Islander	40,710	5,468	7,772	3,793	3,657	6,587	1,859	5,622	5,166	786
Male	25,669	4,371	4,920	3,060	2,242	1,984	1,457	3,715	3,411	509
Female	15,041	1,097	2,852	733	1,415	4,603	402	1,907	1,755	277
AmInd/Alaskan Native	5,674	590	395	382	707	916	472	1,276	762	174
Male	3,789	450	261	323	423	295	419	971	557	90
Female	1,885	140	134	59	284	621	53	305	205	84

Source: "Occupational Employment in Private Industry by Race/Ethnic Group/Sex, and by Industry, United States, 1994, All Industries." U.S. Equal Employment Opportunity Commission, *Job Patterns for Minorities and Women in Private Industry 1994*, p. 4. *Note:* Data for the state of Hawaii are not included.

★ 569 ★

Occupations

Occupations of the Employed: Characteristics, 1994

[**In thousands.** Annual averages of monthly figures. For civilian noninstitutional population 25 to 64 years old. Based on Current Population Survey; see text, section 1, and Appendix III.]

SEX, RACE, AND EDUCATIONAL ATTAINMENT	Total employed	Managerial/ professional	Tech./ sales/ administrative	Service[1]	Precision production[2]	Operators/ fabricators[3]	Farming, forestry, fishing
Male, total[4]	54,434	16,069	10,667	4,544	10,736	10,357	2,061
Less than a high school diploma	6,392	311	456	806	1,727	2,434	659
High school graduates, no college	17,811	1,923	2,864	1,748	5,185	5,288	802
Less than a bachelor's degree	14,183	3,285	3,782	1,433	3,130	2,155	398
College graduates	16,047	10,550	3,565	558	694	480	201
White	47,013	14,458	9,315	3,399	9,618	8,371	1,853
Less than a high school diploma	5,242	270	380	573	1,509	1,953	557
High school graduates, no college	15,267	1,751	2,496	1,265	4,710	4,318	727
Less than a bachelor's degree	12,277	2,957	3,297	1,116	2,807	1,725	374
College graduates	14,227	9,480	3,142	445	592	374	194
Black	5,131	909	892	847	786	1,566	131
Less than a high school diploma	787	26	52	152	139	355	62
High school graduates, no college	1,976	113	274	378	364	796	52
Less than a bachelor's degree	1,417	234	353	246	224	348	14
College graduates	950	536	213	71	60	67	1
Female, total[4]	46,026	14,784	18,746	7,214	1,107	3,627	548
Less than a high school diploma	3,858	195	753	1,579	185	1,022	125
High school graduates, no college	16,069	2,145	7,827	3,392	554	1,930	221

[Continued]

★ 569 ★

Occupations of the Employed: Characteristics, 1994

[Continued]

SEX, RACE, AND EDUCATIONAL ATTAINMENT	Total employed	Managerial/ professional	Tech./ sales/ administrative	Service[1]	Precision production[2]	Operators/ fabricators[3]	Farming, forestry, fishing
Less than a bachelor's degree	13,755	3,839	7,196	1,762	274	551	130
College graduates	12,344	8,605	2,969	481	94	124	71
White	38,690	12,903	16,135	5,513	870	2,755	514
Less than a high school diploma	2,969	162	645	1,130	146	782	104
High school graduates, no college	13,577	1,907	6,952	2,600	433	1,471	213
Less than a bachelor's degree	11,524	3,340	6,029	1,403	219	406	126
College graduates	10,619	7,492	2,509	381	71	96	70
Black	5,453	1,297	1,960	1,353	158	668	17
Less than a high school diploma	641	24	71	357	23	157	10
High school graduates, no college	1,970	170	684	649	88	376	4
Less than a bachelor's degree	1,795	388	952	292	38	122	1
College graduates	1,047	715	254	55	9	14	-

Source: "Occupations of the Employed, by Selected Characteristics, 1994, *Statistical Abstract of the United States*, 1995, p. 416. Primary source: U.S. Bureau of the Census, unpublished data. *Notes:* - Represents or rounds to zero. 1. Includes household workers. 2. Includes craft and repair. 3. Includes laborers. 4. Includes other races, not shown separately.

Unemployment

★ 570 ★

Unemployed Persons: Cause and Race, 1994-95

[Numbers in thousands].

	White		Black	
Reason	Nov. 1994	Nov. 1995	Nov. 1994	Nov. 1995
NUMBER OF UNEMPLOYED				
Total unemployed	5,048	5,261	1,486	1,363
Job losers and persons who completed temporary jobs	2,519	2,613	618	560
On temporary layoff	600	789	139	104
Not on temporary layoff	1,919	1,825	479	456
Permanent job losers	1,393	1,296	301	269
Persons who completed temporary jobs	526	528	177	188
Job leavers	554	702	124	104
Reentrants	1,670	1,638	600	578
New entrants	305	308	144	121
PERCENT DISTRIBUTION				
Total unemployed	100.0	100.0	100.0	100.0
Job losers and persons who completed temporary jobs	49.9	49.7	41.6	41.1

[Continued]

★ 570 ★

Unemployed Persons: Cause and Race, 1994-95
[Continued]

Reason	White		Black	
	Nov. 1994	Nov. 1995	Nov. 1994	Nov. 1995
On temporary layoff	11.9	15.0	9.4	7.6
Not on temporary layoff	38.0	34.7	32.2	33.5
Job leavers	11.0	13.3	8.4	7.6
Reentrants	33.1	31.1	40.4	42.4
New entrants	6.0	5.9	9.7	8.9
UNEMPLOYED AS A PERCENT OF THE CIVILIAN LABOR FORCE				
Job losers and persons who completed temporary jobs	2.3	2.3	4.2	3.7
Job leavers	.5	.6	.9	.7
Reentrants	1.5	1.5	4.1	3.8
New entrants	.3	.3	1.0	.8

Source: "Unemployed Persons by Reason for Unemployment, Sex, Age, and Race," *Employment and Earnings,* December 1995, p. 45. *Note:* Not seasonally adjusted.

★ 571 ★

Unemployment

Unemployed Persons: Duration

Sex, age, race, and marital status	January 1996							
	Thousands of persons						Weeks	
	Total	Less than 5 weeks	5 to 14 weeks	15 weeks and over			Average (mean) duration	Median duration
				Total	15 to 26 weeks	27 weeks and over		
Race								
White, 16 years and over	6,280	2,601	1,925	1,755	867	888	14.7	7.4
Men	3,578	1,462	1,124	992	483	509	15.1	7.4
Women	2,702	1,139	800	763	384	378	14.1	7.4
Black, 16 years and over	1,600	550	456	595	285	309	18.3	9.7
Men	822	281	247	294	144	151	18.0	9.7
Women	778	269	209	300	142	158	18.6	9.8

Source: "Unemployed Persons by Age, Sex, Race, Marital Status, and Duration of Employment," *Employment and Earnings,* February 1996, p. 41. *Note:* Not seasonally adjusted.

★ 572 ★

Unemployment

Unemployed Persons: Marital Status, Race, Age, and Gender, 1994-95

Marital status, race, and age	Men				Women			
	Thousands of persons		Unemployment rates		Thousands of persons		Unemployment rates	
	Nov. 1994	Nov. 1995	Nov. 1994	Nov. 1995	Nov. 1994	Nov. 1995	Nov. 1994	Nov. 1995
Total, 16 years and over	3,700	3,796	5.2	5.3	3,272	3,228	5.4	5.2
Married, spouse present	1,317	1,335	3.1	3.1	1,248	1,223	3.7	3.6
Widowed, divorced, or separated	542	512	6.5	6.3	763	690	6.2	5.6
Single (never married)	1,840	1,949	9.3	10.0	1,261	1,315	8.3	8.5
White, 16 years and over	2,724	2,896	4.5	4.8	2,324	2,364	4.6	4.6
Married, spouse present	1,056	1,092	2.8	2.8	1,019	1,012	3.5	3.4
Widowed, divorced, or separated	380	411	5.5	6.1	563	538	5.8	5.5
Single (never married)	1,287	1,393	8.1	8.8	743	814	6.4	7.0
Black, 16 years and over	727	671	10.2	9.4	758	691	10.2	8.8
Married, spouse present	152	148	4.9	4.5	140	127	5.6	4.8
Widowed, divorce, or separated	122	83	11.3	7.8	162	118	7.7	5.5
Single (never married)	454	441	15.4	15.9	456	446	16.0	14.4
Total, 25 years and over	2,448	2,476	4.1	4.1	2,237	2,171	4.4	4.2
Married, spouse present	1,225	1,234	3.0	2.9	1,095	1,093	3.5	3.4
Widowed, divorced, or separated	524	498	6.5	6.4	708	647	6.0	5.4
Single (never married)	699	745	6.7	7.2	433	430	5.8	5.5
White, 25 years and over	1,802	1,910	3.5	3.7	1,637	1,633	3.8	3.8
Married, spouse present	977	1,004	2.7	2.7	892	895	3.2	3.2
Widowed, divorced, or separated	365	397	5.5	6.1	523	506	5.6	5.3
Single (never married)	460	508	5.6	6.2	222	233	4.1	4.2
Black, 25 years and over	462	428	8.0	7.3	465	412	7.5	6.3
Married, spouse present	148	142	4.9	4.4	124	121	5.2	4.8
Widowed, divorced, or separated	118	84	11.1	8.1	150	115	7.3	5.4
Single (never married)	197	202	11.6	12.7	191	176	10.9	9.2

Source: "Unemployed Persons by Marital Status, Race, Age, and Sex," *Employment and Earnings,* December 1995, p. 42. *Note:* Not seasonally adjusted.

★ 573 ★

Unemployment

Unemployed Workers: Trends, 1980-1994

[**In thousands, except as indicated.** For civilian noninstitutional population 16 years old and over. Annual averages of monthly figures. For data on unemployment insurance, see table 602. See also *Historical Statistics, Colonial Times to 1970,* series D 87-101.]

AGE, SEX, RACE, HISPANIC ORIGIN	1980	1985	1989	1990	1991	1992	1993	1994[1]
UNEMPLOYED								
White[3]	5,884	6,191	4,770	5,091	6,447	7,047	6,547	5,892
16 to 19 years old	1,291	1,074	863	856	977	983	943	960
20 to 24 years old	1,364	1,235	856	844	1,063	1,084	991	952
Black[3]	1,553	1,864	1,544	1,527	1,679	1,958	1,796	1,666
16 to 19 years old	343	357	300	258	270	313	302	300
20 to 24 years old	426	455	322	335	362	401	371	351
Hispanic[3,4]	620	811	750	769	963	1,160	1,104	1,187
16 to 19 years old	145	141	132	131	149	185	173	198
20 to 24 years old	138	171	158	135	172	193	191	220
UNEMPLOYMENT RATE (percent)[5]								
White[3]	6.3	6.2	4.5	4.7	6.0	6.5	6.0	5.3
16 to 19 years old	15.5	15.7	12.7	13.4	16.4	17.1	16.2	15.1
20 to 24 years old	9.9	9.2	7.2	7.2	9.2	9.4	8.7	8.1
Black[3]	14.3	15.1	11.4	11.3	12.4	14.1	12.9	11.5
16 to 19 years old	38.5	40.2	32.4	31.1	36.3	39.8	38.9	35.2
20 to 24 years old	23.6	24.5	18.0	19.9	21.6	23.9	22.0	19.5
Hispanic[3,4]	10.1	10.5	8.0	8.0	9.9	11.4	10.6	9.9
16 to 19 years old	22.5	24.3	19.4	19.5	22.9	27.5	26.2	24.5
20 to 24 years old	12.1	12.6	10.7	9.1	11.6	13.2	13.1	11.8
Married men, wife present[2]	4.2	4.3	3.0	3.4	4.4	5.0	4.4	3.7
White	3.9	4.0	2.8	3.1	4.2	4.7	4.1	3.4
Black	7.4	8.0	5.8	6.2	6.5	8.3	7.2	6.0

Source: "Unemployed Workers-Summary: 1980 to 1994," *Statistical Abstract of the United States,* 1995, p. 420. Primary source: U.S. Bureau of Labor Statistics, *Employment and Earnings,* monthly, January issues; and unpublished data. *Notes:* NA Not available. 1. See footnote 2, table 626. 2. Includes other races, not shown separately. 3. Includes other ages, not shown separately. 4. Persons of Hispanic origin may be of any race. 5. Unemployed as percent of civilian labor force in specified group.

★ 574 ★

Unemployment

Unemployment Rates by Population Group: 1980 and 1992

The unemployment rate, which is the most common measure of unemployment, is the proportion of persons in the Civilian Labor Force (CLF) who are without jobs and are seeking work. As of 1992, there were more than nine million unemployed persons in the nation and they represented 7.4 percent of the CLF. The accompanying table provides annual average unemployment rates from the Current Population Survey (CPS) for 1980 and 1992. Total rates are provided, as well as rates covering whites, blacks, Hispanics and men and women, and youths and adults.

Age and gender	Total, All Groups[1]		Whites		Blacks		Hispanics[2]	
	1980	1992	1980	1992	1980	1992	1980	1992
Total, Both male and female	7.1	7.4	6.3	6.5	14.3	14.1	8.9	11.4
Male	6.9	7.8	6.1	6.9	14.5	15.2	8.5	11.5
Female	7.4	6.9	6.5	6.0	14.0	13.0	9.6	11.3
Total youth, both male and female	17.8	20.0	15.5	17.1	38.5	39.8	16.4	27.5
Male youth	18.3	21.5	16.2	18.4	37.5	42.0	16.8	28.1
Female youth	17.2	18.5	14.8	15.7	39.8	37.2	15.9	26.5
Total adult, both male and female	6.1	6.7	5.4	5.9	12.1	12.5	8.2	10.3
Male adult	5.9	7.0	5.3	6.3	12.4	13.4	7.7	10.4
Female adult	6.4	6.3	5.6	5.4	11.9	11.7	8.9	10.1

Source: "Unemployment Rates by Population Group: U.S. Summary, 1980 and 1992." U.S. Equal Employment Opportunity Commission, Indicators of Equal Employment Opportunity—Status and Trends, p. 42. Primary source: U.S. Department of Labor, Bureau of Labor Statistics, *Bulletin 2307* and unpublished data from the *Current Population Survey* (CPS) *Notes:* 1. Includes such racial minorities as Asian Americans, not shown separately. 2. Hispanics may be of any race.

★ 575 ★

Unemployment

Unemployment Rates: Selected Unemployment Rates, by Race, 1985-1995

[Monthly data seasonally adjusted].

Period	Unemployment rate (percent of civilian labor force in group)											
	All civilian workers	By sex and age			By race			By selected groups				
		Men 20 years and over	Women 20 years and over	Both sexes 16-19 years	White	Black and other	Black	Experienced wage and salary workers	Married men, spouse present	Women who maintain families	Full-time workers[1]	Part-time workers[1]
1985	7.2	6.2	6.6	18.6	6.2	13.7	15.1	6.8	4.3	10.4	7.1	7.5
1986	7.0	6.1	6.2	18.3	6.0	13.1	14.5	6.6	4.4	9.8	6.9	7.4
1987	6.2	5.4	5.4	16.9	5.3	11.6	13.0	5.8	3.9	9.2	6.0	6.9
1988	5.5	4.8	4.9	15.3	4.7	10.4	11.7	5.2	3.3	8.1	5.3	6.4
1989	5.3	4.5	4.7	15.0	4.5	10.0	11.4	5.0	3.0	8.1	5.1	6.2
1990	5.5	4.9	4.8	15.5	4.7	10.1	11.3	5.3	3.4	8.2	5.4	6.3
1991	6.7	6.3	5.7	18.6	6.0	11.1	12.4	6.5	4.4	9.1	6.7	6.9
1992	7.4	7.0	6.3	20.0	6.5	12.7	14.1	7.1	5.0	9.9	7.4	7.4

[Continued]

★ 575 ★

Unemployment Rates: Selected Unemployment Rates, by Race, 1985-1995
[Continued]

Period	Unemployment rate (percent of civilian labor force in group)											
	All civilian workers	By sex and age			By race			By selected groups				
		Men 20 years and over	Women 20 years and over	Both sexes 16-19 years	White	Black and other	Black	Experienced wage and salary workers	Married men, spouse present	Women who maintain families	Full-time workers[1]	Part-time workers[1]
1993	6.8	6.4	5.9	19.0	6.0	11.7	12.9	6.5	4.4	9.5	6.8	7.1
1994[2]	6.1	5.4	5.4	17.6	5.3	10.5	11.5	5.9	3.7	8.9	6.1	6.0
1994: Aug	6.0	5.3	5.3	17.5	5.2	10.6	11.3	5.8	3.5	8.8	6.0	6.2
Sept	5.8	5.1	5.2	17.2	5.1	10.2	10.7	5.7	3.4	8.9	5.8	5.8
Oct	5.7	5.0	5.0	17.1	5.0	10.4	11.1	5.5	3.3	8.9	5.8	5.6
Nov	5.6	4.9	5.0	15.8	4.8	9.8	10.5	5.4	3.2	8.7	5.6	5.4
Dec	5.4	4.7	4.7	17.2	4.8	9.2	9.8	5.3	3.2	8.8	5.3	5.9
1995: Jan	5.7	5.0	4.9	16.7	4.9	9.5	10.2	5.4	3.4	8.9	5.5	6.2
Feb	5.4	4.6	4.8	17.6	4.7	9.4	10.1	5.1	3.0	8.1	5.3	6.0
Mar	5.5	4.7	4.9	16.1	4.7	9.2	9.8	5.2	3.2	7.6	5.4	8.5
Apr	5.8	4.9	5.2	17.5	5.0	9.8	10.7	5.6	3.4	9.0	5.6	6.3
May	5.7	5.1	4.8	17.6	5.0	9.1	9.9	5.6	3.4	8.0	5.6	6.1
June	5.6	4.8	5.0	16.4	4.8	9.8	10.6	5.4	3.4	8.4	5.5	6.3
July	5.7	4.7	5.1	18.2	4.8	10.1	11.1	5.5	3.4	8.5	5.5	6.6
Aug	5.6	4.8	5.0	17.7	4.8	10.2	11.3	5.4	3.3	7.0	5.6	5.9

Source: "Selected Unemployment Rates," *Economic Indicators*, August 1995, p. 12. Primary source: Department of Labor, Bureau of Labor Statistics. *Notes:* Data relate to persons age 16 years and over. 1. Revised definition; for details see *Employment and Earnings*, February 1994. 2. Data beginning January 1994 are not directly comparable with data for earlier periods. See *Employment and Earnings*, February 1994.

★ 576 ★

Unemployment

Unemployment Rates: Trends by Sex and Race: 1970-1991

[In percent. As of **March**. For the civilian noninstitutional population 25 to 64 years of age. Due to a change in the method of reporting educational attainment, 1992 data are not comparable with data for earlier years. See table 663 for data beginning 1992. Based on the Current Population Survey; see text, section 1, and Appendix III.]

ITEM	1970	1975	1980	1984	1985	1986	1987	1988	1989	1990	1991
White: Total	3.1	6.5	4.4	5.7	5.3	5.5	5.0	4.0	3.8	4.0	5.6
Less than 4 years of high school[1]	4.5	10.1	7.8	10.6	10.6	10.9	10.2	8.3	7.7	8.3	11.6
4 years of high school, only	2.7	6.5	4.6	6.4	6.1	6.2	5.5	4.6	4.2	4.4	6.2
College: 1-3 years	2.8	5.1	3.9	4.6	3.9	4.2	4.1	3.2	3.0	3.3	4.6
4 years or more	1.3	2.4	1.8	2.4	2.1	2.2	2.2	1.4	2.0	1.8	2.7
Black: Total[2]	4.7	10.9	9.6	13.3	12.0	10.7	10.6	10.0	9.2	8.6	10.1
Less than 4 years of high school[1]	5.2	13.5	11.7	17.4	15.3	15.3	14.8	14.6	14.6	15.9	15.9
4 years of high school, only	5.2	10.7	9.5	14.5	13.0	11.7	11.7	11.2	9.2	8.6	10.3

[Continued]

★ 576 ★

Unemployment Rates: Trends by Sex and Race: 1970-1991
[Continued]

ITEM	1970	1975	1980	1984	1985	1986	1987	1988	1989	1990	1991
College: 1-3 years	3.5	9.8	9.0	9.7	10.6	8.7	7.6	7.4	6.9	6.5	8.0
4 years or more	0.9	3.9	4.0	6.2	5.4	3.2	4.2	3.3	4.7	1.9	5.2

Source: "Unemployment Rates by Educational Attainment, Sex, and Race: 1970 to 1991," *Statistical Abstract of the United States*, 1995, p. 422. Primary source: U.S. Bureau of Labor Statistics, Bulletin 2307; and unpublished data. *Notes:* 1. Includes persons reporting no school years completed. 2. For 1970 and 1975, data refer to Black and other workers.

★ 577 ★
Unemployment

Unemployment Rates: Unemployed Workers by Month, Race, Hispanic Origin-1

[Unemployment rates by occupation, industry, and selected demographic characteristics, seasonally adjusted.]

Category	1994		1995				
	Nov.	Dec.	Jan.	Feb.	Mar.	Apr.	May
CHARACTERISTIC							
White	4.8	4.8	4.9	4.7	4.7	5.0	5.0
Black and other	9.8	9.2	9.5	9.4	9.2	9.8	9.1
Black	10.5	9.8	10.2	10.1	9.8	10.7	9.9
Hispanic origin	8.8	9.2	10.2	8.9	9.1	8.8	10.0

Source: "Unemployment Rates by Occupation, Industry, and Selected Demographic Characteristics, Seasonally Adjusted," *Employment and Earnings*, December 1995, p. 25.

★ 578 ★

Unemployment

Unemployment Rates: Unemployed Workers by Month, Race, Hispanic Origin-2

[Unemployment rates by occupation, industry, and selected demographic characteristics, seasonally adjusted.].

Category	1995					
	June	July	Aug.	Sept.	Oct.	Nov.
CHARACTERISTIC						
White	4.8	4.8	4.8	4.8	4.8	5.0
Black and other	9.8	10.1	10.2	10.2	9.4	8.9
Black	10.6	11.1	11.3	11.3	9.9	9.4
Hispanic origin	9.0	8.8	9.9	8.9	9.4	9.4

Source: "Unemployment Rates by Occupation, Industry, and Selected Demographic Characteristics, Seasonally Adjusted," *Employment and Earnings,* December 1995, p. 25.

★ 579 ★

Unemployment

Unemployment and Unemployment Rates: Trends by Education, Sex, Race, and Hispanic Origin: 1992-1994

[As of **March**. For the civilian noninstitutional population 25 to 64 years old. See table 630 for civilian labor force and participation rate data Based on Current Population Survey; see text, section 1, and Appendix III.]

YEAR, SEX, AND RACE	UNEMPLOYED (1,000)					UNEMPLOYMENT RATE[1]				
	Total	Less than high school diploma	High school graduates, no degrees	Less than a bachelor's degree	College graduate	Total	Less than high school diploma	High school graduate, no degree	Less than a bachelor's degree	College graduate
Total:[2]										
1992	6,846	1,693	2,851	1,521	782	6.7	13.5	7.7	5.9	2.9
1993	6,596	1,550	2,666	1,492	888	6.4	13.0	7.3	5.5	3.2
1994[3]	6,126	1,463	2,388	1,453	823	5.8	12.6	6.7	5.0	2.9
White:										
1992	5,247	1,285	2,146	1,176	641	6.0	12.9	6.8	5.3	2.7
1993	5,129	1,175	2,025	1,166	763	5.8	12.4	6.5	5.0	3.1
1994[3]	4,598	1,092	1,738	1,109	659	5.2	11.7	5.8	4.5	2.6
Black:										
1992	1,353	361	619	291	81	12.4	17.2	14.1	10.7	4.8
1993	1,201	321	542	266	72	10.9	17.3	12.4	8.7	4.1
1994[3]	1,202	286	546	277	94	10.6	17.4	12.2	8.3	4.9
Hispanic:[4]										
1992	757	408	224	88	36	9.8	13.6	9.6	5.9	4.2

[Continued]

★ 579 ★

Unemployment and Unemployment Rates: Trends by Education, Sex, Race, and Hispanic Origin: 1992-1994

[Continued]

YEAR, SEX, AND RACE	UNEMPLOYED (1,000)					UNEMPLOYMENT RATE[1]				
	Total	Less than high school diploma	High school graduates, no degrees	Less than a bachelor's degree	College graduate	Total	Less than high school diploma	High school graduate, no degree	Less than a bachelor's degree	College graduate
1993	826	449	215	117	46	10.3	14.5	9.1	7.0	5.2
1994[3]	871	465	215	139	52	9.7	13.4	8.3	7.2	5.2

Source: "Unemployment and Unemployment Rates by Educational Attainment, Sex, Race, and Hispanic Origin: 1992 to 1994," *Statistical Abstract of the United States,* 1995, p. 422. Primary source: U.S. Bureau of Labor Statistics, unpublished data. *Notes:* 1. Percent unemployed of the civilian labor force. 2. Includes other races, not shown separately. 3. See footnote 2, table 626. 4. Persons of Hispanic origin may be of any race.

Unions

★ 580 ★

Labor Unions by Selected Characteristics: 1983 and 1994. Part 1

[**Annual averages of monthly data.** Covers employed wage and salary workers 16 years old and over. Excludes self-employed workers whose businesses are incorporated although they technically qualify as wage and salary workers. See headnote table 643 regarding data by occupation and industry. Based on Current Population Survey, see text, section 1, and Appendix III].

CHARACTERISTIC	EMPLOYED WAGE AND SALARY WORKERS					
	Total (1,000)		Percent union members[2]		Percent represented by unions[3]	
	1983	1994[1]	1983	1994[1]	1983	1994[1]
Total[4]	88,290	107,989	20.1	15.5	22.3	17.5
White	77,046	91,290	19.3	14.8	22.3	16.7
Men	42,168	48,351	24.0	17.2	26.9	18.9
Women	34,877	42,939	13.5	12.1	16.7	14.1
Black	8,979	12,229	27.2	20.5	31.7	23.3
Men	4,477	5,834	31.7	23.3	36.1	25.9
Women	4,502	6,395	22.7	18.1	27.4	20.8
Hispanic[5]	(NA)	10,017	(NA)	14.2	(NA)	15.9
Men	(NA)	6,002	(NA)	15.5	(NA)	17.0
Women	(NA)	4,015	(NA)	12.1	(NA)	14.2

Source: "Union Members, by Selected Characteristics: 1983 and 1994." U.S. Bureau of the Census, *Statistical Abstract of the United States,* 115th ed., 1995, p. 445. Primary source: U.S. Bureau of Labor Statistics, *Employment and Earnings,* January Issues. *Notes:* B Data not shown where base is less than 50,000. NA Not available. 1. See footnote 2, table 626. 2. Members of a labor union or an employee association similar to a labor union. 3. Members of a labor union or an employee association similar to a union as well as workers who report no union affiliation but whose jobs are covered by a union or an employee association contract. 4. Includes races not shown separately. For 1994, includes a small number of multiple jobholders whose full- part-time status can not be determined for their principal job. 5. Persons of Hispanic origin may be of any race.

★ 581 ★

Unions

Labor Unions by Selected Characteristics: 1983 and 1994. Part 2

[**Annual averages of monthly data.** Covers employed wage and salary workers 16 years old and over. Excludes self-employed workers whose businesses are incorporated although they technically qualify as wage and salary workers. See headnote table 643 regarding data by occupation and industry. Based on Current Population Survey, see text, section 1, and Appendix III].

| CHARACTERISTIC | MEDIAN USUAL WEEKLY WARNINGS[4] (dol.) | | | | | | | |
| | Total | | Union members[2] | | Represented by unions[3] | | Not represented by unions | |
	1983	1994[1]	1983	1994[1]	1983	1994[1]	1983	1994[1]
Total[5]	313	467	388	592	383	587	288	432
White	319	484	396	609	391	604	295	451
Men	387	547	423	640	421	638	362	513
Women	254	408	314	546	313	538	240	386
Black	261	371	331	493	324	487	222	338
Men	293	400	366	524	360	518	244	359
Women	231	346	292	452	287	446	209	323
Hispanic[6]	(NA)	324	(NA)	470	(NA)	468	(NA)	307
Men	(NA)	343	(NA)	506	(NA)	501	(NA)	316
Women	(NA)	305	(NA)	402	(NA)	413	(NA)	289

Source: "Union Members, by Selected Characteristics: 1983 and 1994." U.S. Bureau of the Census, *Statistical Abstract of the United States,* 115th ed., 1995, p. 445. Primary source: U.S. Bureau of Labor Statistics, *Employment and Earnings,* January Issues. *Notes:* B Data not shown where base is less than 50,000. NA Not available. 1. See footnote 2, table 626. 2. Members of a labor union or an employee association similar to a labor union. 3. Members of a labor union or an employees association similar to a union as well as workers who report no union affiliation but whose jobs are covered by a union or an employee association contract. 4. For full-time employed wage and salary workers: 1983 revised since originally published. 5. Includes races not shown separately. For 1994, includes a small number of multiple jobholders whose full- part-time status can not be determined for their principal job. 6. Persons of Hispanic origin may be of any race.

Work Schedules

★ 582 ★

Varied Schedules: Workers on Flexible and Shift Schedules: 1995 to 1991

[**In thousands, except percent.** As of **May.** For employed persons 16 years old and over who usually work full-time and who were at work during the survey reference week. Based on Current Population Survey; see text, section 1, and Appendix III.]

| CHARACTERISTIC | Total employed[1] | WORK SCHEDULES-PERCENT DISTRIBUTION | | | | | | |
| | | Regular daytime schedules | | Shift workers | | | | |
		Total	Workers on flexible schedules[2]	Total	Evening	Night	Rotating	Other[3]
Total, 1985[4]	73,395	84.1	12.3	15.9	6.3	2.7	4.3	2.6
Total, 1991[4]	80,452	81.8	15.1	17.8	5.1	3.7	3.4	5.7
Race and Hispanic origin:								
White	68,795	82.6	15.5	17.1	4.6	3.4	3.3	5.9
Black	8,943	76.0	12.1	23.3	8.4	5.6	4.7	4.7
Hispanic[5]	6,598	80.3	10.6	19.1	6.4	4.6	2.7	5.5

Source: "Workers on Flexible and Shift Schedules: 1985 and 1991," *Statistical Abstract of the United States,* 1995, p. 410. Primary source: U.S. Bureau of Labor Statistics, *News,* USDL 91-491, August 14, 1992; and unpublished data. *Notes:* 1. Includes a small number of workers who did not report data on shift worked. 2. A flexible schedule allows workers to vary the time they begin and end their work day. 3. Includes employer arranged irregular schedules. 4. Data for 1985 are not strictly comparable to those for 1991 because of the addition of "irregular" category in the May 1991 survey. Includes other races, not shown separately. 5. Persons of Hispanic origin may be of any race.

Work at Home

★ 583 ★

Workers Doing Job-Related Work at Home: 1991

[As of **May.** For persons 16 years old and over doing job-related work at home as part of their primary job in nonagriculture industries.]

CHARACTERISTIC	Total at work (1,000)	PERSONS DOING JOB RELATED WORK AT HOME					
		Total[1] (1,000)	Worked at home for pay				
			Total (1,000)	Worked 8 hours or more			Mean hours worked (number)[3]
				Total (1,000)	Rate[2]	35 hours or more (1,000)	
Total[4]	109,126	19,967	7,432	3,651	3.3	1,069	14.1
Race and Hispanic origin:							
White	94,387	18,520	7,022	3,403	3.8	966	13.8

[Continued]

★ 583 ★

Workers Doing Job-Related Work at Home: 1991

[Continued]

CHARACTERISTIC	Total at work (1,000)	PERSONS DOING JOB RELATED WORK AT HOME					
		Total[1] (1,000)	Worked at home for pay				
			Total (1,000)	Worked 8 hours or more			Mean hours worked (number)[3]
				Total (1,000)	Rate[2]	35 hours or more (1,000)	
Black	11,020	970	239	147	1.3	76	22.8
Hispanic[5]	7,977	667	255	137	1.7	36	13.7

Source: "Workers Doing Job-Related Work at Home: 1991," *Statistical Abstract of the United States,* 1994, p. 406. Primary source: U.S. Bureau of Labor Statistics, *Monthly Labor Review,* February 1994; and unpublished data. *Notes:* 1. Includes those that did not report pay status and unpaid family members. 2. Persons working at home for pay as a percent of the total at work. 3. For definition of mean, see Guide to Tabular Presentation. 4. Includes other industries and occupations, not shown separately. 5. Persons of Hispanic origin may be of any race.

Workers and Computers

★ 584 ★

Workers Using Computers on the Job: 1993

[**In percent.** For workers 18 years old and over. Based on the Current Population Survey and subject to sampling error; see Appendix III and source.]

CHARACTERISTIC	Number using computers[1] (1,000)	Percent of total	TYPE OF APPLICATION						
			Book-keeping inventory	Word processing	Communica-tions[2]	Analysis/ spread-sheets	Data-bases	Desktop publishing	Sales and telemarketing
Total	51,106	45.8	36.1	45.0	38.7	34.5	22.3	16.2	44.4
Race/ethnicity:									
White[3]	43,020	48.7	37.2	45.8	39.3	35.2	23.0	16.7	45.9
Black[3]	4,016	36.2	27.5	38.3	37.3	31.2	16.8	12.9	35.5
Hispanic	2,492	29.3	29.1	45.6	32.1	27.6	18.7	16.0	33.6
Other	1,578	43.9	39.7	39.4	37.2	33.5	22.6	10.2	44.5

Source: "Workers Using Computers on the Job: 1993," *Statistical Abstract of the United States,* 1995, p. 430. Primary source: U.S. National Center for Education Statistics, *Digest of Education Statistics,* 1994. *Notes:* 1. Includes other applications, not shown separately. A person may be counted in more than one application. 2. Includes bulletin boards and electronic mail. 3. Non-Hispanic.

Chapter 9
MISCELLANY

★ 585 ★

Arts Activities: Attendance Rates, 1992

[In percent. For persons 18 years old and over. Excludes elementary and high school performances. Based on 1992 household survey, Public Participation in the Arts, conducted January through December 1992. Data are subject to sampling error; see source.]

Item	ATTENDANCE AT LEAST ONCE IN THE PRIOR 12 MONTHS AT--								Reading litera-ture[1]
	Jazz perfor-mance	Classical music perform-mance	Opera	Musical play	Non-musical play	Ballet	Art museum	Historic park	
Total	11	13	3	17	14	5	27	35	54
Sex: Male	12	12	3	15	12	4	27	35	47
Female	9	13	4	20	15	6	27	34	60
Race: White	10	13	3	18	14	5	28	37	56
Black	16	7	2	14	12	3	19	18	45
Other	6	12	5	11	10	6	29	23	42

Source: "Attendance Rates for Various Arts Activities: 1992," *Statistical Abstracts of the United States: 1995*, p. 263. Primary source: U.S. National Endowment for the Arts, *Arts Participation in America: 1982 to 1992. Note:* 1. Includes novels, short stories, poetry, or plays.

★ 586 ★

Arts and Entertainment

Arts Activities: Participation Rates, 1992

[In percent, except as indicated. Covers activities engaged in at least once in the prior 12 months.]

| ITEM | Adult popu-lation (mil.) | IN THE PAST 12 MONTHS PERCENT ENGAGED AT LEAST ONCE IN-- | | | | | | | |
		Playing classical music	Modern danc-ing[1]	Pottery work[2]	Needle-work[3]	Photo-graphy[4]	Paint-ing[5]	Creative writing	Buying art work
Total	185.8	4	8	8	25	12	10	7	22
Sex: Male	89.0	3	8	8	5	13	9	7	22
Female	96.8	5	8	9	43	10	10	8	22
Race: White	158.8	4	8	9	26	12	10	7	24
Black	21.1	3	8	8	15	11	5	6	12
Other	5.9	5	9	5	24	9	10	11	8

Source: "Participation Rates in Various Arts Activities: 1992," *Statistical Abstracts of the United States: 1995,* p. 263. Primary source: U.S. National Endowment for the Arts, *Arts Participation in America: 1982 to 1992. Notes:* 1. Dancing other than ballet (e.g. folk and tap.) 2. Includes ceramics, jewelry, leatherwork, and metalwork. 3. Includes weaving, crocheting, quilting, and sewing. 4. Includes making movies or video as an artistic activity. 5. Includes drawing, sculpture, and printmaking.

Military and Military Affairs

★ 587 ★

Personnel: Profile of the Ready Reserve, by Gender and Race/Ethnic Origin: 1990-1993

| ITEM | RACE | | | | | PERCENT DISTRIBUTION | | | |
	Total	White	Black	Asian	American Indian	White	Black	Asian	American Indian
1990	1,558,867	1,269,278	271,470	14,608	3,511	81.4	17.4	0.9	0.2
1991	1,154,515	906,748	190,214	12,711	5,652	78.5	16.5	1.1	0.5
1992	1,114,905	725,963	172,770	11,479	4,842	65.1	15.5	1.0	0.4
1993	1,057,676	829,797	173,444	13,350	4,785	78.5	16.4	1.3	0.5
1994, total[1]	1,137,048	771,068	163,427	13,686	4,584	67.8	14.4	1.2	0.4
Male	998,330	681,062	124,683	11,897	3,800	68.2	12.5	1.2	0.4
Officers	153,809	117,107	7,630	1,620	292	76.1	5.0	1.1	0.2
Enlisted	844,521	563,955	117,053	10,277	3,508	66.8	13.9	1.2	0.4
Female	138,718	90,006	38,744	1,789	784	64.9	27.9	1.3	0.6

[Continued]

★ 587 ★

Personnel: Profile of the Ready Reserve, by Gender and Race/Ethnic Origin: 1990-1993

[Continued]

ITEM	RACE					PERCENT DISTRIBUTION			
	Total	White	Black	Asian	American Indian	White	Black	Asian	American Indian
Officers	24,197	19,200	3,731	287	59	79.3	15.4	1.2	0.2
Enlisted	114,521	70,806	35,013	1,502	725	61.8	30.6	1.3	0.6

Source: "Ready Reserve Personnel Profile—Race, and Sex: 1990 to 1994," *Statistical Abstract of the United States: 1995*, p. 367. Primary source: U.S. dept. of defense, *Official Guide and reserve Manpower Strengths and Statistics*, annual. *Note:* 1. Includes unknown sex.

Multimedia Audience-Summary

★ 588 ★

Multimedia Audiences: 1994

[**In percent, except as indicated.** As of **spring.** For persons **18 years old and over.** Represents the number of people viewing/listening during a specified time period. Based on sample and subjects error; see source for details].

ITEM	Total population (1,000)	Television viewing	Television prime time viewing	Cable viewing	Radio listening	Newspaper reading
Total	188,654	92.1	78.4	61.6	84.7	82.9
Male	90,177	91.7	76.9	63.5	86.6	83.0
Female	98,478	92.4	79.8	59.9	83.0	82.8
White	160,581	91.7	78.0	64.0	84.8	83.6
Black	21,415	94.5	81.1	48.1	84.7	82.2
Other	6,658	92.8	79.7	47.0	82.9	68.5
Spanish speaking	16,247	93.6	81.1	49.1	88.0	75.2

Source: "Multimedia Audiences-Summary: 1994." U.S. Bureau of the Census, *Statistical Abstract of the United States*, 115th ed., 1995, p. 703. Primary source: Mediamark Research Inc., New York, NY, *Multimedia Audiences*, fall 1994 (copyright). Published by permission.

Religion

★ 589 ★

Religious Bodies: Characteristics of Black Churches and Organizations

[Represents latest information available from religious bodies with memberships of 200,000 or more; excludes a few groups giving no data. Not all groups follow same calendar year nor count membership the same way; some groups give only approximate figures. Data which appear in italics are "noncurrent," i.e., they are reported for 1990 or earlier. All other data are "current" and were reported in 1991 or 1992.]

RELIGIOUS BODY	Year reported	Churches reported	Member-ship (1,000)	Pastors serving parishes[1]
African American Methodist Episcopal Church[2]	1991	8,000	3,500	(NA)
African American Episcopal Zion Church	1991	3,000	1,200	2,500
Church of God in Christ, The	1991	15,300	5,500	28,988
Church of God in Christ, International, The	1982	300	200	700
National Baptist Convention of America	1987	2,500	3,500	8,000
National Baptist Convention, U.S.A., Inc.	1992	33,000	8,200	32,832
Pentecostal Assemblies of the World[2]	1989	1,005	500	(NA)
Progressive National Baptist Convention, Inc.	1991	1,400	2,500	1,400

Source: "Religious Bodies—Selected Data," *Statistical Abstracts of the United States: 1995*, p. 68. Primary source: Ecumenical Programs in Information and Communications, Inc., Dayton, OH, *Yearbook of American and Canadian Churches*, annual (Copyright). Published by permission. *Notes:* NA Not available. 1. Includes other pastors performing pastoral duties. 2. Figures obtained from the *Directory of African American Religious Bodies, 1991*. Published by permission.

Television Production

★ 590 ★

Production Costs: Prime-Time Black Shows

In order from most expensive to least expensive.

Show	Cost ($)
M.A.N.T.I.S.	1.8 million
Cosby Mysteries	1.27 million
Sweet Justice	1.12 million
Touched By An Angel	1.5 million
Family Matters	720,000
On Our Own	655,000
Me & The Boys	650,000
Fresh Prince Of Bel-Air	625,000

[Continued]

★ 590 ★

Production Costs: Prime-Time Black Shows
[Continued]

Show	Cost ($)
Martin	600,000
Hangin' With Mr. Cooper	590,000
Living Single	540,000

Source: "Production Costs for Prime-Time Black Shows," *Jet 87* (December 19, 1994), p. 60. Primary source: *New York Daily News* (undated article).

Chapter 10
POLITICS AND ELECTIONS

Elected Officials

★ 591 ★

Black Elected Officials: Distribution by Office, 1970-1993, and Region and State, 1993

[As of January 1993, no Black elected officials had been identified in Hawaii, Idaho, Montana, North Dakota, or Utah.]

REGION, DIVISION, AND STATE	Total	U.S. and State legislatures[1]	City and county offices[2]	Law enforcement[3]	Education[4]
1970 (Feb.)	1,469	179	715	213	362
1980 (July)	4,890	326	2,832	526	1,206
1985 (Jan.)	6,016	407	3,517	661	1,431
1990 (Jan.)	7,335	436	4,485	769	1,645
1991 (Jan.)	7,445	473	4,496	847	1,629
1992 (Jan.)	7,517	499	4,557	847	1,614
1993 (Jan.)	7,984	561	4,819	922	1,682
Northeast	777	96	291	126	264
N.E.	109	35	60	4	10
ME	1	-	1	-	-
NH	2	2	-	-	-
VT	2	2	-	-	-
MA	30	8	18	2	2
RI	12	9	3	-	-
CT	62	14	38	2	8
M.A.	668	61	231	122	254
NY	299	30	63	70	136
NJ	211	13	113	-	85
PA	158	18	55	52	33
Midwest	1,361	106	757	171	327
E.N.C.	1,119	78	604	143	294
OH	219	16	124	30	49
IN	72	12	50	4	6
IL	465	25	282	37	121

[Continued]

★ 591 ★

Black Elected Officials: Distribution by Office, 1970-1993, and Region and State, 1993

[Continued]

REGION, DIVISION, AND STATE	Total	U.S. and State legisla-tures[1]	City and county offices[2]	Law enforce-ment[3]	Educa-tion[4]
MI	333	17	133	68	115
WI	30	8	15	4	3
W.N.C.	242	28	153	28	33
MN	16	1	2	10	3
IA	11	1	6	1	3
MO	185	18	134	14	19
SD	3	1	2	-	-
NE	6	1	2	-	3
KS	21	6	7	3	5
South	5,492	328	3,675	518	971
S.A.	2,200	173	1,522	147	358
DE	23	3	14	-	6
MD	140	32	79	23	6
DC	198	4[5]	185	-	9
VA	155	14	126	15	-
WV	21	1	17	3	-
NC	468	28	328	31	81
SC	450	26	269	15	140
GA	545	43	371	32	99
FL	200	22	133	28	17
E.S.C.	1,681	85	1,175	175	246
KY	63	4	47	5	7
TN	168	16	104	24	24
AL	699	23	529	58	89
MS	751	42	495	88	126
W.S.C.	1,611	70	978	196	367
AR	380	13	214	51	102
LA	636	33	346	104	153
OK	123	6	95	1	21
TX	472	18	323	40	91
West	354	31	96	107	120
Mountain	49	11	11	16	11
WY	1	-	-	-	1
CO	20	4	4	10	2
NM	3	-	-	2	1
AZ	15	4	3	3	5
NV	10	3	4	1	2
Pacific	305	20	85	91	109
WA	19	2	9	5	3
OR	10	4	2	4	-

[Continued]

★ 591 ★

Black Elected Officials: Distribution by Office, 1970-1993, and Region and State, 1993

[Continued]

REGION, DIVISION, AND STATE	Total	U.S. and State legisla-tures[1]	City and county offices[2]	Law enforce-ment[3]	Educa-tion[4]
CA	273	13	72	82	106
AK	3	1	2	-	-

Source: "Black Elected Officials, by Office, 1970 to 1993, and by Region and State, 1993," *Statistical Abstract of the United states: 1995*, p. 287. Primary source: Joint Center for Political and Economic Studies, Washington, DC, *Black Elected Officials: A National Roster*, annual, (copyright). *Notes:* - Represents zero. 1. Includes elected State administrators. 2. County commissioners and councilmen, mayors, vice mayors, aldermen, regional officials, and other. 3. Judges, magistrates, constables, marshals, sheriffs, justices of the peace, and other. 4. Members of State education agencies, college boards, school boards, and other. 5. Includes two shadow senators and one shadow representative.

★ 592 ★

Elected Officials

Elected Officials: Characteristics of Members of Congress, 1981-1995. Part 1

[As of beginning of first session of each Congress (January 3). Figures for representatives exclude vacancies.].

MEMBERS OF CONGRESS AND YEAR	Male	Fe-male	Black[1]	Asian, Pacific Island-der[2]	His-panic[3]
REPRESENTATIVES					
87th Cong., 1981	416	19	17	3	6
98th Cong., 1983	413	21	21	3	8
99th Cong., 1985	412	22	20	3	10
100th Cong., 1987	412	23	23	4	11
101st Cong., 1989	408	25	24	5	10
102d Cong., 1991	407	28	25	3	11
103d Cong., 1993[4]	388	47	38	4	17
104th Cong., 1995	388	47	40	4	17
SENATORS					
97th Cong., 1981	98	2	-	3	-
98th Cong., 1983	98	2	-	2	-
99th Cong., 1985	98	2	-	2	-
100th Cong., 1987	98	2	-	2	-
101st Cong., 1989	98	2	-	2	-
102d Cong., 1991	98	2	-	2	-

[Continued]

★ 592 ★

Elected Officials: Characteristics of Members of Congress, 1981-1995. Part 1
[Continued]

MEMBERS OF CONGRESS AND YEAR	Male	Fe-male	Black[1]	Asian, Pacific Island-der[2]	His-panic[3]
103d Cong., 1993[4]	93	7	1	2	-
104th Cong., 1995	92	8	1	2	-

Source: "Members of Congress-Selected Characteristics: 1981 to 1995," *Statistical Abstract of the United States: 1995*, p. 281. Primary source: Except as noted, compiled by U.S. Bureau of Census from data published in *Congressional Directory*, biennial. *Notes:* - Represents zero. 1. Source: Joint Center for Political and Economic Studies, Washington, DC, *Black Elected Officials: A National Roster*, annual (copyright). 2. Source: Library of Congress, Congressional Research Service "Asian Pacific Americans in the United States Congress," Report 94-767 GOV. 3. Source: National Association of Latino Elected and Appointed Officials, Washington, DC, *National Roster of Hispanic Elected Officials*, annual. 4. Includes members elected to fill vacant seats through June 14, 1993.

★ 593 ★

Elected Officials

Elected Officials: Characteristics of Members of Congress, 1981-1995. Part 2

[As of beginning of first session of each Congress (January 3). Figures for representatives exclude vacancies.]

MEMBERS OF CONGRESS AND YEAR	AGE (in years)					SENIORITY				
	Under 40	40 to 49	50 to 59	60 to 69	70 and over	Less than 2 yrs.	2 to 9 yrs.	10 to 19 yrs.	20 to 29 yrs.	30 yrs. or more
REPRESENTATIVES										
87th Cong., 1981	94	142	132	54	13	77	231	96	23	8
98th Cong., 1983	86	146	132	57	14	83	224	88	28	11
99th Cong., 1985	71	154	131	59	19	49	237	104	34	10
100th Cong., 1987	63	153	137	56	26	51	221	114	37	12
101st Cong., 1989	41	163	133	74	22	39	207	139	35	13
102d Cong., 1991	39	152	134	86	24	55	178	147	44	11
103d Cong., 1993[4]	47	151	128	89	15	118	141	132	32	12
104th Cong., 1995	53	155	135	79	13	92	188	110	36	9
SENATORS										
97th Cong., 1981	9	35	36	14	6	19	51	17	11	2
98th Cong., 1983	7	28	39	20	6	5	61	21	10	3
99th Cong., 1985	4	27	38	25	6	8	56	27	7	2
100th Cong., 1987	5	30	36	22	7	14	41	36	7	2
101st Cong., 1989	-	30	40	22	8	23	22	43	10	2
102d Cong., 1991	-	23	46	24	7	5	34	47	10	4

[Continued]

★ 593 ★

Elected Officials: Characteristics of Members of Congress, 1981-1995. Part 2

[Continued]

MEMBERS OF CONGRESS AND YEAR	AGE (in years)					SENIORITY				
	Under 40	40 to 49	50 to 59	60 to 69	70 and over	Less than 2 yrs.	2 to 9 yrs.	10 to 19 yrs.	20 to 29 yrs.	30 yrs. or more
103d Cong., 1993[4]	1	16	48	22	12	15	30	39	11	5
104th Cong., 1995	1	14	41	27	17	12	38	30	15	5

Source: "Members of Congress-Selected Characteristics: 1981 to 1995," *Statistical Abstract of the United States: 1995*, p. 281. Primary source: Except as noted, compiled by U.S. Bureau of Census from data published in *Congressional Directory*, biennial. *Notes:* - Represents zero. 1. Source: Joint Center for Political and Economic Studies, Washington, DC, *Black Elected Officials: A National Roster*, annual (copyright). 2. Source: Library of Congress, Congressional Research Service "Asian Pacific Americans in the United States Congress," Report 94-767 GOV. 3. Source: National Association of Latino Elected and Appointed Officials, Washington, DC, *National Roster of Hispanic Elected Officials*, annual. 4. Includes members elected to fill vacant seats through June 14, 1993.

★ 594 ★
Elected Officials

Elected Officials: Local Officials, by Gender, Race, Hispanic Origin, and Type of Government, 1992

SEX, RACE, AND HISPANIC ORIGIN	Total	GENERAL PURPOSE			SPECIAL PURPOSE	
		County	Municipal	Town, township	School district	Special district
Total	491,669	56,390	135,580	127,009	88,610	84,080
Male	324,487	43,582	94,828	76,258	54,582	55,237
Female	100,597	12,528	26,831	27,713	24,772	8,753
Sex not reported	66,585	280	13,921	23,038	9,256	20,090
White	406,199	52,726	114,898	102,733	74,064	61,778
Black	11,560	1,716	4,566	371	4,233	674
American Indian, Eskimo, Aleut	1,811	147	783	90	564	227
Asian, Pacific Islander	514	80	97	16	184	137
Hispanic	5,871	906	1,701	217	2,471	576
Non-Hispanic	414,213	53,763	118,643	102,993	76,574	62,240
Race, Hispanic origin not reported	71,585	1,721	15,236	23,799	9,565	21,264

Source: "Local Elected Officials, by Sex, Race, Hispanic Origin and Type of Government," *Statistical Abstract of the United States: 1995*, p. 285. Primary source: U.S. Bureau of the Census, *Census of Governments, Popularly Elected Officials in 1992, Preliminary Report* (GC92-2(P).

Male Officials

★ 595 ★

Male County Officials by Race and Ethnicity, Part 1

Position	Total reporting (A)	Total males		Race					
				White		Black		American Indian	
		No. (B)	% of (A)	No.	% of (B)	No.	% of (B)	No.	% of (B)
Chief elected official	1,538	1,389	90.3	1,283	92.4	40	2.9	9	0.6
Chief appointed administrative officer	725	592	81.7	545	92.1	14	2.4	4	0.7
Clerk to the governing board	1,426	424	29.7	384	90.6	8	1.9	2	0.5
Chief financial officer	1,209	644	53.3	590	91.6	10	1.6	4	0.6
County health officer	937	600	64.0	519	86.5	13	2.2	3	0.5
Planning director	783	654	83.5	607	92.8	7	1.1	1	0.2
County engineer	806	793	98.4	735	92.7	7	0.9	1	0.1
Director health/human services	806	441	54.7	385	87.3	15	3.4	2	0.5
Chief law enforcement official	1,544	1,535	99.4	1,404	91.5	19	1.2	10	0.7
Purchasing director	626	377	60.2	336	89.1	14	3.7	4	1.1
Personnel director	754	404	53.6	353	87.4	21	5.2	4	1.0

Source: "Male County Officials by Race and Ethnicity." *The Municipal Yearbook 1995*, p. 268. Published by permission.

★ 596 ★

Male Officials

Male County Officials by Race and Ethnicity, Part 2

Position	Race							
	Asian		Other		Race not reported		Hispanic	
	No.	% of (B)	No.	% of (B)	No.	% of (B)	No.	% of (B)
Chief elected official	0	0.0	9	0.6	48	3.5	21	1.5
Chief appointed administrative officer	3	0.5	9	1.5	17	2.9	12	2.0
Clerk to the governing board	3	0.7	4	0.9	23	5.4	9	2.1
Chief financial officer	8	1.2	3	0.5	29	4.5	10	1.6
County health officer	8	1.3	5	0.8	52	8.7	9	1.5
Planning director	3	0.5	2	0.3	34	5.2	6	0.9
County engineer	4	0.5	6	0.8	40	5.0	12	1.5
Director health/human services	2	0.5	2	0.5	35	7.9	12	2.7
Chief law enforcement official	2	0.1	12	0.8	88	5.7	34	2.2

[Continued]

★ 596 ★

Male County Officials by Race and Ethnicity, Part 2

[Continued]

Position	Race							
	Asian		Other		Race not reported		Hispanic	
	No.	% of (B)	No.	% of (B)	No.	% of (B)	No.	% of (B)
Purchasing director	1	0.3	5	1.3	17	4.5	12	3.2
Personnel director	3	0.7	4	1.0	19	4.7	6	1.5

Source: "Male County Officials by Race and Ethnicity." *The Municipal Yearbook 1995*, p. 268. Published by permission.

★ 597 ★

Male Officials

Male Municipal Officials by Race and Ethnicity, Part 1

Position	Total reporting (A)	Total males		Race					
				White		Black		American Indian	
		No. (B)	% of (A)	No.	% of (B)	No.	% of (B)	No.	% of (B)
Chief elected official	4,311	3,698	85.8	3,307	89.4	87	2.4	17	0.5
Chief appointed administrative officer/ manager	3,403	3,024	88.9	2,679	88.6	36	1.2	13	0.4
Assistant manager/assistant CAO	1,102	725	65.8	606	83.6	32	4.4	1	0.1
City clerk/secretary	3,872	966	24.9	626	64.8	13	1.3	1	0.1
Chief financial officer	2,931	1,875	64.0	1,539	82.1	25	1.3	5	0.3
Director of economic development	1,031	834	80.9	681	81.7	33	4.0	5	0.6
Treasurer	2,824	1,458	51.6	1,120	76.8	13	0.9	8	0.5
Director of public works	3,621	3,575	98.7	3,000	83.9	63	1.8	22	0.6
Engineer	1,849	1,817	98.3	1,535	84.5	13	0.7	5	0.3
Police chief	4,068	4,041	99.3	3,336	82.6	101	2.5	27	0.7
Fire chief	3,446	3,441	99.9	2,850	82.8	55	1.6	17	0.5
Planning director	1,947	1,637	84.1	1,349	82.4	38	2.3	6	0.4
Personnel director	2,031	1,128	55.5	883	78.3	56	5.0	4	0.4
Risk manager	954	658	69.0	549	83.4	20	3.0	0	0.0
Director of parks and recreation	2,128	1,827	85.9	1,470	80.5	41	2.2	7	0.4
Superintendent of parks	1,362	1,301	95.5	1,051	80.8	34	2.6	9	0.7
Director of recreation	1,313	513	39.1	323	63.0	15	2.9	1	0.2
Librarian	1,729	564	32.6	286	50.7	2	0.4	2	0.4
Director of data processing info. serv.	872	622	71.3	496	79.7	11	1.8	0	0.0
Purchasing director	1,356	563	41.5	361	64.1	33	5.9	4	0.7

Source: "Male Municipal Officials by Race and Ethnicity." *The Municipal Yearbook 1995*, p. 188. Published by permission.

Male Officials

Male Municipal Officials by Race and Ethnicity, Part 2

Position	Race							
	Asian		Other		Race not reported		Hispanic	
	No.	% of (B)	No.	% of (B)	No.	% of (B)	No.	% of (B)
Chief elected official	6	0.2	18	0.5	263	7.1	56	1.5
Chief appointed administrative officer/ manager	5	0.2	18	0.6	273	9.0	63	2.1
Assistant manager/assistant CAO	3	0.4	9	1.2	74	10.2	20	2.8
City clerk/secretary	1	0.1	3	0.3	322	33.3	12	1.2
Chief financial officer	19	1.0	13	0.7	274	14.6	33	1.8
Director of economic development	2	0.2	7	0.8	106	12.7	19	2.3
Treasurer	7	0.5	9	0.6	301	20.6	14	1.0
Director of public works	17	0.5	19	0.5	454	12.7	64	1.8
Engineer	17	0.9	21	1.2	226	12.4	23	1.3
Police chief	3	0.1	26	0.6	548	13.6	57	1.4
Fire chief	1	0.0	17	0.5	501	14.6	51	1.5
Planning director	10	0.6	10	0.6	224	13.7	42	2.6
Personnel director	1	0.1	14	1.2	170	15.1	29	2.6
Risk manager	3	0.5	3	0.5	83	12.6	18	2.7
Director of parks and recreation	2	0.1	11	0.6	296	16.2	40	2.2
Superintendent of parks	4	0.3	13	1.0	190	14.6	47	3.6
Director of recreation	0	0.0	8	1.6	166	32.4	12	2.3
Librarian	1	0.2	0	0.0	273	48.4	9	1.6
Director of data processing info. serv.	8	1.3	4	0.6	103	16.6	15	2.4
Purchasing director	1	0.2	5	0.9	159	28.2	17	3.0

Source: "Male Municipal Officials by Race and Ethnicity." *The Municipal Yearbook 1995*, p. 188. Published by permission.

Political Parties

★ 599 ★

Political Party Identification: Adult Attachment, 1972-1994, and Selected Characteristics, 1994

[In percent. Covers citizens of voting-age living in private housing units in the contiguous United States. Data are from the National Election Studies and are based on a sample and subject to sampling variability; for details, see source.]

YEAR AND SELECTED CHARACTERISTIC	Total	Strong Democrat	Weak Democrat	Independent Democrat	Independent	Independent Republican	Weak Republican	Strong Republican	Apolitical
Race:									
White	100	12	19	12	10	13	16	17	1
Black	100	38	23	20	8	4	2	3	1

Source: "Political Party Identification of the Adult Population, by Degree of Attachment, 1972 to 1994, and by Selected Characteristics, 1994," *Statistical Abstract of the United States: 1995*, p. 288. Primary source: Center for Political Studies, University of Michigan, Ann Arbor, MI, unpublished data. Data prior to 1988 published in Warren E. Miller and Santa A. Traugott, *American National Election Studies Data Sourcebook, 1952-1986*, Harvard University Press, Cambridge, MA, 1989 (copyright). Published by permission.

Voters and Voting

★ 600 ★

Voting and Registration: Indicators for 1980 High School Sophomores Registered and Voting, Selected Years, 1984-1992

Student characteristics	Percent registered in 1986	Percent registered in 1992	Percent voted 1984 presidential	Percent voted 1988 in non-presidential	Percent voted 1988 presidential
Total	66.9	65.0	48.8	33.5	52.7
Political beliefs in 1980					
Conservative	75.6	75.5	58.3	42.2	65.7
Moderate	69.9	70.0	56.0	40.3	60.8
Liberal	74.4	71.2	60.3	37.7	62.1
Radical	72.4	67.2	50.3	36.0	52.3
None	57.7	57.6	39.3	27.6	44.4
Highest degree earned by 1992					
Less than high school	46.1	43.0	24.1	14.4	25.3
High school	61.6	61.1	43.0	29.9	46.2
Certificate	67.6	65.1	48.0	35.1	53.0

[Continued]

★ 600 ★

Voting and Registration: Indicators for 1980 High School Sophomores Registered and Voting, Selected Years, 1984-1992
[Continued]

Student characteristics	Percent registered in 1986	Percent registered in 1992	Percent voted 1984 presidential	Percent voted 1988 in non-presidential	Percent voted 1988 presidential
Associate's	69.3	71.2	56.9	39.4	60.4
Bachelor's	80.2	76.0	63.8	43.4	72.0
Master's	87.3	85.3	65.9	49.7	75.6
Professional	79.4	81.2	63.7	42.0	70.6
Doctorate	-	-	-	-	-
Marital status in 1992					
Married	65.5	64.3	47.4	33.2	52.7
Separated	65.2	54.1	41.5	22.7	38.7
Divorced	57.0	55.5	36.9	22.9	40.0
Widowed	-	-	-	-	-
Never married	70.6	68.2	53.4	36.3	56.1
Living in a marriage-like relationship	63.4	62.9	45.5	35.6	47.4
Sex					
Male	67.2	64.2	48.2	32.2	51.5
Female	66.5	65.8	49.4	34.9	53.9
Race-ethnicity					
Native American/ Alaska Native	64.5	65.6	41.4	29.4	40.2
Asian/Pacific Islander	50.6	56.8	33.2	25.7	39.9
Black	73.9	70.7	51.2	36.1	51.3
Hispanic	62.4	63.0	41.3	29.8	43.3
White	66.6	64.5	49.7	33.7	54.6

Source: "Voting Indicators for 1980 High School Sophomores, by Selected Characteristics," *National Center for Educational Statistics, High School and Beyond: 1980 Sophomore Cohort, 1980-1992.* Primary source: U.S. Department of Education, Office of Educational Research and Improvement, National Center for Education Statistics, Statistical Analysis Report, *High School and Beyond: Educational Attainment of 1980 High School Sophomores by 1992; 1992 Descriptive Summary of 1980 High School Sophomores 12 Years Later,* March 1995. *Note:* - Sample too small for a reliable estimate.

★ 601 ★

Voters and Voting

Voting-Age Population: Registered and Voted, 1980-1994. Part 1

[As of November. Covers civilian noninstitutional population 18 years old and over. Includes aliens. Figures are based on Current Population Survey and differ from those in table 461 based on population estimates and official vote counts.]

CHARACTERISTIC	VOTING-AGE POPULATION (mil.)							
	1980	1982	1984	1986	1988	1990	1992	1994
Male	74.1	78.0	80.3	82.4	84.5	86.6	88.6	91.0
Female	83.0	87.4	89.6	91.5	93.6	95.5	97.1	99.3
White	137.7	143.6	146.8	149.9	152.9	155.6	157.8	160.3
Black	16.4	17.6	18.4	19.0	19.7	20.4	21.0	21.8
Hispanic[1]	8.2	8.8	9.5	11.8	12.9	13.8	14.7	17.5

Source: "Voting-Age Population, Percent Reporting Registered and Voted: 1980 to 1994," *Statistical Abstract of the United States: 1995*, p. 289. Primary source: U.S. Bureau of the Census, *Current Population Reports* P20-453 and P20-466; and unpublished data. *Note:* 1. Hispanic persons may be of any race.

★ 602 ★

Voters and Voting

Voting-Age Population: Registered and Voted, 1980-1994. Part 2

[As of November. Covers civilian noninstitutional population 18 years old and over. Includes aliens. Figures are based on Current Population Survey and differ from those in table 461 based on population estimates and official vote counts.]

CHARACTERISTIC	PERCENT REPORTING THEY REGISTERED							
	Presidential year				Congressional election years			
	1980	1984	1988	1992	1982	1986	1990	1994
Male	66.6	67.3	65.2	66.9	63.7	63.4	61.2	60.8
Female	67.1	69.3	67.8	69.3	64.4	65.0	63.1	63.2
White	68.4	69.6	67.9	70.1	65.6	65.3	63.8	64.2
Black	60.0	66.3	64.5	63.9	59.1	64.0	58.8	58.3
Hispanic[1]	36.3	40.1	35.5	35.0	35.3	35.9	32.3	30.0

Source: "Voting-Age Population, Percent Reporting Registered and Voted: 1980 to 1994," *Statistical Abstract of the United States: 1995*, p. 289. Primary source: U.S. Bureau of the Census, *Current Population Reports* P20-453 and P20-466; and unpublished data. *Note:* 1. Hispanic persons may be of any race.

★ 603 ★

Voters and Voting

Voting-Age Population: Registered and Voted, 1980-1994. Part 3

[As of November. Covers civilian noninstitutional population 18 years old and over. Includes aliens. Figures are based on Current Population Survey and differ from those in table 461 based on population estimates and official vote counts.]

| CHARACTERISTIC | PERCENT REPORTING THEY VOTED | | | | | | | |
| | Presidential year | | | | Congressional election years | | | |
	1980	1984	1988	1992	1982	1986	1990	1994
White	60.9	61.4	59.1	63.6	49.9	47.0	46.7	46.9
Black	50.5	55.8	51.5	54.0	43.0	43.2	39.2	37.0
Hispanic[1]	29.9	32.6	28.8	28.9	25.3	24.2	21.0	19.1

Source: "Voting-Age Population, Percent Reporting Registered and Voted: 1980 to 1994," *Statistical Abstract of the United States: 1995,* p. 289. Primary source: U.S. Bureau of the Census, *Current Population Reports* P20-453 and P20-466; and unpublished data. *Note:* 1. Hispanic persons may be of any race.

Women Officials

★ 604 ★

Female County Officials by Race and Ethnicity, Part 1

| Position | Total reporting (A) | Total females | | Race | | | | | |
| | | | | White | | Black | | American Indian | |
		No. (B)	% of (A)	No.	% of (B)	No.	% of (B)	No.	% of (B)
Chief elected official	1,538	149	9.7	137	91.9	5	3.4	2	1.3
Chief appointed administrative officer	725	133	18.3	119	89.5	4	3.0	2	1.5
Clerk to the governing board	1,426	1,002	70.3	937	93.5	19	1.9	9	0.9
Chief financial officer	1,209	565	46.7	541	95.8	5	0.9	2	0.4
County health officer	937	337	36.0	314	93.2	9	2.7	0	0.0
Planning director	783	129	16.5	121	93.8	5	3.9	1	0.8
County engineer	806	13	1.6	12	92.3	0	0.0	0	0.0
Director welfare/human services	806	365	45.3	327	89.6	29	7.9	0	0.0
Chief law enforcement official	1,544	9	0.6	8	88.9	1	11.1	0.	0.0
Purchasing director	626	249	39.8	226	90.8	14	5.6	2	0.8
Personnel director	754	350	46.4	315	90.0	23	6.6	3	0.9

Source: "Female County Officials by Race and Ethnicity." *The Municipal Yearbook 1995,* p. 268. Published by permission.

★ 605 ★

Women Officials

Female County Officials by Race and Ethnicity, Part 2

Position	Race							
	Asian		Other		Race not reported		Hispanic	
	No.	% of (B)	No.	% of (B)	No.	% of (B)	No.	% of (B)
Chief elected official	0	0.0	0	0.0	5	3.4	2	1.3
Chief appointed administrative officer	0	0.0	0	0.0	8	6.0	4	3.0
Clerk to the governing board	2	0.2	11	1.1	24	2.4	24	2.4
Chief financial officer	0	0.0	4	0.7	13	2.3	9	1.6
County health officer	4	1.2	5	1.5	5	1.5	3	0.9
Planning director	1	0.8	0	0.0	1	0.8	1	0.8
County engineer	1	7.7	0	0.0	0	0.0	1	7.7
Director welfare/human services	1	0.3	2	0.5	6	1.6	8	2.2
Chief law enforcement official	0	0.0	0	0.0	0	0.0	0	0.0
Purchasing director	0	0.0	3	1.2	4	1.6	9	3.6
Personnel director	0	0.0	1	0.3	8	2.3	10	2.9

Source: "Female County Officials by Race and Ethnicity." *The Municipal Yearbook 1995*, p. 268. Published by permission.

★ 606 ★

Women Officials

Female Municipal Officials by Race and Ethnicity, Part 1

Position	Total reporting (A)	Total females		Race					
				White		Black		American Indian	
		No. (B)	% of (A)	No.	% of (B)	No.	% of (B)	No.	% of (B)
Chief elected official	4,311	613	14.2	563	91.8	19	3.1	5	0.8
Chief appointed administrative officer/ manager	3,403	379	11.1	342	90.2	13	3.4	2	0.5
Assistant manager/assistant CAO	1,102	377	34.2	347	92.0	14	3.7	1	0.3
City clerk/secretary	3,872	2,906	75.1	2,702	93.0	77	2.6	22	0.8
Chief financial officer	2,931	1,056	36.0	991	93.8	19	1.8	7	0.7
Director of economic development	1,031	197	19.1	182	92.4	10	5.1	1	0.5
Treasurer	2,824	1,366	48.4	1,291	94.5	28	2.0	7	0.5
Director of public works	3,621	46	1.3	42	91.3	4	8.7	0	0.0
Engineer	1,849	32	1.7	30	93.8	0	0.0	0	0.0
Police chief	4,068	27	0.7	23	85.2	3	11.1	1	3.7
Fire chief	3,446	5	0.1	5	100.0	0	0.0	0	0.0
Planning director	1,947	310	15.9	290	93.5	9	2.9	0	0.0
Personnel director	2,031	903	44.5	820	90.8	57	6.3	2	0.2
Risk manager	954	296	31.0	273	92.2	14	4.7	1	0.3

[Continued]

★ 606 ★

Female Municipal Officials by Race and Ethnicity, Part 1
[Continued]

Position	Total reporting (A)	Total females		White		Black		American Indian	
		No. (B)	% of (A)	No.	% of (B)	No.	% of (B)	No.	% of (B)
Director of parks and recreation	2,128	301	14.1	276	91.7	16	5.3	1	0.3˙
Superintendent of parks	1,362	61	4.5	57	93.4	2	3.3	0	0.0
Director of recreation	1,313	800	60.9	722	90.3	43	5.4	9	1.1
Librarian	1,729	1,165	67.4	1,115	95.7	12	1.0	4	0.3
Director of data processing info. serv.	872	250	28.7	227	90.8	14	5.6	3	1.2
Purchasing director	1,356	793	58.5	736	92.8	22	2.8	4	0.5

Source: "Female Municipal Officials by Race and Ethnicity." *The Municipal Yearbook 1995*, p. 188. Published by permission.

★ 607 ★

Women Officials

Female Municipal Officials by Race and Ethnicity, Part 2

Position	Race							
	Asian		Other		Race not reported		Hispanic	
	No.	% of (B)	No.	% of (B)	No.	% of (B)	No.	% of (B)
Chief elected official	2	0.3	5	0.8	19	3.1	14	2.3
Chief appointed administrative officer/ manager	2	0.5	5	1.3	15	4.0	10	2.6
Assistant manager/assistant CAO	0	0.0	6	1.6	9	2.4	10	2.7
City clerk/secretary	11	0.4	24	.8	70	2.4	77	2.6
Chief financial officer	8	0.8	7	0.7	24	2.3	21	2.0
Director of economic development	1	0.5	3	1.5	0	0.0	3	1.5
Treasurer	6	0.4	6	0.4	28	2.0	21	1.5
Director of public works	0	0.0	0	0.0	0	0.0	0	0.0
Engineer	1	3.1	0	0.0	1	3.1	0	0.0
Police chief	0	0.0	0	0.0	0	0.0	1	3.7
Fire chief	0	0.0	0	0.0	0	0.0	0	0.0
Planning director	4	1.3	1	0.3	6	1.9	5	1.6
Personnel director	4	0.4	7	0.8	13	1.4	27	3.0
Risk manager	2	0.7	3	1.0	3	1.0	7	2.4
Director of parks and recreation	1	0.3	3	1.0	4	1.3	4	1.3
Superintendent of parks	0	0.0	1	1.3	1	1.6	1	1.6
Director of recreation	0	0.0	4	0.5	22	2.8	17	2.1
Librarian	8	0.7	3	0.3	23	2.0	9	0.8
Director of data processing info. serv.	1	0.4	1	0.4	4	1.6	4	1.6
Purchasing director	3	0.4	6	0.8	22	2.8	22	2.8

Source: "Female Municipal Officials by Race and Ethnicity." *The Municipal Yearbook 1995*, p. 188. Published by permission.

Chapter 11
POPULATION

Ancestry

★ 608 ★

Top 15 Ancestry Groups: 1990

(In millions. Percent of total population in parentheses).

Ancestry		
German		58
Irish	(16%)	39
English	(13%)	33
Afro-American	(10%)	24
Italian	(6%)	15
American	(5%)	12
Mexican	(5%)	12
French	(4%)	10
Polish	(4%)	9
American Indian	(4%)	9
Dutch	(3%)	6
Scotch-Irish	(2%)	6
Scottish	(2%)	5
Swedish	(2%)	5
Norwegian	(2%)	4

Source: "Top 15 Ancestry Groups: 1990," We Asked... You Told Us: Ancestry." U.S. Department of Commerce, Economics and Statistics Administration, Bureau of the Census, February 1995, p. 1.

Black Households

★ 609 ★

Black Households: Characteristics, March 1994

[Numbers in thousands except for averages and medians].

Characteristics	Total	Age of householder										
		Under 20 years	20 to 24 years	25 to 29 years	30 to 34 years	35 to 39 years	40 to 44 years	45 to 54 years	55 to 64 years	65 to 74 years	75 to 84 years	85 years and over
Total households	11,281	91	682	1,198	1,546	1,504	1,322	1,856	1,315	1,071	553	143
With members of either sex:												
Under 6 years	2,857	57	423	631	608	427	250	243	139	64	17	1
6 to 11 years	2,814	-	73	461	734	556	382	340	154	88	21	4
12 to 17 years	2,585	13	27	83	473	662	505	497	207	93	22	2
18 to 24 years	2,530	88	682	130	74	297	369	571	182	98	32	6
25 to 34 years	3,992	13	101	1,198	1,546	242	128	330	248	146	34	5
35 to 44 years	3,702	5	27	35	173	1,504	1,322	338	130	115	50	2
45 to 64 years	3,740	10	21	54	49	38	90	1,856	1,315	224	73	10
65 to 74 years	1,330	-	5	9	9	20	21	29	66	1,071	90	9
75 years and over	817	-	-	-	-	6	9	22	33	50	553	143
Total members of either sex	32,724	230	1,769	3,439	4,797	4,695	4,257	5,876	3,645	2,644	1,142	230
Under 6 years	3,952	68	618	899	828	527	323	347	230	82	27	2
6 to 11 years	3,623	-	76	609	943	670	489	476	225	107	24	4
12 to 17 years	3,495	16	25	89	611	891	742	670	281	139	29	1
18 to 24 years	3,607	104	865	139	86	392	593	938	267	169	46	9
25 to 34 years	5,481	16	118	1,588	2,043	270	143	561	450	233	50	9
35 to 44 years	4,972	8	28	48	213	1,873	1,809	391	241	247	111	2
45 to 64 years	5,081	17	34	60	64	42	129	2,437	1,841	322	117	17
65 to 74 years	1,559	-	4	7	8	20	20	29	67	1,292	100	12
75 years and over	953	-	-	-	-	10	10	28	42	53	638	173
Households with male members	8,566	63	519	954	1,232	1,241	1,079	1,477	941	691	322	49
Under 6 years	1,658	35	285	372	363	224	131	128	80	35	5	1
6 to 11 years	1,607	-	34	280	416	340	203	193	78	48	10	4
12 to 17 years	1,514	7	8	49	232	402	324	312	104	63	14	-
18 to 24 years	1,281	27	252	33	19	203	212	341	96	70	22	5
25 to 34 years	1,922	13	65	563	742	65	50	198	143	71	10	2
35 to 44 years	1,748	5	8	30	82	733	713	44	57	46	29	-
45 to 64 years	1,930	5	10	13	18	15	42	1,059	696	46	22	4
65 to 74 years	602	-	-	4	1	3	2	9	44	523	13	3
75 years and over	333	-	-	-	-	3	4	8	14	11	258	36
Total male members	15,150	109	790	1,497	2,140	2,174	2,018	2,871	1,720	1,245	508	78
Under 6 years	2,002	33	364	430	422	249	158	181	112	43	8	2
6 to 11 years	1,857	-	37	311	466	356	246	256	114	57	11	4
12 to 17 years	1,756	8	10	47	247	454	398	368	126	81	16	-
18 to 24 years	1,644	33	270	38	21	232	303	472	126	111	31	8
25 to 34 years	2,463	16	81	601	833	86	63	363	274	121	21	5
35 to 44 years	2,205	5	8	43	112	766	766	93	163	162	87	-
45 to 64 years	2,248	13	20	23	38	20	78	1,113	743	131	57	12
65 to 74 years	617	-	-	4	2	4	2	9	45	527	18	6
75 years and over	359	-	-	-	-	7	5	16	18	13	258	42
Households with female members	9,898	80	611	1,059	1,330	1,300	1,166	1,641	1,146	964	474	127
Under 6 years	1,734	42	252	390	364	263	149	142	86	32	14	-
6 to 11 years	1,679	-	44	286	457	320	221	202	88	50	12	-
12 to 17 years	1,458	8	19	43	303	378	277	245	128	45	10	2
18 to 24 years	1,584	70	570	97	55	122	209	317	93	38	12	1
25 to 34 years	2,869	-	37	954	1,198	181	78	162	140	91	26	3
35 to 44 years	2,710	2	21	5	95	1,084	1,037	295	73	72	23	2
45 to 64 years	2,807	5	15	43	31	24	52	1,310	1,079	190	53	5
65 to 74 years	941	-	5	5	7	18	19	20	22	760	79	6
75 years and over	583	-	-	-	-	3	5	14	24	41	373	124
Total female members	17,575	121	980	1,942	2,657	2,521	2,239	3,006	1,925	1,399	633	152
Under 6 years	1,950	35	254	468	406	279	165	166	118	40	18	-

[Continued]

★ 609 ★

Black Households: Characteristics, March 1994
[Continued]

Characteristics	Total	Age of householder										
		Under 20 years	20 to 24 years	25 to 29 years	30 to 34 years	35 to 39 years	40 to 44 years	45 to 54 years	55 to 64 years	65 to 74 years	75 to 84 years	85 years and over
6 to 11 years	1,766	-	40	299	477	313	242	220	111	50	13	-
12 to 17 years	1,739	8	16	41	364	437	344	302	155	58	13	1
18 to 24 years	1,963	71	595	101	64	160	290	466	141	58	14	1
25 to 34 years	3,018	-	37	987	1,211	184	80	197	177	112	29	4
35 to 44 years	2,767	3	20	5	101	1,107	1,043	298	79	84	24	2
45 to 64 years	2,833	4	14	38	27	22	51	1,324	1,097	192	60	5
65 to 74 years	942	-	4	3	6	15	19	20	23	765	81	6
75 years and over	595	-	-	-	-	3	4	12	23	40	381	131

Source: "Households, by Type, Age of Members, Age, Sex, and Race and Hispanic Origin of Householder: March 1994." Rawlings, Steve W., and Arlene F. Saluter, *Household and Family Characteristics: March 1994*, p. 171-72.

★ 610 ★

Black Households

Black Nonfamily Households: Characteristics, March 1994. Part 1

[Numbers in thousands except for averages and medians].

Characteristic	Total	Age of householder				
		Under 20 years	20 to 24 years	25 to 34 years	30 to 39 years	35 to 39 years
BLACK NONFAMILY HOUSEHOLDS						
Total households	3,292	26	172	316	365	326
With members of either sex:						
Under 6 years	21	-	3	8	2	3
6 to 11 years	34	-	-	10	4	8
12 to 17 years	37	7	-	3	6	6
18 to 24 years	232	22	172	14	8	4
25 to 34 years	772	8	36	316	365	18
35 to 44 years	716	-	2	1	27	326
45 to 64 years	987	3	-	6	2	1
65 to 74 years	472	-	-	2	-	-
75 years and over	370	-	-	-	-	-
Total members of either sex	4,076	60	256	431	500	402
Under 6 years	22	-	2	10	1	4
6 to 11 years	35	-	-	10	4	6
12 to 17 years	49	8	-	6	9	7
18 to 24 years	286	33	207	15	9	4
25 to 34 years	929	10	43	381	437	21
35 to 44 years	818	-	4	1	36	355
45 to 64 years	1,087	9	-	5	3	3
65 to 74 years	478	-	-	3	-	-
75 years and over	372	-	-	-	-	-

[Continued]

★ 610 ★

Black Nonfamily Households: Characteristics, March 1994. Part 1

[Continued]

Characteristic	Total	Age of householder				
		Under 20 years	20 to 24 years	25 to 34 years	30 to 39 years	35 to 39 years
Households with male members	1,582	17	103	182	247	222
Under 6 years	9	-	-	4	-	2
6 to 11 years	15	-	-	8	4	-
12 to 17 years	15	3	-	-	3	1
18 to 24 years	114	13	91	4	3	-
25 to 34 years	477	8	27	177	242	10
35 to 44 years	408	-	2	1	7	216
45 to 64 years	414	3	-	-	2	1
65 to 74 years	134	-	-	2	-	-
75 years and over	88	-	-	-	-	-
Total male members	1,889	42	133	207	317	239
Under 6 years	11	-	-	6	-	2
6 to 11 years	15	-	-	8	4	-
12 to 17 years	16	5	-	-	3	1
18 to 24 years	127	18	96	4	3	-
25 to 34 years	550	10	34	186	288	12
35 to 44 years	465	-	4	1	16	220
45 to 64 years	476	9	-	-	3	3
65 to 74 years	136	-	-	3	-	-
75 years and over	91	-	-	-	-	-
Households with female members	2,061	18	109	196	171	148
Under 6 years	12	-	3	4	2	2
6 to 11 years	19	-	-	2	-	8
12 to 17 years	22	3	-	3	3	5
18 to 24 years	146	15	105	10	5	4
25 to 34 years	366	-	9	184	149	8
35 to 44 years	349	-	-	-	20	136
45 to 64 years	605	-	-	6	-	-
65 to 74 years	343	-	-	-	-	-
75 years and over	282	-	-	-	-	-
Total female members	2,187	18	123	224	183	163
Under 6 years	11	-	2	4	1	2
6 to 11 years	20	-	-	2	-	6
12 to 17 years	33	3	-	6	6	6
18 to 24 years	158	15	112	12	6	4
25 to 34 years	379	-	10	195	149	9
35 to 44 years	353	-	-	-	21	135
45 to 64 years	610	-	-	5	-	-
65 to 74 years	342	-	-	-	-	-
75 years and over	281	-	-	-	-	-

Source: "Households, by Type, Age of Members, Age, Sex, and race and Hispanic Origin of Householder: March 1994." Rawlings, Steve W., and Arlene F. Saluter, *Household and Family Characteristics: March 1994*, p. 173.

★ 611 ★
Black Households

Black Nonfamily Households: Characteristics, March 1994. Part 2

[Numbers in thousands except for averages and medians].

Characteristic	Age of householder					
	40 to 44 years	45 to 54 years	55 to 64 years	65 to 74 years	75 to 84 years	85 years and over
BLACK NONFAMILY HOUSEHOLDS						
Total households	317	476	471	458	264	102
With members of either sex:						
Under 6 years	-	3	-	2	-	-
6 to 11 years	5	4	4	-	-	-
12 to 17 years	2	1	9	2	-	-
18 to 24 years	2	7	1	2	-	-
25 to 34 years	17	10	-	2	-	-
35 to 44 years	317	29	10	4	-	-
45 to 64 years	9	476	471	14	1	3
65 to 74 years	-	-	6	458	4	1
75 years and over	-	-	-	5	264	102
Total members of either sex	401	602	538	503	273	111
Under 6 years	-	2	-	2	-	-
6 to 11 years	8	4	2	-	-	-
12 to 17 years	4	2	12	2	-	-
18 to 24 years	2	11	1	2	-	-
25 to 34 years	16	17	-	3	1	-
35 to 44 years	357	42	18	5	-	-
45 to 64 years	13	522	500	20	4	7
65 to 74 years	-	-	5	464	5	1
75 years and over	-	-	-	6	264	103
Households with male members	175	238	179	129	76	16
Under 6 years	-	1	-	2	-	-
6 to 11 years	2	1	-	-	-	-
12 to 17 years	-	1	3	2	-	-
18 to 24 years	-	3	1	-	-	-
25 to 34 years	5	8	-	-	-	-
35 to 44 years	172	7	3	-	-	-
45 to 64 years	4	227	172	2	-	3
65 to 74 years	-	-	4	124	2	1
75 years and over	-	-	-	2	73	14
Total male members	209	297	205	139	79	23
Under 6 years	-	1	-	2	-	-
6 to 11 years	1	2	-	-	-	-
12 to 17 years	-	2	4	2	-	-
18 to 24 years	-	6	1	-	-	-
25 to 34 years	5	15	-	-	1	-
35 to 44 years	195	19	11	-	-	-

[Continued]

★ 611 ★

Black Nonfamily Households: Characteristics, March 1994. Part 2
[Continued]

Characteristic	Age of householder					
	40 to 44 years	45 to 54 years	55 to 64 years	65 to 74 years	75 to 84 years	85 years and over
45 to 64 years	8	252	186	7	2	7
65 to 74 years	-	-	4	126	3	1
75 years and over	-	-	-	4	73	15
Households with female members	172	288	319	360	193	88
Under 6 years	-	2	-	-	-	-
6 to 11 years	3	3	4	-	-	-
12 to 17 years	2	-	6	-	-	-
18 to 24 years	2	4	-	2	-	-
25 to 34 years	11	2	-	2	-	-
35 to 44 years	160	22	7	4	-	-
45 to 64 years	6	269	311	12	1	-
65 to 74 years	-	-	1	339	2	-
75 years and over	-	-	-	3	191	88
Total female members	192	305	333	364	195	88
Under 6 years	-	1	-	-	-	-
6 to 11 years	7	3	2	-	-	-
12 to 17 years	4	-	8	-	-	-
18 to 24 years	2	5	-	2	-	-
25 to 34 years	12	2	-	3	-	-
35 to 44 years	162	23	7	5	-	-
45 to 64 years	5	271	314	13	2	-
65 to 74 years	-	-	1	338	2	-
75 years and over	-	-	-	2	191	88

Source: "Households, by Type, Age of Members, Age, Sex, and race and Hispanic Origin of Householder: March 1994." Rawlings, Steve W., and Arlene F. Saluter, *Household and Family Characteristics: March 1994*, p. 173.

Black Owner Households

★612★

Black Owner Households: Age

[Numbers in thousands except for averages and medians].

Characteristic	Total	Family households				Nonfamily households		
		Total	Married-couple	Other family		Total	Male householder	Female householder
				Male householder	Female householder			
BLACK OWNER HOUSEHOLDS								
Age								
Households	1,188	773	506	36	229	415	84	331
No nonrelatives	1,146	759	501	36	222	387	67	320
Some nonrelatives	42	14	7	-	7	28	17	11
One nonrelative	40	14	7	-	7	26	17	9
Two nonrelatives	2	-	-	-	-	1	-	1
Three to 8 nonrelatives	-	-	-	-	-	-	-	-
Total nonrelatives	64	21	9	1	11	44	19	24
Average per household	.05	.03	.02	.02	.05	.11	.23	.07
Members 18 and Over, Other Than Householder or Spouse								
Households	4,791	3,756	2,487	166	1,102	1,035	330	705
No other members 18 and over	2,914	1,979	1,597	40	342	936	271	664
One other member 18 and over	1,258	1,165	615	87	464	93	54	39
Two or more other members 18 and over	618	612	276	39	297	6	4	1
Related Children Under 18								
Households	4,791	3,756	2,487	166	1,102	1,035	330	705
Without any related children under 18	2,707	1,672	1,179	81	412	1,035	330	705
With related children under 18	2,083	2,083	1,306	85	690	-	-	-
One child under 18	914	914	549	51	314	-	-	-
Two children under 18	729	729	487	18	223	-	-	-
Three children under 18	281	281	174	6	101	-	-	-
Four or more children under 18	160	160	96	9	52	-	-	-
Total related children under 18	3,951	3,951	2,500	152	1,300	-	-	-
Average per household	.82	1.05	1.0	.91	1.18	-	-	-
Average per household with children	1.90	1.90	1.91	1.79	1.88	(B)	(B)	(B)
Own Children Under 18								
Households	4,791	3,756	2,487	166	1,102	1,035	330	705
Without own children under 18	3,150	2,115	1,374	107	634	1,035	330	705
With own children under 18	1,640	1,640	1,113	59	468	-	-	-
One child under 18	742	742	483	36	224	-	-	-
Two children under 18	580	580	397	15	168	-	-	-
Three children under 18	220	220	163	6	52	-	-	-
Four children under 18	78	78	52	2	24	-	-	-
Five children under 18	10	10	10	-	-	-	-	-
Six or more children under 18	9	9	7	-	2	-	-	-
Total own children under 18	2,943	2,943	2,035	101	808	-	-	-

[Continued]

★ 612 ★

Black Owner Households: Age
[Continued]

| Characteristic | Total | Family households | | Other family | | Nonfamily households | | |
		Total	Married-couple	Male householder	Female householder	Total	Male householder	Female householder
Average per household	.61	.78	.82	.61	.73	-	-	-
Average per household with children	1.79	1.79	1.83	(B)	1.73	(B)	(B)	(B)

Source: "Households, by Type, Tenure, and Race and Hispanic Origin of Householder: March 1994." Steve W. Rawlings, and Arlene F. Saluter, *Household and Family Characteristics: March 1994*, p. 147. *Note:* B = Base less than 75,000.

★ 613 ★

Black Owner Households

Black Owner Households: Characteristics. Part 1.

[Numbers in thousands except for averages and medians].

| Characteristic | Total | Family households | | Other family | | Nonfamily households | | |
		Total	Married-couple	Male householder	Female householder	Total	Male householder	Female householder
BLACK OWNER HOUSEHOLDS								
Size of Household								
Households	4,791	3,756	2,487	166	1,102	1,035	330	705
One person	927	-	-	-	-	927	271	655
Two persons	1,338	1,255	760	83	413	82	42	41
Three persons	954	938	581	38	319	16	8	8
Four persons	870	861	632	32	197	9	9	-
Five persons	382	381	290	8	84	-	-	-
Six persons	193	193	137	-	56	-	-	-
Seven or more persons	127	127	88	5	33	-	-	-
Total persons	15,057	13,844	9,267	535	4,042	1,213	427	786
Persons per household	3.14	3.69	3.73	3.22	3.67	1.17	1.29	1.12
Metropolitan-Nonmetropolitan Residence								
Households	4,791	3,756	2,487	166	1,102	1,035	330	705
In MSA's	3,948	3,098	2,059	153	885	850	280	570
Central cities	2,442	1,843	1,137	101	606	599	191	407
Ring	1,506	1,254	923	52	280	251	88	163
MSA's of 2,500,000 or more	1,697	1,335	887	67	381	361	125	236
Central cities	1,046	785	482	49	254	262	89	173
Ring	650	550	405	18	127	100	37	63
MSA's of 1,000,000 to 2,499,999	877	711	469	22	220	166	47	120
Central cities	576	465	261	16	189	111	33	78
Ring	301	246	209	6	31	55	14	41
MSA's of 250,000 to 999,999	969	747	495	47	204	223	79	144
Central cities	578	424	274	28	123	154	57	97
Ring	391	322	222	19	82	69	22	46
MSA's of 249,999 or less	405	305	206	17	80	100	29	71

[Continued]

★ 613 ★

Black Owner Households: Characteristics. Part 1.
[Continued]

Characteristic	Total	Family households		Other family		Nonfamily households		
		Total	Married-couple	Male householder	Female householder	Total	Male householder	Female householder
Central cities	241	169	121	8	41	72	13	59
Ring	163	136	87	9	40	27	15	12
Not in MSA's	843	658	428	13	217	185	51	134
Nonrelatives in Household								
Households	4,791	3,756	2,487	166	1,102	1,035	330	705
No nonrelatives	4,560	3,633	2,442	144	1,048	927	271	655
Some nonrelatives	231	123	46	22	55	108	59	49
One nonrelative	177	95	31	16	48	82	42	41
Two nonrelatives	30	13	6	6	1	16	8	8
Three to 8 nonrelatives	24	14	9	-	6	9	9	-
Total nonrelatives	402	223	88	30	105	178	97	82
Average per household	.08	.06	.04	.18	.10	.17	.29	.12

Source: "Households, by Type, Tenure, and Race and Hispanic Origin of Householder: March 1994." Steve W. Rawlings, and Arlene F. Saluter, *Household and Family Characteristics: March 1994*, p. 147.

★ 614 ★

Black Owner Households

Black Owner Households: Characteristics. Part 2.

[Numbers in thousands except for averages and medians].

Characteristic	Total	Family households		Other family		Nonfamily households		
		Total	Married-couple	Male householder	Female householder	Total	Male householder	Female householder
BLACK OWNER HOUSEHOLDS								
Age of Householder								
Households	4,791	3,756	2,487	166	1,102	1,035	330	705
15 to 19 years	5	5	1	-	4	-	-	-
20 to 24 years	52	43	24	9	10	8	-	8
25 to 29 years	171	136	82	16	38	34	16	19
30 to 34 years	354	307	190	23	93	47	34	13
35 to 39 years	515	456	266	25	165	59	22	37
40 to 44 years	650	553	374	19	160	97	48	50
45 to 49 years	577	466	324	12	129	111	49	62
50 to 54 years	470	398	291	14	93	72	26	46
55 to 59 years	431	352	234	8	111	79	23	56
60 to 64 years	378	265	193	2	70	113	29	84
65 to 74 years	721	507	350	22	134	215	47	167
75 to 84 years	372	233	148	9	76	139	30	109
85 years and over	94	33	10	5	19	61	6	55
Median	50.8	49.0	49.7	42.3	48.1	60.4	49.7	63.7

[Continued]

★ 614 ★

Black Owner Households: Characteristics. Part 2.

[Continued]

Characteristic	Total	Family households				Nonfamily households		
		Total	Married-couple	Other family		Total	Male householder	Female householder
				Male householder	Female householder			
Marital Status of Householder								
Households	4,791	3,756	2,487	166	1,102	1,035	330	705
Married, spouse present	2,487	2,487	2,487	-	-	-	-	-
Married, spouse absent	320	222	-	36	186	98	55	44
Separated	277	190	-	28	162	87	50	38
Other	43	32	-	8	24	11	5	6
Widowed	781	359	-	30	330	422	56	366
Divorced	699	420	-	54	366	279	115	164
Never married	502	267	-	46	221	236	105	131
Units in Structure								
Households[1]	4,791	3,756	2,487	166	1,102	1,035	330	705
One unit	3,803	3,023	2,014	120	888	780	254	527
Two units	135	93	54	5	34	41	7	34
Three or 4 units	64	46	32	3	12	18	5	12
Five to 9 units	67	49	36	5	8	18	10	7
Ten or more units	75	38	14	2	22	38	13	25

Source: "Households, by Type, Tenure, and Race and Hispanic Origin of Householder: March 1994." Steve W. Rawlings, and Arlene F. Saluter, *Household and Family Characteristics: March 1994*, p. 148.

Black Renter Households

★ 615 ★

Black Renter Households: Age

[Numbers in thousands except for averages and medians].

Characteristic	Total	Family households				Nonfamily households		
		Total	Married-couple	Other family		Total	Male householder	Female householder
				Male householder	Female householder			
BLACK RENTER HOUSEHOLDS								
Households With Householder 65 Years and Over								
Households	580	171	53	12	106	409	125	284
No nonrelatives	566	171	52	12	106	396	113	282
Some nonrelatives	14	-	-	-	-	13	11	2
One nonrelative	11	-	-	-	-	10	8	2
Two nonrelatives	-	-	-	-	-	-	-	-
Three to 8 nonrelatives	3	-	-	-	-	3	3	-

[Continued]

★ 615 ★

Black Renter Households: Age

[Continued]

Characteristic	Total	Family households		Other family		Nonfamily households		
		Total	Married-couple	Male householder	Female householder	Total	Male householder	Female householder
Total nonrelatives	20	1	1	-	-	20	17	3
Average per household	.04	-	.01	-	-	.05	.13	.01
Members 18 and Over, Other Than Householder or Spouse								
Households	6,490	4,233	1,227	284	2,722	2,257	1,122	1,135
No other members 18 and over	4,702	2,821	1,025	69	1,726	1,882	875	1,006
One other member 18 and over	1,381	1,050	153	172	724	331	207	125
Two or more other members 18 and over	407	363	48	43	272	44	40	4
Related Children Under 18								
Households	6,490	4,233	1,227	284	2,722	2,257	1,122	1,135
Without related children under 18	3,051	794	389	74	330	2,257	1,122	1,135
With related children under 18	3,439	3,439	837	210	2,392	-	-	-
One child under 18	1,332	1,332	274	122	936	-	-	-
Two children under 18	1,092	1,092	313	60	719	-	-	-
Three children under 18	588	588	152	24	412	-	-	-
Four or more children under 18	427	427	98	3	326	-	-	-
Total related children under 18	6,843	6,843	1,705	331	4,807	-	-	-
Average per household	1.05	1.62	1.39	1.16	1.77	-	-	-
Average per household with children	1.99	1.99	2.04	1.58	2.01	(B)	(B)	(B)
Own Children Under 18								
Households	6,490	4,233	1,227	284	2,722	2,257	1,122	1,135
Without own children under 18	3,338	1,081	416	105	560	2,257	1,122	1,135
With own children under 18	3,152	3,152	811	180	2,162	-	-	-
One child under 18	1,240	1,240	288	108	844	-	-	-
Two children under 18	1,050	1,050	298	48	704	-	-	-
Three children under 18	535	535	146	23	366	-	-	-
Four children under 18	222	222	57	1	165	-	-	-
Five children under 18	61	61	13	-	48	-	-	-
Six or more children under 18	44	44	8	-	36	-	-	-
Total own children under 18	5,940	5,940	1,567	274	4,099	-	-	-
Average per household	.92	1.40	1.28	.96	1.51	-	-	-
Average per household with children	1.88	1.88	1.93	1.53	1.90	(B)	(B)	(B)

Source: "Households, by Type, Tenure, and Race and Hispanic Origin of Householder: March 1994." Steve W. Rawlings, and Arlene F. Saluter, *Household and Family Characteristics: March 1994*, p. 153. *Note:* B = Base less than 75,000.

★ 616 ★
Black Renter Households

Black Renter Households: Characteristics. Part 1

[Numbers in thousands except for averages and medians].

Characteristic	Total	Family households				Nonfamily households		
		Total	Married-couple	Other family		Total	Male householder	Female householder
				Male householder	Female householder			
BLACK RENTER HOUSEHOLDS								
Size of Household								
Households	6,490	4,233	1,227	284	2,722	2,257	1,122	1,135
One person	1,877	-	-	-	-	1,877	875	1,002
Two persons	1,581	1,282	315	103	864	299	174	125
Three persons	1,302	1,244	294	73	877	58	50	8
Four persons	890	872	313	60	498	18	18	-
Five persons	486	480	163	42	276	6	6	-
Six persons	170	170	83	4	83	-	-	-
Seven or more persons	185	185	58	3	124	-	-	-
Total persons	17,667	14,804	4,502	978	9,324	2,863	1,519	1,344
Persons per household	2.72	3.50	3.67	3.44	3.43	1.27	1.35	1.18
Metropolitan-Nonmetropolitan Residence								
Households	6,490	4,233	1,227	284	2,722	2,257	1,122	1,135
In MSA's	5,823	3,741	1,083	257	2,400	2,082	1,009	1,074
Central cities	4,101	2,540	637	152	1,752	1,561	746	815
Ring	1,722	1,201	447	105	649	522	263	259
MSA's of 2,500,000 or more	2,721	1,686	491	109	1,086	1,035	501	533
Central cities	2,021	1,206	297	65	846	813	383	430
Ring	700	478	194	44	240	222	119	103
MSA's of 1,000,000 to 2,499,999	1,446	924	253	46	626	521	272	249
Central cities	909	565	113	24	428	344	171	173
Ring	537	359	140	22	197	178	101	77
MSA's of 250,000 to 999,999	1,218	808	234	71	504	409	178	231
Central cities	870	534	144	45	345	335	152	183
Ring	348	274	90	26	158	74	26	48
MSA's of 249,999 or less	439	322	106	32	185	117	57	60
Central cities	301	232	82	19	132	69	40	29
Ring	137	90	23	13	53	48	17	31
Not in MSA's	667	492	143	27	322	175	114	61
Nonrelatives in Household								
Households	6,490	4,233	1,227	284	2,722	2,257	1,122	1,135
No nonrelatives	5,811	3,934	1,207	173	2,554	1,877	875	1,002
Some nonrelatives	679	299	19	112	168	380	247	133
One nonrelative	550	251	14	86	151	299	174	125
Two nonrelatives	91	34	4	15	15	58	50	8
Three to 8 nonrelatives	38	14	1	10	2	24	24	-

[Continued]

★ 616 ★

Black Renter Households: Characteristics. Part 1
[Continued]

Characteristic	Total	Family households		Other family		Nonfamily households		
		Total	Married-couple	Male householder	Female householder	Total	Male householder	Female householder
Total nonrelatives	1,081	475	35	156	284	606	397	209
Average per household	.17	.11	.03	.55	.10	.27	.35	.18

Source: "Households, by Type, Tenure, and Race and Hispanic Origin of Householder: March 1994." Steve W. Rawlings, and Arlene F. Saluter, *Household and Family Characteristics: March 1994*, p. 153.

★ 617 ★

Black Renter Households

Black Renter Households: Characteristics. Part 2

[Numbers in thousands except for averages and medians].

Characteristic	Total	Family households		Other family		Nonfamily households		
		Total	Married-couple	Male householder	Female householder	Total	Male householder	Female householder
BLACK RENTER HOUSEHOLDS								
Age of Householder								
Households	6,490	4,233	1,227	284	2,722	2,257	1,122	1,135
15 to 19 years	86	60	-	6	54	26	7	18
20 to 24 years	631	466	93	24	350	164	88	76
25 to 29 years	1,027	746	234	51	460	282	143	139
30 to 34 years	1,192	874	243	68	563	318	194	125
35 to 39 years	989	722	199	45	478	266	188	78
40 to 44 years	672	453	146	26	280	219	118	101
45 to 49 years	481	316	103	19	195	165	89	76
50 to 54 years	328	199	65	19	115	129	52	77
55 to 59 years	257	123	50	8	65	134	56	78
60 to 64 years	248	102	40	7	55	145	62	83
65 to 74 years	350	106	24	9	74	243	74	169
75 to 84 years	181	57	24	4	29	125	43	82
85 years and over	49	8	4	-	3	41	8	33
Median	36.8	34.8	36.1	34.5	34.4	41.6	38.4	47.0
Marital Status of Householder								
Households	6,490	4,233	1,227	284	2,722	2,257	1,122	1,135
Married, spouse present	1,227	1,227	1,227	-	-	-	-	-
Married, spouse absent	986	644	-	55	589	342	204	138
Separated	842	553	-	43	510	289	165	124
Other	143	91	-	12	79	53	38	14
Widowed	537	194	-	14	180	343	80	263
Divorced	1,075	608	-	88	520	467	220	247
Never married	2,665	1,561	-	127	1,434	1,105	619	486

[Continued]

★ 617 ★

Black Renter Households: Characteristics. Part 2

[Continued]

Characteristic	Total	Family households				Nonfamily households		
		Total	Married-couple	Other family		Total	Male householder	Female householder
				Male householder	Female householder			
Units in Structure								
Households[1]	6,490	4,233	1,227	284	2,722	2,257	1,122	1,135
One unit	1,536	1,224	422	83	719	312	188	125
Two units	682	519	141	31	347	164	68	95
Three or 4 units	569	362	71	22	268	207	102	105
Five to 9 units	934	637	152	45	440	298	156	142
Ten or more units	2,020	1,021	305	66	650	999	450	549

Source: "Households, by Type, Tenure, and Race and Hispanic Origin of Householder: March 1994." Steve W. Rawlings, and Arlene F. Saluter, *Household and Family Characteristics: March 1994*, p. 154.

Characteristics

★ 618 ★

Native and Foreign-Born: Selected Characteristics of Natives and Foreign-Born Population by Citizenship and Year of Entry, 1994

(Numbers in thousands).

Characteristic	Native	Foreign born						
		Total	Natural-ized citizen	Not a citizen	Year of entry			
					Before 1970	1970 to 1979	1980 to 1989	1990 to 1994
Race and Hispanic origin								
White	199,793	15,428	4,749	10,680	4,313	3,058	5,190	2,867
Black	31,443	1,596	343	1,253	200	342	738	317
Asian or Pacific Islander	2,813	4,630	1,701	2,929	386	1,176	1,992	1,076
Hispanic origin[1]	16,376	10,270	1,879	8,391	1,560	2,334	4,404	1,971

Source: "Selected Characteristics of Natives and the Foreign-Born Population by Citizenship and Year of Entry: 1994," Kristin A. Hansen and Amara Bachu, "The Foreign-Born Population: 1994," *Current Population Reports*, August 1995, p. 5. *Note:* 1. Persons of Hispanic origin may be of any race.

★ 619 ★

Characteristics

Population Changes: Components of Population Changes, 1990 to 1993, and Projections, 1995 and 2000

[The April 1, 1990, census count (248,718,291) includes count resolution corrections processed through March 1994 and does not include adjustments for census coverage errors.]

YEAR	Population at start of period (1,000)	TOTAL (Jan. 1-Dec. 31)					RATE PER 1,000 MIDYEAR POPULATION			
		Net increase[1]		Natural increase		Net migration[3] (1,000)	Net growth rate[1]	Natural increase		Net migration rate[3]
		Total (1,000)	Per-cent[2]	Births (1,000)	Deaths (1,000)			Birth rate	Death rate	
WHITE										
1990	208,376	1,669	0.8	3,265	1,860	306[4]	8.0	15.6	8.9	1.5[4]
1991	210,046	1,966	0.9	3,241	1,869	594[4]	9.3	15.4	8.9	2.8[4]
1992	212,012	1,949	0.9	3,202	1,874	621	9.2	15.0	8.8	2.9
1993	213,961	1,757	0.8	3,169	1,950	539	8.2	14.8	9.1	2.5
Projections:[5]										
1995	217,460	1,718	0.8	3,128	1,892	482	7.9	14.3	8.7	2.2
2000	225,520	1,478	0.7	2,992	1,997	482	6.5	13.2	8.8	2.1
BLACK										
1990	30,377	440	1.4	692	266	27[4]	14.4	22.6	8.7	0.9[4]
1991	30,817	581	1.9	683	270	168[4]	18.7	21.9	8.7	5.4[4]
1992	31,398	541	1.7	674	269	136	17.1	21.3	8.5	4.3
1993	31,939	502	1.6	673	282	111	15.6	20.9	8.8	3.5
Projections:[5]										
1995	32,874	483	1.5	685	283	81	14.6	20.7	8.5	2.4
2000	35,238	463	1.3	695	313	81	13.0	19.6	8.8	2.3
AMERICAN INDIAN, ESKIMO, ALEUT										
1990	2,044	45	2.2	42	8	1[4]	21.8	20.1	4.1	0.6[4]
1991	2,089	35	1.7	39	9	5[4]	16.6	18.4	4.1	2.3[4]
1992	2,124	36	1.7	39	9	5	16.7	18.4	4.2	2.5
1993	2,160	34	1.6	40	11	5	15.5	18.2	4.9	2.1
Projections:[5]										
1995	2,211	30	1.4	40	10	-	13.7	17.9	4.4	0.1
2000	2,364	31	1.3	42	11	-	13.2	17.7	4.6	0.1
ASIAN, PACIFIC ISLANDER										
1990	7,345	382	5.2	149	21	242[4]	50.6	19.8	2.7	32.0[4]
1991	7,727	353	4.6	148	22	227[4]	44.7	18.8	2.8	28.7[4]
1992	8,080	376	4.6	150	24	249	45.4	18.2	2.9	30.1
1993	8,456	358	4.2	157	25	226	41.4	18.2	2.9	26.1
Projections:[5]										
1995	9,527	461	4.8	170	26	317	47.2	17.5	2.7	32.5
2000	11,883	486	4.1	205	36	317	40.1	16.9	2.9	26.1
HISPANIC ORIGIN[6]										
1990	22,122	847	3.8	595	84	292[4]	37.6	26.4	3.7	12.9[4]
1991	22,969	841	3.7	628	85	298[4]	36.0	26.8	3.6	12.8[4]
1992	23,810	913	3.8	646	87	354	37.6	26.6	3.6	14.6
1993	24,723	913	3.7	659	94	348	36.2	26.2	3.7	13.8
Projections:[5]										
1995	26,368	862	3.3	639	100	322	32.1	23.8	3.7	12.0
2000	30,723	888	2.9	690	125	322	28.5	22.1	4.0	10.3

[Continued]

★ 619 ★

Population Changes: Components of Population Changes, 1990 to 1993, and Projections, 1995 and 2000
[Continued]

| YEAR | TOTAL (Jan. 1-Dec. 31) | | | | | | RATE PER 1,000 MIDYEAR POPULATION | | | |
| | Population at start of period (1,000) | Net increase[1] | | Natural increase | | Net migration[3] (1,000) | Net growth rate[1] | Natural increase | | Net migration rate[3] |
		Total (1,000)	Per-cent[2]	Births (1,000)	Deaths (1,000)			Birth rate	Death rate	
WHITE, NON-HISPANIC										
1990	188,160	929	0.5	2,720	1,782	52[4]	4.9	14.4	9.4	0.3[4]
1991	189,089	1,211	0.6	2,667	1,790	334[4]	6.4	14.1	9.4	1.8[4]
1992	190,300	1,132	0.6	2,611	1,793	314	5.9	13.7	9.4	1.6
1993	191,432	938	0.5	2,566	1,864	236	4.9	13.4	9.7	1.2
Projections:[5]										
1995	193,416	936	0.5	2,544	1,800	193	4.8	13.1	9.3	1.0
2000	197,525	674	0.3	2,363	1,882	193	3.4	11.9	9.5	1.0
BLACK NON-HISPANIC										
1990	29,191	372	1.3	659	262	-[4]	12.7	22.4	8.9	-[4]
1991	29,562	522	1.8	646	265	140[4]	17.5	21.7	8.9	4.7[4]
1992	30,084	474	1.6	636	265	102	15.6	21.0	8.7	3.4
1993	30,558	436	1.4	635	277	78	14.2	20.6	9.0	2.5
Projections:[5]										
1995	31,430	432	1.4	649	278	61	13.7	20.5	8.8	1.9
2000	33,536	410	1.2	655	307	61	12.1	19.4	9.1	1.8

Source: "Components of Population Change, by Race and Hispanic Origin, 1990 to 1993, and Projections, 1995 and 2000," *Statistical Abstract of the United States: 1995*, p. 20. Primary source: U.S. Bureau of the Census, *Current Population Reports*, P25-1104; and Population Paper Listing 21. *Notes:* - Represents or rounds to zero. 1. Prior to April 1, 1990, includes "error of closure" (the amount necessary to make the components of change add to the net change between censuses), for which figures are not shown separately. 2. Percent of population at beginning of period. 3. Covers net international migration and movement of Armed forces, federally affiliated civilian citizens, and their dependents. 4. Data reflect movement of Armed forces due to the Gulf War. 5. Based on middle series of assumptions. 6. Persons of Hispanic origin may be of any race.

★ 620 ★

Characteristics

Resident Population: Age and Hispanic Origin: 1980 to 1994. Part 1

[In thousands, except percent. As of April, except 1994 as of July. Hispanic persons may be of any race.]

YEAR AND SEX	Total all years	Under 5 years	5-9 years	10-14 years	15-19 years	20-24 years	25-29 years	30-34 years	35-39 years	40-44 years
HISPANIC ORIGIN										
1980	14,609	1,663	1,537	1,475	1,606	1,586	1,376	1,129	854	712
1990[1]	22,354	2,467	2,178	1,989	2,085	2,320	2,337	2,045	1,642	1,276
1994	26,077	3,096	2,527	2,355	2,198	2,338	2,483	2,460	2,060	1,632
Male	13,219	1,583	1,292	1,202	1,128	1,245	1,334	1,291	1,058	818
Female	12,857	1,513	1,235	1,153	1,070	1,093	1,149	1,168	1,002	814

[Continued]

★ 620 ★

Resident Population: Age and Hispanic Origin: 1980 to 1994. Part 1
[Continued]

YEAR AND SEX	Total all years	Under 5 years	5-9 years	10-14 years	15-19 years	20-24 years	25-29 years	30-34 years	35-39 years	40-44 years
NON-HISPANIC WHITE										
1980	180,906	11,842	12,262	13,703	16,166	16,574	15,358	14,091	11,315	9,437
1990[1]	188,306	12,721	12,516	11,854	12,450	13,524	15,508	16,331	15,162	13,839
1994	192,727	12,764	12,707	12,783	12,033	12,592	13,338	16,056	16,371	15,038
Male	94,091	6,549	6,525	6,569	6,193	6,390	6,680	8,042	8,206	7,508
Female	98,636	6,215	6,183	6,214	5,840	6,202	6,657	8,014	8,165	7,529
BLACK										
1980	26,142	2,399	2,455	2,635	2,944	2,689	2,292	1,865	1,438	1,233
1990[1]	29,275	2,798	2,596	2,525	2,605	2,528	2,650	2,601	2,265	1,811
1994	31,192	2,945	2,791	2,733	2,610	2,539	2,475	2,693	2,608	2,210
Male	14,748	1,492	1,415	1,385	1,322	1,246	1,175	1,255	1,215	1,020
Female	16,444	1,453	1,376	1,348	1,289	1,293	1,301	1,438	1,393	1,190
AMERICAN INDIAN, ESKIMO, ALEUT										
1980	1,326	136	135	145	158	138	116	100	79	66
1990[1]	1,796	185	179	170	165	151	160	156	138	117
1994	1,907	179	188	195	166	159	149	159	150	133
Male	938	91	96	99	84	81	75	78	73	64
Female	969	89	92	96	82	78	74	81	77	69
ASIAN, PACIFIC ISLANDER										
1980	3,563	308	311	285	294	332	378	376	279	221
1990[1]	6,988	586	566	522	581	612	673	700	640	545
1994	8,438	743	646	686	609	697	731	809	772	687
Male	4,080	380	330	347	309	348	354	391	368	318
Female	4,358	363	316	339	300	349	377	418	404	369
1994, PERCENT										
Hispanic origin	100.0	11.9	9.7	9.0	8.4	9.0	9.5	9.4	7.9	6.3
Non-Hispanic:										
White	100.0	6.6	6.6	6.6	6.2	6.5	6.9	8.3	8.5	7.8
Black	100.0	9.4	8.9	8.8	8.4	8.1	7.9	8.6	8.4	7.1
American Indian, Eskimo, Aleut	100.0	9.4	9.8	10.2	8.7	8.4	7.8	8.3	7.9	6.9
Asian, Pacific Islander	100.0	8.8	7.7	8.1	7.2	8.3	8.7	9.6	9.1	8.1

Source: "Resident Population, by Age and Hispanic Origin: 1980 to 1994," *Statistical Abstract of the United States: 1995*, p. 24. Primary source: U.S. Bureau of the Census, *Current Population Reports*, P25-1095; and Population Paper Listing 21. *Notes:* 1. The April 1, 1990, census count (248,718,291) includes count resolution corrections processed through March 1994 and does not include adjustments for census coverage errors.

★ 621 ★

Characteristics

Resident Population: Age and Hispanic Origin: 1980 to 1994. Part 2

[In thousands, except percent. As of April, except 1994 as of July. Hispanic persons may be of any race.]

YEAR AND SEX	45-49 years	50-54 years	55-59 years	60-64 years	65-74 years	75-84 years	85 years and over	5-13 years	14-17 years	18-24 years
HISPANIC ORIGIN										
1980	622	564	454	321	457	203	49	2,715	1,251	2,240
1990[1]	936	750	633	550	715	340	91	3,782	1,574	3,215
1994	1,230	913	738	616	904	405	122	4,424	1,773	3,221
Male	603	438	348	285	398	155	40	2,260	910	1,698
Female	627	475	390	332	506	250	82	2,164	864	1,523
NON-HISPANIC WHITE										
1980	9,104	9,824	9,963	8,775	13,614	6,863	2,014	23,126	12,313	23,267
1990[1]	10,971	9,057	8,548	8,872	15,511	8,767	2,675	22,106	9,224	19,014
1994	13,130	10,522	8,760	8,208	15,797	9,534	3,094	22,935	9,847	17,333
Male	6,514	5,172	4,254	3,910	7,049	3,682	847	11,780	5,075	8,822
Female	6,615	5,350	4,507	4,298	8,748	5,852	2,247	11,155	4,772	8,511
BLACK										
1980	1,127	1,114	1,024	861	1,327	582	157	4,530	2,331	3,862
1990[1]	1,362	1,138	1,08	945	1,465	758	219	4,638	1,975	3,642
1994	1,669	1,287	1,069	950	1,554	797	260	4,962	2,159	3,553
Male	759	577	468	409	646	288	75	2,514	1,098	1,755
Female	910	710	601	541	908	509	185	2,448	1,061	1,798
AMERICAN INDIAN, ESKIMO, ALEUT										
1980	55	49	43	32	46	20	6	249	127	199
1990[1]	90	72	58	48	68	31	9	316	131	217
1994	107	82	64	51	75	37	13	344	143	221
Male	51	39	30	24	34	15	4	175	72	112
Female	55	43	34	27	42	22	9	169	70	109
ASIAN, PACIFIC ISLANDER										
1980	182	158	131	98	136	60	14	540	226	455
1990[1]	384	297	240	210	287	116	27	983	436	862
1994	544	387	304	257	381	152	32	1,197	505	936
Male	253	184	143	112	163	66	13	609	257	469
Female	292	204	161	145	218	86	20	588	248	467
1994, PERCENT										
Hispanic origin	4.7	3.5	2.8	2.4	3.5	1.6	0.5	17.0	6.8	12.4
Non-Hispanic:										
White	6.8	5.5	4.5	4.3	8.2	4.9	1.6	11.9	5.1	9.0
Black	5.4	4.1	3.4	3.0	5.0	2.6	0.8	15.9	6.9	11.4

[Continued]

★ 621 ★

Resident Population: Age and Hispanic Origin: 1980 to 1994. Part 2

[Continued]

YEAR AND SEX	45-49 years	50-54 years	55-59 years	60-64 years	65-74 years	75-84 years	85 years and over	5-13 years	14-17 years	18-24 years
American Indian, Eskimo, Aleut	5.6	4.3	3.4	2.7	3.9	2.0	0.7	18.0	7.5	11.6
Asian, Pacific Islander	6.5	4.6	3.6	3.0	4.5	1.8	0.4	14.2	6.0	11.1

Source: "Resident Population, by Age and Hispanic Origin: 1980 to 1994," *Statistical Abstract of the United States: 1995,* p. 24. Primary source: U.S. Bureau of the Census, *Current Population Reports,* P25-1095; and Population Paper Listing 21. *Notes:* 1. The April 1, 1990, census count (248,718,291) includes count resolution corrections processed through March 1994 and does not include adjustments for census coverage errors.

★ 622 ★

Characteristics

Resident Population: Age, Gender, Race, and Hispanic Origin of the Population: 1950 to 1992. Part 1

[Data are based on decennial census updated by data from multiple sources.]

Sex, race, Hispanic origin, and year	Total resident population	Under 1 year	1-4 years	5-14 years	15-24 years	25-34 years	35-44 years	45-54 years	55-64 years	65-74 years	75-84 years	85 years and over
					Number in thousands							
White male												
1950	67,129	1,400	5,845	10,860	9,689	10,430	9,529	7,836	6,180	3,736	1,406	218
1960	78,367	1,784	7,065	15,659	10,483	9,940	10,564	9,114	6,850	4,702	1,875	331
1970	86,721	1,501	5,873	17,667	15,232	10,775	9,979	10,090	7,958	4,916	2,243	487
1980	94,976	1,487	5,402	14,773	18,123	15,940	11,010	9,774	9,151	6,096	2,600	621
1985	98,635	1,535	5,897	14,013	16,828	17,698	13,538	9,538	9,290	6,628	2,982	688
1988	100,786	1,543	5,968	14,167	15,921	18,170	14,929	10,167	8,990	6,958	3,242	731
1989	101,534	1,569	6,030	14,332	15,565	18,156	15,417	10,455	8,870	7,056	3,335	750
1990	102,143	1,604	6,071	14,467	15,389	18,071	15,819	10,624	8,813	7,127	3,397	760
1991	103,268	1,591	6,189	14,766	15,084	17,892	16,556	10,892	8,763	7,212	3,529	795
1992	104,339	1,617	6,312	14,958	14,922	17,666	16,753	11,631	8,726	7,292	3,641	821
Black male												
1950	7,300	-	-	1,442	1,162	1,105	1,003	772	460	299	-	-
1960	9,114	281	1,082	2,185	1,305	1,120	1,086	891	617	382	137	29
1970	10,748	245	975	2,784	2,041	1,226	1,084	979	739	461	169	46
1980	12,585	269	967	2,614	2,807	1,967	1,235	1,024	854	567	228	53
1985	13,505	276	1,067	2,599	2,768	2,391	1,543	1,069	887	586	257	62
1988	14,056	297	1,103	2,640	2,723	2,550	1,789	1,132	885	602	271	65
1989	14,258	315	1,135	2,671	2,687	2,579	1,883	1,157	881	609	275	66
1990	14,420	322	1,164	2,700	2,669	2,592	1,962	1,175	878	614	277	66
1991	14,753	343	1,225	2,767	2,649	2,602	2,094	1,205	886	631	282	69
1992	15,000	322	1,244	2,820	2,661	2,608	2,188	1,268	890	643	286	70

[Continued]

★ 622 ★

Resident Population: Age, Gender, Race, and Hispanic Origin of the Population: 1950 to 1992.
Part 1
[Continued]

Sex, race, Hispanic origin, and year	Total resident population	Under 1 year	1-4 years	5-14 years	15-24 years	25-34 years	35-44 years	45-54 years	55-64 years	65-74 years	75-84 years	85 years and over
American Indian or Alaskan Native male												
1980												
1985	849	20	75	171	181	144	104	66	47	26	11	3
1988	952	21	82	191	189	166	127	78	52	30	13	3
1989	992	23	85	199	190	176	135	83	53	31	13	3
1990	1,024	24	88	206	192	183	140	86	55	32	13	3
1991	1,050	27	92	213	191	184	146	89	57	34	14	4
1992	1,062	21	90	219	192	185	151	94	58	35	15	4
Asian or Pacific Islander male												
1980												
1985	2,740	52	205	463	499	559	409	244	160	99	43	8
1988	3,291	61	234	544	599	661	517	305	188	120	51	11
1989	3,494	66	246	574	636	696	557	327	198	127	55	11
1990	3,652	68	258	598	665	718	588	347	208	133	57	12
1991	3,909	91	278	643	686	749	638	377	226	145	63	13
1992	4,078	84	291	671	703	773	676	405	240	154	66	14
Hispanic male												
1980	7,280	173	675	1,530	1,646	1,255	761	570	364	201	86	19
1985	9,275	208	783	1,823	2,022	1,852	1,060	674	479	239	111	24
1988	10,558	240	886	2,006	2,234	2,179	1,300	755	525	280	123	30
1989	11,016	626	937	2,074	2,304	2,260	1,394	791	538	298	128	31
1990	11,388	279	980	2,128	2,376	2,310	1,471	818	551	312	131	32
1991	11,890	284	1,046	2,219	2,364	2,421	1,596	868	578	337	140	37
1992	12,292	317	1,114	2,293	2,337	2,490	1,683	925	594	356	145	39

Source: "Resident Population, According to Age, Sex, Detailed Race, and Hispanic Origin: United States, Selected Years 1950-92," *Health, United States, 1994*, pp. 63-64. Primary source: U.S. Bureau of the Census: 1950 Nonwhite Population by Race. Special Report P-E, No. 3B. Washington. U.S. Government Printing Office, 1951; U.S. Bureau of the Census, U.S. Census of Population: 1960, Number of inhabitants, PC(1)- A1, United States Summary, 1964; 1970, Number of Inhabitants, Final Report PC (1)- A1, United States Summary, 1971; U.S. Bureau of the Census: U.S. Population estimates, by age, sex, race, and Hispanic origin: 1980 to 1991. Current Population Reports. Series P-25, No. 1095. Washington. U.S. Government Printing Office, Feb. 1993: U.S. Bureau of the Census: U.S. Population estimates, by age, sex, race, and Hispanic origin: 1992. Census file RESP0792. 1994. *Notes:* The race groups, white and black, include persons of Hispanic and non- Hispanic origin. Conversely, persons of Hispanic origin may be of any race. Population figures are census counts as of April 1 for 1950, 1960, 1970, 1980, and 1990 and estimates as of July 1 for other years. Data for the 1980's are intercensal population estimates. See Appendix I, Department of Commerce. Populations for age groups may not sum to total due to rounding.

Characteristics

Resident Population: Age, Gender, Race, and Hispanic Origin of the Population: 1950 to 1992. Part 2

[Data are based on decennial census updated by data from multiple sources.]

Sex, race, Hispanic origin, and year	Total resident population	Under 1 year	1-4 years	5-14 years	15-24 years	25-34 years	35-44 years	45-54 years	55-64 years	65-74 years	75-84 years	85 years and over
						Number in thousands						
White female												
1950	67,813	1,341	5,599	10,431	9,821	10,851	9,719	7,868	6,168	4,031	1,669	314
1960	80,465	1,714	6,795	15,068	10,596	10,204	11,000	9,364	7,327	5,428	2,441	527
1970	91,028	1,434	5,615	16,912	15,420	11,004	10,349	10,756	8,853	6,366	3,429	890
1980	99,835	1,412	5,127	14,057	17,653	15,896	11,232	10,285	10,325	7,951	4,457	1,440
1985	103,396	1,457	5,599	13,288	16,236	17,435	13,699	9,909	10,378	8,536	5,104	1,756
1988	105,343	1,465	5,666	13,422	15,214	17,850	15,005	10,495	9,968	8,867	5,484	1,906
1989	106,006	1,492	5,724	13,579	14,817	17,830	15,457	10,780	9,793	8,968	5,604	1,961
1990	106,561	1,524	5,862	13,706	14,599	17,757	15,834	10,946	9,698	9,048	5,687	2,001
1991	107,631	1,511	5,877	13,990	14,296	17,568	16,542	11,218	9,586	9,125	5,828	2,090
1992	108,584	1,542	5,996	14,174	14,145	17,312	16,704	11,945	9,500	9,177	5,937	2,152
Black female												
1950	7,745	-	-	1,446	1,300	1,260	1,112	796	443	322	-	-
1960	9,758	283	1,085	2,191	1,404	1,300	1,229	974	663	430	160	38
1970	11,832	243	970	2,773	2,196	1,456	1,309	1,134	868	582	230	71
1980	14,046	266	951	2,578	2,937	2,267	1,488	1,258	1,059	776	360	106
1985	15,064	271	1,045	2,547	2,845	2,711	1,828	1,298	1,121	833	431	133
1988	15,667	291	1,079	2,583	2,771	2,863	2,094	1,366	1,133	864	474	149
1989	15,886	309	1,110	2,613	2,726	2,892	2,195	1,395	1,132	876	486	153
1990	16,063	316	1,137	2,641	2,700	2,905	2,279	1,416	1,135	884	495	156
1991	16,412	334	1,196	2,702	2,669	2,914	2,425	1,456	1,144	905	503	163
1992	16,653	314	1,215	2,748	2,673	2,907	2,519	1,530	1,152	916	512	167
American Indian or Alaskan Native female												
1980												
1985	868	19	73	165	173	149	111	71	52	33	17	5
1988	971	21	80	184	177	170	136	82	58	38	19	6
1989	1,010	23	82	193	178	179	143	88	60	39	20	6
1990	1,041	24	85	200	178	186	148	92	61	41	21	6
1991	1,068	27	89	206	178	184	154	95	63	42	22	7
1992	1,081	21	87	212	180	184	159	100	64	43	22	8
Asian or Pacific Islander female												
1980												
1985	2,866	50	201	445	462	608	459	265	200	117	46	12
1988	3,433	58	226	525	557	699	583	325	240	147	57	15
1989	3,641	63	237	554	593	730	629	349	253	157	61	16
1990	3,805	65	247	578	621	749	664	371	264	166	65	17
1991	4,087	87	265	622	647	783	719	407	281	185	73	19
1992	4,279	80	277	649	670	810	756	443	295	199	79	20
Hispanic female												
1980	7,329	166	648	1,482	1,547	1,249	805	615	411	257	116	30
1985	9,093	199	749	1,755	1,814	1,704	1,092	719	540	317	163	42
1988	10,228	231	849	1,926	1,949	1,958	1,304	803	599	366	192	52
1989	10,632	252	897	1,989	1,986	2,025	1,382	840	617	386	202	56

[Continued]

★ 623 ★

Resident Population: Age, Gender, Race, and Hispanic Origin of the Population: 1950 to 1992.
Part 2
[Continued]

Sex, race, Hispanic origin, and year	Total resident population	Under 1 year	1-4 years	5-14 years	15-24 years	25-34 years	35-44 years	45-54 years	55-64 years	65-74 years	75-84 years	85 years and over
1990	10,966	268	939	2,039	2,028	2,073	1,448	868	632	403	209	59
1991	11,460	270	1,001	2,125	2,050	2,154	1,559	918	659	433	223	69
1992	11,871	304	1,065	2,194	2,050	2,210	1,636	975	677	456	231	73

Source: "Resident Population, According to Age, Sex, Detailed Race, and Hispanic Origin: United States, Selected Years 1950-92," *Health, United States, 1994*, pp. 63-64. Primary source: U.S. Bureau of the Census: 1950 Nonwhite Population by Race. Special Report P-E, No. 3B. Washington. U.S. Government Printing Office, 1951; U.S. Bureau of the Census, U.S. Census of Population: 1960, Number of inhabitants, PC(1)- A1, United States Summary, 1964; 1970, Number of Inhabitants, Final Report PC (1)- A1, United States Summary, 1971; U.S. Bureau of the Census: U.S. Population estimates, by age, sex, race, and Hispanic origin: 1980 to 1991. Current Population Reports. Series P-25, No. 1095. Washington. U.S. Government Printing Office, Feb. 1993: U.S. Bureau of the Census: U.S. Population estimates, by age, sex, race, and Hispanic origin: 1992. Census file RESP0792. 1994. *Notes:* The race groups, white and black, include persons of Hispanic and non- Hispanic origin. Conversely, persons of Hispanic origin may be of any race. Population figures are census counts as of April 1 for 1950, 1960, 1970, 1980, and 1990 and estimates as of July 1 for other years. Data for the 1980's are intercensal population estimates. See Appendix I, Department of Commerce. Populations for age groups may not sum to total due to rounding.

Children and Parents

★ 624 ★

Population Characteristics: Children Under 18 Years Old, by Presence of Parents: 1970 to 1994

[As of March. Excludes persons under 18 years old who maintained households or family groups. Based on Current Population Survey. In thousands, except as indicated. Excludes members of Armed forces except those living off post or with their families on post.]

RACE, HISPANIC ORIGIN, AND YEAR	Number (1,000)	Both parents	PERCENT LIVING WITH--					Father only	Neither parent
			Mother only						
			Total	Divorced	Married spouse absent	Never married	Wid-owed		
ALL RACES[1]									
1970	69,162	85	11	3	5	1	2	1	3
1980	63,427	77	18	8	6	3	2	2	4
1985	62,475	74	21	9	5	6	2	3	3
1990	64,137	73	22	8	5	7	2	3	3
1994	69,508	69	23	8	6	9	1	3	4
WHITE									
1970	58,790	90	8	3	3	(Z)	2	1	2
1980	52,242	83	14	7	4	1	2	2	2
1985	50,836	80	16	8	4	2	1	2	2
1990	51,390	79	16	8	4	3	1	3	2
1994	54,795	76	18	8	4	4	1	3	3

[Continued]

★ 624 ★

Population Characteristics: Children Under 18 Years Old, by Presence of Parents: 1970 to 1994

[Continued]

RACE, HISPANIC ORIGIN, AND YEAR	Number (1,000)	Both parents	PERCENT LIVING WITH--					Father only	Neither parent
			Mother only						
			Total	Divorced	Married spouse absent	Never married	Wid-owed		
BLACK									
1970	9,422	59	30	5	16	4	4	2	10
1980	9,375	42	44	11	16	13	4	2	12
1985	9,479	40	51	11	12	25	3	3	7
1990	10,018	38	51	10	12	27	2	4	8
1994	11,177	33	53	10	12	30	1	4	10
HISPANIC[2]									
1970	4,006[3]	78	(NA)	(NA)	(NA)	(NA)	(NA)	(NA)	(NA)
1980	5,459	75	20	6	8	4	2	2	4
1985	6,057	68	27	7	11	7	2	2	3
1990	7,174	67	27	7	10	8	2	3	3
1994	9,496	63	28	6	9	11	2	4	5

Source: "Children Under 18 Years Old, by Presence of Parents: 1970 to 1994," *Statistical Abstract of the United States: 1995*, p. 66. Primary source: U.S. Bureau of the Census, *Current Population Reports*, P20-450, and earlier reports; and unpublished data. *Notes:* NA Not available. Z Less than 0.5 percent. 1. Includes other races not shown separately. 2. Hispanic persons may be of any race. 3. All persons under 18 years old.

Distribution

★ 625 ★

Population by Region: Resident Population, Region and Division, 1960 to 1994

[As of April 1. For composition of regions, see table 27 of source.]

RACE AND HISPANIC ORIGIN	POPULATION (1,000)					PERCENT DISTRIBUTION				
	United States	North-east	Midwest	South	West	United States	North-east	Midwest	South	West
Total	248,710	50,809	59,669	85,446	52,786	100.0	20.4	24.0	34.4	21.2
White	199,686	42,069	52,018	65,582	40,017	100.0	21.1	26.0	32.8	20.0
Black	29,986	5,613	5,716	15,829	2,828	100.0	18.7	19.1	52.8	9.4
American Indian, Eskimo, Aleut	1,959	125	338	563	933	100.0	6.4	17.2	28.7	47.6
American Indian	1,878	122	334	557	866	100.0	6.5	17.8	29.7	46.1
Eskimo	57	2	2	3	51	100.0	2.9	3.5	4.9	88.8
Aleut	24	2	2	3	17	100.0	8.1	8.1	11.5	72.3

[Continued]

★ 625 ★

Population by Region: Resident Population, Region and Division, 1960 to 1994

[Continued]

RACE AND HISPANIC ORIGIN	POPULATION (1,000)					PERCENT DISTRIBUTION				
	United States	North-east	Midwest	South	West	United States	North-east	Midwest	South	West
Asian or Pacific Islander	7,274	1,335	768	1,122	4,048	100.0	18.4	10.6	15.4	55.7
Chinese	1,645	445	133	204	863	100.0	27.0	8.1	12.4	52.4
Filipino	1,407	143	113	159	991	100.0	10.2	8.1	11.3	70.5
Japanese	848	74	63	67	643	100.0	8.8	7.5	7.9	75.9
Asian Indian	815	285	146	196	189	100.0	35.0	17.9	24.0	23.1
Korean	799	182	109	153	355	100.0	22.8	13.7	19.2	44.4
Vietnamese	615	61	52	169	334	100.0	9.8	8.5	27.4	54.3
Laotian	149	16	28	29	76	100.0	10.7	18.6	19.6	51.0
Cambodian	147	30	13	19	85	100.0	20.5	8.8	13.1	57.7
Thai	91	12	13	24	43	100.0	12.9	14.2	26.0	46.8
Hmong	90	2	37	2	50	100.0	1.9	41.3	1.8	55.0
Pakistani	81	28	15	22	17	100.0	34.3	18.9	26.5	20.4
Hawaiian	211	4	6	12	189	100.0	2.0	2.6	5.8	89.6
Samoan	63	2	2	4	55	100.0	2.4	3.6	6.4	87.6
Guamanian	49	4	3	8	34	100.0	7.3	6.4	16.8	69.5
Other Asian or Pacific Islander	263	49	34	54	126	100.0	18.6	12.9	20.5	48.0
Other races	9,805	1,667	829	2,350	4,960	100.0	17.0	8.5	24.0	50.6
Hispanic origin[1]	22,354	3,754	1,727	6,767	10,106	100.0	16.8	7.7	30.3	45.2
Mexican	13,496	175	1,153	4,344	7,824	100.0	1.3	8.5	32.2	58.0
Puerto Rican	2,728	1,872	258	406	192	100.0	68.6	9.4	14.9	7.0
Cuban	1,044	184	37	735	88	100.0	17.6	3.5	70.5	8.5
Other Hispanic	5,086	1,524	279	1,282	2,002	100.0	30.0	5.5	25.2	39.4
Not of Hispanic origin	226,356	47,055	57,942	78,679	42,680	100.0	20.8	25.6	34.8	18.9

Source: "Resident Population, by Region and Division: 1960 to 1994," *Statistical Abstract of the United States: 1995,* p. 31. Primary source: U.S. Bureau of the Census, *1990 Census of Population, General Population Characteristics, United States* (CP-1-1). *Note:* 1. Persons of Hispanic origin may be of any race.

Household Characteristics

★ 626 ★

All-Black Households: Age

[Numbers in thousands except for averages and medians].

Characteristic	Total	Family households				Nonfamily households		
		Total	Married-couple	Other family		Total	Male householder	Female householder
				Male householder	Female householder			
ALL BLACK HOUSEHOLDS								
Households With Householder 65 Years and Over								
Households	1,767	944	561	49	335	823	208	615
No nonrelatives	1,712	929	553	48	328	783	181	602
Some nonrelatives	56	15	8	-	7	41	28	13
One nonrelative	51	14	8	-	7	36	25	12
Two nonrelatives	2	-	-	-	-	1	-	1
Three to 8 nonrelatives	3	-	-	-	-	3	3	-
Total nonrelatives	85	21	9	1	11	64	36	28
Average per household	.05	.02	.02	.02	.03	.08	.17	.04
Members 18 and Over, Other Than Householder or Spouse								
Households	11,281	7,989	3,714	450	3,825	3,292	1,452	1,840
No other members 18 and over	7,617	4,799	2,622	109	2,068	2,817	1,147	1,671
One other member 18 and over	2,640	2,215	768	259	1,188	425	261	163
Two or more other members 18 and over	1,025	975	324	82	569	50	44	5
Related Children Under 18								
Households	11,281	7,989	3,714	450	3,825	3,292	1,452	1,840
Without any related children under 18	5,758	2,466	1,568	156	742	3,292	1,452	1,840
With related children under 18	5,523	5,523	2,146	295	3,083	-	-	-
One child under 18	2,246	2,246	823	173	1,250	-	-	-
Two children under 18	1,821	1,821	801	79	941	-	-	-
Three children under 18	869	869	326	30	513	-	-	-
Four or more children under 18	587	587	196	13	378	-	-	-
Total related children under 18	10,794	10,794	4,204	482	6,107	-	-	-
Average per household	.96	1.35	1.13	1.07	1.60	-	-	-
Average per household with children	1.95	1.95	1.96	1.64	1.98	(B)	(B)	(B)
Own Children Under 18								
Households	11,281	7,989	3,714	450	3,825	3,292	1,452	1,840
Without own children under 18	6,488	3,196	1,790	212	1,194	3,292	1,452	1,840
With own children under 18	4,793	4,793	1,924	238	2,630	-	-	-
One child under 18	1,983	1,983	771	144	1,068	-	-	-
Two children under 18	1,630	1,630	696	63	871	-	-	-
Three children under 18	755	755	309	29	417	-	-	-
Four children under 18	301	301	110	3	188	-	-	-
Five children under 18	70	70	23	-	48	-	-	-
Six or more children under 18	53	53	16	-	38	-	-	-
Total own children under 18	8,884	8,884	3,602	375	4,907	-	-	-

[Continued]

★ 626 ★

All-Black Households: Age
[Continued]

Characteristic	Total	Family households		Other family		Nonfamily households		
		Total	Married-couple	Male householder	Female householder	Total	Male householder	Female householder
Average per household	.79	1.11	.97	.83	1.28	-	-	-
Average per household with children	1.85	1.85	1.87	1.57	1.87	(B)	(B)	(B)

Source: "Households, by Type, Tenure, and Race and Hispanic Origin of Householder: March 1994." Steve W. Rawlings, and Arlene F. Saluter, *Household and Family Characteristics: March 1994*, p. 141. *Note:* B = Base less than 75,000.

★ 627 ★

Household Characteristics

All-Black Households: Characteristics. Part 1

[Numbers in thousands except for averages and medians].

Characteristic	Total	Family households		Other family		Nonfamily households		
		Total	Married-couple	Male householder	Female householder	Total	Male householder	Female householder
ALL BLACK HOUSEHOLDS								
Size of Household								
Households	11,281	7,969	3,714	450	3,825	3,292	1,452	1,840
One person	2,804	-	-	-	-	2,804	1,147	1,657
Two persons	2,918	2,536	1,074	186	1,277	381	215	166
Three persons	2,256	2,182	875	111	1,196	74	58	16
Four persons	1,760	1,733	945	92	695	27	27	-
Five persons	867	861	452	49	360	6	6	-
Six persons	363	363	220	4	139	-	-	-
Seven or more persons	312	312	147	8	157	-	-	-
Total persons	32,724	28,648	13,769	1,513	13,365	4,076	1,946	2,131
Persons per household	2.90	3.59	3.71	3.36	3.49	1.24	1.34	1.16
Metropolitan-Nonmetropolitan Residence								
Households	11,281	7,969	3,714	450	3,825	3,292	1,452	1,840
In MSA's	9,771	6,839	3,143	410	3,286	2,932	1,288	1,644
Central cities	6,543	4,363	1,773	253	2,357	2,159	937	1,222
Ring	3,226	2,455	1,369	157	928	773	351	422
MSA's of 2,500,000 or more	4,417	3,021	1,378	176	1,467	1,396	627	770
Central cities	3,067	1,993	779	114	1,100	1,074	471	603
Ring	1,351	1,029	599	63	367	322	156	166
MSA's of 1,000,000 to 2,499,999	2,323	1,835	723	67	845	687	319	369
Central cities	1,485	1,030	374	40	617	454	204	251
Ring	838	805	349	28	228	233	115	118
MSA's of 250,000 to 999,999	2,187	1,555	729	118	708	632	257	375
Central cities	1,448	959	418	73	468	489	209	281
Ring	739	596	311	45	240	143	48	94
MSA's of 249,999 or less	844	627	313	49	265	216	86	131

[Continued]

★ 627 ★

All-Black Households: Characteristics. Part 1

[Continued]

Characteristic	Total	Family households				Nonfamily households		
		Total	Married-couple	Other family		Total	Male householder	Female householder
				Male householder	Female householder			
Central cities	543	402	203	27	172	141	54	88
Ring	301	226	111	22	92	75	32	43
Not in MSA's	1,510	1,150	571	40	539	360	164	196
Nonrelatives in Household								
Households	11,261	7,989	3,714	450	3,825	3,292	1,452	1,840
No nonrelatives	10,371	7,567	3,649	316	3,602	2,804	1,147	1,657
Some nonrelatives	910	421	65	134	222	488	306	182
One nonrelative	727	346	45	102	199	381	215	166
Two nonrelatives	121	47	10	21	16	74	58	16
Three to 8 nonrelatives	62	28	10	10	8	33	33	-
Total nonrelatives	1,483	696	124	186	389	785	494	291
Average per household	.13	.09	.03	.41	.10	.24	.34	.16

Source: "Households, by Type, Tenure, and Race and Hispanic Origin of Householder: March 1994." Steve W. Rawlings, and Arlene F. Saluter, *Household and Family Characteristics: March 1994*, p. 141.

★ 628 ★

Household Characteristics

All-Black Households: Characteristics. Part 2

[Numbers in thousands except for averages and medians].

Characteristic	Total	Family households				Nonfamily households		
		Total	Married-couple	Other family		Total	Male householder	Female householder
				Male householder	Female householder			
ALL BLACK HOUSEHOLDS								
Age of Householder								
Households	11,281	7,989	3,714	450	3,825	3,292	1,452	1,840
15 to 19 years	91	65	1	6	58	26	7	18
20 to 24 years	682	510	117	33	359	172	88	84
25 to 29 years	1,198	882	317	67	498	316	158	158
30 to 34 years	1,546	1,181	433	91	657	365	228	137
35 to 39 years	1,504	1,178	465	70	643	326	211	115
40 to 44 years	1,322	1,006	520	45	440	317	166	151
45 to 49 years	1,058	782	427	31	324	276	138	138
50 to 54 years	798	597	356	33	209	201	78	122
55 to 59 years	688	476	284	16	176	213	79	134
60 to 64 years	626	368	233	9	125	258	91	168
65 to 74 years	1,071	613	374	31	208	458	122	337
75 to 84 years	553	290	172	13	105	264	73	191
85 years and over	143	41	14	5	22	102	14	88
Median	42.3	40.9	45.0	36.9	37.6	47.3	41.0	54.9

[Continued]

★ 628 ★

All-Black Households: Characteristics. Part 2
[Continued]

Characteristic	Total	Family households				Nonfamily households		
		Total	Married-couple	Other family		Total	Male householder	Female householder
				Male householder	Female householder			
Marital Status of Householder								
Households	11,281	7,989	3,714	450	3,825	3,292	1,452	1,840
Married, spouse present	3,714	3,714	3,714	-	-	-	-	-
Married, spouse absent	1,306	866	-	91	774	441	258	182
Separated	1,120	743	-	71	672	377	215	162
Other	187	123	-	20	103	64	43	21
Widowed	1,319	553	-	44	509	765	136	630
Divorced	1,775	1,029	-	142	886	746	335	411
Never married	3,167	1,827	-	172	1,655	1,340	724	617
Units in Structure								
Households[1]	11,281	7,989	3,714	450	3,825	3,292	1,452	1,840
One unit	5,340	4,247	2,436	203	1,607	1,093	441	651
Two units	817	612	195	36	381	205	75	130
Three or 4 units	633	408	103	25	280	225	107	117
Five to 9 units	1,001	686	188	50	448	315	166	149
Ten or more units	2,096	1,059	319	67	672	1,037	463	574

Source: "Households, by Type, Tenure, and Race and Hispanic Origin of Householder: March 1994." Steve W. Rawlings, and Arlene F. Saluter, *Household and Family Characteristics: March 1994*, p. 142.

★ 629 ★

Household Characteristics

Households by Type, Age, and Size: March 1994. Part 1

Characteristic	Total	Age of householder				
		Under 20 years	20 to 24 years	25 to 29 years	30 to 34 years	35 to 39 years
UNITED STATES-BLACK						
Households by Type						
All households	11,281	91	682	1,198	1,546	1,504
Family households	7,989	65	510	882	1,181	1,178
Married-couple family	3,714	1	117	317	433	465
Other family, male householder	450	6	33	67	91	70
Other family, female householder	3,825	58	359	498	657	643
Nonfamily households	3,292	26	172	316	365	326
Male householder	1,452	7	88	158	228	211
Female householder	1,840	18	84	158	137	115

[Continued]

★ 629 ★

Households by Type, Age, and Size: March 1994. Part 1

[Continued]

Characteristic	Total	Age of householder				
		Under 20 years	20 to 24 years	25 to 29 years	30 to 34 years	35 to 39 years
Age of Household Members						
All members	32,724	230	1,769	3,439	4,797	4,695
Under 18 years	11,070	84	720	1,596	2,382	2,088
18 to 64 years	19,142	145	1,045	1,836	2,407	2,577
65 years and over	2,512	-	4	7	8	30
Households with members:						
Under 18 years	5,632	67	450	787	1,097	1,057
18 to 64 years	10,130	89	682	1,198	1,546	1,504
65 years and over	1,985	-	5	9	9	26
Average per household	2.90	2.52	2.59	2.87	3.10	3.12
Under 18 years	.98	.93	1.06	1.33	1.54	1.39
18 to 64 years	1.70	1.60	1.53	1.53	1.56	1.71
65 years and over	.22	-	.01	.01	.01	.02
Size of Household						
Households	11,281	91	682	1,198	1,546	1,504
One person	2,804	9	100	232	285	278
Two persons	2,918	41	236	270	319	305
Three persons	2,256	25	173	275	345	318
Four persons	1,760	11	111	237	326	313
Five persons	867	3	47	115	155	161
Six persons	363	2	12	49	43	73
Seven or more persons	312	-	3	20	74	56
Total persons	32,724	230	1,769	3,439	4,797	4,695
Persons per household	2.90	2.52	2.59	2.87	3.10	3.12

Source: "Households, by Type, Age of Members, Age, Region of Residence, Race, and Hispanic Origin of Householder: March 1994," Steve W. Rawlings and Arlene F. Saluter, *Household and Family Characteristics: March 1994*, p. 158.

★ 630 ★
Household Characteristics

Households by Type, Age, and Size: March 1994. Part 2

Characteristic	Age of householder						
	40 to 44 years	45 to 54 years	55 to 64 years	65 to 74 years	75 to 84 years	85 years and over	Median age
UNITED STATES-BLACK							
Households by Type							
All households	1,322	1,856	1,315	1,071	553	143	42.3
Family households	1,006	1,379	844	613	290	41	40.9
Married-couple family	520	783	517	374	172	14	45.0
Other family, male householder	45	63	25	31	13	5	36.9
Other family, female householder	440	533	301	208	105	22	37.6
Nonfamily households	317	476	471	458	264	102	47.3
Male householder	166	216	169	122	73	14	41.0
Female householder	151	260	302	337	191	88	54.9
Age of Household Members							
All members	4,257	5,876	3,645	2,644	1,142	230	(X)
Under 18 years	1,554	1,493	736	328	80	7	(X)
18 to 64 years	2,674	4,327	2,799	971	324	38	(X)
65 years and over	30	57	109	1,345	738	185	(X)
Households with members:							
Under 18 years	792	800	342	188	44	6	37.0
18 to 64 years	1,322	1,856	1,315	452	147	20	40.2
65 years and over	26	51	93	1,071	553	143	72.0
Average per household	3.22	3.17	2.77	2.47	2.06	1.61	(X)
Under 18 years	1.18	.80	.56	.31	.14	.05	(X)
18 to 64 years	2.02	2.33	2.13	.91	.59	.27	(X)
65 years and over	.02	.03	.08	1.26	1.33	1.30	(X)
Size of Household							
Households	1,322	1,856	1,315	1,071	553	143	42.3
One person	279	408	431	428	257	98	49.6
Two persons	298	501	399	320	200	30	44.8
Three persons	259	407	219	162	61	11	39.9
Four persons	240	275	127	104	16	2	38.1
Five persons	134	133	67	33	16	2	38.5
Six persons	68	65	35	16	-	-	40.2
Seven or more persons	44	67	36	9	4	-	40.4
Total persons	4,257	5,876	3,645	2,644	1,142	230	(X)
Persons per household	3.22	3.17	2.77	2.47	2.06	1.61	(X)

Source: "Households, by Type, Age of Members, Age, Region of Residence, Race, and Hispanic Origin of Householder: March 1994," Steve W. Rawlings and Arlene F. Saluter, *Household and Family Characteristics: March 1994*, p. 158. *Note:* X - Not applicable.

★ 631 ★
Household Characteristics

Households by Type, Age, and Size: March 1994. Part 1-1 - Northeast

(Numbers in thousands except for averages and medians).

Characteristic	Total	Age of householder				
		Under 20 years	20 to 24 years	25 to 29 years	30 to 34 years	35 to 39 years
NORTHEAST-BLACK						
Households by Type						
All households	1,935	15	81	201	265	256
Family households	1,298	13	59	132	193	189
Married-couple family	590	-	14	46	64	78
Other family, male householder	67	5	6	7	7	8
Other family, female householder	641	9	39	79	122	104
Nonfamily households	637	2	22	69	72	67
Male householder	241	-	7	24	37	37
Female householder	396	2	15	45	34	30
Age of Household Members						
All members	5,531	44	199	523	815	764
Under 18 years	1,791	15	64	227	384	346
18 to 64 years	3,337	29	133	295	429	415
65 years and over	404	-	2	-	2	2
Households with members:						
Under 18 years	900	11	43	118	172	172
18 to 64 years	1,740	15	81	201	265	256
65 years and over	333	-	3	-	2	2
Average per household	2.86	(B)	2.45	2.60	3.08	2.98
Under 18 years	.93	(B)	.79	1.13	1.45	1.35
18 to 64 years	1.72	(B)	1.63	1.47	1.62	1.62
65 years and over	.21	(B)	.03	-	0.1	0.1
Size of Household						
Households	1,935	15	81	201	265	256
One person	551	2	17	51	53	58
Two persons	486	3	30	55	57	49
Three persons	377	8	16	42	66	50
Four persons	280	-	9	28	49	53
Five persons	122	-	7	14	24	22
Six persons	56	2	2	7	4	13
Seven or more persons	62	-	-	4	11	10

[Continued]

★ 631 ★

Households by Type, Age, and Size: March 1994. Part 1-1 - Northeast
[Continued]

| Characteristic | Total | Age of householder | | | | |
		Under 20 years	20 to 24 years	25 to 29 years	30 to 34 years	35 to 39 years
Total persons	5,531	44	199	523	815	764
Persons per household	2.86	(B)	2.45	2.60	3.08	2.98

Source: "Households, by type, Age of Members, Age, Region of Residence, Race, and Hispanic Origin of Householder: March 1994," Steve W. Rawlings and Arlene F. Sautler, *Household and Family Characteristics: March 1994*, p. 160 *Note:* B - less than 75,000; X - Not applicable.

★ 632 ★

Household Characteristics

Households by Type, Age, and Size: March 1994. Part 1-2 - Northeast

(Numbers in thousands except for averages and medians).

| Characteristic | Age of householder | | | | | | Median age |
	40 to 44 years	45 to 54 years	55 to 64 years	65 to 74 years	75 to 84 years	85 years and over	
NORTHEAST-BLACK							
Households by Type							
All households	233	372	225	166	103	18	43.2
Family households	168	260	139	101	38	5	41.8
Married-couple family	83	146	82	53	25	-	45.7
Other family, male householder	9	11	3	10	2	-	(B)
Other family, female householder	75	104	54	39	12	5	38.4
Nonfamily households	65	112	87	64	64	14	46.7
Male householder	27	41	32	5	16	4	42.8
Female householder	38	70	55	50	48	10	49.1
Age of Household Members							
All members	761	1,145	646	416	186	32	(X)
Under 18 years	308	244	151	42	7	1	(X)
18 to 64 years	448	887	479	171	44	7	(X)
65 years and over	6	14	17	203	134	23	(X)
Households with members:							
Under 18 years	143	140	64	32	3	2	38.1
18 to 64 years	233	372	225	74	14	5	41.1
65 years and over	7	15	17	166	103	18	72.0
Average per household	3.27	3.08	2.87	2.51	1.81	(B)	(X)
Under 18 years	1.32	.86	.67	.25	.07	(B)	(X)
18 to 64 years	1.92	2.38	2.13	1.03	.43	(B)	(X)
65 years and over	.02	.04	.07	1.23	1.31	(B)	(X)

[Continued]

★ 632 ★

Households by Type, Age, and Size: March 1994. Part 1-2 - Northeast

[Continued]

Characteristic	Age of householder						Median age
	40 to 44 years	45 to 54 years	55 to 64 years	65 to 74 years	75 to 84 years	85 years and over	
Size of Household							
Households	233	372	225	166	103	18	43.2
One person	63	93	77	63	63	12	48.2
Two persons	35	106	65	55	26	5	46.5
Three persons	44	68	44	26	9	2	40.5
Four persons	40	60	18	19	4	-	40.1
Five persons	28	22	3	2	-	-	38.6
Six persons	13	14	2	-	-	-	(B)
Seven or more persons	11	8	15	1	1	-	(B)
Total persons	761	1,145	646	416	186	32	(X)
Persons per household	3.27	3.08	2.87	2.51	1.81	(B)	(X)

Source: "Households, by type, Age of Members, Age, Region of Residence, Race, and Hispanic Origin of Householder: March 1994," Steve W. Rawlings and Arlene F. Sautler, *Household and Family Characteristics: March 1994*, p. 160 *Note:* B - less than 75,000; X - Not applicable.

★ 633 ★

Household Characteristics

Households by Type, Age, and Size: March 1994. Part 2-1 - Midwest

(Numbers in thousands except for averages and medians).

Characteristic	Total	Age of householder				
		Under 20 years	20 to 24 years	25 to 29 years	30 to 34 years	35 to 39 years
NORTHEAST-BLACK						
Households by Type						
All households	2,383	18	192	254	359	320
Family households	1,643	12	148	193	273	240
Married-couple family	598	-	7	44	83	64
Other family, male householder	102	-	8	21	21	18
Other family, female householder	944	12	133	127	168	158
Nonfamily households	740	6	44	62	86	80
Male householder	323	4	25	23	54	57
Female householder	417	2	18	39	32	23
Age of Household Members						
All members	6,619	35	472	738	1,093	940
Under 18 years	2,342	15	229	388	546	432
18 to 64 years	3,758	20	242	350	547	499
65 years and over	519	-	-	-	-	8

[Continued]

★ 633 ★

Households by Type, Age, and Size: March 1994. Part 2-1 - Midwest
[Continued]

Characteristic	Total	Age of householder				
		Under 20 years	20 to 24 years	25 to 29 years	30 to 34 years	35 to 39 years
Households with members:						
Under 18 years	1,205	14	144	176	257	238
18 to 64 years	2,141	16	192	254	359	320
65 years and over	415	-	-	-	-	6
Average per household	2.78	(B)	2.46	2.90	3.04	2.93
Under 18 years	.98	(B)	1.20	1.53	1.52	1.35
18 to 64 years	1.58	(B)	1.26	1.38	1.52	1.56
65 years and over	.22	(B)	-	-	-	.03
Size of Household						
Households	2,383	18	192	254	359	320
One person	639	2	25	56	64	68
Two persons	622	11	76	51	83	65
Three persons	463	5	43	51	83	77
Four persons	354	-	35	49	66	55
Five persons	158	-	9	31	32	28
Six persons	89	-	5	13	13	21
Seven or more persons	59	-	-	5	19	6
Total persons	6,619	35	472	738	1,093	940
Persons per household	2.78	(B)	2.46	2.90	3.04	2.93

Source: "Households, by type, Age of Members, Age, Region of Residence, Race, and Hispanic Origin of Householder: March 1994," Steve W. Rawlings and Arlene F. Sautler, *Household and Family Characteristics: March 1994*, p. 162. *Note:* B - less than 75,000; X - Not applicable.

★ 634 ★

Household Characteristics

Households by Type, Age, and Size: March 1994. Part 2-2 - Midwest

(Numbers in thousands except for averages and medians).

Characteristic	Age of householder						Median age
	40 to 44 years	45 to 54 years	55 to 64 years	65 to 74 years	75 to 84 years	85 years and over	
NORTHEAST-BLACK							
Households by Type							
All households	259	349	268	227	111	28	40.9
Family households	193	243	162	130	44	5	39.1
Married-couple family	82	129	92	75	19	4	46.3
Other family, male householder	6	12	6	7	1	-	35.0

[Continued]

★ 634 ★

Households by Type, Age, and Size: March 1994. Part 2-2 - Midwest
[Continued]

Characteristic	Age of householder						
	40 to 44 years	45 to 54 years	55 to 64 years	65 to 74 years	75 to 84 years	85 years and over	Median age
Other family, female householder	105	102	65	49	24	1	36.0
Nonfamily households	66	105	105	97	67	22	47.2
Male householder	33	52	34	23	17	-	39.8
Female householder	33	53	72	73	50	22	56.7
Age of Household Members							
All members	775	1,034	745	570	186	33	(X)
Under 18 years	278	253	141	52	8	-	(X)
18 to 64 years	492	770	569	224	46	-	(X)
65 years and over	5	11	35	294	132	33	(X)
Households with members:							
Under 18 years	137	142	61	29	7	-	35.3
18 to 64 years	259	349	268	98	27	-	38.9
65 years and over	5	12	26	227	111	28	72.1
Average per household	2.99	2.97	2.78	2.51	1.67	(B)	(X)
Under 18 years	1.07	.73	.53	.23	.07	(B)	(X)
18 to 64 years	1.90	2.21	2.12	.99	.41	(B)	(X)
65 years and over	.02	.03	.13	1.30	1.19	(B)	(X)
Size of Household							
Households	259	349	268	227	111	28	40.9
One person	58	95	95	90	65	22	49.0
Two persons	69	86	78	67	32	5	41.9
Three persons	51	73	31	38	11	-	38.3
Four persons	47	53	28	18	3	-	37.5
Five persons	18	14	20	7	-	-	36.4
Six persons	5	14	13	5	-	-	38.4
Seven or more persons	11	13	2	2	-	-	(B)
Total persons	775	1,034	745	570	186	33	(X)
Persons per household	2.99	2.97	2.78	2.51	1.67	(B)	(X)

Source: "Households, by type, Age of Members, Age, Region of Residence, Race, and Hispanic Origin of Householder: March 1994," Steve W. Rawlings and Arlene F. Sautler, *Household and Family Characteristics: March 1994*, p. 162. *Note:* B - less than 75,000; X - Not applicable.

★ 635 ★

Household Characteristics

Households by Type, Age, and Size: March 1994. Part 3-1 - South

(Numbers in thousands except for averages and medians).

Characteristic	Total	Age of householder				
		Under 20 years	20 to 24 years	25 to 29 years	30 to 34 years	35 to 39 years
SOUTH-BLACK						
Households by Type						
All households	6,058	53	342	651	787	820
Family households	4,456	36	264	500	622	666
Married-couple family	2,188	1	79	193	242	276
Other family, male householder	261	2	14	38	60	44
Other family, female householder	2,007	34	170	269	320	345
Nonfamily households	1,601	17	78	151	165	154
Male householder	730	3	39	86	111	98
Female householder	871	13	39	65	54	56
Age of Household Members						
All members	18,132	137	923	1,952	2,478	2,675
Under 18 years	6,111	46	367	901	1,256	1,188
18 to 64 years	10,613	91	554	1,047	1,216	1,469
65 years and over	1,408	-	2	5	6	18
Households with members:						
Under 18 years	3,092	38	226	449	580	580
18 to 64 years	5,431	53	342	651	787	820
65 years and over	1,091	-	2	6	7	16
Average per household	2.99	(B)	2.70	3.00	3.15	3.26
Under 18 years	1.01	(B)	1.07	1.38	1.60	1.45
18 to 64 years	1.75	(B)	1.62	1.61	1.55	1.79
65 years and over	.23	(B)	.01	.01	.01	.02
Size of Household						
Households	6,058	53	342	651	787	820
One person	1,360	5	44	103	140	131
Two persons	1,576	26	109	137	152	168
Three persons	1,258	8	100	164	171	171
Four persons	979	11	59	145	181	181
Five persons	505	3	23	63	80	92
Six persons	201	-	5	28	18	37
Seven or more persons	179	-	3	11	43	40

[Continued]

★ 635 ★

Households by Type, Age, and Size: March 1994. Part 3-1 - South

[Continued]

Characteristic	Total	Age of householder				
		Under 20 years	20 to 24 years	25 to 29 years	30 to 34 years	35 to 39 years
Total persons	18,132	137	923	1,952	2,478	2,675
Persons per household	2.99	(B)	2.70	3.00	3.15	3.26

Source: "Households, by type, Age of Members, Age, Region of Residence, Race, and Hispanic Origin of Householder: March 1994," Steve W. Rawlings and Arlene F. Sautler, *Household and Family Characteristics: March 1994*, p. 164. *Note:* B - less than 75,000; X - Not applicable.

★ 636 ★

Household Characteristics

Households by Type, Age, and Size: March 1994. Part 3-2 - South

(Numbers in thousands except for averages and medians).

Characteristic	Age of householder						
	40 to 44 years	45 to 54 years	55 to 64 years	65 to 74 years	75 to 84 years	85 years and over	Median age
SOUTH-BLACK							
Households by Type							
All households	725	993	701	590	307	90	42.6
Family households	566	789	461	335	187	31	41.2
Married-couple family	303	462	295	216	112	10	45.0
Other family, male householder	24	38	16	10	10	5	36.8
Other family, female householder	239	290	150	109	65	16	38.0
Nonfamily households	159	204	240	256	120	59	48.0
Male householder	92	95	87	72	36	10	41.5
Female householder	67	109	152	184	84	49	57.4
Age of Household Members							
All members	2,384	3,304	1,949	1,469	703	158	(X)
Under 18 years	828	888	373	199	59	6	(X)
18 to 64 years	1,537	2,391	1,530	529	219	31	(X)
65 years and over	19	24	47	741	424	121	(X)
Households with members:							
Under 18 years	442	463	169	109	32	4	37.2
18 to 64 years	725	993	701	246	99	15	40.4
65 years and over	14	18	42	590	307	90	72.1
Average per household	3.29	3.33	2.78	2.49	2.29	1.76	(X)
Under 18 years	1.14	.89	.53	.34	.19	.07	(X)
18 to 64 years	2.12	2.41	2.18	.90	.71	.34	(X)
65 years and over	.03	.02	.07	1.26	1.38	1.35	(X)

[Continued]

★ 636 ★

Households by Type, Age, and Size: March 1994. Part 3-2 - South

[Continued]

Characteristic	Age of householder						
	40 to 44 years	45 to 54 years	55 to 64 years	65 to 74 years	75 to 84 years	85 years and over	Median age
Size of Household							
Households	725	993	701	590	307	90	42.6
One person	136	170	222	236	117	57	51.2
Two persons	172	272	222	176	123	20	45.8
Three persons	147	245	120	82	40	9	40.5
Four persons	126	144	61	58	10	2	37.6
Five persons	80	87	37	22	16	2	39.5
Six persons	45	37	19	11	-	-	41.3
Seven or more persons	19	38	19	5	1	-	39.1
Total persons	2,384	3,304	1,949	1,469	703	158	(X)
Persons per household	3.29	3.33	2.78	2.49	2.29	1.76	(X)

Source: "Households, by type, Age of Members, Age, Region of Residence, Race, and Hispanic Origin of Householder: March 1994," Steve W. Rawlings and Arlene F. Sautler, *Household and Family Characteristics: March 1994*, p. 164. *Note:* B - less than 75,000; X - Not applicable.

★ 637 ★

Household Characteristics

Households by Type, Age, and Size: March 1994. Part 4-1 - West

(Numbers in thousands except for averages and medians).

Characteristic	Total	Age of householder				
		Under 20 years	20 to 24 years	25 to 29 years	30 to 34 years	35 to 39 years
WEST-BLACK						
Households by Type						
All households	904	5	68	92	135	108
Family households	591	4	39	57	93	83
Married-couple family	338	-	18	35	45	47
Other family, male householder	21	-	5	-	3	-
Other family, female householder	232	4	17	22	46	37
Nonfamily households	313	1	28	35	42	24
Male householder	158	-	16	26	26	18
Female householder	155	1	12	9	17	6
Age of Household Members						
All members	2,442	13	176	226	412	317
Under 18 years	826	8	59	80	197	122
18 to 64 years	1,434	6	117	143	215	194
65 years and over	182	-	-	3	-	2

[Continued]

★ 637 ★

Households by Type, Age, and Size: March 1994. Part 4-1 - West

[Continued]

Characteristic	Total	Age of householder				
		Under 20 years	20 to 24 years	25 to 29 years	30 to 34 years	35 to 39 years
Households with members:						
Under 18 years	436	5	37	44	89	67
18 to 64 years	817	5	68	92	135	108
65 years and over	146	-	-	2	-	2
Average per household	2.70	(B)	(B)	2.46	3.04	2.94
Under 18 years	.91	(B)	(B)	.87	1.46	1.13
18 to 64 years	1.59	(B)	(B)	1.56	1.59	1.80
65 years and over	.20	(B)	(B)	.03	-	.02
Size of Household						
Households	904	5	68	92	135	108
One person	254	-	14	22	30	20
Two persons	234	1	22	28	27	23
Three persons	158	4	15	18	24	20
Four persons	147	-	8	15	29	23
Five persons	82	-	9	8	18	19
Six persons	17	-	-	1	8	2
Seven or more persons	12	-	-	-	-	-
Total persons	2,442	13	176	226	412	317
Persons per household	2.70	(B)	(B)	2.46	3.04	2.94

Source: "Households, by Type, Age of Members, Age, Region of Residence, Race, and Hispanic Origin of Householder: March 1994," Steve W. Rawlings and Arlene F. Saluter, *Household and Family Characteristics: March 1994*, p. 166. *Note:* B - less than 75,000; X - Not applicable.

★ 638 ★

Household Characteristics

Households by Type, Age, and Size: March 1994. Part 4-2 - West

(Numbers in thousands except for averages and medians).

Characteristic	Age of householder						
	40 to 44 years	45 to 54 years	55 to 64 years	65 to 74 years	75 to 84 years	85 years and over	Median age
WEST-BLACK							
Households by Type							
All households	105	142	121	88	33	7	42.1
Family households	79	87	82	47	20	-	41.2
Married-couple family	52	46	49	31	16	-	42.4
Other family, male householder	6	3	-	4	-	-	(B)

[Continued]

★ 638 ★

Households by Type, Age, and Size: March 1994. Part 4-2 - West
[Continued]

Characteristic	Age of householder						
	40 to 44 years	45 to 54 years	55 to 64 years	65 to 74 years	75 to 84 years	85 years and over	Median age
Other family, female householder	21	38	33	11	4	-	38.7
Nonfamily households	27	55	39	41	12	7	44.7
Male householder	14	27	16	12	4	-	38.1
Female householder	13	28	23	30	9	7	52.8
Age of Household Members							
All members	337	394	305	189	67	7	(X)
Under 18 years	140	108	71	35	5	-	(X)
18 to 64 years	197	279	222	48	15	-	(X)
65 years and over	-	6	11	106	47	7	(X)
Households with members:							
Under 18 years	71	55	48	19	2	-	38.2
18 to 64 years	105	142	121	34	7	-	40.0
65 years and over	-	6	8	88	33	7	71.0
Average per household	3.20	2.78	2.52	2.14	(B)	(B)	(X)
Under 18 years	1.33	7.6	.59	.40	(B)	(B)	(X)
18 to 64 years	1.87	1.97	1.84	.54	(B)	(B)	(X)
65 years and over	-	.05	.09	1.20	(B)	(B)	(X)
Size of Household							
Households	105	142	121	88	33	7	42.1
One person	23	50	37	39	12	7	49.3
Two persons	22	36	34	22	19	-	43.7
Three persons	17	21	23	16	-	-	39.5
Four persons	27	18	19	8	-	-	39.7
Five persons	8	10	8	3	-	-	36.6
Six persons	6	-	-	-	-	-	(B)
Seven or more persons	3	7	-	-	2	-	(B)
Total persons	337	394	305	189	67	7	(X)
Persons per household	3.20	2.78	2.52	2.14	(B)	(B)	(X)

Source: "Households, by Type, Age of Members, Age, Region of Residence, Race, and Hispanic Origin of Householder: March 1994," Steve W. Rawlings and Arlene F. Saluter, *Household and Family Characteristics: March 1994*, p. 166. *Note:* B - less than 75,000; X - Not applicable.

Marital Status

★ 639 ★

Marital Status: Gender, Race, and Hispanic Origin: 1970 to 1994

[In millions, except percent. As of March, except as noted. Persons 18 years old and over. Excludes members of Armed Forces except those living off post or with their families on post. Except as noted, based on Current Population Survey, see text, section 1, and Appendix III. See *Historical Statistics, Colonial Times to 1970*, series A 160-171, for decennial data.]

MARITAL STATUS, RACE, AND HISPANIC ORIGIN	TOTAL				MALE				FEMALE			
	1970	1980	1990	1994	1970	1980	1990	1994	1970	1980	1990	1994
Total[1]	132.5	159.5	181.8	190.0	62.5	75.7	86.9	91.2	70.0	83.8	95.0	98.6
Never married	21.4	32.3	40.4	44.2	11.8	18.0	22.4	24.7	9.6	14.3	17.9	19.5
Married	95.0	104.6	112.6	115.1	47.1	51.8	55.8	57.0	47.9	52.8	56.7	58.1
Widowed	11.8	12.7	13.8	13.3	2.1	2.0	2.3	2.2	9.7	10.8	11.5	11.1
Divorced	4.3	9.9	15.1	17.4	1.6	3.9	6.3	7.2	2.7	6.0	8.8	10.1
Percent of total	100.0	100.0	100.0	100.0	100.0	100.0	100.0	100.0	100.0	100.0	100.0	100.0
Never married	16.2	20.3	22.2	23.3	18.9	23.8	25.8	27.1	13.7	17.1	18.9	19.7
Married	71.7	65.5	61.9	60.6	756.3	68.4	64.3	62.5	68.5	63.0	59.7	58.8
Widowed	8.9	8.0	7.6	7.0	3.3	2.6	2.7	2.4	13.9	12.8	12.1	11.2
Divorced	3.2	6.2	8.3	9.2	2.5	5.2	7.2	7.9	3.9	7.1	9.3	10.2
Percent standardized for age:[2]												
Never married	14.1	16.5	20.6	23.7	16.5	18.7	23.3	27.8	12.1	14.5	18.2	19.7
Married	74.2	69.3	63.7	60.9	77.6	72.9	66.5	61.9	70.8	65.9	61.2	59.8
Widowed	8.3	7.6	6.9	6.2	3.3	2.7	2.7	2.3	13.0	12.1	10.8	9.9
Divorced	3.4	6.6	8.7	9.3	2.6	5.6	7.6	8.0	4.1	7.6	9.8	10.6
White, total	118.2	139.5	155.5	160.3	55.9	66.7	74.8	77.6	62.2	72.8	80.6	82.6
Never married	18.4	26.4	31.6	33.5	10.2	15.0	18.0	19.3	8.2	11.4	13.6	14.2
Married	85.8	93.8	99.5	100.9	42.7	46.7	49.5	50.2	43.1	47.1	49.9	50.7
Widowed	10.3	10.9	11.7	11.3	1.7	1.6	1.9	1.9	8.6	9.3	9.8	9.4
Divorced	3.7	8.3	12.6	14.5	1.3	3.4	5.4	6.2	2.3	5.0	7.3	8.3
Percent of total	100.0	100.0	100.0	100.0	100.0	100.0	100.0	100.0	100.0	100.0	100.0	100.0
Never married	15.6	18.9	20.3	20.9	18.2	22.5	24.1	24.9	13.2	15.7	16.9	17.1
Married	72.6	67.2	64.0	62.9	76.3	70.0	66.2	64.6	69.3	64.7	61.9	61.4
Widowed	8.7	7.8	7.5	7.1	3.1	2.5	2.6	2.4	13.8	12.8	12.2	11.4
Divorced	3.1	6.0	8.1	9.1	2.4	5.0	7.2	8.0	3.8	6.8	9.0	10.1
Black, total	13.0	16.6	20.3	21.8	5.9	7.4	9.1	9.8	7.1	9.2	11.2	12.0
Never married	2.7	5.1	7.1	8.5	1.4	2.5	3.5	4.1	1.2	2.5	3.6	4.3
Married	8.3	8.5	9.3	9.3	3.9	4.1	4.5	4.5	4.4	4.5	4.8	4.9
Widowed	1.4	1.6	1.7	1.6	0.3	0.3	0.3	0.3	1.1	1.3	1.4	1.3
Divorced	0.6	1.4	2.1	2.3	0.2	0.5	0.8	0.9	0.4	0.9	1.3	1.5
Percent of total	100.0	100.0	100.0	100.0	100.0	100.0	100.0	100.0	100.0	100.0	100.0	100.0
Never married	20.6	30.5	35.1	38.9	24.3	34.3	38.4	42.4	17.4	27.4	32.5	36.2
Married	64.1	51.4	45.8	42.8	66.9	54.6	49.2	45.9	61.7	48.7	43.0	40.4
Widowed	11.0	9.8	8.5	7.4	5.2	4.2	3.7	3.0	15.8	14.3	12.4	11.0

[Continued]

★ 639 ★

Marital Status: Gender, Race, and Hispanic Origin: 1970 to 1994

[Continued]

MARITAL STATUS, RACE, AND HISPANIC ORIGIN	TOTAL				MALE				FEMALE			
	1970	1980	1990	1994	1970	1980	1990	1994	1970	1980	1990	1994
Divorced	4.4	8.4	10.6	10.8	3.6	7.0	8.8	8.7	5.0	9.5	12.0	12.4
Hispanic,[3] total	5.1	7.9	13.6	17.1	2.4	3.8	6.7	8.6	2.6	4.1	6.8	8.5
Never married	0.9	1.9	3.7	5.1	0.5	1.0	2.2	3.0	0.4	0.9	1.5	2.1
Married	3.6	5.2	8.4	10.0	1.8	2.5	4.1	4.8	1.8	2.6	4.3	5.1
Widowed	0.3	0.4	0.5	0.8	0.1	0.1	0.1	0.2	0.2	0.3	0.4	0.6
Divorced	0.2	0.5	1.0	1.3	0.1	0.2	0.4	0.5	0.1	0.3	0.6	0.7
Percent of total	100.0	100.0	100.0	100.0	100.0	100.0	100.0	100.0	100.0	100.0	100.0	100.0
Never married	18.6	24.1	27.2	29.8	21.2	27.3	32.1	35.4	16.2	21.1	22.5	24.2
Married	71.8	65.6	61.7	58.3	73.8	67.1	60.9	56.4	70.0	64.3	62.4	60.2
Widowed	5.6	4.4	4.0	4.4	2.3	1.6	1.5	2.0	8.7	7.1	6.5	6.9
Divorced	3.9	5.8	7.0	7.5	2.7	4.0	5.5	6.2	5.1	7.6	8.5	8.7

Source: "Marital Status of the Population, by Sex, Race, and Hispanic Origin: 1970 to 1994," *Statistical Abstract of the United states: 1995*, p. 54. Primary source: U.S. Bureau of the Census, *1970 Census of Population*, vol. 1, part 1, and *Current Population Reports*, P20-450, and earlier reports; and unpublished data. *Notes:* 1. Includes persons of other races, not shown separately. 2. 1960 age distribution used as standard; standardization improves comparability over time by removing effects of changes in age distribution of population. 3. Hispanic persons may be of any race. 1970 data as of April and based on census.

★ 640 ★

Marital Status

Marital Status: Married Couples of Same or Mixed Races and Origins: 1970 to 1994

[In thousands. As of March, except as noted. Persons 15 years old and over. Persons of Hispanic origin may be of any race. Except as noted, based on Current Population Survey.]

RACE AND ORIGIN OF SPOUSES	1970[1]	1980	1990	1994
Married couples, total	44,598	49,714	53,256	54,251
RACE				
Same race couples	43,922	48,264	50,889	51,204
White/White	40,578	44,910	47,202	47,606
Black/Black	3,344	3,354	3,687	3,598
Interracial couples	310	651	964	1,283
Black/White	65	167	211	296
Black husband/White wife	41	122	150	196
White husband/Black wife	24	45	61	100
White/other race[2]	233	450	720	909
Black/other race[2]	12	34	33	78
All other couples[2]	366	799	1,401	1,764

[Continued]

★ 640 ★

Marital Status: Married Couples of Same or Mixed Races and Origins: 1970 to 1994
[Continued]

RACE AND ORIGIN OF SPOUSES	1970[1]	1980	1990	1994
HISPANIC ORIGIN				
Hispanic/Hispanic	1,368	1,906	3,085	3,755
Hispanic/other origin (not Hispanic)	584	891	1,193	1,283
All other couples (not of Hispanic origin)	42,645	46,917	48,979	49,212

Source: "Married Couples of Same or Mixed Races and Origins: 1970 to 1994," *Statistical Abstract of the United States: 1995*, p. 55. Primary source: U.S. Bureau of the Census, *Current Population Reports*, P20-450, and earlier reports; and unpublished data. *Notes:* 1. As of April and based on Census of Population. 2. Excluding White and Black.

★ 641 ★
Marital Status

Marital Status: Number and Percent of Unmarried Women by Age and Race, 1960 to 1992

[Populations as of July 1 for all years].

Race of women and year	Ages 15-44 years		Percent							
			15-19 years			20-24 years	25-29 years	30-34 years	35-39 years	40-44 years
	Number[1]	Percent	Total	15-17 years	18-19 years					
All races[2]										
1992	27,096	45.9	95.4	98.6	90.7	68.1	41.1	30.2	26.2	26.2
1990	26,588	45.3	95.3	98.6	91.0	66.1	38.8	28.6	25.4	25.9
1985	25,287	44.6	94.0	98.1	88.0	61.3	35.2	26.5	23.1	23.1
1980	22,681	42.8	92.0	97.4	84.4	54.4	29.8	21.9	19.1	18.8
1975	18,315	38.5	89.0	96.4	77.9	44.4	21.1	15.4	15.0	15.3
1970	15,121	35.5	89.2	97.0	77.2	38.6	15.9	12.0	12.2	13.8
1965	12,419	31.8	87.9	-	-	33.4	13.1	9.4	10.7	12.9
1960	10,392	28.8	85.8	-	-	30.8	12.9	11.2	11.8	13.9
White										
1992	20,489	42.5	94.7	98.4	89.3	65.1	37.2	26.2	22.7	23.9
1990	20,372	42.2	94.7	98.3	89.8	63.3	35.4	25.2	22.3	23.6
1985	19,832	41.9	93.1	97.9	86.3	58.2	31.8	24.0	20.8	21.2
1980	18,201	40.5	91.4	97.1	83.3	51.5	27.1	19.7	16.8	17.1
1975	15,002	36.7	88.4	96.1	77.0	42.6	19.1	14.1	13.0	13.9
1970	12,643	34.1	89.1	96.9	77.0	37.2	14.2	10.7	10.6	12.7
1965	10,700	31.3	87.9	-	-	32.9	12.3	8.9	11.3	
1960	8,950	28.1	85.8	-	-	30.2	12.2	10.4	12.2	
Black										
1992	5,305	65.5	98.4	99.6	96.6	82.4	62.3	54.6	49.9	44.7

[Continued]

★ 641 ★

Marital Status: Number and Percent of Unmarried Women by Age and Race, 1960 to 1992
[Continued]

Race of women and year	Ages 15-44 years		Percent								
			15-19 years			20-24 years	25-29 years	30-34 years	35-39 years	40-44 years
	Number[1]	Percent	Total	15-17 years	18-19 years					
1990	5,031	63.6	98.2	100.0	95.7	80.5	58.6	50.2	46.1	44.4
1985	4,627	62.7	98.3	99.3	96.9	78.0	57.1	45.1	41.3	38.8
1980	3,929	58.4	95.9	99.0	91.3	70.8	46.6	37.6	34.9	31.5
1975	2,964	51.0	91.9	97.5	83.2	56.8	36.2	25.6	29.9	25.7
1970	2,252	45.1	90.3	97.9	77.7	47.7	27.2	21.6	23.6	23.6
1965	-	-	-	-	-	-	-	-	-	-
1960	-	-	-	-	-	-	-	-	-	-

Source: "Number and Percent of Women Who Are Unmarried by Age and Race: United States, Selected Years 1960-92," S.J. Ventura, *Births to Unmarried Mothers: United States, 1980-92,* p. 15. Primary source: Number of unmarried women computed based on three-year moving average of percent unmarried by age and race, applied to population estimates published by U.S. Bureau of the Census, as of July 1 for each year. *Notes:* 1. In thousands. 2. Includes races other than white and black.

Mobility

★ 642 ★

Geographical Mobility: Characteristics of Movers Within and Between Metropolitan and Nonmetroplitan Areas, 1993

[Numbers in thousands].

Selected characteristics	From metropolitan to nonmetropolitan			From nonmetropolitan to metropolitan		
	Total	From central cities	From suburbs	Total	To central cities	To suburbs
Race and Hispanic Origin						
White	100.0	43.1	56.9	100.0	34.0	66.0
Black	100.0	77.1	22.9	100.0	47.2	51.9
Hispanic origin (of any race)	100.0	72.3	26.6	100.0	39.1	60.9

Source: "Movers Within and Between Metropolitan and Nonmetropolitan Areas by Selected Characteristics: 1993," *Geographical Mobility: March 1992 to March 1993,* p. xxvii.

★ 643 ★
Mobility

Geographical Mobility: Detailed Mobility of Family Householders: Characteristics. Part 1-1

[Mobility data from March 1992 to March 1993. Numbers in thousands. For meaning of symbols, see text.]

Characteristic	Total population				Same house (nonmovers)		
		MSA's		Outside MSA's	MSA's		Outside MSA's
	Total	Central cities	Balance		Central cities	Balance	
BLACK FAMILY HOUSEHOLDERS							
All Family Householders							
Householders 15 to 54 years old	5,988	3,324	1,792	871	2,576	1,382	717
No own children under 18	1,581	892	512	177	765	398	153
With own children under 18	4,407	2,432	1,280	694	1,811	984	584
Under 6 only	1,085	603	350	132	383	207	83
Under 6 and 6 to 17	1,080	620	271	188	463	225	154
6 to 17 only	2,242	1,209	659	374	966	552	328
Married-Couple Family Households							
Householders 15 to 54 years old	2,640	1,266	965	408	1,015	734	353
No own children under 18	803	400	310	93	331	243	71
With own children under 18	1,837	866	655	316	684	491	282
Under 6 only	453	209	199	45	147	112	36
Under 6 and 6 to 17	437	217	126	95	174	110	84
6 to 17 only	947	440	330	176	362	269	161
Single-Parent Family Households							
Householders 15 to 54 years old	3,348	2,058	827	463	1,561	648	364
No own children under 18	778	492	202	84	434	155	82
With own children under 18	2,570	1,566	625	379	1,127	493	282
Under 6 only	632	393	151	87	235	96	46
Under 6 and 6 to 17	642	404	145	93	288	115	70
6 to 17 only	1,296	769	329	198	603	283	166
Female Single-Parent Family Households							
Householders 15 to 54 years old	3,002	1,868	720	414	1,405	568	327
No own children under 18	607	399	145	63	354	119	60
With own children under 18	2,395	1,470	574	351	1,052	449	267
Under 6 only	561	357	130	74	212	78	39
Under 6 and 6 to 17	620	387	140	92	272	110	69
6 to 17 only	1,214	725	303	185	568	261	159

Source: "Detailed Mobility of Householders, by Race and Hispanic Origin of Householder, Type of Household, and Presence and Ages of Own Children Under 18," *Geographical Mobility: March 1992 to March 1993*, p. 138.

★ 644 ★
Mobility

Geographical Mobility: Detailed Mobility of Family Householders: Characteristics. Part 1-2

[Mobility data from March 1992 to March 1993. Numbers in thousands. For meaning of symbols, see text.]

Characteristic	Total	Movers within same MSA				
		Within central city	Between central cities	Within balance	Central city to balance	Balance to central city
BLACK FAMILY HOUSEHOLDERS						
All Family Householders						
Householders 15 to 54 years old	951	543	14	194	133	67
No own children under 18	189	94	-	57	27	11
With own children under 18	762	449	14	137	106	56
Under 6 only	306	163	8	68	51	17
Under 6 and 6 to 17	182	120	3	21	20	18
6 to 17 only	274	167	4	48	34	21
Married-Couple Family Households						
Householders 15 to 54 years old	355	157	1	106	68	23
No own children under 18	100	48	-	34	15	3
With own children under 18	255	108	1	73	53	21
Under 6 only	113	42	1	39	28	4
Under 6 and 6 to 17	45	26	-	3	9	7
6 to 17 only	98	41	-	30	17	10
Single-Parent Family Households						
Householders 15 to 54 years old	596	386	13	88	65	43
No own children under 18	89	46	-	23	12	8
With own children under 18	507	341	13	65	53	35
Under 6 only	194	121	7	30	23	13
Under 6 and 6 to 17	137	94	3	17	12	11
6 to 17 only	176	126	4	18	18	11
Female Single-Parent Family Households						
Householders 15 to 54 years old	546	363	13	75	57	38
No own children under 18	62	35	-	14	7	5
With own children under 18	484	327	13	61	49	33
Under 6 only	181	113	7	26	23	11
Under 6 and 6 to 17	137	94	3	17	12	11
6 to 17 only	166	120	4	18	14	11

Source: "Detailed Mobility of Householders, by Race and Hispanic Origin of Householder, Type of Household, and Presence and Ages of Own Children Under 18," *Geographical Mobility: March 1992 to March 1993*, p. 138.

★ 645 ★
Mobility

Geographical Mobility: Detailed Mobility of Family Householders: Characteristics. Part 2-1

[Mobility data from March 1992 to March 1993. Numbers in thousands. For meaning of symbols, see text.]

Characteristic	Total population				Same house (nonmovers)		
	Total	MSA's		Outside MSA's	MSA's		Outside MSA's
		Central cities	Balance		Central cities	Balance	
HISPANIC[1] FAMILY HOUSEHOLDERS							
All Family Householders							
Householders 15 to 54 years old	4,321	2,256	1,745	320	1,656	1,316	235
No own children under 18	1,102	577	464	61	424	341	42
With own children under 18	3,219	1,679	1,281	259	1,232	974	193
Under 6 only	877	481	327	69	285	201	37
Under 6 and 6 to 17	914	459	385	70	344	305	58
6 to 17 only	1,428	738	569	120	604	468	98
Married-Couple Family Households							
Householders 15 to 54 years old	2,961	1,406	1,302	253	1,062	1,005	190
No own children under 18	704	342	310	52	243	238	34
With own children under 18	2,257	1,064	992	202	819	768	156
Under 6 only	812	309	253	49	196	157	29
Under 6 and 6 to 17	680	308	315	57	237	255	48
6 to 17 only	966	447	423	95	386	356	79
Single-Parent Family Households							
Householders 15 to 54 years old	1,360	850	443	67	594	310	45
No own children under 18	398	235	153	10	181	104	8
With own children under 18	962	615	290	57	413	207	37
Under 6 only	266	172	74	20	88	44	7
Under 6 and 6 to 17	236	152	70	13	106	51	11
6 to 17 only	462	291	145	25	218	112	19
Female Single-Parent Family Households							
Householders 15 to 54 years old	1,008	659	310	40	473	223	31
No own children under 18	202	127	71	4	110	55	4
With own children under 18	806	531	239	36	363	168	27
Under 6 only	197	133	54	10	71	32	5
Under 6 and 6 to 17	217	145	63	9	99	44	8
6 to 17 only	393	254	122	17	193	93	14

Source: "Detailed Mobility of Householders, by Race and Hispanic Origin of Householder, Type of Household, and Presence and Ages of Own Children Under 18," *Geographical Mobility: March 1992 to March 1993*, p. 139. *Note:* 1. Persons of Hispanic origin may be of any race.

★ 646 ★

Mobility

Geographical Mobility: Detailed Mobility of Family Householders: Characteristics. Part 2-2

[Mobility data from March 1992 to March 1993. Numbers in thousands. For meaning of symbols, see text.]

Characteristic	Total	Movers within same MSA				
		Within central city	Between central cities	Within balance	Central city to balance	Balance to central city
HISPANIC[1] FAMILY HOUSEHOLDERS						
All Family Householders						
Householders 15 to 54 years old	810	410	20	238	99	43
No own children under 18	220	102	10	68	28	12
With own children under 18	589	308	9	171	71	31
Under 6 only	259	144	4	67	31	13
Under 6 and 6 to 17	155	83	1	46	13	11
6 to 17 only	175	81	4	57	26	7
Married-Couple Family Households						
Householders 15 to 54 years old	508	243	14	151	74	26
No own children under 18	138	63	10	33	20	11
With own children under 18	371	180	3	118	54	15
Under 6 only	170	89	2	52	24	5
Under 6 and 6 to 17	106	56	-	34	10	9
6 to 17 only	92	36	2	32	21	2
Single-Parent Family Households						
Householders 15 to 54 years old	301	167	6	87	25	17
No own children under 18	83	39	-	35	8	1
With own children under 18	219	128	6	53	17	16
Under 6 only	89	55	3	15	8	8
Under 6 and 6 to 17	47	28	1	12	4	2
6 to 17 only	83	45	2	25	6	5
Female Single-Parent Family Households						
Householders 15 to 54 years old	212	123	4	56	16	13
No own children under 18	27	14	-	12	1	-
With own children under 18	185	109	4	43	14	13
Under 6 only	65	41	2	10	6	6
Under 6 and 6 to 17	47	28	1	12	4	2
6 to 17 only	74	41	2	21	5	5

Source: "Detailed Mobility of Householders, by Race and Hispanic Origin of Householder, Type of Household, and Presence and Ages of Own Children Under 18," *Geographical Mobility: March 1992 to March 1993*, p. 139. *Note:* 1. Persons of Hispanic origin may be of any race.

★ 647 ★
Mobility

Geographical Mobility: Detailed Mobility of Householders, by Race and Income. Part 1-1

[Mobility data from March 1993. Numbers in thousands. For meaning of symbols, see text.]

Characteristic	Total population				Same house (nonmovers)		
	Total	MSA's		Outside MSA's	MSA's		Outside MSA's
		Central cities	Balance		Central cities	Balance	
BLACK							
Both Sexes							
Householders 15 years and over	11,190	6,481	3,080	1,628	5,173	2,424	1,399
Household income:							
Less than $5,000	1,318	855	262	201	604	197	148
$5,000 to $9,999	2,090	1,265	415	410	993	322	351
$10,000 to $14,999	1,367	796	310	261	608	239	220
$15,000 to $19,999	1,095	654	283	158	510	204	137
$20,000 to $24,999	950	548	242	160	429	201	142
$25,000 to $29,999	827	500	204	123	405	155	115
$30,000 to $34,999	653	341	237	74	274	205	69
$35,000 to $39,999	570	316	197	57	271	154	53
$40,000 to $44,999	511	304	168	40	276	124	36
$45,000 to $49,999	354	212	99	42	192	68	36
$50,000 to $54,999	313	154	139	20	137	107	16
$55,000 to $59,999	248	120	105	23	105	93	22
$60,000 to $64,999	197	92	83	22	83	69	18
$65,000 to $69,999	122	56	52	14	47	45	14
$70,000 to $74,999	109	40	65	5	31	57	5
$75,000 to $79,999	80	45	28	7	41	26	7
$80,000 to $84,999	67	37	26	4	33	17	4
$85,000 to $89,999	55	26	28	1	22	25	1
$90,000 to $94,999	70	35	33	2	30	27	2
$95,000 to $99,999	30	13	17	-	10	14	-
$100,000 and over	163	72	87	3	70	76	3
Median income (dollars)	18,744	17,488	25,669	13,879	18,736	26,607	14,586

Source: "Detailed Mobility of Householders, by Race and Hispanic Origin, Sex, and Household Income," *Geographical Mobility: March 1992 to March 1993*, p. 144.

★ 648 ★

Mobility

Geographical Mobility: Detailed Mobility of Householders, by Race and Income. Part 1-2

[Mobility data from March 1993. Numbers in thousands. For meaning of symbols, see text.]

| Characteristic | Total | Movers within same MSA | | | | |
		Within central cities	Between central cities	Within balance	Central city to balance	Balance to central city
BLACK						
Both Sexes						
Householders 15 years and over	1,582	924	33	313	201	112
Household income:						
Less than $5,000	271	195	6	32	22	15
$5,000 to $9,999	295	206	5	50	23	11
$10,000 to $14,999	203	137	-	21	31	14
$15,000 to $19,999	206	127	4	35	35	5
$20,000 to $24,999	128	81	3	23	10	11
$25,000 to $29,999	109	52	12	26	11	8
$30,000 to $34,999	75	38	-	17	6	15
$35,000 to $39,999	50	20	-	15	8	7
$40,000 to $44,999	56	19	-	24	10	3
$45,000 to $49,999	44	12	3	20	8	2
$50,000 to $54,999	44	9	-	20	11	5
$55,000 to $59,999	20	7	-	5	2	6
$60,000 to $64,999	19	3	-	11	-	5
$65,000 to $69,999	10	4	-	-	7	-
$70,000 to $74,999	13	6	-	7	-	-
$75,000 to $79,999	4	2	-	-	2	-
$80,000 to $84,999	9	-	-	-	9	-
$85,000 to $89,999	4	4	-	-	-	-
$90,000 to $94,999	7	-	-	4	-	3
$95,000 to $99,999	5	-	-	3	-	3
$100,000 and over	10	2	-	2	6	-
Median income (dollars)	15,554	12,205	(B)	24,313	18,451	24,717

Source: "Detailed Mobility of Householders, by Race and Hispanic Origin, Sex, and Household Income," *Geographical Mobility: March 1992 to March 1993*, p. 144. *Note:* B = Base too small to show derived measure.

★ 649 ★

Mobility

Geographical Mobility: Detailed Mobility of Householders, by Race and Income.
Part 2-1

[Mobility data from March 1993. Numbers in thousands. For meaning of symbols, see text.]

Characteristic	Total population				Same house (nonmovers)		
	Total	MSA's		Outside MSA's	MSA's		Outside MSA's
		Central cities	Balance		Central cities	Balance	
BLACK							
Male							
Householders 15 years and over	5,105	2,732	1,606	766	2,203	1,265	672
Household income:							
Less than $5,000	280	183	58	39	118	53	36
$5,000 to $9,999	605	361	110	134	276	83	107
$10,000 to $14,999	519	284	127	108	215	96	92
$15,000 to $19,999	481	268	128	85	221	95	75
$20,000 to $24,999	477	239	147	91	186	126	79
$25,000 to $29,999	402	245	91	66	195	61	64
$30,000 to $34,999	372	187	139	47	142	114	43
$35,000 to $39,999	354	184	126	44	160	106	40
$40,000 to $44,999	321	173	118	31	155	84	28
$45,000 to $49,999	208	121	58	28	106	38	23
$50,000 to $54,999	225	105	101	19	96	68	15
$55,000 to $59,999	178	90	68	20	79	57	18
$60,000 to $64,999	141	62	59	19	56	49	18
$65,000 to $69,999	98	44	40	13	36	37	13
$70,000 to $74,999	88	36	47	5	28	40	5
$75,000 to $79,999	66	34	24	7	30	22	7
$80,000 to $84,999	52	26	24	2	25	15	2
$85,000 to $89,999	44	19	24	1	15	22	1
$90,000 to $94,999	47	13	31	2	11	25	2
$95,000 to $99,999	25	10	15	-	7	12	-
$100,000 and over	123	49	71	3	47	60	3
Median income (dollars)	27,365	25,623	35,175	20,937	27,187	35,210	21,694

Source: "Detailed Mobility of Householders, by Race and Hispanic Origin, Sex, and Household Income," *Geographical Mobility: March 1992 to March 1993*, p. 144.

★ 650 ★

Mobility

Geographical Mobility: Detailed Mobility of Householders, by Race and Income. Part 2-2

[Mobility data from March 1993. Numbers in thousands. For meaning of symbols, see text.]

Characteristic	Total	Movers with same MSA				
		Within central city	Between central cities	Within balance	Central city to balance	Balance to central city
BLACK						
Male						
Householders 15 years and over	658	343	16	156	97	45
Household income:						
Less than $5,000	50	47	-	-	1	2
$5,000 to $9,999	86	64	-	13	9	-
$10,000 to $14,999	73	50	-	10	10	4
$15,000 to $19,999	65	34	4	15	10	2
$20,000 to $24,999	62	41	-	11	6	4
$25,000 to $29,999	58	20	-	13	9	6
$30,000 to $34,999	48	27	-	12	2	7
$35,000 to $39,999	23	8	-	4	6	5
$40,000 to $44,999	40	13	-	16	10	2
$45,000 to $49,999	29	10	3	15	2	-
$50,000 to $54,999	38	4	-	20	11	3
$55,000 to $59,999	15	5	-	4	2	4
$60,000 to $64,999	13	3	-	8	-	2
$65,000 to $69,999	7	4	-	-	4	-
$70,000 to $74,999	13	6	-	7	-	-
$75,000 to $79,999	4	2	-	-	2	-
$80,000 to $84,999	9	-	-	-	9	-
$85,000 to $89,999	4	4	-	-	-	-
$90,000 to $94,999	4	-	-	4	-	-
$95,000 to $99,999	5	-	-	3	-	3
$100,000 and over	10	2	-	2	6	-
Median income (dollars)	24,397	16,691	(B)	39,194	36,782	(B)

Source: "Detailed Mobility of Householders, by Race and Hispanic Origin, Sex, and Household Income," *Geographical Mobility: March 1992 to March 1993*, p. 144. *Note:* B=Base too small to show derived measure.

★ 651 ★

Mobility

Geographical Mobility: Detailed Mobility of Householders, by Race and Income. Part 3-1

[Mobility data from March 1993. Numbers in thousands. For meaning of symbols, see text.]

Characteristic	Total population				Same house (nonmovers)		
	Total	MSA's		Outside MSA's	MSA's		Outside MSA's
		Central cities	Balance		Central cities	Balance	
BLACK							
Female							
Householders 15 years and over	6,085	3,749	1,474	862	2,970	1,160	728
Household income:							
Less than $5,000	1,037	672	204	162	486	144	112
$5,000 to $9,999	1,486	904	306	276	717	239	243
$10,000 to $14,999	849	512	183	153	393	143	128
$15,000 to $19,999	614	385	155	73	289	109	62
$20,000 to $24,999	473	309	95	69	242	75	64
$25,000 to $29,999	425	255	114	57	210	94	51
$30,000 to $34,999	280	155	99	27	132	91	26
$35,000 to $39,999	217	133	71	13	111	48	13
$40,000 to $44,999	190	131	50	9	122	39	9
$45,000 to $49,999	146	91	41	14	87	29	12
$50,000 to $54,999	88	49	38	1	41	38	1
$55,000 to $59,999	71	30	38	4	26	36	4
$60,000 to $64,999	56	30	23	3	27	20	-
$65,000 to $69,999	25	12	11	1	11	8	1
$70,000 to $74,999	21	4	18	-	4	18	-
$75,000 to $79,999	15	11	3	-	11	3	-
$80,000 to $84,999	15	11	3	2	8	3	2
$85,000 to $89,999	11	7	3	-	7	3	-
$90,000 to $94,999	24	22	2	-	19	2	-
$95,000 to $99,999	5	3	1	-	3	1	-
$100,000 and over	39	23	16	-	23	16	-
Median income (dollars)	13,062	12,920	16,431	9,876	13,582	17,463	10,326

Source: "Detailed Mobility of Householders, by Race and Hispanic Origin, Sex, and Household Income," *Geographical Mobility: March 1992 to March 1993*, p. 144.

★ 652 ★

Mobility

Geographical Mobility: Detailed Mobility of Householders, by Race and Income. Part 3-2

[Mobility data from March 1993. Numbers in thousands. For meaning of symbols, see text.]

Characteristic	Movers with same MSA					
	Total	Within central city	Between central cities	Within balance	Central city to balance	Balance to central city
BLACK						
Female						
Householders 15 years and over	924	580	17	156	103	67
Household income:						
Less than $5,000	221	149	6	32	21	13
$5,000 to $9,999	209	142	5	36	14	11
$10,000 to $14,999	129	88	-	11	21	9
$15,000 to $19,999	141	92	-	20	26	3
$20,000 to $24,999	66	40	3	11	5	7
$25,000 to $29,999	51	32	3	13	2	2
$30,000 to $34,999	27	11	-	4	3	8
$35,000 to $39,999	27	11	-	11	3	2
$40,000 to $44,999	15	6	-	8	-	1
$45,000 to $49,999	15	2	-	5	6	2
$50,000 to $54,999	7	5	-	-	-	1
$55,000 to $59,999	6	2	-	2	-	2
$60,000 to $64,999	6	-	-	3	-	3
$65,000 to $69,999	3	-	-	-	3	-
$70,000 to $74,999	-	-	-	-	-	-
$75,000 to $79,999	-	-	-	-	-	-
$80,000 to $84,999	-	-	-	-	-	-
$85,000 to $89,999	-	-	-	-	-	-
$90,000 to $94,999	3	-	-	-	-	3
$95,000 to $99,999	-	-	-	-	-	-
$100,000 and over	-	-	-	-	-	-
Median income (dollars)	11,271	9,981	(B)	14,596	13,909	(B)

Source: "Detailed Mobility of Householders, by Race and Hispanic Origin, Sex, and Household Income," *Geographical Mobility: March 1992 to March 1993*, p. 144. *Note:* B = Base too small to show derived measure.

★ 653 ★
Mobility

Geographical Mobility: Detailed Mobility of Persons 16 Years and Over, by Race, Gender, and Labor Force Status. Part 1-1

[Mobility data from March 1992 to March 1993. Numbers in thousands. For meaning of symbols, see text.]

Characteristic	Total population				Same house (nonmovers)		
	Total	MSA's		Outside MSA's	MSA's		Outside MSA's
		Central cities	Balance		Central cities	Balance	
ALL RACES							
Both Sexes							
Persons 16 years and over	193,792	58,457	92,370	42,966	46,533	78,521	36,488
Civilian labor force	126,393	37,342	62,335	26,715	28,787	51,929	22,125
Employed	116,978	34,085	58,290	24,603	26,543	48,822	20,631
Unemployed	9,415	3,257	4,045	2,112	2,243	3,107	1,494
Armed forces	837	289	412	136	165	239	89
Not in labor force	66,562	20,826	29,622	16,114	17,581	26,353	14,253
Male							
Persons 16 years and over	93,084	27,677	44,734	20,674	21,810	37,826	17,486
Civilian labor force	68,835	20,018	34,243	14,574	15,338	28,456	12,062
Employed	62,981	17,965	31,682	13,335	13,891	26,454	11,155
Unemployed	5,854	2,053	2,561	1,239	1,447	2,002	907
Armed forces	783	263	392	128	152	233	88
Not in labor force	23,466	7,396	10,098	5,971	6,320	9,137	5,337
Female							
Persons 16 years and over	100,709	30,780	47,636	22,292	24,723	40,695	18,961
Civilian labor force	57,558	17,324	28,092	12,141	13,449	23,473	10,064
Employed	53,997	16,120	26,608	11,268	12,652	22,368	9,476
Unemployed	3,561	1,204	1,484	873	797	1,105	587
Armed forces	54	26	20	8	13	7	1
Not in labor force	43,096	13,430	19,524	10,143	11,261	17,216	8,916
WHITE							
Both Sexes							
Persons 16 years and over	164,048	42,642	82,733	38,673	33,882	70,850	32,840
Civilian labor force	108,032	27,901	55,883	24,249	21,363	46,813	20,108
Employed	100,881	25,926	52,469	22,486	20,034	44,174	18,843
Unemployed	7,151	1,975	3,414	1,762	1,329	2,639	1,264
Armed forces	633	188	317	128	111	193	83
Not in labor force	55,383	14,554	26,532	14,297	12,408	23,844	12,649
Male							
Persons 16 years and over	79,344	20,501	40,097	18,746	16,131	34,159	15,862

[Continued]

★ 653 ★

Geographical Mobility: Detailed Mobility of Persons 16 Years and Over, by Race, Gender, and Labor Force Status. Part 1-1

[Continued]

Characteristic	Total population				Same house (nonmovers)		
	Total	MSA's		Outside MSA's	MSA's		Outside MSA's
		Central cities	Balance		Central cities	Balance	
Civilian labor force	59,502	15,323	30,857	13,322	11,708	25,805	11,042
Employed	55,003	14,043	28,682	12,278	10,818	24,086	10,267
Unemployed	4,499	1,280	2,176	1,044	890	1,719	776
Armed forces	604	176	308	120	105	187	82
Not in labor force	19,237	5,002	8,932	5,304	4,318	8,168	4,738
Female							
Persons 16 years and over	83,704	22,141	42,635	19,928	17,751	36,691	16,978
Civilian labor force	48,530	12,578	25,026	10,926	9,654	21,008	9,065
Employed	45,878	11,883	23,787	10,208	9,216	20,089	8,577
Unemployed	2,652	695	1,239	719	439	919	489
Armed forces	28	11	9	8	6	6	1
Not in labor force	36,146	9,552	17,601	8,993	8,091	15,677	7,911

Source: "Detailed Mobility of Persons 16 Years and Over, by Race and Hispanic Origin, Sex, and Labor Force Status," *Geographical Mobility: March 1992 to March 1993*, p. 106.

★ 654 ★

Mobility

Geographical Mobility: Detailed Mobility of Persons 16 Years and Over, by Race, Gender, and Labor Force Status. Part 1-2

[Mobility data from March 1992 to March 1993. Numbers in thousands. For meaning of symbols, see text.]

Characteristic	Movers within same MSA					
	Total	Within central city	Between central cities	Within balance	Central city to balance	Balance to central city
ALL RACES						
Both Sexes						
Persons 16 years and over	18,174	6,849	319	6,958	2,631	1,417
Civilian labor force	13,677	4,923	256	5,371	2,040	1,087
Employed	12,304	4,359	232	4,968	1,866	979
Unemployed	1,274	565	24	403	174	108
Armed forces	138	32	3	35	36	31
Not in labor force	4,358	1,894	60	1,551	555	298

[Continued]

★ 654 ★

Geographical Mobility: Detailed Mobility of Persons 16 Years and Over, by Race, Gender, and Labor Force Status. Part 1-2

[Continued]

Characteristic	Total	Movers within same MSA				
		Within central city	Between central cities	Within balance	Central city to balance	Balance to central city
Male						
Persons 16 years and over	8,862	3,297	145	3,441	1,310	668
Civilian labor force	7,416	2,650	131	2,980	1,099	556
Employed	6,646	2,315	112	2,725	1,000	493
Unemployed	770	335	19	255	99	93
Armed forces	126	28	3	32	35	28
Not in labor force	1,320	620	11	430	175	84
Female						
Persons 16 years and over	9,312	3,552	174	3,517	1,322	749
Civilian labor force	6,261	2,273	125	2,392	941	531
Employed	5,757	2,043	120	2,243	866	486
Unemployed	504	230	5	149	75	45
Armed forces	13	4	-	4	1	4
Not in labor force	3,039	1,274	49	1,121	380	214
WHITE						
Both Sexes						
Persons 16 years and over	14,418	4,813	245	6,089	2,138	1,133
Civilian labor force	11,215	3,660	197	4,767	1,679	911
Employed	10,316	3,339	180	4,430	1,535	831
Unemployed	900	322	16	337	144	80
Armed forces	76	12	3	18	23	19
Not in labor force	3,127	1,141	45	1,304	436	203
Male						
Persons 16 years and over	7,105	2,366	116	3,015	1,060	548
Civilian labor force	6,125	2,006	101	2,638	910	470
Employed	5,569	1,807	87	2,427	825	423
Unemployed	556	198	15	212	84	47
Armed forces	74	12	3	18	22	19
Not in labor force	906	348	11	359	128	59
Female						
Persons 16 years and over	7,313	2,447	129	3,074	1,078	585
Civilian labor force	5,090	1,655	95	2,129	770	441
Employed	4,747	1,532	94	2,003	710	408

[Continued]

★ 654 ★

Geographical Mobility: Detailed Mobility of Persons 16 Years and Over, by Race, Gender, and Labor Force Status. Part 1-2

[Continued]

| Characteristic | Movers within same MSA | | | | | |
	Total	Within central city	Between central cities	Within balance	Central city to balance	Balance to central city
Unemployed	343	123	2	126	60	33
Armed forces	2	-	-	-	1	-
Not in labor force	2,221	792	34	945	307	144

Source: "Detailed Mobility of Persons 16 Years and Over, by Race and Hispanic Origin, Sex, and Labor Force Status," *Geographical Mobility: March 1992 to March 1993,* p. 106.

★ 655 ★

Mobility

Geographical Mobility: Detailed Mobility of Persons 16 Years and Over, by Race, Gender, and Labor Force Status. Part 2-1

[Mobility data from March 1992 to March 1993. Numbers in thousands. For meaning of symbols, see text.]

| Characteristic | Total population | | | | Same house (nonmovers) | | |
| | Total | MSA's | | Outside MSA's | MSA's | | Outside MSA's |
		Central cities	Balance		Central cities	Balance	
BLACK							
Both Sexes							
Persons 16 years and over	22,384	12,720	6,341	3,323	10,317	5,076	2,858
Civilian labor force	13,608	7,479	4,240	1,890	5,935	3,335	1,574
Employed	11,699	6,346	3,753	1,600	5,129	2,974	1,380
Unemployed	1,909	1,133	487	289	806	361	194
Armed forces	168	76	84	8	45	41	6
Not in labor force	8,608	5,165	2,018	1,425	4,337	1,700	1,279
Male							
Persons 16 years and over	10,162	5,662	3,019	1,480	4,566	2,405	1,267
Civilian labor force	6,751	3,639	2,158	954	2,851	1,672	788
Employed	5,617	2,957	1,871	788	2,358	1,462	675
Unemployed	1,135	682	287	166	493	210	113
Armed forces	143	61	74	8	38	41	5
Not in labor force	3,268	1,962	787	519	1,677	693	474
Female							
Persons 16 years and over	12,222	7,058	3,322	1,842	5,752	2,671	1,591
Civilian labor force	6,857	3,840	2,081	935	3,084	1,663	786

[Continued]

★ 655 ★

Geographical Mobility: Detailed Mobility of Persons 16 Years and Over, by Race, Gender, and Labor Force Status. Part 2-1

[Continued]

Characteristic	Total population				Same house (nonmovers)		
	Total	MSA's		Outside MSA's	MSA's		Outside MSA's
		Central cities	Balance		Central cities	Balance	
Employed	6,082	3,389	1,882	812	2,771	1,512	705
Unemployed	775	452	200	123	313	151	81
Armed forces	25	15	10	1	7	-	-
Not in labor force	5,340	3,203	1,231	906	2,660	1,008	805

Source: "Detailed Mobility of Persons 16 Years and Over, by Race and Hispanic Origin, Sex, and Labor Force Status," *Geographical Mobility: March 1992 to March 1993*, p. 106.

★ 656 ★

Mobility

Geographical Mobility: Detailed Mobility of Persons 16 Years and Over, by Race, Gender, and Labor Force Status. Part 2-2

[Mobility data from March 1992 to March 1993. Numbers in thousands. For meaning of symbols, see text.]

Characteristic	Movers within same MSA					
	Total	Within central city	Between central cities	Within balance	Central city to balance	Balance to central city
BLACK						
Both Sexes						
Persons 16 years and over	2,893	1,659	61	557	395	221
Civilian labor force	1,908	1,036	46	399	293	135
Employed	1,580	811	38	353	265	112
Unemployed	329	225	8	46	28	23
Armed forces	48	10	-	16	13	10
Not in labor force	937	613	15	142	89	76
Male						
Persons 16 years and over	1,334	742	27	267	207	91
Civilian labor force	991	516	27	225	158	65
Employed	806	391	23	194	144	53
Unemployed	185	125	4	30	14	12
Armed forces	37	6	-	12	13	6
Not in labor force	305	220	-	30	35	20

[Continued]

★ 656 ★

Geographical Mobility: Detailed Mobility of Persons 16 Years and Over, by Race, Gender, and Labor Force Status. Part 2-2

[Continued]

Characteristic	Movers within same MSA					
	Total	Within central city	Between central cities	Within balance	Central city to balance	Balance to central city
Female						
Persons 16 years and over	1,560	917	34	290	189	130
Civilian labor force	917	520	19	174	135	70
Employed	773	420	15	158	121	59
Unemployed	144	100	3	15	14	11
Armed forces	11	4	-	4	-	3
Not in labor force	631	393	15	113	54	56

Source: "Detailed Mobility of Persons 16 Years and Over, by Race and Hispanic Origin, Sex, and Labor Force Status," *Geographical Mobility: March 1992 to March 1993*, p. 106.

★ 657 ★

Mobility

Geographical Mobility: Detailed Mobility of Persons 16 Years and Over, by Race, Gender, and Labor Force Status. Part 3-1

[Mobility data from March 1992 to March 1993. Numbers in thousands. For meaning of symbols, see text.]

Characteristic	Total population				Same house (nonmovers)		
	Total	MSA's		Outside MSA's	MSA's		Outside MSA's
		Central cities	Balance		Central cities	Balance	
HISPANIC[1]							
Both Sexes							
Persons 16 years and over	15,628	8,107	6,399	1,122	6,126	4,935	837
Civilian labor force	10,204	5,093	4,395	716	3,728	3,342	520
Employed	8,992	4,456	3,901	635	3,293	3,022	460
Unemployed	1,212	637	494	81	436	321	60
Armed forces	44	15	24	5	4	16	5
Not in labor force	5,381	2,999	1,980	401	2,393	1,577	312
Male							
Persons 16 years and over	7,783	3,934	3,291	558	2,917	2,526	416
Civilian labor force	6,132	3,033	2,665	434	2,156	2,004	310
Employed	5,374	2,635	2,355	384	1,877	1,802	275
Unemployed	758	398	310	49	278	202	35
Armed forces	41	13	24	5	4	16	5
Not in labor force	1,610	888	602	120	757	507	101

[Continued]

★ 657 ★

Geographical Mobility: Detailed Mobility of Persons 16 Years and Over, by Race, Gender, and Labor Force Status. Part 3-1

[Continued]

| Characteristic | Total population | | | | Same house (nonmovers) | | |
| | Total | MSA's | | Outside MSA's | MSA's | | Outside MSA's |
		Central cities	Balance		Central cities	Balance	
Female							
Persons 16 years and over	7,845	4,173	3,108	564	3,209	2,409	421
Civilian labor force	4,072	2,060	1,729	283	1,573	1,338	210
Employed	3,617	1,821	1,546	251	1,415	1,220	185
Unemployed	454	239	184	32	157	119	25
Armed forces	2	2	-	-		-	-
Not in labor force	3,771	2,111	1,378	281	1,637	1,070	211

Source: "Detailed Mobility of Persons 16 Years and Over, by Race and Hispanic Origin, Sex, and Labor Force Status," *Geographical Mobility: March 1992 to March 1993,* p. 108. *Note:* 1. Persons of Hispanic origin may be of any race.

★ 658 ★

Mobility

Geographical Mobility: Detailed Mobility of Persons 16 Years and Over, by Race, Gender, and Labor Force Status. Part 3-2

[Mobility data from March 1992 to March 1993. Numbers in thousands. For meaning of symbols, see text.]

| Characteristic | Movers within same MSA | | | | | |
	Total	Within central city	Between central cities	Within balance	Central city to balance	Balance to central city
HISPANIC[1]						
Both Sexes						
Persons 16 years and over	2,588	1,339	43	733	333	140
Civilian labor force	1,855	935	31	541	244	105
Employed	1,598	813	25	461	211	89
Unemployed	257	122	6	79	33	16
Armed forces	9	7	-	2	1	-
Not in labor force	724	398	12	191	88	35
Male						
Persons 16 years and over	1,335	695	19	384	164	72
Civilian labor force	1,167	601	17	341	146	62
Employed	1,010	528	13	288	128	52
Unemployed	157	72	4	53	18	10
Armed forces	9	7	-	2	1	-

[Continued]

★ 658 ★

Geographical Mobility: Detailed Mobility of Persons 16 Years and Over, by Race, Gender, and Labor Force Status. Part 3-2

[Continued]

Characteristic	Total	Movers within same MSA				
		Within central city	Between central cities	Within balance	Central city to balance	Balance to central city
Not in labor force	159	88	3	42	17	10
Female						
Persons 16 years and over	1,253	644	24	349	169	68
Civilian labor force	688	334	14	200	98	42
Employed	589	284	12	173	83	37
Unemployed	99	50	2	27	15	6
Armed forces	-	-	-	-	-	-
Not in labor force	565	309	10	149	71	26

Source: "Detailed Mobility of Persons 16 Years and Over, by Race and Hispanic Origin, Sex, and Labor Force Status," *Geographical Mobility: March 1992 to March 1993*, p. 108. *Note:* 1. Persons of Hispanic origin may be of any race.

★ 659 ★

Mobility

Geographical Mobility: Detailed Mobility of Persons 25 Years and Over, by Race, Age, and Education. Part 1-1

[Mobility data from March 1992 to March 1993. Numbers in thousands. For meaning of symbols, see text.]

Characteristic	Total population				Same house (nonmovers)		
	Total	MSA's		Outside MSA's	MSA's		Outside MSA's
		Central cities	Balance		Central cities	Balance	
ALL RACES							
Persons 25 years and over	162,826	48,439	78,226	36,161	40,031	67,829	31,532
Less than 9th grade	15,128	5,415	5,354	4,360	4,647	4,795	3,960
9th to 12th grade, no diploma	17,067	5,578	6,984	4,504	4,642	6,055	3,918
High school graduate	57,589	15,408	27,391	14,791	12,824	24,025	12,960
Some college or associate degree	37,451	10,858	18,980	7,613	8,812	16,374	6,504
Bachelor's degree	23,619	7,147	13,076	3,396	5,718	11,000	2,877
Graduate or professional degree	11,972	4,033	6,441	1,497	3,388	5,581	1,312
Percent high school graduates	80.2	77.3	84.2	75.5	76.8	84.0	75.0
Persons 25 to 29 years	19,603	6,847	9,068	3,688	4,497	6,409	2,650
Less than 9th grade	725	314	270	141	198	189	100
9th to 12th grade, no diploma	1,878	718	749	410	471	508	302
High school graduate	6,994	2,186	3,091	1,717	1,490	2,259	1,227
Some college or associate degree	5,368	1,858	2,553	957	1,213	1,851	702
Bachelor's degree	3,828	1,395	2,018	415	900	1,353	289

[Continued]

★ 659 ★

Geographical Mobility: Detailed Mobility of Persons 25 Years and Over, by Race, Age, and Education. Part 1-1
[Continued]

Characteristic	Total population				Same house (nonmovers)		
	Total	MSA's		Outside MSA's	MSA's		Outside MSA's
		Central cities	Balance		Central cities	Balance	
Graduate or professional degree	811	377	387	47	225	249	30
Percent high school graduate	86.7	84.9	88.8	85.1	85.1	89.1	84.8
Persons 30 to 34 years	22,261	7,045	10,802	4,413	5,270	8,616	3,549
Less than 9th grade	880	432	300	148	327	233	124
9th to 12th grade, no diploma	2,015	690	797	528	490	600	397
High school graduate	8,042	2,257	3,792	1,994	1,696	3,131	1,644
Some college or associate degree	5,994	1,851	3,011	1,131	1,428	2,453	902
Bachelor's degree	3,969	1,271	2,202	496	927	1,674	401
Graduate or professional degree	1,360	544	700	116	402	526	81
Percent high school graduates	87.0	84.1	89.9	84.7	84.5	90.3	85.3
Persons 35 to 44 years	40,342	11,481	20,175	8,687	9,418	17,346	7,444
Less than 9th grade	1,671	725	607	340	599	483	254
9th to 12th grade, no diploma	2,939	1,009	1,115	815	782	909	670
High school graduate	13,715	3,438	6,633	3,645	2,810	5,669	3,207
Some college or associate degree	11,245	3,146	5,795	2,304	2,598	5,043	1,968
Bachelor's degree	7,088	1,992	4,025	1,071	1,649	3,508	900
Graduate or professional degree	3,684	1,171	2,001	512	980	1,733	446
Percent high school graduates	88.6	84.9	91.5	86.7	85.3	92.0	87.6
Persons 45 to 64 years	49,750	13,960	24,555	11,235	12,355	22,509	10,216
Less than 9th grade	4,401	1,587	1,542	1,271	1,341	1,391	1,138
9th to 12th grade, no diploma	5,419	1,778	2,160	1,481	1,589	1,981	1,342
High school graduate	18,271	4,575	8,915	4,781	4,078	8,254	4,404
Some college or associate degree	10,501	2,790	5,509	2,202	2,454	5,030	1,969
Bachelor's degree	6,337	1,775	3,664	898	1,569	3,351	817
Graduate or professional degree	4,821	1,454	2,766	601	1,324	2,503	547
Percent high school graduates	80.3	75.9	84.9	75.5	76.3	85.0	75.7
Persons 65 years and over	30,870	9,106	13,626	8,138	8,491	12,949	7,673
Less than 9th grade	7,451	2,357	2,636	2,459	2,182	2,499	2,345
9th to 12th grade, no diploma	4,817	1,383	2,164	1,269	1,309	2,058	1,207
High school graduate	10,567	2,952	4,961	2,654	2,749	4,712	2,477
Some college or associate degree	4,343	1,213	2,112	1,018	1,120	1,997	965
Bachelor's degree	2,396	714	1,166	516	673	1,113	471
Graduate or professional degree	1,296	487	587	222	457	570	208
Percent high school graduates	60.3	58.9	64.8	54.2	58.9	64.8	53.7

Source: "Detailed Mobility of Persons 25 Years and Over, by Race and Hispanic Origin, Age, and Educational Attainment," *Geographical Mobility: March 1992 to March 1993*, pp. 94, 96.

★ 660 ★

Mobility

Geographical Mobility: Detailed Mobility of Persons 25 Years and Over, by Race, Age, and Education. Part 1-2

[Mobility data from March 1992 to March 1993. Numbers in thousands. For meaning of symbols, see text.]

Characteristic		Movers within same MSA				
	Total	Within central city	Between central cities	Within balance	Central city to balance	Balance to central city
ALL RACES						
Persons 25 years and over	13,323	4,770	232	5,337	1,978	1,007
Less than 9th grade	977	487	19	310	101	60
9th to 12th grade, no diploma	1,404	637	13	490	194	70
High school graduate	4,448	1,562	57	1,826	656	347
Some college or associate degree	3,403	1,156	85	1,375	520	266
Bachelor's degree	2,218	651	39	961	367	201
Graduate or professional degree	874	277	19	375	140	63
Percent high school graduates	82.1	76.4	86.0	85.0	85.1	87.1
Persons 25 to 29 years	3,659	1,385	58	1,409	506	301
Less than 9th grade	155	71	4	46	21	13
9th to 12th grade, no diploma	388	189	-	147	37	14
High school graduate	1,196	454	19	479	158	87
Some college or associate degree	1,010	380	20	369	152	90
Bachelor's degree	740	227	15	310	107	81
Graduate or professional degree	170	64	-	59	31	16
Percent high school graduate	85.2	81.2	(B)	86.3	88.6	90.9
Persons 30 to 34 years	2,862	996	68	1,115	435	249
Less than 9th grade	139	77	3	46	11	3
9th to 12th grade, no diploma	318	136	9	92	63	16
High school graduate	958	347	7	377	129	98
Some college or associate degree	720	226	24	299	107	64
Bachelor's degree	558	150	19	232	105	52
Graduate or professional degree	170	60	7	70	19	15
Percent high school graduates	84.1	78.6	(B)	87.6	83.0	92.1
Persons 35 to 44 years	3,478	1,191	44	1,440	565	238
Less than 9th grade	194	85	2	81	13	14
9th to 12th grade, no diploma	316	143	2	99	50	23
High school graduate	1,147	383	11	471	204	79
Some college or associate degree	982	335	25	409	145	69
Bachelor's degree	558	166	-	260	99	33
Graduate or professional degree	280	79	5	121	54	20
Percent high school graduates	85.3	80.9	(B)	87.5	88.8	84.7
Persons 45 to 64 years	2,493	896	54	1,021	365	157
Less than 9th grade	279	152	5	72	28	21
9th to 12th grade, no diploma	271	131	3	98	28	11
High school graduate	852	282	19	362	132	57

[Continued]

★ 660 ★

Geographical Mobility: Detailed Mobility of Persons 25 Years and Over, by Race, Age, and Education. Part 1-2

[Continued]

Characteristic	Movers within same MSA					
	Total	Within central city	Between central cities	Within balance	Central city to balance	Balance to central city
Some college or associate degree	548	178	16	234	94	26
Bachelor's degree	312	90	4	138	49	31
Graduate or professional degree	232	63	7	117	34	11
Percent high school graduates	78.0	68.4	(B)	83.3	84.7	79.8
Persons 65 years and over	831	302	8	351	108	63
Less than 9th grade	210	102	5	65	28	10
9th to 12th grade, no diploma	112	38	-	53	15	6
High school graduate	295	96	2	137	34	26
Some college or associate degree	143	37	-	65	23	18
Bachelor's degree	49	17	1	22	6	3
Graduate or professional degree	22	12	-	8	2	-
Percent high school graduates	61.3	53.8	(B)	66.1	59.9	(B)

Source: "Detailed Mobility of Persons 25 Years and Over, by Race and Hispanic Origin, Age, and Educational Attainment," *Geographical Mobility: March 1992 to March 1993*, pp. 94, 96. *Note:* B = Base too small to show derived measure.

★ 661 ★

Mobility

Geographical Mobility: Detailed Mobility of Persons 25 Years and Over, by Race, Age, and Education. Part 2-1

[Mobility data from March 1992 to March 1993. Numbers in thousands. For meaning of symbols, see text.]

Characteristic	Total population				Same house (nonmovers)		
	Total	MSA's		Outside MSA's	MSA's		Outside MSA's
		Central cities	Balance		Central cities	Balance	
BLACK							
Persons 25 years and over	17,786	10,158	4,961	2,667	8,448	4,025	2,332
Less than 9th grade	2,182	1,177	438	568	1,058	396	530
9th to 12th grade, no diploma	3,079	1,891	608	579	1,551	504	495
High school graduate	6,451	3,721	1,780	951	3,070	1,408	820
Some college or associate degree	3,909	2,221	1,311	378	1,800	1,056	315
Bachelor's degree	1,561	797	632	131	658	503	119
Graduate or professional degree	603	351	193	60	313	158	52
Percent high school graduates	70.4	69.8	78.9	57.0	69.1	77.6	56.0
Persons 25 to 29 years	2,614	1,540	735	339	1,097	509	258
Less than 9th grade	37	19	13	5	15	13	3
9th to 12th grade, no diploma	413	258	92	63	179	72	48

[Continued]

★ 661 ★
Geographical Mobility: Detailed Mobility of Persons 25 Years and Over, by Race, Age, and Education. Part 2-1
[Continued]

| Characteristic | Total population | | | | Same house (nonmovers) | | |
| | | MSA's | | Outside MSA's | MSA's | | Outside MSA's |
	Total	Central cities	Balance		Central cities	Balance	
High school graduate	1,112	651	281	180	480	192	136
Some college or associate degree	705	407	231	68	277	154	55
Bachelor's degree	292	167	105	20	119	70	14
Graduate or professional degree	54	38	13	3	27	8	2
Percent high school graduate	82.8	82.0	85.7	80.0	82.4	83.3	80.2
Persons 30 to 34 years	2,785	1,565	859	361	1,201	646	294
Less than 9th grade	80	63	8	8	54	7	8
9th to 12th grade, no diploma	379	232	68	79	156	44	58
High school graduate	1,122	607	334	182	463	267	152
Some college or associate degree	848	474	309	64	371	238	52
Bachelor's degree	298	152	125	21	124	80	19
Graduate or professional degree	59	37	16	7	32	9	5
Percent high school graduates	83.6	81.2	91.2	75.8	82.5	92.1	77.5
Persons 35 to 44 years	4,629	2,500	1,375	755	2,029	1,080	652
Less than 9th grade	173	101	19	54	76	18	45
9th to 12th grade, no diploma	632	346	130	156	261	90	127
High school graduate	1,873	995	543	335	801	399	294
Some college or associate degree	1,231	725	385	121	603	322	101
Bachelor's degree	532	238	230	64	204	193	63
Graduate or professional degree	188	96	68	24	82	59	22
Percent high school graduates	82.6	82.1	89.2	72.2	83.3	90.0	73.6
Persons 45 to 64 years	5,098	3,000	1,478	621	2,677	1,312	565
Less than 9th grade	661	335	177	149	299	148	132
9th to 12th grade, no diploma	1,105	726	200	180	651	182	168
High school graduate	1,797	1,105	521	171	985	463	157
Some college or associate degree	951	506	356	89	447	317	79
Bachelor's degree	356	191	147	18	163	138	16
Graduate or professional degree	228	136	78	15	131	65	13
Percent high school graduates	65.3	64.6	74.5	47.0	64.5	74.9	46.8
Persons 65 years and over	2,660	1,554	514	592	1,445	478	564
Less than 9th grade	1,231	658	221	353	613	211	341
9th to 12th grade, no diploma	550	330	119	101	303	116	94
High school graduate	547	363	101	83	340	87	81
Some college or associate degree	175	110	30	35	102	24	28
Bachelor's degree	83	49	26	8	47	23	8
Graduate or professional degree	74	44	18	11	40	16	11
Percent high school graduates	33.0	36.4	33.9	23.3	36.6	31.7	22.8

Source: "Detailed Mobility of Persons 25 Years and Over, by Race and Hispanic Origin, Age, and Educational Attainment," *Geographical Mobility: March 1992 to March 1993,* pp. 94, 96.

★ 662 ★

Mobility

Geographical Mobility: Detailed Mobility of Persons 25 Years and Over, by Race, Age, and Education. Part 2-2

[Mobility data from March 1992 to March 1993. Numbers in thousands. For meaning of symbols, see text.]

Characteristic	Total	Movers within same MSA				
		Within central city	Between central cities	Within balance	Central city to balance	Balance to central city
BLACK						
Persons 25 years and over	2,067	1,146	46	410	296	168
Less than 9th grade	132	99	-	25	5	3
9th to 12th grade, no diploma	365	261	3	54	29	19
High school graduate	810	413	22	157	130	89
Some college or associate degree	528	287	20	114	80	27
Bachelor's degree	185	72	-	50	39	24
Graduate or professional degree	47	14	2	12	12	7
Percent high school graduates	75.9	68.6	(B)	80.8	88.3	87.0
Persons 25 to 29 years	523	298	15	99	67	44
Less than 9th grade	5	5	-	-	-	-
9th to 12th grade, no diploma	87	60	-	18	2	7
High school graduate	223	120	7	41	29	26
Some college or associate degree	149	90	8	25	25	1
Bachelor's degree	51	23	-	14	8	6
Graduate or professional degree	8	-	-	-	3	5
Percent high school graduate	82.4	78.2	(B)	81.6	(B)	(B)
Persons 30 to 34 years	461	238	17	95	67	45
Less than 9th grade	7	7	-	-	-	-
9th to 12th grade, no diploma	84	61	3	8	8	4
High school graduate	173	90	5	37	17	24
Some college or associate degree	140	66	7	36	20	11
Bachelor's degree	56	14	-	13	22	6
Graduate or professional degree	2	-	2	-	-	-
Percent high school graduates	80.3	71.3	(B)	91.2	(B)	(B)
Persons 35 to 44 years	605	321	4	128	108	44
Less than 9th grade	24	22	-	-	1	1
9th to 12th grade, no diploma	98	59	-	18	15	6
High school graduate	257	133	4	50	56	15
Some college or associate degree	155	84	-	38	21	12
Bachelor's degree	54	17	-	20	9	8
Graduate or professional degree	17	5	-	3	6	3
Percent high school graduates	79.9	74.7	(B)	86.1	85.3	(B)
Persons 45 to 64 years	374	218	10	77	43	26
Less than 9th grade	52	29	-	23	-	-
9th to 12th grade, no diploma	81	66	-	8	4	2
High school graduate	132	59	6	22	26	20

[Continued]

★ 662 ★

Geographical Mobility: Detailed Mobility of Persons 25 Years and Over, by Race, Age, and Education. Part 2-2

[Continued]

Characteristic		Movers within same MSA				
	Total	Within central city	Between central cities	Within balance	Central city to balance	Balance to central city
Some college or associate degree	72	44	5	15	9	-
Bachelor's degree	22	16	-	2	-	4
Graduate or professional degree	15	5	-	7	3	-
Percent high school graduates	64.4	56.5	(B)	59.0	(B)	(B)
Persons 65 years and over	103	71	-	12	11	10
Less than 9th grade	45	36	-	2	4	2
9th to 12th grade, no diploma	15	14	-	1	-	-
High school graduate	25	11	-	7	2	5
Some college or associate degree	12	3	-	-	5	3
Bachelor's degree	2	2	-	-	-	-
Graduate or professional degree	6	4	-	2	-	-
Percent high school graduates	42.2	(B)	(B)	(B)	(B)	(B)

Source: "Detailed Mobility of Persons 25 Years and Over, by Race and Hispanic Origin, Age, and Educational Attainment," *Geographical Mobility: March 1992 to March 1993*, pp. 94, 96. *Note:* B=Base too small to show derived measure.

★ 663 ★

Mobility

Geographical Mobility: Detailed Mobility of Persons 25 Years and Over, by Race, Age, and Education. Part 3-1

[Mobility data from March 1992 to March 1993. Numbers in thousands. For meaning of symbols, see text.]

Characteristic		Total population			Same house (nonmovers)		
		MSA's		Outside MSA's	MSA's		Outside MSA's
	Total	Central cities	Balance		Central cities	Balance	
HISPANIC							
Persons 25 years and over	12,100	6,200	5,041	859	4,898	4,032	679
Less than 9th grade	3,812	2,136	1,381	295	1,723	1,120	244
9th to 12th grade, no diploma	1,865	1,066	683	115	832	526	86
High school graduate	3,242	1,573	1,430	239	1,225	1,126	181
Some college or associate degree	2,092	952	990	150	760	810	123
Bachelor's degree	780	330	411	39	242	332	30
Graduate or professional degree	309	144	145	21	117	118	15
Percent high school graduates	53.1	48.4	59.0	52.2	47.8	59.2	51.4
Persons 25 to 29 years	2,192	1,125	918	149	739	583	84
Less than 9th grade	446	237	174	35	147	111	17
9th to 12th grade, no diploma	411	231	156	24	143	64	14

[Continued]

★ 663 ★

Geographical Mobility: Detailed Mobility of Persons 25 Years and Over, by Race, Age, and Education. Part 3-1

[Continued]

Characteristic	Total population				Same house (nonmovers)		
	Total	MSA's		Outside MSA's	MSA's		Outside MSA's
		Central cities	Balance		Central cities	Balance	
High school graduate	683	347	279	56	230	178	27
Some college or associate degree	470	230	209	30	169	150	25
Bachelor's degree	154	63	89	2	37	55	1
Graduate or professional degree	28	16	11	1	12	5	-
Percent high school graduate	60.9	58.4	64.1	60.3	60.7	66.5	63.3
Persons 30 to 34 years	2,086	1,080	858	148	785	642	105
Less than 9th grade	490	266	191	33	195	147	25
9th to 12th grade, no diploma	347	208	126	14	145	94	10
High school graduate	628	309	263	55	225	196	40
Some college or associate degree	416	195	185	36	150	137	25
Bachelor's degree	153	71	75	7	49	59	4
Graduate or professional degree	51	30	18	3	21	10	1
Percent high school graduates	59.8	56.1	63.1	68.0	56.7	62.6	67.0
Persons 35 to 44 years	3,330	1,623	1,474	233	1,299	1,183	193
Less than 9th grade	878	477	354	47	394	252	39
9th to 12th grade, no diploma	509	281	193	35	225	164	24
High school graduate	929	432	428	69	345	347	59
Some college or associate degree	672	292	326	54	229	278	47
Bachelor's degree	240	107	113	20	80	94	18
Graduate or professional degree	103	36	59	8	27	48	6
Percent high school graduates	58.4	53.4	62.9	64.7	52.4	64.9	67.4
Persons 45 to 64 years	3,271	1,704	1,334	233	1,460	1,198	207
Less than 9th grade	1,242	727	413	103	600	374	91
9th to 12th grade, no diploma	455	266	154	35	240	135	32
High school graduate	831	396	384	50	342	336	47
Some college or associate degree	458	199	231	27	179	210	24
Bachelor's degree	187	70	108	9	58	101	6
Graduate or professional degree	97	46	43	8	41	43	7
Percent high school graduates	481	41.8	57.5	40.6	42.4	57.6	40.6
Persons 65 years and over	1,222	669	457	97	616	426	90
Less than 9th grade	756	430	250	77	386	236	72
9th to 12th grade, no diploma	142	81	55	7	80	50	7
High school graduate	171	88	75	8	83	69	7
Some college or associate degree	77	36	39	2	34	34	2
Bachelor's degree	46	19	25	2	18	24	1
Graduate or professional degree	30	15	14	1	15	12	1
Percent high school graduates	26.5	23.7	33.4	13.5	24.4	32.7	12.7

Source: "Detailed Mobility of Persons 25 Years and Over, by Race and Hispanic Origin, Age, and Educational Attainment," *Geographical Mobility: March 1992 to March 1993*, pp. 96, 98. *Note:* 1. Persons of Hispanic origin may be of any race.

★ 664 ★
Mobility

Geographical Mobility: Detailed Mobility of Persons 25 Years and Over, by Race, Age, and Education. Part 3-2

[Mobility data from March 1992 to March 1993. Numbers in thousands. For meaning of symbols, see text.]

Characteristic		Movers within same MSA				
	Total	Within central city	Between central cities	Within balance	Central city to balance	Balance to central city
HISPANIC						
Persons 25 years and over	1,728	864	26	507	238	93
Less than 9th grade	513	270	12	152	53	27
9th to 12th grade, no diploma	304	160	2	96	32	14
High school graduate	493	246	4	140	79	24
Some college or associate degree	277	133	5	73	51	15
Bachelor's degree	114	44	3	43	15	10
Graduate or professional degree	26	12	-	3	7	4
Percent high school graduates	52.7	50.3	(B)	51.1	64.1	56.4
Persons 25 to 29 years	551	274	6	182	71	19
Less than 9th grade	118	61	1	33	17	5
9th to 12th grade, no diploma	121	64	-	48	7	1
High school graduate	165	93	2	44	26	1
Some college or associate degree	98	43	2	34	13	5
Bachelor's degree	46	12	1	23	4	5
Graduate or professional degree	4	-	-	-	3	2
Percent high school graduate	56.8	54.2	(B)	55.7	(B)	(B)
Persons 30 to 34 years	384	191	5	107	48	33
Less than 9th grade	93	48	3	31	8	3
9th to 12th grade, no diploma	78	37	-	21	9	10
High school graduate	122	60	-	33	16	12
Some college or associate degree	60	29	1	13	12	5
Bachelor's degree	26	12	2	8	2	2
Graduate or professional degree	5	4	-	-	1	-
Percent high school graduates	55.3	55.1	(B)	51.4	(B)	(B)
Persons 35 to 44 years	455	204	4	149	72	26
Less than 9th grade	143	50	2	68	12	11
9th to 12th grade, no diploma	67	39	-	17	10	2
High school graduate	125	54	-	38	24	9
Some college or associate degree	83	43	2	16	17	5
Bachelor's degree	26	12	-	8	5	-
Graduate or professional degree	12	6	-	2	3	-
Percent high school graduates	54.0	56.8	(B)	42.8	(B)	(B)
Persons 45 to 64 years	282	163	10	55	40	14
Less than 9th grade	120	81	5	13	12	7
9th to 12th grade, no diploma	33	20	2	6	6	-
High school graduate	80	38	3	25	12	2

[Continued]

★ 664 ★

Geographical Mobility: Detailed Mobility of Persons 25 Years and Over, by Race, Age, and Education. Part 3-2

[Continued]

Characteristic		Movers within same MSA				
	Total	Within central city	Between central cities	Within balance	Central city to balance	Balance to central city
Some college or associate degree	31	17	-	8	6	-
Bachelor's degree	14	5	-	3	3	2
Graduate or professional degree	4	2	-	-	-	2
Percent high school graduates	45.7	38.1	(B)	(B)	(B)	(B)
Persons 65 years and over	55	32	1	14	8	-
Less than 9th grade	40	30	1	6	3	-
9th to 12th grade, no diploma	4	-	-	4	-	-
High school graduate	1	-	-	-	1	-
Some college or associate degree	6	1	-	2	2	-
Bachelor's degree	3	2	-	-	1	-
Graduate or professional degree	1	-	-	1	-	-
Percent high school graduates	(B)	(B)	(B)	(B)	(B)	(B)

Source: "Detailed Mobility of Persons 25 Years and Over, by Race and Hispanic Origin, Age, and Educational Attainment," *Geographical Mobility: March 1992 to March 1993*, pp. 96, 98. *Notes:* B = Base too small to show derived measure. 1. Persons of Hispanic origin may be of any race.

★ 665 ★

Mobility

Geographical Mobility: Detailed Mobility, by Household and Family Status, Region, and Race and Hispanic Origin. Part 1-1

[Mobility data from March 1992 to March 1993. Numbers in thousands. For meaning of symbols, see text.]

Characteristic	Total population				Same house (nonmovers)		
	Total	MSA's		Outside MSA's	MSA's		Outside MSA's
		Central cities	Balance		Central cities	Balance	
FAMILY HOUSEHOLDERS							
United States	68,144	19,336	32,964	15,844	15,846	28,673	13,657
White	57,858	13,966	29,609	14,283	11,527	25,990	12,324
Black	7,888	4,382	2,266	1,240	3,559	1,821	1,068
Hispanic[1]	5,318	2,761	2,158	399	2,127	1,705	311
Northeast	12,478	3,990	7,768	1,720	3,539	7,157	1,515
White	11,839	2,884	7,262	1,694	2,553	6,716	1,489
Black	1,242	896	336	9	804	293	9
Hispanic[1]	884	648	222	14	526	194	10
Midwest	16,326	4,309	7,163	4,854	3,539	6,302	4,213

[Continued]

★ 665 ★

Geographical Mobility: Detailed Mobility, by Household and Family Status, Region, and Race and Hispanic Origin. Part 1-1

[Continued]

Characteristic	Total population				Same house (nonmovers)		
		MSA's		Outside MSA's	MSA's		Outside MSA's
	Total	Central cities	Balance		Central cities	Balance	
White	14,454	2,971	6,742	4,742	2,458	5,947	4,135
Black	1,621	1,226	341	55	996	283	40
Hispanic[1]	400	244	132	24	180	101	18
South	24,040	6,305	10,763	6,972	5,038	9,114	6,036
White	19,184	4,255	9,220	5,709	3,466	7,919	4,938
Black	4,361	1,907	1,310	1,145	1,477	1,031	1,000
Hispanic[1]	1,676	865	636	176	695	487	130
West	14,299	4,731	7,270	2,298	3,731	6,100	1,894
White	12,381	3,857	6,386	2,138	3,050	5,407	1,761
Black	663	353	279	31	283	214	20
Hispanic[1]	2,358	1,004	1,168	185	726	923	153

Source: "Detailed Mobility of Householders, by Race and Hispanic Origin," *Geographical Mobility: March 1992 to March 1993,* p. 124. *Note:* 1. Persons of Hispanic origin may be of any race.

★ 666 ★

Mobility

Geographical Mobility: Detailed Mobility, by Household and Family Status, Region, and Race and Hispanic Origin. Part 1-2

[Mobility data from March 1992 to March 1993. Numbers in thousands. For meaning of symbols, see text.]

Characteristic	Movers within same MSA					
	Total	Within central city	Between central cities	Within balance	Central city to balance	Balance to central city
FAMILY HOUSEHOLDERS						
United States	5,705	2,085	94	2,283	839	403
White	4,371	1,357	74	1,960	670	310
Black	1,039	595	17	213	141	74
Hispanic[1]	851	433	20	249	106	44
Northeast	808	296	6	399	60	47
White	664	205	6	357	59	38
Black	112	74	1	30	-	7
Hispanic[1]	114	91	1	16	4	2
Midwest	1,230	513	12	486	136	83

[Continued]

★ 666 ★

Geographical Mobility: Detailed Mobility, by Household and Family Status, Region, and Race and Hispanic Origin. Part 1-2

[Continued]

Characteristic		Movers within same MSA				
	Total	Within central city	Between central cities	Within balance	Central city to balance	Balance to central city
White	963	323	12	451	118	59
Black	241	171	-	31	18	21
Hispanic[1]	79	52	2	23	2	2
South	2,046	720	46	771	378	130
White	1,416	390	31	630	268	97
Black	570	304	15	117	102	31
Hispanic[1]	224	89	8	71	41	15
West	1,621	557	30	627	264	143
White	1,328	439	26	522	225	115
Black	117	46	2	34	21	14
Hispanic[1]	434	202	8	140	59	25

Source: "Detailed Mobility of Householders, by Race and Hispanic Origin," *Geographical Mobility: March 1992 to March 1993*, p. 124. *Note:* 1. Persons of Hispanic origin may be of any race.

★ 667 ★
Mobility

Geographical Mobility: Detailed Mobility, by Household and Family Status, Region, and Race and Hispanic Origin. Part 2-1

[Mobility data from March 1992 to March 1993. Numbers in thousands. For meaning of symbols, see text.]

Characteristic		Total population			Same house (nonmovers)		
	Total	MSA's		Outside MSA's	MSA's		Outside MSA's
		Central cities	Balance		Central cities	Balance	
POPULATION IN FAMILY HOUSEHOLDS							
United States	211,552	60,013	103,158	48,381	49,044	89,208	41,415
White	176,050	41,697	91,392	42,961	34,305	79,665	36,771
Black	26,823	14,804	7,625	4,194	11,967	6,228	3,612
Hispanic[1]	19,613	10,095	8,072	1,447	7,817	6,351	1,116
Northeast	42,157	12,340	24,570	5,247	10,980	22,690	4,627
White	36,406	8,545	22,730	5,132	7,591	21,069	4,528
Black	4,285	3,076	1,164	45	2,759	1,031	40
Hispanic[1]	2,879	2,105	723	51	1,728	628	39
Midwest	50,516	13,363	22,311	14,841	10,935	19,568	12,879

[Continued]

★ 667 ★

Geographical Mobility: Detailed Mobility, by Household and Family Status, Region, and Race and Hispanic Origin. Part 2-1

[Continued]

Characteristic	Total population				Same house (nonmovers)		
	Total	MSA's		Outside MSA's	MSA's		Outside MSA's
		Central cities	Balance		Central cities	Balance	
White	44,094	8,790	20,879	14,425	7,265	18,322	12,565
Black	5,472	4,175	1,128	169	3,372	976	132
Hispanic[1]	1,439	929	428	82	674	331	59
South	73,736	19,483	32,920	21,334	15,522	27,658	18,290
White	57,123	12,531	27,548	17,044	10,202	23,459	14,569
Black	14,754	6,411	4,439	3,905	4,949	3,541	3,392
Hispanic[1]	6,084	3,136	2,297	651	2,496	1,736	500
West	45,143	14,827	23,358	6,960	11,608	19,292	5,619
White	38,426	11,830	20,236	6,360	9,247	16,814	5,109
Black	2,112	1,143	894	75	887	681	48
Hispanic[1]	9,211	3,925	4,624	663	2,919	3,656	517

Source: "Detailed Mobility of Householders, by Race and Hispanic Origin," *Geographical Mobility: March 1992 to March 1993*, p. 124. *Note:* 1. Persons of Hispanic origin may be of any race.

★ 668 ★

Mobility

Geographical Mobility: Detailed Mobility, by Household and Family Status, Region, and Race and Hispanic Origin. Part 2-2

[Mobility data from March 1992 to March 1993. Numbers in thousands. For meaning of symbols, see text.]

Characteristic	Movers within same MSA					
	Total	Within central city	Between central cities	Within balance	Central city to balance	Balance to central city
POPULATION IN FAMILY HOUSEHOLDS						
United States	17,811	6,536	273	7,145	2,612	1,245
White	13,248	4,115	200	6,113	2,100	900
Black	3,382	1,989	60	623	428	282
Hispanic[1]	3,067	1,546	51	921	392	158
Northeast	2,379	891	11	1,177	183	117
White	1,921	579	10	1,057	178	95
Black	369	260	1	86	3	19
Hispanic[1]	347	267	1	50	15	14

[Continued]

★ 668 ★

Geographical Mobility: Detailed Mobility, by Household and Family Status, Region, and Race and Hispanic Origin. Part 2-2
[Continued]

Characteristic		Movers within same MSA				
	Total	Within central city	Between central cities	Within balance	Central city to balance	Balance to central city
Midwest	3,753	1,602	38	1,438	410	264
White	2,862	943	38	1,357	350	173
Black	799	589	-	70	56	84
Hispanic[1]	276	194	4	60	12	5
South	6,318	2,259	135	2,390	1,139	395
White	4,249	1,159	80	1,927	804	278
Black	1,844	1,010	52	369	300	112
Hispanic[1]	831	359	27	255	145	46
West	5,360	1,784	89	2,139	879	469
White	4,397	1,434	71	1,771	768	354
Black	370	131	7	98	68	66
Hispanic[1]	1,613	726	18	557	219	93

Source: "Detailed Mobility of Householders, by Race and Hispanic Origin," *Geographical Mobility: March 1992 to March 1993*, p. 124. *Note:* 1. Persons of Hispanic origin may be of any race.

★ 669 ★

Mobility

Geographical Mobility: Detailed Mobility, by Household and Family Status, Region, and Race and Hispanic Origin. Part 3-1

[Mobility data from March 1992 to March 1993. Numbers in thousands. For meaning of symbols, see text.]

Characteristic		Total population			Same house (nonmovers)		
	Total	MSA's		Outside MSA's	MSA's		Outside MSA's
		Central cities	Balance		Central cities	Balance	
SINGLE-PARENT FAMILY HOUSEHOLDERS							
United States	14,973	6,113	5,950	2,910	4,700	4,863	2,333
White	10,257	3,349	4,725	2,183	2,548	3,907	1,736
Black	4,140	2,506	1,003	631	1,973	804	520
Hispanic[1]	1,645	1,022	541	81	751	403	59
Northeast	3,087	1,415	1,362	310	1,209	1,194	251
White	2,348	845	1,196	307	715	1,058	248
Black	665	519	145	2	453	121	2
Hispanic[1]	409	346	63	1	283	50	-

[Continued]

★ 669 ★

Geographical Mobility: Detailed Mobility, by Household and Family Status, Region, and Race and Hispanic Origin. Part 3-1

[Continued]

Characteristic	Total population				Same house (nonmovers)		
	Total	MSA's		Outside MSA's	MSA's		Outside MSA's
		Central cities	Balance		Central cities	Balance	
Midwest	3,498	1,541	1,149	808	1,192	962	647
White	2,450	717	980	753	545	824	607
Black	974	781	155	38	619	128	29
Hispanic[1]	122	77	38	7	48	26	5
South	5,336	1,917	1,997	1,421	1,395	1,554	1,164
White	3,015	846	1,357	812	606	1,059	654
Black	2,201	1,035	587	579	771	464	484
Hispanic[1]	409	237	133	38	174	102	25
West	3,051	1,240	1,441	371	904	1,153	271
White	2,444	941	1,191	311	683	965	227
Black	300	171	116	13	130	90	6
Hispanic[1]	705	362	307	36	245	225	28

Source: "Detailed Mobility of Householders, by Race and Hispanic Origin," *Geographical Mobility: March 1992 to March 1993*, p. 124.
Note: 1. Persons of Hispanic origin may be of any race.

★ 670 ★

Mobility

Geographical Mobility: Detailed Mobility, by Household and Family Status, Region, and Race and Hispanic Origin. Part 3-2

[Mobility data from March 1992 to March 1993. Numbers in thousands. For meaning of symbols, see text.]

Characteristic	Movers within same MSA					
	Total	Within central city	Between central cities	Within balance	Central city to balance	Balance to central city
SINGLE-PARENT FAMILY HOUSEHOLDERS						
United States	2,056	970	36	641	247	162
White	1,297	506	20	499	163	108
Black	645	415	13	100	69	47
Hispanic[1]	316	177	6	90	26	17
Northeast	306	152	1	114	18	21
White	220	93	1	95	18	12
Black	75	51	-	16	-	7
Hispanic[1]	59	45	1	10	2	1

[Continued]

★ 670 ★

Geographical Mobility: Detailed Mobility, by Household and Family Status, Region, and Race and Hispanic Origin. Part 3-2

[Continued]

Characteristic	Total	Movers within same MSA				
		Within central city	Between central cities	Within balance	Central city to balance	Balance to central city
Midwest	466	267	3	129	30	37
White	283	125	3	112	20	24
Black	166	130	-	13	10	12
Hispanic[1]	32	22	1	9	1	-
South	772	353	22	231	122	45
White	395	134	9	161	64	27
Black	346	208	12	58	51	18
Hispanic[1]	62	29	2	18	6	8
West	512	198	11	167	77	59
White	399	154	8	131	61	45
Black	58	25	2	13	9	10
Hispanic[1]	163	82	2	53	18	8

Source: "Detailed Mobility of Householders, by Race and Hispanic Origin," *Geographical Mobility: March 1992 to March 1993*, p. 124. *Note:* 1. Persons of Hispanic origin may be of any race.

★ 671 ★

Mobility

Geographical Mobility: Detailed Mobility, by Household and Family Status, Region, and Race and Hispanic Origin. Part 4-1

[Mobility data from March 1992 to March 1993. Numbers in thousands. For meaning of symbols, see text.]

Characteristic	Total population				Same house (nonmovers)		
	Total	MSA's		Outside MSA's	MSA's		Outside MSA's
		Central cities	Balance		Central cities	Balance	
POPULATION IN SINGLE-PARENT FAMILY HOUSEHOLDS							
United States	43,032	18,026	16,876	8,130	13,768	13,654	6,501
White	27,962	9,096	13,025	5,840	6,848	10,604	4,615
Black	13,301	8,167	3,152	1,982	6,383	2,555	1,642
Hispanic[1]	5,342	3,272	1,819	250	2,397	1,362	185
Northeast	8,829	4,191	3,815	824	3,597	3,341	670
White	6,379	2,307	3,277	796	1,971	2,885	648
Black	2,216	1,729	470	18	1,505	409	13
Hispanic[1]	1,244	1,045	195	4	874	155	3

[Continued]

★ 671 ★

Geographical Mobility: Detailed Mobility, by Household and Family Status, Region, and Race and Hispanic Origin. Part 4-1
[Continued]

| Characteristic | Total population | | | | Same house (nonmovers) | | |
| | Total | MSA's | | Outside MSA's | MSA's | | Outside MSA's |
		Central cities	Balance		Central cities	Balance	
Midwest	9,897	4,571	3,117	2,210	3,556	2,591	1,779
White	6,520	1,881	2,600	2,038	1,423	2,152	1,648
Black	3,143	2,560	477	105	2,047	404	85
Hispanic[1]	357	249	95	14	155	71	9
South	15,533	5,788	5,680	4,065	4,133	4,379	3,310
White	8,109	2,306	3,647	2,155	1,618	2,803	1,719
Black	7,040	3,364	1,845	1,832	2,460	1,468	1,527
Hispanic[1]	1,310	770	424	116	535	320	86
West	8,772	3,476	4,264	1,031	2,482	3,343	742
White	6,955	2,602	3,501	851	1,836	2,764	600
Black	901	514	360	27	370	274	17
Hispanic[1]	2,430	1,208	1,105	117	833	816	87

Source: "Detailed Mobility of Householders, by Race and Hispanic Origin," *Geographical Mobility: March 1992 to March 1993*, p. 126. *Note:* 1. Persons of Hispanic origin may be of any race.

★ 672 ★

Mobility

Geographical Mobility: Detailed Mobility, by Household and Family Status, Region, and Race and Hispanic Origin. Part 4-2

[Mobility data from March 1992 to March 1993. Numbers in thousands. For meaning of symbols, see text.]

| Characteristic | Movers within same MSA | | | | | |
	Total	Within central city	Between central cities	Within balance	Central city to balance	Balance to central city
POPULATION IN SINGLE-PARENT FAMILY HOUSEHOLDERS						
United States	6,037	2,879	104	1,864	696	493
White	3,654	1,391	62	1,448	471	281
Black	2,063	1,350	39	294	190	191
Hispanic[1]	1,027	572	14	295	85	52
Northeast	848	443	1	312	44	49
White	564	230	1	262	44	27
Black	249	188	-	42	-	19
Hispanic[1]	160	122	1	28	6	4

[Continued]

★ 672 ★

Geographical Mobility: Detailed Mobility, by Household and Family Status, Region, and Race and Hispanic Origin. Part 4-2

[Continued]

Characteristic	Movers within same MSA					
	Total	Within central city	Between central cities	Within balance	Central city to balance	Balance to central city
Midwest	1,295	750	8	336	85	116
White	733	310	8	299	57	60
Black	519	406	-	34	27	52
Hispanic[1]	90	70	1	18	1	-
South	2,346	1,107	54	706	329	150
White	1,139	382	20	480	176	81
Black	1,105	694	32	182	130	67
Hispanic[1]	227	115	5	62	22	23
West	1,548	579	41	510	239	178
White	1,217	469	33	408	194	114
Black	191	62	7	36	33	52
Hispanic[1]	551	266	7	187	66	25

Source: "Detailed Mobility of Householders, by Race and Hispanic Origin," *Geographical Mobility: March 1992 to March 1993*, p. 124.
Note: 1. Persons of Hispanic origin may be of any race.

★ 673 ★

Mobility

Geographical Mobility: Detailed Mobility, by Household and Family Status, Region, and Race and Hispanic Origin. Part 5-1

[Mobility data from March 1992 to March 1993. Numbers in thousands. For meaning of symbols, see text.]

Characteristic	Total population				Same house (nonmovers)		
	Total	MSA's		Outside MSA's	MSA's		Outside MSA's
		Central cities	Balance		Central cities	Balance	
FEMALE SINGLE-PARENT FAMILY HOUSEHOLDERS							
United States	11,947	5,043	4,628	2,276	3,875	3,784	1,836
White	7,848	2,584	3,623	1,642	1,969	2,996	1,316
Black	3,680	2,260	862	558	1,766	694	460
Hispanic[1]	1,238	801	386	51	600	294	41
Northeast	2,477	1,193	1,043	241	1,021	917	191
White	1,837	690	910	238	584	808	187
Black	590	470	118	2	407	100	2
Hispanic[1]	358	305	52	1	255	42	-

[Continued]

★ 673 ★

Geographical Mobility: Detailed Mobility, by Household and Family Status, Region, and Race and Hispanic Origin. Part 5-1
[Continued]

Characteristic	Total population				Same house (nonmovers)		
	Total	MSA's		Outside MSA's	MSA's		Outside MSA's
		Central cities	Balance		Central cities	Balance	
Midwest	2,787	1,293	885	608	988	746	485
White	1,872	568	745	559	427	628	449
Black	861	895	132	35	542	112	26
Hispanic[1]	87	58	23	5	32	19	4
South	4,446	1,640	1,646	1,160	1,198	1,283	954
White	2,387	669	1,095	623	484	858	504
Black	1,970	944	517	509	700	410	426
Hispanic[1]	297	180	94	23	132	74	18
West	2,237	917	1,053	267	668	837	207
White	1,752	657	873	222	474	705	176
Black	260	152	95	13	116	73	6
Hispanic[1]	497	258	217	22	180	160	19

Source: "Detailed Mobility of Householders, by Race and Hispanic Origin," *Geographical Mobility: March 1992 to March 1993,* p. 126. *Note:* 1. Persons of Hispanic origin may be of any race.

★ 674 ★
Mobility

Geographical Mobility: Detailed Mobility, by Household and Family Status, Region, and Race and Hispanic Origin. Part 5-2

[Mobility data from March 1992 to March 1993. Numbers in thousands. For meaning of symbols, see text.]

Characteristic	Movers within same MSA					
	Total	Within central city	Between central cities	Within balance	Central city to balance	Balance to central city
FEMALE SINGLE-PARENT FAMILY HOUSEHOLDERS						
United States	1,673	812	34	501	191	134
White	998	388	18	389	116	87
Black	588	387	13	85	61	42
Hispanic[1]	226	134	4	58	16	13
Northeast	248	128	-	92	12	16
White	172	78	-	73	12	9
Black	71	48	-	16	-	7
Hispanic[1]	47	38	-	7	2	-

[Continued]

★ 674 ★

Geographical Mobility: Detailed Mobility, by Household and Family Status, Region, and Race and Hispanic Origin. Part 5-2

[Continued]

Characteristic		Movers within same MSA				
	Total	Within central city	Between central cities	Within balance	Central city to balance	Balance to central city
Midwest	388	232	3	102	18	33
White	223	99	3	93	8	22
Black	153	126	-	7	10	10
Hispanic[1]	24	19	1	3	1	-
South	659	315	20	189	102	33
White	320	113	7	129	52	19
Black	314	193	12	52	43	14
Hispanic[1]	49	25	1	12	4	6
West	378	137	11	119	59	52
White	283	96	8	95	45	38
Black	51	21	2	10	8	10
Hispanic[1]	106	52	2	36	10	7

Source: "Detailed Mobility of Householders, by Race and Hispanic Origin," *Geographical Mobility: March 1992 to March 1993*, p. 126. *Note:* 1. Persons of Hispanic origin may be of any race.

★ 675 ★

Mobility

Geographical Mobility: Detailed Mobility, by Household and Family Status, Region, and Race and Hispanic Origin. Part 6-1

[Mobility data from March 1992 to March 1993. Numbers in thousands. For meaning of symbols, see text.]

Characteristic	Total population				Same house (nonmovers)		
	Total	MSA's		Outside MSA's	MSA's		Outside MSA's
		Central cities	Balance		Central cities	Balance	
POPULATION IN FEMALE SINGLE-PARENT FAMILY HOUSEHOLDS							
United States	34,855	15,057	13,288	6,510	11,527	10,763	5,206
White	21,660	7,052	10,098	4,510	5,330	8,239	3,558
Black	11,927	7,425	2,746	1,756	5,783	2,233	1,456
Hispanic[1]	4,089	2,596	1,320	173	1,927	997	144
Northeast	7,164	3,585	2,928	651	3,078	2,578	522
White	5,014	1,898	2,489	627	1,623	2,201	503
Black	1,991	1,584	389	18	1,369	341	13
Hispanic[1]	1,103	938	161	4	796	130	3

[Continued]

★ 675 ★

Geographical Mobility: Detailed Mobility, by Household and Family Status, Region, and Race and Hispanic Origin. Part 6-1
[Continued]

| Characteristic | Total population | | | | Same house (nonmovers) | | |
| | | MSA's | | Outside MSA's | MSA's | | Outside MSA's |
	Total	Central cities	Balance		Central cities	Balance	
Midwest	8,087	3,898	2,473	1,716	3,035	2,072	1,364
White	5,076	1,494	2,023	1,559	1,138	1,681	1,245
Black	2,836	2,315	422	99	1,842	367	79
Hispanic[1]	263	198	55	9	111	45	7
South	13,111	4,995	4,741	3,375	3,585	3,658	2,742
White	6,523	1,844	2,985	1,694	1,302	2,302	1,338
Black	6,316	3,066	1,638	1,612	2,243	1,303	1,347
Hispanic[1]	991	597	310	84	418	234	70
West	6,493	2,579	3,146	768	1,828	2,456	577
White	5,047	1,815	2,601	631	1,267	2,055	471
Black	784	460	296	27	329	222	17
Hispanic[1]	1,732	862	794	76	602	587	64

Source: "Detailed Mobility of Householders, by Race and Hispanic Origin," *Geographical Mobility: March 1992 to March 1993*, p. 126. *Note:* 1. Persons of Hispanic origin may be of any race.

★ 676 ★

Mobility

Geographical Mobility: Detailed Mobility, by Household and Family Status, Region, and Race and Hispanic Origin. Part 6-2

[Mobility data from March 1992 to March 1993. Numbers in thousands. For meaning of symbols, see text.]

| Characteristic | Movers within same MSA | | | | | |
	Total	Within central city	Between central cities	Within balance	Central city to balance	Balance to central city
POPULATION IN FEMALE SINGLE-PARENT FAMILY HOUSEHOLDS						
United States	4,956	2,436	98	1,465	547	410
White	2,817	1,079	55	1,118	347	217
Black	1,889	1,248	39	261	166	175
Hispanic[1]	769	450	13	204	64	39
Northeast	697	385	-	240	34	39
White	440	197	-	191	34	20
Black	241	180	-	42	-	19
Hispanic[1]	132	107	-	19	6	1

[Continued]

★ 676 ★

Geographical Mobility: Detailed Mobility, by Household and Family Status, Region, and Race and Hispanic Origin. Part 6-2

[Continued]

Characteristic		Movers within same MSA				
	Total	Within central city	Between central cities	Within balance	Central city to balance	Balance to central city
Midwest	1,089	660	8	270	51	100
White	576	242	8	249	23	54
Black	479	391	-	19	27	41
Hispanic[1]	73	63	1	8	1	-
South	2,020	980	52	588	281	119
White	929	328	18	386	143	55
Black	1,000	624	32	167	114	63
Hispanic[1]	185	99	5	46	16	19
West	1,150	412	39	366	182	152
White	871	312	30	293	147	88
Black	170	54	7	32	25	52
Hispanic[1]	380	181	7	130	42	20

Source: "Detailed Mobility of Householders, by Race and Hispanic Origin," *Geographical Mobility: March 1992 to March 1993*, p. 126.
Note: 1. Persons of Hispanic origin may be of any race.

★ 677 ★

Mobility

Geographical Mobility: Detailed Mobility, by Household and Family Status, Region, and Race. Part 1-1

[Mobility data from March 1992 to March 1993. Numbers in thousands. For meaning of symbols, see text.]

Characteristic		Total population			Same house (nonmovers)		
		MSA's		Outside MSA's	MSA's		Outside MSA's
	Total	Central cities	Balance		Central cities	Balance	
TOTAL, 1 YEAR OLD AND OVER							
United States	250,210	75,127	119,140	55,943	59,733	101,122	47,306
White	208,754	53,264	105,745	49,745	42,399	90,435	42,076
Black	31,366	17,748	8,843	4,774	14,207	7,116	4,073
Hispanic[1]	22,232	11,560	9,009	1,663	8,769	6,964	1,258
Northeast	50,003	15,530	28,332	6,142	13,618	25,784	5,309
White	43,130	10,919	26,207	6,004	9,552	23,928	5,197
Black	5,200	3,752	1,387	60	3,345	1,228	47
Hispanic[1]	3,322	2,445	824	53	1,999	705	40
Midwest	60,031	16,931	25,740	17,359	13,441	22,087	14,824

[Continued]

★ 677 ★

Geographical Mobility: Detailed Mobility, by Household and Family Status, Region, and Race. Part 1-1

[Continued]

| Characteristic | Total population | | | | Same house (nonmovers) | | |
| | Total | MSA's | | Outside MSA's | MSA's | | Outside MSA's |
		Central cities	Balance		Central cities	Balance	
White	52,433	11,445	24,121	16,868	9,106	20,708	14,457
Black	6,442	4,977	1,264	201	3,988	1,074	159
Hispanic[1]	1,635	1,035	489	111	726	370	74
South	86,107	23,929	37,826	24,353	18,527	31,163	20,731
White	66,854	15,681	31,695	19,477	12,305	26,473	16,551
Black	17,173	7,618	5,121	4,434	5,807	4,004	3,818
Hispanic[1]	8,859	3,578	2,519	762	2,772	1,874	572
West	54,068	18,737	27,242	8,089	14,146	22,088	6,441
White	46,338	15,219	23,722	7,396	11,436	19,325	5,872
Black	2,551	1,401	1,070	79	1,068	811	49
Hispanic[1]	10,415	4,501	5,177	736	3,271	4,014	573

Source: "Detailed Mobility, by Household and Family Status, Region, and Race and Hispanic Origin," *Geographical Mobility: March 1992 to March 1993*, p. 122. *Note:* 1. Persons of Hispanic origin may be of any race.

★ 678 ★

Mobility

Geographical Mobility: Detailed Mobility, by Household and Family Status, Region, and Race. Part 1-2

[Mobility data from March 1992 to March 1993. Numbers in thousands. For meaning of symbols, see text.]

| Characteristic | Movers within same MSA | | | | | |
	Total	Within central city	Between central cities	Within balance	Central city to balance	Balance to central city
TOTAL, 1 YEAR OLD AND OVER						
United States	23,779	9,018	389	9,133	3,388	1,851
White	18,356	6,028	291	7,901	2,727	1,409
Black	4,198	2,462	82	768	533	353
Hispanic[1]	3,662	1,886	54	1,060	456	207
Northeast	3,220	1,194	15	1,547	270	193
White	2,650	808	11	1,409	262	160
Black	447	315	4	98	5	25
Hispanic[1]	415	313	2	58	23	19
Midwest	5,169	2,222	61	1,883	579	425

[Continued]

★ 678 ★

Geographical Mobility: Detailed Mobility, by Household and Family Status, Region, and Race. Part 1-2

[Continued]

Characteristic		Movers within same MSA				
	Total	Within central city	Between central cities	Within balance	Central city to balance	Balance to central city
White	4,074	1,407	57	1,783	510	317
Black	971	728	1	84	61	96
Hispanic[1]	329	229	3	7	18	8
South	8,276	3,049	194	3,033	1,436	564
White	5,682	1,697	122	2,465	992	406
Black	2,319	1,241	70	462	396	151
Hispanic[1]	992	461	28	284	159	60
West	7,114	2,553	118	2,671	1,103	669
White	5,950	2,115	101	2,243	964	527
Black	462	178	7	124	72	81
Hispanic[1]	1,926	883	18	648	257	120

Source: "Detailed Mobility, by Household and Family Status, Region, and Race and Hispanic Origin," *Geographical Mobility: March 1992 to March 1993*, p. 122. *Note:* 1. Persons of Hispanic origin may be of any race.

★ 679 ★

Mobility

Geographical Mobility: Detailed Mobility, by Household and Family Status, Region, and Race. Part 2-1

[Mobility data from March 1992 to March 1993. Numbers in thousands. For meaning of symbols, see text.]

Characteristic		Total population			Same house (nonmovers)		
		MSA's		Outside MSA's	MSA's		Outside MSA's
	Total	Central cities	Balance		Central cities	Balance	
HOUSEHOLDERS							
United States	96,391	30,276	44,606	21,509	24,140	37,962	18,371
White	82,083	22,456	40,191	19,436	17,979	34,518	16,616
Black	11,190	6,481	3,080	1,628	5,173	2,424	1,399
Hispanic[1]	6,626	3,546	2,586	494	2,686	2,022	383
Northeast	19,437	6,458	10,637	2,342	5,645	9,613	2,015
White	17,046	4,758	9,984	2,304	4,157	9,050	1,981
Black	1,865	1,403	449	13	1,240	394	11
Hispanic[1]	1,160	872	272	15	710	235	11
Midwest	23,307	6,859	9,777	6,671	5,451	8,342	5,723

[Continued]

★ 679 ★

Geographical Mobility: Detailed Mobility, by Household and Family Status, Region, and Race. Part 2-1

[Continued]

| Characteristic | Total population | | | | Same house (nonmovers) | | |
| | | MSA's | | Outside MSA's | MSA's | | Outside MSA's |
	Total	Central cities	Balance		Central cities	Balance	
White	20,638	4,898	9,221	6,519	3,913	7,898	5,611
Black	2,320	1,803	446	71	1,431	356	56
Hispanic[1]	502	306	163	33	213	121	23
South	33,392	9,602	14,437	9,353	7,410	11,948	8,053
White	26,696	6,652	12,359	7,685	5,197	10,387	6,614
Black	6,045	2,745	1,790	1,511	2,083	1,376	1,313
Hispanic[1]	2,085	1,118	748	219	885	589	159
West	20,255	7,357	9,754	3,144	5,635	8,059	2,581
White	17,703	6,149	8,628	2,927	4,712	7,183	2,410
Black	960	531	395	34	420	298	20
Hispanic[1]	2,880	1,249	1,404	227	897	1,097	191

Source: "Detailed Mobility, by Household and Family Status, Region, and Race and Hispanic Origin," *Geographical Mobility: March 1992 to March 1993*, p. 122. *Note:* 1. Persons of Hispanic origin may be of any race.

★ 680 ★

Mobility

Geographical Mobility: Detailed Mobility, by Household and Family Status, Region, and Race. Part 2-2

[Mobility data from March 1992 to March 1993. Numbers in thousands. For meaning of symbols, see text.]

| Characteristic | Movers within same MSA | | | | | |
	Total	Within central city	Between central cities	Within balance	Central city to balance	Balance to central city
HOUSEHOLDERS						
United States	9,197	3,589	164	3,467	1,252	725
White	7,202	2,479	127	3,015	996	585
Black	1,582	924	33	313	201	112
Hispanic[1]	1,103	588	20	299	131	65
Northeast	1,347	513	8	632	111	84
White	1,129	366	6	579	107	71
Black	168	118	2	35	2	11
Hispanic[1]	152	121	1	20	6	3
Midwest	2,102	889	22	783	230	176

[Continued]

★ 680 ★

Geographical Mobility: Detailed Mobility, by Household and Family Status, Region, and Race. Part 2-2

[Continued]

| Characteristic | Movers within same MSA | | | | | |
	Total	Within central city	Between central cities	Within balance	Central city to balance	Balance to central city
White	1,686	585	20	734	204	143
Black	372	277	1	42	22	29
Hispanic[1]	106	66	2	28	5	5
South	3,265	1,239	83	1,167	546	229
White	2,299	743	54	954	373	175
Black	871	456	28	182	153	51
Hispanic[1]	305	149	8	78	49	20
West	2,483	948	51	886	364	234
White	2,088	784	48	748	313	196
Black	172	71	2	54	24	21
Hispanic[1]	540	251	9	173	71	36

Source: "Detailed Mobility, by Household and Family Status, Region, and Race and Hispanic Origin," *Geographical Mobility: March 1992 to March 1993*, p. 122. *Note:* 1. Persons of Hispanic origin may be of any race.

★ 681 ★

Mobility

Geographical Mobility: Detailed Mobility, by Household and Family Status, Region, and Race. Part 3-1

[Mobility data from March 1992 to March 1993. Numbers in thousands. For meaning of symbols, see text.]

| Characteristic | Total population | | | | Same house (nonmovers) | | |
| | Total | MSA's | | Outside MSA's | MSA's | | Outside MSA's |
		Central cities	Balance		Central cities	Balance	
POPULATION IN HOUSEHOLDS							
United States	249,902	75,045	118,964	55,893	59,687	101,030	47,267
White	208,529	53,211	105,614	49,704	42,368	90,375	42,046
Black	31,311	17,740	8,804	4,767	14,203	7,086	4,065
Hispanic[1]	22,206	11,555	8,994	1,657	8,769	6,957	1,254
Northeast	49,936	15,509	28,290	6,137	13,597	25,746	5,305
White	43,089	10,897	26,193	5,999	9,531	23,916	5,193
Black	5,174	3,752	1,362	60	3,345	1,204	47
Hispanic[1]	3,319	2,445	821	53	1,999	703	40
Midwest	59,929	16,884	25,711	17,334	13,424	22,069	14,804

[Continued]

★ 681 ★

Geographical Mobility: Detailed Mobility, by Household and Family Status, Region, and Race. Part 3-1

[Continued]

Characteristic	Total population				Same house (nonmovers)		
	Total	MSA's		Outside MSA's	MSA's		Outside MSA's
		Central cities	Balance		Central cities	Balance	
White	52,353	11,417	24,091	16,844	9,096	20,690	14,439
Black	6,434	4,970	1,264	200	3,983	1,074	158
Hispanic[1]	1,631	1,032	488	111	726	369	73
South	86,034	23,929	37,764	24,341	18,527	31,156	20,722
White	66,795	15,681	31,643	19,472	12,305	26,469	16,458
Black	17,158	7,618	5,113	4,428	5,807	4,001	3,812
Hispanic[1]	6,854	3,578	2,514	762	2,772	1,874	572
West	54,003	18,723	27,199	8,081	14,139	22,060	6,435
White	46,291	15,216	23,687	7,388	11,436	19,301	5,866
Black	2,545	1,401	1,066	79	1,068	807	49
Hispanic[1]	10,402	4,500	5,171	731	3,271	4,010	569

Source: "Detailed Mobility, by Household and Family Status, Region, and Race and Hispanic Origin," *Geographical Mobility: March 1992 to March 1993*, p. 122. *Note:* 1. Persons of Hispanic origin may be of any race.

★ 682 ★

Mobility

Geographical Mobility: Detailed Mobility, by Household and Family Status, Region, and Race. Part 3-2

[Mobility data from March 1992 to March 1993. Numbers in thousands. For meaning of symbols, see text.]

Characteristic	Movers within same MSA					
	Total	Within central city	Balance central cities	Within balance	Central city to balance	Balance central to city
POPULATION IN HOUSEHOLDS						
United States	23,724	8,998	389	9,113	3,374	1,851
White	18,315	6,015	291	7,883	2,717	1,409
Black	4,194	2,461	82	765	533	353
Hispanic[1]	3,657	1,886	54	1,059	452	207
Northeast	3,218	1,194	15	1,546	270	193
White	2,650	808	11	1,409	262	160
Black	446	315	4	97	5	25
Hispanic[1]	414	313	2	57	23	19
Midwest	5,145	2,206	61	1,881	572	425

[Continued]

★ 682 ★

Geographical Mobility: Detailed Mobility, by Household and Family Status, Region, and Race. Part 3-2

[Continued]

Characteristic	Movers within same MSA					
	Total	Within central city	Balance central cities	Within balance	Central city to balance	Balance central to city
White	4,055	1,397	57	1,782	503	317
Black	969	727	1	84	61	96
Hispanic[1]	329	229	4	70	18	8
South	8,255	3,049	194	3,015	1,432	564
White	5,662	1,697	122	2,449	988	406
Black	2,318	1,241	70	460	396	151
Hispanic[1]	968	461	28	284	156	60
West	7,106	2,548	118	2,671	1,100	669
White	5,948	2,113	101	2,243	964	527
Black	462	178	7	124	72	81
Hispanic[1]	1,926	883	18	648	257	120

Source: "Detailed Mobility, by Household and Family Status, Region, and Race and Hispanic Origin," *Geographical Mobility: March 1992 to March 1993*, p. 122. Note: 1. Persons of Hispanic origin may be of any race.

★ 683 ★

Mobility

Geographical Mobility: Detailed Mobility, by Race, Gender, and Age. Part 1-1

[Mobility data from March 1992 to March 1993. Numbers in thousands. For meaning of symbols, see text.]

Characteristic	Total population				Same house (nonmovers)		
	Total	MSA's		Outside MSA's	MSA's		Outside MSA's
		Central cities	Balance		Central cities	Balance	
BLACK							
Both Sexes							
Total, 1 year and over	31,366	17,748	8,843	4,774	14,207	7,116	4,073
1 to 4 years	2,592	1,538	715	339	1,143	532	249
5 to 9 years	2,914	1,621	812	482	1,257	655	409
10 to 14 years	2,922	1,595	807	520	1,258	703	457
15 to 19 years	2,640	1,395	784	461	1,097	675	408
15 to 17 years	1,621	856	462	303	705	414	269
18 and 19 years	1,019	539	322	158	392	261	139
20 to 24 years	2,512	1,441	765	305	1,005	526	218
25 to 29 years	2,614	1,540	735	339	1,097	509	258

[Continued]

★ 683 ★

Geographical Mobility: Detailed Mobility, by Race, Gender, and Age. Part 1-1

[Continued]

Characteristic	Total population				Same house (nonmovers)		
	Total	MSA's		Outside MSA's	MSA's		Outside MSA's
		Central cities	Balance		Central cities	Balance	
30 to 34 years	2,785	1,565	859	361	1,201	646	294
35 to 39 years	2,557	1,395	744	417	1,121	571	342
40 to 44 years	2,072	1,104	630	337	908	509	309
45 to 49 years	2,577	877	540	160	778	467	148
50 to 54 years	1,333	800	381	151	716	329	140
55 to 59 years	1,144	693	309	142	613	285	120
60 to 64 years	1,044	629	248	167	570	231	156
60 and 61 years	476	289	118	69	268	107	68
62 to 64 years	568	340	129	98	303	124	88
65 to 69 years	939	563	193	182	527	176	176
70 to 74 years	763	415	170	179	376	160	171
75 to 79 years	450	268	74	109	250	69	102
80 to 84 years	296	199	39	58	188	36	55
85 years and over	211	110	38	63	104	38	61
Median age	29.0	29.2	28.7	29.1	31.0	29.6	30.6

Source: "Detailed Mobility, by Race and Hispanic Origin, Sex, and Age," *Geographical Mobility: March 1992 to March 1993,* p. 86.

★ 684 ★

Mobility

Geographical Mobility: Detailed Mobility, by Race, Gender, and Age. Part 1-2

[Mobility data from March 1992 to March 1993. Numbers in thousands. For meaning of symbols, see text.]

Characteristic	Movers within same MSA					
	Total	Within central city	Between central cities	Within balance	Central city to balance	Balance to central city
BLACK						
Both Sexes						
Total, 1 year and over	4,198	2,462	82	768	533	353
1 to 4 years	502	301	12	90	63	37
5 to 9 years	418	246	-	68	44	59
10 to 14 years	339	232	6	44	27	30
15 to 19 years	337	214	10	58	22	33
15 to 17 years	168	111	5	26	10	16
18 and 19 years	169	103	5	32	12	17
20 to 24 years	534	324	7	97	81	25

[Continued]

★ 684 ★

Geographical Mobility: Detailed Mobility, by Race, Gender, and Age. Part 1-2
[Continued]

Characteristic	Movers within same MSA					
	Total	Within central city	Between central cities	Within balance	Central city to balance	Balance to central city
25 to 29 years	523	298	15	99	67	44
30 to 34 years	461	238	17	95	67	45
35 to 39 years	365	195	-	94	47	29
40 to 44 years	240	125	4	35	61	15
45 to 49 years	150	80	4	42	21	4
50 to 54 years	88	56	-	11	15	5
55 to 59 years	74	39	3	16	4	13
60 to 64 years	62	44	3	8	3	4
60 and 61 years	22	13	3	3	3	-
62 to 64 years	40	31	-	5	-	4
65 to 69 years	44	30	-	10	4	-
70 to 74 years	35	26	-	-	6	3
75 to 79 years	14	10	-	2	2	-
80 to 84 years	7	2	-	-	1	5
85 years and over	4	2	-	-	-	2
Median age	24.7	23.7	26.7	26.4	27.2	23.4

Source: "Detailed Mobility, by Race and Hispanic Origin, Sex, and Age," *Geographical Mobility: March 1992 to March 1993,* p. 86.

★ 685 ★

Mobility

Geographical Mobility: Detailed Mobility, by Race, Gender, and Age. Part 2-1

[Mobility data from March 1992 to March 1993. Numbers in thousands. For meaning of symbols, see text.]

Characteristic	Total population				Same house (nonmovers)		
	Total	MSA's		Outside MSA's	MSA's		Outside MSA's
		Central cities	Balance		Central cities	Balance	
BLACK							
Male							
Total, 1 year and over	14,717	8,202	4,263	2,252	6,539	3,446	1,915
1 to 4 years	1,297	804	332	161	592	275	121
5 to 9 years	1,492	830	402	259	652	323	217
10 to 14 years	1,486	789	414	283	630	361	250
15 to 19 years	1,319	663	412	244	552	361	219
15 to 17 years	820	405	248	167	337	221	147

[Continued]

★ 685 ★

Geographical Mobility: Detailed Mobility, by Race, Gender, and Age. Part 2-1
[Continued]

Characteristic	Total population			Same house (nonmovers)		
	Total	MSA's		Outside MSA's	MSA's		Outside MSA's
		Central cities	Balance		Central cities	Balance	
18 and 19 years	499	258	164	77	214	140	72
20 to 24 years	1,170	668	353	149	480	264	119
25 to 29 years	1,205	684	383	138	474	253	106
30 to 34 years	1,283	733	403	147	568	303	116
35 to 39 years	1,176	634	338	204	500	238	154
40 to 44 years	933	466	309	159	378	237	142
45 to 49 years	703	379	257	67	322	235	64
50 to 54 years	586	342	179	65	306	153	60
55 to 59 years	516	318	137	61	270	124	47
60 to 64 years	471	291	107	73	265	102	71
60 and 61 years	236	142	53	40	128	50	40
62 to 64 years	235	148	54	32	137	51	31
65 to 69 years	392	227	100	65	206	90	64
70 to 74 years	350	192	68	90	171	63	83
75 to 79 years	166	82	25	59	77	21	56
80 to 84 years	99	64	21	14	60	19	13
85 years and over	73	36	22	15	36	22	13
Median age	27.5	27.5	27.8	26.1	28.8	27.7	26.5

Source: "Detailed Mobility, by Race and Hispanic Origin, Sex, and Age," Geographical Mobility: March 1992 to March 1993, p. 86.

★ 686 ★

Mobility

Geographical Mobility: Detailed Mobility, by Race, Gender, and Age. Part 2-2

[Mobility data from March 1992 to March 1993. Numbers in thousands. For meaning of symbols, see text.]

Characteristic	Movers within same MSA					
	Total	Within central city	Between central cities	Within balance	Central city to balance	Balance to central city
BLACK						
Male						
Total, 1 year and over	1,947	1,134	38	361	261	154
1 to 4 years	232	157	6	30	19	21
5 to 9 years	202	126	-	33	21	23
10 to 14 years	158	101	4	23	11	19
15 to 19 years	129	82	-	21	20	6

[Continued]

★ 686 ★

Geographical Mobility: Detailed Mobility, by Race, Gender, and Age. Part 2-2
[Continued]

| Characteristic | Movers within same MSA | | | | | |
	Total	Within central city	Between central cities	Within balance	Central city to balance	Balance to central city
15 to 17 years	74	53	-	12	9	-
18 and 19 years	56	30	-	9	11	6
20 to 24 years	208	128	4	36	26	13
25 to 29 years	259	131	4	59	43	22
30 to 34 years	210	101	10	44	35	20
35 to 39 years	198	100	-	51	36	12
40 to 44 years	124	54	4	22	38	6
45 to 49 years	69	48	1	17	-	3
50 to 54 years	37	24	-	7	7	-
55 to 59 years	41	23	-	10	1	6
60 to 64 years	26	21	3	3	-	-
60 and 61 years	12	9	3	-	-	-
62 to 64 years	14	12	-	3	-	-
65 to 69 years	24	19	-	2	3	-
70 to 74 years	16	16	-	-	-	-
75 to 79 years	7	3	-	2	2	-
80 to 84 years	5	-	-	-	-	5
85 years and over	-	-	-	-	-	-
Median age	25.8	24.0	(B)	28.1	28.8	23.3

Source: "Detailed Mobility, by Race and Hispanic Origin, Sex, and Age," *Geographical Mobility: March 1992 to March 1993*, p. 86. *Note:* B = Base less than 75,000.

★ 687 ★
Mobility

Geographical Mobility: Detailed Mobility, by Race, Gender, and Age. Part 3-1

[Mobility data from March 1992 to March 1993. Numbers in thousands. For meaning of symbols, see text.]

| Characteristic | Total population | | | | Same house (nonmovers) | | |
| | Total | MSA's | | Outside MSA's | MSA's | | Outside MSA's |
		Central cities	Balance		Central cities	Balance	
BLACK							
Female							
Total, 1 year and over	16,649	9,546	4,581	2,522	7,669	3,671	2,158
1 to 4 years	1,295	734	382	179	551	257	129
5 to 9 years	1,423	791	410	222	605	332	192

[Continued]

★ 687 ★

Geographical Mobility: Detailed Mobility, by Race, Gender, and Age. Part 3-1

[Continued]

Characteristic	Total population				Same house (nonmovers)		
	Total	MSA's		Outside MSA's	MSA's		Outside MSA's
		Central cities	Balance		Central cities	Balance	
10 to 14 years	1,436	806	393	237	627	342	207
15 to 19 years	1,320	732	371	218	545	314	189
15 to 17 years	800	450	214	136	368	193	122
18 and 19 years	520	281	157	82	177	121	67
20 to 24 years	1,342	773	412	156	525	262	100
25 to 29 years	1,409	856	353	200	623	256	151
30 to 34 years	1,502	832	456	214	633	343	178
35 to 39 years	1,382	762	406	214	621	333	188
40 to 44 years	1,139	638	322	179	530	272	167
45 to 49 years	874	498	282	94	456	231	84
50 to 54 years	746	458	202	86	409	176	80
55 to 59 years	628	375	172	81	342	161	73
60 to 64 years	573	339	140	94	306	130	85
60 and 61 years	240	147	65	28	140	57	28
62 to 64 years	333	192	75	66	166	73	57
65 to 69 years	547	336	94	117	321	86	112
70 to 74 years	413	222	102	89	205	97	87
75 to 79 years	285	186	49	49	173	47	45
80 to 84 years	197	135	18	45	128	17	42
85 years and over	137	73	16	48	68	16	48
Median age	30.3	30.5	29.6	31.1	32.8	31.1	33.1

Source: "Detailed Mobility, by Race and Hispanic Origin, Sex, and Age," *Geographical Mobility: March 1992 to March 1993,* p. 86.

★ 688 ★

Mobility

Geographical Mobility: Detailed Mobility, by Race, Gender, and Age. Part 3-2

[Mobility data from March 1992 to March 1993. Numbers in thousands. For meaning of symbols, see text.]

Characteristic	Movers within same MSA					
	Total	Within central city	Between central cities	Within balance	Central city to balance	Balance to central city
BLACK						
Female						
Total, 1 year and over	2,251	1,329	45	407	272	199
1 to 4 years	270	144	6	60	44	16

[Continued]

★ 688 ★

Geographical Mobility: Detailed Mobility, by Race, Gender, and Age. Part 3-2

[Continued]

Characteristic	Total	Movers within same MSA				
		Within central city	Between central cities	Within balance	Central city to balance	Balance to central city
5 to 9 years	215	120	-	35	23	37
10 to 14 years	181	131	2	21	16	12
15 to 19 years	208	132	10	37	2	27
15 to 17 years	94	58	5	14	1	16
18 and 19 years	113	73	5	23	1	11
20 to 24 years	326	196	3	61	55	12
25 to 29 years	264	167	11	40	23	22
30 to 34 years	252	137	6	51	33	25
35 to 39 years	167	95	-	43	11	17
40 to 44 years	116	71	-	12	23	9
45 to 49 years	81	32	3	25	21	2
50 to 54 years	51	33	-	5	8	5
55 to 59 years	33	14	3	6	2	7
60 to 64 years	36	23	-	5	3	4
60 and 61 years	10	4	-	3	3	-
62 to 64 years	25	19	-	3	-	4
65 to 69 years	19	12	-	7	1	-
70 to 74 years	19	11	-	-	6	3
75 to 79 years	7	7	-	-	-	-
80 to 84 years	3	2	-	-	1	-
85 years and over	4	2	-	-	-	2
Median age	23.9	23.5	(B)	24.2	24.7	23.5

Source: "Detailed Mobility, by Race and Hispanic Origin, Sex, and Age," Geographical Mobility: March 1992 to March 1993, p. 86. Note: B = Base less than 75,000.

★ 689 ★

Mobility

Geographical Mobility: Detailed Mobility, by Selected Characteristics. Part 1-1

[Mobility data from March 1992 to March 1993. Numbers in thousands. For meaning of symbols, see text.]

Characteristic	Total population				Same house (nonmovers)		
	Total	MSA's		Outside MSA's	MSA's		Outside MSA's
		Central cities	Balance		Central cities	Balance	
Race and Hispanic Origin							
White	208,754	53,264	105,745	49,745	42,399	90,435	42,076
Black	31,366	17,748	8,843	4,774	14,207	7,116	4,073
Hispanic	22,232	11,560	9,009	1,663	8,769	6,964	1,258

Source: "Detailed Mobility, by Selected Characteristics," *Geographical Mobility: March 1992 to March 1993*, p. 76.

★ 690 ★

Mobility

Geographical Mobility: Detailed Mobility, by Selected Characteristics. Part 1-2

[Mobility data from March 1992 to March 1993. Numbers in thousands. For meaning of symbols, see text.]

Characteristic	Movers within same MSA					
	Total	Within central city	Between central cities	Within balance	Central city to balance	Balance to central city
Race and Hispanic Origin						
White	18,358	6,028	291	7,901	2,727	1,409
Black	4,198	2,462	82	768	533	353
Hispanic	3,662	1,886	54	1,060	456	207

Source: "Detailed Mobility, by Selected Characteristics," *Geographical Mobility: March 1992 to March 1993*, p. 76.

★ 691 ★

Mobility

Geographical Mobility: Detailed Mobility, by Selected Characteristics. Part 2-1

Characteristic	Movers between MSA's					Movers from outside MSA's to MSA's		
	Total	Between central cities	Between balances	Central city to balance	Balance to central city	Total	To central cities	To balances of MSA's
Race and Hispanic Origin								
White	5,581	1,220	1,942	1,493	926	1,380	469	911
Black	913	411	159	194	148	106	50	55
Hispanic[1]	682	224	132	213	113	92	36	56

Source: "Detailed Mobility, by Selected Characteristics," *Geographical Mobility: March 1992 to March 1993*, p. 77. *Note:* 1. Persons of Hispanic origin may be of any race.

★ 692 ★

Mobility

Geographical Mobility: Detailed Mobility, by Selected Characteristics. Part 2-2

Characteristic	Movers from MSA's to outside MSA's			Movers, outside MSA's at both dates			Movers from abroad			
	Total	From central cities	From balances of MSA's	Total	Within same county	To different county	Total	To central cities of MSA's	To balances of MSA's	To outside MSA's
Race and Hispanic Origin										
White	1,690	729	961	5,906	4,327	1,578	931	521	337	73
Black	118	91	27	577	463	114	56	33	18	5
Hispanic[1]	94	68	25	298	254	43	414	272	129	13

Source: "Detailed Mobility, by Selected Characteristics," *Geographical Mobility: March 1992 to March 1993*, p. 77. *Note:* 1. Persons of Hispanic origin may be of any race.

★ 693 ★
Mobility

Geographical Mobility: Frequency Distribution of Selected Characteristics by Type of Move, 1993

Selected Characteristics	Total persons	Same house (non-movers)	Total movers	Different house in the United States						Movers from abroad
				Total	Same county	Different county				
						Total	Same state	Different state		
Total, 1 year and over	100.0	100.0	100.0	100.0	100.0	100.0	100.0	100.0		100.0
Race and Hispanic Origin										
White	83.4	84.0	80.5	80.8	78.4	85.1	86.3	83.7		71.3
Black	12.5	12.2	14.2	14.5	16.5	10.9	10.4	11.5		4.3
Hispanic origin (of any race)	8.9	8.2	12.5	11.8	14.4	7.2	7.8	6.5		31.7

Source: "Frequency Distribution of Selected Characteristics by Type of Move: 1993," *Geographical Mobility: March 1992 to March 1993*, p. xvi.

★ 694 ★
Mobility

Geographical Mobility: General Mobility of Family Householders, by Race, Hispanic Origin and Type of Householder, and Presence of Children. Part 1

[Mobility data from March 1992 to March 1993. Numbers in thousands. For meaning of symbols, see text.]

Characteristic	Total	Same house (non-movers)	Different house in United States										Movers from abroad
			Total	Same county	Different county								
					Total	Same State	Different State						
							Total	Same region			Different region	
								Total	Same division	Different division		
BLACK FAMILY HOUSEHOLDERS												
All Households												
Householders 15 to 54 years old	5,988	4,676	1,297	985	312	166	147	102	92	10	45	15
No own children under 18	1,581	1,316	264	187	77	489	29	19	18	1	10	1
With own children under 18	4,407	3,360	1,033	798	235	118	118	83	74	8	35	14
Under 6 only	1,085	673	403	311	92	55	37	23	23	-	14	8
Under 6 and 6 to 17	1,080	842	238	197	41	22	18	13	10	4	5	-
6 to 17 only	2,242	1,845	392	289	103	40	62	46	41	5	16	5
Married-Couple Households												
Householders 15 to 54 years old	2,640	2,102	527	336	191	102	89	63	55	7	26	11
No own children under 18	803	645	156	99	57	36	21	15	15	-	6	1
With own children under 18	1,837	1,457	371	237	134	66	68	48	41	7	20	9
Under 6 only	453	296	152	95	57	31	26	19	19	-	7	6
Under 6 and 6 to 17	437	369	69	44	25	16	9	7	4	4	1	-
6 to 17 only	947	793	150	98	53	19	34	22	18	3	12	4

[Continued]

★ 694 ★

Geographical Mobility: General Mobility of Family Householders, by Race, Hispanic Origin and Type of Householder, and Presence of Children. Part 1

[Continued]

Characteristic	Total	Same house (non-movers)	Different house in United States										Movers from abroad
			Total	Same county	Different county								
					Total	Same State	Different State					
							Total	Same region			Different region	
								Total	Same division	Different division		
Single-Parent Households													
Householders 15 to 54 years old	3,348	2,574	770	649	121	63	58	39	37	3	19	4
No own children under 18	778	671	107	87	20	12	9	4	3	1	4	-
With own children under 18	2,570	1,903	663	561	101	52	50	35	34	1	14	4
Under 6 only	632	377	252	216	35	24	11	4	4	-	7	3
Under 6 and 6 to 17	642	473	169	153	16	6	10	6	6	-	3	-
6 to 17 only	1,296	1,052	242	192	50	12	29	24	23	1	4	2
Female Single-Parent Households													
Householders 15 to 54 years old	3,002	2,301	696	592	104	51	53	39	36	3	14	4
No own children under 18	607	533	74	63	10	4	6	4	3	1	2	-
With own children under 18	2,395	1,768	623	529	94	47	46	35	33	1	12	4
Under 6 only	561	329	229	199	30	22	8	4	4	-	4	3
Under 6 and 6 to 17	620	451	169	153	16	6	10	6	6	-	3	-
6 to 17 only	1,214	988	224	177	47	19	28	24	23	1	4	2

Source: "General Mobility, of Family Householders, by Race and Hispanic Origin of Householder, Type of Household, and Presence and Ages of Own Children," *Geographical Mobility: March 1992 to March 1993*, p. 32.

★ 695 ★

Mobility

Geographical Mobility: General Mobility of Family Householders, by Race, Hispanic Origin and Type of Householder, and Presence of Children. Part 2

[Mobility data from March 1992 to March 1993. Numbers in thousands. For meaning of symbols, see text.]

Characteristic	Total	Same house (non-movers)	Different house in United States										Movers from abroad
			Total	Same county	Different county								
					Total	Same State	Different State					
							Total	Same region			Different region	
								Total	Same division	Different division		
HISPANIC FAMILY HOUSEHOLDERS													
All Households													
Householders 15 to 54 years old	4,321	3,207	1,050	838	212	135	77	36	26	9	41	64
No own children under 18	1,102	808	275	220	55	43	12	4	4	-	8	19
With own children under 18	3,219	2,399	776	619	157	93	65	31	22	9	33	44
Under 6 only	877	523	341	274	67	42	25	11	8	3	14	14
Under 6 and 6 to 17	914	708	201	160	41	23	18	10	5	5	8	6
6 to 17 only	1,428	1,169	234	185	49	27	22	10	10	1	11	25
Married-Couple Households													
Householders 15 to 54 years old	2,961	2,257	666	537	129	82	47	23	17	6	24	38
No own children under 18	704	514	181	142	39	30	10	4	4	-	6	9

[Continued]

★ 695 ★

Geographical Mobility: General Mobility of Family Householders, by Race, Hispanic Origin and Type of Householder, and Presence of Children. Part 2

[Continued]

Characteristic	Total	Same house (non-movers)	Different house in United States									Movers from abroad
			Total	Same county	Different county							
					Total	Same State	Different State				Different region	
							Total	Same region				
								Total	Same division	Different division		
With own children under 18	2,257	1,743	485	395	90	52	37	19	13	6	18	29
Under 6 only	612	382	222	178	44	27	17	8	4	3	10	8
Under 6 and 6 to 17	680	540	136	113	23	16	7	3	1	2	4	4
6 to 17 only	966	821	127	105	23	10	13	9	8	1	4	18
Single-Parent Households												
Householders 15 to 54 years old	1,360	950	384	301	83	54	30	13	10	3	17	26
No own children under 18	398	294	94	77	16	13	3	1	-	-	2	11
With own children under 18	962	656	291	223	67	40	27	12	9	3	15	15
Under 6 only	266	140	120	96	23	16	8	4	4	-	4	6
Under 6 and 6 to 17	235	168	65	47	17	7	11	6	4	3	4	2
6 to 17 only	462	348	106	80	27	18	9	2	2	-	7	7
Female Single-Parent Households												
Householders 15 to 54 years old	1,008	727	269	208	61	35	26	12	9	3	14	12
No own children under 18	202	169	31	27	3	1	3	-	-	-	2	2
With own children under 18	806	558	238	181	58	34	23	11	9	3	12	10
Under 6 only	197	108	83	66	17	12	5	4	4	-	1	6
Under 6 and 6 to 17	217	151	63	46	17	7	10	6	3	3	4	2
6 to 17 only	393	299	92	68	24	16	8	2	2	-	6	2

Source: "General Mobility, of Family Householders, by Race and Hispanic Origin of Householder, Type of Household, and Presence and Ages of Own Children," *Geographical Mobility: March 1992 to March 1993*, p. 32. *Note:* 1. Persons of Hispanic origin may be of any race.

★ 696 ★

Mobility

Geographical Mobility: General Mobility of Householder, by Race, Gender, and Household Income. Part 1-1

[Mobility data from March 1992 to March 1993. Numbers in thousands. For meaning of symbols, see text.]

Characteristic	Total	Same house (non-movers)	Different house in United States				
			Total	Same county	Different county	
					Total	Same State
BLACK						
Both Sexes						
Householder 15 years and over	11,190	8,997	2,169	1,577	592	311
Household income						
Less than $5,000	1,318	949	368	279	89	48
$5,000 to $9,999	2,090	1,666	417	320	96	50

[Continued]

★ 696 ★

Geographical Mobility: General Mobility of Householder, by Race, Gender, and Household Income. Part 1-1

[Continued]

Characteristic	Total	Same house (non-movers)	Different house in United States			
			Total	Same county	Different county	
					Total	Same State
$10,000 to $14,999	1,367	1,067	296	224	71	33
$15,000 to $19,999	1,095	850	244	210	34	19
$20,000 to $24,999	950	771	179	125	54	27
$25,000 to $29,999	827	675	144	108	36	14
$30,000 to $34,999	653	548	104	68	36	16
$35,000 to $39,999	570	478	92	37	55	29
$40,000 to $44,999	511	436	72	49	23	14
$45,000 to $49,999	354	296	58	38	20	12
$50,000 to $54,999	313	259	54	40	14	9
$55,000 to $59,999	248	220	29	18	11	8
$60,000 to $64,999	197	171	26	18	7	6
$65,000 to $69,999	122	105	17	4	13	4
$70,000 to $74,999	109	93	16	10	6	4
$75,000 to $79,999	80	74	6	4	2	-
$80,000 to $84,999	67	55	12	3	10	6
$85,000 to $89,999	55	49	6	4	2	-
$90,000 to $94,999	70	59	11	4	7	5
$95,000 to $99,999	30	24	5	3	3	3
$100,000 and over	163	150	13	10	3	3
Median income (dollars)	18,744	19,803	15,086	14,225	20,432	20,972

Source: "General Mobility of Householders, by Race and Hispanic Origin, Sex, and Householder Income," *Geographical Mobility: March 1992 to March 1993*, p. 35. *Note:* B=Base too small to show derived measure.

★ 697 ★

Mobility

Geographical Mobility: General Mobility of Householder, by Race, Gender, and Household Income. Part 1-2

[Mobility data from March 1992 to March 1993. Numbers in thousands. For meaning of symbols, see text.]

Characteristic	Different house in United States Different county Different State				Different region	Movers from abroad
	Total	Same region				
		Total	Same division	Different division		
BLACK						
Both Sexes						
Householder 15 years and over	281	171	150	21	110	24
Household income						
Less than $5,000	42	28	27	1	14	1
$5,000 to $9,999	46	22	21	1	24	8
$10,000 to $14,999	38	26	23	3	12	5
$15,000 to $19,999	15	11	8	3	4	-
$20,000 to $24,999	28	19	18	2	8	-
$25,000 to $29,999	22	16	9	7	7	7
$30,000 to $34,999	20	9	9	-	11	-
$35,000 to $39,999	25	13	9	4	12	-
$40,000 to $44,999	9	4	4	-	5	3
$45,000 to $49,999	8	4	4	-	4	-
$50,000 to $54,999	4	1	1	-	3	-
$55,000 to $59,999	2	2	2	-	-	-
$60,000 to $64,999	2	-	-	-	2	-
$65,000 to $69,999	9	9	9	-	1	-
$70,000 to $74,999	2	-	-	-	2	-
$75,000 to $79,999	2	2	2	-	-	-
$80,000 to $84,999	4	3	3	-	1	-
$85,000 to $89,999	2	2	2	-	-	-
$90,000 to $94,999	1	-	-	-	1	-
$95,000 to $99,999	-	-	-	-	-	-
$100,000 and over	-	-	-	-	-	-
Median income (dollars)	19,842	19,337	17,875	(B)	20,589	(B)

Source: "General Mobility of Householders, by Race and Hispanic Origin, Sex, and Householder Income," *Geographical Mobility: March 1992 to March 1993*, p. 35. *Note:* B=Base too small to show derived measure.

★ 698 ★

Mobility

Geographical Mobility: General Mobility of Householder, by Race, Gender, and Household Income. Part 2-1

| Characteristic | Total | Same house (non-movers) | Different house in United States | | | |
| | | | Total | Same county | Different county | |
					Total	Same State
BLACK						
Male						
Householders 15 years and over	5,105	4,140	948	634	314	167
Household income:						
Less than $5,000	280	206	74	49	25	6
$5,000 to $9,999	605	466	135	100	35	18
$10,000 to $14,999	519	402	11	80	31	17
$15,000 to $19,999	481	391	90	63	27	17
$20,000 to $24,999	477	391	87	59	28	13
$25,000 to $29,999	402	320	77	52	25	13
$30,000 to $34,999	372	299	73	47	26	9
$35,000 to $39,999	354	307	47	21	26	10
$40,000 to $44,999	321	267	51	35	16	10
$45,000 to $49,999	208	167	40	26	14	11
$50,000 to $54,999	225	180	45	34	12	9
$55,000 to $59,999	178	154	23	16	7	5
$60,000 to $64,999	141	123	18	10	7	6
$65,000 to $69,999	98	85	12	4	8	4
$70,000 to $74,999	88	72	16	10	6	4
$75,000 to $79,999	66	60	6	4	2	-
$80,000 to $84,999	52	43	9	3	7	6
$85,000 to $89,999	44	38	6	4	2	-
$90,000 to $94,999	47	38	8	4	4	3
$95,000 to $99,999	25	19	5	3	3	3
$100,000 and over	123	111	13	10	3	3
Median income (dollars)	27,365	28,334	23,672	22,088	27,286	29,605

Source: "General Mobility of Householders, by Race and Hispanic Origin, Sex, and Household Income," *Geographical Mobility: March 1992 to March 1993,* p. 35.

★ 699 ★

Mobility

Geographical Mobility: General Mobility of Householder, by Race, Gender, and Household Income. Part 2-2

Characteristic	Different house in United States Different county				Different region	Movers from abroad
	Different State					
		Same region				
	Total	Total	Same division	Different division		
BLACK						
Male						
Householders 15 years and over	147	91	78	13	56	17
Household income:						
Less than $5,000	19	16	16	-	3	-
$5,000 to $9,999	17	9	9	-	9	3
$10,000 to $14,999	13	8	7	2	5	5
$15,000 to $19,999	10	7	4	3	3	-
$20,000 to $24,999	14	8	6	2	6	-
$25,000 to $29,999	12	11	7	3	2	6
$30,000 to $34,999	17	9	9	-	8	-
$35,000 to $39,999	16	8	4	4	8	-
$40,000 to $44,999	7	4	4	-	3	3
$45,000 to $49,999	3	-	-	-	3	-
$50,000 to $54,999	2	1	1	-	1	-
$55,000 to $59,999	2	2	2	-	-	-
$60,000 to $64,999	2	-	-	-	2	-
$65,000 to $69,999	5	4	4	-	1	-
$70,000 to $74,999	2	-	-	-	2	-
$75,000 to $79,999	2	2	2	-	-	-
$80,000 to $84,999	1	-	-	-	1	-
$85,000 to $89,999	2	2	2	-	-	-
$90,000 to $94,999	1	-	-	-	1	-
$95,000 to $99,999	-	-	-	-	-	-
$100,000 and over	-	-	-	-	-	-
Median income (dollars)	24,839	23,085	22,099	(B)	(B)	(B)

Source: "General Mobility of Householders, by Race and Hispanic Origin, Sex, and Household Income," *Geographical Mobility: March 1992 to March 1993,* p. 35. *Note:* B = Base too small to show derived measure.

★ 700 ★

Mobility

Geographical Mobility: General Mobility of Householder, by Race, Gender, and Household Income. Part 3-1

[Mobility data from March 1992 to March 1993. Numbers in thousands. For meaning of symbols, see text.]

Characteristic	Total	Same house (non-movers)	Different house in United States			
			Total	Same county	Different county	
					Total	Same State
BLACK						
Female						
Householders 15 years and over	6,085	4,857	1,221	943	278	144
Household income:						
Less than $5,000	1,037	742	294	230	64	42
$5,000 to $9,999	1,486	1,200	282	220	61	32
$10,000 to $14,999	849	664	184	144	40	16
$15,000 to $19,999	614	460	154	147	7	2
$20,000 to $24,999	473	381	92	66	27	13
$25,000 to $29,999	425	356	68	56	11	1
$30,000 to $34,999	280	249	31	21	10	7
$35,000 to $39,999	217	172	45	16	28	20
$40,000 to $44,999	190	170	21	14	6	5
$45,000 to $49,999	146	128	18	12	6	1
$50,000 to $54,999	88	80	8	7	2	-
$55,000 to $59,999	71	65	6	2	3	3
$60,000 to $64,999	56	48	8	8	-	-
$65,000 to $69,999	25	20	5	-	5	-
$70,000 to $74,999	21	21	-	-	-	-
$75,000 to $79,999	15	15	-	-	-	-
$80,000 to $84,999	15	12	3	-	3	-
$85,000 to $89,999	11	11	-	-	-	-
$90,000 to $94,999	24	21	3	-	3	3
$95,000 to $99,999	5	5	-	-	-	-
$100,000 and over	39	39	-	-	-	-
Median income (dollars)	13,062	13,662	10,941	10,741	11,653	9,698

Source: "General Mobility of Householders, by Race and Hispanic Origin, Sex, and Household Income," *Geographical Mobility: March 1992 to March 1993*, p. 35.

★ 701 ★
Mobility

Geographical Mobility: General Mobility of Householder, by Race, Gender, and Household Income. Part 3-2

[Mobility data from March 1992 to March 1993. Numbers in thousands. For meaning of symbols, see text.]

Characteristic	Different house in United States					Movers from abroad
	Different county					
	Different State					
	Total	Same region			Different region	
		Total	Same division	Different division		
BLACK						
Female						
Householders 15 years and over	134	80	72	8	54	7
Household income:						
Less than $5,000	23	11	10	1	11	1
$5,000 to $9,999	29	13	12	1	16	4
$10,000 to $14,999	25	18	16	1	7	-
$15,000 to $19,999	5	4	4	-	1	-
$20,000 to $24,999	13	12	12	-	2	-
$25,000 to $29,999	10	5	1	4	5	2
$30,000 to $34,999	4	-	-	-	4	-
$35,000 to $39,999	9	5	5	-	4	-
$40,000 to $44,999	2	-	-	-	2	-
$45,000 to $49,999	5	4	4	-	1	-
$50,000 to $54,999	2	-	-	-	2	-
$55,000 to $59,999	-	-	-	-	-	-
$60,000 to $64,999	-	-	-	-	-	-
$65,000 to $69,999	5	5	5	-	-	-
$70,000 to $74,999	-	-	-	-	-	-
$75,000 to $79,999	-	-	-	-	-	-
$80,000 to $84,999	3	3	3	-	-	-
$85,000 to $89,999	-	-	-	-	-	-
$90,000 to $94,999	-	-	-	-	-	-
$95,000 to $99,999	-	-	-	-	-	-
$100,000 and over	-	-	-	-	-	-
Median income (dollars)	13,117	14,289	(B)	(B)	(B)	(B)

Source: "General Mobility of Householders, by Race and Hispanic Origin, Sex, and Household Income," *Geographical Mobility: March 1992 to March 1993*, p. 35. *Note:* B = Base too small to show derived measure.

★ 702 ★

Mobility

Geographical Mobility: General Mobility of Persons 16 Years and Over, by Race, Gender, and Labor Force Status

[Mobility data from March 1992 to March 1993. Numbers in thousands.]

Characteristic	Total	Same house (non-movers)	Different house in United States										Movers from abroad
			Total	Same county	Different county								
					Total	Same State	Different State						
							Total	Same region			Different region	
								Total	Same division	Different division		
WHITE													
Both sexes													
Persons 16 years and over	164,048	137,571	25,738	15,913	9,824	5,329	4,496	2,387	1,544	843	2,108	739
Civilian labor force	108,032	88,283	19,374	12,257	7,117	4,040	3,077	1,650	1,027	623	1,428	375
Employed	100,881	83,051	17,529	11,189	6,340	3,682	2,658	1,429	887	542	1,229	301
Unemployed	7,151	5,232	1,846	1,069	777	357	420	221	139	82	199	74
Armed Forces	633	387	211	80	130	17	113	40	19	21	74	36
Not in labor force	55,383	48,902	6,153	3,576	2,577	1,272	1,305	698	498	199	607	329
Male													
Persons 16 years and over	79,344	66,152	12,790	7,842	4,948	2,664	2,285	1,194	797	406	1,091	402
Civilian labor force	59,502	48,555	10,713	6,681	4,031	2,271	1,760	928	598	330	832	234
Employed	55,003	45,170	9,650	6,046	3,603	2,074	1,529	797	517	280	732	183
Unemployed	4,499	3,385	1,063	635	428	197	232	131	81	50	101	51
Armed Forces	604	374	198	79	119	14	105	36	17	19	69	33
Not in labor force	19,237	17,223	1,879	1,061	798	378	419	230	172	58	189	136
Female													
Persons 16 years and over	84,704	71,419	12,948	8,072	4,876	2,665	2,211	1,193	756	437	1,017	337
Civilian labor force	48,530	39,728	8,661	5,576	3,086	1,769	1,317	722	428	294	595	141
Employed	45,878	37,881	7,879	5,142	2,737	1,608	1,129	632	370	262	497	118
Unemployed	2,652	1,847	782	434	349	160	188	90	58	32	98	23
Armed Forces	28	13	12	1	11	3	8	4	2	2	4	3
Not in labor force	36,146	31,679	4,274	2,495	1,779	894	886	467	326	141	418	193
BLACK													
Both Sexes													
Persons 16 years and over	22,384	18,252	4,086	2,907	1,179	599	580	351	280	71	229	46
Civilian labor force	13,608	10,843	2,738	1,903	834	419	415	247	192	54	168	27
Employed	11,699	9,483	2,201	1,554	648	323	324	195	153	42	129	15
Unemployed	1,909	1,360	536	350	186	96	91	52	39	12	39	13
Armed Forces	168	92	74	45	30	14	16	8	6	2	7	2
Not in labor force	8,608	7,317	1,274	959	315	165	150	96	81	15	54	17
Male													
Persons 16 years and over	10,162	8,238	1,904	1,313	591	304	287	174	140	34	113	19
Civilian labor force	6,751	5,311	1,427	980	448	228	219	129	107	22	90	14
Employed	5,617	4,495	1,115	784	331	169	162	92	74	17	70	7
Unemployed	1,135	816	312	196	116	59	57	38	33	5	19	7
Armed Forces	143	84	57	34	23	14	9	2	-	2	7	1
Not in labor force	3,268	2,843	420	300	121	62	59	43	33	10	16	4
Female													
Persons 16 years and over	12,222	10,014	2,181	1,594	587	294	293	177	139	38	116	27

[Continued]

★ 702 ★

Geographical Mobility: General Mobility of Persons 16 Years and Over, by Race, Gender, and Labor Force Status
[Continued]

Characteristic	Total	Same house (non-movers)	Different house in United States — Total	Same county	Different county — Total	Same State	Different State — Total	Same region — Total	Same division	Different division	Different region	Movers from abroad
Civilian labor force	6,857	5,533	1,310	924	387	191	196	117	85	32	79	14
Employed	6,082	4,988	1,086	770	316	154	162	103	79	25	59	8
Unemployed	775	545	224	154	70	37	33	14	6	7	20	6
Armed Forces	25	8	17	11	6	-	6	6	6	-	-	-
Not in labor force	5,340	4,473	854	659	194	103	91	53	48	5	38	13

Source: "General Mobility of Persons 16 Years and Over, by Race, Hispanic Origin, Sex, and Labor Force Status," *Geographical Mobility: March 1992 to March 1993*, p. 15.

★ 703 ★

Mobility

Geographical Mobility: General Mobility of Persons 25 Years and Over, by Race, Age, and Education

[Mobility data from March 1992 to March 1993. Numbers in thousands.]

Characteristic	Total	Same house (non-movers)	Different house in United States — Total	Same county	Different county — Total	Same State	Different State — Total	Same region — Total	Same division	Different division	Different region	Movers from abroad
BLACK												
Persons 25 years and over	17,786	14,805	2,951	2,062	888	459	429	259	208	50	170	30
Less than 9th grade	2,182	1,984	194	149	46	20	26	16	12	4	10	4
9th to 12th grade, no diploma	3,079	2,549	521	378	143	89	55	28	23	5	26	8
High school graduate	6,451	5,298	1,144	833	312	126	185	118	91	27	68	9
Some college or associate degree	3,909	3,171	734	515	218	125	94	63	53	10	31	4
Bachelor's degree	1,561	1,280	277	153	123	75	49	24	19	5	25	4
Graduate or professional degree	603	523	80	34	46	26	21	11	11	-	10	-
Percent high school graduates	70.4	69.4	75.8	74.5	78.7	76.5	81.2	82.9	83.1	(B)	78.6	(B)
Persons 25 to 29 years	2,614	1,864	743	527	216	104	111	56	48	8	55	8
Less than 9th grade	37	31	6	6	-	-	-	-	-	-	-	-
9th to 12th grade, no diploma	413	299	111	86	25	10	15	9	9	-	6	3
High school graduate	1,112	808	299	241	58	22	36	17	16	2	18	5
Some college or associate degree	705	486	219	144	75	44	31	17	14	3	14	-
Bachelor's degree	292	202	90	48	42	18	25	11	8	3	13	-
Graduate or professional degree	54	37	17	1	16	11	5	1	1	-	4	-
Percent high school graduates	82.8	82.3	84.2	82.4	88.5	90.2	86.8	(B)	(B)	(B)	(B)	(B)
Persons 30 to 34 years	2,785	2,141	638	455	182	107	75	39	35	4	36	7
Less than 9th grade	80	69	10	7	3	-	3	1	-	1	2	1
9th to 12th grade, no diploma	379	258	118	84	35	29	6	6	6	-	-	2
High school graduate	1,122	882	239	193	46	14	32	9	8	2	22	1
Some college or associate degree	848	662	185	135	51	23	27	19	18	1	8	1
Bachelor's degree	298	223	73	37	36	34	2	2	2	-	-	2
Graduate or professional degree	59	46	13	-	13	8	5	1	1	-	4	-
Percent high school graduates	83.6	84.7	79.9	80.0	79.5	73.3	88.3	(B)	(B)	(B)	(B)	(B)

[Continued]

★ 703 ★

Geographical Mobility: General Mobility of Persons 25 Years and Over, by Race, Age, and Education
[Continued]

Characteristic	Total	Same house (non-movers)	Different house in United States									Movers from abroad
			Total	Same county	Different county							
					Total	Same State	Different State					
							Total	Same region			Different region	
								Total	Same division	Different division		
Persons 35 to 44 years	4,629	3,760	860	598	262	129	133	96	68	28	37	9
Less than 9th grade	173	140	33	31	2	1	1	1	-	1	-	-
9th to 12th grade, no diploma	632	478	150	103	47	30	16	3	-	3	13	4
High school graduate	1,873	1,494	378	253	126	53	73	57	42	16	16	1
Some college or associate degree	1,231	1,025	203	153	51	28	23	18	13	5	4	2
Bachelor's degree	532	460	70	44	25	14	11	9	7	2	3	2
Graduate or professional degree	188	163	25	14	11	3	8	6	6	-	2	-
Percent high school graduates	82.6	83.6	78.6	77.5	81.2	75.6	86.6	95.0	(B)	(B)	(B)	(B)
Persons 45 to 64 years	5,098	4,553	537	368	170	93	77	48	38	10	28	7
Less than 9th grade	661	579	78	55	24	14	10	6	5	1	3	3
9th to 12th grade, no diploma	1,105	1,001	104	88	16	6	10	6	4	1	4	-
High school graduate	1,797	1,605	189	121	67	34	34	25	17	8	9	2
Some college or associate degree	951	843	106	66	40	29	11	8	8	-	3	1
Bachelor's degree	356	316	40	22	18	7	11	2	2	-	9	-
Graduate or professional degree	228	208	20	15	5	3	2	2	2	-	-	-
Percent high school graduates	65.3	65.3	66.0	61.1	76.8	78.2	75.0	(B)	(B)	(B)	(B)	(B)
Persons 65 years and over	2,660	2,487	173	115	58	25	33	20	19	1	13	-
Less than 9th grade	1,231	1,165	66	49	17	5	13	8	6	1	5	-
9th to 12th grade, no diploma	550	513	37	16	21	13	8	4	4	-	4	-
High school graduate	547	507	40	25	15	4	11	8	8	-	3	-
Some college or associate degree	175	155	20	19	2	-	2	-	-	-	2	-
Bachelor's degree	83	79	4	2	3	3	-	-	-	-	-	-
Graduate or professional degree	74	68	6	4	2	2	-	-	-	-	-	-
Percent high school graduates	33.0	32.5	40.3	42.8	(B)	(B)	(B)	(B)	(B)	(B)	(B)	(B)

Source: "General Mobility of Persons 25 Years and Over, by Race and Hispanic Origin, Age, and Educational Attainment," *Geographical Mobility: March 1992 to March 1993*, p. 10. *Note:* B = Base too small to show derived measure.

★ 704 ★

Mobility

Geographical Mobility: General Mobility, By Selected Characteristics. Part 1

[Mobility data from March 1992 to March 1993. Numbers in thousands. For meaning of symbols, see text.]

Characteristic	Total	Same house (non-movers)	Different house in United States				
			Total	Same county	Different county		
					Total	Same State
Race and Hispanic Origin						
White	208,754	174,910	32,913	20,547	12,365	6,677
Black	31,366	25,397	5,913	4,325	1,588	808
Hispanic	22,232	16,991	4,827	3,779	1,048	606

Source: "General Mobility, by Selected Characteristics," *Geographical Mobility: March 1992 to March 1993*, p. 1.

★ 705 ★

Mobility

Geographical Mobility: General Mobility, By Selected Characteristics. Part 2

[Mobility data from March 1992 to March 1993. Numbers in thousands. For meaning of symbols, see text.]

Characteristic	Different house in United States Different county Different State					Movers from abroad
	Total	Same region			Different region	
		Total	Same division	Different division		
Race and Hispanic Origin						
White	5,688	3,046	1,956	1,091	2,642	931
Black	780	492	401	90	288	56
Hispanic	442	214	149	64	228	414

Source: "General Mobility, by Selected Characteristics," *Geographical Mobility: March 1992 to March 1993*, p. 1.

★ 706 ★

Mobility

Geographical Mobility: General Mobility, by Household and Family Status, Region, Race, and Hispanic Origin. Part 1

[Mobility data from March 1992 to March 1993. Numbers in thousands.]

Characteristic	Total	Same house (non-movers)	Different house in United States										Movers from abroad
			Total	Same county	Different county								
					Total	Same State	Different State					Different region	
							Total	Same region			Different region	
								Total	Same division	Different division		
TOTAL, 1 YEAR OLD AND OVER													
United States	250,210	208,162	40,743	26,212	14,532	7,735	6,797	3,728	2,499	1,229	3,069		1,305
White	208,754	174,910	32,913	20,547	12,365	6,677	5,688	3,046	1,956	1,091	2,642		931
Black	31,366	25,397	5,913	4,325	1,588	808	780	492	401	90	288		56
Hispanic[1]	22,232	16,991	4,827	3,779	1,048	606	442	214	149	64	228		414
Northeast	50,003	44,711	5,063	3,268	1,795	959	836	523	432	90	313		230
White	43,130	38,677	4,277	2,736	1,541	835	705	425	347	78	281		176
Black	5,200	4,619	561	421	139	83	56	38	31	7	18		20
Hispanic[1]	3,322	2,745	503	368	135	85	50	42	35	7	8		74
Midwest	60,031	50,353	9,480	6,050	3,430	1,932	1,497	657	459	197	841		198
White	52,433	44,271	8,031	4,906	3,124	1,819	1,305	552	371	180	754		131
Black	6,442	5,221	1,209	969	240	100	140	83	74	9	57		13
Hispanic[1]	1,635	1,170	420	317	103	42	60	26	22	4	35		45
South	86,107	70,422	15,173	9,203	5,970	3,127	2,843	1,698	1,134	563	1,145		513
White	86,854	55,329	11,172	6,412	4,760	2,517	2,243	1,311	824	487	933		352
Black	17,173	13,629	3,522	2,494	1,028	531	498	346	276	70	151		23
Hispanic[1]	6,859	5,218	1,472	1,080	392	205	187	58	44	15	129		169
West	54,068	42,676	11,028	7,692	3,337	1,716	1,620	851	473	378	769		364
White	46,338	36,633	9,433	6,493	2,940	1,506	1,434	759	413	346	675		272
Black	2,551	1,928	621	441	180	94	86	25	20	5	61		1
Hispanic[1]	10,415	7,857	2,432	2,014	418	273	144	88	49	39	56		126

Source: "General Mobility, by Household and Family Status, Region, and Race and Hispanic Origin," *Geographical Mobility: March 1992 to March 1993*, p. 24.

★ 707 ★
Mobility

Geographical Mobility: General Mobility, by Household and Family Status, Region, Race, and Hispanic Origin. Part 2

[Mobility data from March 1992 to March 1993. Numbers in thousands.]

Characteristic	Total	Same house (non-movers)	Different house in United States										Movers from abroad
			Total	Same county	Different county								
					Total	Same State	Different State					
							Total	Same region			Different region	
								Total	Same division	Different division		
HOUSEHOLDERS													
United States	96,391	80,473	15,548	9,945	5,603	3,015	2,588	1,408	937	470	1,180	370
White	82,083	69,114	12,712	7,912	4,799	2,608	2,191	1,169	742	427	1,022	258
Black	11,190	6,997	2,169	1,577	592	311	281	171	150	21	110	24
Hispanic[1]	6,626	5,091	1,456	1,122	334	212	122	65	44	21	57	79
Northeast	19,437	17,272	2,088	1,364	724	376	348	219	169	50	129	77
White	17,046	15,188	1,799	1,161	637	335	302	186	143	43	116	59
Black	1,865	1,646	210	156	54	28	26	17	15	3	9	9
Hispanic[1]	1,160	956	181	134	47	33	13	11	10	2	2	23
Midwest	23,307	19,515	3,735	2,386	1,350	782	568	253	177	77	315	57
White	20,638	17,422	3,182	1,959	1,223	731	493	216	145	71	277	33
Black	2,320	1,842	468	370	98	46	52	26	26	-	26	10
Hispanic[1]	502	358	137	101	37	16	21	12	10	2	9	7
South	33,392	27,411	5,833	3,531	2,302	1,243	1,060	614	415	199	446	148
White	26,696	22,199	4,388	2,539	1,850	999	850	482	305	177	369	109
Black	6,045	4,771	1,268	884	384	210	174	119	101	18	55	6
Hispanic[1]	2,065	1,593	455	332	124	69	55	21	13	8	34	37
West	20,255	16,275	3,892	2,664	1,227	615	613	322	176	145	294	89
White	17,703	14,304	3,342	2,253	1,069	543	547	286	150	137	260	56
Black	960	738	222	167	55	27	29	8	8	-	20	-
Hispanic[1]	2,880	2,185	683	556	127	94	33	20	11	10	12	12

Source: "General Mobility, by Household and Family Status, Region, and Race and Hispanic Origin," *Geographical Mobility: March 1992 to March 1993*, p. 24. *Note:* 1. Persons of Hispanic origin may be of any race.

★ 708 ★

Mobility

Geographical Mobility: General Mobility, by Household and Family Status, Region, Race, and Hispanic Origin. Part 3

[Mobility data from March 1992 to March 1993. Numbers in thousands.]

Characteristic	Total	Same house (non-movers)	Different house in United States										Movers from abroad
			Total	Same county	Different county								
					Total	Same State	Different State				Different region	
							Total	Same region				
								Total	Same division	Different division		
POPULATION HOUSEHOLDS													
United States	249,902	207,984	40,632	26,160	14,472	7,694	6,779	3,712	2,487	1,225	3,067	1,285
White	208,529	174,789	32,821	20,510	12,311	6,636	5,675	3,035	1,947	1,087	2,640	919
Black	31,311	25,354	5,903	4,320	1,583	808	775	487	397	90	288	55
Hispanic[1]	22,206	16,979	4,820	3,777	1,043	603	441	213	148	64	228	407
Northeast	49,936	44,648	5,059	3,265	1,793	959	834	521	432	89	313	230
White	43,089	38,639	4,275	2,736	1,539	835	704	423	347	76	281	176
Black	5,174	4,596	559	419	139	83	56	38	31	7	18	20
Hispanic[1]	3,319	2,743	502	367	135	85	50	42	35	7	8	74
Midwest	59,929	50,297	9,443	6,029	3,414	1,923	1,491	650	455	195	841	189
White	52,353	44,225	7,998	4,890	3,108	1,809	1,299	546	367	179	753	130
Black	6,434	5,215	1,207	967	240	100	140	83	74	9	57	11
Hispanic[1]	1,631	1,169	420	317	103	42	60	26	22	4	35	42
South	86,034	70,405	15,116	9,184	5,932	3,096	2,836	1,691	1,127	563	1,145	513
White	66,795	55,322	11,121	6,395	4,726	2,485	2,241	1,308	822	487	933	352
Black	17,158	13,619	3,516	2,492	1,024	531	493	342	271	70	151	23
Hispanic[1]	6,854	5,218	1,467	1,080	388	202	186	57	43	15	129	169
West	54,003	42,634	11,015	7,682	3,334	1,716	1,617	850	472	378	767	354
White	46,291	36,603	9,427	6,489	2,938	1,506	1,432	758	412	346	673	261
Black	2,545	1,924	621	441	180	94	86	25	20	5	61	1
Hispanic[1]	10,402	7,850	2,431	2,013	418	273	144	88	49	39	56	122

Source: "General Mobility, by Household and Family Status, Region, and Race and Hispanic Origin," *Geographical Mobility: March 1992 to March 1993*, p. 24. *Note:* 1. Persons of Hispanic origin may be of any race.

★ 709 ★

Mobility

Geographical Mobility: General Mobility, by Race. Part 1

[Mobility data from March 1992 to March 1993. Numbers in thousands.]

Characteristic	Total	Same house (non-movers)	Different house in United States										Movers from abroad
			Total	Same county	Different county								
					Total	Same State	Different State				Different region	
							Total	Same region				
								Total	Same division	Different division		
BLACK													
Both sexes													
Total, 1 year and over	31,366	25,397	5,913	4,325	1,588	808	780	494	401	90	288	56
1 to 4 years	2,592	1,924	664	541	122	63	59	41	39	2	18	4
5 to 9 years	2,914	2,320	594	455	139	75	64	42	38	5	21	1
10 to 14 years	2,922	2,418	500	374	126	56	70	52	41	11	18	4
15 to 19 years	2,640	2,180	454	352	101	59	42	24	20	4	18	6
15 to 17 years	1,621	1,388	231	192	39	20	19	12	10	2	8	1
18 and 19 years	1,019	792	223	161	62	40	23	12	10	2	10	4
20 to 24 years	2,512	1,749	751	540	211	95	116	73	56	17	43	12
25 to 29 years	2,614	1,864	743	527	216	104	111	56	48	8	55	8
30 to 34 years	2,785	2,141	638	455	162	107	75	39	35	4	36	7
35 to 39 years	2,557	2,034	520	377	144	71	73	56	37	19	17	3
40 to 44 years	2,072	1,727	340	221	118	58	60	40	31	8	21	6
45 to 49 years	1,577	1,393	183	143	40	31	9	6	5	1	3	1
50 to 54 years	1,333	1,184	144	89	54	22	32	22	17	6	10	5
55 to 59 years	1,144	1,018	125	71	54	32	22	15	11	4	7	1
60 to 64 years	1,044	958	86	64	22	9	13	5	5	-	8	-
60 and 61 years	476	443	33	22	11	4	7	4	4	-	3	-
62 to 64 years	588	515	53	43	10	4	6	2	2	-	5	-
65 to 69 years	939	878	61	42	19	12	7	1	1	-	6	-
70 to 74 years	763	706	57	43	14	2	12	12	12	-	-	-
75 to 79 years	450	421	30	17	13	9	4	1	1	-	3	-
80 to 84 years	296	279	18	9	9	3	6	5	3	1	2	-
85 years and over	211	203	8	4	4	-	4	2	2	-	2	-
Median age	29.0	30.6	25.0	24.1	27.2	27.7	26.8	26.1	25.8	28.3	27.4	(B)

Source: "General Mobility, by Race and Hispanic Origin, Sex, and Age," *Geographical Mobility: March 1992 to March 1993*, p. 5. *Note:* B = Base too small to show derived measure.

★ 710 ★

Mobility

Geographical Mobility: General Mobility, by Race. Part 2

[Mobility data from March 1992 to March 1993. Numbers in thousands.]

Characteristic	Total	Same house (non-movers)	Different house in United States									Movers from abroad
			Total	Same county	Different county							
					Total	Same State	Different State					
							Total	Same region			Different region	
								Total	Same division	Different division		
BLACK												
Male												
Total, 1 year and over	14,717	11,899	2,794	1,968	806	420	386	242	200	42	144	23
1 to 4 years	1,297	987	308	256	51	25	26	15	12	2	11	2
5 to 9 years	1,492	1,192	299	223	76	46	30	23	19	3	7	1
10 to 14 years	1,486	1,242	243	175	68	32	37	26	24	2	11	1
15 to 19 years	1,319	1,132	187	129	58	35	23	16	14	2	7	1
15 to 17 years	820	705	114	85	29	15	14	9	7	2	5	1
18 and 19 years	499	426	73	44	29	20	9	7	7	-	2	-
20 to 24 years	1,170	862	302	197	106	39	66	38	32	6	29	5
25 to 29 years	1,205	834	369	249	120	58	62	38	30	8	24	2
30 to 34 years	1,283	987	293	206	87	52	35	14	14	1	21	2
35 to 39 years	1,176	892	281	210	71	43	28	19	8	11	9	2
40 to 44 years	933	758	172	115	57	28	29	18	14	3	11	4
45 to 49 years	703	622	81	63	19	14	5	3	3	-	1	-
50 to 54 years	586	519	64	41	23	12	11	9	9	-	2	3
55 to 59 years	516	442	73	40	33	19	14	10	7	4	4	1
60 to 64 years	471	437	34	26	7	3	4	4	4	-	1	-
60 and 61 years	236	218	18	12	6	2	4	4	4	-	1	-
62 to 64 years	235	219	16	14	1	1	-	-	-	-	-	-
65 to 69 years	392	360	32	24	8	6	3	-	-	-	3	-
70 to 74 years	350	317	33	23	11	2	8	8	8	-	-	-
75 to 79 years	166	155	11	7	4	2	2	1	1	-	1	-
80 to 84 years	99	91	8	5	4	3	1	1	1	-	-	-
85 years and over	73	71	2	-	2	-	2	-	-	-	2	-
Median age	27.5	28.2	25.8	25.3	26.8	27.8	25.9	25.6	24.8	(B)	26.5	(B)

Source: "General Mobility, by Race and Hispanic Origin, Sex, and Age," *Geographical Mobility: March 1992 to March 1993*, p. 5. *Note:* B = Base too small to show derived measure.

★ 711 ★

Mobility

Geographical Mobility: General Mobility, by Race. Part 3

Characteristic	Total	Same house (non-movers)	Different house in United States									Movers from abroad
			Total	Same county	Different county							
					Total	Same State	Different State				Different region	
							Total	Same region				
								Total	Same division	Different division		
BLACK												
Female												
Total, 1 year and over	16,649	13,498	3,119	2,337	782	388	394	250	201	49	144	33
1 to 4 years	1,295	937	356	285	71	38	33	26	26	-	7	2
5 to 9 years	1,423	1,128	294	232	63	29	34	20	18	1	14	-
10 to 14 years	1,436	1,176	257	199	58	24	34	27	17	10	7	3
15 to 19 years	1,320	1,049	267	223	44	24	19	8	6	2	11	5
15 to 17 years	800	683	117	106	10	5	6	2	2	-	3	1
18 and 19 years	520	366	150	117	33	19	14	6	3	2	8	4
20 to 24 years	1,342	887	449	343	106	56	49	36	24	11	14	6
25 to 29 years	1,409	1,030	373	277	96	47	49	18	18	-	32	6
30 to 34 years	1,502	1,153	344	249	95	55	40	24	22	3	16	5
35 to 39 years	1,382	1,142	239	167	72	29	44	37	29	8	7	1
40 to 44 years	1,139	969	168	106	61	30	32	22	17	5	10	2
45 to 49 years	874	771	102	80	21	16	5	3	2	1	2	1
50 to 54 years	746	666	79	48	31	10	21	13	8	6	8	1
55 to 59 years	628	576	52	31	21	13	7	5	5	-	3	-
60 to 64 years	573	521	53	38	14	5	9	2	2	-	7	-
60 and 61 years	240	225	15	10	5	2	3	-	-	-	3	-
62 and 64 years	333	296	3	28	9	3	6	2	2	-	5	-
65 to 69 years	547	518	39	18	11	6	5	1	1	-	4	-
70 to 74 years	413	389	24	21	3	-	3	3	3	-	-	-
75 to 79 years	285	266	19	10	9	7	2	-	2	-	2	-
80 to 84 years	197	188	9	4	5	-	5	4	2	1	2	-
85 years and over	137	132	6	4	2	-	2	2	2	-	-	-
Median age	30.3	32.4	24.3	23.3	27.6	27.5	27.8	27.4	27.6	(B)	28.0	(B)

Source: "General Mobility, by Race and Hispanic Origin, Sex, and Age," *Geographical Mobility: March 1992 to March 1993,* p. 5. *Note:* B=Base too small to show derived measure.

★ 712 ★

Mobility

Geographical Mobility: Inmigrants, Outmigrants, and Net Migration for Large MSA's: Characteristics-1

[Mobility data from March 1992 to March 1993. Numbers in thousands. For meaning of symbols, see text.]

MSA's	Persons 1 year and over living in U.S. at both dates	Total		Race		
		Male	Female	White	Black	Hispanic[1]
NEW YORK-NORTHERN NEW JERSEY-LONG ISLAND, NY-NJ-CT CMSA						
Inmigrants	213	114	100	155	27	24
Outmigrants	389	186	204	293	63	75
Net migration	-176	-72	-104	-138	-37	-51
LOS ANGELES-ANAHEIM-RIVERSIDE, CA CMSA						
Inmigrants	285	147	138	226	30	43
Outmigrants	526	259	266	453	26	75
Net migration	-240	-112	-128	-227	4	-31
CHICAGO-GARY-LAKE COUNTY-IL-IN-WI CMSA						
Inmigrants	159	84	75	118	41	5
Outmigrants	183	98	85	163	15	19
Net migration	-24	-14	-10	-45	26	-14
SAN FRANCISCO-OAKLAND-SAN JOSE, CA CMSA						
Inmigrants	107	55	52	89	8	2
Outmigrants	164	87	77	137	16	17
Net migration	-57	-32	-25	-48	-8	-15
PHILADELPHIA-WILMINGTON-TRENTON, PA-NJ-DE-MD CMSA						
Inmigrants	89	39	51	75	12	1
Outmigrants	123	69	53	116	2	3
Net migration	-33	-31	-3	-40	9	-1

[Continued]

★ 712 ★

Geographical Mobility: Inmigrants, Outmigrants, and Net Migration for Large MSA's: Characteristics-1

[Continued]

MSA's	Persons 1 year and over living in U.S. at both dates	Total		Race		
		Male	Female	White	Black	Hispanic[1]
DETROIT, ANN ARBOR, MI CMSA						
Inmigrants	71	36	36	59	9	3
Outmigrants	91	38	52	70	17	5
Net migration	-19	-3	-17	-11	-8	-2
BOSTON-LAWRENCE-SALEM, MA-NH CMSA						
Inmigrants	70	33	37	54	4	5
Outmigrants	72	44	28	69	-	1
Net migration	-2	-11	8	-16	4	4
DALLAS-FORT WORTH, TX CMSA						
Inmigrants	193	106	87	131	43	45
Outmigrants	115	70	45	103	11	9
Net migration	78	36	42	28	32	36
HOUSTON-GALVESTON-BRAZORIA, TX CMSA						
Inmigrants	128	66	63	117	11	23
Outmigration	90	36	55	79	7	16
Net migration	38	30	8	37	4	7
WASHINGTON, DC-MD-VA MSA						
Inmigrants	95	47	48	59	31	7
Outmigrants	115	51	63	76	37	6
Net migration	-119	-4	-15	-17	-6	1

Source: "Inmigrants, Outmigrants, and Net Migration for Large Metropolitan Statistical Areas (MSA's), by Sex, Race and Hispanic Origin, and Age," *Geographical Mobility: March 1992 to March 1993*, p. 164. *Note:* 1. Persons of Hispanic origin may be of any race.

★ 713 ★

Mobility

Geographical Mobility: Inmigrants, Outmigrants, and Net Migration for Large MSA's: Characteristics-2

[Mobility data from March 1992 to March 1993. Numbers in thousands. For meaning of symbols, see text.]

MSA's	Age								
	1 to 4 years	5 to 9 years	10 to 14 years	15 to 19 years	20 to 24 years	25 to 29 years	30 to 44 years	45 to 64 years	65 years and over
NEW YORK-NORTHERN NEW JERSEY-LONG ISLAND, NY-NJ-CT CMSA									
Inmigrants	12	11	9	10	45	29	49	31	16
Outmigrants	31	12	15	22	34	61	109	65	32
Net migration	-19	-10	-5	-12	11	-32	-60	-34	-15
LOS ANGELES-ANAHEIM-RIVERSIDE, CA CMSA									
Inmigrants	9	20	16	19	49	17	75	75	5
Outmigrants	48	38	33	37	78	49	141	68	34
Net migration	-39	-18	-17	-18	-28	-32	-66	7	-30
CHICAGO-GARY-LAKE COUNTY-IL-IN-WI CMSA									
Inmigrants	18	6	10	10	33	21	26	17	18
Outmigrants	14	17	15	9	29	14	46	29	10
Net migration	4	-12	-5	1	4	6	-20	-11	8
SAN FRANCISCO-OAKLAND-SAN JOSE, CA CMSA									
Inmigrants	9	7	-	9	16	19	39	4	4
Outmigrants	12	12	4	8	36	17	59	12	5
Net migration	-3	-5	-4	2	-19	3	-19	-9	-2
PHILADELPHIA-WILMINGTON-TRENTON, PA-NJ-DE-MD CMSA									
Inmigrants	4	2	5	3	9	14	28	15	9
Outmigrants	9	-	12	11	11	4	39	24	12
Net migration	-5	2	-7	-8	-1	10	-11	-10	-4
DETROIT, ANN ARBOR, MI CMSA									
Inmigrants	8	5	1	4	17	15	18	3	2
Outmigrants	6	-	7	2	17	14	18	23	3
Net migration	-	4	-5	2	-	1	-	-21	-1

[Continued]

★ 713 ★

Geographical Mobility: Inmigrants, Outmigrants, and Net Migration for Large MSA's: Characteristics-2
[Continued]

MSA's	Age								
	1 to 4 years	5 to 9 years	10 to 14 years	15 to 19 years	20 to 24 years	25 to 29 years	30 to 44 years	45 to 64 years	65 years and over
BOSTON-LAWRENCE-SALEM, MA-NH CMSA									
Inmigrants	3	5	3	1	6	17	26	4	6
Outmigrants	-	-	-	7	23	19	12	9	3
Net migration	3	5	3	-6	-17	-2	14	-5	4
DALLAS-FORT WORTH, TX CMSA									
Inmigrants	16	19	14	17	13	21	55	29	7
Outmigrants	6	5	4	14	27	14	36	6	2
Net migration	10	14	10	3	-14	7	20	23	4
HOUSTON-GALVESTON-BRAZORIA, TX CMSA									
Inmigrants	17	10	5	6	23	32	24	9	2
Outmigration	4	5	7	8	10	8	33	11	3
Net migration	13	5	-1	-2	12	25	-9	-3	-1
WASHINGTON, DC-MD-VA MSA									
Inmigrants	14	13	-	-	17	10	33	8	1
Outmigrants	8	7	10	3	15	16	40	13	1
Net migration	5	6	-10	-3	2	-7	-7	-5	-

Source: "Inmigrants, Outmigrants, and Net Migration for Large Metropolitan Statistical Areas (MSA's), by Sex, Race and Hispanic Origin, and Age," *Geographical Mobility: March 1992 to March 1993*, p. 164.

★ 714 ★

Mobility

Geographical Mobility: Inmigrants, Outmigrants, and Net Migration for Regions, by Select Characteristics-1

Characteristic	Northeast			Midwest		
	Inmigrants	Outmigrants	Net migration	Inmigrants	Outmigrants	Net migration
BLACK						
Age and Sex						
Total, 1 year and over	18	82	-64	57	55	2
1 to 14 years	2	13	-12	12	11	1
15 to 19 years	2	3	-1	4	3	1
20 to 24 years	2	9	-7	14	2	12

[Continued]

Geographical Mobility: Inmigrants, Outmigrants, and Net Migration for Regions, by Select Characteristics-1
[Continued]

Characteristic	Northeast			Midwest		
	Inmigrants	Outmigrants	Net migration	Inmigrants	Outmigrants	Net migration
25 to 29 years	7	16	-9	8	24	-16
30 to 44 years	6	23	-17	11	11	-
45 to 64 years	-	13	-13	3	3	-
65 to 74 years	-	4	-4	3	-	3
75 years and over	-	2	-2	3	1	2
Male	13	40	-27	29	17	12
1 to 14 years	2	6	-5	6	1	5
15 to 19 years	-	-	-	2	2	-
20 to 24 years	2	6	-4	9	-	9
25 to 29 years	5	9	-5	5	9	-4
30 to 44 years	5	15	-10	5	4	-
45 to 64 years	-	2	-2	-	-	-
65 to 74 years	-	-	-	3	-	3
75 years and over	-	2	-2	-	1	-1
Female	5	42	-37	28	-38	-10
1 to 14 years	-	7	-7	6	10	-4
15 to 19 years	2	3	-1	2	1	1
20 to 24 years	-	3	-3	5	2	3
25 to 29 years	2	6	-4	3	15	-12
30 to 44 years	1	8	-7	6	7	-1
45 to 64 years	-	11	-11	3	3	-
65 to 74 years	-	4	-4	-	-	-
75 years and over		-	-	3	-	3
Relationship to Householder						
Householder, spouse present	2	6	-4	5	9	-3
Other family householder	-	7	-7	7	3	4
Nonfamily householder	7	18	-12	14	13	1
Spouse of householder	2	6	-4	6	7	-1
Other relatives of householder	8	38	-30	23	21	2
All other	-	7	-7	2	3	-
Marital Status						
Single (never married)	10	48	-38	37	32	6
Married, spouse present	4	13	-9	11	16	-5
Married, spouse absent	4	13	-9	-	1	-1
Widowed	-	2	-2	6	1	-1
Divorced	-	6	-6	3	5	-3

Source: "Inmigrant, Outmigrants, and Net Migration for Regions, by Selected Characteristics," *Geographical Mobility: March 1992 to March 1993,* p. 59. *Note:* X = Not applicable. B = Base less than 75,000.

★ 715 ★

Mobility

Geographical Mobility: Inmigrants, Outmigrants, and Net Migration for Regions, by Select Characteristics-2

Characteristic	South			West		
	Inmigrants	Outmigrants	Net migration	Inmigrants	Outmigrants	Net migration
BLACK						
Age and Sex						
Total, 1 year and over	151	96	55	61	55	7
1 to 14 years	24	29	-5	20	4	16
15 to 19 years	7	5	2	5	7	-2
20 to 24 years	20	16	5	7	16	-9
25 to 29 years	34	12	22	6	4	2
30 to 44 years	38	26	12	19	14	5
45 to 64 years	20	4	16	5	8	-3
65 to 74 years	4	3	1	-	-	-
75 years and over	3	2	2	-	2	-2
Male	70	56	14	32	31	1
1 to 14 years	9	19	-10	13	4	9
15 to 19 years	1	3	-1	3	2	2
20 to 24 years	13	12	2	5	11	-7
25 to 29 years	14	5	9	-	1	-1
30 to 44 years	23	13	10	9	9	-1
45 to 64 years	6	3	3	3	4	-2
65 to 74 years	-	3	-3	-	-	-
75 years and over	3	-	3	-	-	-
Female	81	40	41	29	23	6
1 to 14 years	15	11	4	7	-	7
15 to 19 years	6	2	4	1	5	-4
20 to 24 years	7	4	3	2	5	-3
25 to 29 years	20	6	14	6	4	3
30 to 44 years	15	14	1	10	4	6
45 to 64 years	14	2	13	3	4	-1
65 to 74 years	4	-	4	-	-	-
75 years and over	-	2	-2	-	2	-2
Relationship to Householder						
Householder, spouse present	18	7	11	3	6	-4
Other family householder	12	11	1	6	4	2
Nonfamily householder	25	19	6	11	7	5
Spouse of householder	14	11	2	6	3	3
Other relatives of householder	71	47	24	30	27	3
All other	11	1	10	4	7	-3

[Continued]

★ 715 ★

Geographical Mobility: Inmigrants, Outmigrants, and Net Migration for Regions, by Select Characteristics-2

[Continued]

Characteristic	South			West		
	Inmigrants	Outmigrants	Net migration	Inmigrants	Outmigrants	Net migration
Marital Status						
Single (never married)	80	61	19	40	27	14
Married, spouse present	42	18	24	9	20	-11
Married, spouse absent	12	9	3	7	-	7
Widowed	3	4	-1	-	2	-2
Divorced	14	4	10	5	6	-1

Source: "Inmigrant, Outmigrants, and Net Migration for Regions, by Selected Characteristics," *Geographical Mobility: March 1992 to March 1993*, p. 59. *Note:* X=Not applicable. B=Base less than 75,000.

★ 716 ★

Mobility

Geographical Mobility: Inmigration, Outmigration, and Net Migration for MSA's and Nonmetropolitan Areas: Characteristics. Part 1

[Mobility data from March 1992 to March 1993. Numbers in thousands. For meaning of symbols, see text.]

United States and regions	Persons 1 year and over living in U.S. at both dates	Total		Race		
		Male	Female	White	Black	Hispanic[1]
UNITED STATES						
Inside MSA's:						
Inmigrants	1,531	765	766	1,380	106	92
Outmigrants	1,848	917	931	1,690	118	94
Net migration	-318	-152	-165	-310	-13	-2
Central cities of MSA's:						
Inmigrants	3,550	1,813	1,737	2,804	551	356
From balance of MSA's	3,010	1,519	1,491	2,335	501	320
From outside MSA's	541	295	246	469	50	36
Outmigrants	6,043	3,002	3,041	4,950	818	737
To balance of MSA's	5,198	2,580	2,618	4,221	727	669
To outside MSA's	845	422	423	729	91	68
Net migration	-2,493	-1,189	-1,304	-2,146	-267	-381
Balance of MSA's:						
Inmigrants	6,188	3,051	3,138	5,132	783	725
From central cities	5,198	2,580	2,618	4,221	727	669

[Continued]

★ 716 ★

Geographical Mobility: Inmigration, Outmigration, and Net Migration for MSA's and Nonmetropolitan Areas: Characteristics.
Part 1
[Continued]

United States and regions	Persons 1 year and over living in U.S. at both dates	Total		Race		
		Male	Female	White	Black	Hispanic[1]
From outside MSA's	990	470	520	911	55	56
Outmigrants	4,013	2,014	1,999	3,296	528	346
To central cities	3,010	1,519	1,491	2,335	501	320
To outside MSA's	1,003	495	508	961	27	25
Net migration	2,175	1,037	1,139	1,836	254	379
Outside MSA's:						
Inmigrants	1,848	917	931	1,690	118	94
Outmigrants	1,531	765	766	1,380	106	92
Net migration	318	152	165	310	13	2

Source: "Inmigration, Outmigration and Net Migration for Metropolitan Statistical Area (MSA's) and Nonmetropolitan Areas, by Sex, Race, Hispanic Origin, Age, and Region of Current Residence." *Geographical Mobility: March 1992 to March 1993,* p. 72. *Note:* 1. Persons of Hispanic origin may be of any race.

★ 717 ★
Mobility

Geographical Mobility: Inmigration, Outmigration, and Net Migration for MSA's and Nonmetropolitan Areas: Characteristics.
Part 2

[Mobility data from March 1992 to March 1993. Numbers in thousands. For meaning of symbols, see text.]

United States and regions	Persons 1 year and over living in U.S. at both dates	Total		Race		
		Male	Female	White	Black	Hispanic[1]
UNITED STATES						
NORTHEAST						
Inside MSA's:						
Inmigrants	142	69	73	131	7	-
Outmigrants	220	105	115	217	-	6
Net migration	-79	-37	-42	-87	7	-6
Central cities of MSA's:						
Inmigrants	387	184	203	314	44	33
From balance of MSA's	329	152	177	266	37	33

[Continued]

★ 717 ★

Geographical Mobility: Inmigration, Outmigration, and Net Migration for MSA's and Nonmetropolitan Areas: Characteristics. Part 2

[Continued]

United States and regions	Persons 1 year and over living in U.S. at both dates	Total		Race		
		Male	Female	White	Black	Hispanic[1]
From outside MSA's	59	33	26	48	7	-
Outmigrants	609	302	308	556	24	40
To balance of MSA's	522	263	259	471	24	37
To outside MSA's	87	38	49	85	-	3
Net migration	-222	-117	-105	-242	20	-7
Balance of MSA's:						
Inmigrants	605	300	305	554	24	37
From central cities	522	263	259	471	24	37
From outside MSA's	83	36	47	83	-	-
Outmigrants	461	219	243	399	37	36
To central cities	329	152	177	266	37	33
To outside MSA's	133	67	66	133	-	3
Net migration	143	81	63	155	-13	1
Outside MSA's:						
Inmigrants	220	105	115	217	-	6
Outmigrants	142	69	73	131	7	-
Net migration	79	37	42	87	-7	6

Source: "Inmigration, Outmigration and Net Migration for Metropolitan Statistical Area (MSA's) and Nonmetropolitan Areas, by Sex, Race, Hispanic Origin, Age, and Region of Current Residence." *Geographical Mobility: March 1992 to March 1993*, p. 72. *Note:* 1. Persons of Hispanic origin may be of any race.

★ 718 ★
Mobility

Geographical Mobility: Inmigration, Outmigration, and Net Migration for MSA's and Nonmetropolitan Areas: Characteristics. Part 3

[Mobility data from March 1992 to March 1993. Numbers in thousands. For meaning of symbols, see text.]

United States and regions	Persons 1 year and over living in U.S. at both dates	Total		Race		
		Male	Female	White	Black	Hispanic[1]
UNITED STATES						
MIDWEST						
Inside MSA's:						
Inmigrants	427	219	208	410	15	7
Outmigrants	459	240	219	427	16	29
Net migration	-32	-21	-11	-17	-1	-21
Central cities of MSA's:						
Inmigrants	714	371	343	549	148	14
From balance of MSA's	594	309	284	444	134	8
From outside MSA's	121	62	59	106	14	5
Outmigrants	1,072	566	506	938	102	51
To balance of MSA's	856	454	402	749	85	25
To outside MSA's	216	112	104	188	16	26
Net migration	-358	-194	-163	-388	46	-38
Balance of MSA's:						
Inmigrants	1,162	611	551	1,054	87	27
From central cities	856	454	402	749	85	25
From outside MSA's	306	157	149	305	2	2
Outmigrants	837	438	399	683	134	11
To central cities	534	309	284	444	134	8
To outside MSA's	244	129	115	239	-	3
Net migration	325	173	152	371	-47	17
Outside MSA's:						
Inmigrants	459	340	219	427	16	29
Outmigrants	427	219	208	410	15	7
Net migration	32	21	11	17	1	21

Source: "Inmigration, Outmigration and Net Migration for Metropolitan Statistical Area (MSA's) and Nonmetropolitan Areas, by Sex, Race, Hispanic Origin, Age, and Region of Current Residence." *Geographical Mobility: March 1992 to March 1993,* p. 72. *Note:* 1. Persons of Hispanic origin may be of any race.

★ 719 ★

Mobility

Geographical Mobility: Inmigration, Outmigration, and Net Migration for MSA's and Nonmetropolitan Areas: Characteristics. Part 4

[Mobility data from March 1992 to March 1993. Numbers in thousands. For meaning of symbols, see text.]

United States and regions	Persons 1 year and over living in U.S. at both dates	Total		Race		
		Male	Female	White	Black	Hispanic[1]
UNITED STATES						
SOUTH						
Inside MSA's:						
Inmigrants	613	307	306	517	81	41
Outmigrants	799	391	408	691	97	26
Net migration	-187	-85	-102	-173	-16	15
Central cities of MSA's:						
Inmigrants	1,199	606	593	920	247	124
From balance of MSA's	1,020	493	527	776	217	109
From outside MSA's	179	113	66	144	29	14
Outmigrants	2,616	1,280	1,336	1,921	593	242
To balance of MSA's	2,222	1,077	1,145	1,602	523	224
To outside MSA's	394	202	191	319	70	18
Net migration	-1,417	-674	-743	-1,001	-346	-118
Balance of MSA's:						
Inmigrants	2,656	1,271	1,384	1,975	575	250
From central cities	2,222	1,077	1,145	1,602	523	224
From outside MSA's	434	194	240	373	52	27
Outmigrants	1,426	682	744	1,147	244	117
To central cities	1,020	493	527	776	217	109
To outside MSA's	406	189	216	372	27	7
Net migration	1,230	589	641	827	330	134
Outside MSA's:						
Inmigrants	799	391	408	691	97	26
Outmigrants	613	307	306	517	81	41
Net migration	187	85	102	173	16	-15

Source: "Inmigration, Outmigration and Net Migration for Metropolitan Statistical Area (MSA's) and Nonmetropolitan Areas, by Sex, Race, Hispanic Origin, Age, and Region of Current Residence." *Geographical Mobility: March 1992 to March 1993,* p. 73. *Note:* 1. Persons of Hispanic origin may be of any race.

★ 720 ★

Mobility

Geographical Mobility: Inmigration, Outmigration, and Net Migration for MSA's and Nonmetropolitan Areas: Characteristics. Part 5

[Mobility data from March 1992 to March 1993. Numbers in thousands. For meaning of symbols, see text.]

United States and regions	Persons 1 year and over living in U.S. at both dates	Total		Race		
		Male	Female	White	Black	Hispanic[1]
UNITED STATES						
WEST						
Inside MSA's:						
Inmigrants	350	170	179	322	3	44
Outmigrants	369	180	189	355	5	33
Net migration	-20	-10	-10	-32	-2	11
Central cities of MSA's:						
Inmigrants	1,250	652	598	1,021	113	186
From balance of MSA's	1,067	564	503	850	112	170
From outside MSA's	183	88	95	171	1	17
Outmigrants	1,747	855	891	1,536	99	404
To balance of MSA's	1,599	786	813	1,398	94	384
To outside MSA's	148	70	78	137	5	20
Net migration	-496	-203	-293	-515	13	-218
Balance of MSA's:						
Inmigrants	1,765	868	897	1,549	96	410
From central cities	1,599	786	813	1,398	94	384
From outside MSA's	167	83	84	151	2	27
Outmigrants	1,288	675	614	1,067	112	182
To central cities	1,067	564	503	850	112	170
To outside MSA's	221	110	111	217	-	13
Net migration	477	194	283	482	-16	228
Outside MSA's:						
Inmigrants	369	180	189	355	5	33
Outmigrants	350	170	179	322	3	44
Net migration	20	10	10	32	2	-11

Source: "Inmigration, Outmigration and Net Migration for Metropolitan Statistical Area (MSA's) and Nonmetropolitan Areas, by Sex, Race, Hispanic Origin, Age, and Region of Current Residence." *Geographical Mobility: March 1992 to March 1993*, p. 73. *Note:* 1. Persons of Hispanic origin may be of any race.

★ 721 ★

Mobility

Geographical Mobility: Migration Flows Between Regions, by Selected Characteristics-1

[Mobility data from March 1992 to March 1993. Numbers in thousands. For meaning of symbols, see text.]

Characteristic	From Northeast to-			From Midwest to-		
	Midwest	South	West	Northeast	South	West
BLACK						
Age and Sex						
Total, 1 year and over	9	71	2	2	40	13
1 to 14 years	-	12	1	-	10	1
15 to 19 years	-	3	-	-	1	2
20 to 24 years	6	3	-	-	1	1
25 to 29 years	3	12	-	2	18	4
30 to 44 years	-	22	1	-	7	4
45 to 64 years	-	13	-	-	2	1
65 to 74 years	-	4	-	-	-	-
75 years and over	-	2	-	-	1	-
Male	6	34	-	2	11	4
1 to 14 years	-	6	-	-	1	-
15 to 19 years	-	-	-	-	1	1
20 to 24 years	4	2	-	-	-	-
25 to 29 years	2	7	-	2	7	-
30 to 44 years	-	15	-	-	1	3
45 to 64 years	-	2	-	-	-	-
65 to 74 years	-	-	-	-	-	-
75 years and over	-	2	-	-	1	-
Female	3	37	2	-	29	9
1 to 14 years	-	6	1	-	9	1
15 to 19 years	-	3	-	-	-	1
20 to 24 years	2	1	-	-	1	1
25 to 29 years	2	5	-	-	12	4
30 to 44 years	-	7	1	-	6	1
45 to 64 years	-	11	-	-	2	1
65 to 74 years	-	4	-	-	-	-
75 years and over	-	-	-	-	-	-
Relationship to Householder						
Householder, spouse present	-	6	-	-	7	1
Other family householder	-	6	1	-	3	-
Nonfamily householder	3	15	-	2	7	4
Spouse of householder	-	6	-	-	6	1
Other relative of householder	4	32	1	-	14	3
All other	2	5	-	-	-	3

[Continued]

★ 721 ★

Geographical Mobility: Migration Flows Between Regions, by Selected Characteristics-1

[Continued]

Characteristic	From Northeast to-			From Midwest to-		
	Midwest	South	West	Northeast	South	West
Martial Status						
Single (never married)	9	39	1	2	21	8
Married, spouse present	-	13	-	-	13	3
Married, spouse absent	-	12	1	-	-	1
Widowed	-	2	-	-	1	-
Divorced	-	6	-	-	4	1

Source: "Migration Flows Between Regions, by Selected Characteristics," *Geographical Mobility: March 1992 to March 1993,* p. 66.

★ 722 ★

Mobility

Geographical Mobility: Migration Flows Between Regions, by Selected Characteristics-2

[Mobility data from March 1992 to March 1993. Numbers in thousands. For meaning of symbols, see text.]

Characteristic	From South to-			From West to-		
	Northeast	Midwest	West	Northeast	Midwest	South
BLACK						
Age and Sex						
Total, 1 year and over	16	33	47	-	15	40
1 to 14 years	2	10	18	-	2	2
15 to 19 years	2	-	3	-	4	3
20 to 24 years	2	8	5	-	-	16
25 to 29 years	5	5	2	-	1	4
30 to 44 years	6	6	14	-	5	9
45 to 64 years	-	-	4	-	3	6
65 to 74 years	-	3	-	-	-	-
75 years and over	-	2	-	-	2	-
Male	11	16	29	-	6	25
1 to 14 years	2	4	13	-	2	2
15 to 19 years	-	-	3	-	2	-
20 to 24 years	2	5	5	-	-	11
25 to 29 years	3	3	-	-	1	-
30 to 44 years	5	2	6	-	2	7
45 to 64 years	-	-	3	-	-	4
65 to 74 years	-	3	-	-	-	-
75 years and over	-	-	-	-	-	-

[Continued]

★ 722 ★

Geographical Mobility: Migration Flows Between Regions, by Selected Characteristics-2

[Continued]

Characteristic	From South to-			From West to-		
	Northeast	Midwest	West	Northeast	Midwest	South
Female	5	17	18	-	8	15
1 to 14 years	-	6	5	-	-	-
15 to 19 years	2	-	-	-	2	3
20 to 24 years	-	3	1	-	-	5
25 to 29 years	2	2	2	-	-	4
30 to 44 years	1	4	8	-	2	2
45 to 64 years	-	-	2	-	3	1
65 to 74 years	-	-	-	-	-	-
75 years and over	-	2	-	-	2	-
Relationship to Householder						
Householder, spouse present	2	3	1	-	2	4
Other family householder	-	5	6	-	2	2
Nonfamily householder	5	8	7	-	3	4
Spouse of householder	2	4	5	-	2	1
Other relative of householder	8	13	26	-	5	22
All other	-	-	1	-	1	6
Martial Status						
Single (never married)	8	22	31	-	6	20
Married, spouse present	4	7	6	-	4	16
Married, spouse absent	4	-	5	-	-	-
Widowed	-	4	-	-	2	-
Divorced	1	1	4	-	3	4

Source: "Migration Flows Between Regions, by Selected Characteristics," *Geographical Mobility: March 1992 to March 1993,* p. 66.

★ 723 ★

Mobility

Geographical Mobility: Mobility and Region of Residence, by Race. Part 1

[Mobility data from March 1992 to March 1993. Numbers in thousands. For meaning of symbols, see text.]

	Current residence									
	Black					Hispanic[1]				
		Inside MSA's					Inside MSA's			
Previous residence	Total	Total	Central cities of MSA's	Balance of MSA's	Outside MSA's	Total	Total	Central cities of MSA's	Balance of MSA's	Outside MSA's
UNITED STATES IN 1993										
Total, 1 year old and over	31,366	26,592	17,748	8,843	4,774	22,232	20,569	11,560	9,009	1,663
Same house	25,397	21,324	14,207	7,116	4,073	16,991	15,732	8,769	6,964	1,258
Different house in U.S.	5,913	5,217	3,508	1,709	696	4,827	4,436	2,519	1,917	391
Same county	4,325	3,862	2,783	1,079	463	3,779	3,525	2,078	1,446	254
Different county	1,588	1,355	725	630	233	1,048	911	441	470	137
Same State	808	686	288	398	122	606	548	250	297	58
Central cities of MSA's	380	357	157	200	24	334	310	147	164	24
Balance of MSA's	275	261	102	160	14	210	195	78	117	15
Outside MSA's	152	68	30	38	84	62	43	26	17	20
Different State	780	670	437	233	111	442	363	190	173	79
Northeast	120	100	38	61	20	109	106	49	57	4
Central cities of MSA's	93	74	28	46	19	59	58	30	28	1
Balance of MSA's	25	23	10	14	1	47	46	19	26	1
Outside MSA's	2	2	-	2	-	3	2	-	2	1
Midwest	138	132	89	43	6	56	41	29	12	15
Central cities of MSA's	82	79	41	38	3	34	28	22	6	6
Balance of MSA's	48	48	43	5	-	8	5	1	2	-
Outside MSA's	8	5	5	-	3	14	5	1	4	9
South	443	384	264	120	59	118	87	40	48	30
Central cities of MSA's	285	253	201	52	32	71	55	25	30	16
Balance of MSA's	110	104	47	58	6	21	16	6	10	4
Outside MSA's	48	27	16	11	21	27	16	9	8	10
West	79	54	46	8	25	159	129	73	56	30
Central cities of MSA's	53	40	38	2	14	97	75	49	26	21
Balance of MSA's	16	10	8	2	6	32	27	23	5	5
Outside MSA's	11	4	-	4	6	30	26	1	26	3
Movers from abroad	56	51	33	18	5	414	401	272	129	13

Source: "Mobility and Region of Residence, by Race and Hispanic Origin," *Geographical Mobility: March 1992 to March 1993,* p. 75. *Note:* 1. Persons of Hispanic origin may be of any race.

★ 724 ★

Mobility

Geographical Mobility: Mobility and Region of Residence, by Race. Part 2

[Mobility data from March 1992 to March 1993. Numbers in thousands. For meaning of symbols, see text.]

Previous residence	Current residence									
	Black					Hispanic[1]				
	Total	Inside MSA's			Outside MSA's	Total	Inside MSA's			Outside MSA's
		Total	Central cities of MSA's	Balance of MSA's			Total	Central cities of MSA's	Balance of MSA's	
NORTHEAST IN 1993										
Total, 1 year old and over	5,200	5,140	3,752	1,387	60	3,322	3,269	2,445	824	53
Same house	4,619	4,573	3,345	1,228	47	2,745	2,705	1,999	705	40
Different house in U.S.	561	547	389	158	13	503	490	382	108	13
Same county	421	408	321	87	13	368	362	298	64	6
Different county	139	139	68	71	-	135	128	84	44	7
Same State	83	83	38	46	-	85	83	59	24	3
Central cities of MSA's	33	33	23	10	-	69	69	53	16	-
Balance of MSA's	49	49	13	36	-	16	14	6	8	3
Outside MSA's	2	2	2	-	-	-	-	-	-	-
Different State	56	56	31	26	-	50	45	25	20	5
Northeast	38	38	15	23	-	42	39	21	18	3
Central cities of MSA's	24	24	14	11	-	28	27	15	12	1
Balance of MSA's	13	13	1	12	-	13	12	6	6	1
Outside MSA's	-	-	-	-	-	1	-	-	-	1
Midwest	2	2	2	-	-	-	-	-	-	-
Central cities of MSA's	2	2	2	-	-	-	-	-	-	-
Balance of MSA's	-	-	-	-	-	-	-	-	-	-
Outside MSA's	-	-	-	-	-	-	-	-	-	-
South	16	16	14	3	-	7	5	4	1	2
Central cities of MSA's	3	3	3	-	-	4	2	2	-	2
Balance of MSA's	9	9	6	3	-	3	3	2	1	-
Outside MSA's	5	5	5	-	-	-	-	-	-	-
West	-	-	-	-	-	1	1	-	1	-
Central cities of MSA's	-	-	-	-	-	1	1	-	1	-
Balance of MSA's	-	-	-	-	-	-	-	-	-	-
Outside MSA's	-	-	-	-	-	-	-	-	-	-
Movers from abroad	20	20	18	2	-	74	74	64	10	-

Source: "Mobility and Region of Residence, by Race and Hispanic Origin," *Geographical Mobility: March 1992 to March 1993*, p. 75. *Note:* 1. Persons of Hispanic origin may be of any race.

Geographical Mobility: Mobility and Region of Residence, by Race. Part 3

[Mobility data from March 1992 to March 1993. Numbers in thousands. For meaning of symbols, see text.]

	Current residence								
	Black					Hispanic[1]			
		Inside MSA's			Outside MSA's		Inside MSA's		Outside MSA's
Previous residence	Total	Total	Central cities of MSA's	Balance of MSA's		Total	Total	Central cities of MSA's	Balance of MSA's	
MIDWEST IN 1993									
Total, 1 year old and over	6,442	6,242	4,977	1,264	201	1,635	1,524	1,035	489	111
Same house	5,221	5,062	3,988	1,074	159	1,170	1,096	725	370	74
Different house in U.S.	1,209	1,167	978	188	42	420	383	276	107	37
Same county	969	950	810	140	19	317	311	234	77	6
Different county	240	217	169	48	23	103	72	42	30	31
Same State	100	87	59	28	13	42	30	14	16	12
Central cities of MSA's	60	53	41	12	7	28	16	9	7	12
Balance of MSA's	31	31	15	16	-	9	9	-	9	-
Outside MSA's	9	3	3	-	6	6	5	5	-	1
Different State	140	130	110	20	10	60	42	28	14	18
Northeast	9	9	4	5	-	6	6	-	6	-
Central cities of MSA's	6	6	4	2	-	1	1	-	1	-
Balance of MSA's	2	2	-	2	-	3	3	-	3	-
Outside MSA's	2	2	-	2	-	2	2	-	2	-
Midwest	83	83	72	11	-	26	22	19	2	4
Central cities of MSA's	46	46	35	11	-	21	18	16	2	3
Balance of MSA's	37	37	37	-	-	3	3	3	-	-
Outside MSA's	-	-	-	-	-	2	1	-	1	1
South	33	33	31	2	-	8	5	4	2	2
Central cities of MSA's	21	21	19	2	-	5	4	4	-	2
Balance of MSA's	2	2	2	-	-	2	2	-	2	-
Outside MSA's	11	11	11	-	-	-	-	-	-	-
West	15	5	3	2	10	22	10	5	4	12
Central cities of MSA's	13	3	3	-	10	18	8	5	3	10
Balance of MSA's	2	2	-	2	-	4	1	-	1	2
Outside MSA's	1	-	-	-	1	-	-	-	-	-
Movers from abroad	13	13	11	2	-	45	44	33	11	1

Source: "Mobility and Region of Residence, by Race and Hispanic Origin," *Geographical Mobility: March 1992 to March 1993*, p. 75. *Note:* 1. Persons of Hispanic origin may be of any race.

★ 726 ★

Mobility

Geographical Mobility: Mobility and Region of Residence, by Race. Part 4

[Mobility data from March 1992 to March 1993. Numbers in thousands. For meaning of symbols, see text.]

Previous residence	Current residence									
	Black					Hispanic[1]				
		Inside MSA's					Inside MSA's			
	Total	Total	Central cities of MSA's	Balance of MSA's	Outside MSA's	Total	Total	Central cities of MSA's	Balance of MSA's	Outside MSA's
SOUTH IN 1993										
Total, 1 year old and over	17,173	12,739	7,618	5,121	4,434	6,659	6,097	3,576	2,519	762
Same house	13,629	9,810	5,807	4,004	3,818	5,218	4,647	2,772	1,874	572
Different house in U.S.	3,522	2,911	1,807	1,104	611	1,472	1,293	718	575	179
Same county	2,494	2,083	1,389	694	411	1,080	952	533	419	128
Different county	1,028	829	418	410	199	392	341	186	155	51
Same State	531	421	162	259	110	205	185	87	98	21
Central cities of MSA's	253	236	81	156	17	113	103	48	55	10
Balance of MSA's	136	122	56	66	14	62	61	34	27	1
Outside MSA's	142	63	25	38	79	31	21	5	16	10
Different State	498	406	257	151	90	187	157	99	58	30
Northeast	71	53	19	33	18	62	61	28	33	1
Central cities of MSA's	61	44	11	33	17	3	31	15	16	-
Balance of MSA's	10	9	9	-	1	31	30	13	17	1
Outside MSA's	-	-	-	-	-	-	-	-	-	-
Midwest	40	35	14	21	6	19	10	4	6	9
Central cities of MSA's	24	22	3	18	2	6	2	2	1	3
Balance of MSA's	8	8	6	2	-	3	3	1	2	-
Outside MSA's	8	5	5	-	3	10	4	1	3	6
South	346	286	195	93	59	58	41	26	15	17
Central cities of MSA's	242	210	171	38	32	20	16	13	3	4
Balance of MSA's	75	69	24	45	6	12	9	4	4	4
Outside MSA's	29	9	-	9	21	26	16	9	8	9
West	40	33	28	4	7	48	45	41	4	3
Central cities of MSA's	22	20	20	-	1	35	33	33	-	2
Balance of MSA's	14	8	8	-	6	13	12	8	4	2
Outside MSA's	4	4	-	4	-	-	-	-	-	-
Movers from abroad	23	17	4	13	5	169	158	88	70	11

Source: "Mobility and Region of Residence, by Race and Hispanic Origin," *Geographical Mobility: March 1992 to March 1993,* p. 77. *Note:* 1. Persons of Hispanic origin may be of any race.

★ 727 ★

Mobility

Geographical Mobility: Mobility and Region of Residence, by Race. Part 5

[Mobility data from March 1992 to March 1993. Numbers in thousands. For meaning of symbols, see text.]

Previous residence	Current residence									
	Black					Hispanic[1]				
	Total	Inside MSA's			Outside MSA's	Total	Inside MSA's			Outside MSA's
		Total	Central cities of MSA's	Balance of MSA's			Total	Central cities of MSA's	Balance of MSA's	
WEST IN 1993										
Total, 1 year old and over	2,551	2,471	1,401	1,070	79	10,415	9,679	4,501	5,177	736
Same house	1,928	1,879	1,068	811	49	7,857	7,284	3,271	4,014	573
Different house in U.S.	621	592	333	259	30	2,432	2,269	1,143	1,126	162
Same county	441	422	263	158	19	2,014	1,899	1,014	886	115
Different county	180	170	70	100	10	418	370	130	240	48
Same State	94	94	30	64	-	273	251	91	160	23
Central cities of MSA's	34	34	13	22	-	124	122	36	86	2
Balance of MSA's	60	60	17	42	-	123	111	39	73	12
Outside MSA's	-	-	-	-	-	26	17	16	1	9
Different State	86	76	40	36	10	144	119	39	81	25
Northeast	2	-	-	-	2	-	-	-	-	-
Central cities of MSA's	2	-	-	-	2	-	-	-	-	-
Balance of MSA's	-	-	-	-	-	-	-	-	-	-
Outside MSA's	-	-	-	-	-	-	-	-	-	-
Midwest	13	12	1	11	1	11	10	6	4	2
Central cities of MSA's	10	10	1	8	1	8	8	4	4	-
Balance of MSA's	3	3	-	3	-	2	2	2	-	-
Outside MSA's	-	-	-	-	-	2	-	-	-	2
South	47	47	23	24	-	45	36	7	30	9
Central cities of MSA's	19	19	7	12	-	41	33	7	27	8
Balance of MSA's	25	25	16	9	-	3	3	-	3	-
Outside MSA's	3	3	1	2	-	1	-	-	-	1
West	25	17	15	2	8	88	74	26	47	15
Central cities of MSA's	19	17	15	2	3	43	33	11	22	10
Balance of MSA's	-	-	-	-	-	15	14	14	-	1
Outside MSA's	6	-	-	-	6	30	26	1	26	3
Movers from abroad	1	1	-	1	-	126	125	88	37	1

Source: "Mobility and Region of Residence, by Race and Hispanic Origin," *Geographical Mobility: March 1992 to March 1993*, p. 77. *Note:* 1. Persons of Hispanic origin may be of any race.

★ 728 ★

Mobility

Geographical Mobility: Movers Within and Between States and Regions by Selected Characteristics-1

[Mobility data from March 1992 to March 1993. Numbers in thousands. For meaning of symbols, see text.]

Characteristic	Movers living in Northeast in 1993			Movers living in Midwest in 1993		
	Total	Within same State	Between States, same region	Total	Within same State	Between States, same region
BLACK						
Age and Sex						
Total, 1 year and over	580	505	38	1,222	1,069	83
1 to 14 years	151	145	2	356	317	25
15 to 19 years	59	52	3	99	91	-
20 to 24 years	68	57	7	170	144	9
25 to 29 years	90	76	3	139	113	16
30 t0 44 years	137	110	14	282	250	19
45 to 64 years	60	51	6	124	113	7
65 to 74 years	11	9	1	29	21	5
75 years and over	5	3	2	23	19	1
Male	266	226	17	554	487	31
1 to 14 years	74	71	1	171	157	7
15 to 19 years	17	16	1	20	18	-
20 to 24 years	35	26	6	69	55	2
25 to 29 years	44	39	1	67	55	5
30 to 44 years	67	50	6	132	119	9
45 to 64 years	23	19	3	65	62	3
65 to 74 years	4	4	-	24	17	5
75 years and over	2	2	-	5	5	-
Female	314	278	21	668	582	52
1 to 14 years	77	74	1	185	160	18
15 to 19 years	41	36	2	79	73	-
20 to 24 years	34	32	1	101	89	7
25 to 29 years	46	37	3	72	58	10
30 to 44 years	70	60	8	149	131	11
45 to 64 years	36	32	3	59	52	4
65 to 74 years	7	6	1	5	5	-
75 years and over	3	2	2	19	14	1
Relationship of Householder						
Householder, spouse present	47	38	4	104	84	10
Other family householder	90	84	5	198	179	9
Nonfamily householder	83	62	8	175	152	7
Spouse of householder	52	41	4	111	92	13
Other relative of householder	267	247	7	578	513	41
All other	42	32	10	55	48	3

[Continued]

★ 728 ★

Geographical Mobility: Movers Within and Between States and Regions by Selected Characteristics-1
[Continued]

Characteristic	Movers living in Northeast in 1993			Movers living in Midwest in 1993		
	Total	Within same State	Between States, same region	Total	Within same State	Between States, same region
Marital Status						
Single (never married)	394	357	20	809	712	52
Married, spouse present	99	79	8	219	180	23
Married, spouse absent	50	33	7	80	77	2
Widowed	15	14	2	49	41	2
Divorced	22	21	1	65	59	4

Source: "Movers Within and Between States, for Regions, by Selected Characteristics," *Geographical Mobility: March 1992 to March 1993*, p. 52.

★ 729 ★
Mobility

Geographical Mobility: Movers Within and Between States and Regions by Selected Characteristics-2

[Mobility data from March 1992 to March 1993. Numbers in thousands. For meaning of symbols, see text.]

Characteristic	Movers living in South in 1993			Movers living in West in 1993		
	Total	Within same State	Between States, same region	Total	Within same State	Between States, same region
BLACK						
Age and Sex						
Total, 1 year and over	3,545	3,025	346	622	535	25
1 to 14 years	1,049	922	98	210	179	10
15 to 19 years	260	232	21	41	37	-
20 to 24 years	462	384	51	63	50	6
25 to 29 years	458	387	35	63	55	2
30 t0 44 years	899	758	98	195	172	4
45 to 64 years	321	264	33	40	32	3
65 to 74 years	68	58	6	11	11	-
65 years and over	27	19	4	-	-	-
Male	1,683	1,430	176	314	264	18
1 to 14 years	502	442	49	107	87	6
15 to 19 years	127	111	15	23	20	-
20 to 24 years	169	132	24	34	24	6
25 to 29 years	227	183	30	33	31	2
30 to 44 years	461	402	35	93	84	1

[Continued]

★ 729 ★

Geographical Mobility: Movers Within and Between States and Regions by Selected Characteristics-2
[Continued]

Characteristic	Movers living in South in 1993			Movers living in West in 1993		
	Total	Within same State	Between States, same region	Total	Within same State	Between States, same region
45 to 64 years	150	123	17	19	14	3
65 to 74 years	32	29	3	5	5	-
75 years and over	15	10	2	-	-	-
Female	1,861	1,594	170	308	271	7
1 to 14 years	547	481	49	103	91	4
15 to 19 years	133	121	6	18	17	-
20 to 24 years	292	252	28	28	26	-
25 to 29 years	231	204	5	30	24	-
30 to 44 years	438	356	63	101	88	3
45 to 64 years	172	141	15	21	18	-
65 to 74 years	36	29	3	6	6	-
75 years and over	12	10	2	-	-	-
Relationship of Householder						
Householder, spouse present	373	298	52	72	64	5
Other family householder	481	441	28	74	68	-
Nonfamily householder	420	355	39	76	62	3
Spouse of householder	352	282	53	66	56	3
Other relative of householder	1,666	1,426	158	284	239	14
All other	253	221	16	50	46	-
Marital Status						
Single (never married)	2,188	1,912	184	375	317	17
Married, spouse present	754	594	108	142	125	8
Married, spouse absent	222	191	18	47	40	-
Widowed	78	64	11	9	9	-
Divorced	302	263	25	50	45	-

Source: "Movers Within and Between States, for Regions, by Selected Characteristics," *Geographical Mobility: March 1992 to March 1993,* p. 52.

★ 730 ★

Mobility

Geographical Mobility: Movers Within the Same MSA/PMSA by Selected Characteristics, 1993

[Numbers in thousands].

Selected characteristics	Movers with same MSA/PMSA				
	Total	Within central city(s)	Central city(s) to suburbs	Suburbs to central city(s)	Within suburbs
Race and Hispanic Origin					
White	100.0	34.4	14.9	7.7	43.0
Black	100.0	60.6	12.7	8.4	18.3
Hispanic origin (of any race)	100.0	53.0	12.5	5.7	28.9

Source: "Movers Within the Same MSA/PSA by Selected Characteristics: 1993," *Geographical Mobility: March 1992 to March 1993*, p. xxvi.

★ 731 ★

Mobility

Geographical Mobility: Rates by Selected Characteristics, 1993

[Numbers in thousands].

Selected characteristics	Total persons	Same house (non-movers)	Total movers	Different house in the United States					Movers from abroad
				Total	Same county	Different county			
						Total	Same state	Different state	
Total, 1 year and over	250,210	208,162	42,048	40,744	26,212	14,532	7,735	6,797	1,305
Race and Hispanic Origin									
White	208,754	174,910	33,844	32,913	20,547	12,365	6,677	5,688	931
Black	31,366	25,397	5,969	5,913	4,325	1,588	808	780	56
Hispanic origin (of any race)	22,232	16,991	5,241	4,827	3,779	1,048	606	442	414

Source: "Geographical Mobility Rates by Selected Characteritsics: 1993," *Geographical Mobility: March 1992 to March 1993*, p. xii.

★ 732 ★

Mobility

Geographical Mobility: Size and Type of Area at Both Dates, by Race. Part 1-1

Current residence	Persons 1 year and over	Previous residence MSAs of-					
		All sizes	2,500,000 or more	1,000,000 to 2,500,000	500,000 to 1,000,000	250,000 to 500,000	Less than 250,000
ALL RACES							
United States	250,210	32,523	12,032	7,269	4,444	4,075	4,703
Inside MSA's	194,266	30,675	11,562	6,949	4,151	3,813	4,200
2,500,000 or more	79,631	11,239	10,192	323	278	211	236
1,000,000 to 2,500,000	44,987	7,705	566	5,985	639	241	274
500,000 to 1,000,000	25,729	4,282	311	254	3,022	532	164
250,000 to 500,000	21,004	2,568	288	177	88	2,677	337
Less than 250,000	22,915	3,881	205	212	124	152	3,188
Outside MSA's	55,943	1,848	471	319	293	262	503
Places of 25,000 or more	3,275	126	47	8	26	22	23
Places of 2,500 to 25,000	22,306	764	172	119	115	128	231
Outside places of 2,500 or more	30,362	958	252	192	153	112	249
WHITE							
United States	208,754	25,627	9,149	5,842	3,477	3,223	3,936
Inside MSA's	159,009	23,937	8,735	5,550	3,210	2,983	3,459
2,500,000 or more	62,251	8,377	7,606	248	196	152	175
1,000,000 to 2,500,000	37,653	6,183	462	4,761	543	153	264
500,000 to 1,000,000	20,813	3,323	246	209	2,294	438	136
250,000 to 500,000	18,226	2,890	246	158	81	2,131	274
Less than 250,000	20,066	3,163	175	173	86	109	2,610
Outside MSA's	49,745	1,690	415	292	266	240	477
Places of 25,000 or more	2,809	113	39	8	23	21	22
Places of 2,500 to 25,000	19,544	677	136	103	106	119	213
Outside places of 2,500 or more	27,393	900	240	181	137	100	242

Source: "Size and Type of Area of Both Dates, by Race and Hispanic Origin," *Geographical Mobility: March 1992 to March 1993,* p. 71.

★ 733 ★

Mobility

Geographical Mobility: Size and Type of Area at Both Dates, by Race.
Part 1-2

Current residence	Previous residence				Abroad
		Outside MSA's			
	Total	Places of 25,000 or more	Places of 2,500 to 25,000	Outside places of 2,500 or more	
ALL RACES					
United States	8, 220	684	2,854	4,683	1,305
Inside MSA's	1,531	113	528	891	1,206
2,500,000 or more	266	37	89	141	620
1,000,000 to 2,500,000	337	39	135	163	181
500,000 to 1,000,000	297	7	83	207	145
250,000 to 500,000	271	11	89	171	115
Less than 250,000	360	18	132	209	144
Outside MSA's	6,690	571	2,326	3,792	99
Places of 25,000 or more	546	359	67	119	11
Places of 2,500 to 25,000	3,301	127	1,638	1,537	52
Outside places of 2,500 or more	2,843	85	621	2,137	37
WHITE					
United States	7,286	590	2,492	4,203	931
Inside MSA's	1,380	100	459	821	858
2,500,000 or more	217	27	66	124	422
1,000,000 to 2,500,000	321	39	133	149	125
500,000 to 1,000,000	242	4	58	180	104
250,000 to 500,000	255	11	80	164	97
Less than 250,000	345	18	122	205	109
Outside MSA's	5,906	490	2,033	3,382	73
Places of 25,000 or more	451	285	59	108	5
Places of 2,500 to 25,000	2,926	122	1,438	1,366	37
Outside places of 2,500 or more	2,529	84	536	1,909	30

Source: "Size and Type of Area of Both Dates, by Race and Hispanic Origin," *Geographical Mobility: March 1992 to March 1993*, p. 71.

★ 734 ★

Mobility

Geographical Mobility: Size and Type of Area at Both Dates, by Race. Part 2-1

[Mobility data from March 1992 to March 1993. Numbers in thousands. For meaning of symbols, see text.]

Current residence	Persons 1 year and over	Previous residence MSAs of-					
		All sizes	2,500,000 or more	1,000,000 to 2,500,000	500,000 to 1,000,000	250,000 to 500,000	Less than 250,000
BLACK							
United States	31,366	5,230	2,030	1,149	789	625	637
Inside MSA's	26,592	5,111	1,989	1,125	771	609	617
2,500,000 or more	12,148	2,029	1,820	59	69	29	52
1,000,000 to 2,500,000	6,085	1,205	67	981	87	66	5
500,000 to 1,000,000	3,718	742	53	31	591	59	9
250,000 to 500,000	2,254	518	25	17	6	422	48
Less than 250,000	2,386	617	24	37	19	33	503
Outside MSA's	4,774	118	41	24	18	16	20
Places of 25,000 or more	343	7	5	-	2	-	-
Places of 2,500 to 25,000	2,139	69	29	16	4	5	15
Outside places of 2,500 or more	2,292	42	6	9	12	11	5
HISPANIC[1]							
United States	22,232	4,437	2,686	690	205	461	396
Inside MSA's	20,569	4,344	2,661	668	192	436	385
2,500,000 or more	12,959	2,619	2,508	49	12	23	28
1,000,000 to 2,500,000	2,847	664	58	559	32	3	12
500,000 to 1,000,000	1,449	280	31	17	144	80	9
250,000 to 500,000	1,834	472	33	29	3	326	81
Less than 250,000	1,480	308	31	14	1	6	256
Outside MSA's	1,663	94	24	21	13	24	10
Places of 25,000 or more	171	9	-	1	-	7	1
Places of 2,500 to 25,000	983	55	15	8	11	14	6
Outside places of 2,500 or more	509	30	9	12	2	4	3

Source: "Size and Type of Area of Both Dates, by Race and Hispanic Origin," *Geographical Mobility: March 1992 to March 1993,* p. 71. *Note:* 1. Persons of Hispanic origin may be of any race.

★ 735 ★

Mobility

Geographical Mobility: Size and Type of Area at Both Dates, by Race.
Part 2-2

[Mobility data from March 1992 to March 1993. Numbers in thousands. For meaning of symbols, see text.]

Current residence		Previous residence Outside MSAs			
	Total	Places of 25,000 or more	Places of 2,500 to 25,000	Outside places of 2,500 or more	Abroad
BLACK					
United States	683	75	286	323	56
Inside MSA's	106	10	50	46	51
2,500,000 or more	31	7	13	11	24
1,000,000 to 2,500,000	2	-	-	2	8
500,000 to 1,000,000	51	3	23	25	7
250,000 to 500,000	14	-	7	8	5
Less than 250,000	7	-	7	-	7
Outside MSA's	577	65	236	277	5
Places of 25,000 or more	71	59	5	7	-
Places of 2,500 to 25,000	268	4	169	95	-
Outside places of 2,500 or more	238	1	62	176	5
HISPANIC[1]					
United States	390	33	157	199	414
Inside MSA's	92	3	26	63	401
2,500,000 or more	11	1	5	5	236
1,000,000 to 2,500,000	34	-	-	34	51
500,000 to 1,000,000	2	-	1	2	27
250,000 to 500,000	16	1	2	13	46
Less than 250,000	18	1	18	9	41
Outside MSA's	298	30	131	136	13
Places of 25,000 or more	27	18	1	7	-
Places of 2,500 to 25,000	183	11	121	51	13
Outside places of 2,500 or more	88	-	9	78	-

Source: "Size and Type of Area of Both Dates, by Race and Hispanic Origin," *Geographical Mobility: March 1992 to March 1993*, p. 71. *Note:* 1. Persons of Hispanic origin may be of any race.

★ 736 ★

Mobility

Geographical Mobility: Sunbelt Mobility, by Selected Characteristics-1

[Mobility data from March 1992 to March 1993. Numbers in thousands. For meaning of symbols, see text.]

| Characteristic | Current residence in sunbelt | | | | | |
| | Total | Same house (non-movers) | Movers within sunbelt | | | |
			Total	Same county	Different county, same State	Different State
Race and Hispanic Origin						
White	73,907	60,178	12,118	8,529	2,402	1,187
Black	15,489	12,252	2,981	2,365	412	203
Hispanic	14,048	10,688	2,990	2,515	350	125

Source: "Sunbelt Mobility, by Selected Characteristics," *Geographical Mobility: March 1992 to March 1993,* p. 165.

★ 737 ★

Mobility

Geographical Mobility: Sunbelt Mobility, by Selected Characteristics-2

[Mobility data from March 1992 to March 1993. Numbers in thousands. For meaning of symbols, see text.]

| Characteristic | Current residence in sunbelt Inmigrants to sunbelt | | | | Out-migrants from sunbelt | Net migration for sunbelt |
	Total	Same State	Different State	From abroad		
Race and Hispanic Origin						
White	1,612	114	1,058	440	1,242	370
Black	258	20	213	23	110	145
Hispanic	370	12	111	247	82	267

Source: "Sunbelt Mobility, by Selected Characteristics," *Geographical Mobility: March 1992 to March 1993,* p. 165.

Projections

★ 738 ★

Population Projections: Hispanic and Non-Hispanic Population. By Age and Gender: 1995 to 2025

[As of **July 1**. Resident population. Data are for middle series; for assumptions, see table 3.]

AGE, SEX, AND RACE	POPULATION (1,000)					PERCENT DISTRIBUTION		
	1995	2000	2005	2010	2025	2000	2010	2025
Hispanic origin, total[1]	26,798	31,166	35,702	40,525	56,927	100.0	100.0	100.0
Under 5 years old	3,090	3,293	3,579	3,983	5,337	10.6	9.8	9.4
5 to 13 years old	4,560	5,542	6,196	6,651	9,020	17.8	16.4	15.8
14 to 17 years old	1,817	2,102	2,582	2,909	3,750	6.7	7.2	6.6
18 to 24 years old	3,204	3,547	4,070	4,863	6,300	11.4	12.0	11.1
25 to 34 years old	5,021	5,145	5,301	5,834	8,464	16.5	14.4	14.9
35 to 44 years old	3,894	4,830	5,396	5,519	7,043	15.5	13.6	12.4
45 to 54 years old	2,274	3,046	3,930	4,828	5,668	9.8	11.9	10.0
55 to 64 years old	1,407	1,734	2,281	3,020	5,266	5.6	7.5	9.3
65 to 74 years old	955	1,137	1,333	1,637	3,609	3.6	4.0	6.3
75 to 84 years old	436	586	767	914	1,744	1.9	2.3	3.1
85 years old and over	141	203	267	367	725	0.7	0.9	1.3
Male	13,610	15,777	18,022	20,410	28,531	50.6	50.4	50.1
Female	13,188	15,388	17,679	20,115	28,396	49.4	49.6	49.9
Non-Hispanic White, total	193,900	197,872	200,842	203,441	209,863	100.0	100.0	100.0
Under 5 years old	13,020	11,936	11,326	11,273	11,267	6.0	5.5	5.4
5 to 13 years old	23,032	23,506	22,605	21,141	21,096	11.9	10.4	10.1
14 to 17 years old	9,892	10,507	10,751	10,564	9,494	5.3	5.2	4.5
18 to 24 years old	17,413	17,245	18,458	19,001	16,691	8.7	9.3	8.0
25 to 34 years old	29,455	25,852	24,077	24,421	25,531	13.1	12.0	12.2
35 to 44 years old	31,542	32,741	29,965	26,370	26,262	16.5	13.0	12.5
45 to 54 years old	23,777	27,760	30,735	31,928	24,094	14.0	15.7	11.5
55 to 64 years old	17,064	18,751	22,605	26,459	28,104	9.5	13.0	13.4
65 to 74 years old	15,938	15,174	14,837	16,503	26,348	7.7	8.1	12.6
75 to 84 years old	9,629	10,674	11,153	10,768	15,129	5.4	5.3	7.2
85 years old and over	3,138	3,726	4,331	5,013	5,846	1.9	2.5	2.8
Male	94,716	96,846	98,472	99,903	103,362	48.9	49.1	49.3
Female	99,184	101,025	102,370	103,538	106,501	51.1	50.9	50.7
Non-Hispanic Black, total	31,648	33,741	35,793	37,930	44,705	100.0	100.0	100.0
Under 5 years old	3,076	3,033	3,109	3,289	3,790	9.0	8.7	8.5
5 to 13 years old	5,027	5,519	5,678	5,735	6,704	16.4	15.1	15.0
14 to 17 years old	2,187	2,312	2,587	2,676	2,955	6.9	7.1	6.6
18 to 24 years old	3,593	3,705	3,990	4,400	4,769	11.0	11.6	10.7
25 to 34 years old	5,196	4,953	4,886	5,084	6,214	14.7	13.4	13.9
35 to 44 years old	4,863	5,338	5,207	4,967	5,526	15.8	13.1	12.4
45 to 54 years old	2,996	3,781	4,584	5,023	4,647	11.2	13.2	10.4

[Continued]

★ 738 ★

Population Projections: Hispanic and Non-Hispanic Population. By Age and Gender: 1995 to 2025

[Continued]

AGE, SEX, AND RACE	POPULATION (1,000)					PERCENT DISTRIBUTION		
	1995	2000	2005	2010	2025	2000	2010	2025
55 to 64 years old	2,049	2,274	2,752	3,480	4,561	6.7	9.2	10.2
65 to 74 years old	1,583	1,626	1,698	1,903	3,593	4.8	5.0	8.0
75 to 84 years old	814	880	945	978	1,447	2.6	2.6	3.2
85 years old and over	263	319	356	397	500	0.9	1.0	1.1
Male	14,958	15,939	16,891	17,890	21,089	47.2	47.2	47.2
Female	16,689	17,802	18,901	20,040	23,616	52.8	52.8	52.8
Non-Hispanic American Indian, Eskimo, Aleut, total	1,927	2,055	2,190	2,336	2,796	100.0	100.0	100.0
Under 5 years old	188	185	198	214	246	9.0	9.2	8.8
5 to 13 years old	347	361	359	372	453	17.6	15.9	16.2
14 to 17 years old	144	164	176	170	205	8.0	7.3	7.3
18 to 24 years old	222	232	265	286	310	11.3	12.2	11.1
25 to 34 years old	310	304	313	341	430	14.8	14.6	14.4
35 to 44 years old	284	302	293	290	363	14.7	12.4	13.0
45 to 54 years old	189	225	255	272	269	10.9	11.6	9.6
55 to 64 years old	117	134	161	191	226	6.5	8.2	8.1
65 to 74 years old	76	82	91	106	174	4.0	4.5	6.2
75 to 84 years old	38	46	53	58	92	2.2	2.5	3.3
85 years old and over	13	20	27	34	55	1.0	1.5	2.0
Male	948	1,010	1,075	1,146	1,370	49.1	49.1	49.0
Female	979	1,045	1,115	1,190	1,426	50.9	50.9	51.0
Non-Hispanic Asian, Pacific Islander, total	9,161	11,407	13,759	16,199	24,046	100.0	100.0	100.0
Under 5 years old	807	984	1,122	1,258	1,732	8.6	7.8	7.2
5 to 13 years old	1,295	1,617	2,006	2,314	3,184	1.42	14.3	13.2
14 to 17 years old	552	727	850	1,070	1,492	6.4	6.6	6.2
18 to 24 years old	1,034	1,181	1,454	1,670	2,515	10.4	10.3	10.5
25 to 34 years old	1,688	1,983	2,215	2,499	3,687	17.4	15.4	15.3
35 to 44 years old	1,567	1,914	2,214	2,513	3,394	16.8	15.5	14.1
45 to 54 years old	988	1,357	1,715	2,048	2,857	11.9	12.6	11.9
55 to 64 years old	604	795	1,071	1,403	2,298	7.0	8.7	9.6
65 to 74 years old	412	532	663	829	1,637	4.7	5.1	6.8
75 to 84 years old	170	251	346	441	861	2.2	2.7	3.6
85 years old and over	42	66	102	157	389	0.6	1.0	1.6
Male	4,453	5,529	6,660	7,838	11,660	48.5	48.4	48.5
Female	4,708	5,879	7,099	8,361	12,386	51.5	51.6	51.5

Source: "Projections of Resident Population, by Age, Sex, and Race: 1995 to 2025," *Statistical Abstract of the United States: 1995,* p. 26. Primary source: U.S. Bureau of the Census, *Current Population Reports,* P25-1104. *Note:* 1. Persons of Hispanic origin may be of any race.

★ 739 ★

Projections

Population Projections: Race and Status, 1995 to 2010

[**In thousands. As of July 1.** Data shown are for series A, the preferred series model; for explanation of methodology, see text, section 1.]

REGION, DIVISION, AND STATE	WHITE			BLACK			AMERICAN INDIAN, ESKIMO, ALEUT			ASIAN, PACIFIC ISLANDER		
	1995	2000	2010	1995	2000	2010	1995	2000	2010	1995	2000	2010
U.S.	218,333	226,268	240,293	33,118	35,475	40,227	2,229	2,382	2,718	9,756	12,121	17,188
Northeast	43,381	43,218	43,268	6,263	6,570	7,267	118	108	98	1,678	1,989	2,669
N.E.	12,183	12,120	12,408	691	718	810	32	31	31	291	348	506
ME	1,217	1,220	1,283	5	5	5	6	6	6	8	9	14
NH	1,109	1,137	1,236	7	8	10	2	3	3	14	18	31
VT	570	582	609	2	3	4	2	2	2	4	5	9
MA	5,445	5,373	5,387	340	352	393	11	10	10	180	215	307
RI	927	917	933	44	46	51	4	4	4	25	31	46
CT	2,915	2,891	2,960	293	304	347	7	6	6	60	70	99
M.A.	31,198	31,098	30,860	5,572	5,852	6,547	86	77	67	1,387	1,641	2,163
NY	14,025	13,819	13,542	3,249	3,391	3,705	57	50	43	846	977	1,257
NJ	6,405	6,445	6,526	1,156	1,242	1,434	14	13	11	356	435	591
PA	10,768	10,834	10,792	1,167	1,219	1,318	15	14	13	185	229	315
Midwest	54,306	55,391	56,441	6,249	6,689	7,526	382	411	460	1,055	1,345	1,900
E.N.C.	37,392	38,006	38,350	5,277	5,653	6,379	165	170	174	776	976	1,354
OH	9,806	9,943	9,948	1,253	1,335	1,483	22	22	22	122	152	206
IN	5,275	5,444	5,587	476	514	582	14	15	15	55	72	102
IL	9,603	9,713	9,801	1,843	1,957	2,181	23	22	21	383	476	648
MI	7,958	8,000	7,979	1,417	1,520	1,737	61	63	64	140	176	253
WI	4,750	4,906	5,035	288	327	396	45	48	52	76	100	145
W.N.C.	16,914	17,385	18,091	972	1,036	1,147	217	241	286	279	369	546
MN	4,344	4,498	4,669	104	111	122	58	64	75	113	151	232
IA	2,763	2,816	2,841	57	65	78	8	8	8	33	41	53
MO	4,629	4,737	4,970	581	609	664	20	20	21	56	72	105
ND	600	601	622	4	4	5	28	31	37	5	7	11
SD	663	685	702	3	4	4	62	74	97	5	7	11
NE	1,550	1,598	1,669	64	69	76	14	15	16	17	22	31
KS	2,365	2,450	2,588	159	174	198	27	29	33	50	69	103
South	72,121	75,813	82,386	17,378	18,708	21,297	606	630	677	1,624	2,094	3,024
S.A.	35,962	37,772	40,805	9,960	10,868	12,615	185	194	208	911	1,173	1,691
DE	570	589	603	132	149	181	3	3	3	14	18	28
MD	3,500	3,546	3,631	1,368	1,514	1,776	13	13	14	196	249	361
DC	178	176	195	369	349	365	1	1	1	11	12	16
VA	5,127	5,367	5,743	1,284	1,391	1,592	15	15	15	220	275	378
WV	1,756	1,770	1,768	54	53	50	3	3	3	11	14	20
NC	5,378	5,682	6,125	1,594	1,715	1,916	90	98	109	88	123	190

[Continued]

★ 739 ★

Population Projections: Race and Status, 1995 to 2010
[Continued]

REGION, DIVISION, AND STATE	WHITE			BLACK			AMERICAN INDIAN, ESKIMO, ALEUT			ASIAN, PACIFIC ISLANDER		
	1995	2000	2010	1995	2000	2010	1995	2000	2010	1995	2000	2010
SC	2,561	2,677	2,902	1,131	1,207	1,344	9	9	9	31	39	56
GA	5,025	5,346	5,857	1,955	2,139	2,485	13	12	12	109	140	199
FL	11,867	12,619	13,981	2,073	2,351	2,906	38	40	42	231	303	443
E.S.C.	12,690	13,231	14,042	3,166	3,331	3,634	44	45	46	120	155	219
KY	3,535	3,646	3,769	286	307	345	6	6	6	24	30	40
TN	4,327	4,563	4,899	845	905	1,014	11	11	11	46	59	83
AL	3,140	3,284	3,529	1,083	1,139	1,243	18	18	19	33	44	65
MS	1,688	1,738	1,845	952	980	1,032	9	10	10	17	22	31
W.S.C.	23,469	24,810	27,539	4,252	4,509	5,048	377	391	423	593	766	1,114
AR	2,047	2,139	2,311	386	395	412	15	17	18	20	27	41
LA	2,909	2,953	3,119	1,371	1,427	1,550	19	19	20	60	78	119
OK	2,699	2,770	2,979	244	251	269	276	290	320	52	71	115
TX	15,814	16,948	19,130	2,251	2,436	2,817	67	65	65	461	590	839
West	48,525	51,846	58,198	3,228	3,508	4,137	1,123	1,233	1,483	5,399	6,693	9,596
Mountain	14,004	15,248	16,974	436	485	556	589	669	818	354	490	748
MT	798	847	908	2	2	3	55	62	74	6	8	12
ID	1,118	1,242	1,392	5	6	8	18	21	24	15	21	31
WY	467	498	564	4	5	5	12	14	17	4	6	3
CO	3,431	3,733	4,090	156	174	200	34	36	38	89	117	166
NM	1,460	1,574	1,760	32	33	35	159	181	231	25	35	56
AZ	3,606	3,894	4,379	123	131	143	251	285	348	91	127	204
UT	1,843	2,017	2,272	14	16	18	33	39	50	54	77	122
NV	1,281	1,443	1,609	100	118	144	27	31	36	70	99	148
Pacific	34,521	36,598	41,224	2,792	3,023	3,581	534	564	665	5,045	6,203	8,847
WA	4,915	5,360	6,071	164	174	187	101	112	131	318	424	635
OR	2,929	3,139	3,508	54	60	70	47	52	60	111	153	238
CA	25,701	26,987	30,357	2,512	2,719	3,245	277	276	314	3,908	4,906	7,169
AK	477	516	543	26	28	29	102	116	150	29	39	59
HI	499	596	745	36	42	50	7	8	10	679	681	746

Source: "Population Projections, by Race-States: 1995 to 2010," *Statistical Abstract of the United States: 1995,* p. 36. Primary source: U.S. Bureau of the Census, *Current Population Reports,* series P25- 1111.

★ 740 ★

Projections

Resident Population: Projected Trends, 1995 to 2025

[As of **July 1.** Data are for middle series; for assumptions, see table 3.]

AGE, SEX, AND RACE	POPULATION (1,000)					PERCENT DISTRIBUTION		
	1995	2000	2005	2010	2025	2000	2010	2025
White, total	218,334	226,267	233,343	240,297	261,531	100.0	100.0	100.0
Under 5 years old	15,841	14,945	14,587	14,893	16,117	6.6	6.2	6.2
5 to 13 years old	27,167	28,534	28,244	27,184	29,258	12.6	11.3	11.2
14 to 17 years old	11,544	12,409	13,078	13,203	12,874	5.5	5.5	4.9
18 to 24 years old	20,339	20,477	22,149	23,396	22,396	9.0	9.7	8.6
25 to 34 years old	34,027	30,534	28,900	29,715	33,202	13.5	12.4	12.7
35 to 44 years old	35,081	37,139	34,879	31,394	32,634	16.4	13.1	12.5
45 to 54 years old	25,852	30,535	34,313	36,330	29,259	13.5	15.1	11.2
55 to 64 years old	18,355	20,339	24,688	29,213	32,913	9.0	12.2	12.6
65 to 74 years old	16,822	16,220	16,058	17,998	29,634	7.2	7.5	11.3
75 to 84 years old	10,035	11,219	11,866	11,612	16,726	5.0	4.8	6.4
85 years old and over	3,271	3,917	4,581	5,357	6,518	1.7	2.2	2.5
Male	107,140	111,245	114,911	118,505	129,322	49.2	49.3	49.4
Female	111,195	115,022	118,433	121,792	132,209	50.8	50.7	50.6
Black, total	33,117	35,469	37,793	40,224	48,005	100.0	100.0	100.0
Under 5 years old	3,243	3,214	3,310	3,518	4,102	9.1	8.7	8.5
5 to 13 years old	5,285	5,836	6,025	6,114	7,238	16.5	15.2	15.1
14 to 17 years old	2,285	2,431	2,741	2,842	3,182	6.9	7.1	6.6
18 to 24 years old	3,764	3,900	4,222	4,687	5,140	11.0	11.7	10.7
25 to 34 years old	5,475	5,235	5,176	5,409	6,698	14.8	13.4	14.0
35 to 44 years old	5,088	5,610	5,506	5,268	5,933	15.8	13.1	12.4
45 to 54 years old	3,122	3,954	4,811	5,297	4,956	11.1	13.2	10.3
55 to 64 years old	2,124	2,370	2,880	3,654	4,858	6.7	9.1	10.1
65 to 74 years old	1,629	1,686	1,772	1,997	3,815	4.8	5.0	7.9
75 to 84 years old	835	907	981	1,025	1,547	2.6	2.5	3.2
85 years old and over	268	326	367	413	535	0.9	1.0	1.1
Male	15,697	16,802	17,886	19,027	22,713	47.4	47.3	47.3
Female	17,420	18,667	19,906	21,197	25,291	52.6	52.7	52.7
American Indian, Eskimo, Aleut, total	2,226	2,380	2,543	2,719	3,278	100.0	100.0	100.0
Under 5 years old	222	215	231	252	287	9.0	9.3	8.8
5 to 13 years old	410	428	420	435	533	18.0	16.0	16.3
14 to 17 years old	167	192	210	198	243	8.1	7.3	7.4
18 to 24 years old	256	271	312	342	364	11.4	12.6	11.1
25 to 34 years old	364	356	363	399	473	15.0	14.7	14.4
35 to 44 years old	327	352	345	340	432	14.8	12.5	13.2
45 to 54 years old	212	256	294	317	313	10.8	11.7	9.5
55 to 64 years old	129	149	180	218	268	6.3	8.0	8.2
65 to 74 years old	84	90	102	118	202	3.8	4.3	6.2
75 to 84 years old	41	50	58	63	104	2.1	2.3	3.2
85 years old and over	14	21	28	36	59	0.9	1.3	1.8

[Continued]

★ 740 ★

Resident Population: Projected Trends, 1995 to 2025
[Continued]

AGE, SEX, AND RACE	POPULATION (1,000)					PERCENT DISTRIBUTION		
	1995	2000	2005	2010	2025	2000	2010	2025
Male	1,103	1,177	1,256	1,342	1,614	49.5	49.4	49.2
Female	1,123	1,203	1,287	1,377	1,664	50.5	50.6	50.8
Asian, Pacific Islander, total	9,756	12,125	14,608	17,191	25,524	100.0	100.0	100.0
Under 5 years old	876	1,056	1,205	1,354	1,866	8.7	7.9	7.3
5 to 13 years old	1,400	1,751	2,153	2,479	3,425	14.4	14.4	13.4
14 to 17 years old	594	779	918	1,143	1,600	6.4	6.6	6.3
18 to 24 years old	1,105	1,262	1,553	1,795	2,685	10.4	10.4	10.5
25 to 34 years old	1,805	2,112	2,353	2,656	3,927	17.4	15.4	15.4
35 to 44 years old	1,655	2,023	2,344	2,657	3,591	16.7	15.5	14.1
45 to 54 years old	1,038	1,425	1,802	2,155	3,005	11.8	12.5	11.8
55 to 64 years old	633	833	1,120	1,468	2,417	6.9	8.5	9.5
65 to 74 years old	429	555	692	864	1,710	4.6	5.0	6.7
75 to 84 years old	178	261	360	458	897	2.2	2.7	3.5
85 years old and over	44	69	106	163	402	0.6	0.9	1.6
Male	4,756	5,877	7,068	8,312	12,363	48.5	48.4	48.4
Female	5,011	6,248	7,540	8,878	13,161	51.5	51.6	51.6

Source: "Projections of Resident Population, by Age, Sex, and Race: 1995 to 2025," *Statistical Abstract of the United States: 1995,* p. 25. Primary source: U.S. Bureau of the Census, *Current Population Reports,* P25-1104.

Resident Population

★ 741 ★

Characteristics: Percent Distribution and Median Age, 1850-1994 and Projections, 1995-2050

[**In percent, except as indicated.** For definition of median, see Guide to Tabular Presentation.]

DATE	SEX		RACE			Hispanic origin[1]	Median age (years)
	Male	Female	White	Black	Other		
1850 (June 1)[2]	51.0	49.0	84.3	15.7	(NA)	(NA)	18.9
1900 (June 1)[2]	51.1	48.9	87.9	11.6	0.5	(NA)	22.9
1910 (Apr. 15)[2]	51.5	48.5	88.9	10.7	0.4	(NA)	24.1
1920 (Jan. 1)[2]	51.0	49.0	89.7	9.9	0.4	(NA)	25.3
1930 (Apr. 1)[3]	50.6	49.4	89.8	9.7	0.5	(NA)	26.4
1940 (Apr. 1)[2]	50.2	49.8	89.8	9.8	0.4	(NA)	29.0
1950 (Apr. 1)[2]	49.7	50.3	89.5	10.0	0.5	(NA)	30.2
1950 (Apr. 1)	49.7	50.3	89.3	9.9	0.7	(NA)	30.2

[Continued]

★ 741 ★

Characteristics: Percent Distribution and Median Age, 1850-1994 and Projections, 1995-2050

[Continued]

DATE	SEX		RACE			Hispanic origin[1]	Median age (years)
	Male	Female	White	Black	Other		
1960 (Apr. 1)	49.3	50.7	88.6	10.5	0.9	(NA)	29.5
1970 (Apr. 1)	48.7	51.3	87.6	11.1	1.3	(NA)	28.0
1980 (Apr. 1)[3,4]	48.6	51.4	85.9	11.8	2.3	6.4	30.0
1990 (Apr. 1)[3,5]	48.7	51.3	83.9	12.3	3.8	9.0	32.8
1991 (July 1)[6]	48.8	51.2	83.7	12.3	4.0	9.3	33.1
1992 (July 1)[6]	48.8	51.2	83.5	12.4	4.1	9.5	33.4
1993 (July 1)[6]	48.8	51.2	83.3	12.5	4.2	9.8	33.7
1994 (July 1)[6]	48.8	51.2	83.1	12.5	4.3	10.0	34.0
1995 (July 1)[7]	58.8	51.2	82.9	12.6	4.5	10.2	34.0
2000 (July 1)[7]	48.9	51.1	81.9	12.8	5.3	11.3	35.5
2025 (July 1)[7]	49.1	50.9	77.3	14.2	8.5	16.8	38.1
2050 (July 1)[7]	49.0	51.0	72.8	15.7	11.4	22.5	39.0

Source: Resident Population-Percent Distribution and Median Age, 1850 to 1994, and Projections 1995 to 2050," *Statistical Abstract of the United States: 1995,* p. 13. Primary source: U.S. Bureau of the Census. *U.S. Census of Population: 1940,* vol. II, part 1, and vol. IV, part 1; *1950,* vol. II, part 1; *1970,* vol. I, part B; *Current Population Reports,* P25-1104; and unpublished data. *Notes:* NA Not available. 1. Persons of Hispanic origin may be of any race. 2. Excludes Alaska and Hawaii. 3. The race data shown have been modified: see text, section 1 for explanation. 4. See footnote 4, table 1. 5. See footnote, 6, table 12. 6. Estimated. 7. Middle series projection; see table 3.

★ 742 ★

Resident Population

Characteristics: Selected Characteristics of the Population, 1790-1994 and Projections, 1995-2050

[**In thousands.** See also *Historical Statistics, Colonial Times to 1970,* series A 73-81 and A 143-149.]

DATE	SEX		RACE					Hispanic origin[1]
			White	Black	Other			
	Male	Female			Total	American Indians and Alaska Natives	Asian and Pacific Islanders	
1790 (Aug. 2)[2]	(NA)	(NA)	3,172	757	(NA)	(NA)	(NA)	(NA)
1800 (Aug. 4)[2]	(NA)	(NA)	4,306	1,002	(NA)	(NA)	(NA)	(NA)
1850 (June 1)[2]	11,838	11,354	19,553	3,639	(NA)	(NA)	(NA)	(NA)
1900 (June 1)[2]	38,816	37,178	66,809	8,834	351	(NA)	(NA)	(NA)
1910 (Apr. 15)[2]	47,332	44,640	81,732	9,828	413	(NA)	(NA)	(NA)
1920 (Jan. 1)[2]	53,900	51,810	94,821	10,463	427	(NA)	(NA)	(NA)
1930 (Apr. 1)[2]	62,137	60,638	110,287	11,891	597	(NA)	(NA)	(NA)
1940 (Apr. 1)[2]	66,062	65,608	118,215	12,866	589	(NA)	(NA)	(NA)
1950 (Apr. 1)[2]	74,833	75,864	134,942	15,042	713	(NA)	(NA)	(NA)

[Continued]

★ 742 ★

Characteristics: Selected Characteristics of the Population, 1790-1994 and Projections, 1995-2050

[Continued]

DATE	SEX		RACE					Hispanic origin[1]
			White	Black	Other			
					Total	American Indians and Alaska Natives	Asian and Pacific Islanders	
	Male	Female						
1950 (Apr. 1)	75,187	76,139	135,150	15,045	1,131	(NA)	(NA)	(NA)
1960 (Apr. 1)	88,331	90,992	158,832	18,872	1,620	(NA)	(NA)	(NA)
1970 (Apr. 1)[3]	98,926	104,309	178,098	22,581	2,557	(NA)	(NA)	(NA)
1980 (Apr. 1)[4,5]	110,053	116,493	194,713	26,683	5,150	1,420	3,729	14,609
1990 (Apr. 1)[4,6]	121,244	127,474	208,710	30,486	9,523	2,065	7,458	22,354
1991 (July 1)[7]	122,947	129,184	211,015	31,111	10,006	2,107	7,899	23,381
1992 (July 1)[7]	124,430	130,597	212,953	21,659	10,415	2,142	8,273	24,270
1993 (July 1)[7]	125,800	131,983	214,789	32,180	10,814	2,177	8,637	25,191
1994 (July 1)[7]	127,076	133,265	216,470	32,672	11,199	2,210	8,989	26,077
1995 (July 1)[8]	128,685	134,749	218,334	33,117	11,982	2,226	9,756	26,798
2000 (July 1)[8]	135,101	141,140	226,267	35,469	14,505	2,380	12,125	31,166
2005 (July 1)[8]	141,121	147,165	233,343	37,793	17,151	2,543	14,608	35,702
2010 (July 1)[8]	147,187	153,245	240,297	40,224	19,910	2,719	17,191	40,525
2015 (July 1)[8]	153,517	159,599	247,542	42,797	22,777	2,904	19,873	45,719
2020 (July 1)[8]	159,897	166,045	254,791	45,409	25,743	3,090	22,653	51,217
2025 (July 1)[8]	166,012	172,326	261,531	48,005	28,802	3,278	25,524	56,927
2050 (July 1)[8]	192,098	199,933	285,591	61,586	44,854	4,346	40,508	88,071

Source: Resident Population-Selected Characteristics, 1790 to 1994, and Projections, 1995 to 2050," *Statistical Abstract of the United States: 1995,* p. 14. Primary source: U.S. Bureau of the Census, *U.S. Census of Population: 1940,* vol. II, part 1, and vol. IV, part 1; *1950,* vol. II, part 1; *1960,* vol. I, part 1; *1970,* vol. I, part B; *Current Population Reports,* P25-1095 and P25-1104; and unpublished data. *Notes:* NA Not available. 1. Persons of Hispanic origin may be of any race. 2. Excludes Alaska and Hawaii. 3. The revised 1970 resident population count is 203,302,031; which incorporated changes due to errors found after tabulations were completed. The race and sex data shown here reflect the official 1970 census count. 4. The race data shown have been modified; see text, section 1, for explanation. 5. See footnote 4, table 1. 6. The April 1, 1990, census count (248,718,291) includes count resolution corrections processed through March 1994 and does not include adjustments for census coverage errors. 7. Estimated. 8. Middle series projection; see table 3.

★ 743 ★

Resident Population

Resident Population: Age and Race: 1980 to 1994. Part 1

[**In thousands, except percent.** As of **April,** except **1994** as of **July.** See headnote, table 18 and, for 1980 data, footnote 4, table 1.]

YEAR, SEX, AND RACE	Total, all years	Under 5 years	5-9 years	10-14 years	15-19 years	20-24 years	25-29 years	30-34 years	35-39 years	40-44 years	45-49 years
ALL RACES											
1980	226,546	16,348	16,700	18,242	21,168	21,319	19,521	17,561	13,965	11,669	11,090
1990[1]	248,718	18,757	18,035	17,060	17,886	19,135	21,328	21,833	19,846	17,589	13,744
1994	260,341	19,727	18,859	18,753	17,616	18,326	19,177	22,177	21,961	19,699	16,679
Male	127,076	10,094	9,657	9,602	9,036	9,311	9,619	11,058	10,920	9,728	8,181
Female	133,265	9,633	9,201	9,150	8,580	9,015	9,558	11,119	11,040	9,970	8,498

[Continued]

★ 743 ★

Resident Population: Age and Race: 1980 to 1994. Part 1
[Continued]

YEAR, SEX, AND RACE	Total, all years	Under 5 years	5-9 years	10-14 years	15-19 years	20-24 years	25-29 years	30-34 years	35-39 years	40-44 years	45-49 years
WHITE											
1980	194,713	13,414	13,717	15,095	17,681	18,072	16,658	15,157	12,122	10,110	9,693
1990[1]	208,710	14,960	14,502	13,670	14,354	15,640	17,638	18,190	16,652	15,001	11,826
1994	216,470	15,592	14,997	14,921	14,035	14,722	15,593	18,292	18,237	16,516	14,249
Male	106,139	7,995	7,695	7,661	7,222	7,527	7,894	9,218	9,165	8,250	7,064
Female	110,331	7,597	7,302	7,260	6,814	7,195	7,699	9,074	9,072	8,266	7,185
BLACK											
1980	26,683	2,459	2,509	2,691	3,007	2,749	2,342	1,904	1,469	1,260	1,150
1990[1]	30,486	2,939	2,711	2,629	2,715	2,656	2,780	2,718	2,360	1,882	1,413
1994	32,675	3,119	2,939	2,864	2,733	2,668	2,619	2,837	2,733	2,308	1,740
Male	15,491	1,581	1,491	1,452	1,385	1,313	1,250	1,330	1,280	1,069	793
Female	17,181	1,538	1,448	1,412	1,349	1,355	1,369	1,507	1,453	1,239	946
AMERICAN INDIAN, ESKIMO, ALEUT											
1980	1,420	149	147	156	170	149	125	107	84	69	58
1990[1]	2,065	220	209	197	191	179	188	181	157	132	99
1994	2,210	212	223	229	193	187	178	187	174	151	120
Male	1,094	108	113	116	98	96	92	93	85	73	58
Female	1,116	105	109	113	95	91	87	94	88	78	62
ASIAN, PACIFIC ISLANDER											
1980	3,729	326	328	300	310	349	396	393	291	230	188
1990[1]	7,458	638	612	564	626	661	722	745	678	574	405
1994	8,989	804	700	739	655	750	787	861	816	723	571
Male	4,352	411	358	374	332	375	383	417	390	336	266
Female	4,637	393	342	365	323	374	404	444	426	388	306
PERCENT											
Total, 1994	100.0	7.6	7.2	7.2	6.8	7.0	7.4	8.5	8.4	7.6	6.4
White	100.0	7.2	6.9	6.9	6.5	6.8	7.2	8.5	8.4	7.6	6.6
Black	100.0	9.5	9.0	8.8	8.4	8.2	8.0	8.7	8.4	7.1	5.3
American Indian, Eskimo, Aleut	100.0	9.6	10.1	10.4	8.7	8.5	8.1	8.5	7.9	6.8	5.4
Asian, Pacific Islander	100.0	8.9	7.8	8.2	7.3	8.3	8.8	9.6	9.1	8.0	6.4

Source: "Resident Population, by Age and Race: 1980 to 1994," *Statistical Abstract of the United States: 1995,* p. 21. Primary source: U.S. Bureau of the Census, *Current Population Reports,* p25-1095; and Population Paper Listing 21. *Notes:* 1. The April 1, 1990, census count (248,718,291) includes count resolution processed through March 1994, and does not include adjustments for census coverage errors.

★ 744 ★

Resident Population

Resident Population: Age and Race: 1980 to 1994. Part 2

[**In thousands, except percent. As of April,** except **1994** as of **July.** See headnote, table 18 and, for 1980 data, footnote 4, table 1.]

YEAR, SEX, AND RACE	50-54 years	55-59 years	60-64 years	65-74 years	75-84 years	85 years and over	5-13 years	14-17 years	18-24 years
ALL RACES									
1980	11,710	11,615	10,088	15,581	7,729	2,240	31,159	16,247	30,022
1990[1]	11,313	10,487	10,625	18,046	10,012	3,022	31,826	13,340	26,950
1994	13,191	10,936	10,082	18,712	10,925	3,522	33,863	14,428	25,263
Male	6,410	5,244	4,740	8,290	4,206	980	17,339	7,412	12,856
Female	6,781	5,692	5,342	10,422	6,719	2,542	16,524	7,016	12,407
WHITE									
1980	10,360	10,394	9,078	14,045	7,057	2,060	25,692	13,491	25,361
1990[1]	9,744	9,131	9,381	16,175	9,085	2,761	25,557	10,664	21,946
1994	11,355	9,436	8,773	16,631	9,911	3,209	26,947	11,459	20,269
Male	5,572	4,573	4,172	7,419	3,827	885	13,829	5,902	10,373
Female	5,782	4,863	4,601	9,213	6,064	2,324	13,118	5,5557	9,896
BLACK									
1980	1,135	1,041	874	1,344	588	159	4,628	2,380	3,948
1990[1]	1,178	1,041	972	1,498	772	223	4,838	2,056	3,818
1994	1,340	1,110	964	1,600	815	265	5,214	2,259	3,730
Male	602	487	424	665	295	76	2,644	1,150	1,846
Female	738	623	560	935	521	188	2,571	1,109	1,884
AMERICAN INDIAN, ESKIMO, ALEUT									
1980	52	45	34	48	21	6	270	136	216
1990[1]	79	64	53	73	34	9	368	151	257
1994	91	71	57	83	40	14	407	167	259
Male	43	34	26	37	16	4	207	85	132
Female	47	37	30	46	24	9	200	82	126
ASIAN, PACIFIC ISLANDER									
1980	163	135	101	143	63	15	570	239	478
1990[1]	312	252	220	300	122	29	1,063	469	930
1994	406	318	268	398	159	34	1,294	543	1,005
Male	192	150	117	170	69	14	659	276	505
Female	214	168	151	228	90	21	636	267	501
PERCENT									
Total, 1994	5.1	4.2	3.9	7.2	4.2	1.4	13.0	5.5	9.7
White	5.2	4.4	4.1	7.7	4.6	1.5	12.4	5.3	9.4
Black	4.1	3.4	3.0	4.9	2.5	0.8	16.0	6.9	11.4
American Indian, Eskimo, Aleut	4.1	3.2	2.6	3.7	1.8	0.6	18.4	7.5	11.7

[Continued]

★ 744 ★

Resident Population: Age and Race: 1980 to 1994. Part 2

[Continued]

YEAR, SEX, AND RACE	50-54 years	55-59 years	60-64 years	65-74 years	75-84 years	85 years and over	5-13 years	14-17 years	18-24 years
Asian, Pacific Islander	4.5	3.5	3.0	4.4	1.8	0.4	14.4	6.0	11.2

Source: "Resident Population, by Age and Race: 1980 to 1994," *Statistical Abstract of the United States: 1995*, p. 21. Primary source: U.S. Bureau of the Census, *Current Population Reports*, p25-1095; and Population Paper Listing 21. *Notes:* 1. The April 1, 1990, census count (248,718,291) includes count resolution processed through March 1994, and does not include adjustments for census coverage errors.

★ 745 ★

Resident Population

Resident Population: Hispanic Origin Status, 1980-1994, and Projections, 1995-2050

[**In thousands, except as indicated.** As of **July**, except as indicated. These data are consistent with the 1980 and 1990 decennial enumerations and have been modified from the official census counts; see text, section 1, for explanation. See headnote, table 3. Minus sign (-) indicates decrease.]

YEAR	Total	Hispanic origin[1]	NOT OF HISPANIC ORIGIN			
			White	Black	American Indian, Eskimo, Aleut	Asian, Pacific Islander
1980 (April)[2]	226,546	14,609	180,906	26,142	1,326	3,563
1980	227,225	14,869	181,140	26,215	1,336	3,665
1981	229,466	15,560	181,974	26,532	1,377	4,022
1982	231,664	16,240	182,782	26,856	1,420	4,367
1983	233,792	16,935	183,561	27,159	1,466	4,671
1984	235,825	17,640	184,243	27,444	1,512	4,986
1985	237,924	18,368	184,945	27,738	1,558	5,315
1986	240,133	19,154	185,678	28,040	1,606	5,655
1987	242,289	19,946	186,353	28,351	1,654	5,985
1988	244,499	20,786	167,012	28,669	1,703	6,329
1989	246,819	21,648	187,713	29,005	1,755	6,698
1990 (April)[3]	248,718	22,354	188,306	29,275	1,796	6,988
1990	249,402	22,549	188,601	29,374	1,802	7,076
1991	252,131	23,381	189,690	29,825	1,829	7,406
1992	255,028	24,270	190,830	30,310	1,856	7,761
1993	257,783	25,191	191,841	30,764	1,882	8,105
1994	260,341	26,077	192,727	31,192	1,907	8,438
PROJECTIONS						
Lowest series:						
1995	262,051	26,402	193,295	31,514	1,924	8,915
2000	270,259	29,473	195,240	33,112	2,033	10,400
2005	276,316	32,373	195,520	34,419	2,137	11,867

[Continued]

★ 745 ★

Resident Population: Hispanic Origin Status, 1980-1994, and Projections, 1995-2050

[Continued]

YEAR	Total	Hispanic origin[1]	NOT OF HISPANIC ORIGIN			
			White	Black	American Indian, Eskimo, Aleut	Asian, Pacific Islander
2010	281,180	35,223	194,860	35,547	2,237	13,311
2020	289,553	41,235	192,130	37,503	2,424	16,261
2030	292,902	47,049	185,402	38,624	2,576	19,250
2040	290,351	52,450	174,123	39,009	2,704	22,066
2050	285,502	57,643	161,382	38,933	2,807	24,738
Middle series:						
1995	263,434	26,798	193,900	31,648	1,927	9,161
2000	276,241	31,166	197,872	33,741	2,055	11,407
2005	288,286	35,702	200,842	35,793	2,190	13,759
2010	300,431	40,525	203,441	37,930	2,336	16,199
2020	325,942	51,217	208,280	42,459	2,641	21,345
2030	349,993	62,810	210,480	46,934	2,960	26,810
2040	371,505	75,130	209,148	51,489	3,314	32,424
2050	392,031	88,071	205,849	56,346	3,701	38,064
Highest series:						
1995	264,715	27,150	194,465	31,779	1,929	9,392
2000	281,957	32,699	200,482	34,354	2,063	12,359
2005	299,941	38,767	206,306	37,089	2,210	15,569
2010	319,536	45,494	212,559	40,094	2,376	19,013
2020	363,213	61,104	226,025	46,813	2,741	26,530
2030	410,991	79,684	238,947	54,209	3,154	34,998
2040	463,579	101,872	251,077	62,453	3,647	44,529
2050	522,098	128,255	262,855	71,675	4,221	55,093
PERCENT DISTRIBUTION						
Middle series:						
1995	100.0	10.2	73.6	12.0	0.7	3.5
2000	100.0	11.3	71.6	12.2	0.7	4.1
2005	100.0	12.4	69.7	12.4	0.8	4.8
2010	100.0	13.5	67.7	12.6	0.8	5.4
2020	100.0	15.7	63.9	13.0	0.8	6.5
2030	100.0	17.9	60.1	13.4	0.8	7.7
2040	100.0	20.2	56.3	13.9	0.9	8.7
2050	100.0	22.5	52.5	14.4	0.9	9.7
PERCENT CHANGE (middle series)						
1995-2000	4.9	16.3	2.0	6.6	6.6	24.5
2000-2010	8.8	30.0	2.8	12.4	13.7	42.0

[Continued]

★ 745 ★

Resident Population: Hispanic Origin Status, 1980-1994, and Projections, 1995-2050

[Continued]

YEAR	Total	Hispanic origin[1]	NOT OF HISPANIC ORIGIN			
			White	Black	American Indian, Eskimo, Aleut	Asian, Pacific Islander
2010-2020	8.5	26.4	2.4	11.9	13.1	31.8
2020-2030	7.4	22.6	1.1	10.5	12.1	25.6
2030-2040	6.1	19.6	-0.6	9.7	12.0	20.9
2040-2050	5.5	17.2	-1.6	9.4	11.7	17.4

Source: Resident Population, by Hispanic Origin Status, 1980 to 1994, and Projections, 1995-2050," *Statistical Abstract of the United States: 1995,* p. 19. Primary source: U.S. Bureau of the Census, *Current Population Reports,* P25-1095 and P25-1104; and Population Paper Listing 21. *Notes:* 1. Persons of Hispanic origin may be of any race. 2. See footnote 4 table 1. 3. The April 1, 1990, census count (248,718,291) includes count (248,718,291) includes count resolution corrections through March 1994 and does not include adjustments for census coverage errors.

★ 746 ★

Resident Population

Resident Population: Race, 1980-1994, and Projections, 1995-2050

[**In thousands, except as indicated.** As of **July,** except as indicated. These data are consistent with the 1980 and 1990 decennial enumerations and have been modified from the official census counts; see text, section 1, for explanation. See headnote, table 3.]

YEAR	Total	White	Black	American Indian, Eskimo, Aleut	Asian, Pacific Islander
1980 (April)[1]	226,546	194,713	26,683	1,420	3,729
1980	227,225	195,185	26,771	1,433	3,837
1981	229,466	196,635	27,133	1,483	4,214
1982	231,664	198,037	27,508	1,537	4,581
1983	233,792	199,420	27,867	1,596	4,909
1984	235,825	200,708	28,212	1,656	5,249
1985	237,924	202,031	28,569	1,718	5,608
1986	240,133	203,430	28,942	1,783	5,978
1987	242,289	204,770	29,325	1,851	6,343
1988	244,499	206,129	29,723	1,923	6,724
1989	246,819	207,540	30,143	2,001	7,134
1990 (April)[2]	248,718	208,710	30,486	2,065	7,458
1990	249,402	209,180	30,599	2,073	7,550
1991	252,131	211,015	31,111	2,107	7,899
1992	255,028	212,953	31,658	2,142	8,273
1993	257,783	214,789	32,180	2,177	8,637
1994	260,341	216,470	32,672	2,210	8,989

[Continued]

★ 746 ★

Resident Population: Race, 1980-1994, and Projections, 1995-2050

[Continued]

YEAR	Total	White	Black	American Indian, Eskimo, Aleut	Asian, Pacific Islander
PROJECTIONS					
Lowest series:					
1995	262,051	217,381	32,954	2,222	9,493
2000	270,259	222,143	34,715	2,354	11,047
2005	276,316	225,080	36,175	2,480	12,581
2010	281,180	227,026	37,456	2,604	14,094
2020	289,553	229,790	39,735	2,837	17,191
2030	292,902	228,386	41,161	3,029	20,326
2040	290,351	222,048	41,828	3,191	23,284
2050	285,502	214,054	42,026	3,323	26,099
Middle series:					
1995	263,434	218,334	33,117	2,226	9,756
2000	276,241	226,267	35,469	2,380	12,125
2005	288,286	233,343	37,793	2,543	14,608
2010	300,431	240,297	40,224	2,719	17,191
2020	325,942	254,791	45,409	3,090	22,653
2030	349,993	267,457	50,596	3,473	28,467
2040	371,505	277,232	55,917	3,894	34,461
2050	392,031	285,591	61,586	4,346	40,508
Highest series:					
1995	264,715	219,210	33,274	2,228	10,002
2000	281,957	230,232	36,195	2,390	13,140
2005	299,941	241,516	39,314	2,569	16,541
2010	319,536	253,813	42,751	2,773	20,200
2020	363,213	281,304	50,475	3,223	28,212
2030	410,991	310,917	59,073	3,729	37,271
2040	463,579	342,960	68,767	4,336	47,516
2050	522,098	378,408	79,722	5,039	58,930
PERCENT DISTRIBUTION					
Middle series:					
1995	100.0	82.9	12.6	0.8	3.7
2000	100.0	81.9	12.8	0.9	4.4
2005	100.0	80.9	13.1	0.9	5.1
2010	100.0	80.0	13.4	0.9	5.7
2020	100.0	78.2	13.9	0.9	7.0
2030	100.0	76.4	14.5	1.0	8.1
2040	100.0	74.6	15.1	1.0	9.3
2050	100.0	72.8	15.7	1.1	10.3

[Continued]

★ 746 ★

Resident Population: Race, 1980-1994, and Projections, 1995-2050

[Continued]

YEAR	Total	White	Black	American Indian, Eskimo, Aleut	Asian, Pacific Islander
PERCENT CHANGE (middle series)					
1995-2000	4.9	3.6	7.1	6.9	24.3
2000-2010	8.8	6.2	13.4	14.2	41.8
2010-2020	8.5	6.0	12.9	13.6	31.8
2020-2030	7.4	5.0	11.4	12.4	25.7
2030-2040	6.1	3.7	10.5	12.1	21.1
2040-2050	5.5	3.0	10.1	11.6	17.5

Source: Resident Population, by Race, 1980 to 1994, and Projections, 1995- 2050," *Statistical Abstract of the United States: 1995*, p. 18. Primary source: U.S. Bureau of the Census, *Current Population Reports*, P25-1095 and P25-1104; and Population Paper Listing 21. *Notes:* 1. See footnote 4 table 1. 2. The April 1, 1990, census count (248,718,291) includes count (248,718,291) includes count resolution corrections processed through March 1994 and does not include adjustments for census coverage errors.

★ 747 ★

Resident Population

Resident Population: Race, Hispanic Origin, and Single Years of Age: 1994. Part 1

[In thousands, except as indicated. As of July 1. Resident population. For derivation of estimates, see text, section 1.]

AGE	Total	RACE			
		White	Black	American Indian, Eskimo, Aleut	Asian, Pacific Islander
Total	260,341	216,470	32,672	2,210	8,989
Under 5 yrs. old	19,727	15,592	3,119	212	804
Under 1 yr. old	3,870	3,041	619	42	168
1 yr. old	3,878	3,060	616	41	161
2 yrs. old	3,956	3,132	619	41	163
3 yrs. old	3,990	3,163	623	42	163
4 yrs. old	4,032	3,195	642	47	148
5-9 yrs. old	18,859	14,997	2,939	223	700
5 yrs. old	3,884	3,063	630	47	144
6 yrs. old	3,792	3,011	595	45	141
7 yrs. old	3,747	2,985	582	43	136
8 yrs. old	3,595	2,874	544	43	135
9 yrs. old	3,841	3,063	588	45	144
10-14 yrs. old	18,753	14,921	2,864	229	739

[Continued]

★747★

Resident Population: Race, Hispanic Origin, and Single Years of Age: 1994. Part 1
[Continued]

AGE	Total	RACE			
		White	Black	American Indian, Eskimo, Aleut	Asian, Pacific Islander
10 yrs. old	3,744	2,984	567	46	147
11 yrs. old	3,770	3,010	566	46	148
12 yrs. old	3,768	2,994	580	46	149
13 yrs. old	3,722	2,962	562	47	151
14 yrs. old	3,748	2,971	588	45	145
15-19 yrs. old	17,616	14,035	2,733	193	655
15 yrs. old	3,602	2,849	572	43	138
16 yrs. old	3,515	2,802	544	40	129
17 yrs. old	3,562	2,837	555	39	131
18 yrs. old	3,349	2,677	515	35	122
19 yrs. old	3,588	2,870	547	37	133
20-24 yrs. old	18,236	14,722	2,668	187	750
20 yrs. old	3,480	2,781	529	36	135
21 yrs. old	3,492	2,778	533	37	144
22 yrs. old	3,605	2,891	528	37	149
23 yrs. old	3,839	3,094	547	39	159
24 yrs. old	3,910	3,178	531	39	163
25-29 yrs. old	19,177	15,593	2,619	178	787
25 yrs. old	3,756	3,060	501	36	158
26 yrs. old	3,680	2,984	508	35	153
27 yrs. old	3,778	3,076	513	35	154
28 yrs. old	3,674	2,990	503	33	148
29 yrs. old	4,829	3,483	594	38	174
30-34 yrs. old	22,177	18,292	2,837	187	861
30 yrs. old	4,354	3,573	573	37	171
31 yrs. old	4,332	3,563	558	37	174
32 yrs. old	4,431	3,663	563	37	169
33 yrs. old	4,433	3,677	550	36	170
34 yrs. old	4,626	3,817	594	38	178
35-39 yrs. old	21,961	18,237	2,733	174	816
35 yrs. old	4,523	3,743	571	37	171
36 yrs. old	4,439	3,696	545	35	163
37 yrs. old	4,472	3,713	560	35	164
38 yrs. old	4,055	3,375	497	32	152
39 yrs. old	4,472	3,710	560	35	167
40-44 yrs. old	19,699	16,516	2,308	151	723
40 yrs. old	4,223	3,528	507	33	155
41 yrs. old	4,013	3,366	464	32	151
42 yrs. old	3,922	3,303	452	30	138

[Continued]

★ 747 ★

Resident Population: Race, Hispanic Origin, and Single Years of Age: 1994. Part 1
[Continued]

AGE	Total	RACE			
		White	Black	American Indian, Eskimo, Aleut	Asian, Pacific Islander
43 yrs. old	3,716	3,103	438	30	146
44 yrs. old	3,825	3,217	448	27	133

Source: "Resident Population, by Race, Hispanic Origin and Single Years of Age: 1994," *Statistical Abstract of the United States: 1995,* p. 22.

★ 748 ★

Resident Population

Resident Population: Race, Hispanic Origin, and Single Years of Age: 1994. Part 2

AGE	NOT OF HISPANIC ORIGIN			
	White	Black	American Indian Eskimo, Aleut	Asian Pacific Islander
45-59 yrs. old	13,130	1,669	107	544
45 yrs. old	2,844	391	23	124
46 yrs. old	2,800	354	22	114
47 yrs. old	3,088	360	23	115
48 yrs. old	2,074	255	18	92
49 yrs. old	2,323	309	20	100
50-54 yrs. old	10,522	1,287	82	387
50 yrs. old	2,298	282	19	88
51 yrs. old	2,371	267	17	81
52 yrs. old	2,032	253	16	74
53 yrs. old	1,941	240	15	72
54 yrs. old	1,880	246	15	72
55-59 yrs. old	8,760	1,069	64	304
55 yrs. old	1,808	237	14	67
56 yrs. old	1,825	226	13	63
57 yrs. old	1,742	215	13	62
58 yrs. old	1,632	187	11	54
59 yrs. old	1,754	204	13	59
60-64 yrs. old	8,208	950	51	257
60 yrs. old	1,597	191	11	54
61 yrs. old	1,581	187	11	52
62 yrs. old	1,597	189	10	50

[Continued]

★ 748 ★

Resident Population: Race, Hispanic Origin, and Single Years of Age: 1994. Part 2

[Continued]

AGE	NOT OF HISPANIC ORIGIN			
	White	Black	American Indian Eskimo, Aleut	Asian Pacific Islander
63 yrs. old	1,695	185	10	50
64 yrs. old	1,737	197	10	51
65-69 yrs. old	8,312	878	42	217
65 yrs. old	1,689	197	9	48
66 yrs. old	1,720	187	9	45
67 yrs. old	1,670	179	8	43
68 yrs. old	1,589	163	8	41
69 yrs. old	1,643	155	8	40
70-74 yrs. old	7,485	676	33	164
70 yrs. old	1,592	149	8	38
71 yrs. old	1,534	142	7	36
72 yrs. old	1,558	135	7	34
73 yrs. old	1,461	127	6	30
74 yrs. old	1,340	123	5	27
75-79 yrs. old	5,724	487	23	98
75 yrs. old	1,274	114	5	23
76 yrs. old	1,196	98	5	20
77 yrs. old	1,130	94	4	19
78 yrs. old	1,097	90	4	18
79 yrs. old	1,028	91	4	17
80-84 yrs. old	3,810	309	15	54
80 yrs. old	917	75	4	14
81 yrs. old	844	70	3	12
82 yrs. old	753	57	3	10
83 yrs. old	688	54	3	10
84 yrs. old	609	53	2	9
85-89 yrs. old	2,008	158	8	21
90-94 yrs. old	828	76	4	8
95-99 yrs. old	218	20	1	3
100 yrs. old and over	40	7	-	1
Median age (yr.)	33.2	29.1	27.2	30.7

Source: "Resident Population, by Race, Hispanic Origin and Single Years of Age: 1994," *Statistical Abstract of the United States: 1995,* p. 23. Primary source: U.S. Bureau of the Census, unpublished data. *Notes:* - Represents or rounds to zero.

Social and Economic Characteristics

★ 749 ★

Social and Economic Characteristics: Black and White Population: 1980 to 1994

[As of **March, except labor force status, annual average.** Excludes members of Armed Forces except those living off post or with their families on post. Data for 1980 and 1990 are based on 1980 census population controls; 1994 data based on 1990 census population controls. Based on Current Population Survey; see text, section 1, and Appendix III.]

| CHARACTERISTIC | NUMBER (1,000) | | | | | | PERCENT DISTRIBUTION | | | |
| | White | | | Black | | | White | | Black | |
	1980	1990	1994	1980	1990	1994	1980	1994	1980	1994
Total persons	191,905	206,963	215,221	26,033	30,392	33,040	100.0	100.0	100.0	100.0
Under 5 years old	13,307	15,161	16,055	2,444	2,932	3,357	6.9	7.5	9.4	10.2
5 to 14 years old	28,828	28,405	30,391	5,190	5,546	6,183	15.0	14.1	19.9	18.7
15 to 44 years old	88,570	96,656	97,917	12,247	14,660	15,907	46.2	45.5	47.0	48.1
45 to 64 years old	39,302	40,282	43,278	4,112	4,766	5,082	20.5	20.1	15.8	15.4
65 years old and over	21,898	26,479	27,580	2,040	2,487	2,510	11.4	128	7.8	7.6
YEARS OF SCHOOL COMPLETED										
Persons 25 years old and over	114,763	134,687	139,740	12,927	16,751	18,103	100.0	100.0	100.0	100.0
Elementary: 0 to 8 years	18,739	14,131	11,796	3,559	2,701	1,860	16.3	8.4	27.5	10.3
High school: 1 to 3 years	15,064	14,080	13,340[1]	2,748	2,969	3,048[1]	13.1	9.5[1]	21.3	16.8[1]
4 years	43,149	52,449	48,236[2]	3,980	6,239	6,549[2]	37.6	34.5[2]	30.8	36.2[2]
College: 1 to 3 years	17,350	24,350	34,331[3]	1,618	2,952	4,310[3]	15.1	24.6[3]	12.5	23.8[3]
4 years or more	20,460	29,677	32,057[4]	1,024	1,890	2,337[4]	17.8	22.9[4]	7.9	12.9[4]
LABOR FORCE STATUS[5]										
Civilians 16 years old and over	146,122	160,415	165,555	17,824	21,300	22,879	100.0	100.0	100.0	100.0
Civilian labor force	93,600	107,177	111,082	10,865	13,493	14,502	64.1	67.1	61.0	63.4
Employed	87,715	102,087	105,190	9,313	11,966	12,835	60.0	63.5	52.2	56.1
Unemployed	5,884	5,091	5,892	1,553	1,527	1,666	4.0	3.6	8.7	7.3
Unemployment rate[8]	6.3	4.7	5.3	14.3	11.3	11.5	(X)	(X)	(X)	(X)
Not in labor force	52,523	53,237	54,473	6,959	7,808	8,377	35.9	32.9	39.0	36.6
FAMILY TYPE										
Total families	52,243	56,590	57,870	6,184	7,470	7,989	100.0	100.0	100.0	100.0
With own children[7]	26,474	26,718	27,624	3,820	4,378	4,794	50.7	47.7	61.8	60.0
Married couple	44,751	46,981	47,443	3,433	3,750	3,714	85.7	82.0	55.5	46.5
With own children[7]	22,415	21,579	21,874	1,927	1,972	1,925	42.9	37.8	31.2	24.1
Female householder,										
no spouse present	6,052	7,306	8,130	2,495	3,275	3,825	11.6	14.0	40.3	47.9
With own children[7]	3,558	4,199	4,742	1,793	2,232	2,630	6.8	8.2	29.0	32.9
Male householder, no										
spouse present	1,441	2,303	2,297	256	446	450	2.8	4.0	4.1	5.6
With own children[7]	500	939	1,008	99	173	238	1.0	1.7	1.6	3.0
FAMILY INCOME IN PREVIOUS YEARS										
IN CONSTANT (1993) DOLLARS										
Total families	52,243	56,590	57,870	6,184	7,470	7,989	100.0	100.0	100.0	100.0
Less than $5,000	908	1,188	1,432	405	665	856	1.7	2.5	6.5	10.7
$5,000 to $9,999	2,110	2,264	2,765	872	964	1,205	4.0	4.8	14.1	15.1
$10,000 to $14,999	3,097	3,339	3,818	787	896	911	5.9	6.6	12.7	11.4
$15,000 to $24,999	7,906	7,923	8,756	1,326	1,389	1,485	15.1	15.1	21.4	18.6
$25,000 to $34,999	7,963	8,262	8,719	871	1,031	1,093	15.2	15.1	14.1	13.7
$35,000 to $49,999	12,244	11,318	10,865	972	1,091	1,035	23.4	18.8	15.7	13.0

[Continued]

★ 749 ★

Social and Economic Characteristics: Black and White Population: 1980 to 1994
[Continued]

CHARACTERISTIC	NUMBER (1,000)						PERCENT DISTRIBUTION			
	White			Black			White		Black	
	1980	1990	1994	1980	1990	1994	1980	1994	1980	1994
$50,000 or more	18,015	22,296	21,515	952	1,434	1,404	34.5	37.2	15.3	17.8
Median income (dol.)[8]	39,911	41,922	39,308	22,601	23,550	21,548	(X)	(X)	(X)	(X)
Families below poverty level[9]	3,581	4,409	5,452	1,722	2,077	2,499	6.9	9.4	27.8	31.3
Persons below poverty level[9]	17,214	20,785	26,226	8,050	9,302	10,877	9.0	12.2	31.0	33.1
HOUSING TENURE										
Total occupied units	70,766	80,163	82,387	8,586	10,486	11,281	100.0	100.0	100.0	100.0
Owner-occupied	49,913	54,094	55,879	4,173	4,445	4,791	70.5	67.8	48.6	42.5
Renter-occupied	19,581	24,685	24,955	4,257	5,862	6,268	27.7	30.3	49.6	55.6
No cash rent	1,272	1,384	1,553	156	178	222	1.8	1.9	1.8	2.0

Source: "Social and Economic Characteristics of the White and Black Population: 1980 to 1994," *Statistical Abstract of the United States: 1995,* p. 48. Primary source: Except as noted, U.S. Bureau of the Census, *Current Population Reports,* P20-480, and earlier reports; P60-188; and unpublished data. *Notes:* X Not applicable. 1. Represents those who completed ninth to twelfth grade, but have no high school diploma. 2. High school graduate. 3. Some college or associate degree. 4. Bachelor's or advanced degree. 5. Source: U.S. Bureau of Labor Statistics, *Employment and Earnings,* January issues. Data beginning 1994 not directly comparable with earlier years. See text, section 13, and February 1994 issue of *Employment and Earnings.* 6. Total unemployment as percent of civilian labor force. 7. Children under 18 years old. 8. For definition of median, see Guide to Tabular Presentation. 9. For explanation of poverty level, see text, section 14.

Chapter 12
SOCIAL AND HUMAN SERVICES

Child Support and Alimony

★ 750 ★

Child Support: Selected Characteristics of Custodial Parents: 1991

[For definition of mean, see Guide to Tabular Presentation].

RECIPIENCY STATUS OF PARENT	Unit	Total[1]	AGE			RACE		Hispanic[2]	CURRENT MARITAL STATUS			
			18 to 29 years	30 to 39 years	40 years and over	White	Black		Divorced	Married[3]	Never married	Separated
ALL CUSTODIAL PARENTS												
All parents, total	1,000	11,502	3,197	5,058	3,154	8,319	2,886	1,160	3,599	3,428	2,685	1,705
Payments agreed to or awarded	1,000	6,190	1,321	2,997	1,862	5,035	1,009	410	2,477	2,208	712	755
Percent of total	Percent	54	41	59	59	61	35	35	69	64	27	44
Supposed to receive child support in 1991	1,000	5,326	1,175	2,647	1,499	4,357	834	356	2,190	1,909	600	597
Percent received payment	Percent	75	70	75	79	77	69	65	76	75	74	74
Mean child support	Dollars	2,961	1,790	3,052	3,625	3,131	2,079	2,165	3,544	2,799	1,537	2,707
Percent of total income	Percent	15	16	16	14	16	15	15	15	15	14	19
Parents with incomes below the poverty level in 1991	1,000	3,720	1,529	1,555	575	2,134	1,478	591	935	410	1,487	874
Payments agreed to or awarded	1,000	1,438	545	664	224	962	438	152	514	221	362	333
Percent of total	Percent	39	36	43	39	45	30	26	55	54	24	38
Supposed to receive child support in 1991	1,000	1,257	486	577	191	858	364	138	472	194	313	274
Percent received payment	Percent	68	69	69	65	66	74	61	67	68	73	67
Mean child support	Dollars	1,910	1,390	2,042	2,919	1,839	2,106	2,580	2,453	1,492	1,500	1,786
Percent of total income	Percent	33	26	32	62	33	34	51	36	37	26	36
ALL CUSTODIAL MOTHERS												
All mothers, total	1,000	9,918	3,022	4,379	2,429	6,966	2,698	1,043	3,052	2,707	2,565	1,514
Payments agreed to or awarded	1,000	5,542	1,269	2,691	1,571	4,459	958	368	2,221	1,888	693	702
Percent of total	Percent	56	42	61	65	64	36	35	73	70	27	46
Supposed to receive child support in 1991	1,000	4,883	1,132	2,446	1,299	3,976	791	324	2,027	1,679	583	563
Percent received payment	Percent	76	71	76	82	78	70	68	77	76	74	74
Mean child support	Dollars	3,011	1,816	3,127	3,719	3,193	2,102	2,200	3,623	2,831	1,534	2,753
Percent of total income	Percent	17	17	17	16	17	15	16	16	18	14	20
Mothers with incomes below the poverty level in 1991	1,000	3,513	1,472	1,455	528	1,979	1,433	563	877	338	1,449	836
Payments agreed to or awarded	1,000	1,368	534	621	207	896	433	140	486	187	359	328

[Continued]

★ 750 ★

Child Support: Selected Characteristics of Custodial Parents: 1991
[Continued]

RECIPIENCY STATUS OF PARENT	Unit	Total[1]	AGE			RACE		Hispanic[2]	CURRENT MARITAL STATUS			
			18 to 29 years	30 to 39 years	40 years and over	White	Black		Divorced	Married[3]	Never married	Separated
Percent of total	Percent	39	36	43	39	45	30	25	55	55	25	39
Supposed to receive child support in 1991	1,000	1,200	474	539	184	804	361	126	448	169	311	268
Percent received payment	Percent	70	70	72	67	68	74	67	69	73	72	68
Mean child support	Dollars	1,922	1,399	2,058	2,939	1,869	2,083	2,580	2,474	1,477	1,515	1,786
Percent of total income	Percent	34	26	33	62	34	33	51	36	40	26	36

Source: "Child Support-Selected Characteristics of Custodial Parents: 1991." U.S. Bureau of the Census, *Statistical Abstract of the United States*, 115th ed., 1995, p. 391. Primary source: U.S. Bureau of the Census, *Current Population Reports*, P60-187. *Notes:* 1. Includes other items not shown separately. 2. Hispanic persons may be of any race. 3. Remarried parents whose previous marriage ended in divorce and persons in first marriage.

Government Assistance Programs

★ 751 ★

Participants in Selected Means-Tested Government Assistance Programs: 1987 to 1991

[**Average monthly participation.** Covers noninstitutionalized population. Persons are considered participants in Aid to Families with Dependent Children (AFDC), General Assistance, and the Food Stamp Program if they are the primary recipient or if they are covered under another person's allotment. Persons receiving Supplemental Security Income (SSI) payments are considered to be participants in an assistance program as are persons covered by Medicaid or living in public or subsidized rental housing. Based on the Survey of Income and Program Participation; for details on sample survey, see source].

YEAR AND SELECTED CHARACTERISTIC	NUMBER OF PARTICIPANTS (1,000)					PERCENT OF POPULATION PARTICIPATING				
	Major meanstested assistance programs[1]	AFDC or General Assistance	Food stamps	Medicaid	Housing assistance	Major meanstested assistance programs[1]	AFDC or General Assistance	Food stamps	Medicaid	Housing assistance
1987	27,412	10,385	17,365	17,474	9,222	11.4	4.3	7.2	7.3	3.8
1990	28,461	10,573	17,136	19,110	10,694	11.5	4.3	6.9	7.7	4.3
1991, total	30,859	11,556	18,870	21,379	10,951	12.4	4.6	7.6	8.6	4.4
White	19,104	5,950	10,902	12,930	6,145	9.1	2.8	5.2	6.1	2.9
Black	10,302	4,836	7,029	7,282	4,332	33.4	15.7	22.8	23.6	14.1
Hispanic origin[2]	5,740	2,166	3,672	3,966	1,995	26.3	9.9	16.9	18.2	9.2

Source: "Persons Participating in Selected Means-Tested Government Assistance Programs, by Selected Characteristics: 1987 to 1991." U.S. Bureau of the Census, *Statistical Abstract of the United States*, 115th ed., 1995, p. 378. Primary source: U.S. Bureau of the Census, *Current Population Reports*, P70-41. *Notes:* 1. Covers AFDC, General Assistance, SSI, food stamps, Medicaid, and housing assistance. 2. Persons of Hispanic origin may be of any race.

★ 752 ★

Government Assistance Programs

Public Assistance: Food Stamp Mothers and Nonfood Stamp Mothers: Characteristics: Summer 1993

Mothers 15 to 44 years old by food stamp recipiency status and selected socioeconomic characteristics: summer 1993.

Characteristic	Receiving food stamps					Not receiving food stamps				
	Mothers		Births per 1,000 mothers	Mean age of mothers in years--		Mothers		Births per 1,000 mothers	Mean age of mothers in years--	
	Number (thousands)	Confidence interval[1]		at time of survey	at first birth	Number (thousands)	Confidence interval[1]		at time of survey	at first birth
Total	5,303	245	2,577	30.1	19.9	30,473	505	2,101	34.2	22.5
Race										
White	3,176	192	2,536	30.2	20.4	25,250	476	2,089	34.3	22.8
Black	1,903	150	2,653	29.9	19.1	3,826	210	2,125	33.4	20.5
Hispanic Origin										
Hispanic[2]	1,060	112	3,020	30.6	20.0	3,129	191	2,378	33.0	21.2
Not Hispanic	2,424	221	2,466	30.0	19.9	27,344	489	2,069	34.3	22.7

Source: "Food Stamp Mothers Versus Nonfood Stamp Mothers," "Mothers Who receive Foodstamps—Fertility and Socioeconomic Characteristics," *Statistical Brief*, U.S. Department of Commerce, Bureau of the Census, August 1995, p. 4. *Notes:* 1. represents the 90-percent confidence interval (1.6 standard error) or the estimated population. 2. Persons of Hispanic origin may be of any race.

★ 753 ★

Government Assistance Programs

Public Assistance: Percentage of Persons Aged 25-35 Receiving AFDC or Public Assistance by Years of Schooling: 1972-92

Year	Years of schooling completed					
	White		Black		Hispanic	
	9-11 years	12 years	9-11 years	12 years	9-11 years	12 years
1972	6.0	2.2	23.2	12.2	9.6	3.4
1973	5.6	2.1	25.9	12.1	16.2	5.5
1974	8.0	2.4	25.0	10.7	14.2	3.8
1975	7.0	2.4	27.8	10.0	10.6	3.4
1976	7.5	2.3	27.0	11.4	15.0	4.7
1977	8.0	2.6	26.4	12.4	13.1	6.6
1978	7.7	2.3	28.1	12.4	13.7	6.9
1979	7.9	2.5	26.8	12.0	15.1	5.4
1980	8.5	3.2	25.3	12.9	14.2	4.5
1981	9.5	2.9	29.1	14.9	13.3	5.0
1982	10.3	2.6	25.8	13.6	14.2	5.4
1983	10.7	2.6	26.8	13.4	15.5	5.2
1984	10.6	25.7	30.3	12.6	10.6	5.7

[Continued]

★ 753 ★

Public Assistance: Percentage of Persons Aged 25-35
Receiving AFDC or Public Assistance by Years of
Schooling: 1972-92
[Continued]

| Year | Years of schooling completed | | | | | |
| | White | | Black | | Hispanic | |
	9-11 years	12 years	9-11 years	12 years	9-11 years	12 years
1985	9.5	3.1	30.7	11.9	13.2	5.2
1986	11.2	2.9	25.7	11.8	10.6	6.8
1987	7.8	2.9	28.5	12.4	10.7	5.9
1988	9.2	2.8	28.9	11.6	14.0	4.8
1989	8.5	2.9	30.3	10.9	12.0	4.4
1990	10.6	3.2	30.9	13.0	13.2	5.3
1991	11.9	4.0	28.6	13.1	15.1	6.0
1992	11.3	4.0	35.6	13.2	15.0	7.2

Source: "Percentage of Persons Aged 25-34 Who Received Income from AFDC or Public Assistance by Years of Schooling Completed: 1972-92," "Welfare Recipiency, by Educational Attainment," *Indicator of the Month,* U.S. Department of Education, National Center for Education Statistics, July 1995. Primary source: U.S. Department of Commerce, Bureau of the Census, March Current Population Surveys. *Notes:* Beginning in 1992, the Current Population Survey changed the questions used to obtain the educational attainment of respondents. Table reads: In 1992, among persons aged 25-34 with 9-11 years of schooling, 17.1 percent received income from AFDC or public assistance. Among persons with 12 years of schooling, 5.6 received such income.

Pension Coverage of Workers

★ 754 ★

Pensions Plan Coverage: Workers by Selected Characteristics: 1993

[Covers workers as of **March 1994** who had earnings in year 1993. Based on Current Population Survey; see text, section 1, and Appendix III].

| SEX AND AGE | NUMBER WITH COVERAGE (1,000) | | | | PERCENT OF TOTAL WORKERS | | | |
	Total[1]	White	Black	Hispanic[2]	Total[1]	White	Black	Hispanic[2]
Total	53,742	46,571	5,364	2,964	39.2	39.9	36.6	24.8
Male	29,923	26,440	2,506	1,739	40.8	41.8	35.6	24.4
Under 65 years old	29,331	25,913	2,451	1,713	41.6	42.7	35.6	24.5
15 to 24 years old	1,437	1,242	156	128	11.5	11.6	11.6	8.2
25 to 44 years old	17,190	15,100	1,466	1,133	45.0	46.5	36.9	27.5
45 to 64 years old	10,704	9,571	829	452	54.0	54.6	53.0	34.2
65 years old and over	592	528	55	25	21.5	21.0	34.5	20.4
Female	23,819	20,131	2,858	1,225	37.3	37.5	37.5	25.4
Under 65 years old	23,331	19,707	2,799	1,215	37.8	38.1	37.6	25.6
15 to 24 years old	1,193	1,030	137	104	10.5	10.8	10.4	9.6

[Continued]

★ 754 ★

Pensions Plan Coverage: Workers by Selected Characteristics: 1993
[Continued]

SEX AND AGE	NUMBER WITH COVERAGE (1,000)				PERCENT OF TOTAL WORKERS			
	Total[1]	White	Black	Hispanic[2]	Total[1]	White	Black	Hispanic[2]
25 to 44 years old	13,833	11,573	1,717	783	42.1	42.7	40.0	29.5
45 to 64 years old	8,305	7,103	945	328	47.6	47.4	51.4	32.7
65 years old and over	488	424	59	11	22.6	21.8	32.4	14.4

Source: "Pension Plan Coverage for Workers, by Selected Characteristics: 1993." U.S. Bureau of the Census, *Statistical Abstract of the United States,* 115th ed., 1995, p. 383. Primary source: U.S. Bureau of the Census, unpublished data. *Notes:* 1. Includes other races, not shown separately. 2. Hispanic persons may be of any race.

Uninsured

★ 755 ★

Percent of Persons Under 65 Years of Age Who are Uninsured, by Family Income: 1993

	Percentage
Less than $14,000	35.3
$14,000-$24,999	27.5
$25,000-$34,999	13.8
$35,000-$49,999	7.8
$50,000 or more	4.6
Black	23.2
White	16.2
Mexican American	39.5
Puerto Rican	21.0
Cuban	16.9
Other Hispanic	31.1

Source: "Percent of Persons Under 65 Years of Age Who are Uninsured by Family Income, Race, and Hispanic Origin: United States, 1993." U.S. Bureau of the Census, *Statistical Abstract of the United States,* 115th ed., 1995, p. 36. Primary source: Centers of Disease Control and Prevention, National Center for Health Statistics, National Health Interview Survey. See related *Health, United States, 1994,* table 135.

★ 756 ★

Uninsured

Percent of Persons Under 65 Years of Age Who are Uninsured: Characteristics: 1993

	Percentage
0-14 years	21.6
15-44 years	62.9
45-64 years	15.6
Black	16.9
White	77.0
Mexican American	13.4
Other Hispanic	6.0
Less than $14,000	35.9
$14,000-$24,999	32.1
$25,000-$49,999	24.1
$50,000 or more	8.1

Source: "Percent of Persons Under 65 Years of Age Who are Uninsured by Family Income, Race, and Hispanic Origin: United States, 1993." U.S. Bureau of the Census, *Statistical Abstract of of the United States*, 115th ed., 1995, p. 37. Primary source: Centers for Disease Control and Prevention, National Center for Health Statistics, National Health Interview. *Notes:* Percents include persons not covered by private insurance, Medicaid, Medicare, and military plans.

Volunteer Workers

★ 757 ★

Adult Volunteer Workers: 1993

[Covers persons 18 years and over. Volunteers are persons who worked in some way to help others for no monetary pay during the previous year. See headnote, table 620].

AGE, SEX, RACE, AND HISPANIC ORIGIN	Percent of population volunteering	Average hours volunteered per week	EDUCATIONAL ATTAINMENT AND HOUSEHOLD INCOME	Percent of population volunteering	Average hours volunteered per week	TYPE OF ACTIVITY	Percent of volunteers involved in activity
White	51.1	4.2	$50,000-$59,999	56.9	4.1	Recreation - adults	5.4
Black	29.1	3.7	$60,000-$74,999	66.6	6.1	Religion	24.1
			$75,000-$99,999	58.1	(B)	Work-related organizations	6.9
Hispanic[1]	32.4	(B)	$100,000 or more	67.5	(B)	Youth development	11.7

Source: "Percent of Adult Population Doing Volunteer Work: 1993." U.S. Bureau of the Census, *Statistical Abstract of the United States*, 115th ed., 1995, p. 386. Primary source: Hodgkinson, Virginia, Murray Weitzman, and the Gallup Organization, Inc. *Giving and Volunteering in the United States: 1994 Edition*. (Copyright and published by INDEPENDENT SECTOR, Washington, DC, fall 1994). *Notes:* B Base figure too small to meet statistical standards for reliability. 1. Hispanic persons may be of any race.

Work Disability

★ 758 ★

Persons With Work Disability: Selected Characteristics, 1992

[In thousands, except percent. As of March. Covers civilian noninstitutional population and members of Armed Forces living off post or with their families on post. Persons are classified as having a work disability if they (1) have a health problem or disability which prevents them from working or which limits the kind or amount of work they can do; (2) have a service-connected disability or ever retired or left a job for health reasons; (3) did not work in survey reference week or previous year because of long term illness or disability; or (4) are under age 65, and are covered by Medicare or receive Supplemental Security Income. Based on Current Population Survey].

Age and participation status in assistance programs	Total[1]	White	Black	Hispanic[2]
Persons with work disability	14,959	11,819	2,670	1,192
16 to 24 years old	1,196	916	237	123
25 to 34 years old	2,727	2,057	562	208
35 to 44 years old	3,226	2,568	560	288
45 to 54 years old	3,154	2,508	560	254
55 to 64 years old	4,656	3,769	750	318
Percent work disabled of total population	9.3	8.7	13.8	8.5
16 to 24 years old	3.9	3.6	5.2	3.5
25 to 34 years old	6.4	5.8	10.4	4.9
35 to 44 years old	8.2	7.7	12.6	9.1
45 to 54 years old	11.7	10.8	20.1	14.0
55 to 64 years old	22.0	20.6	34.7	25.4
Percent of work disabled--				
Receiving Social Security income	28.2	28.3	28.2	24.2
Receiving food stamps	22.8	19.1	39.1	31.7
Covered by Medicaid	29.7	25.6	47.2	44.1
Residing in public housing	4.8	3.2	12.1	7.0
Residing in subsidized housing	3.9	3.2	7.1	5.5

Source: "Persons With Work Disability, by Selected Characteristics: 1992." *Statistical Abstract of the United States,* 1994, p. 382. Primary source: U.S. Bureau of the Census, unpublished data. *Notes:* 1. Includes other races not shown separately. 2. Hispanic persons may be of any race.

Work Disability and Assistance Programs

★ 759 ★

Work Disability: Selected Characteristics of Persons, 1993

[In thousands, except percent. As of March. Covers civilian noninstitutional population and members of Armed Forces living off post or with their families on post. Persons are classified as having a work disability if they (1) have a health problem or disability which prevents them from working or which limits the kind or amount of work they can do; (2) have a service-connected disability or ever retired or left a job for health reasons; (3) did not work in survey reference week or previous year because of long-term illness or disability; or (4) are under age 65, and are covered by Medicare or receive Supplemental Security Income. Based on Current Population Survey; see text, section 1, and Appendix III].

AGE AND PARTICIPATION STATUS IN ASSISTANCE PROGRAMS	Total[1]	Male	Female	White	Black	Hispanic[2]
Persons with work disability	16,777	8,548	8,229	12,912	3,223	1,578
16 to 24 years old	1,467	759	708	1,009	382	148
25 to 34 years old	2,843	1,460	1,383	2,106	600	307
35 to 44 years old	3,802	1,956	1,846	2,903	737	376
45 to 54 years old	3,902	2,034	1,867	3,047	715	361
55 to 64 years old	4,763	2,338	2,425	3,848	789	387
Percent work disabled of total population	10.1	10.4	9.8	9.3	15.8	9.5
16 to 24 years old	4.5	4.6	4.3	3.9	7.9	3.4
25 to 34 years old	6.8	7.0	6.6	6.1	11.0	6.1
35 to 44 years old	9.2	9.5	8.8	8.4	14.6	10.2
45 to 54 years old	13.2	14.1	12.4	12.1	23.5	16.3
55 to 64 years old	23.0	23.5	22.4	21.3	38.8	28.3
Percent of work disabled-						
Receiving Social Security income	28.3	29.1	27.5	29.3	25.9	23.4
Receiving food stamps	25.7	19.8	31.8	20.9	43.5	37.2
Covered by Medicaid	32.8	26.3	39.6	28.3	48.9	46.5
Residing in public housing	6.2	4.1	8.3	4.3	13.2	7.6
Residing in subsidized housing	3.5	2.2	4.8	2.8	6.5	4.9

Source: "Persons With Work Disability, by Selected Characteristics: 1993." U.S. Bureau of the Census, *Statistical Abstract of the United States,* 115th ed., 1995, p. 386. Primary source: U.S. Bureau of the Census, unpublished data. *Notes:* 1. Includes other races not shown separately. 2. Hispanic persons may be of any race.

Chapter 13
SPORTS AND LEISURE

Leisure

★ 760 ★

Activities: Percent of Persons Participating in Various Leisure Activities: 1992

[**In percent, except as indicated.** Covers activities engaged in at least once in the prior 12 months].

| ITEM | Adult population (mil.) | ATTENDANCE AT-- | | | PARTICIPATION IN-- | | | | |
		Movies	Sports events	Amusement park	Exercise program	Playing sports	Outdoor activities[1]	Home improvement/ repair	Gardening
Total	185.8	59	37	50	60	39	34	48	55
Race: White	158.8	60	38	51	61	40	37	50	57
Black	21.1	54	32	45	51	32	10	32	39
Other	5.9	62	20	46	51	38	28	31	42

Source: "Participation in Various Leisure Activities: 1992," *Statistical Abstract of the United States: 1995*, 1995, p. 257. Primary source: U.S. National Endowment for the Arts, *Arts Participation in America: 1982 to 1992. Note:* 1. Camping, hiking, and canoeing.

★ 761 ★

Leisure

Expenditures: Money Spent per Consumer Unit for Entertainment and Reading, by Race: 1985-1993

[Data are **annual averages. In dollars, except as indicated.** Based on Consumer Expenditures Survey].

YEAR AND CHARACTERISTIC	ENTERTAINMENT AND READING		ENTERTAINMENT				Reading
	Total	Percent of total expenditures	Total	Fees and admissions	Television, radios, and sound equipment	Other equipment and services[1]	
Race:							
White and other	1,911	6.0	1,734	448	610	676	177
Black	855	4.1	772	155	427	190	83

Source: "Expenditures per Consumer Unit for Entertainment and Reading: 1985 to 1993," *Statistical Abstract of the United States: 1995,* 1995, p. 254. Primary source: U.S. Bureau of Labor Statistics, *Consumer Expenditure Survey,* annual. *Notes:* 1. Other equipment and services includes pets, toys, and playground equipment, and sports, exercise, and photographic equipment.

★ 762 ★

Leisure

Hunting/Guns: Percent of Gun Ownership, by Race: 1974-1993

[**In percent.** For the 50 States and DC, except prior to 1984 excludes Alaska and Hawaii. Represents respondents indicating there is a gun in the home or garage. Based on samples of noninstitutionalized English speaking persons 18 years old and older].

CHARACTERISTIC	1974	1976	1980	1984	1987	1990	1991	TYPE OF FIREARM, 1993			
								Total[1]	Pistol	Shotgun	Rifle
Total	46	47	48	45	46	43	40	42	24	27	23
Race:											
White	48	58	50	48	49	45	42	45	25	29	26
Black/other	32	37	29	30	33	29	29	26	17	14	9

Source: "Gun Ownership: 1974 to 1993," *Statistical Abstract of the United States: 1995,* 1995, p. 262. Primary source: U.S. Bureau of Justice Statistics, *Sourcebook of Criminal Justice Statistics,* annual. *Note:* 1. Includes other types of firearms, not shown separately.

Leisure Sports

★ 763 ★

Golf: Black Participation in Leisure Golf During the 1980s: 1980-1989

Year	African American Population[1]	African American Golf Partici- pants[1]	African American Golf Participation Rate (%)	African Ameri- can Participa- tion Rate per 1,000 African Americans	African American % of all Golf Players
1980	17,363	315	1.8	18.1	2.4
1981	17,258	697	4.0	40.4	5.3
1982	17,270	379	2.2	21.9	2.9
1983	17,832	376	2.1	21.1	2.7
1984	17,974	554	3.1	30.8	3.7
1985	18,302	503	2.7	27.5	3.3
1986	18,715	626	3.3	33.4	3.2
1987	19,130	915	4.8	47.8	4.8
1988	19,434	1,416	7.3	72.9	6.2
1989	19,771	1,015	5.1	51.3	4.6

Source: Adapted by the editors from "African American Golf Participation in the 80's" News Release by Rod Warnick, University of Massachusetts at Amherst, August 7, 1991, [no p. No.]. Primary source: Simmons Market Research Bureau, Inc. Volume P-10, *Sports and Leisure*, 1980-1989. Compiled by Rod Warnick, Ph.D., Associate Professor, Leisure Studies and Resources Program, University of Massachusetts at Amherst, MA 01003-0069. Published by permission. *Note:* 1. In thousands.

★ 764 ★

Leisure Sports

Golf: Growth in Black Participation in Leisure Golf: 1984-1989

Year	Participants
1984	554
1985	503
1986	626
1987	915
1988	1,416
1989	1,015

Source: "African American Golf Participation in the 80's," News Release by Rod Warnick, University of Massachusetts at Amherst, August 7, 1991, [no p. No.]. Primary source: Simmons Market Research Bureau, Inc. Compiled by: Rod Warwick, University of Massachusetts. Published by permission.

Sports

★ 765 ★

College Basketball: College Sports' Top 95-96 Players

Position	No. Players	No. Black American Players
Point guards	30	25
Shooting guards	30	20
Small forwards	30	22
Power forwards	30	22
Centers	30	24

Source: Adapted and compiled by the editors from "CS' Top 30 Point Guards,...Shooting Guards, ...Small forwards, ...Power Forwards, ...[and] Centers," *College Sports*, November, 1995, pp. 42-49. Published by permission.

★ 766 ★

Sports

College Basketball: All-Time Final Four Super Teams

Years	No. Players	No. Black American Players
ALL-DECADE TEAMS		
All-Time Team	5	4
1980-1987	10	8
1970s	10	7
1960s	10	4
1950s	10	5
1939-40s	10	0
CONSENSUS ALL-AMERICANS[1]	75	32

Source: Adapted and compiled by the editors from "All-Decade Teams" and "Consensus All-Americans in the Final Four," *NCAA Final Four: Final Four Records* Book, 1994, p. 19. Published by permission. *Note:* 1. In the year their team played in the Final Four.

★ 767 ★

Sports

College Basketball: Institutions with Black Head Coaches in the NCAA Division I Men's Basketball Tournament: 1995

Ball State University
Georgetown University
North Carolina A&T University
Temple University
Texas Southern University
Tulane University
University of Arkansas
University of Memphis
University of Oklahoma
University of Tulsa

Source: Compiled by the editors from various media sources, March, 1995.

★ 768 ★

Sports

College Football: *Football Digest*'s College All-Americans: 1995

Team	Offense		Defense	
	No. Players	No. Black Americans	No. Players	No. Black Americans
First team	13	8	12	8
Second team	13	6	12	10
Total	26	14	24	18
%	100.0	53.8	100.0	75.0

Source: Adapted and compiled by the editors from "*Football Digest's* 1995 All- American First Team [and] Second Team," *Football Digest*, February, 1996, pp. 85, 87. Published by permission.

★ 769 ★

Sports

NCAA Affiliates: NCAA Awards: 1995

Award Category	Total Awards	Number Black-Americans
Silver Anniversary Award	6	1
Today's Top Eight Award	8	2

Source: Adapted by the editors from "1995 NCAA Honor Roll," *NCAA.* Program Book of the 1995 Division I Men's Basketball Championship First & Second Rounds, [no p. no.]. Published by permission. Primary source: *NCAA.* Program Book of the 1995 Division I Men's Basketball Championship First & Second Rounds.

★ 770 ★

Sports

NCAA Affiliates: Percent of African-American Players and Head Coaches in NCAA Football and Men's Basketball: 1992

Sport	Total percent
Players	
NCAA football (1992)	40
NCAA basketball (1992)	60
Head Coaches	
NCAA football (1992)	3
NCAA Men's basketball (1992)	19

Source: "Percentages of African-Americans in the Three Major Professional Team Sports," Angela Lumpkin, Sharon Kay Stoll, & Jennifer M. Beller, *Sport Ethics: Applications for Fair Play,* 1993, p. 151. Primary source: *1993 Racial Report Card,* Center for the Study of Sport in Society. Published by permission. *Note:* NCAA = National Collegiate Athletic Association.

★ 771 ★

Sports

Professional Baseball: 1995 Batting and Pitching Leaders

Category	AMERICAN LEAGUE		NATIONAL LEAGUE	
	Number Players	Number Black American players	Number Players	Number Black American Players
BATTING				
Batting average	10	3	10	4
Home runs	13	4	13	4
Runs batted in	12	3	14	4
Runs	12	3	10	4
Singles	10	3	11	4
Doubles	13	2	13	6
Triples	14	2	11	3
Total bases	10	4	12	2
Hits	12	6	10	3
Walks	11	1	12	4
Stolen bases	12	4	10	5
Slugging percentage	11	3	12	4
On-base percentage	14	5	10	4
Extra-base hits	10	3	21	8
Hit by pitch	10	1	6	1
PITCHING				
Earned run average	10	0	10	0
Wins	12	0	12	0
Strikeouts	10	0	10	0
Innings pitched	15	0	10	0
Complete games	7	0	8	0
Shutouts	8	0	12	0
Saves	12	1	10	1

Source: Adapted and compiled by the editors from "1995 American League Batting Leaders," "1995 A.L. Pitching Leaders," "1995 National League Batting Leaders," and "1995 N.L. Pitching Leaders," *Baseball Digest*, January, 1996, pp. 70-73. Published by permission.

★ 772 ★

Sports

Professional Baseball: 1995 Home Run Leaders

Category	Number Players	Number Black Americans
Players with three-homer games	7	2
Players with the most solo home runs	28	6
Players with the most 2-run home runs	19	5
Players with the most 3-run home runs	21	4
Players with the most grand slams	19	2
Players with most home runs with runners on base	19	4
Players who drove in most runs with homes	21	6

Source: Adapted and compiled by the editors from "Players with Three-Homer Games, 1995," and "1995 Home Run Breakdown," *Baseball Digest*, February, 1966, pp. 82-83 and 91.

★ 773 ★

Sports

Professional Baseball: 1995 League Leaders

Category	AMERICAN LEAGUE		NATIONAL LEAGUE	
	Number Players	Number Black Americans	Number Players	Number Black Americans
Players who reached base most often	41	10	22	7
Players with highest run production average	16	3	17	6
Players who were toughest to strike out	24	4	20	4
Highest base stealing percentages	24	5	38	19

Source: Adapted and compiled by the editors from "Players who were Toughest to Strike Out, 1995," "Highest Base Stealing Percentages, 1995," "Players who Reached Base Most Often, 1995," and "Players with Highest Run Production Average," *Baseball Digest*, February, 1996, pp. 86-90. Published by permission.

★ 774 ★

Sports

Professional Baseball: 1995 Players who Led the Pack in Selected Categories

Category	American League		National League	
	No. Players	No. Black Americans	No. Players	No. Black Americans
Biggest batting gains	10	3	10	4
Biggest batting declines	10	3	10	1
Toughest to strike out	24	4	20	3
Highest base stealing percentages	24	5	38	19

Source: Adapted and compiled by the editors from "Biggest Batting Gainers and Losers, 1995," "Players who were Toughest to Strike Out, 1995," and "Highest Base Stealing Percentages, 1995," *Baseball Digest*, February, 1996, pp. 33, 86, 87. Published by permission.

★ 775 ★

Sports

Professional Baseball: African-American Head Coaches and Player Positions in Major League Baseball: 1993

Professional League	Position	Players Number	Total Percent
Major League Baseball (1993)	Pitcher	5	16
	Catcher	1	
	First base	19	
	Second base	13	
	Third base	12	
	Shortstop	8	
	Outfield	50	
Major League Baseball (1993)	-	-	14

Source: "Percentages of African-Americans in the Three Major Professional Team Sports," Angela Lumpkin, Sharon Kay Stoll, & Jennifer M. Beller, *Sport Ethics: Applications for Fair Play*, 1993, p. 151. Primary source: *1993 Racial Report Card*, Center for the Study of Sport in Society. Published by permission.

★ 776 ★

Sports

Professional Baseball: Individual World Series Leaders: 1903-1994

Category	Number Players	Number Black American Players
BATTING		
Games	11	1
Hits	12	1
Doubles	7	0
Triples	15	0
Home runs	12	2
Runs batted in	11	1
Runs	14	3
Batting average	15	2
Stolen bases	12	3
PITCHING		
Wins	13	1
Winning percentage[1]	10	0
Earned run average	11	0
Shutouts	10	1
Innings pitched	12	1
Games	14	0
Strikeouts	11	1

Source: Adapted and compiled by the editors from "World Series Individual Leaders, 1903-1994," *Baseball Digest,* October, 1995, pp. 91-92. Published by permission. *Note:* 1. 3 or more decisions.

★ 777 ★

Sports

Professional Baseball: Leaders in Single World Series

Category	Range	Number Players	Number Black Americans	Range
BATTING				
Runs	8-10	19	4	8-10
Hits	12-13	16	3	12-13
Doubles	5-6	2	0	---
Triples	3-4	6	0	---
Home runs	4-5	9	2	4-5
Stolen bases	5-7	10	5	5-7
Bases on balls	8-11	10	3	8-9

[Continued]

★ 777 ★

Professional Baseball: Leaders in Single World Series
[Continued]

Category	Range	Number Players	Number Black Americans	Range
PITCHING				
Saves	3	2	0	---
Shutouts	2-3	5	0	---
Wins	3	12	1	3
Strikeouts	20-35	14	3	26-35

Source: Adapted and compiled by the editors from "Single World Series Leaders," *Baseball Digest,* October, 1995, pp. 93-94. Published by permission.

★ 778 ★

Sports

Professional Baseball: MVP, Cy Young, and Rookie-of-the-Year Awards, by Decade-I

Years	MVP (1931-1995)			
	American		National	
	Number	Black American	Number	Black American
1990-1995	6	4	6	4
1980-1989	10	0	10	3
1970-1979	10	5	10	5
1960-1969	10	2	10	5
1950-1959	10	0	10	8
1940-1949	10	0	10	1
1931-1939	9	0	9	0

Source: Adapted and compiled by the editors from "Most Valuable Player Award Voting, 1931-1994," "Cy Young Award Voting, 1947-1994," "Rookie-of-the-Year Award Voting, 1947-1994," *Baseball Digest,* November, 1995, pp. 80-88; and "1995 A.L. and N.L. Award Winners," *Baseball Digest,* February, 1996, p. 91. Published by permission.

★ 779 ★
Sports

Professional Baseball: MVP, Cy Young, and Rookie-of-the-Year Awards, by Decade-II

Years	CY YOUNG (1956-1995)				ROOKIE-OF-THE-YEAR (1949-1995)			
	American		National		American		National	
	Number	Black American	Number	Black American	Number	Black American	Number	Black American
1990-1995	6	0	6	0	6	0	5	1
1980-1989	10	0	10	1	10	0	10	4
1970-1979	10	1	10	2	10	1	10	1
1960-1969	3	0	2	1	10	1	10	2
Combined League Selection								
				11-1				
1950-1959	--	--	--	--	10	0	10	4
1940-1949	--	--	--	--	1	0	1	1
1931-1939	--	--	--	--	--	--	--	--

Source: Adapted and compiled by the editors from "Most Valuable Player Award Voting, 1931-1994," "Cy Young Award Voting, 1947-1994," "Rookie-of-the-Year Award Voting, 1947-1994," *Baseball Digest*, November, 1995, pp. 80-88; and "1995 A.L. and N.L. Award Winners," *Baseball Digest*, February, 1996, p. 91. Published by permission.

★ 780 ★
Sports

Professional Baseball: Most World Series Home Runs for All Series

Category	Number Players	Number Black American Players
Players	40	9
%	100.0	22.5
Avg. # Series	5.6	4.3
Avg. # home runs	6.2	4.4

Source: Adapted and compiled by the editors from "Most Home Runs, Total Series," *Baseball Digest*, October 1994, p. 86. Published by permission.

★ 781 ★

Sports

Professional Baseball: Personnel Whose Uniform Numbers Have Been Retired, by League and Team

Category	Number Players	Number Black Americans
AMERICAN LEAGUE		
Baltimore	5	2
Boston	4	0
California	3	0
Chicago	7	1
Cleveland	5	1
Detroit	3	0
Kansas City	2	0
Milwaukee	3	1
Minnesota	3	0
New York	14	2
Oakland	2	0
Seattle	0	0
Texas	0	0
Toronto	0	0
NATIONAL LEAGUE		
Atlanta	5	1
Chicago	2	2
Cincinnati	2	0
Colorado	0	0
Florida	1	0
Houston	4	0
Los Angeles	8	3
Montreal	2	0
New York	3	0
Philadelphia	4	0
Pittsburgh	8	3
St. Louis	5	3
San Diego	1	0
San Francisco	6	2

Source: Adapted and compiled by the editors from "Retired Uniform Numbers," *Baseball Digest*, January, 1996, p. 13. Published by permission.

★ 782 ★

Sports

Professional Baseball: Players 15 Years or More with One Team

Position	Number Players	Number Black American Players
First basemen	3	1
Second basemen	5	1
Shortstops	7	0
Third basemen	6	0
Outfielders	16	3
Catchers	3	0
Pitchers	15	1
Total		
N	55	6
%	100.0	10.9

Source: Adapted and complied by the editors from "Players who have Spent their Entire Career with One Team (Minimum of 15 Years)," *Baseball Digest*, March, 1994, p. 12.

★ 783 ★

Sports

Professional Baseball: Players with the Most RBIs per 100 At-Bats

Category	Number of players	Range	Number Black Americans	Range
Top Non-Active Players	52	18.0-26.3	7	18.1-19.4
Top Active Players	10	18.2-21.3	2	18.2-20.6
Other high RBI-producing Players[1]	19	15.3-17.8	8	16.0-17.5

Source: Adapted and compiled by the editors from "Major League Players with Most RBI per 100 At-Bats, Career," *Baseball Digest*, July, 1995, p. 81. Published by permission. *Note:* 1. Includes both active and non-active players.

★ 784 ★
Sports

Professional Baseball: Prolific Home Run Hitters Among Retired and Active Players

Player category	Number Players	Number Black American Players
Retired (Minimum 200 homers)	41	9
Active (Minimum 100 homers)	12	7
Total		
N	53	16
%	100.0	30.2

Source: Adapted and compiled by the editors from "Major Leaguers with Best Home Run Frequency," *Baseball Digest*, March, 1994, p. 83. Published by permission.

★ 785 ★
Sports

Professional Baseball: Season Leaders in Regular Games: 1990-1993

Category	AMERICAN LEAGUE				NATIONAL LEAGUE			
	Number Players	Range	Number Black American Players	Range	Number Players	Range	Number Black American Players	Range
Batting average	93	.308-.422	3	.316-.339	94	.313-.424	13	.370-.313
Runs batted in	99	74-184	14	109-139	97	72-159	17	105-149
Home runs	105	7-60	16	32-51	106	7-56	21	35-52

Source: Adapted and compiled by the editors from "Year-by-Year Leaders, American and National Leaders: Records Since 1990," *Baseball Digest*, September, 1994, pp. 88-91. Published by permission.

★ 786 ★
Sports

Professional Baseball: World Series 400 Hitters, by Decade: 1900-1993

Years	Number Players	Number Black American Players
1990-1995	5	0
1980-1989	10	3
1970-1979	13	2
1960-1969	10	2
1950-1959	10	1
1940-1949	5	0
1930-1939	13	0
1920-1929	16	0
1910-1919	12	0
1900-1909	3	0
Total		
N	97	8
%	100.0	8.2

Source: Adapted and compiled by the editors from "400 Hitters Playing in All Games of Series (10 or More at Bats)," *Baseball Digest,* October, 1995, pp. 80-81. Published by permission.

★ 787 ★
Sports

Professional Baseball: World Series Honors: 1955-1995

Years	World Series Number Pitchers	MVP pitchers Number Black American Pitchers	World Series Number Players	MVP Number Black Americans
1990-1995	3	0	6	0
1985-1989	4	0	5	1
1980-1984	0	0	5	0
1975-1979	0	0	5	2
1970-1974	1	0	5	1
1965-1969	3	1	5	2
1960-1964	4	1	5	1
1955-1959	5	9	5	0

[Continued]

★ 787 ★

Professional Baseball: World Series Honors: 1955-1995
[Continued]

Years	World Series Number Pitchers	MVP pitchers Number Black American Pitchers	World Series Number Players	MVP Number Black Americans
Total				
N	20	2	41	7
%	100.0	10.0	100.0	17.1

Source: Adapted and compiled by the editors from "Pitchers who have Won World Series MVP Honors" and "World Series Most Valuable Players," *Baseball Digest,* February, 1996, pp. 26, and 28. Published by permission.

★ 788 ★

Sports

Professional Baseball: World Series Leading Batters, by Decade: 1900-1993

Years	AMERICAN LEAGUE		NATIONAL LEAGUE	
	Number Players	Number Black American Players	Number Players	Number Black American Players
1990-1993	4	1	5	1
1980-1989	10	4	11	1
1970-1979	10	3	10	1
1960-1969	11	1	10	2
1950-1959	10	0	12	2
1940-1949	10	1	10	0
1930-1939	11	0	10	0
1920-1929	10	0	11	0
1910-1919	10	0	11	0
1903-1909	7	0	6	0
Total				
N	93	10	96	7
%	100.0	10.8	100.0	7.3

Source: Adapted and compiled by the editors from "Leading Batters, World Series (Playing in All Games, Each Series)," *Baseball Digest,* October, 1994, pp. 82-83. Published by permission.

★ 789 ★

Sports

Professional Baseball: World Series Pitchers Who Had 10 or More Strikeouts in a Series Game, by Decade: 1903-1980

Years	Number Pitchers	Number Black American Pitchers
1980	1	0
1971-1973	3	0
1962-1968	11	5
1952-1958	5	0
1944-1949	5	1
1932-1936	3	0
1921-1929	6	0
1911-1912	2	0
1903-1909	6	0
Total		
N	42	6
%	100.0	14.3

Source: Adapted and compiled by the editors from "Ten or More Strikeouts by Pitcher in One World Series Game," *Baseball Digest,* October, 1995, p. 84. Published by permission.

★ 790 ★

Sports

Professional Basketball: 1994-95 Holders of NBA Highs and Lows, by Category

Award	No. Players	No. Black American Players
Most minutes played, season	1	1
Most minutes played, game	1	1
Most points, game	1	1
Most field goals made, game	4	
Most field goals attempts, game	1	1
Most free throws made, game	1	1
Most free throw attempts, game	1	1
Most rebounds, game	1	1
Most offensive rebounds, game	3	3
Most defensive rebounds, game	1	1
Most offensive rebounds, season	1	0
Most defensive rebounds, season	1	1

[Continued]

★ 790 ★

Professional Basketball: 1994-95 Holders of NBA Highs and Lows, by Category
[Continued]

Award	No. Players	No. Black American Players
Most assists, game	2	1
Most blocked shots, game	1	0
Most steals, game	8	1
Most personal fouls, season	1	0
Most games disqualified, season	1	0

Source: Adapted and compiled by the editors from "Final NBA Individual Highs and Lows," *Petersen's Pro Basketball*, 1995-96, 1995, p. 162. Published by permission. *Notes:* 1. At least one Black American, who was most recent leader; all names not given in Source.

★ 791 ★

Sports

Professional Basketball: 1994-95 NBA Season Leaders, by Category

Category	No. Players	No. Black American Players
ALL PLAYERS		
Scoring average	20	20
Rebounds per game	20	18
Assists per game	20	18
Individual assist/turnover ratio	10	2
Individual steal/turnover ratio	10	4
ROOKIES		
Scoring average	7	7
Rebounds per game	7	5
Assists per game	7	3
INDIVIDUALS		
Scoring	1	1
Rebounding	1	1
Assists	1	0
Steals	1	1
Blocks	1	0
Field goal percentage	1	0
Free throw percentage	1	1
3-point field goal percentage	1	0

Source: Adapted and compiled by the editors from "Final NBA Leaders," "NBA Rookie Leaders," and "NBA Stat Leaders," *Petersen's Pro Basketball*, 1995-96, 1995, p. 155. Published by permission.

★ 792 ★

Sports

Professional Basketball: 1994-95 Top Tenners, by Category

Category	No. Players	No. Black American Players
Scoring average (min. 70 games or 1400 points)	10	10
Field-goal percentage (minimum 300 made)	10	8
Free-throw percentage (minimum 125 made)	10	7
Assists (minimum 70 games or 400 assists)	10	9
Rebounds (min. 70 games or 800 rebounds)	10	9
Steals (minimum 70 games or 125 steals)	10	9
Blocked shots (min. 70 games or 100 blocked shots)	10	8
3-point-field goal percentage (min. 50 made)	10	6

Source: Adapted and compiled by the editors from "1994-95 Individual Leaders," *The Sporting News 1995-96 Pro Basketball Yearbook*, September, 1995, pp. 116-119. Published by permission.

★ 793 ★

Sports

Professional Basketball: ABA Career Leaders, by Category: 1968-1976

Category	No. Players	No. Black American Players
Most Valuable Player	10	10
Rookie of the Year	10	7
Scoring Leaders	9	4
Rebounding leaders	9	5
Assist leaders	9	0

Source: Adapted and compiled by the editors from "American Basketball Association All-Time Statistics", *Basketball Digest*, January, 1996, p. 84. Published by permission.

★ 794 ★

Sports

Professional Basketball: African-American Head Coaches and Player Positions in the National Basketball Association: 1993

Professional League	Position	Players	Total Percent
National Basketball Association (1993)	Center	55	77
	Forward	80	
	Guard	88	
Head Coaches			
National Basketball Association (1993)	-	-	26

Source: "Percentages of African-Americans in the Three Major Professional Team Sports," Angela Lumpkin, Sharon Kelly Stoll, & Jennifer M. Beller, *Sports Ethics: Applications for Fair Play*, 1993, p. 151. Primary source: *1993 Racial Report Card*. Center for the Study of Sport in Society. Published by permission.

★ 795 ★

Sports

Professional Basketball: All-Star Game Statistics and Records

Category	Number Players	Number Black American Players
ALL-STAR GAME STATISTICS		
Scoring average (Min. 3 games or 60 points)	10	5
Field goal percentage (Min. 15 made)	10	8
Free throw percentage (Min. 10 made)	10	6
ALL-STAR GAME RECORDS: INDIVIDUAL (SINGLE GAME)		
Most minutes played	4	3
Most points scored	1	1
Most field goals made	2	2
Most field goal attempts	1	0
Most free throws made	2	2
Most free throw attempts	1	1
Most 3-pt. field goals made	2	1
Most 3-pt. field goal attempts	2	1
Most rebounds	1	1
Most offensive rebounds	2	1
Most defensive rebounds	1	1
Most assists	2	2
Most steals	1	0
Most blocked shots	3	3

[Continued]

★ 795 ★

Professional Basketball: All-Star Game Statistics and Records
[Continued]

Category	Number Players	Number Black American Players
Most personal fouls	12	7
ALL-STAR GAME RECORDS: CAREER		
Games	9	5
Minutes	10	7
Points	10	8
Field goals made	10	8
Field goals attempted	10	6
Free throws made	10	7
Free throws attempted	10	6
Three-point field goals made	8	5
Three-point field goals attempted	11	7
Rebounds	10	7
Assists	10	6
Personal fouls	10	7
Steals	10	7
Blocked shots	10	8
Disqualifications	12	4

Source: Adapted and compiled by the editors from "NBA All-Star Game Statistics" and "All-Star Game Records," *Basketball Digest,* February, 1996, pp. 82-84. Published by permission.

★ 796 ★
Sports

Professional Basketball: Basketball Hall-of-Famers, by Decade of Election: 1959-1995

Years	No. Players	No. Black American Players
1990-1995	25	10
1980-1989	26	9
1970-1979	25	5
1960-1969	23	1
1959	4	0

Source: Adapted and compiled by the editors from "Members of the Basketball Hall of Fame", *Basketball Digest,* Summer, 1995, pp. 56-57. Published by permission.

★ 797 ★

Sports

Professional Basketball: Continental Basketball Association Records and Leaders, by Category

Category	No. Categories	No. Players	No. Black American Players
Regular season game records	14	17	2
Regular season season records	20	20	3
Leaders			
Points		15	4
Rebounds		15	6
Assists		15	3

Source: Adapted and compiled by the editors from "Continental Basketball Association Statistics," *Basketball Digest*, January, 1996, p. 85. Published by permission.

★ 798 ★

Sports

Professional Basketball: NBA Award Winners: 1994-95

Award	No. Players	No. Black American Players
Most Valuable Player	1	1
Co-Rookies of the Year	2	2
Most Improved Player	1	1
Defensive Player of the Year	1	0
Sixth Man Award	1	1
NBA Finals Most Valuable Player	1	1
IBM Award	1	1
Schick NBA Rookie of the Year	1	1
Bausch and Lomb Award	1	1
ALL-DEFENSIVE TEAM		
First team	5	5
Second team	5	3
ALL-ROOKIE TEAM		
First team	5	5
Second team	5	5

Source: Adapted and compiled by the editors from "1994-95 Award Winners," *The Sporting News 1995-96 Pro Basketball Yearbook*, September, 1995, pp. 116- 119; and "1994-95 NBA Honor Roll," *Petersen's Pro Basketball*, 1995-96, 1995, p. 162. Published by permission.

★ 799 ★
Sports

Professional Basketball: NBA Career Leaders, by Category

Category	No. Players	No. Black American Players
Most points	10	8
Most games played	11	10
Most minutes played	10	9
Most rebounds	10	9
Most blocked shots	10	7
Most field goals made	10	8
Most field games attempted	10	8
Most free throws made	10	7
Most free throws attempted	10	7
Most steals	10	8
Most personal fouls	10	6
Most assists	10	7
Most disqualifications	10	3
Most 3-point field goals made	10	6
Most 3-point field goals attempted	10	7

Source: Adapted and compiled by the editors from "All-Time NBA Leaders", *Basketball Digest*, December, 1995, pp. 94-96. Published by permission.

★ 800 ★
Sports

Professional Basketball: NBA Playoff Leaders, by Category, through 1995

Category	Number	Number Black Americans
Scoring Average	10	7
Field Goal Percentage	10	7
Free Throw Percentage	10	2
3-Point Field Goal Percentage	10	8
Years	5	4
Games	10	7
Minutes	10	6
Field Goals Made	10	7
Field Goals Attempted	10	7
Free Throws Made	10	6
Free Throws Attempted	10	6
3-Point Field Goals Made	10	6

[Continued]

★ 800 ★

Professional Basketball: NBA Playoff Leaders, by Category, through 1995

[Continued]

Category	Number	Number Black Americans
3-Point Field Goals Attempted	10	7
Rebounds	10	9
Assists	10	5
Personal Fouls	10	6
Steals	10	9
Blocked Shots	10	8
Disqualifications	8	3
Coaching Victories	30	4

Source: Compiled by the editors from "NBA Career Playoff Statistics," *Basketball Digest,* March 1996, pp. 82-84. Primary source: "NBA Career Playoff Statistics," *Basketball Digest,* March, 1996, pp. 82-84. Published by permission.

★ 801 ★

Sports

Professional Basketball: Top Statistical Leaders in Men's NCAA Tournaments: 1957-1995

Category	No. ranked	No. Black Americans
Scoring average	10	4
Field goal percentage	10	4
3-point field goal percentage	9	5
Free throw percentage	16	5
Rebounding average	10	7
Assists average	10	4
Blocked shots average	10	8
Steals average	10	6
Total	85	43
%	100.0	50.6

Source: Compiled and adapted by the editors from "NCAA Tournament Statistical Leaders" *Basketball Digest,* April 1996, pp. 84-85. Published by permission. *Notes:* Years when leads were achieved range from 1952-1995, except for Assists and Steals, for which records were kept in 1984, and Blocked shots, for which records were first kept in 1986.

★ 802 ★

Sports

Professional Football: AFC and NFC Individual Leaders: 1995

Category	AFC		NFC	
	No. Players	No. Black Americans	No. Players	No. Black Americans
Touchdowns	13	10	10	10
Kicking	13	0	13	0
Receptions	21	16	24	23
Receiving yards	20	9	20	20
Rushing	20	17	20	20
Passing	15	1	20	20
Total yards from scrimmage	20	20	15	2
Punt returns	10	10	10	10
Kickoff returns	10	9	10	10
Interceptions	15	11	9	8
Sacks	11	9	10	8
Punting	15	0	15	1
Total	183	112	176	132
%	100.0	61.2	100.0	75.0

Source: Compiled and adapted by the editors from "1995 Individual Leaders" *Football Digest*, April 1996, pp. 89-94. Published by permission.

★ 803 ★

Sports

Professional Football: African-American Head Coaches and Player Positions in the National Football League: 1992

Professional League	Position	Players (No.)	Total Percent
National Football League (1992)	Quarterback	6	68
	Running back	92	
	Wide receiver	88	
	Offensive center	19	
	Offensive guard	55	
	Tight end	59	
	Offensive tackle	46	
	Kicker	7	
	Punter	10	
	Cornerback	98	
	Safety	88	
	Linebacker	71	
	Defensive end	78	

[Continued]

★ 803 ★

Professional Football: African-American Head Coaches and Player Positions in the National Football League: 1992
[Continued]

Professional League	Position	Players (No.)	Total Percent
	Defensive tackle	67	
	Defensive back	92	
	Nose tackle	60	
Major League Baseball (1993)	Pitcher	5	16
	Catcher	1	
	First base	19	
	Second base	13	
	Third base	12	
	Shortstop	8	
	Outfield	50	
National Basketball Association (1993)	Center	55	
	Forward	80	
	Guard	83	
NCAA football (1992)	-	-	40
NCAA basketball (1992)	-	-	60
Head Coaches			
National Football League (1992)	-	-	7
National Basketball Association (1993)	-	-	26
Major League Baseball (1993)	-	-	14
NCAA football (1992)	-	-	3
NCAA Men's basketball (1992)	-	-	19

Source: "Percentages of African-Americans in the Three Major Professional Team Sports," Angela Lumpkin, Sharon Kay Stoll, & Jennifer M. Beller, *Sport Ethics: Applications for Fair Play*, 1993, p. 151. Primary source: *1993 Racial Report Card.* Center for the Study of Sport in Society. Published by permission.

★ 804 ★
Sports

Professional Football: All-Madden Hall of Fame (1992-1995) and 1995 All-Madden Team

Category	Number Players	Number Black American Players
ALL-MADDEN HALL OF FAME		
1992	1	0
1993	1	0
1994	1	1

[Continued]

★ 804 ★

Professional Football: All-Madden Hall of Fame (1992-1995) and 1995 All-Madden Team

[Continued]

Category	Number Players	Number Black American Players
1995	3	2
ALL-MADDEN TEAM		
Running backs	8	8
Offensive linemen	8	6
Defensive linemen	5	4
Linebackers	3	2
Defensive backs	7	7
Receivers	7	7
Quarterbacks	3	0
Kickers	2	0

Source: Compiled by the editors from on-the-air transmissions, Fox Television Network, January 21, 1996. Primary source: Fox Television Network.

★ 805 ★

Sports

Professional Football: Decade Players of the Year According to *Football Digest*: 1973-1995

Decade	No. Players	No. Black Americans
1990-1995	6	4
1980-1989	10	3
1973-1979	7	4
Total	23	11
%	100.0	47.8

Source: Compiled and adapted by the editors from "Football Digest's Players of the Year," *Football Digest*, April 1996, p. 20. Published by permission.

★ 806 ★

Sports

Professional Football: First Team All Pros, According to *Football Digest*: 1995

Position	No. Players	No. Black Americans
Offense		
Quarterback	1	0
Running back	2	2
Fullback	1	1
Wide receiver	2	2
Tight end	1	0
Tackle	2	1
Guard	2	2
Center	1	1
Defense		
End	2	2
Tackle	2	1
Outside linebacker	2	1
Inside linebacker	2	1
Cornerback	2	1
Safety	2	2
Special Teams		
Kicker	1	0
Punter	1	1
Special teamer	1	1
Total	28	20
%	100.0	71.4

Source: Compiled and adapted by the editors from "Football Digest's 1995 All-Pro First Team," *Football Digest*, April 1996, p. 35. Published by permission.

★ 807 ★

Sports

Professional Football: NFL Passing, Rushing, and Receiving Yearly Leaders, by Decade: 1932-1994

Years	Passing[1]		Rushing		Receiving	
	No. Players	No. Black Americans	No. Players	No. Black Americans	No. Players	No. Black Americans
1990-1994	5	0	5	5	5	5
1980-1989	10	0	10	9	10	7
1970-1979	10	0	10	10	10	8
1960-1969	20[2]	0	20[2]	9	20[2]	9
1950-1959	10	0	10	4	10	0

[Continued]

★ 807 ★

Professional Football: NFL Passing, Rushing, and Receiving Yearly Leaders, by Decade: 1932-1994
[Continued]

Years	Passing[1]		Rushing		Receiving	
	No. Players	No. Black Americans	No. Players	No. Black Americans	No. Players	No. Black Americans
1940-1949	10	0	10	0	10	0
1932-1939	8	0	8	0	8	0

Source: Adapted and compiled by the editors from "Yearly Leaders," *Football Digest*, November, 1995, pp. 86-88. Published by permission. *Notes:* 1. Based on efficiency rating. 2. Separate records for American Football Conference and National Football Conference.

★ 808 ★

Sports

Professional Football: NFL Scoring, Field Goal, and Punt Return Yearly Leaders, by Decade: 1932-1994

Years	Scoring		Field Goals		Punt Returns	
	No. Players	No. Black Americans	No. Players	No. Black Americans	No. Players	No. Black Americans
1990-1994	5	0	8	0	5	5
1980-1989	11	2	10	0	10	8
1970-1979	10	1	12	0	10	4
1960-1969	20[1]	5	20[1]	0	20[1]	12
1950-1959	11	2	11	0	10	3
1940-1949	11	0	14	0	9	0
1932-1939	9	0	12	0	[2]	[2]

Source: Adapted and compiled by the editors from "Yearly Leaders," *Football Digest*, November, 1995, pp. 88-90. Published by permission. *Notes:* 1. Separate records for American Football Conference and National Football Conference. 2. Records begin in 1941.

★ 809 ★

Sports

Professional Football: NFL Scoring, Kickoff Return, Punting, and Interception Yearly Leaders, by Decade: 1932-1994

Years	Kickoff Returns		Punting		Interceptions	
	No. Players	No. Black Americans	No. Players	No. Black Americans	No. Players	No. Black Americans
1990-1994	5	5	5	1	8	8
1980-1989	10	9	10	0	10	7
1970-1979	10	8	10	0	11	3
1960-1969	20[1]	13	20[1]	0	20[1]	7
1950-1959	10	2	10	0	14	4
1940-1949	8	0	10	0	14	0
1932-1939	[2]	[2]	10	[2]	[2]	0

Source: Adapted and compiled by the editors from "Yearly Leaders," *Football Digest*, November, 1995, pp. 90, 92. Published by permission. *Notes:* 1. Separate records for American Football Conference and National Football Conference. 2. Records begin in 1940s decade.

★ 810 ★

Sports

Professional Football: NFL Single Season Individual All-Time Records, by Record Category

Category	No. Players	No. Black Americans
Rushing yards	28	24
Passing yards	28	4
Passing touchdowns	30	1
Receptions	31	26
Receiving yards	28	17
Interceptions	30	9
Field goals	31	0
Touchdowns	33	23

Source: Adapted and compiled by the editors from "All-Time Individual Single- Season Team Records," *Football Digest*, January, 1996, pp. 90-95. Published by permission.

★ 811 ★

Sports

Professional Football: Super Bowl Fumbles, Yards Gained, and Sacks Records

Category	No. Players	No. Black Americans
Fumbles: Touchdowns		
Most touchdowns, game	5	4
Combined net yards gained		
Most yards gained, career	3	3
Most yards gained, game	3	3
Sacks		
Most sacks, career (compiled since 1983)	5	5
Most sacks, game	9	8

Source: Adapted and compiled by the editors from "All-Time Super Bowl Records," *Football Digest*, February, 1996, p. 94. Published by permission.

★ 812 ★

Sports

Professional Football: Super Bowl Passing and Pass Receiving Records

Category	No. Players	No. Black Americans
Passing		
Highest passing rating, career (40 attempts)	3	0
Passing: Attempts		
Most passes attempted, career	3	0
Most passes attempted, game	4	0
Passing: Completions		
Most passes completed, career	3	0
Most passes completed, game	3	0
Passing: Completed percentage		
Highest completion percentage, career (40 attempts)	3	0
Highest completion percentage, game (20 attempts)	3	0
Passing: Yards gained		
Most yards gained, career	3	0
Most yards gained, game	3	1
Longest pass completion	5	1
Passing: Touchdowns		
Most touchdown passes, career	3	0
Most touchdown passes, game	5	1
Pass Receiving		
Most receptions, career	4	4

[Continued]

★ 812 ★

Professional Football: Super Bowl Passing and Pass Receiving Records
[Continued]

Category	No. Players	No. Black Americans
Most receptions, game	5	4
Pass receiving: Yards gained		
Most yards gained, career	3	3
Most yards gained, game	3	3
Longest reception	5	3
Pass Receiving: Average gain		
Highest average gain, career (8 receptions)	3	3
Highest average gain, game (3 receptions)	3	3
Pass Receiving: Touchdowns		
Most touchdowns, career	15	11
Most touchdowns, game	10	7

Source: Adapted and compiled by the editors from "All-Time Super Bowl Records," *Football Digest*, February, 1996, pp. 93-94. Published by permission.

★ 813 ★
Sports

Professional Football: Super Bowl Service, Scoring, and Rushing Records

Category	No. Players	No. Black Americans
Service: Most games played, career	7	2
Scoring		
Most points, career	5	4
Most points, game	6	3
Most touchdowns, Career	9	9
Most touchdowns, game	20	13
Most field goals, career	15	0
Most field goals, game	9	0
Longest field goal	4	0
Rushing: Yards gained		
Most yards gained, career	3	2
Most yards gained, game	3	2
Longest run from scrimmage	4	2
Rushing: Average gain		
Highest average gain, Career (20 attempts)	3	2

[Continued]

★ 813 ★

Professional Football: Super Bowl Service, Scoring, and Rushing Records
[Continued]

Category	No. Players	No. Black Americans
Rushing: touchdowns		
Most touchdowns, career	17	9
Most touchdowns, game	10	6

Source: Adapted and compiled by the editors from "All-Time Super Bowl Records," *Football Digest*, February, 1996, pp. 92-93. Published by permission.

Chapter 14
THE FAMILY

Children

★814★

1980 High School Sophomores in 1992: Percent Distribution of Number of Children of 1980 High School Sophomore Cohort, by Race/Ethnic Origin: 1992

	None	One	Two	Three or four	Five or more
Total	48.9	21.3	20.1	9.4	0.2
Race-ethnicity					
Native American/Alaska Native	33.5	16.4	31.9	17.8	0.4
Asian/Pacific Islander	62.4	23.1	8.5	6.0	0.0
Black	36.7	25.8	21.9	15.2	0.4
White	51.9	20.3	19.6	8.0	0.2
Hispanic-Mexican	41.7	23.4	19.9	15.0	0.0
Hispanic-Cuban	51.4	20.8	19.9	7.9	0.0
Hispanic-Puerto Rican	44.5	21.8	23.9	9.6	0.2
Hispanic-other	41.7	24.4	21.9	12.1	0.0

Source: "Percentage of 1980 High Sophomores, by the Number of Children Parented Through 1992 and Selected Characteristics," *Educational Attainment of 1980 High School Sophomores by 1992*, March 1995, p. 64. Primary source: U.S. Department of Education, Office of Educational Research and Improvement, National Center for Education Statistics. Statistical Analysis Report. *High School and Beyond: Educational Attainment of 1980 High School Sophomores by 1992; 1992 Descriptive Summary of 1980 High School Sophomores 12 Years Later.* NCES 95-304. Washington, DC: U.S. Government Printing Office, March, 1995. National Center for Education Statistics, High School & Beyond: 1980 Sophomore Cohort, 1980-1992.

★ 815 ★

Children

Living Arrangements: Parent(s) with Whom Children Under 18 Live, by Age of Parent(s) and Race/Ethnic Origin: 1994-I

[**In thousands.** As of **March.** Covers only those persons under 18 years old who are living with one or both parents. Characteristics are shown for the householder or reference person in married-couple situations].

CHARACTERISTIC OF PARENT	All races[1] total	WHITE			
		Total	Living with-		
			Both parents	Mother only	Father only
Children under 18 years old	66,674	52,300	41,766	9,724	1,710
Age:					
15 to 24 years old	4,011	2,706	1,295	1,276	135
25 to 29 years old	8,350	6,202	4,171	1,794	237
30 to 34 years old	14,654	11,431	8,875	2,223	333
35 to 39 years old	16,925	14,019	11,326	2,268	424
40 to 44 years old	12,514	10,441	8,817	1,320	304
45 to 54 years old	8,947	7,449	6,431	797	221
55 to 64 years old	1,077	799	710	41	49
65 years old and over	196	153	142	5	7

Source: "Living Arrangements of Children Under 18 Years Old, by Selected Characteristic of Parent: 1994," *Statistical Abstract of the United States: 1995,* 1995, p. 65. Primary source: U.S. Bureau of the Census, unpublished data. *Notes:* 1. Includes other races, not shown separately.

★ 816 ★

Children

Living Arrangements: Parent(s) with Whom Children Under 18 Live, by Age of Parent(s) and Race/Ethnic Origin: 1994-II

[**In thousands.** As of **March.** Covers only those persons under 18 years old who are living with one or both parents. Characteristics are shown for the householder or reference person in married-couple situations].

CHARACTERISTIC OF PARENT	BLACK				HISPANIC[2]			
	Total	Living with-			Total	Living with-		
		Both parents	Mother only	Father only		Both parents	Mother only	Father only
Children under 18 years old	10,106	3,722	5,967	417	9,041	6,022	2,646	373
Age:								
15 to 24 years old	1,133	118	994	22	777	337	376	64
25 to 29 years old	1,779	497	1,207	76	1,560	932	568	60
30 to 34 years old	2,580	780	1,663	137	2,183	1,415	682	87
35 to 39 years old	2,018	817	1,123	78	1,899	1,287	536	76
40 to 44 years old	1,404	749	611	43	1,474	1,155	281	38
45 to 54 years old	952	587	310	54	973	748	184	41

[Continued]

★ 816 ★

Living Arrangements: Parent(s) with Whom Children Under 18 Live, by Age of Parent(s) and Race/Ethnic Origin: 1994-II
[Continued]

CHARACTERISTIC OF PARENT	BLACK				HISPANIC[2]			
		Living with-				Living with-		
	Total	Both parents	Mother only	Father only	Total	Both parents	Mother only	Father only
55 to 64 years old	208	153	49	8	164	140	18	5
65 years old and over	31	21	9	1	10	6	-	3

Source: "Living Arrangements of Children Under 18 Years Old, by Selected Characteristic of Parent: 1994," *Statistical Abstract of the United States: 1995,* 1995, p. 65. Primary source: U.S. Bureau of the Census, unpublished data. *Notes:* 1. Includes other races, not shown separately. 2. Persons of Hispanic origin may be of any race.

★ 817 ★
Children

Living Arrangements: Parent(s) with Whom Children Under 18 Live, by Educational Attainment and Employment Status of Parent(s), and Race/Ethnic Origin: 1994-I

[**In thousands. As of March.** Covers only those persons under 18 years old who are living with one or both parents. Characteristics are shown for the householder or reference person in married-couple situations].

CHARACTERISTICS OF PARENT	All races[1] total	WHITE			
			Living with-		
		Total	Both parents	Mother only	Father only
Children under 18 years old	66,674	53,200	41,766	9,724	1,710
Educational attainment:					
Less than 9th grade	4,117	3,481	2,546	810	126
9th to 12th grade, no diploma	7,948	5,464	3,373	1,791	299
High school graduate[3]	21,659	16,740	12,685	3,416	640
Some college, no degree or associate degree	17,757	14,296	11,146	2,725	424
Bachelor's degree	9,832	8,500	7,701	673	126
Graduate or professional degree	5,362	4,719	4,315	309	95
Employment status[4]					
In the civilian labor force	54,878	45,451	37,678	6,291	1,482
Employed	51,127	42,977	36,035	5,615	1,328
Both parents employed	27,284	23,933	23,933	(X)	(X)
Unemployed	3,751	2,473	1,643	676	154
Not in the labor force	10,796	7,008	3,364	3,422	222

Source: "Living Arrangements of Children Under 18 Years Old, by Selected Characteristic of Parent: 1994," *Statistical Abstract of the United States: 1995,* 1995, p. 65. Primary source: U.S. Bureau of the Census, unpublished data. *Notes:* X Not applicable. 1. Includes other races, not shown separately. 2. Persons of Hispanic origin may be of any race. 3. Includes equivalency. 4. Excludes children whose parent is in the Armed Forces.

★ 818 ★

Children

Living Arrangements: Parent(s) with Whom Children Under 18 Live, by Educational Attainment and Employment Status of Parent(s), and Race/Ethnic Origin: 1994-II

[In thousands. As of March. Covers only those persons under 18 years old who are living with one or both parents. Characteristics are shown for the householder or reference person in married-couple situations].

CHARACTERISTICS OF PARENT	BLACK				HISPANIC[2]			
	Total	Living with-			Total	Living with-		
		Both parents	Mother only	Father only		Both parents	Mother only	Father only
Children under 18 years old	10,106	3,722	5,967	417	9,041	6,022	2,646	373
Educational attainment:								
Less than 9th grade	268	116	126	26	2,716	1,967	653	96
9th to 12th grade, no diploma	2,085	405	1,618	62	1,951	1,083	789	79
High school graduate[3]	4,140	1,534	2,404	202	2,252	1,427	716	108
Some college, no degree or associate degree	2,689	1,049	1,543	96	1,513	1,032	405	76
Bachelor's degree	692	441	225	26	398	336	57	5
Graduate or professional degree	232	177	51	5	211	176	26	9
Employment status[4]								
In the civilian labor force	6,826	3,012	3,469	345	6,699	5,129	1,252	318
Employed	5,736	2,739	2,692	304	6,042	4,710	1,057	275
Both parents employed	2,021	2,021	(X)	(X)	2,322	2,322	(X)	(X)
Unemployed	1,090	273	777	40	657	419	195	44
Not in the labor force	3,102	543	2,490	69	2,251	802	1,394	55

Source: "Living Arrangements of Children Under 18 Years Old, by Selected Characteristic of Parent: 1994," *Statistical Abstract of the United States: 1995*, 1995, p. 65. Primary source: U.S. Bureau of the Census, unpublished data. *Notes:* X Not applicable. 1. Includes other races, not shown separately. 2. Persons of Hispanic origin may be of any race. 3. Includes equivalency. 4. Excludes children whose parent is in the Armed Forces.

★ 819 ★

Children

Living Arrangements: Parent(s) with Whom Children Under 18 Live, by Family Income, Home Tenure, and Race/Ethnic Origin: 1994-I

[In thousands. As of March. Covers only those persons under 18 years old who are living with one or both parents. Characteristics are shown for the householder or reference person in married-couple situations].

CHARACTERISTIC OF PARENT	All races[1] total	WHITE			
		Total	Living with-		
			Both parents	Mother only	Father only
Children under 18 years old	66,674	53,200	41,766	9,724	1,710
Family income					
Under $5,000	3,651	2,049	492	1,414	143

[Continued]

★ 819 ★

Living Arrangements: Parent(s) with Whom Children Under 18 Live, by Family Income, Home Tenure, and Race/Ethnic Origin: 1994-I

[Continued]

CHARACTERISTIC OF PARENT	All races[1] total	WHITE			
		Total	Living with-		
			Both parents	Mother only	Father only
$5,000 to $9,999	5,607	3,375	1,102	2,127	146
$10,000 to $14,999	4,870	3,371	1,885	1,304	180
$15,000 to $24,999	9,579	7,320	4,988	1,884	448
$25,000 to $29,999	4,603	3,762	3,010	585	166
$30,000 to $39,999	8,790	7,282	5,943	1,085	254
$40,000 to $49,999	7,655	6,694	6,059	468	167
$50,000 and over	21,921	19,349	18,288	857	204
Tenure:[5]					
Owned	41,506	36,136	31,348	3,863	925
Rented	25,168	17,064	10,418	5,861	785

Source: "Living Arrangements of Children Under 18 Years Old, by Selected Characteristic of Parent: 1994," *Statistical Abstract of the United States: 1995,* 1995, p. 65. Primary source: U.S. Bureau of the Census, unpublished data. *Notes:* X Not applicable. 1. Includes other races, not shown separately. 2. Persons of Hispanic origin may be of any race. 3. Includes equivalency. 4. Excludes children whose parent is in the Armed Forces. 5. Refers to the tenure of the householder (who may or may not be the child's parent).

★ 820 ★
Children

Living Arrangements: Parent(s) with Whom Children Under 18 Live, by Family Income, Home Tenure, and Race/Ethnic Origin: 1994-II

[**In thousands.** As of **March.** Covers only those persons under 18 years old who are living with one or both parents. Characteristics are shown for the householder or reference person in married-couple situations].

CHARACTERISTIC OF PARENT	BLACK				HISPANIC[2]			
	Total	Living with-			Total	Living with-		
		Both parents	Mother only	Father only		Both parents	Mother only	Father only
Children under 18 years old	10,106	3,722	5,967	417	9,041	6,022	2,646	373
Family income								
Under $5,000	1,428	106	1,261	60	666	164	461	42
$5,000 to $9,999	1,980	195	1,737	48	1,207	398	781	28
$10,000 to $14,999	1,170	199	916	55	1,242	741	438	63
$15,000 to $24,999	1,767	626	1,038	103	2,094	1,482	500	112
$25,000 to $29,999	629	316	270	42	791	655	99	28
$30,000 to $39,999	1,092	659	408	25	1,143	906	191	45
$40,000 to $49,999	682	480	156	46	678	575	76	27
$50,000 and over	1,357	1,140	181	36	1,221	1,090	103	27

[Continued]

★ 820 ★

Living Arrangements: Parent(s) with Whom Children Under 18 Live, by Family Income, Home Tenure, and Race/Ethnic Origin: 1994-II

[Continued]

CHARACTERISTIC OF PARENT	BLACK				HISPANIC[2]			
	Total	Living with-			Total	Living with-		
		Both parents	Mother only	Father only		Both parents	Mother only	Father only
Tenure:[5]								
Owned	3,569	2,156	1,289	125	3,523	2,897	510	116
Rented	6,537	1,566	4,678	293	5,518	3,125	2,137	257

Source: "Living Arrangements of Children Under 18 Years Old, by Selected Characteristic of Parent: 1994," *Statistical Abstract of the United States: 1995,* 1995, p. 65. Primary source: U.S. Bureau of the Census, unpublished data. *Notes:* X Not applicable. 1. Includes other races, not shown separately. 2. Persons of Hispanic origin may be of any race. 3. Includes equivalency. 4. Excludes children whose parent is in the Armed Forces. 5. Refers to the tenure of the householder (who may or may not be the child's parent).

★ 821 ★

Children

Poverty: Trends in Children Living in Poverty, by Race/Ethnic Origin: 1970-1993

[Persons as of **March of the following year.** Covers only related children in families under 18 years old. Based on Current Population Survey].

YEAR	NUMBER BELOW POVERTY LEVEL (1,000)				PERCENT BELOW POVERTY LEVEL			
	All races[1]	White	Black	Hispanic[2]	All races[1]	White	Black	Hispanic[2]
1970	10,235	6,138	3,922	(NA)	14.9	10.5	41.5	(NA)
1975	10,882	6,748	3,884	1,619	16.8	12.5	41.4	33.1
1980	11,114	6,817	3,906	1,718	17.9	13.4	42.1	33.0
1981	12,068	7,429	4,170	1,874	19.5	14.7	44.9	35.4
1982	13,139	8,282	4,388	2,117	21.3	16.5	47.3	38.9
1983[3]	13,427	8,534	4,273	2,251	21.8	17.0	46.2	37.7
1984	12,929	8,086	4,320	2,317	21.0	16.1	46.2	38.7
1985	12,483	7,838	4,057	2,512	20.1	15.6	43.1	38.6
1986	12,257	7,714	4,037	2,413	19.8	15.3	42.7	37.1
1987[4]	12,275	7,398	4,234	2,606	19.7	14.7	44.4	38.9
1988	11,935	7,095	4,148	2,576	19.0	14.0	42.8	37.3
1989	12,001	7,164	4,257	2,496	19.0	14.1	43.2	35.5
1990	12,715	7,696	4,412	2,750	19.9	15.1	44.2	37.7
1991	13,658	8,316	4,637	2,977	21.1	16.1	45.6	39.8
1992[5]	14,521	8,752	5,015	3,440	21.6	16.5	46.3	39.0
1993	14,961	9,123	5,030	3,666	22.0	17.0	45.9	39.9

Source: "Children Below Poverty Level, by Race and Hispanic Origin: 1970 to 1993," *Statistical Abstract of the United States: 1995,* 1995, p. 480. Primary source: U.S. Bureau of the Census, *Current Population Reports,* P60-188. *Notes:* NA Not available. 1. Includes other races not shown separately. 2. Persons of Hispanic origin may be of any race. 3. Beginning 1983, data based on revised Hispanic population controls and not directly comparable with prior years. 4. Beginning 1987, data based on revised processing procedures and not directly comparable with prior years. 5. Beginning 1992, based on 1990, population controls.

★ 822 ★
Children

Relationships: Age of Own Black Children in Families, by Age of Householder: 1994. Part 1

[Numbers in thousands, except for averages and medians].

Characteristic	Total	Age of Householder				
		Under 20 years	20 to 24 years	25 to 29 years	30 to 34 years	35 to 39 years
BLACK-ALL FAMILIES						
Age of Own Children						
Families	7,969	65	510	882	1,181	1,178
With own children of any age	6,234	57	425	762	1,082	1,096
Under 25 years	5,456	57	424	761	1,077	1,096
Under 18 years	4,793	57	421	761	1,077	1,020
Under 12 years	3,647	57	421	751	975	704
Under 6 years	2,266	57	409	614	592	355
Under 3 years	1,306	53	325	355	317	163
Under 1 year	417	25	108	107	89	62
Six to 17 years	3,687	-	63	472	895	900
Total own children	12,804	68	653	1,522	2,292	2,216
Under 25 years	10,967	68	652	1,518	2,280	2,215
Under 18 years	8,884	68	649	1,518	2,265	1,880
Under 12 years	5,966	68	649	1,453	1,691	1,039
Under 6 years	3,005	68	587	867	778	413
Under 3 years	1,460	56	358	402	352	184
Under 1 year	420	19	101	110	94	64
Six to 17 years	5,879	-	63	651	1,488	1,466
Own Children, Selected Ages						
Families with own children						
under 18	4,793	57	421	761	1,077	1,020
Under 6 only	1,105	57	358	289	183	120
Some under 6 and some 6 to 17	1,161	-	51	325	410	235
Six to 17 only	2,526	-	12	147	485	665
Total members	17,727	126	1,212	2,610	3,883	3,791
Average per family	3.70	(B)	2.88	3.43	3.60	3.72

Source: "Families, by Type, Age of Own children, and Age, Race, and Hispanic Origin of Householder: March 1994," Rawlings, S.W., and Saluter, A.F., *Household and Family Characteristics: March 1994*, p. 21. *Note:* B = Base less than 75,000.

★ 823 ★
Children

Relationships: Age of Own Black Children in Families, by Age of Householder: 1994. Part 2

[Numbers in thousands, except for averages and medians].

Characteristic	Age of Householder						
	40 to 44 years	45 to 54 years	55 to 64 years	65 to 74 years	75 to 84 years	85 years and over	Median age
BLACK-ALL FAMILIES							
Age of Own Children							
Families	1,006	1,379	844	613	290	41	40.9
With own children of any age	851	1,069	482	300	95	16	38.6
Under 25 years	837	914	229	49	10	2	36.9
Under 18 years	711	606	118	20	1	2	35.4
Under 12 years	418	265	47	10	-	-	33.1
Under 6 years	159	59	15	7	-	-	30.5
Under 3 years	63	19	8	3	-	-	28.9
Under 1 year	17	8	-	-	-	-	28.5
Six to 17 years	656	577	109	13	1	2	37.3
Total own children	1,935	2,278	1,014	614	186	25	(X)
Under 25 years	1,898	1,816	407	96	16	1	(X)
Under 18 years	1,335	937	198	31	1	1	(X)
Under 12 years	621	357	74	11	-	-	(X)
Under 6 years	191	74	21	7	-	-	(X)
Under 3 years	70	26	8	4	-	-	(X)
Under 1 year	22	9	-	-	-	-	(X)
Six to 17 years	1,144	863	178	24	1	1	(X)
Own Children, Selected Ages							
Families with own children under 18	711	606	118	20	1	2	35.4
Under 6 only	55	29	9	7	-	-	27.4
Some under 6 and some 6 to 17	104	30	7	-	-	-	32.5
Six to 17 only	552	547	103	13	1	2	39.7
Total members	2,932	2,511	572	78	4	9	(X)
Average per family	4.13	4.15	4.85	(B)	(B)	(B)	(X)

Source: "Families, by Type, Age of Own children, and Age, Race, and Hispanic Origin of Householder: March 1994," Rawlings, S.W., and Saluter, A.F., *Household and Family Characteristics: March 1994*, p. 21. *Note:* B = base less than 75,000. X = not applicable. - Data not available.

★ 824 ★

Children

Relationships: Age of Own Black Children in Family Groups, by Householder's Educational Attainment: 1994

[Numbers in thousands except for averages and medians].

Characteristic	All householders						Householders under 45 years old					
	Total	Less than 9th grade	High school 9th to 12th grade, no diploma	High school graduate	College Some college	College Bachelor's or higher degree	Total	Less than 9th grade	High school 9th to 12th grade, no diploma	High school graduate	College Some college	College Bachelor's or higher degree
Age of Own Children												
Families	7,989	719	1,416	2,914	2,022	918	4,822	85	733	1,944	1,496	565
With own children of any age	6,234	369	1,118	2,360	1,727	661	4,272	72	676	1,728	1,359	438
Under 25 years	5,456	182	900	2,176	1,586	612	4,252	71	674	1,716	1,356	435
Under 18 years	4,793	130	800	1,914	1,419	530	4,046	70	654	1,630	1,276	416
Under 12 years	3,647	75	588	1,458	1,120	406	3,324	40	533	1,359	1,041	351
Under 6 years	2,266	29	411	97	662	257	2,185	19	394	877	648	248
Under 3 years	1,306	15	266	524	357	144	1,276	10	257	513	353	144
Under 1 year	417	3	88	157	112	58	409	3	88	150	110	58
Six to 17 years	3,687	123	604	1,507	1,079	374	2,985	66	466	1,243	947	263
Total own children	12,804	843	2,624	4,867	3,211	1,260	8,687	168	1,617	3,618	2,496	787
Under 25 years	10,967	434	2,063	4,408	2,905	1,157	8,631	168	1,604	3,596	2,483	780
Under 18 years	8,884	258	1,702	3,649	2,394	881	7,715	134	1,452	3,251	2,175	703
Under 12 years	5,966	114	1,156	2,434	1,687	575	5,523	64	1,068	2,296	1,582	512
Under 6 years	3,005	36	624	1,237	818	291	2,903	21	597	1,201	803	281
Under 3 years	1,460	19	295	611	390	144	1,423	12	285	597	385	144
Under 1 year	420	3	79	163	119	55	410	3	79	156	117	55
Six to 17 years	5,879	223	1,078	2,412	1,576	590	4,812	113	854	2,050	1,373	422
Own Children, Selected Ages												
Families with own children under 18	4,793	130	800	1,914	1,419	530	4,046	70	654	1,630	1,276	416
Under 6 only	1,105	7	195	407	339	156	1,061	4	188	386	329	153
Some under 6 and some 6 to 17	1,161	22	216	500	322	101	1,124	15	206	490	318	95
Six to 17 only	2,526	101	388	1,007	757	273	1,861	51	260	753	628	169
Total family members	17,727	573	3,246	7,088	4,865	1,954	14,554	278	2,547	5,936	4,314	1,479
Average per family	3.70	4.40	4.06	3.70	3.43	3.69	3.60	(B)	3.89	3.64	3.38	3.55

Source: "Families, by Type, Age of Own Children, and Educational Attainment, Race, and Hispanic Origin of Householder: March 1994," Rawlings, S.W., and Saluter, A.F., *Household and Family Characteristics: March 1994*, p. 63.

★ 825 ★
Children

Relationships: Age of Own Children in All Black Families and Families with Householders Under 45, by Family Type: 1994

[Numbers in thousands except for averages and medians].

Characteristic	All family householders				Family householders under 45			
	Total	Married-couple families	Other families		Total	Married-couple families	Other families	
			Male householder	Female householder			Male householder	Female householder
BLACK								
Total	7,989	3,714	450	3,825	4,822	1,853	313	2,656
Families With Own Children in Each Specified Age Group								
Under 25 years	5,456	2,186	266	3,004	4,252	1,507	210	2,536
18 to 24 only	663	262	28	373	206	49	14	143
12 to 17 only	767	291	44	42	521	148	31	342
6 to 11 only	642	227	51	364	537	166	37	334
3 to 5 only	332	96	15	220	318	86	14	218
Under 3 only	446	181	57	208	436	178	55	204
Under 18	4,793	1,924	238	2,630	4,046	1,458	196	2,392
12 to 17	2,200	914	69	1,217	1,650	562	48	1,040
6 to 17	3,687	1,515	154	2,018	2,985	1,071	115	1,799
6 to 11	2,366	971	102	1,293	2,098	793	84	1,222
3 to 11	3,143	1,237	129	1,777	2,837	1,037	110	1,690
3 to 5	1,484	551	50	884	1,421	509	45	867
Families With Own children in Each Specified Age group and No Others								
With children aged--								
18 to 24, and 12 to 17	379	192	9	178	201	78	-	122
18 to 24, and 6 to 11	99	50	1	48	67	27	1	38
18 to 24, and 3 to 5	16	9	-	7	6	4	-	2
18 to 24, and under 3	3	3	-	-	-	-	-	-
18 to 24, 12 to 17, and 6 to 11	126	62	2	62	95	34	2	59
18 to 24, 12 to 17, and 3 to 5	21	9	-	12	19	7	-	12
18 to 24, 12 to 17, and under 3	7	6	-	2	7	6	-	2
18 to 24, 12 to 17, 3 to 5, and under 3	-	-	-	-	-	-	-	-
18 to 24, 12 to 17, 6 to 11, and 3 to 5	8	3	-	5	4	-	-	4
18 to 24, 12 to 17, 6 to 11, under 3	5	-	-	5	5	-	-	5
18 to 24, 12 to 17, 6 to 11, 3 to 5, and under 3	9	2	-	6	9	2	-	6
18 to 24, 6 to 11, and 3 to 5	6	-	-	6	6	-	-	6
18 to 24, 6 to 11, and under 3	1	-	-	1	1	-	-	1
18 to 24, 6 to 11, 3 to 5, and under 3	-	-	-	-	-	-	-	-
18 to 24, 3 to 5, and under 3	2	-	-	2	-	-	-	-
12 to 17, and 6 to 11	513	229	14	270	441	182	14	244
12 to 17 and 3 to 5	83	26	-	57	80	22	-	57
12 to 17 and under 3	48	13	-	34	44	11	-	33
12 to 17, 6 to 11, and 3 to 5	128	40	-	88	121	33	-	88
12 to 17, 6 to 11, and under 3	45	17	-	28	45	17	-	28
12 to 17, 6 to 11, 3 to 5, and under 3	45	17	-	28	44	15	-	28
12 to 17, 3 to 5, and under 3	16	7	-	9	16	7	-	9
6 to 11 and 3 to 5	366	178	14	173	357	173	11	173
6 to 11 and under 3	227	102	10	115	225	102	10	113

[Continued]

★ 825 ★

Relationships: Age of Own Children in All Black Families and Families with Householders Under 45, by Family Type: 1994

[Continued]

Characteristic	All family householders				Family householders under 45			
	Total	Married-couple families	Other families		Total	Married-couple families	Other families	
			Male householder	Female householder			Male householder	Female householder
6 to 11, 3 to 5, and under 3	145	44	8	94	143	41	8	94
3 to 5 and under 3	307	119	12	176	301	119	12	170

Source: "Families, by Type, Age of Own Children, and Race and Hispanic Origin of Householder: March 1994," Rawlings, S.W., and Saluter, A.F., *Household and Family Characteristics: March 1994*, p. 83.

★ 826 ★

Children

Relationships: Age of Own Children in Black Families, in Relation to Family Type and Residence Area: 1994

Characteristic	United States				Metropolitan				Nonmetropolitan			
	Total	Married-couple families	Other families		Total	Married-couple families	Other families		Total	Married-couple families	Other families	
			Male house-holder	Female house-holder			Male house-holder	Female house-holder			Male house-holder	Female house-holder
BLACK FAMILIES												
Own Children, Selected Ages												
Families with own children under 18	4,793	1,924	238	2,630	4,146	1,647	218	2,281	647	277	20	349
Under 6 only	1,105	409	84	613	973	358	75	540	133	51	9	73
Some under 6 and some 6 to 17	1,161	464	33	664	1,021	401	29	591	140	64	3	73
6 to 17 only	2,526	1,050	122	1,354	2,152	888	114	1,150	374	162	8	204
Total family members	17,727	8,379	659	8,689	16,368	7,190	613	7,565	2,359	1,189	46	1,124
Average per family	3.70	4.36	2.76	3.30	3.71	4.37	2.81	3.32	3.65	4.29	(B)	3.22
Own Children Under 18												
Families	7,989	3,714	450	3,825	6,839	3,143	410	3,286	1,150	571	40	539
Without own children under 18	3,196	1,790	212	1,194	2,692	1,496	192	1,004	504	294	20	190
With own children under 18	4,793	1,924	238	2,630	4,146	1,647	218	2,281	647	277	20	349
One own child under 18	1,983	771	144	1,068	1,711	660	132	920	271	111	12	148
Two own children under 18	1,630	696	63	871	1,423	610	59	754	207	86	5	117
Three own children under 18	755	309	29	417	657	272	25	359	98	37	3	58
Four own children under 18	301	110	3	188	237	68	2	166	64	41	1	22
Five own children under 18	70	23	-	48	64	21	-	44	6	2	-	4
Six or more own children under 18	53	16	-	38	53	16	-	38	-	-	-	-
Total own children under 18	8,884	3,602	375	4,907	7,731	3,091	349	4,292	1,152	511	26	616
Average per family	1.11	.97	.83	1.28	1.13	.98	.85	1.31	1.00	.89	(B)	1.14
Average per family with children	1.85	1.87	1.57	1.87	1.86	1.88	1.60	1.88	1.78	1.84	(B)	1.76
Own Children Under 6												
Families	7,989	3,714	450	3,825	6,839	3,143	410	3,286	1,150	571	40	539
Without own children under 6	5,722	2,841	334	2,548	4,845	2,384	306	2,155	878	457	28	393
With own children under 6	2,266	873	117	1,277	1,994	759	104	1,131	272	115	12	145

[Continued]

★ 826 ★

Relationships: Age of Own Children in Black Families, in Relation to Family Type and Residence Area: 1994

[Continued]

Characteristic	United States				Metropolitan				Nonmetropolitan			
	Total	Married-couple families	Other families		Total	Married-couple families	Other families		Total	Married-couple families	Other families	
			Male house-holder	Female house-holder			Male house-holder	Female house-holder			Male house-holder	Female house-holder
One own child under 6	1,494	610	76	808	1,315	533	67	715	179	77	9	93
Two own children under 6	588	210	38	340	511	182	35	294	77	28	3	46
Three own children under 6	145	35	3	107	137	34	3	100	8	2	-	7
Four or more children under 6	40	18	-	22	32	10	-	22	8	8	-	-
Total own children under 6	3,005	1,133	157	1,715	2,657	989	144	1,525	348	144	13	190
Average per family	.38	.31	.35	.45	.39	.31	.35	.46	.30	.25	(B)	.35
Average per family with children	1.33	1.30	1.35	1.34	1.33	1.30	1.38	1.35	1.28	1.26	(B)	1.31
Own Children Under 3												
Families	7,989	3,714	450	3,825	6,839	3,143	410	3,286	1,150	571	40	539
Without own children under 3	6,683	3,203	363	3,117	5,690	2,699	334	2,657	992	504	29	459
With own children under 3	1,306	511	87	708	1,148	444	76	628	158	67	11	80
One own child under 3	1,074	442	76	557	936	383	68	485	138	58	8	72
Two or more children under 3	232	69	11	151	212	60	8	143	20	9	3	8
Total own children under 3	1,460	561	97	802	1,295	495	84	716	164	67	12	86
Average per family	.18	.15	.21	.21	.19	.16	.21	.22	.14	.12	(B)	.16
Average per family with children	1.12	1.10	1.11	1.13	1.13	1.12	1.11	1.14	1.04	(B)	(B)	1.08

Source: "Families, by Type, Age, Metropolitan-Nonmetropolitan Residence, and Race and Hispanic Origin of Householder: March 1994," Rawlings, S.W., and Saluter, A.F., *Household and Family Characteristics: March 1994*, pp. 3-4. *Note:* B = Base less than 75,000.

★ 827 ★

Children

Relationships: Own Black Children Under 18, in Families, by Subfamily Type: 1994

[Numbers in thousands, except for averages and medians].

Characteristic	All subfamilies				Related subfamilies				Unrelated subfamilies			
	Total	Married-couple	Father-child	Mother-child	Total	Married-couple	Father-child	Mother-child	Total	Married-couple	Father-child	Mother-child
Own Children Under 18												
Total	867	99	48	719	778	95	40	644	89	4	9	76
Without own children under 18	45	45	-	-	43	43	-	-	2	2	-	-
With own children under 18	822	54	48	719	735	52	40	644	87	2	9	76
One own child under 18	570	28	45	497	501	25	37	439	69	2	9	58
Two own children under 18	165	14	3	148	152	14	3	135	13	-	-	13
Three own children under 18	55	7	-	48	49	7	-	43	5	-	-	5
Four own children under 18	21	5	-	17	21	5	-	17	-	-	-	-
Five own children under 18	11	1	-	10	11	1	-	10	-	-	-	-
Six or more own children under 18	-	-	-	-	-	-	-	-	-	-	-	-
Total own children under 18	1,107	92	48	967	1,010	89	40	880	97	3	8	87
Average per subfamily	1.28	.93	(B)	1.35	1.30	.94	(B)	1.37	1.10	(B)	(B)	1.15
Average per subfamily with children	1.35	(B)	(B)	1.35	1.37	(B)	(B)	1.7	1.12	(B)	(B)	1.15

Source: "Subfamilies, by Type, Race, and Hispanic Origin of Reference Person: March 1994," Rawlings, S.W., and Saluter, A.F., *Household and Family Characteristics: March 1994*, p. 129. *Note:* B = Base less than 75,000.

Family Types

★ 828 ★

Heads/Householders: Trends in Married Couple, Male-Headed, and Female- Headed Households, by Race/Ethnic Origin: 1970-1994

(Numbers in thousands).

Type of family	1994	1993[1]	1993	1990	1982	1970	Average annual percent change		
							1990-94	1980-90	1970-80
ALL RACES									
Family households	68,490	68,216	68,144	66,090	59,550	51,456	0.9	1.0	1.5
Married-couple families	53,171	53,090	53,171	52,317	49,112	44,728	0.4	0.6	0.9
Male householder, no wife present	2,913	3,065	3,026	2,884	1,733	1,228	0.3	5.1	3.4
Female householder, no husband present	12,406	12,061	11,947	10,890	8,705	5,500	3.3	2.2	4.6
WHITE									
Family households	57,870	57,669	57,858	56,590	52,243	46,166	0.6	0.8	1.2
Married-couple families	47,443	47,383	47,601	46,981	44,751	41,029	0.2	0.5	0.9
Male householder, no wife present	2,297	2,418	2,409	2,303	1,441	1,038	-0.1	4.7	3.3
Female householder, no husband present	8,130	7,868	7,848	7,306	6,052	4,099	2.7	1.9	3.9
BLACK									
Family households	7,989	7,982	7,888	7,470	6,184	4,856	1.7	1.9	2.4
Married-couple families	3,714	3,777	3,748	3,750	3,433	3,317	-0.2	0.9	0.3
Male householder, no wife present	450	467	460	446	256	181	0.2	5.6	3.5
Female householder, no husband present	3,825	3,738	3,680	3,275	2,495	1,358	3.9	2.7	6.1
ASIAN OR PACIFIC ISLANDER[2]									
Family households	1,737	1,760	1,662	1,531	818	(NA)	3.2	6.3	(NA)
Married-couple families	1,426	1,409	1,335	1,256	691	(NA)	3.2	6.0	(NA)
Male householder, no wife present	79	106	95	86	39	(NA)	-2.1	7.9	(NA)
Female householder, no husband present	232	245	232	188	88	(NA)	5.3	7.6	(NA)
HISPANIC[3]									
Family households	5,940	5,733	5,318	4,840	3,029	2,004	5.1	4.7	4.1

[Continued]

★ 828 ★

Heads/Householders: Trends in Married Couple, Male-Headed, and Female- Headed Households, by Race/Ethnic Origin: 1970-1994

[Continued]

Type of family	1994	1993¹	1993	1990	1982	1970	Average annual percent change		
							1990-94	1980-90	1970-80
Married-couple families	4,033	3,940	3,674	3,395	2,282	1,615	4.3	4.0	3.5
Male householder, no wife present	410	445	407	329	138	82	5.5	8.7	5.2
Female householder, no husband present	1,498	1,348	1,238	1,116	610	307	7.4	6.0	6.9

Source: "Family Households, by Type, Race and Hispanic Origin of Householder: 1970-1994," Rawlings, S.W., and Saluter, A.F., *Household and Family Characteristics: March 1994*, p. xiii. *Notes:* NA Not available. 1. Revised using population controls based on the 1990 Census. 2. 1980 data for Asian or Pacific Islander from 1980 Census of Population, Vol. I, Table 141. 3. Persons of Hispanic origin may be of any race. 1970 Hispanic data from 1970 Census of Population, Vol. II, 4A, Table 6.

★ 829 ★
Family Types

Relationships: Age and Gender in Black Female-Headed Families, by Age of Householder: 1994

[Numbers in thousands except for averages and medians].

Characteristic	Total	Age of householder										
		Under 20 years	20 to 24 years	25 to 29 years	30 to 34 years	35 to 39 years	40 to 44 years	45 to 54 years	55 to 64 years	65 to 74 years	75 to 84 years	85 years and over
BLACK--OTHER FAMILIES, FEMALE HOUSEHOLDER												
With members of either sex:												
Total families	3,825	58	359	496	657	643	440	533	301	208	105	22
Under 6 years	1,636	56	334	370	319	198	100	126	85	38	9	1
6 to 11 years	1,510	-	57	331	426	282	158	128	73	44	9	1
12 to 17 years	1,415	4	17	58	341	423	241	173	94	49	12	2
18 to 24 years	1,283	56	359	23	34	204	200	248	89	45	19	5
25 to 34 years	1,803	-	15	498	657	19	26	177	130	69	12	2
35 to 44 years	1,294	2	14	3	1	643	440	26	64	59	39	2
45 to 64 years	1,001	-	8	25	27	2	13	533	301	53	34	5
65 to 74 years	261	-	3	-	5	8	4	11	2	208	11	8
75 years and over	168	-	-	-	-	5	5	14	9	9	105	22
Families with male members	2,756	37	250	375	449	480	332	390	123	155	61	14
Under 6 years	929	35	228	217	181	91	47	65	48	16	-	1
6 to 11 years	869	-	27	195	244	170	85	78	38	26	5	1
12 to 17 years	843	-	3	36	181	250	163	120	49	34	6	-
18 to 24 years	535	2	5	13	10	154	123	141	38	34	10	5
25 to 34 years	271	-	7	9	14	14	20	106	67	28	2	2
35 to 44 years	108	2	-	3	-	7	4	13	32	27	20	-
45 to 64 years	83	-	3	5	6	-	6	7	10	30	17	-
65 to 74 years	13	-	-	-	-	1	-	-	.	5	5	2
75 years and over	15	-	-	-	-	2	-	4	4	-	2	3
Families with female members	3,825	58	359	498	657	643	440	533	301	208	105	22
Under 6 years	1,022	41	201	232	194	128	61	80	51	24	9	-
6 to 11 years	927	-	35	226	272	157	90	78	42	24	3	-
12 to 17 years	788	4	14	28	210	253	120	72	52	27	6	2
18 to 24 years	838	54	359	10	24	71	98	146	51	16	10	-
25 to 34 years	1,399	-	8	498	657	4	6	91	80	46	9	-
35 to 44 years	1,203	3	14	-	1	643	440	12	32	34	21	2
45 to 64 years	948	-	8	22	21	2	7	533	301	28	20	5

[Continued]

★ 829 ★

Relationships: Age and Gender in Black Female-Headed Families, by Age of Householder: 1994
[Continued]

Characteristic	Total	Age of householder										
		Under 20 years	20 to 24 years	25 to 29 years	30 to 34 years	35 to 39 years	40 to 44 years	45 to 54 years	55 to 64 years	65 to 74 years	75 to 84 years	85 years and over
65 to 74 years	253	-	3	-	5	8	4	11	2	208	6	6
75 years and over	162	-	-	-	-	3	5	10	9	9	105	22

Source: "Families, by Type, Age and Sex of Members, and Age, Race, and Hispanic Origin of Householder: March 1994," Rawlings, S.W., and Saluter, A.F., *Household and Family Characteristics: March 1994*, pp. 76-77.

★ 830 ★
Family Types

Relationships: Age and Gender in Black Male-Headed Families, by Age of Householder: 1994

[Numbers in thousands except for averages and medians].

Characteristic	Total	Age of householder										
		Under 20 years	20 to 24 years	25 to 29 years	30 to 34 years	35 to 39 years	40 to 44 years	45 to 54 years	55 to 64 years	65 to 74 years	75 to 84 years	85 years and over
BLACK--OTHER FAMILIES, MALE HOUSEHOLDER												
With members of either sex:												
Total families	450	6	33	67	91	70	45	63	25	31	13	5
Under 6 years	148	-	15	34	51	22	9	13	2	1	-	-
6 to 11 years	129	-	4	18	39	23	11	20	6	4	-	3
12 to 17 years	88	2	-	3	17	20	13	17	4	9	2	-
18 to 24 years	98	6	33	6	8	6	11	16	6	5	1	-
25 to 34 years	218	2	7	67	91	12	-	13	5	14	4	3
35 to 44 years	149	-	6	5	6	70	45	7	2	8	-	-
45 to 64 years	132	4	7	11	2	4	3	63	25	4	7	2
65 to 74 years	55	-	2	4	3	5	10	-	-	31	-	-
75 years and over	27	-	-	-	-	-	4	-	2	3	13	5
Families with male members	450	6	33	67	91	70	45	63	25	31	13	5
Under 6 years	80	-	7	21	33	7	7	4	-	1	-	-
6 to 11 years	94	-	-	13	22	19	10	20	4	2	-	3
12 to 17 years	45	2	-	3	10	10	8	7	2	4	-	-
18 to 24 years	85	6	33	6	4	6	7	13	4	5	1	-
25 to 34 years	202	2	4	67	91	9	-	11	3	10	4	-
35 to 44 years	136	-	5	5	4	70	45	1	2	2	-	2
45 to 64 years	100	2	3	-	-	-	1	63	25	-	3	2
65 to 74 years	34	-	-	1	-	2	-	-	-	31	-	-
75 years and over	22	-	-	-	-	-	4	-	-	-	13	5
Families with female members	255	3	20	39	55	44	24	31	8	22	4	3
Under 6 years	96	-	8	20	34	19	3	9	2	1	-	-
6 to 11 years	43	-	4	5	19	8	1	-	2	2	-	-
12 to 17 years	48	-	-	-	8	14	6	11	2	5	2	-
18 to 24 years	18	1	3	-	4	-	5	4	2	-	-	-
25 to 34 years	33	-	3	5	4	2	-	5	2	8	-	3
35 to 44 years	19	-	2	-	2	-	2	7	-	6	-	-
45 to 64 years	35	3	5	11	2	4	1	1	-	4	3	-
65 to 74 years	21	-	2	2	3	3	10	-	-	-	-	-
75 years and over	6	-	-	-	-	-	-	-	2	3	-	-

Source: "Families, by Type, Age and Sex of Members, and Age, Race, and Hispanic Origin of Householder: March 1994," Rawlings, S.W., and Saluter, A.F., *Household and Family Characteristics, March 1994*, p. 77.

★ 831 ★

Family Types

Relationships: Age and Gender in Black Married-Couple Families, by Age of Householder: 1994

[Numbers in thousands except for averages and medians].

Characteristic	Total	Age of householder										
		Under 20 years	20 to 24 years	25 to 29 years	30 to 34 years	35 to 39 years	40 to 44 years	45 to 54 years	55 to 64 years	65 to 74 years	75 to 84 years	85 years and over
BLACK--MARRIED-COUPLE FAMILIES												
With members of either sex:												
Total families	3,714	1	117	317	433	465	520	783	517	374	172	14
Under 6 years	1,035	1	69	219	232	204	139	95	44	23	8	-
6 to 11 years	1,118	-	12	99	262	237	204	186	67	40	12	-
12 to 17 years	1,023	-	6	15	107	211	246	301	99	31	8	-
18 to 24 years	880	1	117	74	18	76	155	296	85	46	11	1
25 to 34 years	1,341	-	25	317	433	174	77	121	113	61	19	-
35 to 44 years	1,500	1	5	22	119	465	520	262	51	44	10	-
45 to 64 years	1,596	-	7	9	9	27	61	783	517	152	31	-
65 to 74 years	535	-	-	3	1	7	6	18	54	374	72	-
75 years and over	250	-	-	-	-	1	-	7	23	33	172	14
Families with male members	3,714	1	117	317	433	465	520	783	517	374	172	14
Under 6 years	624	-	49	129	146	121	76	55	25	16	5	-
6 to 11 years	611	-	7	63	144	145	102	92	34	19	4	-
12 to 17 years	593	-	4	5	36	140	150	179	50	20	8	-
18 to 24 years	512	-	105	10	2	38	82	180	53	30	11	-
25 to 34 years	887	-	12	285	377	22	21	63	71	33	4	-
35 to 44 years	1,058	1	-	19	60	435	484	05	19	17	8	-
45 to 64 years	1,303	-	4	5	1	9	27	759	483	12	2	-
65 to 74 years	414	-	-	-	1	-	2	9	35	363	4	-
75 years and over	208	-	-	-	-	1	-	4	9	9	170	14
Families with female members	3,714	1	117	317	433	465	520	783	517	374	172	14
Under 6 years	586	1	37	134	129	114	84	48	27	8	4	-
6 to 11 years	677	-	5	47	160	147	127	121	37	24	9	-
12 to 17 years	592	-	2	13	80	105	149	161	66	13	2	-
18 to 24 years	545	1	95	64	15	45	102	161	40	21	1	1
25 to 34 years	1,006	-	13	251	356	157	57	63	57	35	17	-
35 to 44 years	1,106	-	5	4	63	299	426	248	32	28	2	-
45 to 64 years	1,213	-	3	3	8	18	38	502	467	145	28	-
65 to 74 years	325	-	-	3	-	7	4	9	18	214	70	-
75 years and over	132	-	-	-	-	-	-	3	13	24	77	14

Source: "Families, by Type, Age and Sex of Members, and Age, Race, and Hispanic Origin of Householder: March 1994," Rawlings, S.W., and Saluter, A.F., *Household and Family Characteristics: March 1994*, pp. 75-76.

★ 832 ★

Family Types

Relationships: Age and Gender of All Black Family Members, by Age of Householder: 1994

[Numbers in thousands except for averages and medians].

Characteristic	Total	Age of householder										
		Under 20 years	20 to 24 years	25 to 29 years	30 to 34 years	35 to 39 years	40 to 44 years	45 to 54 years	55 to 64 years	65 to 74 years	75 to 84 years	85 years and over
BLACK--ALL FAMILIES												
With members of either sex:												
Total families	7,989	65	510	882	1,181	1,178	1,006	1,379	844	613	290	41
Under 6 years	2,818	57	418	623	603	424	248	235	132	62	17	1

[Continued]

★ 832 ★

Relationships: Age and Gender of All Black Family Members, by Age of Householder: 1994

[Continued]

Characteristic	Total	Age of householder										
		Under 20 years	20 to 24 years	25 to 29 years	30 to 34 years	35 to 39 years	40 to 44 years	45 to 54 years	55 to 64 years	65 to 74 years	75 to 84 years	85 years and over
6 to 11 years	2,756	-	73	448	727	542	373	334	146	88	20	4
12 to 17 years	2,525	6	23	77	465	654	500	491	197	88	22	2
18 to 24 years	2,261	63	510	103	59	285	367	560	180	96	31	6
25 to 34 years	3,163	2	47	882	1,181	204	104	311	248	143	34	5
35 to 44 years	2,943	3	25	31	26	1,178	1,006	295	117	111	50	2
45 to 64 years	2,729	4	21	44	38	33	77	1,379	844	210	71	7
65 to 74 years	851	-	5	6	9	20	21	29	56	613	84	8
75 years and over	446	-	-	-	-	6	9	22	33	45	290	41
Families with male members	6,920	44	400	759	973	1,014	897	1,236	755	561	246	33
Under 6 years	1,633	35	285	368	361	219	130	125	73	33	5	1
6 to 11 years	1,575	-	34	272	410	334	197	190	76	48	10	4
12 to 17 years	1,481	2	7	45	227	400	321	306	100	58	14	-
18 to 24 years	1,132	9	143	29	16	197	212	334	95	69	22	5
25 to 34 years	1,359	2	23	361	482	45	41	181	141	71	10	2
35 to 44 years	1,302	3	5	27	64	512	533	30	53	46	29	-
45 to 64 years	1,486	2	10	10	6	9	34	829	518	43	22	2
65 to 74 years	461	-	-	1	1	3	2	9	35	399	9	2
75 years and over	245	-	-	-	-	3	4	8	14	9	185	22
Families with female members	7,793	62	497	854	1,145	1,152	985	1,347	827	604	281	39
Under 6 years	1,706	42	246	386	358	262	148	137	80	32	14	-
6 to 11 years	1,647	-	44	279	451	312	218	199	82	50	12	-
12 to 17 years	1,426	4	17	41	298	372	274	244	121	45	10	2
18 to 24 years	1,402	55	457	74	43	116	205	311	93	36	11	1
25 to 34 years	2,438	-	24	755	1,016	164	62	160	140	89	26	3
35 to 44 years	2,327	2	21	4	66	942	868	267	64	68	23	2
45 to 64 years	2,196	3	15	36	31	24	46	1,037	769	177	52	5
65 to 74 years	598	-	5	5	7	18	19	20	21	421	77	6
75 years and over	300	-	-	-	-	3	5	14	24	36	182	36

Source: "Families, by Type, Age and Sex of Members, and Age, Race, and Hispanic Origin of Householder: March 1994," Rawlings, S.W., and Saluter, A.F., *Household and Family Characteristics: March 1994*, p.75.

★ 833 ★

Family Types

Relationships: Age of Black Family Members, in Relation to Family Type and Residence Area: 1994

[Numbers in thousands except for averages and medians].

Characteristic	United States				Metropolitan				Nonmetropolitan			
	Total	Married-couple families	Other families		Total	Married-couple families	Other families		Total	Married-couple families	Other families	
			Male house-holder	Female house-holder			Male house-holder	Female house-holder			Male house-holder	Female house-holder
BLACK FAMILIES												
Members Under 18												
Families	7,969	3,714	450	3,825	6,839	3,143	410	3,286	1,150	571	40	539
No members under 18	2,457	1,561	156	739	2,076	1,313	137	626	381	248	19	114
One member under 18	2,252	828	173	1,251	1,928	699	161	1,067	324	129	12	183
Two members under 18	1,825	802	79	943	1,588	698	73	817	236	105	5	126
Three members under 18	869	326	30	513	763	284	27	453	106	43	3	60
Four members under 18	379	131	13	235	298	88	12	198	81	43	1	37
Five members under 18	117	41	-	76	96	38	-	59	20	3	-	17
Six or more members under 18	91	24	-	68	90	24	-	66	2	-	-	2

[Continued]

★ 833 ★

Relationships: Age of Black Family Members, in Relation to Family Type and Residence Area: 1994

[Continued]

Characteristic	United States				Metropolitan				Nonmetropolitan			
	Total	Married-couple families	Other families		Total	Married-couple families	Other families		Total	Married-couple families	Other families	
			Male house-holder	Female house-holder			Male house-holder	Female house-holder			Male house-holder	Female house-holder
Total members under 18	10,807	4,213	482	6,111	9,360	3,602	455	5,303	1,447	611	28	809
Average per family	1.35	1.13	1.07	1.60	1.37	1.15	1.11	1.61	1.26	1.07	(B)	1.50
Members 18 to 64												
Families	7,989	3,714	450	3,825	6,839	3,143	410	3,286	1,150	571	40	539
No members 18 to 64	351	276	7	68	267	213	6	48	84	63	1	20
One member 18 to 64	2,917	241	265	2,411	2,501	196	239	2,066	416	45	26	345
Two members 18 to 64	3,412	2,344	141	927	2,930	1,998	130	802	482	346	11	125
Three members 18 to 64	952	595	32	325	821	506	29	285	131	89	3	40
Four members 18 to 64	279	195	5	78	254	179	5	70	25	17	-	8
Five or members 18 to 64	77	62	-	16	66	51	-	15	12	11	-	1
Total members 18 to 64	15,496	8,344	761	6,391	13,354	7,136	688	5,531	2,142	1,208	73	860
Average per family	1.94	2.25	1.69	1.67	1.95	2.27	1.68	1.68	1.86	2.12	(B)	1.60
Members 65 and Over												
Families	7,989	3,714	450	3,825	6,839	3,143	410	3,286	1,150	571	40	539
No members 65 and over	6,840	3,041	376	3,424	5,913	2,610	342	2,961	927	431	34	462
One member 65 and over	693	282	66	345	580	231	61	289	113	52	5	56
Two members 65 and over	434	375	8	51	325	288	7	30	109	87	1	21
Three or more members 65 and over	22	17	-	5	20	15	-	5	2	2	-	-
Total members 65 and over	1,647	1,088	84	475	1,310	857	77	376	337	231	7	99
Average per family	.21	.29	.19	.12	.19	.27	.19	.11	.29	.40	(B)	.18

Source: "Families, by Type, Age, Metropolitan-Nonmetropolitan Residence, and Race and Hispanic Origin of Householder: March 1994," Rawlings, S.W., and Saluter, A.F., *Household and Family Characteristics: March 1994*, p. 3. *Note:* B = Base less than 75,000.

★ 834 ★

Family Types

Relationships: Size of Black Families in Relation to Family Type and Householder's Educational Attainment: 1994

[Numbers in thousands except for averages and medians].

Characteristic	All householders						Householders under 45 years old					
	Total	Less than 9th grade	High school		College		Total	Less than 9th grade	High school		College	
			9th to 12th grade, no diploma	High school graduate	Some college	Bachelor's or higher degree			9th to 12th grade, no diploma	High school graduate	Some college	Bachelor's or higher degree
BLACK--ALL FAMILIES												
Size of family												
Families	7,989	719	1,416	2,914	2,022	918	4,822	85	733	1,944	1,496	565
Two persons	2,701	332	415	917	682	356	1,343	28	154	525	431	204
Three persons	2,184	151	384	814	585	250	1,339	13	179	539	448	160

[Continued]

★ 834 ★

Relationships: Size of Black Families in Relation to Family Type and Householder's Educational Attainment: 1994

[Continued]

Characteristic	All householders						Householders under 45 years old					
	Total	Less than 9th grade	High school		College		Total	Less than 9th grade	High school		College	
			9th to 12th grade, no diploma	High school graduate	Some college	Bachelor's or higher degree			9th to 12th grade, no diploma	High school graduate	Some college	Bachelor's or higher degree
Four persons	1,688	93	287	658	461	190	1,176	14	181	492	371	118
Five persons	790	81	148	301	191	69	548	18	96	225	160	48
Six persons	338	33	82	115	67	40	234	7	58	84	59	25
Seven or more persons	289	29	100	109	37	13	182	3	65	79	26	9
Total persons	27,950	2,661	5,390	10,200	6,681	3,018	16,633	321	2,786	6,786	4,907	1,833
Average per family	3.50	3.70	3.81	3.50	3.30	3.29	3.45	3.78	3.80	3.49	3.28	3.24

BLACK--MARRIED-COUPLE FAMILIES

Size of Family

Characteristic	All householders						Householders under 45 years old					
Families	3,714	396	480	1,336	891	610	1,853	18	136	742	602	354
Two persons	1,088	204	152	342	212	178	316	2	20	121	89	84
Three persons	882	65	110	330	220	157	404	4	20	151	135	95
Four persons	957	49	105	374	268	162	626	6	44	260	217	99
Five persons	439	42	55	149	129	64	288	3	24	106	111	44
Six persons	209	23	29	80	39	37	139	4	16	59	35	24
Seven or more persons	139	13	30	62	23	11	79	-	12	45	16	7
Total persons	13,645	1,363	1,876	4,992	3,249	2,165	7,162	76	581	2,954	2,279	1,273
Average per family	3.67	3.44	3.91	3.74	3.64	3.55	3.87	(B)	4.27	3.98	3.78	3.59

BLACK--OTHER FAMILIES, FEMALE HOUSEHOLDER

Size of Family

Characteristic	All householders						Householders under 45 years old					
Families	3,825	272	866	1,392	1,028	266	2,656	53	560	1,054	814	175
Two persons	1,362	96	220	496	396	154	866	18	117	344	287	99
Three persons	1,193	77	269	417	349	81	844	6	155	328	299	54
Four persons	657	39	165	247	182	24	498	9	125	204	144	16
Five persons	340	34	89	150	62	5	253	13	68	119	49	4
Six persons	129	10	54	35	28	2	95	3	42	25	24	1
Seven or more persons	144	16	70	47	11	-	100	3	53	34	10	-
Total persons	12,977	1,135	3,303	4,641	3,163	735	8,568	205	2,085	3,391	2,429	458
Average per family	3.39	4.17	3.82	3.33	3.08	2.76	3.23	(B)	3.72	3.22	.98	2.62

BLACK--OTHER FAMILIES, MALE HOUSEHOLDER

Size of Family

Characteristic	All householders						Householders under 45 years old					
Families	450	50	70	186	103	42	313	14	37	148	79	36
Two persons	251	32	43	79	73	24	160	8	17	59	55	21
Three persons	109	8	5	68	17	11	91	3	4	60	14	10
Four persons	74	5	17	37	10	4	52	-	11	28	10	2
Five persons	11	5	4	2	-	-	7	2	4	1	-	-
Six persons	-	-	-	-	-	-	-	-	-	-	-	-
Seven or persons	6	-	-	-	3	2	3	-	-	-	-	2
Total persons	1,327	163	211	566	269	118	903	40	120	442	200	102
Average per family	2.95	(B)	(B)	3.05	2.61	(B)	2.88	(B)	(B)	2.99	2.52	(B)

Source: "Families, by Type, Age of Own Children, and Educational Attainment, Race, and Hispanic Origin of Householder: March 1994," Rawlings, S.W., and Saluter, A.F., *Household and Family Characteristics: March 1994*, pp. 63-65. *Note:* B = Base less than 75,000.

★ 835 ★

Family Types

Relationships: Size of Black Families, in Relation to Family Type and Age of Householder: 1994. Part 1

[Numbers in thousands except for averages and medians].

Characteristic	Total	Age of householder				
		Under 20 years	20 to 24 years	25 to 29 years	30 to 34 years	35 to 39 years
BLACK--ALL FAMILIES						
Size of family						
Families	7,989	65	510	882	1,181	1,178
Two persons	2,701	32	209	234	286	289
Three persons	2,184	22	150	272	329	320
Four persons	1,688	11	97	211	328	299
Five persons	790	-	41	104	128	148
Six persons	338	-	10	45	46	66
Seven or more persons	289	-	3	18	63	56
Total persons	27,950	156	1,446	2,904	4,132	4,205
Average per family	3.50	(B)	2.84	3.29	3.50	3.57
BLACK--MARRIED-COUPLE FAMILIES						
Size of Family						
Families	3,714	1	117	317	433	465
Two persons	1,088	-	37	71	60	55
Three persons	882	1	41	95	83	87
Four persons	957	-	24	92	179	170
Five persons	439	-	15	29	65	82
Six persons	209	-	-	26	24	45
Seven or more persons	139	-	-	5	23	26
Total persons	13,645	2	367	1,093	1,676	1,900
Average per family	3.67	(B)	3.13	3.45	3.87	4.09
BLACK--OTHER FAMILIES, FEMALE HOUSEHOLDER						
Size of Family						
Families	3,825	58	359	498	657	643
Two persons	1,362	29	153	133	186	194
Three persons	1,193	19	100	149	226	215
Four persons	657	11	67	112	119	122
Five persons	340	-	26	73	63	62
Six persons	129	-	10	19	22	21
Seven or more persons	144	-	2	13	40	30

[Continued]

★ 835 ★

Relationships: Size of Black Families, in Relation to Family Type and Age of Householder: 1994. Part 1

[Continued]

Characteristic	Total	Age of householder				
		Under 20 years	20 to 24 years	25 to 29 years	30 to 34 years	35 to 39 years
Total persons	12,977	134	990	1,622	2,193	2,098
Average per family	3.39	(B)	2.76	3.26	3.34	3.26
BLACK--OTHER FAMILIES, MALE HOUSEHOLDER						
Size of Family						
Families	450	6	33	67	91	70
Two persons	251	4	19	30	40	40
Three persons	109	3	9	28	20	18
Four persons	74	-	5	6	31	7
Five persons	11	-	-	2	-	5
Six persons	-	-	-	-	-	-
Seven or more persons	6	-	-	-	-	-
Total persons	1,327	20	89	189	264	207
Average per family	2.95	(B)	(B)	(B)	2.89	(B)

Source: "Families, by Type, Age of Own Children, Race, and Hispanic Origin of Householder: March 1994," Rawlings, S.W., and Saluter, A.F., *Household and Family Characteristics: March 1994*, pp. 21-24. *Note:* B=Base less than 75,000.

★ 836 ★

Family Types

Relationships: Size of Black Families, in Relation to Family Type and Age of Householder: 1994. Part 2

[Numbers in thousands except for averages and medians].

Characteristic	Total	Age of householder					
		40 to 44 years	45 to 54 years	55 to 64 years	65 to 74 years	85 years and over	Median age
BLACK--ALL FAMILIES							
Size of family							
Families	1,006	1,379	844	613	290	41	40.9
Two persons	193	461	380	294	194	26	45.2
Three persons	246	399	210	165	60	11	40.0
Four persons	231	264	134	100	14	1	38.3
Five persons	127	130	63	30	16	2	39.1
Six persons	67	61	27	16	-	-	40.1
Seven or more persons	43	64	30	9	4	-	40.6

[Continued]

★ 836 ★

Relationships: Size of Black Families, in Relation to Family Type and Age of Householder: 1994. Part 2
[Continued]

| Characteristic | Total | Age of householder | | | | | |
		40 to 44 years	45 to 54 years	55 to 64 years	65 to 74 years	85 years and over	Median age
Total persons	3,790	5,179	3,031	2,126	862	120	(X)
Average per family	3.77	3.76	3.59	3.47	2.97	(B)	(X)
BLACK--MARRIED-COUPLE FAMILIES							
Size of Family							
Families	520	783	517	374	172	14	45.0
Two persons	93	204	241	186	128	13	56.0
Three persons	98	220	127	110	21	1	46.5
Four persons	161	195	80	49	7	-	40.4
Five persons	98	84	35	18	14	-	41.5
Six persons	44	42	17	11	-	-	41.0
Seven or more persons	26	38	18	1	3	-	43.1
Total persons	2,125	3,007	1,794	1,192	461	30	(X)
Average per family	4.08	3.84	3.47	3.18	2.68	(B)	(X)
BLACK--OTHER FAMILIES, FEMALE HOUSEHOLDER							
Size of Family							
Families	440	533	301	208	105	22	37.6
Two persons	172	218	118	90	59	11	39.7
Three persons	135	169	83	53	37	7	37.4
Four persons	67	60	49	42	6	1	35.8
Five persons	29	45	28	10	2	2	35.6
Six persons	23	20	10	5	-	-	38.3
Seven or more persons	15	22	13	8	1	-	37.8
Total persons	1,531	1,978	1,169	832	359	72	(X)
Average per family	3.48	3.71	3.8	4.00	3.42	(B)	(X)
BLACK--OTHER FAMILIES, MALE HOUSEHOLDER							
Size of Family							
Families	45	63	25	31	13	5	36.9
Two persons	28	39	21	18	11	2	39.1
Three persons	12	11	-	2	2	3	33.5
Four persons	3	9	4	9	-	-	(B)

[Continued]

★ 836 ★

Relationships: Size of Black Families, in Relation to Family Type and Age of Householder: 1994. Part 2

[Continued]

Characteristic	Total	Age of householder					
		40 to 44 years	45 to 54 years	55 to 64 years	65 to 74 years	85 years and over	Median age
Five persons	-	1	-	2	-	-	(B)
Six persons	-	-	-	-	-	-	(B)
Seven or more persons	2	3	-	-	-	-	(B)
Total persons	134	194	68	102	42	18	(X)
Average per family	(B)	(B)	(B)	(B)	(B)	(B)	(X)

Source: "Families, by Type, Age of Own Children, Race, and Hispanic Origin of Householder: March 1994," Rawlings, S.W., and Saluter, A.F., *Household and Family Characteristics: March 1994*, pp. 21-24. *Note:* B = Base less than 75,000. X = Not applicable.

★ 837 ★

Family Types

Relationships: Size of Black Family Members, in Relation to Family Type and Residence Area: 1994

[Numbers in thousands except for averages and medians].

Characteristic	United States				Metropolitan				Nonmetropolitan			
	Total	Married-couple families	Other families		Total	Married-couple families	Other families		Total	Married-couple families	Other families	
			Male house-holder	Female house-holder			Male house-holder	Female house-holder			Male house-holder	Female house-holder
BLACK FAMILIES												
Size of family												
Families	7,989	3,714	450	3,825	6,839	3,143	410	3,286	1,150	571	40	539
Two persons	2,701	1,088	251	1,362	2,271	901	222	1,148	430	187	28	214
Three persons	2,184	882	109	1,193	1,887	752	102	1,033	297	130	7	160
Four persons	1,688	957	74	657	1,482	841	70	572	206	117	4	85
Five persons	790	439	11	340	682	376	10	296	107	63	1	43
Six persons	338	209	-	129	263	155	-	107	75	53	-	22
Seven or more persons	289	139	6	144	253	118	6	129	35	21	-	15
Total persons	27,950	13,645	1,327	12,977	24,024	11,595	1,219	11,209	3,926	2,050	108	1,768
Average per family	3.50	3.67	2.95	3.39	3.51	3.69	2.97	3.41	3.41	3.59	(B)	3.28

Source: "Families, by Type, Age, Metropolitan-Nonmetropolitan Residence, and Race and Hispanic Origin of Householder: March 1994," Rawlings, S.W., and Saluter, A.F., *Household and Family Characteristics: March 1994*, p. 3. *Note:* B = base less than 75,000.

★ 838 ★

Family Types

Single Parents: Age Characteristics of Members of Black Single-Parent Families, by Gender of Parent: 1994. Part 1

[Family group includes own children under 18. Numbers in thousands except for averages and medians].

Characteristic	Total, one-parent family groups	Maintained by father					
		Total	Never married	Married, wife absent		Widowed	Divorced
				Separated	Other		
BLACK--ALL FAMILY GROUPS							
Members 18 and Over, Other Than Householder or Reference Person							
Total	3,636	287	128	36	12	10	101
No other members 18 and over	2,112	108	29	20	2	5	52
One other member 18 and over	1,038	143	74	16	7	5	41
Two or more other members 18 and over	487	36	26	-	3	-	7
Members Under 18							
Total	3,636	287	126	36	12	10	101
No members under 18	-	-	-	-	-	-	-
One member under 18	1,619	184	79	25	8	8	65
Two members under 18	1,114	68	38	7	2	-	21
Three members under 18	526	30	11	2	2	-	15
Four members under 18	239	5	1	2	-	2	-
Five members under 18	79	-	-	-	-	-	-
Six or more members under 18	60	-	-	-	-	-	-
Total members under 18	6,699	434	179	60	20	19	155
Average per family	1.84	1.51	1.41	(B)	(B)	(B)	1.54
Members 18 to 64							
Total	3,636	287	128	36	12	10	101
No members 18 to 64	73	7	6	-	-	-	1
One member 18 to 64	3,036	255	120	34	6	8	86
Two members 18 to 64	399	21	3	2	4	1	11
Three members 18 to 64	103	4	-	-	2	-	2
Four members 18 to 64	24	-	-	-	-	-	-
Five or more members 18 to 64	2	-	-	-	-	-	-
Total members 18 to 64	4,388	316	129	38	20	11	118
Average per family	1.21	1.10	1.00	(B)	(B)	(B)	1.17

[Continued]

★ 838 ★

Single Parents: Age Characteristics of Members of Black Single-Parent Families, by Gender of Parent: 1994. Part 1

[Continued]

Characteristic	Total, one-parent family groups	Maintained by father					
		Total	Never married	Married, wife absent		Widowed	Divorced
				Separated	Other		
Members 65 and Over							
Total	3,636	287	128	36	12	10	101
No members 65 and over	3,599	284	128	36	12	8	100
One member 65 and over	35	3	-	-	-	2	1
Two members 65 and over	2	-	-	-	-	-	-
Three or more members 65 and over	-	-	-	-	-	-	-
Total members 65 and over	43	5	-	-	-	4	1
Average per family	.01	.02	-	(B)	(B)	(B)	.01

Source: "One-Parent Family Groups, by Marital Status, Sex, Race, and Hispanic Origin of Parent: March 1994," Rawlings, S.W., and Saluter, A.F., *Household and Family Characteristics: March 1994*, pp. 117-118. *Note:* B = Base less than 75,000.

★ 839 ★

Family Types

Single Parents: Age Characteristics of Members of Black Single-Parent Families, by Gender of Parent: 1994. Part 2

[Family group includes own children under 18. Numbers in thousands except for averages and medians].

Characteristic	Maintained by mother					
	Total	Never married	Married, husband absent		Widowed	Divorced
			Separated	Other		
BLACK--ALL FAMILY GROUPS						
Members 18 and Over, Other Than Householder or Reference Person						
Total	3,350	1,967	565	102	93	622
No other members 18 and over	2,004	1,161	352	69	40	382
One other member 18 and over	895	528	150	20	25	173
Two or more other members 18 and over	450	278	63	14	29	67

[Continued]

★ 839 ★

Single Parents: Age Characteristics of Members of Black Single-Parent Families, by Gender of Parent: 1994. Part 2

[Continued]

Characteristic		Maintained by mother				
	Total	Never married	Married, husband absent		Widowed	Divorced
			Separated	Other		
Members Under 18						
Total	3,350	1,967	565	102	93	622
No members under 18	-	-	-	-	-	-
One member under 18	1,435	901	190	25	39	279
Two members under 18	1,046	600	192	41	34	179
Three members under 18	496	274	92	19	10	101
Four members under 18	234	130	51	9	5	39
Five members under 18	79	35	26	1	1	14
Six or more members under 18	60	27	13	7	4	9
Total members under 18	6,265	3,440	1,207	252	200	1,165
Average per family	1.87	1.75	2.14	2.46	2.14	1.88
Members 18 to 64						
Total	3,350	1,967	565	102	93	622
No members 18 to 64	67	62	1	-	3	-
One member 18 to 64	2,781	1,722	441	91	51	476
Two members 18 to 64	377	135	93	10	23	116
Three members 18 to 64	99	40	21	2	13	24
Four members 18 to 64	24	6	9	-	3	6
Five or more members 18 to 64	2	2	-	-	-	-
Total members 18 to 64	4,072	2,197	761	118	165	831
Average per family	1.22	1.12	1.35	1.15	1.76	1.34
Members 65 and Over						
Total	3,350	1,967	565	102	93	622
No members 65 and over	3,315	1,951	563	102	83	616
One member 65 and over	32	14	3	-	10	5
Two members 65 and over	2	2	-	-	-	-
Three or more members 65 and over	-	-	-	-	-	-
Total members 65 and over	38	21	3	-	10	5
Average per family	.01	.01	-	-	.10	.01

Source: "One-Parent Family Groups, by Marital Status, Sex, Race, and Hispanic Origin of Parent: March 1994," Rawlings, S.W., and Saluter, A.F., *Household and Family Characteristics: March 1994*, pp. 117-118. *Note:* B = Base less than 75,000.

★ 840 ★

Family Types

Single Parents: Age of Householder in Black Single-Parent Families, by Gender of Parent: 1994. Part 1

[Family group includes own children under 18. Numbers in thousands except for averages and medians].

Characteristic	Total, one-parent family groups	Maintained by father					
		Total	Never married	Married, wife absent		Widowed	Divorced
				Separated	Other		
BLACK--ALL FAMILY GROUPS							
Metropolitan-Nonmetropolitan Residences							
Age of Householder or Reference Person							
Total	3,636	287	128	36	12	10	101
15 to 19 years	190	9	8	-	1	-	-
20 to 24 years	542	12	12	-	-	-	-
25 to 29 years	664	60	49	5	2	-	4
30 to 34 years	849	77	32	10	-	-	35
35 to 39 years	702	56	21	10	3	4	18
40 to 44 years	382	28	3	6	2	3	13
45 to 49 years	169	22	2	3	-	-	17
50 to 54 years	88	14	2	2	4	2	5
55 to 59 years	36	8	-	-	-	1	7
60 to 64 years	5	-	-	-	-	-	-
65 to 74 years	7	1	-	-	-	-	1
75 to 84 years	-	-	-	-	-	-	-
85 years and over	2	-	-	-	-	-	-
Median	32.5	34.0	29.5	(B)	(B)	(B)	38.0
BLACK--ALL FAMILY HOUSEHOLDS							
Age of Householder or Reference Person							
Total	2,869	238	94	32	11	8	94
15 to 19 years	56	-	-	-	-	-	-
20 to 24 years	348	12	12	-	-	-	-
25 to 29 years	518	40	29	5	2	-	4
30 to 34 years	709	76	31	10	-	-	35
35 to 39 years	622	48	18	8	3	4	15
40 to 44 years	335	19	2	4	2	3	9
45 to 49 years	160	22	2	3	-	-	17
50 to 54 years	75	12	2	2	4	-	5
55 to 59 years	32	8	-	-	-	1	7

[Continued]

★ 840 ★

Single Parents: Age of Householder in Black Single-Parent Families, by Gender of Parent: 1994. Part 1
[Continued]

Characteristic	Total, one-parent family groups	Maintained by father					
		Total	Never married	Married, wife absent		Widowed	Divorced
				Separated	Other		
60 to 64 years	5	-	-	-	-	-	-
65 to 74 years	7	1	-	-	-	-	1
75 to 84 years	-	-	-	-	-	-	-
85 years and over	2	-	-	-	-	-	-
Median	33.6	34.4	31.0	(B)	(B)	(B)	37.5
BLACK--ALL RELATED SUBFAMILIES							
Age of Householder or Reference Person							
Total	683	40	29	5	1	2	3
15 to 19 years	131	9	8	-	1	-	-
20 to 24 years	178	-	-	-	-	-	-
25 to 29 years	129	20	20	-	-	-	-
30 to 34 years	126	1	1	-	-	-	-
35 to 39 years	62	2	-	2	-	-	-
40 to 44 years	34	5	-	3	-	-	3
45 to 49 years	9	-	-	-	-	-	-
50 to 54 years	11	2	-	-	-	2	-
55 to 59 years	4	-	-	-	-	-	-
60 to 64 years	-	-	-	-	-	-	-
65 to 74 years	-	-	-	-	-	-	-
75 to 84 years	-	-	-	-	-	-	-
85 years and over	-	-	-	-	-	-	-
Median	26.3	(B)	(B)	(B)	(B)	(B)	(B)
BLACK--ALL UNRELATED SUBFAMILIES							
Age of Householder or Reference Person							
Total	84	9	5	-	-	-	4
15 to 19 years	3	-	-	-	-	-	-
20 to 24 years	16	-	-	-	-	-	-
25 to 29 years	17	-	-	-	-	-	-
30 to 34 years	15	-	-	-	-	-	-
35 to 39 years	17	6	3	-	-	-	3
40 to 44 years	14	3	2	-	-	-	1
45 to 49 years	-	-	-	-	-	-	-

[Continued]

★ 840 ★

Single Parents: Age of Householder in Black Single-Parent Families, by Gender of Parent: 1994. Part 1

[Continued]

Characteristic	Total, one-parent family groups	Maintained by father					
		Total	Never married	Married, wife absent		Widowed	Divorced
				Separated	Other		
50 to 54 years	2	-	-	-	-	-	-
55 to 59 years	-	-	-	-	-	-	-
60 to 64 years	-	-	-	-	-	-	-
65 to 74 years	-	-	-	-	-	-	-
75 to 84 years	-	-	-	-	-	-	-
85 years and over	-	-	-	-	-	-	-
Median	32.0	(B)	(B)	(B)	(B)	(B)	(B)

Source: "One-Parent Family Groups, by Marital Status, Sex, Race, and Hispanic Origin of Parent: March 1994," Rawlings, S.W., and Saluter, A.F., *Household and Family Characteristics: March 1994*, pp. 117-118, 120-121. *Note:* B = Base less than 75,000.

★ 841 ★

Family Types

Single Parents: Age of Householder in Black Single-Parent Families, by Gender of Parent: 1994. Part 2

[Family group includes own children under 18. Numbers in thousands except for averages and medians].

Characteristic		Maintained by mother				
	Total	Never married	Married, husband absent		Widowed	Divorced
			Separated	Other		
BLACK--ALL FAMILY GROUPS						
Metropolitan-Nonmetropolitan Residences						
Age of Householder or Reference Person						
Total	3,350	1,967	565	102	93	622
15 to 19 years	180	180	-	-	-	-
20 to 24 years	530	465	29	14	3	19
25 to 29 years	604	456	91	17	-	40
30 to 34 years	772	428	144	22	12	167
35 to 39 years	646	257	147	31	17	194
40 to 44 years	354	123	88	8	22	113
45 to 49 years	147	27	46	5	5	64
50 to 54 years	74	23	13	3	16	20

[Continued]

★ 841 ★

Single Parents: Age of Householder in Black Single-Parent Families, by Gender of Parent: 1994. Part 2

[Continued]

Characteristic	Maintained by mother					
	Total	Never married	Married, husband absent		Widowed	Divorced
			Separated	Other		
55 to 59 years	28	6	6	3	9	4
60 to 64 years	5	-	-	-	5	-
65 to 74 years	6	-	1	-	4	-
75 to 84 years	-	-	-	-	-	-
85 years and over	2	2	-	-	-	-
Median	32.3	28.7	35.6	34.7	43.4	37.2
BLACK--ALL FAMILY HOUSEHOLDS						
Age of Householder or Reference Person						
Total	2,630	1,419	500	81	84	547
56 to 19 years	56	-	-	-	-	
20 to 24 years	336	297	20	7	-	12
25 to 29 years	478	350	82	10	-	36
30 to 34 years	633	337	126	17	9	144
35 to 39 years	574	226	130	27	13	178
40 to 44 years	315	105	82	8	22	99
45 to 49 years	138	24	42	5	5	62
50 to 54 years	63	21	11	3	16	13
55 to 59 years	24	2	6	3	9	4
60 to 64 years	5	-	-	-	5	-
65 to 74 years	6	-	1	-	4	-
75 to 84 years	-	-	-	-	-	-
85 years and over	2	2	-	-	-	-
Median	33.5	30.1	35.8	36.0	44.4	37.3
BLACK--ALL RELATED SUBFAMILIES						
Age of Householder or Reference Person						
Total	644	502	56	22	8	55
15 to 19 years	122	122	-	-	-	-
20 to 24 years	178	154	6	7	3	7
25 to 29 years	109	91	10	6	-	2
30 to 34 years	124	86	17	4	3	15
35 to 39 years	60	26	13	5	2	14
40 to 44 years	28	14	6	-	-	8
45 to 49 years	9	3	4	-	-	2

[Continued]

★ 841 ★

Single Parents: Age of Householder in Black Single-Parent Families, by Gender of Parent: 1994. Part 2

[Continued]

Characteristic	Maintained by mother					
	Total	Never married	Married, husband absent		Widowed	Divorced
			Separated	Other		
50 to 54 years	9	2	-	-	-	7
55 to 59 years	4	4	-	-	-	-
60 to 64 years	-	-	-	-	-	-
65 to 74 years	-	-	-	-	-	-
75 to 84 years	-	-	-	-	-	-
85 years and over	-	-	-	-	-	-
Median	26.0	24.2	(B)	(B)	(B)	(B)
BLACK--ALL UNRELATED SUBFAMILIES						
Age of Householder or Reference Person						
Total	76	45	9	-	2	20
15 to 19 years	3	3	-	-	-	-
20 to 24 years	16	14	2	-	-	-
25 to 29 years	17	14	-	-	-	3
30 to 34 years	15	5	1	-	-	9
35 to 39 years	12	4	4	-	2	2
40 to 44 years	11	5	-	-	-	6
45 to 49 years	-	-	-	-	-	-
50 to 54 years	2	-	2	-	-	-
55 to 59 years	-	-	-	-	-	-
60 to 64 years	-	-	-	-	-	-
65 to 74 years	-	-	-	-	-	-
75 to 84 years	-	-	-	-	-	-
85 years and over	-	-	-	-	-	-
Median	30.6	(B)	(B)	(B)	(B)	(B)

Source: "One-Parent Family Groups, by Marital Status, Sex, Race, and Hispanic Origin of Parent: March 1994," Rawlings, S.W., and Saluter, A.F., *Household and Family Characteristics: March 1994*, pp. 117-118, 120-121. *Note:* B = Base less than 75,000.

★ 842 ★

Family Types

Single Parents: Characteristics of Black and White One-Parent Families: 1970-1994

(Numbers in thousands).

Subject	1994	1993[1]	1993	1990	1980	1970	Average annual percent change		1970-80
							1990-94	1980-90	
WHITE									
One-parent family group	7,335	7,242	7,167	6,389	4,664	2,638	3.5	3.1	5.7
Maintained by mother	6,144	5,971	5,901	5,310	4,122	2,330	3.6	2.5	5.7
Never married	1,708	1,534	1,478	1,139	379	73	10.1	11.0	16.5
Spouse absent	1,302	1,307	1,288	1,206	1,033	796	1.9	1.5	2.6
Separated	1,044	1,105	1,091	1,015	840	477	0.7	1.9	5.7
Divorced	2,809	2,820	2,825	2,553	2,201	930	2.4	1.5	8.6
Widowed	324	310	311	411	511	531	-5.9	-2.2	-0.4
Maintained by father	1,191	1,271	1,265	1,079	542	307	2.5	6.9	5.7
Never married	315	366	356	253	32	18	5.5	(B)	(B)
Spouse absent[2]	209	240	239	169	141	196	5.3	1.8	-3.3
Divorced	607	602	606	5912	88	(NA)	0.7	7.2	(NA)
Widowed	60	64	64	65	82	93	(B)	-2.3	-1.3
BLACK									
One-parent family group	3,636	3,498	3,377	3,081	2,114	1,148	4.1	3.8	6.1
Maintained by mother	3,350	3,249	3,135	2,860	1,984	1,063	4.0	3.7	6.2
Never married	1,967	1,946	1,871	1,572	665	173	5.6	8.6	13.5
Spouse absent	667	632	611	570	667	570	3.9	-1.6	1.6
Separated	565	550	532	502	616	479	3.0	-2.0	2.5
Divorced	622	578	562	574	477	172	2.0	1.9	10.2
Widowed	93	92	91	144	174	148	-10.9	-1.9	1.6
Maintained by father	287	250	242	221	129	85	6.5	5.4	4.2
Never married	128	135	130	74	30	4	(B)	(B)	(B)
Spouse absent[2]	48	39	38	38	37	50	(B)	(B)	(B)
Divorced	101	63	61	93	43	(NA)	(B)	(B)	(B)
Widowed	10	14	13	18	19	30	(B)	(B)	(B)

Source: "One-Parent Family Groups, by Race, Hispanic Origin, and Marital Status of Householder or Reference Person: 1970 to 1994," Rawlings, S.W., and Saluter, A.F., *Household and Family Characteristics: March 1994*, p. xviii. *Notes:* Family groups comprise family households, related subfamilies and unrelated subfamilies. B Base less than 75,000. NA Not available. 1. Revised using population controls based on 1990 Census. 2. Data for 1970 includes divorced fathers.

★ 843 ★

Family Types

Single Parents: Family Size in Black Single-Parent Families, by Gender of Parent: 1994. Part 1

[Family group includes own children under 18. Numbers in thousands except for averages and medians].

Characteristic	Total, one-parent family groups	Maintained by father					
		Total	Never married	Married, wife absent		Widowed	Divorced
				Separated	Other		
BLACK--ALL FAMILY GROUPS							
Size of Family Group							
Total	3,636	287	128	36	12	10	101
Two persons	1,467	174	84	23	4	5	58
Three persons	1,067	64	30	9	2	3	20
Four persons	595	43	14	2	6	-	21
Five persons	292	6	1	2	-	2	1
Six persons	105	-	-	-	-	-	-
Seven or more persons	111	-	-	-	-	-	-
Total persons	11,130	755	308	98	41	34	274
Average number of persons	3.06	2.63	2.40	(B)	(B)	(B)	2.73
BLACK--ALL FAMILY HOUSEHOLDS							
Size of Family Group							
Total	2,869	238	94	32	11	8	94
Two persons	925	129	50	18	3	3	54
Three persons	916	61	29	9	2	3	18
Four persons	547	43	14	2	6	-	21
Five persons	275	6	1	2	-	2	1
Six persons	95	-	-	-	-	-	-
Seven or more persons	111	-	-	-	-	-	-
Total persons	9,348	659	244	89	38	30	258
Average number of persons	3.26	2.76	2.59	(B)	(B)	(B)	2.74
BLACK--ALL RELATED SUBFAMILIES							
Metropolitan-Nonmetropolitan Residence							
Size of Family Group							
Total	683	40	29	5	1	2	3

[Continued]

★ 843 ★

Single Parents: Family Size in Black Single-Parent Families, by Gender of Parent: 1994. Part 1

[Continued]

Characteristic	Total, one-parent family groups	Maintained by father					
		Total	Never married	Married, wife absent		Widowed	Divorced
				Separated	Other		
Two persons	46	37	29	5	1	2	-
Three persons	138	3	-	-	-	-	3
Four persons	43	-	-	-	-	-	-
Five persons	17	-	-	-	-	-	-
Six persons	10	-	-	-	-	-	-
Seven or more persons	-	-	-	-	-	-	-
Total persons	1,603	79	854	9	3	4	9
Average number of persons	2.35	(B)	(B)	(B)	(B)	(B)	(B)
BLACK--ALL UNRELATED SUBFAMILIES							
Size of Family Group							
Total	84	9	5	-	-	-	4
Two persons	86	9	5	-	-	-	4
Three persons	13	-	-	-	-	-	-
Four persons	5	-	-	-	-	-	-
Five persons	-	-	-	-	-	-	-
Six persons	-	-	-	-	-	-	-
Seven or more persons	-	-	-	-	-	-	-
Total persons	179	17	10	-	-	-	7
Average number of persons	2.12	(B)	(B)	(B)	(B)	(B)	(B)

Source: "One-Parent Family Groups, by Marital Status, Sex, Race, and Hispanic Origin of Parent: March 1994," Rawlings, S.W., and Saluter, A.F., *Household and Family Characteristics: March 1994*, pp. 117-119, 121. *Note:* B = Base less than 75,000.

★ 844 ★
Family Types

Single Parents: Family Size in Black Single-Parent Families, by Gender of Parent: 1994. Part 2

[Family group includes own children under 18. Numbers in thousands except for averages and medians].

Characteristic		Maintained by mother				
	Total	Never married	Married, husband absent		Widowed	Divorced
			Separated	Other		
BLACK--ALL FAMILY GROUPS						
Size of Family Group						
Total	3,350	1,967	565	102	93	622
Two persons	1,293	896	148	23	23	202
Three persons	1,003	543	187	35	30	209
Four persons	552	277	108	25	16	126
Five persons	286	147	67	8	15	48
Six persons	105	54	32	1	4	14
Seven or more persons	111	50	24	9	6	22
Total persons	10,375	5,658	1,971	370	375	2,002
Average number of persons	3.10	2.88	3.49	3.62	4.01	3.22
BLACK--ALL FAMILY HOUSEHOLDS						
Size of Family Group						
Total	2,630	1,419	500	81	84	547
Two persons	796	497	112	16	16	155
Three persons	855	438	165	26	30	197
Four persons	504	247	108	22	16	111
Five persons	269	137	65	7	12	48
Six persons	95	50	25	1	4	14
Seven or more persons	111	50	24	9	6	22
Total persons	8,689	4,425	1,799	307	350	1,809
Average number of persons	3.30	3.12	3.60	3.81	4.17	3.31
BLACK--ALL RELATED SUBFAMILIES						
Metropolitan-Nonmetropolitan Residence						
Size of Family Group						
Total	644	502	56	22	8	55
Two persons	439	362	28	7	5	37

[Continued]

★ 844 ★

Single Parents: Family Size in Black Single-Parent Families, by Gender of Parent: 1994. Part 2

[Continued]

Characteristic	Maintained by mother					
	Total	Never married	Married, husband absent		Widowed	Divorced
			Separated	Other		
Three persons	135	96	20	9	-	9
Four persons	43	30	-	4	-	9
Five persons	17	10	2	2	3	-
Six persons	10	4	6	-	-	-
Seven or more persons	-	-	-	-	-	-
Total persons	1,524	1,143	154	64	22	142
Average number of persons	2.37	2.28	(B)	(B)	(B)	(B)
BLACK--ALL UNRELATED SUBFAMILIES						
Size of Family Group						
Total	76	45	9	-	2	20
Two persons	58	37	8	-	2	11
Three persons	13	9	1	-	-	3
Four persons	5	-	-	-	-	5
Five persons	-	-	-	-	-	-
Six persons	-	-	-	-	-	-
Seven or more persons	-	-	-	-	-	-
Total persons	162	90	18	-	3	51
Average number of persons	2.15	(B)	(B)	(B)	(B)	(B)

Source: "One-Parent Family Groups, by Marital Status, Sex, Race, and Hispanic Origin of Parent: March 1994," Rawlings, S.W., and Saluter, A.F., *Household and Family Characteristics: March 1994*, pp. 117-119, 121. *Note:* B = Base less than 75,000.

★ 845 ★

Family Types

Subfamilies: Age of Reference Person in Black Subfamilies: 1994

(Numbers in thousands except for averages and medians).

Characteristic	All subfamilies				Related subfamilies				Unrelated subfamilies			
	Total	Married-couple	Father-child	Mother-child	Total	Married-couple	Father-child	Mother-child	Total	Married-couple	Father-child	Mother-child
BLACK SUBFAMILIES												
Age of Reference Person												
Total	867	99	48	719	778	95	40	644	89	4	9	76
15 to 19 years	134	-	9	125	131	-	9	122	3	-	-	3
20 to 24 years	214	20	-	194	195	17	-	178	19	2	-	16

[Continued]

★ 845 ★

Subfamilies: Age of Reference Person in Black Subfamilies: 1994
[Continued]

Characteristic	All subfamilies				Related subfamilies				Unrelated subfamilies			
	Total	Married-couple	Father-child	Mother-child	Total	Married-couple	Father-child	Mother-child	Total	Married-couple	Father-child	Mother-child
25 to 29 years	178	32	20	126	159	30	20	109	19	2	-	17
30 to 34 years	147	7	1	139	132	7	1	124	15	-	-	15
35 to 39 years	95	16	7	72	77	16	2	60	17	-	6	12
40 to 44 years	52	4	8	39	38	4	5	28	14	-	3	11
45 to 49 years	11	2	-	9	11	2	-	9	-	-	-	-
50 to 54 years	18	5	2	11	16	5	2	9	2	-	-	2
55 to 59 years	6	1	-	4	6	1	-	4	-	-	-	-
60 to 64 years	2	2	-	-	2	2	-	-	-	-	-	-
65 to 74 years	5	5	-	-	5	5	-	-	-	-	-	-
75 to 84 years	6	6	-	-	6	6	-	-	-	-	-	-
85 years and over	-	-	-	-	-	-	-	-	-	-	-	-
Median	27.4	29.7	(B)	26.6	27.0	30.2	(B)	26.0	31.3	(B)	(B)	30.6

Source: "Subfamilies, by Type, Race, and Hispanic Origin of Reference Person: March 1994," Rawlings, S.W., and Saluter, A.F., *Household and Family Characteristics: March 1994*, p. 129. *Note:* B = base less than 75,000.

★ 846 ★

Family Types

Subfamilies: Family Groups with Children Under 18, by Family Type and Race/Ethnic Origin 1994

(Numbers in thousands).

Subject	All family groups		Family households		All subfamilies		Related subfamilies		Unrelated subfamilies	
	Number	Percent	Number	Percent	Number	Percent	Number	Percent	Number	Percent
ALL RACES										
Family groups with children	37,008	100.0	34,081	100.0	2,989	100.0	2,305	100.0	684	100.0
Two-parent groups	25,598	69.2	25,058	73.5	540	18.1	505	21.9	34	5.0
One-parent groups	11,410	30.8	8,961	26.3	2,449	81.9	1,800	78.1	650	95.0
Maintained by mother	9,854	26.6	7,647	22.4	2,207	73.8	1,636	71.0	571	83.5
Maintained by father	1,556	4.2	1,314	3.9	242	8.1	164	7.1	78	11.4
WHITE										
Family groups with children	29,645	100.0	27,642	100.0	2,004	100.0	1,443	100.0	561	100.0
Two-parent groups	22,310	75.3	21,884	79.2	426	21.3	402	27.9	24	4.3
One-parent groups	7,335	24.7	5,758	20.8	1,578	78.7	1,041	72.1	536	95.5
Maintained by mother	6,144	20.7	4,748	17.2	1,396	69.7	925	64.1	470	83.8
Maintained by father	1,191	4.0	1,010	3.7	182	9.1	116	8.0	66	11.8
BLACK										
Family groups with children	5,614	100.0	4,793	100.0	822	100.0	735	100.0	87	100.0
Two-parent groups	1,978	35.2	1,924	40.1	54	6.6	52	7.1	2	2.3
One-parent groups	3,636	64.8	2,869	59.9	767	93.3	683	92.9	84	96.6
Maintained by mother	3,350	59.7	2,630	54.9	719	87.5	644	87.6	76	87.4
Maintained by father	287	5.1	238	5.0	48	5.8	40	5.4	9	10.3

[Continued]

★ 846 ★

Subfamilies: Family Groups with Children Under 18, by Family Type and Race/Ethnic Origin 1994

[Continued]

Subject	All family groups		Family households		All subfamilies		Related subfamilies		Unrelated subfamilies	
	Number	Percent	Number	Percent	Number	Percent	Number	Percent	Number	Percent
HISPANIC[1]										
Family groups with children	4,369	100.0	3,790	100.0	579	100.0	444	100.0	135	100.0
Two-parent groups	2,786	63.8	2,609	68.8	177	30.6	154	34.7	23	17.0
One-parent groups	1,583	36.2	1,181	31.2	402	69.4	290	65.3	112	83.0
Maintained by mother	1,364	31.2	1,006	26.5	358	61.8	258	58.1	100	74.1
Maintained by father	219	5.0	175	4.6	44	7.6	32	7.2	12	8.9

Source: "Family Groups with Children Under 18, by Type, Race and Hispanic Origin of Householder or Reference Person: 1994," Rawlings, S.W., and Saluter, A.F., *Household and Family Characteristics: March 1994*, p. xvi. *Notes:* Family groups comprise family households, related subfamilies, and unrelated subfamilies. 1. May be of any race.

★ 847 ★
Family Types

Subfamilies: Number Parents Present in Families with Children Under 18, by Race/Ethnic Origin: 1970-1994

(Numbers in thousands).

Subject	1994	1993[1]	1993	1990	1980	1970	Average annual percent change		
							1990-94	1980-90	1980-70
ALL RACES									
Family groups with children	37,008	36,533	36,058	34,670	32,150	29,631	1.6	0.8	0.8
Two-parent family groups	25,598	25,384	25,157	24,921	25,231	25,823	0.7	-0.1	-0.2
One-parent family groups	11,410	11,149	10,901	9,749	6,920	3,808	3.9	3.4	6.0
Maintained by mother	9,854	9,566	9,339	8,398	6,230	3,415	4.0	3.0	6.0
Maintained by father	1,556	1,583	1,562	1,351	690	393	3.5	6.7	5.6
WHITE									
Family groups with children	29,645	29,355	29,225	28,294	27,294	26,115	1.2	0.4	0.4
Two-parent family groups	22,310	22,113	22,058	21,905	22,628	23,477	0.5	-0.3	-0.4
One-parent family groups	7,335	7,242	7,167	6,389	4,664	2,638	3.5	3.1	5.7
Maintained by mother	6,144	5,971	5,901	5,310	4,122	2,330	3.6	2.5	5.7
Maintained by father	1,191	1,271	1,265	1,079	542	307	2.5	6.9	5.7
BLACK									
Family groups with children	5,614	5,545	5,364	5,087	4,074	3,219	2.5	2.2	2.4
Two-parent family groups	1,978	2,047	1,987	2,006	1,961	2,071	-0.4	0.2	-0.5
One-parent family groups	3,636	3,498	3,377	3,081	2,114	1,148	4.1	3.8	6.1
Maintained by mother	3,350	3,249	3,135	2,860	1,984	1,063	4.0	3.7	6.2
Maintained by father	287	250	242	221	129	85	6.5	5.4	4.2

[Continued]

★ 847 ★

Subfamilies: Number Parents Present in Families with Children Under 18, by Race/Ethnic Origin: 1970-1994

[Continued]

Subject	1994	1993[1]	1993	1990	1980	1970	Average annual percent change		
							1990-94	1980-90	1980-70
HISPANIC[2]									
Family groups with children	4,369	4,181	3,838	3,429	2,194	(NA)	6.1	4.5	(NA)
Two-parent family groups	2,786	2,697	2,494	2,289	1,626	(NA)	4.9	3.4	(NA)
One-parent family groups	1,583	1,484	1,344	1,140	568	(NA)	8.2	7.0	(NA)
Maintained by mother	1,364	1,279	1,157	1,003	526	(NA)	7.7	6.5	(NA)
Maintained by father	219	205	187	138	42	(NA)	11.5	11.9	(NA)

Source: "Family Groups with Children Under 18, by Race and Hispanic Origin of Householder or Reference Person: 1970 to 1994," Rawlings, S.W., and Saluter, A.F., *Household and Family Characteristics: March 1994*, p. xv. *Notes:* Family group comprises family households, related subfamilies and unrelated subfamilies. NA Not available. 1. Revised using population controls based on the 1990 Census. 2. May be of any race.

★ 848 ★

Family Types

Subfamilies: Percentage Distribution of Family Type in Families with Children, by Race/Ethnic Origin: 1970-1994

(In percent)

	1994	1990	1980	1970
All races				
Two-parent groups	69.2	71.9	78.5	87.1
One-parent (mother/child)	26.6	24.2	19.4	11.5
One-parent (father/child)	4.2	3.9	2.1	1.3
White				
Two-parent groups	75.3	77.4	82.9	89.9
One-parent (mother/child)	20.7	18.8	15.1	8.9
One-parent (father/child)	4.0	3.8	2.0	1.2
Black				
Two-parent groups	35.2	39.4	48.1	64.3
One-parent (mother/child)	59.7	56.2	48.7	33.0
One-parent (father/child)	5.1	4.3	3.2	2.6
Hispanic[1]				
Two-parent groups	63.8	66.8	74.1	
One-parent (mother/child)	31.2	29.3	24.0	
One-parent (father/child)	5.0	4.0	1.9	

Source: "Composition of Family Groups with Children, by Race and Hispanic Origin: 1970-1994," Rawlings, S.W., and Saluter, A.F., *Household and Family Characteristics: March 1994*, p. xvii. *Notes:* Family groups comprise family households and subfamilies. Hispanic data not available for 1970. 1. Hispanic may be of any race.

★ 849 ★

Family Types

Subfamilies: Size of Black Subfamilies, by Subfamily Type: 1994

(Numbers in thousands except for averages and medians).

Characteristic	All subfamilies				Related subfamilies				Unrelated subfamilies			
	Total	Married-couple	Father-child	Mother-child	Total	Married-couple	Father-child	Mother-child	Total	Married-couple	Father-child	Mother-child
BLACK SUBFAMILIES												
Size of Subfamily												
Total	867	99	48	719	778	95	40	644	89	4	9	76
Two persons	587	45	45	497	519	43	37	439	68	2	9	58
Three persons	178	28	3	148	163	25	3	135	15	2	-	13
Four persons	62	14	-	48	57	14	-	43	5	-	-	5
Five persons	23	7	-	17	23	7	-	17	-	-	-	-
Six persons	15	5	-	10	15	5	-	10	-	-	-	-
Seven or more persons	1	1	-	-	1	1	-	-	-	-	-	-
Total persons	2,073	290	96	1,686	1,883	279	79	1,524	190	11	17	162
Average per subfamily	2.39	2.93	(B)	2.35	2.42	2.94	(B)	2.37	2.15	(B)	(B)	2.15

Source: "Subfamilies, by Type, Race, and Hispanic Origin of Reference Person: March 1994," Rawlings, S.W., and Saluter, A.F., *Household and Family Characteristics: March 1994*, p. 129. *Note:* B = base less than 75,000.

Income

★ 850 ★

Money Income: Family Income at Selected Points in the Income Distribution in Constant (1993) Dollars, in 1980 and 1993, by Race

ITEM	All families, 1980	1993		
		All families	RACE	
			White	Black
Number (1,000)	60,309	68,506	57,881	7,993
INCOME AT SELECTED POSITIONS (dollars)				
Upper limit of each fifth:				
Lowest	17,535	16,952	19,017	8,000
Second	29,645	30,000	32,024	16,010
Third	41,988	45,020	47,293	27,742
Fourth	58,871	66,794	69,039	46,502
Lower limit of top 5 percent	92,158	113,182	117,278	83,600

[Continued]

★ 850 ★

Money Income: Family Income at Selected Points in the Income Distribution in Constant (1993) Dollars, in 1980 and 1993, by Race
[Continued]

ITEM	All families, 1980	1993 All families	1993 RACE White	1993 RACE Black
PERCENT DISTRIBUTION OF AGGREGATE INCOME				
Lowest fifth	5.2	4.2	4.7	3.0
Second fifth	11.5	10.1	10.5	7.9
Third fifth	17.5	15.9	16.1	14.5
Fourth fifth	24.3	23.6	23.4	24.1
Highest fifth	41.5	46.2	45.4	50.6
Top 5 percent	15.3	19.1	18.8	20.3

Source: "Money Income of Families—Percent Distribution of Aggregate Income Received by Quintile and Income at Selected Positions, in Constant (1993) Dollars: 1980 and 1993," *Statistical Abstract of the United States: 1995,* 1995, p. 475. Primary source: U.S. Bureau of the Census, *Current Population Reports,* P60-188; and unpublished data.

★ 851 ★
Income

Money Income: Median Family Income, by Region, Family Type, Number Earners and Race/Ethnic Origin: 1993

CHARACTERISTIC	NUMBER (1,000) All families[1]	NUMBER (1,000) White	NUMBER (1,000) Black	NUMBER (1,000) Hispanic[2]	MEDIAN INCOME (dollars) All families[1]	MEDIAN INCOME (dollars) White	MEDIAN INCOME (dollars) Black	MEDIAN INCOME (dollars) Hispanic[2]
All families	68,506	57,881	7,993	5,946	36,959	39,300	21,542	23,654
Region:								
Northeast	13,456	11,690	1,298	1,001	40,987	42,526	25,002	19,580
Midwest	16,210	14,258	1,643	405	37,942	40,158	20,794	27,501
South	24,438	19,461	4,461	1,915	33,365	36,504	20,372	23,651
West	14,402	12,472	591	2,624	38,881	39,614	26,182	24,781
Type of family:								
Married-couple families	53,181	47,452	3,715	4,038	43,005	43,675	35,218	28,454
Wife in paid labor force	32,194	28,539	2,417	2,121	51,204	51,630	44,805	35,973
Wife not in paid labor force	20,988	18,913	1,298	1,917	30,218	30,878	22,207	20,721
Male householder, wife absent	2,914	2,298	450	410	26,467	28,269	19,478	21,717
Female householder, husband absent	12,411	8,131	3,828	1,498	17,443	20,000	11,909	12,047
With related children, under 18	36,456	29,234	5,525	4,153	36,200	39,837	18,671	22,117
Married couple	26,121	22,670	2,147	2,747	45,548	46,376	36,659	28,499
Male householder, wife absent	1,577	1,202	295	239	22,348	24,272	18,857	17,835
Female householder, husband absent	8,758	5,361	3,084	1,167	13,472	16,020	10,375	10,497

[Continued]

★ 851 ★

Money Income: Median Family Income, by Region, Family Type, Number Earners and Race/ Ethnic Origin: 1993

[Continued]

CHARACTERISTIC	NUMBER (1,000)				MEDIAN INCOME (dollars)			
	All families[1]	White	Black	Hispanic[2]	All families[1]	White	Black	Hispanic[2]
Number of earners:								
No earners	10,546	8,622	1,574	860	15,515	17,656	6,858	8,362
One earner	19,301	15,556	2,999	2,044	26,193	28,574	16,571	17,121
Two earners	30,137	26,336	2,620	2,248	47,424	48,332	37,124	32,172
Three earners	6,367	5,486	651	538	57,745	58,651	49,489	40,724
Four or more earners	2,155	1,882	149	256	72,673	73,269	59,678	49,876

Source: "Money Income of Families—Median Income, by Race and Hispanic Origin: 1993," *Statistical Abstract of the United States: 1995,* 1995, p. 476. Primary source: U.S. Bureau of the Census, *Current Population Reports,* P60-188; and unpublished data. *Notes:* 1. Includes other races not shown separately. 2. Persons of Hispanic origin may be of any race.

★ 852 ★

Income

Money Income: Percent Distribution of Family Income, by Region and Race/Ethnic Origin: 1993

ITEM	Number of families (1,000)	PERCENT DISTRIBUTION								Median income (dollars)
		Under $5,000	$5,000 to $9,999	$10,000 to $14,999	$15,000 to $24,999	$25,000 to $34,999	$35,000 to $49,999	$50,000 to $75,999	$75,000 and over	
All families[1]	68,506	3.5	6.1	7.2	15.5	14.8	17.9	19.4	15.5	36,959
White, total	57,881	2.5	4.8	6.6	15.1	15.1	18.8	20.6	16.6	39,300
Northeast	11,690	2.6	4.6	5.7	13.5	13.5	18.3	21.5	20.3	42,526
Midwest	14,258	2.2	4.2	5.8	14.9	15.6	20.7	21.8	14.8	40,158
South	19,461	2.7	5.1	7.6	16.4	16.0	18.4	19.0	14.9	36,504
West	12,472	2.4	5.1	6.7	14.9	14.5	17.7	20.8	17.8	39,614
Black, total	7,993	10.7	15.1	11.4	18.6	13.7	12.9	10.9	6.6	21,542
Northeast	1,298	11.0	14.1	9.6	15.3	14.1	14.0	13.4	8.5	25,002
Midwest	1,643	12.7	18.0	10.0	17.3	13.1	12.2	9.7	6.8	20,794
South	4,461	10.2	15.0	12.6	20.2	13.3	13.2	10.2	5.4	20,372
West	591	8.8	10.0	10.0	17.6	17.1	10.8	15.1	11.2	26,182
Hispanic,[2] total	5,946	5.8	12.1	12.5	22.2	16.6	14.0	11.4	5.4	23,654
Northeast	1,001	9.1	19.3	11.9	19.5	13.6	12.7	8.5	5.5	19,580
Midwest	405	4.2	10.9	10.6	20.2	17.5	18.0	13.6	5.2	27,501
South	1,915	6.1	10.9	13.3	23.1	16.9	12.4	11.1	6.2	23,651
West	2,624	4.6	10.4	12.3	22.9	17.3	14.9	12.4	4.9	24,781

Source: "Money Income of Families—Percent Distribution, by Income Level and Selected Characteristics: 1993," *Statistical Abstract of the United States: 1995,* 1995, p. 476. Primary source: U.S. Bureau of the Census, *Current Population Reports,* P60-188; and unpublished data. *Notes:* 1. Includes other races not shown separately. 2. Persons of Hispanic origin may be of any race.

★ 853 ★

Income

Money Income: Percent of Family in Each Income Quintile and Top 5%, by Race/Ethnic Origin: 1993

CHARACTERISTIC	Number (1,000)	PERCENT DISTRIBUTION						
		Total	Lowest fifth	Second fifth	Third fifth	Fourth fifth	Highest fifth·	Top 5 percent
All families	68,506	100.0	20.0	20.0	20.0	20.0	20.0	5.0
White	57,881	100.0	16.9	19.9	20.7	21.2	21.4	5.5
Black	7,993	100.0	41.4	21.6	15.9	12.1	9.0	1.5
Hispanic origin[1]	5,946	100.0	35.3	26.3	18.4	11.9	8.1	1.5

Source: "Money Income of Families—Percent Distribution, by Income Quintile and Top 5 Percent: 1993," *Statistical Abstract of the United States: 1995*, 1995, p. 475. Primary source: U.S. Bureau of the Census, Current Population Survey, unpublished data. *Note:* 1. Persons of Hispanic origin may be of any race.

★ 854 ★

Income

Money Income: Trends in Distribution of Family Income, in Constant (1993) Dollars, by Race/Ethnic Origin: 1970-1993

[Constant dollars based on CPI-U-XI deflator. Families as of **March** of following year. Beginning with 1980 based on householder concept and restricted to primary families. Based on Current Population Survey].

YEAR	Number of families (1,000)	PERCENT DISTRIBUTION							Median income (dollars)
		Under $10,000	$10,000-$14,999	$15,000-$24,999	$25,000-$34,999	$35,000-$49,999	$50,000-$74,999	$75,000 and over	
ALL FAMILIES[1]									
1970	52,227	8.2	7.3	16.6	19.6	23.6	17.3	7.5	34,523
1975	56,245	7.6	7.9	16.6	17.7	23.0	18.7	8.4	35,274
1980	60,309	8.0	7.1	16.1	15.6	22.2	20.0	10.9	36,912
1985	63,558	9.0	7.0	15.5	15.5	19.9	19.9	13.3	37,246
1990	66,322	8.3	6.5	14.8	14.6	19.8	20.0	15.9	39,086
1991	67,173	9.0	6.8	14.8	15.3	19.3	19.7	15.0	38,129
1992	68,216	9.5	7.1	15.2	14.6	19.1	19.9	14.7	37,668
1993	68,506	9.6	7.2	15.5	14.8	17.9	19.4	15.5	36,959
WHITE									
1970	46,535	7.0	6.7	15.8	19.8	24.5	18.2	8.0	35,814
1975	49,873	6.3	7.3	16.1	17.9	23.7	19.7	9.0	36,686
1980	52,710	6.4	6.3	15.6	15.9	23.1	21.1	11.8	38,458
1985	54,991	7.3	6.3	15.0	15.6	20.6	20.8	14.4	39,149
1990	56,803	6.3	5.9	14.4	14.9	20.5	21.1	16.9	40,813
1991	57,224	6.7	6.3	14.4	15.5	20.1	20.8	16.2	40,085
1992	57,669	7.1	6.4	14.8	14.9	19.8	21.2	15.8	39,828

[Continued]

★ 854 ★

Money Income: Trends in Distribution of Family Income, in Constant (1993) Dollars, by Race/Ethnic Origin: 1970-1993

[Continued]

YEAR	Number of families (1,000)	PERCENT DISTRIBUTION							Median income (dollars)
		Under $10,000	$10,000-$14,999	$15,000-$24,999	$25,000-$34,999	$35,000-$49,999	$50,000-$74,999	$75,000 and over	
1993	57,881	7.3	6.6	15.1	15.1	18.8	20.6	16.6	39,300
BLACK									
1970	4,928	20.1	13.0	23.9	17.2	15.1	8.8	1.9	21,969
1975	5,586	19.6	14.2	20.9	16.8	16.5	9.6	2.3	22,572
1980	6,317	20.7	13.9	21.2	14.2	15.2	11.4	3.5	22,253
1985	6,921	22.8	11.9	19.9	14.5	15.1	11.5	4.3	22,543
1990	7,471	22.9	11.3	18.6	13.1	15.7	11.5	7.0	23,685
1991	7,716	25.0	10.7	18.1	14.2	15.2	11.3	5.6	22,861
1992	7,982	25.7	11.8	18.4	13.0	14.4	10.8	5.8	21,735
1993	7,993	25.8	11.4	18.6	13.7	12.9	10.9	6.6	21,542
HISPANIC ORIGIN[2]									
1970	2,499	14.9	12.9	23.3	18.9	18.4	9.0	2.7	24,557
1975	3,235	14.5	12.1	22.2	17.0	17.6	12.3	4.3	25,838
1980	4,206	16.7	13.0	19.8	16.7	15.9	12.5	5.4	25,552
1985	4,981	16.1	12.5	20.0	16.0	17.1	11.8	6.5	25,905
1990	5,177	17.5	11.8	20.1	16.8	15.4	12.1	6.4	25,351
1991	5,733	17.5	12.4	21.8	15.6	15.5	11.5	5.7	24,260
1992	5,946	17.9	12.5	22.2	16.6	14.0	11.4	5.5	23,654
1993	5,946	17.9	12.5	22.2	16.6	14.0	11.4	5.5	23,654

Source: "Money Income of Families—Percent Distribution, by Income Level, Race, and Hispanic Origin, in Constant (1993) Dollars: 1970 to 1993," *Statistical Abstract of the United States: 1995,* 1995, p. 474. *Notes:* 1. Includes other races not shown separately. 2. Persons of Hispanic origin may be of any race.

★ 855 ★

Income

Money Income: Trends in Family Median Income, in Current and Constant (1993) Dollars, by Race/Ethnic Origin: 1970-1993

[Constant dollars based on CPI-U-XI deflator. Families as of **March** of following year. Beginning with 1980 based on householder concept and restricted to primary families. Based on Current Population Survey].

YEAR	MEDIAN INCOME IN CURRENT DOLLARS					MEDIAN INCOME IN CONSTANT (1993) DOLLARS				
	All families[1]	White	Black	Asian, Pacific Islander	Hispanic[2]	All families[1]	White	Black	Asian, Pacific Islander	Hispanic[2]
1970	9,867	10,236	6,279	(NA)	(NA)	34,523	35,814	21,969	(NA)	(NA)
1975	13,719	14,268	8,779	(NA)	9,551	35,274	36,686	22,572	(NA)	24,557
1980	21,023	21,904	12,674	(NA)	14,716	36,912	38,458	22,253	(NA)	25,838
1981	22,388	23,517	13,266	(NA)	16,401	35,905	37,716	21,276	(NA)	26,303
1982	23,433	24,603	13,598	(NA)	16,227	35,419	37,188	20,553	(NA)	24,527

[Continued]

★ 855 ★

Money Income: Trends in Family Median Income, in Current and Constant (1993) Dollars, by Race/Ethnic Origin: 1970-1993

[Continued]

YEAR	MEDIAN INCOME IN CURRENT DOLLARS					MEDIAN INCOME IN CONSTANT (1993) DOLLARS				
	All families[1]	White	Black	Asian, Pacific Islander	Hispanic[2]	All families[1]	White	Black	Asian, Pacific Islander	Hispanic[2]
1983[3]	24,580	25,757	14,506	(NA)	16,956	35,661	37,368	21,045	(NA)	24,600
1984	26,433	27,686	15,431	(NA)	18,832	36,762	38,505	21,461	(NA)	26,191
1985	27,735	29,152	16,786	(NA)	19,027	37,246	39,149	22,543	(NA)	25,552
1986	29,458	30,809	17,605	(NA)	19,995	38,838	40,620	23,210	(NA)	26,362
1987[4]	30,970	32,385	18,406	(NA)	20,300	39,394	41,194	23,413	(NA)	25,822
1988	32,191	33,915	19,329	36,560	21,769	39,320	41,426	23,610	44,657	26,590
1989	34,213	35,975	20,209	40,351	23,446	39,869	41,922	23,550	47,022	27,322
1990	35,353	36,915	21,423	42,246	23,431	39,086	40,813	23,685	46,707	25,905
1991	35,939	37,783	21,548	40,974	23,895	38,129	40,085	22,861	43,471	25,351
1992	36,812	38,909	21,161	42,556	23,901	37,914	40,074	21,794	43,830	24,616
1992[5]	36,573	38,670	21,103	42,255	23,555	37,668	39,828	21,735	43,520	24,260
1993	36,959	39,300	21,542	44,456	23,654	36,959	39,300	21,542	44,456	23,654

Source: "Money Income of Families—Median Income, by Race and Hispanic Origin, in Current and Constant (1993) Dollars: 1970 to 1993," *Statistical Abstract of the United States: 1995,* 1995, p. 474. Primary source: U.S. Bureau of the Census, *Current Population Reports,* P60-188; and unpublished data. *Notes:* NA Not available. 1. Includes other races not shown separately. 2. Persons of Hispanic origin may be of any race. 3. Beginning 1983, data based on revised Hispanic population controls and not directly comparable with prior years. 4. Beginning 1987, data on revised processing procedures and not directly comparable with prior years. 5. Based on 1990 census population controls.

★ 856 ★

Income

Poverty: Families in Poverty in 1993, by Family Size, Householder's Education and Work Experience, and Race/Ethnic Origin

[Families as of **March 1994**. Based on Current Population Survey].

CHARACTERISTIC	NUMBER BELOW POVERTY LEVEL (1,000)				PERCENT BELOW POVERTY LEVEL			
	All races[1]	White	Black	Hispanic[2]	All races[1]	White	Black	Hispanic[2]
Total	8,393	5,452	2,499	1,625	12.3	9.4	31.3	27.3
Size of family:								
Two persons	2,688	1,874	718	343	9.5	7.5	26.6	21.9
Three persons	2,020	1,274	649	357	12.6	9.7	29.7	25.9
Four persons	1,723	1,105	516	370	11.9	9.1	30.6	27.4
Five persons	1,095	689	327	273	17.3	13.2	41.3	30.2
Six persons	451	279	136	138	22.0	18.0	40.2	34.8
Seven persons or more	415	231	153	144	34.6	28.6	52.9	41.1
Average size	3.57	3.50	3.66	4.21	(X)	(X)	(X)	(X)
Avg. number of children per family with children	2.22	2.18	2.28	2.56	(X)	(X)	(X)	(X)
Education of householder[3]								
No high school diploma	3,109	2,033	882	969	25.1	20.6	44.4	37.2
High school diploma, no college	2,492	1,557	840	329	11.7	8.6	31.4	23.5
Some college, less than bachelor's degree	1,295	875	367	116	8.0	6.3	19.7	11.5
Bachelor's degree or more	355	255	47	42	2.3	1.8	5.3	8.4

[Continued]

★ 856 ★

Poverty: Families in Poverty in 1993, by Family Size, Householder's Education and Work Experience, and Race/Ethnic Origin
[Continued]

CHARACTERISTIC	NUMBER BELOW POVERTY LEVEL (1,000)				PERCENT BELOW POVERTY LEVEL			
	All races[1]	White	Black	Hispanic[2]	All races[1]	White	Black	Hispanic[2]
Work experience of householder:								
Total[4]	7,616	4,925	2,286	1,537	15.4	11.7	42.5	35.2
Worked during year	3,992	2,746	1,074	848	8.1	6.5	20.0	19.4
Year-round, full-time	1,265	924	278	323	3.4	2.8	7.5	10.7
Not year-round, full-time	2,727	1,822	796	524	23.4	19.1	47.8	39.3
Did not work	3,624	2,179	1,212	689	46.0	37.5	72.5	63.0

Source: "Families Below Poverty Level, by Selected Characteristics: 1993," *Statistical Abstract of the United States: 1995*, 1995, p. 484. *Notes:* X Not applicable. 1. Includes other races not shown separately. 2. Hispanic persons may be of any race. 3. Householder 25 years old and over. 4. Persons 16 years old and over.

★ 857 ★
Income

Poverty: Trends in Percent of Families Below Poverty Level, by Race/Ethnic Origin: 1960 - 1993

[Families as of **March of the following year**. Based on Current Population Survey].

YEAR	NUMBER BELOW POVERTY LEVEL (1,000)				PERCENT BELOW POVERTY LEVEL			
	All races[1]	White	Black	Hispanic[2]	All races[1]	White	Black	Hispanic[2]
1960	8,243	6,115	(NA)	(NA)	18.1	14.9	(NA)	(NA)
1970	5,260	3,708	1,481	(NA)	10.1	8.0	29.5	(NA)
1972	5,075	3,441	1,529	477	9.3	7.1	29.0	20.6
1973	4,828	3,219	1,527	468	8.8	6.6	28.1	19.8
1974	4,922	3,352	1,479	526	8.8	6.8	26.9	21.2
1975	5,450	3,383	1,513	627	9.7	7.7	27.1	25.1
1976	5,311	3,560	1,617	598	9.4	7.1	27.9	23.1
1977	5,311	3,540	1,637	591	9.3	7.0	28.2	21.4
1978	5,280	3,523	1,622	559	9.1	6.9	27.5	20.4
1979[3]	5,461	3,581	1,722	614	9.2	6.9	27.8	20.3
1980	6,217	4,195	1,826	751	10.3	8.0	28.9	23.2
1981	6,851	4,670	1,972	792	11.2	8.8	30.8	24.0
1982	7,512	5,118	2,158	916	12.2	9.6	33.0	27.2
1983[4]	7,647	5,220	2,161	981	12.3	9.7	32.3	25.9
1984	7,277	4,925	2,094	991	11.6	9.1	30.9	25.2
1985	7,223	4,983	1,983	1,074	11.4	9.1	28.7	25.5
1986	7,023	4,811	1,987	1,085	10.9	8.6	28.0	24.7
1987[5]	7,005	4,567	2,117	1,168	10.7	8.1	29.4	25.5
1988	6,874	4,471	2,089	1,141	10.4	7.9	28.2	23.7
1989	6,784	4,409	2,077	1,133	10.3	7.8	27.8	23.4
1990	7,098	4,622	2,193	1,244	10.7	8.1	29.3	25.0
1991	7,712	5,022	2,343	1,373	11.5	8.8	30.4	26.5

[Continued]

★ 857 ★

Poverty: Trends in Percent of Families Below Poverty Level, by Race/Ethnic Origin:
1960 - 1993
[Continued]

YEAR	NUMBER BELOW POVERTY LEVEL (1,000)				PERCENT BELOW POVERTY LEVEL			
	All races[1]	White	Black	Hispanic[2]	All races[1]	White	Black	Hispanic[2]
1992[6]	8,144	5,255	2,484	1,529	11.9	9.1	31.1	26.7
1993	8,393	5,452	2,499	1,625	12.3	9.4	31.3	27.3

Source: "Families Below Poverty Level and Below 125 Percent of Poverty Level: 1960 to 1993," *Statistical Abstract of the United States: 1995,* 1995, p. 484. Primary source: U.S. Bureau of the Census, *Current Population Reports,* P60-188. *Notes:* NA Not available. 1. Includes other races not shown separately. 2. Persons of Hispanic origin may be of any race. 3. Population controls based on 1980 census. 4. Beginning 1983, data based on revised Hispanic population controls and not directly comparable with prior years. 5. Beginning 1987, data based on revised processing procedures and not directly comparable with prior years. 6. Beginning 1992, based on 1990 population controls.

★ 858 ★
Income

Relationships: Family Median Income, by Family Type
and Householder's Race: 1993

Householder	With children	Without children
Black		
Married-couple	$36,670	$32,810
Female householder, no spouse present	$10,380	$23,360
White, not Hispanic		
Married-couple	$48,630	$41,440
Female householder, no spouse present	$17,890	$29,400

Source: "Median Family Income, by Type of Family and Race of Householder: 1993," *Population Profile of the United States: 1995,* 1995, p. 45.

★ 859 ★

Income

Relationships: Married Couples' Median Income, by Work Experience of Husbands and Wives and Race/Ethnic Origin: 1993

[**March 1994**. Based on Current Population Survey].

WORK EXPERIENCE OF HUSBAND	NUMBER (1,000)				MEDIAN INCOME (dollars)			
	Total	Wife worked		Wife did not work	Total	Wife worked		Wife did not work
		Total	Worked year-round full-time			Total	Worked year-round, full-time	
All families[1]	53,181	34,411	18,657	18,770	43,005	50,798	56,078	28,779
Husband worked	42,072	31,419	17,170	10,653	49,450	52,494	57,891	37,482
Worked year-round, full-time	33,357	25,423	14,325	7,934	52,869	56,017	60,711	41,776
Husband did not work	11,109	2,992	1,487	8,117	23,128	30,131	34,661	20,987
White	47,452	30,574	16,231	16,878	43,675	51,205	58,519	29,571
Husband worked	37,634	28,069	14,993	9,565	49,988	52,863	58,269	38,601
Worked year-round, full-time	29,808	22,690	12,470	7,118	53,356	56,341	61,062	42,456
Husband did not work	9,818	2,505	1,238	7,313	23,822	30,777	35,421	21,709
Black	3,715	2,562	1,617	1,153	35,218	44,446	51,192	20,953
Husband worked	2,763	2,171	1,427	592	43,181	47,815	53,146	29,354
Worked year-round, full-time	2,214	1,759	1,210	455	47,002	51,442	55,517	30,966
Husband did not work	953	392	190	561	17,211	25,712	29,380	13,962
Hispanic[2]	4,038	2,236	1,166	1,802	28,454	35,919	43,856	19,989
Husband worked	3,395	2,047	1,078	1,349	31,198	37,282	45,587	21,681
Worked year-round, full-time	2,483	1,543	885	939	35,357	42,191	48,607	25,254
Husband did not work	643	190	88	453	17,042	21,431	28,779	14,714

Source: "Median Income of Married-Couple Families, by Work Experience of Husbands and Wives: 1993," *Statistical Abstract of the United States: 1995*, 1995, p. 479. Primary source: U.S. Bureau of the Census, *Current Population Reports*, P60-188. *Notes:* 1. Includes other races not shown separately. 2. Persons of Hispanic origin may be of any race.

★ 860 ★

Income

Relationships: Trends in Median Family Earnings, by Family Type, Number Earners, and Race/Ethnic Origin: 1980-1993

[**In current dollars of usual weekly earnings.** Annual averages of quarterly figures based on Current Population Survey. For families with wage and salary earners].

CHARACTERISTIC	NUMBER OF FAMILIES (1,000)				MEDIAN WEEKLY EARNINGS (dollars)			
	1980	1985	1990	1993	1980	1985	1990	1993
Total families with earners[1]	41,162	41,616	43,759	44,383	400	522	653	707
WHITE								
Total families with earners[1]	35,786	35,848	37,239	37,458	411	543	681	739
Married-couple families	30,316	29,899	30,361	30,288	438	589	745	816
One earner[2]	13,437	12,097	10,856	10,790	311	395	473	492
Husband	11,152	9,496	8,162	7,755	343	452	535	583
Wife	1,740	1,925	2,044	2,383	160	218	270	313
Two or more earners	16,878	17,802	19,505	19,497	542	723	892	984
Husband and wife only	11,448	12,394	14,148	14,546	511	691	855	954
Families maintained by women	4,140	4,616	5,127	5,355	233	311	382	415
Families maintained by men	1,331	1,333	1,751	1,816	374	475	539	547
BLACK								
Total families with earners[1]	4,503	4,668	5,082	5,268	299	378	459	490
Married-couple families	2,802	2,671	2,724	2,698	366	487	601	674
One earner[2]	1,103	902	893	909	210	257	304	344
Husband	769	580	527	539	244	292	345	381
Wife	279	257	290	287	151	206	243	321
Two or more earners	1,700	1,769	1,831	1,789	472	622	748	846
Husband and wife only	1,238	1,258	1,297	1,285	461	603	713	819
Families maintained by women	1,438	1,703	1,986	2,168	192	259	314	334
Families maintained by men	263	294	372	403	307	360	397	413
HISPANIC ORIGIN[3]								
Total families with earners[1]	(NA)	(NA)	3,624	3,879	(NA)	(NA)	496	505
Married-couple families	(NA)	(NA)	2,599	2,800	(NA)	(NA)	555	566
One earner[2]	(NA)	(NA)	1,050	1,177	(NA)	(NA)	322	334
Husband	(NA)	(NA)	814	912	(NA)	(NA)	356	365
Wife	(NA)	(NA)	164	183	(NA)	(NA)	236	262
Two or more earners	(NA)	(NA)	1,549	1,622	(NA)	(NA)	716	744
Husband and wife only	(NA)	(NA)	924	1,032	(NA)	(NA)	672	733
Families maintained by women	(NA)	(NA)	691	749	(NA)	(NA)	326	353
Families maintained by men	(NA)	(NA)	334	330	(NA)	(NA)	468	432

Source: "Families with Earners—Number and Earnings: 1980 to 1993," *Statistical Abstract of the United States:1995,* 1995, p. 434. Primary source: U.S. Bureau of Labor Statistics, Bulletin 2307; and *Employment and Earnings,* monthly, January issues. *Notes:* NA Not available.. 1. Excludes families in which there is no wage or salary earner or in which the husband, wife, or other person maintaining the family is either self-employed or in the Armed Forces. 2. Includes other earners, not shown separately. 3. Persons of Hispanic origin may be of any race.

Marriage Characteristics

★ 861 ★

1980 High School Sophomores in 1992: Percent Distribution of Number of Marriages of 1980 High School Sophomore Cohort, by Race/Ethnic Origin: 1992

Student characteristics	Never married	One	Two	Three or four
Total	37.9	56.8	5.1	0.3
Race-ethnicity				
Native American/Alaska Native	36.5	51.5	11.7	0.3
Asian/Pacific Islander	49.4	46.8	3.8	0.0
Black	55.2	41.7	3.1	0.1
White	34.7	59.5	5.4	0.4
Hispanic-Mexican	40.4	56.3	3.2	0.0
Hispanic-Cuban	37.7	58.2	4.2	0.0
Hispanic-Puerto Rican	44.6	51.2	3.7	0.5
Hispanic-other	36.0	59.2	4.8	0.0

Source: "Percentage of 1980 High Sophomores, by the Number of Times They had been Married by 1992 and Selected Distribution Characteristics," *Educational Attainment of 1980 High School Sophomores by 1992*, March 1995, p. 63. Primary source: U.S. Department of Education, Office of Educational Research and Improvement, National Center for Education Statistics. Statistical Analysis Report. *High School and Beyond: Educational Attainment of 1980 High School Sophomores by 1992; 1992 Descriptive Summary of 1980 High School Sophomores 12 Years Later.* NCES 95-304. Washington, DC: U.S. Government Printing Office, March, 1995.

★ 862 ★

Marriage Characteristics

Age of Spouses: Age of Husband in Black Married-Couple Families, by Age of Wife: 1994. Part 1

(Numbers in thousands except for averages and medians).

Characteristic	Total	Age of wife					
		Under 25 years	25 to 34 years	35 to 44 years	45 to 54 years	55 to 59 years	60 and 61 years
ALL RACES							
Total	54,251	2,897	12,297	14,231	10,295	3,789	1,363
BLACK							
Total	3,813	211	896	1,084	726	261	118

[Continued]

★ 862 ★

Age of Spouses: Age of Husband in Black Married-Couple Families, by Age of Wife: 1994. Part 1
[Continued]

Characteristic	Total	Age of wife					
		Under 25 years	25 to 34 years	35 to 44 years	45 to 54 years	55 to 59 years	60 and 61 years
Age of husband:							
Under 25 years	138	99	23	11	2	2	-
25 to 34 years	744	97	545	101	2	-	-
35 to 44 years	1,022	10	281	669	62	-	-
45 to 54 years	765	4	33	281	408	34	-
55 to 59 years	312	-	1	18	167	89	28
60 and 61 years	98	-	10	-	25	48	10
62 to 64 years	118	-	-	1	26	35	23
65 to 69 years	241	-	3	3	21	31	38
70 to 74 years	163	-	-	-	8	16	8
75 to 79 years	126	-	-	-	3	3	9
80 to 84 years	67	-	-	-	1	2	3
85 years and over	19	-	-	-	2	-	-
Median	45.0	25.6	32.8	41.4	52.3	60.2	64.7

Source: "Married-Couples, by Age of Husband, Age of Wife, and Race and Hispanic Origin of Householder or Subfamily Reference Person: March 1994," Rawlings, S.W., and Saluter, A.F., *Household and Family Characteristics: March 1994*, p. 132.

★ 863 ★

Marriage Characteristics

Age of Spouses: Age of Husband in Black Married-Couple Families, by Age of Wife: 1994. Part 2

(Numbers in thousands except for averages and medians).

Characteristic	Age of wife						Median
	62 to 64 years	65 to 69 years	70 to 74 years	75 to 79 years	80 to 84 years	85 years and over	
ALL RACES							
Total	1,988	3,041	2,283	1,212	599	255	43.4
BLACK							
Total	95	194	115	70	36	7	42.4
Age of husband:							
Under 25 years	-	-	-	-	-	-	21.9
25 to 34 years	-	-	-	-	-	-	30.1
35 to 44 years	-	-	-	-	-	-	38.3
45 to 54 years	1	2	-	-	-	1	46.6
55 to 59 years	3	4	1	-	2	-	53.2

[Continued]

★ 863 ★

Age of Spouses: Age of Husband in Black Married-Couple Families, by Age of Wife: 1994. Part 2

[Continued]

Characteristic	Age of wife						
	62 to 64 years	65 to 69 years	70 to 74 years	75 to 79 years	80 to 84 years	85 years and over	Median
60 and 61 years	3	-	2	-	-	-	56.5
62 to 64 years	15	13	1	-	3	-	59.6
65 to 69 years	49	84	13	-	-	-	63.5
70 to 74 years	13	66	39	12	-	-	67.7
75 to 79 years	9	15	48	30	10	-	72.6
80 to 84 years	1	10	12	20	16	1	(B)
85 years and over	-	-	-	7	5	5	(B)
Median	67.5	69.7	75.2	(B)	(B)	(B)	(X)

Source: "Married-Couples, by Age of Husband, Age of Wife, and Race and Hispanic Origin of Householder or Subfamily Reference Person: March 1994," Rawlings, S.W., and Saluter, A.F., *Household and Family Characteristics: March 1994*, p. 132. *Note:* B = base less than 75,000. X = Not applicable.

★ 864 ★

Marriage Characteristics

Marital Status: Marital Status in Black Subfamilies: 1994

(Numbers in thousands except for averages and medians).

Characteristic	All subfamilies				Related subfamilies				Unrelated subfamilies			
	Total	Married-couple	Father-child	Mother-child	Total	Married-couple	Father-child	Mother-child	Total	Married-couple	Father-child	Mother-child
BLACK SUBFAMILIES												
Marital Status of Reference Person												
Total	867	99	48	719	778	95	40	644	89	4	9	76
Married, spouse present	99	99	-	-	95	95	-	-	4	4	-	-
Married, spouse absent	93	-	6	87	84	-	6	78	9	-	-	9
Separated	70	-	5	65	61	-	5	56	9	-	-	9
Other	23	-	1	22	23	-	1	22	-	-	-	-
Widowed	12	-	2	10	10	-	2	8	2	-	-	2
Divorced	81	-	6	75	58	-	3	55	23	-	4	20
Never married	582	-	34	548	531	-	29	502	51	-	5	45

Source: "Subfamilies, by Type, Race, and Hispanic Origin of Reference Person: March 1994," Rawlings, S.W., and Saluter, A.F., *Household and Family Characteristics: March 1994*, p. 129.

★ 865 ★

Marriage Characteristics

Race of Spouses: Race of Wife, by Race of Husband in Married-Couple Families, by Subfamily Type and Race/Ethnic Origin: 1994

[Numbers in thousands except for averages and medians].

Characteristic	Total	Race of wife			Origin of wife	
		White	Black	Other	Hispanic[1]	Other
ALL MARRIED COUPLES						
Race of Husband						
Total	54,251	48,167	3,718	2,366	4,475	49,776
White	48,251	47,606	100	544	4,094	44,157
Black	3,852	196	3,598	59	92	3,761
Other	2,148	365	19	1,764	289	1,859
Origin of husband						
Hispanic[1]	4,320	3,979	72	269	3,755	564
Other	49,931	44,188	3,646	2,098	719	49,212
FAMILY HOUSEHOLDS						
Race of Husband						
Total	53,171	47,334	3,615	2,222	4,166	49,005
White	47,407	46,782	96	528	3,813	43,594
Black	3,751	194	3,499	59	88	3,663
Other	2,013	359	19	1,635	265	1,748
Origin of Husband						
Hispanic[1]	4,023	3,708	70	244	3,472	551
Other	49,148	43,626	3,545	1,977	694	48,454
RELATED SUBFAMILIES						
Race of Husband						
Total	1,014	783	99	132	274	740
White	791	775	4	12	251	540
Black	97	2	95	-	4	93
Other	126	5	-	120	19	107
Origin of Husband						
Hispanic[1]	266	244	2	20	252	14
Other	748	538	97	113	22	726

[Continued]

★ 865 ★

Race of Spouses: Race of Wife, by Race of Husband in Married-Couple Families, by Subfamily Type and Race/Ethnic Origin: 1994
[Continued]

Characteristic	Total	Race of wife			Origin of wife	
		White	Black	Other	Hispanic[1]	Other
UNRELATED SUBFAMILIES						
Race of Husband						
Total	66	50	4	12	35	32
White	52	49	-	4	29	23
Black	4	-	4	-	-	4
Other	10	1	-	9	6	4
Origin of Husband						
Hispanic[1]	31	27	-	5	31	-
Other	35	23	4	8	3	32

Source: "Married-Couples, by Age of Husband, Age of Wife, and Race and Hispanic Origin of Householder or Subfamily Reference Person: March 1994," Rawlings, S.W., and Saluter, A.F., *Household and Family Characteristics: March 1994*, p. 131. *Note:* 1. May be of any race.

Chapter 15
VITAL STATISTICS

Abortions

★ 866 ★

Abortions, by Selected Characteristics: 1985-1991

[Number of abortions from surveys conducted by source: characteristics from the U.S. Centers for Disease Control's (CDC) annual abortion surveillance summaries, with adjustments for changes in States reporting data to the CDC each year.]

CHARACTERISTIC	NUMBER (1,000)			PERCENT DISTRIBUTION			ABORTION RATIO[1]		
	1985	1990[1]	1991	1985	1990[1]	1991	1985	1990[1]	1991
Total abortions	1,589	1,609	1,557	100	100	100	297	280	275
Race of woman:									
White	1,076	1,039	982	68	65	63	265	241	233
Black and other	513	570	574	32	35	37	397	396	398

Source: "Abortions, by Selected Characteristics: 1985 to 1991," *Statistical Abstract of the United States*, 1995, p. 84. Primary source: S.K. Henshaw and J. Van Vort, eds., *Abortion Factbook, 1992 Edition: Readings, Trends, and State and Local Data to 1988.* The Alan Guttmacher Institute, New York, NY, 1992 (copyright): S.K. Henshaw and J. Van Vort, *Abortion Services in the United States, 1991 and 1992; Family Perspective, 26:100, 1994;* and unpublished data. *Notes:* NA Not available. 1. Number of abortions per 1,000 abortions and live births. Live births are those which occurred from July 1 of year shown through June 30 of the following year (to match time of conception with abortions).

★ 867 ★

Abortions

Legal Abortion Ratios and Patient Characteristics: 1973-1992

[Data are based on reporting by State health departments and by facilities].

	Abortions per 100 live births		
	Total	Race	
		White	All other
1973	19.6	17.5	28.9
1975	27.2	22.7	46.5
1980	35.9	31.3	54.7
1983	34.9	29.5	56.0
1984	36.4	30.8	58.2
1985	35.4	29.6	57.6
1986	35.4	30.0	55.8
1987	35.6	30.0	55.7
1988	35.2	25.7	45.5
1989	34.6	24.8	46.1
1990	34.6	25.2	47.5
1991	33.9	23.9	45.4
1992[1]	33.5	23.3	46.0

Source: "Legal Abortion Ratios, According to Selected Patient Characteristics: United States, Selected Years 1973-92." National Center for Health Statistics, *Health, United States, 1994*, p. 79. Primary source: Centers for Disease Control and Prevention: Abortion Surveillance, 1973-81. Public Health Service, DHHS, Atlanta, Ga., May 1977-Nov. 1985; CDC Surveillance Summaries. Abortion Surveillance, United States, 1982-83, Vol. 36, No. 1SS, Public Health Service, DHHS, Atlanta, Ga., Feb. 1987; 1984 and 1985, Vol. 38, No. SS-2, Sept. 1989; 1986 and 1987, Vol. 39, No. SS-2, June 1990; 1988, Vol. 40, No. SS-2, July 1991; 1989 , Vol. 41, No. Ss-5, Sept. 1992; 1990, Vol. 42, No. SS-6, Dec. 1993; 1991, in press; and Abortion Surveillance: Preliminary Analysis, United States, 1992, Vol. 43, No. 50. Public Health Service, DHHS, Atlanta, Ga., Dec. 23, 1994. *Notes:* 1. Data for 1992 are from 33 States, the District of Columbia, and New York City.

Birth Control

★ 868 ★

Methods of Contraception for Women 15-44 Years Old: 1982, 1988, and 1990

[Data are based on household interviews of samples of women in the childbearing ages].

Method of contraception and age	All races			White			Black		
	1982	1988	1990	1982	1988	1990	1982	1988	1990
	Number of women in thousands								
15-44 years	54,099	57,900	58,381	45,367	47,076	47,342	6,985	7,679	7,846
15-19 years	9,521	9,179	8,483	7,815	7,313	6,533	1,416	1,409	1,344

[Continued]

★ 868 ★

Methods of Contraception for Women 15-44 Years Old: 1982, 1988, and 1990
[Continued]

Method of contraception and age	All races			White			Black		
	1982	1988	1990	1982	1988	1990	1982	1988	1990
20-24 years	10,629	9,413	9,154	8,855	7,401	7,344	1,472	1,364	1,327
25-34 years	19,644	21,726	21,728	16,485	17,682	17,501	2,479	2,865	2,923
35-44 years	14,305	17,582	19,016	12,212	14,681	15,964	1,618	2,041	2,251
Percent of women using contraception									
All methods									
15-44 years	55.7	60.3	59.3	56.7	61.8	59.9	52.0	56.7	58.0
15-19 years	24.2	32.1	31.5	23.4	32.2	29.7	30.0	35.1	42.9
20-24 years	55.8	59.0	55.3	56.6	60.2	55.6	52.5	61.1	58.4
25-34 years	66.7	66.3	63.2	67.7	67.7	63.2	64.0	63.8	65.7
35-44 years	61.6	68.3	68.9	63.1	70.2	70.2	52.3	58.9	57.0
Percent of contracepting women									
Female sterilization									
15-44 years	23.2	27.5	29.5	22.1	26.1	27.7	30.0	38.1	41.8
15-19 years	-	1.5[1]	-	-	1.6[1]	-	-	1.6[1]	-
20-24 years	4.5	4.6	8.0	3.8[1]	3.9	8.1	9.8	9.1	9.3[1]
25-34 years	22.1	25.0	25.6	20.2	23.2	22.7	33.5	39.9	43.3
35-44 years	43.5	47.6	47.8	41.9	44.7	44.5	56.8	70.5	78.1
Male sterilization									
15-44 years	10.9	11.7	12.6	12.2	13.6	14.8	1.4[1]	0.9[1]	1.5[1]
15-19 years	0.4[1]	0.2[1]	-	0.5[1]	0.3[1]	-	-	-	-
20-24 years	3.6[1]	1.8[1]	1.8[1]	4.2[1]	2.3[1]	2.2[1]	0.5[1]	-	-
25-34 years	10.1	10.2	9.3	11.3	11.7	10.8	1.4[1]	1.1[1]	2.7[1]
35-44 years	19.9	20.8	22.9	21.6	23.7	25.7	3.1[1]	1.5[1]	1.5[1]
Birth control pill									
15-44 years	28.0	30.7	28.5	26.7	29.8	28.8	38.0	38.0	27.9
15-19 years	63.9	58.8	52.0	62.1	55.9	53.2	70.8	74.2	42.6
20-24 years	55.1	68.2	55.4	53.5	67.9	57.1	65.0	70.3	51.7
25-34 years	25.7	32.6	34.7	24.8	32.4	36.3	33.7	35.7	30.0
35-44 years	3.7	4.3	6.8	3.7	4.5	7.0	5.1[1]	4.2[1]	3.7[1]

[Continued]

★ 868 ★

Methods of Contraception for Women 15-44 Years Old: 1982, 1988, and 1990
[Continued]

Method of contraception and age	All races			White			Black		
	1982	1988	1990	1982	1988	1990	1982	1988	1990
Intrauterine device									
15-44 years	7.1	2.0	1.4	6.9	1.8	1.4	9.1	3.1	1.4[1]
15-19 years	1.3[1]	-	-	0.5[1]	-	-	4.9[1]	-	-
20-24 years	4.2	0.3[1]	0.8[1]	3.5[1]	0.3[1]	0.9[1]	6.2[1]	0.9[1]	-
25-34 years	9.7	2.1	0.7[1]	9.4	1.7	0.6[1]	13.0	4.1[1]	1.6[1]
35-44 years	6.9	3.1	2.6	7.0	3.0	2.5	6.5[1]	4.3[1]	2.4[1]
Diaphragm									
15-44 years	8.1	5.7	2.8	8.8	6.2	2.8	3.5	1.9	1.6[1]
15-19 years	6.0[1]	1.0[1]	-	7.1[1]	1.3[1]	-	1.8[1]	-	-
20-24 years	10.2	3.7	0.6[1]	11.3	4.1	0.7[1]	2.8[1]	1.6[1]	0.5[1]
25-34 years	10.3	7.3	3.6	11.3	8.0	3.9	3.0[1]	1.7[1]	2.1[1]
35-44 years	4.0	6.0	3.5	3.8	6.2	2.9	6.0[1]	3.3[1]	2.1[1]
Condom									
15-44 years	12.0	14.6	17.7	12.7	14.9	17.0	6.2	10.3	19.2
15-19 years	20.8	32.8	44.0	22.6	34.2	43.3	12.6[1]	22.7	52.4
20-24 years	10.7	14.5	25.3	11.4	15.8	23.1	6.4[1]	9.6	29.9
25-34 years	11.4	13.7	17.3	12.0	14.0	17.1	5.3	9.4	13.2
35-44 years	11.3	11.2	9.8	12.0	11.3	10.3	4.5[1]	7.0	6.7

Source: "Legal Abortion ratios, According to Selected Patient Characteristics: United States, Selected Years 1982, 1988, and 1990." National Center for Health Statistics, *Health, United States, 1994*, p. 82. Primary source: Centers for Disease Control and Prevention, National Center for Health Statistics, Division of Vital Statistics: Data from the National Survey of Family Growth. *Note:* 1. Relative standard error greater than 30 percent.

Birth Projections

★ 869 ★

Birth Projections: Lifetime Births Expected by Women 18 to 34 Years Old: 1992

[As of **June.** Covers women in the civilian noninstitutional population. Based on Current Population Survey; see text, section 1, and Appendix III].

CHARACTERISTIC	Women reporting on birth expectations (1,000)	RATE PER 1,000 WOMEN			PERCENTAGE EXPECTING-	
		Birth to date	Future births expected	Lifetime births expected	No lifetime births	No future births
Total[1]	24,223	1,135	963	2,098	9.3	48.3
White	20,141	1,077	1,014	2,091	9.3	46.1
Black	3,217	1,508	628	2,136	9.3	63.4
Hispanic[2]	2,357	1,493	838	2,331	5.7	51.4

Source: "Lifetime Births Expected by Women, 18 to 34 Years Old, by Selected Characteristics: 1992," *Statistical Abstract of the United States,* 1994, p. 81. Primary source: U.S. Bureau of the Census, *Current Population Reports,* series P20- 470. *Notes:* 1. Includes other races not shown separately. 2. Persons of Hispanic origin may be of any race.

★ 870 ★
Birth Projections

Birth Projections: Percent Distribution Per 1,000 Wives: 1971-1992. Part 1

[Based on samples of the female population of the United States; see source for details. See Appendix III.]

CONTRACEPTIVE STATUS AND METHOD	All women[1]	AGE			RACE		
		15-24 years	25-34 years	35-44 years	Non-Hispanic		Hispanic
					White	Black	
All women (1,000)	58,381	17,637	21,728	19,016	42,968	7,510	5,500
PERCENT DISTRIBUTION							
Sterile	32.1	3.8	26.4	64.6	32.9	34.0	27.5
Surgically sterile	30.2	3.1	24.8	61.1	31.2	31.4	23.9
Noncontraceptively sterile[2]	5.2	0.3	2.7	12.5	5.4	6.5	3.2
Contraceptively sterile[3]	25.0	2.8	22.1	48.6	25.8	24.9	20.7
Nonsurgically sterile[4]	1.9	0.7	1.6	3.5	1.7	2.6	3.6
Pregnant, postpartum	5.4	7.0	7.9	1.2	5.2	5.5	7.7
Seeking pregnancy	4.0	1.8	7.6	2.0	3.7	4.7	5.1
Other nonusers	24.2	46.4	17.1	12.0	23.6	22.1	28.3
Never had intercourse	9.4	26.4	2.8	1.3	8.7	7.0	16.4
No intercourse in last month	7.0	7.7	7.1	6.4	7.2	7.5	5.1

[Continued]

★ 870 ★

Birth Projections: Percent Distribution Per 1,000 Wives: 1971-1992. Part 1

[Continued]

CONTRACEPTIVE STATUS AND METHOD	All women[1]	AGE			RACE		
		15-24 years	25-34 years	35-44 years	Non-Hispanic		Hispanic
					White	Black	
Had intercourse in last month	7.8	12.3	7.2	4.3	7.7	7.6	6.8
Nonsurgical contraceptors	34.3	41.2	41.3	20.1	34.6	33.8	31.7
Pill	16.9	23.9	22.0	4.7	17.3	16.7	16.4
IUD	0.8	0.2	0.4	1.8	0.8	0.8	1.0
Diaphragm	1.7	0.2	2.3	2.4	1.8	1.0	0.8
Condom	10.5	13.9	11.0	6.7	10.3	11.4	8.9
Periodic abstinence	1.6	1.0	2.0	1.6	1.6	0.7	1.9
Natural family planning	0.2	0.1	0.4	0.2	0.2	-	-
Withdrawal	0.6	0.6	0.6	0.5	0.6	0.4	0.4
Other methods[5]	2.3	1.4	3.0	2.4	2.2	2.8	2.3

Source: "Contraceptive Use by Women, 15 to 44 Years Old: 1990," *Statistical Abstract of the United States*, 1994, p. 82. Primary source: U.S. National Center for Health Statistics, *Advance Data from Vital and Health Statistics*, No. 182. *Notes:* - Represents or rounds to zero. 1. Includes other races, not shown separately. 2. Persons who had sterilizing operation and who gave as one reason that they had medical problems with their female organs. 3. Includes all other sterilization operations and sterilization of the husband or current partner. 4. Persons sterile from illness, accident, or congenital conditions. 5. Douches, suppository, and less frequently used methods.

★ 871 ★

Birth Projections

Birth Projections: Percent Distribution Per 1,000 Wives: 1971-1992. Part 2

[See headnote, table 100].

YEAR	LIFETIME BIRTHS TO ALL WIVES[1] AGED-			LIFETIME BIRTHS TO WHITE WIVES AGED-		
	18 to 24 yrs. old	25 to 29 yrs. old	30 to 34 yrs. old	18 to 24 yrs. old	25 to 29 yrs. old	30 to 34 yrs. old
1971	2,375	2,619	2,989	2,353	2,577	2,936
1975	2,173	2,260	2,610	2,147	2,233	2,564
1980	2,134	2,166	2,248	2,130	2,146	2,223
1985	2,183	2,236	2,167	2,177	2,227	2,139
1990	2,244	2,285	2,277	2,218	2,272	2,257
1992	2,279	2,271	2,218	2,274	2,259	2,208

Source: "Lifetime Births Expected per 1,000 Wives: 1971 to 1992," *Statistical Abstract of the United States*, 1994, p. 81. *Notes:* NA Not available. 1. Includes other races not shown separately.

★ 872 ★

Birth Projections

Birth Projections: Percent Distribution Per 1,000 Wives: 1971-1992. Part 3

[See headnote, table 100].

YEAR	LIFETIME BIRTHS TO ALL BLACK WIVES AGED-			LIFETIME BIRTHS TO HISPANIC[2] WIVES AGED-		
	18 to 24 yrs. old	25 to 29 yrs. old	30 to 34 yrs. old	18 to 24 yrs. old	25 to 29 yrs. old	30 to 34 yrs. old
1971	2,623	3,112	3,714	(NA)	(NA)	(NA)
1975	2,489	2,587	3,212	2,223	2,607	3,238
1980	2,155	2,426	2,522	2,428	2,495	2,909
1985	2,242	2,259	2,521	2,367	2,628	2,712
1990	2,509	2,443	2,579	2,404	2,482	2,824
1992	2,353	2,389	2,362	2,511	2,437	2,600

Source: "Lifetime Births Expected per 1,000 Wives: 1971 to 1992," *Statistical Abstract of the United States,* 1994, p. 81. *Notes:* NA Not available. 1. Includes other races not shown separately. 2. Persons of Hispanic origin may be of any race.

★ 873 ★

Birth Projections

Lifetime Births Expected by Married Women: Trends, Part 1

[Data are based on household interviews of samples of currently married women of the civilian noninstitutionalized population].

Race and year	Expected births per currently married women					
	All ages 18-34 years	18-19 years	20-21 years	22-24 years	25-29 years	30-34 years
All races						
1967	3.1	2.7	2.9	2.9	3.0	3.3
1971	2.6	2.3	2.4	2.4	2.6	3.0
1975	2.3	2.2	2.2	2.2	2.3	2.6
1980	2.2	2.1	2.2	2.1	2.2	2.2
1985	2.2	2.1	2.2	2.2	2.2	2.2
1986	2.3	2.2	2.2	2.3	2.3	2.2
1987	2.2	2.1	2.2	2.2	2.2	2.2
1988	2.2	2.1	2.2	2.	2.3	2.2
1990	2.3	2.1	2.2	2.3	2.3	2.3
1992	2.2	2.3	2.3	2.3	2.3	2.2
White						
1967	3.0	2.7	3.0	2.8	3.0	3.2
1971	2.6	2.3	2.4	2.4	2.6	2.9
1975	2.3	2.2	2.1	2.1	2.2	2.6
1980	2.2	2.1	2.2	2.1	2.1	2.2

[Continued]

★ 873 ★

Lifetime Births Expected by Married Women: Trends, Part 1
[Continued]

Race and year	Expected births per currently married women					
	All ages 18-34 years	18-19 years	20-21 years	22-24 years	25-29 years	30-34 years
1985	2.2	2.0	2.2	2.2	2.2	2.1
1986	2.2	2.1	2.2	2.3	2.2	2.2
1987	2.2	2.0	2.2	2.2	2.2	2.2
1988	2.2	2.1	2.2	2.2	2.3	2.2
1990	2.3	2.1	2.2	2.3	2.3	2.3
1992	2.2	2.3	2.3	2.3	2.3	2.2
Black						
1967	3.5	[1]	2.5	3.0	3.4	4.3
1971	3.1	[1]	2.4	2.8	3.1	3.7
1975	2.8	[1]	2.6	2.5	2.6	3.2
1980	2.4	[1]	2.2	2.1	2.4	2.5
1985	2.4	[1]	[1]	2.4	2.3	2.6
1986	2.4	[1]	[1]	2.4	2.3	2.6
1987	2.3	[1]	[1]	2.2	2.3	2.3
1988	2.3	[1]	[1]	2.2	2.3	2.3
1990	2.5	2.1	2.4	2.6	2.4	2.6
1992	2.4	[1]	[1]	2.1	2.4	2.4

Source: "Lifetime Births Expected by Currently Married Women and Percent of Expected Births Already Born, According to Age and Race: United States, Selected Years 1967-92," National Center for Health Statistics, *Health, United States, 1994,* p. 69. Primary source: U.S. Bureau of the Census: Population characteristics. Current Population Reports Series P-20, Nos 301, 375, 406, 436, 454, and 470. Washington. U.S. Government Printing Office, Nov. 1976, Oct. 1982, June 1986, May 1989, Oct. 1991, and June 1993. Data from the Current Population Survey (CPS). *Notes:* Data for 1989 and 1991 are not available because surveys were not conducted in those years. 1. Estimates based on 50 or fewer subjects are not shown.

★ 874 ★

Birth Projections

Lifetime Births Expected by Married Women: Trends, Part 2

[Data are based on household interviews of samples of currently married women of the civilian noninstitutionalized population].

Race and year	Percent of expected births already born					
	All ages 18-34 years	18-19 years	20-21 years	22-24 years	25-29 years	30-34 years
All races						
1967	70.2	26.9	33.2	47.8	76.1	92.7
1971	69.4	25.3	32.5	46.7	74.4	93.7
1975	68.8	27.5	30.7	43.9	70.9	93.0
1980	67.0	29.5	32.9	44.9	64.7	89.7
1985	64.2	27.0	30.9	41.8	60.2	84.4
1986	64.7	29.0	30.4	41.8	59.5	84.8

[Continued]

★ 874 ★

Lifetime Births Expected by Married Women: Trends, Part 2
[Continued]

Race and year	Percent of expected births already born					
	All ages 18-34 years	18-19 years	20-21 years	22-24 years	25-29 years	30-34 years
1987	66.5	27.8	36.4	43.0	62.0	83.8
1988	65.3	25.0	33.4	40.9	58.9	83.6
1990	64.5	29.9	33.1	44.2	57.5	81.1
1992	66.3	27.9	36.1	45.0	59.4	82.2
White						
1967	68.9	24.2	30.1	46.2	75.1	92.9
1971	68.9	23.7	31.4	45.3	74.1	93.8
1975	68.5	24.9	29.4	42.3	70.5	93.2
1980	66.3	28.6	31.8	43.5	64.0	90.0
1985	63.3	25.7	30.6	40.4	59.4	84.1
1986	63.8	28.6	28.7	40.5	58.6	84.8
1987	65.6	27.0	36.0	42.0	60.9	83.6
1988	64.4	24.0	32.6	38.9	58.2	83.2
1990	63.6	26.8	30.0	43.1	56.2	80.8
1992	65.4	27.4	33.6	42.7	58.1	82.2
Black						
1967	82.8	[1]	65.7	67.9	87.9	92.3
1971	74.8	[1]	43.0	57.5	81.0	93.4
1975	76.4	[1]	43.3	61.0	78.2	91.8
1980	74.7	[1]	46.1	58.9	73.8	90.9
1985	77.1	[1]	[1]	62.3	72.8	91.4
1986	75.7	[1]	[1]	59.7	70.2	90.0
1987	77.8	[1]	[1]	55.4	76.6	89.7
1988	75.5	[1]	[1]	61.4	70.1	89.9
1990	74.1	49.0	54.8	56.6	71.9	85.0
1992	79.3	[1]	[1]	76.1	73.3	85.9

Source: "Lifetime Births Expected by Currently Married Women and Percent of Expected Births Already Born, According to Age and Race: United States, Selected Years 1967-92," National Center for Health Statistics, *Health, United States, 1994*, p. 69. Primary source: U.S. Bureau of the Census: Population characteristics. Current Population Reports Series P-20, Nos 301, 375, 406, 436, 454, and 470. Washington. U.S. Government Printing Office, Nov. 1976, Oct. 1982, June 1986, May 1989, Oct. 1991, and June 1993. Data from the Current Population Survey (CPS). *Notes:* Data for 1989 and 1991 are not available because surveys were not conducted in those years. 1. Estimates based on 50 or fewer subjects are not shown.

Birth Rates

★ 875 ★

Birth Rates: Estimated Birth Rate for Unmarried Women by Education, Age, Race, and Hispanic Origin of Mother, 1992

[Rates are live births to unmarried women per 1,000 unmarried women in specified group: see Technical notes.]

Race, Hispanic origin, and age of mother	Total	Years of school completed				
		0-8 years	9-11 years	12 years	13-15 years	16 years or more
All races[1]						
15-44 years[2]	45.2	82.3	59.2	70.2	21.2	10.8
15-17 years	30.4	28.2	28.4	244.1	6.3	...
18-24 years	68.1	259.1	127.2	111.9	19.8	11.0
25-29 years	56.5	210.8	109.4	77.1	40.2	11.1
30-34 years	37.9	82.8	71.7	46.7	26.7	15.5
35-39 years	18.8	58.4	28.8	20.9	13.6	11.6
40-44 years[3]	4.1	15.1	6.3	4.0	2.6	3.3
White						
15-44 years[2]	35.2	85.5	47.9	55.8	14.4	7.9
15-17 years	21.6	24.2	19.4	168.8	5.1	...
18-24 years	52.3	256.9	116.8	85.3	13.2	6.9
25-29 years	45.4	256.5	122.6	61.8	28.1	7.3
30-34 years	31.5	102.1	62.7	39.5	19.4	12.4
35-39 years	16.2	59.9	32.2	17.6	10.0	10.1
40-44 years[3]	3.6	17.0	5.8	3.3	2.0	3.0
Black						
15-44 years[2]	86.5	76.1	101.0	111.9	54.7	31.6
15-17 years	78.0	46.5	79.9	671.7	15.3	...
18-24 years	145.4	228.0	168.3	200.2	66.6	76.7
25-29 years	98.2	78.8	97.5	123.1	85.0	46.2
30-34 years	57.7	32.3	88.2	64.8	49.2	32.2
35-39 years	25.8	47.3	24.4	28.2	27.0	16.8
40-44 years[3]	5.4	9.2	6.3	5.8	4.4	5.0
Hispanic[4]						
15-44 years[2]	95.4	169.1	100.7	111.0	33.2	29.0
15-17 years	51.0	66.0	44.2	419.5	12.2	...
18-24 years	130.9	306.4	196.6	140.3	28.6	28.5
25-29 years	138.3	302.3	185.6	131.4	59.3	34.4
30-34 years	91.8	153.9	99.7	105.6	40.0	38.7

[Continued]

★ 875 ★

Birth Rates: Estimated Birth Rate for Unmarried Women by Education, Age, Race, and Hispanic Origin of Mother, 1992

[Continued]

Race, Hispanic origin, and age of mother	Total	Years of school completed				
		0-8 years	9-11 years	12 years	13-15 years	16 years or more
35-39 years	48.1	87.4	61.4	37.6	25.0	20.0
40-44 years[3]	14.5	33.8	12.5	10.0	6.1	8.9

Source: "Estimated Birth Rate for Unmarried Women by Educational Attainment, Age, Race, and Hispanic Origin of Mother: United States, 1992," S.J. Ventura, *Births to Unmarried Mothers: United States, 1980-92,* p. 7. *Notes:* 1. Includes race other than white and black. 2. Rates computed by relating total births, regardless of age of mother, to unmarried women aged 15-44 years in specified group. 3. Rates computed by relating births to unmarried mothers aged 40 years and over to unmarried women aged 40-44 years in specified group. 4. Persons of Hispanic origin may be of any race. For method of estimation, see Technical notes.

★ 876 ★

Birth Rates

Birth Rates: First Birth Rates for Unmarried Women by Age and Race of Mother, 1980-92

[Rates are first live births per 1,000 unmarried women in specified group.]

Race and year	15-44 years[1]	Age of mother							
		15-19 years			20-24 years	25-29 years	30-34 years	35-39 years	40-44 years[2]
		Total	15-17 years	18-19 years					
All races[3]									
1992	21.6	33.8	25.9	46.4	30.8	15.9	8.7	4.0	0.9
1991	21.7	34.1	26.4	45.7	30.9	15.9	8.7	3.9	0.8
1990	21.2	32.5	25.3	42.6	29.5	15.9	8.7	3.8	0.7
1989	20.5	31.0	24.7	39.8	27.7	15.0	8.3	3.5	0.7
1988	19.2	28.4	22.9	36.9	25.5	13.9	7.7	3.3	0.6
1987	18.4	26.7	21.5	35.4	24.6	13.0	7.3	3.0	0.6
1986	17.7	25.7	20.1	34.9	23.5	12.3	5.5	2.7	0.5
1985	17.2	25.0	19.7	33.5	22.2	11.6	6.1	2.4	0.4
1984	16.4	23.9	19.3	31.0	20.5	10.7	5.6	2.2	0.4
1983	16.2	23.6	19.4	29.9	19.8	10.1	5.2	2.0	0.3
1982	16.3	22.9	18.9	29.0	19.8	10.1	5.0	1.8	0.3
1981	16.3	22.4	18.4	28.7	19.7	10.0	4.6	1.6	0.3
1980	16.6	22.3	18.3	28.8	19.8	9.7	4.6	1.5	0.3
White									
1992	18.4	27.0	19.4	39.2	26.9	14.3	8.3	4.0	0.9
1991	18.4	27.0	19.6	38.1	26.6	14.2	8.2	3.8	0.8
1990	17.6	25.2	18.4	34.7	24.9	13.9	8.1	3.8	0.7

[Continued]

★ 876 ★

Birth Rates: First Birth Rates for Unmarried Women by Age and Race of Mother, 1980-92
[Continued]

Race and year	15-44 years[1]	Age of mother							
		15-19 years			20-24 years	25-29 years	30-34 years	35-39 years	40-44 years[2]
		Total	15-17 years	18-19 years					
1989	16.4	23.3	17.5	31.4	22.6	12.7	7.5	3.5	0.7
1988	15.1	21.2	16.0	28.9	20.3	11.6	7.0	3.2	0.6
1987	14.2	19.7	14.9	27.4	19.4	10.8	6.6	2.9	0.5
1986	13.6	18.5	13.7	26.7	18.4	10.3	6.0	2.6	0.5
1985	13.0	17.7	13.4	24.9	17.2	9.7	5.5	2.3	0.4
1984	12.0	16.4	12.6	22.3	15.4	8.7	5.0	2.1	0.3
1983	11.7	16.0	12.6	21.2	14.7	8.1	4.6	1.8	0.3
1982	11.7	15.5	12.1	20.4	14.7	8.1	4.4	1.7	0.3
1981	11.5	14.9	11.7	20.0	14.5	7.9	3.9	1.5	0.2
1980	11.4	14.3	11.2	19.7	14.3	7.7	3.7	1.3	0.3
Black									
1992	34.9	70.5	61.5	84.2	51.2	22.3	9.9	3.6	0.7
1991	36.4	72.6	63.3	85.9	53.0	22.5	10.2	3.7	0.8
1990	37.4	71.9	62.3	84.9	52.3	23.9	10.5	3.6	0.7
1989	38.7	72.6	63.4	85.8	52.4	23.7	10.5	3.6	0.7
1988	37.6	67.9	59.8	80.3	50.2	22.5	9.8	3.5	0.7
1987	36.8	65.3	57.6	77.0	48.9	21.3	9.3	3.2	0.6
1986	35.9	64.2	55.7	76.9	47.1	19.6	8.6	2.9	0.5
1985	35.6	63.8	55.5	75.8	45.2	18.3	7.9	2.8	0.5
1984	35.3	63.0	55.4	73.6	43.3	17.7	7.4	2.6	0.5
1983	36.0	62.9	55.8	73.0	42.2	17.5	7.1	2.5	0.4
1982	36.9	62.4	55.2	72.8	42.7	17.9	7.1	2.3	0.4
1981	38.4	62.4	55.0	73.7	43.4	18.2	7.1	2.2	0.5
1980	40.1	65.3	58.1	76.8	44.6	17.3	7.3	2.0	0.4

Source: "First Birth Rates for Unmarried Women by Age and Race of Mother, United States, 1980-92," S.J. Ventura, *Births to Unmarried Mothers: United States, 1980-92,* p. 31. *Notes:* 1. Rates computed by relating first births to unmarried women, regardless of age of mother, to unmarried women aged 15-44 years. 2. Rates computed by relating first births to unmarried women aged 40 and over to unmarried women aged 40-44 years. 3. Includes races other than white and black.

★ 877 ★

Birth Rates

Birth Rates: First Birth Rates for Unmarried Women by Age of Mother, 1940-92, and Age of Mother and Race, 1940, 1950, and 1955-92

[Rates are live births to unmarried women per 1,000 unmarried women in specified group.]

Race and year	15-44 years[1]	Age of mother								
		15-19 years			20-24 years	25-29 years	30-34 years	35-39 years	40-44 years[2]
		Total	15-17 years	18-19 years					
Black[5]										
Race of mother:										
					Reported/inferred[3]					
1992	86.5	105.9	78.0	147.8	144.3	98.2	57.7	25.8	5.4
1991	89.5	108.5	80.4	148.7	147.5	100.9	60.1	25.6	5.4
1990	90.5	106.0	78.8	143.7	144.8	105.3	61.5	25.5	5.1
1989	90.7	104.5	78.9	140.9	142.4	102.9	60.5	24.9	5.0
1988	86.5	96.1	73.5	130.5	133.6	97.2	57.4	24.1	5.0
1987	82.6	90.9	69.9	123.0	126.1	91.6	53.1	22.4	4.7
1986	79.0	88.5	67.0	121.1	118.0	84.6	50.0	20.6	4.4
1985	77.0	87.6	66.8	117.9	113.1	79.3	47.5	20.4	4.3
1984	75.2	86.1	66.5	113.6	107.9	77.8	43.8	19.4	4.3
1983	76.2	85.5	66.8	111.9	107.2	79.7	43.8	19.4	4.8
1982	77.9	85.1	66.3	112.7	109.3	82.7	44.1	19.5	5.2
1981	79.4	85.0	65.9	114.2	110.7	83.1	45.5	19.6	5.6
1980	81.1	87.9	68.8	118.2	112.3	81.4	46.7	19.0	5.5
Race of child:										
					Estimated[4]					
1980	83.2	90.3	70.6	121.8	116.0	82.9	47.0	18.5	5.5
1979	83.0	91.0	71.0	123.3	114.1	80.0	44.8	19.3	5.9
1978	81.1	87.9	68.8	119.6	114.4	79.6	43.9	18.5	6.2
1977	82.6	90.9	73.0	121.7	110.1	78.6	45.7	19.0	6.6
1976	81.6	89.7	73.5	117.9	107.2	78.0	45.0	19.2	7.0
1975	84.2	93.5	76.8	123.8	108.0	75.7	50.0	20.5	7.2
1974	85.5	93.8	78.6	122.2	109.8	80.3	51.8	24.3	6.7
1973	88.6	94.9	81.2	120.5	116.0	84.5	57.8	27.6	7.7
1972	91.6	98.2	82.8	128.2	121.2	88.3	57.4	30.4	8.5
1971	96.1	98.6	80.7	135.2	130.6	99.6	68.6	32.7	10.1

[Continued]

★ 877 ★

Birth Rates: First Birth Rates for Unmarried Women by Age of Mother, 1940-92, and Age of Mother and Race, 1940, 1950, and 1955-92

[Continued]

Race and year	15-44 years[1]	Age of mother								
		15-19 years			20-24 years	25-29 years	30-34 years	35-39 years	40-44 years[2]
		Total	15-17 years	18-19 years					
1970	95.5	96.9	77.9	136.4	131.5	100.9	71.8	32.9	10.4
1969	90.6	90.3	72.0	128.4	125.3	99.5	70.1	34.3	10.1

Source: "Birth Rates for Unmarried Women by Age of Mother: United States, 1940- 42, and by Age of Mother and Race, 1940, 1950, and 1955-92," *Births to Unmarried Mothers: United States, 1980-92,* p. 30. *Notes:* Rates for 1981-89 have been revised and differ, therefore, from rates published in *Vital Statistics of the United States,* Vol. I, Natality, for 1991 and earlier years; see Technical notes. 1. Rates computed by relating births to unmarried women, regardless of age of mother, to unmarried women age 15-44 years. 2. Rates computed by relating births to unmarried women aged 40 and over to unmarried women aged 40-44 years. Rates by race for years prior to 1969 are computed by relating births to unmarried women aged 35 years and over to unmarried women aged 35-44 years. 3. Data for States in which marital status was not reported have been inferred from other items on the birth certificate and included with data from the reporting States; see Technical notes. 4. Births to unmarried women are estimated for the United States from data from registration areas in which marital status of mother was reported; see Technical notes. 5. Data also included in "all other" group.

Births

★ 878 ★

Births: Number and Percent Distribution of Births by Adequacy of Prenatal Care to Marital Status and Race of Mother, 1992

Adequacy of care[1]	All races[2]		White		Black	
	Married	Unmarried	Married	Unmarried	Married	Unmarried
Number						
Number of births	2,840,138	1,224,876	2,479,692	721,986	214,664	458,969
Percent distribution[3]						
Total	100.0	100.0	100.0	100.0	100.0	100.0
Adequate	78.0	51.7	79.2	55.1	69.1	46.9
Intermediate	17.8	33.7	16.9	32.7	23.6	35.2
Inadequate	4.2	14.6	3.8	12.3	7.3	17.9

Source: "Number of Births and Percent Distribution by Adequacy of Prenatal Care, According to Marital Status and Race of Mother: United States, 1992," S.J. Ventura, *Births to Unmarried Mothers: United States, 1980-92,* p. 20. *Notes:* 1. Adequacy of care as directed by Kessner index. See Technical notes. 2. Includes races other than white and black. 3. Based on births for which all items comprising adequacy of care were reported.

★ 879 ★
Births

Births: Percent Low Birthweight, by Smoking Status, Age, and Race of Mother: 1992

[Low birthweight is defined as weight of less than 2,500 grams (5 lb. 8 oz.) Excludes California, Indiana, New York, and South Dakota, which did not require reporting of tobacco use during pregnancy.]

| Smoking Measure And Race of Mother | All ages | Under 15 years | 15-19 years | | | 20-24 years | 25-29 years | 30-34 years | 35-39 years | 40-49 years |
			Total	15-17 years	18-19 years					
All races[1], total	7.3	13.4	9.6	10.5	9.1	7.4	6.3	6.6	7.7	8.7
Smoker	11.5	13.2	11.0	11.4	10.8	10.1	11.2	12.9	15.6	16.9
Nonsmoker	6.3	13.4	9.2	10.2	8.6	6.6	5.3	5.5	6.4	7.6
Not stated	9.1	14.2	11.8	13.1	11.1	9.4	8.2	8.0	9.7	9.2
White, total	5.9	9.9	7.9	8.5	7.5	6.0	5.2	5.5	6.5	7.4
Smoker	9.7	12.6	10.4	11.0	10.1	8.8	9.1	10.3	12.6	14.2
Nonsmoker	5.0	9.3	6.9	7.8	6.5	5.1	4.4	4.7	5.5	6.6
Not stated	7.2	(B)	9.8	10.3	9.6	7.3	6.5	6.4	8.3	7.9
Black, total	13.4	15.9	13.5	13.9	13.2	12.3	13.1	14.8	16.2	16.7
Smoker	22.1	(B)	16.7	16.1	17.0	18.8	22.4	25.7	28.6	29.1
Nonsmoker	11.9	16.0	13.2	13.6	12.8	11.3	10.9	11.6	12.8	14.3
Not stated	16.8	14.3	16.2	17.8	15.0	15.6	17.0	18.5	19.4	16.7

Source: "Percent Low Birthweight, by Smoking Status, Age and Race of Mother: 1992," *Statistical Abstract of the United States,* 1994, p. 83. Primary source: U.S. National Center for Health Statistics, *Monthly Vital Statistics Reports. Notes:* B Base figure too small to meet statistical standards for reliability of a derived figure. 1. Includes other races other than White and Black.

★ 880 ★
Births

Births: Percent of Births to Mother with Adequate Prenatal Care by Education, Age, Race, and Marital Status of Mother, 1992

| Age and years of school completed by mother | All races[1] | | White | | Black | |
	Married	Unmarried	Married	Unmarried	Married	Unmarried
Under 20 years[2]	57.6	47.4	58.5	51.3	50.4	41.9
0-8 years	44.4	38.4	44.7	40.0	40.3	35.4
9-11 years	55.3	46.5	56.2	51.0	46.7	40.5
12 years	64.2	52.5	65.6	57.1	53.8	46.3
13-15 years	67.6	53.7	69.1	57.3	60.9	49.5
16 years or more	---	---	---	---	---	---
20 years and over[2]	79.1	53.6	80.4	56.6	70.0	49.2
0-8 years	47.5	39.4	47.2	39.3	51.7	38.9
9-11 years	60.0	45.5	61.0	50.0	50.2	38.0
12 years	77.4	55.5	79.2	60.3	65.0	49.6

[Continued]

★ 880 ★

Births: Percent of Births to Mother with Adequate Prenatal Care by Education, Age, Race, and Marital Status of Mother, 1992

[Continued]

Age and years of school completed by mother	All races[1]		White		Black	
	Married	Unmarried	Married	Unmarried	Married	Unmarried
13-15 years	83.5	62.5	84.9	65.8	74.9	59.2
16 years or more	88.6	72.5	89.5	75.6	83.1	67.2

Source: "Percent of Births to Mothers with Adequate Prenatal Care by Education, Age, Race, and Marital Status of Mother: United States, 1992," S.J. Ventura, *Births to Unmarried Mothers: United States, 1980-92,* p. 20. *Notes:* 1. Includes races other than white and black. 2. Includes births to mothers with educational attainment not reported.

★ 881 ★

Births

Births: Percent of Mothers Gaining Less Than 16 Pounds During Pregnancy, by Education, Age, Marital Status, and Race, 1992

Age and years of school completed by mother	Married			Unmarried		
	All races[1]	White	Black	All races[1]	White	Black
Under 20 years of age[2]	8.1	7.7	12.6	11.4	8.2	15.6
0-8 years	12.8	12.4	18.9	14.1	11.5	17.9
9-11 years	8.5	8.1	14.0	11.5	8.1	16.1
12 years	6.5	6.0	11.0	10.0	7.0	14.1
13-15 years	6.1	5.8	9.0	9.0	7.2	11.4
16 years or more	---	---	---	---	---	---
20 years of age and over[2]	8.4	7.9	13.6	13.8	11.1	17.4
0-8 years	16.3	15.3	21.8	18.7	16.7	24.5
9-11 years	13.4	12.7	20.3	16.6	12.8	21.9
12 years	9.7	9.2	14.9	13.3	10.4	17.0
13-15 years	7.8	7.4	12.3	11.1	9.0	13.6
16 years or more	4.9	4.5	9.5	8.7	6.7	12.1

Source: "Percent of Births to Mothers Gaining Less Than 16 Pounds During Pregnancy by Education, Age, Marital Status, and Race of Mother: Total of 46 Reporting States and the District of Columbia, 1992," S.J. Ventura, *Births to Unmarried Mothers: United States, 1980-92,* p. 21. *Notes:* Excludes data for California, which did not require reporting of weight gain on the birth certificate. 1. Includes races other than white and black. 2. Includes births to mothers with educational attainment not reported.

★ 882 ★

Births

Births: Percent of Mothers Who Smoked During Pregnancy by Age, Marital Status, and Race, 1992

Age and years of school completed by mother	Married			Unmarried		
	All races[1]	White	Black	All races[1]	White	Black
All ages[2]	13.3	13.9	8.8	25.9	34.0	16.1
0-8 years	13.0	13.6	11.2	21.9	26.8	11.5
9-11 years	31.1	32.7	19.9	30.3	39.6	19.2
12 years	17.5	18.6	9.7	25.6	34.7	15.2
13-15 years	10.0	10.6	6.7	20.6	27.5	13.1
16 years or more	3.6	3.7	3.2	12.9	15.6	9.5
Under 20 years of age[2]	19.3	20.6	4.5	17.8	27.5	5.9
0-8 years	21.7	22.3	9.3	18.8	28.0	5.4
9-11 years	23.9	25.3	6.3	19.6	30.2	6.9
12 years	14.4	15.6	2.6	15.2	23.9	4.1
13-15 years	7.4	8.1	-	8.5	14.0	2.1
16 years or more	---	---	---	---	---	---
20 years of age and over[2]	12.9	13.5	9.0	29.7	37.1	21.0
0-8 years	11.3	11.7	11.6	25.1	25.9	26.4
9-11 years	33.7	35.5	23.7	42.2	49.4	33.7
12 years	17.7	18.7	10.1	28.5	37.9	18.2
13-15 years	10.1	10.6	6.8	21.6	28.7	14.1
16 years or more	3.6	3.7	3.2	12.9	15.6	9.5

Source: "Percent of Mothers Who Smoked During Pregnancy by Education, Age, Marital Status, and Race of Mother: Total of 46 Reporting States and the District of Columbia, 1992," S.J. Ventura, *Births to Unmarried Mothers: United States, 1980-92*, p. 21. *Notes:* Excludes data for California, Indiana, New York, and South Dakota, which did not require reporting of tobacco use on the birth certificate. 1. Includes races other than white and black. 2. Includes births with educational attainment not reported.

★ 883 ★

Births

Live Births and Crude Birth Rates: Trends

[Data are based on the National Vital Statistics System].

| Race and year | Live births | Crude birth rate[1] | 10-14 years | 15-19 years | | | 20-24 years | 25-29 years | 30-34 years | 35-39 years | 40-44 years | 45-49 years |
				Total	15-17 years	18-19 years						
				Age of mother								
						Live births per 1,000 women						
All races												
1950	3,632,000	24.1	1.0	81.6	40.7	132.7	196.6	166.1	103.7	52.9	15.1	1.2
1960	4,257,850	23.7	0.8	89.1	43.9	166.7	258.1	197.4	112.7	56.2	15.5	0.9
1970	3,731,386	18.4	1.2	68.3	38.8	114.7	167.8	145.1	73.3	31.7	8.1	0.5
1980	3,612,258	15.9	1.1	53.0	32.5	82.1	115.1	112.9	61.9	19.8	3.9	0.2
1981	3,629,238	15.8	1.1	52.2	32.0	80.0	112.2	111.5	61.4	20.0	3.8	0.2
1982	3,680,537	15.9	1.1	52.4	32.3	79.4	111.6	111.0	64.1	21.2	3.9	0.2
1983	3,638,933	15.6	1.1	51.4	31.8	77.4	107.8	108.5	64.9	22.0	3.9	0.2
1984	3,669,141	15.6	1.2	50.6	31.0	77.4	106.8	108.7	67.0	22.9	3.9	0.2
1985	3,760,561	15.8	1.2	51.0	31.0	79.6	108.3	111.0	69.1	24.0	4.0	0.2
1986	3,756,547	15.6	1.3	50.2	30.5	79.6	107.4	109.8	70.1	24.4	4.1	0.2
1987	3,809,394	15.7	1.3	50.6	31.7	78.5	107.9	111.6	72.1	26.3	4.4	0.2
1988	3,909,510	16.0	1.3	53.0	33.6	79.9	110.2	114.4	74.8	28.1	4.8	0.2
1989	4,040,958	16.4	1.4	57.3	36.4	84.2	113.8	117.6	77.4	29.9	5.2	0.2
1990	4,158,212	16.7	1.4	59.9	37.5	88.6	116.5	120.2	80.8	31.7	5.5	0.2
1991	4,110,907	16.3	1.4	62.1	38.7	94.4	115.7	118.2	79.5	32.0	5.5	0.2
1992	4,065,014	15.9	1.4	60.7	37.8	94.5	114.6	117.4	80.2	32.5	5.9	0.3
Provisional data:												
1992	4,084,000	16.0	-	-	-	-	-	-	-	-	-	-
1993	4,039,000	15.7	-	-	-	-	-	-	-	-	-	-
Race of child:[2] White												
1950	3,108,000	23.0	0.4	70.0	31.3	120.5	190.4	165.1	102.6	51.4	14.5	1.0
1960	3,600,744	22.7	0.4	79.4	35.5	154.6	252.8	194.9	109.6	54.0	14.7	0.8
1970	3,091,264	17.4	0.5	57.4	29.2	101.5	163.4	145.9	71.9	30.0	7.5	0.4
1980	2,898,732	14.9	0.6	44.7	25.2	72.1	109.5	112.4	60.4	18.5	3.4	0.2
Race of mother:[3] White												
1980	2,936,351	15.1	0.6	45.4	25.5	73.2	111.1	113.8	61.2	18.8	3.5	0.2
1981	2,947,679	15.0	0.5	44.9	25.4	71.5	108.3	112.3	61.0	19.0	3.4	0.2
1982	2,984,817	15.1	0.6	45.0	25.5	70.8	107.7	111.9	64.0	20.4	3.6	0.2
1983	2,946,468	14.8	0.6	43.9	25.0	68.8	103.8	109.4	65.3	21.3	3.6	0.2
1984	2,967,100	14.8	0.6	42.9	24.3	68.4	102.7	109.8	67.7	22.2	3.6	0.2
1985	3,037,913	15.0	0.6	43.3	24.4	70.4	104.1	112.3	69.9	23.3	3.7	0.2
1986	3,019,175	14.8	0.6	42.3	23.8	70.1	102.7	110.8	70.9	23.9	3.8	0.2
1987	3,043,828	14.9	0.6	42.5	24.6	68.9	102.3	112.3	73.0	25.9	4.1	0.2
1988	3,102,083	15.0	0.6	44.4	26.0	69.6	103.7	114.8	75.4	27.7	4.5	0.2
1989	3,192,355	15.4	0.7	47.9	28.1	72.9	106.9	117.8	78.1	29.7	4.9	0.2
1990	3,290,273	15.8	0.7	50.8	29.5	78.0	109.8	120.7	81.7	31.5	5.2	0.2
1991	3,241,273	15.4	0.8	52.8	30.7	83.5	109.0	118.8	80.5	31.8	5.2	0.2
1992	3,201,678	15.0	0.8	51.8	30.1	83.8	108.2	118.4	81.4	32.2	5.7	0.2

[Continued]

★ 883 ★

Live Births and Crude Birth Rates: Trends
[Continued]

| Race and year | Live births | Crude birth rate[1] | 10-14 years | 15-19 years | | | 20-24 years | 25-29 years | 30-34 years | 35-39 years | 40-44 years | 45-49 years |
				Total	15-17 years	18-19 years						
Race of child:[2] Black												
1960	602,264	31.9	4.3	156.1	-	-	295.4	218.6	137.1	73.9	21.9	1.1
1970	572,362	25.3	5.2	140.7	101.4	204.9	202.7	136.3	79.6	41.9	12.5	1.0
1980	589,616	22.1	4.3	100.0	73.6	138.8	146.3	109.1	62.9	24.5	5.8	0.3
Race of mother:[3] Black												
1980	568,080	21.3	4.3	97.8	72.5	135.1	140.0	103.9	59.9	23.5	5.6	0.3
1981	564,955	20.8	4.0	94.5	69.3	131.0	136.5	102.3	57.4	23.1	5.6	0.3
1982	568,506	20.7	4.0	94.3	69.7	128.9	135.4	101.3	57.5	23.3	5.1	0.4
1983	562,624	20.2	4.1	93.9	69.6	127.1	131.9	98.4	56.2	23.3	5.1	0.3
1984	568,138	20.1	4.4	94.1	69.2	128.1	132.2	98.4	56.7	23.3	4.8	0.2
1985	581,824	20.4	4.5	95.4	69.3	132.4	135.0	100.2	57.9	23.9	4.6	0.3
1986	592,910	20.5	4.7	95.8	69.3	135.1	137.3	101.1	59.3	23.8	4.8	0.3
1987	611,173	20.8	4.8	97.6	72.1	135.8	142.7	104.3	60.6	24.6	4.8	0.2
1988	638,562	21.5	4.9	102.7	75.7	142.7	149.7	108.2	63.1	25.6	5.1	0.3
1989	673,124	22.3	5.1	111.5	81.9	151.9	156.8	114.4	66.3	26.7	5.4	0.3
1990	684,336	22.4	4.9	112.8	82.3	152.9	160.2	115.5	68.7	28.1	5.5	0.3
1991	682,602	21.9	4.8	115.5	84.1	158.6	160.9	113.1	67.7	28.3	5.5	0.2
1992	673,633	21.3	4.7	112.4	81.3	157.9	158.0	111.2	67.5	28.8	5.6	0.2

Source: "Live Births, Crude Birth Rates by Age of Mother, According to Race: United States, Selected Years 1950-93," National Center for Health Statistics, *Health, United States, 1994*, p. 66. Primary source: Centers for Disease Control and Prevention, National Center for Health Statistics: Ventura SJ, Martin JA, Taffel SM, et al. Advance report of final natality statistics, 1992. Monthly Vital Statistics Report; Vol 43 No 5, suppl. Hyattsville, Md. 1994; and Annual summary of births; marriages, divorces, and deaths: United States, 1993. Monthly Vital Statistics Report; Vol 42 No 13. Hyattsville, Md.: Public Health Service. 1994. *Notes:* Data are based on births adjusted for underregistration for 150 and on registered births for all other years. Beginning in 1970, births to nonresidents of the United States are excluded. Final data for the 1980's are based on intercensal population estimates. Provisional rates for 1992- 93 were calculated using 1990's-based postcensal population estimates. See Appendix I, National Center for Health Statistics and Department of Commerce. 1. Live births per 1,000 population. 2. Live births are tabulated by race of child. 3. Live births are tabulated by race of mother.

★ 884 ★

Births

Live Births by Race and Hispanic Origin of Mother: 1970-82

[Data are based on the National Vital Statistics System].

| Race of mother and Hispanic origin of mother | Total number of live births | | | | | | | | |
	1970	1975	1980	1985	1988	1989	1990	1991	1992
All races	3,731,386	3,144,198	3,612,258	3,760,561	3,909,510	4,040,958	4,158,212	4,110,907	4,065,014
White	3,109,956	2,576,818	2,936,351	3,037,913	3,102,083	3,192,355	3,290,273	3,241,273	3,201,678
Black	561,992	496,829	568,080	581,824	638,562	673,124	684,336	682,602	673,633
American Indian or Alaskan Native	22,264	22,690	29,389	34,037	37,088	39,478	39,051	38,841	39,453
Asian or Pacific Islander	-	-	74,355	104,606	129,035	133,075	141,635	145,372	150,250
Chinese	7,044	7,778	11,671	16,405	21,322	20,982	22,737	22,498	25,061
Japanese	7,744	6,725	7,482	8,035	8,658	8,689	8,674	8,500	9,098
Filipino	8,066	10,359	13,968	20,058	23,207	24,585	25,770	26,227	28,959
Hawaiian and part Hawaiian	-	-	-	-	-	5,609	6,099	5,888	5,883
Other Asian or Pacific Islander	-	-	-	-	-	73,210	78,355	82,259	81,249

[Continued]

★ 884 ★

Live Births by Race and Hispanic Origin of Mother: 1970-82

[Continued]

Race of mother and Hispanic origin of mother	Total number of live births								
	1970	1975	1980	1985	1988	1989	1990	1991	1992
Hispanic origin (selected States)[1,2]	-	-	307,163	372,814	449,604	532,249	595,073	623,085	643,271
Mexican American	-	-	215,439	242,976	271,170	327,233	385,640	411,233	432,047
Puerto Rican	-	-	33,671	35,147	46,232	56,229	58,807	59,833	59,569
Cuban	-	-	7,163	10,024	10,189	10,842	11,311	11,058	11,472
Central and South American	-	-	21,268	40,985	57,610	72,443	83,008	86,908	89,031
Other and unknown Hispanic	-	-	29,622	43,682	64,403	65,502	56,307	54,053	51,152
Non-Hispanic white (selected States)[1]	-	-	1,245,221	1,394,729	1,664,239	2,526,367	2,626,500	2,589,878	2,527,207
Non-Hispanic black (selected States)[1]	-	-	299,646	336,029	434,843	611,269	661,701	666,758	657,450

Source: "Live Births, According to Detailed Race of Mother and Hispanic Origin of Mother: United States, Selected Years 1970-92." National Center for Health Statistics, *Health, United States, 1994,* p. 70. Primary source: Centers for Disease Control and Prevention, National Center for Health Statistics: Data computed by the Division of Health and Utilization Analysis from data compiled by the Division of Vital Statistics. *Notes:* The race groups, white and black, include persons of Hispanic and non- Hispanic origin. Conversely, persons of Hispanic origin may be of any race. 1. rend data for Hispanics and non-Hispanics are affected by expansion of the reporting area for an Hispanic-origin item on the birth certificate and by immigration. These two factors affect numbers of events, composition of the Hispanic population, and maternal and infant health characteristics. The number of States in the reporting area increased from 22 in 1980, to 23 and the District of Columbia (DC) in 1983-87, 30 and DC in 1988, 47 and DC in 1989, 48 and DC in 1990, and 49 and DC in 1991-92 (see Appendix I, National Vital Statistics System). 2. Includes mothers of all races.

★ 885 ★

Births

Live Births in Metropolitan Areas

Age	Race/ethnicity				
	White, non-Hispanic	Black, non-Hispanic	Hispanic	Other[1]	Total
Percentage					
<18	3.0	7.6	8.2	4.3	4.8
18-24	28.0	46.2	43.9	36.9	34.4
25-29	28.6	23.9	25.7	21.1	27.0
30-34	30.1	16.0	15.1	25.1	24.8
35+	10.3	6.2	7.1	12.6	9.1
All ages	100.0	100.0	100.0	100.0	100.0
Racial/ethnic group (percent)	60.6	17.3	18.3	3.8	100.0
Number of women delivering					
<18	62,776	46,018	52,205	5,696	166,695
18-24	593,157	280,326	280,957	49,128	1,203,568
25-29	607,756	145,207	164,413	28,053	945,430
30-34	639,530	97,179	96,755	33,447	866,911
35+	218,438	37,575	45,560	16,759	318,333
All ages	2,121,658	606,305	639,891	133,083	3,500,937

Source: "Annualized National Estimates of Women Delivering Liveborn Infants in Metropolitan Areas of the United States, by Age and Race/Ethnicity of Mothers," National Institute on Drug Abuse, *Drug Use Among Racial/Ethnic Minorities,* p. 69. Primary source: *National Pregnancy and Health Survey,* National Institute on Drug Abuse, 1994. *Note:* 1. Includes Asian, Pacific Islander, Eskimo, Aleut, and American Indian.

★ 886 ★

Births

Live Births: Drinking Status of Mother During Pregnancy: 1992

[In thousands, except percents. Excludes California, New York, and South Dakota, which did not require reporting of alcohol use during pregnancy.]

Drinking Status, Drinking Measure, And Race of Mother	All ages	Under 15 years	Age of mother			20-24 years	25-29 years	30-34 years	35-39 years	40-49 years
			15-19 years							
			Total	15-17 years	18-19 years					
All races[1], total	3,164.4	10.0	409.4	151.5	257.9	850.6	916.9	683.8	253.6	40.1
Drinker	78.7	0.1	5.4	1.7	3.7	16.6	22.9	22.7	9.6	1.4
Nondrinker	2,993.1	9.6	392.5	145.4	247.1	810.1	867.8	640.0	235.7	37.4
Not stated	92.6	0.3	11.5	4.4	7.1	23.8	26.2	21.1	8.2	1.4
White, total	2,487.5	3.9	268.4	91.6	176.8	637.8	755.0	578.1	211.5	32.8
Drinker	57.5	(Z)	3.7	1.2	2.6	11.1	16.2	17.7	7.7	1.1
Nondrinker	2,359.3	3.7	257.2	87.8	169.4	609.5	718.0	543.1	197.1	30.6
Not stated	70.7	0.1	7.4	2.6	4.8	17.2	20.8	17.3	6.7	1.1
Black, total	566.1	5.8	129.7	55.7	74.0	186.5	129.1	79.4	30.5	5.0
Drinker	18.3	(Z)	1.3	0.4	0.9	4.8	5.9	4.4	1.7	0.2
Nondrinker	529.6	5.6	124.8	53.8	71.0	176.0	118.8	72.1	27.7	4.6
Not stated	18.2	0.2	3.7	1.6	2.1	5.8	4.4	2.9	1.1	0.2
Percent: Drinker[1]	2.6	8.0	1.4	1.2	1.5	2.0	2.6	3.4	3.9	3.5
White	2.4	1.2	1.4	1.3	1.5	1.8	2.2	3.2	3.7	3.5
Black	3.3	0.5	1.0	0.7	1.2	2.6	4.7	5.8	5.8	4.1

Source: "Live Births—Drinking Status of Mother Who Drank During Pregnancy, According to Age and Race of Mother: 1992," *Statistical Abstract of the United States,* 1994, p. 83. Primary source: U.S. National Center for Health Statistics, *Monthly Vital Statistics Reports. Notes:* Z Less than 50. 1. Includes other races other than White and Black.

★ 887 ★

Births

Live Births: Education of Mothers Who Smoked During Pregnancy: 1992

[In thousands, except percents. Excludes California, Indiana, New York, and South Dakota, which did not require reporting of tobacco use during pregnancy.]

Smoking Measure And Race of Mother	Total	Years of school completed by mother					
		0-8 years	9-11 years	12 years	13-15 years	16 years or more	Not stated
All races[1]	3,080	144	516	1,144	646	581	49
White	2,414	116	350	878	521	514	34
Black	557	20	149	231	106	41	11
Percent: Smoker[1]	16.9	16.8	30.6	20.1	12.0	3.9	17.2
White	17.9	18.3	35.9	22.1	12.6	4.0	17.5
Black	13.8	11.4	19.3	13.5	10.1	4.7	20.3
Percent Distribution							
All races[1]: Smoker	100.0	100.0	100.0	100.0	100.0	100.0	100.0

[Continued]

★ 887 ★

Live Births: Education of Mothers Who Smoked During Pregnancy: 1992
[Continued]

Smoking Measure And Race of Mother	Total	Years of school completed by mother					
		0-8 years	9-11 years	12 years	13-15 years	16 years or more	Not stated
10 cigarettes or less	61.9	55.9	60.5	61.2	64.8	73.9	63.7
11-20 cigarettes	32.8	35.6	33.5	33.8	30.7	22.5	30.8
21 cigarettes or more	5.4	8.5	6.0	5.1	4.4	3.6	5.6
White: Smoker	100.0	100.0	100.0	100.0	100.0	100.0	100.0
10 cigarettes or less	58.6	53.5	56.3	58.0	62.3	73.0	59.9
11-20 cigarettes	35.5	37.3	37.0	36.5	32.8	23.1	33.7
21 cigarettes or more	5.9	9.2	6.8	5.5	4.9	3.8	6.5
Black: Smoker	100.0	100.0	100.0	100.0	100.0	100.0	100.0
10 cigarettes or less	78.3	72.3	77.6	79.2	79.1	81.0	74.1
11-20 cigarettes	19.0	23.9	19.3	18.4	18.9	17.7	23.0
21 cigarettes or more	2.6	3.9	3.1	2.3	2.0	1.2	2.9

Source: "Live Births - Mothers Who Smoked During Pregnancy, According to Educational Attainment and Race of Mother: 1992," *Statistical Abstract of the United States,* 1994, p. 83. Primary source: U.S. National Center for Health Statistics, *Monthly Vital Statistics Reports. Note:* 1. Includes races other than White and Black.

★ 888 ★

Births

Low-birth Live Births among Mothers Twenty Years of Age and Over, by Race, Hispanic Origin, and Educational Attainment: 1989-92

[Data are based on the National Vital Statistics System].

Mother's education, race of mother, and Hispanic origin of mother	Percent of births weighing less than 2,500 grams			
	1989	1990	1991	1992
Less than 12 years of education				
All races	9.0	8.6	8.7	8.4
White	7.3	7.0	7.1	6.9
Black	17.0	16.5	17.0	16.5
American Indian or Alaskan Native	7.3	7.4	7.4	7.1
Asian or Pacific Islander	6.6	6.4	6.5	6.2
Chinese	5.4	5.2	5.0	4.4
Japanese	4.0	10.6	7.5	7.0
Filipino	6.9	7.2	7.4	6.8
Hawaiian and part Hawaiian	11.0	10.7	7.1	9.5
Other Asian or Pacific Islander	6.8	6.4	6.7	6.4
Hispanic origin (selected States)[1,2]	6.0	5.7	5.8	5.8
Mexican American	5.3	5.2	5.3	5.3
Puerto Rican	11.3	10.3	11.2	10.4
Cuban	9.4	7.9	7.1	7.8

[Continued]

★ 888 ★

Low-birth Live Births among Mothers Twenty Years of Age and Over, by Race, Hispanic Origin, and Educational Attainment: 1989-92
[Continued]

Mother's education, race of mother, and Hispanic origin of mother	Percent of births weighing less than 2,500 grams			
	1989	1990	1991	1992
Central and South American	5.8	5.8	5.7	5.8
Other and unknown Hispanic	8.2	8.0	8.1	7.8
Non-Hispanic white (selected States)[1]	8.4	8.3	8.4	8.3
Non-Hispanic black (selected States)[1]	17.6	16.7	17.2	16.7
12 years of education				
All races	7.1	7.1	7.3	7.2
White	5.7	5.8	5.9	5.9
Black	13.4	13.1	13.5	13.3
American Indian or Alaskan native	5.6	6.1	5.9	6.0
Asian or Pacific Islander	6.4	6.5	6.5	6.8
Chinese	5.1	4.9	5.5	5.7
Japanese	7.4	6.2	6.4	7.4
Filipino	6.8	7.6	6.9	7.4
Hawaiian or part Hawaiian	7.0	6.7	6.7	7.0
Other Asian or Pacific Islander	6.5	6.7	6.7	6.8
Hispanic origin (selected States)[1,2]	5.9	6.0	6.0	6.0
Mexican American	5.2	5.5	5.4	5.5
Puerto Rican	8.8	8.3	8.4	8.3
Cuban	5.3	5.2	6.1	6.6
Central and South American	5.7	5.8	5.6	5.7
Other and unknown Hispanic	6.1	6.6	6.8	7.1
Non-Hispanic white (selected States)[1]	5.7	5.7	5.9	5.9
Non-Hispanic black (selected States)[1]	13.6	13.2	13.6	13.4
13 or more years of education				
All races	5.5	5.4	5.6	5.6
White	4.6	4.6	4.7	4.8
Black	11.2	11.1	11.4	11.2
American Indian or Alaskan Native	5.6	4.7	4.9	5.6
Asian or Pacific Islander	6.1	6.0	6.2	6.2
Chinese	4.5	4.4	4.9	4.7
Japanese	6.6	6.0	5.6	6.9
Filipino	7.2	7.0	7.1	7.3
Hawaiian and part Hawaiian	6.3	4.7	4.9	5.4
Other Asian or Pacific Islander	6.1	6.2	6.4	6.2
Hispanic origin (selected States)[1,2]	5.5	5.5	5.5	5.5
Mexican American	5.1	5.2	5.0	5.1
Puerto Rican	7.4	7.4	7.5	7.5

[Continued]

★ 888 ★

Low-birth Live Births among Mothers Twenty Years of Age and Over, by Race, Hispanic Origin, and Educational Attainment: 1989-92

[Continued]

Mother's education, race of mother, and Hispanic origin of mother	Percent of births weighing less than 2,500 grams			
	1989	1990	1991	1992
Cuban	4.9	5.0	4.8	5.1
Central and South American	5.2	5.6	5.7	5.1
Other and unknown Hispanic	5.4	5.2	5.7	5.4
Non-Hispanic white (selected States)[1]	4.6	4.5	4.7	4.7
Non-Hispanic black (selected States)[1]	11.2	11.1	11.4	11.2

Source: "Low-birthweight Live Births among Mothers 20 Years of Age and Over, by Mother's Detailed Race, Hispanic Origin, and Educational Attainment: Selected States, Selected Years 1989-92," National Center for Health Statistics, *Health, United States, 1994*, p. 72. Primary source: Centers for Disease Control and Prevention, National Center for Health Statistics: Data computed by the Division of Health and Utilization Analysis from data compiled by the Division of Vital Statistics. *Notes:* Includes data for 48 States and the District of Columbia (DC) in 1989-91 and all 50 States and DC in 1992. Excludes data for births to residents of New York and Washington (1989-91), which did not require the reporting of education of mother on the birth certificate (see Appendix I). In 1989-91 New York and Washington accounted for 13-19 percent of Chinese and Other Asian or Pacific Islander births, and 5-6 percent of Filipino, Japanese and American Indian births compared with 9-10 percent of white births and black births. the race groups, white and black, include persons of Hispanic and non-Hispanic origin. Conversely, persons of Hispanic origin may be of any race. 1. Data shown only for States with an Hispanic-origin item and education of mother on their birth certificate 2. Includes mothers of all races.

★ 889 ★

Births

Low-birth Live Births by Race and Hispanic Origin of Mother and Smoking Status: 1970-92. Part 1

[Data are based on the National Vital Statistics System].

Birth weight, race of mother, Hispanic origin of mother, and smoking status of mother	Percent of live births[1]					
	1970	1975	1980	1983	1984	1985
Low birthweight (less than 2,500 grams)						
All mothers	7.93	7.38	6.84	6.82	6.72	6.75
White	6.85	6.27	5.72	5.69	5.61	5.65
Black	13.90	13.19	12.69	12.82	12.58	12.65
American Indian or Alaskan Native	7.97	6.41	6.44	6.17	6.15	5.86
Asian or Pacific Islander	-	-	6.68	6.57	6.57	6.16
Chinese	6.67	5.29	5.21	5.07	5.05	4.98
Japanese	9.03	7.47	6.60	6.05	5.91	6.21
Filipino	10.02	8.08	7.40	7.28	7.78	6.95
Hawaiian or part Hawaiian	-	-	-	-	-	-
Other Asian or Pacific Islander	-	-	-	-	-	-
Hispanic origin (selected States)[2,3]	-	-	6.12	6.29	6.15	6.16
Mexican American	-	-	5.62	5.77	5.68	5.77
Puerto Rican	-	-	8.95	8.90	8.88	8.69
Cuban	-	-	5.62	5.65	5.86	6.02
Central and South American	-	-	5.76	6.20	5.81	5.68

[Continued]

★ 889 ★

Low-birth Live Births by Race and Hispanic Origin of Mother and Smoking Status: 1970-92. Part 1
[Continued]

Birth weight, race of mother, Hispanic origin of mother, and smoking status of mother	Percent of live births[1]					
	1970	1975	1980	1983	1984	1985
Other and unknown Hispanic	-	-	6.96	7.23	6.89	6.83
Non-Hispanic white (selected States)[2]	-	-	5.67	5.64	5.53	5.60
Non-Hispanic black (selected States)[2]	-	-	12.71	12.83	12.54	12.61
Cigarette smoker[4]	-	-	-	-	-	-
Nonsmoker[4]	-	-	-	-	-	-
Very low birthweight (less than 1,500 grams)						
All mothers	1.17	1.16	1.15	1.19	1.19	1.21
White	0.95	0.92	0.90	0.93	0.93	0.94
Black	2.40	2.40	2.48	2.60	2.60	2.71
American Indian or Alaskan Native	0.98	0.95	0.92	1.07	1.02	1.01
Asian or Pacific Islander	-	-	0.92	0.88	0.93	0.85
Chinese	0.80	0.52	0.66	0.77	0.70	0.57
Japanese	1.48	0.89	0.94	0.96	0.81	0.84
Filipino	1.08	0.93	0.99	0.98	0.97	0.86
Hawaiian and part Hawaiian	-	-	-	-	-	-
Other Asian or Pacific Islander	-	-	-	-	-	-
Hispanic origin (selected States)[2,3]	-	-	0.98	1.03	1.01	1.01
Mexican American	-	-	0.92	0.96	0.93	0.97
Puerto Rican	-	-	1.29	1.46	1.49	1.30
Cuban	-	-	1.02	0.97	1.04	1.18
Central and South American	-	-	0.99	0.99	1.04	1.01
Other and unknown Hispanic	-	-	1.01	1.08	1.05	0.96
Non-Hispanic white (selected States)[2]	-	-	0.86	0.90	0.88	0.90
Non-Hispanic black (selected States)[2]	-	-	2.46	2.57	2.56	2.66

[Continued]

★ 889 ★

Low-birth Live Births by Race and Hispanic Origin of Mother and Smoking Status: 1970-92. Part 1

[Continued]

Birth weight, race of mother, Hispanic origin of mother, and smoking status of mother	Percent of live births[1]					
	1970	1975	1980	1983	1984	1985
Cigarette smoker[4]	-	-	-	-	-	-
Nonsmoker[4]	-	-	-	-	-	-

Source: "Low-birthweight Live Births, According to Mother's Detailed Race, Hispanic Origin, and Smoking Status, Selected Years 1970-92." National Center for Health Statistics, *Health, United States, 1994*, p. 71. Primary source: Centers for Disease Control and Prevention, National Center for Health Statistics: Data computed by the Division of Health and Utilization Analysis from data compiled by the Division of Vital Statistics. *Notes:* The race groups, white and black, include persons of Hispanic and non- Hispanic origin. Conversely, persons of Hispanic origin may be of any race. 1. Excludes live births with unknown birthweight. Percent based on live births with known birthweight. 2. Trend data for Hispanics and non-Hispanics are affected by expansion of the reporting area for an Hispanic-origin item on the birth certificate and by immigration. These two factors affect numbers of events, composition of the Hispanic population, and maternal and infant health characteristics. The number of States in the reporting area increased from 22 in 1980, to 23 and the District of Columbia (DC) in 1983-87, 30 and DC in 1988, 47 and DC in 1990, and 49 and DC in 1991-92 (see Appendix I, National Vital Statistics System). 3. Includes mothers of all races. 4. Percent based on live births with known smoking status of mother and known birthweight. Includes data for 43 States and the District of Columbia (DC) in 1989, 45 States and DC in 1990, and 46 States and DC in 1991-92. Excludes data for California, Indiana, New York, and South Dakota (1989- 92), Oklahoma (1989-90), and Louisiana and Nebraska (1989), which did not require the reporting of mother's tobacco use during pregnancy on the birth certificate (see Appendix I).

★ 890 ★

Births

Low-birth Live Births by Race and Hispanic Origin of Mother and Smoking Status: 1970-92. Part 2

[Data are based on the National Vital Statistics System].

Birth weight, race of mother, Hispanic origin of mother, and smoking status of mother	Percent of live births[1]						
	1986	1987	1988	1989	1990	1991	1992
Low birthweight (less than 2,500 grams)							
All mothers	6.81	6.90	6.93	7.05	6.97	7.12	7.08
White	5.66	5.70	5.67	5.72	5.70	5.80	5.80
Black	12.77	12.98	13.26	13.51	13.25	13.55	13.31
American Indian or Alaskan Native	5.94	6.15	6.00	6.26	6.11	6.15	6.22
Asian or Pacific Islander	6.47	6.41	6.31	6.51	6.45	6.54	6.57
Chinese	4.85	5.02	4.63	4.89	4.69	5.10	4.98
Japanese	6.03	6.49	6.69	6.67	6.16	5.90	7.00
Filipino	7.42	7.30	7.15	7.35	7.30	7.31	7.43
Hawaiian or part Hawaiian	-	-	-	7.29	7.24	6.73	6.89
Other Asian or Pacific Islander	-	-	-	6.61	6.65	6.74	6.68
Hispanic origin (selected States)[2,3]	6.13	6.24	6.17	6.18	6.06	6.15	6.10
Mexican American	5.62	5.74	5.60	5.60	5.55	5.60	5.61
Puerto Rican	9.22	9.30	9.42	9.50	8.99	9.42	9.19

[Continued]

★ 890 ★

Low-birth Live Births by Race and Hispanic Origin of Mother and Smoking Status: 1970-92. Part 2
[Continued]

Birth weight, race of mother, Hispanic origin of mother, and smoking status of mother	Percent of live births[1]						
	1986	1987	1988	1989	1990	1991	1992
Cuban	5.46	5.89	5.94	5.77	5.67	5.57	6.10
Central and South American	5.69	5.74	5.58	5.81	5.84	5.87	5.77
Other and unknown Hispanic	6.87	6.91	6.85	6.74	6.87	7.25	7.24
Non-Hispanic white (selected States)[2]	5.58	5.63	5.62	5.62	5.61	5.72	5.73
Non-Hispanic black (selected States)[2]	12.85	13.10	13.28	13.61	13.32	13.62	13.40
Cigarette smoker[4]	-	-	-	11.36	11.25	11.41	11.49
Nonsmoker[4]	-	-	-	6.02	6.14	6.36	6.35
Very low birthweight (less than 1,500 grams)							
All mothers	1.21	1.24	1.24	1.28	1.27	1.29	1.29
White	0.93	0.94	0.93	0.95	0.95	0.96	0.96
Black	2.73	2.79	2.86	2.95	2.92	2.96	2.96
American Indian or Alaskan Native	0.99	1.13	1.00	1.00	1.01	1.07	0.95
Asian or Pacific Islander	0.86	0.83	0.84	0.90	0.87	0.85	0.91
Chinese	0.63	0.65	0.57	0.61	0.51	0.65	0.67
Japanese	0.86	0.80	0.92	0.86	0.73	0.62	0.85
Filipino	0.87	0.94	0.91	1.12	1.05	0.97	1.05
Hawaiian and part Hawaiian	-	-	-	1.13	0.97	1.02	1.02
Other Asian or Pacific Islander	-	-	-	0.89	0.92	0.87	0.93
Hispanic origin (selected States)[2,3]	1.02	1.06	1.01	1.05	1.03	1.02	1.04
Mexican American	0.94	0.96	0.89	0.94	0.92	0.92	0.94
Puerto Rican	1.47	1.63	1.61	1.71	1.62	1.66	1.70
Cuban	1.09	0.97	1.17	1.13	1.20	1.15	1.24
Central and South American	1.04	1.02	0.97	1.05	1.05	1.02	1.02
Other and unknown Hispanic	1.08	1.15	1.11	1.04	1.09	1.09	1.10
Non-Hispanic white (selected States)[2]	0.89	0.94	0.89	0.93	0.93	0.94	0.94
Non-Hispanic black (selected States)[2]	2.68	2.73	2.82	2.97	2.93	2.97	2.97

[Continued]

★ 890 ★

Low-birth Live Births by Race and Hispanic Origin of Mother and Smoking Status: 1970-92. Part 2

[Continued]

Birth weight, race of mother, Hispanic origin of mother, and smoking status of mother	Percent of live births[1]						
	1986	1987	1988	1989	1990	1991	1992
Cigarette smoker[4]	-	-	-	1.75	1.73	1.73	1.74
Nonsmoker[4]	-	-	-	1.16	1.18	1.21	1.22

Source: "Low-birthweight Live Births, According to Mother's Detailed Race, Hispanic Origin, and Smoking Status, Selected Years 1970-92." National Center for Health Statistics, *Health, United States, 1994*, p. 71. Primary source: Centers for Disease Control and Prevention, National Center for Health Statistics: Data computed by the Division of Health and Utilization Analysis from data compiled by the Division of Vital Statistics. *Notes:* The race groups, white and black, include persons of Hispanic and non- Hispanic origin. Conversely, persons of Hispanic origin may be of any race. 1. Excludes live births with unknown birthweight. Percent based on live births with known birthweight. 2. Trend data for Hispanics and non-Hispanics are affected by expansion of the reporting area for an Hispanic-origin item on the birth certificate and by immigration. These two factors affect numbers of events, composition of the Hispanic population, and maternal and infant health characteristics. The number of States in the reporting area increased from 22 in 1980, to 23 and the District of Columbia (DC) in 1983-87, 30 and DC in 1988, 47 and DC in 1990, and 49 and DC in 1991-92 (see Appendix I, National Vital Statistics System). 3. Includes mothers of all races. 4. Percent based on live births with known smoking status of mother and known birthweight. Includes data for 43 States and the District of Columbia (DC) in 1989, 45 States and DC in 1990, and 46 States and DC in 1991-92. Excludes data for California, Indiana, New York, and South Dakota (1989- 92), Oklahoma (1989-90), and Louisiana and Nebraska (1989), which did not require the reporting of mother's tobacco use during pregnancy on the birth certificate (see Appendix I).

★ 891 ★

Births

Maternal Age and Marital Status for Live Births by Race and Hispanic Origin of Mother: 1970-92. Part 1

[Data are based on the National Vital Statistics System].

Age, marital status, race of mother, and Hispanic origin of mother	Percent of live births					
	1970	1975	1980	1983	1984	1985
Age of mother less than 18 years						
All mothers	6.3	7.6	5.8	5.0	4.8	4.7
White	4.8	6.0	4.5	3.9	3.7	3.7
Black	14.8	16.3	12.5	11.2	10.8	10.6
American Indian or Alaskan Native	7.5	11.2	9.4	8.7	7.9	7.6
Asian or Pacific Islander	-	-	1.5	1.6	1.6	1.6
Chinese	1.1	0.4	0.3	0.3	0.2	0.3
Japanese	2.0	1.7	1.0	0.7	0.8	0.9
Filipino	3.7	2.4	1.6	1.8	2.0	1.6
Hawaiian and part Hawaiian	-	-	-	-	-	-
Other Asian or Pacific Islander	-	-	-	-	-	-
Hispanic origin (selected States)[1,2]	-	-	7.4	7.0	6.7	6.4
Mexican American	-	-	7.7	7.5	7.2	6.9
Puerto Rican	-	-	10.0	9.3	8.5	8.5
Cuban	-	-	3.8	2.6	2.5	2.2
Central and South American	-	-	2.4	2.6	2.4	2.4
Other and unknown Hispanic	-	-	6.5	7.1	7.0	7.0

[Continued]

★ 891 ★

Maternal Age and Marital Status for Live Births by Race and Hispanic Origin of Mother: 1970-92. Part 1

[Continued]

Age, marital status, race of mother, and Hispanic origin of mother	Percent of live births					
	1970	1975	1980	1983	1984	1985
Non-Hispanic white (selected States)[1]	-	-	4.0	3.4	3.2	3.2
Non-Hispanic black (selected States)[1]	-	-	12.7	11.2	10.9	10.7
Age of mother 18-19 years						
All mothers	11.3	11.3	9.8	8.7	8.3	8.0
White	10.4	10.3	9.0	7.9	7.4	7.1
Black	16.6	16.9	14.5	13.6	13.3	12.9
American Indian or Alaskan Native	12.8	15.2	14.6	13.3	13.1	12.4
Asian or Pacific Islander	-	-	3.9	3.7	3.4	3.4
Chinese	3.9	1.7	1.0	0.6	0.5	0.6
Japanese	4.1	3.3	2.3	2.3	2.3	1.9
Filipino	7.1	5.0	4.0	3.8	3.5	3.7
Hawaiian and part Hawaiian	-	-	-	-	-	-
Other Asian or Pacific Islander	-	-	-	-	-	-
Hispanic origin (selected States)[1,2]	-	-	11.6	10.6	10.3	10.1
Mexican American	-	-	12.0	10.9	10.8	10.6
Puerto Rican	-	-	13.3	13.2	12.8	12.4
Cuban	-	-	9.2	6.8	5.7	4.9
Central and South American	-	-	6.0	6.0	5.7	5.8
Other and unknown Hispanic	-	-	10.8	11.2	10.9	10.5
Non-Hispanic white (selected States)[1]	-	-	8.5	7.4	6.8	6.6
Non-Hispanic black (selected States)[1]	-	-	14.7	13.5	13.4	12.9
Unmarried mothers						
All mothers	10.7	14.3	18.4	20.3	21.0	22.0
White	5.5	7.1	11.2	12.9	13.6	14.7
Black	37.5	49.5	56.1	59.2	60.3	61.2
American Indian or Alaskan Native	22.4	32.7	39.2	45.3	46.1	46.8
Asian or Pacific Islander	-	-	7.3	8.6	9.2	9.5
Chinese	3.0	1.6	2.7	3.3	3.4	3.0
Japanese	4.6	4.6	5.2	7.2	6.9	7.9
Filipino	9.1	6.9	8.6	10.3	10.8	11.4
Hawaiian and part Hawaiian	-	-	-	-	-	-
Other Asian or Pacific Islander	-	-	-	-	-	-
Hispanic origin (selected States)[1,2]	-	-	23.6	27.5	28.3	29.5
Mexican American	-	-	20.3	23.8	24.2	25.7
Puerto Rican	-	-	46.3	49.5	50.8	51.1
Cuban	-	-	10.0	16.1	16.2	16.1
Central and South American	-	-	27.1	33.0	34.0	34.9

[Continued]

★ 891 ★

Maternal Age and Marital Status for Live Births by Race and Hispanic Origin of Mother: 1970-92. Part 1
[Continued]

Age, marital status, race of mother, and Hispanic origin of mother	Percent of live births					
	1970	1975	1980	1983	1984	1985
Other and unknown Hispanic	-	-	22.4	28.2	30.0	31.1
Non-Hispanic white (selected States)[1]	-	-	9.6	11.0	11.5	12.4
Non-Hispanic black (selected States)[1]	-	-	57.3	60.5	61.5	62.1

Source: "Maternal Age and Marital Status for Live Births, According to Detailed race of Mother and Hispanic Origin of United States, Selected Years 1970- 92." National Center for Health Statistics, *Health, United States, 1994,* p. 75 Primary source: Centers for Disease Control and Prevention, National Center for Health Statistics: Data computed by the Division of Health and Utilization Analysis from data compiled by the Division of Vital Statistics. *Notes:* National estimates for 1970 and 1975 for unmarried mothers based on births occurring in States reporting marital status (see Appendix I). The race groups, white and black, include persons of Hispanic and non-Hispanic origin. Conversely, persons of Hispanic origin may be of any race. 1. Trend data for Hispanics and non-Hispanics are affected by expansion of the reporting area for an Hispanic-origin item on the birth certificate and by immigration. These two factors affect numbers of events, composition of the Hispanic population, and maternal and infant health characteristics. The number of States in the reporting area increased from 22 in 1980, to 23 and the District of Columbia (DC) in 1983-87, 30 and DC in 1988, 47 and DC in 1989, 48 and DC in 1990, and 49 and DC in 1991-92 (see Appendix I, National Vital Statistics System). 2. Includes mothers of all races.

★ 892 ★

Births

Maternal Age and Marital Status for Live Births by Race and Hispanic Origin of Mother: 1970-92. Part 2

[Data are based on the National Vital Statistics System].

Age, marital status, race of mother, and Hispanic origin of mother	Percent of live births						
	1986	1987	1988	1989	1990	1991	1992
Age of mother less than 18 years							
All mothers	4.8	4.8	4.8	4.8	4.7	4.9	4.9
White	3.7	3.7	3.7	3.6	3.6	3.8	3.9
Black	10.6	10.7	10.6	10.5	10.1	10.3	10.3
American Indian or Alaskan Native	8.0	7.9	7.8	7.5	7.2	7.9	8.0
Asian or Pacific Islander	1.7	1.8	1.8	2.0	2.1	2.1	2.0
Chinese	0.2	0.2	0.3	0.3	0.4	0.3	0.3
Japanese	0.9	0.9	0.8	0.9	0.8	1.0	0.9
Filipino	1.7	1.8	1.7	1.9	2.0	2.0	1.9
Hawaiian and part Hawaiian	-	-	-	5.9	6.5	6.8	7.0
Other Asian or Pacific Islander	-	-	-	2.4	2.4	2.4	2.3
Hispanic origin (selected States)[1,2]	6.5	6.6	6.6	6.7	6.6	6.9	7.1
Mexican American	6.9	7.0	7.0	6.9	6.9	7.2	7.3
Puerto Rican	8.4	8.7	9.2	9.4	9.1	9.5	9.6
Cuban	2.3	2.1	2.2	2.7	2.7	2.6	2.5
Central and South American	2.4	2.7	2.7	3.0	3.2	3.5	3.6
Other and unknown Hispanic	7.3	7.7	7.6	8.0	8.0	8.3	8.9
Non-Hispanic white (selected States)[1]	3.2	3.2	3.2	3.0	3.0	3.1	3.1

[Continued]

★ 892 ★

Maternal Age and Marital Status for Live Births by Race and Hispanic Origin of Mother: 1970-92. Part 2

[Continued]

Age, marital status, race of mother, and Hispanic origin of mother	Percent of live births						
	1986	1987	1988	1989	1990	1991	1992
Non-Hispanic black (selected States)[1]	10.6	10.7	10.8	10.5	10.2	10.3	10.4
Age of mother 18-19 years							
All mothers	7.8	7.6	7.7	8.1	8.1	8.1	7.8
White	7.0	6.8	6.9	7.2	7.3	7.2	7.0
Black	12.6	12.2	12.3	12.9	13.0	12.8	12.4
American Indian or Alaskan Native	12.1	11.8	11.4	12.1	12.3	12.4	11.9
Asian or Pacific Islander	3.4	3.3	3.4	3.7	3.7	3.7	3.6
Chinese	0.5	0.6	0.5	0.7	0.8	0.8	0.7
Japanese	1.9	1.6	1.8	1.8	2.0	1.7	1.7
Filipino	3.4	3.4	3.8	4.0	4.1	4.0	3.7
Hawaiian and part Hawaiian	-	-	-	11.3	11.9	11.3	11.4
Other Asian or Pacific Islander	-	-	-	4.1	3.9	4.1	4.1
Hispanic origin (selected States)[1,2]	9.9	9.7	9.8	10.0	10.2	10.3	10.1
Mexican American	10.5	10.3	10.3	10.5	10.7	10.9	10.7
Puerto Rican	12.5	11.8	12.2	12.6	12.6	12.2	11.8
Cuban	4.5	4.1	3.9	4.3	5.0	4.5	4.6
Central and South American	5.7	5.3	5.4	5.6	5.9	6.0	5.9
Other and unknown Hispanic	10.0	10.5	10.8	11.2	11.1	11.4	11.1
Non-Hispanic white (selected States)[1]	6.4	6.2	6.6	6.5	6.6	6.5	6.3
Non-Hispanic black (selected States)[1]	12.6	12.2	12.4	13.0	13.0	12.9	12.5
Unmarried mothers							
All mothers	23.4	24.5	25.7	27.1	28.0	29.5	30.1
White	15.9	16.9	18.0	19.2	20.4	21.8	22.6
Black	62.4	63.4	64.7	65.7	66.5	67.9	68.1
American Indian or Alaskan Native	48.8	51.1	51.7	52.7	53.6	55.3	55.3
Asian or Pacific Islander	10.0	11.0	11.5	12.4	13.2	13.9	14.7
Chinese	3.5	4.5	3.9	4.2	5.0	5.5	6.1
Japanese	7.9	7.9	8.8	9.4	9.6	9.8	9.8
Filipino	12.0	12.7	3.6	14.8	15.9	16.8	16.8
Hawaiian and part Hawaiian	-	-	-	42.7	45.0	45.0	45.7
Other Asian or Pacific Islander	-	-	-	12.0	12.6	13.5	14.9
Hispanic origin (selected States)[1,2]	31.6	32.6	34.0	35.5	36.7	38.5	39.1
Mexican American	27.9	28.9	30.6	31.7	33.3	35.3	36.3
Puerto Rican	52.6	53.0	53.3	55.2	55.9	57.5	57.5
Cuban	15.8	16.1	16.3	17.5	18.2	19.5	20.2
Central and South American	38.0	37.1	36.4	38.9	41.2	43.1	43.9
Other and unknown Hispanic	31.9	34.2	35.5	37.0	37.2	37.9	37.6

[Continued]

★ 892 ★

Maternal Age and Marital Status for Live Births by Race and Hispanic Origin of Mother: 1970-92. Part 2

[Continued]

Age, marital status, race of mother, and Hispanic origin of mother	Percent of live births						
	1986	1987	1988	1989	1990	1991	1992
Non-Hispanic white (selected States)[1]	13.5	14.3	15.2	16.1	16.9	18.0	18.5
Non-Hispanic black (selected States)[1]	63.3	64.2	64.8	66.0	66.7	68.2	68.3

Source: "Maternal Age and Marital Status for Live Births, According to Detailed race of Mother and Hispanic Origin of United States, Selected Years 1970- 92." National Center for Health Statistics, *Health, United States, 1994*, p. 75 Primary source: Centers for Disease Control and Prevention, National Center for Health Statistics: Data computed by the Division of Health and Utilization Analysis from data compiled by the Division of Vital Statistics. *Notes:* National estimates for 1970 and 1975 for unmarried mothers based on births occurring in States reporting marital status (see Appendix I). The race groups, white and black, include persons of Hispanic and non-Hispanic origin. Conversely, persons of Hispanic origin may be of any race. 1. Trend data for Hispanics and non-Hispanics are affected by expansion of the reporting area for an Hispanic-origin item on the birth certificate and by immigration. These two factors affect numbers of events, composition of the Hispanic population, and maternal and infant health characteristics. The number of States in the reporting area increased from 22 in 1980, to 23 and the District of Columbia (DC) in 1983-87, 30 and DC in 1988, 47 and DC in 1989, 48 and DC in 1990, and 49 and DC in 1991-92 (see Appendix I, National Vital Statistics System). 2. Includes mothers of all races.

★ 893 ★

Births

Maternal Education for Live Births: Characteristics and Trends: 1970-92. Part 1

[Data are based on the National Vital Statistics System].

Education, race of mother, and Hispanic origin of mother	Percent of live births[1]					
	1970	1975	1980	1983	1984	1985
Education of mother less than 12 years						
All mothers	30.8	28.6	23.7	21.7	20.9	20.6
White	27.1	25.1	20.8	18.7	18.1	17.8
Black	51.2	45.3	36.4	34.5	33.4	32.6
American Indian or Alaskan Native	60.5	52.7	44.2	41.3	40.0	39.0
Asian or Pacific Islander	-	-	21.0	21.7	20.2	19.4
Chinese	23.0	16.5	15.2	18.2	18.2	15.5
Japanese	11.8	9.1	5.0	4.0	3.5	4.8
Filipino	26.4	22.3	16.4	15.0	13.4	13.9
Hawaiian and part Hawaiian	-	-	-	-	-	-
Other Asian or Pacific Islander	-	-	-	-	-	-
Hispanic origin (selected States)[2,3]	-	-	51.1	46.5	44.9	44.5
Mexican American	-	-	62.8	59.4	58.7	59.0
Puerto Rican	-	-	55.3	50.0	48.2	46.6
Cuban	-	-	24.1	24.6	22.4	21.1
Central and South American	-	-	41.2	39.5	37.1	37.0
Other and unknown Hispanic	-	-	40.1	38.9	36.0	36.5

[Continued]

★ 893 ★

Maternal Education for Live Births: Characteristics and Trends: 1970-92. Part 1
[Continued]

Education, race of mother, and Hispanic origin of mother	Percent of live births[1]					
	1970	1975	1980	1983	1984	1985
Non-Hispanic white (selected States)[2]	-	-	18.3	16.7	15.9	15.8
Non-Hispanic black (selected States)[2]	-	-	37.4	35.4	34.2	33.5
Education of mother 16 years or more						
All mothers	8.6	11.4	14.0	15.8	16.4	16.7
White	9.6	12.7	15.5	17.6	18.3	18.6
Black	2.8	4.3	6.2	6.7	6.9	7.0
American Indian or Alaskan Native	2.7	2.2	3.5	3.4	3.6	3.7
Asian or Pacific Islander	-	-	30.8	30.0	30.4	30.3
Chinese	34.0	37.8	41.5	38.0	36.4	35.2
Japanese	20.7	30.6	36.8	38.8	39.8	38.1
Filipino	28.1	36.6	37.1	35.8	35.8	35.2
Hawaiian and part Hawaiian	-	-	-	-	-	-
Other Asian or Pacific Islander	-	-	-	-	-	-
Hispanic origin (selected States)[2,3]	-	-	4.2	5.2	5.7	6.0
Mexican American	-	-	2.2	2.8	2.9	3.0
Puerto Rican	-	-	3.0	3.9	4.3	4.6
Cuban	-	-	11.6	12.4	13.7	15.0
Central and South American	-	-	6.1	6.6	7.6	8.1
Other and unknown Hispanic	-	-	5.5	6.4	7.0	7.2
Non-Hispanic white (selected States)[2]	-	-	16.4	18.3	18.9	19.3
Non-Hispanic black (selected States)[2]	-	-	5.7	6.3	6.5	6.7

Source: "Maternal Education for Live Births, According to Detailed Race of Mother and Hispanic Origin of Mother: United States, Selected Years 1970- 92." National Center for Health Statistics, *Health, United States, 1994*, p. 74. Primary source: Centers for Disease Control and Prevention, National Center for Health Statistics: Data computed by the Division of Health and Utilization Analysis from data compiled by the Division of Vital Statistics. *Notes:* Excludes births that occurred in States not reporting education. The race groups, white and black, include persons of Hispanic and non-Hispanic origin. Conversely, persons of Hispanic origin may be of any race. 1. Excludes live births for whom education of mother is unknown. 2. Trend data for Hispanics and non-Hispanics are affected by expansion of the reporting area for an Hispanic-origin item on the birth certificate and by immigration. These two factors affect numbers of events, composition of the HIspanic population, and maternal and infant health characteristics. Data shown only for States with an Hispanic-origin item and education of mother item on their birth certificates. The number of States reporting both items increased from 20 in 1980, to 21 and the District of Columbia (DC) in 1983-87, 26 and DC in 1988, 45 and DC in 1989, 47 and DC in 1990- 91, and 49 and DC in 1992 (see Appendix I, National Vital Statistics System). 3. Includes mothers of all races.

★ 894 ★

Births

Maternal Education for Live Births: Characteristics and Trends: 1970-92. Part 2

[Data are based on the National Vital Statistics System].

Education, race of mother, and Hispanic origin of mother	Percent of live births[1]						
	1986	1987	1988	1989	1990	1991	1992
Education of mother less than 12 years							
All mothers	20.4	20.2	20.4	23.2	23.8	23.9	23.6
White	17.7	17.4	17.6	21.6	22.4	22.5	22.3
Black	31.9	31.6	31.4	30.4	30.2	30.4	30.0
American Indian or Alaskan Native	39.2	38.5	37.9	37.2	36.4	36.3	35.9
Asian or Pacific Islander	17.9	17.9	17.9	19.5	20.0	19.7	19.0
Chinese	12.3	13.5	14.2	14.9	15.8	15.7	15.2
Japanese	4.0	3.1	3.5	3.3	3.5	3.0	2.4
Filipino	12.6	12.3	11.8	10.2	10.3	10.1	9.3
Hawaiian and part Hawaiian	-	-	-	17.3	19.3	19.4	18.6
Other Asian or Pacific Islander	-	-	-	26.8	26.8	26.0	25.7
Hispanic origin (selected States)[2,3]	43.4	42.8	42.5	52.8	53.9	54.3	54.1
Mexican American	58.9	58.4	56.9	61.3	61.4	61.7	61.3
Puerto Rican	44.8	44.3	45.2	43.7	42.7	41.9	41.0
Cuban	19.7	18.7	18.1	17.9	17.8	16.7	15.6
Central and South American	35.9	34.1	31.8	43.6	44.2	44.5	43.6
Other and unknown Hispanic	33.7	34.3	34.1	34.5	33.3	34.4	34.7
Non-Hispanic white (selected States)[2]	15.7	15.3	16.7	15.3	15.2	15.0	14.5
Non-Hispanic black (selected States)[2]	32.6	32.2	31.8	29.9	30.0	30.3	29.8
Education of mother 16 years or more							
All mothers	17.1	17.6	17.7	17.4	17.5	18.1	18.9
White	19.2	19.8	20.1	19.2	19.3	19.9	20.7
Black	7.1	7.1	7.1	7.2	7.2	7.3	7.8
American Indian or Alaskan Native	3.8	3.7	3.7	4.3	4.4	4.0	4.7
Asian or Pacific Islander	31.4	32.0	31.7	31.2	31.0	31.8	32.5
Chinese	36.8	36.8	36.4	40.5	40.3	41.7	44.0
Japanese	41.3	41.8	42.3	43.6	44.1	45.0	46.6
Filipino	35.4	36.9	35.5	36.0	34.5	34.1	35.8
Hawaiian and part Hawaiian	-	-	-	6.6	6.8	6.7	8.0
Other Asian or Pacific Islander	-	-	-	26.9	27.3	28.6	28.0
Hispanic origin (selected States)[2,3]	6.5	6.6	7.0	5.1	5.1	5.2	5.4
Mexican American	3.3	3.2	3.7	3.2	3.3	3.3	3.5
Puerto Rican	4.9	5.4	5.3	6.3	6.5	6.8	7.3
Cuban	15.4	17.3	18.2	19.2	20.4	21.9	22.5
Central and South American	8.4	8.8	10.1	8.2	8.6	9.1	9.2

[Continued]

★ 894 ★

Maternal Education for Live Births: Characteristics and Trends: 1970-92. Part 2

[Continued]

Education, race of mother, and Hispanic origin of mother	Percent of live births[1]						
	1986	1987	1988	1989	1990	1991	1992
Other and unknown Hispanic	8.7	7.6	8.0	7.7	8.5	8.2	8.5
Non-Hispanic white (selected States)[2]	19.8	20.4	20.4	22.0	22.6	23.3	24.4
Non-Hispanic black (selected States)[2]	6.9	6.8	6.9	7.2	7.3	7.3	7.8

Source: "Maternal Education for Live Births, According to Detailed Race of Mother and Hispanic Origin of Mother: United States, Selected Years 1970- 92." National Center for Health Statistics, *Health, United States, 1994,* p. 74. Primary source: Centers for Disease Control and Prevention, National Center for Health Statistics: Data computed by the Division of Health and Utilization Analysis from data compiled by the Division of Vital Statistics. *Notes:* Excludes births that occurred in States not reporting education. The race groups, white and black, include persons of Hispanic and non-Hispanic origin. Conversely, persons of Hispanic origin may be of any race. 1. Excludes live births for whom education of mother is unknown. 2. Trend data for Hispanics and non-Hispanics are affected by expansion of the reporting area for an Hispanic-origin item on the birth certificate and by immigration. These two factors affect numbers of events, composition of the HIspanic population, and maternal and infant health characteristics. Data shown only for States with an Hispanic-origin item and education of mother item on their birth certificates. The number of States reporting both items increased from 20 in 1980, to 21 and the District of Columbia (DC) in 1983-87, 26 and DC in 1988, 45 and DC in 1989, 47 and DC in 1990- 91, and 49 and DC in 1992 (see Appendix I, National Vital Statistics System). 3. Includes mothers of all races.

★ 895 ★

Births

Women Giving Birth: Black Children Ever Born Per 1,000 Women and Percent Childless: Characteristics. Part 1

[Numbers in thousands. For meaning of symbols, see table of contents.]

Characteristic	Women 15 to 24 years old			Women 25 to 34 years old			Women 35 to 44 years old		
	Number of women	Children ever born per 1,000 women	Percent childless	Number of women	Children ever born per 1,000 women	percent childless	Number of women	Children ever born per 1,000 women	Percent childless
REGION									
All Marital Classes									
Total	2,832	534	67.3	2,960	1,693	26.5	2,732	2,092	15.2
Northeast	463	401	74.3	564	1,424	33.0	479	1,892	16.9
Midwest	573	753	56.7	552	2,013	19.1	519	1,992	16.7
South	1,616	488	69.0	1,606	1,699	26.3	1,520	2,199	13.0
West	179	589	67.9	237	1,550	30.5	214	2,028	23.4
Women Ever Married									
Total	283	1,173	29.2	1,447	1,875	17.1	1,939	2,296	8.6
Northeast	32	(B)	(B)	211	1,697	19.2	302	2,195	8.0
Midwest	34	(B)	(B)	235	2,085	12.0	334	2,121	10.2
South	186	1,066	25.8	875	1,887	17.4	1,135	2,382	7.1
West	29	(B)	(B)	126	1,701	21.8	169	2,239	16.5

[Continued]

Women Giving Birth: Black Children Ever Born Per 1,000 Women and Percent Childless: Characteristics. Part 1
[Continued]

Characteristic	Women 15 to 24 years old			Women 25 to 34 years old			Women 35 to 44 years old		
	Number of women	Children ever born per 1,000 women	Percent childless	Number of women	Children ever born per 1,000 women	percent childless	Number of women	Children ever born per 1,000 women	Percent childless
Women Never Married									
Total	2,549	463	71.6	1,513	1,519	35.5	793	1,595	31.5
Northeast	430	388	75.2	353	1,261	41.2	178	1,377	32.0
Midwest	539	662	59.9	317	1,960	24.3	185	1,756	28.6
South	1,430	412	74.7	732	1,473	36.9	385	1,660	30.6
West	150	444	72.8	112	1,380	40.3	45	(B)	(B)

Source: "Children Ever Born Per 1,000 Women and Percent Childless, by Selected Characteristics," *Fertility of American Women: June 1994*, p. 7. *Note:* B = Base too small to show derived measures.

Women Giving Birth: Black Children Ever Born Per 1,000 Women and Percent Childless: Characteristics. Part 2

[Numbers in thousands. For meaning of symbols, see table of contents.]

Characteristic	Women 15 to 24 years old			Women 25 to 34 years old			Women 35 to 44 years old		
	Number of women	Children ever born per 1,000 women	Percent childless	Number of women	Children ever born per 1,000 women	percent childless	Number of women	Children ever born per 1,000 women	Percent childless
All Marital Classes									
Total	2,832	534	67.3	2,960	1,693	26.5	2,732	2,092	15.2
Not a high school graduate	1,335	429	76.4	495	2,499	13.7	39.3	2,911	10.1
High school, 4 years	643	919	43.6	1,199	1,893	22.4	1,066	2,167	10.7
College: 1 or more years	854	408	71.1	1,265	1,188	35.5	1,273	1,777	20.6
Some college, no degree	671	399	71.9	606	1,415	28.8	599	1,917	16.6
Associate degree	83	630	48.4	262	1,239	29.5	252	2,003	15.7
Bachelor's degree	89	328	82.3	315	854	46.5	304	1,461	28.5
Graduate or professional degree	11	(B)	(B)	82	632	60.9	117	1,399	30.8
Women Ever Married									
Total	283	1,173	29.2	1,447	1,875	17.1	1,939	2,296	8.6
Not a high school graduate	44	(B)	(B)	216	2,537	8.0	238	3,160	6.6
High school, 4 years	112	1,149	19.0	553	2,122	13.9	726	2,331	6.5
College: 1 or more years	127	863	42.1	677	1,463	22.8	975	2,058	10.7
Some college, no degree	76	1,041	34.7	297	1,764	18.4	455	2,209	7.2
Associate degree	26	(B)	(B)	136	1,369	20.0	195	2,193	9.6
Bachelor's degree	16	(B)	(B)	201	1,162	29.3	238	1,750	17.1
Graduate or professional degree	9	(B)	(B)	43	(B)	(B)	87	1,814	13.3

[Continued]

★ 896 ★

Women Giving Birth: Black Children Ever Born Per 1,000 Women and Percent Childless: Characteristics. Part 2

[Continued]

Characteristic	Women 15 to 24 years old			Women 25 to 34 years old			Women 35 to 44 years old		
	Number of women	Children ever born per 1,000 women	Percent childless	Number of women	Children ever born per 1,000 women	percent childless	Number of women	Children ever born per 1,000 women	Percent childless
Women Never Married									
Total	2,549	463	71.6	1,513	1,519	35.5	793	1,595	31.5
Not a high school graduate	1,291	371	78.4	279	2,468	18.2	155	2,528	15.6
High school, 4 years	531	870	48.6	646	1,698	29.8	340	1,815	19.7
College: 1 or more years	728	329	76.1	588	871	50.1	298	857	53.2
Some college, no degree	595	317	76.6	308	1,080	38.9	145	999	46.4
Associate degree	57	(B)	(B)	126	1,100	39.7	58	(B)	(B)
Bachelor's degree	71	(B)	(B)	114	306	76.8	66	(B)	(B)
Graduate or professional degree	2	(B)	(B)	40	(B)	(B)	30	(B)	(B)

Source: "Children Ever Born Per 1,000 Women and Percent Childless, by Selected Characteristics," *Fertility of American Women: June 1994*, p. 7. *Note:* B = Base too small to show derived measures.

★ 897 ★

Births

Women Giving Birth: Black Children Ever Born Per 1,000 Women and Percent Childless: Characteristics. Part 3

[Numbers in thousands. For meaning of symbols, see table of contents.]

Characteristic	Women 15 to 24 years old			Women 25 to 34 years old			Women 35 to 44 years old		
	Number of women	Children ever born per 1,000 women	Percent childless	Number of women	Children ever born per 1,000 women	percent childless	Number of women	Children ever born per 1,000 women	Percent childless
METROPOLITAN RESIDENCE									
All Marital Classes									
Total	2,832	534	67.3	2,960	1,693	26.5	2,732	2,092	15.2
Metropolitan	2,424	527	68.0	2,561	1,682	27.1	2,345	2,043	15.7
In central cities	1,511	569	65.3	1,652	1,787	26.1	1,408	2,046	15.1
Outside central cities	914	457	72.4	906	1,491	28.8	937	2,039	16.7
Nonmetropolitan	406	577	63.7	399	1,764	23.2	387	2,391	12.2
Women Ever Married									
Total	283	1,173	29.2	1,447	1,875	17.1	1,939	2,296	8.6
Metropolitan	214	1,097	34.9	1,253	1,857	18.4	1,666	2,245	8.8
In central cities	129	1,068	34.3	770	1,903	19.8	960	2,219	8.6
Outside central cities	86	1,141	35.8	483	1,783	16.3	705	2,280	9.0
Nonmetroplitan	89	(B)	(B)	194	1,995	8.9	274	2,603	7.5

[Continued]

★ 897 ★

Women Giving Birth: Black Children Ever Born Per 1,000 Women and Percent Childless: Characteristics. Part 3

[Continued]

Characteristic	Women 15 to 24 years old			Women 25 to 34 years old			Women 35 to 44 years old		
	Number of women	Children ever born per 1,000 women	Percent childless	Number of women	Children ever born per 1,000 women	percent childless	Number of women	Children ever born per 1,000 women	Percent childless
Women Never Married									
Total	2,549	463	71.6	1,513	1,519	35.5	793	1,595	31.5
Metropolitan	2,210	471	71.2	1,306	1,514	35.3	679	1,548	32.7
In central cities	1,382	522	68.2	882	1,685	31.6	448	1,647	28.8
Outside central cities	828	386	76.2	426	1,160	43.0	231	1,302	40.5
Nonmetroplitan	339	406	74.2	205	1,547	36.8	113	1,880	23.6

Source: "Children Ever Born Per 1,000 Women and Percent Childless, by Selected Characteristics," *Fertility of American Women: June 1994*, p. 8.

★ 898 ★

Births

Women Giving Birth: Black Children Ever Born Per 1,000 Women and Percent Childless: Characteristics. Part 4

[Numbers in thousands. For meaning of symbols, see table of contents.]

Characteristic	Women 15 to 24 years old			Women 25 to 34 years old			Women 35 to 44 years old		
	Number of women	Children ever born per 1,000 women	Percent childless	Number of women	Children ever born per 1,000 women	Percent childless	Number of women	Children ever born per 1,000 women	Percent childless
LABOR FORCE STATUS									
All Marital Classes									
Total	2,832	534	67.3	2,600	1,693	26.5	2,732	2,092	15.2
In labor force	1,553	532	65.8	2,149	1,469	30.7	2,058	1,993	15.7
Employed	1,077	454	69.4	1,906	1,373	32.2	1,913	1,978	15.9
Unemployed	476	707	57.6	244	2,216	18.6	144	2,195	12.8
Not in labor force	1,279	536	69.2	810	2,288	15.6	674	2,395	13.9
Women Ever Married									
Total	263	1,173	29.2	1,447	1,875	17.1	1,939	2,296	8.6
In labor force	194	1,004	36.1	1,142	1,735	18.7	1,509	2,195	8.7
Employed	143	777	44.0	1,024	1,657	19.4	1,429	2,184	6.7
Unemployed	51	(B)	(B)	118	2,406	12.3	80	2,391	8.4
Not in labor force	89	1,545	9.7	305	2,403	11.3	430	2,646	8.3
Women Never Married									
Total	2,549	463	71.6	1,513	1,519	35.5	793	1,595	31.5
In labor force	1,359	464	69.8	1,006	1,168	44.3	548	1,437	35.0
Employed	935	405	73.3	882	1,043	47.1	484	1,370	37.1
Unemployed	424	595	61.9	126	2,041	24.4	64	(B)	(B)
Not in labor force	1,191	461	73.6	505	2,218	18.1	244	1,950	23.7

[Continued]

★ 898 ★

Women Giving Birth: Black Children Ever Born Per 1,000 Women and Percent Childless: Characteristics. Part 4

[Continued]

Characteristic	Women 15 to 24 years old			Women 25 to 34 years old			Women 35 to 44 years old		
	Number of women	Children ever born per 1,000 women	Percent childless	Number of women	Children ever born per 1,000 women	Percent childless	Number of women	Children ever born per 1,000 women	Percent childless
OCCUPATION									
All Marital Classes									
Total employed	1,077	454	69.4	1,906	1,373	32.2	1,913	1,978	15.9
Managerial and professional	82	420	70.5	423	1,044	42.9	535	1,583	24.9
Technical, sales, and administrative support	623	349	73.8	801	1,210	32.5	648	1,904	15.4
Service occupations	259	583	66.5	389	1,791	25.9	457	2,222	12.2
Farming, forestry, and fishing	9	(B)	(B)	10	(B)	(B)	10	(B)	(B)
Precision production, craft, and repair	18	(B)	(B)	66	(B)	(B)	42	(B)	(B)
Operators, fabricators, and laborers	87	775	49.7	216	1,804	24.5	222	2,542	5.0
Women Ever Married									
Total employed	143	777	44.0	1,024	1,657	19.4	1,429	2,184	87
Managerial and professional	19	(B)	(B)	265	1,374	27.3	426	1,827	13.4
Technical, sales, and administrative support	73	(B)	(B0	408	1,498	21.0	496	2,179	7.0
Service, occupations	36	(B)	(B)	194	2,061	12.1	315	2,420	7.3
Farming, forestry, and fishing	-	(B)	(B)	10	(B)	(B)	7	(B)	(B)
Precision production, craft and repair	6	(B)	(B)	47	(B)	(B)	25	(B)	(B)
Operators, fabricators, and laborers	7	(B)	(B)	99	1,880	6.5	159	2,539	5.8
Women Never Married									
Total employed	935	405	73.3	882	1,043	47.1	484	1,370	37.1
Managerial and professional	63	(B)	(B)	158	490	69.1	109	625	70.4
Technical, sales, and administrative support	550	319	76.5	393	911	44.4	151	1,000	42.9
Service occupations	221	516	70.7	195	1,521	39.6	142	1,781	23.1
Farming, forestry, and fishing	9	(B)	(B)	-	(B)	(B)	3	(B)	(B)
Precision production, craft, and repair	11	(B)	(B)	19	(B)	(B)	17	(B)	(B)
Operators, fabricators, and laborers	79	755	54.2	117	1,371	39.8	63	(B)	(B)

Source: "Children Ever Born Per 1,000 Women and Percent Childless, by Selected Characteristics," *Fertility of American Women: June 1994,* p. 8. *Note:* B = Base too small to show derived measure.

Births

Women Giving Birth: Black Women Who Have Had a Child in the Last Year Per 1,000 Women: Characteristics. Part 1

[Numbers in thousands. For meaning of symbols, see table of contents.]

Characteristic	Number of women	Percent childless	Women who have had a child in the last year		
			Number	Total births per 1,000 women	First births per 1,000 women
AGE					
Total	8,524	36.5	567	66.5	24.3
15 to 29 years old	4,269	55.6	420	98.3	44.1
15 to 19 years old	1,417	84.7	87	61.3	50.0
20 to 24 years old	1,416	50.0	189	133.5	53.3
25 to 29 years old	1,436	32.5	144	100.2	29.1
30 to 44 years old	4,255	17.3	147	34.6	4.4
30 to 34 years old	1,523	21.0	101	66.2	9.3
35 to 39 years old	1,477	16.1	30	20.5	3.1
40 to 44 years old	1,254	14.3	16	12.9	-
MARITAL STATUS					
Total	8,524	36.5	567	66.5	24.3
Currently married	2,731	13.3	193	70.5	26.1
Married, husband present	2,075	15.0	159	76.6	33.5
Married, husband absent[1]	656	8.0	34	51.5	2.7
Widowed or divorced	938	14.2	21	22.8	-
Never married	4,855	53.8	353	72.7	27.9
EDUCATIONAL ATTAINMENT					
Total	8,524	36.5	567	66.5	24.3
Not a high school graduate	2,223	50.7	165	74.4	29.8
High school, 4 years	2,908	22.8	236	81.3	22.2
College: 1 or more years	3,393	38.9	165	48.8	22.4
Some college, no degree	1,876	40.3	82	43.7	19.6
Associate degree	597	26.3	40	66.2	32.8
Bachelor's degree	709	43.3	38	53.4	19.1
Graduate or professional degree	211	46.3	6	29.0	29.0

Source: "Women Who Had a Child in the Last Year Per 1,000 Women, by Selected Characteristics," *Fertility of American Women: June 1994,* p. 14. *Notes:* - Represents zero or rounds to zero. 1. Includes separated women.

★ 900 ★

Births

Women Giving Birth: Black Women Who Have Had a Child in the Last Year Per 1,000 Women: Characteristics. Part 2

[Numbers in thousands. For meaning of symbols, see table of contents.]

Characteristic	Number of women	Percent childless	Women who have had a child in the last year		
			Number	Total births per 1,000 women	First births per 1,000 women
LABOR FORCE STATUS					
Total	8,524	36.5	567	66.5	24.3
In labor force	5,760	34.8	266	46.2	18.8
Employed	4,897	34.0	177	36.1	13.4
Unemployed	864	39.1	90	103.8	49.6
Not in labor force	2,763	40.0	301	108.8	35.6
OCCUPATION					
Total employed	4,897	34.0	177	36.1	13.4
Managerial and professional	1,040	35.9	36	35.1	15.6
Technical, sales, and administrative support	2,072	39.5	63	30.6	17.2
Service occupations	1,105	29.7	51	46.6	7.2
Farming, forestry, and fishing	30	(B)	-	(B)	(B)
Precision production, craft, and repair	126	23.3	9	72.6	37.0
Operators, fabricators, and laborers	525	20.4	16	31.0	2.1
FAMILY INCOME					
Total income	8,524	36.5	567	66.5	24.3
Under $10,000	2,425	27.5	210	86.5	24.9
$10,000 to $19,999	1,766	35.5	133	75.5	23.3
$20,000 to $24,999	634	33.6	55	87.3	40.8
$25,000 to $29,999	670	43.1	36	54.0	16.0
$30,000 to $34,999	473	39.7	37	79.2	39.1
$35,000 to $49,999	968	42.2	43	44.6	21.3
$50,000 to $74,999	694	42.3	21	30.4	20.8
$75,000 and over	316	54.4	6	19.4	11.1
Income not reported	578	43.7	24	41.9	20.2
REGION OF RESIDENCE					
Total	8,524	36.5	567	66.5	24.3
Northeast	1,506	40.6	80	52.9	18.2
Midwest	1,643	31.5	122	74.1	24.1
South	4,744	36.6	316	66.6	26.0
West	630	38.7	50	78.7	26.5
METROPOLITAN RESIDENCE					
Total	8,524	36.5	567	66.5	24.3

[Continued]

★ 900 ★

Women Giving Birth: Black Women Who Have Had a Child in the Last Year Per 1,000 Women: Characteristics. Part 2

[Continued]

Characteristic	Number of women	Percent childless	Women who have had a child in the last year		
			Number	Total births per 1,000 women	First births per 1,000 women
Metropolitan	7,330	37.0	457	82.3	21.6
In central cities	4,572	35.6	297	64.9	23.4
Outside central cities	2,758	39.1	160	58.0	18.6
Nonmetroplitan	1,194	33.5	110	92.4	40.8

Source: "Women Who Had a Child in the Last Year Per 1,000 Women, by Selected Characteristics," *Fertility of American Women: June 1994,* p. 14. *Notes:* B Base too small to show derived measure. - Represents zero or rounds to zero.

★ 901 ★

Births

Women Giving Birth: Characteristics of Women Who Had a Child in the Last Year: 1992

[As of **June.** Covers civilian noninstitutional population. Since the number of women who had a birth during the 12-month period was tabulated and not the actual numbers of births, some small underestimation of fertility for this period may exist due to the omission of: (1) Multiple births, (2) Two or more live births spaced within the 12-month period (the woman is counted only once). (3)Women who had births in the period and who did not survive to the survey date. (4) Women who were in instititions and therefore not in the survey universe. These losses may be somewhat offset by the inclusion in the CPS of births to immigrants who did not have their children born in the United States and births to nonresident women. These births would not have been recorded in the vital registration system. Based on Current Population Survey (CPS); see text, section 1, and Appendix III.]

CHARACTERISTIC	TOTAL, 15 TO 44 YEARS OLD			15 TO 29 YEARS OLD			30 TO 44 YEARS OLD		
	Number of women (1,000)	Women who have had a child in the last year		Number of women (1,000)	Women who have had a child in the last year		Number of women (1,000)	Women who have had a child in the last year	
		Total births per 1,000 women	First births per 1,000 women		Total births per 1,000 women	First births per 1,000 women		Total births per 1,000 women	First births per 1,000 women
Total[1]	58,614	63	25	27,312	86	41	31,302	43	11
White	48,157	62	25	22,102	82	41	25,056	44	11
Black	8,017	69	22	4,070	106	39	3,947	31	5
Asian or Pacific Islander	1,827	64	26	832	69	30	996	59	16
Hispanic[2]	5,555	95	35	2,915	125	60	2,640	62	8

Source: "Characteristics of Women Who Have Had a Child in the Last Year: 1992," *Statistical Abstract of the United States,* 1994, p. 79. Primary source: U.S. Bureau of the Census, *Current Population Reports,* P20-375, P20- 454, and P20-470. *Notes:* 1. Includes women of other races and women with family income not reported, not shown separately. 2. Persons of Hispanic origin may be of any race. 3. Includes separated women.

★ 902 ★

Births

Women Giving Birth: Distribution of Women and Average Number of Children Ever Born: Characteristics. Part 1

[Percent distribution. Numbers in thousands. For meaning of symbols, see table of contents.]

| Characteristic | Total women | Women by number of children ever born | | | | | | | | Children ever born | |
		Total	None	One	Two	Three	Four	Five and six	Seven or more	Total number	Per 1,000 women
ALL RACES											
All Marital Classes											
15 to 44 years	60,066	100.0	42.0	17.9	23.0	11.5	3.7	1.6	.3	74,644	1,242
15 to 19 years	8,798	100.0	91.5	6.9	1.3	.2	.1	-	-	913	104
20 to 24 years	9,310	100.0	65.3	20.9	9.5	3.3	.8	.2	-	5,051	542
25 to 29 years	9,785	100.0	43.6	23.2	20.2	9.2	2.8	.9	.1	10,541	1,077
30 to 34 years	11,131	100.0	26.3	21.0	30.4	15.1	4.4	2.4	.4	17,836	1,602
35 to 39 years	11,093	100.0	19.6	16.8	35.5	19.0	5.9	2.5	.6	20,710	1,867
40 to 44 years	9,972	100.0	17.5	17.1	25.2	18.9	7.0	3.3	.8	19,593	1,965
Women Ever Married											
15 to 44 years	37,355	100.0	19.1	22.5	33.8	16.8	5.2	2.2	.5	65,954	1,766
15 to 19 years	393	100.0	49.2	43.5	6.8	.4	-	-	-	230	584
20 to 24 years	3,189	100.0	37.4	36.4	19.2	5.6	1.0	.3	.1	3,120	978
25 to 29 years	6,283	100.0	28.9	29.0	26.7	11.5	3.0	9	.1	8,420	1,340
30 to 34 years	8,898	100.0	17.5	22.8	34.9	17.3	4.8	2.3	.4	15,912	1,788
35 to 39 years	9,584	100.0	13.3	17.0	39.2	20.9	6.4	2.5	.7	19,406	2,025
40 to 44 years	9,009	100.0	12.1	17.6	38.2	20.5	7.4	3.4	.8	18,863	2,094
Women Never Married											
15 to 44 years	22,733	100.0	79.8	10.3	5.2	2.7	1.2	.7	.1	8,690	382
15 to 19 years	8,405	100.0	93.5	5.2	1.0	.2	.1	-	-	683	81
20 to 24 years	6,121	100.0	79.8	12.9	4.4	2.1	.7	.2	-	1,930	315
25 to 29 years	3,502	100.0	70.0	13.0	8.4	5.2	2.5	.8	.2	2,121	606
30 to 34 years	2,233	100.0	61.4	14.1	12.3	6.4	2.8	2.6	.3	1,924	862
35 to 39 years	1,509	100.0	59.9	15.5	12.3	7.0	2.5	2.4	.3	1,302	863
40 to 44 years	963	100.0	68.4	12.6	7.9	4.4	3.4	1.9	1.3	730	758
WHITE											
All Marital Classes											
15 to 44 years	48,531	100.0	42.7	17.4	23.7	11.3	3.2	1.4	.3	58,675	1,209
15 to 19 years	6,906	100.0	92.9	6.0	.9	.1	.1	-	-	587	85
20 to 24 years	7,350	100.0	67.5	20.3	8.9	2.7	.5	.1	-	3,603	490
25 to 29 years	7,848	100.0	45.3	22.9	20.8	8.3	2.0	.7	.1	7,958	1,014
30 to 34 years	9,097	100.0	27.3	20.7	31.5	14.8	3.5	1.8	.3	13,999	1,539
35 to 39 years	9,062	100.0	20.3	16.5	36.2	18.8	5.6	2.1	.6	16,630	1,831
40 to 44 years	8,249	100.0	18.0	16.4	36.6	18.9	6.5	2.9	.6	15,899	1,927

[Continued]

★ 902 ★

Women Giving Birth: Distribution of Women and Average Number of Children Ever Born: Characteristics. Part 1

[Continued]

| Characteristic | Total women | Women by number of children ever born | | | | | | | | Children ever born | |
		Total	None	One	Two	Three	Four	Five and six	Seven or more	Total number	Per 1,000 women
Women Ever Married											
15 to 44 years	31,863	100.0	19.6	22.4	34.5	16.5	4.7	1.9	.4	55,152	1,731
15 to 19 years	346	100.0	46.4	46.9	6.2	.5	-	-	-	210	607
20 to 24 years	2,762	100.0	37.7	36.5	19.4	5.3	.9	.2	.1	2,667	966
25 to 29 years	5,367	100.9	29.5	28.5	27.6	11.0	2.6	.8	.1	7,072	1,318
30 to 34 years	7,643	100.0	18.0	22.7	36.0	17.1	3.9	2.0	.3	13,350	1,747
35 to 39 years	8,155	100.0	13.9	17.0	39.6	20.6	6.1	2.2	.6	16,229	1,990
40 to 44 years	7,591	100.0	12.5	17.1	39.3	20.4	7.0	3.1	.6	15,624	2,058
Women Never Married											
15 to 44 years	16,668	100.0	87.1	7.9	3.1	1.2	.4	.2	.1	3,523	211
15 to 19 years	6,560	100.0	95.4	3.8	.6	.1	.1	-	-	377	57
20 to 24 years	4,589	100.0	85.4	10.6	2.5	1.2	.2	.1	-	935	204
25 to 29 years	2,481	100.0	79.5	10.6	6.2	2.3	.6	.5	.1	886	357
30 to 34 years	1,453	100.0	76.6	10.3	8.1	2.9	1.2	.9	-	649	447
35 to 39 years	927	100.0	76.6	11.2	7.1	3.0	1.5	.5	-	401	433
40 to 44 years	659	100.0	81.9	8.3	4.3	2.3	1.1	1.1	1.0	275	418

Source: "Distribution of Women and Average Number of Children Ever Born, by Race, Age, and Marital Status," *Fertility of American Women: June 1994*, p. 1.

★ 903 ★
Births

Women Giving Birth: Distribution of Women and Average Number of Children Ever Born: Characteristics. Part 2

[Percent distribution. Numbers in thousands. For meaning of symbols, see table of contents.]

| Characteristic | Total women | Women by number of children ever born | | | | | | | | Children ever born | |
		Total	None	One	Two	Three	Four	Five and six	Seven or more	Total number	Per 1,000 women
BLACK											
All Marital Classes											
15 to 44 years	8,524	100.0	36.5	21.8	19.5	12.7	6.0	2.9	.7	12,239	1,436
15 to 19 years	1,417	100.0	84.7	11.9	3.0	.4	-	-	-	271	192
20 to 24 years	1,416	100.0	50.0	26.6	13.6	6.5	2.7	.7	-	1,241	876
25 to 29 years	1,436	100.0	32.5	25.6	19.2	13.9	6.8	1.7	.3	2,065	1,438
30 to 34 years	1,523	100.0	21.0	23.5	23.9	15.7	9.3	6.0	.6	2,946	1,934
35 to 39 years	1,477	100.0	16.0	20.2	31.1	21.1	6.5	4.0	1.0	2,963	2,005
40 to 44 years	1,254	100.0	14.3	22.7	26.0	18.9	10.7	5.2	2.2	2,753	2,195

[Continued]

Women Giving Birth: Distribution of Women and Average Number of Children Ever Born: Characteristics. Part 2

[Continued]

Characteristic	Total women	Women by number of children ever born								Children ever born	
		Total	None	One	Two	Three	Four	Five and six	Seven or more	Total number	Per 1,000 women
Women Ever Married											
15 to 44 years	3,669	100.0	13.6	24.8	28.6	19.2	8.8	4.1	1.0	7,495	2,043
15 to 19 years	22	(B)	(B)	(B)	(B)	(B)	(B)	(B)	(B)	13	(B)
20 to 24 years	261	100.0	26.8	41.1	19.8	8.8	2.5	1.0	-	319	1,222
25 to 29 years	618	100.0	22.2	31.5	24.8	14.3	5.3	1.9	-	956	1,548
30 to 34 years	829	100.0	13.4	25.1	26.1	17.5	11.9	5.5	.4	1,757	2,120
35 to 39 years	948	100.0	7.7	18.3	36.1	25.0	8.0	3.8	1.0	2,141	2,259
40 to 44 years	991	100.0	9.4	22.3	28.5	21.2	10.9	5.5	2.2	2,310	2,330
Women Never Married											
15 to 44 years	4,855	100.0	53.8	19.4	12.6	7.9	3.9	2.0	.4	4,743	977
15 to 19 years	1,395	100.0	85.1	11.7	2.8	.4	-	-	-	259	186
20 to 24 years	1,154	100.0	55.2	23.3	12.1	6.0	2.8	.6	-	921	798
25 to 29 years	818	100.0	40.2	21.1	15.0	13.7	8.0	1.6	.5	1,109	1,354
30 to 34 years	695	100.0	30.0	21.7	21.2	13.6	6.2	6.5	.9	1,189	1,712
35 to 39 years	530	100.0	31.0	23.7	22.2	14.1	3.9	4.3	.9	821	1,551
40 to 44 years	263	100.0	32.5	24.0	16.6	10.4	10.0	4.3	2.2	443	1,685
HISPANIC[1]											
All Marital Classes											
15 to 44 years	6,492	100.0	36.6	17.2	21.2	15.1	5.3	3.7	.9	9,896	1,524
15 to 19 years	1,114	100.0	84.8	11.9	2.6	.4	.2	-	-	216	194
20 to 24 years	1,209	100.0	50.2	29.5	15.2	4.0	.2	.7	.2	946	782
25 to 29 years	1,146	100.0	30.9	22.0	25.4	15.5	3.4	2.5	.3	1,699	1,482
30 to 34 years	1,209	100.0	18.9	13.6	28.4	25.8	6.9	5.5	1.0	2,560	2,117
35 to 39 years	1,038	100.0	13.6	11.5	29.8	23.4	12.9	6.4	2.4	2,527	2,435
40 to 44 years	776	100.0	13.0	11.3	28.8	24.8	10.8	9.0	2.3	1,948	2,510
Women Ever Married											
15 to 44 years	3,958	100.0	13.4	19.7	30.2	22.5	7.8	6.1	1.3	8,523	2,154
15 to 19 years	95	100.0	31.2	53.9	14.9	-	-	-	-	80	838
20 to 24 years	525	100.0	21.3	42.8	27.6	6.2	.5	1.1	.4	675	1,287
25 to 29 years	777	100.0	17.4	25.0	31.2	19.9	3.8	2.5	.2	1,377	1,772
30 to 34 years	961	100.0	10.9	13.4	30.6	30.5	7.7	5.8	1.1	2,258	2,350
35 to 39 years	904	100.0	9.3	11.3	31.7	25.2	13.6	6.3	2.8	2,324	2,572
40 to 44 years	696	100.0	9.1	11.4	30.4	26.5	11.7	9.0	1.9	1,808	2,599

[Continued]

★ 903 ★

Women Giving Birth: Distribution of Women and Average Number of Children Ever Born: Characteristics. Part 2
[Continued]

| Characteristic | Total women | Women by number of children ever born | | | | | | | | Children ever born | |
		Total	None	One	Two	Three	Four	Five and six	Seven or more	Total number	Per 1,000 women
Women Never Married											
15 to 44 years	2,535	100.0	72.9	13.2	7.3	3.4	1.4	1.5	.3	1,374	542
15 to 19 years	1,018	100.0	89.8	8.0	1.5	.5	.3	-	-	136	134
20 to 24 years	684	100.0	72.3	19.4	5.6	2.4	-	.4	-	271	395
25 to 29 years	369	100.0	59.4	15.7	13.1	6.2	2.8	2.5	.4	322	872
30 to 34 years	248	100.0	50.0	14.6	19.7	7.5	3.7	4.1	.4	302	1,216
35 to 39 years	134	100.0	42.4	13.5	17.3	11.2	8.7	6.9	-	203	1,510
40 to 44 years	80	100.0	46.6	9.8	15.2	10.2	3.2	8.8	6.2	140	1,745

Source: "Distribution of Women and Average Number of Children Ever Born, by Race, Age, and Marital Status," *Fertility of American Women: June 1994*, p. 1. *Notes:* 1. Persons of Hispanic origin may be of any race. B = Base too small to show drived measure.

★ 904 ★
Births

Women Giving Birth: Number and Percent of Births to Unmarried Women by Race and Hispanic Origin of Mother, 1992. Part 1

| Years of school completed by mother, Hispanic origin, and race[1] | Age of mother | | | | |
	All ages[2]	15-17 years	18 years	19 years	20 years
Total[3,4]	30.1	79.2	69.2	61.0	53.3
Hispanic[3]	39.1	69.0	60.6	54.4	49.7
Non-Hispanic[3,5]	28.5	82.2	71.5	62.6	54.2
White[3]	18.5	71.6	59.7	49.9	41.2
Black[3]	68.3	95.7	92.5	89.0	84.2
0-8 years[4]	44.0	73.4	56.9	51.4	48.8
Hispanic	41.5	63.1	54.1	50.0	48.6
Non-Hispanic[5]	48.7	79.8	60.3	53.7	49.0
White	40.4	67.7	52.5	46.9	42.9
Black	86.3	96.9	92.1	89.1	88.1
9-11 years[4]	59.2	80.6	70.3	63.6	58.4
Hispanic	51.1	71.2	62.2	57.2	53.6
Non-Hispanic[5]	62.0	82.9	72.5	65.5	59.9
White	48.5	72.5	60.0	52.0	46.6
Black	87.9	95.7	93.7	91.8	88.9

[Continued]

★ 904 ★

Women Giving Birth: Number and Percent of Births to Unmarried Women by Race and Hispanic Origin of Mother, 1992. Part 1
[Continued]

Years of school completed by mother, Hispanic origin, and race[1]	Age of mother				
	All ages[2]	15-17 years	18 years	19 years	20 years
12 years[4]	32.4	76.5	70.1	60.3	51.5
Hispanic	35.4	67.9	62.2	53.7	47.0
Non-Hispanic[5]	32.0	78.3	71.3	61.2	52.2
White	21.3	68.4	60.1	48.6	38.8
Black	69.7	93.8	91.4	87.5	82.9
13-15 years[4]	19.4	67.1	68.7	60.9	50.6
Hispanic	24.9	63.9	63.3	53.7	45.9
Non-Hispanic[5]	18.9	67.6	69.6	61.9	51.1
White	11.7	57.4	58.4	49.3	38.6
Black	52.4	90.2	88.3	86.6	80.1
16 years or more[4]	5.4	-	-	-	42.8
Hispanic	12.9	-	-	-	40.2
Non-Hispanic[5]	5.1	-	-	-	43.5
White	3.4	-	-	-	31.9
Black	25.5	-	-	-	75.2

Source: "Percent of Births to Unmarried Women by Age, Education, and Hispanic Origin of Mother and by Race of Mother for Mothers of Non-Hispanic Origin: United States, 1992," S.J. Ventura, *Births to Unmarried Mothers: United States, 1980-92*, p. 12. *Notes:* 1. Totals for years of school completed by mother include origin not stated and races other than white and black. 2. Includes births to mothers under age 15 years. 3. Includes figures for educational attainment not stated. 4. Includes origin not stated. 5. Includes races other than white and black.

★ 905 ★

Births

Women Giving Birth: Number and Percent of Births to Unmarried Women by Race and Hispanic Origin of Mother, 1992. Part 2

Years of school completed by mother, Hispanic origin, and race[1]	Age of mother						
	21 years	22 years	23 years	24 years	25-29 years	30-34 years	35 years and over
Total[3,4]	46.6	40.3	34.3	29.7	19.8	14.3	15.6
Hispanic[3]	45.3	41.8	38.5	36.2	30.8	27.2	28.9
Non-Hispanic[3,5]	46.9	39.9	33.4	28.2	17.9	12.6	13.7
White[3]	33.8	28.1	22.7	18.2	10.7	7.5	8.9
Black[3]	79.6	74.5	69.7	65.3	55.1	46.7	44.3

[Continued]

★ 905 ★

Women Giving Birth: Number and Percent of Births to Unmarried Women by Race and Hispanic Origin of Mother, 1992. Part 2
[Continued]

Years of school completed by mother, Hispanic origin, and race[1]	Age of mother						
	21 years	22 years	23 years	24 years	25-29 years	30-34 years	35 years and over
0-8 years[4]	45.2	42.5	39.2	38.2	34.8	30.7	30.6
Hispanic	45.6	43.7	41.1	40.0	37.3	33.4	33.3
Non-Hispanic[5]	44.3	39.8	34.5	33.6	28.3	23.4	24.2
White	38.5	34.5	30.2	29.2	23.7	18.0	18.0
Black	82.6	78.4	76.7	73.9	68.0	58.3	56.3
9-11 years[4]	55.0	52.4	49.9	48.1	45.2	42.7	41.1
Hispanic	50.2	47.7	45.4	43.2	40.7	38.0	38.2
Non-Hispanic[5]	56.6	54.1	51.8	50.2	47.3	44.8	42.4
White	42.8	41.2	39.2	37.2	34.4	31.8	31.2
Black	87.4	85.5	83.0	83.1	79.1	73.8	65.9
12 years[4]	44.6	38.7	33.7	30.0	23.1	19.4	21.2
Hispanic	42.6	38.4	34.9	33.0	28.3	26.4	27.6
Non-Hispanic[5]	44.9	38.8	33.5	29.6	22.4	18.5	20.4
White	31.6	26.5	22.5	18.9	13.8	11.5	13.3
Black	78.4	73.6	70.2	67.0	60.5	55.1	52.5
13-15 years[4]	40.9	32.3	25.9	21.4	14.3	11.8	13.7
Hispanic	37.6	32.4	28.7	25.5	19.9	18.3	22.0
Non-Hispanic[5]	41.3	32.4	25.6	20.9	13.8	11.3	13.1
White	29.2	21.8	16.6	12.7	7.9	6.6	8.5
Black	73.3	66.2	59.3	53.9	44.1	39.6	40.3
16 years or more[4]	33.3	27.7	17.8	11.5	4.8	3.8	6.3
Hispanic	33.7	33.0	24.6	20.2	12.2	10.4	12.7
Non-Hispanic[5]	33.3	27.3	17.3	10.9	4.4	3.5	6.0
White	23.1	19.4	10.9	6.8	2.6	2.4	4.8
Black	70.2	65.1	54.5	42.4	25.6	18.5	20.9

Source: "Percent of Births to Unmarried Women by Age, Education, and Hispanic Origin of Mother and by Race of Mother for Mothers of Non-Hispanic Origin: United States, 1992," S.J. Ventura, *Births to Unmarried Mothers: United States, 1980-92,* p. 12. *Notes:* 1. Totals for years of school completed by mother include origin not stated and races other than white and black. 2. Includes births to mothers under age 15 years. 3. Includes figures for educational attainment not stated. 4. Includes origin not stated. 5. Includes races other than white and black.

★ 906 ★

Births

Women Giving Birth: Number and Percent of Births to Unmarried Women by Race and Hispanic and Non-Hispanic Origin of Mother, 1992

Race and Hispanic origin	Number of births	Percent of all births
All races	1,224,876	30.1
White	721,986	22.6
Black	458,969	68.1
American Indian	21,825	55.3
Chinese	1,537	6.1
Japanese	890	9.8
Hawaiian	2,688	45.7
Filipino	4,879	16.8
Other Asian or Pacific Islander	12,102	14.9
All Hispanic[1]	251,737	39.1
Mexican[1]	156,809	36.3
Puerto Rican[1]	34,275	57.5
Cuban[1]	2,323	20.2
Central and South American[1]	39,115	43.9
Other and unknown Hispanic[1]	19,215	37.6
Non-Hispanic[2]	958,804	28.5
White	468,739	18.5
Black	449,351	68.3
Origin not stated	11,267	28.2

Source: "Number and Percent of Births to Unmarried Women by Race and Hispanic Origin of Mother and by Race of Mother for Mothers of Non-Hispanic Origin: United States, 1992," S.J. Ventura, *Births to Unmarried Mothers: United States, 1980-92*, p. 11. *Notes:* Figures by Hispanic origin exclude data for New Hampshire, which did not require the reporting of Hispanic origin on the birth certificate. 1. Persons of Hispanic origin may be of any race. 2. Includes races other than white and black.

★ 907 ★

Births

Women Giving Birth: Number of Births to Unmarried Women by Age of Mother and Race: 1940 and 1950-92. Part 1

Race and year	All ages	Under 15 years	Age of mother					
			15-19 years					
			Total	15 years	16 years	17 years	18 years	19 years
Reported/inferred[1]								
Race of mother: Black[2]								
1992	458,969	6,296	135,994	12,059	20,158	27,985	35,422	40,370
1991	463,750	6,298	139,325	11,701	20,402	28,714	36,902	41,606
1990	455,304	6,240	139,442	11,732	19,894	28,476	36,875	42,465
1989	442,395	6,458	138,718	11,797	20,735	28,840	37,398	39,948
1988	413,157	6,057	129,333	11,498	19,680	28,470	33,914	35,771
1987	387,468	5,681	122,502	11,188	19,722	26,134	31,207	34,251
1886	369,786	5,762	119,357	11,310	18,749	24,499	31,022	33,777
1985	356,205	5,753	118,058	10,653	17,881	24,695	30,867	33,962
1984	342,524	5,599	117,844	10,285	18,179	24,842	31,026	33,512
1983	333,183	5,324	119,216	10,383	18,636	25,527	31,542	33,128
1982	327,998	5,272	120,243	10,685	19,025	26,218	31,798	32,529
1981	321,383	5,323	121,738	11,016	19,543	26,662	31,553	32,964
1980	318,799	5,691	126,276	12,137	20,602	27,809	32,457	33,271
1980	327,000	5,800	129,700	12,400	21,100	28,600	33,400	34,200
1979	315,800	6,100	130,100	12,300	21,800	28,800	33,200	33,900
1976	293,400	5,900	125,200	12,000	21,100	28,100	32,300	31,700
1977	281,600	6,500	127,200	12,900	22,600	28,900	31,900	30,800
1976	258,800	6,600	122,700	13,200	22,900	28,000	30,200	28,400
1975	249,600	7,200	123,800	13,800	23,200	28,500	30,600	27,600
1974	238,800	7,100	121,200	14,200	23,300	28,600	29,300	25,900
1973	234,500	7,500	119,800	14,600	23,700	28,700	27,900	25,000
1972	233,300	7,100	119,900	14,600	23,900	28,100	28,700	24,500
1971	229,000	6,900	114,900	13,600	22,600	26,900	27,000	24,800
1970	215,100	6,800	107,800	13,000	20,900	24,500	25,600	23,900
1969	189,400	6,100	95,000	11,500	17,900	21,800	23,200	20,700

Source: "Number of Births to Unmarried Women by Age of Mother and Race: United States, 1940 and 1950-92," S.J. Ventura, *Births to Unmarried Mothers: United States, 1980-92,* pp. 38-39. *Notes:* Figures by age may not add to estimated totals for years 1980 because of rounding. 1. Data for States in which marital status were not reported have been inferred from other items on the birth certificate and included with data from that reporting States; see Technical notes. 2. Data also included in "all other" group.

★ 908 ★

Births

Women Giving Birth: Number of Births to Unmarried Women by Age of Mother and Race: 1940 and 1950-92. Part 2

Race and year	Age of mother				
	20-24 years	25-29 years	30-34 years	35-39 years	40 years and over
Black[2]					
	Reported/inferred[1]				
Race of mother:					
1992	162,561	86,853	46,860	17,608	2,797
1991	163,532	89,198	46,370	16,357	2,670
1990	157,819	89,614	44,930	14,946	2,313
1989	153,551	86,846	41,468	13,333	2,021
1988	146,697	80,125	37,290	11,833	1,822
1987	139,771	74,133	33,112	10,511	1,578
1886	134,360	69,623	29,892	9,387	1,385
1985	130,032	65,126	27,262	8,650	1,324
1984	124,541	61,091	24,580	7,579	1,290
1983	120,905	57,122	22,586	6,735	1,295
1982	119,113	54,500	21,366	6,229	1,255
1981	116,568	51,170	19,712	5,633	1,239
1980	114,538	47,594	18,160	5,338	1,202
1980	118,300	48,500	18,300	5,200	1,200
1979	113,100	44,000	16,100	5,200	1,200
1976	103,500	38,900	14,000	4,800	1,200
1977	94,600	35,000	12,600	4,700	1,200
1976	82,400	30,800	10,700	4,400	1,200
1975	75,600	27,100	10,500	4,200	1,200
1974	69,700	24,900	10,200	4,400	1,200
1973	67,500	23,400	10,400	4,500	1,400
1972	67,000	22,600	10,500	4,800	1,500
1971	67,000	22,400	10,900	5,300	1,500
1970	61,800	21,300	10,700	5,100	1,600
1969	53,500	18,900	9,400	4,900	1,600

Source: "Number of Births to Unmarried Women by Age of Mother and Race: United States, 1940 and 1950-92," S.J. Ventura, *Births to Unmarried Mothers: United States, 1980-92,* pp. 38-39. *Notes:* Figures by age may not add to estimated totals for years 1980 because of rounding. 1. Data for States in which marital status were not reported have been inferred from other items on the birth certificate and included with data from that reporting States; see Technical notes. 2. Data also included in "all other" group.

★ 909 ★

Births

Women Giving Birth: Percent of Births to Mothers with Less Than 12 Years of School, 1992

Age and marital status of mother	All births[1,2]	Hispanic	Non-Hispanic		
			Total[2]	White	Black
All ages[3]	23.6	54.1	17.9	14.5	29.8
Married	15.1	47.4	10.0	9.4	11.5
Unmarried	43.3	64.5	37.8	37.1	38.3
15-17 years	91.6	93.5	91.0	90.1	92.1
Married	90.4	93.3	89.0	89.0	88.6
Unmarried	91.9	93.6	91.4	90.6	92.2
18 years	58.3	72.6	54.5	54.5	54.4
Married	59.5	73.9	54.2	55.0	46.3
Unmarried	57.7	71.8	54.6	54.1	55.0
19 years	42.5	63.2	37.4	37.5	36.7
Married	41.8	62.8	35.5	36.2	27.7
Unmarried	43.0	63.6	38.5	38.8	37.8
20-24 years	28.0	53.9	21.9	20.7	24.1
Married	23.1	50.0	17.0	16.9	13.8
Unmarried	35.2	59.2	29.2	30.4	27.5
25 years and over	12.8	46.1	7.8	5.9	15.2
Married	9.4	41.1	5.3	4.5	7.9
Unmarried	29.9	58.3	21.5	20.0	23.3

Source: "Percent of Births to Mothers Who Completed Less Than 12 Years of School by Age, Marital Status, and Hispanic Origin of Mother and by Race of Mother for Mothers of Non-Hispanic Origin: United States, 1992," S.J. Ventura, *Births to Unmarried Mothers: United States, 1980-92*, p. 8. *Notes:* Figures by Hispanic origin exclude data for New Hampshire, which did not require the reporting of Hispanic origin on the birth certificate. Only 0.25 percent of all nonmarital births in 1992 were to New Hampshire residents. 1. Includes origin not stated. 2. Includes races other than white and black. 3. Includes births to mothers under 15 years of age.

★ 910 ★

Births

Women Giving Birth: Percentage of Unmarried Women Who Had a Child in the Last Year: 1990-1994

[Numbers in thousands].

Characteristics	July 1993 to June 1994			July 1989 to June 1990		
	Total	Unmarried women[1]		Total	Unmarried women[1]	
		Number	Percent		Number	Percent
RACE						
All Races						
Total, 15 to 44 years	3,890	1,007	25.9	3,913	913	23.3
15 to 19 years	397	288	72.5	338	229	67.8
20 to 24 years	938	383	40.8	1,038	355	34.2
25 to 29 years	1,054	163	15.5	1,192	180	15.1
30 to 44 years	1,501	172	11.5	1,346	148	11.0
White						
Total, 15 to 44 years	3,107	580	18.7	3,148	543	17.2
15 to 19 years	294	194	66.0	227	134	59.0
20 to 24 years	702	215	30.6	784	205	26.1
25 to 29 years	856	87	10.2	1,012	121	12.0
30 to 44 years	1,255	84	6.7	1,125	83	7.4
Black						
Total, 15 to 44 years	567	375	66.1	615	349	56.7
15 to 19 years	87	78	89.7	96	86	89.6
20 to 24 years	189	152	80.4	211	141	66.8
25 to 29 years	144	69	47.9	135	58	43.0
30 to 44 years	147	78	51.7	172	64	37.2
Asian and Pacific Islander						
Total, 15 to 44 years	112	18	16.1	101	9	9.4
HISPANIC ORIGIN						
Hispanic[2]						
Total, 15 to 44 years	644	177	27.5	491	114	23.2
15 to 19 years	108	71	65.7	43	28	(B)
20 to 24 years	161	50	31.1	154	42	27.3
25 to 29 years	181	28	15.5	147	25	17.0
30 to 44 years	195	28	14.4	146	19	13.0
Not of Hispanic origin						
Total, 15 to 44 years	3,245	830	25.6	3,422	799	23.3
15 to 19 years	290	217	74.8	294	201	68.4
20 to 24 years	777	334	43.0	883	314	35.6

[Continued]

★ 910 ★

Women Giving Birth: Percentage of Unmarried Women Who Had a Child in the Last Year: 1990-1994

[Continued]

Characteristics	July 1993 to June 1994			July 1989 to June 1990		
	Total	Unmarried women[1]		Total	Unmarried women[1]	
		Number	Percent		Number	Percent
25 to 29 years	872	135	15.5	1,045	155	14.8
30 to 44 years	1,306	144	11.0	1,199	128	10.8

Source: "Percentage of Women Who Have Had a Child in the Last Year Who Were Unmarried: June 1990 and 1994," *Fertility of American Women: June 1994*, p. 2. Primary source: June Current Population Survey, 1990 and 1994. *Notes:* 1. Women widowed, divorced or never married at the survey data. 2. Persons of Hispanic origin may be of any race.

★ 911 ★

Births

Women Giving Birth: Ratios of Births to Unmarried Women by Age of Mother and Race: 1940 and 1950-92. Part 1

[Ratios are live births to unmarried women per 1,000 total live births in specified group.]

Race and year	All ages	Age of mother							
		Under 15 years	15-19 years						
			Total	15 years	16 years	17 years	18 years	19 years
Reported/inferred[1]									
Race of mother: Black[3]									
1992	681.3	976.4	926.4	970.0	961.3	945.4	923.4	888.5
1991	679.4	981.1	923.0	972.5	960.2	947.9	922.1	878.4
1990	665.3	984.5	919.7	975.8	959.5	945.3	918.0	874.5
1989	657.2	984.5	920.5	979.2	968.4	949.6	915.1	868.5
1988	647.0	989.9	919.8	983.8	972.3	951.3	916.2	857.1
1987	634.0	990.5	913.9	982.3	980.0	945.5	907.0	850.3
1886	623.7	990.2	907.0	979.7	967.5	939.3	899.3	842.4
1985	612.2	987.7	902.2	981.1	965.0	940.1	894.9	834.2
1984	602.9	985.7	896.2	977.7	963.1	936.1	890.5	822.9
1983	592.2	985.2	890.0	981.2	961.7	932.6	884.5	808.8
1982	576.9	984.1	874.8	972.7	954.4	921.4	865.7	786.4
1981	568.9	989.4	867.4	977.3	951.7	915.0	857.4	773.8
1980	561.2	958.8	856.8	973.1	943.1	904.4	843.4	759.2
Race of child: Black[3]									
Estimated[2]									
1980	554.6	1000.0	862.6	985.7	954.9	914.0	850.2	758.3
1979	546.5	993.6	851.4	971.2	945.1	900.0	833.5	749.2
1976	532.0	972.3	829.1	958.1	927.3	877.1	808.9	724.6
1977	517.4	987.5	819.6	957.7	922.6	870.1	792.4	704.0
1976	503.0	990.8	797.1	956.0	917.0	857.6	761.1	663.1
1975	487.9	984.3	768.7	947.7	896.4	826.0	726.2	627.9

[Continued]

★ 911 ★

Women Giving Birth: Ratios of Births to Unmarried Women by Age of Mother and Race: 1940 and 1950-92. Part 1

[Continued]

Race and year	All ages	Under 15 years	Age of mother						
			15-19 years						
			Total	15 years	16 years	17 years	18 years	19 years
1974	470.9	973.8	737.1	937.2	875.4	790.5	689.9	588.4
1973	457.5	964.3	709.8	914.6	849.2	769.8	648.5	560.7
1972	439.1	964.3	695.7	916.3	839.0	743.5	644.2	537.5
1971	405.3	949.9	669.3	897.8	826.3	732.2	611.9	513.2
1970	375.8	934.8	627.4	883.0	785.8	688.9	570.0	477.7
1969	348.7	917.3	586.6	851.0	754.6	645.3	530.6	438.6

Source: "Number of Births to Unmarried Women by Age of Mother and Race: United States, 1940 and 1950-92," S.J. Ventura, *Births to Unmarried Mothers: United States, 1980-92*, p. 44. *Notes:* 1. Data for States in which marital status was not reported have been inferred from other items on the birth certificate and included with data from the reporting States; see Technical notes. 2. Births to unmarried women are estimated for the United States from data for registration areas in which marital status of mother was reported; see Technical notes. 3. Data also included in "all other" group.

★ 912 ★
Births

Women Giving Birth: Ratios of Births to Unmarried Women by Age of Mother and Race: 1940 and 1950-92. Part 2

[Ratios are live births to unmarried women per 1,000 total live births in specified group.]

Race and year	Age of mother				
	20-24 years	25-29 years	30-34 years	35-39 years	40 years and over
Race of mother: Black[3]					
1992	752.4	549.8	467.0	447.0	421.2
1991	747.0	547.1	465.4	437.8	426.7
1990	726.4	532.7	451.5	419.9	399.6
1989	712.3	519.2	437.6	405.9	371.7
1988	698.9	505.3	423.2	388.7	377.2
1987	685.2	486.4	402.5	372.8	365.1
1886	672.2	472.5	384.3	355.5	342.1
1985	653.5	452.2	370.1	351.1	344.3
1984	637.7	438.2	352.3	334.8	333.9
1983	620.7	419.4	336.9	317.5	322.2
1982	598.8	400.1	322.3	308.2	312.8
1981	584.4	385.6	307.5	297.7	307.1
1980	569.5	367.5	295.7	284.0	295.0
Race of child: Black					
1980	564.4	357.5	284.3	264.9	286.1
1979	549.0	338.1	272.3	269.9	275.2
1976	526.1	319.9	261.7	261.7	279.3

[Continued]

★ 912 ★

Women Giving Birth: Ratios of Births to Unmarried Women by Age of Mother and Race: 1940 and 1950-92. Part 2

[Continued]

Race and year	Age of mother				
	20-24 years	25-29 years	30-34 years	35-39 years	40 years and over
1977	494.8	297.4	249.7	254.5	258.1
1976	460.6	284.9	239.9	251.2	252.8
1975	429.8	268.4	241.0	238.9	231.0
1974	400.9	261.7	237.8	241.1	226.7
1973	286.3	257.0	233.4	229.0	231.8
1972	369.5	240.5	221.9	216.3	220.2
1971	338.8	221.3	204.5	207.0	185.2
1970	312.8	202.7	196.4	186.0	183.4
1969	290.2	190.2	176.4	174.1	170.9

Source: "Number of Births to Unmarried Women by Age of Mother and Race: United States, 1940 and 1950-92," S.J. Ventura, *Births to Unmarried Mothers: United States, 1980-92*, p. 44. *Notes:* 1. Data for States in which marital status was not reported have been inferred from other items on the birth certificate and included with data from the reporting States; see Technical notes. 2. Births to unmarried women are estimated for the United States from data for registration areas in which marital status of mother was reported; see Technical notes. 3. Data also included in "all other" group.

★ 913 ★

Births

Women Giving Birth: Unmarried Women by Child's Race and Mother's Age: 1970-1992

RACE OF CHILD AND AGE OF MOTHER	1970	1980	1985	1990	1992
NUMBER (1,000)					
Total live births	399	666	828	1,165	1,225
White	175	320	433	647	722
Black	215	326	366	473	459
Under 15 years old	10	9	9	11	11
15 to 19 years old	190	263	271	350	354
20 to 24 years old	127	237	300	404	436
25 to 29 years old	41	100	152	230	233
30 to 34 years old	19	41	67	118	128
35 years old and over	12	16	28	53	63
PERCENT DISTRIBUTION					
Total[1]	100.0	100.0	100.0	100.0	100.0
White	43.9	48.1	52.3	55.6	58.9
Black	54.0	48.9	44.1	40.6	37.5

[Continued]

★ 913 ★

Women Giving Birth: Unmarried Women by Child's Race and Mother's Age: 1970-1992

[Continued]

RACE OF CHILD AND AGE OF MOTHER	1970	1980	1985	1990	1992
Under 15 years	2.4	1.4	1.1	0.9	0.9
15 to 19 years	47.8	39.5	32.7	30.0	28.9
20 to 24 years	31.8	35.6	36.3	34.7	35.6
25 to 29 years	10.2	15.0	18.4	19.7	19.1
30 to 34 years	4.8	6.2	8.1	10.1	10.4
35 years and over	3.1	2.4	3.4	4.5	5.1
AS PERCENT OF ALL BIRTHS IN RACIAL GROUPS					
Total[1]	10.7	18.4	22.0	28.0	30.1
White	5.7	11.0	14.5	20.1	22.6
Black	37.6	55.2	60.1	65.2	68.1
BIRTH RATE[2]					
Total[1,3]	26.4	29.4	32.8	43.8	45.2
White[3]	13.9	17.6	21.8	31.8	35.2
Black[3]	95.5	82.9	79.0	93.9	86.5

Source: "Births to Unmarried Women, by Race of Child and Age of Mother: 1970 to 1992," *Statistical Abstract of the United States,* 1994, p. 77. *Notes:* 1. Includes other races, not shown separately. 2. Race per 1,000 unmarried women (never-married, widowed, and divorced) estimated as of July 1. 3. Covers women aged 15 to 44 years.

★ 914 ★

Births

Women Giving Birth: Unmarried Women by Women's Age and Race, 1992

Race and age of mother	Number			Percent distribution[3]			First birth rate[2]
	All births[1]	First	2nd and higher	All births	First	2nd and higher	
All races[4]	1,224,876	580,513	637,706	100.0	47.7	52.3	21.6
Under 15 years	11,161	10,722	371	100.0	96.7	3.3	---
15-19 years	353,878	267,026	85,303	100.0	75.8	24.2	33.8
15-17 years	148,583	126,096	21,810	100.0	85.3	14.7	25.9
18-19 years	205,295	140,930	63,493	100.0	68.9	31.1	46.4
20-24 years	435,727	195,110	238,377	100.0	45.0	55.0	30.8
25-29 years	233,467	65,446	166,503	100.0	28.2	71.8	15.9
30-34 years	127,982	29,097	98,050	100.0	22.9	77.1	8.7
35-39 years	52,447	10,966	41,113	100.0	21.1	78.9	4.0
40-44 years	10,214	2,146	7,989	100.0	21.2	78.8	0.9
White	721,986	376,188	342,048	100.0	52.4	47.6	18.4

[Continued]

★ 914 ★

Women Giving Birth: Unmarried Women by Women's Age and Race, 1992

[Continued]

Race and age of mother	Number			Percent distribution[3]			First birth rate[2]
	All births[1]	First	2nd and higher	All births	First	2nd and higher	
Under 15 years	4,553	4,405	125	100.0	97.2	2.8	---
15-19 years	206,830	168,313	37,634	100.0	81.7	18.3	27.0
15-17 years	83,848	74,997	8,471	100.0	89.9	10.1	19.4
18-19 years	122,982	93,316	29,163	100.0	76.2	23.8	39.2
20-24 years	258,268	130,983	126,051	100.0	51.0	49.0	26.9
25-29 years	137,639	43,215	93,564	100.0	31.6	68.4	14.3
30-34 years	75,696	19,702	55,531	100.0	26.2	73.8	8.3
35-39 years	32,218	7,945	24,040	100.0	24.8	75.2	4.0
40-44 years	6,782	1,625	5,103	100.0	24.2	75.8	0.9
Black	458,969	184,004	272,302	100.0	40.3	59.7	34.9
Under 15 years	6,296	6,021	231	100.0	96.3	3.7	---
15-19 years	135,994	90,210	45,170	100.0	66.6	33.4	70.5
15-17 years	60,202	47,198	12,732	100.0	78.8	21.2	61.5
18-19 years	75,792	43,012	32,438	100.0	57.0	43.0	84.2
20-24 years	162,561	57,358	104,277	100.0	35.5	64.5	51.2
25-29 years	86,853	19,590	66,665	100.0	22.7	77.3	22.3
30-34 years	46,860	7,995	38,520	100.0	17.2	82.8	9.9
35-39 years	17,608	2,446	15,045	100.0	14.0	86.0	3.6
40-44 years	2,797	384	2,394	100.0	13.8	86.2	0.7

Source: "Number and Percent Distribution of Live Birth to Unmarried Women by Live-Birth Order and First Birth Rate for Births to Unmarried Women, According to Age and Race of Mother: United States, 1992," S.J. Ventura, *Births to Unmarried Mothers: United States, 1980-92,* p. 6. *Notes:* 1. Includes live-birth order not stated. 2. First births per 1,000 unmarried women in specified group. 3. Based only on records for which live-birth order is stated. 4. Includes races other than white and black.

★ 915 ★

Births

Women Giving Birth: Women Who Had a Child in the Last Year Per 1,000 Women: Characteristics, June 1994

[Numbers in thousands. For meaning of symbols, see table of contents.]

Characteristics	Total, 15 to 44 years old Women who had a child in the last year			15 to 29 years old Women who had a child in the last year			30 to 44 years old Women who had a child in the last year		
	Number of women	Total births per 1,000	First births per 1,000	Number of women	Total births per 1,000	First births per 1,000	Number of women	Total births per 1,000	First births per 1,000
Total, all women	60,088	64.7	27.4	27,893	85.6	46.3	32,195	46.6	11.0
RACE									
White	48,531	64.0	28.3	22,104	83.8	47.3	26,427	47.5	12.3
Black	8,524	66.5	24.3	4,269	98.3	44.1	4,255	34.6	4.4
Asian and Pacific Islander	1,860	60.2	20.8	915	56.9	31.8	946	63.4	10.1

[Continued]

★ 915 ★

Women Giving Birth: Women Who Had a Child in the Last Year Per 1,000 Women: Characteristics, June 1994

[Continued]

Characteristics	Total, 15 to 44 years old Women who had a child in the last year			15 to 29 years old Women who had a child in the last year			30 to 44 years old Women who had a child in the last year		
	Number of women	Total births per 1,000	First births per 1,000	Number of women	Total births per 1,000	First births per 1,000	Number of women	Total births per 1,000	First births per 1,000
HISPANIC									
Hispanic[1]	6,492	99.2	42.4	3,469	129.6	65.2	3,023	64.4	16.2
Not Hispanic	53,596	60.6	25.6	24,424	79.4	43.7	29,172	44.8	10.5

Source: "Women Who Have Had a Child in the Last Year Per 1,000 Women, by Age, Birth Order, and Selected Characteristics: June 1993," *Fertility of American Women: June 1994,* p. vii. *Note:* 1. Persons of Hispanic origin may be of any race.

★ 916 ★

Births

Women Giving Birth: Women Who Had a Child in the Last Year and Children Ever Born: June 1994

[Numbers in thousands].

Characteristic	Number of women	Percent childless	Women who have had a child last year		Children born per 1,000 women
			Number	Births per 1,000 women	
TOTAL	60,088	42	3,890	64.7	1,231
Race					
White	3,896	29.2	405	103.9	1,671
Black	575	41.5	45	78.1	1,179
Asian and Pacific Islander	1,370	46.2	87	64.7	1,113
Hispanic origin					
Hispanic[1]	3,079	26.3	372	120.8	1,827
Not Hispanic	3,160	41.9	208	65.8	1,206

Source: "Women Who Have Had a Child in the Last Year and Children Ever Born Per 1,000 Women, by Age and Place of Birth: June 1994," *Fertility of American Women: June 1994,* p. xii. Primary source: June Current Population Survey, 1994. *Note:* 1. Persons of Hispanic origin may be of any race.

★ 917 ★

Births

Women Giving Birth: Women Who Had a Child in the Last Year and Their Percentage Employed: Selected Characteristics, 1990 and 1994

[Numbers in thousands].

Characteristic	July 1993 to June 1994		July 1989 to June 1990	
	Number	Percent in labor force	Number	Percent in labor force
Total	3,890	53.1	3,913	52.8
RACE				
White	3,107	55.4	3,148	54.5
Black	567	47.0	615	46.9
Asian or Pacific Islander	112	37.7	101	48.0
HISPANIC ORIGIN				
Hispanic[1]	644	37.7	491	43.8
Not Hispanic	3,245	56.2	3,422	54.1

Source: "Women Who Have Had a Child in the Last Year and Their Percentage in the Labor Force, Selected Characteristics: June 1990 and 1994," *Fertility of American Women: June 1994,* p. xvii. Primary source: June Current Population Survey, 1990 and 1994. *Note:* 1. Persons of Hispanic origin may be of any race.

★ 918 ★

Births

Women Without Children: Childless Women and Children Ever Born: 1992

[See headnote, table 100].

CHARACTERISTIC	Total number of women (1,000)	WOMEN BY NUMBER OF CHILDREN EVER BORN (percent)				CHILDREN EVER BORN	
		Total	None	One	Two or more	Total number (1,000)	Per 1,000 women
ALL RACES[1]							
Women ever married	37,260	100	18	23	59	65,874	1,768
15 to 19 years old	339	100	44	46	10	228	673
20 to 24 years old	3,064	100	38	34	28	3,046	994
25 to 29 years old	6,780	100	28	30	43	9,237	1,362
30 to 34 years old	9,050	100	17	23	60	15,988	1,767
35 to 39 years old	9,337	100	12	19	69	18,866	2,020
40 to 44 years old	8,690	100	11	18	71	18,509	2,130
Women never married	21,354	100	81	10	9	7,440	348

[Continued]

★ 918 ★

Women Without Children: Childless Women and Children Ever Born: 1992
[Continued]

CHARACTERISTIC	Total number of women (1,000)	WOMEN BY NUMBER OF CHILDREN EVER BORN (percent)				CHILDREN EVER BORN	
		Total	None	One	Two or more	Total number (1,000)	Per 1,000 women
15 to 19 years old	7,847	100	95	4	1	511	65
20 to 24 years old	6,023	100	80	13	7	1,827	303
25 to 29 years old	3,259	100	70	13	17	1,926	591
30 to 34 years old	2,199	100	64	15	22	1,728	786
35 to 39 years old	1,300	100	65	13	22	1,016	782
40 to 44 years old	726	100	75	11	15	433	596
WHITE							
Women ever married	32,165	100	19	23	58	55,482	1,725
15 to 19 years old	313	100	45	47	8	200	638
20 to 24 years old	2,708	100	40	35	26	2,546	940
25 to 29 years old	5,929	100	28	30	41	7,827	1,320
30 to 34 years old	7,799	100	17	23	60	13,650	1,750
35 to 39 years old	7,993	100	13	19	68	15,753	1,971
40 to 44 years old	7,422	100	12	17	72	15,507	2,089
Women never married	15,993	100	88	7	5	3,006	188
15 to 19 years old	6,191	100	96	3	4	272	44
20 to 24 years old	4,674	100	87	9	4	814	174
25 to 29 years old	2,287	100	80	10	10	832	364
30 to 34 years old	1,476	100	77	13	10	641	434
35 to 39 years old	837	100	82	8	10	307	367
40 to 44 years old	529	100	88	6	6	140	265
BLACK							
Women ever married	3,585	100	11	23	66	7,686	2,144
15 to 19 years old	16	100	(B)	(B)	(B)	16	(B)
20 to 24 years old	238	100	22	28	50	384	1,609
25 to 29 years old	608	100	19	27	54	1,072	1,763
30 to 34 years old	858	100	12	22	66	1,707	1,988
35 to 39 years old	934	100	7	22	71	2,255	2,416
40 to 44 years old	930	100	7	22	72	2,251	2,421
Women never married	4,432	100	53	20	27	4,215	951
15 to 19 years old	1,297	100	88	9	4	226	174
20 to 24 years old	1,097	100	47	29	23	966	881
25 to 29 years old	813	100	41	23	37	1,028	1,264
30 to 34 years old	634	100	31	21	49	1,039	1,639

[Continued]

★ 918 ★

Women Without Children: Childless Women and Children Ever Born: 1992

[Continued]

CHARACTERISTIC	Total number of women (1,000)	WOMEN BY NUMBER OF CHILDREN EVER BORN (percent)				CHILDREN EVER BORN	
		Total	None	One	Two or more	Total number (1,000)	Per 1,000 women
35 to 39 years old	412	100	30	24	47	677	1,645
40 to 44 years old	179	100	34	26	41	278	1,555

Source: "Childless Women and Children Ever Born, by Race, Age, and Marital Status," *Statistical Abstract of the United States*, 1994, p. 80. Primary source: U.S. Bureau of the Census, *Current Population Reports*, series P20- 470. *Notes:* B Base figure too small to meet statistical standards for reliability. 1. Includes other races, not shown separately.

Births and Birth Rates

★ 919 ★

Births and Birth Rates: Trends: 1970-1992

[Births in thousands and beginning 1980, by race of child. Excludes births to nonresidents of the United States. For population bases used to derive these data, see text, section 2, and Appendix III. See also *Historical Statistics, Colonial Times to 1970*, series B 1,B 5-10, and B 12- 20.]

ITEM	1970	1980	1984	1985	1986	1987	1988	1989	1990	1991	1992
Live births[1]	3,731	3,612	3,669	3,761	3,757	3,809	3,910	4,041	4,158	4,111	4,065
White	3,091	2,936	2,967	3,038	3,019	3,044	3,102	3,192	3,290	3,241	3,202
Black	572	568	568	582	593	611	639	673	684	683	674
American Indian	26	29	33	34	34	35	37	39	39	39	39
Asian or Pacific Islander	(NA)	74	99	105	108	117	129	133	142	145	150
Male	1,915	1,853	1,879	1,928	1,925	1,951	2,002	2,069	2,129	2,102	2,082
Female	1,816	1,760	1,790	1,833	1,832	1,858	1,907	1,971	2,029	2,009	1,963
Males per 100 females	106	105	105	105	105	105	105	105	105	105	105
Birth rate per 1,000 population	18.4	15.9	15.6	15.8	15.6	15.7	16.0	16.4	16.7	16.3	15.9
White	17.4	15.1	14.8	15.0	14.8	14.9	15.0	15.4	15.8	15.4	15.0
Black	25.3	21.3	20.1	20.4	20.5	20.8	21.5	22.3	22.4	21.9	21.3
American Indian	(NA)	20.7	20.1	19.8	19.2	19.1	19.3	19.7	18.9	18.3	18.4
Asian or Pacific Islander	(NA)	19.9	18.8	18.7	18.0	18.4	19.2	18.7	19.0	18.2	18.0
Male	19.4	16.8	16.4	16.7	16.5	16.5	16.8	17.2	17.6	17.1	16.7
Female	17.4	15.1	14.8	15.0	14.9	14.9	15.2	15.6	15.9	15.6	15.2
Plural birth ratio[2]	(NA)	19.3	20.3	21.0	21.6	22.0	22.4	23.0	23.3	23.9	24.4
White	(NA)	18.5	19.8	20.4	21.2	21.6	22.0	22.5	22.9	23.4	24.0
Black	(NA)	24.1	24.2	25.3	24.9	25.4	25.8	26.9	27.0	27.8	28.2

[Continued]

★ 919 ★

Births and Birth Rates: Trends: 1970-1992

[Continued]

ITEM	1970	1980	1984	1985	1986	1987	1988	1989	1990	1991	1992
Birth rate per 1,000 women[3]	87.9	68.4	65.4	66.2	65.4	65.7	67.2	69.2	70.9	69.6	68.9
White[3]	84.1	64.8	63.2	64.1	63.1	63.3	64.5	66.4	68.3	67.0	66.5
Black[3]	115.4	84.7	78.2	78.8	78.9	60.1	82.6	86.2	86.8	85.2	83.2
American Indian[3]	(NA)	82.7	79.8	78.6	75.9	75.6	76.8	79	76.2	75.1	75.4
Asian or Pacific Islander[3]	(NA)	73.2	69.2	68.4	66	67.1	70.2	68.2	69.6	67.6	67.2

Source: "Births and Birth Rates: 1970 to 1992," *Statistical Abstract of the United States*, 1994, p. 74. Primary source: U.S. National Center for Health Statistics, *Vital Statistics of the United States*, annual; *Monthly Vital Statistics Report*; and unpublished data. *Notes:* NA Not available. 1. Includes other races not shown separately. 2. Number of multiple births per 1,000 live births. 3. Per 1,000 women, 15 to 44 years old in specified group. The rate for age of mother 45 to 49 years old computed by relating births to mothers 45 years old and over to women 45 to 49 years old.

Birthweight

★ 920 ★

Birthweight: Percent Low Birthweight by Age, Marital Status, and Race of Mother, 1992. Part 1

[Low birthweight includes birthweight of less than 2,500 grams (5 lb 8 oz.).]

Age and years of school completed by mother	All races[1]		White		Black	
	Married	Unmarried	Married	Unmarried	Married	Unmarried
Under 20 years of age[2]	7.4	10.2	7.0	8.1	12.1	13.4
0-8 years	8.0	10.7	7.8	8.5	14.4	15.3
9-11 years	7.8	10.4	7.4	8.4	12.6	13.5
12 years	6.9	9.4	6.4	7.2	11.4	12.6
13-15 years	6.5	8.5	6.0	6.4	10.6	11.5
16 years or more	...	...	...	...	...	...
20 years of age and over[2]	5.6	10.5	5.1	7.9	10.7	15.0
0-8 years	5.5	7.7	5.3	6.9	10.7	15.6
9-11 years	7.3	11.7	6.8	8.7	14.2	17.3
12 years	5.9	10.6	5.4	8.0	11.1	14.5
13-15 years	5.3	9.7	4.7	7.1	10.0	13.1
16 years or more	4.8	8.8	4.4	6.8	9.2	12.8

Source: "Percent Low Birthweight by Age, Marital Status, and Race of Mother: United States, 1992," S.J. Ventura, *Births to Unmarried Mothers: United States, 1980-92*, p. 23. *Notes:* 1. Includes races other than white and black. 2. Includes births to mothers with educational attainment not reported.

★ 921 ★
Birthweight

Birthweight: Percent Low Birthweight by Age, Marital Status, and Race of Mother, 1992. Part 2

Race and marital status	All ages	Age of mother								
		Under 15 years	15-17 years	18 years	19 years	20-24 years	25-29 years	30-34 years	35-39 years	40-49 years
All races[1]	7.1	13.2	10.1	9.0	8.5	7.1	6.2	6.5	7.7	8.5
Married	5.7	10.6	8.3	7.4	6.9	5.7	5.1	5.5	6.5	7.5
Unmarried	10.4	13.4	10.6	9.7	9.5	9.2	10.7	12.8	14.0	13.0
White	5.8	10.2	8.3	7.5	7.1	5.8	5.1	5.5	6.4	7.4
Married	5.2	9.7	7.9	7.1	6.5	5.2	4.7	5.0	6.0	6.8
Unmarried	7.9	10.3	8.5	7.7	7.6	7.1	7.8	9.2	10.7	10.8
Black	13.3	15.9	13.7	13.2	12.6	12.2	13.1	14.7	16.2	16.0
Married	10.8	13.8	13.3	12.2	11.4	10.3	10.0	11.0	12.5	13.8
Unmarried	14.5	15.9	13.8	13.3	12.7	12.8	15.6	19.0	20.7	19.1

Source: "Percent Low Birthweight by Age, Marital Status, and Race of Mother: United States, 1992," S.J. Ventura, *Births to Unmarried Mothers: United States, 1980-92*, p. 22. *Note:* 1. Includes races other than white and black.

★ 922 ★
Birthweight

Birthweight: Percent Low Birthweight by Age, Smoking Status, Marital Status, and Race of Mother, 1992

[Low birthweight includes birthweight of less than 2,500 grams (5 lb. 8 oz).]

Age and smoking status of mother	All races[1]		White		Black	
	Married	Unmarried	Married	Unmarried	Married	Unmarried
Under 20 years[2]	7.6	10.6	7.2	8.4	12.5	13.7
Smoker	10 .1	11.4	10.1	10.6	16.4	16.8
Nonsmoker	7.0	10.4	6.5	7.4	12.2	13.4
20 years and over[2]	5.7	11.1	5.2	8.3	10.8	15.0
Smoker	9.4	14.8	8.8	11.0	19.8	23.5
Nonsmoker	5.1	9.4	4.6	6.8	9.8	12.6

Source: "Percent Low Birthweight by Age, Smoking Status, Marital Status, and Race of Mother: United States and the District of Columbia, 1992," S.J. Ventura, *Births of Unmarried Mothers: United States, 1980-92*, p. 22. *Notes:* Excludes data from California, Indiana, New York, and South Dakota, which did not require reporting of tobacco use on the birth certificate. 1. Includes races other than white and black. 2. Includes births with smoking status not reported.

★ 923 ★

Birthweight

Low-Birthweight Live Births by Geographical Division and State: 1980-82, 1985-87, and 1990-92

[Data are based on the National Vital Statistics System].

Geographic division and State	Percent of live births weighing less than 2,500 grams								
	All races			White			Black		
	1980-82	1985-87	1990-92	1980-82	1985-87	1990-92	1980-82	1985-87	1990-92
United States	6.80	6.82	7.05	5.68	5.67	5.77	12.67	12.80	13.37
New England	6.08	5.89	5.99	5.66	5.40	5.42	12.27	12.29	11.74
Maine	5.61	5.21	5.20	5.61	5.16	5.19	[1]	[1]	[1]
New Hampshire	5.20	5.04	5.01	5.20	5.02	4.97	[1]	[1]	[1]
Vermont	6.02	5.45	5.51	6.02	5.45	5.48	[1]	[1]	[1]
Massachusetts	5.99	5.77	5.90	5.60	5.31	5.34	11.33	11.42	10.55
Rhode Island	6.10	6.25	6.15	5.62	5.80	5.67	11.88[1]	11.98[1]	10.51[1]
Connecticut	6.79	6.62	6.79	5.91	5.71	5.72	13.51	13.47	13.74
Middle Atlantic	7.03	7.06	7.44	5.78	5.69	5.92	12.83	13.06	13.76
New York	7.34	7.30	7.69	6.04	5.82	6.12	12.41	12.71	13.41
New Jersey	7.09	6.88	7.18	5.59	5.46	5.63	13.23	12.90	13.39
Pennsylvania	6.51	6.80	7.20	5.54	5.64	5.79	13.52	14.09	14.96
East North Central	6.69	6.73	7.26	5.50	5.49	5.73	13.45	13.45	14.34
Ohio	6.71	6.62	7.32	5.73	5.70	6.07	13.09	12.28	13.91
Indiana	6.33	6.43	6.64	5.65	5.80	5.92	12.17	12.00	12.40
Illinois	7.27	7.33	7.69	5.48	5.51	5.65	13.98	14.10	14.66
Michigan	6.88	6.95	7.61	5.64	5.48	5.67	13.51	14.15	14.94
Wisconsin	5.22	5.36	5.98	4.69	4.71	5.05	12.90	12.73	13.98
West North Central	5.67	5.77	6.06	5.15	5.20	5.40	12.74	12.88	13.06
Minnesota	5.12	4.98	5.19	4.89	4.67	4.78	12.79[1]	13.29	13.19
Iowa	4.93	5.16	5.59	4.77	5.00	5.36	11.91[1]	11.78[1]	12.29[1]
Missouri	6.67	6.84	7.31	5.61	5.72	6.00	12.85	13.00	13.55
North Dakota	4.74	4.90	5.13	4.66	4.77	5.03	[1]	[1]	[1]
South Dakota	5.17	5.32	5.22	4.82	5.06	5.11	[1]	[1]	[1]
Nebraska	5.51	5.43	5.50	5.09	5.05	5.12	13.53[1]	12.55[1]	11.77[1]
Kansas	6.10	6.23	6.30	5.55	5.63	5.76	12.40	12.93	11.89
South Atlantic	7.91	7.80	8.04	6.00	5.93	5.97	12.57	12.58	13.05
Delaware	7.60	7.14	7.70	5.51	5.52	5.77	14.43	12.49	13.68
Maryland	7.75	7.72	8.05	5.76	5.53	5.56	12.54	12.84	13.33
District of Columbia	13.15	13.00	14.93	6.01[1]	5.23	5.89	14.74	15.24	17.29
Virginia	7.32	6.98	7.27	5.74	5.55	5.60	12.31	11.60	12.43
West Virginia	6.82	6.99	7.05	6.63	6.81	6.82	11.60[1]	11.79[1]	12.97[1]
North Carolina	7.93	7.89	8.27	6.06	6.04	6.22	12.32	12.51	13.05
South Carolina	8.79	8.58	8.97	6.11	6.04	6.26	12.84	12.69	13.26
Georgia	8.53	8.14	8.60	6.16	6.10	6.09	12.70	12.08	12.97
Florida	7.48	7.60	7.43	5.94	5.98	5.91	12.05	12.84	12.31
East South Central	7.84	7.92	8.39	6.17	6.30	6.54	12.28	12.32	13.21
Kentucky	6.93	6.98	7.03	6.44	6.47	6.50	11.84	12.27	12.05
Tennessee	7.97	7.98	8.50	6.38	6.50	6.73	13.52	13.02	14.17

[Continued]

★ 923 ★

Low-Birthweight Live Births by Geographical Division and State: 1980-82, 1985-87, and 1990-92
[Continued]

Geographic division and State	Percent of live births weighing less than 2,500 grams								
	All races			White			Black		
	1980-82	1985-87	1990-92	1980-82	1985-87	1990-92	1980-82	1985-87	1990-92
Alabama	7.91	8.03	8.53	5.73	5.96	6.27	11.93	12.09	12.83
Mississippi	8.70	8.81	9.72	5.83	6.08	6.62	11.88	12.03	13.08
West South Central	7.21	7.19	7.40	6.00	6.00	6.06	12.67	12.57	13.31
Arkansas	7.49	7.78	8.18	5.87	6.40	6.55	12.47	12.27	13.47
Louisiana	8.48	8.66	9.32	5.90	5.88	6.11	12.81	12.95	13.79
Oklahoma	6.73	6.55	6.62	6.23	6.02	6.02	12.39	11.77	11.91
Texas	6.90	6.85	7.00	5.99	5.98	6.01	12.64	12.44	13.11
Mountain	6.52	6.62	6.83	6.35	6.42	6.58	12.48	13.68	14.10
Montana	5.59	5.68	5.92	5.53	5.65	5.97	[1]	[1]	[1]
Idaho	5.26	5.44	5.65	5.23	5.41	5.62	[1]	[1]	[1]
Wyoming	7.01	7.17	7.23	6.95	7.14	7.14	[1]	[1]	[1]
Colorado	7.98	7.79	8.24	7.67	7.40	7.73	13.93	14.90	16.07
New Mexico	7.58	7.09	7.23	7.64	7.20	7.31	10.95[1]	12.25[1]	12.70[1]
Arizona	6.06	6.29	6.41	5.85	6.09	6.18	11.45	12.80	12.25
Utah	5.36	5.62	5.79	5.31	5.56	5.75	[1]	[1]	[1]
Nevada	6.66	7.08	7.20	6.10	6.26	6.44	12.17[1]	13.51[1]	14.41
Pacific	5.75	5.87	5.76	5.13	5.19	5.10	11.67	12.77	12.45
Washington	5.14	5.27	5.23	4.83	4.91	4.89	11.52	11.85	11.59
Oregon	4.89	5.20	5.03	4.68	5.01	4.82	11.27[1]	12.74[1]	11.24
California	5.90	6.01	5.85	5.23	5.27	5.16	11.73	12.90	12.57
Alaska	5.07	4.77	4.81	4.58	4.30	4.28	8.51[1]	10.05[1]	9.79[1]
Hawaii	7.09	6.79	7.02	6.00	5.44	5.55	10.37[1]	9.63[1]	11.45[1]

Source: "Low-Birthweight Live Births, According to Race of Mother, Geographical Division, and State: United States, Average Annual 1980-82, 1985-87, and 1990-92." National Center for Health Statistics, *Health, United States, 1994*, p. 77. Primary source: Centers for Disease Control and Prevention, National Center for Health Statistics: data computed by the Division of Health and Utilization Analysis from data compiled by the Division of Vital Statistics. *Notes:* 1. Data for States with fewer than 5,000 live births for the 3-year period are considered unreliable. Data for States with fewer than 1,000 live births are considered highly unreliable and are not shown.

★ 924 ★

Birthweight

Very Low-Birthweight Live Births by Geographical Division and State: 1980-82, 1985-87, and 1990-92

[Data are based on the National Vital Statistics System].

Geographic division and State	Percent of live births weighing less than 1,500 grams								
	All races			White			Black		
	1980-82	1985-87	1990-92	1980-82	1985-87	1990-92	1980-82	1985-87	1990-92
United States	1.16	1.22	1.29	0.91	0.94	0.96	2.52	2.74	2.95
New England	1.10	1.03	1.11	0.99	0.90	0.95	2.86	2.87	2.81
Maine	1.31	0.84	0.86	1.31	0.84	0.87	[1]	[1]	[1]
New Hampshire	0.94	0.86	0.87	0.94	0.86	0.84	[1]	[1]	[1]
Vermont	0.90	0.91	0.82	0.90	0.92	0.82	[1]	[1]	[1]
Massachusetts	1.04	0.98	1.08	0.92	0.85	0.95	2.65	2.62	2.35
Rhode Island	1.07	1.14	1.16	0.98	1.05	1.01	2.36[1]	2.54[1]	2.74[1]
Connecticut	1.25	1.26	1.36	1.00	1.00	1.04	3.18	3.26	3.50
Middle Atlantic	1.20	1.31	1.43	0.92	0.96	1.02	2.55	2.85	3.19
New York	1.26	1.34	1.46	0.96	0.97	1.03	2.45	2.73	3.07
New Jersey	1.22	1.29	1.41	0.90	0.94	1.04	2.55	2.81	3.03
Pennsylvania	1.10	1.26	1.39	0.87	0.95	0.99	2.79	3.18	3.64
East North Central	1.20	1.25	1.37	0.93	0.94	0.99	2.79	2.95	3.14
Ohio	1.15	1.19	1.34	0.93	0.97	1.03	2.63	2.55	3.00
Indiana	1.06	1.09	1.18	0.88	0.93	0.97	2.56	2.52	2.81
Illinois	1.37	1.40	1.47	0.96	0.96	1.00	2.94	3.06	3.12
Michigan	1.26	1.35	1.50	0.97	0.95	1.00	2.82	3.33	3.40
Wisconsin	0.96	0.98	1.09	0.85	0.81	0.87	2.59	2.82	3.03
West North Central	0.95	0.99	10.6	0.84	0.86	0.90	2.48	2.65	2.81
Minnesota	0.90	0.88	0.93	0.84	0.83	0.85	3.38[1]	2.60	2.76
Iowa	0.82	0.84	0.95	0.79	0.82	0.88	2.22[1]	1.88[1]	2.81[1]
Missouri	1.10	1.21	1.28	0.88	0.93	0.93	2.41	2.75	2.91
North Dakota	0.85	0.80	0.90	0.82	0.78	0.87	[1]	[1]	[1]
South Dakota	0.80	0.99	0.90	0.75	0.92	0.88	[1]	[1]	[1]
Nebraska	0.88	0.86	0.93	0.79	0.77	0.84	2.55[1]	2.54[1]	2.46[1]
Kansas	1.02	1.02	1.12	0.90	0.88	0.99	2.43	2.62	2.66
South Atlantic	1.46	1.51	1.59	1.00	1.02	1.02	2.59	2.79	2.96
Delaware	1.56	1.54	1.60	1.03	0.99	1.02	3.27	3.39	3.46
Maryland	1.56	1.71	1.70	1.04	1.07	0.99	2.83	3.27	3.24
District of Columbia	2.91	3.23	3.55	1.25[1]	1.03	1.12	3.29	3.90	4.20
Virginia	1.31	1.26	1.42	0.96	0.90	0.96	2.44	2.44	2.88
West Virginia	1.05	1.19	1.16	1.03	1.11	1.11	1.76[1]	3.35[1]	2.62[1]
North Carolina	1.47	1.54	1.65	1.02	1.07	1.07	2.53	2.75	3.01
South Carolina	1.60	1.62	1.70	1.02	1.02	1.06	2.49	2.60	2.74
Georgia	1.58	1.57	1.68	1.00	1.06	1.01	2.60	2.57	2.84
Florida	1.33	1.42	1.44	0.96	1.01	1.04	2.46	2.79	2.76
East South Central	1.28	1.39	1.53	0.91	1.01	1.06	2.26	2.42	2.77
Kentucky	1.08	1.19	1.20	0.94	1.07	1.06	2.42	2.38	2.56
Tennessee	1.29	1.41	1.56	0.96	1.04	1.09	2.45	2.66	3.07

[Continued]

★ 924 ★

Very Low-Birthweight Live Births by Geographical Division and State: 1980-82, 1985-87, and 1990-92

[Continued]

Geographic division and State	Percent of live births weighing less than 1,500 grams								
	All races			White			Black		
	1980-82	1985-87	1990-92	1980-82	1985-87	1990-92	1980-82	1985-87	1990-92
Alabama	1.32	1.43	1.63	0.86	0.93	1.05	2.16	2.41	2.73
Mississippi	1.47	1.54	1.76	0.83	0.94	0.97	2.18	2.24	2.60
West South Central	1.15	1.23	1.26	0.89	0.95	0.93	2.33	2.55	2.72
Arkansas	1.14	1.31	1.32	0.80	1.02	0.98	2.17	2.31	2.45
Louisiana	1.39	1.63	1.74	0.84	0.95	0.93	2.31	2.68	2.88
Oklahoma	1.06	1.03	1.08	0.93	0.89	0.96	2.46	2.38	2.27
Texas	1.09	1.16	1.17	0.90	0.95	0.93	2.36	2.51	2.72
Mountain	0.92	0.96	1.01	0.88	0.90	0.95	2.62	2.60	2.65
Montana	0.88	0.85	0.85	0.86	0.80	0.84	[1]	[1]	[1]
Idaho	0.68	0.86	0.85	0.68	0.84	0.84	[1]	[1]	[1]
Wyoming	0.93	0.98	0.83	0.93	0.96	0.81	[1]	[1]	[1]
Colorado	1.03	1.00	1.13	0.97	0.91	1.02	2.47	2.78	2.96
New Mexico	0.98	0.98	0.97	0.99	0.98	0.98	2.28[1]	2.74[1]	2.59[1]
Arizona	0.96	1.07	1.09	0.90	1.01	1.04	2.73	2.66	2.53
Utah	0.78	0.75	0.85	0.78	0.74	0.84	[1]	[1]	[1]
Nevada	1.03	1.00	1.06	0.85	0.87	0.92	2.94[1]	2.35[1]	2.49
Pacific	0.98	1.02	0.99	0.86	0.89	0.86	2.29	2.71	2.68
Washington	0.85	0.89	0.83	0.80	0.81	0.77	1.98	2.58	2.60
Oregon	0.81	0.84	0.83	0.78	0.80	0.81	1.99[1]	2.68[1]	1.87[1]
California	1.01	1.06	1.02	0.88	0.91	0.88	2.32	2.73	2.70
Alaska	0.84	0.86	0.90	0.75	0.79	0.77	2.26[1]	1.88[1]	2.20[1]
Hawaii	1.05	1.06	1.00	0.94	0.91	0.85	1.66[1]	2.69[1]	3.24[1]

Source: "Very Low-birthweight Live Births, According to Race of Mother, Geographical Division, and State: United States, Average Annual 1880-82, 1885-87, and 1990-92." National Center for Health Statistics, *Health, United States, 1994,* p. 78. Primary source: Centers for Disease Control and Prevention, National Center for Health Statistics: data computed by the Division of Health and Utilization Analysis from data compiled by the Division of Vital Statistics. *Notes:* 1. Data for States with fewer than 5,000 live births for the 3-year period are considered unreliable. Data for States with fewer than 1,000 live births are considered highly unreliable and are not shown.

Breastfeeding

★ 925 ★

Breastfeeding by Mothers 14-55 Years of Age: 1970-71 to 1986-87

[Data are based on household interviews of samples of women in the childbearing ages].

Selected characteristics of mother	1970-71	1972-73	1974-75	1976-77	1978-79	1980-81	1982-83	1984-85	1986-87
				Percent of babies breastfed					
Total	24.9	29.1	34.2	42.0	44.4	52.5	57.3	55.5	55.0
Race									
White	26.4	30.4	37.3	45.9	48.1	57.2	62.3	59.9	60.3
Black	10.8	14.6	17.1	19.5	24.5	24.5	27.0	22.9	23.5
Total	49.5	53.4	61.7	61.7	66.5	66.0	66.6	61.6	54.2
Race									
White	49.0	52.5	60.8	63.6	66.9	66.3	65.6	62.6	53.1
Black	55.7	48.8	74.5	59.5	61.3	55.4	60.4	49.9	53.2

Source: "Breastfeeding by Mothers 15-44 Years of Age by Year of Baby's Birth, According to Selected Characteristics of Mother: United States, 1970-71 to 1986-87." National Center for Health Statistics, *Health, United States, 1994*, p. 83. Primary source: Centers for Disease Control and Prevention, National Center for Health Statistics, Division of Vital Statistics, Data from the National Survey of Family Growth, Cycle III 1982, Cycle IV 1988. *Notes:* Data on breastfeeding during 1970-81 are based on responses to questions in the National Survey of Family Growth, Cycle III conducted in 1982. Data for 1982-87 are based on the National Survey of family growth Cycle IV conducted in 1988.

Death Rates

★ 926 ★

Causes of Deaths: Accidents and Violence, 1990-1992

[Rates are per 100,000 population. Excludes deaths of nonresidents of the United States. Beginning 1980, deaths classified according to the ninth revision of the *International Classification of Diseases*. For earlier years, classified according to the revisions in use at the time; see text, section 2. See Appendix III.]

| CAUSE OF DEATH AND AGE | WHITE | | | | | | BLACK | | | | | |
| | Male | | | Female | | | Male | | | Female | | |
	1990	1991	1992	1990	1991	1992	1990	1991	1992	1990	1991	1992
Total[1]	81.2	78.7	76.2	32.1	31.5	30.4	142.0	143.9	134.5	38.6	38.4	36.7
Motor vehicle accidents	26.1	24.4	22.4	11.4	10.8	10.2	28.1	25.6	24.0	9.4	8.7	8.8
All other accidents	23.6	23.3	23.4	12.4	12.6	12.4	32.7	34.2	30.9	13.4	13.5	12.7
Suicide	22.0	21.7	12.2	5.3	5.2	5.1	12.0	12.1	12.0	2.3	1.9	2.0
Homicide	9.0	9.3	9.1	2.8	3.0	2.8	69.2	72.0	67.5	13.5	14.2	13.1
15 to 24 years old	107.3	104.2	97.4	30.5	31.2	28.4	208.0	231.9	222.2	34.9	37.0	34.9
25 to 34 years old	97.4	94.2	90.4	26.0	24.7	23.6	218.1	213.8	193.6	48.1	47.7	46.1
35 to 44 years old	82.3	78.5	80.3	24.4	23.5	23.5	176.6	171.8	159.8	38.5	40.0	38.9
45 to 54 years old	73.5	72.9	69.8	25.3	25.2	24.2	138.5	132.4	132.9	30.7	33.1	29.5
55 to 64 years old	79.5	75.6	73.0	29.4	26.6	25.7	129.9	124.7	118.7	36.1	32.5	31.8
65 years old and over	150.7	147.4	145.4	80.1	79.6	78.6	175.5	182.2	165.7	81.6	78.6	72.6
65 to 74 years old	99.7	94.8	94.0	40.5	39.0	38.7	141.8	142.6	130.8	50.4	48.1	43.9
75 to 84 years old	195.7	190.5	186.2	89.4	87.1	83.9	206.1	213.5	201.4	95.8	89.7	89.5
85 years old and over	428.3	433.3	421.4	232.4	234.8	234.2	359.1	373.9	340.0	213.0	209.8	178.4

Source: "Death Rates from Accidents and Violence: 1990 to 1992," *Statistical Abstract of the United States, 1995*, p. 99. *Note:* 1. Includes persons under 15 years old, not shown separately.

★ 927 ★

Death Rates

Death Rates: Age Adjusted by Cause: Trends. Part 1

[Data are based on the National Vital Statistics System.]

Sex, race, and cause of death	1950[1]	1960[1]	1970	1980	1985	1988	1989	1990	1991	1992
	Deaths per 100,000 resident population									
White male										
All causes	963.1	917.7	893.4	745.3	693.3	671.3	652.2	644.3	634.4	620.9
Natural causes	860.1	825.8	788.6	651.2	613.4	592.2	575.3	567.6	560.0	548.8
Disease of heart	381.1	375.4	347.6	277.5	246.2	223.0	208.7	202.0	196.1	190.3
Ischemic heart disease	-	-	-	218.0	182.1	157.6	150.2	145.3	139.7	134.8

[Continued]

★ 927 ★

Death Rates: Age Adjusted by Cause: Trends. Part 1
[Continued]

Sex, race, and cause of death	1950[1]	1960[1]	1970	1980	1985	1988	1989	1990	1991	1992
Cerebrovascular disease	87.0	80.3	68.8	41.9	33.0	30.3	28.4	27.7	26.9	26.3
Malignant neoplasms	130.9	141.6	154.3	160.5	160.4	159.6	159.4	160.3	159.5	157.3
Respiratory system	21.6	34.6	49.9	58.0	58.7	58.8	58.3	59.0	58.1	56.7
Colorectal	19.8	18.9	18.9	18.3	17.8	16.8	16.5	16.5	16.0	15.7
Prostate	13.1	12.4	12.3	13.2	13.4	14.2	14.7	15.3	15.3	15.1
Chronic obstructive pulmonary diseases	6.0	13.8	24.0	26.7	28.7	28.2	27.2	27.4	27.4	26.8
Pneumonia and influenza	27.1	31.0	26.0	16.2	17.5	18.2	17.1	17.5	16.6	15.8
Chronic liver disease and cirrhosis	11.6	14.4	18.8	15.7	12.7	12.3	12.1	11.5	11.2	11.1
Diabetes mellitus	11.3	11.6	12.7	9.5	9.2	9.7	11.1	11.3	11.5	11.6
Nephritis, nephrotic syndrome, and nephrosis	-	-	-	4.9	5.4	5.3	4.8	4.6	4.7	4.8
Septicemia	-	-	-	2.8	4.3	4.6	4.2	4.2	4.1	3.9
Human immunodeficiency virus infection	-	-	-	-	-	10.0	13.2	15.0	16.7	18.1
External causes	103.0	91.9	104.8	94.1	80.0	79.1	76.9	76.7	74.4	72.1
Unintentional injuries	80.9	70.5	76.2	62.3	50.5	50.0	47.8	46.4	43.9	41.9
Motor vehicle crashes	35.9	34.0	40.1	34.8	27.6	28.4	26.7	26.3	24.2	22.2
Suicide	18.1	17.5	18.21	18.9	19.9	19.9	19.7	20.1	19.9	19.5
Homicide and legal intervention	3.9	3.9	7.3	10.9	8.1	7.8	8.1	8.9	9.4	9.3
Drug-induced causes	-	-	-	3.2	4.0	4.9	4.8	4.2	4.6	5.5
Alcohol-induced causes	-	-	-	10.8	9.2	9.5	9.9	9.9	9.7	9.9
Black male										
All causes	1,373.1	1,246.1	1,318.6	1,112.8	1,053.4	1,083.0	1,082.8	1,061.3	1,048.8	1,026.9
Natural causes	1,209.2	1,093.4	1,095.4	942.6	920.7	938.1	936.0	915.2	900.3	886.7
Disease of heart	415.5	381.2	375.9	327.3	310.8	301.7	289.7	275.9	272.7	264.1
Ischemic heart disease	-	-	-	196.0	170.4	155.1	152.2	147.1	144.5	138.2
Cerebrovascular disease	146.2	141.2	122.5	77.5	62.7	60.8	57.3	56.1	54.9	52.0
Malignant neoplasms	126.1	158.5	198.0	229.9	239.9	240.4	246.2	248.1	242.4	238.1
Respiratory system	16.9	36.6	60.8	82.0	87.7	88.7	90.8	91.0	88.4	86.7
Colorectal	13.8	15.0	17.3	19.2	20.2	20.1	20.7	21.6	20.4	20.5
Prostate	16.9	22.2	25.4	29.1	31.2	32.0	33.1	35.3	35.3	35.8
Chronic obstructive pulmonary diseases	-	-	-	20.9	24.8	27.4	26.5	26.5	25.9	24.8
Pneumonia and influenza	63.8	70.2	53.8	28.0	27.5	29.2	29.3	28.7	26.2	25.0
Chronic liver disease and cirrhosis	8.8	14.8	33.1	30.6	23.8	21.3	21.2	20.0	17.4	17.2
Diabetes mellitus	11.5	16.2	21.2	17.7	18.2	20.8	24.1	23.6	24.6	24.2
Nephritis, nephrotic syndrome, and nephrosis	-	-	-	14.2	14.5	14.0	14.7	12.9	12.8	12.5
Septicemia	-	-	-	8.0	12.2	12.8	11.8	11.6	11.6	11.4
Human immunodeficiency virus infection	-	-	-	-	-	31.6	40.3	44.2	52.9	61.8
External causes	163.9	152.7	223.2	170.2	132.6	144.9	146.8	146.0	148.5	140.2
Unintentional injuries	105.7	100.0	119.5	82.0	67.6	70.4	68.8	62.4	61.0	56.7
Motor vehicle crashes	39.8	38.2	50.1	32.9	28.0	30.1	29.8	28.9	26.2	25.0
Suicide	7.0	7.8	9.9	11.1	11.5	11.9	12.6	12.4	12.5	12.4
Homicide and legal intervention	51.1	44.9	82.1	71.9	50.2	58.6	61.9	68.7	72.5	68.1

[Continued]

★ 927 ★

Death Rates: Age Adjusted by Cause: Trends. Part 1

[Continued]

Sex, race, and cause of death	1950[1]	1960[1]	1970	1980	1985	1988	1989	1990	1991	1992
Drug-induced causes	-	-	-	5.8	8.9	12.9	11.4	8.4	9.7	10.6
Alcohol-induced causes	-	-	-	32.4	27.7	27.3	27.7	26.6	22.9	22.3

Source: "Age-adjusted Death Rates for Selected Causes of Death, According to Sex and Race: United States, Selected Years 1950-92," *Health, United States, 1994*, pp. 97-98. Primary source: Centers for Disease Control and Prevention, National Center for Health Statistics: Vital Statistics Rates in the United States, 1940-1960, by R.D. Grove and A.M. Hetzel, DHEW Pub. No. (PHS) 1677. Public Health Service. Washington. U.S. Government Printing Office, 1968; Vital statistics of the United States, Vol. II, Mortality, Part A, for data years 1960-92. Public Health Service. Washington. U.S. Government Printing Office; Data computed by the Division of Health and Utilization Analysis from data compiled by the Division of Vital Statistics and from table 1. *Notes:* For data years shown, the code number for cause of death are based on the then current International Classification of Diseases, which are described in Appendix II, tables IV and V. Categories for the coding and classification of human immunodeficiency virus infection were introduced in the United States beginning with mortality data for 1987. Data for the 1980's are based on intercensal population estimates. See Appendix I, department of Commerce. 1. Includes deaths of nonresidents of the United States. 2. Male only.

★ 928 ★

Death Rates: Age Adjusted by Cause: Trends. Part 2

[Data are based on the National Vital Statistics System].

Sex, race, and cause of death	1950[1]	1960[1]	1970	1980	1985	1988	1989	1990	1991	1992
				Deaths per 100,000 resident population						
White female										
All causes	645.0	555.0	501.7	411.1	391.0	385.3	376.0	369.9	366.3	359.9
Natural causes	607.7	522.7	463.8	380.0	363.9	358.0	349.3	344.2	341.1	335.8
Disease of heart	223.6	197.1	167.8	134.6	121.7	114.1	106.6	103.1	100.7	98.1
Ischemic heart disease	-	-	-	97.4	82.9	74.7	71.0	68.6	66.4	64.1
Cerebrovascular disease	79.7	68.7	56.2	35.2	27.9	25.5	24.2	23.8	22.8	22.5
Malignant neoplasms	119.4	109.5	107.6	107.7	110.5	110.4	111.1	111.2	111.2	110.3
Respiratory system	4.6	5.1	10.1	18.2	22.7	24.9	25.9	26.5	26.8	27.4
Colorectal	19.0	17.0	15.3	13.3	12.3	11.5	11.1	10.9	10.8	10.5
Breast	22.5	22.4	23.4	22.8	23.4	23.1	23.1	22.9	22.5	21.7
Chronic obstructive pulmonary diseases	2.8	3.3	5.3	9.2	12.9	14.5	15.2	15.2	16.1	16.1
Pneumonia and influenza	18.9	19.0	15.0	9.4	9.9	10.7	10.4	10.6	10.2	9.7
Chronic liver disease and cirrhosis	5.8	6.6	8.7	7.0	5.6	5.1	5.0	4.8	4.8	4.6
Diabetes mellitus	16.4	13.7	12.8	8.7	8.1	8.4	9.6	9.5	9.6	9.6
Nephritis, nephrotic syndrome, and nephrosis	-	-	-	2.9	3.4	3.3	3.0	3.0	3.0	3.0
Septicemia	-	-	-	1.8	3.0	3.5	3.1	3.1	3.1	3.1
Human immunodeficiency virus infection	-	-	-	-	-	0.7	0.9	1.1	1.3	1.6
External causes	37.3	32.3	37.9	31.1	27.1	27.3	26.7	25.7	25.2	24.0
Unintentional injuries	30.6	25.5	27.2	21.4	18.4	18.9	18.6	17.6	17.0	16.1
Motor vehicle crashes	10.6	11.1	14.4	12.3	10.8	11.6	11.6	11.0	10.4	9.6
Suicide	5.3	5.3	7.2	5.7	5.3	5.1	4.8	4.8	4.8	4.6
Homicide and legal intervention	1.4	1.5	2.2	3.2	2.9	2.9	2.8	2.8	3.0	2.8
Drug-induced causes	-	-	-	2.6	2.5	2.7	2.6	2.5	2.6	2.7
Alcohol-induced causes	-	-	-	3.5	2.8	2.7	2.8	2.8	2.7	2.6

[Continued]

★ 928 ★

Death Rates: Age Adjusted by Cause: Trends. Part 2
[Continued]

Sex, race, and cause of death	1950[1]	1960[1]	1970	1980	1985	1988	1989	1990	1991	1992
Black female										
All causes	1,106.7	916.9	814.4	631.1	594.8	601.0	594.3	581.6	575.1	568.4
Natural causes	1,054.8	867.3	757.9	588.4	559.8	562.2	556.3	545.1	538.4	533.3
Disease of heart	349.5	292.6	251.7	201.1	188.3	183.3	175.6	168.1	165.5	162.4
Ischemic heart disease	-	-	-	116.1	101.6	94.1	92.3	88.8	88.3	84.9
Cerebrovascular disease	155.6	139.5	107.9	61.7	50.6	47.1	45.5	42.7	41.0	39.9
Malignant neoplasms	131.9	127.8	123.5	129.7	131.8	133.5	133.5	137.2	136.3	136.6
Respiratory system	4.1	5.5	10.9	19.5	22.8	25.2	26.0	27.5	27.4	28.5
Colorectal	15.0	15.4	16.1	15.3	16.2	15.1	15.1	15.5	15.2	14.8
Breast	19.3	21.3	21.5	23.3	25.5	27.5	26.5	27.5	27.6	27.0
Chronic obstructive pulmonary diseases	-	-	-	6.3	8.8	10.2	11.1	10.7	11.3	11.2
Pneumonia and influenza	50.4	43.9	29.2	12.7	12.5	13.6	14.0	13.7	13.5	12.2
Chronic liver disease and cirrhosis	5.7	8.9	17.8	14.4	10.2	9.5	8.7	8.7	8.2	6.9
Diabetes mellitus	22.7	27.3	30.9	22.1	21.3	22.5	24.6	25.4	25.7	25.8
Nephritis, nephrotic syndrome, and nephrosis	-	-	-	10.3	10.6	10.5	9.7	9.4	8.6	8.7
Septicemia	-	-	-	5.4	8.1	9.1	8.5	8.0	7.9	8.1
Human immunodeficiency virus infection	-	-	-	-	-	6.2	8.1	9.9	12.0	14.3
External causes	51.9	49.6	56.5	42.7	35.0	38.7	38.0	36.6	36.6	35.0
Unintentional injuries	38.5	35.9	35.3	25.1	20.9	22.4	21.9	20.4	19.9	19.3
Motor vehicle crashes	10.3	10.0	13.8	8.4	8.2	9.4	9.3	9.3	8.7	8.7
Suicide	1.7	1.9	2.9	2.4	2.1	2.5	2.4	2.4	1.9	2.1
Homicide and legal intervention	11.7	11.8	15.0	13.7	10.9	12.8	12.7	13.0	13.9	13.0
Drug-induced causes	-	-	-	2.7	3.3	4.4	4.1	3.4	3.9	3.6
Alcohol-induced causes	-	-	-	10.6	8.0	7.9	7.8	7.7	6.8	6.3

Source: "Age-adjusted Death Rates for Selected Causes of Death, According to Sex and Race: United States, Selected Years 1950-92," *Health, United States, 1994,* pp. 97-98. Primary source: Centers for Disease Control and Prevention, National Center for Health Statistics: Vital Statistics Rates in the United States, 1940-1960, by R.D. Grove and A.M. Hetzel, DHEW Pub. No. (PHS) 1677. Public Health Service. Washington. U.S. Government Printing Office, 1968; Vital statistics of the United States, Vol. II, Mortality, Part A, for data years 1960-92. Public Health Service. Washington. U.S. Government Printing Office; Data computed by the Division of Health and Utilization Analysis from data compiled by the Division of Vital Statistics and from table 1. *Notes:* For data years shown, the code number for cause of death are based on the then current International Classification of Diseases, which are described in Appendix II, tables IV and V. Categories for the coding and classification of human immunodeficiency virus infection were introduced in the United States beginning with mortality data for 1987. Data for the 1980's are based on intercensal population estimates. See Appendix I, department of Commerce. 1. Includes deaths of nonresidents of the United States.

★ 929 ★

Death Rates

Death Rates: Age, Gender, and Race: 1970-1993

[Number of deaths per 100,000 population in specified group.]

SEX, YEAR, AND RACE	All ages[1]	Under 1 yr. old	1-4 yr. old	5-14 yr. old	15-24 yr. old	25-34 yr. old	35-44 yr. old	45-54 yr. old	55-64 yr. old	65-74 yr. old	75-84 yr. old	85 yr. old and over
MALE[2]												
1970	1,090	2,410	93	51	189	215	403	959	2,283	4,874	10,010	17,822
1980	977	1,429	73	37	172	196	299	767	1,815	4,105	8,817	18,801
1990	918	1,083	52	29	147	204	310	610	1,553	3,492	7,889	18,057
1992	902	957	48	27	142	202	319	592	1,482	3,374	7,483	17,740
1993[3]	927	965	49	27	144	211	328	603	1,480	3,415	7,720	18,099
White: 1970	1,087	2,113	84	48	171	177	344	883	2,203	4,810	10,099	18,552
1980	983	1,230	66	35	167	171	257	699	1,729	4,036	8,830	19,097
1990	931	896	46	26	131	176	268	549	1,467	3,398	7,845	18,268
1992	917	781	43	25	122	176	277	533	1,399	3,287	7,441	17,956
1993[3]	944	795	44	26	122	186	282	541	1,391	3,335	7,672	18,229
Black: 1970	1,187	4,299	151	67	321	560	957	1,778	3,257	5,803	9,455	12,222
1980	1,034	2,587	111	47	209	407	690	1,480	2,873	5,131	9,232	16,099
1990	1,006	2,112	86	41	252	431	700	1,261	2,618	4,946	9,130	16,955
1992	978	1,958	78	41	269	413	697	1,223	2,494	4,747	8,745	16,717
1993[3]	1,005	1,962	77	35	283	410	732	1,277	2,538	4,761	8,969	18,169
FEMALE[2]												
1970	808	1,864	75	32	68	102	231	517	1,099	2,580	6,678	15,518
1980	785	1,142	55	24	58	76	159	413	934	2,145	5,440	14,747
1990	812	856	41	19	49	74	138	343	879	1,991	4,883	14,274
1992	807	771	39	18	47	74	141	326	855	1,971	4,731	13,901
1993[3]	834	727	40	20	49	74	144	333	864	2,009	4,826	14,512
White: 1970	813	1,615	66	30	62	84	193	463	1,015	2,471	6,699	15,980
1980	806	963	49	23	56	65	138	373	876	2,067	5,402	14,980
1990	847	690	36	18	46	62	117	309	823	1,924	4,839	14,401
1992	844	619	33	16	44	61	117	294	799	1,909	4,696	14,016
1993[3]	874	611	35	18	45	63	117	296	810	1,929	4,788	14,669
Black: 1970	829	3,369	129	44	112	231	533	1,044	1,986	3,861	6,692	10,707
1980	733	2,124	84	31	71	150	324	768	1,561	3,057	6,212	12,367
1990	748	1,736	68	28	69	160	299	639	1,453	2,866	5,688	13,310
1992	736	1,610	69	26	68	159	314	621	1,405	2,797	5,483	13,264
1993[3]	758	1,418	64	31	72	147	332	659	1,393	2,968	5,650	13,634

Source: "Death Rates, by Age, Sex, and Race: 1970 to 1993," *Statistical Abstract of the United States, 1995*, p. 88. Primary source: U.S. National Center for Health Statistics, *Vital Statistics of the United States*, annual; *Monthly Vital Statistics Report*; and unpublished data. *Notes:* 1. Includes unknown age. 2. Includes other races not shown separately. 3. Includes deaths of nonresidents. Based on a 10-percent sample of deaths.

★ 930 ★
Death Rates

Death Rates: Age-Adjusted Death Rates by Race, Gender, Region, and Urbanization, 1980-82, 1984-86, and 1990-92. Part 1

[Data are based on the National Vital Statistics System.]

Sex, Region, and Urbanization[1]	Deaths per 100,000 resident population								
	All races			White			Black		
	1980-82	1984-86	1990-92	1980-82	1984-86	1990-92	1980-82	1984-86	1990-92
Male									
All regions:									
Large core metropolitan	794.6	762.3	725.2	746.3	712.6	665.4	1,104.4	1,091.3	1,114.7
Large fringe metropolitan	691.2	657.9	587.9	683.2	650.1	576.5	928.0	901.4	868.3
Medium/small metropolitan	748.4	710.9	653.0	722.7	685.2	622.4	1,071.0	1,037.9	1,016.8
Urban nonmetropolitan	763.6	727.8	679.1	740.4	704.9	653.1	1,074.0	1,046.3	1,037.0
Rural	764.5	729.5	688.3	738.5	704.3	659.1	1,017.1	995.3	996.8
Northeast:									
Large core metropolitan	828.1	811.5	782.7	772.8	752.9	713.9	1,099.9	1,103.3	1,111.9
Large fringe metropolitan	701.6	666.2	591.8	693.4	657.9	581.8	930.8	904.9	844.8
Medium/small metropolitan	731.7	696.0	622.7	721.9	684.3	608.1	1,003.1	1,007.5	961.5
Urban nonmetropolitan	730.7	704.9	629.6	730.6	704.9	629.2	857.7	885.9	828.5
Rural	715.7	706.8	617.5	715.8	709.5	616.1	[2]	[2]	[2]
South:									
Large core metropolitan	812.5	773.7	758.3	732.0	692.9	658.5	1,152.7	1,121.6	1,174.1
Large fringe metropolitan	701.7	667.9	603.4	686.5	653.3	581.8	912.8	882.4	863.7
Medium/small metropolitan	790.4	746.5	694.9	740.9	698.6	640.2	1,101.0	1,063.0	1,047.2
Urban nonmetropolitan	831.5	795.7	752.5	789.8	753.8	704.7	1,091.8	1,068.4	1,064.9
Rural	822.1	793.0	756.4	787.7	757.7	716.8	1,019.4	1,002.1	1,004.1
Midwest:									
Large core metropolitan	837.6	798.3	755.2	770.4	725.7	658.3	1,124.3	1,107.1	1,134.4
Large fringe metropolitan	705.2	673.4	597.3	694.7	663.0	582.5	984.7	960.9	942.8
Medium/small metropolitan	723.6	690.8	627.4	709.5	676.1	608.4	995.7	975.8	958.4
Urban nonmetropolitan	704.4	667.9	622.3	701.6	665.6	618.9	924.5	871.4	858.2
Rural	708.9	671.1	632.4	695.3	659.4	617.4	[2]	[2]	[2]
West:									
Large core metropolitan	716.4	685.7	642.4	711.7	681.3	638.7	994.6	992.1	991.8
Large fringe metropolitan	629.2	600.5	544.2	636.4	607.2	548.7	824.6	831.5	814.3
Medium/small metropolitan	683.1	652.8	605.8	689.1	658.1	609.8	923.1	864.5	850.1
Urban nonmetropolitan	705.8	662.2	612.8	697.5	654.1	604.7	932.8	820.3	772.0
Rural	704.2	637.7	584.4	699.0	637.2	579.6	[2]	[2]	[2]

Source: "Age-adjusted Death Rates, According to Race, Sex, Region, and Urbanization: United States, Average Annual 1980-82, 1984-86, and 1990-92," *Health, United States, 1994,* pp. 106-107. Primary source: Centers for Disease Control and Prevention,National Center for Health Statistics: Data computed by the Division of Health and Utilization Analysis using the Compressed Mortality File. See Appendix I, National Vital Statistics System. *Notes:* 1. Urbanization categories for county of residence of decedent are based on classification of counties by the Department of Agriculture. 2. Age-adjusted death rate with 6 or more age-specific rates based on fewer than 20 deaths.

★ 931 ★
Death Rates

Death Rates: Age-Adjusted Death Rates by Race, Gender, Region, and Urbanization, 1980-82, 1984-86, and 1990-92. Part 2

[Data are based on the National Vital Statistics System.]

Sex, Region, and Urbanization[1]	Deaths per 100,000 resident population								
	All races			White			Black		
	1980-82	1984-86	1990-92	1980-82	1984-86	1990-92	1980-82	1984-86	1990-92
Female									
All regions:									
Large core metropolitan	448.0	433.2	406.2	418.2	404.3	372.6	616.3	598.3	590.5
Large fringe metropolitan	403.7	391.2	359.2	397.5	385.6	352.3	559.1	536.6	516.6
Medium/small metropolitan	417.0	404.3	381.4	399.0	386.3	362.8	611.9	601.1	575.3
Urban nonmetropolitan	410.8	402.5	387.7	394.5	386.1	371.6	596.3	596.6	578.3
Rural	401.3	393.1	382.6	383.6	376.2	365.6	558.1	551.2	535.2
Northeast:									
Large core metropolitan	465.0	454.1	430.5	432.0	421.3	391.4	604.6	591.6	581.3
Large fringe metropolitan	413.3	399.1	362.2	407.6	393.9	355.5	548.4	528.5	504.1
Medium/small metropolitan	411.6	398.7	368.0	405.5	391.7	359.1	569.7	571.9	557.3
Urban nonmetropolitan	410.8	405.2	371.6	410.1	404.5	370.8	582.6	[2]	537.8
Rural	405.7	394.3	366.7	406.4	394.7	367.1	[2]	[2]	[2]
South:									
Large core metropolitan	447.4	431.7	409.3	398.0	384.5	354.0	638.5	614.1	610.8
Large fringe metropolitan	399.3	387.6	360.5	387.1	376.9	347.4	552.5	523.8	511.2
Medium/small metropolitan	432.1	418.5	397.4	397.9	385.4	365.1	620.8	609.8	581.4
Urban nonmetropolitan	433.5	426.6	415.9	402.4	395.2	386.2	596.3	598.2	580.1
Rural	422.6	421.0	410.7	396.2	395.7	387.0	558.0	552.1	535.0
Midwest:									
Large core metropolitan	466.8	451.7	429.3	425.9	410.7	379.9	628.5	609.8	601.3
Large fringe metropolitan	407.8	398.1	368.1	400.3	390.6	359.2	588.3	585.3	562.3
Medium/small metropolitan	406.7	394.6	371.1	395.8	384.1	358.9	602.3	579.0	561.1
Urban nonmetropolitan	383.3	373.2	359.3	380.6	370.7	356.2	603.1	577.6	574.0
Rural	377.4	363.0	354.9	368.8	356.1	345.7	[2]	[2]	[2]
West:									
Large core metropolitan	414.2	399.4	368.4	409.5	396.0	364.8	575.0	563.7	555.7
Large fringe metropolitan	378.1	365.9	337.6	380.6	369.4	341.4	565.6	506.5	494.7
Medium/small metropolitan	391.0	379.9	364.7	392.9	380.8	365.9	541.1	555.4	543.4
Urban nonmetropolitan	397.0	384.6	369.5	391.5	380.0	365.5	576.3	551.9	504.9
Rural	383.1	362.0	348.3	379.2	360.6	347.1	[2]	[2]	[2]

Source: "Age-adjusted Death Rates, According to Race, Sex, Region, and Urbanization: United States, Average Annual 1980-82, 1984-86, and 1990-92," *Health, United States, 1994,* pp. 106-107. Primary source: Centers for Disease Control and Prevention, National Center for Health Statistics: Data computed by the Division of Health and Utilization Analysis using the Compressed Mortality File. See Appendix I, National Vital Statistics System. *Notes:* 1. Urbanization categories for county of residence of decedent are based on classification of counties by the Department of Agriculture. 2. Age-adjusted death rate with 6 or more age-specific rates based on fewer than 20 deaths.

★ 932 ★

Death Rates

Death Rates: Cause of Death, 1980-1992

[Deaths per 100,000 population in specified group. Except as noted, excludes deaths of nonresidents of the United States.]

YEAR, RACE, and AGE	Total[1]	Heart disease	Malignant neoplasms	Accidents and adverse effects	Cerebrovascular diseases	Chronic obstructive pulmonary diseases[2]	Pneumonia, flu	Suicide	Chronic liver disease, cirrhosis	Diabetes mellitus	Homicide and legal intervention
WHITE											
Both sexes:											
1980, age-adjusted	559.4	350.8	189.0	46.3	76.3	26.9	24.8	12.7	13.0	14.8	7.0
1990, age-adjusted	492.8	305.4	211.6	36.9	59.7	38.4	33.9	13.5	10.3	18.5	5.8
1991, age-adjusted	486.8	301.9	213.1	35.3	58.7	39.8	32.8	13.3	10.1	18.8	6.1
1992, age-adjusted	477.5	297.5	213.5	34.0	58.4	40.0	31.7	13.0	10.0	19.0	5.9
Male:											
1980, age-adjusted	745.3	384.0	208.7	66.3	63.3	37.9	25.1	19.9	17.3	12.8	10.9
1990, age-adjusted	644.3	312.7	227.7	50.3	47.0	44.3	31.4	22.0	13.6	16.5	9.0
1991, age-adjusted	634.4	307.6	228.9	47.7	46.3	44.9	30.6	21.7	13.4	16.9	9.3
1992, age-adjusted	620.9	302.4	228.6	45.9	46.1	44.4	29.7	21.2	13.3	17.2	9.1
Female:											
1980, age-adjusted	411.1	319.2	170.3	27.2	88.8	16.4	24.6	5.9	8.8	16.8	3.2
1990, age-adjusted	369.9	298.4	196.1	24.0	71.8	32.8	36.3	5.3	7.1	20.5	2.8
1991, age-adjusted	366.3	296.5	198.0	23.4	70.5	35.0	35.0	5.2	7.1	20.6	3.0
1992, age-adjusted	359.9	292.9	199.0	22.6	70.3	35.8	33.6	5.1	6.8	20.7	2.8
BLACK											
Both sexes:											
1980, age-adjusted	842.5	274.0	169.1	50.6	75.6	12.7	21.2	6.0	18.0	20.8	38.6
1990, age-adjusted	789.2	246.4	187.2	40.7	57.1	18.6	24.8	6.9	12.3	26.6	39.8
1991, age-adjusted	780.7	243.9	185.9	40.0	55.7	18.7	23.7	6.7	11.1	27.3	41.6
1992, age-adjusted	767.5	238.8	184.5	37.3	53.8	18.5	22.3	6.8	10.5	27.3	38.9
Male:											
1980, age-adjusted	1,112.8	301.0	205.5	77.1	73.1	19.3	26.9	10.3	24.0	16.0	66.6
1990, age-adjusted	1,061.3	256.8	221.9	60.7	53.1	25.2	28.9	12.0	16.6	21.1	69.2
1991, age-adjusted	1,048.8	253.9	217.5	59.8	52.1	24.5	26.7	12.1	14.5	22.1	72.0
1992, age-adjusted	1,026.9	246.9	214.4	54.9	49.5	23.8	25.5	12.0	14.5	21.8	67.5
Female:											
1980, age-adjusted	631.1	249.7	136.5	26.9	77.9	6.8	16.1	2.2	12.6	25.2	13.5
1990, age-adjusted	581.6	237.0	156.1	22.8	60.7	12.6	21.2	2.3	8.5	31.5	13.5
1991, age-adjusted	575.1	235.0	157.4	22.2	59.0	13.4	20.9	1.9	8.1	32.0	14.2
1992, age-adjusted	568.4	231.6	157.6	21.5	57.8	13.7	19.5	2.0	6.8	32.3	13.1

Source: "Death Rates, by Selected Causes and Age: 1980 to 1992," *Statistical Abstract of the United States, 1995*, p. 95. Primary source: U.S. National Center for Health Statistics, *Vital Statistics of the United States*, annual; and *Monthly Vital Statistics Report. Notes:* NA Not available. 1. Includes other causes not shown separately. 2. Includes allied conditions.

★ 933 ★
Death Rates

Death Rates: Causes, by Gender, Race, and Hispanic Origin: Trends, 1950-92. Part 1

[Data are based on the National Vital Statistics System.]

Sex, Race, Hispanic origin, and age	1950[1]	1960[1]	1970	1980	1985	1988	1989	1990	1991	1992
					Deaths per 100,000 resident population					
White male										
All ages, age adjusted	963.1	917.7	893.4	745.3	693.3	671.3	652.2	644.3	634.4	620.9
All ages, crude	1,089.5	1,098.5	1,086.7	983.3	963.6	957.9	936.5	930.9	926.2	917.2
Under 1 year	3,400.5	2,694.1	2,113.2	1,230.3	1,056.5	964.2	940.7	896.1	860.8	780.9
1-4 years	135.5	104.9	83.6	66.1	52.8	51.5	48.3	45.9	45.5	42.6
5-14 years	67.2	52.7	48.0	35.0	30.1	29.2	28.4	26.4	26.5	24.7
15-24 years	152.4	143.7	170.8	167.0	134.2	135.8	128.6	131.3	128.2	121.5
25-34 years	185.3	163.2	176.6	171.3	158.8	172.6	177.0	176.1	176.1	175.7
35-44 years	380.9	332.6	343.5	257.4	243.1	259.5	263.4	268.2	269.1	277.1
45-54 years	984.5	932.2	882.9	698.9	611.7	568.6	556.0	548.7	544.6	533.3
55-64 years	2,304.4	2,225.2	2,202.6	1,728.5	1,625.8	1,546.7	1,504.1	1,467.2	1,443.7	1,398.5
65-74 years	4,864.9	4,848.4	4,810.1	4,035.7	3,770.7	3,588.1	3,455.1	3,397.7	3,349.7	3,287.0
75-84 years	10,526.3	10,299.6	10,098.8	8,829.8	8,486.1	8,196.7	7,913.4	7,844.9	7,641.5	7,440.9
85 years and over	22,116.3	21,750.0	18,551.7	19,097.3	18,980.1	19,020.8	18,241.7	18,268.3	18,020.9	17,956.2
Black male										
All ages, age adjusted	1,373.1	1,246.1	1,318.6	1,112.8	1,053.4	1,083.0	1,082.8	1,061.3	1,048.8	1,026.9
All ages, crude	1,260.3	1,181.7	1,186.6	1,034.1	989.3	1,026.1	1,026.7	1,008.0	998.7	977.5
Under 1 year	-	5,306.8	4,298.9	2,586.7	2,219.9	2,189.6	2,172.1	2,112.4	1,957.4	1,957.9
1-4 years	-	208.5	150.5	110.5	90.1	92.1	90.0	85.8	88.4	77.6
5-14 years	95.1	75.1	67.1	47.4	42.3	43.7	43.5	41.2	42.4	41.2
15-24 years	289.7	212.0	320.6	209.1	173.6	222.4	234.5	252.2	278.1	269.4
25-34 years	503.5	402.5	559.5	407.3	351.9	417.4	425.6	430.8	425.5	413.3
35-44 years	878.1	762.0	956.6	689.8	630.2	706.7	718.1	699.6	702.4	697.2
45-54 years	1,905.0	1,624.8	1,777.5	1,479.9	1,292.9	1,296.9	1,311.5	1,261.0	1,256.8	1,223.3
55-64 years	3,773.2	3,316.4	3,256.9	2,873.0	2,779.8	2,712.7	2,699.9	2,618.4	2,533.9	2,493.8
65-74 years	5,310.3	5,798.7	5,803.2	5,131.1	5,172.4	5,147.7	5,129.7	4,946.1	4,850.7	4,746.7
75-84 years	-	8,605.1	9,454.9	9,231.6	9,262.3	9,454.6	9,163.3	9,129.5	9,013.0	8,744.5
85 years and over	-	14,844.8	12,222.3	16,098.8	15,774.2	16,643.1	16,751.5	16,954.9	16,663.8	16,717.1
American Indian or Alaskan Native male[2]										
All ages, age adjusted	-	-	-	732.5	602.6	585.7	622.8	573.1	562.6	579.6
All ages, crude	-	-	-	597.1	492.5	485.0	510.7	476.4	471.2	487.7
Under 1 year	-	-	-	1,598.1	1,080.0	1,047.6	1,139.1	1,056.6	737.0	1,057.5
1-4 years	-	-	-	82.7	105.3	75.6	88.2	77.4	58.7	74.7
5-14 years	-	-	-	43.7	39.2	34.6	34.7	33.4	30.0	37.0
15-24 years	-	-	-	311.1	214.4	222.2	216.8	219.8	187.4	191.2
25-34 years	-	-	-	360.6	275.0	266.3	272.2	256.1	271.7	260.1
35-44 years	-	-	-	556.8	363.5	349.6	354.8	365.4	338.4	344.1
45-54 years	-	-	-	871.3	687.9	662.8	648.2	619.9	588.8	624.6
55-64 years	-	-	-	1,547.5	1,319.1	1,301.9	1,424.5	1,211.3	1,340.4	1,384.0

[Continued]

★ 933 ★

Death Rates: Causes, by Gender, Race, and Hispanic Origin: Trends, 1950-92. Part 1

[Continued]

Sex, Race, Hispanic origin, and age	1950[1]	1960[1]	1970	1980	1985	1988	1989	1990	1991	1992
65-74 years	-	-	-	2,968.4	2,692.3	2,693.3	2,867.7	2,461.7	2,502.9	2,604.0
75-84 years	-	-	-	5,607.0	5,572.7	4,746.2	5,492.3	5,389.2	5,278.6	5,239.7
85 years and over	-	-	-	12,635.2	8,900.0	11,366.7	13,033.3	11,243.9	10,000.0	9,381.3
Asian or Pacific Islander male[3]										
All ages, age adjusted	-	-	-	416.6	396.9	385.4	378.9	377.8	360.2	364.1
All ages, crude	-	-	-	375.3	344.6	339.0	334.5	334.3	3256	332.7
Under 1 year	-	-	-	816.5	750.0	642.6	745.5	605.3	426.4	477.7
1-4 years	-	-	-	50.9	43.4	29.5	40.7	45.0	30.9	29.9
5-14 years	-	-	-	23.4	22.5	22.8	20.2	20.7	18.5	20.7
15-24 years	-	-	-	80.8	76.0	69.9	67.0	76.0	69.8	76.1
25-34 years	-	-	-	83.5	77.3	80.6	78.2	79.6	81.2	77.7
35-44 years	-	-	-	128.3	14.4	115.7	124.4	130.8	123.5	119.0
45-54 years	-	-	-	342.3	284.8	292.1	293.9	287.1	270.6	282.9
55-64 years	-	-	-	881.1	869.4	857.4	817.7	789.1	745.1	766.8
65-74 years	-	-	-	2,236.1	2,102.0	2,019.2	1,932.3	2,041.4	1,927.6	1,962.5
75-84 years	-	-	-	5,389.5	5,551.2	5,364.7	5,125.5	5,008.6	4,927.0	4,819.7
85 years and over	-	-	-	13,753.6	12,750.0	12,290.9	13,254.5	12,446.3	12,707.7	12,628.8
Hispanic male[4]										
All ages, age adjusted	-	-	-	-	524.8	528.2	558.1	531.2	518.5	506.1
All ages, crude	-	-	-	-	374.6	382.2	430.6	411.6	407.1	402.2
Under 1 year	-	-	-	-	1,041.8	982.9	1,058.5	921.8	844.2	763.9
1-4 years	-	-	-	-	53.8	45.7	54.6	53.8	49.6	45.7
5-14 years	-	-	-	-	23.0	24.6	26.7	26.0	25.8	24.6
15-24 years	-	-	-	-	147.5	143.0	156.2	159.3	1632	165.9
25-34 years	-	-	-	-	202.0	219.5	242.8	234.0	221.1	223.2
35-44 years	-	-	-	-	290.3	333.8	367.7	341.8	331.8	341.3
45-54 years	-	-	-	-	495.4	531.2	568.2	533.9	518.5	512.0
55-64 years	-	-	-	-	1,129.2	1,152.0	1,162.9	1,123.7	1,107.9	1,061.1
65-74 years	-	-	-	-	2,488.9	2,393.3	2,505.7	2,368.2	2,347.0	2,322.3
75-84 years	-	-	-	-	5,724.6	5,383.5	5,684.2	5,369.1	5,226.7	4,924.1
85 years and over	-	-	-	-	11,856.1	12,217.0	12,583.1	12,272.1	11,609.9	10,895.4

Source: Centers for Disease Control and Prevention, National Center for Health Statistics: Vital Statistics of the United States, Vol. II, Mortality, Part A, for data years 1950-92. Public Health Service. Washington. U.S. Government Printing Office; Data computed by the Division of Health and Utilization Analysis from data compiled by the Division of Vital Statistics and from national population estimates for race groups from table 1 and State or U.S. aggregate population estimates for Hispanics provided by the Census Bureau. *Notes:* Data for the 1980's are based on intercensal population estimates. See Appendix I, Department of Commerce. The race groups, white, black, Asian, or Pacific Islander, and American Indian or Alaskan Native, include persons of Hispanic and non-Hispanic origin. Conversely, persons of Hispanic origin may be of any race. Consistency of race and Hispanic origin identification between the death certificate (source of data for numerator of death races) and data from the Census Bureau (denomination) is high for individual white, black, and Hispanic persons; however, persons identified as American Indian or Asian in data from the Census Bureau are sometimes misreported as white on the death certificate, causing death rates to be underestimated by 22-30 percent for American Indians and by about 12 percent for Asians. (Sorlie PD, Rogot E, and Johnson NJ; Validity of demographic characteristics on the death certificate, *Epidemiology* 3(2):181-184, 1992). 1. Includes deaths of nonresidents of the United States. 2. Interpretation of trends should take into account that population estimates for American Indians increased by 45 percent between 1980 and 1990, partly due to better enumeration techniques in the 1990 decennial census and to the increased tendency for people to identify themselves as American Indian in 1990. 3. Interpretation of trends should take into account that the Asian population in the United States more than doubled between 1980 and 1990, primarily due to immigration. 4. Excludes data from States lacking an Hispanic-origin item on their death certificates. See Appendix I.

Death Rates: Causes, by Gender, Race, and Hispanic Origin: Trends, 1950-92. Part 2

[Data are based on the National Vital Statistics System.]

Sex, Race, Hispanic origin, and age	1950[1]	1960[1]	1970	1980	1985	1988	1989	1990	1991	1992
					Deaths per 100,000 resident population					
White female										
All ages, age adjusted	645.0	555.0	501.7	411.1	391.0	385.3	376.0	369.9	366.3	359.9
All ages, crude	803.3	800.9	812.6	806.1	840.1	865.3	851.8	846.9	847.7	844.3
Under 1 year	2,566.8	2,007.7	1,614.6	962.5	799.3	754.1	739.5	690.0	659.2	618.7
1-4 years	112.2	85.2	66.1	49.3	40.0	40.7	38.8	36.1	37.6	33.3
5-14 years	45.1	34.7	29.9	22.9	19.5	18.7	19.0	17.9	17.2	16.2
15-24 years	71.5	54.9	61.6	55.5	48.1	48.8	48.4	45.9	46.6	43.9
25-34 years	112.8	85.0	84.1	65.4	59.4	62.7	63.1	61.5	61.7	60.5
35-44 years	235.8	191.1	193.3	138.2	121.9	120.1	118.5	117.4	117.3	117.3
45-54 years	546.4	458.8	462.9	372.7	341.7	320.4	310.8	309.3	306.0	294.0
55-64 years	1,293.8	1,078.9	1,014.9	876.2	869.1	858.7	837.5	822.7	821.9	799.2
65-74 years	3,242.8	2,779.3	2,470.7	2,066.6	2,027.1	1,995.9	1,948.5	1,923.5	1,909.4	1,909.1
75-84 years	8,481.5	7,696.6	6,698.7	5,401.7	5,111.6	5,040.4	4,910.6	4,839.1	4,752.8	4,696.4
85 years and over	19,679.5	19,477.7	15,980.2	14,979.6	14,745.4	15,019.1	14,526.1	14,400.6	14,188.1	14,015.9
Black female										
All ages, age adjusted	1,106.7	916.9	814.4	631.1	594.8	601.0	594.3	581.6	575.1	568.4
All ages, crude	1,002.0	905.0	829.2	733.3	734.2	764.6	763.2	747.9	744.5	736.2
Under 1 year	-	4,162.2	3,368.8	2,123.7	1,821.4	1,834.0	1,839.8	1,735.5	1,580.8	1,609.7
1-4 years	-	173.3	129.4	84.4	71.1	71.2	72.9	67.6	70.8	68.7
5-14 years	72.8	53.8	43.8	30.5	28.6	30.6	29.0	27.5	25.8	26.0
15-24 years	213.1	107.5	111.9	70.5	59.6	69.3	68.0	68.7	72.6	67.8
25-34 years	393.3	273.2	231.0	150.0	137.6	157.8	161.0	159.5	158.6	158.8
35-44 years	758.1	568.5	533.0	323.9	276.5	304.8	298.6	298.6	303.5	314.4
45-54 years	1,576.4	1,177.0	1,043.9	768.2	667.6	655.3	640.6	639.4	633.2	620.5
55-64 years	3,089.4	2,510.9	1,986.2	1,561.0	1,532.5	1,513.3	1,478.3	1,452.6	1,399.7	1,405.4
65-74 years	4,000.2	4,064.2	3,860.9	3,057.4	2,967.8	2,948.1	2,936.0	2,865.7	2,854.1	2,796.6
75-84 years	-	6,730.0	6,691.5	6,212.1	6,078.0	5,991.4	5,930.2	5,688.3	5,707.3	5,483.0
85 years and over	-	13,052.6	10,706.6	12,367.2	12,703.0	13,461.1	13,509.2	13,309.5	13,258.9	13,264.1
American Indian or Alaskan Native female[2]										
All ages, age adjusted	-	-	-	414.1	353.3	343.2	353.4	335.1	335.9	343.1
All ages, crude	-	-	-	380.1	342.5	339.9	351.3	330.4	343.9	348.9
Under 1 year	-	-	-	1,352.6	910.5	923.8	995.7	688.7	763.0	821.2
1-4 years	-	-	-	87.5	54.8	66.2	65.9	37.8	37.1	69.3
5-14 years	-	-	-	33.5	23.0	23.4	24.4	25.5	16.0	16.0
15-24 years	-	-	-	90.3	72.8	77.4	75.8	69.0	68.5	65.4
25-34 years	-	-	-	178.5	121.5	109.4	92.2	102.3	100.5	103.3
35-44 years	-	-	-	286.0	185.6	150.7	175.5	156.4	159.1	157.8
45-54 years	-	-	-	491.4	415.5	373.2	380.7	380.9	342.1	329.1
55-64 years	-	-	-	837.1	851.9	824.1	833.3	805.9	815.9	912.4

[Continued]

★ 934 ★

Death Rates: Causes, by Gender, Race, and Hispanic Origin: Trends, 1950-92. Part 2
[Continued]

Sex, Race, Hispanic origin, and age	1950[1]	1960[1]	1970	1980	1985	1988	1989	1990	1991	1992
65-74 years	-	-	-	1,765.5	1,630.3	1,636.8	1,712.8	1,679.4	1,673.8	1,743.2
75-84 years	-	-	-	3,612.9	3,200.0	3,389.5	3,495.0	3,073.2	3,440.9	3,307.1
85 years and over	-	-	-	8,567.4	7,740.0	7,183.3	7,733.3	8,201.1	7,842.9	6,878.7
Asian or Pacific Islander female[3]										
All ages, age adjusted	-	-	-	224.6	228.5	226.5	225.2	228.9	218.3	220.5
All ages, crude	-	-	-	222.5	224.9	227.4	229.4	234.3	231.1	235.8
Under 1 year	-	-	-	755.8	622.0	555.2	534.9	518.2	348.3	400.2
1-4 years	-	-	-	35.4	36.8	34.1	39.7	32.0	29.8	23.8
5-14 years	-	-	-	21.5	19.1	17.7	19.0	13.0	11.6	11.4
15-24 years	-	-	-	32.3	30.7	28.9	27.2	28.8	28.4	30.6
25-34 years	-	-	-	45.4	36.5	37.1	39.2	37.5	34.5	38.7
35-44 years	-	-	-	89.7	77.8	69.8	72.7	69.9	77.1	69.6
45-54 years	-	-	-	214.1	184.9	204.6	188.3	182.7	186.0	185.5
55-64 years	-	-	-	440.8	468.0	480.8	468.0	483.4	471.9	476.3
65-74 years	-	-	-	1,027.7	1,130.8	1,058.5	1,052.2	1,089.2	1,073.5	1,095.0
75-84 years	-	-	-	2,833.6	2,873.9	3,014.0	2,945.9	3,127.9	2,812.3	2,873.1
85 years and over	-	-	-	7,923.3	9,808.3	9,280.0	10,143.8	10,254.0	9,794.7	9,561.8
Hispanic female[4]										
All ages, age adjusted	-	-	-	-	286.6	285.1	296.5	284.9	276.8	268.6
All ages, crude	-	-	-	-	251.9	259.0	295.1	285.4	282.5	277.7
Under 1 year	-	-	-	-	793.0	781.3	887.0	746.6	691.7	644.2
1-4 years	-	-	-	-	42.3	42.2	45.4	42.1	44.3	37.5
5-14 years	-	-	-	-	16.0	16.6	17.3	17.3	17.0	17.2
15-24 years	-	-	-	-	36.3	38.1	41.9	40.6	43.5	40.2
25-34 years	-	-	-	-	56.3	60.7	69.4	62.9	61.3	63.3
35-44 years	-	-	-	-	100.0	109.4	116.4	109.3	109.6	111.0
45-54 years	-	-	-	-	251.3	246.3	249.2	253.3	250.1	237.1
55-64 years	-	-	-	-	620.3	628.8	631.7	607.5	614.0	598.2
65-74 years	-	-	-	-	1,449.3	1,440.9	1,476.2	1,453.8	1,378.3	1,354.2
75-84 years	-	-	-	-	3,549.8	3,450.8	3,586.4	3,351.3	3,224.4	3,149.7
85 years and over	-	-	-	-	10,216.9	9,607.5	10,232.5	10,098.7	9,385.8	8,772.4

Source: Centers for Disease Control and Prevention, National Center for Health Statistics: Vital Statistics of the United States, Vol. II, Mortality, Part A, for data years 1950-92. Public Health Service. Washington. U.S. Government Printing Office; Data computed by the Division of Health and Utilization Analysis from data compiled by the Division of Vital Statistics and from national population estimates for race groups from table 1 and State or U.S. aggregate population estimates for Hispanics provided by the Census Bureau. *Notes:* Data for the 1980's are based on intercensal population estimates. See Appendix I, Department of Commerce. The race groups, white, black, Asian, or Pacific Islander, and American Indian or Alaskan Native, include persons of Hispanic and non-Hispanic origin. Conversely, persons of Hispanic origin may be of any race. Consistency of race and Hispanic origin identification between the death certificate (source of data for numerator of death races) and data from the Census Bureau (denomination) is high for individual white, black, and Hispanic persons; however, persons identified as American Indian or Asian in data from the Census Bureau are sometimes misreported as white on the death certificate, causing death rates to be underestimated by 22-30 percent for American Indians and by about 12 percent for Asians. (Sorlie PD, Rogot E, and Johnson NJ; Validity of demographic characteristics on the death certificate, *Epidemiology* 3(2):181-184, 1992). 1. Includes deaths of nonresidents of the United States. 2. Interpretation of trends should take into account that population estimates for American Indians increased by 45 percent between 1980 and 1990, partly due to better enumeration techniques in the 1990 decennial census and to the increased tendency for people to identify themselves as American Indian in 1990. 3. Interpretation of trends should take into account that the Asian population in the United States more than doubled between 1980 and 1990, primarily due to immigration. 4. Excludes data from States lacking an Hispanic-origin item on their death certificates. See Appendix I.

★ 935 ★

Death Rates

Death Rates: Infant, Maternal, and Neonatal Death Rates and Fetal Mortality Ratios, by Race: 1970-1992. Part 1

[Deaths per 1,000 live births, except as noted. Excludes deaths of nonresidents of the U.S. Beginning 1980, race for live births tabulated according to race of mother, for infant and neonatal mortality rates. Beginning 1989, race for live births tabulated according to race of mother, for maternal mortality rates and mortality rates. See also Appendix III and *Historical Statistics, Colonial Times to 1970*, series B 136-147.]

ITEM	1970	1980	1982	1983	1984	1985	1986
Infant deaths[1]	20.0	12.6	11.5	11.2	10.8	10.6	10.4
White	17.8	10.9	9.9	9.6	9.3	9.2	8.8
Black and other	30.9	20.2	18.3	17.8	17.1	16.8	16.7
Black	32.6	22.2	20.5	20.0	19.2	19.0	18.9
Maternal deaths[2]	21.5	9.2	7.9	8.0	7.8	7.8	7.2
White	14.4	6.7	5.8	5.9	5.4	5.2	4.9
Black and other	55.9	19.8	16.4	16.3	16.9	18.1	16.0
Black	59.8	21.5	18.2	18.3	19.7	20.4	18.8
Fetal deaths[3]	14.2	9.2	8.9	8.5	8.2	7.9	7.7
White	12.4	8.2	7.9	7.5	7.4	7.0	6.8
Black and other	22.6	13.4	12.7	12.4	11.5	11.3	11.2
Neonatal deaths[4]	15.1	8.5	7.7	7.3	7.0	7.0	6.7
White	13.8	7.4	6.7	6.3	6.1	6.0	5.7
Black and other	21.4	13.2	12.0	11.4	10.9	11.0	10.8
Black	22.8	14.6	13.6	12.9	12.3	12.6	12.3

Source: "Infant, Maternal, and Neonatal Mortality Rates and Fetal Mortality Ratios, by Race: 1970 to 1992," *Statistical Abstract of the United States, 1995*, p. 90. *Notes:* NA Not available. 1. Represents deaths of infants under 1 year old, exclusive of fetal deaths. 2. Per 100,000 live births from deliveries and complications of pregnancy, childbirth, and the puerperium. Beginning 1979, deaths are classified according to the ninth revision of the *International Classification of diseases*; earlier years classified according to the revision in use at the time. 3. Includes only those deaths with stated or presumed period of gestation of 20 weeks or more. 4. Represents deaths of infants under 28 days old, exclusive of fetal deaths.

★ 936 ★
Death Rates

Death Rates: Infant, Maternal, and Neonatal Death Rates and Fetal Mortality Ratios, by Race: 1970-1992. Part 2

[Deaths per 1,000 live births, except as noted. Excludes deaths of nonresidents of the U.S. Beginning 1980, race for live births tabulated according to race of mother, for infant and neonatal mortality rates. Beginning 1989, race for live births tabulated according to race of mother, for maternal mortality rates and mortality rates. See also Appendix III and *Historical Statistics, Colonial Times to 1970*, series B 136-147.]

ITEM	1987	1988	1989	1990	1991	1992
Infant deaths[1]	10.1	10.0	9.8	9.2	8.9	8.5
White	8.5	8.4	8.1	7.6	7.3	6.9
Black and other	16.5	16.1	16.3	15.5	15.1	14.4
Black	18.8	18.5	18.6	18.0	17.6	16.8
Maternal deaths[2]	6.6	8.4	7.9	8.2	7.9	7.8
White	5.1	5.9	5.6	5.4	5.8	5.0
Black and other	12.0	17.4	16.5	19.1	15.6	18.2
Black	14.2	19.5	18.4	22.4	18.3	20.8
Fetal deaths[3]	7.7	7.5	7.5	7.5	7.3	(NA)
White	6.7	6.4	6.4	6.4	6.2	(NA)
Black and other	11.5	11.4	11.7	11.9	11.4	(NA)
Neonatal deaths[4]	6.5	6.3	6.2	5.8	5.6	5.4
White	5.4	5.3	5.1	4.8	4.5	4.3
Black and other	10.7	10.3	10.3	9.9	9.5	9.2
Black	12.3	12.1	11.9	11.6	11.2	10.8

Source: "Infant, Maternal, and Neonatal Mortality Rates and Fetal Mortality Ratios, by Race: 1970 to 1992," *Statistical Abstract of the United States, 1995*, p. 90. *Notes:* NA Not available. 1. Represents deaths of infants under 1 year old, exclusive of fetal deaths. 2. Per 100,000 live births from deliveries and complications of pregnancy, childbirth, and the puerperium. Beginning 1979, deaths are classified according to the ninth revision of the *International Classification of diseases*; earlier years classified according to the revision in use at the time. 3. Includes only those deaths with stated or presumed period of gestation of 20 weeks or more. 4. Represents deaths of infants under 28 days old, exclusive of fetal deaths.

★ 937 ★
Death Rates

Death Rates: Provisional Death Rates For All Causes, 1992-93

[Data are based on a 10 percent sample of death certificates from the National Vital Statistics System.]

Sex and age	Deaths per 100,000 resident population					
	All races		White		Black	
	1992	1993	1992	1993	1992	1993
Both sexes						
All ages, age adjusted	504.9	514.0	477.7	486.0	767.4	786.6
All ages, crude	853.3	879.3	879.4	908.3	854.0	874.9
Under 1 year	864.5	848.7	705.4	704.7	1,718.8	1,695.4
1-4 years	42.9	44.5	38.0	39.6	65.9	70.3
5-14 years	22.6	23.6	20.8	21.9	33.4	33.2
15-24 years	97.4	97.6	84.7	84.3	171.3	177.4
25-34 years	135.0	142.6	115.5	125.2	277.1	270.9
35-44 years	233.0	234.9	201.7	199.8	487.2	518.3
45-54 years	452.2	464.6	409.3	416.6	876.3	939.5
55-64 years	1,161.0	1,156.6	1,092.6	1,088.9	1,917.2	1,892.0
65-74 years	2,580.1	2,629.8	2,513.1	2,553.9	3,550.6	3,709.3
75-84 years	5,794.2	5,930.4	5,747.7	5,891.3	6,785.3	6,840.9
85 years and over	14,909.1	15,523.3	15,007.7	15,658.6	14,692.0	14,958.8
Male						
All ages, age adjusted	656.0	667.7	620.9	631.2	1,026.1	1,051.1
All ages, crude	902.1	927.2	917.0	943.9	979.5	1,004.7
Under 1 year	918.6	965.1	754.8	794.7	1,830.2	1,962.3
1-4 years	47.4	49.0	42.9	44.3	68.3	76.6
5-14 years	27.5	27.4	25.5	26.1	40.8	35.4
15-24 years	144.8	144.1	124.1	121.7	270.7	282.8
25-34 years	199.9	211.4	172.9	186.2	413.2	409.5
35-44 years	324.9	327.9	285.0	282.2	682.5	732.4
45-54 years	587.1	602.7	530.8	540.7	1,186.1	1,277.3
55-64 years	1,482.1	1,480.1	1,396.4	1,391.3	2,512.4	2,537.8
65-74 years	3,360.2	3,414.8	3,271.1	3,334.7	4,760.9	4,760.7
75-84 years	7,537.7	7,719.5	7,478.6	7,672.1	9,034.8	8,969.1
85 years and over	17,656.0	18,099.4	17,865.9	18,229.2	17,014.3	18,169.0
Female						
All ages, age adjusted	381.2	387.5	360.2	366.1	570.0	583.1
All ages, crude	806.7	833.7	843.2	874.0	741.1	757.8
Under 1 year	807.7	727.2	653.4	611.0	1,601.3	1,417.5
1-4 years	38.1	39.7	32.8	34.6	63.4	64.0
5-14 years	17.4	19.6	15.9	17.6	25.9	31.0
15-24 years	47.9	49.2	43.2	44.9	72.3	72.4
25-34 years	70.1	73.7	57.0	62.9	155.0	146.5

[Continued]

★ 937 ★

Death Rates: Provisional Death Rates For All Causes, 1992-93
[Continued]

Sex and age	Deaths per 100,000 resident population					
	All races		White		Black	
	1992	1993	1992	1993	1992	1993
35-44 years	142.7	143.5	118.1	117.1	317.7	332.3
45-54 years	323.2	332.6	290.9	295.7	619.4	659.4
55-64 years	872.1	864.4	813.6	810.1	1,457.5	1,393.1
65-74 years	1,966.2	2,008.9	1,910.7	1,929.2	2,699.8	2,967.7
75-84 years	4,727.7	4,825.6	4,686.3	4,787.9	5,529.2	5,650.0
85 years and over	13,838.7	14,511.6	13,919.2	14,669.1	13,718.6	13,633.7

Source: "Provisional Death Rates for All Causes, According to Sex, Race, and Age: United States, 1992-93," *Health, United States, 1994,* p. 142. Primary source: Centers for Disease Control and Prevention, National Center for Health Statistics: Annual summary of births, marriages, divorces, and deaths, United States, 1992 and 1993. Monthly Vital Statistics Report, Vols. 41 and 42, No. 13. DHHS Pub. Nos. (PHS) 93-1120 and 94-1120. 1993 and 1994. Public Health Service. Hyattsville, Md. *Notes:* Data exclude deaths of nonresidents of the United States. Provisional data for 1992-93 were calculated using 1990's-based postcensal population estimates. See Appendix I, National Center for Health Statistics and Department of Commerce.

★ 938 ★
Death Rates

Death Rates: Trends in Deaths by Sex, Race, and Age, 1987-92

[Data are based on the National Vital Statistics System.]

Sex, race, Hispanic origin, and age	Deaths per 100,000 population						
	1987	1988	1989	1990	1991	1992	1990-92
White male							
All ages, age adjusted	8.4	10.0	13.2	15.0	16.7	18.1	16.6
All ages, crude	8.7	10.4	13.9	15.8	17.8	19.3	17.6
Under 1 year	1.3	1.5	1.7	*	*	*	0.9
1-4 years	0.4	0.4	*	*	0.4	0.5	0.4
5-14 years	0.2	0.2	0.2	*	0.3	0.3	0.2
15-24 years	1.7	1.8	2.0	1.7	1.7	1.5	1.6
25-34 years	17.0	19.8	26.2	28.8	32.3	34.9	32.0
35-44 years	21.8	26.9	36.1	42.5	46.9	51.2	46.9
45-54 years	13.6	16.5	22.5	25.8	28.8	31.6	28.8
55-64 years	6.0	6.6	9.1	10.0	11.8	12.5	11.4
65-74 years	2.3	2.6	2.8	3.1	3.5	3.9	3.5
75-84 years	1.2	1.4	1.2	1.0	1.1	1.4	1.2
85 years and over	*	*	*	*	*	*	*
Black male							
All ages, age adjusted	25.4	31.6	40.3	44.2	52.9	61.8	53.1
All ages, crude	23.8	29.9	38.4	42.3	50.4	59.5	50.8
Under 1 year	7.3	8.8	8.6	9.3	9.3	10.3	9.6

[Continued]

★ 938 ★

Death Rates: Trends in Deaths by Sex, Race, and Age, 1987-92
[Continued]

Sex, race, Hispanic origin, and age	Deaths per 100,000 population						
	1987	1988	1989	1990	1991	1992	1990-92
1-4 years	2.4	3.3	3.5	3.6	3.8	4.5	4.0
5-14 years	*	*	*	1.1	0.9	0.9	1.0
15-24 years	5.3	5.9	6.8	5.7	6.9	7.2	6.6
25-34 years	52.9	64.0	77.4	84.1	90.0	104.5	92.9
35-44 years	71.0	89.0	116.9	127.1	152.7	176.7	153.0
45-54 years	35.7	45.7	60.6	67.1	95.2	109.2	91.0
55-64 years	16.9	20.1	27.1	34.5	38.9	54.0	42.5
65-74 years	*	7.0	10.2	10.6	16.5	22.1	6.5
75-84 years	*	*	*	*	*	*	4.4
85 years and over	*	*	*	*	*	*	*
White female							
All ages, age adjusted	0.6	0.7	0.9	1.1	1.3	1.6	1.3
All ages, crude	0.6	0.7	0.9	1.1	1.4	1.6	1.4
Under 1 year	*	*	1.7	*	*	*	0.7
1-4 years	0.4	0.4	0.5	0.5	0.5	0.5	0.5
5-14 years	*	*	*	*	0.2	*	0.1
15-24 years	0.1	0.3	0.4	0.4	0.4	0.5	0.4
25-34 years	1.4	1.7	2.2	2.4	3.0	3.6	3.0
35-44 years	1.0	1.4	1.6	2.3	2.9	3.7	3.0
45-54 years	0.5	0.6	0.9	1.0	1.6	1.9	1.5
55-64 years	0.4	0.5	0.5	0.7	0.8	1.0	0.8
65-74 years	0.5	0.6	0.6	0.6	0.7	0.6	0.6
75-84 years	0.6	0.4	0.4	*	0.5	*	0.3
85 years and over	*	*	*	*	*	*	*
Black female							
All ages, age adjusted	4.7	6.2	8.1	9.9	12.0	14.3	12.1
All ages, crude	4.8	6.4	8.3	10.2	12.2	14.7	12.4
Under 1 year	11.7	7.6	13.3	14.6	11.4	12.7	12.9
1-4 years	2.5	2.8	2.5	3.0	4.1	3.6	3.6
5-14 years	*	*	*	0.9	*	0.8	0.8
15-24 years	1.4	1.7	2.1	2.7	3.7	3.5	3.3
25-34 years	12.2	15.6	19.4	21.4	25.3	28.6	25.1
35-44 years	10.7	15.3	21.0	26.6	29.4	41.0	32.6
45-54 years	3.4	5.1	7.7	10.0	15.9	15.6	13.9
55-64 years	*	2.6	2.9	4.4	7.5	9.4	7.1
65-74 years	*	*	*	2.8	2.3	3.2	2.8

[Continued]

★ 938 ★

Death Rates: Trends in Deaths by Sex, Race, and Age, 1987-92
[Continued]

Sex, race, Hispanic origin, and age	Deaths per 100,000 population						
	1987	1988	1989	1990	1991	1992	1990-92
75-84 years	*	*	*	*	*	*	1.4
85 years and over	*	*	*	*	*	*	*

Source: "Death Rates for Human Immunodeficienncy Virus (HIV) Infection, According to Sex, Detailed Race, Hispanic Origin,and Age: United States, Selected Years 1987-92," *Health, United States, 1994*, p. 126. Primary source: Centers for Disease Control and Prevention, National Center for Health Statistics: Vital Statistics of the United States, Vol. II, Mortality, Part A, for data years 1950-92. Public Health Service. Washington. U.S. Government Printing Office; Data computed by the Division of Health and Utilization Analysis from data compiled by the Division of Vital Statistics and from national population estimates for race groups from table 1 and State or U.S. aggregate population estimates for Hispanics provided by the Census Bureau. *Notes:* Categories for the coding and classification of human immunodeficiency virus infection were introduced in the United states beginning with mortality data for 1987. Data for the 1980's are based on intercensal population estimates. See Appendix I, department of Commerce. (Sorlie PD, Rogot E, and Johnson NJ: Validity of demographic characteristics on the death certificate, *Epidemiology* 3(2): 181-184, 1992.) * Age-specific death rates based on fewer than 20 deaths.

★ 939 ★
Death Rates

Death Rates: Trends in Deaths by Breast Malignancies, 1950-1992

[Data are based on the National Vital Statistics System.]

Sex, race, and age	Deaths per 100,000 resident population									
	1950[1]	1960[1]	1970	1980	1985	1988	1989	1990	1991	1992
All races										
All ages, age adjusted	22.2	22.3	23.1	22.7	23.3	23.3	23.1	23.1	22.7	21.9
All ages, crude	24.7	26.1	28.4	30.6	32.8	33.6	33.9	34.0	33.7	33.0
Under 25 years	[2]	[2]	[2]	[2]	0.0	[2]	[2]	[2]	[2]	[2]
25-34 years	3.8	3.8	3.9	3.3	3.0	3.1	3.0	2.9	3.0	2.9
35-44 years	20.8	20.2	20.4	17.9	17.5	17.6	17.8	17.8	16.9	16.1
45-54 years	46.9	51.4	52.6	48.1	47.1	45.8	45.3	45.4	44.3	42.8
55-64 years	70.4	70.8	77.6	80.5	84.2	82.8	79.7	78.6	79.1	73.6
65-74 years	94.0	90.0	93.8	101.1	107.8	109.8	111.6	111.7	108.6	109.3
75-84 years	139.8	129.9	127.4	126.4	136.2	140.8	145.1	146.3	145.1	140.8
85 years and over	195.5	191.9	157.1	169.3	178.5	188.2	190.5	196.8	197.9	195.5
White										
All ages, age adjusted	22.5	22.4	23.4	22.8	23.4	23.1	23.1	22.9	22.5	21.7
All ages, crude	25.7	27.2	29.9	32.3	34.7	35.4	35.8	35.9	35.5	34.8
Under 25 years	[2]	[2]	[2]	[2]	[2]	[2]	[2]	[2]	[2]	[2]
25-34 years	3.7	3.6	3.7	3.0	2.8	2.8	2.8	2.6	2.8	2.6
35-44 years	20.8	19.7	20.2	17.3	16.8	16.6	17.2	17.1	15.9	15.1
45-54 years	47.1	51.2	53.0	48.1	46.8	44.8	44.1	44.3	43.0	41.3
55-64 years	70.9	71.8	79.3	81.3	84.7	83.0	80.4	78.5	78.9	73.4

[Continued]

★ 939 ★

Death Rates: Trends in Deaths by Breast Malignancies, 1950-1992

[Continued]

Sex, race, and age	Deaths per 100,000 resident population									
	1950[1]	1960[1]	1970	1980	1985	1988	1989	1990	1991	1992
65-74 years	96.3	91.6	95.9	103.7	109.9	111.8	113.2	113.3	109.8	110.9
75-84 years	143.6	132.8	129.6	128.4	138.8	142.7	147.7	148.2	146.8	143.0
85 years and over	204.2	199.7	161.9	171.7	180.9	189.9	192.7	198.0	199.5	197.6
Black										
All ages, age adjusted	19.3	21.3	21.5	23.3	25.5	27.5	26.5	27.5	27.6	27.0
All ages, crude	16.4	18.7	19.7	22.9	25.9	28.5	27.7	29.0	29.3	28.7
Under 25 years	[2]	[2]	[2]	[2]	[2]	[2]	[2]	[2]	[2]	[2]
25-34 years	4.9	6.1	5.9	5.3	4.5	5.4	5.2	5.3	5.0	5.1
35-44 years	21.0	24.8	24.4	24.1	26.1	28.8	25.1	25.8	26.7	26.1
45-54 years	46.5	54.4	52.0	52.7	55.5	60.5	61.4	60.5	59.5	61.2
55-64 years	64.3	63.2	64.7	79.9	90.4	93.4	85.3	93.1	93.2	87.4
65-74 years	67.0	72.3	77.3	84.3	100.7	105.1	109.9	112.2	114.9	112.3
75-84 years	-	87.5	101.8	114.1	117.6	133.1	129.2	140.5	143.3	133.1
85 years and over	-	92.1	112.1	149.9	159.4	187.2	184.3	201.5	193.3	188.7

Source: "Death Rates for Malignant Neoplasms of Breast for Females, According to Race and Age: United States, Selected Years 1970-92," *Health, United States, 1994*, p. 123. Primary source: Centers for Disease Control and Prevention, National Center for Health Statistics: Vital Statistics of the United states, Vol. II, Mortality, Part A, for data years 1950-92. Public Health Service. Washington. U.S. Government Printing Office; Data computed by the Division of Health and Utilization Analysis from data compiled by the Division of Vital Statistics and from table 1. *Notes:* For data years shown, the code numbers for cause of death are based on the then current International Classification of Diseases, which are described in Appendix II, tables IV and V. Data for the 1980's are based on intercensal population estimates. See Appendix I, Department of Commerce. 1. Includes deaths of nonresidents of the United States. 2. Based on fewer than 20 deaths.

★ 940 ★

Death Rates

Death Rates: Trends in Deaths by Cerebrovascular Diseases, 1950-1992. Part 1

[Data are based on the National Vital Statistics System.]

Sex, Race, Hispanic origin, and age	1950[1]	1960[1]	1970	1980	1985	1988	1989	1990	1991	1992	1990-92
	Deaths per 100,000 resident population										
White male											
All ages, age adjusted	87.0	80.3	68.8	41.9	33.0	30.3	28.4	27.7	26.9	26.3	27.0
All ages, crude	100.5	102.7	93.5	63.3	52.7	50.3	47.8	47.0	46.3	46.1	46.5
Under 1 year	5.9	4.3	4.5	3.8	3.7	3.2	2.9	3.1	3.5	4.1	3.6
1-4 years	1.1	0.8	1.2	0.4	[5]	0.3	[5]	[5]	[5]	[5]	0.3
5-14 years	0.5	0.7	0.8	0.2	0.2	0.3	0.2	0.2	0.2	0.2	0.2
15-24 years	1.6	1.7	1.6	1.0	0.7	0.7	0.5	0.6	0.6	0.6	0.6
25-34 years	3.4	3.5	3.2	2.0	1.8	1.8	1.7	1.8	1.5	1.6	1.6
35-44 years	13.1	11.3	11.8	6.5	5.5	5.5	5.0	4.9	5.2	5.0	5.0
45-54 years	53.7	40.9	35.6	21.7	18.1	16.2	15.0	15.4	15.2	15.2	15.3
55-64 years	182.2	139.0	119.9	64.2	54.6	50.9	48.0	45.8	44.2	44.2	44.7
65-74 years	569.7	501.0	420.0	240.4	186.4	167.4	156.3	153.2	150.5	143.0	148.9
75-84 years	1,556.3	1,564.8	1,361.6	854.8	650.0	590.4	554.8	540.7	516.4	499.5	518.4

[Continued]

★ 940 ★

Death Rates: Trends in Deaths by Cerebrovascular Diseases, 1950-1992. Part 1

[Continued]

Sex, Race, Hispanic origin, and age	1950[1]	1960[1]	1970	1980	1985	1988	1989	1990	1991	1992	1990-92
85 years and over	3,127.1	3,734.8	3,018.1	2,236.9	1,765.6	1,685.4	1,591.3	1,549.8	1,499.5	1,521.7	1,523.3
Black male											
All ages, age adjusted	146.2	141.2	122.5	77.5	62.7	60.8	57.3	56.1	54.9	52.0	54.3
All ages, crude	122.0	122.9	108.8	73.1	59.2	57.6	54.3	53.1	52.1	49.5	51.5
Under 1 year	-	8.5	12.3	11.2	10.1	9.4	7.6	10.2	7.3	12.1	9.8
1-4 years	-	1.9	5	5	5	5	5	5	5	5	0.7
5-14 years	5	5	0.8	5	5	5	5	5	5	5	0.3
15-24 years	3.3	3.7	3.0	2.1	1.3	0.9	1.0	0.9	5	0.9	0.8
25-34 years	12.0	12.8	14.6	7.7	5.8	6.9	4.9	4.6	4.5	4.0	4.4
35-44 years	59.3	47.4	52.7	29.2	25.4	25.1	24.0	22.7	22.6	22.3	22.5
45-54 years	211.9	166.1	136.1	82.1	71.1	67.4	67.6	68.4	67.1	58.2	64.4
55-64 years	522.8	439.9	343.4	189.8	160.7	160.3	150.1	141.8	137.4	139.4	139.5
65-74 years	783.6	899.2	780.1	472.8	379.7	357.1	335.0	327.2	317.3	302.4	315.5
75-84 years	-	1,475.2	1,445.7	1,067.6	814.4	799.3	723.3	723.7	719.9	661.6	701.4
85 years and over	-	2,700.0	1,963.1	1,873.2	1,429.0	1,403.1	1,454.5	1,430.5	1,415.9	1,340.7	1,395.1
American Indian or Alaskan Native male[2]											
All ages, age adjusted	-	-	-	5	5	5	5	5	5	5	20.4
All ages, crude	-	-	-	23.2	18.5	18.0	19.5	16.0	15.9	16.8	16.3
45-54 years	-	-	-	5	5	5	5	5	5	5	13.0
55-64 years	-	-	-	72.0	5	46.2	49.1	39.8	36.8	51.9	42.9
65-74 years	-	-	-	170.5	200.0	133.3	171.0	120.3	117.6	140.1	126.7
75-84 years	-	-	-	535.1	372.7	392.3	430.8	325.9	328.6	310.6	321.4
85 years and over	-	-	-	1,384.7	733.3	900.0	966.7	949.8	875.0	760.6	872.7
Asian or Pacific Islander male[3]											
All ages, age adjusted	-	-	-	5	28.0	27.5	26.9	26.9	29.1	26.4	27.5
All ages, crude	-	-	-	28.7	24.0	24.0	23.5	23.4	26.0	23.8	24.4
45-54 years	-	-	-	17.0	13.9	18.0	19.6	15.6	20.7	17.5	18.0
55-64 years	-	-	-	59.9	48.8	52.1	50.0	51.8	56.6	57.9	55.6
65-74 years	-	-	-	197.9	155.6	153.3	140.2	167.9	169.0	149.7	161.7
75-84 years	-	-	-	619.5	583.7	507.8	489.1	485.7	487.3	454.7	475.8
85 years and over	-	-	-	1,399.0	1,387.5	1,381.8	1,436.4	1,196.6	1,576.9	1,283.2	1,359.0
Hispanic male[4]											
All ages, age adjusted	-	-	-	-	27.7	25.3	23.8	22.7	24.1	21.9	22.9
All ages, crude	-	-	-	-	17.2	15.8	16.4	15.6	16.8	15.7	16.0
45-54 years	-	-	-	-	23.6	21.3	20.2	20.0	24.2	20.1	21.4
55-64 years	-	-	-	-	63.9	55.1	50.4	49.4	52.9	49.3	50.5
65-74 years	-	-	-	-	163.5	135.6	136.6	126.4	140.3	116.6	127.6

[Continued]

★ 940 ★

Death Rates: Trends in Deaths by Cerebrovascular Diseases, 1950-1992. Part 1

[Continued]

Sex, Race, Hispanic origin, and age	1950[1]	1960[1]	1970	1980	1985	1988	1989	1990	1991	1992	1990-92
75-84 years	-	-	-	-	396.7	438.6	379.3	356.6	366.3	357.9	360.3
85 years and over	-	-	-	-	1,152.1	932.6	890.2	866.3	879.2	790.5	842.9

Source: "Death Rates for Cerebrovascular, According to Sex, Detailed Race, Hispanic Origin, and Age: United States, Selected Years 1950-92," *Health, United States, 1994*, pp. 116-18. Primary source: Centers for Disease Control and Prevention, National Center for Health Statistics: Vital Statistics of the United States, Vol. II, Mortality, Part A, for data years 1950-92. Public Health Service. Washington. U.S. Government Printing Office; Data computed by the Division of Health and Utilization Analysis from data compiled by the Division of Vital Statistics and from national population estimates for race groups from table 1 and State or U.S. aggregate population estimates for Hispanics provided by the Census Bureau. *Notes:* For data years shown, the code numbers for cause of death are based on the then current International Classification of Diseases, which are described in Appendix II, tables IV and V. Data for the 1980's are based on intercensal population estimates. See Appendix I, Department of Commerce. Age groups chosen to show data for American Indians, Asians, Hispanics, and non-Hispanic whites were selected to minimize the presentation of unstable age-specific death rates based on small numbers of deaths and for consistency among comparison groups. The race groups, white, black, Asian or Pacific Islander, and American Indian or Alaskan Native, include persons of Hispanic and non-Hispanic origin. Conversely, persons of Hispanic origin may be of any race. Consistency of race and Hispanic origin identification between the death certificate (source of data for numerator of death rates) and data from the Census Bureau (denominator) is high for individual white, black, and Hispanic persons; however, persons identified as American Indian or Asian in data from the Census Bureau are sometimes misreported as white on the death certificate, causing death rates to be underestimated by 22-30 percent for American Indians and by about 12 percent for Asians. (Sorlie PD, Rogot E, and Johnson NJ: Validity of demographic characteristics on the death certificate, *Epidemology* 3(2): 181-184, 1992) 1. Includes deaths of nonresidents of the United States. 2. Interpretation of trends should take into account that population estimates for American Indians increased by 45 percent between 1980 and 1990, partly due to better enumeration techniques in the 1990 decennial census and to the increased tendency for people to identify themselves as American Indian in 1990. 3. Interpretation of trends should take into account that the Asian population in the United States more than doubled between 1980 and 1990, primarily due to immigration. 4. Excludes data from States lacking and Hispanic-origin item on their death certificates. See Appendix I. 5. Age-specific death rate based on fewer than 20 deaths. For age- adjusted death rates, 6 or more age-specific rates were based on fewer than 20 deaths.

★ 941 ★

Death Rates

Death Rates: Trends in Deaths by Cerebrovascular Diseases, 1950-1992. Part 2

[Data are based on the National Vital Statistics System.]

Sex, Race, Hispanic origin, and age	1950[1]	1960[1]	1970	1980	1985	1988	1989	1990	1991	1992	1990-92
					Deaths per 100,000 resident population						
White female											
All ages, age adjusted	79.7	68.7	56.2	35.2	27.9	25.5	24.2	23.8	22.8	22.5	23.0
All ages, crude	103.3	110.1	109.8	88.8	78.4	75.4	72.6	71.8	70.5	70.3	70.8
Under 1 year	2.9	2.6	3.2	3.3	2.3	2.9	2.6	2.6	3.2	2.4	2.7
1-4 years	0.6	0.5	0.6	0.4	5	5	5	0.3	5	5	0.3
5-14 years	0.4	0.6	0.6	0.3	0.3	0.2	0.2	0.2	0.2	0.1	0.2
15-24 years	1.2	1.4	1.1	0.7	0.7	0.6	0.5	0.5	0.5	0.4	0.5
25-34 years	2.9	3.4	3.4	2.0	1.6	1.6	1.6	1.7	1.5	1.4	1.5
35-44 years	13.6	10.1	11.5	6.7	5.3	4.6	4.4	4.4	4.4	4.5	4.4
45-54 years	55.0	33.8	30.5	18.7	15.5	14.0	13.3	13.5	13.1	12.4	13.0
55-64 years	156.9	103.0	78.1	48.7	40.0	37.3	35.9	35.8	34.1	34.4	34.8
65-74 years	498.1	383.3	303.2	172.8	137.9	125.3	117.8	116.3	110.5	109.5	112.1
75-84 years	1,471.3	1,444.7	1,176.8	730.3	552.9	503.8	471.0	457.6	439.1	434.1	443.4
85 years and over	3,017.9	3,795.7	3,167.6	2,367.8	1,944.9	1,798.5	1,729.6	1,691.4	1,640.8	1,608.1	1,645.7
Black female											
All ages, age adjusted	155.6	139.5	107.9	61.7	50.6	47.1	45.5	42.7	41.0	39.9	41.2
All ages, crude	128.3	127.7	112.2	77.9	68.6	66.3	64.5	60.7	59.0	57.8	59.1
Under 1 year	-	5	9.1	5	5	8.2	5	5	7.2	6.4	6.5
1-4 years	-	5	5	5	5	5	5	5	5	5	5
5-14 years	5	1.0	0.8	5	5	5	5	5	5	5	0.3
15-24 years	4.2	3.4	3.0	1.7	1.5	1.1	1.3	1.1	1.3	5	1.1
25-34 years	15.9	17.4	14.3	7.0	5.7	5.4	5.8	5.5	5.0	4.8	5.1
35-44 years	75.0	57.4	49.1	21.6	19.1	18.3	16.7	18.6	16.0	17.5	17.4
45-54 years	248.9	166.2	119.4	61.9	50.8	44.4	45.7	44.1	41.4	41.1	42.2

[Continued]

★ 941 ★

Death Rates: Trends in Deaths by Cerebrovascular Diseases, 1950-1992. Part 2
[Continued]

Sex, Race, Hispanic origin, and age	1950[1]	1960[1]	1970	1980	1985	1988	1989	1990	1991	1992	1990-92
55-64 years	57.7	452.0	272.4	138.7	113.6	109.2	103.3	97.0	95.9	88.3	93.7
65-74 years	754.4	830.5	673.5	362.2	285.6	271.4	255.1	236.8	224.6	218.0	226.4
75-84 years	-	1,413.1	1,338.3	918.6	753.8	671.1	669.3	596.0	575.2	569.4	580.0
85 years and over	-	2,578.9	2,210.5	1,896.3	1,657.1	1,609.4	1,530.7	1,496.5	1,494.5	1,451.8	1,480.5
American Indian or Alaskan Native female[2]											
All ages, age adjusted	-	-	-	5	5	5	5	5	5	5	18.3
All ages, crude	-	-	-	22.1	21.8	20.6	17.9	19.3	20.3	20.0	19.9
45-54 years	-	-	-	5	5	5	5	5	5	5	13.5
55-64 years	-	-	-	5	40.4	46.6	43.3	40.7	38.1	37.3	38.6
65-74 years	-	-	-	128.3	121.2	102.6	69.2	100.5	102.4	101.5	101.6
75-84 years	-	-	-	404.2	317.6	305.3	290.0	282.0	350.0	306.7	313.8
85 years and over	-	-	-	1,123.6	1,000.0	766.7	800.0	776.2	657.1	713.8	700.0
Asian or Pacific Islander female[3]											
All ages, age adjusted	-	-	-	5	23.6	22.5	22.5	23.4	22.3	21.1	22.3
All ages, crude	-	-	-	26.5	23.3	23.0	23.2	24.3	24.1	23.1	23.8
45-54 years	-	-	-	20.3	15.1	21.2	19.5	19.7	18.2	18.3	18.7
55-64 years	-	-	-	44.5	49.0	37.5	48.2	42.5	42.7	44.4	43.2
65-74 years	-	-	-	136.1	130.8	116.3	107.0	124.0	118.9	113.0	118.4
75-84 years	-	-	-	449.6	387.0	400.0	357.4	396.6	371.2	319.9	359.4
85 years and over	-	-	-	1,545.2	1,383.3	1,333.3	1,387.5	1,395.0	1,352.6	1,295.0	1,361.8
Hispanic female[4]											
All ages, age adjusted	-	-	-	-	20.6	19.3	19.6	19.5	17.9	17.1	18.1
All ages, crude	-	-	-	-	18.3	17.4	19.9	20.2	18.8	18.3	19.1
45-54 years	-	-	-	-	15.8	17.4	18.2	15.2	15.1	12.7	14.3
55-64 years	-	-	-	-	35.8	36.0	38.9	38.8	34.1	36.0	36.3
65-74 years	-	-	-	-	108.6	107.6	99.1	102.9	97.7	90.4	96.8
75-84 years	-	-	-	-	339.8	311.9	324.5	309.5	284.0	282.9	291.6
85 years and over	-	-	-	-	1,191.5	900.0	957.2	1,060.4	880.9	823.4	912.8

Source: "Death Rates for Cerebrovascular, According to Sex, Detailed Race, Hispanic Origin, and Age: United States, Selected Years 1950-92," *Health, United States, 1994*, pp. 116-18. Primary source: Centers for Disease Control and Prevention, National Center for Health Statistics: Vital Statistics of the United States, Vol. II, Mortality, Part A, for data years 1950-92. Public Health Service. Washington. U.S. Government Printing Office; Data computed by the Division of Health and Utilization Analysis from data compiled by the Division of Vital Statistics and from national population estimates for race groups from table 1 and State or U.S. aggregate population estimates for Hispanics provided by the Census Bureau. *Notes:* For data years shown, the code numbers for cause of death are based on the then current International Classification of Diseases, which are described in Appendix II, tables IV and V. Data for the 1980's are based on intercensal population estimates. See Appendix I, Department of Commerce. Age groups chosen to show data for American Indians, Asians, Hispanics, and non-Hispanic whites were selected to minimize the presentation of unstable age-specific death rates based on small numbers of deaths and for consistency among comparison groups. The race groups, white, black, Asian or Pacific Islander, and American Indian or Alaskan Native, include persons of Hispanic and non-Hispanic origin. Conversely, persons of Hispanic origin may be of any race. Consistency of race and Hispanic origin identification between the death certificate (source of data for numerator of death rates) and data from the Census Bureau (denominator) is high for individual white, black, and Hispanic persons; however, persons identified as American Indian or Asian in data from the Census Bureau are sometimes misreported as white on the death certificate, causing death rates to be underestimated by 22-30 percent for American Indians and by about 12 percent for Asians. (Sorlie PD, Rogot E, and Johnson NJ: Validity of demographic characteristics on the death certificate, *Epidemiology* 3(2): 181-184, 1992) 1. Includes deaths of nonresidents of the United States. 2. Interpretation of trends should take into account that population estimates for American Indians increased by 45 percent between 1980 and 1990, partly due to better enumeration techniques in the 1990 decennial census and to the increased tendency for people to identify themselves as American Indian in 1990. 3. Interpretation of trends should take into account that the Asian population in the United States more than doubled between 1980 and 1990, primarily due to immigration. 4. Excludes data from States lacking and Hispanic-origin item on their death certificates. See Appendix I. 5. Age-specific death rate based on fewer than 20 deaths. For age-adjusted death rates, 6 or more age-specific rates were based on fewer than 20 deaths.

Death Rates: Trends in Deaths by Chronic Obstructive Pulmonary Diseases, 1950-1992

[Data are based on the National Vital Statistics System.]

Sex, race, and age	Deaths per 100,000 population											
	1980	1982	1983	1984	1985	1986	1987	1988	1989	1990	1991	1992
White male												
All ages, age adjusted	26.7	26.3	27.8	27.7	28.7	28.3	27.7	28.2	27.2	27.4	27.4	26.8
All ages, crude	37.9	38.3	41.1	41.6	43.7	43.6	43.3	44.5	43.4	44.3	44.9	44.4
Under 1 year	1.3	1.8	1.4	1.3	2.0	1.8	1.6	1.5	1.6	1.3	1	1
1-4 years	1	1	0.4	1	1	1	1	1	1	0.3	1	0.3
5-14 years	0.1	0.2	0.2	0.2	0.2	0.2	0.2	0.2	0.3	0.2	0.3	0.2
15-24 years	0.3	0.4	0.3	0.3	0.2	0.4	0.4	0.3	0.4	0.3	0.4	0.4
25-34 years	0.4	0.5	0.4	0.4	0.4	0.4	0.4	0.5	0.5	0.5	0.6	0.5
35-44 years	1.2	1.2	1.3	1.3	1.3	1.4	1.6	1.4	1.3	1.3	1.4	1.5
45-54 years	11.4	10.5	10.9	10.1	10.5	10.2	9.0	9.5	8.7	8.6	8.4	8.3
55-64 years	60.0	57.1	59.9	61.0	60.6	59.8	60.3	60.9	60.2	58.7	57.8	56.6
65-74 years	218.4	210.4	220.0	217.2	225.2	220.6	209.6	215.8	204.5	208.1	206.7	204.6
75-84 years	459.8	470.2	502.5	502.5	525.5	522.4	521.2	521.3	502.2	513.5	511.8	494.1
85 years and over	611.2	625.2	703.2	736.1	798.1	785.7	779.1	829.0	824.9	847.0	867.4	862.5
Black male												
All ages, age adjusted	20.9	20.6	22.7	23.4	24.8	25.6	25.2	27.4	26.5	26.5	25.9	24.8
All ages, crude	19.3	19.1	21.4	21.9	23.4	24.1	23.9	25.9	25.2	25.2	24.5	23.8
Under 1 year	1	1	1	1	1	1	1	1	1	1	1	1
1-4 years	1	1	1	1	1	1	1	1	1	1	1	1
5-14 years	0.8	1	1.0	0.9	1.0	1.2	1.6	0.9	1.0	1.4	1.1	1.0
15-24 years	1.1	1.7	1.2	1.1	1.7	1.6	1.7	1.6	1.4	1.4	1.9	1.9
25-34 years	1.9	2.0	2.3	1.4	2.1	1.7	2.3	2.6	2.8	2.4	2.5	2.3
35-44 years	5.8	5.6	5.2	5.0	5.3	5.1	5.6	6.5	6.5	5.3	5.5	4.7
45-54 years	19.7	18.5	16.8	20.8	19.5	20.5	17.8	19.9	18.1	18.8	19.8	15.1
55-64 years	66.6	59.4	72.6	66.6	69.6	71.5	65.9	71.3	66.6	67.4	66.7	64.8
65-74 years	142.0	151.0	156.5	169.9	178.2	190.7	188.8	202.3	192.8	184.5	183.2	175.1
75-84 years	229.8	224.5	271.7	294.4	321.8	317.2	325.8	374.5	373.5	390.9	357.8	354.5
85 years and over	271.6	272.4	346.7	326.2	374.2	423.8	440.6	441.5	481.8	498.0	482.6	559.8
White female												
All ages, age adjusted	9.2	10.1	11.3	11.8	12.9	13.3	13.7	14.5	15.2	15.2	16.1	16.1
All ages, crude	16.4	18.6	21.3	22.9	25.5	26.7	28.1	30.2	31.9	32.8	35.0	35.8
Under 1 year	1	1	1	1	1	1	1	1	1	1	1	1
1-4 years	1	1	1	0.4	1	1	1	1	1	1	1	1
5-14 years	0.2	0.2	0.2	0.2	0.2	0.2	0.2	1	0.2	0.2	0.2	0.2
15-24 years	0.2	0.3	0.3	0.3	0.4	0.3	0.3	0.3	0.4	0.4	0.4	0.4
25-34 years	0.3	0.4	0.4	0.4	0.4	0.5	0.4	0.5	0.5	0.5	0.5	0.4
35-44 years	1.3	1.3	1.3	1.2	1.3	1.3	1.5	1.3	1.3	1.2	1.3	1.3
45-54 years	7.6	7.8	8.6	8.0	9.1	8.6	8.5	8.2	8.8	8.3	8.4	7.5

[Continued]

★ 942 ★

Death Rates: Trends in Deaths by Chronic Obstructive Pulmonary Diseases, 1950-1992
[Continued]

Sex, race, and age	Deaths per 100,000 population											
	1980	1982	1983	1984	1985	1986	1987	1988	1989	1990	1991	1992
55-64 years	28.7	29.6	32.9	34.7	37.8	38.0	38.8	40.7	43.7	41.9	44.7	43.2
65-74 years	71.0	80.6	90.5	94.8	101.1	106.7	108.2	115.6	118.6	118.8	127.0	127.7
75-84 years	104.0	120.0	137.2	150.9	171.0	179.0	187.4	205.9	216.2	226.3	238.3	246.9
85 years and over	144.2	153.6	175.7	194.2	217.6	224.9	248.4	262.6	278.1	298.4	311.6	330.7
Black female												
All ages, age adjusted	6.3	7.4	7.7	8.1	8.8	9.0	9.6	10.2	11.1	10.7	11.3	11.2
All ages, crude	6.8	7.9	8.5	9.2	10.0	10.2	11.2	11.7	13.1	12.6	13.4	13.7
Under 1 year	1	1	1	1	1	1	1	1	1	1	1	1
1-4 years	1	1	1	1	1	1	1	1	1	1	1	1
5-14 years	1	1	1	1	1.1	1	1	0.8	1	1	0.9	1
15-24 years	0.8	0.8	1.0	0.9	1.1	1.1	1.2	0.9	0.8	0.9	1.2	1.1
25-34 years	1.8	1.3	1.8	1.8	1.4	1.6	1.6	1.7	1.8	1.9	2.1	1.3
35-44 years	3.4	4.0	4.3	4.4	2.8	3.4	4.2	4.6	4.2	3.8	4.1	4.3
45-54 years	9.3	11.2	11.3	10.0	11.2	11.2	12.1	13.3	12.8	14.0	15.0	13.3
55-64 years	20.8	25.7	25.7	27.8	30.6	31.4	31.6	35.0	37.4	33.4	34.0	32.1
65-74 years	32.7	37.3	37.5	43.9	48.3	53.4	55.4	58.9	68.5	64.7	70.4	73.5
75-84 years	41.1	49.7	58.4	65.2	76.6	68.2	82.6	77.6	99.2	96.0	96.0	105.6
85 years and over	63.2	59.3	93.5	96.9	94.0	96.4	118.1	113.4	130.7	133.0	142.3	169.0

Source: "Death Rates for Chronic Pulmonary Diseases, According to Sex, Race, and Age: United States, Selected Years 1970-92," *Health, United States, 1994,* p. 124. Primary source: Centers for Disease Control and Prevention, National Center for Health Statistics: Vital Statistics of the United states, Vol. II, Mortality, Part A, for data years 1950-92. Health Service. Washington. U.S. Government Printing Office; Data computed by the Division of Health and Utilization Analysis from data compiled by the Division of Vital Statistics and from table 1. *Notes:* For data years shown, the code numbers for cause of death are based on the then current International Classification of Diseases, which are described in Appendix II, tables IV and V. data for the 1980's are based on intercensal population estimates. See Appendix I, Department of Commerce. 1. Based on fewer than 20 deaths.

★ 943 ★
Death Rates

Death Rates: Trends in Deaths by Firearm-Related Injuries, 1970-92

[Data are based on the National Vital Statistics System.]

Sex, race, and age	Deaths per 100,000 population											
	1970	1980	1983	1984	1985	1986	1987	1988	1989	1990	1991	1992
White male												
All ages, age adjusted	18.2	21.1	19.4	19.6	19.4	20.0	19.2	19.3	19.5	20.5	20.7	20.4
All ages, crude	17.6	21.8	20.5	20.8	20.7	21.4	20.7	20.7	20.8	21.8	21.7	21.3
Under 1 year	1	1	1	1	1	1	1	1	1	1	1	1
1-4 years	0.8	0.7	0.6	0.8	0.6	0.5	0.5	0.6	0.7	0.6	0.5	0.4
5-14 years	2.1	2.3	2.1	2.6	2.7	2.5	2.5	2.4	2.7	2.4	2.5	2.5
15-24 years	16.9	28.4	23.4	23.8	24.1	25.6	23.9	25.3	26.5	29.5	32.0	32.4
25-34 years	24.3	31.1	27.8	27.0	26.3	27.0	25.8	26.0	26.2	27.8	27.5	27.0

[Continued]

★ 943 ★

Death Rates: Trends in Deaths by Firearm-Related Injuries, 1970-92
[Continued]

Sex, race, and age	Deaths per 100,000 population											
	1970	1980	1983	1984	1985	1986	1987	1988	1989	1990	1991	1992
35-44 years	24.1	27.1	24.3	23.5	23.3	23.2	22.1	22.5	22.2	23.3	22.4	22.6
45-54 years	25.7	23.8	23.5	23.9	23.0	23.6	22.7	21.5	22.4	22.0	22.7	21.2
55-64 years	29.5	22.7	23.6	24.7	24.2	24.5	24.6	23.6	22.7	23.7	23.0	22.7
65-74 years	29.1	27.8	28.3	31.1	30.5	32.0	31.3	30.3	30.7	29.0	27.9	27.5
75-84 years	32.0	34.0	40.4	41.7	45.0	47.6	48.8	49.3	44.7	49.8	46.2	42.8
85 years and over	27.7	36.1	40.6	38.5	40.8	44.6	47.7	46.2	51.6	52.4	54.2	49.9
Black male												
All ages, age adjusted	73.4	61.8	44.6	42.6	42.2	47.1	46.4	51.0	55.0	61.5	66.4	64.5
All ages, crude	60.8	57.7	42.9	41.2	41.3	46.9	46.5	51.7	55.4	61.9	66.0	63.9
Under 1 year	[1]	[1]	[1]	[1]	[1]	[1]	[1]	[1]	[1]	[1]	[1]	[1]
1-4 years	3.3	2.1	[1]	[1]	2.2	1.9	[1]	1.8	[1]	[1]	[1]	2.7
5-14 years	6.1	3.3	2.5	2.6	2.8	3.0	4.3	5.0	5.4	5.8	6.5	7.1
15-24 years	97.3	77.9	59.1	55.8	61.3	72.1	81.3	99.0	115.3	138.0	162.2	162.3
25-34 years	145.6	128.4	86.3	82.8	79.8	93.1	84.8	97.1	98.8	108.6	112.3	108.3
35-44 years	104.2	92.3	65.7	64.0	59.2	62.5	62.1	60.7	60.9	66.1	62.6	58.6
45-54 years	83.9	63.4	46.0	43.0	40.8	45.7	36.7	34.4	36.6	39.1	41.5	37.6
55-64 years	54.3	46.5	37.3	34.4	32.1	27.1	27.0	25.9	27.9	28.4	27.3	24.3
65-74 years	36.0	31.2	27.1	27.0	29.2	31.6	28.0	25.1	29.1	24.8	25.4	21.3
75-84 years	20.2	26.8	26.7	26.3	23.0	25.2	27.7	26.9	24.7	22.4	28.4	22.7
85 years and over	[1]	[1]	[1]	[1]	[1]	[1]	[1]	[1]	31.8	[1]	[1]	[1]
White female												
All ages, age adjusted	4.0	4.2	4.0	3.9	3.9	3.9	3.8	3.7	3.6	3.7	3.7	3.6
All ages, crude	3.7	4.1	4.0	4.0	4.0	3.9	3.9	3.8	3.7	3.8	3.7	3.6
Under 1 year	[1]	[1]	[1]	[1]	[1]	[1]	[1]	[1]	[1]	[1]	[1]	[1]
1-4 years	0.6	0.5	0.4	0.4	0.5	0.4	[1]	0.4	0.4	[1]	0.4	0.4
5-14 years	0.6	0.7	0.6	0.8	0.7	0.6	0.8	0.7	0.7	0.7	0.7	0.8
15-24 years	3.4	5.1	4.7	5.0	4.4	4.7	4.3	4.1	4.3	4.8	4.8	4.7
25-34 years	6.7	6.0	5.9	5.3	5.7	5.5	5.6	5.5	5.2	5.5	5.2	4.9
35-44 years	7.1	6.6	5.7	5.7	5.5	5.4	5.3	5.2	4.9	5.0	5.0	4.9
45-54 years	5.7	5.9	5.7	5.4	5.4	5.4	5.3	5.1	4.7	4.9	5.0	4.7
55-64 years	4.0	4.4	4.9	4.5	4.7	4.5	4.4	4.3	4.4	4.1	3.7	3.8
65-74 years	2.7	3.1	3.8	3.4	3.7	3.8	3.9	3.7	3.3	3.7	3.8	3.5
75-84 years	1.7	1.7	2.2	2.5	2.7	2.7	3.1	3.1	2.7	3.0	2.6	2.9
85 years and over	[1]	[1]	[1]	1.5	1.9	[1]	1.9	2.1	1.2	1.2	1.6	1.6
Black female												
All ages, age adjusted	11.4	9.1	6.5	6.5	6.6	7.0	7.3	7.6	7.4	7.8	8.0	8.1
All ages, crude	10.0	8.8	6.4	6.4	6.5	7.1	7.3	7.7	7.4	7.8	7.9	8.0

[Continued]

★ 943 ★

Death Rates: Trends in Deaths by Firearm-Related Injuries, 1970-92
[Continued]

Sex, race, and age	Deaths per 100,000 population											
	1970	1980	1983	1984	1985	1986	1987	1988	1989	1990	1991	1992
Under 1 year	[1]	[1]	[1]	[1]	[1]	[1]	[1]	[1]	[1]	[1]	[1]	[1]
1-4 years	2.5	[1]	[1]	[1]	[1]	[1]	[1]	[1]	[1]	[1]	[1]	1.7
5-14 years	1.6	1.1	1.0	1.4	1.0	1.5	1.0	2.2	1.6	2.4	1.7	2.3
15-24 years	15.2	12.3	9.2	8.8	8.3	10.0	11.6	11.2	12.6	13.3	15.3	15.3
25-34 years	21.2	18.3	12.4	12.0	12.8	13.8	14.0	14.7	13.2	14.6	15.2	15.4
35-44 years	17.4	12.8	10.0	9.7	9.4	9.6	9.1	10.9	9.5	9.7	8.7	8.9
45-54 years	13.2	9.1	7.1	5.5	7.4	5.9	7.0	5.8	5.7	5.5	5.6	4.6
55-64 years	6.2	7.1	3.2	5.2	3.9	4.8	4.4	4.4	5.2	3.9	3.5	3.6
65-74 years	4.6	3.9	2.5	3.9	2.9	4.0	3.9	3.7	3.2	3.2	2.8	3.1
75-84 years	[1]	[1]	[1]	[1]	6.0	[1]	[1]	[1]	[1]	[1]	[1]	[1]
85 years and over	[1]	[1]	[1]	[1]	[1]	[1]	[1]	[1]	[1]	[1]	[1]	[1]

Source: "Death Rates for Firearm-Related Injuries, According to Sex, Race, and Age: United States, Selected Years 1970-92," *Health, United States, 1994,* pp. 138-39. Primary source: Centers for Disease Control and Prevention, National Center for Health Statistics: Data computed by the Division of Health and Utilization Analysis from data compiled by the Division of Vital Statistics and from table 1. *Notes:* International Classification of Diseases code numbers for causes of death included in firearm injuries are described in Appendix II, tables IV and V. Data for the 1980's are based on intercensal population estimates. See Appendix I, department of Commerce. 1. Based on fewer than 20 deaths.

★ 944 ★

Death Rates

Death Rates: Trends in Deaths by Heart Diseases, 1950-1992. Part 1

[Data are based on the National Vital Statsitics System.]

Sex, Race, Hispanic origin, and age	1950[1]	1960[1]	1970	1980	1985	1988	1989	1990	1991	1992	1990-92
	Deaths per 100,000 resident population										
White male											
All ages, age adjusted	381.1	375.4	347.6	277.5	246.2	223.0	208.7	202.0	196.1	190.3	196.0
All ages, crude	433.0	454.6	438.3	384.0	360.3	338.9	320.5	312.7	307.6	302.4	307.5
Under 1 year	4.1	6.9	12.0	22.5	24.2	22.0	19.0	17.5	16.7	16.3	16.8
1-4 years	1.1	1.0	1.5	2.1	1.7	2.0	1.7	1.5	1.7	1.4	1.5
5-14 years	1.7	1.1	0.8	0.9	0.8	10	0.8	0.9	0.7	0.7	0.8
15-24 years	5.8	3.6	3.0	2.9	2.9	3.0	2.6	2.6	2.8	2.7	2.7
25-34 years	20.1	17.6	12.3	9.1	9.3	9.3	9.1	8.4	8.9	8.8	8.7
35-44 years	110.6	107.5	94.6	61.8	52.7	46.6	43.5	42.6	41.9	42.6	42.4
45-54 years	423.6	413.2	365.7	269.8	225.5	187.7	176.4	170.6	166.9	161.4	166.2
55-64 years	1,081.7	1,056.0	979.3	730.6	640.1	571.2	537.9	516.7	499.4	483.2	499.8
65-74 years	2,308.3	2,297.9	2,177.2	1,729.7	1,522.7	1,381.1	1,278.0	1,230.5	1,198.6	1,159.9	1,196.1
75-84 years	4,907.3	4,839.9	4,617.6	3,883.2	3,527.0	3,255.6	3,067.0	2,983.4	2,858.2	2,761.0	2,865.0
85 years and over	9,950.5	10,135.8	8,818.0	8,958.0	8,481.7	8,160.9	7,660.7	7,558.7	7,411.2	7,290.1	7,416.5
Black male											
All ages, age adjusted	415.5	381.2	375.9	327.3	310.8	301.7	289.7	275.9	272.7	264.1	270.8
All ages, crude	348.4	330.6	330.3	301.0	288.6	281.6	268.8	256.8	253.9	246.9	252.5
Under 1 year	-	13.9	33.5	42.8	48.6	43.4	34.3	43.7	33.5	34.8	37.3
1-4 years	-	3.8	3.9	6.3	4.5	4.6	4.7	4.0	5.1	4.5	4.6

[Continued]

★ 944 ★

Death Rates: Trends in Deaths by Heart Diseases, 1950-1992. Part 1
[Continued]

Sex, Race, Hispanic origin, and age	1950[1]	1960[1]	1970	1980	1985	1988	1989	1990	1991	1992	1990-92
5-14 years	6.4	3.0	1.4	1.3	1.6	1.8	1.4	1.3	1.6	1.6	1.5
15-24 years	18.0	8.7	8.3	8.3	7.2	7.9	6.3	6.4	7.3	7.4	7.0
25-34 years	51.9	43.1	41.6	30.3	29.5	28.1	25.8	24.5	24.8	24.8	24.7
35-44 years	198.1	168.1	189.2	136.6	119.8	109.6	104.5	100.0	100.0	96.9	98.9
45-54 years	624.1	514.0	512.8	433.4	385.2	357.0	363.4	328.9	329.6	318.7	325.6
55-64 years	1,434.0	1,236.8	1,135.4	987.2	935.3	912.1	880.7	824.0	810.3	784.0	806.0
65-74 years	2,140.1	2,281.4	2,237.8	1,847.2	1,839.2	1,772.4	1,700.0	1,632.9	1,614.3	1,548.0	1,597.7
75-84 years	-	3,533.6	3,783.4	3,578.8	3,436.6	3,448.3	3,191.6	3,107.1	3,063.1	2,960.9	3,042.9
85 years and over	-	6,037.9	5,367.6	6,819.5	6,393.5	6,640.0	6,368.2	6,479.6	6,240.6	6,298.7	6,337.6
American Indian or Alaskan Native male[2]											
All ages, age adjusted	-	-	-	180.9	162.2	146.4	161.6	144.6	140.8	146.6	144.4
All ages, crude	-	-	-	130.6	117.9	110.1	119.4	108.0	109.0	114.3	110.5
45-54 years	-	-	-	238.1	209.1	184.6	179.5	173.8	129.2	176.3	159.6
55-64 years	-	-	-	496.3	438.3	425.0	479.2	411.0	447.4	425.6	428.2
65-74 years	-	-	-	1,009.4	984.6	850.0	971.0	839.1	817.6	854.7	840.6
75-84 years	-	-	-	2,062.2	2,118.2	1,700.0	1,938.5	1,788.8	1,807.1	1,890.6	1,831.0
85 years and over	-	-	-	4,413.7	2,766.7	4,033.3	4,733.3	3,860.3	3,850.0	3,245.4	3,709.1
Asian or Pacific Islander male[3]											
All ages, age adjusted	-	-	-	136.7	123.4	114.8	108.1	102.6	102.9	103.8	103.2
All ages, crude	-	-	-	119.8	103.5	98.0	92.7	88.7	90.6	93.4	91.0
45-54 years	-	-	-	112.0	81.1	70.5	75.8	70.4	70.0	71.2	70.6
55-64 years	-	-	-	306.7	291.2	273.4	249.5	226.1	231.4	235.0	231.2
65-74 years	-	-	-	852.4	753.5	713.3	606.3	623.5	605.5	611.2	612.7
75-84 years	-	-	-	2,010.9	2,025.6	1,905.9	1,834.5	1,642.2	1,709.5	1,667.2	1,675.8
85 years and over	-	-	-	5,923.0	4,937.5	4,645.5	5,181.8	4,617.8	4,623.1	4,810.3	4,705.1
Hispanic male[4]											
All ages, age adjusted	-	-	-	-	152.3	142.4	144.8	136.3	129.9	126.2	130.6
All ages, crude	-	-	-	-	92.1	86.9	97.3	91.0	88.9	87.7	89.2
45-54 years	-	-	-	-	128.0	122.6	128.7	116.4	107.2	109.6	110.9
55-64 years	-	-	-	-	398.8	378.2	365.0	363.0	335.1	334.5	343.8
65-74 years	-	-	-	-	972.6	901.2	900.0	829.9	822.1	798.1	816.0

[Continued]

★ 944 ★

Death Rates: Trends in Deaths by Heart Diseases, 1950-1992. Part 1
[Continued]

Sex, Race, Hispanic origin, and age	1950[1]	1960[1]	1970	1980	1985	1988	1989	1990	1991	1992	1990-92
75-84 years	-	-	-	-	2,160.8	1,971.3	2,091.6	1,971.3	1,859.0	1,752.2	1,856.8
85 years and over	-	-	-	-	4,791.2	4,742.0	5,005.2	4,711.9	4,618.1	4,162.2	4,479.4

Source: "Death Rates for Diseases of Heart, According to Sex, Detailed Race, Hispanic Origin, and Age: United States, Selected Years 1950-92," *Health, United States, 1994*, pp. 113-15. Primary source: Centers for Disease Control and Prevention, National Center for Health Statistics: Vital Statistics of the United States, Vol. II, Mortality, Part A, for data years 1950-92. Public Health Service. Washington. U.S. Government Printing Office; Data computed by the Division of Health and Utilization Analysis from data compiled by the Division of Vital Statistics and from national population estimates for race groups from table 1 and State or U.S. aggregate population estimates for Hispanics provided by the Census Bureau. *Notes:* For data years shown, the code numbers for cause of death are based on the then current International Classification of Diseases, which are described in Appendix II, tables IV and V. Data for the 1980's are based on intercensal population estimates. See Appendix I, Department of Commerce. Age groups chosen to show data for American Indians, Asians, Hispanics, and non-Hispanic whites were selected to minimize the presentation of unstable age-specific death rates based on small numbers of deaths and for consistency among comparison groups. The race groups, white, black, Asian or Pacific Islander, and American Indian or Alaskan Native, include persons of Hispanic and non-Hispanic origin. Conversely, persons of Hispanic origin may be of any race. Consistency of race and Hispanic origin identification between the death certificate (source of data for numerator of death rates) and data from the Census Bureau (denominator) is high for individual white, black, and Hispanic persons; however, persons identified as American Indian or Asian in data from the Census Bureau are sometimes misreported as white on the death certificate, causing death rates to be underestimated by 22-30 percent for American Indians and by about 12 percent for Asians. (Sorlie PD, Rogot E, and Johnson NJ: Validity of demographic characteristics on the death certificate, *Epidemiology* 3(2): 181-184, 1992) 1. Includes deaths of nonresidents of the United States. 2. Interpretation of trends should take into account that population estimates for American Indians increased by 45 percent between 1980 and 1990, partly due to better enumeration techniques in the 1990 decennial census and to the increased tendency for people to identify themselves as American Indian in 1990. 3. Interpretation of trends should take into account that the Asian population in the United States more than doubled between 1980 and 1990, primarily due to immigration. 4. Excludes data from States lacking and Hispanic-origin item on their death certificates. See Appendix I.

★ 945 ★
Death Rates

Death Rates: Trends in Deaths by Heart Diseases, 1950-1992. Part 2

[Data are based on the National Vital Statistics System.]

Sex, Race, Hispanic origin, and age	1950[1]	1960[1]	1970	1980	1985	1988	1989	1990	1991	1992	1990-92
					Deaths per 100,000 resident population						
White female											
all ages, age adjusted	223.6	197.1	167.8	134.6	121.7	114.1	106.6	103.1	100.7	98.1	100.6
All ages, crude	289.4	306.5	313.8	319.2	321.8	319.9	305.1	298.4	296.5	292.9	295.9
Under 1 year	2.7	4.3	7.0	15.7	18.6	17.4	14.7	14.5	13.1	13.9	13.8
1-4 years	1.1	0.9	1.2	2.1	1.6	2.2	1.3	1.6	1.7	1.5	1.6
5-14 years	1.9	0.9	0.7	0.8	0.9	0.7	0.7	0.7	0.7	0.6	0.6
15-24 years	5.3	2.8	1.7	1.7	1.7	1.7	1.5	1.4	1.6	1.6	1.5
25-34 years	12.2	8.2	5.5	3.9	3.9	3.9	3.9	3.7	4.1	4.1	4.0
35-44 years	40.5	28.6	23.9	16.4	14.4	12.6	12.1	11.4	12.1	11.8	11.8
45-54 years	141.9	103.4	91.4	71.2	62.5	55.0	51.0	50.2	48.8	47.3	48.7
55-64 years	460.2	383.0	317.7	248.1	227.1	215.3	198.3	192.4	188.2	180.9	187.2
65-74 years	1,400.9	1,229.8	1,044.0	796.7	713.3	656.2	604.7	583.6	567.4	557.8	569.5
75-84 years	3,925.2	3,629.7	3,143.5	2,493.6	2,207.5	2,065.1	1,954.5	1,874.3	1,814.7	1,756.7	1,814.4
85 years and over	9,087.4	9,280.8	7,839.9	7,501.6	7,170.0	7,081.4	6,711.3	6,563.4	6,447.3	6,337.0	6,446.5
Black female											
All ages, age adjusted	349.5	292.6	251.7	201.1	188.3	183.3	175.6	168.1	165.5	162.4	165.3
All ages, crude	289.9	268.5	261.0	249.7	250.3	254.6	246.2	237.0	235.0	231.6	234.5
Under 1 year	-	12.0	31.3	43.6	41.0	40.2	39.2	35.8	30.8	32.8	33.1
1-4 years	-	2.8	4.2	4.4	5.3	4.2	3.2	3.8	4.0	3.2	3.7
5-14 years	8.8	3.0	1.8	1.7	1.8	1.0	1.7	1.4	1.3	1.3	1.3
15-24 years	19.8	10.0	6.0	4.6	4.6	4.4	4.2	4.4	3.9	4.0	4.1

[Continued]

★ 945 ★

Death Rates: Trends in Deaths by Heart Diseases, 1950-1992. Part 2
[Continued]

Sex, Race, Hispanic origin, and age	1950[1]	1960[1]	1970	1980	1985	1988	1989	1990	1991	1992	1990-92
25-34 years	52.0	35.9	24.7	15.7	13.2	13.4	13.3	13.4	13.5	14.0	13.6
35-44 years	185.0	125.3	99.8	61.7	50.1	50.3	46.6	43.6	46.1	47.2	45.7
45-54 years	526.8	360.7	290.9	202.4	176.2	173.4	159.6	155.3	152.8	153.8	154.0
55-64 years	1,210.7	952.3	710.5	530.1	510.7	486.8	470.3	442.0	423.3	432.5	432.6
65-74 years	1,659.4	1,680.5	1,553.2	1,2103	1,149.9	1,087.0	1,054.1	1,017.5	1,003.4	953.7	991.2
75-84 years	-	2,926.9	2,964.1	2,707.2	2,533.4	2,514.8	2,380.0	2,250.9	2,246.0	2,135.8	2,210.3
85 years and over	-	5,650.0	5,003.8	5,796.5	5,686.5	5,989.3	5,898.7	5,766.1	5,700.0	5,763.1	5,742.9
American Indian or Alaskan Native female[2]											
All ages, age adjusted	-	-	-	5	83.7	5	82.7	5	5	74.5	73.7
All ages, crude	-	-	-	80.3	84.3	80.0	85.1	77.5	75.9	80.4	78.0
45-54 years	-	-	-	65.2	59.2	58.5	65.9	62.0	49.5	46.9	52.4
55-64 years	-	-	-	193.5	230.8	181.0	193.3	197.0	181.0	197.4	191.5
65-74 years	-	-	-	577.2	472.7	497.4	502.6	492.8	440.5	472.7	469.0
75-84 years	-	-	-	1,364.3	1,258.8	1,247.4	1,290.0	1,050.3	1,040.9	1,115.7	1,070.8
85 years and over	-	-	-	2,893.3	3,180.0	2,733.3	3,100.0	2,868.7	2,942.9	2,41.9	2,704.8
Asian or Pacific Islander female[3]											
All ages, age adjusted	-	-	-	55.8	59.6	57.8	56.9	58.3	54.8	56.4	56.5
All ages, crude	-	-	-	57.0	60.3	60.2	60.0	62.0	60.6	63.7	62.2
45-54 years	-	-	-	28.6	23.8	24.0	24.6	17.5	22.6	20.8	20.4
55-64 years	-	-	-	92.9	103.0	107.1	100.0	99.0	92.9	89.8	93.7
65-74 years	-	-	-	313.3	341.0	317.0	317.2	323.9	300.5	309.3	310.9
75-84 years	-	-	-	1,053.2	1,056.5	1,073.7	1,006.6	1,130.9	1,009.6	1,086.3	1,071.9
85 years and over	-	-	-	3,211.0	4,208.3	3,893.3	4,156.2	4,161.2	3,921.1	4,040.6	4,087.3
Hispanic female[4]											
All ages, age adjusted	-	-	-	-	86.5	80.9	80.5	76.0	72.1	69.2	72.3
All ages, crude	-	-	-	-	75.0	73.8	84.1	79.4	77.9	76.2	77.8
45-54 years	-	-	-	-	46.6	40.6	43.2	43.5	36.7	39.3	39.7
55-64 years	-	-	-	-	184.8	179.1	159.2	153.2	154.4	138.9	148.7
65-74 years	-	-	-	-	534.0	504.6	471.6	460.4	414.4	413.1	428.2
75-84 years	-	-	-	-	1,456.5	1,333.4	1,382.2	1,259.7	1,243.6	1,178.3	1,225.8
85 years and over	-	-	-	-	4,523.4	4,244.2	4,709.2	4,440.3	4,155.3	3,881.7	4,138.7

Source: "Death Rates for Diseases of Heart, According to Sex, Detailed Race, Hispanic Origin, and Age: United States, Selected Years 1950-92," *Health, United States, 1994,* pp. 113-15. Primary source: Centers for Disease Control and Prevention, National Center for Health Statistics: Vital Statistics of the United States, Vol. II, Mortality, Part A, for data years 1950-92. Public Health Service. Washington. U.S. Government Printing Office; Data computed by the Division of Health and Utilization Analysis from data compiled by the Division of Vital Statistics and from national population estimates for race groups from table 1 and State or U.S. aggregate population estimates for Hispanics provided by the Census Bureau. *Notes:* For data years shown, the code numbers for cause of death are based on the then current International Classification of Diseases, which are described in Appendix II, tables IV and V. Data for the 1980's are based on intercensal population estimates. See Appendix I, Department of Commerce. Age groups chosen to show data for American Indians, Asians, Hispanics, and non-Hispanic whites were selected to minimize the presentation of unstable age-specific death rates based on small numbers of deaths and for consistency among comparison groups. The race groups, white, black, Asian or Pacific Islander, and American Indian or Alaskan Native, include persons of Hispanic and non-Hispanic origin. Conversely, persons of Hispanic origin may be of any race. Consistency of race and Hispanic origin identification between the death certificate (source of data for numerator of death rates) and data from the Census Bureau (denominator) is high for individual white, black, and Hispanic persons; however, persons identified as American Indian or Asian in data from the Census Bureau are sometimes misreported as white on the death certificate, causing death rates to be underestimated by 22-30 percent for American Indians and by about 12 percent for Asians. (Sorlie PD, Rogot E, and Johnson NJ: Validity of demographic characteristics on the death certificate, *Epidemology* 3(2): 181-184, 1992) 1. Includes deaths of nonresidents of the United States. 2. Interpretation of trends should take into account that population estimates for American Indians increased by 45 percent between 1980 and 1990, partly due to better enumeration techniques in the 1990 decennial census and to the increased tendency for people to identify themselves as American Indian in 1990. 3. Interpretation of trends should take into account that the Asian population in the United States more than doubled between 1980 and 1990, primarily due to immigration. 4. Excludes data from States lacking and Hispanic-origin item on their death certificates. See Appendix I. 5. Age-specific death rate based on fewer than 20 deaths. For age- adjusted death rates, 6 or more age-specific rates were based on fewer than 20 deaths.

★ 946 ★
Death Rates

Death Rates: Trends in Deaths by Homicide and Legal Intervention, 1950-92. Part 1

[Data are based on the National Vital Statistics System.]

Sex, Race, Hispanic origin, and age	1950[1]	1960[1]	1970	1980	1985	1988	1989	1990	1991	1992	1990-92
	Deaths per 100,000 resident population										
White male											
All ages, age adjusted	3.9	3.9	7.3	10.9	8.1	7.8	8.1	8.9	9.4	9.3	9.2
All ages, crude	3.9	3.6	6.8	10.9	8.2	7.9	8.2	9.0	9.3	9.1	9.1
Under 1 year	4.3	3.8	2.9	4.3	3.8	5.8	5.8	6.4	7.6	6.4	6.8
1-4 years	0.4	0.6	1.4	2.0	1.9	2.2	1.9	1.8	2.1	2.1	2.0
5-14 years	0.4	0.4	0.5	0.9	1.1	1.0	1.0	1.1	1.2	1.2	1.2
15-24 years	3.7	4.4	7.9	15.5	11.0	11.2	12.3	15.4	16.9	17.5	16.6
25-44 years	-	-	-	17.4	12.9	12.1	12.4	13.3	13.4	13.1	13.3
25-34 years	5.4	6.2	13.0	18.9	14.0	13.5	14.0	15.1	15.5	15.1	15.2
35-44 years	6.4	5.5	11.0	15.5	11.5	10.5	10.6	11.4	11.2	10.9	11.2
45-64 years	-	-	-	9.9	7.5	6.9	7.3	7.0	7.6	7.1	7.2
45-54 years	5.5	5.0	9.0	11.9	8.6	7.7	8.6	8.3	8.7	8.1	8.4
55-64 years	4.4	4.3	7.7	7.8	6.3	6.1	5.7	5.5	6.1	5.9	5.8
65-74 years	4.1	3.4	5.6	6.9	4.5	4.2	4.0	4.1	4.0	3.6	3.9
75-84 years	3.5	2.7	5.1	6.3	4.5	4.3	3.9	3.9	3.8	4.0	3.9
85 years and over	1.8	2.7	6.4	6.4	3.9	5.2	5.2	4.9	4.4	5.1	4.8
Black male											
All ages, age adjusted	51.1	44.9	82.1	71.9	50.2	58.6	61.9	68.7	72.5	68.1	69.7
All ages, crude	47.3	36.6	67.6	66.6	49.0	59.1	62.3	69.2	72.0	67.5	69.6
Under 1 year	-	10.3	14.3	18.6	16.7	19.5	21.9	21.4	22.4	22.4	22.1
1-4 years	-	1.7	5.1	7.2	6.6	7.6	8.0	7.6	7.9	7.6	7.7
5-14 years	1.8	1.4	4.2	2.9	3.3	4.3	5.1	5.1	5.4	5.9	5.5
15-24 years	58.9	46.4	102.5	84.3	65.9	101.4	114.2	138.3	158.9	154.4	150.5
25-44 years	-	-	-	130.1	87.5	96.8	98.4	106.2	103.9	95.7	102.0
25-34 years	110.5	92.0	158.5	145.1	95.6	110.9	114.9	125.4	125.0	116.1	122.2
35-44 years	83.7	77.5	126.2	110.3	74.9	76.9	75.9	82.3	77.6	71.4	76.9
45-64 years	-	-	-	70.8	46.3	39.7	40.9	41.7	43.5	38.6	41.3
45-54 years	54.6	54.8	100.5	83.8	51.4	45.8	46.7	47.7	50.6	46.9	48.4
55-64 years	35.7	31.8	59.8	55.6	40.0	31.9	33.4	34.0	33.9	26.7	31.5
65-74 years	18.7	19.1	40.6	33.9	29.2	28.7	29.2	24.3	31.2	26.7	27.4
75-84 years	-	16.1	19.0	27.6	21.4	30.6	28.7	29.2	29.8	23.1	27.3
85 years and over	-	[5]	[5]	[5]	[5]	33.8	37.9	[5]	[5]	31.6	26.3
American Indian or Alaskan Native male[2]											
All ages, age adjusted	-	-	-	[5]	[5]	[5]	[5]	[5]	[5]	[5]	17.5

[Continued]

★ 946 ★

Death Rates: Trends in Deaths by Homicide and Legal Intervention, 1950-92. Part 1

[Continued]

Sex, Race, Hispanic origin, and age	1950[1]	1960[1]	1970	1980	1985	1988	1989	1990	1991	1992	1990-92
All ages, crude	-	-	-	23.4	19.0	18.7	17.8	17.3	18.4	16.2	17.3
15-24 years	-	-	-	36.0	27.1	30.7	24.7	27.7	29.8	25.5	27.7
25-44 years	-	-	-	39.7	30.2	32.7	28.7	26.0	30.0	24.4	26.8
45-64 years	-	-	-	22.1	21.2	[5]	[5]	15.5	17.1	[5]	14.5
Asian or Pacific Islander male[3]											
All ages, age adjusted	-	-	-	[5]	[5]	[5]	[5]	[5]	[5]	[5]	8.4
All ages, crude	-	-	-	8.3	6.0	6.7	8.0	7.9	9.0	8.7	8.6
15-24 years	-	-	-	9.3	8.6	9.8	11.9	14.9	15.9	18.6	16.5
25-44 years	-	-	-	11.3	8.9	8.8	11.0	9.7	12.0	9.9	10.6
45-64 years	-	-	-	10.4	5.4	8.1	6.8	7.0	9.3	7.4	7.9
Hispanic male[4]											
All ages, age adjusted	-	-	-	-	[5]	24.1	26.8	29.8	30.5	29.6	29.9
All ages, crude	-	-	-	-	27.6	25.1	28.0	31.5	31.8	30.8	31.4
15-24 years	-	-	-	-	42.9	39.5	45.5	56.2	63.4	68.0	62.5
25-44 years	-	-	-	-	47.3	39.9	43.7	47.2	44.4	42.0	44.5
45-64 years	-	-	-	-	19.9	19.9	21.5	20.9	21.9	17.6	20.1

Source: "Death Rates for Motor Vehicle Crashes, According to Race and Age: United States, Selected Years 1950-92," *Health, United States, 1994*, pp. 132-34. Primary source: Centers for Disease Control and Prevention, National Center for Health Statistics: Vital Statistics of the United States, Vol. II, Mortality, Part A, for data years 1950-92. Public Health Service. Washington. U.S. Government Printing Office; Data computed by the Division of Health and Utilization Analysis from data compiled by the Division of Vital Statistics and from national population estimates for race groups from table 1 and State or U.S. aggregate population estimates for Hispanics provided by the Census Bureau. *Notes:* For data years shown, the code numbers for cause of death are based on the then current International Classification of Diseases, which are described in Appendix II, tables IV and V. Data for the 1980's are based on intercensal population estimates. See Appendix I, Department of Commerce. Age groups chosen to show data for American Indians, Asians, Hispanics, and non-Hispanic whites were selected to minimize the presentation of unstable age-specific death rates based on small numbers of deaths and for consistency among comparison groups. The race groups, white, black, Asian or Pacific Islander, and American Indian or Alaskan Native, include persons of Hispanic and non-Hispanic origin. Conversely, persons of Hispanic origin may be of any race. Consistency of race and Hispanic origin identification between the death certificate (source of data for numerator of death rates) and data from the Census Bureau (denominator) is high for individual white, black, and Hispanic persons; however, persons identified as American Indian or Asian in data from the Census Bureau are sometimes misreported as white on the death certificate, causing death rates to be underestimated by 22-30 percent for American Indians and by about 12 percent for Asians. (Sorlie PD, Rogot E, and Johnson NJ: Validity of demographic characteristics on the death certificate, *Epidemiology* 3(2): 181-184, 1992) 1. Includes deaths of nonresidents of the United States. 2. Interpretation of trends should take into account that population estimates for American Indians increased by 45 percent between 1980 and 1990, partly due to better enumeration techniques in the 1990 decennial census and to the increased tendency for people to identify themselves as American Indian in 1990. 3. Interpretation of trends should take into account that the Asian population in the United States more than doubled between 1980 and 1990, primarily due to immigration. 4. Excludes data from States lacking and Hispanic-origin item on their death certificates. See Appendix I. 5. Age-specific death rate based on fewer than 20 deaths. For age- adjusted death rates, 6 or more age-specific rates were based on fewer than 20 deaths.

Death Rates: Trends in Deaths by Homicide and Legal Intervention, 1950-92. Part 2

[Data are based on the National Vital Statistics System.]

Sex, Race, Hispanic origin, and age	1950[1]	1960[1]	1970	1980	1985	1988	1989	1990	1991	1992	1990-92
					Deaths per 100,000 resident population						
White female											
All ages, age adjusted	1.4	1.5	2.2	3.2	2.9	2.9	2.8	2.8	3.0	2.8	2.9
All ages, crude	1.4	1.4	2.1	3.2	2.9	2.9	2.8	2.8	3.0	2.8	2.9
Under 1 year	3.9	3.5	2.9	4.3	4.3	6.2	5.8	5.1	5.7	5.5	5.4
1-4 years	0.6	0.5	1.2	1.5	1.7	1.6	1.5	1.4	1.6	1.5	1.5
5-14 years	0.4	0.3	0.5	1.0	0.8	0.8	0.9	0.8	0.7	0.8	0.8
15-24 years	1.3	1.5	2.7	4.7	3.6	3.9	3.8	4.0	4.4	4.1	4.2
25-44 years	-	-	-	4.2	4.1	3.9	3.8	3.8	3.9	3.8	3.9
25-34 years	1.9	2.0	3.4	4.3	4.4	4.5	4.2	4.3	4.4	4.2	4.3
35-44 years	2.2	2.2	3.2	4.1	3.6	3.3	3.3	3.2	3.5	3.4	3.4
45-64 years	-	-	-	2.6	2.6	2.3	2.2	2.3	2.6	2.2	2.4
45-54 years	1.6	1.9	2.2	3.0	2.9	2.5	2.6	2.6	3.0	2.7	2.8
55-64 years	1.3	1.5	2.0	2.1	2.3	2.0	1.7	1.8	2.1	1.6	1.8
65-74 years	1.1	1.1	1.7	2.5	2.2	2.3	2.1	1.8	2.0	1.9	1.9
75-84 years	1.2	1.2	2.5	3.3	3.1	2.9	2.6	2.8	2.6	2.3	2.6
85 years and over	1.9	1.5	1.9	4.0	3.2	3.0	2.0	2.5	2.9	2.6	2.7
Black female											
All ages, age adjusted	11.7	11.8	15.0	13.7	10.9	12.8	12.7	13.0	13.9	13.0	13.3
All ages, crude	11.5	10.4	13.3	13.5	11.1	13.3	13.1	13.5	14.2	13.1	13.6
Under 1 year	-	13.8	10.7	12.8	10.7	23.7	23.6	22.8	24.6	17.8	21.8
1-4 years	-	5	6.3	6.4	6.3	6.3	7.3	7.2	7.3	7.4	7.3
5-14 years	1.2	1.0	2.0	2.2	2.0	3.2	3.0	3.6	2.8	3.4	3.3
15-24 years	16.5	11.9	17.7	18.4	14.2	17.5	17.4	18.9	21.6	19.4	19.9
25-44 years	-	-	-	22.3	17.8	21.0	19.7	20.9	21.5	20.7	21.1
25-34 years	26.6	24.9	25.6	25.8	20.0	25.8	23.5	25.3	26.4	25.7	25.8
35-44 years	17.8	20.5	25.1	17.7	14.7	14.4	14.6	15.6	15.7	14.9	15.4
45-64 years	-	-	-	10.8	7.9	7.6	8.5	6.5	8.3	6.9	7.2
45-54 years	8.5	12.7	17.5	12.5	9.2	8.0	8.7	7.3	9.5	8.0	8.2
55-64 years	3.6	6.8	8.1	8.9	6.5	7.1	8.4	5.6	6.7	5.5	5.9
65-74 years	3.4	3.3	7.7	8.6	7.3	9.3	8.4	6.8	6.5	6.3	6.5
75-84 years	-	5	5	6.7	7.4	9.5	9.5	11.3	12.5	9.4	11.1
85 years and over	-	5	5	5	5	13.4	16.3	19.2	5	5	12.1
American Indian or Alaskan Native female[2]											
All ages, age adjusted	-	-	-	5	5	5	5	5	5	5	5.2

[Continued]

★ 947 ★

Death Rates: Trends in Deaths by Homicide and Legal Intervention, 1950-92. Part 2
[Continued]

Sex, Race, Hispanic origin, and age	1950[1]	1960[1]	1970	1980	1985	1988	1989	1990	1991	1992	1990-92
All ages, crude	-	-	-	7.7	4.5	5.1	7.1	4.9	5.9	4.9	5.2
15-24 years	-	-	-	5	5	5	11.2	5	5	5	6.0
25-44 years	-	-	-	13.7	5	6.5	9.3	6.9	9.7	7.3	8.0
45-64 years	-	-	-	5	5	5	5	5	5	5	4.6
Asian or Pacific Islander female[3]											
All ages, age adjusted	-	-	-	5	5	5	5	5	5	5	3.0
All ages, crude	-	-	-	3.1	2.8	3.2	2.8	2.8	3.6	2.8	3.1
15-24 years	-	-	-	5	5	5	5	5	4.3	3.6	3.7
25-44 years	-	-	-	4.6	2.9	4.8	3.8	3.8	4.9	3.4	4.0
45-64 years	-	-	-	5	5	5	5	5	3.9	3.0	3.3
Hispanic female[4]											
All ages, age adjusted	-	-	-	-	5	5	5	4.6	4.8	4.6	4.7
All ages, crude	-	-	-	-	4.3	4.0	4.5	4.7	4.9	4.6	4.7
15-24 years	-	-	-	-	5.7	5.6	6.0	8.1	8.5	7.0	7.8
25-44 years	-	-	-	-	6.8	5.9	6.8	6.1	6.4	7.0	6.5
45-64 years	-	-	-	-	3.2	3.0	3.4	3.3	3.8	2.9	3.3

Source: "Death Rates for Motor Vehicle Crashes, According to Race and Age: United States, Selected Years 1950-92," *Health, United States, 1994,* pp. 132-34. Primary source: Centers for Disease Control and Prevention, National Center for Health Statistics: Vital Statistics of the United States, Vol. II, Mortality, Part A, for data years 1950-92. Public Health Service. Washington. U.S. Government Printing Office; Data computed by the Division of Health and Utilization Analysis from data compiled by the Division of Vital Statistics and from national population estimates for race groups from table 1 and State or U.S. aggregate population estimates for Hispanics provided by the Census Bureau. *Notes:* For data years shown, the code numbers for cause of death are based on the then current International Classification of Diseases, which are described in Appendix II, tables IV and V. Data for the 1980's are based on intercensal population estimates. See Appendix I, Department of Commerce. Age groups chosen to show data for American Indians, Asians, Hispanics, and non-Hispanic whites were selected to minimize the presentation of unstable age-specific death rates based on small numbers of deaths and for consistency among comparison groups. The race groups, white, black, Asian or Pacific Islander, and American Indian or Alaskan Native, include persons of Hispanic and non-Hispanic origin. Conversely, persons of Hispanic origin may be of any race. Consistency of race and Hispanic origin identification between the death certificate (source of data for numerator of death rates) and data from the Census Bureau (denominator) is high for individual white, black, and Hispanic persons; however, persons identified as American Indian or Asian in data from the Census Bureau are sometimes misreported as white on the death certificate, causing death rates to be underestimated by 22-30 percent for American Indians and by about 12 percent for Asians. (Sorlie PD, Rogot E, and Johnson NJ: Validity of demographic characteristics on the death certificate, *Epidemology* 3(2): 181-184, 1992) 1. Includes deaths of nonresidents of the United States. 2. Interpretation of trends should take into account that population estimates for American Indians increased by 45 percent between 1980 and 1990, partly due to better enumeration techniques in the 1990 decennial census and to the increased tendency for people to identify themselves as American Indian in 1990. 3. Interpretation of trends should take into account that the Asian population in the United States more than doubled between 1980 and 1990, primarily due to immigration. 4. Excludes data from States lacking and Hispanic-origin item on their death certificates. See Appendix I. 5. Age-specific death rate based on fewer than 20 deaths. For age- adjusted death rates, 6 or more age-specific rates were based on fewer than 20 deaths.

★ 948 ★

Death Rates

Death Rates: Trends in Deaths by Malignant Neoplasms, 1950-1992. Part 1

[Data are based on the National Vital Statistics System.]

Sex, Race, Hispanic origin, and age	1950[1]	1960[1]	1970	1980	1985	1988	1989	1990	1991	1992	1990-92
					Deaths per 100,000 resident population						
White male											
All ages, age adjusted	130.9	141.6	154.3	160.5	160.4	159.6	159.4	160.3	159.5	157.3	159.0
All ages, crude	147.2	166.1	185.1	208.7	218.1	222.8	224.9	227.7	228.9	228.6	228.4
Under 1 year	9.6	7.9	4.3	3.5	3.1	2.4	2.9	2.2	1.9	2.7	2.3
1-14 years	13.1	13.1	8.5	5.4	4.4	4.0	3.9	3.7	3.6	3.3	3.5
5-14 years	7.6	8.0	7.0	5.2	4.0	3.8	3.7	3.5	3.7	3.5	3.6
15-24 years	9.9	10.3	10.6	7.8	6.4	5.8	5.5	5.7	6.0	6.0	5.9
25-34 years	17.7	18.8	16.2	13.6	13.1	11.7	11.6	12.3	12.0	11.9	12.1
35-44 years	44.5	46.3	50.1	41.1	39.8	37.2	35.9	35.8	36.3	35.6	35.9
45-54 years	150.8	164.1	172.0	175.4	162.0	154.6	151.0	149.9	146.7	142.8	146.3
55-64 years	409.4	450.9	498.1	497.4	512.0	514.1	511.8	508.2	505.0	490.8	501.4
65-74 years	798.7	887.3	997.0	1,070.7	1,076.5	1,075.5	1,083.3	1,090.7	1,091.5	1,082.7	1,088.3
75-84 years	1,367.6	1,413.7	1,592.7	1,779.7	1,817.1	1,838.6	1,853.6	1,883.2	1,866.4	1,854.3	1,867.6
85 years and over	1,732.7	1,791.4	1,772.2	2,375.6	2,449.1	2,560.7	2,603.7	2,715.1	2,733.0	2,783.6	2,744.7
Black male											
All ages, age adjusted	12.61	158.5	198.0	229.9	239.9	240.4	246.2	248.1	242.4	238.1	242.8
All ages, crude	106.6	136.7	171.6	205.5	214.9	215.7	220.6	221.9	217.5	214.4	217.9
Under 1 year	-	5	5	5	5	5	5	5	5	5	2.6
1-14 years	-	7.9	7.6	5.1	3.4	3.4	3.0	3.6	4.7	2.2	3.5
5-14 years	5.8	4.4	4.8	3.7	3.7	3.2	3.4	3.4	3.0	2.9	3.1
15-24 years	7.9	9.7	9.4	8.1	6.4	6.2	6.9	6.1	5.4	5.7	5.7
25-34 years	18.0	18.4	18.8	14.1	14.9	14.2	15.2	15.7	15.3	15.1	15.4
35-44 years	55.7	72.9	81.3	73.8	69.9	66.0	63.0	64.3	63.4	62.3	63.3
45-54 years	211.7	244.7	311.2	333.0	315.9	305.7	308.0	302.6	297.1	279.2	292.7
55-64 years	490.8	579.7	689.2	812.5	851.3	821.0	840.5	859.2	811.9	808.9	826.5
65-74 years	636.4	938.5	1,168.9	1,417.2	1,532.8	1,572.8	1,621.3	1,613.9	1,587.2	1,570.1	1,590.0
75-84 years	-	1,053.3	1,624.8	2,029.6	2,229.6	2,353.1	2,436.7	2,478.3	2,500.7	2,442.2	2,473.6
85 years and over	-	1,155.2	1,387.0	2,393.9	2,629.0	2,929.2	3,040.9	3,238.3	3,233.3	3,292.9	3,255.2
American Indian or Alaskan Native male[2]											
All ages, age adjusted	-	-	-	5	87.1	85.9	97.7	83.5	98.0	94.0	92.1
All ages, crude	-	-	-	58.1	62.8	62.4	71.2	61.4	72.7	71.4	68.6
25-34 years	-	-	-	5	5	5	11.4	5	5	5	6.2
35-44 years	-	-	-	5	28.8	21.3	25.2	22.8	15.8	20.6	19.7
45-54 years	-	-	-	86.9	89.4	97.4	74.7	86.9	94.4	92.4	91.1
55-64 years	-	-	-	213.4	276.6	275.0	311.3	246.2	303.5	316.6	289.4
65-74 years	-	-	-	613.0	584.6	620.0	683.9	530.6	685.3	628.9	618.8
75-84 years	-	-	-	936.4	963.6	830.8	1,107.7	1,038.4	1,214.3	1,033.1	1,095.2
85 years and over	-	-	-	1,471.2	1,133.3	1,333.3	1,833.3	1,654.4	1,275.0	1,419.9	1,463.6
Asian or Pacific Islander male[3]											
All ages, age adjusted	-	-	-	96.4	101.0	97.0	98.2	99.6	92.9	97.7	96.7
All ages, crude	-	-	-	81.9	82.6	80.2	80.7	82.7	78.8	84.0	81.9
25-34 years	-	-	-	6.3	10.0	9.5	9.5	9.2	7.7	7.6	8.2

[Continued]

★ 948 ★

Death Rates: Trends in Deaths by Malignant Neoplasms, 1950-1992. Part 1

[Continued]

Sex, Race, Hispanic origin, and age	1950[1]	1960[1]	1970	1980	1985	1988	1989	1990	1991	1992	1990-92
35-44 years	-	-	-	29.4	25.7	29.0	30.0	27.7	28.2	25.3	27.0
45-54 years	-	-	-	108.2	98.0	95.4	92.7	92.6	89.9	90.7	91.0
55-64 years	-	-	-	298.5	315.0	300.5	305.1	274.6	256.6	284.6	272.3
65-74 years	-	-	-	581.2	631.3	601.7	647.2	687.2	624.8	648.1	652.0
75-84 years	-	-	-	1,147.6	1,251.2	1,192.2	1,140.0	1,229.9	1,139.7	1,214.0	1,195.2
85 years and over	-	-	-	1,798.7	1,800.0	1,736.4	1,745.5	1,837.0	1,884.6	1,893.3	1,879.5
Hispanic male[4]											
All ages, age adjusted	-	-	-	-	92.1	90.8	101.1	99.8	97.7	95.1	97.4
All ages, crude	-	-	-	-	56.1	55.1	66.8	65.5	65.7	64.9	65.4
25-34 years	-	-	-	-	9.7	7.6	9.1	8.0	8.4	9.7	8.7
35-44 years	-	-	-	-	23.0	23.9	25.3	22.5	25.9	23.5	24.0
45-54 years	-	-	-	-	83.4	87.2	89.7	96.6	86.9	78.3	86.8
55-64 years	-	-	-	-	259.0	271.5	299.3	294.0	291.3	276.9	287.2
65-74 years	-	-	-	-	599.1	579.0	662.9	655.5	643.2	657.1	652.0
75-84 years	-	-	-	-	1,216.6	1,147.9	1,292.9	1,233.4	1,217.4	1,171.8	1,206.4
85 years and over	-	-	-	-	1,700.7	1,730.7	1,848.8	2,019.4	1,814.7	1,765.2	1,858.1

Source: "Death Rates for Malignant Neoplasms, According to Sex, Detailed Race, Hispanic Origin, and Age: United States, Selected Years 1950-92," *Health, United States, 1994,* pp. 119-21. Primary source: Centers for Disease Control and Prevention, National Center for Health Statistics: Vital Statistics of the United States, Vol. II, Mortality, Part A, for data years 1950-92. Public Health Service. Washington. U.S. Government Printing Office; Data computed by the Division of Health and Utilization Analysis from data compiled by the Division of Vital Statistics and from national population estimates for race groups from table 1 and State or U.S. aggregate population estimates for Hispanics provided by the Census Bureau. *Notes:* For data years shown, the code numbers for cause of death are based on the then current International Classification of Diseases, which are described in Appendix II, tables IV and V. Data for the 1980's are based on intercensal population estimates. See Appendix I, Department of Commerce. Age groups chosen to show data for American Indians, Asians, Hispanics, and non-Hispanic whites were selected to minimize the presentation of unstable age-specific death rates based on small numbers of deaths and for consistency among comparison groups. The race groups, white, black, Asian or Pacific Islander, and American Indian or Alaskan Native, include persons of Hispanic and non-Hispanic origin. Conversely, persons of Hispanic origin may be of any race. Consistency of race and Hispanic origin identification between the death certificate (source of data for numerator of death rates) and data from the Census Bureau (denominator) is high for individual white, black, and Hispanic persons; however, persons identified as American Indian or Asian in data from the Census Bureau are sometimes misreported as white on the death certificate, causing death rates to be underestimated by 22-30 percent for American Indians and by about 12 percent for Asians. (Sorlie PD, Rogot E, and Johnson NJ: Validity of demographic characteristics on the death certificate, *Epidemiology* 3(2): 181-184, 1992) 1. Includes deaths of nonresidents of the United States. 2. Interpretation of trends should take into account that population estimates for American Indians increased by 45 percent between 1980 and 1990, partly due to better enumeration techniques in the 1990 decennial census and to the increased tendency for people to identify themselves as American Indian in 1990. 3. Interpretation of trends should take into account that the Asian population in the United States more than doubled between 1980 and 1990, primarily due to immigration. 4. Excludes data from States lacking and Hispanic-origin item on their death certificates. See Appendix I. 5. Age-specific death rate based on fewer than 20 deaths. For age-adjusted death rates, 6 or more age-specific rates were based on fewer than 20 deaths.

★ 949 ★

Death Rates

Death Rates: Trends in Deaths by Malignant Neoplasms, 1950-1992. Part 2

[Data are based on the National Vital Statistics System.]

Sex, Race, Hispanic origin, and age	1950[1]	1960[1]	1970	1980	1985	1988	1989	1990	1991	1992	1990-92
	Deaths per 100,000 resident population										
White female											
All ages, age adjusted	119.4	109.5	107.6	107.7	110.5	110.4	111.1	111.2	111.2	110.3	110.9
All ages, crude	139.9	139.8	149.4	170.3	184.4	190.5	194.2	196.1	198.0	199.0	197.7
Under 1 year	7.8	6.8	5.4	2.7	3.1	2.3	3.2	2.2	1.8	2.4	2.1
1-14 years	11.3	9.7	6.9	3.6	3.5	3.7	3.0	3.2	3.3	3.0	3.2

[Continued]

★ 949 ★

Death Rates: Trends in Deaths by Malignant Neoplasms, 1950-1992. Part 2

[Continued]

Sex, Race, Hispanic origin, and age	1950[1]	1960[1]	1970	1980	1985	1988	1989	1990	1991	1992	1990-92
5-14 years	6.3	6.2	5.4	3.7	3.1	2.7	3.0	2.9	2.7	2.7	2.7
15-24 years	7.5	6.5	6.2	4.7	4.3	4.1	4.2	4.0	4.0	4.1	4.0
25-34 years	20.9	18.8	16.3	13.5	12.7	11.7	12.2	11.9	12.2	12.2	12.1
35-44 years	74.5	66.6	62.4	50.9	47.3	46.6	46.0	46.2	44.7	43.9	44.9
45-54 years	185.8	175.7	177.3	166.4	161.6	152.8	149.9	150.9	147.5	142.1	146.7
55-64 years	362.5	329.0	338.6	355.5	376.3	376.1	375.0	368.5	374.7	364.0	369.1
65-74 years	616.5	562.1	554.7	605.2	644.9	660.0	671.2	675.1	673.8	684.5	677.8
75-84 years	1,026.6	939.3	903.5	905.4	938.2	967.4	995.5	1,011.8	1,018.7	1,029.0	1,020.0
85 years and over	1,348.3	1,304.9	1,126.6	1,266.8	1,285.4	1,323.2	1,348.3	1,372.3	1,391.7	1,390.9	1,385.2
Black female											
All ages, age adjusted	131.9	127.8	123.5	129.7	131.8	133.5	133.5	137.2	136.3	136.6	136.7
All ages, crude	111.8	113.8	117.3	136.5	145.2	150.9	151.8	156.1	157.4	157.6	157.1
Under 1 year	-	5	5	5	5	5	5	5	5	5	5
1-14 years	-	6.9	5.7	3.9	2.5	3.8	3.7	3.4	3.2	2.9	3.2
5-14 years	3.9	4.8	4.0	3.4	3.0	2.9	2.9	2.4	2.6	2.8	2.6
15-24 years	8.8	6.9	6.4	5.7	4.4	4.9	4.9	4.8	5.2	4.6	4.9
25-34 years	34.3	31.0	20.9	18.3	17.2	17.8	16.1	18.7	16.2	17.8	17.5
35-44 years	119.8	102.4	94.6	73.5	69.0	70.5	66.7	67.4	69.2	69.8	68.8
45-54 years	277.0	254.8	228.6	230.2	212.4	202.9	205.3	209.9	199.9	204.5	204.7
55-64 years	484.6	442.7	404.8	450.4	474.9	468.9	459.1	482.4	464.9	466.4	471.2
65-74 years	477.3	541.6	615.8	662.4	704.2	746.9	769.4	773.2	786.3	790.0	783.3
75-84 years	-	696.3	763.3	923.9	986.3	1,017.7	1,029.8	1,059.9	1,118.5	1,068.7	1,082.4
85 years and over	-	728.9	791.5	1,159.9	1,284.2	1,365.8	1,383.0	1,431.3	1,500.0	1,502.0	1,478.6
American Indian or Alaskan Native female[2]											
All ages, age adjusted	-	-	-	62.1	60.5	64.5	68.3	69.6	71.0	71.5	70.7
All ages, crude	-	-	-	50.4	52.5	57.4	60.6	62.1	64.7	66.0	64.3
25-34 years	-	-	-	5	5	5	5	5	5	5	5
35-44 years	-	-	-	36.9	23.4	21.3	23.1	31.0	23.4	30.2	28.1
45-54 years	-	-	-	96.9	90.1	92.7	94.3	104.5	106.3	87.8	99.0
55-64 years	-	-	-	198.4	192.3	219.0	210.0	213.3	234.9	237.8	228.6
65-74 years	-	-	-	350.8	378.8	394.7	446.2	438.9	442.9	475.0	453.2
75-84 years	-	-	-	446.4	505.9	563.2	645.0	554.3	622.7	617.9	600.0
85 years and over	-	-	-	786.5	700.0	783.3	666.7	843.7	928.6	700.8	804.8
Asian or Pacific Islander female[3]											
All ages, age adjusted	-	-	-	59.8	62.8	65.8	64.5	63.6	65.9	64.5	64.7
All ages, crude	-	-	-	54.1	57.5	61.6	61.4	60.5	64.4	64.2	63.1
25-34 years	-	-	-	9.5	9.9	7.4	8.4	7.3	9.2	10.7	9.1
35-44 years	-	-	-	38.7	33.1	28.1	32.6	29.8	35.6	28.4	31.3
45-54 years	-	-	-	99.8	91.3	103.7	88.8	93.9	91.6	93.2	92.9
55-64 years	-	-	-	174.7	195.5	216.7	187.4	196.2	211.4	205.1	204.3
65-74 years	-	-	-	301.9	330.8	329.3	361.8	346.2	348.1	347.4	347.5
75-84 years	-	-	-	522.1	589.1	638.6	645.9	641.4	620.5	607.0	620.7
85 years and over	-	-	-	800.0	908.3	1,033.3	1,125.0	971.7	1,042.1	1,099.2	1,054.5
Hispanic female[4]											
All ages, age adjusted	-	-	-	-	64.1	63.1	69.8	70.0	68.8	68.3	69.0

[Continued]

★ 949 ★

Death Rates: Trends in Deaths by Malignant Neoplasms, 1950-1992. Part 2

[Continued]

Sex, Race, Hispanic origin, and age	1950[1]	1960[1]	1970	1980	1985	1988	1989	1990	1991	1992	1990-92
All ages, crude	-	-	-	-	49.8	50.2	60.5	60.7	60.4	60.9	60.7
25-34 years	-	-	-	-	9.7	8.1	10.3	9.7	9.1	9.8	9.6
35-44 years	-	-	-	-	30.9	31.6	31.9	34.8	31.3	34.0	33.4
45-54 years	-	-	-	-	90.1	88.0	93.1	100.5	95.6	91.4	95.6
55-64 years	-	-	-	-	199.4	197.4	212.4	205.4	218.9	218.5	214.5
65-74 years	-	-	-	-	356.3	355.4	407.7	404.8	392.3	382.8	392.9
75-84 years	-	-	-	-	599.7	602.1	674.5	663.0	630.0	630.7	640.6
85 years and over	-	-	-	-	906.1	868.4	1,037.9	1,022.7	991.7	949.8	985.4

Source: "Death Rates for Malignant Neoplasms, According to Sex, Detailed Race, Hispanic Origin, and Age: United States, Selected Years 1950-92," *Health, United States, 1994,* pp. 119-21. Primary source: Centers for Disease Control and Prevention, National Center for Health Statistics: Vital Statistics of the United States, Vol. II, Mortality, Part A, for data years 1950-92. Public Health Service. Washington. U.S. Government Printing Office; Data computed by the Division of Health and Utilization Analysis from data compiled by the Division of Vital Statistics and from national population estimates for race groups from table 1 and State or U.S. aggregate population estimates for Hispanics provided by the Census Bureau. *Notes:* For data years shown, the code numbers for cause of death are based on the then current International Classification of Diseases, which are described in Appendix II, tables IV and V. Data for the 1980's are based on intercensal population estimates. See Appendix I, Department of Commerce. Age groups chosen to show data for American Indians, Asians, Hispanics, and non-Hispanic whites were selected to minimize the presentation of unstable age-specific death rates based on small numbers of deaths and for consistency among comparison groups. The race groups, white, black, Asian or Pacific Islander, and American Indian or Alaskan Native, include persons of Hispanic and non-Hispanic origin. Conversely, persons of Hispanic origin may be of any race. Consistency of race and Hispanic origin identification between the death certificate (source of data for numerator of death rates) and data from the Census Bureau (denominator) is high for individual white, black, and Hispanic persons; however, persons identified as American Indian or Asian in data from the Census Bureau are sometimes misreported as white on the death certificate, causing death rates to be underestimated by 22-30 percent for American Indians and by about 12 percent for Asians. (Sorlie PD, Rogot E, and Johnson NJ: Validity of demographic characteristics on the death certificate, *Epidemiology* 3(2): 181-184, 1992) 1. Includes deaths of nonresidents of the United States. 2. Interpretation of trends should take into account that population estimates for American Indians increased by 45 percent between 1980 and 1990, partly due to better enumeration techniques in the 1990 decennial census and to the increased tendency for people to identify themselves as American Indian in 1990. 3. Interpretation of trends should take into account that the Asian population in the United States more than doubled between 1980 and 1990, primarily due to immigration. 4. Excludes data from States lacking and Hispanic-origin item on their death certificates. See Appendix I. 5. Age-specific death rate based on fewer than 20 deaths. For age-adjusted death rates, 6 or more age-specific rates were based on fewer than 20 deaths.

★ 950 ★

Death Rates

Death Rates: Trends in Deaths by Motor Vehicle Accidents, 1950-1992. Part 1

[Data are based on the National Vital Statistics System.]

Sex, Race, Hispanic origin, and age	1950[1]	1960[1]	1970	1980	1985	1988	1989	1990	1991	1992	1990-92
	Deaths per 100,000 resident population										
White male											
All ages, age adjusted	35.9	34.0	40.1	34.8	27.6	28.4	26.7	26.3	24.2	22.2	24.2
All ages, crude	35.1	31.5	39.1	35.9	28.3	28.9	27.2	26.7	24.4	22.4	24.5
Under 1 year	9.1	8.8	9.1	7.0	4.6	6.0	5.1	4.8	4.1	4.2	4.4
1-14 years	-	-	-	9.8	8.3	8.2	7.6	6.6	6.5	6.2	6.4
1-4 years	13.2	11.3	12.2	9.5	7.7	7.0	6.9	6.1	5.8	6.0	6.0
5-14 years	12.0	10.3	12.6	9.8	8.6	8.8	7.9	6.8	6.8	6.3	6.6
15-24 years	58.3	62.7	75.2	73.8	56.5	58.6	52.5	52.5	48.3	42.3	47.8
25-34 years	39.1	38.6	47.0	46.6	35.8	36.7	35.4	35.4	31.7	29.1	32.1
35-44 years	30.9	28.4	35.2	30.7	24.3	24.8	23.9	23.7	21.2	20.3	21.7
45-64 years	-	-	-	25.2	20.8	21.2	21.1	20.6	19.0	17.7	19.1
45-54 years	31.6	29.7	34.6	26.3	21.0	21.7	20.9	20.7	19.1	17.9	19.2

[Continued]

★ 950 ★

Death Rates: Trends in Deaths by Motor Vehicle Accidents, 1950-1992. Part 1

[Continued]

Sex, Race, Hispanic origin, and age	1950[1]	1960[1]	1970	1980	1985	1988	1989	1990	1991	1992	1990-92
55-64 years	41.9	34.4	39.0	23.9	20.7	20.7	21.2	20.6	18.9	17.4	19.0
65 years and over	-	-	-	32.7	29.9	32.7	32.5	31.4	30.5	30.0	30.7
65-74 years	59.1	45.5	46.2	25.8	22.0	24.8	24.2	23.5	21.9	22.2	22.5
75-84 years	86.4	66.8	69.2	43.6	41.2	43.4	43.1	41.1	41.4	39.7	40.7
85 years and over	79.3	61.9	65.5	57.3	57.0	59.9	62.9	65.3	59.9	57.0	60.6
Black male											
All ages, age adjusted	39.8	38.2	50.1	32.9	28.0	30.1	29.8	28.9	26.2	25.0	26.7
All ages, crude	37.2	33.1	44.3	31.1	27.1	29.4	28.9	28.1	25.6	24.0	25.9
Under 1 year	-	5	10.6	7.8	5	7.7	7.6	5	5	5	5.3
1-14 years	-	-	-	11.4	9.7	9.7	9.0	8.9	8.6	7.8	8.4
1-4 years	-	12.7	16.9	13.7	10.9	9.3	9.0	10.1	8.9	6.8	8.6
5-14 years	9.7	10.4	16.1	10.5	9.2	9.8	9.0	8.4	8.5	8.2	8.4
15-24 years	41.6	46.4	58.1	34.9	32.0	37.8	36.4	36.1	35.0	32.4	34.5
25-34 years	57.4	51.0	70.4	44.9	37.7	39.1	38.6	39.5	35.0	30.4	34.9
35-44 years	45.9	43.6	59.5	41.2	34.7	36.2	36.4	33.5	30.9	28.0	30.7
45-64 years	-	-	-	39.5	32.9	32.8	35.9	33.3	27.4	30.3	30.3
45-54 years	49.9	48.1	61.4	39.1	30.1	32.6	36.2	34.1	27.0	30.0	30.3
55-64 years	58.8	47.3	62.1	40.3	36.3	33.1	35.4	32.5	27.9	30.8	30.4
65 years and over	-	-	-	42.4	35.2	44.0	37.9	36.3	35.4	34.8	35.6
65-74 years	48.5	46.1	54.9	41.8	31.7	40.5	33.3	33.2	31.5	31.9	32.2
75-84 years	-	51.8	51.6	46.5	42.0	45.4	44.4	40.8	37.9	40.9	39.9
85 years and over	-	5	45.7	5	38.7	70.8	53.0	48.3	60.9	37.3	48.8
American Indian or Alaskan Native male[2]											
All ages, age adjusted	-	-	-	5	52.3	5	5	5	48.2	5	47.5
All ages, crude	-	-	-	74.6	51.7	51.7	48.3	47.6	45.7	43.5	45.6
1-14 years	-	-	-	15.1	16.2	9.9	12.3	11.6	9.8	10.4	10.6
15-24 years	-	-	-	126.1	77.3	88.4	77.4	75.2	63.4	63.0	67.2
25-34 years	-	-	-	107.0	84.0	77.7	75.6	78.2	76.1	66.0	73.5
35-44 years	-	-	-	82.8	55.8	57.5	54.1	57.0	52.7	55.8	55.1
45-64 years	-	-	-	77.4	52.2	43.8	46.3	45.9	53.4	48.7	49.3
65 years and over	-	-	-	97.0	5	76.1	50.0	43.0	57.7	46.5	49.4
Asian or Pacific Islander male[3]											
All ages, age adjusted	-	-	-	5	16.2	15.0	13.4	15.8	12.9	12.5	13.7
All ages, crude	-	-	-	17.1	16.0	14.8	13.3	15.8	12.8	12.2	13.5
1-14 years	-	-	-	8.2	5.2	4.5	4.8	6.3	5.1	4.6	5.3

[Continued]

★ 950 ★

Death Rates: Trends in Deaths by Motor Vehicle Accidents, 1950-1992. Part 1
[Continued]

Sex, Race, Hispanic origin, and age	1950[1]	1960[1]	1970	1980	1985	1988	1989	1990	1991	1992	1990-92
15-24 years	-	-	-	27.2	28.1	26.2	20.8	25.7	18.7	20.2	21.5
25-34 years	-	-	-	18.8	18.4	16.5	14.7	17.0	16.2	13.8	15.6
35-44 years	-	-	-	13.1	12.0	11.0	11.1	12.2	10.3	8.7	10.4
45-64 years	-	-	-	13.7	13.4	13.8	13.7	15.1	11.3	12.1	12.8
65 years and over	-	-	-	37.3	37.3	33.0	25.9	33.6	29.0	28.1	30.1
Hispanic male[4]											
All ages, age adjusted	-	-	-	-	25.3	28.1	29.9	29.1	25.9	24.1	26.3
All ages, crude	-	-	-	-	25.6	27.9	29.8	29.2	25.7	23.7	26.1
1-14 years	-	-	-	-	7.7	7.8	7.8	7.2	6.9	6.7	6.9
15-24 years	-	-	-	-	44.9	45.8	49.2	48.2	44.4	41.6	44.8
25-34 years	-	-	-	-	31.2	36.6	39.2	41.0	33.7	30.8	35.0
35-44 years	-	-	-	-	26.3	28.4	30.5	28.0	24.5	25.3	25.9
45-64 years	-	-	-	-	25.9	26.0	28.5	28.9	25.8	23.0	25.8
65 years and over	-	-	-	-	22.9	39.9	42.0	35.3	32.1	26.9	31.2

Source: "Death Rates for Motor Vehicle Crashes, According to Race and Age: United States, Selected Years 1950-92," *Health, United States, 1994,* pp. 129-31. Primary source: Centers for Disease Control and Prevention, National Center for Health Statistics: Vital Statistics of the United States, Vol. II, Mortality, Part A, for data years 1950-92. Public Health Service. Washington. U.S. Government Printing Office; Data computed by the Division of Health and Utilization Analysis from data compiled by the Division of Vital Statistics and from national population estimates for race groups from table 1 and State or U.S. aggregate population estimates for Hispanics provided by the Census Bureau. *Notes:* For data years shown, the code numbers for cause of death are based on the then current International Classification of Diseases, which are described in Appendix II, tables IV and V. Data for the 1980's are based on intercensal population estimates. See Appendix I, Department of Commerce. Age groups chosen to show data for American Indians, Asians, Hispanics, and non-Hispanic whites were selected to minimize the presentation of unstable age-specific death rates based on small numbers of deaths and for consistency among comparison groups. The race groups, white, black, Asian or Pacific Islander, and American Indian or Alaskan Native, include persons of Hispanic and non-Hispanic origin. Persons of Hispanic origin may be of any race. Consistency of race and Hispanic origin identification between the death certificate (source of data for numerator of death rates) and data from the Census Bureau (denominator) is high for individual white, black, and Hispanic persons; however, persons identified as American Indian or Asian in data from the Census Bureau are sometimes misreported as white on the death certificate, causing death rates to be underestimated by 22-30 percent for American Indians and by about 12 percent for Asians. (Sorlie PD, Rogot E, and Johnson NJ: Validity of demographic characteristics on the death certificate, *Epidemiology* 3(2): 181-184, 1992) 1. Includes deaths of nonresidents of the United States. 2. Interpretation of trends should take into account that population estimates for American Indians increased by 45 percent between 1980 and 1990, partly due to better enumeration techniques in the 1990 decennial census and to the increased tendency for people to identify themselves as American Indian in 1990. 3. Interpretation of trends should take into account that the Asian population in the United States more than doubled between 1980 and 1990, primarily due to immigration. 4. Excludes data from States lacking and Hispanic-origin item on their death certificates. See Appendix I. 5. Age-specific death rate based on fewer than 20 deaths. For age-adjusted death rates, 6 or more age-specific rates were based on fewer than 20 deaths.

★ 951 ★

Death Rates

Death Rates: Trends in Deaths by Motor Vehicle Accidents, 1950-1992. Part 2

[Data are based on the National Vital Statistics System.]

Sex, Race, Hispanic origin, and age	1950[1]	1960[1]	1970	1980	1985	1988	1989	1990	1991	1992	1990-92
	Deaths per 100,000 resident population										
White female											
All ages, age adjusted	10.6	11.1	14.4	12.3	10.8	11.6	11.6	11.0	10.4	9.6	10.3
All ages, crude	10.9	11.2	14.8	12.8	11.4	12.2	12.1	11.6	10.8	10.2	10.9
Under 1 year	7.8	7.5	10.2	7.1	3.9	5.5	4.9	4.7	3.6	2.9	3.7
1-14 years	-	-	-	6.2	5.4	5.5	5.4	4.8	4.5	3.8	4.4
1-4 years	10.1	8.3	9.6	7.7	5.8	6.2	6.1	5.2	5.5	4.1	4.9
5-14 years	5.6	5.3	6.9	5.7	5.2	5.2	5.1	4.7	4.1	3.7	4.2
15-24 years	12.6	15.6	22.7	23.0	20.0	21.6	21.1	19.5	19.6	17.7	19.0
25-34 years	9.0	9.0	12.7	12.2	10.1	11.8	12.1	11.6	10.6	9.8	10.7
35-44 years	8.1	8.9	12.3	10.6	9.4	9.2	9.6	9.2	8.4	8.1	8.5
45-64 years	-	-	-	10.4	9.5	10.1	9.9	9.9	8.7	8.5	9.0
45-54 years	10.8	11.4	14.3	10.2	9.0	9.6	9.6	9.4	8.5	8.1	8.7
55-64 years	15.0	15.3	16.1	10.5	9.9	10.6	10.2	10.5	9.1	8.9	9.5
65 years and over	-	-	-	15.3	16.2	17.6	17.9	17.4	16.7	16.5	16.9
65-74 years	20.9	19.3	22.1	13.4	14.3	14.5	15.3	14.0	13.4	13.4	13.6
75-84 years	25.4	23.8	28.1	19.0	19.7	22.4	22.0	22.4	21.6	20.8	21.6
85 years and over	22.3	22.2	18.1	15.3	15.3	18.0	17.7	19.1	17.7	17.3	18.0
Black female											
All ages, age adjusted	10.3	10.0	13.8	8.4	8.2	9.4	9.3	9.3	8.7	8.7	8.9
All ages, crude	10.2	9.7	13.4	8.3	8.3	9.5	9.4	9.4	8.7	8.8	9.0
Under 1 year	-	8.1	11.9	5	8.1	5	7.8	7.0	7.2	8.8	7.5
1-14 years	-	-	-	6.3	5.1	6.3	5.2	5.3	5.0	5.8	5.4
1-4 years	-	8.8	12.6	9.5	6.8	7.5	6.3	7.7	6.4	8.7	7.6
5-14 years	6.2	5.9	9.3	5.2	4.4	5.7	4.7	4.3	4.4	4.5	4.4
15-24 years	11.5	9.9	13.4	8.0	9.1	10.8	10.2	9.9	10.0	9.5	9.8
25-34 years	10.7	9.8	13.3	10.6	9.3	11.3	12.1	11.1	10.4	9.6	10.4
35-44 years	11.1	11.0	16.1	8.3	9.1	10.0	10.3	9.4	9.2	9.8	9.5
45-64 years	-	-	-	9.2	9.0	9.6	9.3	10.7	9.4	9.5	9.9
45-54 years	10.6	11.8	16.4	9.1	8.3	9.2	8.7	9.6	9.0	8.5	9.0
55-64 years	14.0	14.0	17.0	9.3	9.7	10.1	10.0	12.2	9.9	10.9	11.0
65 years and over	-	-	-	9.5	11.2	11.2	12.3	13.5	11.4	10.5	11.8
65-74 years	12.7	14.2	16.3	8.5	9.7	9.8	12.9	13.7	10.9	10.0	11.5
75-84 years	-	5	14.4	11.1	14.6	13.5	13.0	15.0	12.3	12.5	13.2
85 years and over	-	5	5	5	5	5	5	5	5	5	9.0
American Indian or Alaskan Native female[2]											
All ages, age adjusted	-	-	-	5	5	5	5	5	5	5	18.6

[Continued]

★ 951 ★

Death Rates: Trends in Deaths by Motor Vehicle Accidents, 1950-1992. Part 2

[Continued]

Sex, Race, Hispanic origin, and age	1950[1]	1960[1]	1970	1980	1985	1988	1989	1990	1991	1992	1990-92
All ages, crude	-	-	-	32.0	20.6	20.2	19.4	17.3	18.4	17.9	17.9
1-14 years	-	-	-	15.0	9.2	12.1	9.5	8.1	5.4	7.0	6.8
15-24 years	-	-	-	42.3	29.5	33.3	27.5	31.4	32.0	28.3	30.5
25-34 years	-	-	-	52.5	30.2	26.5	25.7	18.8	27.2	21.7	22.6
35-44 years	-	-	-	38.1	27.0	19.1	23.8	18.2	22.7	16.3	19.0
45-64 years	-	-	-	32.6	19.5	16.4	22.4	17.6	17.1	26.1	20.4
65 years and over	-	-	-	5	5	5	5	5	5	5	16.5
Asian or Pacific Islander female[3]											
All ages, age adjusted	-	-	-	5	5	8.7	8.5	9.2	7.1	7.5	7.9
All ages, crude	-	-	-	8.2	7.9	8.4	8.5	9.0	7.0	7.4	7.8
1-14 years	-	-	-	7.4	5.0	4.5	5.8	3.6	5	2.3	2.6
15-24 years	-	-	-	7.4	7.4	12.2	9.8	11.4	9.6	9.4	10.1
25-34 years	-	-	-	7.3	8.4	5.9	6.4	7.3	5.0	6.8	6.4
35-44 years	-	-	-	8.6	7.0	8.1	8.4	7.5	6.5	6.5	6.8
45-64 years	-	-	-	8.5	8.6	9.6	8.5	11.8	10.0	9.5	10.4
65 years and over	-	-	-	18.6	20.5	20.5	21.8	24.3	17.0	20.1	20.3
Hispanic female[4]											
All ages, age adjusted	-	-	-	-	8.3	8.5	9.5	9.2	9.0	8.1	8.8
All ages, crude	-	-	-	-	7.9	8.2	9.4	8.9	8.9	7.9	8.6
1-14 years	-	-	-	-	4.8	4.5	5.5	4.8	5.9	3.8	4.8
15-24 years	-	-	-	-	10.1	11.9	13.3	11.6	12.7	11.6	12.0
25-34 years	-	-	-	-	7.5	8.1	9.7	9.4	9.0	8.3	8.9
35-44 years	-	-	-	-	8.8	7.7	9.3	8.0	8.0	7.9	8.0
45-64 years	-	-	-	-	9.4	9.4	9.5	11.4	9.2	8.6	9.7
65 years and over	-	-	-	-	14.8	13.5	14.7	14.9	13.7	14.1	14.2

Source: "Death Rates for Motor Vehicle Crashes, According to Race and Age: United States, Selected Years 1950-92," *Health, United States, 1994*, pp. 129-31. Primary source: Centers for Disease Control and Prevention, National Center for Health Statistics: Vital Statistics of the United States, Vol. II, Mortality, Part A, for data years 1950-92. Public Health Service. Washington. U.S. Government Printing Office; Data computed by the Division of Health and Utilization Analysis from data compiled by the Division of Vital Statistics and from national population estimates for race groups from table 1 and State or U.S. aggregate population estimates for Hispanics provided by the Census Bureau. *Notes:* For data years shown, the code numbers for cause of death are based on the then current International Classification of Diseases, which are described in Appendix II, tables IV and V. Data for the 1980's are based on intercensal population estimates. See Appendix I, Department of Commerce. Age groups chosen to show data for American Indians, Asians, Hispanics, and non-Hispanic whites were selected to minimize the presentation of unstable age-specific death rates based on small numbers of deaths and for consistency among comparison groups. The race groups, white, black, Asian or Pacific Islander, and American Indian or Alaskan Native, include persons of Hispanic and non-Hispanic origin. Conversely, persons of Hispanic origin may be of any race. Consistency of race and Hispanic origin identification between the death certificate (source of data for numerator of death rates) and data from the Census Bureau (denominator) is high for individual white, black, and Hispanic persons; however, persons identified as American Indian or Asian in data from the Census Bureau are sometimes misreported as white on the death certificate, causing death rates to be underestimated by 22-30 percent for American Indians and by about 12 percent for Asians. (Sorlie PD, Rogot E, and Johnson NJ: Validity of demographic characteristics on the death certificate, *Epidemology* 3(2): 181-184, 1992) 1. Includes deaths of nonresidents of the United States. 2. Interpretation of trends should take into account that population estimates for American Indians increased by 45 percent between 1980 and 1990, partly due to better enumeration techniques in the 1990 decennial census and to the increased tendency for people to identify themselves as American Indian in 1990. 3. Interpretation of trends should take into account that the Asian population in the United States more than doubled between 1980 and 1990, primarily due to immigration. 4. Excludes data from States lacking and Hispanic-origin item on their death certificates. See Appendix I. 5. Age-specific death rate based on fewer than 20 deaths. For age- adjusted death rates, 6 or more age-specific rates were based on fewer than 20 deaths.

★ 952 ★
Death Rates

Death Rates: Trends in Deaths by Respiratory System Malignancies, 1950-1992

[Data are based on the National Vital Statistics System.]

Sex, race, and age	Deaths per 100,000 resident population									
	1950[1]	1960[1]	1970	1980	1985	1988	1989	1990	1991	1992
White male										
All ages, age adjusted	21.6	34.6	49.9	58.0	58.7	58.8	58.3	59.0	58.1	56.7
All ages, crude	24.1	39.6	58.3	73.4	77.6	79.5	79.6	81.0	80.7	79.5
Under 25 years	0.1	0.1	0.1	0.1	0.1	0.1	0.1	0.1	0.1	0.1
25-34 years	1.2	1.6	1.4	0.9	0.7	0.8	0.7	0.9	0.7	0.7
35-44 years	7.9	10.4	15.4	11.2	9.5	8.5	7.9	8.0	7.6	7.5
45-54 years	39.1	53.0	67.6	74.3	65.5	61.1	59.0	57.9	55.1	52.9
55-64 years	95.9	149.8	199.3	215.0	223.3	225.4	221.8	222.5	218.0	28.0
65-74 years	119.4	225.1	344.8	418.4	425.2	428.8	430.1	438.2	437.0	431.7
75-84 years	109.1	191.9	360.7	516.1	561.7	578.7	580.6	593.6	591.4	585.0
85 years and over	102.7	133.9	221.8	391.5	463.8	499.3	517.7	540.4	556.6	549.2
Black male										
All ages, age adjusted	16.9	36.6	60.8	82.0	87.7	88.7	90.8	91.0	88.4	86.7
All ages, crude	14.3	31.1	51.2	70.8	75.5	76.7	78.0	77.8	75.8	74.7
Under 25 years	[2]	[2]	[2]	[2]	[2]	[2]	[2]	[2]	[2]	[2]
25-34 years	2.1	2.6	2.9	1.9	1.9	1.3	1.2	2.1	1.1	1.7
35-44 years	9.4	20.7	32.6	26.9	22.4	20.3	19.4	20.0	18.2	18.5
45-54 years	41.1	75.0	123.5	142.8	133.1	124.2	128.0	125.0	125.1	114.9
55-64 years	78.8	161.8	250.3	340.3	373.2	352.9	364.9	377.5	348.1	346.4
65-74 years	65.2	184.6	322.2	499.4	565.9	610.1	622.8	613.4	607.9	599.9
75-84 years	-	126.3	290.6	499.6	579.0	666.8	684.7	669.9	694.0	683.6
85 years and over	-	110.3	154.4	337.7	409.7	569.2	507.6	535.7	546.4	552.6
White female										
All ages, age adjusted	4.6	5.1	10.1	18.2	22.7	24.9	25.9	26.5	26.8	27.4
All ages, crude	5.4	6.4	13.1	26.5	34.8	39.7	41.9	43.4	44.6	46.2
Under 25 years	[2]	0.1	0.1	0.1	0.1	[2]	[2]	[2]	[2]	[2]
25-34 years	0.5	0.6	0.6	0.5	0.6	0.5	0.5	0.6	0.7	0.6
35-44 years	2.2	3.4	6.0	6.8	5.7	5.7	5.3	5.2	5.2	5.3
45-54 years	6.5	9.8	22.1	33.9	36.2	35.3	34.4	35.2	33.5	32.2
55-64 years	15.5	16.7	39.3	74.2	94.7	104.2	107.4	108.0	108.6	109.6
65-74 years	27.2	26.5	45.4	108.1	149.0	168.1	180.3	185.3	189.6	199.0
75-84 years	40.0	36.5	56.8	99.3	138.7	170.4	188.2	199.0	211.0	221.3
85 years and over	44.0	45.2	57.4	96.8	103.2	129.3	131.5	143.2	154.1	160.9
Black female										
All ages, age adjusted	4.1	5.5	10.9	19.5	22.8	25.2	26.0	27.5	27.4	28.5

[Continued]

★ 952 ★

Death Rates: Trends in Deaths by Respiratory System Malignancies, 1950-1992

[Continued]

Sex, race, and age	Deaths per 100,000 resident population									
	1950[1]	1960[1]	1970	1980	1985	1988	1989	1990	1991	1992
All ages, crude	3.4	4.9	10.1	19.3	23.5	26.5	27.8	29.2	29.7	30.9
Under 25 years	[2]	[2]	[2]	[2]	[2]	[2]	[2]	[2]	[2]	[2]
25-34 years	[2]	0.8	[2]	[2]	1.0	[2]	1.0	0.8	0.8	0.9
35-44 years	2.7	3.4	10.5	7.9	7.6	6.5	7.8	7.9	7.8	8.6
45-54 years	8.8	12.8	25.3	46.4	41.5	42.4	42.7	43.4	43.3	42.3
55-64 years	15.3	20.7	36.4	83.8	107.8	113.9	111.2	122.8	113.6	119.3
65-74 years	16.4	20.7	49.3	91.7	120.6	149.5	161.3	169.9	174.5	187.4
75-84 years	-	33.1	52.6	81.1	105.6	139.9	151.2	153.8	175.6	173.1
85 years and over	-	44.7	47.6	90.5	117.3	112.1	132.0	138.1	158.9	158.3

Source: "Death Rates for Malignant Neoplasms of Respiratory System, According to Sex, Detailed Race, Hispanic Origin, and Age: United States, Selected Years 1950-92," *Health, United States, 1994*, p. 122. Primary source: Centers for Disease Control and Prevention, National Center for Health Statistics: Vital Statistics of the United states, Vol. II, Mortality, Part A, for data years 1950-92. Public Health Service. Washington. U.S. Government Printing Office; Data computed by the Division of Health and Utilization Analysis from data compiled by the Division of Vital Statistics and from table 1. *Notes:* For data years shown, the code numbers for cause of death are based on the then current International Classification of Diseases, which are described in Appendix II, tables IV and V. Data for the 1980's are based on intercensal population estimates. See Appendix I, Department of Commerce. 1. Includes deaths of nonresidents of the United States. 2. Based on fewer than 20 deaths.

★ 953 ★

Death Rates

Death Rates: Trends in Suicides, 1950-92. Part 1

[Data are based on the National Vital Statistics System.]

Sex, race, Hispanic origin, and age	Death per 100,000 resident population										
	1950[1]	1960[1]	1970	1980	1985	1988	1989	1990	1991	1992	1990-92
White male											
All ages, age adjusted	18.1	17.5	18.2	18.9	19.9	19.9	19.7	20.1	19.9	19.5	19.9
All ages, crude	19.0	17.6	18.0	19.9	21.6	21.8	21.5	22.0	21.7	21.2	21.6
Under 1 year	-	-	-	-	-	-	-	-	-	-	-
1-4 years	-	-	-	-	-	-	-	-	-	-	-
5-14 years	0.3	0.5	0.5	0.7	1.3	1.1	1.1	1.1	1.2	1.3	1.2
15-24 years	6.6	8.6	13.9	21.4	22.3	22.7	22.5	23.2	23.0	22.7	23.0
25-44 years	-	-	-	24.6	24.8	25.3	24.8	25.4	25.4	25.1	25.3
25-34 years	13.8	14.9	19.9	25.6	25.6	26.1	25.5	25.6	26.1	25.1	25.6
35-44 years	22.4	21.9	23.3	23.5	23.7	24.3	24.1	25.3	24.7	25.2	25.1
45-64 years	-	-	-	25.0	27.0	25.2	25.5	26.0	26.0	24.9	25.6
45-54 years	34.1	33.7	29.5	24.2	25.2	23.4	24.4	24.8	25.3	24.0	24.7
55-64 years	45.9	40.2	35.0	25.8	28.8	27.3	26.9	27.5	26.8	26.0	26.8
65 years and over	-	-	-	37.2	43.7	45.7	44.3	44.2	42.7	41.0	42.7
65-74 years	53.2	42.0	38.7	32.5	35.8	36.2	36.0	34.2	32.6	32.0	32.9
75-84 years	61.9	55.7	45.5	45.5	57.0	61.4	55.3	60.2	56.1	53.0	56.4
85 years and over	61.9	61.3	45.8	52.8	60.9	66.5	72.9	70.3	75.1	67.6	71.0

[Continued]

★ 953 ★

Death Rates: Trends in Suicides, 1950-92. Part 1

[Continued]

Sex, race, Hispanic origin, and age	Death per 100,000 resident population										
	1950[1]	1960[1]	1970	1980	1985	1988	1989	1990	1991	1992	1990-92
Black male											
All ages, age adjusted	7.0	7.8	9.9	11.1	11.5	11.9	12.6	12.4	12.5	12.4	12.4
All ages, crude	6.3	6.4	8.0	10.3	11.0	11.7	12.4	12.0	12.1	12.0	12.0
Under 1 year	-	-	-	-	-	-	-	-	-	-	-
1-4 years	-	-	-	-	-	-	-	-	-	-	-
5-14 years	[5]	[5]	[5]	[5]	[5]	[5]	0.9	0.8	1.0	1.0	1.0
15-24 years	4.9	4.1	10.5	12.3	13.3	14.5	16.6	15.1	16.4	18.0	16.5
25-44 years	-	-	-	19.2	17.8	19.8	20.3	19.6	18.5	18.9	19.0
25-34 years	9.3	12.4	19.2	21.8	19.9	22.5	22.5	21.9	21.1	20.7	21.2
35-44 years	10.4	12.8	12.6	15.6	14.6	15.9	17.4	16.9	15.2	16.9	16.3
45-64 years	-	-	-	11.8	12.9	11.8	11.2	13.1	13.7	11.4	12.7
45-54 years	10.4	10.8	13.8	12.0	13.6	11.8	11.1	14.8	14.3	12.4	13.8
55-64 years	16.5	16.2	10.6	11.7	12.2	11.6	11.5	10.8	13.0	10.1	11.3
65 years and over	-	-	-	11.4	15.8	14.9	16.9	14.9	16.3	14.1	15.1
65-74 years	10.0	11.3	8.7	11.1	16.7	14.1	17.1	14.7	13.8	11.8	13.4
75-84 years	-	6.6	8.9	10.5	15.6	17.7	14.9	14.4	21.6	18.5	18.2
85 years and over	-	6.9	[5]	[5]	[5]	[5]	[5]	[5]	[5]	[5]	18.1
American Indian or Alaskan Native male[2]											
All ages, age adjusted	-	-	-	[5]	[5]	[5]	[5]	[5]	[5]	[5]	19.4
All ages, crude	-	-	-	20.9	20.3	20.2	19.9	20.9	18.5	17.6	19.0
15-24 years	-	-	-	45.3	42.0	41.8	43.7	49.1	37.7	40.6	42.5
25-44 years	-	-	-	31.2	30.2	27.9	30.6	27.8	27.3	24.7	26.6
45-64 years	-	-	-	[5]	[5]	15.4	[5]	[5]	16.4	[4]	13.0
65 years and over	-	-	-	[5]	[5]	[5]	[5]	[5]	[5]	[5]	[5]
Asian or Pacific Islander male[3]											
All ages, age adjusted	-	-	-	[5]	[5]	[5]	7.9	8.8	9.0	8.5	8.7
All ages, crude	-	-	-	8.8	8.4	7.7	7.7	8.7	8.6	8.4	8.6
15-24 years	-	-	-	10.8	14.2	8.5	11.6	13.5	12.8	13.7	13.3
25-44 years	-	-	-	11.0	9.3	10.2	8.6	10.6	9.2	9.9	9.9
45-64 years	-	-	-	13.0	10.4	9.7	8.9	9.7	12.3	9.2	10.4
65 years and over	-	-	-	18.6	16.7	15.4	19.2	16.8	19.9	16.6	17.8

[Continued]

★ 953 ★

Death Rates: Trends in Suicides, 1950-92. Part 1

[Continued]

Sex, race, Hispanic origin, and age	Death per 100,000 resident population										
	1950[1]	1960[1]	1970	1980	1985	1988	1989	1990	1991	1992	1990-92
Hispanic male[4]											
All ages, age adjusted	-	-	-	-	10.4	10.8	13.4	12.4	12.6	12.2	12.4
All ages, crude	-	-	-	-	9.8	10.2	12.2	11.4	11.6	11.3	11.5
15-24 years	-	-	-	-	13.8	14.1	15.6	14.7	15.3	16.3	15.4
25-44 years	-	-	-	-	14.8	14.5	16.8	16.2	16.1	15.3	15.8
45-64 years	-	-	-	-	12.3	12.7	17.5	16.1	17.1	15.8	16.3
65 years and over	-	-	-	-	14.7	20.9	28.5	23.4	23.0	21.5	22.6

Source: "Death Rates for Suicide, According to Sex, Detailed Race, Hispanic Origin, and Age: United States, Selected Years 1950-92," Health United States, 1994, pp. 135-37. Primary source: Centers for Disease Control and Prevention, National Center for Health Statistics: Vital Statistics of the United States, Vol. II, Mortality, Part A, for data years 1950-92. Public Health Service. Washington. U.S. Government Printing Office; Data computed by the Division of Health and Utilization Analysis from data compiled by the Division of Vital Statistics and from national population estimates for race groups from table 1 and State or U.S. aggregate population estimates for Hispanics provided by the Census Bureau. Notes: For data years shown, the code numbers for cause of death are based on the then current International Classification of Diseases, which are described in Appendix II, tables IV and V. Data for the 1980's are based on intercensal population estimates. See Appendix I, Department of Commerce. Age groups chosen to show data for American Indians, Asians, Hispanics, and non-Hispanic whites were selected to minimize the presentation of unstable age-specific death rates based on small numbers of deaths and for consistency among comparison groups. The race groups, white, black, Asian or Pacific Islander, and American Indian or Alaskan Native, include persons of Hispanic and non-Hispanic origin. Conversely, persons of Hispanic origin may be of any race. Consistency of race and Hispanic origin identification between the death certificate (source of data for numerator of death rates) and data from the Census Bureau (denominator) is high for individual white, black, and Hispanic persons; however, persons identified as American Indian or Asian in data from the Census Bureau are sometimes misreported as white on the death certificate, causing death rates to be underestimated by 22-30 percent for American Indians and by about 12 percent for Asians. (Sorlie PD, Rogot E, and Johnson NJ: Validity of demographic characteristics on the death certificate, Epidemiology 3(2):181-194, 1992.) 1. Includes deaths of nonresidents of the United States. 2. Interpretation of trends should take into account that population estimates for American Indians increased by 45 percent between 1980 and 1990, partly due to better enumeration techniques in the 1990 decennial census and to the increased tendency for people to identify themselves as American Indian in 1990. 3. Interpretation of trends should take into account that the Asian population in the United States more than doubled between 1980 and 1990, primarily due to immigration. 4. Excludes data from States lacking an Hispanic-origin item on their death certificates. 5. Age-specific death rate based on fewer than 20 deaths. For age-adjusted death rates, 5 or more age-specific rates were based on fewer than 20 deaths.

★ 954 ★

Death Rates

Death Rates: Trends in Suicides, 1950-92. Part 2

[Data are based on the National Vital Statistics System.]

Sex, race, Hispanic origin, and age	Death per 100,000 resident population										
	1950[1]	1960[1]	1970	1980	1985	1988	1989	1990	1991	1992	1990-92
White female											
All ages, age adjusted	5.3	5.3	7.2	5.7	5.3	5.1	4.8	4.8	4.8	4.6	4.7
All ages, crude	5.5	5.3	7.1	5.9	5.6	5.5	5.3	5.3	5.2	5.1	5.2
Under 1 year	-	-	-	-	-	-	-	-	-	-	-
1-4 years	-	-	-	-	-	-	-	-	-	-	-
5-14 years	5	5	0.1	0.2	0.5	0.4	0.3	0.4	0.4	0.5	0.4
15-24 years	2.7	2.3	4.2	4.6	4.7	4.5	4.3	4.2	4.2	3.8	4.1
25-44 years	-	-	-	8.1	7.0	6.8	6.6	6.6	6.4	6.3	6.5
25-34 years	5.2	5.8	9.0	7.5	6.4	6.2	6.0	6.0	5.8	5.4	5.7
35-44 years	8.2	8.1	13.0	9.1	7.7	7.5	7.2	7.4	7.2	7.2	7.3
45-64 years	-	-	-	9.6	8.7	8.3	8.0	7.7	7.8	7.6	7.7

[Continued]

★ 954 ★

Death Rates: Trends in Suicides, 1950-92. Part 2
[Continued]

Sex, race, Hispanic origin, and age	Death per 100,000 resident population										
	1950[1]	1960[1]	1970	1980	1985	1988	1989	1990	1991	1992	1990-92
45-54 years	10.5	10.9	13.5	10.2	9.1	8.7	8.1	7.5	8.3	7.9	7.9
55-64 years	10.7	10.9	12.3	9.1	8.4	8.0	8.0	8.0	7.1	7.2	7.4
65 years and over	-	-	-	6.4	6.9	7.0	6.3	6.8	6.3	6.4	6.5
65-74 years	10.6	8.8	9.6	7.0	7.3	7.3	6.4	7.2	6.4	6.3	6.6
75-84 years	8.4	9.2	7.2	5.7	7.0	7.2	6.1	6.7	6.0	6.6	6.4
85 years and over	8.9	6.1	5.8	5.8	4.8	5.4	6.3	5.4	6.6	6.3	6.1
Black female											
All ages, age adjusted	1.7	[5]	2.9	2.4	2.1	2.5	2.4	2.4	1.9	2.1	2.1
All ages, crude	1.5	1.6	2.6	2.2	2.1	2.4	2.4	2.3	1.9	2.0	2.1
Under 1 year	-	-	-	-	-	-	-	-	-	-	-
1-4 years	-	-	-	-	-	-	-	-	-	-	-
5-14 years	[5]	[5]	0.2	[5]	[5]	[5]	[5]	[5]	[5]	[5]	[5]
15-24 years	[5]	[5]	3.8	2.3	2.0	2.6	2.9	2.3	1.6	2.2	2.0
25-44 years	-	-	-	4.3	3.2	3.7	3.8	3.8	3.1	3.3	3.4
25-34 years	2.6	3.0	5.7	4.1	3.0	3.9	3.8	3.7	3.3	3.3	3.4
35-44 years	2.0	3.0	3.7	4.6	3.6	3.4	3.8	4.0	2.9	3.3	3.4
45-64 years	-	-	-	2.5	2.8	3.3	2.9	2.9	2.6	2.6	2.7
45-54 years	3.5	3.1	3.7	2.8	3.3	4.0	3.2	3.2	3.0	3.0	3.1
55-64 years	[5]	3.0	[5]	3.2	2.2	2.6	2.6	2.6	2.1	2.0	2.2
65 years and over	-	-	-	[5]	2.7	1.6	1.8	1.9	2.0	1.8	1.9
65-74 years	[5]	[5]	[5]	[5]	[5]	[5]	[5]	2.6	2.4	[5]	2.4
75-84 years	-	[5]	[5]	[5]	[5]	[5]	[5]	[5]	[5]	[5]	[5]
85 years and over	-	[5]	[5]	[5]	[5]	[5]	[5]	[5]	[5]	[5]	[5]
American Indian or Alaskan Native female[2]											
All ages, age adjusted	-	-	-	[5]	[5]	[5]	[5]	[5]	[5]	[5]	3.8
All ages, crude	-	-	-	4.7	4.4	3.7	3.5	3.7	3.5	3.8	3.6
15-24 years	-	-	-	[5]	[5]	[5]	[5]	[5]	[5]	[5]	6.7
25-44 years	-	-	-	10.7	[5]	6.9	[5]	[5]	5.9	5.8	5.7
45-64 years	-	-	-	[5]	[5]	[5]	[5]	[5]	[5]	[5]	[5]
65 years and over	-	-	-	[5]	[5]	[5]	[5]	[5]	[5]	[5]	[5]
Asian or Pacific Islander female[3]											
All ages, age adjusted	-	-	-	[5]	[5]	[5]	[5]	[5]	[5]	[5]	3.5
All ages, crude	-	-	-	4.7	4.3	3.2	3.9	3.4	3.5	3.8	3.6

[Continued]

★ 954 ★

Death Rates: Trends in Suicides, 1950-92. Part 2

[Continued]

Sex, race, Hispanic origin, and age	Death per 100,000 resident population										
	1950[1]	1960[1]	1970	1980	1985	1988	1989	1990	1991	1992	1990-92
15-24 years	-	-	-	5	5.8	5	4.2	3.9	5	5.5	4.1
25-44 years	-	-	-	5.4	4.2	4.2	4.6	3.8	4.1	4.1	4.0
45-64 years	-	-	-	7.9	5.4	5	5.3	5.0	5.5	4.9	5.1
65 years and over	-	-	-	5	13.6	11.4	9.8	8.5	8.7	7.7	8.3
Hispanic female[4]											
All ages, age adjusted	-	-	-	-	5	5	2.6	5	2.4	5	2.3
All ages, crude	-	-	-	-	1.6	1.8	2.4	2.2	2.2	2.0	2.2
15-24 years	-	-	-	-	2.1	2.5	3.0	3.1	3.2	2.2	2.9
25-44 years	-	-	-	-	2.1	2.9	3.4	3.1	3.3	2.8	3.1
45-64 years	-	-	-	-	3.2	1.8	3.9	2.5	3.2	2.9	2.9
65 years and over	-	-	-	-	5	5	5	5	5	3.6	2.8

Source: "Death Rates for Suicide, According to Sex, Detailed Race, Hispanic Origin, and Age: United States, Selected Years 1950-92," *Health United States, 1994,* pp. 135-37. Primary source: Centers for Disease Control and Prevention, National Center for Health Statistics: Vital Statistics of the United States, Vol. II, Mortality, Part A, for data years 1950-92. Public Health Service. Washington. U.S. Government Printing Office; Data computed by the Division of Health and Utilization Analysis from data compiled by the Division of Vital Statistics and from national population estimates for race groups from table 1 and State or U.S. aggregate population estimates for Hispanics provided by the Census Bureau. *Notes:* For data years shown, the code numbers for cause of death are based on the then current International Classification of Diseases, which are described in Appendix II, tables IV and V. Data for the 1980's are based on intercensal population estimates. See Appendix I, Department of Commerce. Age groups chosen to show data for American Indians, Asians, Hispanics, and non-Hispanic whites were selected to minimize the presentation of unstable age-specific death rates based on small numbers of deaths and for consistency among comparison groups. The race groups, white, black, Asian or Pacific Islander, and American Indian or Alaskan Native, include persons of Hispanic and non-Hispanic origin. Conversely, persons of Hispanic origin may be of any race. Consistency of race and Hispanic origin identification between the death certificate (source of data for numerator of death rates) and data from the Census Bureau (denominator) is high for individual white, black, and Hispanic persons; however, persons identified as American Indian or Asian in data from the Census Bureau are sometimes misreported as white on the death certificate, causing death rates to be underestimated by 22-30 percent for American Indians and by about 12 percent for Asians. (Sorlie PD, Rogot E, and Johnson NJ: Validity of demographic characteristics on the death certificate, *Epidemiology* 3(2):181-194, 1992.) 1. Includes deaths of nonresidents of the United States. 2. Interpretation of trends should take into account that population estimates for American Indians increased by 45 percent between 1980 and 1990, partly due to better enumeration techniques in the 1990 decennial census and to the increased tendency for people to identify themselves as American Indian in 1990. 3. Interpretation of trends should take into account that the Asian population in the United States more than doubled between 1980 and 1990, primarily due to immigration. 4. Excludes data from States lacking an Hispanic-origin item on their death certificates. 5. Age-specific death rate based on fewer than 20 deaths. For age- adjusted death rates, 5 or more age-specific rates were based on fewer than 20 deaths.

★ 955 ★

Death Rates

Maternal Deaths: Maternal Mortality Rates, 1950-1992

[Data based on the National Vital Statistics System].

Race and age	Deaths per 100,000 live births									
	1950[1]	1960[1]	1970	1980	1985	1988	1989	1990	1991	1992
All races										
All ages, age adjusted	73.7	32.1	21.5	9.4	7.6	8.0	7.3	7.6	7.2	7.3
All ages, crude	83.3	37.1	21.5	9.2	7.8	8.4	7.9	8.2	7.9	7.8
Under 20 years	70.7	22.7	18.9	7.6	6.9	7.0	5.8	7.5	6.8	7.1
20-24 years	47.6	20.7	13.0	5.8	5.4	7.2	6.4	6.1	5.9	6.9
25-29 years	63.5	29.8	17.0	7.7	6.4	6.1	6.7	6.0	5.9	4.8

[Continued]

★ 955 ★

Maternal Deaths: Maternal Mortality Rates, 1950-1992

[Continued]

Race and age	Deaths per 100,000 live births									
	1950[1]	1960[1]	1970	1980	1985	1988	1989	1990	1991	1992
30-34 years	107.7	50.3	31.6	13.6	8.9	9.3	10.0	9.5	8.8	9.2
35 years and over[2]	222.0	104.3	81.9	36.3	25.0	21.9	15.3	20.7	19.0	16.9
White										
All ages, age adjusted	53.1	22.4	14.4	6.7	4.9	5.5	5.4	5.1	5.0	4.7
All ages, crude	61.1	26.0	14.3	6.6	5.1	5.8	5.6	5.4	5.8	5.0
Under 20 years	44.9	14.8	13.8	5.8	[3]	[3]	[3]	[3]	[3]	[3]
20-24 years	35.7	15.3	8.4	4.2	3.3	5.4	4.9	3.9	3.8	4.7
25-29 years	45.0	20.3	11.1	5.4	4.6	4.5	4.8	4.8	4.2	3.1
30-34 years	75.9	34.3	18.7	9.3	5.1	7.0	6.4	5.0	7.2	6.3
35 years and over[2]	174.1	73.9	59.3	25.5	17.5	12.2	9.7	12.6	14.3	9.4
Black										
All ages, age adjusted	-	92.0	65.5	24.9	22.1	20.9	18.6	21.7	18.1	20.1
All ages, crude	-	103.6	60.9	22.4	21.3	20.5	18.4	22.4	18.3	20.8
Under 20 years	-	54.8	32.3	13.1	[3]	[3]	[3]	[3]	[3]	13.7
20-24 years	-	56.9	41.9	13.9	14.6	15.2	13.5	14.7	13.2	15.3
25-29 years	-	92.8	65.2	22.4	19.4	15.1	17.9	14.9	16.6	15.8
30-34 years	-	150.6	117.8	44.0	38.0	28.4	33.8	44.2	23.1	30.9
35 years and over[2]	-	299.5	207.5	100.6	77.2	90.7	57.5	79.7	61.9	65.2

Source: "Maternal Mortality Rates for Complications of Pregnancy, Childbirth, and the Puerperium, According to Race and Age: United States 1950-92," *Health, United States, 1994*, p. 128. Primary source: Centers for Disease Control and Prevention, National Center for Health Statistics: Vital Statistics of the United States, Vol. II, Mortality, Part A, for data years 1950-92. Public Health Service. Washington. U.S. Government Printing Office; Vital Statistics of the United States, Vol. I, Natality, for data years 1950-92. Public Health Service. Washington. U.S. Government Printing Office; Data computed by the Division of Health and Utilization Analysis from data compiled by the Division of Vital Statistics. *Notes:* For data years shown, the code numbers for cause of death are based on the then current International Classification of DIseases, which are described in Appendix II, tables IV and V. For 1950 and 1960, rates are based on live births by race of child; for all other years, rates are based on live births by race of mother. See Appendix II, Race. 1. Includes deaths of nonresidents of the United States. 2. Rates computed by relating deaths of women 35 years and over to live births to women 35-49 years. 3. Based on fewer than 20 deaths.

Deaths

★ 956 ★

AIDS Deaths: Trends, 1982-1994

[Data are shown by year of death and are subject to substantial retrospective changes. For data on AIDS cases reported, see table 213. Based on reporting by State health departments.]

CHARACTERISTIC	NUMBER									PERCENT DISTRIBUTION	
	Total, 1982-1994[1]	1985	1988	1989	1990	1991	1992	1993	1994	1994	1982-1994
Total[2]	258,658	6,689	19,979	26,266	29,781	34,491	37,619	40,015	31,212	100.0	100.0
Race/ethnicity:											
White	137,602	4,015	10,956	14,439	16,450	18,619	19,392	19,877	14,929	47.8	53.2
Black	82,556	1,754	6,061	7,941	8,989	10,706	12,493	14,084	11,453	36.7	31.9
Hispanic	36,244	889	2,798	3,647	4,105	4,828	5,404	5,691	4,488	14.4	14.0
Indian	537	6	25	40	49	87	73	117	97	0.3	0.2
Asian	1,750	29	129	180	195	240	246	281	280	0.9	0.7

Source: "Acquired Immunodeficiency Syndrome (AIDS) Deaths, by Selected Characteristics: 1982-1994," *Statistical Abstract of the United States*, 1995, p. 97. Primary source: U.S. Centers for Disease Control, *Surveillance Report*, annual. *Notes:* 1. Includes deaths prior to 1982. 2. Includes other race/ethnicity groups not shown separately.

★ 957 ★

Deaths

Causes of Death: Death by Firearms, by Race and Gender: 1980-1992

[Age-adjusted rates per 100,000].

YEAR	ALL RACES			WHITE			ALL OTHER					
							Total			Black		
	Both sexes	Male	Female	Both sexes	Male	Female	Both sexes	Male	Female	Both sexes	Male	Female
NUMBER												
1980	33,780	28,322	5,458	24,849	20,714	4,135	8,931	7,608	1,323	8,505	7,265	1,240
1985	31,566	26,382	5,184	24,507	20,389	4,118	7,059	5,993	1,066	6,565	5,584	981
1990	37,155	31,736	5,419	26,299	22,249	4,050	10,856	9,487	1,369	10,175	8,922	1,253
1991	38,317	32,882	5,435	26,455	22,448	4,007	11,862	10,434	1,428	11,025	9,733	1,292
1992	37,776	32,425	5,351	26,120	22,208	3,912	11,656	10,217	1,439	10,906	9,581	1,325
RATE[1]												
1980	14.8	25.3	4.8	12.4	21.1	4.2	29.1	53.0	8.1	33.5	61.8	9.1
1985	12.7	21.8	4.2	11.4	19.4	3.9	19.7	35.4	5.7	23.2	42.2	6.5

[Continued]

★ 957 ★

Causes of Death: Death by Firearms, by Race and Gender: 1980-1992

[Continued]

YEAR	ALL RACES			WHITE			ALL OTHER					
							Total			Black		
	Both sexes	Male	Female	Both sexes	Male	Female	Both sexes	Male	Female	Both sexes	Male	Female
1990	14.6	25.4	4.2	11.9	20.5	3.7	26.9	48.9	6.5	33.4	61.5	7.8
1991	15.2	26.4	4.2	12.0	20.7	3.7	29.0	52.9	6.6	35.9	66.4	8.0
1992	14.9	25.9	4.1	11.8	20.4	3.6	28.0	50.9	6.6	35.1	64.5	8.0

Source: "Deaths and Death Rates by Injury by Firearms, by Race and Sex: 1980 to 1992," *Statistical Abstract of the United States, 1995*, p. 101. Primary source: U.S. National Center for Health Statistics, *Monthly Vital Statistics Reports. Note:* 1. Age-adjusted death rates. For method of computation see source.

★ 958 ★

Deaths

Causes of Death: Deaths and Death Rates for Alcohol-Induced Causes, by Race and Gender: 1980-1992

YEAR	ALL RACES			WHITE			ALL OTHER					
							Total			Black		
	Both sexes	Male	Female	Both sexes	Male	Female	Both sexes	Male	Female	Both sexes	Male	Female
NUMBER												
1980	19,765	14,447	5,318	14,815	10,936	3,879	4,950	3,511	1,439	4,451	3,170	1,281
1985	17,741	13,216	4,525	13,216	9,922	3,294	4,525	3,294	1,231	4,114	3,030	1,084
1990	19,757	14,842	4,915	14,904	11,334	3,570	4,853	3,508	1,345	4,337	3,172	1,165
1991	19,233	14,467	4,766	14,825	11,286	3,539	4,408	3,181	1,227	3,883	2,816	1,067
1992	19,568	14,926	4,642	15,143	11,701	3,442	4,425	3,225	1,200	3,809	2,800	1,009
RATE[1]												
1980	8.4	13.0	4.3	6.9	10.8	3.5	18.8	29.5	10.0	20.4	32.4	10.6
1985	7.0	11.0	3.4	5.8	9.2	2.8	14.6	23.5	7.2	16.8	27.7	8.0
1990	7.2	11.4	3.4	6.2	9.9	2.8	13.6	22.0	6.8	16.1	26.6	7.7
1991	6.8	10.9	3.2	6.0	9.7	2.7	11.8	19.2	5.9	13.9	22.9	6.8
1992	6.8	11.0	3.1	6.1	9.9	2.6	11.6	18.9	5.6	13.4	22.3	6.3

Source: "Deaths and Death Rates for Alcohol-Induced Causes, by Race and Sex: 1980 to 1992," *Statistical Abstract of the United States, 1995*, p. 101. Primary source: U.S. National Center for Health Statistics, *Monthly Vital Statistics Reports. Note:* 1. Age-adjusted death rates. For method of computation see source.

★ 959 ★

Deaths

Causes of Death: Deaths and Death Rates for Drug-Induced Causes, by Race and Gender: 1980-1992

[Age-adjusted rates per 100,000].

YEAR	ALL RACES			WHITE			ALL OTHER					
							Total			Black		
	Both sexes	Male	Female	Both sexes	Male	Female	Both sexes	Male	Female	Both sexes	Male	Female
NUMBER												
1980	6,900	3,771	3,129	5,814	3,088	2,726	1,086	683	403	1,006	648	358
1985	8,663	5,342	3,321	6,946	4,172	2,774	1,717	1,170	547	1,600	1,107	493
1990	9,463	5,897	3,566	7,603	4,646	2,957	1,860	1,251	609	1,703	1,155	548
1991	10,388	6,593	3,795	8,204	5,129	3,075	2,184	1,464	720	2,037	1,385	652
1992	11,703	7,766	3,937	9,360	6,124	3,236	2,343	1,642	701	2,148	1,533	615
RATE[1]												
1980	3.0	3.4	2.6	2.9	3.2	2.6	3.7	4.9	2.5	4.1	5.8	2.7
1985	3.5	4.5	2.6	3.3	4.0	2.5	4.9	7.2	2.9	5.9	8.9	3.3
1990	3.6	4.6	2.6	3.3	4.2	2.5	4.6	6.7	2.8	5.7	8.4	3.4
1991	3.8	5.0	2.7	3.6	4.6	2.6	5.2	7.5	3.2	6.6	9.7	3.9
1992	4.3	5.9	2.8	4.1	5.5	2.7	5.5	8.3	3.1	6.8	10.6	3.6

Source: "Deaths and Death Rates for Drug-Induced Causes, by Race and Sex: 1980 to 1992," *Statistical Abstract of the United States, 1995*, p. 101. Primary source: U.S. National Center for Health Statistics, *Monthly Vital Statistics Reports. Note:* 1. Age-adjusted death rate. For method of computation see source.

★ 960 ★

Deaths

Causes of Death: Trends and Characteristics of Death by Suicide, 1980-1992. Part 1

AGE	Total[1] 1980	1990	1992	MALE					
				White			Black		
				1980	1990	1992	1980	1990	1992
All ages[2]	11.9	12.4	12.0	19.9	22.0	21.2	10.3	12.0	12.0
10 to 14 years old	0.8	1.5	1.7	1.4	2.3	2.6	0.5	1.6	2.0
15 to 19 years old	8.5	11.1	10.8	15.0	19.3	18.4	5.6	11.5	14.8
20 to 24 years old	16.1	15.1	14.9	27.8	26.8	26.6	20.0	19.0	21.2
25 to 34 years old	16.0	15.2	14.5	25.6	25.6	25.1	21.8	21.9	20.7
35 to 44 years old	15.4	15.3	15.1	23.5	25.3	25.2	15.6	16.9	16.9
45 to 54 years old	15.9	14.8	14.7	24.2	24.8	24.0	12.0	14.8	12.4
55 to 64 years old	15.9	16.0	14.8	25.8	27.5	26.0	11.7	10.8	10.1

[Continued]

★ 960 ★

Causes of Death: Trends and Characteristics of Death by Suicide, 1980-1992. Part 1
[Continued]

| AGE | Total[1] 1980 | 1990 | 1992 | MALE | | | | | |
| | | | | White | | | Black | | |
				1980	1990	1992	1980	1990	1992
65 to 74 years old	16.9	17.9	16.5	32.5	34.2	32.0	11.1	14.7	11.8
75 to 84 years old	19.1	24.9	22.8	45.5	60.2	53.0	10.5	14.4	18.5
85 years and over	19.2	22.2	21.9	52.8	70.3	67.6	18.9	(B)	(B)

Source: "Suicide Rates, by Sex, Race, and Age Group: 1980 to 1992," *Statistical Abstract of the United States, 1995*, p. 100. Primary source: U.S. National Center for Health Statistics, *Monthly Vital Statistics Report*; and unpublished data. *Notes:* B Base figure too small to meet statistical standards for reliability of a derived figure. 1. Includes other races not shown separately. 2. Includes other age groups not shown separately.

★ 961 ★
Deaths

Causes of Death: Trends and Characteristics of Death by Suicide, 1980-1992. Part 2

| AGE | FEMALE | | | | | |
| | White | | | Black | | |
	1980	1990	1992	1980	1990	1992
All ages[2]	5.9	5.3	5.1	2.2	2.3	2.0
10 to 14 years old	0.3	0.9	1.1	0.1	(B)	(B)
15 to 19 years old	3.3	4.0	3.7	1.6	1.9	1.9
20 to 24 years old	5.9	4.4	4.0	3.1	2.6	2.4
25 to 34 years old	7.5	6.0	5.4	4.1	3.7	3.2
35 to 44 years old	9.1	7.4	7.2	4.6	4.0	3.2
45 to 54 years old	10.2	7.5	7.9	2.8	3.2	3.0
55 to 64 years old	9.1	8.0	7.2	2.3	2.6	2.0
65 to 74 years old	7.0	7.2	6.3	1.7	2.6	(B)
75 to 84 years old	5.7	6.7	6.6	1.4	(B)	(B)
85 years and over	5.8	5.4	6.3	0.1	(B)	(B)

Source: "Suicide Rates, by Sex, Race, and Age Group: 1980 to 1992," *Statistical Abstract of the United States, 1995*, p. 100. Primary source: U.S. National Center for Health Statistics, *Monthly Vital Statistics Report*; and unpublished data. *Notes:* B Base figure too small to meet statistical standards for reliability of a derived figure. 1. Includes other races not shown separately. 2. Includes other age groups not shown separately.

★ 962 ★

Deaths

Causes of Deaths: Age and Leading Cause: 1992

[Excludes deaths of nonresidents of the United States. Deaths classified according to ninth revision of *International Classification of Diseases*. See also Appendix III and *Historical Statistics, Colonial Times to 1970*, series B 149-166.]

AGE AND LEADING CAUSE OF DEATH	NUMBER OF DEATHS			DEATH RATE PER 100,000 POPULATION		
	Total	Male	Female	Total	Male	Female
All Ages[1]						
All races[2]	2,175,613	1,122,336	1,053,277	852.9	901.6	806.5
White	1,873,781	956,957	916,824	880.0	917.2	844.3
Black	269,219	146,630	122,589	850.5	977.5	736.2

Source: "Deaths, by Age and Leading Cause: 1992," *Statistical Abstract of the United States, 1995*, p. 94. Primary source: U.S. National Center for Health Statistics, *Vital Statistics of the United States*, annual; and unpublished data. *Notes:* 1. Includes those deaths with age not stated. 2. Includes other races not shown separately.

★ 963 ★

Deaths

Causes of Deaths: Characteristics: 1992

[In thousands. Excludes deaths of nonresidents of the U.S. Deaths classified according to the ninth revision of *International Classification of Diseases*. See also Appendix III.]

AGE, SEX AND RACE	Total[1]	Heart disease	Cancer	Accidents and adverse effects	Cerebrovascular diseases	Chronic obstructive pulmonary diseases[2]	Pneumonia, flu	Suicide	Chronic liver disease, cirrhosis	Diabetes mellitus	Homicide and legal intervention
WHITE											
Both sexes, total[3]	880	633.5	454.5	72.4	124.4	85.2	67.5	27.6	21.3	40.4	12.5
Under 1 year old	702	0.5	0.1	0.5	0.1	(Z)	0.4	(Z)	(Z)	(Z)	0.2
1 to 4 years old	38	0.2	0.4	1.8	(Z)	(Z)	0.1	(Z)	(Z)	(Z)	0.2
5 to 14 years old	21	0.2	0.9	2.5	0.1	0.1	0.1	0.3	(Z)	(Z)	0.3
15 to 24 years old	84	0.6	1.5	11.5	0.1	0.1	0.2	3.9	(Z)	0.1	3.2
25 to 34 years old	119	2.3	4.2	11.3	0.5	0.2	0.4	5.4	0.5	0.5	3.4
35 to 44 years old	197	9.1	13.3	9.6	1.6	0.5	0.8	5.4	2.7	1.2	2.4
45 to 54 years old	412	24.4	33.6	6.0	3.3	1.9	1.2	3.7	3.6	2.3	1.2
55 to 64 years old	1,086	59.4	77.4	5.2	7.1	9.0	2.7	3.0	4.9	5.2	0.7
65 to 74 years old	2,519	135.8	141.8	7.1	20.5	26.6	8.7	2.9	5.6	11.2	0.4
75 to 84 years old	5,740	204.8	128.6	9.2	44.0	32.6	21.8	2.3	3.2	12.8	0.3
85 years old and over	15,104	196.2	52.8	7.7	47.1	14.2	31.0	0.7	0.7	7.2	0.1

[Continued]

★ 963 ★

Causes of Deaths: Characteristics: 1992

[Continued]

AGE, SEX AND RACE	Total[1]	Heart disease	Cancer	Accidents and adverse effects	Cerebrovascular diseases	Chronic obstructive pulmonary diseases[2]	Pneumonia, flu	Suicide	Chronic liver disease, cirrhosis	Diabetes mellitus	Homicide and legal intervention
BLACK											
Both sexes, total[3]	851	75.6	58.4	11.8	17.0	5.9	7.1	2.1	3.3	8.7	12.3
Under 1 year old	1,786	0.2	(Z)	0.3	0.1	(Z)	0.2	(Z)	(Z)	(Z)	0.1
1 to 4 years old	73	0.1	0.1	0.6	(Z)	(Z)	0.1	(Z)	(Z)	(Z)	0.2
5 to 14 years old	34	0.1	0.2	0.7	(Z)	(Z)	(Z)	(Z)	(Z)	(Z)	0.3
15 to 24 years old	168	0.3	0.3	1.7	(Z)	0.1	0.1	0.5	(Z)	(Z)	4.6
25 to 34 years old	279	1.1	0.9	2.0	0.2	0.1	0.2	0.6	0.2	0.2	3.8
35 to 44 years old	492	3.3	3.1	2.1	0.9	0.2	0.5	0.5	0.8	0.4	1.9
45 to 54 years old	894	6.4	6.7	1.2	1.4	0.4	0.4	0.2	0.8	0.8	0.7
55 to 64 years old	1,880	12.0	12.6	1.0	2.3	0.9	0.7	0.1	0.8	1.7	0.3
65 to 74 years old	3,601	18.7	17.3	0.9	3.9	1.8	1.3	0.1	0.6	2.5	0.2
75 to 84 years old	6,652	19.4	12.5	0.9	4.8	1.6	1.8	0.1	0.2	2.1	0.1
85 years old and over	14,279	14.0	4.8	0.5	3.4	0.7	1.8	(Z)	(Z)	1.0	(Z)

Source: "Deaths, by Selected Causes and Selected Characteristics: 1992," *Statistical Abstract of the United States, 1995*, p. 93. Primary source: U.S. National Center for Health Statistics, *Vital Statistics of the United States*, annual. *Notes:* Z Fewer than 50. 1. Includes allied conditions. 2. Includes other races not shown separately. 3. Includes those deaths with age not stated.

★ 964 ★

Deaths

Causes of Deaths: Firearm Mortality Among Children, Youth, and Young Adults: 1992

[Death rate per 100,000 population. Deaths classified according to the ninth revision of the *International Classification of Diseases*.]

ITEM	Under 5 years old	5 to 9 years old	10 to 14 years old	15 to 19 years old	20 to 24 years old	25 to 29 years old	30 to 34 years old
MALE							
Total: White	0.5	0.5	4.6	29.1	34.6	29.0	26.0
Black	1.4	1.5	11.5	140.5	184.3	129.4	94.8
Accidents: White	0.1	0.3	1.6	2.9	1.6	1.0	0.8
Black	0.2	0.6	2.0	6.3	4.7	2.2	1.2
Suicide: White	(X)	(X)	1.5	13.6	17.7	15.3	14.9
Black	(X)	(X)	1.1	9.0	14.4	13.4	10.5
Homicide: White	0.3	0.3	1.4	11.8	14.9	12.3	10.1

[Continued]

★ 964 ★

Causes of Deaths: Firearm Mortality Among Children, Youth, and Young Adults: 1992

[Continued]

ITEM	Under 5 years old	5 to 9 years old	10 to 14 years old	15 to 19 years old	20 to 24 years old	25 to 29 years old	30 to 34 years old
Black	1.1	0.9	8.2	123.6	164.4	113.4	82.9
FEMALE							
Total: White	0.4	0.3	1.0	4.6	5.1	4.9	5.5
Black	1.5	0.5	3.0	12.7	17.7	16.5	13.9
Accidents: White	0.1	0.1	0.1	0.2	0.2	0.1	0.1
Black	0.4	0.1	0.2	0.2	(X)	0.1	0.1
Suicide: White	(X)	(X)	0.4	2.1	2.0	2.4	2.8
Black	(X)	(X)	0.1	0.8	0.7	1.9	0.7
Homicide: White	0.3	0.2	0.5	2.2	2.7	2.3	2.4
Black	1.1	0.4	2.7	11.2	16.8	14.4	13.1

Source: "Firearm Mortality Among Children, Youth, and Young Adults. 1 to 34 Years Old: 1992," *Statistical Abstract of the United States,* 1995, p. 100. Primary source: U.S. National Center for Health Statistics, *Advance Data from Vital and Health Statistics,* No. 231. *Note:* X Not applicable.

★ 965 ★

Deaths

Deaths and Death Rates: Age, Gender, and Race: 1970-1993

[Rates are per 1,000 population for specified groups. Excludes deaths of nonresidents of the United States and fetal deaths. For explanation of age-adjustment, see text, section 2. The standard population for this table is the total population of the United States enumerated in 1940. See Appendix III. See also *Historical Statistics, Colonial Times to 1970,* series B 167-173 and B 181-192.]

SEX AND RACE	1970	1980	1984	1985	1986	1987	1988	1989	1990	1991	1992	1993
Deaths[1] (1,000)	1,921	1,990	2,039	2,086	2,105	2,123	2,168	2,150	2,148	2,170	2,176	2,268
Male[1] (1,000)	1,078	1,075	1,077	1,098	1,104	1,108	1,126	1,114	1,113	1,122	1,122	1,167
Female[1] (1,000)	843	915	963	989	1,001	1,015	1,042	1,036	1,035	1,048	1,053	1,101
White (1,000)	1,682	1,739	1,782	1,819	1,831	1,843	1,877	1,854	1,853	1,869	1,874	1,951
Male (1,000)	942	934	935	950	953	953	965	951	951	956	957	994
Female (1,000)	740	805	847	869	879	890	911	903	902	912	917	957
Black (1,000)	226	233	236	244	250	255	264	268	266	270	269	281
Male (1,000)	128	130	129	134	137	140	144	146	145	147	147	153
Female (1,000)	98	103	107	111	113	115	120	121	120	122	123	128
Death rates[1]	9.5	8.8	8.6	8.8	8.8	8.8	8.8	8.7	8.6	8.6	8.5	8.8
Male[1]	10.9	9.8	9.4	9.5	9.4	9.4	9.5	9.3	9.2	9.1	9.0	9.3
Female[1]	8.1	7.9	7.9	8.1	8.1	8.2	8.3	8.2	8.1	8.1	8.1	8.3

[Continued]

★ 965 ★

Deaths and Death Rates: Age, Gender, and Race: 1970-1993
[Continued]

SEX AND RACE	1970	1980	1984	1985	1986	1987	1988	1989	1990	1991	1992	1993
White	9.5	8.9	8.9	9.0	9.0	9.0	9.1	8.9	8.9	8.9	8.8	9.1
Male	10.9	9.8	9.5	9.6	9.6	9.5	9.6	9.4	9.3	9.3	9.2	9.4
Female	8.1	8.1	8.2	8.4	8.4	8.5	8.7	8.5	8.5	8.5	8.4	8.7
Black	10.0	8.8	8.4	8.5	8.6	8.7	8.9	8.9	8.8	8.6	8.5	8.7
Male	11.9	10.3	9.7	9.9	10.0	10.1	10.3	10.3	10.1	10.0	9.8	10.0
Female	8.3	7.3	7.2	7.3	7.4	7.5	7.6	7.6	7.5	7.4	7.4	7.6
Age-adjusted death rates[1]	7.1	5.9	5.5	5.5	5.4	5.4	5.4	5.3	5.2	5.1	5.0	5.1
Male[1]	9.3	7.8	7.2	7.2	7.2	7.1	7.1	6.9	6.8	6.7	6.6	6.7
Female[1]	5.3	4.3	4.1	4.1	4.1	4.0	4.1	4.0	3.9	3.9	3.8	3.9
White	6.8	5.6	5.3	5.2	5.2	5.1	5.1	5.0	4.9	4.9	4.8	4.9
Male	8.9	7.5	6.9	6.9	6.8	6.7	6.7	6.5	6.4	6.3	6.2	6.3
Female	5.0	4.1	3.9	3.9	3.9	3.8	3.9	3.8	3.7	3.7	3.6	3.7
Black	10.4	8.4	7.8	7.9	8.0	8.0	8.1	8.1	7.9	7.8	7.7	7.9
Male	13.2	11.1	10.4	10.5	10.6	10.6	10.8	10.8	10.6	10.5	10.3	10.5
Female	8.1	6.3	5.9	5.9	5.9	5.9	6.0	5.9	5.8	5.8	5.7	5.8

Source: "Deaths and Death Rates, by Age, Sex, and Race: 1970 to 1993," *Statistical Abstract of the United States, 1995,* p. 88. Primary source: U.S. National Center for Health Statistics, *Vital Statistics of the United States,* annual; and *Monthly Vital Statistics Report. Note:* 1. Includes other races, not shown separately.

★ 966 ★

Deaths

Deaths: Leading Causes of Deaths and Number of Deaths, 1980 and 1982. Part 1

[Data are based on the National Vital Statistics System.]

Race, Sex, and Cause of Death	1980		1992		
	Rank order	Deaths	Cause of death	Rank order	Deaths
White male					
All causes		933,878	All causes		956,957
Diseases of heart	1	364,679	Diseases of heart	1	315,483
Malignant neoplasms	2	198,188	Malignant neoplasms	2	238,499
Unintentional injuries	3	62,963	Cerebrovascular diseases	3	48,073
Cerebrovascular diseases	4	60,095	Unintentional injuries	4	47,879
Chronic obstructive pulmonary diseases	5	35,977	Chronic obstructive pulmonary diseases	5	46,355
Pneumonia and influenza	6	23,810	Pneumonia	6	30,951
Suicide	7	18,901	Suicide	7	22,126
Chronic liver disease and cirrhosis	8	16,407	Human immunodeficiency virus infection	8	20,161
Diabetes mellitus	9	12,125	Diabetes mellitus	9	17,951
Atherosclerosis	10	10,543	Chronic liver disease and cirrhosis	10	13,910
Black male					
All causes		130,138	All causes		146,630
Diseases of heart	1	37,877	Diseases of heart	1	37,040
Malignant neoplasms	2	25,861	Malignant neoplasms	2	32,155

[Continued]

★ 966 ★

Deaths: Leading Causes of Deaths and Number of Deaths, 1980 and 1982. Part 1
[Continued]

Race, Sex, and Cause of Death	1980		1992		
	Rank order	Deaths	Cause of death	Rank order	Deaths
Unintentional injuries	3	9,701	Homicide and legal intervention	3	10,131
Cerebrovascular diseases	4	9,194	Human immunodeficiency virus infection	4	8,925
Homicide and legal intervention	5	8,385	Unintentional injuries	5	8,238
Certain conditions originating in the perinatal period	6	3,869	Cerebrovascular diseases	6	7,421
Pneumonia and influenza	7	3,386	Pneumonia and influenza	7	3,822
Chronic liver disease and cirrhosis	8	3,020	Chronic obstructive pulmonary diseases	8	3,569
Chronic obstructive pulmonary diseases	9	2,429	Certain conditions originating in the perinatal period	9	3,469
Diabetes mellitus	10	2,010	Diabetes mellitus	10	3,271
American Indian or Alaskan Native male					
All causes		4,193	All causes		5,181
Unintentional injuries	1	946	Diseases of heart	1	1,214
Diseases of heart	2	917	Unintentional injuries	2	872
Malignant neoplasms	3	408	Malignant neoplasms	3	759
Chronic liver disease and cirrhosis	4	239	Chronic liver disease and cirrhosis	4	220
Homicide and legal intervention	5	164	Suicide	5	187
Cerebrovascular diseases	6	163	Cerebrovascular diseases	6	179
Pneumonia and influenza	7	148	Diabetes mellitus	7	174
Suicide	8	147	Homicide and legal intervention	8	172
Certain conditions originating in the perinatal period	9	107	Pneumonia and influenza	9	171
Diabetes mellitus	10	86	Chronic obstructive pulmonary diseases	10	120
Asian or Pacific Islander male					
All causes		6,809	All causes		13,568
Diseases of heart	1	2,174	Diseases of heart	1	3,808
Malignant neoplasms	2	1,485	Malignant neoplasms	2	3,425
Unintentional injuries	3	556	Cerebrovascular diseases	3	972
Cerebrovascular diseases	4	521	Unintentional injuries	4	873
Pneumonia and influenza	5	227	Pneumonia and influenza	5	521
Suicide	6	159	Chronic obstructive pulmonary diseases	6	421
Chronic obstructive pulmonary diseases	7	158	Homicide and legal intervention	7	356
Homicide and legal intervention	8	151	Suicide	8	341
Certain conditions originating in the perinatal period	9	128	Diabetes mellitus	9	276

[Continued]

★ 966 ★

Deaths: Leading Causes of Deaths and Number of Deaths, 1980 and 1982. Part 1
[Continued]

Race, Sex, and Cause of Death	1980		1992		
	Rank order	Deaths	Cause of death	Rank order	Deaths
Diabetes mellitus	10	103	Human immunodeficiency virus infection	10	187
Hispanic male[1]					
	---	---	All causes		49,434
	---	---	Diseases of heart	1	10,785
	---	---	Malignant neoplasms	2	7,980
	---	---	Unintentional injuries	3	5,407
	---	---	Human immunodeficiency virus infection	4	3,816
	---	---	Homicide and legal intervention	5	3,789
	---	---	Cerebrovascular diseases	6	1,929
	---	---	Chronic liver disease and cirrhosis	7	1,806
	---	---	Suicide	8	1,390
	---	---	Diabetes mellitus	9	1,361
	---	---	Pneumonia and influenza	10	1,347

Source: "Years of Potential Life Lost Before Age 65 for Selected Causes of Death, According to Sex and Race: United States, Selected Years 1970-92," *Health, United States, 1994*, pp. 101-102. Primary source: Centers for Disease Control and Prevention, National Center for Health Statistics: Vital Statistics of the United States, Vol. II, Mortality, Part A, for data years 1980 and 1992. Public Health Service. Washington. U.S. government Printing Office; Data computed by the Division of Health and Utilization Analysis from data compiled by the Division of Vital Statistics. *Notes:* For data years shown, the code numbers for cause of death are based on the *International Classification of Diseases, Ninth Revision*, described in Appendix II, table V. Categories for the coding and classification of human immunodeficiency virus infection were introduced in the United States beginning with mortality data for 1987. 1. Excludes data from States lacking an Hispanic-origin item on their death certificates.

★ 967 ★
Deaths

Deaths: Leading Causes of Deaths and Number of Deaths, 1980 and 1982. Part 2

[Data are based on the National Vital Statistics System.]

Race, Sex, and Cause of Death	1980		1992		
	Rank order	Deaths	Cause of death	Rank order	Deaths
White female					
All causes		804,729	All causes		916,824
Diseases of heart	1	318,668	Disease of heart	1	318,004
Malignant neoplasms	2	169,974	Malignant neoplasms	2	216,032
Cerebrovascular diseases	3	88,639	Cerebrovascular diseases	3	76,298
Unintentional injuries	4	27,159	Chronic obstructive pulmonary diseases	4	38,876
Pneumonia and influenza	5	24,559	Pneumonia and influenza	5	36,505
Diabetes mellitus	6	16,743	Unintentional injuries	6	24,513
Atherosclerosis	7	16,526	Diabetes mellitus	7	22,491
Chronic obstructive pulmonary diseases	8	16,398	Atherosclerosis	8	9,737
Chronic liver disease and cirrhosis	9	8,833	Nephritis, nephrotic syndrome, and nephrosis	9	9,119
Certain conditions originating in the perinatal period	10	6,512	Septicemia	10	9,057
Black female					
All causes		102,997	All causes		122,589
Diseases of heart	1	35,079	Diseases of heart	1	38,560
Malignant neoplasms	2	19,176	Malignant neoplasms	2	26,246

[Continued]

★ 967 ★

Deaths: Leading Causes of Deaths and Number of Deaths, 1980 and 1982. Part 2
[Continued]

Race, Sex, and Cause of Death	1980		1992		
	Rank order	Deaths	Cause of death	Rank order	Deaths
Cerebrovascular diseases	3	10,941	Cerebrovascular diseases	3	9,623
Unintentional injuries	4	3,779	Diabetes mellitus	4	5,382
Diabetes mellitus	5	3,534	Unintentional injuries	5	3,582
Certain conditions originating in the perinatal period	6	3,092	Pneumonia and influenza	6	3,252
Pneumonia and influenza	7	2,262	Certain conditions originating in the perinatal period	7	2,707
Homicide and legal intervention	8	1,898	Human immunodeficiency virus infection	8	2,453
Chronic liver disease and cirrhosis	9	1,770	Chronic obstructive pulmonary diseases	9	2,288
Nephritis, nephhrotic syndrome, and nephrosis	10	1,722	Homicide and legal intervention	10	2,187
American Indian or Alaskan Native female					
All causes		2,730	All causes		3,772
Diseases of heart	1	577	Diseases of heart	1	869
Malignant neoplasms	2	362	Malignant neoplasms	2	714
Unintentional injuries	3	344	Unintentional injuries	3	315
Chronic liver disease and cirrhosis	4	171	Diabetes mellitus	4	229
Cerebrovascular diseases	5	159	Cerebrovascular diseases	5	216
Diabetes mellitus	6	124	Chronic liver disease and cirrhosis	6	173
Pneumonia and influenza	7	109	Pneumonia and influenza	7	131
Certain conditions originating in the perinatal period	8	92	Chronic obstructive pulmonary diseases	8	101
Nephritis, nephrotic syndrome, and nephrosis	9	56	Nephritis, nephrotic syndrome, and nephrosis	9	64
Homicide and legal intervention	10	55	Congenital anomalies	10	58
Asian or Pacific Islander female					
All causes		4,262	All causes		10,092
Diseases of heart	1	1,091	Malignant neoplasms	1	2,748
Malignant neoplasms	2	1,037	Diseases of heart	2	2,728
Cerebrovascular diseases	3	507	Cerebrovascular diseases	3	987
Unintentional injuries	4	254	Unintentional injuries	4	505
Diabetes mellitus	5	124	Pneumonia and influenza	5	366
Certain conditions originating in the perinatal period	6	118	Diabetes mellitus	6	293
Pneumonia and influenza	7	115	Chronic obstructive pulmonary diseases	7	208
Congenital anomalies	8	104	Suicide	8	161
Suicide	9	90	Congenital anomalies	9	157

[Continued]

★ 967 ★

Deaths: Leading Causes of Deaths and Number of Deaths, 1980 and 1982. Part 2
[Continued]

Race, Sex, and Cause of Death	1980		1992		
	Rank order	Deaths	Cause of death	Rank order	Deaths
Homicide and legal intervention	10	60	Nephritis, nephrotic syndrome, and nephrosis	10	124
Hispanic female[1]					
	---	---	All causes		32,961
	---	---	Diseases of heart	1	9,044
	---	---	Malignant neoplasms	2	7,235
	---	---	Cerebrovascular diseases	3	2,177
	---	---	Diabetes mellitus	4	1,683
	---	---	Unintentional injuries	5	1,562
	---	---	Pneumonia and influenza	6	1,068
	---	---	Certain conditions originating in the perinatal period	7	845
	---	---	Chronic obstructive pulmonary diseases	8	750
	---	---	Congenital anomalies	9	696
	---	---	Human immunodeficiency virus infection	10	658

Source: "Years of Potential Life Lost Before Age 65 for Selected Causes of Death, According to Sex and Race: United States, Selected Years 1970-92," *Health, United States, 1994,* pp. 101-102. Primary source: Centers for Disease Control and Prevention, National Center for Health Statistics: Vital Statistics of the United States, Vol. II, Mortality, Part A, for data years 1980 and 1992. Public Health Service. Washington. U.S. government Printing Office; Data computed by the Division of Health and Utilization Analysis from data compiled by the Division of Vital Statistics. *Notes:* For data years shown, the code numbers for cause of death are based on the *International Classification of Diseases, Ninth Revision,* described in Appendix II, table V. Categories for the coding and classification of human immunodeficiency virus infection were introduced in the United States beginning with mortality data for 1987. 1. Excludes data from States lacking an Hispanic-origin item on their death certificates.

★ 968 ★
Deaths

Deaths: Years of Potential Life Lost Before Age 65 for Selected Causes: Trends, 1970-92. Part 1

[Data are based on the National Vital Statistics System].

Sex, race, and cause of death	1970	1980	1984	1985	1986	1987	1988	1989	1990	1991	1992
	Years lost before age 65 per 100,000 population under 65 years of age										
White male											
All causes	9,757.4	7,611.5	6,670.3	6,697.6	6,770.4	6,632.2	6,646.2	6,559.9	6,503.1	6,405.8	6,244.7
Diseases of heart	1,607.4	1,179.1	1,061.1	1,034.8	1,004.2	967.2	928.9	874.6	847.7	837.8	833.3
Ischemic heart disease	-	869.7	734.5	707.8	664.8	629.3	590.7	564.6	545.5	529.5	522.0
Cerebrovascular diseases	215.0	122.6	108.3	104.5	100.2	101.2	100.8	93.7	93.9	92.9	94.9
Malignant neoplasms	1,036.9	935.1	884.7	887.5	881.0	861.5	854.4	842.9	843.1	842.2	832.1
Respiratory system	287.8	286.0	270.8	266.8	261.9	262.6	259.0	251.7	251.6	243.1	237.9
Colorectal	81.2	73.5	72.0	71.2	69.0	70.9	68.8	65.6	66.1	66.6	65.9
Prostate	14.4	15.2	15.5	15.0	15.8	15.2	15.5	16.1	16.2	15.6	14.8
Chronic obstructive pulmonary diseases	88.8	64.2	63.8	63.2	64.0	63.3	63.0	61.7	60.3	60.6	59.4
Pneumonia and influenza	353.2	88.7	75.5	77.6	81.6	77.0	81.4	80.0	76.3	78.1	70.5
Chronic liver disease and cirrhosis	209.8	166.9	141.7	136.8	134.2	136.9	140.6	139.8	132.5	131.9	133.7
Diabetes mellitus	75.3	52.5	52.7	53.9	55.8	58.8	62.0	67.7	65.7	57.0	70.8
Human immunodeficiency virus infection	-	-	-	-	-	254.3	302.2	401.7	451.2	507.0	546.3
Unintentional injuries	2,261.3	2,071.0	1,639.4	1,606.9	1,647.6	1,576.3	1,563.9	1,468.9	1,420.1	1,328.6	1,237.4
Motor vehicle crashes	1,296.5	1,301.7	1,019.3	985.2	1,032.7	999.2	989.2	907.4	886.8	801.9	721.6
Suicide	369.6	509.0	526.4	529.4	548.0	533.1	529.9	520.7	532.3	528.6	515.8

[Continued]

★ 968 ★

Deaths: Years of Potential Life Lost Before Age 65 for Selected Causes: Trends, 1970-92. Part 1
[Continued]

Sex, race, and cause of death	1970	1980	1984	1985	1986	1987	1988	1989	1990	1991	1992
Homicide and legal intervention	201.9	365.4	278.6	275.0	292.6	265.4	267.8	279.9	313.3	327.0	321.6
Black male											
All causes	20,283.5	14,381.9	12,308.9	12,675.5	13,287.7	13,564.8	14,059.5	14,412.5	14,365.8	14,432.4	13,944.9
Diseases of heart	2,022.2	1,661.4	1,538.7	1,561.7	1,556.2	1,514.6	1,514.2	1,458.8	1,387.8	1,398.3	1,378.9
Ischemic heart disease	-	800.9	697.3	684.9	642.8	621.1	602.7	598.2	552.5	561.0	537.4
Cerebrovascular diseases	595.6	349.3	302.6	295.8	295.1	288.2	300.7	283.2	279.9	272.5	267.2
Malignant neoplasms	1,216.0	1,175.8	1,167.9	1,141.3	1,121.7	1,093.8	1,109.2	1,125.0	1,131.9	1,102.3	1,075.5
Respiratory system	376.7	400.4	390.9	386.0	375.3	366.0	360.6	368.6	378.2	356.3	352.2
Colorectal	80.8	76.7	81.9	79.4	76.8	83.9	82.5	80.7	83.8	79.7	80.2
Prostate	35.2	34.1	30.5	33.1	29.4	28.4	31.1	30.2	30.5	29.9	33.0
Chronic obstructive pulmonary diseases	146.8	110.8	107.8	114.6	116.9	122.4	122.5	120.3	121.9	126.7	113.9
Pneumonia and influenza	1,308.9	315.2	244.2	254.9	249.3	261.3	274.1	275.1	261.4	239.9	222.3
Chronic liver disease and cirrhosis	463.5	391.9	289.5	305.8	282.0	296.8	276.0	269.4	242.4	208.5	201.7
Diabetes mellitus	144.0	102.2	106.4	106.1	108.2	108.6	126.4	139.6	133.7	140.0	140.6
Human immunodeficiency virus infection	-	-	-	-	-	719.7	892.7	1,124.3	1,224.5	1,416.5	1,647.1
Unintentional injuries	3,500.6	2,308.9	1,874.9	1,891.1	1,979.9	1,985.0	2,003.8	1,945.8	1,807.4	1,810.8	1,589.9
Motor vehicle crashes	1,466.1	1,022.4	872.7	893.7	967.7	943.2	964.3	938.7	919.9	847.1	771.0
Suicide	237.5	323.8	324.1	336.9	340.2	356.1	369.2	394.0	376.3	374.1	386.1
Homicide and legal intervention	2,234.6	2,274.9	1,664.0	1,689.1	1,956.0	1,924.0	2,148.2	2,287.7	2,580.7	2,712.3	2,567.5

Source: "Years of Potential Life Lost Before Age 65 for Selected Causes of Death, According to Sex and Race: United States, Selected Years 1970-92," *Health United States, 1994,* pp. 99-100. Primary source: Centers for Disease Control and Prevention, National Center for Health Statistics; Vital Statistics of the United States, Vol. II, Mortality, Part A, for data years 1970-92. Public Health Service. Washington. U.S. Government Printing Office; Data computed by the Division of Health and Utilization Analysis from data compiled by the Division of Vital Statistics and from table 1. *Notes:* For data years shown, the code numbers for cause of death are based on the International Classification of Diseases, Ninth Revision, described in Appendix II, table V. International Classification of Diseases codes for human immunodeficiency virus infection not available for use with the National Vital Statistics System until 1987. Years of potential life lost before age 65 provides a measure of the impact of mortality on the population under 65 years of age. See Appendix II for method of calculation. Data for the 1980's are based on intercensal population estimates. See Appendix I, Department of Commerce.

★ 969 ★
Deaths

Deaths: Years of Potential Life Lost Before Age 65 for Selected Causes: Trends, 1970-92. Part 2

[Data are based on the National Vital Statistics System].

Sex, race, and cause of death	1970	1980	1984	1985	1986	1987	1988	1989	1990	1991	1992
	Years lost before age 65 per 100,000 population under 65 years of age										
White female											
All causes	5,527.4	3,983.2	3,594.0	3,542.3	3,519.0	3,484.4	3,475.0	3,433.9	3,330.7	3,287.7	3,177.3
Diseases of heart	497.4	401.2	377.2	369.4	363.8	357.2	344.1	317.3	309.6	311.3	305.4
Ischemic heart disease	-	227.9	202.4	195.4	185.5	181.5	171.9	160.8	155.9	156.1	152.1
Cerebrovascular diseases	180.1	111.6	98.5	93.0	90.5	89.8	87.2	82.8	84.5	83.3	79.9
Malignant neoplasms	974.6	858.3	847.7	846.4	834.4	827.1	828.8	831.9	829.1	824.6	816.2
Respiratory system	89.8	132.6	141.8	144.9	142.8	145.8	149.4	148.7	150.2	148.7	149.1
Colorectal	77.0	64.0	59.3	57.9	56.9	56.4	54.1	51.8	52.2	53.3	51.0
Breast	233.4	211.7	214.8	215.1	213.4	212.7	215.4	217.2	217.5	213.3	205.6

[Continued]

Deaths: Years of Potential Life Lost Before Age 65 for Selected Causes: Trends, 1970-92. Part 2
[Continued]

Sex, race, and cause of death	1970	1980	1984	1985	1986	1987	1988	1989	1990	1991	1992
Chronic obstructive pulmonary diseases	46.5	43.0	47.3	51.8	50.7	52.4	51.6	55.2	52.7	55.0	51.1
Pneumonia and influenza	247.2	64.0	50.3	52.1	51.8	49.4	51.6	52.0	50.5	50.2	46.9
Chronic liver disease and cirrhosis	114.7	79.1	60.9	58.9	56.9	54.5	54.2	51.3	51.3	50.9	48.9
Diabetes mellitus	65.1	45.4	42.4	43.2	46.4	44.6	47.7	52.1	52.0	52.8	51.6
Human immunodeficiency virus infection	-	-	-	-	-	19.0	23.9	31.2	35.0	44.3	51.7
Unintentional injuries	755.6	647.8	542.9	532.4	542.5	543.1	541.4	534.9	494.2	479.3	438.0
Motor vehicle crashes	466.5	437.3	371.2	364.2	372.8	383.1	383.9	377.4	351.6	330.2	297.0
Suicide	157.2	145.4	143.0	137.7	140.6	137.7	132.5	127.3	126.3	124.2	119.4
Homicide and legal intervention	69.7	109.3	100.1	98.1	102.7	100.3	99.7	97.6	97.5	101.7	96.3
Black female											
All causes	12,188.8	7,927.2	6,958.2	6,961.4	7,108.0	7,211.7	7,455.1	7,542.7	7,382.2	7,275.9	7,162.7
Diseases of heart	1,297.7	937.2	853.1	856.7	868.6	832.0	845.7	811.5	782.4	776.9	796.7
Ischemic heart disease	-	382.7	333.2	325.1	310.0	296.2	296.9	287.7	272.3	273.5	278.3
Cerebrovascular diseases	564.7	289.0	250.9	248.8	240.9	243.2	241.5	234.9	235.8	224.5	220.4
Malignant neoplasms	1,044.8	968.4	954.1	936.8	975.7	971.6	960.7	939.9	972.7	953.0	983.5
Respiratory system	89.3	132.8	133.2	137.6	139.5	145.5	137.9	144.8	149.0	147.8	154.6
Colorectal	81.4	70.3	67.0	74.7	69.3	71.7	72.4	65.7	72.9	68.9	70.8
Breast	209.3	210.9	247.0	236.4	260.2	263.8	271.5	257.3	264.1	268.8	271.2
Chronic obstructive pulmonary diseases	93.3	62.5	71.1	74.5	72.3	78.3	86.0	80.4	80.6	92.7	84.3
Pneumonia and influenza	888.7	187.4	142.6	141.1	154.2	145.9	154.0	163.3	145.6	153.3	127.5
Chronic liver disease and cirrhosis	295.6	210.9	149.0	146.7	139.3	139.9	131.1	118.9	122.7	115.2	89.7
Diabetes mellitus	179.7	109.3	99.6	100.8	105.4	103.0	113.5	113.8	125.8	127.0	126.4
Human immunodeficiency virus infection	-	-	-	-	-	170.7	218.0	280.9	336.7	392.5	462.3
Unintentional injuries	1,169.9	718.5	600.4	616.8	649.3	634.9	692.3	662.3	614.4	602.3	590.1
Motor vehicle crashes	478.4	296.8	269.4	283.1	293.3	304.5	328.2	315.2	305.6	292.2	298.0
Suicide	81.9	70.3	66.0	59.1	66.1	66.9	74.2	75.0	69.8	54.7	60.3
Homicide and legal intervention	460.3	492.0	421.3	399.8	447.7	467.4	495.8	481.4	509.8	534.9	498.8

Source: "Years of Potential Life Lost Before Age 65 for Selected Causes of Death, According to Sex and Race: United States, Selected Years 1970-92," *Health United States, 1994*, pp. 99-100. Primary source: Centers for Disease Control and Prevention, National Center for Health Statistics; Vital Statistics of the United States, Vol. II, Mortality, Part A, for data years 1970-92. Public Health Service. Washington. U.S. Government Printing Office; Data computed by the Division of Health and Utilization Analysis from data compiled by the Division of Vital Statistics and from table 1. *Notes:* For data years shown, the code numbers for cause of death are based on the International Classification of Diseases, Ninth Revision, described in Appendix II, table V. International Classification of Diseases codes for human immunodeficiency virus infection not available for use with the National Vital Statistics System until 1987. Years of potential life lost before age 65 provides a measure of the impact of mortality on the population under 65 years of age. See Appendix II for method of calculation. Data for the 1980's are based on intercensal population estimates. See Appendix I, Department of Commerce.

Fertility

★ 970 ★

Fertility Indicators: Characteristics of Never-Married Women 14 to 44 Years Old: 1990 and 1994

[Numbers in thousands].

Characteristics	1994				1990			
	Total	Number of mothers	Mothers as a percent of total	Children ever born per 1,000 women	Total	Number of mothers	Mothers as a percent of total	Children ever born per 1,000 women
Total	22,733	4,603	20.2	378	20,739	3,756	18.1	323
RACE								
White	16,668	2,158	12.9	210	15,707	1,710	10.9	170
Black	4,855	2,244	46.2	964	4,189	1,955	46.7	929
Asian and Pacific Islander	726	67	9.2	179	653	42	6.4	100
HISPANIC ORIGIN								
Hispanic[1]	2,535	687	27.1	531	1,935	505	26.1	507
Not Hispanic	20,198	3,916	19.4	359	18,804	3,251	17.3	305

Source: "Fertility Indicators for Never-Married Women 15 to 44 Years old by Selected Characteristics," *Fertility of American Women: June 1994,* p. xviii. Primary source: June Current Population surveys, 1990 and 1994. *Notes:* NA = not applicable. 1. Persons of Hispanic origin may be of any race.

★ 971 ★
Fertility

Fertility Rates and Live-Birth Order: 1950-93

[Data are based on the National Vital Statistics System].

Race and year	Live births per 1,000 women 15-44 years of age					
	Total	Live-birth order				
		1	2	3	4	5 or higher
Race of child:[1] White						
1950	102.3	33.3	32.3	17.9	8.4	10.4
1960	113.2	30.8	29.2	22.7	14.1	16.4
1970	84.1	32.9	23.7	13.3	6.8	7.4
1980	64.7	28.4	21.0	9.5	3.4	2.4

[Continued]

★ 971 ★

Fertility Rates and Live-Birth Order: 1950-93

[Continued]

Race and year	Live births per 1,000 women 15-44 years of age					
	Total	Live-birth order				
		1	2	3	4	5 or higher
Race of mother:[2] White						
1980	65.6	28.8	21.3	9.6	3.4	2.4
1981	64.8	28.4	21.1	9.5	3.4	2.3
1982	64.8	28.0	21.6	9.6	3.4	2.2
1983	63.4	27.2	21.2	9.5	3.3	2.1
1984	63.2	26.8	21.4	9.6	3.3	2.1
1985	64.1	27.0	21.8	9.9	3.4	2.1
1986	63.1	26.6	21.3	9.8	3.4	2.1
1987	63.3	26.5	21.3	10.0	3.5	2.1
1988	64.5	26.8	21.6	10.4	3.6	2.1
1989	66.4	27.6	21.9	10.7	3.8	2.2
1990	68.3	28.4	22.4	11.1	4.0	2.4
1991	67.0	27.8	22.0	10.8	4.0	2.4
1992	66.5	27.3	22.0	10.8	4.0	2.4
Race of child:[1] Black						
1960	153.5	33.6	29.3	24.0	18.6	48.0
1970	115.4	43.3	27.1	16.1	10.0	18.9
1980	88.1	35.2	25.7	14.5	6.7	6.0
Race of mother:[2] Black						
1980	84.9	33.7	24.7	14.0	6.5	5.9
1981	82.0	32.3	24.2	13.7	6.3	5.5
1982	80.9	31.7	23.9	13.8	6.3	5.2
1983	78.7	31.1	23.1	13.2	6.1	5.1
1984	78.1	30.9	23.0	13.2	6.0	4.9
1985	78.8	31.0	23.4	13.4	6.1	4.8
1986	78.9	31.0	23.4	13.5	6.1	4.8
1987	80.1	31.2	23.8	13.9	6.3	4.9
1988	82.6	31.8	24.6	14.4	6.6	5.1
1989	86.2	32.9	25.4	15.3	7.1	5.5
1990	86.8	32.4	25.6	15.6	7.4	5.8

[Continued]

★ 971 ★

Fertility Rates and Live-Birth Order: 1950-93

[Continued]

Race and year	Live births per 1,000 women 15-44 years of age					
	Total	Live-birth order				
		1	2	3	4	5 or higher
1991	85.2	31.5	25.0	15.4	7.4	6.0
1992	83.2	30.6	24.3	15.0	7.2	6.1

Source: "Fertility Rates According to Live-Birth Order and Race: United States, Selected Years 1950-93." National Center for Health Statistics, *Health, United States, 1994*, p. 68. Primary source: Centers for Disease Control and Prevention, National Center for Health Statistics: Ventura SJ, Martin JA, Taffel SM, et al. Advance report of final natality statistics, 1992. Monthly Vital Statistics Report; Vol43, No 5, suppl. Hyattsville, Md. 1994; and Annual summary of birth, marriages, divorces, and deaths: United States, 1993. Monthly Vital Statistics Report; Vol 42 No 13. Hyattsville, Md.: Public Health Service. 1994. *Notes:* Data are based on births adjusted for underregistration for 1950 and on registered births for all other years. Beginning in 1970, births to nonresidents of the United States are excluded. Figures for live-birth order not stated are distributed. Final data for the 1980's are based on intercensal population estimates. Provisional rates for 1992-93 were calculated using 1990's-based postcensal population estimates. See Appendix I, National Center for Health Statistics and Department of Commerce. 1. Live births are tabulated by race of child. 2. Live births are tabulated by race of mother.

★ 972 ★

Fertility

Fertility Rates: Totals, and Intrinsic Rate of Natural Increase: 1960-1992

[Based on race of child and registered births only, thru 1979. Beginning 1980, based on race of mother. Beginning 1970, excludes births to nonresidents of United States. The total fertility rate is the number of births that 1,000 women would have in their lifetimes if, at each year of age, they experienced the birth rates occurring in the specified year. A total fertility rate of 2,110 represents "replacement level" fertility for the total population under current mortality conditions (assuming no net migration). The intrinsic rate of natural increase is the rate that would eventually prevail if a population were to experience, at each year of age, the birth rates and death rates occurring in the specified year and if those rates remained unchanged over a long period of time. Minus sign (-) indicates decrease.]

ANNUAL AVERAGE AND YEAR	TOTAL FERTILITY RATE			INTRINSIC RATE OF NATURAL INCREASE		
	Total	White	Black and other	Total	White	Black and other
1960-64	3,449	3,326	4,326	18.6	17.1	27.7
1965-69	2,622	2,512	3,362	8.2	6.4	18.6
1970-74	2,094	1,997	2,680	-0.7	-2.5	9.1
1975-79	1,774	1,685	2,270	-6.6	-8.5	3.0
1980-84	1,819	1,731	2,262	-5.4	-7.3	3.0
1985-88	1,870	1,769	2,339	-4.2	-6.3	4.3
1970	2,480	2,385	3,067	6.0	4.5	14.4
1971	2,267	2,161	2,920	2.6	0.8	12.6
1972	2,010	1,907	2,628	-2.0	-3.9	8.6

[Continued]

★ 972 ★

Fertility Rates: Totals, and Intrinsic Rate of Natural Increase: 1960-1992
[Continued]

ANNUAL AVERAGE AND YEAR	TOTAL FERTILITY RATE			INTRINSIC RATE OF NATURAL INCREASE		
	Total	White	Black and other	Total	White	Black and other
1973	1,879	1,783	2,443	-4.5	-6.5	5.7
1974	1,835	1,749	2,339	-5.4	-7.2	4.0
1975	1,774	1,686	2,276	-6.7	-8.6	3.0
1976	1,738	1,652	2,223	-7.4	-9.3	2.1
1977	1,790	1,703	2,279	-6.2	-8.1	3.2
1978	1,760	1,668	2,265	-6.8	-8.8	2.9
1979	1,808	1,716	2,310	-5.7	-7.7	3.0
1980	1,840	1,773	2,177	-5.1	-7.0	4.0
1981	1,812	1,748	2,118	-5.6	-7.4	3.0
1982	1,828	1,767	2,107	-5.2	-7.0	3.0
1983	1,799	1,741	2,066	-5.8	-7.5	2.2
1984	1,807	1,749	2,071	-5.6	-7.3	2.1
1985	1,844	1,787	2,109	-4.8	-6.5	2.7
1986	1,838	1,776	2,136	-4.9	-6.7	2.8
1987	1,872	1,805	2,198	-4.1	-6.1	4.0
1988	1,934	1,857	2,298	-2.9	-5.1	5.7
1989	2,014	1,931	2,433	-1.4	-3.6	7.4
1990	2,081	2,003	2,480	-0.1	-2.3	8.3
1991	2,073	1,996	2,480	-0.2	-2.4	8.2
1992	2,065	1,994	2,442	-0.4	-2.5	7.5

Source: "Total Fertility Rate and Intrinsic Rate of Natural Increase: 1960 to 1992" *Statistical Abstract of the United States, 1994*, p. 76. Primary source: U.S. National Center for Health Statistics, *Vital Statistics of the United States*, annual; and unpublished data.

★ 973 ★

Fertility

Fertility Rates: Trends and Projections, 1994, 2010

[For definition of total fertility rate, see headnote, table 91. Birth rates represent live births per 1,000 women in age group indicated. Projections are based on middle fertility assumptions. For explanations of methodology, see text, section 1.]

AGE GROUP	ALL RACES[1]		WHITE		BLACK		AMERICAN INDIAN, ESKIMO, ALEUT		ASIAN AND PACIFIC ISLANDERS		HISPANIC[2]	
	1994	2010	1994	2010	1994	2010	1994	2010	1994	2010	1994	2010
Total fertility rate	2,079	2,119	1,976	2,009	2,470	2,469	2,779	2,759	2,513	2,406	2,900	2,777
Birth rates:												
10 to 14 years old	1.4	1.6	0.7	0.9	4.9	5.0	2.0	2.1	0.8	0.8	2.3	2.3
15 to 19 years old	60.0	62.4	50.0	52.9	113.3	113.8	102.9	105.2	33.4	31.6	99.5	95.4

[Continued]

★ 973 ★

Fertility Rates: Trends and Projections, 1994, 2010
[Continued]

AGE GROUP	ALL RACES[1]		WHITE		BLACK		AMERICAN INDIAN, ESKIMO, ALEUT		ASIAN AND PACIFIC ISLANDERS		HISPANIC[2]	
	1994	2010	1994	2010	1994	2010	1994	2010	1994	2010	1994	2010
20 to 24 years old	118.0	120.0	110.0	112.4	160.9	161.1	188.6	187.0	100.1	95.6	180.5	172.6
25 to 29 years old	118.8	120.2	118.0	118.8	112.8	113.5	141.4	141.6	160.7	153.4	149.7	143.7
30 to 34 years old	80.1	82.0	80.2	80.9	67.8	68.4	78.1	78.4	134.2	128.4	95.7	91.5
35 to 39 years old	31.6	31.8	31.0	30.6	28.0	27.5	34.0	33.5	61.2	57.9	43.0	40.5
40 to 44 years old	5.4	5.5	5.2	5.1	5.3	5.1	7.2	7.0	12.7	12.0	9.2	8.5
45 to 49 years old	0.3	0.3	0.2	0.2	0.3	0.3	0.4	0.4	1.3	1.2	0.6	0.5

Source: "Projected Fertility Rates, by Race and Age Group: 1994 and 2010," *Statistical Abstract of the United States, 1994,* p. 76. Primary source: U.S. Bureau of the Census, *Current Population Reports,* P25-1104. *Notes:* 1. Includes races not shown separately. 2. Persons of Hispanic origin may be of any race.

Fetal and Infant Deaths

★ 974 ★

Fetal Death Rates: Mortality Rates by Race, Geographic Division and States: Trends

[Data are based on the National Vital Statistics System.]

Geographic division and State	Fetal deaths[2] per 1,000 live births plus fetal deaths								
	All races			White[1]			Black[1]		
	1980-82	1985-87	1990-92	1980-82	1985-87	1990-92	1980-82	1985-87	1990-92
United States	9.0	7.7	7.4	8.0	6.8	6.3	14.2	12.9	13.1
New England	7.3	6.4	6.0	7.1	6.0	5.5	11.4	11.8	11.4
Maine	7.0	5.9	5.2	7.0	6.0	5.1	[3]	[3]	[3]
New Hampshire	6.4	5.8	5.4	6.4	5.8	5.3	[3]	[3]	[3]
Vermont	7.1	6.2	6.1	7.0	6.2	5.9	[3]	[3]	[3]
Massachusetts	7.0	6.3	5.7	6.8	5.9	5.3	10.4	11.6	10.9
Rhode Island	9.9	7.3	5.5	9.6	6.9	5.5	15.9[3]	13.6[3]	7.1[3]
Connecticut	7.8	6.7	7.0	7.3	6.0	6.1	11.7	11.8	12.8
Middle Atlantic	10.3	9.0	9.4	9.4	7.9	7.8	14.8	14.2	16.5
New York	11.3	9.6	10.4	10.4	8.4	8.3	15.0	14.6	18.2
New Jersey	8.3	8.0	7.8	7.2	6.9	6.2	12.9	12.7	14.5
Pennsylvania	10.1	8.8	8.9	9.2	7.9	8.0	16.2	14.4	14.1
East North Central	8.2	7.0	6.7	7.4	6.2	5.8	12.7	11.1	10.7
Ohio	8.3	7.4	7.1	7.7	6.7	6.2	12.2	11.2	11.3
Indiana	8.3	7.6	7.1	7.8	6.8	6.4	12.6	13.3	12.5
Illinois	9.1	7.7	7.5	7.7	6.5	6.0	14.3	12.1	12.6

[Continued]

★974★

Fetal Death Rates: Mortality Rates by Race, Geographic Division and States: Trends
[Continued]

Geographic division and State	Fetal deaths[2] per 1,000 live births plus fetal deaths								
	All races			White[1]			Black[1]		
	1980-82	1985-87	1990-92	1980-82	1985-87	1990-92	1980-82	1985-87	1990-92
Michigan	7.2	5.7	5.1	6.6	5.2	4.7	10.5	8.3	6.6
Wisconsin	7.3	6.3	6.2	7.0	5.7	5.5	13.3	12.7	11.6
West North Central	7.7	6.4	6.3	7.3	6.1	5.8	14.2	11.1	11.1
Minnesota	6.6	6.2	6.2	6.5	6.1	5.9	12.5[3]	10.2	11.1
Iowa	7.2	6.1	6.4	7.1	6.0	6.2	11.0[3]	9.5[3]	13.4[3]
Missouri	8.8	6.6	6.5	7.8	5.9	5.5	14.9	10.8	11.5
North Dakota	7.7	6.1	6.7	7.4	5.9	6.4	[3]	[3]	[3]
South Dakota	7.7	6.3	6.2	6.8	5.9	5.6	[3]	[3]	[3]
Nebraska	8.3	7.3	6.8	8.0	7.0	6.4	13.3[3]	13.0[3]	10.8[3]
Kansas	8.0	6.5	5.5	7.5	6.0	5.2	13.5	12.8	9.1
South Atlantic	11.1	9.4	9.0	9.2	7.5	6.8	16.0	14.2	14.6
Delaware	8.8	7.4	6.5	7.8	5.8	5.4	12.5	12.6	9.4
Maryland	8.8	8.2	8.5	7.1	6.5	6.3	13.1	12.4	13.6
District of Columbia	13.2	12.2	13.3	10.3[3]	6.7	6.5	13.8	14.0	15.7
Virginia	12.5	10.1	8.2	10.8	8.5	6.6	18.2	15.9	13.7
West Virginia	9.3	7.9	7.6	9.2	7.8	7.3	14.5[3]	11.9[3]	13.9[3]
North Carolina	10.1	8.5	8.5	8.3	7.1	6.5	14.4	12.0	13.3
South Carolina	12.4	10.3	10.1	9.0	7.6	7.4	17.5	14.7	14.4
Georgia	14.2	11.7	12.0	11.6	9.3	8.3	18.9	16.3	18.3
Florida	9.9	8.4	8.0	8.4	6.7	6.3	14.3	14.0	13.3
East South Central	10.5	9.1	8.2	8.6	7.3	6.2	15.7	13.9	13.3
Kentucky	9.4	8.1	7.2	8.9	7.5	6.7	13.6	13.9	12.0
Tennessee	8.8	7.0	5.7	7.7	6.1	4.7	12.7	9.7	8.9
Alabama	11.3	10.6	9.8	8.9	8.2	7.3	15.8	15.3	14.5
Mississippi	13.5	11.3	11.2	9.4	7.5	6.5	18.0	15.7	16.1
West South Central	8.4	7.4	6.8	7.5	6.6	5.9	12.3	11.0	10.7
Arkansas	8.7	7.9	7.7	7.3	6.9	6.1	13.1	11.2	12.8
Louisiana	9.8	8.4	8.0	7.7	6.4	6.0	13.6	11.7	10.7
Oklahoma	8.6	7.7	7.6	7.7	7.3	7.2	15.5	11.9	10.8
Texas	7.9	7.0	6.4	7.5	6.5	5.7	10.7	10.3	10.2
Mountain	8.0	6.9	6.1	7.8	6.7	6.0	14.6	11.5	10.5
Montana	6.5	7.3	7.4	6.4	6.9	7.2	[3]	[3]	[3]
Idaho	7.4	6.7	6.2	7.4	6.6	6.1	[3]	[3]	[3]
Wyoming	8.3	6.9	7.2	8.4	6.8	7.3	[3]	[3]	[3]
Colorado	9.8	8.3	6.8	9.5	8.1	6.6	16.8	11.9	10.9
New Mexico	7.7	4.9	4.1	7.4	4.9	4.2	15.2[3]	7.2[3]	4.3[3]
Arizona	7.8	6.5	6.0	7.3	6.2	5.7	14.3	11.6	10.4
Utah	7.1	6.7	5.7	7.0	6.6	5.7	[3]	[3]	[3]
Nevada	8.0	7.2	7.0	7.6	6.8	6.4	12.6[3]	11.1[3]	12.4

[Continued]

★ 974 ★

Fetal Death Rates: Mortality Rates by Race, Geographic Division and States: Trends

[Continued]

Geographic division and State	Fetal deaths[2] per 1,000 live births plus fetal deaths								
	All races			White[1]			Black[1]		
	1980-82	1985-87	1990-92	1980-82	1985-87	1990-92	1980-82	1985-87	1990-92
Pacific	7.7	6.7	6.3	7.3	6.2	5.9	12.2	12.2	11.5
Washington	7.4	5.9	5.8	7.3	5.7	5.4	13.5	10.8	12.4
Oregon	6.8	6.2	6.0	6.8	6.3	5.9	8.6[3]	8.0[3]	10.1[3]
California	7.7	6.7	6.3	7.3	6.3	6.0	12.1	12.4	11.6
Alaska	7.4	6.7	5.3	6.6	6.2	5.3	15.1[3]	8.6[3]	5.6[3]
Hawaii	11.4	8.5	7.0	12.0	7.8	8.6	19.1[3]	13.5[3]	10.5[3]

Source: "Fetal Death Rates, According to Race, Geographic Division, and State: United States, Average Annual 1980-92, 1985-87, and 1990-92" *Health, United States, 1994,* p. 92. Primary source: Centers for Disease Control and Prevention, National Center for Health Statistics: Data computed by the Division of Health and Utilization Analysis from data compiled by the Division of Vital Statistics. *Notes:* 1. Fetal deaths and live births are tabulated by race of mother. 2. Deaths of fetuses 20 weeks or more gestation. 3. Data for States with fewer than 5,000 live births for the 3-year period are considered unreliable. Data for States with fewer than 1,000 live births are considered highly unreliable and are not shown.

★ 975 ★

Fetal and Infant Deaths

Infant Deaths: Mortality Rates by Race and State: 1980-1992

[Deaths per 1,000 live births, by place of residence. Represents deaths of infants under 1 year old, exclusive of fetal deaths. Excludes deaths of nonresidents of the United States. See Appendix III and *Historical Statistics, Colonial Times to 1970,* series B 143-147, for U.S. totals.]

DIVISION AND STATE	TOTAL[1]			WHITE		BLACK	
	1980	1990	1992	1990	1992	1990	1992
U.S.	12.6	9.2	8.5	7.7	6.9	18.0	16.8
N.E.	10.5	7.2	6.8	6.8	6.0	14.0	14.9
ME	9.2	6.2	5.6	6.2	5.5	(NA)	(NA)
NH	9.9	7.1	5.9	7.2	5.8	(NA)	(NA)
VT	10.7	6.4	7.2	6.5	7.3	(NA)	(NA)
MA	10.5	7.0	6.5	6.7	5.8	11.9	13.4
RI	11.0	8.1	7.4	8.3	6.9	(NA)	(NA)
CT	11.2	7.9	7.6	6.6	6.2	17.6	17.2
M.A.	12.8	9.5	8.8	7.5	6.8	18.7	17.5
NY	12.5	9.6	8.8	7.7	7.1	18.1	15.8
NJ	12.5	9.0	8.4	6.8	5.9	18.4	18.7
PA	13.2	9.6	9.0	7.8	6.9	20.5	20.4
E.N.C.	13.0	10.1	9.5	8.0	7.4	21.0	19.6
OH	12.8	9.8	9.4	8.2	7.9	19.5	18.0
IN	11.9	9.6	9.4	8.9	8.0	17.4	20.3
IL	14.8	10.7	10.1	7.7	7.4	22.4	19.8
MI	12.8	10.7	10.2	7.9	7.0	21.6	22.1
WI	10.3	8.2	7.2	7.2	6.4	19.0	13.5

[Continued]

★ 975 ★

Infant Deaths: Mortality Rates by Race and State: 1980-1992

[Continued]

DIVISION AND STATE	TOTAL[1]			WHITE		BLACK	
	1980	1990	1992	1990	1992	1990	1992
W.N.C.	11.3	8.4	8.0	7.5	7.0	18.9	17.3
MN	10.0	7.3	7.1	6.7	6.2	23.7	17.5
IA	11.8	8.1	8.0	7.8	7.7	21.9	19.4
MO	12.4	9.4	8.5	7.8	6.9	18.2	15.9
ND	12.1	8.0	7.8	7.9	7.4	(NA)	(NA)
SD	10.9	10.1	9.3	8.6	7.7	(NA)	(NA)
NE	11.5	8.3	7.4	7.2	6.7	18.9	19.8
KS	10.4	8.4	8.7	7.7	7.5	17.7	21.7
S.A.	14.5	10.7	9.8	8.0	7.1	17.9	16.4
DE	13.9	10.1	8.6	7.3	5.8	20.1	18.0
MD	14.0	9.5	9.8	6.5	6.7	17.1	16.5
DC	25.0	20.7	19.6	12.1	13.1	24.6	22.0
VA	13.6	10.2	9.5	7.5	6.9	19.5	17.7
WV	11.8	9.9	9.2	9.6	8.9	(NA)	(NA)
NC	14.5	10.6	10.0	8.3	7.3	16.5	16.5
SC	15.6	11.7	10.4	8.3	7.1	17.3	16.0
GA	14.5	12.4	10.3	9.1	7.1	18.3	15.9
FL	14.6	9.6	8.8	7.6	7.0	16.8	15.1
E.S.C.	14.5	10.4	9.9	8.1	7.5	16.4	16.2
KY	12.9	8.5	8.3	8.0	7.9	14.3	12.7
TN	13.5	10.3	9.4	8.0	7.0	17.9	17.4
AL	15.1	10.8	10.5	8.3	7.6	16.0	16.2
MS	17.0	12.1	11.9	8.5	8.0	16.2	16.1
W.S.C.	12.7	8.7	8.3	7.4	7.1	15.3	14.2
AR	12.7	9.2	10.3	8.0	8.6	13.9	16.2
LA	14.3	11.1	9.4	7.3	6.9	16.7	13.0
OK	12.7	9.2	8.8	9.4	7.9	14.3	16.8
TX	12.2	8.1	7.8	7.1	6.8	14.7	14.2
Mountain	11.0	8.6	7.6	8.3	7.2	18.5	16.7
MT	12.4	9.0	7.5	8.6	6.7	(NA)	(NA)
ID	10.7	8.7	8.8	8.7	8.8	(NA)	(NA)
WY	9.8	8.6	8.9	8.8	9.0	(NA)	(NA)
CO	10.1	8.8	7.6	8.4	7.2	19.4	14.6
NM	11.5	9.0	7.6	9.3	6.8	(NA)	(NA)
AZ	12.4	8.8	8.4	8.2	7.8	20.6	16.7
UT	10.4	7.5	5.9	7.4	6.0	(NA)	(NA)
NV	10.7	8.4	6.7	8.1	5.9	14.2	16.6
Pacific	11.2	7.9	7.0	7.6	6.4	17.1	16.7
WA	11.8	7.8	6.8	7.6	6.4	20.6	15.9
OR	12.2	8.3	7.1	8.1	6.8	(NA)	23.0
CA	11.1	7.9	7.0	7.6	6.3	16.8	16.8

[Continued]

★ 975 ★

Infant Deaths: Mortality Rates by Race and State: 1980-1992

[Continued]

DIVISION AND STATE	TOTAL[1]			WHITE		BLACK	
	1980	1990	1992	1990	1992	1990	1992
AK	12.3	10.5	8.6	8.5	7.3	(NA)	(NA)
HI	10.3	6.7	6.3	5.1	(NA)	(NA)	(NA)

Source: "Infant Mortality Rates, by Race-States: 1980 to 1992," *Statistical Abstract of the United States,* 1995, p. 91. Primary source: U.S. National Center for Health Statistics, *Vital Statistics of the United States,* annual; and unpublished data. *Notes:* NA Not available. 1. Includes other races, not shown separately.

Infant Mortality

★ 976 ★

Infant Mortality Rates by Race, Region, and State: 1980-82, 1985-87, and 1990-92

[Data are based on the National Vital Statistics System].

Geographic division and State	All races			White[1]			Black[1]		
	1980-82	1985-87	1990-92	1980-82	1985-87	1990-92	1980-82	1985-87	1990-92
	Infant deaths per 1,000 live births								
United States	12.0	10.4	8.9	10.4	8.8	7.3	21.2	18.9	17.5
New England	10.4	8.6	6.9	9.8	7.9	6.3	20.7	20.0	14.2
Maine	9.7	8.7	6.2	9.8	8.7	6.1	[2]	[2]	[2]
New Hampshire	10.2	8.7	6.4	10.2	8.6	6.3	[2]	[2]	[2]
Vermont	9.2	9.0	6.5	9.2	8.9	6.5	[2]	[2]	[2]
Massachusetts	10.1	8.3	6.7	9.6	7.4	6.2	19.1	19.6	12.5
Rhode Island	10.9	8.7	7.8	10.5	8.3	7.4	19.4[2]	14.5[2]	14.9[2]
Connecticut	11.5	9.2	7.6	10.1	7.8	6.3	22.4	21.3	16.5
Middle Atlantic	12.2	10.5	9.1	10.4	8.7	7.1	20.9	18.9	18.1
New York	12.4	10.7	9.3	10.5	9.0	7.3	20.0	17.5	17.2
New Jersey	11.7	9.9	8.7	9.5	7.9	6.3	21.1	19.3	18.5
Pennsylvania	12.2	10.5	9.2	10.8	8.7	7.3	23.0	22.3	20.1
East North Central	12.5	10.8	9.8	10.5	8.9	7.7	24.3	21.0	20.2
Ohio	12.2	10.1	9.6	10.7	8.9	7.9	22.6	17.5	18.4
Indiana	11.7	10.8	9.4	10.5	9.6	8.2	22.0	21.2	19.0
Illinois	14.1	11.8	10.5	11.1	9.1	7.6	25.9	22.2	21.2
Michigan	12.7	11.2	10.4	10.3	8.8	7.4	25.3	22.9	21.8
Wisconsin	10.0	9.0	7.9	9.3	8.2	7.1	20.0	17.9	15.5

[Continued]

★ 976 ★

Infant Mortality Rates by Race, Region, and State: 1980-82, 1985-87, and 1990-92
[Continued]

Geographic division and State	All races			White[1]			Black[1]		
	1980-82	1985-87	1990-92	1980-82	1985-87	1990-92	1980-82	1985-87	1990-92
West North Central	11.0	9.5	8.4	10.1	8.7	7.3	21.8	18.6	19.0
Minnesota	9.9	8.9	7.3	9.4	8.5	6.5	27.8[2]	20.8	21.0
Iowa	10.7	9.0	8.1	10.4	8.8	7.8	26.5[2]	18.0[2]	18.3[2]
Missouri	12.3	10.4	9.4	10.9	9.0	7.5	20.7	18.3	18.6
North Dakota	11.3	8.6	8.0	10.6	8.2	7.5	[2]	[2]	[2]
South Dakota	10.9	11.0	9.6	9.1	8.9	8.0	[2]	[2]	[2]
Nebraska	10.5	9.4	7.7	9.9	8.7	6.9	22.4[2]	20.0[2]	18.9[2]
Kansas	10.7	9.2	8.7	9.9	8.5	7.7	21.9	18.4	19.8
South Atlantic	13.8	11.8	10.2	10.8	9.1	7.4	21.2	19.0	17.2
Delaware	13.8	12.7	10.2	10.3	10.1	7.6	25.9	21.4	18.8
Maryland	12.8	11.7	9.5	10.1	8.9	6.6	19.8	18.7	16.1
District of Columbia	23.8	20.4	20.4	13.3[2]	11.0	10.9	26.1	23.7	24.0
Virginia	13.0	10.9	9.9	11.0	8.7	7.2	20.1	18.6	18.5
West Virginia	12.1	10.3	9.1	11.8	9.8	8.9	21.9[2]	23.3[2]	14.9[2]
North Carolina	13.8	11.7	10.5	11.1	9.2	7.8	20.2	18.2	16.7
South Carolina	16.0	13.4	11.1	11.7	9.7	7.8	22.6	19.4	16.6
Georgia	13.6	12.6	11.4	10.2	9.7	7.9	19.9	18.5	17.5
Florida	13.6	10.9	9.1	10.7	8.6	7.1	22.4	18.8	16.1
East South Central	13.6	11.8	10.2	11.0	9.4	7.8	20.7	18.5	16.5
Kentucky	12.3	10.3	8.6	11.7	9.7	8.0	19.9	16.1	14.2
Tennessee	12.7	11.4	9.9	10.7	8.9	7.4	20.1	19.8	18.0
Alabama	14.0	12.7	10.9	10.7	9.6	8.0	20.2	18.8	16.5
Mississippi	16.0	13.3	11.8	10.6	9.3	7.9	21.8	17.9	15.9
West South Central	12.0	10.1	8.5	10.5	8.7	7.2	19.1	16.6	14.7
Arkansas	11.6	10.8	9.9	9.4	9.4	8.3	18.5	15.3	15.5
Louisiana	13.7	11.9	10.4	10.0	8.4	7.4	20.0	17.4	14.6
Oklahoma	12.3	10.3	9.2	11.5	9.7	8.6	20.1	17.8	16.2
Texas	11.5	9.5	7.8	10.5	8.6	6.9	18.3	16.1	14.5
Mountain	10.5	9.5	8.1	10.1	9.1	7.6	20.4	18.5	18.3
Montana	11.1	10.0	7.9	10.5	9.1	7.0	[2]	[2]	[2]
Idaho	10.0	10.7	8.7	10.0	10.6	8.7	[2]	[2]	[2]
Wyoming	10.1	10.8	8.5	9.9	10.7	8.4	[2]	[2]	[2]
Colorado	9.7	9.3	8.3	9.5	8.9	7.7	16.8	19.3	17.4
New Mexico	10.9	9.4	8.2	10.6	9.0	7.8	21.6[2]	23.6[2]	23.4[2]
Arizona	11.1	9.5	8.6	10.4	8.9	7.9	20.6	18.1	19.2
Utah	10.4	9.0	6.5	10.3	9.0	6.4	[2]	[2]	[2]
Nevada	10.7	9.1	8.1	9.8	8.6	7.3	22.5[2]	17.0[2]	17.4
Pacific	10.5	9.3	7.5	9.9	8.7	6.9	18.9	18.6	16.8
Washington	11.0	10.1	7.4	10.5	9.8	7.0	21.1	17.6	16.9
Oregon	11.2	9.9	7.5	11.0	9.7	7.2	20.3[2]	22.5[2]	21.5[2]
California	10.4	9.2	7.5	9.8	8.5	6.9	18.7	18.6	16.8

[Continued]

★ 976 ★

Infant Mortality Rates by Race, Region, and State: 1980-82, 1985-87, and 1990-92

[Continued]

Geographic division and State	All races			White[1]			Black[1]		
	1980-82	1985-87	1990-92	1980-82	1985-87	1990-92	1980-82	1985-87	1990-92
Alaska	12.0	10.7	9.3	9.5	8.9	7.7	26.1[2]	17.4[2]	13.2[2]
Hawaii	9.6	9.0	6.8	7.4	6.2	4.4	17.3[2]	20.8[2]	18.7[2]

Source: "Infant Mortality Rates According to Race, Geographic Division, and State: United States, Average Annual 1980-82, 1985-87, and 1990-92." National Center for Health Statistics, *Health, United States, 1994*, p. 89. Primary source: Centers for Disease Control and Prevention, National Center for Health Statistics: Data computed by the Division of Health and Utilization Analysis from data compiled by the division of Vital Statistics. *Notes:* 1. Deaths are tabulated by race of decedent; live births are tabulated by race of mother. 2. Data for States with fewer than 5,000 live births for the 3-year period are considered unreliable. Data for States with fewer than 1,000 live births are considered highly unreliable and are not shown.

★ 977 ★

Infant Mortality

Infant Mortality Rates by Race: 1970-92

Year	All mothers	White	Black
1970	20.0	17.6	33.3
1971	19.1	17.0	30.9
1972	18.5	16.2	30.3
1973	17.7	15.6	28.8
1974	16.7	14.7	27.5
1975	16.1	14.0	27.0
1976	15.2	13.2	26.4
1977	14.1	12.2	24.4
1978	13.8	11.9	23.9
1979	13.1	11.3	22.6
1980	12.6	10.9	22.2
1981	11.9	10.3	20.8
1982	11.5	9.9	20.5
1983	11.2	9.6	20.0
1984	10.8	9.3	19.2
1985	10.6	9.2	19.0
1986	10.4	8.8	18.9
1987	10.1	8.5	18.8
1988	10.0	8.4	18.5
1989	9.8	8.1	18.6
1990	9.2	7.6	18.0
1991	8.9	7.3	17.6
1992	8.5	6.9	16.8

Source: "Infant Mortality Rates by Race: United States, 1970-92." National Center for Health Statistics, *Health, United States, 1994*, p. 16. Primary source: Centers for Disease Control and Prevention, National Center for Health Statistics, National Vital Statistics System. *Notes:* Infant mortality rates by race are calculated with infant deaths tabulated by race of decedent and live births tabulated by race of mother (see Appendix II, Race). These data are plotted on the log scale.

★ 978 ★
Infant Mortality

Infant Mortality Rates for Mothers Twenty Years of Age and Over: Characteristics: 1983-88

[Data are based on the National Linked Files of Live Births and Infant Deaths].

Race of mother and Hispanic origin of mother	Birth cohort							
	1983	1984	1985	1986	1987	1988	1983-85	1986-88
	Infant deaths per 1,000 live births							
Less than 12 years of education								
All mothers	16.2	15.4	15.4	15.0	14.6	14.7	15.7	14.8
White	13.8	13.3	13.2	12.7	12.4	12.3	13.4	12.5
Black	22.9	21.0	21.4	20.9	20.4	20.8	21.8	20.7
American Indian or Alaskan Native	16.4	14.0	16.7	18.1	15.7	14.8	15.7	16.2
Asian or Pacific Islander[1]	10.6	11.6	9.3[4]	10.6[4]	7.4	9.3	10.5	9.1
Hispanic origin[2,3]	11.2	11.3	11.0	11.5	9.6	10.6	11.1	10.6
Mexican American	8.7	9.9	10.8	10.1	8.7	8.8	9.8	9.2
Puerto Rican	15.2	14.9	11.9	14.4	11.2	13.9	14.0	13.2
Cuban	4	4	4	4	4	4	4	4
Central or South American	4	4	8.6[4]	10.3[4]	9.5[4]	8.7[4]	8.4	9.5
Other and unknown Hispanic	10.3	11.6[4]	11.7	11.0[4]	9.3	11.4[4]	11.2	10.6
Non-Hispanic white[2]	14.2	13.4	13.9	13.1	13.0	13.0	13.9	13.0
Non-Hispanic black[2]	23.5	21.8	21.5	21.1	20.1	21.9	22.3	21.1
12 years of education								
All mothers	10.5	10.3	10.3	10.0	9.7	9.8	10.4	9.9
White	9.0	8.7	8.7	8.4	8.1	8.1	8.8	8.2
Black	17.7	17.7	17.7	17.3	16.8	16.8	17.7	16.9
American Indian or Alaskan Native	15.0	13.6	10.7	12.6	11.5	11.2	13.0	11.8
Asian or Pacific Islander[1]	9.9	10.2	8.2	8.4	7.8	7.6	9.4	7.9
Hispanic origin[2,3]	9.0	9.8	9.4	8.0	8.3	8.8	9.4	8.4
Mexican American	8.0[4]	7.4[4]	8.9	6.9	8.7	9.5	8.1	8.5
Puerto Rican	10.7	12.5	11.6	10.3	9.1	10.7	11.6	10.1
Cuban	4	4	4	4	4		8.3[4]	6.5[4]
Central or South American	4	10.1[4]	8.1[4]	7.6[4]	7.8	6.7	9.0	7.3
Other and unknown Hispanic	9.2	9.1	8.8	7.9	7.6	8.4	9.0	8.0
Non-Hispanic white[2]	9.1	8.4	8.5	8.5	8.1	8.1	8.6	8.2
Non-Hispanic black[2]	17.6	17.9	18.3	17.7	17.1	17.2	17.9	17.3
13 or more years of education								
All mothers	8.2	7.8	7.7	7.6	7.1	7.0	7.9	7.3
White	7.2	6.9	6.7	6.5	6.2	6.0	6.9	6.2
Black	15.4	14.9	15.9	15.5	14.5	14.5	15.4	14.8
American Indian or Alaskan Native	4	4	4	4	4	4	10.3	8.4

[Continued]

★ 978 ★

Infant Mortality Rates for Mothers Twenty Years of Age and Over: Characteristics: 1983-88
[Continued]

Race of mother and Hispanic origin of mother	Birth cohort							
	1983	1984	1985	1986	1987	1988	1983-85	1986-88
Asian or Pacific Islander[1]	6.6	7.5	6.2	6.4	6.1	5.7	6.8	6.0
Hispanic origin[2,3]	9.1	7.0	6.6	7.4	6.6	7.0	7.5	7.0
Mexican American	[4]	[4]	[4]	[4]	[4]	[4]	7.9	6.5
Puerto Rican	[4]	[4]	[4]	[4]	[4]	6.8[4]	8.3	6.8
Cuban	[4]	[4]	[4]	[4]	[4]	[4]	5.4	5.8
Central or South American	[4]	[4]	[4]	[4]	[4]	7.8[4]	7.3	7.6
Other and unknown Hispanic	[4]	[4]	[4]	[4]	[4]	[4]	7.9	7.8
Non-Hispanic white[2]	7.1	6.9	6.7	6.4	6.1	6.1	6.9	6.2
Non-Hispanic black[2]	15.0	14.1	15.2	15.3	14.3	14.7	14.8	14.8

Source: "Infant Mortality Rates for Mothers 20 Years of Age and Over, According to Educational Attainment, Detailed Race of Mother, and Hispanic Origin of Mother: Selected states, 1983-88 Birth Cohorts." National Center for Health Statistics, *Health, United States, 1994,* p. 85. Primary source: Centers for Disease Control and Prevention, National Center for Health Statistics: Data computed by the Division of Health and Utilization Analysis from data compiled by the Division of Vital Statistics for the National Linked Files of Live Births and Infant Deaths. *Notes:* Includes data for 47 States and the District of Columbia (DC) in 1983- 87, and 46 States and DC in 1988. Excludes data for California, Texas, and Washington (1983-88) and New York (1988), which did not require the reporting of maternal education on the birth certificate (see Appendix I). The race groups, white and black, include persons of Hispanic and non- Hispanic origin. Conversely, persons of Hispanic origin may be of any race. 1. The States not reporting maternal education on the birth certificate accounted for 49-51 percent of the Asian or Pacific Islander births in the United States in 1983-87 and 59 percent in 1988. 2. Includes mothers of all races. 3. Data shown only for States with an Hispanic-origin item on their birth certificates. In 1983-87, 21 States and the District of Columbia (DC), and in 1988, 26 States and DC included both item. The States not reporting maternal education on the birth certificate during 1983-88, together accounted for 28-85 percent of the births in each Hispanic subgroup (except Cuban) in the Hispanic reporting area. 4. Infant mortality rates for groups with fewer than 10,000 births are considered unreliable. Infant mortality rates for groups with fewer than 7,500 births are considered highly unreliable and are not shown.

★ 979 ★

Infant Mortality

Infant, Neonatal, and Postneonatal Mortality Rates by Race and Hispanic Origin of Mother, 1960 and 1983-88

[Data are based on the National Linked Files of Live Births and Infant Deaths].

Race of mother and Hispanic origin of mother	Birth cohort								
	1960[1]	1983	1984	1985	1986	1987	1988	1983-85	1986-88
	Infant deaths per 1,000 live births								
All mothers	25.1	10.9	10.4	10.4	10.1	9.8	9.6	10.6	9.8
White	22.2	9.3	8.9	8.9	8.5	8.2	8.0	9.0	8.2
Black	42.1	19.2	18.2	18.6	18.2	17.8	17.8	18.7	17.9
American Indian or Alaskan Native	-	15.2	13.4	13.1	13.9	13.0	12.7	13.9	13.2
Asian or Pacific Islander	-	8.3	8.9	7.8	7.8	7.3	6.8	8.3	7.3
Chinese	-	9.5	7.2	5.8	5.9	6.2	5.5	7.4	5.8
Japanese	-	[4]	6.4[4]	6.0[4]	7.2[4]	6.6[4]	7.0[4]	6.0	6.9
Filipino	-	8.4	8.5	7.7	7.2	6.6	6.9	8.2	6.9
Hawaiian and part Hawaiian	-	[4]	[4]	[4]	[4]	[4]	[4]	11.3	11.1
Other Asian or Pacific Islander	-	8.1	9.4	8.5	8.3	7.6	7.0	8.6	7.6

[Continued]

Infant, Neonatal, and Postneonatal Mortality Rates by Race and Hispanic Origin of Mother, 1960 and 1983-88
[Continued]

Race of mother and Hispanic origin of mother	Birth cohort								
	1960[1]	1983	1984	1985	1986	1987	1988	1983-85	1986-88
Hispanic origin[2,3]	-	9.5	9.3	8.8	8.4	8.2	8.3	9.2	8.3
Mexican American	-	9.1	8.9	8.5	7.9	8.0	7.9	8.8	7.9
Puerto Rican	-	12.9	12.9	11.1	11.7	9.9	11.6	12.3	11.1
Cuban	-	7.5[4]	8.1[4]	8.5	7.5[4]	7.1	7.2	8.0	7.3
Central or South American	-	8.5	8.3	8.0	7.8	7.8	7.2	8.2	7.6
Other and unknown Hispanic	-	10.6	9.6	9.5	9.2	8.7	9.1	9.9	9.0
Non-Hispanic white[3]	-	9.2	8.7	8.7	8.4	8.1	8.0	8.9	8.1
Non-Hispanic black[3]	-	19.1	18.1	18.3	18.0	17.4	18.1	18.5	17.9

Neonatal deaths per 1,000 live births

	1960[1]	1983	1984	1985	1986	1987	1988	1983-85	1986-88
All mothers	18.4	7.1	6.8	6.8	6.5	6.2	6.1	6.9	6.3
White	16.9	6.1	5.8	5.8	5.5	5.2	5.0	5.9	5.2
Black	27.3	12.5	11.9	12.3	11.9	11.8	11.5	12.2	11.7
American Indian or Alaskan Native	-	7.5	6.4	6.1	6.1	6.2	5.4	6.7	5.9
Asian or Pacific Islander	-	5.2	5.7	4.8	4.8	4.5	4.3	5.2	4.5
Chinese	-	5.5	4.4	3.3	3.1	3.7	3.1	4.3	3.3
Japanese	-	[4]	3.6[4]	3.1[4]	4.7[4]	4.0[4]	4.5[4]	3.4	4.4
Filipino	-	5.6	5.3	5.1	4.9	4.1	4.4	5.3	4.5
Hawaiian and part Hawaiian	-	[4]	[4]	[4]	[4]	[4]	[4]	7.4	7.1
Other Asian or Pacific Islander	-	5.0	6.2	5.4	5.1	4.6	4.4	5.5	4.7
Hispanic origin[2,3]	-	6.2	6.2	5.7	5.5	5.3	5.2	6.0	5.3
Mexican American	-	5.9	5.8	5.4	5.1	5.1	4.8	5.7	5.0
Puerto Rican	-	8.7	8.6	7.6	7.6	6.7	7.3	8.3	7.2
Cuban	-	5.0[4]	6.4[4]	6.2	5.1[4]	5.3	5.5	5.9	5.3
Central or South American	-	5.8	5.9	5.6	5.2	5.0	4.8	5.7	5.0
Other and unknown Hispanic	-	6.4	6.5	5.6	6.0	5.6	5.9	6.2	5.8
Non-Hispanic white[3]	-	6.0	5.7	5.7	5.4	5.0	5.0	5.8	5.1
Non-Hispanic black[3]	-	12.1	11.5	11.9	11.5	11.3	11.5	11.8	11.4

Postneonatal deaths per 1,000 live births

	1960[1]	1983	1984	1985	1986	1987	1988	1983-85	1986-88
All mothers	6.7	3.8	3.6	3.6	3.6	3.5	3.5	3.7	3.5
White	5.3	3.2	3.1	3.1	3.0	3.0	3.0	3.1	3.0
Black	14.8	6.7	6.3	6.3	6.3	6.1	6.3	6.4	6.2
American Indian or Alaskan Native	-	7.7	7.0	7.0	7.8	6.8	7.4	7.2	7.3
Asian or Pacific Islander	-	3.1	3.1	2.9	3.0	2.8	2.6	3.1	2.8
Chinese	-	[4]	[4]	2.5[4]	2.8[4]	2.5[4]	2.4	3.1	2.5
Japanese	-	[4]	[4]	[4]	[4]	[4]	[4]	2.6	2.5
Filipino	-	2.8[4]	3.2[4]	2.7[4]	2.3	2.5	2.5	2.9	2.4
Hawaiian and part Hawaiian	-	[4]	[4]	[4]	[4]	[4]	[4]	[4]	4.0[4]
Other Asian or Pacific Islander	-	3.0	3.2	3.0	3.2	2.9	2.6	3.1	2.9

[Continued]

★ 979 ★

Infant, Neonatal, and Postneonatal Mortality Rates by Race and Hispanic Origin of Mother, 1960 and 1983-88

[Continued]

Race of mother and Hispanic origin of mother	Birth cohort								
	1960[1]	1983	1984	1985	1986	1987	1988	1983-85	1986-88
Hispanic origin[2,3]	-	3.3	3.1	3.2	2.9	2.9	3.1	3.2	3.0
Mexican American	-	3.2	3.2	3.2	2.8	2.9	3.1	3.2	2.9
Puerto Rican	-	4.2	4.3	3.5	4.2	3.2	4.2	4.0	3.9
Cuban	-	[4]	[4]	[4]	[4]	[4]	[4]	2.2	2.0
Central or South American	-	2.6	2.4	2.4	2.6	2.8	2.4	2.5	2.6
Other and unknown Hispanic	-	4.1	3.1	3.9	3.2	3.2	3.2	3.7	3.2
Non-Hispanic white[3]	-	3.2	3.0	3.0	3.0	3.0	3.0	3.1	3.0
Non-Hispanic black[3]	-	7.0	6.6	6.4	6.5	6.2	6.6	6.7	6.4

Source: "Infant, Neonatal, and Postneonatal Mortality Rates, According to Detailed Race of Mother and Hispanic Origin of Mother: United States, 1960 and 1983-88 Birth Cohorts." National Center for Health Statistics, *Health, United States, 1994*, p. 84. Primary source: Centers for Disease Control and Prevention, National Center for Health Statistics: Data computed by the Division of Health and Utilization Analysis from data compiled by the Division of Vital Statistics for the National Linked Files of Live Births and Infant Deaths. *Notes:* 1. Data are shown by race of child in 1960. 2. Includes mothers of all races. 3. Data shown only for States with an Hispanic-origin item on their birth certificates. In 1983-87, 23 States and the District of Columbia (DC) and in 1988, 30 States and DC included this item. 4. Infant and neonatal mortality rates for groups with fewer than 10,000 births are considered unreliable. Postneonatal mortality rates for groups with fewer than 20,000 births are considered unreliable. Infant and neonatal mortality rates for groups with fewer than 7,500 births are considered highly unreliable and are not shown. Postneonatal mortality rates for groups with fewer than 15,000 births are considered highly unreliable and are not shown.

Infant, Fetal, and Perinatal Deaths

★ 980 ★

Infant, Fetal, and Perinatal Deaths: Mortality Rates by Race: Trends

[Data are based on the National Vital Statistics System.]

Race and year	Deaths per 1,000 live births						
	Infant mortality rate[1]				Fetal death rate[2]	Late fetal death rate[3]	Perinatal mortality rate[4]
	Total	Neonatal		Postneonatal			
		Under 28 days	Under 7 days				
Race of child:[6] White							
1950[5]	26.8	19.4	17.1	7.4	16.6	13.3	30.1
1960[5]	22.9	17.2	15.6	5.7	13.9	10.8	26.2
1970	17.8	13.8	12.5	4.0	12.3	8.6	21.0
1980	11.0	7.5	6.2	3.5	8.1	5.7	11.9
Race of mother:[7] White							
1980	10.9	7.4	6.1	3.5	8.1	5.7	11.8
1981	10.3	7.0	5.8	3.4	8.0	5.4	11.2
1982	9.9	6.7	5.6	3.2	7.8	5.4	10.9

[Continued]

★ 980 ★

Infant, Fetal, and Perinatal Deaths: Mortality Rates by Race: Trends
[Continued]

Race and year	Deaths per 1,000 live births						
	Infant mortality rate[1]				Fetal death rate[2]	Late fetal death rate[3]	Perinatal mortality rate[4]
	Total	Neonatal		Postneonatal			
		Under 28 days	Under 7 days				
1983	9.6	6.3	5.3	3.3	7.4	5.0	10.2
1984	9.3	6.1	5.1	3.2	7.3	4.8	9.8
1985	9.2	6.0	5.0	3.2	6.9	4.5	9.5
1986	8.8	5.7	4.7	3.1	6.7	4.3	9.0
1987	8.5	5.4	4.5	3.1	6.6	4.2	8.6
1988	8.4	5.3	4.3	3.1	6.4	4.0	8.3
1989	8.1	5.1	4.2	2.9	6.4	4.0	8.2
1990	7.6	4.8	3.9	2.8	6.4	3.8	7.7
1991	7.3	4.5	3.7	2.8	6.2	3.7	7.4
1992	6.9	4.3	3.5	2.6	6.2	3.7	7.2
Race of child:[6] Black							
1950[5]	43.9	27.8	23.0	16.1	32.1	-	-
1960[5]	44.3	27.8	23.7	16.5	-	-	-
1970	32.6	22.8	20.3	9.9	23.2	-	34.5
1980	21.4	14.1	11.9	7.3	14.4	8.9	20.7
Race of mother:[7] Black							
1980	22.2	14.6	12.3	7.6	14.7	9.1	21.3
1981	20.8	14.0	11.8	6.8	14.0	8.3	20.0
1982	20.5	13.6	11.6	6.9	14.0	8.3	19.7
1983	20.0	12.9	11.1	7.0	13.7	7.8	18.7
1984	19.2	12.3	10.6	6.8	12.9	7.3	17.9
1985	19.0	12.6	10.8	6.4	12.8	7.2	17.9
1986	18.9	12.3	10.6	6.6	12.7	7.1	17.6
1987	18.8	12.3	10.5	6.4	13.1	7.1	17.5
1988	18.5	12.1	10.3	6.5	13.0	6.9	17.1
1989	18.6	11.9	10.1	6.7	13.1	6.8	16.8
1990	18.0	11.6	9.7	6.4	13.3	6.7	16.4

[Continued]

★ 980 ★

Infant, Fetal, and Perinatal Deaths: Mortality Rates by Race: Trends
[Continued]

Race and year	Deaths per 1,000 live births						
	Infant mortality rate[1]			Fetal death rate[2]	Late fetal death rate[3]	Perinatal mortality rate[4]
		Neonatal					
	Total	Under 28 days	Under 7 days	Postneonatal			
1991	17.6	11.2	9.4	6.3	12.8	6.4	15.7
1992	16.8	10.8	9.0	6.0	13.3	6.4	15.4

Source: "Infant Mortality Rates, Fetal Death Rates, and Perinatal Mortality Rates, According to Race: United States, Selected Years 1950-93, *Health, United States, 1994,* pp. 87-88. Primary source: Centers for Disease Control and Prevention, National Center for Health Statistics: Vital Statistics of the United States, Vol. II, Mortality, Part A, for data years 1950-82. Public Health Service. Washington. U.S. Government Printing Office. Annual summary of births, marriages, divorces, and deaths: United States, 1992 and 1993. Monthly Vital Statistics Report; Vols 41 and 42 No. 13. Hyattsville, Md.: Public Health Service. 1993 and 1994; Advance report of final mortality statistics, 1992. Monthly Vital Statistics Report; Vol 43 No 6, suppl. Hyattsville, Md.: Public Health Service. 1994. Data computed by the Division of Health and Utilization Analysis from data compiled by the Division of Vital Statistics. *Notes:* 1. Rates are infant (under 1 year of age), neonatal (under 28 days), early neonatal (7 days), and postneonatal (28-365 days) deaths per 1,000 live births in specified group. 2. Number of fetal deaths of 20 weeks or more gestation per 1,000 live births plus fetal deaths. 3. Number of fetal deaths of 28 weeks or more gestation per 1,000 live births plus fetal deaths. 4. Number of late fetal deaths plus infant deaths within 7 days of birth per 1,000 live births plus late fetal deaths. 5. Includes births and deaths of nonresidents of the United States. 6. Infant deaths and fetal deaths are tabulated by race of decedent; live births are tabulated by race of child. 7. Infant deaths are tabulated by race of decedent; fetal deaths and live births are tabulated by race of mother.

Life Expectancy

★ 981 ★

Life Expectancy: Expectancy of Life at Birth, 1970-1993, and Projections, 1995-2010

[In years. Excludes deaths of nonresidents of the United States. See also *Historical Statistics, Colonial Times to 1970,* series B 107-115.]

YEAR	TOTAL			WHITE			BLACK AND OTHER			BLACK		
	Total	Male	Female	Total	Male	Female	Total	Male	Female	Total	Male	Female
1970	70.8	67.1	74.7	71.7	68.0	75.6	65.3	61.3	69.4	64.1	60.0	68.3
1975	72.6	68.8	76.6	73.4	69.5	77.3	68.0	63.7	72.4	66.8	62.4	71.3
1980	73.7	70.0	77.4	74.4	70.7	78.1	69.5	65.3	73.6	68.1	63.8	72.5
1981	74.1	70.4	77.8	74.8	71.1	78.4	70.3	66.2	74.4	68.9	64.5	73.2
1982	74.5	70.8	78.1	75.1	71.5	78.7	70.9	66.8	74.9	69.4	65.1	73.6
1983	74.6	71.0	78.1	75.2	71.6	78.7	70.9	67.0	74.7	69.4	65.2	73.5
1984	74.7	71.1	78.2	75.3	71.8	78.7	71.1	67.2	74.9	69.5	65.3	73.6
1985	74.7	71.1	78.2	75.3	71.8	78.7	71.0	67.0	74.8	69.3	65.0	73.4
1986	74.7	71.2	78.2	75.4	71.9	78.8	70.9	66.8	74.9	69.1	64.8	73.4
1987	74.9	71.4	78.3	75.6	72.1	78.9	71.0	66.9	75.0	69.1	64.7	73.4
1988	74.9	71.4	78.3	75.6	72.2	78.9	70.8	66.7	74.8	68.9	64.4	73.2
1989	75.1	71.7	78.5	75.9	72.5	79.2	70.9	66.7	74.9	68.8	64.3	73.3
1990	75.4	71.8	78.8	76.1	72.7	79.4	71.2	67.0	75.2	69.1	64.5	73.6
1991	75.5	72.0	78.9	76.3	72.9	79.6	71.5	67.3	75.5	69.3	64.6	73.8
1992	75.8	72.3	79.1	76.5	73.2	79.8	71.8	67.7	75.7	69.6	65.0	73.9
1993	75.5	72.1	78.9	76.3	73.0	79.5	71.5	67.4	75.5	69.3	64.7	73.7

[Continued]

★ 981 ★

Life Expectancy: Expectancy of Life at Birth, 1970-1993, and Projections, 1995-2010
[Continued]

YEAR	TOTAL			WHITE			BLACK AND OTHER			BLACK		
	Total	Male	Female	Total	Male	Female	Total	Male	Female	Total	Male	Female
Projections:[1] 1995	76.3	72.8	79.7	77.0	73.7	80.3	72.5	68.2	76.8	70.3	65.8	74.8
2000	76.7	73.2	80.2	77.6	74.3	80.9	72.9	68.3	77.5	70.2	65.3	75.1
2005	77.3	73.8	80.7	78.2	74.9	81.4	73.6	69.1	78.1	70.7	65.9	75.5
2010	77.9	74.5	81.3	78.8	75.6	82.0	74.3	69.9	78.7	71.3	66.5	76.0

Source: "Expectations of Life at Birth, 1970 to 1993, and Projections, 1995 to 2010," *Statistical Abstract of the United States, 1995*, p. 86. Primary source: Except as noted, U.S. National Center for Health Statistics, *Vital Statistics of the United States*, annual, and *Monthly Vital Statistics Reports. Notes:* 1. Based on middle mortality assumptions; for details, see source. Source: U.S. Bureau of the Census, *Current Population Reports*, P25-1104.

★ 982 ★

Life Expectancy

Life Expectancy: Life and Death Expectancy By Gender and Age: 1992

AGE IN 1990 (years)	EXPECTATION OF LIFE IN YEARS					EXPECTED DEATHS PER 1,000 ALIVE AT SPECIFIED AGE[1]				
	Total	White		Black		Total	White		Black	
		Male	Female	Male	Female		Male	Female	Male	Female
At birth	75.8	73.2	79.8	65.0	73.9	8.51	7.68	6.10	18.36	15.23
1	75.4	72.8	79.3	65.2	74.1	0.62	0.63	0.46	1.11	0.88
2	74.5	71.8	78.3	64.3	73.1	0.46	0.45	0.36	0.79	0.71
3	73.5	70.9	77.3	63.4	72.2	0.35	0.34	0.28	0.60	0.58
4	72.5	69.9	76.3	62.4	71.2	0.29	0.28	0.22	0.50	0.46
5	71.6	68.9	75.4	61.4	70.3	0.25	0.25	0.19	0.45	0.37
6	70.6	67.9	74.4	60.5	69.3	0.23	0.23	0.16	0.43	0.30
7	69.6	66.9	73.4	59.5	68.3	0.21	0.22	0.15	0.40	0.25
8	68.6	65.9	72.4	58.5	67.3	0.18	0.20	0.13	0.34	0.22
9	67.6	65.0	71.4	57.5	66.3	0.16	0.17	0.12	0.26	0.20
10	66.6	64.0	70.4	56.5	65.4	0.14	0.14	0.12	0.18	0.20
11	65.6	63.0	69.4	55.5	64.4	0.14	0.15	0.12	0.17	0.22
12	64.6	62.0	68.4	54.6	63.4	0.19	0.21	0.15	0.29	0.24
13	63.7	61.0	67.4	53.6	62.4	0.30	0.35	0.20	0.58	0.28
14	62.7	60.0	66.5	52.6	61.4	0.44	0.54	0.26	1.00	0.32
15	61.7	59.1	65.5	51.7	60.4	0.61	0.76	0.34	1.46	0.38
16	60.7	58.1	64.5	50.7	59.5	0.76	0.96	0.41	1.90	0.44
17	59.8	57.2	63.5	49.8	58.5	0.88	1.11	0.46	2.28	0.51
18	58.8	56.2	62.5	48.9	57.5	0.95	1.20	0.48	2.55	0.57
19	57.9	55.3	61.6	48.1	56.6	0.98	1.25	0.47	2.75	0.63
20	56.9	54.3	60.6	47.2	55.6	1.00	1.28	0.45	2.93	0.69
21	56.0	53.4	59.6	46.3	54.6	1.03	1.32	0.44	3.13	0.76
22	55.1	52.5	58.7	45.5	53.7	1.06	1.36	0.44	3.28	0.84
23	54.1	51.6	57.7	44.6	52.7	1.08	1.39	0.44	3.37	0.92
24	53.2	50.6	56.7	43.8	51.8	1.11	1.42	0.46	3.42	1.02
25	52.2	49.7	55.7	42.9	50.8	1.13	1.44	0.48	3.44	1.12

[Continued]

★ 982 ★

Life Expectancy: Life and Death Expectancy By Gender and Age: 1992
[Continued]

AGE IN 1990 (years)	EXPECTATION OF LIFE IN YEARS					EXPECTED DEATHS PER 1,000 ALIVE AT SPECIFIED AGE[1]				
	Total	White		Black		Total	White		Black	
		Male	Female	Male	Female		Male	Female	Male	Female
26	51.3	48.8	54.8	42.1	49.9	1.16	1.46	0.50	3.48	1.22
27	50.4	47.8	53.8	41.2	48.9	1.19	1.51	0.52	3.56	1.32
28	49.4	46.9	52.8	40.4	48.0	1.24	1.58	0.54	3.72	1.42
29	48.5	46.0	51.8	39.5	47.1	1.31	1.67	0.57	3.93	1.51
30	47.5	45.1	50.9	38.7	46.1	1.38	1.77	0.60	4.16	1.61
31	46.6	44.1	49.9	37.8	45.2	1.45	1.87	0.64	4.40	1.72
32	45.7	43.2	48.9	37.0	44.3	1.53	1.97	0.68	4.65	1.85
33	44.7	42.3	48.0	36.2	43.4	1.61	2.06	0.73	4.90	1.99
34	43.8	41.4	47.0	35.3	42.4	1.70	2.15	0.78	5.17	2.15
35	42.9	40.5	46.0	34.5	41.5	1.80	2.25	0.84	5.46	2.32
36	42.0	39.6	45.1	33.7	40.6	1.91	2.36	0.90	5.77	2.50
37	41.0	38.7	44.1	32.9	39.7	2.01	2.47	0.97	6.10	2.68
38	40.1	37.8	43.2	32.1	38.8	2.11	2.58	1.04	6.44	2.87
39	39.2	36.9	42.2	31.3	37.9	2.22	2.69	1.11	6.80	3.06
40	38.3	36.0	41.2	30.5	37.1	2.33	2.81	1.19	7.17	3.27
41	37.4	35.1	40.3	29.7	36.2	2.47	2.96	1.28	7.58	3.49
42	36.5	34.2	39.3	28.9	35.3	2.61	3.12	1.39	8.00	3.72
43	35.6	33.3	38.4	28.2	34.4	2.77	3.29	1.52	8.46	3.94
44	34.7	32.4	37.5	27.4	33.6	2.94	3.48	1.67	8.95	4.16
45	33.8	31.5	36.5	26.7	32.7	3.14	3.71	1.83	9.48	4.41
46	32.9	30.6	35.6	25.9	31.9	3.36	3.97	2.01	10.06	4.69
47	32.0	29.7	34.7	25.2	31.0	3.63	4.27	2.23	10.63	5.02
48	31.1	28.8	33.7	24.4	30.2	3.94	4.61	2.47	11.18	5.41
49	30.2	28.0	32.8	23.7	29.3	4.29	5.01	2.75	11.75	5.85
50	29.3	27.1	31.9	23.0	28.5	4.68	5.45	3.05	12.33	6.33
51	28.5	26.3	31.0	22.3	27.7	5.11	5.96	3.39	13.00	6.85
52	27.6	25.4	30.1	21.5	26.8	5.60	6.53	3.75	13.86	7.45
53	26.8	24.6	29.2	20.8	26.0	6.15	7.18	4.14	15.00	8.17
54	25.9	23.7	28.3	20.1	25.3	6.76	7.91	4.56	16.36	8.96
55	25.1	22.9	27.5	19.5	24.5	7.43	8.71	5.01	17.85	9.84
56	24.3	22.1	26.6	18.8	23.7	8.15	9.59	5.51	19.38	10.74
57	23.5	21.3	25.7	18.2	23.0	8.93	10.57	6.06	20.92	11.64
58	22.7	20.6	24.9	17.6	22.2	9.79	11.67	6.68	22.40	12.52
59	21.9	19.8	24.1	16.9	21.5	10.71	12.89	7.36	23.87	13.40
60	21.1	19.1	23.2	16.3	20.8	11.71	14.20	8.10	25.41	14.30
61	20.4	18.3	22.4	15.8	20.1	12.77	15.60	8.90	27.08	15.28
62	19.7	17.6	21.6	15.2	19.4	13.91	17.11	9.74	28.83	16.37
63	18.9	16.9	20.8	14.6	18.7	15.12	18.76	10.63	30.69	17.61
64	18.2	16.2	20.0	14.1	18.0	16.42	20.53	11.57	32.66	18.98
65	17.5	15.5	19.3	13.5	17.4	17.81	22.43	12.57	34.68	20.43

[Continued]

★ 982 ★

Life Expectancy: Life and Death Expectancy By Gender and Age: 1992

[Continued]

AGE IN 1990 (years)	EXPECTATION OF LIFE IN YEARS					EXPECTED DEATHS PER 1,000 ALIVE AT SPECIFIED AGE[1]				
	Total	White		Black		Total	White		Black	
		Male	Female	Male	Female		Male	Female	Male	Female
70	14.2	12.4	15.6	11.0	14.3	26.54	33.64	19.55	49.07	28.93
75	11.2	9.6	12.2	8.9	11.4	39.26	50.60	30.19	65.43	38.70
80	8.5	7.2	9.2	6.8	8.6	59.53	77.27	48.24	89.10	55.92
85 and over	6.2	5.3	6.6	5.1	6.3	1,000.00	1,000.00	1,000.00	1,000.00	1,000.00

Source: "Expectancy of Life and Expected Deaths, by Race, Sex, and Age: 1992," *Statistical Abstract of the United States, 1995,* p. 87. Primary source: U.S. National Center for Health Statistics, *Vital Statistics of the United States,* annual; and unpublished data. *Notes:* 1. Based on the proportion of the cohort who are alive at the beginning of an indicated age interval who will die before reaching the end of that interval. For example, out of every 1,000 people alive and exactly 50 years old at the beginning of the period, between 4 and 5 (4.86) will die before reaching their 51st birthdays.

★ 983 ★

Life Expectancy

Life Expectancy: Selected Life Table Values: 1979 to 1992

[See also *Historical Statistics, Colonial Times to 1970,* series B 116- 125].

AGE AND SEX	TOTAL[1]			WHITE			BLACK		
	1979-1981	1990	1992	1979-1981	1990	1992	1979-1981	1990	1992
AVERAGE EXPECTATION OF LIFE IN YEARS									
At birth: Male	70.1	71.8	72.3	70.8	72.7	73.2	64.1	64.5	65.0
Female	77.6	78.8	79.1	78.2	79.4	79.8	72.9	73.6	73.9
Age 20: Male	51.9	53.3	53.7	52.5	54.0	54.3	46.4	46.7	47.2
Female	59.0	59.8	60.1	59.4	60.3	60.6	54.9	55.3	55.6
Age 40: Male	33.6	35.1	35.5	34.0	35.6	36.0	29.5	30.1	30.5
Female	39.8	40.6	40.9	40.2	41.0	41.2	36.3	36.8	37.1
Age 50: Male	25.0	26.4	26.8	25.3	26.7	27.1	22.0	22.5	23.0
Female	30.7	31.3	31.6	31.0	31.6	31.9	27.8	28.2	28.5
Age 65: Male	14.2	15.1	15.4	14.3	15.2	15.5	13.3	13.2	13.5
Female	18.4	18.9	19.2	18.6	19.1	19.3	17.1	17.2	17.4
EXPECTED DEATHS PER 1,000 ALIVE AT SPECIFIED AGE[2]									
At birth: Male	13.9	10.3	9.4	12.3	8.6	7.7	23.0	19.7	18.4
Female	11.2	8.2	7.6	9.7	6.6	6.1	19.3	16.3	15.2
Age 20: Male	1.8	1.6	1.5	1.8	1.4	1.3	2.2	2.7	2.9
Female	0.6	0.5	0.5	0.6	0.5	0.5	0.7	0.7	0.7
Age 40: Male	3.0	3.1	3.3	2.6	2.7	2.8	6.9	7.1	7.2
Female	1.6	1.4	1.4	1.4	1.2	1.2	3.2	3.1	3.3
Age 50: Male	7.8	6.2	6.0	7.1	5.6	5.5	14.9	12.8	12.3

[Continued]

★ 983 ★

Life Expectancy: Selected Life Table Values: 1979 to 1992

[Continued]

AGE AND SEX	TOTAL[1]			WHITE			BLACK		
	1979-1981	1990	1992	1979-1981	1990	1992	1979-1981	1990	1992
Female	4.2	3.5	3.4	3.8	3.2	3.1	7.7	6.6	6.3
Age 65: Male	28.2	12.9	23.3	27.4	23.0	22.4	38.5	36.8	34.7
Female	14.3	13.5	13.2	13.6	12.8	12.6	21.6	21.4	20.4
NUMBER SURVIVING TO SPECIFIED AGE PER 1,000 BORN ALIVE									
Age 20: Male	973	979	980	975	981	983	961	963	964
Female	982	986	987	984	988	989	972	976	977
Age 40: Male	933	938	939	940	946	948	885	880	883
Female	965	971	972	969	975	976	941	944	945
Age 50: Male	890	899	901	901	912	913	801	801	804
Female	941	950	951	947	957	958	896	904	904
Age 65: Male	706	741	748	724	760	767	551	571	582
Female	835	851	855	848	864	868	733	751	755

Source: "Selected Life Table Values: 1979 to 1992," *Statistical Abstract of the United States, 1995,* p. 86. Primary source: U.S. National Center for Health Statistics, *U.S. Life Tables and Acturarial Tables, 1959-61, 1969-71,* and *1979-81; Vital Statistics of the United States,* annual; and unpublished data. *Notes:* 1. Includes other races not shown separately. 2. See footnote 1, table 116.

★ 984 ★

Life Expectancy

Life Expectancy: Trends, 1900-1993

[Data are based on the National Vital Statistics System.]

Specified age and year	All races			White			Black		
	Both sexes	Male	Female	Both sexes	Male	Female	Both sexes	Male	Female
				Remaining life expectancy in years					
At birth									
1900[1,2]	47.3	46.3	48.3	47.6	46.6	48.7	33.0[3]	32.5[3]	33.5[3]
1950[2]	68.2	65.6	71.1	69.1	66.5	72.2	60.7	58.9	62.7
1960[2]	69.7	66.6	73.1	70.6	67.4	74.1	63.2	60.7	65.9
1970	70.8	67.1	74.7	71.7	68.0	75.6	64.1	60.0	68.3
1980	73.7	70.0	77.4	74.4	70.7	78.1	68.1	63.8	72.5
1984	74.7	71.1	78.2	75.3	71.8	78.7	69.5	65.3	73.6
1985	74.7	71.1	78.2	75.3	71.8	78.7	69.3	65.0	73.4
1986	74.7	71.2	78.2	75.4	71.9	78.8	69.1	64.8	73.4
1987	74.9	71.4	78.3	75.6	72.1	78.9	69.1	64.7	73.4
1988	74.9	71.4	78.3	75.6	72.2	78.9	68.9	64.4	73.2

[Continued]

★ 984 ★

Life Expectancy: Trends, 1900-1993
[Continued]

Specified age and year	All races			White			Black		
	Both sexes	Male	Female	Both sexes	Male	Female	Both sexes	Male	Female
1989	75.1	71.7	78.5	75.9	72.5	79.2	68.8	64.3	73.3
1990	75.4	71.8	78.8	76.1	72.7	79.4	69.1	64.5	73.6
1991	75.5	72.0	78.9	76.3	72.9	79.6	69.3	64.6	73.8
1992	75.8	72.3	79.1	76.5	73.2	79.8	69.6	65.0	73.9
Provisional data:									
1992	75.7	72.3	79.0	76.5	73.2	79.7	69.8	65.5	73.9
1993	75.5	72.1	78.9	76.3	73.0	79.5	69.3	64.7	73.7
At 65 years									
1900-1902[1,2]	11.9	11.5	12.2	-	11.5	12.2	-	10.4	11.4
1950[2]	13.9	12.8	15.0	-	12.8	15.1	13.9	12.9	14.9
1960[2]	14.3	12.8	15.8	14.4	12.9	15.9	13.9	12.7	15.1
1970	15.2	13.1	17.0	15.2	13.1	17.1	14.2	12.5	15.7
1980	16.4	14.1	18.3	16.5	14.2	18.4	15.1	13.0	16.8
1984	16.8	14.5	18.6	16.8	14.6	18.7	15.4	13.2	17.2
1985	16.7	14.5	18.5	16.8	14.5	18.7	15.2	13.0	16.9
1986	16.8	14.6	18.6	16.9	14.7	18.7	15.2	13.0	17.0
1987	16.9	14.7	18.7	17.0	14.8	18.8	15.2	13.0	17.0
1988	16.9	14.7	18.6	17.0	14.8	18.7	15.1	12.9	16.9
1989	17.1	15.0	18.8	17.2	15.1	18.9	15.2	13.0	16.9
1990	17.2	15.1	18.9	17.3	15.2	19.1	15.4	13.2	17.2
1991	17.4	15.3	19.1	17.5	15.4	19.2	15.5	13.4	17.2
1992	17.5	15.4	19.2	17.6	15.5	19.3	15.7	13.5	17.4
Provisional data:									
1992	17.5	15.5	19.1	-	-	-	-	-	-
1993	17.3	15.3	18.9	-	-	-	-	-	-
At 75 years									
1980	10.4	8.8	11.5	10.4	8.8	11.5	9.7	8.3	10.7
1984	10.7	9.0	11.8	10.7	9.0	11.8	10.3	8.9	11.4
1985	10.6	9.0	11.7	10.6	9.0	11.7	10.1	8.7	11.1
1986	10.7	9.1	11.7	10.7	9.1	11.8	10.1	8.6	11.1
1987	10.7	9.1	11.8	10.7	9.1	11.8	10.1	8.6	11.1
1988	10.6	9.1	11.7	10.7	9.1	11.7	10.0	8.5	11.0
1989	10.9	9.3	11.9	10.9	9.3	11.9	10.1	8.6	11.0
1990	10.9	9.4	12.0	11.0	9.4	12.0	10.2	8.6	11.2
1991	11.1	9.5	12.1	11.1	9.5	12.1	10.2	8.7	11.2
1992	11.2	9.6	12.2	11.2	9.6	12.2	10.4	8.9	11.4

[Continued]

★ 984 ★

Life Expectancy: Trends, 1900-1993

[Continued]

Specified age and year	All races			White			Black		
	Both sexes	Male	Female	Both sexes	Male	Female	Both sexes	Male	Female
Provisional data:									
1992	11.1	9.5	12.1	-	-	-	-	-	-
1993	10.9	9.4	12.0	-	-	-	-	-	-

Source: "Life Expectancy at Birth, At Age 65 Years of Age, and At 75 Years of Age, According to by Race and Sex: United States, Selected Years 1900-93," *Health, United States, 1994*, p. 96. Primary source: U.S. Bureau of the Census: U.S. Life Tables 1980, 1901, 1910, and 1901-1910, by J.W. Glover. Washington. U.S. Government Printing Office, 1921; Centers for Disease Control and Prevention, National Center for Health Statistics: Vital Statistics Rates in the United States, 1940-1960, by R.D. Grove and A.M. Hetzel. DHEW Pub. No. (PHS) 1677. Public Health Service. Washington. U.S. Government Printing Office, 1968; Kochanek KD and Hudson BL. Advance report of final mortality statistics, 1992. Monthly Vital Statistics Report; Vol 43 No 6, suppl. Hyattsville, Md. 1994; Annual summary of births, marriages, divorces, and deaths: United States, 1992 and 1993. Monthly Vital Statistics Report; Vols 41 and 42 No 13. Hyattsville, Md.; Public Health Service. 1993 and 1994; Unpublished data from the Division of Vital Statistics: Data for 1960 and earlier years for the black population were computed by the Office of Research and Methodology from data compiled by the Division of Vital Statistics. *Notes:* Final data for the 1980's are based on intercensal population estimates. Provisional data for 1992-93 were calculated using 1990's-based postcensal population estimates. See Appendix I, National Center for Health Statistics and Department of Commerce. 1. Death registration only. The death registration area increased from 10 States and the District of Columbia in 1900 to the coterminous United States in 1933. 2. Includes deaths of nonresidents of the United States. 3. Figure is for the all other population.

★ 985 ★

Life Expectancy

Life Expectancy: Trends, 1970-92

Year	White male	Black male	White female	Black female
1970	68.0	60.0	75.6	68.3
1971	68.3	60.5	75.8	68.9
1972	68.3	60.4	75.9	69.1
1973	68.5	60.9	76.1	69.3
1974	69.0	61.7	76.7	70.3
1975	69.5	62.4	77.3	71.3
1976	69.9	62.9	77.5	71.6
1977	70.2	63.4	77.9	72.0
1978	70.4	63.7	78.0	72.4
1979	70.8	64.0	78.4	72.9
1980	70.7	63.8	78.1	72.5
1981	71.1	64.5	78.4	73.2
1982	71.5	65.1	78.7	73.6
1983	71.6	65.2	78.7	73.5
1984	71.8	65.3	78.7	73.6
1985	71.8	65.0	78.7	73.4
1986	71.9	64.8	78.8	73.4
1987	72.1	64.7	78.9	73.4
1988	72.2	64.4	78.9	73.2
1989	72.5	64.3	79.2	73.3
1990	72.7	64.5	79.4	73.6

[Continued]

★ 985 ★

Life Expectancy: Trends, 1970-92
[Continued]

Year	White male	Black male	White female	Black female
1991	72.9	64.6	79.6	73.8
1992	73.2	65.0	79.8	73.9

Source: "Life Expectancy at Birth by Race and Sex: United States, 1970-92," *Health United States, 1994,* pp. 15,50. Primary source: Centers for Disease Control and Prevention, National Center for Health Statistics, National Vital Statistics System.

Live Births

★ 986 ★

Birth Rates: Live Order and Race, 1970-1992

[Births per 1,000 women 15 to 44 years old in specified racial group. Live-birth order refers to number of children born alive. Figures for births of order not stated are distributed. See also headnote, table 89, and *Historical Statistics, Colonial Times to 1970*, series B 20-27.]

LIVE-BIRTH ORDER	1970	1980	1990	1991	1992
ALL RACES[1]					
Total	87.9	68.4	70.9	69.6	68.9
First birth	34.2	29.5	29.0	28.3	27.8
Second birth	24.2	21.8	22.8	22.4	22.3
Third birth	13.6	10.3	11.7	11.4	11.3
Fourth birth	7.2	3.9	4.5	4.5	4.4
Fifth birth	3.8	1.5	1.7	1.7	1.7
Sixth and seventh	3.2	1.0	1.0	1.0	1.0
Eighth and over	1.8	0.4	0.3	0.3	0.3
WHITE					
Total	84.1	65.6	68.3	67.0	66.5
First birth	32.9	28.8	28.4	27.8	27.3
Second birth	23.7	21.3	22.4	22.0	22.0
Third birth	13.3	9.6	11.1	10.8	10.8
Fourth birth	6.8	3.4	4.0	4.0	4.0
Fifth birth	3.4	1.3	1.4	1.4	1.4
Sixth and seventh	2.7	0.8	0.8	0.8	0.8
Eighth and over	1.2	0.3	0.2	0.2	0.2
BLACK					
Total	115.4	84.9	86.8	85.2	83.2

[Continued]

★ 986 ★

Birth Rates: Live Order and Race, 1970-1992
[Continued]

LIVE-BIRTH ORDER	1970	1980	1990	1991	1992
First birth	43.3	33.7	32.4	31.5	30.6
Second birth	27.1	24.7	25.6	25.0	24.3
Third birth	16.1	14.0	15.6	15.4	15.0
Fourth birth	10.0	6.5	7.4	7.4	7.2
Fifth birth	6.4	2.9	3.2	3.3	3.3
Sixth and seventh	7.0	2.1	2.0	2.1	2.2
Eighth and over	5.6	0.9	0.5	0.6	0.6

Source: "Birth Rates, by Live-Birth Order and Race: 1970-1992," *Statistical Abstract of the United States, 1994*, p. 76. Primary source: U.S. National Center for Health Statistics, *Vital Statistics of the United States*, annual; and *Monthly Vital Statistics Reports. Note:* 1. Includes other races not shown separately.

★ 987 ★
Live Births

Live Births: Percent and Characteristics, 1990, 1992

[Represents registered births. Excludes births to nonresidents of the United States. Hispanic origin data are available from only 23 States and the District of Columbia in 1985 and 48 States and DC in 1990.]

RACE AND HISPANIC ORIGIN	NUMBER OF BIRTHS (1,000)		BIRTHS TO TEENAGE MOTHERS, PERCENT OF TOTAL		BIRTHS TO UNMARRIED MOTHERS, PERCENT OF TOTAL		PERCENT OF MOTHERS BEGINNING PRENATAL CARE DURING--				PERCENT OF BIRTHS WITH LOW BIRTH WEIGHT[1]	
							First trimester		Third trimester or no care			
	1990	1992	1990	1992	1990	1992	1990	1992	1990	1992	1990	1992
Total	4,158	4,065	12.8	12.7	26.6	30.1	74.2	77.7	6.0	5.2	7.0	7.1
White	3,290	3,202	10.9	10.9	16.9	22.6	77.7	80.8	4.9	4.2	5.7	5.8
Black	684	674	23.1	22.7	66.7	68.1	60.7	63.9	10.9	9.9	13.3	13.3
American Indian, Eskimo, Aleut	39	39	19.5	20.0	53.6	55.3	57.9	62.1	12.9	11.0	6.1	6.2
Asian and Pacific Islander[2]	142	150	5.7	5.6	(NA)	14.7	(NA)	76.6	(NA)	4.9	(NA)	6.6
Filipino	26	29	6.1	5.6	15.9	16.8	77.1	78.7	4.5	4.3	7.3	7.4
Chinese	23	25	1.2	1.0	5.0	6.1	81.3	83.8	3.4	2.9	4.7	5.0
Japanese	9	9	2.9	2.6	9.6	9.8	87.0	88.2	2.9	2.4	6.2	7.0
Hawaiian	6	6	18.4	18.4	45.0	45.7	65.8	69.9	8.7	7.0	7.2	6.9
Hispanic origin[3]	595	643	16.8	17.1	36.7	39.1	60.2	64.2	12.0	9.5	6.1	6.1
Mexican	386	432	17.7	18.0	33.3	36.3	57.8	62.1	13.2	10.5	5.5	5.6
Puerto Rican	59	60	21.7	21.4	55.9	57.5	63.5	67.8	10.6	8.0	9.0	9.2
Cuban	11	11	7.7	7.1	18.2	20.2	84.8	86.8	2.8	2.1	5.7	6.1
Central and South American	83	89	9.0	9.6	41.2	43.9	61.5	66.8	10.9	7.9	5.8	5.8

Source: "Live Births, by Race and Type of Hispanic Origin—Selected Characteristics," *Statistical Abstract of the United States, 1994*, p. 73. Primary source: U.S. National Center for Health Statistics, *Vital Statistics of the United States*, annual, *Monthly Vital Statistics Report*; and unpublished data. *Notes:* NA Not available. 1. Births less than 2,500 rams (5 lb.- 8 oz). 2. Includes other races not shown separately. 3. Hispanic persons may be of any race. Includes other types, not shown separately.

★ 988 ★

Live Births

Live Births: State of Birth, 1992

[Registered births. Excludes births to nonresidents of the United States. By race of mother.]

DIVISION AND STATE	All races[1]	WHITE Total	WHITE Non-Hispanic	BLACK Total	BLACK Non-Hispanic	His-panic[2]	Birth rate[3]	Fertility rate[4]
United States	4,065,014	3,201,678	2,527,207	673,633	657,450	643,271	15.9	68.9
Northeast	761,509	606,595	491,957	126,004	116,253	92,287	14.9	(NA)
New England	189,088	167,197	132,905	16,203	13,614	15,682	14.3	(NA)
Maine	16,057	15,762	15,033	82	75	101	13.0	56.3
New Hampshire	15,990	15,714	(NA)	109	(NA)	(NA)	14.3	59.5
Vermont	7,737	7,629	6,672	34	32	30	13.5	56.6
Massachusetts	87,231	75,141	67,564	8,647	7,141	8,522	14.6	60.8
Rhode Island	14,500	12,673	10,408	1,186	1,017	1,553	14.5	62.5
Connecticut	47,573	40,278	33,228	6,145	5,349	5,476	14.5	63.2
Middle Atlantic	572,421	439,396	359,052	109,801	102,639	76,605	15.1	(NA)
New York	287,887	212,579	154,439	60,990	55,549	53,047	15.9	68.1
New Jersey	119,909	90,823	74,348	23,406	22,103	17,609	15.3	66.8
Pennsylvania	164,625	135,996	130,265	25,405	24,987	5,949	13.7	61.6
Midwest	914,172	753,638	698,065	137,587	135,667	45,183	15.1	(NA)
East North Central	652,542	523,958	480,964	115,392	114,346	38,291	15.3	(NA)
Ohio	162,247	134,344	131,703	25,994	25,880	2,583	14.7	63.9
Indiana	84,140	73,914	71,956	9,426	9,392	1,941	14.9	64.0
Illinois	191,396	142,842	115,760	42,923	42,346	27,333	16.5	71.4
Michigan	144,089	112,169	102,987	29,742	29,463	4,302	15.3	65.2
Wisconsin	70,670	60,689	58,558	7,307	7,265	2,132	14.2	62.4
West North Central	261,630	229,680	217,101	22,195	21,321	6,892	14.6	(NA)
Minnesota	65,607	59,187	52,515	2,916	2,132	1,377	14.7	63.7
Iowa	38,469	36,567	35,724	1,184	1,167	853	13.7	63.2
Missouri	76,301	61,908	60,901	13,315	13,282	1,018	14.7	65.5
North Dakota	8,811	7,831	7,657	75	73	119	13.9	63.6
South Dakota	11,018	9,110	9,008	79	74	109	15.6	73.0
Nebraska	23,397	21,403	20,013	1,312	1,306	1,105	14.6	66.0
Kansas	38,027	33,674	31,283	3,314	3,287	2,311	15.1	68.2
South	1,388,111	1,006,482	833,487	346,605	346,605	174,970	15.7	(NA)
South Atlantic	681,787	467,543	425,656	198,740	196,151	3,567	15.1	(NA)
Delaware	10,656	7,901	7,504	2,553	2,502	426	15.4	65.2
Maryland	77,815	49,619	46,492	25,426	24,549	2,980	15.8	65.3
District of Columbia	10,960	1,607	1,319	8,803	8,521	893	18.7	71.2
Virginia	97,198	70,137	66,370	23,854	23,737	3,890	15.2	62.6
West Virginia	22,170	21,248	21,185	815	812	75	12.3	54.6
North Carolina	103,967	70,772	68,482	30,333	30,262	2,379	15.2	64.7
South Carolina	56,192	33,977	33,379	21,604	21,535	625	15.6	65.5
Georgia	111,116	68,819	65,794	40,382	40,279	2,932	16.4	66.9
Florida	191,713	143,463	115,131	44,970	43,954	29,367	14.2	68.0

[Continued]

★ 988 ★

Live Births: State of Birth, 1992
[Continued]

DIVISION AND STATE	All races[1]	WHITE		BLACK		His-panic[2]	Birth rate[3]	Fertility rate[4]
		Total	Non-Hispanic	Total	Non-Hispanic			
East South Central	232,395	165,390	163,868	64,744	64,660	1,552	15.0	(NA)
Kentucky	53,840	48,227	47,840	5,188	5,167	372	14.3	61.5
Tennessee	73,614	55,279	54,700	17,510	17,490	595	14.6	62.5
Alabama	62,260	40,180	39,774	21,522	21,488	444	15.0	64.8
Mississippi	42,681	21,704	21,554	20,524	20,515	141	16.3	70.2
West South Central	473,929	373,549	243,963	86,173	85,794	129,851	17.2	(NA)
Arkansas	34,820	26,289	25,828	8,152	8,133	472	14.5	66.2
Louisiana	70,707	39,757	38,900	29,841	29,751	977	16.5	69.8
Oklahoma	47,557	37,305	35,320	5,164	5,124	2,045	14.8	66.5
Texas	320,845	270,198	143,915	43,016	42,786	126,357	18.1	76.1
West	1,001,222	834,963	503,698	60,385	58,925	330,831	18.2	(NA)
Mountain	246,417	219,655	165,971	8,549	8,294	53,949	17.1	(NA)
Montana	11,472	9,981	9,458	49	36	189	14.0	63.6
Idaho	17,362	16,834	15,065	58	55	1,758	16.3	73.5
Wyoming	6,723	6,326	5,852	65	61	482	14.5	62.9
Colorado	54,535	49,644	39,512	3,008	2,919	10,303	15.7	65.0
New Mexico	27,922	23,159	10,331	513	489	12,957	17.7	77.0
Arizona	68,829	59,432	37,790	2,448	2,399	21,862	18.0	80.4
Utah	37,200	35,317	33,062	245	208	2,282	20.5	88.5
Nevada	22,374	18,962	14,901	2,163	2,127	4,116	16.7	73.6
Pacific	754,805	615,308	337,727	51,836	50,631	276,882	18.5	(NA)
Washington	79,450	70,081	61,224	3,145	2,993	7,182	15.4	66.1
Oregon	42,035	39,068	35,577	955	943	3,561	14.1	62.7
California	601,730	492,487	228,252	46,509	45,510	263,525	19.5	83.1
Alaska	11,726	7,934	7,590	542	531	373	20.0	82.0
Hawaii	19,864	5,738	5,084	685	654	2,241	17.2	75.2

Source: "Live Births, by State: 1992," *Statistical Abstract of the United States, 1994,* p. 75. Primary source: U.S. National Center for Health Statistics, *Vital Statistics of the United States,* annual, and *Monthly Vital Statistics Report. Notes:* NA Not available. 1. Includes other races not shown separately. 2. Persons of Hispanic origin may be of any race. Births by Hispanic origin of mother. 3. Per 1,000 estimated population. 4. Per 1,000 women aged 15-44 years estimated.

Marital Status

★ 989 ★

Marriage and Divorce: Characteristics of Marriage Experience for Women: 1980 and 1990

[In percent. As of June. Based on Current Population Survey.]

MARITAL STATUS AND AGE	ALL RACES		WHITE		BLACK		HISPANIC[1]	
	1980	1990	1980	1990	1980	1990	1980	1990
EVER MARRIED								
20 to 24 years old	49.5	38.5	52.2	41.3	33.3	23.5	55.4	45.8
25 to 29 years old	78.6	69.0	81.0	73.2	62.3	45.0	80.2	69.6
30 to 34 years old	89.9	82.2	91.6	85.6	77.9	61.1	88.3	83.0
35 to 39 years old	94.3	89.4	95.3	91.4	87.4	74.9	91.2	88.9
40 to 44 years old	95.1	92.0	95.8	93.4	89.7	82.1	94.2	92.8
45 to 49 years old	95.9	94.4	96.4	95.1	92.5	89.7	94.4	91.7
50 to 54 years old	95.3	95.5	95.8	96.1	92.1	91.9	95.0	91.8
DIVORCED AFTER FIRST MARRIAGE								
20 to 24 years old	14.2	12.5	14.7	12.8	10.5	9.6	9.4	6.8
25 to 29 years old	20.7	19.2	21.0	19.8	20.2	17.8	13.9	13.5
30 to 34 years old	26.2	28.1	25.8	28.6	31.4	26.6	21.1	19.9
35 to 39 years old	27.2	34.1	26.7	34.6	32.9	35.8	21.9	29.7
40 to 44 years old	26.1	35.8	25.5	35.2	33.7	45.1	19.7	26.6
45 to 49 years old	23.1	35.2	22.7	35.5	29.0	39.8	23.9	24.6
50 to 54 years old	21.8	29.5	21.0	28.5	29.0	39.2	22.5	22.9
REMARRIED AFTER DIVORCE								
20 to 24 years old	45.5	38.1	47.0	39.3	(B)	(B)	(B)	(B)
25 to 29 years old	53.4	51.8	56.4	52.8	27.9	44.4	(B)	49.5
30 to 34 years old	60.9	59.6	63.3	61.4	42.0	42.0	58.3	45.9
35 to 39 years old	64.9	65.0	66.9	66.5	50.6	54.0	45.2	51.2
40 to 44 years old	67.4	67.1	68.6	69.5	58.4	50.3	(B)	53.9
45 to 49 years old	69.2	65.9	70.4	67.2	62.7	55.0	(B)	51.0
50 to 54 years old	72.0	63.0	72.6	65.4	72.7	50.2	(B)	62.2
REDIVORCED AFTER REMARRIAGE								
20 to 24 years old	8.5	13.1	(NA)	(NA)	(NA)	(NA)	(NA)	(NA)
25 to 29 years old	15.6	17.8	(NA)	(NA)	(NA)	(NA)	(NA)	(NA)
30 to 34 years old	19.1	22.7	(NA)	(NA)	(NA)	(NA)	(NA)	(NA)
35 to 39 years old	24.7	28.5	(NA)	(NA)	(NA)	(NA)	(NA)	(NA)
40 to 44 years old	28.4	30.6	(NA)	(NA)	(NA)	(NA)	(NA)	(NA)

[Continued]

★ 989 ★

Marriage and Divorce: Characteristics of Marriage Experience for Women: 1980 and 1990

[Continued]

MARITAL STATUS AND AGE	ALL RACES		WHITE		BLACK		HISPANIC[1]	
	1980	1990	1980	1990	1980	1990	1980	1990
45 to 49 years old	25.1	36.4	(NA)	(NA)	(NA)	(NA)	(NA)	(NA)
50 to 54 years old	29.0	34.5	(NA)	(NA)	(NA)	(NA)	(NA)	(NA)

Source: "Marriage Experience for Women, by Age and Race: 1980 and 1990," *Statistical Abstract of the United States, 1995*, p. 104. Primary source: U.S. Bureau of the Census, *Current Population Reports*, P23-180. *Notes:* B = Base is less than 75,000. NA Not available. 1. Persons of Hispanic origin may be of any race.

★ 990 ★

Marital Status

Marriage and Divorce: Dissolution of Marriage and Remarriage of Women: 1988

[For women 15 to 44 years old. Based on 1988 National Survey of Family Growth; see Appendix III. Marriage dissolution includes death of spouse, separation because of marital discord, and divorce.]

ITEM	Number (1,000)	YEARS UNTIL REMARRIAGE (cumulative percent)					
		All	1	2	3	4	5
ALL RACES[1]							
Year of dissolution of first marriage:							
All years	11,577	56.8	20.6	32.8	40.7	46.2	49.7
1980-84	3,504	47.5	16.3	28.1	36.4	41.1[2]	45.4[2]
1975-79	3,235	65.3	21.9	36.0	44.7	52.7	55.4
1970-74	1,887	83.2	24.9	38.6	47.9	56.4	61.2
1965-69	1,013	89.9	32.6	48.7	60.2	65.0	72.8
WHITE							
Year of dissolution of first marriage:							
All years	10,103	59.9	21.9	35.2	43.5	49.4	53.0
1980-84	3,030	51.4	18.2	31.1	40.3	45.2[2]	49.8[2]
1975-79	2,839	69.5	23.2	38.5	46.9	55.6	58.4
1970-74	1,622	87.5	24.9	39.8	49.8	59.3	64.3
1965-69	893	91.0	34.7	52.3	64.9	69.3	76.9
BLACK							
Year of dissolution of first marriage:							
All years	1,166	34.0	10.9	16.5	19.6	22.7	25.0
1980-84	380	19.7	4.7[3]	10.6[3]	12.9[3]	14.8[2]	14.8[2]
1975-79	301	32.3	11.4[3]	15.6[3]	18.5	22.2	24.9
1970-74	227	59.0	22.3	29.4	35.3	38.7	42.2

[Continued]

★ 990 ★

Marriage and Divorce: Dissolution of Marriage and Remarriage of Women: 1988

[Continued]

ITEM	Number (1,000)	YEARS UNTIL REMARRIAGE (cumulative percent)					
		All	1	2	3	4	5
1965-69	98	81.2	20.9[3]	27.3[3]	31.3[3]	40.8	52.1
Hispanic,[4] all years	942	44.7	12.5	16.6	22.7	27.8	29.9

Source: "First Marriage Dissolution and Years Until Remarriage for Women," by Race and Hispanic Origin: 1988," *Statistical Abstract of the United States, 1995,* p. 104. Primary source: National Center for Health Statistics, *Advance Data from Vital and Health Statistics,* No. 194. *Notes:* 1. Includes other races. 2. The percent having remarried is biased downward because the women had not completed the indicated number of years since dissolution of first marriage at the time of the survey. 3. Figure does not meet standard of reliability or precision. 4. Hispanic persons may be of any race.

Neonatal Deaths

★ 991 ★

Neonatal Deaths: Mortality Rates by Race, Geographic Division and States: Trends

[Data are based on the National Vital Statistics System.]

Geographic division and State	All races			White[1]			Black[1]		
	1980-82	1985-87	1990-92	1980-82	1985-87	1990-92	1980-82	1985-87	1990-92
	Neonatal deaths per 1,000 live births								
United States	8.1	6.7	5.6	7.0	5.7	4.6	14.1	12.4	11.2
New England	7.6	6.1	4.8	7.2	5.6	4.3	15.2	14.8	10.2
Maine	6.3	5.7	4.2	6.4	5.7	4.2	2	2	2
New Hampshire	7.5	5.9	3.7	7.5	5.9	3.7	2	2	2
Vermont	5.4	6.0	3.8	5.5	6.0	3.9	2	2	2
Massachusetts	7.4	5.8	4.7	7.0	5.3	4.3	13.6	14.0	8.9
Rhode Island	8.6	6.2	5.6	8.4	5.8	5.2	11.5[2]	11.6[2]	11.5[2]
Connecticut	8.7	6.9	5.5	7.6	5.8	4.6	17.5	16.4	11.8
Middle Atlantic	8.6	7.2	6.1	7.5	6.1	4.9	13.8	12.4	11.8
New York	8.6	7.3	6.3	7.5	6.3	5.1	13.4	11.4	11.2
New Jersey	8.0	6.7	5.8	6.9	5.5	4.4	13.1	12.4	11.7
Pennsylvania	8.8	7.2	6.1	7.9	6.0	4.9	15.7	15.0	13.2
East North Central	8.6	7.1	6.3	7.3	5.9	4.9	16.3	14.0	12.8
Ohio	8.4	6.4	6.0	7.4	5.7	5.0	15.2	11.0	11.5
Indiana	7.9	7.1	5.9	7.2	6.3	5.1	14.1	14.6	12.7
Illinois	9.7	8.0	6.9	7.9	6.3	5.2	16.8	14.4	13.2
Michigan	8.9	7.6	6.8	7.2	5.8	4.7	18.2	16.6	14.7
Wisconsin	6.6	5.5	4.7	6.3	4.9	4.3	11.9	11.7	8.0
West North Central	7.1	5.8	5.0	6.7	5.4	4.4	13.9	11.2	11.2

[Continued]

★ 991 ★

Neonatal Deaths: Mortality Rates by Race, Geographic Division and States: Trends
[Continued]

Geographic division and State	All races			White[1]			Black[1]		
	1980-82	1985-87	1990-92	1980-82	1985-87	1990-92	1980-82	1985-87	1990-92
Minnesota	6.2	5.4	4.4	6.0	5.2	4.1	18.1[2]	12.4	12.2
Iowa	6.9	5.7	4.6	6.7	5.5	4.4	16.1[2]	10.3[2]	11.2[2]
Missouri	8.1	6.5	5.7	7.3	5.7	4.6	13.0	11.1	11.1
North Dakota	7.2	4.8	5.0	7.0	4.7	5.0	[2]	[2]	[2]
South Dakota	6.8	5.8	5.3	6.1	5.3	4.8	[2]	[2]	[2]
Nebraska	6.8	5.9	4.3	6.5	5.5	3.9	14.3[2]	11.5[2]	10.2[2]
Kansas	7.3	5.6	5.2	6.7	5.2	4.6	14.7	11.3	11.4
South Atlantic	9.5	7.9	6.8	7.5	6.1	4.8	14.5	12.9	11.6
Delaware	10.1	9.2	6.9	7.5	7.5	5.4	19.2	15.0	12.0
Maryland	9.2	8.1	6.3	7.3	6.0	4.3	14.3	13.4	10.9
District of Columbia	17.8	15.5	14.4	10.2[2]	8.0	8.1	19.4	18.1	16.8
Virginia	9.4	7.4	6.6	7.8	5.8	4.6	14.9	13.0	13.2
West Virginia	8.0	6.9	5.6	7.8	6.6	5.5	15.0[2]	15.9[2]	8.9[2]
North Carolina	9.4	7.8	7.1	7.5	6.1	5.1	14.1	12.4	11.7
South Carolina	10.8	9.1	7.3	7.9	6.6	5.1	15.3	13.3	10.9
Georgia	8.9	8.5	7.5	6.8	6.6	5.0	12.6	12.3	11.8
Florida	9.2	7.1	6.0	7.4	5.6	4.7	14.8	12.1	10.2
East South Central	9.0	7.7	6.4	7.3	6.1	4.7	13.6	12.1	10.8
Kentucky	8.0	6.6	4.9	7.5	6.2	4.5	13.3	10.8	8.5
Tennessee	8.7	7.4	6.2	7.2	5.6	4.5	13.9	13.3	11.7
Alabama	9.2	8.5	7.2	7.3	6.6	5.3	12.7	12.2	11.0
Mississippi	10.6	8.3	7.4	7.2	5.8	4.6	14.2	11.3	10.4
West South Central	7.8	6.3	5.1	6.9	5.5	4.3	12.3	10.3	8.7
Arkansas	6.8	6.2	5.4	5.8	5.6	4.5	10.1	8.3	8.7
Louisiana	9.2	7.7	6.3	6.8	5.6	4.6	13.3	11.1	8.8
Oklahoma	7.6	6.2	5.1	7.1	5.9	4.7	12.5	11.2	9.0
Texas	7.6	6.0	4.7	7.0	5.4	4.1	11.9	10.0	8.7
Mountain	6.6	5.5	4.5	6.5	5.3	4.3	13.4	11.7	10.3
Montana	6.8	5.1	3.6	6.7	4.7	3.4	[2]	[2]	[2]
Idaho	5.9	6.4	5.0	6.0	6.3	4.9	[2]	[2]	[2]
Wyoming	6.7	6.1	3.7	6.7	6.2	3.6	[2]	[2]	[2]
Colorado	6.3	5.6	4.7	6.1	5.3	4.3	11.5	11.8	10.7
New Mexico	6.6	5.6	4.7	6.8	5.4	4.7	13.0[2]	14.4[2]	11.7[2]
Arizona	7.1	5.8	5.1	7.1	5.5	4.7	14.5	12.7	11.9
Utah	6.4	4.9	3.5	6.4	4.9	3.5	[2]	[2]	[2]
Nevada	6.5	4.9	4.0	6.0	4.6	3.6	13.8[2]	10.3[2]	8.3
Pacific	6.6	5.7	4.5	6.3	5.3	4.2	11.9	11.3	10.1
Washington	6.5	5.6	3.9	6.3	5.4	3.7	11.4	10.8	10.7
Oregon	6.7	5.2	4.0	6.6	5.1	3.9	13.4[2]	11.5[2]	11.3[2]
California	6.6	5.7	4.6	6.3	5.3	4.3	11.9	11.4	10.1

[Continued]

★ 991 ★

Neonatal Deaths: Mortality Rates by Race, Geographic Division and States: Trends
[Continued]

Geographic division and State	All races			White[1]			Black[1]		
	1980-82	1985-87	1990-92	1980-82	1985-87	1990-92	1980-82	1985-87	1990-92
Alaska	7.0	5.6	4.2	5.9	4.9	3.7	17.1[2]	8.7[2]	5.6[2]
Hawaii	6.7	5.9	4.2	5.3	3.9	3.0	9.4[2]	13.2[2]	10.1[2]

Source: "Neonatal Mortality Rates, According to Race, Geographic Division, and State: United States, Average Annual 1980-82, 1985-87, and 1990-92," *Health, United States, 1994*, p. 90. Primary source: Centers for Disease Control and Prevention, National Center for Health Statistics: Data computed by the Division of Health and Utilization Analysis from data compiled by the Division of Vital Statistics. *Notes:* 1. Deaths are tabulated by race of decedent; live births are tabulated by race of mother. 2. Data for States with fewer than 5,000 live births for the 3-year period are considered unreliable. Data for States with fewer than 1,000 live births are considered highly unreliable and are not shown.

Postneonatal Deaths

★ 992 ★

Postneonatal Deaths: Mortality Rates by Race, Geographic Division and States: Trends

[Data are based on the National Vital Statistics System.]

Geographic division and State	All races			White[1]			Black[1]		
	1980-82	1985-87	1990-92	1980-82	1985-87	1990-92	1980-82	1985-87	1990-92
	Postneonatal deaths per 1,000 live births								
United States	4.0	3.6	3.3	3.4	3.1	2.7	7.1	6.5	6.3
New England	2.8	2.5	2.1	2.7	2.3	2.0	5.5	5.2	4.1
Maine	3.4	3.0	2.0	3.4	3.0	2.0	[2]	[2]	[2]
New Hampshire	2.7	2.8	2.7	2.7	2.8	2.6	[2]	[2]	[2]
Vermont	3.8	3.0	2.6	3.8	2.9	2.7	[2]	[2]	[2]
Massachusetts	2.7	2.4	2.0	2.5	2.2	1.8	5.5	5.7	3.6
Rhode Island	2.3	2.5	2.2	2.1	2.4	2.2	[2]	3.0[2]	3.4[2]
Connecticut	2.7	2.3	2.2	2.4	2.0	1.8	4.9	4.9	4.7
Middle Atlantic	3.6	3.3	3.0	2.9	2.6	2.2	7.1	6.5	6.3
New York	3.8	3.4	3.0	3.1	2.7	2.2	6.6	6.0	5.9
New Jersey	3.6	3.2	2.8	2.6	2.4	1.9	8.0	6.9	6.8
Pennsylvania	3.4	3.3	3.1	2.9	2.7	2.5	7.3	7.4	6.9
East North Central	3.9	3.7	3.6	3.2	3.1	2.8	8.1	7.0	7.3
Ohio	3.8	3.6	3.6	3.3	3.2	2.9	7.4	6.5	7.0
Indiana	3.8	3.6	3.5	3.3	3.3	3.1	7.8	6.6	6.3
Illinois	4.4	3.9	3.6	3.2	2.8	2.4	9.1	7.8	8.0
Michigan	3.8	3.5	3.6	3.2	3.0	2.7	7.1	6.3	7.1
Wisconsin	3.4	3.5	3.2	3.1	3.3	2.7	8.0	6.2	7.5
West North Central	3.8	3.7	3.4	3.4	3.3	2.9	7.9	7.4	7.8

[Continued]

★ 992 ★

Postneonatal Deaths: Mortality Rates by Race, Geographic Division and States: Trends
[Continued]

Geographic division and State	All races			White[1]			Black[1]		
	1980-82	1985-87	1990-92	1980-82	1985-87	1990-92	1980-82	1985-87	1990-92
Minnesota	3.7	3.5	2.9	3.4	3.3	2.4	9.7[2]	8.4[2]	8.8[2]
Iowa	3.8	3.4	3.4	3.6	3.2	3.3	10.4[2]	7.7[2]	7.1[2]
Missouri	4.1	3.8	3.7	3.5	3.3	2.9	7.7	7.2	7.4
North Dakota	4.1	3.8	2.9	3.6	3.5	2.4	[2]	[2]	[2]
South Dakota	4.1	5.2	4.3	3.0	3.7	3.2	[2]	[2]	[2]
Nebraska	3.7	3.6	3.5	3.4	3.2	3.0	8.1[2]	8.5[2]	8.7[2]
Kansas	3.5	3.7	3.5	3.2	3.3	3.1	7.1[2]	7.1[2]	8.4[2]
South Atlantic	4.3	3.8	3.4	3.3	3.0	2.6	6.7	6.1	5.6
Delaware	3.7	3.4	3.3	2.8	2.6	2.2	6.6[2]	6.4[2]	6.8[2]
Maryland	3.6	3.6	3.2	2.8	2.9	2.3	5.5	5.3	5.2
District of Columbia	6.0	4.9	6.1	3.1[2]	3.0[2]	2.8[2]	6.7	5.6	7.2
Virginia	3.6	3.5	3.2	3.2	2.9	2.6	5.1	5.6	5.3
West Virginia	4.1	3.4	3.4	4.0	3.2	3.4	6.9[2]	7.4[2]	[2]
North Carolina	4.4	3.9	3.4	3.6	3.1	2.7	6.0	5.8	5.0
South Carolina	5.2	4.2	3.8	3.8	3.1	2.7	7.3	6.1	5.7
Georgia	4.8	4.1	3.9	3.4	3.0	2.8	7.3	6.3	5.8
Florida	4.3	3.8	3.2	3.2	2.9	2.4	7.7	6.7	5.9
East South Central	4.6	4.1	3.8	3.7	3.3	3.1	7.1	6.4	5.8
Kentucky	4.3	3.6	3.7	4.1	3.5	3.5	6.6	5.2	5.7
Tennessee	4.1	4.0	3.8	3.5	3.3	3.0	6.2	6.5	6.3
Alabama	4.8	4.2	3.7	3.4	3.0	2.7	7.5	6.5	5.5
Mississippi	5.4	4.9	4.5	3.4	3.5	3.4	7.6	6.6	5.6
West South Central	4.2	3.8	3.5	3.6	3.2	2.9	6.8	6.3	6.0
Arkansas	4.8	4.5	4.5	3.6	3.8	3.8	8.5	7.0	6.8
Louisiana	4.5	4.1	4.0	3.2	2.8	2.8	6.7	6.3	5.8
Oklahoma	4.7	4.1	4.1	4.4	3.8	3.8	7.6	6.6	7.2
Texas	3.9	3.5	3.1	3.6	3.2	2.7	6.4	6.1	5.8
Mountain	3.9	4.0	3.6	3.6	3.8	3.3	7.0	6.7	8.0
Montana	4.2	4.9	4.2	3.7	4.4	3.6	[2]	[2]	[2]
Idaho	4.0	4.3	3.7	4.0	4.3	3.7	[2]	[2]	[2]
Wyoming	3.3	4.7	4.8	3.2	4.5	4.8	[2]	[2]	[2]
Colorado	3.4	3.7	3.6	3.4	3.6	3.4	5.2[2]	7.5[2]	6.7[2]
New Mexico	4.3	3.8	3.5	3.8	3.6	3.1	[2]	[2]	[2]
Arizona	4.0	3.7	3.5	3.3	3.4	3.2	6.1[2]	5.4[2]	7.3[2]
Utah	4.0	4.1	3.0	3.9	4.1	3.0	[2]	[2]	[2]
Nevada	4.2	4.1	4.1	3.8	4.0	3.7	8.7[2]	6.7[2]	9.1[2]
Pacific	3.9	3.7	3.0	3.7	3.4	2.8	6.9	7.3	6.7
Washington	4.5	4.5	3.4	4.2	4.3	3.3	9.7[2]	6.9[2]	6.1[2]
Oregon	4.5	4.7	3.5	4.4	4.6	3.4	[2]	[2]	10.2[2]
California	3.7	3.5	2.9	3.5	3.2	2.7	6.8	7.2	6.7

[Continued]

★ 992 ★

Postneonatal Deaths: Mortality Rates by Race, Geographic Division and States: Trends
[Continued]

Geographic division and State	All races			White[1]			Black[1]		
	1980-82	1985-87	1990-92	1980-82	1985-87	1990-92	1980-82	1985-87	1990-92
Alaska	5.0	5.1	5.1	3.6	4.0	4.0	[2]	[2]	[2]
Hawaii	2.9	3.2	2.6	2.1	2.3	1.3	[2]	[2]	[2]

Source: "Postneonatal Mortality Rates, According to Race, Geographic Division, and State: United States, Average Annual 1980-82, 1985-87, and 1990-92," *Health, United States, 1994,* p. 91. Primary source: Centers for Disease Control and Prevention, National Center for Health Statistics: Data computed by the Division of Health and Utilization Analysis from data compiled by the Division of Vital Statistics. *Notes:* 1. Deaths are tabulated by race of decedent; live births are tabulated by race of mother. 2. Data for States with fewer than 10,000 live births for the 3-year period are considered unreliable. Data for States with fewer than 2,500 live births are considered highly unreliable and are not shown.

Pregnancies

★ 993 ★

Pregnancies: Age of Woman and Race: 1991

ITEM	Total	Under 15 years old	15 to 19 years old	20 to 24 years old	25 to 29 years old	30 to 34 years old	35 to 39 years old	40 years old and over
PREGNANCIES:								
Non-Hispanic:								
White, pregnancies	3,964	8	489	1,007	1,145	884	368	63
Live births	2,635	3	250	637	834	640	235	36
Induced abortions	774	4	164	264	163	106	58	16
Fetal losses	556	1	75	107	148	138	76	11
Black, pregnancies	1,344	14	272	439	320	202	81	15
Live births	673	6	149	216	160	98	37	6
Induced abortions	507	7	101	178	119	67	29	7
Fetal losses	164	1	22	45	41	37	15	3
Hispanic:								
Pregnancies	965	5	177	306	250	149	64	14
Live births	623	2	105	199	170	100	39	8
Induced abortions	208	1	40	73	50	28	13	4
Fetal losses	134	1	32	33	30	22	12	2
RATE PER 1,000 WOMEN								
Non-Hispanic:								
White, pregnancies	91.8	1.3	84.7	151.4	154.7	107.6	47.3	8.6
Live births	61.0	0.5	43.4	95.7	112.7	77.9	30.2	4.8
Induced abortions	17.9	0.7	28.4	39.6	22.0	12.9	7.4	2.2
Fetal losses	12.9	0.2	13.0	16.0	20.0	16.8	9.7	1.6

[Continued]

★ 993 ★

Pregnancies: Age of Woman and Race: 1991

[Continued]

ITEM	Total	Under 15 years old	15 to 19 years old	20 to 24 years old	25 to 29 years old	30 to 34 years old	35 to 39 years old	40 years old and over
Black, pregnancies	174.8	11.0	216.7	337.2	232.3	142.7	63.9	14.4
Live births	87.6	4.9	118.9	166.1	116.3	69.3	28.9	5.7
Induced abortions	65.9	5.1	80.5	136.4	86.3	47.1	23.0	6.2
Fetal losses	21.3	0.9	17.2	34.7	29.7	26.3	12.1	2.4
Hispanic:								
Pregnancies	167.4	4.8	180.2	285.6	224.3	143.9	74.8	19.8
Live births	108.1	2.4	106.7	186.3	152.8	96.1	44.9	11.1
Induced abortions	36.2	1.4	40.4	68.1	44.4	27.1	15.5	5.2
Fetal losses	23.2	1.0	33.1	31.2	27.1	20.7	14.4	3.6

Source: "Pregnancies, by Outcome, Age of Woman, and race: 1991," *Statistical Abstract of the United States, 1994*, p. 82. Primary source: U.S. National Center for Health Statistics, *Monthly Vital Statistics Report*, vol. 43, No. 12.

Prenatal Care

★ 994 ★

Mothers with Early Prenatal Care by Race of Mother: 1970-92

Year	All mothers	White	Black
1970	68.0	72.3	44.2
1971	-	-	-
1972	-	-	-
1973	-	-	-
1974	-	-	-
1975	72.4	75.8	55.5
1976	-	-	-
1977	-	-	-
1978	-	-	-
1979	-	-	-
1980	76.3	79.2	62.4
1981	76.3	79.3	62.1
1982	76.1	79.2	61.1
1983	76.2	79.3	61.2
1984	76.5	79.6	61.9
1985	76.2	79.3	61.5
1986	75.9	79.1	61.2
1987	76.0	79.3	60.8

[Continued]

★ 994 ★

Mothers with Early Prenatal Care by Race of Mother:
1970-92
[Continued]

Year	All mothers	White	Black
1988	75.9	79.3	60.7
1989	75.5	78.9	60.0
1990	75.8	79.2	60.6
1991	76.2	79.5	61.9
1992	77.7	80.8	63.9

Source: "Mothers with Early Prenatal Care by Race of Mother: United States, 1970-92." National Center for Health Statistics, *Health, United States, 1994*, p. 17. Primary source: Centers for Disease Control and Prevention, National Center for Health Statistics, National Vital Statistics System. *Notes:* Early prenatal care is care beginning in the first trimester of pregnancy. Excludes births that occurred in States not reporting prenatal care (see Appendix I). Percent based on live births for whom trimester when prenatal care began is known. These data are plotted on the log scale.

★ 995 ★

Prenatal Care

Prenatal Care for Live Births by Race and Hispanic Origin of
Mother: 1970-92. Part 1

[Data are based on the National Vital Statistics System].

Prenatal care, race of mother and Hispanic origin of mother	Percent of live births[1]					
	1970	1975	1980	1983	1984	1985
Prenatal care began during 1st trimester						
All mothers	68.0	72.4	76.3	76.2	76.5	76.2
White	72.3	75.8	79.2	79.3	79.6	79.3
Black	44.2	55.5	62.4	61.2	61.9	61.5
American Indian or Alaskan Native	38.2	45.4	55.8	56.6	57.4	57.5
Asian or Pacific Islander	-	-	73.7	73.9	74.7	74.1
Chinese	71.8	76.7	82.6	80.4	81.5	82.0
Japanese	78.1	82.7	86.1	86.6	87.0	84.7
Filipino	60.6	70.6	77.3	77.4	77.8	76.5
Hawaiian and part Hawaiian	-	-	-	-	-	-
Other Asian or Pacific Islander	-	-	-	-	-	-
Hispanic origin (selected States)[2,3]	-	-	60.2	61.0	61.5	61.2
Mexican American	-	-	59.6	60.2	60.4	60.0
Puerto Rican	-	-	55.1	55.1	57.4	58.3
Cuban	-	-	82.7	81.2	82.2	82.5
Central and South American	-	-	58.8	59.3	61.1	60.6
Other and unknown Hispanic	-	-	66.4	66.6	66.7	65.8
Non-Hispanic white (selected States)[2]	-	-	81.2	81.3	81.6	81.4

[Continued]

★ 995 ★

Prenatal Care for Live Births by Race and Hispanic Origin of Mother: 1970-92. Part 1

[Continued]

Prenatal care, race of mother and Hispanic origin of mother	Percent of live births[1]					
	1970	1975	1980	1983	1984	1985
Non-Hispanic black (selected States)[2]	-	-	60.7	59.9	60.6	60.1
Prenatal care began during 3d trimester or no prenatal care						
All mothers	7.9	6.0	5.1	5.6	5.6	5.7
White	6.3	5.0	4.3	4.6	4.7	4.8
Black	16.6	10.5	8.9	9.8	9.7	10.2
American Indian or Alaskan Native	28.9	22.4	15.2	14.4	13.8	12.9
Asian or Pacific Islander	-	-	6.5	6.5	6.4	6.5
Chinese	6.5	4.4	3.7	4.6	4.2	4.4
Japanese	4.1	2.7	2.1	2.4	2.6	3.1
Filipino	7.2	4.1	4.0	4.1	4.3	4.8
Hawaiian and part Hawaiian	-	-	-	-	-	-
Other Asian or Pacific Islander	-	-	-	-	-	-
Hispanic origin (selected States)[2,3]	-	-	12.0	12.5	12.6	12.4
Mexican American	-	-	11.8	12.7	13.0	12.9
Puerto Rican	-	-	16.2	17.4	16.3	15.5
Cuban	-	-	3.9	4.0	4.0	3.7
Central and South American	-	-	13.1	13.3	12.6	12.5
Other and unknown Hispanic	-	-	9.2	9.0	9.1	9.4
Non-Hispanic white (selected States)[2]	-	-	3.5	3.9	3.9	4.0
Non-Hispanic black (selected States)[2]	-	-	9.7	10.7	10.6	10.9

Source: "Prenatal Care for Live Births, According to Detailed Race of Mother and Hispanic Origin of Mother: United States, Selected Years 1970-92." National Center for Health Statistics, *Health, United states, 1994,* p. 73. Primary source: Centers for Disease Control and Prevention, National Center for Health Statistics: Data computed by the Division of Health and Utilization Analysis from data compiled by the Division of Vital Statistics. *Notes:* Data for 1970 and 1975 exclude births that occurred in States not reporting prenatal care (see Appendix I). The race groups, white and black, include persons of Hispanic and non-Hispanic origin. Conversely, persons of Hispanic origin may be of any race. 1. Excludes live births for whom trimester prenatal care began is unknown. 2. Trend data for Hispanics and non-Hispanics are affected by expansion of the reporting area for an Hispanic-origin item on the birth certificate and by immigration. These two factors affect numbers of events, composition of the Hispanic population, and maternal and infant health characteristics. The number of States in the reporting area increased from 22 in 1980, to 23 and the District of Columbia (DC) in 1983-87, 30 and DC in 1988, 47 and DC in 1989, 48 and DC in 1990, and 49 and DC in 1991-92 (see Appendix I, National Vital Statistics System). 3. Includes mothers of all races.

★ 996 ★
Prenatal Care

Prenatal Care for Live Births by Race and Hispanic Origin of Mother: 1970-92. Part 2

[Data are based on the National Vital Statistics System].

Prenatal care, race of mother and Hispanic origin of mother	Percent of live births[1]						
	1986	1987	1988	1989	1990	1991	1992
Prenatal care began during 1st trimester							
All mothers	75.9	76.0	75.9	75.5	75.8	76.2	77.7
White	79.1	79.3	79.3	78.9	79.2	79.5	80.8
Black	61.2	60.8	60.7	60.0	60.6	61.9	63.9
American Indian or Alaskan Native	58.2	57.6	58.1	57.9	57.9	59.9	62.1
Asian or Pacific Islander	74.9	75.0	75.5	74.8	75.1	75.3	76.6
Chinese	82.2	81.5	82.3	81.5	81.3	82.3	83.8
Japanese	85.7	86.6	86.3	86.2	87.0	87.7	88.2
Filipino	78.2	77.9	78.4	77.6	77.1	77.1	78.7
Hawaiian and part Hawaiian	-	-	-	66.8	65.8	68.1	69.9
Other Asian or Pacific Islander	-	-	-	71.1	71.9	71.9	72.8
Hispanic origin (selected States)[2,3]	60.3	61.0	61.3	59.5	60.2	61.0	64.2
Mexican American	58.9	60.0	58.3	56.7	57.8	58.7	62.1
Puerto Rican	57.2	57.4	63.2	62.7	63.5	65.0	67.8
Cuban	81.8	83.1	83.4	83.2	84.8	85.4	86.8
Central and South American	58.8	59.1	62.8	60.8	61.5	63.4	66.8
Other and unknown Hispanic	66.6	65.5	67.3	66.0	66.4	65.6	68.0
Non-Hispanic white (selected States)[2]	81.5	81.7	81.8	82.7	83.3	83.7	84.9
Non-Hispanic black (selected States)[2]	60.1	60.0	60.4	59.9	60.7	61.9	64.0
Prenatal care began during 3d trimester or no prenatal care							
All mothers	6.0	6.1	6.1	6.4	6.1	5.8	5.2
White	5.0	5.0	5.0	5.2	4.9	4.7	4.2
Black	10.7	11.2	11.0	11.9	11.3	10.7	9.9
American Indian or Alaskan Native	12.9	13.1	13.2	13.4	12.9	12.2	11.0
Asian or Pacific Islander	6.2	6.3	5.9	6.1	5.8	5.7	4.9
Chinese	4.2	4.2	3.4	3.6	3.4	3.4	2.9
Japanese	3.1	2.8	3.3	2.7	2.9	2.5	2.4
Filipino	4.5	4.9	4.8	4.7	4.5	5.0	4.3
Hawaiian and part Hawaiian	-	-	-	8.7	8.7	7.5	7.0
Other Asian or Pacific Islander	-	-	-	7.5	7.1	6.8	5.9
Hispanic origin (selected States)[2,3]	13.0	12.7	12.1	13.0	12.0	11.0	9.5
Mexican American	13.4	13.0	13.9	14.6	13.2	12.2	10.5
Puerto Rican	17.4	17.1	10.2	11.3	10.6	9.1	8.0
Cuban	4.2	3.9	3.6	4.0	2.8	2.4	2.1
Central and South American	13.8	13.5	9.9	11.9	10.9	9.5	7.9

[Continued]

★ 996 ★

Prenatal Care for Live Births by Race and Hispanic Origin of Mother: 1970-92. Part 2

[Continued]

Prenatal care, race of mother and Hispanic origin of mother	Percent of live births[1]						
	1986	1987	1988	1989	1990	1991	1992
Other and unknown Hispanic	9.0	9.3	8.8	9.3	8.5	8.2	7.5
Non-Hispanic white (selected States)[2]	4.1	4.1	4.1	3.7	3.4	3.2	2.8
Non-Hispanic black (selected States)[2]	11.4	11.8	11.0	12.0	11.2	10.7	9.8

Source: "Prenatal Care for Live Births, According to Detailed Race of Mother and Hispanic Origin of Mother: United States, Selected Years 1970-92." National Center for Health Statistics, *Health, United states, 1994*, p. 73. Primary source: Centers for Disease Control and Prevention, National Center for Health Statistics: Data computed by the Division of Health and Utilization Analysis from data compiled by the Division of Vital Statistics. *Notes:* Data for 1970 and 1975 exclude births that occurred in States not reporting prenatal care (see Appendix I). The race groups, white and black, include persons of Hispanic and non-Hispanic origin. Conversely, persons of Hispanic origin may be of any race. 1. Excludes live births for whom trimester prenatal care began is unknown. 2. Trend data for Hispanics and non-Hispanics are affected by expansion of the reporting area for an Hispanic-origin item on the birth certificate and by immigration. These two factors affect numbers of events, composition of the Hispanic population, and maternal and infant health characteristics. The number of States in the reporting area increased from 22 in 1980, to 23 and the District of Columbia (DC) in 1983-87, 30 and DC in 1988, 47 and DC in 1989, 48 and DC in 1990, and 49 and DC in 1991-92 (see Appendix I, National Vital Statistics System). 3. Includes mothers of all races.

Reference Sources

Bachu, Amara. *Fertility of American Women: June 1994*. U.S. Bureau of the Census. Current Population Reports, P20-482. Washington, D.C.: U.S. Government Printing Office, 1995.

Baseball Digest. Monthly. Century Publishing Co., 990 Grove Street, Evanston, Ill. 60201-4370.

Basketball Digest. Monthly November through July. Century Publishing Co., 990 Grove Street, Evanston, Ill. 60201-4370.

Black Enterprise. Monthly. Earl Graves Publishing Co., Inc., 130 Fifth Avenue, New York, N.Y. 10011. Most issues contain statistical data on blacks and business; however, each issue gives a concentration on statistical tables and charts.

College Entrance Examination Board. Educational Testing Service. *College-Bound Seniors, National Report: 1994 Profile of SAT and Achievement Test Takers*. New York: ETS, 1994.

College Sports. Monthly. College Sports Publishing, L.P., Route 22 East, One Salem Square, Suite 201 East, Whitehouse Station, N.J. 08889.

Crisis. Monthly January, April, July and October; bimonthly February/March, May/June, August/September, and November/December. Crisis Publishing Co., Inc., 4805 Mt. Hope Drive, Baltimore, Md. 21215.

Football Digest. Monthly September through April and bimonthly June and August. Century Publishing Co., 990 Grove Street, Evanston, Ill. 60201-4370.

Hansen, Kristin A. *Geographical Mobility: March 1992 to March 1993*. U.S. Bureau of the Census. Current Population Reports, P20-481. Washington, D.C.: U.S. Government Printing Office, 1994.

Hansen, Kristin, and Amara Bachu. "The Foreign-Born Population: 1994." U.S. Bureau of the Census. *Current Population Reports*. P20-486. Washington, D.C.: U.S. Government Printing Office, August 1995.

International City/County Management Association. *The Management Year Book, 1995*. Washington, D.C.: ICMA, 1995.

Jet. Weekly. Johnson Publishing Co., 820 South Michigan Avenue, Chicago, Ill. 60605.

Lumpkin, A., S. K. Stoll, and J. Beller. *Sports Ethics: Applications for Fair Play*. New York: Mosby, 1994.

Maguire, Kathleen, and Ann L. Pastore, eds. *Sourcebook of Criminal Justice Statistics 1994*. U.S. Department of Justice. Bureau of Justice Statistics. Washington, D.C.: U.S. Government Printing Office, 1995.

National Center for Health Statistics. *Health, United States, 1994*. Hyattsville, Md.: Public Health Service, 1995.

National Science Foundation. *Academic Science and Engineering: R & D Expenditures, Fiscal Year 1992*. Detailed Statistical Tables, NSF 94-324. Arlington, Va.: NSF, 1994.

NCAA. *Program Book of the 1995 Men's Division I Basketball Championship First and Second Rounds*. n.p. Sold at NCAA Tournament sites.

NCAA FINAL FOUR. *The Official 1995 Final Four Records Book*. The National Collegiate Athletic Association, 6201 College Boulevard, Overland Park, Kans. 66211-2422.

New York Daily News, n.d. 220 East 42nd Street, New York, N.Y. 10017

New York Times. Daily. 229 West 43rd Street, New York, N.Y. 10036.

1995 Petersen's Pro Basketball. Annual. Petersen Publishing Co., 6420 Wilshire Boulevard, Los Angeles, Calif., 90048- 5515.

104th Congress, 1st Session. *Economic Indicators, August 1995*. Prepared for the Joint Economic Committee by the Council on Economic Advisers. Washington, D.C.: U.S. Government Printing Office, 1995.

The Sporting News 1995-96 Pro Basketball Yearbook. Published annually in September. The Sporting News Publishing Co., 1212 North Lindbergh Boulevard, St. Louis, Mo. 63132.

The Sporting News 1995 Pro Football Yearbook. Published annually in July. The Sporting News Publishing Co., 1212 North Lindbergh Boulevard, St. Louis, Mo. 63132.

The Tennessean. Daily. 1100 Broadway, Nashville, Tenn. 37203.

Time. Published weekly except for two combined issues at year-end by Time, Inc., Time & Life Building, Rockefeller Center, New York, N.Y. 10020-1393.

U.S. Bureau of the Census. Current Population Reports, Series P23-189. *Population Profile of the United States: 1995.* Washington, D.C.: U.S. Government Printing Office, 1995.

U.S. Bureau of the Census. *Statistical Abstract of the United States: 1995.* 115th ed. Washington, D.C.: U.S. Government Printing Office, 1995.

U.S. Department of Commerce. Bureau of the Census. *American Housing Survey for the United States in 1993.* H150-93. Current Housing Reports. Washington, D.C.: U.S. Government Printing Office, February 1995.

U.S. Department of Commerce, Economics and Statistical Administration, Bureau of the Census. *1992 Economic Census: Survey of Minority-Owned Business Enterprises—Black.* MB92-1. Washington, D.C.: U.S. Government Printing Office, January 1996.

—. *Statistical Brief: Housing in Metropolitan Areas Black Households.* SB/95-5. March 1995.

—. *Statistical Brief: Mothers Who Receive Food Stamps Fertility and Socioeconomic Characteristics.* SB/95- 22. August 1995.

—. *Statistical Brief: Poverty's Revolving Door.* SB/95-20. Washington, D.C.: U.S. Government Printing Office, August 1995.

—. "We Asked . . . You Told Us: Ancestry." Census Questionnaire Content, 1990. CQC 14.

U.S. Department of Education. Office of Educational Research and Improvement. National Center for Education Statistics. *The Condition of Education, 1995.* Washington, D.C.: U.S. Government Printing Office, 1995.

—. Findings from *The Condition of Education 1994: No. 2. The Educational Progress of Black Students.* NCES 95-765. Washington, D.C.: U.S. Government Printing Office, 1995.

—. *Enrollment in Higher Education: Fall 1984 through Fall 1993.* NCES 95-238. Washington, D.C.: U.S. Government Printing Office, April 1995.

—. *Making the Cut: Who Meets Highly Selective College Entrance Criteria?* NCES 95-732. Washington, D.C.: U.S. Government Printing Office, April 1995.

—. *Minority Undergraduate Participation in Postsecondary Education.* CES 95-166. Washington, D.C.: U.S. Government Printing Office, June 1995.

—. *Profile of Older Undergraduates: 1989-90.* NCES 95-167. Washington, D.C.: U.S. Government Printing Office, April 1995.

—. *State Comparisons of Education Statistics: 1969-70 to 1993-94.* NCES 95-122. Washington, D.C.: U.S. Government Printing Office, June 1995.

—. *Understanding Racial-Ethnic Differences in Secondary School Science and Mathematics Achievement.* NCES 95-710. Washington, D.C.: U.S. Government Printing Office, February 1995.

U.S. Department of Education. Office of Educational Research and Improvement. National Center for Education Statistics. Indicator of the Month. *Adult Literacy.* NCES 95-721. Washington, D.C. 20208-5650, January 1995.

U.S. Department of Education. Office of Educational Research and Improvement. National Center for Education Statistics. Statistical Analysis Report. *High School and Beyond: Educational Attainment of 1980 High School Sophomores by 1992; 1992 Descriptive Summary of 1980 High School Sophomores 12 Years Later.* NCES 95-304. Washington, D.C.: U.S. Government Printing Office, March 1995.

U.S. Department of Health and Human Services. Public Health Service. National Institute of Health. National Institute on Drug Abuse. *Drug Use among Ethnic Minorities.* NIH Publication No. 95-3888. Washington, D.C.: U.S. Government Printing Office, 1995.

U.S. Department of Health and Human Services. Public Health Service. Substance Abuse and Mental Health Services Administration. Office of Applied Studies. *National Household Survey on Drug Abuse: Main Findings 1993.* DHHS Publication No. (SMA) 95-3020. Rockville, Md.: June 1995.

U.S. Department of Health and Human Services. Social Security Administration. Office of Research and Statistics. *Income of the Aged Chartbook, 1992.* SSA Publication No. 13-11727. December 1994.

U.S. Department of Justice. Bureau of Justice Statistics. *Bulletin: Prisoners in 1994.* NCJ-151654. Office of Justice Programs, Washington, DC 20531, August 1995.

—. *Selected Findings: Domestic Violence, Violence Between Intimates.* NCJ-149259. Office of Justice Programs, Washington, DC 20531, November 1994.

—. *Special Report: National Crime Victimization Survey.* NCJ-154348. Office of Justice Programs, Washington, D.C. 2051, August 1995.

U.S. Department of Labor, Bureau of Labor Statistics. *Employment and Earnings*. Washington, D.C.: U.S. Government Printing Office, December 1995, February 1996.

U.S. Equal Employment Opportunity Commission. *Indicators of Equal Employment Opportunity—Status and Trends*. Washington, D.C.: U.S. Government Printing Office, September 1993.

—. *Job Patterns for Minorities and Women in Private Industry 1994*. Washington, D.C., EEOC, 1995.

Ventura, Stephanie J. Births to Unmarried Mothers: United States, 1980-92. National Center for Health Statistics, Vital Health Stat 21 (53). Washington, D.C.: U.S. Government Printing Office, 1995.

Warnick, Rod. "African American Golf Participation in the 80s: One Year After Shoal Creek." News release. University of Massachusetts at Amherst, Amherst, MA 01003- 0069, August 7, 1991.

INDEX

Page numbers immediately follow the index terms. Values in brackets are table numbers.

Abortions, pp. 879-880 [866-867]
Abuse
— children, p. 109 [123]
Accidents, pp. 984, 987 [950-951]
Achievement
— high school graduates, p. 143 [170]
— mathematics, pp. 144-145 [171-172]
— reading, p. 146 [173]
— science, p. 147 [174]
— writing, p. 148 [175]
Activities
— leisure, p. 791 [760]
Activity
— limitation, p. 247 [299]
Adolescents
— with AIDS, p. 230 [279-280]
Adult education
— reasons for participation, p. 140 [166]
Adults
— literacy, p. 224 [272-273]
— with AIDS, p. 230 [279-280]
Age
— and college enrollment, p. 195 [231]
— and educational enrollment, p. 223 [271]
— and poverty, p. 468 [435]
— at first drug use, p. 14 [23]
— children, pp. 831-832, 834-835 [822-823, 825-826]
— householders, pp. 831-832, 844-845 [822-823, 835-836]
— murderers, p. 101 [110]
— of family members, pp. 838-841, 848-849 [829-833, 838-839]
— of family reference person, p. 860 [845]
— of murder victims, p. 105 [116]
— of single parents, pp. 851, 853 [840-841]
— of spouses, pp. 874-875 [862-863]
— parents, p. 826 [815-816]
— undergraduates, p. 215 [260]
AIDS
— deaths, p. 963 [938]
— diagnosed cases, p. 231 [281]
— in adults/adolescents, p. 230 [279-280]
— source of transmission, p. 232 [282]
Alcohol
— abuse, p. 250 [303]
— daily use, p. 10 [16]
— heavy use, pp. 16-17, 33, 40 [25, 27, 49, 57]
— use, pp. 12, 16, 20, 30, 32-33, 36-37, 40 [19-20, 25, 31, 46, 48-49,

Alcohol continued:
51-52, 57]
All-Black households, pp. 642-644 [626-628]
Ancestry groups, p. 618 [608]
Arrests
— charge, p. 110 [124]
— drug, p. 121 [143]
Arts, pp. 599-600 [585-586]
Arts activities, pp. 599-600 [585-586]
Aspirations
— educational, p. 6 [9]
Assault
— victims, p. 107 [120]
Attainment
— educational, pp. 141-142 [167, 169]
Attitudes
— drug-related, pp. 1-2 [1-2]
— educational aspirations, p. 6 [9]
— race-related, pp. 3-5 [3-7]
— school-related, p. 5 [8]
— toward black colleges, p. 4 [5]
— toward desegregation, p. 5 [8]
— toward employment, p. 4 [6]
— toward helping others, p. 3 [4]
— toward mathematics, p. 7 [10]
— toward racism, p. 5 [7]
— toward science, p. 7 [10]
— political, p. 3 [3]
Barbiturates
— use, pp. 43-44 [61-62]
Baseball
— award winners, pp. 801-802 [778-779]
— batting averages, p. 806 [786]
— home run leaders, p. 798 [772]
— home runs, pp. 802, 805 [780, 784]
— League leaders, pp. 797-798 [771, 773]
— players, p. 804 [782]
— professional, pp. 797-808 [771-789]
— retired uniform numbers, p. 803 [781]
— runs batted in, p. 804 [783]
— strikeouts, p. 808 [789]
— World Series, pp. 800, 806 [777, 787]
Basketball
— college, pp. 794-796, 815 [765-767, 770, 801]
— head coaches, p. 795 [767]
— NBA All-Star game, p. 811 [795]

Basketball continued:
— professional, pp. 808-814 [790-800]
Batters
— World Series, p. 807 [788]
Batting averages
— World Series, p. 806 [786]
Behavior
— crime-related, pp. 7-10 [11-15]
— drug-related, pp. 10-34, 36-50 [16-68]
— health-related, p. 250 [303]
— risk, pp. 37-39 [53-55]
— youth, pp. 37-39 [53-55]
Birth control, p. 883 [870]
Birth order, p. 1033 [986]
Birth projections, pp. 883-886 [869-874]
Birth rates, pp. 888-889, 891, 896, 934, 940, 1033 [875-877, 883, 913, 919, 986]
— first, p. 889 [876]
Births, pp. 883-886, 889, 891-900, 902, 904, 906, 908, 910, 912-916, 918-922, 924-925, 927-933, 935-938, 940-942, 1034-1035, 1045, 1047 [869, 871-874, 876-912, 914-922, 987-988, 995-996]
— by state, p. 1035 [988]
— characteristics, p. 896 [883]
— geographical area, pp. 897, 902, 904 [884, 889-890]
Birthweight, pp. 893, 900, 941-943, 945 [879, 888, 920-924]
— geographical area, pp. 943, 945 [923-924]
Black colleges
— attitudes toward, p. 4 [5]
Black households, pp. 619-620, 622 [609-611]
Black owner households, pp. 624-626 [612-614]
Black renter households, pp. 627, 629-630 [615-617]
Breastfeeding, p. 947 [925]
Business, pp. 57, 92, 95 [78, 104-105]
— sales, p. 56 [76]
Business growth, p. 57 [77]
Business size, pp. 55-56 [73-75]
Business types, pp. 73-76, 78, 80-82, 84-85, 88, 91 [91-102]
Businesses, pp. 52, 54, 62, 65-66, 70-72 [70-72, 81-84, 86-89]
— leading, p. 69 [85]
— legal form, p. 72 [90]
— location, pp. 58, 60, 73-76, 78, 80-82, 84 [79-80, 91-99]
Cancer
— breast, p. 237 [287]
— incidence rates, pp. 235-236 [285-286]
— prostate, p. 237 [287]
— survival rates, p. 234 [284]
Causes of death, pp. 1003, 1005 [966-967]
Central cities, p. 271 [329]
Child support, p. 783 [750]
Childless women, p. 938 [918]
Children, p. 639 [624]
— 1980 high school sophomore cohort, p. 825 [814]
— abuse, p. 109 [123]
— age, pp. 831-835 [822-826]
— in families, pp. 836, 863 [827, 848]
— in poverty, p. 830 [821]
— living arrangements, pp. 826-829 [815-820]
— neglect, p. 109 [123]

Children continued:
— under 18, pp. 836, 861-862 [827, 846-847]
— vaccinations, p. 252 [305]
Children in households, pp. 338, 341, 344, 346, 355, 358, 360 [359-362, 365-367]
Cholesterol
— level, p. 237 [288]
Cigarette smokers, pp. 902, 904 [889-890]
Cigarettes
— daily consumption, p. 15 [24]
— use, pp. 21, 31, 40-42, 46-49, 269 [32, 47, 57-59, 64-67, 328]
Civilian labor force, p. 470 [438]
Civilians employed, pp. 485-486, 488-489, 494, 502, 512-513 [456-459, 464, 471, 481-482]
Coaches
— basketball, p. 795 [767]
Cocaine
— Emergency Room treatment, p. 256 [310]
— emergency treatment for, pp. 259-260 [314-315]
— use, pp. 13, 22, 31, 36-37, 39-40, 43, 116 [21-22, 33, 47, 51-52, 56-57, 60, 133]
Cocaine/crack-cocaine
— ease of attainment, pp. 1-2 [1-2]
College
— recommended for, p. 149 [176]
College students
— employment status, p. 214 [258]
— family income, p. 203 [242]
— female, pp. 181-182, 184-185, 199 [216, 218, 220-221, 236]
— full-time, pp. 179, 182, 184 [214, 217, 220]
— male, pp. 182-185, 200 [218-221, 237]
— older undergraduates, pp. 209-212 [247-253]
— part-time, pp. 180, 185 [215, 221-222]
— reasons for choice of college, p. 216 [261]
— undergraduates, p. 215 [260]
Colleges and universities
— 2-Year, p. 163 [196]
— 4-Year, p. 164 [197]
— by State, pp. 160-161 [192-193]
— enrollment, pp. 160-161 [192-193]
— enrollment by level of institution, p. 162 [194]
— number, pp. 160-161 [192-193]
— private, p. 177 [212]
— public, p. 177 [212]
— public/private, p. 162 [195]
Computers
— student use, p. 221 [269]
— use at work, p. 598 [584]
Conditions
— acute, p. 233 [283]
— cholesterol, p. 237 [288]
— excess weight, p. 240 [290]
Consumers
— buying power, p. 451 [413]
— expenditures, p. 452 [414]
Contraception, p. 880 [868]
Correctional officers
— age group, p. 112 [128]
County officials, pp. 609, 615-616 [595-596, 604-605]

Numbers following p. or pp. are page references. Numbers in [ ] are table references.

Courts
— sentences for crime, p. 132 [158]
Crack
— use, p. 23 [34]
Crack-cocaine
— use, pp. 36-37, 43, 116 [51-52, 60, 133]
Crack/freebase
— use, p. 13 [21-22]
Crime
— death sentences, p. 136 [162]
— drug arrests, p. 121 [143]
— drug-related, p. 98 [106]
— juvenile offenders, p. 99 [108]
— juveniles, pp. 98, 127 [107, 151]
— law enforcement, pp. 110-116, 118-119, 131 [124-132, 134, 137, 139, 157]
— legal justice, pp. 123-126, 128-131, 134-137, 139 [145-150, 152-157, 160-165]
— murder, pp. 100-102, 105-106 [109-112, 116, 118]
— personal, p. 107 [120]
— prisoners, p. 119 [138]
— sentences, pp. 132, 134 [158-159]
— suicide, p. 103 [113]
— victims, pp. 103-109 [114-115, 117, 119-123]
Criminals
— killers of law enforcement officers, p. 111 [125]
Curriculum
— high school, p. 149 [177]
Death rates, pp. 948, 950, 952-956, 958, 962-963, 965-966, 968, 970-971, 973, 975, 977, 979, 981-982, 984, 987, 989-990, 992, 994, 997-998, 1002, 1007-1008 [927-934, 937-955, 958-959, 965, 968-969]
Deaths, pp. 997-998, 1000, 1002 [958-959, 962-963, 965]
— by accident, pp. 229, 948, 1001 [278, 926, 964]
— by age, pp. 955, 1000 [932, 962]
— by AIDS, p. 996 [956]
— by alcohol-induced causes, p. 997 [958]
— by cause, pp. 955, 1000 [932, 962-963]
— by drug-induced causes, p. 998 [959]
— by firearm, pp. 996, 1001 [957, 964]
— drug-related, p. 228 [277]
— firearm injuries, p. 971 [943]
— legal intervention, pp. 977, 979 [946-947]
— suicide, p. 229 [278]
Defendants
— convicted, p. 128 [153]
— failure to appear in court, p. 126 [149]
Degrees
— associate, pp. 165-166, 176, 213 [199-200, 209, 256]
— bachelor's, pp. 168-169, 176, 213 [201-202, 209, 255]
— doctoral, pp. 165, 170-171, 177 [198, 203-204, 211]
— first professional, pp. 172-173, 176 [205-206, 210]
— master's, pp. 174-175, 177 [207-208, 211]
Dentists
— time interval since last visit, p. 254 [307]
— visits, p. 254 [307]
Desegregation
— attitudes toward, p. 5 [8]

Disability
— days, pp. 248-249 [300-301]
Disabled workers, p. 789 [758]
Discouraged workers, p. 470 [438]
Diseases
— AIDS, pp. 230-232 [279-282]
— cancer, pp. 234-237 [284-287]
Displaced workers, p. 471 [439]
Divorce, pp. 1037-1038 [989-990]
Doctorates
— field, p. 165 [198]
Driving
— under the influence, p. 34 [50]
Dropouts
— age, p. 152 [182]
— and family income, p. 151 [180]
— employment status, p. 222 [270]
— gender, p. 152 [183]
— high school, p. 152 [182-183]
— in relation to population, p. 151 [181]
— number/percent, p. 151 [181]
— rate, p. 151 [180]
Drug history
— State prisoners, p. 117 [135]
Drugs
— abuse, pp. 250, 269 [303, 327]
— alcohol, pp. 10, 16-17, 20 [16, 25, 27, 31]
— arrests, p. 121 [143]
— at at first use, p. 14 [23]
— by injection, p. 13 [21-22]
— cigarettes, pp. 15, 21 [24, 32]
— cocaine, p. 22 [33]
— contributing to crime, p. 98 [106]
— contributing to death, pp. 228-229 [277-278]
— convictions, p. 131 [157]
— crack, p. 23 [34]
— ease of attainment, pp. 1-2 [1-2]
— effects of, p. 19 [30]
— Emergency Room treatment, pp. 254-258, 261 [308-312, 316]
— hallucinogens, p. 23 [35]
— heroin, p. 25 [38]
— ice, p. 27 [40]
— illicit, pp. 16, 28 [26, 43]
— inhalants, p. 24 [36]
— marijuana, p. 24 [37]
— needle use, p. 27 [41]
— neighborhood sales, p. 28 [42]
— nonmedical use, p. 18 [28-29]
— PCP, p. 25 [38]
— psychotherapeutic, p. 18 [28-29]
— smokeless tobacco, p. 26 [39]
— steroids, p. 27 [40]
— use, pp. 11-14, 16, 27-32, 36-37, 39-45, 50, 116 [17-23, 26, 40, 43-45, 47-48, 51-52, 56-63, 68, 133]
— used by pregnant women, p. 251 [304]
— used by women of childbearing age, pp. 29-30 [44-45]
Earners
— family, p. 873 [860]

Index

Numbers following p. or pp. are page references. Numbers in [ ] are table references.

Education
— 1980 high school sophomore cohort, pp. 217-220 [262-267]
— adult, p. 140 [166]
— and employment, p. 222 [270]
— attainment, pp. 141-142 [167, 169]
— dropouts, pp. 151-152, 222 [180-183, 270]
— elementary and secondary, pp. 7, 143-148, 150, 152-157, 159 [10, 170-175, 178-179, 182-187, 189, 191]
— enrollment, pp. 155-156, 195, 223, 225 [186-187, 231, 271, 274]
— high school courses, p. 149 [177]
— high school graduates, pp. 157, 222 [188, 270]
— higher, pp. 160-166, 168-191, 193-195, 197-204, 206-207, 209-216 [192-230, 232-261]
— level of attainment, p. 141 [168]
— preprimary, p. 220 [268]
— private, p. 159 [191]
— public, pp. 153, 155-156 [184, 186-187]
— school choice, p. 157 [189]
— segregation/integration, p. 158 [190]
— smokers, pp. 47, 49 [65, 67]
— student computer use, p. 221 [269]
— students, p. 149 [176]
— test scores, pp. 225-226 [275-276]
Education and labor force, p. 503 [472]
Education of mothers, pp. 910, 912 [893-894]
Educational attainment
— and income, p. 460 [424-425]
— level, p. 141 [168]
— of householders, pp. 833, 842 [824, 834]
— parents, pp. 827-828 [817-818]
Elderly householder, pp. 291, 293, 295, 298, 300, 302, 304, 307, 309, 311, 313, 316, 318, 320, 322, 325, 327, 330, 332 [338-356]
Elected officials, p. 608 [594]
— characteristics, pp. 606-607 [592-593]
— local, p. 608 [594]
— office, p. 604 [591]
— region and state, p. 604 [591]
— representatives, pp. 606-607 [592-593]
— senators, pp. 606-607 [592-593]
Elementary and secondary education
— teachers, p. 154 [185]
Emergency rooms
— visits, p. 259 [313]
Emergency treatment
— drug-related, pp. 254-258, 261 [308-312, 316]
Employment, pp. 71, 473, 495-498, 500-501, 514-585 [87, 441, 465-470, 483-568]
— attitudes toward, p. 4 [6]
— by industry, p. 472 [440]
— characteristics, p. 472 [440]
— public schools, p. 153 [184]
— trends, p. 472 [440]
Employment rates, pp. 474, 479, 567 [442-443, 449-450, 546]
Employment status
— and education, p. 222 [270]
— college students, p. 214 [258]
— parents, pp. 827-828 [817-818]

Enrollment
— 2-year colleges, pp. 181-183, 185, 195 [216-217, 219, 222, 232]
— 4-year colleges, pp. 181-183, 185, 195 [216-217, 219, 222, 232]
— and age, p. 223 [271]
— education, p. 223 [271]
— elementary and secondary, pp. 155-156, 188-191 [186-187, 225-228]
— first-professional, pp. 177-178, 198 [212-213, 234]
— graduate, pp. 177-178, 198 [212-213, 234]
— HBCUs, p. 204 [243]
— high school, p. 225 [274]
— higher education, pp. 162, 177-191, 193-195, 197-199, 204, 214, 225 [194-195, 212-235, 243, 258, 274]
— preprimary, p. 220 [268]
— private colleges and universities, pp. 179-180, 197 [214-215, 233]
— public colleges and universities, pp. 179-180, 197 [214-215, 233]
— undergraduate, pp. 177-178, 198 [212-213, 234]
Entertainment
— expenditures, p. 792 [761]
Executions
— civil court, p. 124 [147]
Expectations
— of black president/vice president, p. 3 [3]
Expenditures
— consumer buying power, p. 451 [413]
— consumers, p. 452 [414]
— entertainment, p. 792 [761]
— health care, p. 253 [306]
— reading, p. 792 [761]
Faculty
— higher education, pp. 200-201 [238-239]
Families, p. 349 [363]
— 1980 high school sophomore cohort, p. 874 [861]
— age of householder, pp. 851, 853 [840-841]
— age of members, pp. 838-840, 848-849 [829-832, 838-839]
— age of reference person, p. 860 [845]
— children, pp. 825-836, 861-863 [814-827, 846-848]
— earners, p. 873 [860]
— female-headed, pp. 838, 840 [829, 831]
— gender of members, pp. 839-840 [830, 832]
— income, pp. 454-455, 864-868, 871, 873 [416-417, 850-855, 858, 860]
— male-headed, p. 839 [830]
— marital status, pp. 856, 876 [842, 864]
— married-couples, pp. 837, 840, 872, 874-875, 877 [828, 831, 859, 862-863, 865]
— members, pp. 841, 847 [833, 837]
— poverty, pp. 869-870 [856-857]
— single-parent, pp. 838-839, 848-849, 851, 853, 856-857, 859 [829-830, 838-844]
— size, pp. 842, 844-845, 857, 859, 864 [834-836, 843-844, 849]
— subfamilies, p. 860 [845]
— type, pp. 835, 837, 841, 847, 856, 861-864 [826, 828, 833, 837, 842, 846-849]
Families employed, pp. 504-505, 507-508 [473-476]
Families in households, pp. 338, 341, 344, 346, 352, 355, 358, 360 [359-362, 364-367]
Families unemployed, pp. 504-505, 507-508 [473-476]
Farm operators, p. 92 [103]
Farms and farming, p. 92 [103]
Federal employment rates, p. 478 [448]

Numbers following p. or pp. are page references. Numbers in [ ] are table references.

Federal government employment rates, p. 479 [449]
Female households
— poverty, p. 466 [433]
Fertility, p. 1010 [970-971]
Fertility rates, pp. 1010, 1012-1013 [971-973]
— projections, p. 1013 [973]
Fetal death rates, pp. 1014, 1024 [974, 980]
Financial institutions, pp. 52, 54 [70-72]
Flexible schedules, p. 597 [582]
Football
— college, pp. 795-796 [768, 770]
— Madden awards, p. 817 [804]
— professional, pp. 816-823 [802-813]
— Super Bowl, pp. 819, 822-823 [807, 811-813]
Franchisors, pp. 70, 72 [86, 89]
Full-time workers
— income, p. 460 [425]
Gender
— of family members, pp. 838-840 [829-832]
Golf
— leisure, p. 793 [763-764]
Government assistance programs, pp. 784-785 [751-753]
Graduates
— college, p. 142 [169]
— high school, pp. 142, 225 [169, 274]
Guns
— handgun victimization rate, p. 104 [115]
— ownership, p. 792 [762]
— type owned, p. 792 [762]
Hallucinogens
— use, pp. 23, 45 [35, 63]
HBCUs
— enrollment, p. 204 [243]
Health
— activity limitation, p. 247 [299]
— acute conditions, p. 233 [283]
— deaths, p. 229 [278]
— disability days, pp. 248-249 [300-301]
— diseases, p. 230 [279-280]
— emergency treatment, pp. 259-260 [314-315]
— insurance, pp. 243-247 [293-298]
— medical care, pp. 242, 254, 259-260, 264-268 [291-292, 307, 314-315, 319-326]
— self-ratings, p. 249 [302]
— status, pp. 247, 249 [299, 302]
Health care
— expenditures, p. 253 [306]
Health care facilities
— nursing home, p. 242 [292]
— short-stay hospitals, p. 242 [291]
Health insurance
— coverage, pp. 245-246 [296-297]
— type, pp. 245-246 [296-297]
Health-related behavior
— vaccinations, p. 252 [305]
Heroin
— ease of attainment, pp. 1-2 [1-2]
— Emergency Room treatment, p. 257 [311]
— use, pp. 25, 43-44 [38, 61-62]

High school
— curriculum, p. 149 [177]
— students, pp. 149, 225 [176, 274]
High school graduates
— achievement, p. 143 [170]
— employment status, p. 222 [270]
— method of completion, p. 157 [188]
High school students
— crime victims, p. 106 [119]
— drug use, pp. 11-13, 41-45 [17-22, 58-63]
— mathematics courses, p. 150 [178-179]
Higher education
— aspirations, p. 6 [9]
— colleges and universities, pp. 160-161 [192-193]
— cost, p. 202 [241]
— degrees, pp. 165-166, 168-177 [198-211]
— enrollment, pp. 162-164, 177-191, 193-195, 197-200, 204, 214, 225 [194-197, 212-237, 243, 258, 274]
— faculty, pp. 200-201 [238-239]
— funding, pp. 204, 206-207 [244-246]
— majors, p. 201 [240]
— older undergraduates, pp. 209-212 [247-253]
— persistence in, pp. 212-214 [254-257]
— science and engineering, pp. 204, 206-207 [244-246]
— students, pp. 203, 216 [242, 261]
— time of degree, p. 215 [259]
— undergraduates, p. 215 [260]
Home runs
— baseball, pp. 802, 805 [780, 784]
Home tenure
— parents, pp. 828-829 [819-820]
Homicide
— rate, p. 108 [122]
— victims, pp. 103, 108 [114, 122]
Homicides, pp. 977, 979 [946-947]
Hospices
— care, p. 262 [317]
Hospitals
— emergency rooms, p. 259 [313]
— outpatient departments, p. 263 [318]
— short-stay, p. 242 [291]
Household composition, p. 365 [369]
Household fuels, p. 363 [368]
Household vehicles, pp. 367-368 [370-371]
Householders, pp. 424, 662-673, 675-679, 681-682, 684-685, 687-711, 713-714, 720-723, 734, 736-737, 739-741, 743-747, 749-755, 758-762 [398-399, 643-692, 698-701, 712-729, 732-737]
— age, pp. 831-832, 844-845 [822-823, 835-836]
— educational attainment, p. 842 [834]
— equipment, p. 336 [358]
— family income, pp. 390, 393, 395, 397, 400, 403 [383-388]
— female, p. 837 [828]
— income, p. 406 [389]
— male, p. 837 [828]
— mobility, pp. 373-374 [374-375]
Households, pp. 619-620, 622, 624-627, 629-630, 642-645, 647-651, 653-656 [609-617, 626-638]
— characteristics, pp. 619-620, 622 [609-611]
— crime victims, p. 105 [117]

Numbers following p. or pp. are page references. Numbers in [ ] are table references.

Housing, pp. 408, 410, 434 [390-391, 405]
— amenities, p. 377 [377]
— black occupied, pp. 272, 334, 377, 417 [330, 357, 377, 395]
— conditions, p. 375 [376]
— costs, pp. 273, 276, 278, 281, 283, 286, 289 [331-337]
— equipment, p. 334 [357]
— improvements, p. 388 [382]
— metropolitan areas, pp. 408, 410 [390-391]
— mobility, pp. 369, 371 [372-373]
— mortgages, pp. 412, 414 [392-393]
— quality, p. 377 [377]
— size, pp. 378, 381, 384 [378-380]
— tenure, pp. 426, 429, 431 [402-404]
— value, pp. 410, 435-436, 439, 441, 444, 446, 448 [391, 406-412]
Husbands
— age, pp. 874-875 [862-863]
— race, p. 877 [865]
Hypertension
— incidence, p. 238 [289]
Illness
— hypertension, p. 238 [289]
Income
— aggregate, p. 453 [415]
— and dropout rate, p. 151 [180]
— and educational attainment, p. 460 [424-425]
— distribution, pp. 455-458 [417, 419, 421-422]
— expenditures, p. 451 [413]
— family, pp. 864-868, 871-873 [850-855, 858-860]
— family households, pp. 454-455 [416-417]
— full-time workers, pp. 460-461 [425-426]
— mean, p. 460 [424]
— median, p. 454 [416]
— minimum-wage workers, p. 461 [427]
— nonfamily households, pp. 454-455 [416-417]
— older adults, p. 457 [420]
— parents, pp. 828-829 [819-820]
— per capita, p. 459 [423]
— poverty, pp. 464-469, 869-870 [430-435, 437, 856-857]
— quintiles, p. 456 [418]
— regions, pp. 865-866 [851-852]
— salaries, pp. 462-463 [428-429]
— Social Security, p. 468 [436]
— source, p. 457 [420]
— top 5%, p. 456 [418]
Infant mortality, pp. 960-961, 1016, 1018, 1020-1022 [935-936, 975-979]
Infant mortality rates, pp. 1018, 1020-1022, 1024 [976-980]
Inhalants
— use, pp. 24, 32, 45 [36, 48, 63]
Inmates
— drug-related offenses, p. 98 [106]
— drug use, p. 116 [133]
Insurance
— health, pp. 243-247 [293-298]
— Medicaid, p. 247 [298]
Insurance companies, pp. 65-66 [82-83]
Integration
— elementary and secondary schools, p. 158 [190]
Investment banks, p. 54 [72]

Jail
— inmates, pp. 116, 120 [133, 140]
Judges
— U.S. Courts of Appeal, p. 123 [145]
— U.S. district courts, p. 123 [146]
Juvenile
— criminal offenses, pp. 99, 103 [108, 113]
Juveniles
— court cases, p. 127 [151]
— court cases outcomes, p. 128 [152]
— crime, pp. 98, 127 [107, 151]
Labor, pp. 516-585 [485-568]
Labor and employment, pp. 470, 474-484, 591 [438, 442-455, 574]
Labor force, pp. 493, 485-486, 488-491, 495-498, 500-503, 510-513, 938 [456-463, 465-472, 477, 479-482, 917]
Labor force and education, p. 493 [462-463]
Labor force projections, pp. 512-513 [481-482]
Law enforcement
— arrests, p. 110 [124]
— correctional officers, p. 112 [128]
— officers slain, pp. 111-112 [125-127]
— prison staff, pp. 113-114 [129, 131]
— prisoners, pp. 116-120, 122, 131 [133-141, 144, 157]
— staff, pp. 114-115 [130, 132]
Legal justice
— defenders, p. 128 [153]
— executions, p. 124 [147]
— felony offenders, p. 125 [148]
— judges, p. 123 [145-146]
— juveniles, p. 128 [152]
— length of time to parole, p. 137 [164]
— offenders, p. 129 [154]
— parole, p. 139 [165]
— pretrials, p. 130 [155-156]
— rearrests, p. 126 [150]
— released defendants, p. 126 [149]
— sentences, pp. 132, 134-136 [158-162]
— time served, p. 136 [163]
Leisure
— activities, p. 791 [760]
— expenditures, p. 792 [761]
Life expectancy, pp. 1027, 1029-1030, 1032 [982-985]
Literacy
— adult, p. 224 [272-273]
— prose, p. 224 [272-273]
Live births, pp. 896-897, 900, 902, 904, 906, 908, 1010, 1045, 1047 [883-884, 888-892, 971, 995-996]
— geographical area, pp. 943, 945 [923-924]
Living arrangements
— children, pp. 826-829 [815-820]
Local government employment, pp. 475-477 [444-447]
Local government employment rates, p. 474 [443]
LSD
— use, p. 45 [63]
Majors
— college students, p. 201 [240]
— older undergraduates, p. 211 [251]
Male municipal officials, pp. 610-611 [597-598]

Numbers following p. or pp. are page references. Numbers in [ ] are table references.

Majors
— college students, p. 201 [240]
— older undergraduates, p. 211 [251]
Male municipal officials, pp. 610-611 [597-598]
Marijuana
— ease of attainment, pp. 1-2 [1-2]
— use, pp. 12, 24, 31, 36-37, 39-40, 45 [19-20, 37, 47, 51-52, 56-57, 63]
Marital status, pp. 658-660 [639-641]
— families, p. 876 [864]
Marriage, pp. 1037-1038 [989-990]
Marriages
— 1980 high school sophomore cohort, p. 874 [861]
Married couples
— income, p. 872 [859]
— mixed races, p. 659 [640]
Maternal mortality, p. 994 [955]
Maternal mortality rates, pp. 960-961 [935-936]
Mathematics
— achievement, p. 144 [171]
— attitude toward, p. 7 [10]
— courses taken, pp. 149-150 [177-178]
— proficiency, p. 145 [172]
— semesters taken, p. 150 [179]
Medicaid
— coverage, p. 247 [298]
Medical care
— dentists, p. 254 [307]
— drug-related, pp. 254-258, 261 [308-312, 316]
— emergency, pp. 259-260 [313-315]
— home, p. 262 [317]
— hospice, p. 262 [317]
— nursing home, p. 242 [292]
— outpatient, p. 263 [318]
— personal home, p. 242 [292]
— physicians, pp. 264-268 [319-326]
— short-stay hospitals, p. 242 [291]
— substance abuse treatment, p. 269 [327]
— vaccinations, p. 252 [305]
Migration, pp. 740-741, 743-747 [716-722]
Military
— personnel, p. 600 [587]
Mobility, pp. 661-673, 675-679, 681-682, 684-685, 687-711, 713-717, 719-725, 727-734, 736-737, 739-741, 743-747, 749-755, 757-762 [642-737]
Mobility rates, pp. 661, 715, 757 [642, 693, 730-731]
Morphine
— Emergency Room treatment, p. 257 [311]
Mothers
— expectant, p. 269 [328]
Movers
— characteristics, pp. 661, 715-717, 719-725, 727-733, 737, 739, 754-755, 757 [642, 693-711, 714-715, 728-730]
Multiple job holders, pp. 510-511 [478-480]
Municipal officials, pp. 610-611, 616-617 [597-598, 606-607]
Murder
— age of offenders, p. 101 [110]
— at place of employment, p. 106 [118]
— offenders, pp. 101-102 [111-112]

Murder continued:
— rate per 100,000 population, p. 100 [109]
— victims, pp. 102, 105-106 [112, 116, 118]
NBA
— playoff leaders, p. 814 [800]
NCAA
— awards, p. 796 [769]
— participation in, p. 796 [770]
Needles
— used with drugs, p. 27 [41]
Neglect
— children, p. 109 [123]
Neighborhoods, p. 417 [395]
— and drug effects, p. 19 [30]
— drug sales, p. 28 [42]
Neonatal death rates, p. 1039 [991]
Neonatal mortality, p. 1022 [979]
Neonatal mortality ratios, pp. 960-961 [935-936]
Newspaper reading, p. 601 [588]
Nonagricultural employees, p. 515 [484]
Occupational distribution, p. 566 [545]
Occupations, pp. 489, 514, 516-586 [459, 483, 485-569]
— private industry, pp. 516-585 [485-568]
Offenders
— convicted, p. 129 [154]
— felony, p. 125 [148]
— incarcerated, p. 129 [154]
— juvenile, pp. 98, 127-128 [107, 151-152]
— sentences, pp. 134-135 [160-161]
Offenses
— juvenile, p. 98 [107]
— juvenile offenders, p. 99 [108]
Older adults
— income, p. 457 [420]
Older persons
— poverty, p. 467 [434]
Older undergraduates
— degree programs, p. 209 [247]
— full-time/part-time, p. 212 [253]
— type of institution, p. 210 [250]
Opiates
— use, pp. 43-44 [61-62]
Owner-occupied housing, p. 434 [405]
Owners, p. 349 [363]
Parents
— age, p. 826 [815-816]
— custodial, p. 783 [750]
— educational attainment, pp. 827-828 [817-818]
— employment status, pp. 827-828 [817-818]
— family income, pp. 828-829 [819-820]
— home tenure, pp. 828-829 [819-820]
— single, pp. 848-849, 851, 853, 857, 859 [838-841, 843-844]
Parole
— length of time to, p. 137 [164]
— method of discharge, p. 139 [165]
PCP
— use, p. 25 [38]
Pension plan, p. 786 [754]
Perinatal mortality rates, p. 1024 [980]

Numbers following p. or pp. are page references. Numbers in [ ] are table references.

Personnel
— military, p. 600 [587]
Physicians
— drug prescriptions, p. 267 [324]
— office visits, pp. 264-267 [319, 321-325]
— patient contacts, p. 264 [320]
— time since last contact, p. 268 [326]
Pitchers
— World Series, p. 808 [789]
Plumbing, p. 334 [357]
Police
— officers slain, pp. 111-112 [125-127]
Political party identification, p. 612 [599]
Population, pp. 618-620, 622, 624-627, 629-630, 632-633, 635-636, 638-640, 642-645, 647-651, 653-656, 658-659, 763, 765, 767-770, 772-773, 775, 777, 779, 781 [608-617, 619-640, 738-749]
— by region, p. 640 [625]
— economic characteristics, p. 781 [749]
— foreign-born, p. 631 [618]
— social characteristics, p. 781 [749]
Population characteristics, pp. 631-633, 635-636, 638-639, 658-659, 768-770, 772-773, 775, 777, 779, 781 [618-624, 639-640, 741-749]
Population projections, pp. 632, 763, 765, 767-769, 773, 775 [619, 738-742, 745-746]
— by race, pp. 763, 767 [738, 740]
Population trends, pp. 632-633, 635-636, 638, 640, 763, 767, 770, 772, 777, 779 [619-623, 625, 738, 740, 743-744, 747-748]
Postneonatal death rates, p. 1041 [992]
Postneonatal mortality, p. 1022 [979]
Postsecondary education
— vocational, p. 214 [257]
Poverty
— and Social Security, p. 468 [436]
— at 65 and over, p. 467 [434]
— children in, p. 830 [821]
— duration, p. 464 [430]
— families, pp. 869-870 [856-857]
— female households, p. 466 [433]
— individual, pp. 464-465, 468 [431-432, 435]
— number/percent, p. 466 [433]
— regions, p. 468 [435]
— transition to and from, p. 469 [437]
Pregnancies, p. 1043 [993]
Pregnancy
— and drug use, p. 251 [304]
Prenatal care, pp. 892-893, 1044-1045, 1047 [878, 880, 994-996]
Preprimary education
— enrollment, p. 220 [268]
Pretrials
— outcomes, p. 130 [155-156]
Prime-time black shows, p. 602 [590]
Prisoners
— criminal history, p. 119 [138]
— drug history, p. 117 [135]
— Federal, pp. 116-117, 119-120, 122 [134, 136, 139, 141, 144]
— jail, pp. 116, 120 [133, 140]
— newly committed, p. 118 [137]

Prisoners continued:
— place of confinement, p. 116 [134]
— State, pp. 117, 119-122 [135-136, 138, 141-142, 144]
— violent, p. 121 [142]
Prisons
— correctional officers, p. 112 [128]
— Federal, pp. 114-115 [130, 132]
— staff, pp. 113-115 [129-132]
Private school
— teachers, p. 159 [191]
Private sector employment, pp. 479, 481-484 [450, 452-455]
Private sector employment rates, p. 480 [451]
Public school
— employment categories, p. 153 [184]
Race
— of spouses, p. 877 [865]
Racism
— attitudes toward, p. 5 [7]
Radio listening, p. 601 [588]
Rape
— victims, p. 107 [120]
Reading
— expenditures, p. 792 [761]
— proficiency, p. 146 [173]
Rearrests
— of defendants, p. 126 [150]
Recommendations
— for college, p. 149 [176]
Regions
— income, pp. 865-866 [851-852]
— poverty, p. 468 [435]
— prison staff, p. 114 [131]
— sentences for crime, p. 134 [159]
Religion, p. 602 [589]
Religious bodies, p. 602 [589]
Renter-occupied housing, p. 434 [405]
Renters, pp. 349, 410 [363, 391]
Robbery
— victims, p. 107 [120]
Salaries
— Federal employees, pp. 462-463 [428-429]
— local Government employees, p. 463 [429]
— State employees, p. 463 [429]
Sales, pp. 57, 92, 95 [78, 104-105]
SAT scores
— characteristics of examinees, p. 226 [276]
— trends, p. 225 [275]
Schoolchildren
— drug use, pp. 31-32 [47-48]
Schools
— drug-related behavior, p. 11 [17-18]
— elementary and secondary, pp. 157-158 [189-190]
— private, p. 159 [191]
— public, p. 153 [184]
Science
— attitude toward, p. 7 [10]
— courses taken, p. 149 [177]
— proficiency, p. 147 [174]

Numbers following p. or pp. are page references. Numbers in [ ] are table references.

Science and engineering
— higher education funding, pp. 204, 206-207 [244-246]
Segregation
— elementary and secondary schools, p. 158 [190]
Sentences
— crime, pp. 132, 134 [158-159]
— criminal, p. 135 [161]
— death, p. 136 [162]
Shift schedules, p. 597 [582]
Single mothers, p. 1010 [970]
Single-parent householders, pp. 692-699 [669-676]
— women, pp. 696-699 [673-676]
Size
— of families, pp. 842, 844-845 [834-836]
— of family members, p. 847 [837]
Smokeless tobacco
— use, pp. 41-42 [58-59]
Smokers, pp. 893, 895, 899, 942 [879, 882, 887, 922]
— education, pp. 47, 49 [65, 67]
Smoking
— during pregnancy, p. 269 [328]
— trends, pp. 46-49 [64-67]
Social Security
— and poverty, p. 468 [436]
Sports
— baseball, pp. 797-808 [771-774, 776-789]
— basketball, pp. 794-795, 808-815 [765-767, 790-793, 795-801]
— college, p. 796 [770]
— football, pp. 795, 816-823 [768, 802, 804-813]
— golf, p. 793 [763-764]
— NCAA, p. 796 [769]
— professional, pp. 799, 811, 816 [775, 794, 803]
Spouses
— age, pp. 874-875 [862-863]
— race, p. 877 [865]
State employment, pp. 475-477 [444-447]
State government and employment rates, p. 474 [443]
States
— associate degrees awarded, pp. 165-166 [199-200]
— bachelor's degrees awarded, pp. 168-169 [201-202]
— colleges and universities, pp. 160-161 [192-193]
— doctoral degrees awarded, pp. 170-171 [203-204]
— higher education enrollment, pp. 186-191 [223-228]
— master's degrees awarded, pp. 172-175 [205-208]
Steroids
— illegal use, p. 13 [21-22]
— use, pp. 41-42 [58-59]
Stimulants
— use, pp. 43-44 [61-62]
Students
— computer use, p. 221 [269]
— high school, pp. 7-10, 149, 225 [11-15, 176, 274]
— higher education, pp. 203, 216 [242, 261]
— employed, pp. 490-491 [460-461]
— unemployed, pp. 490-491 [460-461]
Subfamilies, pp. 420, 422 [396-397]
— size, p. 864 [849]
Substance abuse
— treatment, pp. 250, 269 [303, 327]

Suburban householders, pp. 425-426 [400-401]
Suicide, pp. 990, 992 [953-954]
— attempts, p. 9 [13-14]
— drug-related, p. 229 [278]
— rates by age group, p. 103 [113]
— thoughts, p. 9 [13-14]
Teachers
— elementary and secondary, p. 154 [185]
— private schools, p. 159 [191]
Telephone subscribers, p. 416 [394]
Television production costs, p. 602 [590]
Television viewing, p. 601 [588]
Tenure status
— higher education faculty, p. 201 [239]
Test scores
— mathematics, p. 145 [172]
— reading, p. 146 [173]
— SAT, pp. 225-226 [275-276]
— science, p. 147 [174]
— writing, p. 148 [175]
Tobacco
— smokeless, p. 26 [39]
Tranquilizers
— use, pp. 43-44 [61-62]
Undergraduates
— age, p. 215 [260]
— older, pp. 209-212 [247-253]
Unemployed, pp. 590, 594 [573, 579]
Unemployment, pp. 473, 504-505, 507-508, 587-589, 593-594 [441, 473-476, 570-572, 577-578]
Unemployment rates, pp. 591-592, 594 [574-576, 579]
Uninsured, pp. 787-788 [755-756]
Unions, pp. 595-596 [580-581]
Unmarried mothers, pp. 888-889, 891, 924-925, 927-929, 931-935 [875-877, 904-908, 910-914]
Vaccinations
— children, p. 252 [305]
Values
— 1980 high school sophomore cohort, p. 51 [69]
Vehicles
— annual mileage, p. 367 [370]
— fuel consumption, p. 367 [370]
— fuel expenditures, p. 367 [370]
Victims
— children, p. 109 [123]
— crime, pp. 106, 108 [119, 121]
— handgun, p. 104 [115]
— homicide, pp. 103, 108 [114, 122]
— household, p. 105 [117]
— intimates, p. 121 [142]
— of murder, pp. 102, 105-106 [112, 116, 118]
— of personal crimes, p. 107 [120]
— of violence, p. 121 [142]
Violence
— victims, p. 108 [121]
Visits
— emergency rooms, p. 259 [313]
— hospital outpatient departments, p. 263 [318]
Volunteer workers, p. 788 [757]

Numbers following p. or pp. are page references. Numbers in [ ] are table references.

Index

Voters, p. 612 [600]
Voters and voting, pp. 614-615 [601-603]
Voting patterns, p. 612 [600]
Wages
— hourly rate, p. 461 [427]
Weapons
— high school students, p. 10 [15]
Weight
— excess, p. 240 [290]
Wives
— age, pp. 874-875 [862-863]
— race, p. 877 [865]
Women, pp. 1037-1038 [989-990]
— victims of violence, p. 108 [121]
Women county officials, pp. 615-616 [604-605]
Women employed, pp. 476, 481, 510 [446, 452, 477]
Women municipal officials, pp. 616-617 [606-607]
Women's employment rates, p. 479 [449-450]
Work disability, p. 790 [759]
Work hours
— older undergraduates, p. 210 [249]
Work schedules, p. 597 [582]
Workers
— full-time, p. 461 [426]
— minimum-wage, p. 461 [427]
Workers at home, p. 597 [583]
World Series
— batting averages, p. 806 [786]
— leaders, p. 800 [776-777]
— leading batters, p. 807 [788]
— strikeouts, p. 808 [789]
Writing
— proficiency, p. 148 [175]
Youth
— drug use, pp. 36-37, 39, 50 [51-52, 56, 68]

Numbers following p. or pp. are page references. Numbers in [ ] are table references.